FOR REFERENCE

Do Not Take From This Room

Nineteenth-Century
Literature Criticism

Guide to Gale Literary Criticism Series

For criticism on	Consult these Gale series
Authors now living or who died after December 31, 1959	*CONTEMPORARY LITERARY CRITICISM (CLC)*
Authors who died between 1900 and 1959	*TWENTIETH-CENTURY LITERARY CRITICISM (TCLC)*
Authors who died between 1800 and 1899	*NINETEENTH-CENTURY LITERATURE CRITICISM (NCLC)*
Authors who died between 1400 and 1799	*LITERATURE CRITICISM FROM 1400 TO 1800 (LC)* *SHAKESPEAREAN CRITICISM (SC)*
Authors who died before 1400	*CLASSICAL AND MEDIEVAL LITERATURE CRITICISM (CMLC)*
Authors of books for children and young adults	*CHILDREN'S LITERATURE REVIEW (CLR)*
Dramatists	*DRAMA CRITICISM (DC)*
Poets	*POETRY CRITICISM (PC)*
Short story writers	*SHORT STORY CRITICISM (SSC)*
Black writers of the past two hundred years	*BLACK LITERATURE CRITICISM (BLC)*
Hispanic writers of the late nineteenth and twentieth centuries	*HISPANIC LITERATURE CRITICISM (HLC)*
Native North American writers and orators of the eighteenth, nineteenth, and twentieth centuries	*NATIVE NORTH AMERICAN LITERATURE (NNAL)*
Major authors from the Renaissance to the present	*WORLD LITERATURE CRITICISM, 1500 TO THE PRESENT (WLC)*

ISSN 0732-1864

Volume 70

Nineteenth-Century Literature Criticism

Excerpts from Criticism of the
Works of Novelists, Poets, Playwrights,
Short Story Writers, Philosophers, and Other
Creative Writers Who Died between 1800
and 1899, from the First Published Critical
Appraisals to Current Evaluations

Janet Witalec
Editor

GALE

DETROIT · LONDON

STAFF

This book is printed on acid-free paper that meets the minimum requirements of American National Standard for Information Sciences—Permanence Paper for Printed Library Materials, ANSI Z39.48-1984.

Library of Congress Catalog Card Number 84-643008
ISBN 0-7876-1910-8
ISSN 0732-1864
Printed in the United States of America

10 9 8 7 6 5 4 3 2 1

Contents

Preface vii

Acknowledgments xi

Preface

Since its inception in 1981, *Nineteenth-Century Literature Criticism* has been a valuable resource for students and librarians seeking critical commentary on writers of this transitional period in world history. Designated an "Outstanding Reference Source" by the American Library Association with the publication of its first volume, *NCLC* has since been purchased by over 6,000 school, public, and university libraries. The series has covered more than 300 authors representing 29 nationalities and over 17,000 titles. No other reference source has surveyed the critical reaction to nineteenth-century authors and literature as thoroughly as *NCLC*.

Scope of the Series

NCLC is designed to introduce students and advanced readers to the authors of the nineteenth century, and to the most significant interpretations of these authors' works. The great poets, novelists, short story writers, playwrights, and philosophers of this period are frequently studied in high school and college literature courses. By organizing and reprinting commentary written on these authors, *NCLC* helps students develop valuable insight into literary history, promotes a better understanding of the texts, and sparks ideas for papers and assignments. Each entry in *NCLC* presents a comprehensive survey of an author's career or an individual work of literature and provides the user with a multiplicity of interpretations and assessments. Such variety allows students to pursue their own interests; furthermore, it fosters an awareness that literature is dynamic and responsive to many different opinions.

Every fourth volume of *NCLC* is devoted to literary topics that cannot be covered under the author approach used in the rest of the series. Such topics include literary movements, prominent themes in nineteenth-century literature, literary reaction to political and historical events, significant eras in literary history, prominent literary anniversaries, and the literatures of cultures that are often overlooked by English-speaking readers.

NCLC continues the survey of criticism of world literature begun by Gale's *Contemporary Literary Criticism (CLC)* and *Twentieth-Century Literary Criticism (TCLC),* both of which excerpt and reprint commentary on authors of the twentieth century. For additional information about *TCLC, CLC,* and Gale's other criticism series, users should consult the Guide to Gale Literary Criticism Series preceding the title page in this volume.

Coverage

Each volume of *NCLC* is carefully compiled to present:

- criticism of authors, or literary topics, representing a variety of genres and nationalities
- both major and lesser-known writers and literary works of the period
- 4-8 authors or 4-6 topics per volume
- individual entries that survey critical response to an author's work or a topic in literary history, including early criticism to reflect initial reactions, later criticism to represent any rise or decline in reputation, and current retrospective analyses.

Organization

An author entry consists of the following elements: author heading, biographical and critical introduction, list of principal works, excerpts of criticism (each preceded by a bibliographic citation and an annotation), and a bibliography of further reading.

- The **Author Heading** consists of the name under which the author most commonly wrote, followed by birth and death dates. If an author wrote consistently under a pseudonym, the pseudonym will be listed in the author heading and the real name given in parentheses on the first line of the biographical and critical introduction. Also located at the beginning of the introduction to the author entry are any name variations under which an author wrote, including transliterated forms for an author whose language uses a nonroman alphabet.

- The **Biographical and Critical Introduction** outlines the author's life and career, as well as the critical issues surrounding his or her work. References are provided to past volumes of *NCLC* in which further information about the author may be found.

- Most *NCLC* entries include a **Portrait** of the author. Many entries also contain reproductions of materials pertinent to an author's career, including manuscript pages, title pages, dust jackets, letters, and drawings, as well as photographs of important people, places, and events in an author's life.

- The list of **Principal Works** is chronological by date of first publication and identifies the genre of each work. In the case of foreign authors with both foreign-language publications and English translations, the English-language version is given in brackets. Unless otherwise indicated, dramas are dated by first performance, not first publication.

- **Criticism** in each author entry is arranged chronologically to provide a perspective on changes in critical evaluation over the years. All titles of works by the author featured in the entry are printed in boldface type to enable the user to easily locate discussion of particular works. Also for purposes of easier identification, the critic's name and the publication date of the essay are given at the beginning of each piece of criticism. Unsigned criticism is preceded by the title of the journal in which it appeared. Publication information (such as publisher names and book prices) and some parenthetical numerical references (such as page and line references to specific editions of works) have been deleted at the editors' discretion to provide smoother reading of the text. Footnotes that appear with previously published pieces of criticism are reprinted at the end of each essay or excerpt. In the case of excerpted criticism, only those footnotes that pertain to the excerpted text are included.

- A complete **Bibliographic Citation** provides original publication information for each piece of criticism.

- Critical excerpts are prefaced by **Annotations** providing the reader with a summary of the critical intent of the piece. Also included, when appropriate, is information about the critic's reputation, individual approach to literary criticism, and particular expertise in an author's works, as well as information about the relative importance of the critical excerpt. In some cases, the annotations cross-reference excerpts by critics who discuss each other's commentary.

- An annotated list of **Further Reading** appearing at the end of each entry suggests secondary sources on the author. In some cases it includes essays for which the editors could not obtain reprint rights.

Cumulative Indexes

- Each volume of *NCLC* contains a cumulative **Author Index** listing all authors who have appeared in Gale's Literary Criticism Series, along with cross-references to such biographical series as *Contemporary Authors* and *Dictionary of Literary Biography*. Useful for locating authors within the various series, this index is particularly valuable for those authors who are identified with a certain period but who, because of their death dates, are placed in another, or for those authors whose careers span two periods. For example, Fyodor Dostoevsky is found in *NCLC*, yet Leo Tolstoy, another major nineteenth-century Russian novelist, is found in *TCLC* because he died after 1899.

- Each *NCLC* volume includes a cumulative **Nationality Index** which lists all authors who have appeared in *NCLC*, arranged alphabetically under their respective nationalities.

- Each new volume in Gale's Literary Criticism Series includes a cumulative **Topic Index**, which lists all literary topics treated in *NCLC, TCLC, LC 1400-1800*, and the *CLC* Yearbook.

- Each new volume of *NCLC*, with the exception of the Topics volumes, contains a **Title Index** listing the titles of all literary works discussed in the volume. In response to numerous suggestions from librarians, Gale has also produced a **Special Paperbound Edition** of the *NCLC* title index. This annual cumulation lists all titles discussed in the series since its inception. Additional copies of the index are available on request. Librarians and patrons have welcomed this separate index: it saves shelf space, is easy to use, and is recyclable upon receipt of the following year's cumulation. Titles discussed in the Topics volume entries are not included in the *NCLC* cumulative index.

Citing *Nineteenth-Century Literature Criticism*

When writing papers, students who quote directly from any volume in Gale's Literary Criticism Series may use the following general forms to footnote reprinted criticism. The first example pertains to material drawn from periodicals, the second to material reprinted from books:

[1]T.S. Eliot, "John Donne," *The Nation and Athenaeum*, 33 (9 June 1923), 321-32; excerpted and reprinted in *Literature Criticism from 1400-1800*, Vol. 10, ed. James E. Person, Jr. (Detroit: Gale Research, 1989), pp. 28-9.

[2]Clara G. Stillman, *Samuel Butler: A Mid-Victorian Modern* (Viking Press, 1932); excerpted and reprinted in *Twentieth-Century Literary Criticism*, Vol. 33, ed. Paula Kepos (Detroit: Gale Research, 1989), pp. 43-5.

Suggestions Are Welcome

In response to suggestions, several features have been added to *NCLC* since the series began, including annotations to excerpted criticism, a cumulative index to authors in all Gale literary criticism series, entries devoted to criticism on a single work by a major author, more illustrations, and a title index listing all literary works discussed in the series.

Readers who wish to suggest authors, single works, or topics to appear in future volumes, or who have other suggestions, are cordially invited to write: The Editors, *Nineteenth-Century Literature Criticism*, 835 Penobscot Bldg., 645 Griswold St., Detroit, MI 48226-4094; call toll-free at 1-800-347-GALE; or fax to 1-313-961-6599.

Acknowledgments

The editors wish to thank the copyright holders of the excerpted criticism included in this volume and the permissions managers of many book and magazine publishing companies for assisting us in securing reproduction rights. We are also grateful to the staffs of the Detroit Public Library, the Library of Congress, the University of Detroit Mercy Library, Wayne State University Purdy/Kresge Library Complex, and the University of Michigan Libraries for making their resources available to us. Following is a list of the copyright holders who have granted us permission to reproduce material in this volume of NCLC. Every effort has been made to trace copyright, but if omissions have been made, please let us know.

COPYRIGHTED EXCERPTS IN *NCLC*, VOLUME 70, WERE REPRODUCED FROM THE FOLLOWING PERIODICALS:

Anglia, v. LXXXIX, 1971. © Max Niemeyer Tübingen 1971. Reproduced by permission of the publisher.—*Biography: An Interdisciplinary Quarterly,* v. 18, Fall, 1995. Reproduced by permission.—*Criticism,* v. XXXVII, Fall, 1995. Copyright © 1995 by Wayne State University Press, Detroit, Michigan 48201-1309. Reproduced by permission.—*Eigse: A Journal of Irish Studies,* v. VIII, 1956. Reproduced by permission of The National University of Ireland.—*Éire-Ireland,* v. XIX, Summer, 1984. Copyright © 1984 by the Irish American Cultural Institute. Reproduced by permission of the publisher.—*Irish University Review,* v. 4, Autumn, 1974; v. 11, Autumn, 1981. © 1974, 1981 Irish University Review. Both reproduced by permission of the publisher.—*Keats-Shelley Review,* n. 10, Spring, 1996. Reproduced by permission.—*Latin American Literary Review,* v. XXII, January-June, 1994. Reproduced by permission.—*MLN,* v. 101, March, 1986. Copyright © 1986. Reproduced by permission of The Johns Hopkins University Press.—*Nineteenth-Century Literature,* v. 44, March, 1990 for "Interpretive Historicism: 'Signs of the Times' and Culture and Anarchy in Their Contexts" by Wendell V. Harris; v. 50, June, 1995 for "The Education of Cousin Phillis" by Philip Rogers. © 1990, 1995 by The Regents of the University of California. Both reproduced by permission of the publisher and the respective authors.—*The Southern Review,* Louisana State University, v. 31, July, 1995 for "Orpheus in Ireland: On Brian Merriman's The Midnight Court" by Seamus Heaney. Copyright, 1995, by the author. Reproduced by permission of the author.—*Studies in Philology,* v. LXXXIII, Spring, 1986. Copyright © 1986 by the University of North Carolina Press. Reproduced by permission of the publisher.—*Studies in the Novel,* v. 21, Spring, 1989. Copyright 1989 by North Texas State University. Reproduced by permission.—*Texas Studies in Literature and Language,* v. XI, Spring, 1969 for "Ishmael as Prophet: Heroes and Hero-Worship and the Self-Expressive Basis of Carlyle's Art" by David J. Delaura. Copyright © 1969 by the University of Texas Press. All rights reserved. Reproduced by permission of the University of Texas Press and the author.—*Victorian Studies,* v, 36, Winter, 1993. Reproduced by permission of the Trustees of Indiana University.—*Victorians Institute Journal,* v. 23, 1995. Reproduced by permission.

COPYRIGHTED EXCERPTS IN *NCLC*, VOLUME 70, WERE REPRODUCED FROM THE FOLLOWING BOOKS:

Beane, Carol. From "Black Character: Toward a Dialectical Presentation in Three South American Novels" in *Voices from Under: Black Narrative in Latin America and the Caribbean.* Edited by William Luis. Greenwood Press, 1984. Copyright © 1984 by William Luis. All rights reserved.

Victorian Novel. Oxford University Press, 1992. Copyright © 1992 by Oxford University Press, Inc. All rights reserved. Reproduced by permission of Oxford University Press, Inc.—Stoneman, Patsy. From *Elizabeth Gaskell.* The Harvester Press, 1987. © Patsy Stoneman, 1987. All rights reserved. Reproduced by permission of the author.—Vida, Elizabeth M. From an introduction to *Romantic Affinities: German Authors and Carlyle: A Study in the History of Ideas.* University of Toronto Press, 1993. © University of Toronto Press Incorporated 1993. Reproduced by permission.—Watson, Roderick. From "Carlyle: The World as Text and the Text as Voice" in *The History of Scottish Literature, Volume 3.* Edited by Douglas Gifford. Aberdeen University Press, 1988. © The Contributors 1988. All rights reserved. Reproduced by permission of the author.—Webb, Timothy. From "Correcting the Irritability of His Temper: The Evolution of Leigh Hunt's 'Autobiography'" in *Romantic Revisions.* Edited by Robert Brinkley and Keith Hanley. Cambridge University Press, 1992. © Cambridge University Press 1992. Reproduced with the permission of Cambridge University Press and the author.—Williams, Raymond. From *Culture and Society, 1780-1950.* Columbia University Press, 1983. Copyright © 1983 Columbia University Press. All rights reserved. Reproduced by permission of the publisher.—Yeats, W. B. From an introduction to *The Midnight Court and The Adventures of a Luckless Fellow, by Brian Merriman and Denis Fellow.* Translated by Percy Arland Ussher. AMS Press, 1982. Reproduced A.P. Watt Ltd. on behalf of the Literary Estate of W. B. Yeats.

PHOTOGRAPHS AND ILLUSTRATIONS APPEARING IN *NCLC,* VOLUME 70, WERE RECEIVED FROM THE FOLLOWING SOURCES:

A title page for "Cúirt an Mheán Oíche, The Midnight Court" by Brian Merriman, 1982 edition, photograph. Courtesy of the Graduate Library, University of Michigan. Reproduced by permission.—A title page for "Lord Byron and his Contemporaries" by (James Henry) Leigh Hunt, 1828 edition, photograph. The Department of Rare Books and Special Collections, The University of Michigan Library. Reproduced by permission.—A title page for "María" by Jorge Ricardo Isaccs, 1898 edition, photograph. Courtesy of the Graduate Library, University of Michigan. Reproduced by permission.—A title page for "Mary Barton" by Elizabeth Cleghorn Gaskell, 1912 edition, photograph. Courtesy of the Graduate Library, University of Michigan. Reproduced by permission.—A title page for "On Heroes, Hero Worship and the Heroic in History" by Thomas Carlyle, 1841 edition, photograph. The Department of Rare Books and Special Collections, The University of Michigan Library. Reproduced by permission.—A title page for "Ruth" by Elizabeth Cleghorn Gaskell, 1853 edition, photograph. The Department of Rare Books and Special Collections, The University of Michigan Library. Reproduced by permission.—A title page for "Sartor Resartus" by Thomas Carlyle, 1836 edition, photograph. The Department of Rare Books and Special Collections, The University of Michigan Library. Reproduced by permission.—A title page for "The Autobiography of Leigh Hunt" by (James Henry) Leigh Hunt, 1828 edition, photograph. The Department of Rare Books and Special Collections, The University of Michigan Library. Reproduced by permission.—Carlyle, Thomas, photograph. The Library of Congress.—Gaskell, Elizabeth C., illustration. The Library of Congress.—Hunt, (James Henry) Leigh, painting by M. Gillies was engraved for The Eclectic, December, 1946, photograph. Archive Photos, Inc. Reproduced by permission.

Thomas Carlyle

1795-1881

Scottish philosopher, social critic, essayist, historian, biographer, translator, and editor.

For additional information on Carlyle's life and works, see *NCLC*, Volume 22.

INTRODUCTION

Carlyle achieved literary notoriety for his penetrating and often scathing criticism of Victorian society. His writings demonstrate his opposition to the Victorian emphasis on the logical and mechanical nature of the universe and his feelings against democracy in Britain. In conveying these views, Carlyle developed a writing style so distinct that it has been referred to as "Carlylese," and such works as *Sartor Resartus* (1833-34) and *The French Revolution* (1837) are often regarded as revolutionary in both their prose and their content. Carlyle's methods and themes met with mixed and extreme reactions in his time and continue to fascinate twentieth-century scholars.

Biographical Information

Carlyle was born in 1795 in Ecclefechan, Scotland, to James Carlyle, a stonemason, and Margaret Aitken Carlyle. He studied mathematics at Edinburgh University, but he left before earning his degree. Making a break with his Calvinist upbringing and family tradition, Carlyle chose not to become a clergyman, instead earning his living as a tutor at Annan and then as a schoolmaster at Kirkcaldy School. After returning to Edinburgh in 1818, Carlyle wrote occasional book reviews but grew increasingly depressed by his uncertainty regarding his vocation and religion. In the early 1820s, Carlyle appears to have undergone a spiritual conversion, which he later described in *Sartor Resartus* as a realization of a sense of individual freedom. In 1826, he married Jane Welsh, whom he had courted for some time. After publishing several essays, Carlyle attempted with much difficulty to place *Sartor Resartus*. It was finally accepted by *Fraser's Magazine* in 1833. Following a move to Chelsea, Carlyle began work on *The French Revolution*. It was published in 1837 and brought Carlyle recognition as a major literary figure. Most of Carlyle's major works were produced before the death of his wife—these works include *On Heroes, Hero-Worship and the Heroic in History* (originally a series of lectures, published in 1841), *Past and Present* (1843), *Latter-Day Pamphlets* (1850), *The Life of John Sterling* (1851), and *History of Friedrich II. of Prussia, Called Frederick the Great* (1858-65).

Carlyle was devastated by the death of his wife in 1866, and his literary output after her death is small. Carlyle died in 1881.

Major Works

The publication of *Sartor Resartus* established Carlyle as a social critic, though the work was received with much confusion because of its unique literary style. The title of the work means "the tailor re-tailored" and highlights the main theme of the work: that social customs and religious and political institutions are merely the "clothing" of essential realities. The book is presented as the efforts of a nameless editor, aided by a German colleague, to summarize the life and theories of the German Professor Diogenes Teufelsdröckh (devil's dung). Teufelsdröckh's philosophy stresses that just as clothes go out of fashion, so do ideas and institutions, and they also must be reenvisioned or retailored. Therefore, the significance of being able to see through these symbols, or clothes, is emphasized throughout the work. Carlyle's literary style in this volume presents as many challenges to the reader as does his format in that it heavily employs allusion, metaphor, and other techniques that have been described as "eccentricities" and "syntactical aberrations."

In addition to this philosophy, sometimes characterized as a religious vision without a personal God, Carlyle also developed distinct ideas about the political, social, and economic troubles of his day. In *The French Revolution*, Carlyle sympathized with the revolutionaries to some extent but despised anarchy and appeared to fear the rule of the people. In *On Heroes and Hero-Worship*, Carlyle presented the view that the vast majority of people are unsuited to rule and instead need heroes to provide solid leadership. Additionally, in the essay "Chartism" (1839), Carlyle used the Chartist movement as an example of a threatening revolution in England and advocated British imperialism as the antidote for England's problems—problems that, in Carlyle's view, stemmed from democracy and attempts at reform. Similarly, in *Past and Present*, Carlyle questioned democracy and analyzed the problems of workers in England. Some have suggested that in this work Carlyle foresaw the growth and development of the Labor Party in England.

Critical Reception

Just as readers and critics in Carlyle's time found *Sartor Resartus* perplexing, modern scholars disagree on Carlyle's intention in this work. The "Clothes Philosophy" has been discussed at length by critics, and many have a common understanding of its emphasis on symbolism, the idea that the world's institutions cloak a deeper, divine reality. Yet it is the method Carlyle used to convey this message—particularly the interplay between the Editor and the anonymous colleague—that is problematic for many critics. Lee C. R. Baker, for example, argues that the Editor's apparent skepticism about embracing Teufelsdröckh's philosophy (which would seem to undercut Carlyle's aim of getting the reader to embrace this philosophy) is actually ironic. The use of irony is necessary, Baker states, in order to help "bring forth the reader's own understanding of the Clothes Philosophy." D. Franco Felluga, however, maintains that efforts like Baker's to impose order or a "stable system of thought" on *Sartor* are attempts to "retailor" the work. Felluga argues that Carlyle's goal is to expose "all systems as limiting and false."

The French Revolution examines this period of history in a manner that took Carlyle's contemporary critics off guard. A review in the *Athenaeum* in 1837 charges Carlyle with carrying "quaintness, neologism and a whimsical coxcombery" through three volumes of "misplaced persiflage and flippant pseudo-philosophy." Modern scholars have been a bit more kind. Robert W. Kusch reviews Carlyle's marriage of metaphor and theme throughout the work and praises this union as Carlyle's "artistry at its best." With *On Heroes, Hero-Worship, and the Heroic in History*, it is the message,

more than the method, that has attracted critical attention. Ernst Cassirer explains that Carlyle sought to "stabilize the social and political order" in England and was convinced that hero worship was the best way to achieve this aim. Tracing the effects of Carlyle's views into the twentieth century, Cassirer links him to National Socialism and even to Hitler, and claims that for Carlyle history was identified with great men without whom there would be only stagnation. David J. Delaura takes another view of *Heroes*, arguing that the unity of the lectures stems from Carlyle's efforts to "define the characteristics, the message, and the social role of the prophet." In examining these features, Delaura argues, Carlyle revealed himself as the hero of *Heroes*, as a prophet, "at times *the* prophet whose wise and healing word the age looked for."

PRINCIPAL WORKS

Wilhelm Meister's Apprenticeship [translator; from *Wilhem Meisters Lehrjahre* by Johann Wolfgang von Goethe] (novel) 1824
The Life of Friedrich Schiller (biography) 1825
"Burns" (essay) 1828
"Signs of the Times" (essay) 1829
"Boswell's *Life of Johsnon*" (essay) 1832
Sartor Resartus (prose) 1836
The French Revolution (history) 1837
"Sir Walter Scott" (essay) 1838
**Critical and Miscellaneous Essays*. 4 vols. (essays) 1838-39
"Chartism" (essay) 1839
On Heroes, Hero-Worship, and the Heroic in History (lectures) 1841
Past and Present (prose) 1843
Oliver Cromwell's Letters and Speeches. 2 vols. [editor] (letters and speeches) 1845
Latter-Day Pamphlets (prose) 1850
The Life of John Sterling (biography) 1851
"Occasional Discourse on the Nigger Question" (essay) 1853
The Collected Works of Thomas Carlyle. 16 vols. (prose, history, essays, biography, and translations) 1857-58
History of Friedrich II. of Prussia, Called Frederick the Great. 6 vols. (biography) 1858-65
"Shooting Niagra: And After?" (essay) 1867
Reminiscences (memoir) 1881
The Correspondence of Thomas Carlyle and Ralph Waldo Emerson, 1834-1872. 2 vols. (letters) 1883
Early Letters of Thomas Carlyle. 2 vols. (letters) 1883
Letters and Memorials of Jane Welsh Carlyle. 3 vols. [editor, with James Anthony Froude] (letters and memoirs) 1883
Correspondence between Goethe and Carlyle (letters) 1887
The Works of Thomas Carlyle. 30 vols. (prose, history, essays, biographies, and translations) 1896-99

The Love Letters of Thomas Carlyle and Jane Welsh. 2 vols. (letters) 1909

Letters of Thomas Carlyle to John Stuart Mill, John Sterling, and Robert Browning (letters) 1923

*This work was originally published in the periodical *Fraser's Magazine* in 1833-34.

**The essays in this collection were first published in periodicals.

CRITICISM

The Athenaeum (review date 1837)

SOURCE: A review of *The French Revolution,* in *The Athenaeum,* May 20, 1837, pp. 353-55.

[*In the following review, the anonymous critic offers a negative assessment of* The French Revolution, *describing Carlyle's history as "flippant pseudo-philosophy" and condemning his use of German idiomatic expressions and style.*]

Originality of thought is unquestionably the best excuse for writing a book; originality of style is a rare and a refreshing merit; but it is paying rather dear for one's whistle, to qualify for obtaining it in the university of Bedlam. Originality, without justness of thought, is but novelty of error; and originality of style, without sound taste and discretion, is sheer affectation. Thus, as ever, the *corruptio optimi* turns out to be *pessima;* the abortive attempt to be more than nature has made us, and to add a cubit to our stature, ends by placing us below what we might be, if contented with being simply and unaffectedly ourselves. There is not, perhaps, a more decided mark of the decadence of literature, than the frequency of such extravagance; especially, if it eventually becomes popular. The youth of literature is distinguished by a progressive approach to simplicity and to good taste; but the culminating point once attained; the good and the beautiful, as the Italian poet sings, become commonplace and tiresome,—"caviare to the general"; and the sound canons of criticism and of logic are capriciously deserted, to produce no matter what, provided it be new. Let it not, however, be thought that we advocate the theory of a permanent Augustan age, and "giving our days and nights to Addison." Language is a natural fluent; and to arrest its course is as undesirable as it is difficult. Style, to be good, must bear a certain relation to the mind from which it emanates; and when new ideas and new sciences change the national character, the modes of national expression must change also. Our received ideas, therefore, of classical styles are narrow and unphilosophic; and are derived from the fact, that as far as regards the dead languages, the classical era was followed, not by an increasing, but

a decreasing civilization; and that the silver and brazen ages of the Greek and Latin tongues were produced by a deterioration of mind as well as of language. When, however, great changes arrive suddenly and unprepared, they produce, not reforms merely, but revolutions; and in revolutions, literary as well as political, there occurs between the overthrow of the old and the creation of the new, an epoch of transition in which all monstrous and misshapen things are produced in the unguided search of an unknown and unimagined beauty. In such an epoch of transition we believe a large portion of the literature of Germany still to exist; in such an epoch is the literature of *la jeune France;* but when an English writer is found to adopt the crudities and extravagancies of these nascent schools of thought, and to copy their mannerisms without rhyme, reason, taste, or selection, we can only set it down to an imperfection of intellect, to an incapacity for feeling, truth, and beauty, or to a hopeless determination to be singular, at any cost or sacrifice.

The applicability of these remarks to the History of the French Revolution now before us, will be understood by such of our readers as are familiar with Mr. Carlyle's contributions to our periodical literature. But it is one thing to put forth a few pages of quaintness, neologism, and a whimsical coxcombry; and another, to carry such questionable qualities through three long volumes of misplaced persiflage and flippant pseudo-philosophy. To such a pitch of extravagance and absurdity are these peculiarities exalted in the volumes before us, that we should pass them over in silence, as altogether unworthy of criticism, if we did not know that the rage for German literature may bring such writing into fashion with the ardent and unreflecting; at least, in cases where the faults we deprecate are not pushed, as in the present instance, to a transcendental excess. Under that impression, however, we must take occasion to protest against all and sundry attempts to engraft the idiom of Germany into the king's English, or to transfuse the vague verbiage and affected sentimentality of a sect of Germans into our simple and intelligible philosophy. As yet, the barriers which separate prose from verse, in our language, are firm and unbroken; as yet, our morals and metaphysics are not quite Pindaric; and our narrative may be understood by any plain man who has learned to read. We are not habitually in the clouds, rapt and inspired; and we can read the great majority of our native authors without thinking of a strait waistcoat.

With respect to language, in particular, every nation must be permitted to "speak for itself;" and the pedantry of engrafting on any language foreign modes of expression, is unmitigated folly. Words may successfully be naturalized when they express new ideas; but foreign grammatical idioms are ever ill-assorted patches, which disfigure, and cannot adorn, the cloth to which they are appended. The German compound substantive, for instance, will always appear ludicrous in our simple monosyllabic tongue; and when introduced into prose, is worse than ludicrous,—it is mischievous. It is often sufficiently difficult to detect a confusion of idea, even when that idea is expressed at full, in a sentence of many words; but a compound substantive is merely the sign of such a sentence, the sign of a sign; and its full and precise meaning can only be obtained by intense and laborious study. Such words are misleading and dangerous; and the proper raw material for the construction of *galimatias*. By their use, an author, may fancy himself sublime, when he is only ridiculous; he may conceit himself original, when he is only uttering a commonplace truism in a new way.

This last remark brings us at once to the matter of the book. What need have we of a new History of the French Revolution? We have the contemporary history of that gigantic event in superabundance; and the time is not yet arrived for christening ourselves Posterity. We have looked carefully through these volumes; and, their peculiarity of style and the looseness of their reasoning apart, we have not found a fact in them that is not better told in Mignet, and twenty other unpretending historians. There is, moreover, in them the deadly *crambe repetita* of referring the faults and the failures of the Revolution to the speculative opinions, or "philosophism," as the author calls it, of the eighteenth century. "Faith," he says, "is gone out; scepticism is come in. Evil abounds and accumulates; no one has faith to withstand it, to amend it, to begin by amending himself." Now, faith and scepticism had nothing directly to do with the affair; it was want, and misery, and oppression in the lower classes, utter corruption and incapacity in the higher, that made the revolt. Or if the faith in a state religion must be admitted to be necessary to ensure a tame submission to wrong, the leaders in that infidelity were the church dignitaries, who polluted their own altars. Society has subsisted under all modifications of popular belief; but the faith necessary to its prosperity, is a faith in truth, in honour, honesty, patriotism, and public virtue; and this had, in revolutionary France, been choked in the highest classes by the precepts and the examples of the hierarchy, while it lived and flamed in the confiding masses that trusted too implicitly to any knave who affected the garb of patriotism. Had the people possessed a little less faith in the virtues of the Church and State authorities, they would have prevented the revolution, by nipping its causes in the bud. Louis XIV., the Regent, and Louis XV., would never have existed such as they were; and events would have taken another direction.

The faults which we have been compelled thus to denounce, are the more provoking, as they are not unmingled with many finely conceived passages, and many just and vigorous reflections. The author's mind is so little accustomed to weigh carefully its own philosophy, and is so thoroughly inconsistent with itself, that the grossest absurdity in speculation does not prevent his perceiving and adopting truths in the closest relation of opposition to it. Thus, while he attributes evils innumerable to infidelity and philosophism, and openly preaches passive obedience, religious and politi-

cal, he does not the less wisely sum up the material causes of the revolt, and put forth many just views of men and things, and of the multiplied errors committed both "within and without the walls of Troy." So, too, as to style, amidst an all-pervading absurdity of mannerism, there are passages of great power, and occasionally of splendid, though impure eloquence. Had the author been bred in another school, we should say that he might have written well and usefully; if we did not think that his admiration of that school must be in some way connected with defects in the native constitution of his mind. Having, however, expressed our unfavourable opinion thus freely, it becomes a duty to back our assertions by proof, and to give extracts as well of excellencies as of defects. In the following passage we have inconsistency of thought, vagueness of expression, and quaintness of style, all mixed together:—

> Meanwhile it is singular how long the rotten will hold together, provided you do not handle it roughly. For whole generations it continues standing, 'with a ghastly affectation of life,' after all life and truth has fled out of it: so loath are men to quit their old ways; and, conquering indolence and inertia, venture on new. Great truly is the Actual; is the Thing that has rescued itself from bottomless deeps of theory and possibility, and stands there as a definite indisputable Fact, whereby men do work and live, or once did so. Wisely shall men cleave to that, while it will endure; and quit it with regret, when it gives way under them. Rash enthusiast of Change, beware! Hast thou well considered all that Habit does in this life of ours; how all Knowledge and all Practice hang wondrous over infinite abysses of the Unknown, Impracticable; and our whole being is, an infinite abyss, *overarched* by Habit, as by a thin Earth-rind, laboriously built together?

If things naturally hold together when they are rotten, the inference is in favour and not against a voluntary effect of change, and then, what are "realities rescued from the bottomless depths of theory," but downright jargon and no-meaning?

Next, look, we pray thee, reader, at the following, on the siege of Gibraltar:—

> Neither, while the War yet lasts, will Gibraltar surrender. Not, though Crillon, Nassau-Siegen, with the ablest projectors extant, are there; and Prince Conde and Prince d'Artois have hastened to hell. Wondrous leather-roofed Floating-batteries, set afloat by French-Spanish *Pacte de Famille,* give gallant summons: to which, nevertheless, Gibraltar answers Plutonically, with mere torrents of redhot iron,—as if stone Calpe had become a throat of the Pit; and utters such a Doom's-blast of a *No,* as all men must credit.

There is an historical style with a vengeance! Pistol's "he hears with ears" is plain English to it. The author's estimate of Necker is not high:—

> We saw Turgot cast forth from the Controllership with

shrieks,—for want of a Fortunatus' Purse. As little could M. de Clugny manage the duty; or indeed do anything, but consume his wages; attain 'a place in History,' where as an ineffectual shadow thou beholdest him still lingering; and let the duty manage itself. Did Genevese Necker *possess* such a Purse then? He possessed Banker's skill, Banker's honesty; *credit* of all kinds, for he had written Academic Prize Essays, struggled for India Companies, given dinners to Philosophes, and 'realized a fortune in twenty years.' He possessed further a taciturnity and solemnity; of depth, or else of dulness. How singular for Celadon Gibbon, false swain as he had proved; whose father, keeping most probably his own gig, 'would not hear of such a union,'—to find now his forsaken Demoiselle Curchod sitting in the high places of the world, as Minister's Madame, and 'Necker not jealous.'

A new young Demoiselle, one day to be famed as a Madame and De Stael, was romping about the knees of the Decline and Fall; the lady Necker founds Hospitals; gives solemn Philosophe dinner-parties, to cheer her exhausted Controller General. Strange things have happened; by clamour of Philosophism, management of Marquis de Pezay, and Poverty constraining even Kings. And so Necker, Atlas-like, sustains the burden of the Finances, for five years long. Without wages, for he refused such; cheered only by Public Opinion, and the ministering of his noble Wife. With many thoughts in him, it is hoped; which however he is shy of uttering. His *Compte Rendu*, published by the royal permission, fresh sign of a New Era, shows wonders: which what but the genius of some Atlas-Necker can prevent from becoming portents? In Necker's head too there is a whole pacific French Revolution, of its kind; and in that taciturn dull depth, or deep dulness, ambition enough.

Meanwhile, alas, his Fortunatus' Purse turns out to be little other than the old '*vectigal* of Parsimony.' Nay, he too has to produce his scheme of taxing: Clergy, Noblesse to be taxed; Provincial Assemblies, and the rest,—like a mere Turgot! The expiring M. de Maurepas must gyrate one other time. Let Necker also depart; not unlamented.

Great in a private station, Necker looks on from the distance; abiding his time. 'Eighty thousand copies' of his new Book, which he calls *Administration des Finances,* will be sold in few days. He is gone; but shall return, and that more than once, borne by a whole shouting Nation. Singular Controller-General of the Finances: *once Clerk in Thelusson's Bank!!!*

The following sketch, with all its mannerisms, its affected present tense, and its absurdities, is lively and pregnant:—

For the present, however, consider Longehamp; now when Lent is ending, and the glory of Paris and France has gone forth, as in annual wont. Not to assist at *Tenebris* Masses, but to sun itself and show itself, and salute the Young Spring. Manifold, bright-tinted, glittering with gold; all through the Bois de Boulogne, in long-drawn variegated

rows;—like long-drawn living flower-borders, tulips, dahlias, lilies of the valley; all in their moving flower-pots (of new-gilt carriages): pleasure of the eye, and pride of life! So rolls and dances the Procession; steady, of firm assurance, as if it rolled on adamant and the foundation of the world: not on mere heraldic parchment,—under which smoulders a lake of fire. Dance on, ye foolish ones; ye sought not wisdom, neither have ye found it. Ye and your fathers have sown the wind, ye shall reap the whirlwind. Was it not, from of old, written: *The wages of sin is death?*

But at Longchamp, as elsewhere, we remark for one thing, that dame and cavalier are waited on each by a kind of human familiar, named *jokei.* Little elf, or imp; though young, already withered; with its withered air of premature vice, of knowingness, of completed elfhood: useful in various emergencies. The name *jokei* (jockey) comes from the English; as the thing also fancies that it does. Our Anglomania, in fact, is grown considerable; prophetic of much. If France is to be free, why shall she not, now when mad war is hushed, love neighbouring Freedom? Cultivated men, your Dukes de Liancourt, de la Rochefoucault, admire the English Constitution, the English National Character; would import what of it they can.

Of what is lighter, especially if it be light as wind, how much easier the freightage! Non-Admiral Duke de Chartres (not yet d'Orleans or Egalite) flies to and fro across the Strait; importing English Fashions: this he, as hand-and-glove with an English Prince of Wales, is surely qualified to do. Carriages and saddles; top-boots, and *rédingotes,* as we call riding-coats. Nay the very mode of riding: for now no man on a level with his age but will trot *á l' Anglaise,* rising in the stirrups; scornful of the old sitfast method, in which, according to Shakespeare, 'butter and eggs' go to market. Also, he can urge the fervid wheels, this brave Chartres of ours: no whip in Paris is rasher and surer than the unprofessional one of Monseigneur.

Elf*jokeis* we have seen; but see now real Yorkshire jockies, and what they ride on, and train English racers for French Races. These likewise we owe first (under the Providence of the Devil) to Monseigneur. Prince d'Artois also has his stud of racers. Prince d'Artois has withal the strangest horseleech: a moonstruck, much-enduring individual, of Neuchatel in Switzerland,—named *Jean Paul Marat.* A problematic Chevalier d'Eon, now in petticoats now in breeches, is no less problematic in London than in Paris; and causes bets and lawsuits. Beautiful days of international communion! Swindlery and Blackguardism have stretched hands across the Channel, and saluted mutually: on the race-course of Vincennes or Sablons, behold, in English curricle-and-four, wafted glorious among the principalities and rascalities, an English Dr. Dodd,—for whom also the too early gallows gapes.

Duke de Chartres was a young Prince of great promise, as young princes often are; which promise unfortunately has belied itself. With the huge Orleans Property, with Duke de Penthievre for Father-in-law (and now the young

Brother-in-law Lamballe killed by excesses),—he will one day be the richest man in France. Meanwhile, 'his hair is all falling out, his blood is quite spoiled,'—by early transcendentalism of debauchery. Carbuncles stud his face; dark studs on a ground of burnished copper. A most signal failure, this young Prince! The stuff prematurely burnt out of him; little left but foul smoke and ashes of expiring sensualities: what might have been Thought, Insight, and even Conduct, gone now, or fast going,—to confused darkness, broken by bewildering dazzlements; to obstreperous crochets; to activities which you may call semi-delirious, or even semi-galvanic! Paris affects to laugh at his charioteering; but he heeds not such laughter.

In the author's remarks on the Girondins there is much truth buried in mere jargon:—

In fact, one thing strikes us in these poor Girondins: their fatal shortness of vision; nay fatal poorness of character, for that is the root of it. They are as strangers to the People they would govern; to the thing they have come to work in. Formulas, Philosophies, Respectabilities, what has been written in Books, and admitted by the cultivated classes: *this* inadequate *Scheme* of Nature's working is all that Nature, let her work as she will, can reveal to these men. So they perorate and speculate; and call on the Friends of Law, when the question is not Law of No-Law, but Life or No-Life. Pedants of the Revolution, if not Jesuits of it! Their Formalism is great; great also is their Egoism. France rising to fight Austria has been raised only by Plot of the tenth of March, to kill Twenty-two of *them!* This Revolution Prodigy, unfolding itself into terrific stature and articulation, by its own laws and Nature's, not by the laws of Formula, has become unintelligibles, incredible as an impossibility, the 'waste chaos of a Dream.' A Republic founded on what they call the Virtues; on what we call the Decencies and Respectabilities; this they will have, and nothing but this. Whatsoever other Republic Nature and Reality send, shall be considered as not sent; as a kind of Nightmare Vision, and thing non-extant; disowned by the Laws of Nature, and of Formula. Alas! Dim for the best eyes is this Reality; and as for these men, they will not look at it with eyes at all, but only through 'facetted spectacles' of Pedantry, wounded Vanity; which yield the most portentous spectrum. Carping and complaining for ever of Plots and Anarchy, they will do one thing: prove, to demonstration, that the Reality will not translate into their Formula; that they and their Formula are incompatible with the Reality; and, in its dark wrath, the Reality will extinguish it and them! What a man *kens* he *cans.* But the beginning of a man's doom is that vision be withdrawn from him; that he see not the reality, but a false spectrum of the reality; and, following that, step darkly, with more or less velocity, downwards to the utter Dark; to Ruin, which is the great Sea of Darkness, whether all falsehoods, winding or direct, continually flow!

Such then is the History of the French Revolution, as seen and declared by Mr. Carlyle; for in similar strains he jogs on till he arrives at Bonaparte's war on the Sections of Paris, with which he concludes; summing up in the following vague, unsatisfactory, childish, "most lame and impotent conclusion"—

The ship is *over* the bar, then, free she bounds shoreward,—

amid shouting and vivats! Citoyen Buonaparte is "named General of the Interior, by acclamation;' quelled Sections have to disarm in such humour as they may; sacred right of Insurrection is gone for ever! The Sieyea Constitution can disembark itself, and begin marching. The miraculous Convention Ship has got to land:—and is there, shall we figuratively say, changed, as Epic Ships are wont, into a kind of *Sea Nymph,* never to sail more! to roam the waste Azure, a Miracle in History!

'It is false,' says Napoleon, 'that we fired first with blank charge; it had been a waste of life to do that.' Most false: the firing was with sharp and sharpest shot: to all men it is plain that here was no sport; the rabbets and plinths of Saint-Roch Church show splintered by it, to this hour—Singular: in old Broglie's time, six years ago, this Whiff of Grapeshot was promised; but it could not be given then; could not have profited then. Now; however the time is come for it, and the man: and behold, you have it; and the thing we specifically call *French Revolution* is blown into space by it, and become a thing that was!—

Homer's Epos, it is remarked, is like a Bas-relief sculpture: it does not conclude, but merely ceases. Such, indeed, is the Epos of Universal History itself. Directorates, Consulates, Emperorships, Restorations, Citizen-Kingships succeed this Business in due series, in due genesis one out of the other. Nevertheless the First-parent of all these may be said to have gone to air in the way we see. A Baboeuf Insurrection, next year, will die in the birth; stifled by the Soldiery. A Senate, if tinged with Royalism, can be purged by the Soldiery; and an Eighteenth of Fruetidor transacted by the mere shew of bayonets. Nay Soldiers' bayonets can be used *à posteriori* on a Senate, and make it leap out of window, still bloodless; and produce an Eighteenth of Brumaire. Such changes must happen: but they are managed by intriguings, caballings, and then by orderly word of command; almost like mere changes of Ministry. Not in general by sacred right of Insurrection, but by milder methods growing ever milder, shall the Events of French History be henceforth brought to pass.

It is admitted that this Directorate, which owned, at its starting, these three things, an 'old table, a sheet of paper, and an inkbottle,' and no visible money or arrangement whatever, did wonders: that France, since the Reign of Terror hushed itself, has been a new France, awakened like a giant out of torpor; and has gone on, in the Internal Life of it, with continual progress. As for the External form and forms of Life,—what can we say except that out of the Eater there comes Strength: out of the Unwise there comes *not* wisdom; Shams are burnt up; nay, what as yet is the peculiarity of France, the very Cant of them is burnt up. The new Realities are not yet come: ah no, only Phantasms, Paper models, tentative Prefigurements of such! In France there are now Four Million Landed Properties; that black portent of an Agrarian Law is as it were *realized!* What is still stranger, we understand all Frenchmen have 'the right of duel;' the Hackney-coachman with the Peer, if insult be given: such is the law of Public

Opinion. Equality at least in death! The Form of Government is by Citizen King, frequently shot at, not yet shot.

Readers, have we made out our case?

Frederick William Roe (essay date 1910)

SOURCE: "The English Essays," in *Thomas Carlyle as a Critic of Literature*, The Columbia University Press, 1910, pp. 114-38.

[*In the following essay, Roe discusses the only three essays Carlyle wrote on "English subjects," including Burns, Boswell's Life of Johnson, and Sir Walter Scott. Roe praises the critical method employed by Carlyle but acknowledges that in the case of the essay on Johnson, Carlyle assesses the man and his ideas rather than his literary influence.*]

Carlyle wrote but three essays on English subjects, **"Burns,"** **"Boswell's Life of Johnson"** and **"Sir Walter Scott."** He proposed to write others, notably one on Byron and another on "Fashionable Novels," but they never appeared, chiefly because Napier, the successor to Jeffrey as editor of the *Edinburgh Review,* to whom they were offered, was warned that Carlyle was a man to be feared as an intense radical and a hysterical worshipper of German divinities. The three essays, which therefore constitute his deliberate appreciation of English authors, cover a decade of time and roughly mark the end of three critical periods in Carlyle's literary fortunes. The essay on Burns was the first work executed at Craigenputtock, whither in 1828 he had moved from Edinburgh in order to toil and think and be beyond the reach of interruptions. His critical interest was now at its height, and he had entered the field of letters far enough to be recognized as a new force. But as we have said so often, reviewing in no long time gave way to prophesying; *Sartor* succeeded **"Signs of the Times,"** and **"Characteristics"** followed *Sartor.* Carlyle became restless to deliver his personal message to the world. His letters during this period show that he was considering great moral subjects,—Luther and the German reformation, John Knox and the Scottish reformation. Finally in 1831 he went up to London to try his fortunes with *Sartor,* but the publishers would not print it. Carlyle remained in the metropolis through the winter, a lonely crabbed mystic, sneering and sneered at, a man whose literary and material fortunes still hung in the balance. In the spring before returning to Craigenputtock, at the request of James Fraser, the publisher, he wrote a review of Boswell's *Life of Johnson.* This great essay, like the second one on Goethe written a few months later, may in one sense be regarded as the lyrical cry of a lonely prophet who felt that he must preach heroism to an unheroic, distracted age. After this essay was written there followed another period of struggle, uncertainty and ill-fortune. Carlyle became absorbed in a study of the French Revolution and

in 1834 he moved to London where he could get books to carry on his work. Amidst the harrowing labor of these years the voice of the critic became silent. But in 1837 when the *History* was completed, this voice was heard once more, not indeed passionate and melodious, as it had been a decade ago, but still strong and commanding, fit to win attention even from those who denied its authority. The essay on Sir Walter Scott, published in 1838, was the last of the critical essays, and with it the career of Carlyle the critic may be said to have come to a close.

Burns

Of all the essays from Carlyle's pen that on Burns is the best known and most admired. As Dr. Garnett so well said, it is the "very voice of Scotland." In Burns Carlyle found a subject that fired his heart, a native poet whose songs and whose tragical life alike stirred him to passionate sympathy. To his eyes the Ayrshire poet appeared not as a vulgar wonder to be stared at from the heights of literary Edinburgh, but as Scotland's most original genius and as one of the song-makers of the world. The affinities between Burns and Carlyle were numerous and special. Both were sons of Scottish peasants, both were poor, proud, independent, gifted and ambitious. Like Carlyle, Burns was born to wage war with a hostile environment, unlike him he was destined to be defeated because his will was not as Carlyle's, the will of a Titan. His tragical fate, together with his origin and environment, moved the critic to love and pity. Instead of the turbid stream of declamation that was sometimes poured into the later essays, there flows through this interpretation of Burns a tenderness almost feminine and a spirit of devotion almost sentimental. Even down to his closing years Carlyle would recite or hum over to himself the verses of Burns with the deep delight born of real community of spirit.

He makes no apology for giving up two-thirds of his essay to the life of Burns. "It is not chiefly as a poet," says Carlyle, "but as a man, that he interests us and affects us."[1] Here was a tragical career peculiarly alluring to the moralist, here was a gifted genius gone to ruin because he failed to reconcile the ideal with the actual, failed, that is, to put into practice the great Goethean doctrine of renunciation. Into his account of Burns's waverings between inner and outer conditions Carlyle has put the sum-total of his own ethical philosophy. He measures the "inward springs and relations" of Burns's character in terms of the high ideals he applies to all other men. Burns, he says, was born a true poet and therefore should have been a prophet and teacher to his age.[2] He should have fitted himself by rigorous discipline, by self-denying toil, to deliver his message to his generation. But a man born to be a *vates* or seer must live a whole life, he cannot be anything by halves. The grand error in Burns's life was "the want of unity in his purposes, of consistency in his aims." It was "a hapless attempt to mingle in friendly union the common spirit of the world with the spirit of poetry, which is of a far different and altogether irreconcilable nature. Burns was nothing wholly."[3]

In discussing the want of harmony between the clay soil of Mossgiel and the soul of Burns, Carlyle takes large account of circumstances, the poet's material condition and the influences of the period. He recognizes the pressure of the external fact in the form of poverty, lack of education, early temptations to depart from the right path. He thinks too that Burns's religious quarrels were a "circumstance of fatal import."[4] But of all the outer forces that helped to wreck the poet's life, Carlyle regards the visits to Edinburgh as strongest. These did him great and lasting injury and maddened his heart "still more with the fever of worldly ambition." Had the patrons of genius left Burns to himself "the wounds of the heart would have been healed, vulgar ambition would have died away." "These men, as we believe, were proximately the means of his ruin."[5] But it would have been contrary to Carlyle's philosophy of life to place the final blame elsewhere than upon Burns himself. "His was no bankruptcy of the purse," says the moralist, "but of the soul."[6] It lay in the power of the poet to have lived true to his higher self, to have listened to the voice of the poetic spirit within him, to have made all else save himself and his art a small matter.[7] For the reason that Burns did not live upon this high level, did not bend his soul to the work of revealing the divine idea, Carlyle pronounces his life a fragment.

The general truth of this concluding judgment may pass unchallenged. Burns's life was partial and incomplete. It is idle too to question Carlyle's opinion that the cause of failure lay ultimately with the poet himself. Those whose philosophy of life differs from that of Carlyle may place the blame upon a cruel environment, but, as our entire study has shown, his opinion follows necessarily from the ideals which he held. We may, however, point out that he does not treat the great critical period in Burns's life, the visits to Edinburgh, with strict justice. Cynicism and prejudice seem to have deflected his judgment. It was inevitable that Carlyle should seize upon this picturesque and dramatic episode and make much of it. It was equally inevitable, perhaps, with his hatred of "gigmanity," that he should add to his final opinion a special condemnation of the upper classes. We may admit at once that the poet's two visits to Edinburgh unsettled him for a time. He saw, as he had not seen before, the pitiless divisions between the upper and lower strata of society, and he learned for the first time that genius without habitual refinement is not a sure guarantee of social equality. But the subsequent tenor of Burns's life shows very plainly that his Edinburgh visits did not madden him with the fever of worldly ambition. The higher classes moreover did help him to answer the question what next to do. More than all else we must not overlook, as Carlyle appears to have done, the fact that Burns's ostracism from society at Edinburgh and later at Dumfries really came as the result of his own evil courses. The convivial poet, alternating between the tables of the high and the taverns of the low, and fast descending to the lowest, could not expect to retain the favor and social patronage of refined people. Such important phases of the ethical question at all events Carlyle does not seem to have treated quite candidly, or rather he is prone to give to the Edinburgh visits an active part in the tragedy of Burns's life, when at most it was seductively passive.

As with the life, so with the writings of Burns. His moral nature was at war with itself and therefore his work remains without the unity of a great idea—remains "a poor mutilated fraction of what was in him; brief, broken glimpses of a genius that could never show itself complete."[8] "We can look on but few of these pieces," says Carlyle, speaking of the poetry of Burns, "as, in strict critical language, deserving the name of Poems: they are rhymed eloquence, rhymed pathos, rhymed sense; yet seldom essentially melodious, aerial, poetical."[9] Burns therefore is "not perhaps absolutely a great poet"; he "never rose, except by natural effort and for short intervals into the region of great ideas."[10] Since the poet attained no mastery in his art, the critic thinks it would be "at once unprofitable and unfair" to try him, his imperfect fragments, by the "strict rules of Art."[11] In these opinions, however, the final judgment is implicit. Burns is not a great poet because he has no idea to reveal, because he speaks no word of authentic truth. But if not absolutely great, he is "a poet of Nature's own making,"[12] and "one of the most considerable British men of the eighteenth century."[13] His work has an enduring quality, a rare excellence that merits high appreciation. The source of its sustained vitality, Carlyle finds to be sincerity, graphic phrasal power, vigor and fineness of mind, as shown in the poet's love, indignation and humor. Nowhere else in the considerable mass of Burns criticism is there an interpretation so sympathetic, so illuminated with flashes of inspired comment as this which Carlyle has given us in a few short pages. The treatment is critical in the best sense. Carlyle's insight, knowledge and sympathy are nowhere used to better results, and he evidences an appreciation of the phrasal beauty and emotional value of poetry all too rare in his critical essays.

Perhaps the strongest proofs of his original capacity for criticism are the few paragraphs on *Tam O'Shanter, The Jolly Beggars* and the songs of Burns. Here criticism shows itself to be truly a creative art, as Carlyle said it was. *Tam O'Shanter,* he says, is "not so much a poem, as a piece of sparkling rhetoric." Its parts, its naturalism and supernaturalism, are not properly fused; it is not strictly comic, but farcical; it is not organically, but artificially, alive. Carlyle, we observe, is here applying his test of unity or central truth, with negative results; and to him therefore Burns's *Tam O'Shanter* lacks universal, symbolic significance; is not poetry but rhymed farce.[14] He measures *The Jolly Beggars* by the same standard. This poem rises "into the domain of Art," because it "seems thoroughly compacted; melted together, refined," because its characters are at once "Scottish, yet ideal," because it expresses a "universal sympathy with man." It has, in other words, inner and outer correspondence, a universal appeal, and is a self-supporting whole, "the highest merit in a poem." In these few passages we have a theory of art of Aristotelian breadth applied to concrete material with suggestive results.[15] The songs are considered "by far the best that Britain has yet produced." Carlyle ranks Burns as "the first of all of our Songwriters," and thinks that Burns's chief influence as an author will ultimately rest upon his songs. The second paragraph in this section is the very poetry of criticism, worthy to be classed with the appreciations of Charles Lamb at their best. Had Carlyle chosen to develop the vein that shows itself here, it should seem that he might have become one of England's two or three great critics.[16]

It is when we consider the treatment of the poet's relation to the literature of his own day that we must deduct something from our praise of Carlyle as a critic, especially in his use of the historical method. He touches lightly, though masterfully, upon the literary revival in Scotland and upon Burns's share in it. "In this brilliant resuscitation of our 'fervid genius,'" he says, "there was nothing Scottish, nothing indigenous." Culture was exclusively French and attenuated. But after Burns's day a spirit of nationalism sprang up, and literature became native, domestic, democratic. In this change Scott's influence is acknowledged, but the influence of Burns also, says Carlyle, "may have been considerable," for "his example, in the fearless adoption of domestic subjects, could not but operate from afar." Historical criticism in so far is sound. But Carlyle makes a mistake in regarding the work of Burns as the beginning of a new movement rather than as the culmination of an old. His casual and depreciating notices of Ramsay and Ferguson, the predecessors of Burns, and his apologetic reference to the Scottish dialect, together with various remarks on Burns's lack of proper education, indicate that he did not correctly appreciate the relation of the poet to the vernacular school of poetry. Had Burns written exclusively in English, following the models and literary influences of that day, he would now belong to the school of Shenstone, Thomson and Pope; for his English poetry is admitted on nearly all sides to be his weakest—stiff, imitative, Augustan. The true way is to interpret the poetry of Burns as the flowering of a spirit transmitted through Ferguson and Ramsay from the older Scottish Makers. Burns was greatly indebted to this vernacular literature, for language, meters, subjects, even for ideas, phrases and entire verses. What now seems fulsome praise of Ramsay and Ferguson in the preface to the Kilmarnock Edition of his poems, was a sincere, if grandiloquent, tribute to the lesser poets who kindled his own purer flame.[17] The truth is, Carlyle gives little hint of Burns the craftsman, a subject that would compel consideration of the poet's predecessors in vernacular song, of his ways of handling that older literature, and of his magical power of creating an immortal song from some rude, popular jingle. Burns was an uneven and often a slovenly craftsman, but at his best he was a deliberate and consummate artist, sifting his material with anxious care and fashioning it to suit his high technical demands. Carlyle's essay, therefore, while great as an interpretation of the life of the poet and of the substance of his poetry, must be supplemented by the work[18] of later scholars and critics, if Burns is to receive his full measure of justice.

Boswell and Johnson

In the second English essay, **"Boswell's Life of Johnson,"** Carlyle is both critic and prophet. The changed style and thought proclaim the prophet. Peculiarities of language which found full expression for the first time in *Sartor* appear in this essay in considerable profusion. Hero-worship, the prophet's special message, is thrust forward in two or three expressions and in connection with the main subject itself. Johnson and his biographer, Boswell, are indeed cogent illustrations of a doctrine increasing in favor with Carlyle; for in them he found both hero and hero-worshipper, each by a kind of divine attraction, drawn to the other for the edification of succeeding generations. From this point of view, moreover, it is difficult to avoid regarding the entire essay as a tract for the times. In 1832 reform agitation was at its height. The conditions of English life, political and social, were alarming to many minds. The tide of innovation was strong and men feared that the old landmarks were in danger of being swept away. Carlyle, then in London, watched the current of affairs with eager interest, in fact with apprehension; for reform never meant to him, what it did to the utilitarians, a change in external conditions merely. Unless reform reached the individual and lifted him to a better life, Carlyle distrusted and condemned it, he even feared it. The only way the individual can be bettered, he said, is by contact with another greater individual; soul is kindled only by soul. His remedy for the distracted times of 1832, therefore, was the gospel of hero-worship.

But the prophet does not quite usurp the place of the critic. No other essay displays deeper discernment or more thorough knowledge of subject than this, and it is only below the first **"Goethe"** and the **"Burns"** in sympathy. In epithet and phrase, from the first page to the last, there are flashes of keenest insight. Illuminating suggestions on literature and life are strewn lavishly along the way. We find Carlyle, moreover, measuring Boswell and Johnson, the men and their work, by precisely the same standards which he applied in earlier essays to Richter and to Goethe. The critical method remains unchanged, because the principles upon which it was established are in 1832 what they were in 1828.

A telling proof of the sustained vitality of Carlyle's critical powers is his treatment of Boswell. To say aught in

1832 in defense of Johnson's biographer was to fly in the face of all literary opinion. From 1768 when Gray, commenting on Boswell's first literary venture, the book on Corsica, said that "any fool may write a most valuable book if he will only tell what he heard and saw with veracity,"[19] down to 1831 when Macaulay in the *Edinburgh Review* launched his notorious paradox that Boswell would never have been a great writer if he had not been a great fool, Boswell had been the object of unmeasured ridicule. His only title to public recognition seems to have been his many-sided folly. Carlyle clearly saw the position which Boswell occupied before the British public, but he refused to believe that a great biography had been written by a fool, or that good work could be done by reason of weaknesses or vices. His entire theory of life and of literature was against such a false paradox. He did not shut his eyes to Boswell's follies and foibles, he saw them with a keener vision than did Macaulay, and his portrait of the exterior Bozzy ranks as a masterpiece in a gallery of great paintings. But to laugh at a man's fantastic freaks and to catalogue them is not the same as to interpret the man. Macaulay's Boswell was not for Carlyle the biographer of Johnson. In the place of a false paradox he supplied a true one. Here he said is a man who "has provided us a greater *pleasure* than any other individual . . . ; perhaps has done us a great *service* and can be especially attributed to more than two or three; . . . yet no written or spoken eulogy of James Boswell anywhere exists." This situation existed because critics had seen the visible vices of Boswell, but had no insight into his hidden virtues. Boswell is correctly understood, says Carlyle, only when we think of him as a disciple, a hero-worshipper. He had in him a "love of excellence" invisible to the general eye. In an unspiritual eighteenth century when "Reverence for Wisdom" had well-nigh vanished from the earth, Boswell was raised up to be "a real martyr to this high everlasting truth" that "Hero-worship lives perennially in the human bosom." True to his biographical method, Carlyle finds in this interpretation a key to the greatness of Boswell's work. "Boswell wrote a good Book because he had a heart and an eye to discern Wisdom, and an utterance to render it forth; because of his free insight, his lively talent, above all, of his Love and childlike Openmindedness. None but a *reverent* man could have found his way from Boswell's environment to Johnson's." The critic mentions insight and talent as a part of the biographer's equipment, but he lays stress upon certain *unconscious* powers, like reverence and love, as the greater part. Carlyle indeed finds in Boswell a capital illustration of his theory of art as an unconscious process. "We do the man's intellectual endowment great wrong," he says, "if we measure it by its mere logical outcome; though here too, there is not wanting a light ingenuity, a figurativeness and fanciful sport, with glimpses of insight far deeper than the common. But Boswell's grand intellectual talent was, as such ever is, an *unconscious* one." He is, therefore, "one of Nature's own Artists," and his book is great because of its "import of *Reality*," because it is "wholly *credible*." Upon these terms Carlyle's

praise of the *Life* becomes poetical, one of the sunny spots of interpretation that proves the illuminating presence of the critic. His final judgment is expressed in a sentence: "In worth as a Book we have rated it beyond any other product of the eighteenth century: all Johnson's Writings stand on a quite inferior level to it."[20]

This interpretation of Boswell is one of the highest services that the criticism of Carlyle has done for English literature. Because of it, England's greatest biographer has been lifted from a place of ridicule and contempt to one in which his real greatness is recognized. Since 1832, critical opinion has not only regarded the *Life of Johnson* as the first of biographies, but it has more and more come to understand that Boswell himself is one of England's truest literary artists who knew perfectly well the richness of his material and who knew how to shape it in obedience to the aim of a supremely self-conscious purpose. But if Carlyle's portrait, brilliant as it is, had remained untouched by later criticism, we should to-day fail to understand the real Boswell. The fact is, Carlyle attempts to strain his theory of Hero-Worship farther than it will go. When he says, for example, that it was reverence for wisdom which drew Boswell to Johnson, he has to place both Boswell and Johnson in a somewhat false position in order to support his claim. He seems to forget that when Tom Davies introduced them in 1763 Johnson was not so much "a poor rusty coated scholar," as the foremost literary figure in England. All of Johnson's important work, except the *Shakespeare* and the *Lives,* was done; he had received a pension the previous year for literary merit alone, and he was to establish the famous "Club" a year later. With all his peculiarities, Johnson was a man to know. Now Boswell, beyond most men of his time or of any other, had "a rage for literature," as Hume called it; or, to use the phrase of Horace Walpole, he had "a rage of knowing anybody that was ever talked of." He deliberately sought out literary celebrities. He visited Voltaire at Ferney, Rousseau at Mortier, and in London he was never vainer than when dining with Reynolds, Garrick, Goldsmith, Beauclerk or Hume. To be with the great Cham himself, greatest of them all, was Boswell's highest felicity; then it was that the satellite shone most brightly. So far from having all to lose in seeking out Johnson, as Carlyle implies, Boswell had everything to gain. Nor does Carlyle's explanation of Boswell's art tell the whole truth. Hero-worship and Carlyle's general theory of art, as, in the deepest sense, an unconscious process, led him to keep out of sight the skilled and untiring craftsmanship that went to the making of the *Life.* Of course, in the deepest sense the art of Boswell, like that of any other craftsman, was unconscious; for he could not have explained, nor can we explain, why the gift of biography came to him and not, let us say, to Hawkins. Love and reverence for Johnson were also an indispensable part of Boswell's equipment. But unless he had cultivated these gifts, as we know he did, with the greatest patience and in obedience to the most deliberately determined ideals, he would not have produced a masterpiece which the reading world has never ceased to praise. The *Life* of itself proclaims the craftsmanship of Boswell in every chapter. But we know from numerous external sources how he labored for seven years, collecting materials, sifting, selecting, quizzing this person and that, ceaselessly searching for the least bit of information that would add to the completeness and lifelikeness of his portrait. If we think of these efforts, we may find it difficult to believe that Boswell's love and reverence, unsupported by a hundred follies and foibles and all manner of disgusting assiduities, would ever have been equal to the great and prolonged task which he set himself to do. The true interpretation of Boswell is best reached, perhaps, by a compromise between Macauley and Carlyle. It was by reason of his follies as well as his virtues—if one keeps to these terms—that Boswell realized his artistic ideals. He was neither the unqualified fool of Macaulay's portrait, nor the martyr-hero of Carlyle's; he was something of both, it is true, but he was also a craftsman of the first rank, working by conscious processes, toward self-appointed ends.

But whatever be the true interpretation of the processes by which Boswell achieved his art, there can be no two opinions of its accomplishment. For Carlyle at any rate the case was clear; he found Boswell's work good because it revealed to him a personality which aroused his deepest interest and sympathy. We have already implied in the previous section of this chapter that the unique and profound relationship between Carlyle and Burns was spiritual; and now at the risk of confusing language we wish to point out that the remarkable sympathy between Carlyle and Johnson was largely intellectual. Affinity with Burns moreover was partly a matter of pity; it was the feeling of the strong man toward the weak. Affinity with Johnson was wholly due to the liking of one strong man for another. The mind of Carlyle indeed touches that of Johnson at so many points that at times it is hard to avoid fancying that a great spirit of the eighteenth century became reincarnated in the nineteenth. Johnson, like Carlyle, was a stoic, a hater of cant and sham, a man who renounced happiness as his rule of life. Both were passionately interested in human nature, delighting in biography and believing in the power of a really great man to turn his abilities to any account. In political principles as in ethical, the two men were singularly alike. To Johnson the doctrine of political equality was mere moonshine. He despised the teachings of Rousseau and he regarded agitators of the Wilkes type with contempt. He cherished a superior disregard of the people and (to use the words of Mrs. Piozzi) he expressed "a zeal for insubordination warm even to bigotry." While these political opinions would apply more obviously to the Carlyle of 1850 than to the Carlyle of 1832, they are in reality true of him at any period of his manhood, for he was ever as full of "intuitive aversions" as was Johnson. We might extend the parallel into the less tangible realm of temperament, for each life was overshadowed with

melancholy or lighted at intervals with flashes of saturnine and ironic humor, and in each there dwelt a religious seriousness toward every human interest. Both Johnson and Carlyle were "characters" in their time, bold, independent, dominating, original; and both will live for future generations as men rather than as writers. In all or in nearly all of Carlyle's writing there is the "deep lyric tone" which he confesses to find in Johnson the man. It is because of this manifold and intimate sympathy that Carlyle, after Boswell, is the most inspired interpreter of Johnson. His essay, though not so well balanced as some earlier ones, deserves the praise of Edward Fitzgerald, who thought that it judged Johnson "for good and all."

The interpretation of Johnson rests upon essentially the same ideals of biography as those set forth in the essay on Burns. It is not the outer but the inner Johnson that is presented; not the eccentric, deformed giant of Macaulay's pages, but the "best intellect in England," a man belonging to the "keener order of intellects" such as Hume and Voltaire, a man "not ranking among the highest, or even the high, yet distinctly admitted into that sacred band." That is to say, Johnson is a priest and prophet whose life Carlyle frankly holds up as an answer to the question how to live, as the text to a sermon on hero-worship. The heroic aspects of Johnson's life are therefore brought forward and exhibited in the most favorable light, while the essentially literary sides are left somewhat obscured. Carlyle sings a kind of paean over the early struggles of Johnson, and from the facts concerning Johnson's first days in London he selects material for some of his strongest paragraphs.

As Carlyle saw it, the life problem of Johnson was two-fold, how to live and how to live by speaking only the truth. The problem was made doubly difficult, because the age was transitional in literature, in politics, in religion; and because Johnson himself possessed a contradictory temperament. "It is not the least curious of the incoherences which Johnson had to reconcile," says Carlyle "that though by nature contemptuous and incredulous he was, at that time of day, to find his safety and glory in defending with his whole might the traditions of the elders." But Johnson kept a straight path through these tangled times, because he had "a knowledge of the transcendental, immeasureable character of Duty, the essence of all Religion." This is his great glory, this is the central fact of his life beside which all others are secondary and circumstantial. In thus placing Johnson the moralist high above Johnson the man of letters, Carlyle exalts the hero at the expense of the man. He scarcely more than glances at the interesting figure who gathered the wits about him at the "Club" and who was celebrated as the first talker of London, the perennially delightful personality whom the world knows to-day through the pages of Boswell.

We may infer from Carlyle's slight notice of Johnson as a man of letters that his interest in Johnson's writings is likewise slight. Such is indeed the ease. Intent upon interpreting Johnson as a moralist, the critic cares only for the spirit which shows through the *Ramblers,* the *Idlers* and the *Lives.* This spirit he finds to be an expression of Johnson's moral nature. Johnson "by act and word" was a Tory, "the preserver and transmitter of whatsoever was genuine in the spirit of Toryism." The motive of his life was duty, or truth in the transcendental sense; the work of his life was Toryism.[21] In a time of change, when even the foundations of society were in danger of being swept away, Johnson served England by resisting the rising tide of innovation. The moral endowment by which he effected this work was mainly courage, a belief in the "everlasting Truth, that man is ever a Revelation of God to man," and, lastly, mercy and affection. Johnson's affection, Carlyle points out, manifested itself both as courtesy and as prejudice. Prejudice, again, was the virtue by which Johnson accomplished his mission—the mission of serving as the "John Bull of spiritual Europe."

Sound and solid for the most part as is this appreciation, it suffers not a little from Carlyle's determination to see in Johnson only the hero. It is because prejudice was so colossal in Johnson and because he set himself in wilful and violent opposition to nearly every tendency of enlightenment of his times, that most critics cannot place him as high as Carlyle has done; for we are to remember that Johnson was a tory, not alone in politics, but in religion and literature. He was not, moreover, a greater influence than Burke in checking the revolutionary spirit in England. Johnson died four years before the fall of the Bastile, having shown scarcely more than a churlish indifference to France, while Boswell, at work on the biography from 1784 to 1791, has no word concerning the social and political convulsion across the Channel.[22] But we should remember that Carlyle himself was at all times prejudiced against political agitators and was not likely to distinguish beween a Burke and a Wilkes. We should remember also that this interpretation of Johnson was written for readers of 1832 by a man who, though a radical in the philosophical, literary and religious sense, was on precisely the same fundamental principles a determined reactionary in politics and political economy. It was inevitable therefore that he should lift up the heroic figure of Johnson as an example to the men who were drifting through the distracted days of 1832-3.

Of literary criticism in the restricted sense the essay has little more than a suggestion, though the suggestion indicates clearly enough how Carlyle regarded and ranked Johnson's work. "To Johnson's Writings, good and solid, and still profitable as they are, we have already rated his Life and Conversation as superior." "His Doings and Writings are not *Shows* but *Performances.* Not a line, not a sentence is dishonestly done, is other than it pretends to be." Measured by Carlyle's standard Johnson is not a poet. "Into the region of Poetic Art he indeed never rose; there was no *ideal* without him avowing itself in his work." He could not reveal through his writings, as true poets can through theirs, the Divine

Idea. Johnson was a prophet because his character was a medium for transcendental duty; but he was neither a seer nor a poet because his intellect could not transmit truth. From such judgment there is nothing to deduct. Critical opinion from the time of Burke and Coleridge does not differ essentially from Carlyle's as to the value of Johnson's writings. Even the late Dr. Birbeck Hill has declared that Johnson lives not in his writings but in his talk.[23] Carlyle's sin in his interpretation of Johnson the writer is one of omission. He has failed to take account of Johnson as a literary influence, just as he failed to consider, except in a few sentences, Johnson as a man of letters. And it was in the literary sense, of course, not in the political, that Johnson was the dictator of the British public. We must go to other interpreters and critics, therefore, for an account of Johnson's place in literature from Pope to Wordsworth, even as we must turn to Boswell if we wish to know Johnson as a literary personality. But if we are content to know him as a moralist, as a great ethical force in the total English life of the eighteenth century, we shall find that Carlyle is Johnson's truest interpreter.

Scott

The essay on Sir Walter Scott has increased the number of Carlyle's enemies and apologists. His enemies, or rather those who dislike the man and distrust his criticism, refer to this essay as a spiteful attack of one Scotchman upon his more favored and famous countryman. Mr. Lang, Scott's most recent biographer, asserts that Carlyle was embittered against Scott "on a matter of an unanswered letter."[24] On the other hand Froude apologizes for Carlyle's unsympathetic tone on the ground that he was not yet recovered from the exhaustive labors on the *French Revolution.*[25] So much has been said at one time or another in way of censure or extenuation that we are justified in the present study in briefly reviewing the facts regarding the genesis of the essay and the relations of Carlyle with Scott.

Carlyle was teaching mathematics at Annan Academy when Scott's novels began to appear. He declared that *Waverley* was the best novel that had been published "these thirty years,"[26] and he read many others with youthful pleasure and admiration. His attitude toward them, however, was not at all different from that toward nearly everything he read at this time. But during the next five or six years a great change took place. Carlyle's intellectual life was expanded and deepened by hard struggle with fortune and by a study of Goethe. In his crystallizing philosophy of life there was little or no place for minor poetry and fiction. It is perfectly consistent with this new turn, that Carlyle should make the following entry in his note-book:

> Sir Walter Scott is the great *Restaurateur* of Europe: he might have been numbered among their Conscript Fathers; he has chosen the worser part, and is only a huge Publicanus. What is his novel, any of them? A

bout of champagne, claret, port or even ale drinking. Are we wiser, better, holier, stronger? No! We *have been* amused. O Sir Walter, thou knowest too well, that *Virtus laudatur et alget.*

A few months later occurs this entry:

Not one of Scott's Fairservices or Deanses, etc., is *alive.* As far as prose could go, he has gone; and we have fair *outsides;* but within all is hollow.[27]

These private opinions were written down many months before there was a word of correspondence with Goethe concerning medals, and ten years before the essay was composed, and yet they might serve as texts for nearly everything that Carlyle ever said against the life and work of Scott.[28]

With this attitude of Carlyle's before us, let us turn to the unlucky episode of the unanswered letter. Goethe had long been an admirer of the author of *Waverley.* In testimony of his esteem he sent in 1828 two medals to Carlyle to be delivered to Scott. It was very natural for the German poet to suppose that the two Scotchmen were acquainted, though he had indeed expressed surprise to Eckermann that Scott had had nothing to say of Carlyle. Obviously Carlyle was flattered to be chosen the messenger between the most famous writer of Germany and the most famous writer of Great Britain, and he wrote Goethe that he expected to present the medals to Sir Walter in person.[29] Unhappily the meeting never took place, for Scott was in London at the time.[30] Carlyle was disappointed not to see Scott and probably piqued not to hear from him. But was he so resentful and even so embittered as to allow his private feelings to condition his published criticism of Scott ten years later? Partisan friends of Sir Walter will probably continue to say that he was, even if they have to disregard the early note-book comments which we have quoted. They will continue to assert that Carlyle vented a "private bitterness," to use Mr. Lang's phrase, though to do so they will have to overlook entirely the complete conformity of the individual judgments in the essay to Carlyle's theory of literature and philosophy of life. On the other hand those who know Carlyle's habits of thought from 1827 to 1837, and have examined the literary relations of Scott and Carlyle during these years will always find it hard to believe that the essay contains a critical opinion that it would not have contained had there been no incident of an unanswered letter. Carlyle's central position toward Scott did not change after the incident, as certain privately expressed opinions fully show.[31] What he believed in 1827 he believed and expressed in 1837. If Carlyle's essay is to be interpreted fairly, therefore, we should regard it not as a piece of work inspired by resentment or jealousy, but as a deliberate criticism based upon ideals consistently held and consistently applied to literature for a period of ten years or more. In structure the essay is not so regular as many others,

but in the main it shows an application of the biographical method to the interpretation of Scott's life and work. Carlyle, however, raises the question of Scott's greatness before he comes to systematic criticism. His answer furnishes us with a key to his whole position. Popularity, even the select popularity of Scott, he says, is no measure of greatness. The standard is quite other than that: it is spiritual power and the genius to reveal an idea that makes a man great. Scott is unspiritual because he has no deep passion and expresses no ideas. On the other hand he is "one of the healthiest of men." In a sick and artificial age this robust borderer was appointed by destiny "to be the song-singer and pleasant tale-teller to Britain and Europe. This is the history of the life and achievement of *our* Sir Walter Scott."[32] Carlyle's formula thus becomes clear at the start. Scott is not great, because he does not reveal the "Divine Idea" either in life or in work. He is, however, healthy in nearly all of his relations, and healthiness is the word by which his life and work are properly appreciated.[33]

Subsequent judgments are made on the basis of this preliminary estimate. Carlyle passes in rapid review the earlier periods of Scott's life, giving an undue prominence perhaps to certain "questionable doings" connected with the "Liddesdale *raids.*" He regards the portentous Ballantyne connection as natural in a worldly man like Scott. He criticises Scott's poetry in a desultory manner and seems to consider it as an incident in the author's career and an explanation of this worldly success rather than as literature which merits serious appreciation. At all events, though he does not deny real worth of a kind in the metrical romances, Carlyle explains their immense vogue more on external than on internal grounds. His interest reaches its highest point when he discusses the culminating period of Scott's life, the period of the Waverley Novels. This was the critical time in the career of Scott, when it was to be seen whether he was guided by inner ideals or external considerations. Carlyle's judgment of Scott's character at this point is significant. Though he pronounces the picture presented in the copious extracts from Lockhart's *Life* to be "very beautiful," he unequivocally asserts that Scott, at this period, "with all his health, was *infected.*" Scott wrote impromptu novels to buy farms with and his tragedy was due not to bankruptcy, but to false ambition. "His way of life," says Carlyle, "was not wise." Thus as in the case of Burns, the critic pierces to the soul of Scott and interprets his failure solely upon spiritual grounds. This searching judgment of course carries with it the corollary that the Waverley Novels were in large measure the product of a commercialized mind.

It was inevitable that this appreciation of the life and work of Scott should have aroused the anger of those who honored him as one of the most lovable and manly of men and as the most delightful story-teller of their day. But Carlyle's judgment is the expression of higher standards than the average critic is wont to apply to life and literature. He measured Scott in 1837 by exactly the same standards which he had applied to Richter in 1827 and to Johnson in 1832. However manly or delightful Scott was he was not great or noble because he did not dedicate his character and his art to the expression of truth. In saying or implying this opinion, Carlyle of course does not mean to suggest, as some seem to have supposed, that truth is a barren formula or thesis, or that it is synonymous with the Thirty-nine Articles. We have gone with him too far to suspect him of such shallow thinking. He hated the doctrinaire even more heartily than do some of his unfriendly critics. But he never departed from his belief that the life of a truly great man, whether poet or prophet, must be felt to be under the direction of some central purpose or idea, through which it becomes related to the vast invisible potentialities of the universe. Whether you call this inner force an idea, or a message, it is something which the great man will ever strive to utter and for the sake of which he is willing to sacrifice all else in life.

Scott was not born for this kind of greatness. His mind was not spiritual in this lofty sense. It was not even intellectual, if by intellectuality we mean a passionate interest in abstract truth or in the deeper things of character and art, such as Browning had, for example. To Scott the world was not the vesture of an idea, as it was to Carlyle. Dreamer though he was, his dreams were always of a romantic, never of a mystical world. He was a mediævalist through and through, but he delighted in the mediævalism of Ariosto, not of Dante. He was also an unaffected man of the world. "I have been no sigher in the Shades," he said. "I love the virtues of rough-and-round men." He was human on every side, his nature was patriotic, paternal, social. What philosophy he pretended to have, he exercised in managing his everyday life. Carlyle is not indeed indifferent to these splendid qualities in Sir Walter. He praises the good sense and sanity, the manliness, bravery and genial humanity of Scott, in passages of great beauty and power. But running through this golden character he saw a streak of baser metal, which in his opinion lowered its worth. He could no more approve of the building of Abbotsford than he could approve of the ethics of Bentham or the political principles of the American people. Scott and Carlyle as men lived in different worlds and according to different standards.

In art as well as in life their realms were widely sundered. Scott's literary ideals, as expressed in his own writings and in Lockhart's *Life,* are well known. He wrote to amuse, not to edify or to convey transcendental truth. He would not have understood, or if he had understood he would not have taken seriously, the Fichtean notion of the man of letters as a revealer of the "Divine Idea." He had no illusions concerning his position as a writer. Like Molière he felt that his art served its ends if it brought applause from his audience. He considered literature a profession, not a martyrdom. He regarded his ability to write books very much as a man to-day regards his business ability, as a means with which he may make a success of life both financially and socially. Authorship as a calling to which one solemnly dedicates himself was farthest from Scott's thought; that, as he said, was for the Shakespeares and the Molières, but not for him. With these ideals, accompanied with such gifts as he had, Scott was for Carlyle a minor writer, not an artist of the first rank. And for minor writers the criticism of Carlyle has virtually no place, because they do not add new meanings to our conception of life. While Carlyle's interpretation of Scott reaches therefore negative conclusions and is expressed, we must own, in a spirit sometimes needlessly harsh, it is as a whole entirely in harmony with his literary and critical doctrine.

The individual opinions or estimates which follow upon Carlyle's general judgment are nearly all adverse, and some of them are so unbalanced as to indicate that his want of sympathy with the literature of amusement and with the kind of life that Scott lived got the better of his judgment. When, for example, he lumps Scott's characters together and says that they are created "from the skin inwards," he sees no difference between the conventional heroes and heroines of the Waverley Novels and the genuine, if not heroic, figures drawn from humble life. When, again, he says that these novels are melodramatic and mechanically constructed, he lays the blame partly upon Scott's habits of extempore composition, without giving him any recognition for the labor of those early years when Scott was filling his mind with an inexhaustible store of material for his books. The truth is that Carlyle is too ready to explain not only Scott's shortcomings as a man but his limitations as a literary artist upon the ground of his worldly ambitions as shown conspicuously in the building at Abbotsford. The critic gives way to the moralist, for in this instance he fails properly and fairly to correlate Scott's mind and temperament with his work, or carefully to consider Scott's whole view of literary craftsmanship. Undoubtedly Scott's financial affairs and worldly ambitions influenced his work in literature. But considering his habitual attitude toward his art, before and after Abbotsford was built, it is safer to say that his work would not have been essentially different had there been no decorating of walls and no collecting of old armor.

But Carlyle's waning interest in literature considered apart from ideas is responsible for many gaps in his appreciation of Scott. Scott's greatness as a story-teller, his amazing fertility in invention, his skill as a scene-painter are passed over. So, too, are his place and influence in the history of English literature. Carlyle does indeed refer lightly to Scott's relation to the "buff-belted watch-tower period of literature." But this is quite inadequate in the case of a far-extending influence like Scott's. The essay therefore in spite of numerous flashes of inspired opinion and many brilliant word-pictures is never likely to satisfy the reading world as an interpretation of Scott. As an analysis of the man it over-emphasizes his worldliness and in consequence fails to bring into proper relief the really great moral qualities of his character. As a critique of the author it fails even more decidedly because it is so largely incomplete and negative and because it explains Scott's defects as a writer too largely in terms of his moral weakness in building Abbotsford. But as a Carlyle document the essay is invaluable and it is likely to live as long as an interest in Carlyle endures. It is on all sides an exact expression of the man. In the study of Carlyle as critic it is of peculiar importance, for it is the best illustration we have of the application of his ideas of life, literature and criticism to a distinguished writer whose works he regarded as of minor value, fit only to amuse the indolent or languid mind.

Notes

[1] *Essays,* II, 6; cf. 29.

[2] *Ibid.,* 46.

[3] *Ibid.,* 47.

[4] *Ibid.,* 33.

[5] *Ibid.,* 37-40.

[6] *Ibid.,* 39.

[7] *Ibid.,* 46, 49, 51.

[8] *Ibid.,* 8.

[9] *Ibid.,* 23.

[10] *Ibid.,* 13, 18.

[11] *Ibid.,* 5, 8.

[12] *Ibid.,* 13.

[13] *Ibid.,* 4.

[14] Considering the time of its deliverance, this criticism shows Carlyle's independence of judgment perhaps better than any other that we can point to. All the critics before him, Jeffrey, Scott, Lockhart, Hazlitt, Byron, Wordsworth, regarded *Tam* as Burns's masterpiece. So did Burns. (Wallace, *Life,* III, 254.)

[15] *The Jolly Beggars* was not much noticed by the early critics. It was not indeed published in complete form till 1802. Scott praises it highly. Matthew Arnold with Carlyle ranks it higher than *Tam O'Shanter.*

[16] In relating this bit of criticism of the songs to Carlyle's general theories, we should not forget that to him a song belongs after all to the outlying province of poetry, is "a brief simple species of composition" (*Ibid.,* 23-26). "Had

Carlyle been able to take the modern point of view of the student of *genres* and if he had considered the power of the lyric in all ages to go, as scarcely any other form of art does, straight to the heart of man, and then had noted that Burns had gone to the heart of Scotland and indeed of the world, he might have had doubts with regard to his denial of Burns's greatness as a poet" (comment made upon my manuscript).

[17] Though Carlyle speaks in an apologizing tone of the Scotch dialect, all the songs and poems that he cites, except two, are from the Scotch.

[18] *E. g.,* the *Centenary Edition* of Burns by Henley and Henderson.

[19] Gray, *Works,* III, 310.

[20] *Essays,* IV, 73-83.

[21] It should be understood that though he preaches duty and truth, Carlyle does not unconditionally preach the "Doctrine of Standing-Still." He does not glorify stagnation either in the individual or in the state. He says that "Johnson's aim was in itself an impossible one; this of stemming the eternal Flood of time. The strongest man can but retard the current partially and for a short hour."

[22] Johnson's indirect influence must have been strong and far-reaching, making itself felt through literature and conversation to the remotest parts of Great Britain.

[23] *Dr. Johnson, His Friends and his Critics,* 129.

[24] *Life of Scott,* 129.

[25] Froude, *Life,* III, 103.

[26] *Early Letters,* 10.

[27] *Two Note-Books,* 71, 126, years 1826 and 1827.

[28] In 1827 Jeffrey offered to introduce Carlyle to Scott, if Carlyle would present himself at the court room. Carlyle declined, but he wrote his brother, apropos of this incident, that Scott was no "mongrel," but a sufficient "hodman." *Letters,* 23, 67.

[29] *Goethe and Carlyle Corr.,* 83.

[30] "Walter Scott, I did not see, because he was in London; nor hear of, perhaps because he was a busy or uncourteous man; so I left his Goethe-medals to be be given him by Jeffrey" (*Letters,* 115). In correction of Norton's note to this passage it may be said that Carlyle must have known of Scott's financial troubles (*Early Letters,* 344). It was unfortunate that Carlyle never met Scott. He had more than one opportunity and he might have been won

by Scott's personality. A regard for the man might have softened Carlyle's tone in the essay. But I do not believe that friendly relations would have caused Carlyle to alter opinions growing out of fundamental beliefs. Such relations did not alter them in the case of John Sterling.

[31] *Two Note-Books,* 214-215; Froude, *Life,* II, 251.

[32] *Essays,* VI, 38.

[33] To show how repeatedly these standards are applied to man and author, I subjoin two groups of passages. (1) *Want of ideas, want of spirituality;* (*a*) "Friends to precision will probably deny his title to the name 'great.' One knows not what idea worthy of the name of great, what purpose, instinct or tendency, that could be called great, Scott was ever inspired with." (*b*) "The great Mystery of Existence was not great to him." (*c*) "A great man is ever, as the Transcendentalists speak, possessed with an *idea.*" (*d*) "Perhaps no literary man of any generation has less value than Scott for the immaterial part of his mission in any sense." (*e*) "Our highest literary man . . . had, as it were, no message whatever to deliver to the world." (*f*) "The candid judge will, in general, require that a speaker, in so extremely serious a universe as this of ours, have something to speak about." (*g*) Scott's letters "do not, in any case whatever, proceed from the innermost parts of the mind," . . . "the man of the world is always visible in them." (*h*) The *Waverley Novels* "are altogether addressed to the everyday mind; for any other mind there is next to no nourishment in them;" "not profitable for doctrine, for reproof, for edification, for building up or elevating in any shape;" "they do not form themselves on deep interests, but on comparatively trivial ones." (2) *Healthiness;* (*a*) Not a great man but "the healthiest of men." (*b*) "Were one to preach a sermon on Health, Scott ought to be the text." (*c*) The happiest circumstance of all is, that Scott had in himself a right healthy soul." (*d*) "Scott's healthiness showed itself decisively in all things, and nowhere more decisively than in this: the way in which he took his fame." (*e*) "If no skyborn messenger—a substantial, peaceable, terrestrial man." (*f*) "Letters they are of a most humane man of the world." (*g*) "Scott's rapidity is great, is a proof and consequence of the solid health of the man, bodily and spiritual." (*h*) " . . . in general *healthiness* of mind, these Novels prove Scott to have been amongst the foremost of writers." In connection with so many praises of Scott's health this passage should not be forgotten: "Alas, Scott with all his health, was *infected.*"

Stanley T. Williams (essay date 1922)

SOURCE: "Carlyle's Past and Present: A Prophecy," in *The South Atlantic Quarterly,* Vol. XXI, No. 1, January, 1922, pp. 30-40.

[*In the following essay, Williams analyzes Carlyle's* Past and Present, *arguing that it provides "a piercing glance into the feudal age," an "acute critique upon contemporary England," and a glimpse into the future in which Carlyle foresees the rise of the Labor Party.*]

One day when Mr. Arthur Henderson was stating in no uncertain terms what would be acceptable to the British Labor Party, a member of the audience was moved to quote to his neighbor a sentence from Carlyle's *Past and Present:* "Some 'Chivalry of Labour,' some noble humanity and practical divineness of labor, will yet be realized on this earth." Recent strikes, then, had made the Labor Party "chivalrous," if not "divine;" the speaker's tone was that of complacence, of realized prophecy. "Chivalrous" and "divine" are not the adjectives applied by all men to the Labor Party; but every faction would admit one other epithet, that of *powerful.* Every history of industrialism, of socialism, or merely of political history indicates the growth of the Labor Party; its progress since 1843, the date of the appearance of *Past and Present,* has been almost incalculable. Curiously enough Carlyle's book ends with a section called *Horoscope,* a somewhat incoherent and passionate effort to read the future of labor in the light of the past and his own present-day England. *Past and Present* deals as much with the unknown future as with the known past. Carlyle dogmatizes on the twelfth century, but he speculates concerning the twentieth.

Horoscope is a protracted oracle. Carlyle was oppressed by the industrial tyranny of the forties; and he prophesied the eventual emancipation of the workingman. Nebulous, repetitive, and rhapsodical in style, even as the ancient Delphic oracles, *Horoscope* has, nevertheless, "blest islets of the intelligible" which are pertinent today. For example, "an actual * * * industrial aristocracy, real not imaginary aristocracy, is indispensable and indubitable for us;" or "we shall again have * * * instead of mammon-feudalism and unsold cotton shirts and preservation of the game, noble just industrialism;" or "a question arises here: whether in some ulterior, perhaps some far distant stage of this 'Chivalry of Labour,' your masterworker may not find it possible, and needful, to grant his workers permanent *interest* in his enterprise and theirs?"

Past and Present abounds in such prevision. Carlyle's neology has become our terminology: "Cash-payment;" "gospel of mammonism;" "captains of industry." Though these phrases were created by Carlyle, they are now, as Mr. Frederick Harrison says, household words.

This aspect of Carlyle's genius is especially noticeable in *Past and Present.* It has been the cause of many references to him as a prophet, a seer, and a Jeremiah. But Mr. R. H. Hutton warns us against attributing to Carlyle a definite "message." Carlyle was, Mr. Hutton maintains, always negative; his thought centered upon the *simulacra* of his time; he was a specialist in the diseases of the commonwealth. This is certainly true. Carlyle was not a prophet either in the mystical sense—a Tiresias who saw truly but with "what labour oh, what pain!"—nor according to the modern notion of a prophet an inspired leader who bestows upon his people new philosophies. But Carlyle's imagination, flaming in a few fields of thought, in some ways illumined the future. Carlyle really *foresaw* the rise of the Labor Party, though, of course, he did not guess its extent. And *Past and Present* is an example of this power.

Past and Present is a piercing glance into the feudal age, and a no less acute critique upon contemporary England. The book is enriched by Carlyle's wisdom, and ennobled by his most eloquent and most untrammelled manner. Mr. John Morley, re-reading it in 1891, exclaimed: "What energy, what inexhaustible vigour, what incomparable humor, what substantial justice of insight, and what sublimity of phrase and image!" Of these qualities and of the high originality of design much has been written, yet in 1921 something yet remains to be said concerning the relation of Carlyle's present to our own.

A student of political history once told me that the social disorders of the thirties and forties had never seemed real to him until he read *Past and Present.* When Carlyle pushed across the table to his mother the manuscript of the *French Revolution* he cried: "Never has a book come more *flamingly* from the heart of a man." His comment might have included *Past and Present.* Yet, in spite of the apparently careless fervor of the book, the method used in its composition was that of the literary artist. Over the historian's account of the Manchester insurrection we nod; over Carlyle's, even today, we instinctively clench our fists. For here "persons influence us, voices melt us, looks subdue us, deeds inflame us." Manchester is become, derisively, "Peterloo." The riot becomes in Carlyle's pages a series of stirring images: "Woolwich grapeshot will sweep clear all the streets;" "there lie poor sallow work-worn weavers, and complain no more now." Tennyson hints mildly at some misery connected with "spirit, alum, and chalk;" Carlyle tells one unforgettable anecdote; that of the parents found guilty of poisoning three children to defraud a burial society of 38s, due upon the death of each child. This was a story likely to make some impression even upon the British Philistine; resignation to human suffering did not seem so easy; it seemed a parallel to Carlyle's relentless descriptions of the tanneries at Meudon with their human skins. Concrete, personal detail is characteristic of Carlyle's literary method in *Past and Present.*

Such detail is not always ghastly. To emphasize the talkiness of parliament Carlyle says much of "oceans of horse-hair, continents of parchment;" to accentuate the sin of indifference he relates sardonically the history of the men of the dead sea, who "listened with real tedium to Moses, with light grinning, or with splenetic sniffs and sneers." *Past and Present* is crammed with detail, yet the central purpose of the book is maintained; like a single strand strung with brilliant beads of allusion, of anecdote, of minute detail.

One phase of Carlyle's use of detail is imaginative allusion. As a reader Carlyle had despoiled all literature; he once boasted that while at Craigenputtock he had read everything; and *Past and Present* is a mosaic of allusion. Sometimes an allusion—such as the Behemoth of Chaos—caps a sentence, and is not employed again. More often the illustration echoes through the book: "The day's wages of John Milton's day's work, named *Paradise Lost* and Milton's *Works,* were Ten Pounds, paid by installments, and a rather close escape upon the gallows." An ingenious variation is the use of a myth to point the idea of a chapter or a succession of chapters. Thus *Midas* and *The Sphinx* are chapter captions; in each case there is constructed an elaborate application to England. In the first the "baleful fiat of enchantment" prevents the conversion of the nation's wealth into prosperity; and in the second, England, since she has failed to answer the spiritual questions of life, is being torn to pieces. It is impossible to exaggerate the multiplicity of Carlyle's allusions and examples. *Horoscope,* in particular, is like a stream bearing the *membra disiecta* of literature and history: Columbus, Thersites, Mahomet, Cromwell, Wallace, Igdrasil, Byron and Pilate, King John, Hydra-Coil, Jotuns, Rhadamanthus, Burns and Kilkenny Cate!" "The Iliad and Lakenheath eels!" The writer's juxtaposition is hardly closer than Carlyle's. Such an inundation at first stimulates, then fatigues, but the total effect is that of eloquence and brilliance of manner.

Carlyle's allusions are most pungent when fictitious. He refers solemnly to personages who were without being until they sprang full-formed from his own brain. Who, pray, are Colacorde, Blusterowski and Schnüspel? It is entertaining to know that Schnüspel, the distinguished novelist, is Charles Dickens, but it is as pleasant to know that we cannot label Colacorde and Blusterowski. Their flavour lies not in who they are, but in what they connote. Every aviary has birds whose ludicrousness is surpassed only by their absurd self-esteem. Like them Blusterowski is a grotesque, and grotesques Carlyle loved. Jabesh Windbag is perfect without analysis; so is Sauerteig of the *Houndsditch Indicator,* and Bobus Higgins, "sausage-maker on the great scale." In the matter of elections, says Carlyle, "what can the incorruptiblest *Bobuses* elect, if it be not some Bobissimus?" No one would give readily these Carlylean gargoyles.

All other stylistic devices known to Carlyle are commandeered in *Past and Present* for his attack on the strongholds of English apathy. The book has an amazing exuberance of feeling and expression. Nowhere is it more evident that Carlyle thinks and writes with his whole body. Through four long parts he belabors, unwearying, the numbskulls of his generation. His hyperbole is excessive, but he convinces by his honesty, and by the profusion of his illustration, comment, and exhortation; for these qualities are the essence of *Past and Present,* differentiating it from the commonplace pamphlets of the time.

If the style of *Past and Present* is unique, the underlying conception of the book is no less so. One illusion of a materialistic present is a sense of superiority to the past. A popular form of Victorian complacency was loud felicitation over the escape from feudalism. Carlyle tried to show, as did Ruskin later, that in some respects the present was worse than the past. An examination of certain aspects of twelfth century life would prove this. With imagination as his guide Carlyle turned to the fact of the twelfth century as described in a manuscript. The structure of his book followed logically. The *Proem* gives the clue to his purpose; to paint with all his skill a true picture of social conditions in England. The second book, *The Ancient Monk,* indicates twelfth century England's freedom from these evils. The third part, *The Modern Worker,* a development of ideas suggested in the *Proem,* is a relentless contrast between the nineteenth and twelfth centuries. *Horoscope,* the fourth part, is concentrated Carlylean forboding. Throughout *Past and Present* every lesson for the present is pointed by an experience from the past; a method at variance with modern radicalism which adorns its precepts by morals from an unknown future. In reversion to the past Carlyle outdoes the most conservative historians. "The past," he once remarked, "is a dim, indubitable fact; the Future, too, is one, only *dimmer.*"

The part of *Past and Present* called *The Ancient Monk* is based literally on a "dim, indubitable fact," a manuscript of the twelfth century, *Chronica Jocelini de Brakelonda, de rebus gestis Samsonis Abbatis.* * * * Portions of this part are merely interlineations of the original. Carlyle's picture of Bury St. Edmund's, then, is not romance, but reality, fortified by authority and scholarship. *The Ancient Monk* commands respect because it is truthful in both letter and spirit.

The most obvious danger in using the *Chronica* was pedantry. Carlyle was addressing not German scholars, but English business men. The practical value of his book would not be enhanced by Latin syntax, however erudite. But if heaviness was the English reader's *bete noir,* it was also Carlyle's. He avoids the shoal of pedantry by never forgetting how near it is and how dangerous; and by ridiculing unceasingly the foibles of bastard learning. "I have traced," said an acquaintance of mine triumphantly, "the ancient expression 'cold feet' as far as the early Piedmontese dialect." "That superb change," exclaimed another, "of m to n in the early provencal." "My thesis," declared a third, "deals with the cells in the hind legs of grasshoppers." Darwin once stated that of all minds that he knew Carlyle's was least fitted for scientific enquiry. Certainly no one was ever more scornful of the idiosyncrasies of scholarship. He never tires of scoring ped-

antry. Whenever he refers to the *Chronica* he jeers: "Giant Pedantry will step in with its huge *Dugdale* and other enormous *Monasticons* under its arm!" Or he indulges in a burlesque pedantic note on "Beodric" and "Weorth." Or, still more frequently, he lifts above all such researches the notice: "Dry Rubbish Shot Here."

If Carlyle's Scylla was pedantry then his Charybdis was dilettantism; and from this reef, too, he resolutely steers his course. Englishmen were interested in the middle ages—Scott's novels had been a powerful influence—but their interest was colored by the rosy mist of romance. The twelfth and thirteenth centuries were one vast field of the cloth of gold, on which played at life crusaders, Paladine, troubadours, true-hearted knights and fair-haired maidens. "How glorious," thought the Victorian, and later read with a shock of disapproval more accurate tales of blood, lust, and mediaeval social conditions. Carlyle despised this fool as heartily as he did the pedant. This reader, he declared, believed without effort that the ring found in the river Trent belonged to the Countess of Leicester. Why not, if it happened in the age of chivalry?

Carlyle achieves a *via media.* In his attitude towards the past he is never pedant, and never dilettante. The twelfth century is not dry rubbish, nor is it a glowing canvas of color. In Carlyle's hands it becomes fact made vivid by imagination. The election of Abbot Samson is a beautiful illustration of Carlyle's method, especially if compared with the original. "And now there remains on our list two only, Samson Subsacrista and the Prior. Which of these two? It were hard to say—by Monks who may get themselves foot-gyved and thrown into limbo for speaking! We humbly request that the Bishop of Winchester and Geoffrey the Chancellor may again enter, and help us to decide. 'Which do you want?' asks the bishop. Venerable Dennis made a speech, 'commending the persons of the Prior and Samson; but always in the corner of his discourse, *in angulo sui sermonis,* brought Samson in. 'Either of them is good,' said venerable Dennis, almost trembling; 'but we would have the better, if it pleased God.' 'Which of the two *do* you want?' inquires the Bishop pointedly. 'Samson!' answered Dennis: 'Samson!' echoed all of the rest that durst speak or echo anything." Jocelyn's record reads: *Et responsum est precise a pluribus et a majori parte, 'Volumus Samsonem,' nullo reclamante.* "The total effect of this method is an amazing sense of the reality of the life at Bury St. Edmund's. "Let us know always," reiterates Carlyle, "that it *was* a world, and not a void infinite of gray haze with fantasms swimming in it." And again: "That it is a *fact* and no dream, that we see it there, and gaze into the very eyes of it. Smoke rises daily from those culinary chimney-throats; there are living human beings there, who chant, loud-braying, their matins, nones, vespers."

Carlyle has thus visualized for his readers a society which may be compared, point for point, with that of the nineteenth century. None so actual has been done by other social idealists. The dreamy Utopias of Sir Thomas More, of William Morris, or of Samuel Butler, or of the many others do not warrant practical discussion. They belong to romance. But this twelfth century, if limited, was real; it merited consideration in the fifties; perhaps it does now. Carlyle's next step is to contrast relentlessly the two social orders, Bury St. Edmund's and Victorian England. "How silent * * * lie all cotton trades and such like; not a steeple chimney yet got on end from sea to sea." Landlord Edmund had no complaints from his tenants; or partridge seasons; or Corn Bills, or sliding scales.

Why should he have had? Society was in its childhood. Here Carlyle is merely picturesque. But in the vital points of contrast he is stimulating. The points are three, the old familiar fetiches of Carlyle, government, religion and leadership. Carlyle is not reticent concerning his horror of them as they are in the nineteenth century, and his worship of them as they were in the twelfth century. One sees at once that Bury St. Edmund's under Abbot Samson is a tiny corner of a Carlylean social heaven. Here at least was a segment of a working feudal aristocracy. Here was a government untainted by *laissez-faire;* one that took care of its people. The business of a government, Carlyle was wont to shriek, is to govern. Even a Gurth is entitled to his parings. Give the negro plenty of "sweet-pumpkin" and govern *him.* This is well-known Carlylese, repeated a thousand times in *Past and Present.* Abbot Samson ruled and cared for those under him; among his people were no Chartisms or Manchester insurrections. Let the nineteenth century ponder on this sequence of cause and effect; a government that governs and a contented people.

Yet still more remarkable was a religion with faith. The religion of Carlyle's era has been described as one which church members would be amazed to hear doubted, or see practiced. Ruskin's famous threnody in *Modern Painters,* on the death of faith is a typical nineteenth century lament. "My heart was lightened," writes Clough, "when I said 'Christ is not risen.'" "We have forgotten God," is Carlyle's oft-repeated cry. But the faith of Abbot Samson is like that of the Apostles, silent, unquestioning. Carlyle notes that under Samson there were no "spectral Puseyisms or Methodisms." "Methodism with its eyes on its own navel." Introspective religions were unborn. Here were religious men who *believed.* Let the nineteenth century meditate also on this.

But, after all, the third point of contrast is most striking, leadership at Bury St. Edmund's. Carlyle did not expect either the British government or the British religion to change *instanter;* he did not suggest institutional revolution. But he did believe that the kind of leadership in state and church could be altered, if light was vouchsafed the British people; what he did suggest was spiritual revolution. Real leaders could be selected. Thus the greatest contrast between the twelfth

and nineteenth centuries was not in institutions but in men. Abbot Samson is plainly balanced against George III. The twelfth century worships a Samson or a St. Edmund, the nineteenth a defender of the faith who is deaf, sightless and insane, or Dickens, a distinguished novelist, or Hudson, a railroad engineer. The test of leadership in one century is worth, in the other the ballot box.

For this is clearly the old doctrine of "the hero," Carlyle's only and faint constructive theory. We are to find "the hero," that wisest and best, that blend of vigor, silence, obedience, loyalty, with his surplusage of spiritual force, that—it must be said—*ignis fatuuus!* In this romantic, political, economic tract called *Past and Present* Carlyle would persuade the nineteenth century that in the twelfth century the rainbow's end was reached, "the hero" was found.

He did not persuade the nineteenth century. In spite of admiration for *Past and Present* the nineteenth century was never convinced that Carlyle's notion of "the hero" was a practical remedy. Carlyle as a political critic is one person; Carlyle as a constructive political theorist is another. Vivid and beautiful as *The Ancient Monk* is, a child could impugn its practical application. One palpable falseness of analogy is that Samson's community was considerably fewer in numbers than the twenty-seven millions of Englishmen for whom *Past and Present* was written. There were other fractions of a feudal aristocratic society coeval with Samson's régime whose history would make different reading from that of Bury St. Edmund's. Moreover, Carlyle seems to suggest that the individualistic religious growth of seven centuries can be forgotten. Can the nineteenth century believe, as did the monks of St. Edmund, in a heaven like that of Thomas à Kempis? What Carlyle calls "diseased introspection" is an inevitable by-product of the thought of Luther, Wycliffe and Wesley, and of the scientific revelations of the nineteenth century. The perplexity is at least honest; not so much could be said of a return to blind mediaeval faith. We ought, it is true, to find better leaders or "heroes;" democracy is probably not the last stage of economic process, the ballot box may be a *faute de mieux.* Yet we cannot select our leaders as the Bishop of Winchester did Samson. There is hardly a detail of Samson's household management which is transferable to our own.

In fact, Carlyle cannot tell us what to do. Never expect him to do so. What he can do is to tell us, in the most profound sense, what is the matter. This service *Past and Present* performs in 1921 as it did in 1843. Throughout the century it was praised. "There is nothing like it," wrote Clough. Its eloquence was partly responsible for Kingsley's novel, *Yeast.* It roused thousands of Englishmen from inertia to a fresh consideration of social conditions. The very pessimism of the book stung critics out of their complacency. What if Carlyle did, as Henry James said, "scold like" an angry governess. He made men look about them more thoughtfully. "I hope," Carlyle wrote his mother, "it will be a rather useful kind of book. It goes rather in a fiery strain about the present condition of men in general, and the strange pass they are coming to; and I calculate it may awaken here and there a slumbering blockhead to rub his eyes and consider what he is about in God's creation." This was the sum of the matter; a word from Carlyle was a call to action. There is no surrender to *laissez-faire*. "Ay, by God, Donald, we must help them to man it!" He seems to say: "Ich bin ein Mensch begoren. Und das muss ein Kämpfer sein." Every sentence in *Past and Present* is a plea against acquiesence. As Ruskin declares: "What can you say of Carlyle but that he was born in the clouds and struck by the lightning?"

Today Carlyle's idealism seems like the frantic arguments of a man attempting to prove established facts. No better idea of the change in social thought can be had than by realizing that the reforms desired by Carlyle were then considered visionary. Imagine a place now for factory inspectors; for protection against typhus; or for organization of labor. Yet these are but a few of the changes urged by Carlyle, as if he were a minority of one; now they are *faits accomplis*. Of the laborers of England he asks: "Where are they to find a supportable existence," or "*cash-payment* is not the sole relation of human beings!" Such reforms as insurance for workingmen, model tenements for families, the right to strike, hardly occur to Carlyle as present issues. Yet these are the commonplaces of today. And these were to come by action of the state; not through "Morrison's Pills," as Carlyle dubbed opportunist legislation, but through thoughtful constructive government. State supervision of insurance, of railroads, and factories have arrived in a manner exceeding Carlyle's wildest dreams.

Indeed what the modern reader feels about the advance of labor since 1843 is that a new *Past and Present* is needed. No longer is it so necessary to denounce the gospels of mammonism, dilettantism, of oppression of workmen, of extortion by capital. The boot is on the other leg. Labor's emancipation is more complete than even Carlyle would have guessed likely. Possibly a book proclaiming the rights of the employer would be as pertinent today as was *Past and Present* in 1843. During the war there appeared in an English newspaper, in adjacent columns, accounts of the imprisonment of trivial offenders, and also of the release of notorious strike leaders. The union of all labor parties of the world, without respect to nationalism, is possible. In the newspapers of today appears the notice of a strike which will hold motionless every industrial activity in the British Isles. Carlyle's pious allusion to the land belonging to "the Almighty God, and to all His children of men that have ever worked well on it" is now an acknowledged principle among some millions of Communists, though indeed there is no certainty that God is included, or the test of working on the land required by this extraordinary party. The wheel has come full circle. In three-quarters of a century men shrink not from the gospel of mammonism, but from the gospel of bolshevism.

Carlyle, as has been said, was not, in any supernatural sense, a prophet. Yet, apart from the mood of monition ever natural to him there is vision in his thoughts of the future of workingmen. The French Revolution was to him a continual memento; he honestly feared that some similar fate would befall the industrial leaders of England. When he speaks of England "very ominously, shuddering reeling, on the cliff's edge!" he is more than rhetorical. He saw clearly that things would change with "the millions who rejoiced in potatoes." Of his insistence upon the spiritual truths which underlay the necessity for such changes much might be said. Who can deny that Carlyle is in some degree responsible for governments whose "business is to govern. "He was a leader in the battle against *laissez-faire*. It is enough to notice once more the significance of *The Modern Worker* as a knife-edge of economic progress. Contrast the condition of labor mirrored there with its status today. But more than this, *Past and Present* is, in some respects, a prophecy.

Ernst Cassirer (essay date 1946)

SOURCE: "The Preparation: Carlyle," in *The Myth of the State*, Yale University Press, 1946, pp. 189-223.

[*In the following essay, Cassirer studies Carlyle's views on hero-worship, noting that Carlyle regarded hero-worship as a means of stabilizing the social and political disorder of his time. Cassirer also reviews the influence of Goethe and Fichte on Carlyle.*]

Carlyle's Lectures on Hero Worship

When Thomas Carlyle on May 22, 1840, began his lectures *On Heroes, Hero Worship and the Heroic in History* he spoke to a large and distinguished audience. A "mob of London society" had assembled to listen to the speaker. The lectures created a sort of sensation; but nobody could have foreseen that this social event was pregnant with great political consequences. Carlyle spoke to Englishmen of the Victorian era. His audience was between two and three hundred in number and "aristocratic in rank and intellect." As Carlyle says in one of his letters "bishops and all kinds of people had appeared; they heard something new and seemed greatly astonished and greatly pleased. They laughed and applauded."[1] But assuredly none of the hearers could think for a moment that the ideas expressed in these lectures contained a dangerous explosive. Nor did Carlyle himself feel this way. He was no revolutionary; he was a conservative. He wished to stabilize the social and political order and he was convinced that for such a stabilization he could recommend no better means than hero worship. He never meant to preach a new political evangelism. To him hero worship was the oldest and firmest element in man's social and cultural life. He saw in it "an everlasting hope for the management of the world." "Had all traditions, arrangements, creeds, societies that men ever instituted, sunk away, this would remain . . . it shines like a pole-star through smoke-clouds, dust-clouds, and all manner of down-rushing and conflagration."[2]

The effect produced by Carlyle's lectures was, however, far different from the author's expectations. As Carlyle pointed out, the modern world had passed through three great revolutions. First came the Reformation of Luther, then the Puritan revolution, and at last the French Revolution. The French Revolution was properly the third act of Protestantism. This third act we may well call the final one: "for lower than that savage *Sans-culottism* men cannot go."[3] When Carlyle spoke thus he could not know that the very ideas he propounded in his lectures were also the beginning of a new revolution. A hundred years later these ideas had been turned into the most efficient weapons in the political struggle. In the Victorian era nobody could have divined the role that Carlyle's theory was to play in the twentieth century.

In recent literature there is a strong tendency to connect Carlyle's views with our own political problems—to see in him one of those men who had done most for the future "March of Fascism." In 1928 B. H. Lehman wrote a book—*Carlyle's Theory of the Hero. Its Sources, Development, History, and Influence on Carlyle's Work.*[4] This was a merely historical analysis. But it was soon followed by other studies in which Carlyle was, more or less, made responsible for the whole ideology of National Socialism. After Hitler's rise to power H. F. C. Grierson published a lecture that, three years previously, he had delivered on "Carlyle and the Hero" under a new title, *Carlyle and Hitler.* "I have been tempted," he says, "to give it a new, shall I say metonymous, title, so entirely do the recent happenings in Germany illustrate the conditions which lead up to, or at least make possible, the emergence of the Hero, as Carlyle chiefly thought of him, and the feelings, religious and political . . . which raise the wave that washes him into power."[5] It seemed to be not only natural but almost inevitable to attribute to Carlyle all those ideas of political leadership that developed much later and under a quite different "climate of opinion." To the long list of books and articles in which he had studied the philosophy and genealogy of modern imperialism Ernest Seillière added, in 1939, a book on Carlyle. He finds in his works all the characteristics of an "esthetic mysticism" and the first traces of "racial mysticism," and later on, in his book on Frederick the Great, the open defense of Prussian militarism. "The more that, meditating on life's lessons and on the true character of human nature, he approached Toryism, the more room he made for politicians and the military among the delegates of the Most High: it was the Prussian tendency

in the heart of German romanticism."[6] Accordingly this Prussification of Carlyle's romanticism was the last and decisive step which led him to a deification of the political leaders and to an identification of might and right.[7]

There is much truth in this description of the effects of Carlyle's theory. Nevertheless it seems to me to be an oversimplification of the matter. Carlyle's conception of the "hero" is very complicated, both in its meaning and in its historical presuppositions. To do full justice to his theory we must study all the diverse and often contradictory elements that formed Carlyle's character, his life, and his work. Carlyle was not a systematic thinker. He did not even try to construct a coherent philosophy of history. To him history was no system—it was a great panorama. History, he declared in his essay on biography, is the essence of innumerable biographies.[8] To read into Carlyle's work, therefore, a definite philosophical construction of the historical process, taken as a whole, or a definite political program is precarious and illusive. Instead of jumping to conclusions about his doctrines we must first try to understand the motives that lay at the bottom of them without a clear insight into which many, if not

ON HEROES,

HERO-WORSHIP, & THE HEROIC

IN HISTORY.

Six Lectures.

REPORTED, WITH EMENDATIONS AND ADDITIONS.

By THOMAS CARLYLE.

LONDON:

JAMES FRASER, REGENT STREET.

M.DCCC.XLI.

most, of his ideas remain obscure and ambiguous. Carlyle's conception of history and politics always depends on his own personal history; it is much more biographical than systematic or methodical.

Undoubtedly Carlyle developed in his lectures the idea of "leadership" into its most radical consequences. He identified the whole of historical life with the life of great men. Without them there would be no history; there would be stagnation, and stagnation means death. A mere sequence of events does not constitute history. It consists in deeds and actions, and there are no deeds without a doer, without a great, immediate, personal impulse. "Hero Worship," exclaimed Carlyle, "heartfelt prostrate admiration, submission, burning, boundless, for a noblest godlike form of man—is not that the germ of Christianity itself?"[9] This idea was, in a sense, the alpha and omega, the beginning and the end, of his whole philosophy of life and history. He had spoken likewise in his first work. "Well was it written by theologians," he says in **Sartor Resartus,** "a King rules by divine right. He carries in him an authority from God, or man will never give it him. . . . He who is to be my ruler, whose will is to be higher than my will, was chosen for me in Heaven. Neither except in such obedience to the Heaven-chosen is freedom so much as conceivable."[10]

This seems simply to be the language of a theologian who had lost his implicit faith in any dogmatic religion and who, therefore, tried to replace the worship of God by a worship of men. The medieval form of hierarchy was changed into the modern form of "hero-archy." Carlyle's hero is, indeed, a transformed saint, a secularized saint. He need not be a priest or prophet; he may be a poet, a king, a man of letters. But without such temporal saints, Carlyle declares, we cannot live. If hero-archy ever could die out we should have to despair of the world altogether. Without sovereigns, true sovereigns, temporal and spiritual, I see nothing possible but an anarchy, the hatefullest of all things.[11]

But what *is* a hero? There must be a certain standard by which we can recognize him. We must have a touchstone for testing the heroic men, for discerning true gold from base metals. Carlyle knows, of course, that in the history of religion there are true and false prophets and in political life, real and would-be heroes. Is there any criterion by which we know the one from the others? There are heroes who are the representatives of the Divine Idea—there are others who are mere sham heroes. This is a necessary and indestructible feature of human history. For the mass, or, as Carlyle says, "the valets," must have heroes of their own.

> Know the men that are to be trusted: alas, this is yet, in these days, very far from us. The sincere alone can recognize sincerity. Not a Hero only is needed, but a world fit for him; a world not of *Valets* . . . The Valet-World has to be governed by the Sham-Hero. . . . It

is his; he is its! In brief, one of two things: We shall either learn to know a Hero, a true Governor and Captain, somewhat better, when we see him; or else go on to be for ever governed by the Unheroic.[12]

All this is clear and unmistakable. There is nothing that Carlyle hates and abhors more than the "mechanical" theories of political life that he ascribes to the eighteenth century and the philosophers of the Enlightenment. But notwithstanding all his spiritualism he becomes, in matters of politics, one of the most resolute advocates of passive obedience. Carlyle's political theory is, at bottom, nothing short of a disguised and transformed Calvinism. True spontaneity is reserved to the few elect. As to the others, the mass of the reprobates, they have to submit under the will of these elect, the born rulers.

So far we have only received, however, a rhetorical not a philosophical answer. Even if we accept all the premises of Carlyle's theory, the principal question still remains to be answered. Of course, it would be too much to expect from Carlyle a clear definition of what he understands by a hero. Such a definition would be a logical act, and Carlyle speaks with a great contempt of all logical methods. Logic can never penetrate into the secret of reality. The healthy understanding is not the logical and argumentative, but the intuitive. "Consider the old Schoolmen, and their pilgrimage towards truth: the faithfullest endeavour, incessant unwearied motion, often great natural vigour; only no progress: nothing but antic feats of one limb poised against the other; . . . at best gyrated swiftly, with some pleasure, like Spinning Dervishes, and ended where they began."[13] Logic is good, but is not the best; by logic we shall not succeed in understanding life, let alone its highest form: a heroic life. "To know, to get into the truth of anything, is ever a mystic act—of which the best Logics can but babble on the surface."[14] "To attempt *theorizing* on such matters would profit little; they are matters which refuse to be *theoremed* and diagramed; which Logic ought to know that she *cannot* speak of."[15]

But if knowledge, by its nature and essence, is a mystic act, it seems to be a hopeless attempt, to communicate it, to express it in the poor symbols of our human speech, especially, if this communication has to be made in a series of public lectures—delivered before the "mob of London society." How did Carlyle overcome this difficulty; how could he solve this almost impossible task? He could only give an illustration, not a demonstration of his fundamental thesis. It must be admitted that this illustration was vivid and impressive. He had always looked upon history not as an arid textbook, but as a picture gallery. We cannot understand history by mere concepts, we can only understand it by portraits. In his lectures Carlyle tried to cover the whole field of human history. He went from the first rudimentary stages of human civilization to contemporary history and literature. All this had to be combined into one great intuition. Such a synthesis can never be performed by the understanding; it requires other and higher powers. "Not our logical, mensurative faculty, but our imaginative one is king over us; I might say, priest and prophet to lead us heavenward; or magician and wizard to lead us hellward."[16]

Of this imaginative faculty Carlyle made ample use in his lectures. His style is, indeed, that of a prophet who leads us heavenward and of a wizard who leads us hellward. In his description the two directions are sometimes quite undistinguishable. The understanding, he declared, is indeed thy window . . . ; but fantasy is thy eye, with its colour-giving retina, healthy or diseased.[17] Singular men, he had said in a previous essay,[18] are mystic windows through which we glance deeper into the hidden ways of nature. One "mystic window" after another was opened to the hearers of Carlyle's lectures. He could only speak by examples. He felt under no obligation to answer the question: *What* is a hero? But he tried to show, *who* the great heroic men were. His list is long and variegated. Yet he does not admit any specific differences in the heroic character. This character is one and indivisible; it always remains the same. From Norse Odin to English Samuel Johnson, from the divine founder of Christianity to Voltaire, the hero has been worshiped, in one or another form.[19]

By this method the hero of Carlyle became a Proteus that could assume every shape. In every new lecture he shows us a new face. He appears as a mythical god, as a prophet, a priest, a man of letters, a king. He has no limits; nor is he bound to any special sphere of activity.

> At bottom the great man, as he comes from the hand of nature, is ever the same kind of thing: Odin, Luther, Johnson, Burns: I hope to make it appear that these are all originally of one stuff. . . . I confess, I have no notion of a truly great man that would not be *all* sorts of men. . . . I cannot understand how a Mirabeau, with that great glowing heart, with the fire that was in it, with the bursting tears that were in it, could not have written verses, tragedies, poems, and touched all hearts in that way, had his course of life and education led him thitherward.[20]

That was a rather paradoxical thesis. Even the strongest imagination will have some difficulties in discovering an identity between a mythical god like Odin and a Rousseau whom Carlyle described as "a morbid, excitable, spasmodic man."[21] And we cannot very well think of a Samuel Johnson, a pedant and schoolmaster, as the writer of the *Divina commedia* or of the plays of Shakespeare. But Carlyle was carried away by the stream of his own eloquence. He spoke of all his heroes with the same enthusiasm. In his "transcendent admiration"[22] of the great men he sometimes seems to lose every sense of proportion. The differences of our lower empirical world were almost forgotten; the most disparate historical characters were put on the same level.

In a writer like Carlyle who had devoted his whole life to

historical studies and who in this field possessed a real authority this attitude was rather surprising. But we must not forget the special circumstances under which his lectures were given. Carlyle's style had always been much more oratorical than philosophical. But never before had he made as ample use of mere rhetorical means as in these lectures. As a master in the art of criticism he knew very well how to distinguish between real eloquence and ordinary rhetoric. In the difference between oratory and rhetoric, he declared, we find, as indeed everywhere, that superiority of what is called the natural over the artificial. The orator persuades and carries all with him, he knows not how; the rhetorician can prove that he ought to have persuaded and carried all with him. "So stands it, in short, with all the forms of intellect, whether as directed to the finding of truth, or to the fit imparting thereof."[23] But this time Carlyle had forgotten this precept. Perhaps he was, unconsciously, influenced by the attitude of his audience that seems to have been very susceptible to the form of his rhetorical style. He spoke to a special public "aristocratic in rank and intellect." He had carefully to weigh his words. He chose his effects and was always sure of them. He tried to capture, to increase and stimulate the interest of his hearers. And he succeeded in this task. Only a few, among them one of his best friends and the most competent critic, John Stuart Mill, seem to have kept their clear critical judgment. When Carlyle spoke of Bentham's theory and declared it to be the most beggarly and falsest view of man, Mill rose from his seat to interrupt the orator and to protest against this description. But the greater part of the audience reacted in quite a different way. The course "On Heroes" became Carlyle's last and greatest public triumph. "The good people sat breathless, or broke out into all kinds of testimonies of good will."[24]

Carlyle himself was critical enough not to be deceived by this success. He was by no means blind to the grave defects of his lectures. He judged them very severely. "Nothing which I have ever written pleases me so ill. They have nothing *new*, nothing that to me is not *old*. The style of them requires to be low-pitched, as like talk as possible."[25] But even the book, as it was published later, is open to the same objections. A great admirer of Carlyle declared that, compared with his masterpieces, the book *On Heroes* is "almost flimsy."[26] It would, therefore, be unfair to judge Carlyle's *thoughts* on hero worship by this book alone. In this regard his previous works were widely superior. To be sure *Sartor Resartus* has not only all the merits but all the defects of his style. It is written in a bizarre and grotesque language; it offends and defies all rules of sound composition. But it is sincere in every word; it bears the stamp of Carlyle's personality. In his book on hero worship, which, unfortunately, became his best known and most influential book, he tried much more to persuade than to convince. He had declared the hero to be the "universal man." It was, however, a hard task to prove this universality, not only in the case of a Samuel Johnson or John

Knox but even in the case of Luther or Cromwell. Carlyle's exaggerations and inconsistencies are obvious. Yet we should not too much insist upon these inconsistencies. A historian of the rank of Carlyle may lay claim to being judged according to his own conception of a true historical method.

> The artist in history may be distinguished from the artisan in history; for here, as in all other provinces, there are artists and artisans; men who labour mechanically in a department, without eye for the Whole, not feeling that there is a Whole; and men who inform and ennoble the humblest department with an Idea of the Whole, and habitually know that only in the Whole is the Partial to be truly discerned. The proceedings and the duties of these two, in regard to history, must be altogether different.[27]

"The Whole" of which Carlyle speaks is not a metaphysical but an individual whole. He is a classical witness to that philosophical attitude that was later styled existential philosophy. We find in him all the characteristics of the type of thought represented by Kierkegaard and his attack against the Hegelian system. We know very little of a thinker, he declares, as long as we know only his concepts. We must know the man before we can understand and appreciate his theories. From German romantic writers, especially from Friedrich H. Jacobi, Carlyle borrowed the term *Lebensphilosophie.*

> However it may be with metaphysics and other abstract science originating in the Head (*Verstand*) alone, no Life-Philosophy (*Lebensphilosophie*) . . . which originates equally in the Character (*Gemüt*), and equally speaks thereto, can attain its significance till the Character itself is known and seen; till the author's View of the World (*Weltansicht*) and how he actively and passively came by such view, are clear: in short till a biography of him has been philosophico-poetically written, and philosophico-poetically read.[28]

In accordance with this maxim Carlyle suddenly interrupted his description of the "philosophy of clothes" that he gave in **Sartor Resartus** in order to insert all sorts of biographical details. In a chapter, "Romance," he tells us a love story of his early youth. He proceeds to that great intellectual crisis in which he saw his "fire baptism." This was not a mere diversion; it was a necessary element of Carlyle's method as a writer and as a thinker. He refused to draw a line of demarcation between a philosophical system and its author. What he called his philosophy always contained an autobiographical element. There can be no doubt of the authenticity of the scene in **Sartor Resartus** in which Carlyle describes the beginning of his *vita nuova,* of his moral and philosophical life. "I remember it well and could go straight to the place where the incident recurred. . . . It is from this hour that I incline to date my spiritual New-birth, or Baphometic Fire-baptism; perhaps I directly thereupon began to be a man."[29]

Philosophical systems belong, roughly speaking, to two different types. They follow an empirical or a rational, an inductive or a deductive method. They are based on facts or they are derived from a priori principles. In order to judge them we must either begin with a study of empirical data or with an analysis of general truths. Yet in the case of Carlyle neither way can lead us to a true insight into the character of his philosophy. His was not an empirical philosophy nor was it a speculative system. He never tried to give more than a "Life-Philosophy," and he never meant to separate this philosophy from his personal experience. In metaphysics as such, as a general system, he could see no more than a perennial disease. In all ages the same questions, the questions of death and immortality, of the origin of evil, of freedom and necessity, have appeared under new forms. Ever and anon must the attempt to shape for ourselves some theorem of the universe be repeated. But all these attempts are doomed to failure; "for what theorem of the Infinite can the Finite render complete?" The mere existence and necessity of a philosophy is an evil. Man is not born to solve the riddles of the universe. What he can do and what he ought to do is to understand himself, his destiny, and his duties. He stands as in the center of nature: "his fraction of time encircled by eternity, his handbreadth of space encircled by infinitude: how shall he forbear asking himself, What am I; and Whence; and Whither?"[30] We must first have Carlyle's answer to all these questions before we can understand any part of his philosophy or any of his theories about man's historical and social life.

The Personal Background of Carlyle's Theory

There is little relation between the ideas of Carlyle and Descartes. They are diametrically opposed both in their results and in their principles; they belong to different hemispheres of the *globus intellectualis.* Nevertheless there is one point of contact—their personal approach to philosophy. Both assert that philosophy begins not with certainty but with doubt. Doubt, in itself, is not to be feared. It is not a subversive but a constructive element in our intellectual life. Metaphysics cannot dispense with it. But ethics is not the same as metaphysics. The ethical life of man begins when he ceases to remain in this "center of indifference" which, in a sense, is the only possible standpoint for metaphysics. Man must learn how to oppose to the "Everlasting No" the "Everlasting Yea." "Having no hope," says Carlyle, speaking of his youth,

> neither had I any definite fear. . . . And yet, strangely enough, I lived in a continual, indefinite, pining fear; tremendous, pusillanimous, apprehensive of I knew not what . . . Full of such humour, and perhaps the miserablest man . . . all at once, there arose a thought in me, and I asked myself: "What *art* thou afraid of? Wherefore, like a coward, dost thou forever pip and whimper, and go cowering and trembling? Despicable biped! what is the sum-total of the worst that lies before thee? Death? Well, Death; and say the pangs of Tophet too, and all that the Devil and Man may, will, or can

do against thee! Hast thou not a heart; canst thou not suffer whatsoever it be; . . . Let it come, then; I will meet it and defy it!" And as I so thought, there rushed like a stream of fire over my whole soul; and I shook base fear away from me forever. I was strong, of unknown strength; a spirit, almost a god. Ever from that time, the temper of my misery was changed: not fear or whining sorrow was it, but indignation and grim fire-eyed defiance.[31]

Whenever Carlyle, in his later life and work, preached this new gospel of the "Everlasting Yea," he never forgot to mention the name of Goethe. Without this great example, he declared, he could not have found his own way. Goethe's *Wilhelm Meister* had convinced him that "doubt, of whatever kind, can be ended by action alone."[32] Action not speculative thought, ethics not metaphysics is the only means of overcoming doubt and negation. In this way alone we can pass from a science of denial and destruction to a science of affirmation and reconstruction.[33] Such a "science of reconstruction" Carlyle had found in Goethe. It was not the poet Goethe, however, who aroused his highest admiration and was in the focus of his interest. He always spoke of Goethe as a great thinker rather than as a great poet. He even went so far as to call him, in the age of Kant, "*the* Thinker of our time."[34] "We come nearer our meaning," said Carlyle in his second essay on Goethe, "if we say that in Goethe we discover by far the most striking instance, in our time, of a writer who is, in strict speech, what philosophy can call a Man. He is neither noble nor plebeian, neither liberal nor servile, nor infidel nor devotee; but the best excellence of *all* these, joined in pure union, 'a clear and universal Man.'" He stands forth, not only as the literary ornament, but in many respects too as the Teacher and exemplar of his age.[35] His primary faculty, the foundation of all others, was Intellect, depth and force of vision. "A completed man: the trembling sensibility, the wild enthusiasm of a Mignon, can assort with the scornful world-mockery of a Mephistopheles; and each side of manysided life receives its due from him."[36]

From the point of view of literary criticism this characterization may seem to be onesided. The greatest of all lyrical poets was changed by Carlyle into a great teacher, a sage and a didactic poet. Nevertheless it was a great step forward that Carlyle saw Goethe's work in this light. Here he even surpassed the first German apostles of Goethe. To be sure the romantic writers, Novalis, Friedrich Schlegel, Tieck, were much more susceptible to the charm of Goethe's poetry than was Carlyle. But they did not sympathize with his ethical ideals; they even saw in them a constant danger to the poet Goethe. When Goethe began to publish *Wilhelm Meisters Lehrjahre* those romantic writers were unanimous in their admiration and enthusiasm. Yet when, in the progress of the work, the didactic intention came to the fore, when Goethe began to develop his ideals on education, they were deeply disappointed. Goethe, the man whom Novalis had called

"den Statthalter des poetischen Geistes auf Erden," seemed suddenly to have deserted the cause of poetry: he praised the most prosaic and trivial aspect of human life. On the other hand Goethe's work was also open to the opposite objection. Herder, Goethe's friend and the greatest among the German critics, could never become quite reconciled with the moral atmosphere of the first books of *Wilhelm Meisters Lehrjahre*. Characters like Marianne or Philine were intolerable to him; he found in the book a moral indifferentism and a laxity that seemed to him to be unworthy of a great poet.[37]

It was the great merit of Carlyle to see through both errors. One of the paradoxes in the history of modern literature is that this Puritan became the interpreter and defender of Goethe's moral character. If we take into consideration Carlyle's religious and cultural background this was no easy task. Obviously there was no agreement between the ideas of Goethe and Carlyle. The latter had laid aside all dogmatic religion; but he had never completely broken with his Calvinistic credo. Many things in *Wilhelm Meister* must have been repugnant to him. In a letter to James Johnstone he confessed that he felt nothing but disgust for the "players and libidinous actresses" in the story.[38] But after a short time he overcame these moral scruples, for he had found the key to the whole. He began to understand Goethe, and this led him to a better understanding of himself and the great crisis of his early life. "I then felt, and still feel," he wrote later on in his ***Reminiscences,*** "endlessly indebted to Goethe . . . ; he, in his fashion, I perceived, had travelled the steep rocky road before me—the first of the moderns."[39] He himself had been "in the very midst of Wertherism, the bleakness and darkness of death."[40]

Carlyle was perhaps the first modern critic who interpreted the subtitle to *Wilhelm Meisters Wanderjahre—Die Entsagenden*—in its right sense. He saw in Goethe's work resignation; but to him this resignation was, at the same time, the highest ethical affirmation. It was not denial but reconstruction. To complain about man's unhappiness, he declared, is mere sentimentalism. "A gifted Byron rises in his wrath; and feeling too surely that he for his part is not 'happy,' declares the same in very violent language, as a piece of news that may be interesting. It evidently has surprised him much. One dislikes to see a man and poet reduced to proclaim on the streets such tidings."[41] Man's unhappiness comes of his greatness; it is the surest proof of an Infinite in him, which with all cunning he cannot quite bury under the Finite. Carlyle spoke here in the style of Pascal. "The fraction of life can be increased in value not so much by increasing your numerator as by lessening your denominator. Nay, unless my Algebra deceive me, *Unity* itself divided by *Zero* will give *Infinity*. Make thy claim of wages a zero then; thou hast the world under thy feet. . . . Close thy Byron; open thy Goethe."[42]

This emphasis on man's activity, on his practical life and

practical duties, is the unromantic feature in Carlyle's philosophy. He was a typical romanticist both in his ideas and in their style and expression. But his Philosophy of Life was far different from all the romantic writers. His was a practical not a magical idealism. In his essay on Novalis he spoke of time and space as the deepest of all illusionary appearances. They are not external but internal entities; they are mere forms of man's spiritual being.[43] But this illusionary character of human knowledge disappears as soon as we approach the sphere of action and our ethical life. Only in this sphere do we stand upon firm and unshakeable ground. All skepticism and all theoretical "solipsism" are overcome. We have reached the true reality; we have recognized "the infinite nature of duty."[44] Metaphysics, as such, cannot solve the riddle. We cannot break the spell of skepticism by mere speculation. "There is no more fruitless endeavour than this same, which the metaphysician proper toils in: to educe conviction out of negation. . . . Metaphysical speculation, as it begins in No or Nothingness, so it must needs end in Nothingness; circulates and must circulate in endless vortices, creating, swallowing—itself."[45]

This conviction of the fundamentally ethical character of reality had a double influence upon Carlyle's romanticism. It led not only to a change in his thoughts but also to a change in his style. In **Sartor Resartus** Carlyle deliberately imitated all the characters of the romantic style. Jean Paul became his great model. His manner of writing seemed to defy all logical rules; it was bizarre, fantastic, incoherent. There is, however, one feature of the romantic style that was inconsistent with Carlye's nature and temperament. We find in him the grotesque humor of Jean Paul, but we do not find the romantic irony. "That faculty of irony," wrote Carlyle in his first essay on Jean Paul Friedrich Richter, "of caricature, which often passes by the name of humour, but consists chiefly in a certain superficial distortion or reversal of objects, and ends at best in laughter, bears no resemblance to the humour of Richter. . . . It is but a poor fraction of humour; or rather, it is the body to which the soul is wanting; any life it has being false, artificial, and irrational."[46] Carlyle could not be ironical. He always spoke in dead earnest. "No Mirabeau, Napoleon, Burns, Cromwell," he said in his lectures on **Hero Worship**, "no man adequate to do anything, but is first of all in right earnest about it. . . . Fearful and wonderful, real as life, real as death, is this universe to him. . . . At all moments the Flame-image glares in upon him; undeniable, there, there!—I wish you to take this as my primary definition of a great man."[47]

To most of the romantic writers this aspect of Carlyle's theory would hardly have been understandable. When Friedrich Schlegel, in his novel *Lucinde*, gave his delineation of a truly romantic life his description ended in praise of idleness. Idleness that commonly is denounced as a vice is, in fact, one of the highest virtues. It is the clue to a poetic conception of the universe; the

medium for all imaginative life. Carlyle always spoke of Friedrich Schlegel with great sympathy. But nothing was more remote from his character and from his doctrine than this theory. He called himself a mystic but his mysticism never led him to any kind of quietism. It was not based upon devotional contemplation. "Virtue, *Vir-tus,* manhood, *hero*-hood . . . is first of all . . . courage and the faculty to *do*."[48] "Labour is life. . . . Properly thou hast no other knowledge but what thou hast got by working: the rest is yet all a hypothesis of knowledge; a thing to be argued of in schools, a thing floating in the clouds, in endless logic-vortices, till we try it and fix it."[49] If this is not worship the more pity for worship. The categorical imperative of Carlyle is Produce, Produce! "Were it but the pitifullest fraction of a product, produce it, in God's name! . . . Work while it is called today; for the night cometh, wherein no man can work."[50]

These last words, like so many others in Carlyle's writings, are a direct quotation from Goethe.[51] In Goethe, not in Novalis or Friedrich Schlegel, could Carlyle find the confirmation of his device *Laborare est orare*.[52] Goethe was to him the Oedipus of the modern world who had solved the riddle of the Sphinx. "From our point of view," he said, "does Goethe rise on us as the Uniter, and victorious Reconciler of the distracted, clashing elements of the most distracted and divided age that the world has witnessed since the introduction of the Christian religion."[53]

In one of his *Maxims and Reflections* Goethe says: "Wie kann man sich selbst kennen lernen? Durch Betrachten niemals, wohl aber durch Handeln. Versuche, deine Pflicht zu tun, und du weisst gleich, was an dir ist." "Was aber ist deine Pflicht? Die Forderung des Tages."[54] This maxim became to Carlyle the true metaphysics of life, the kernel of his "Life-Philosophy." Self-contemplation, as a mere theoretical act "is infallibly a symptom of disease. . . . There is a self-seeking; an unprofitable looking behind us to measure the way we have made: whereas the sole concern is to walk continually forward, and make more way."[55] For this purpose it is enough to know "the claims of the day"; to fulfil "the task that lies nearest." "Do the duty which lies nearest thee, which thou knowest to be a duty! Thy second duty will already become clearer. . . . You discover, with amazement enough, like the Lothario in *Wilhelm Meister,* that your 'America is here or nowhere.'"[56] "Our works are the mirror wherein the spirit first sees its natural lineaments. Hence, too, the folly of that impossible precept, *Know thyself;* till it be translated into this partially possible one, *Know what thou canst work at.*"[57]

This active and energetic conception of man's life necessarily has its repercussion upon our conception of nature. Both questions are closely interwoven; they are only different aspects of one and the same problem. Man will always form his image of nature after his own image. If he fails to see in himself an original and creative power, nature too becomes to him a mere passive thing—a dead mechanism. According to Carlyle this was the fate of the French Encyclopedists and the "philosophers" of the eighteenth century. Their theory of nature was the exact counterpart of their theory of man. Holbach's *Système de la nature* and Lamettrie's *L'homme machine* are closely akin. They express the same skeptical, destructive, negative spirit. The true hero of this philosophy was not Faust, the active and striving man, but Mephisto, "der Geist der stets verneint." Mephisto's maxim is the same as Voltaire's *"N'en croyez rien."* "The shrewd, all-informed intellect he has, is an attorney intellect; it can contradict, but it cannot affirm. With lynx vision he descries at a glance the ridiculous, the unsuitable, the bad; but for the solemn, the noble, the worthy, he is blind as his ancient mother."[58]

How could, indeed, man find greatness in nature after he had lost sight of his own greatness? How could he see in it a great living force when he himself was no longer alive but a mere automaton? On the other hand the dynamism that we have discovered in ourselves becomes the clue to a new conception of nature. Nature is no great engine moved by outward mechanical forces. It is the symbol and vesture of the Infinite, "the infinite garment of God." That is the very core of that "philosophy of clothes" which Carlyle develops in **Sartor Resartus.** "Alles Vergängliche ist nur ein Gleichnis"—all visible things are emblems. Before this great vision the illusion of a dead nature disappears. "System of Nature! To the wisest man, wide as his vision, nature remains of quite infinite depth." It is incomprehensible and inscrutable as long as we try to stretch it into the Procrustean bed of our poor words or our scientific concepts. We may speak of the "volume of nature"; but "it is a volume written in celestial hieroglyphs, in the true sacred-writing, of which even prophets are happy that they can read here a line and there a line."[59] We must oppose this true synthetic view of nature to the analytical view of the eighteenth century. Then, and then alone, we shall understand the "open secret."[60] We shall no longer see in the physical world a "frightful machine of death" nor hear in it a "monotonous din of a huge mill—a mill as such without millwright or miller."[61]

In all this Carlyle seems simply to reproduce and paraphrase the ideas of Goethe. Yet, on the other hand, he could never accept these ideas in their real and original meaning. Even after he had abandoned his Puritan faith he needed a more personal ideal of the Divine and Infinite than he could find in Goethe's works. There is a constant tendency in Carlyle's writings to suppress or to minimize all the pagan features of Goethe's religion. His own was a moral religion not a religion of nature. In his first lectures on hero worship he tried to do full justice to the different forms of polytheism. The worship of the great natural powers, he said, was the first and inevitable step in religious history. But he could not even understand this step without, unconsciously, modifying the very character of polytheism. Odin,

the highest god of German mythology, became to him simply a man, a great king or priest. We must not think of Odin as a personification of a natural force, but as a real person. He was, first and foremost, a teacher. Had he not solved, for the Norse people, "the sphinx-enigma of this universe"? Existence had become "articulate, melodious by him, he first had made Life alive. We may call this Odin, the origin of Norse mythology: Odin, or whatever name the first Norse thinker bore while he was a man among men."[62]

That was the personal reaction of Carlyle toward paganism, a reaction far different from that of Goethe who sometimes called himself a "decided pagan" and who, in his essay on Winckelmann, had become the interpreter and defender of Winckelmann's paganism.[63] Carlyle was no longer a "theist" in the traditional sense. But if he needed no personal god, he needed, at least, a personal hero. Worship of a natural power was at bottom unintelligible to him. He was deeply impressed by Goethe's doctrine of the "three reverences," the worship of all that is around, above, and below us. But he could never admit a comparison between Goethe's "ethnic religion" and his own religious convictions. To him such a religion was, at best, the "infant thought of man opening itself with awe and wonder, on this ever stupendous universe"—a rude childlike way of recognizing the divineness of nature.[64]

In Eckermann's *Conversations with Goethe* there is a passage that is very suitable to illustrate the fundamental difference between Goethe's religious views and those of Carlyle. He begins by declaring that there are, obviously, some discrepancies and even contradictions between the various texts upon which the Christian revelation is based. Nevertheless we may regard all four gospels as thoroughly genuine. There is in them the reflection of a greatness which emanated from the person of Jesus. "If I am asked," he continues,

> whether it is in my nature to pay Him devout reverence, I say—certainly! I bow before Him as the divine manifestation of the highest principle of morality. If I am asked whether it is in my nature to revere the Sun, I again say—certainly! For he is likewise a manifestation of the highest Being, and indeed the most powerful that we children of earth are allowed to behold. I adore in him the light and the productive power of God; by which we all live, move, and have our being—we, and all the plants and animals with us.[65]

Carlyle never felt or spoke in this way. To put the reverence of Christ on the same level as the adoration of the Sun would have appeared to him a sacrilege.

There was, however, still another and stronger reason why Carlyle, in his religious conceptions and ideals, could not confine himself to Goethe's works. "I believe in God!" says Goethe in one of his *Maxims.* "That is a fine, a worthy thing to say; but to recognize God where and as he reveals himself, is the only true bliss on earth."[66] According to this dictum Goethe declared himself to be a "pantheist," a "polytheist," and a "theist" at the same time. "As a naturalist," he said, "I am a pantheist; as an artist a polytheist, in my ethical life I am a monotheist."[67]

> Wie Natur im Vielgebilde
> Einen Gott nur offenbart;
> So im weiten Kunstgefilde
> Webt ein Sinn der ew'gen Art;
> Dieses ist der Sinn der Wahrheit,
> Der sich nur mit Schönem schmückt
> Und getrost der höchsten Klarheit
> Hellsten Tags entgegenblickt.[68]

Yet in this description of the manifestation of the Divine there was one thing missing. Goethe spoke of nature and art, but he did not speak of history. He never could esteem history in the same way as nature or art. He did not regard it as an immediate revelation of the Divine—he found it human, all too human. For Goethe historical knowledge was widely inferior to our knowledge of nature. Nature is one great infinite Whole; history gives us, at best, scattered limbs of human life. "Literature," says Goethe, "is the fragment of fragments. The least of what has been spoken was written, the least of what has been written has remained."[69] And even if all sources had been preserved—what would we know of history? What we call historical "facts" are, in most cases, mere legends. Every writer gives us his own distorted image of political events and human characters—according to his taste, his sympathies and antipathies, his national prejudices.[70] Carlyle could not speak of history in so disparaging and skeptical a way. He saw in it, even more than in nature or in art, the "visible garment of God." Great men were to him the inspired speaking and acting texts of that divine book of revelations, whereof a chapter is completed from epoch to epoch, and by some named history. To these inspired texts the more numerous merely talented men are only exegetic commentaries for better or worse. "For my study," he exclaimed, "the inspired texts themselves!"[71] To a true historian history is not, as Goethe says in *Faust,* "ein Kehrichtfass und eine Rumpelkammer." He has not only the power of relating the past; he revivifies it, he makes it present. The genuine historian speaks and acts like Gulliver's conjuror: he brings back "the brave Past, that we might look into it, and scrutinise it at will."[72] For such views Carlyle could find no support in Goethe's works. As a *historian* he had to make a fresh start; he had to find and to pave his own way—and, for this purpose, he had if not completely to change at least to modify his "Life-Philosophy." It was this modification that led him to his theory of hero worship and the heroic in history.

The metaphysical Background of Carlyle's Theory and His Conception of History

When Carlyle looked for a guide who could lead him through the labyrinth of history as Goethe had led him through the realms of nature and art, where was he to find him? There was one man who, if anyone, seemed to be fit for this service: Herder. But we have no evidence that Herder ever exerted a decisive influence upon Carlyle's thought. There was, however, another thinker for whom Carlyle had felt a keen interest and a strong admiration from the beginning. In one of his earliest essays, on the state of German literature (1827), he spoke of Fichte as a cold, colossal, adamantine spirit, standing erect and clear, like an elder Cato among degenerate men. So robust an intellect and a soul so calm, so lofty, massive, and immovable, had not mingled in philosophical discussion since the time of Luther. We may accept or reject his opinions; but his character as a thinker can be slightly valued only by such as know it ill. He ranks with a class of men who were common only in better ages than ours.[73]

When judging thus Carlyle hardly thought of Fichte's metaphysics. The first expositions of his metaphysical system that Fichte had given in his *Wissenschaftslehre* are among the most difficult books of philosophical literature. Carlyle would scarcely have been able to study and master them. What he read rather were Fichte's popular books, *Das Wesen des Gelehrten* and, in all probability, *Die Bestimmung des Menschen* and *Die Grundzüge des gegenwärtigen Zeitalters.* Here he could not find the whole of Fichte's metaphysics; but he found the "elder Cato" who spoke of the present age as the "Age of absolute indifference towards all truth, and of entire and unrestrained licentiousness:—the State of completed Sinfulness."[74] As a thinker whose whole interest was concentrated upon moral problems Carlyle must have been deeply impressed by such a judgment. Was it possible to find a remedy for what Fichte had described as the mortal disease of our modern world?

But could Carlyle accept Fichte's views without becoming unfaithful to the man to whom he felt indebted not only as a disciple to his master but as a son to his "spiritual father"?[75] Was it possible to reconcile the Life-Philosophies of Goethe and Fichte? Obviously they are not of the same type. Fichte's "subjective idealism" was, in its very principle, quite incompatible with Goethe's "objective idealism." But of this difference Carlyle does not seem to have been aware. His was not a logical or discursive but an intuitive mind. While he was no mere eclectic who freely borrowed from the most disparate sources, still he easily accepted any theory as long as he could adapt it to his ethical and religious requirements.

And in this respect there was, indeed, a point of contact between the views of Fichte and Goethe. Time and again Carlyle refers to Goethe's words that "doubt of whatever kind can be ended by action alone." This fundamental thesis he could also find in Fichte. Fichte's *Bestimmung des Menschen* is divided into three books. The first is entitled "Doubt," the second "Knowledge," the third "Faith." According to Fichte knowledge is never a mere theoretical act. By logical inferences, by our power of arguing and reasoning, we never can hope to touch reality and truth—let alone, to penetrate into their essence. This way can only lead us to a radical skepticism. If this were the only gateway to truth we should be forever condemned to live as in a dream. What we call the material world has only a shadowy existence; it is a product of the Ego that "posits" the Non-Ego. But there is another way that leads us beyond this world of shadows. The only reality that is clear, certain, unshakable, and admits of no doubt is the reality of our moral life—a "practical" not a merely "theoretical" reality. Here, and here alone, we stand on firm ground. The certainty of the moral law, of the categorical imperative, is the first thing that is given to us—the condition and the foundation of all other knowledge. Not by our intellect but by our will do we grasp reality.

"The reality in which thou didst formerly believe, a material world existing independently of thee, of which thou didst fear to become the slave," says the Spirit in Fichte's *Bestimmung des Menschen,*

> has vanished; for this whole material world arises only through knowledge, and is itself our knowledge; but knowledge is not reality, just because it is knowledge . . . Thou dost now seek, and with good right as I well know, something real lying beyond mere appearance, another reality than that which has thus been annihilated. But in vain wouldst thou labour to create this reality by means of thy knowledge or out of thy knowledge or to embrace it by thy understanding. If thou hast no other organ by which to apprehend it, thou wilt never find it. But thou hast such an organ. . . . Not merely to know, but according to thy knowledge to do, is thy vocation. . . . Not for idle contemplation of thyself, not for brooding over devout sensations—no, for action art thou here; thine action, and thine action alone, determines thy worth.[76]

All this recurs in Carlyle's writings and is often expressed in the very terms of Fichte. "Not what I Have but what I Do," he says, "is my Kingdom."[77] "Knowledge? The knowledge that will hold good in working, cleave thou to that; for Nature herself accredits that, says Yea to that."[78] If there is any firm and indubitable knowledge it does not belong to the external world, but to our inner life—and to the fixed center of this inner life, the consciousness of ourselves. "Never shall I forget that inward occurrence . . ." says Carlyle, quoting from Jean Paul,

> wherein I witnessed the birth of my Self-consciousness, of which I can still give the place and time. One forenoon, I was standing, a very young child, in the outer door, and looking leftward at the stack of the fuel-wood, when all at once the internal vision, "I am a Me" (*ich bin ein Ich*), came like a flash from heaven before me, and in gleaming light ever afterwards continued; then had my Me, for the first time, seen itself, and forever.[79]

But what is this "Self"? "Who am *I;* the thing that can say 'I' (*das Wesen, das sich Ich nennt*)?"[80] How and where can we find it? Obviously it is not a thing among things—

an object that can be discovered and described by scientific methods. It cannot be calculated and measured. It is not "given" in the same way as a physical thing; it must be "done." As Fichte said, it is not a *Tatsache* but a *Tathandlung;* it is not a fact but an act. Without the performance of this act the knowledge of ourselves and, accordingly, the knowledge of any outward reality, is impossible.

With all this Carlyle had found something that he could not find in Goethe's works. Fichte's *Wesen des Gelehrten,* a work that he quoted over and over again, had given a philosophical basis for his conception of the historical world. According to Fichte the historical world is not a mere by-product, a secondary phenomenon, embraced by and, in a sense, forlorn in the great universe of nature. In his system the relation between nature and history had been reversed. As long as we restrict ourselves to the phenomena of nature, declared Fichte, we cannot find the truth nor grasp the "Absolute." The very possibility of a philosophy of nature was passionately and emphatically denied by Fichte. When Schelling developed his philosophy of nature, he was accused by Fichte of high treason to the cause of transcendental idealism. Do not allow yourselves to be blinded and led astray, said Fichte in his second lecture addressing his students, by a philosophy assuming the name *Natur-Philosophie*. Very far from being a step toward truth, that philosophy is but a return to an old and already widespread error.[81]

In this conception of history and the "spiritual" world as the truly, nay only, "Absolute," Carlyle found the first decisive impulse to his theory of heroism and hero worship. Fichte could provide him with a whole *metaphysics* of hero worship.

We must content ourselves with a general delineation of Fichte's system.[82] It may be described as a system of "subjective" idealism. But the term "subjective" is always ambiguous and misleading. It requires a fixation and determination. Fichte's "transcendental subject"—the *Ich* that posits the *Nicht-Ich*—is neither the empirical subject; nor does it coincide with those types of subjectivity that we find in previous philosophical systems. It is neither the logical subject of Descartes nor the psychological subject of Berkeley. It belongs to a different order, the purely ethical order; to the realm of "ends" rather than to the realm of "nature"; to the realm of "values" rather than to that of "being." The first fundamental reality, the condition and prerequisite of anything else that we call "real," is the moral subject. We find this subject not by logical processes such as speculation, contemplation, or demonstration but by an act of our free WILL. In Fichte's philosophy Descartes' *Cogito, ergo sum* is changed to the maxim: *Volo, ergo sum*. But Fichte is neither a "solipsist" nor is he an egotist. The "I" finds itself by a free act—by an original *Tathandlung*. Activity is its very essence and meaning. But it cannot act without a material to act upon. It demands a "world" as the scene of its activity.

And in this world it finds other acting and working subjects. It has to respect their rights and their original freedom. Hence it has to restrict its own activity in order to give room to the activity of others. This restriction is not enforced on us by an external power. Its necessity is not that of a physical thing; it is a moral necessity. According to the moral law, the true absolute, we have to coöperate with other subjects and we have to build up a social order. The free act by which we find ourselves is to be completed by another act, by which we recognize other free subjects. This act of recognition is our first and fundamental duty.

Duty and obligation are, therefore, the elements of what we call the "real" world. Our world is the material of our duty, represented in a sensuous form. "Unsere Welt ist das versinnlichte Materiale unserer Pflicht; dies ist das eigentliche Reelle in den Dingen, der wahre Grundstoff aller Erscheinung. Der Zwang, mit welchem der Glaube an die Realität derselben sich uns aufdringt, ist ein moralischer Zwang; der einzige, welcher für das freie Wesen möglich ist."[83]

Yet in this great edifice of our moral world the cornerstone is still missing. Fichte's philosophy begins with the axiom that the basic element of reality, the stuff and material out of which it has been formed, is the moral energy of man. But where do we find this energy? There are some individuals who are so weak that they can hardly raise themselves to the idea of freedom. They have no conception of what a free personality is and means. They do not know and they do not understand that they have a personal, independent being and value, that they are "the thing that can say 'I.'"[84] On the other hand we find other individuals in which the moral energy, the consciousness of the "I," appears in its full vigor.

When speaking of the historical and cultural world, we must bear in mind this fundamental difference. The philosophers of the eighteenth century were resolute individualists. They inferred their doctrines of the equal *rights* of men from their implicit faith in the equality of *reason*. Descartes began his *Discourse on Method* by the words: "Good sense is, of all things among men, the most equally distributed; for everyone thinks himself so abundantly provided with it that those even who are the most difficult to satisfy in everything else, do not usually desire a larger measure of this quality than they already possess." Fichte broke with this conception. In his later works, he sees in the thesis of the equality of reason a mere intellectualistic prejudice. If reason means practical reason, if it means the moral will, it is by no means equally distributed. It is not to be found everywhere; it is actually concentrated in a few great personalities. In them the real meaning of the historical process manifests itself in its full and incomparable strength. These are the "heroes," the first pioneers of human culture. "Who, then, in the first place," asks Fichte,

> gave to the countries of Modern Europe their present habitable shape, and made them worthy to be the dwelling-place of cultivated men? History answers the

question. It was pious and holy men, who, believing it to be God's Will that the timid fugitive of the woods should be elevated to civilized life . . . went forth into the desert wilderness . . . Who has united rude races together, and reduced opposing tribes under the dominion of law? . . . Who has maintained them in this condition, and protected existing states from dissolution through internal disorder, or destruction by outward power? Whatever name they may have borne, it was Heroes, who had left their Age far behind them, giants among surrounding men in material and spiritual power.[85]

I do not mean to say that Carlyle accepted this metaphysical doctrine of Fichte in all its details. Perhaps he could not even understand Fichte's system of transcendental idealism in its full meaning and purport. He had no clear grasp of its theoretical premises or of its implications. Fichte spoke as a metaphysician, Carlyle spoke as a psychologist and historian. Fichte tried to convince by arguments; Carlyle usually contented himself with speaking to the sentiments of his readers and hearers. He simply declared hero worship to be a fundamental instinct in human nature, which if it were ever rooted out would lead to despair for mankind.[86]

Looking back at the results of our historical and systematic analysis we are now in a better position to judge the meaning and the influence of Carlyle's theory of hero worship. Perhaps no other philosophical theory has done so much to prepare the way for the modern ideals of political leadership. Had not Carlyle explicitly and emphatically declared that the hero as king, the commander over men, "is practically the summary for us of *all* the figures of heroism?" "Priest, Teacher, whatsoever of earthly or of spiritual dignity we can fancy to reside in a man, embodies itself here, to *command* over us, to furnish with constant practical teaching, to tell us for the day and hour what we are to do."[87] That was clear and plain spoken. The modern defenders of fascism did not fail to see their opportunity here and they could easily turn Carlyle's words into political weapons. But to charge Carlyle with all the consequences that have been drawn from his theory would be against all the rules of historical objectivity. In this regard I cannot accept the judgment that I find in recent literature on the subject.[88] What Carlyle meant by "heroism" or "leadership" was by no means the same as what we find in our modern theories of fascism. According to Carlyle there are two criteria by which we can easily distinguish the true hero from the sham hero: his "insight" and his "sincerity." Carlyle could never think or speak of lies as necessary or legitimate weapons in the great political struggles. If a man, like Napoleon in his later period, begins to lie, he immediately ceases to be a hero. "'False as a bulletin' became a proverb in Napoleon's time. He makes what excuse he could for it: that it was necessary to mislead the enemy, to keep up his own men's courage, and so forth. On the whole, there are no excuses. . . . A lie is *no*-thing; you cannot of nothing make something; you make *nothing* at last, and lose your labour into the bargain."[89] When Carlyle spoke of his heroes it was always his first concern to convince us that they despised all manner of deception. There can be no greater mistake than to speak of men like Mahomet or Cromwell as liars. "From of old, I will confess, this theory of Cromwell's falsity has been incredible to me. Nay I cannot believe the like, of any great man whatever."[90] "I will believe most things sooner than that. One would be entirely at a loss what to think of this world at all, if quackery so grew and were sanctioned here."[91]

There is still one other feature that distinguishes Carlyle's theory from the later types of hero worship. What he most admired in his heroes was not only the sincerity of feeling but also clearness of thought. Great energy of action and great will-power always imply an intellectual element. The strength of will and character would remain powerless without an equal power of thought. The equipoise between these two elements is the distinctive mark of the true hero. He is the man who lives among things, not among the shows of things. While others walk in formulas and hearsays, contented enough to dwell there, the hero is alone with his own soul and the reality of things.[92] Carlyle spoke as a mystic but his mysticism was no mere irrationalism. All his heroes—the prophets, the priests, the poets—are at the same time described as deep and genuine thinkers. In Carlyle's description even Odin, a mythical god, appears as a "thinker." "The first Norse 'man of genius,' as we should call him! Innumerable men had passed by, across this Universe, with a dumb vague wonder, such as the very animals may feel; or with a painful, fruitlessly inquiring wonder, such as men only feel;—till the great Thinker came, the *original* man, the Seer, whose shaped spoken thought awakes the slumbering capability of all into thought. It is ever the way with the thinker, the spiritual hero."[93] Thought, if it is deep, sincere, genuine, has the power to work wonders. In *Sartor Resartus* Carlyle speaks of "the grand thaumaturgic art of thought." "Thaumaturgic I name it; for hitherto all Miracles have been wrought thereby, and henceforth innumerable will be wrought."[94] Poetry, too, would be a very poor thing without this "thaumaturgic art of thought," for it is a very inadequate conception of poetry to see nothing in it except a play of imagination. Dante, Shakespeare, Milton and Goethe were great, deep, and genuine thinkers—and this was one of the most prolific sources of their poetical imagination. Imagination without thought would be barren; it could produce nothing but mere shadows and illusions. "At bottom," says Carlyle, "it is the Poet's first gift, as it is all men's, that he have intellect enough."[95]

It is, therefore, the rare and happy union of all the productive and constructive forces in man that, on Carlyle's theory, constitutes the character of the hero. And among all these forces the *moral* force obtains the highest rank and plays the preponderant role. In his philosophy "morality" means the power of affirmation over against the power of denial and negation. What really matters is not so much the thing affirmed as the act of affirmation itself and the strength of this act.

Here too Carlyle could have appealed to Goethe who relates in his autobiography that, when, in his youth, his friends tried to convert him to a special credo, he constantly repelled their efforts.

> In Faith, I said, every thing depends on the fact of believing; what is believed is perfectly indifferent. Faith is a profound sense of security in regard to both the present and the future; and this assurance springs from confidence in an immense, all-powerful, and inscrutable Being. The firmness of this confidence is the one great point; but what we think of this Being depends on our other faculties, or even on circumstances, and is wholly indifferent. Faith is a holy vessel into which every one stands ready to pour his feeling, his understanding, his imagination, as perfectly as he can.[96]

Here we have a striking expression of Carlyle's own religious feelings after he had abandoned his orthodox faith in the Calvinistic dogma. In his lectures on heroes he laid the whole stress not upon the kind but upon the intensity of religious feeling. The degree of it was to him the only standard. Hence he could speak with the same sympathy of Dante's catholicism and Luther's protestantism, of old Norse mythology and the Islam or Christian religion. What Carlyle admired most in Dante was that intensity. Dante, he said, does not come before us as a large catholic mind, rather as a narrow and even sectarian mind. He is world-great not because he is world-wide but because he is world-deep. "I know nothing so intense as Dante."[97]

Yet Carlyle was not always able to live up to this universal, all-embracing ideal of religion. There remained in him certain instinctive sympathies or antipathies that influenced his judgment. This becomes particularly clear in his attitude toward the eighteenth century. When Carlyle tried to describe the character of the historical process in a short formula he spoke of it as "the war of Belief against Unbelief."[98] "The special, sole and deepest theme of the World's and Man's history," Goethe had said in a note to his *West-Oestlicher Divan,*

> whereto all other themes are subordinated, remains the conflict of unbelief and belief. All epochs wherein belief prevails, under what form it may, are splendid, heart-elevating, fruitful for contemporaries and posterity. All epochs, on the contrary, wherein unbelief, under what form soever, maintains its sorry victory, should they even for a moment glitter with a sham splendour, vanish from the eyes of posterity; because no one chooses to burden himself with study of the unfruitful.[99]

Carlyle quoted these words with whole-hearted assent at the end of his essay on Diderot.[100] But he did not understand them in the same sense as Goethe. His conception of "belief" or "unbelief" was very different. According to

Goethe every productive period in human history is *ipso facto* to be regarded as a period of belief. The term has no theological not even a specific religious connotation but simply expresses the preponderance of the positive over the negative powers. Goethe could never speak of the eighteenth century, therefore, as a period of disbelief. He too had felt a strong personal aversion for the general tendency expressed in the Great Encyclopedia. "Whenever we heard the encyclopedists mentioned," he says in his autobiography,

> or opened a volume of their immense work, we felt as if we were going between the innumerable moving spools and looms of a great factory, where, what with the mere creaking and rattling; what with all the mechanism, embarrassing both eyes and senses; what with the mere incomprehensibility of an arrangement, the parts of which work into each other in the most manifold way; what with the contemplation of all that is necessary to prepare a piece of cloth—we feel disgusted with the very coat which we wear upon our backs.[101]

Yet, in spite of this feeling, Goethe never thought or spoke of the period of the Enlightenment as an unproductive age. He criticized Voltaire severely; but he always professed a profound admiration for his work. Diderot was regarded by Goethe as a genius and he translated his *Neveu de Rameau* and edited and commented on his *Essai sur la peinture.*[102]

All this was inadmissible and even unintelligible to Carlyle. As a historian Carlyle was somewhat in a better position than Goethe. His interest in historical problems was much more intense; his knowledge of facts was more comprehensive. Yet, on the other hand, he could only understand history in terms of his own personal experience. His "Life-Philosophy" was the clue to his historical work. In the great crisis of his youth he had found the way that led him from denial and despair to affirmation and reconstruction—from the "Everlasting No" to the "Everlasting Yea." Henceforth he conceived and interpreted the whole history of the human race in the same way. In his imagination, the imagination of a puritan, history became a great religious drama—the perpetual conflict between the powers of good and evil. "Are not all true men that live, or that ever lived, soldiers of the same army, enlisted, under Heaven's captaincy, to do battle against the same enemy, the empire of Darkness and Wrong?"[103] So Carlyle never could simply "write" history. He had to canonize or anathematize; he must extol to the skies or damn. His historical portraits are very impressive. But we miss in them all those delicate shades that we admire in the works of other great historians. He always paints in black and white. And from his point of view the eighteenth century was doomed from the very beginning. Voltaire of whom Goethe spoke as this "universal source of light"[104] was and remained to Carlyle the spirit of darkness. If we believe Carlyle's description Voltaire lacked all power of imagination and, therefore,

all productivity. The whole eighteenth century invented nothing; not one of man's virtues, not one of man's powers is due to it. The "philosophers" could only criticize, quarrel, rend to pieces. The age of Louis XV was "an age without nobleness, without high virtue or high manifestations of talent; an age of shallow clearness, of polish, self conceit, scepticism and all forms of *persiflage.*"[105]

In this judgment Carlyle simply followed the example of the romantic writers. But he spoke with an increasingly fanatic hatred. A man like Friedrich Schlegel would hardly have denied that the eighteenth century, with all its limitations, was an age of talents. Here Carlyle did not speak as a historian or literary critic but as a theological zealot. He described the work of the Encyclopedists as the "Acts and Epistles of the Parisian Church of Antichrist."[106] He completely failed to see the positive element in the cultural life of the Enlightenment. The most fearful disbelief is the disbelief in yourself. Can we charge the thinkers of the Enlightenment, the writers of the Great Encyclopedia with this disbelief? Indeed it would be much more correct to accuse them of the very opposite fault, of an overconfidence in their own powers and the power of human reason in general.

On the other hand it is hardly possible to see in Carlyle's aversion for the ideals of the French Revolution a definite political or social program. His interest always remained biographical rather than social, although he became more interested later in the social problems of his own age. His principal concern was the individual men not the forms of civil government or social life. The attempts made in recent literature to connect him with St.-Simonism or to read into his work a sociological conception of history are futile.[107] Ernest Seillière has tried to prove in his book *L'actualité de Carlyle* that Carlyle belongs to the long list of thinkers whom he formerly had studied in his great work on the philosophy of imperialism.[108] Other authors have described Carlyle as the "father of British Imperialism."[109] There is, however, a clear and unmistakable difference between Carlyle's views, even his views on colonial policy[110] and other forms of British imperialism. Even Carlyle's nationalism had its specific color. He saw the real greatness of a nation in the intensity and depth of its moral life and its intellectual achievements and not in its political aspirations. He spoke very bluntly and boldly. "Which Englishman we ever made, in this land of ours," he asked his aristocratic audience speaking of Shakespeare,

> which million of Englishmen, would we not give up rather than the Stratford peasant? There is no regiment of highest dignitaries that we would sell him for. He is the grandest thing we have yet done. For our honour among foreign nations, as an ornament to our English Household, what item is there that we would not surrender rather than him? Consider now, if they asked us, Will you give up your Indian Empire or your Shakespeare, you English; never have had any Indian

Empire, or never have had any Shakespeare? Really it were a grave question. Official persons would answer doubtless in official language; but we, for our part too, should not we be forced to answer: Indian Empire, or no Indian Empire; we cannot do without Shakespeare! Indian Empire will go, at any rate, some day; but this Shakespeare does not go, he lasts forever with us; we cannot give up our Shakespeare.[111]

That sounds vastly different from the imperialism and nationalism of the twentieth century. However we may object to Carlyle's theory of hero worship, a man who spoke thus ought never to be charged with being an advocate of contemporary National Socialistic ideas and ideals. It is true, that Carlyle did not refrain from saying that "might makes right." But he always understood the very term "might" in a moral rather than in a physical sense. Hero worship always meant to him the worship of a moral force. He seems often to have a deep distrust of human nature. But he is confident and optimistic enough to assume and assert that "man never yields himself wholly to brute force, but always to moral greatness."[112] If we ignore this principle of his thought we destroy his whole conception of history, of culture, of political and social life.

Notes

[1] A detailed description of Carlyle's lectures has been given by A. MacMeehan in the introduction to his edition (Boston, Ginn & Co., 1891). See also *The Correspondence of Thomas Carlyle and Ralph Emerson, 1834-1872* (Boston, 1894), I, 293 f. 2 vols.

[2] *On Heroes, Hero Worship and the Heroic in History,* Lect. VI, p. 195. Centenary ed., V, 202. I quote the lectures from the edition of H. D. Gray in Longman's English Classics (New York, Longmans, Green & Co., 1896). The other works of Carlyle are quoted from the Centenary edition, "The Works of Thomas Carlyle" (30 vols.) first published by H. D. Traill (London, Chapman & Hall, 1831 ff.), then superseded by a new American edition (New York, Charles Scribner's Sons, 1900).

[3] *On Heroes,* Lect. VI, p. 229. Centenary ed., V, 237.

[4] Durham, N. C., Duke University Press.

[5] H. F. C. Grierson, *Carlyle and Hitler* (Cambridge, England, University Press, 1933).

[6] E. Seillière, *Un précurseur du National-Socialisme: L'actualité de Carlyle* (Paris, Editions de la Nouvelle Revue Critique, 1939), p. 173.

[7] *Idem,* pp. 203 ff.

[8] "Biography" (1832), *Critical and Miscellaneous Essays,* III, 46. Centenary ed., Vol. XXVIII.

[9] *On Heroes,* Lect. I, p. 11. Centenary ed., V, 11.

[10] *Sartor Resartus,* Bk. III, chap. VII, I, 198.

[11] *On Heroes,* Lect. IV, p. 120. Centenary ed., V, 124.

[12] *Idem,* Lect. VI, p. 209. Centenary ed., V, 216 f.

[13] "Characteristics," *Essays,* III, 6.

[14] *On Heroes,* II, 56. Centenary ed., V, 57.

[15] *Idem,* I, 25. Centenary ed., V, 26.

[16] *Sartor Resartus,* Bk. III, chap. III, I, 176.

[17] *Idem,* I, 177.

[18] "Peter Nimmo, a Rhapsody."

[19] *On Heroes,* Lect. I, p. 14 f. Centenary ed., V, 15.

[20] *Idem,* Lect. II, 41 f., Centenary ed., V, 43; Lect. III, 76 f., Centenary ed., V, 78 f.

[21] *Idem,* Lect. V, 178. Centenary ed., V, 184.

[22] *Idem,* Lect. I, 11. Centenary ed., V, 11.

[23] "Characteristics," *Essays,* III, 7.

[24] See Carlyle's letters to Margaret Carlyle and to his brother Dr. John Carlyle. Cf. J. A. Froude, *Thomas Carlyle. A History of His Life in London* (New York, Charles Scribner's Sons, 1908), I, 155 ff.

[25] See Froude, *idem,* I, 167.

[26] See MacMeehan, *op. cit.,* pp. xxxv ff.

[27] "On History," *Essays,* II, 90.

[28] *Sartor Resartus,* Bk. I, chap. XI, I, 59.

[29] *Idem,* Bk. II, chap. VII, I, 135.

[30] "Characteristics," *Essays,* III, 25.

[31] *Sartor Resartus,* Bk. II, chap. VIII, I, 134 f.

[32] *Past and Present,* Bk. III, chap. XI, X, 198. See Carlyle's trans. of *Wilhelm Meisters Lehrjahre,* Bk. V, chap. XVI, XXIII, 386.

[33] *Sartor Resartus,* Bk. I, chap. III, I, 14.

[34] "Diderot," *Essays,* III, 248.

[35] "Goethe," *Essays,* I, 208.

[36] "Death of Goethe," *Essays*, II, 382.

[37] See R. Haym, *Herder* (Berlin, R. Gaertner, 1880), II, 618 f.

[38] Letter of September 21, 1823. See *Early Letters*, ed. Charles E. Norton (London, Macmillan & Co., 1886), p. 286.

[39] *Reminiscences*, ed. Charles E. Norton (Everyman's Library, London, J. M. Dent & Sons; New York, E. P. Dutton & Co., 1932), p. 282.

[40] *Lectures on the History of Literature*, ed. J. Reay Greene (New York, Charles Scribner's Sons, 1892), pp. 192 ff.

[41] *Past and Present*, Bk. III, chap. IV, X, 154.

[42] *Sartor Resartus*, Bk. II, chap. IX, I, 152 f.

[43] "Novalis," *Essays*, II, 24 ff.

[44] *On Heroes*, Lect. II, p. 73. Centenary ed., V, 75.

[45] "Characteristics," *Essays*, III, 27.

[46] "Jean Paul Friedrich Richter," *Essays*, I, 16 f.

[47] *On Heroes*, Lect. II, p. 44. Centenary ed., V, 45.

[48] *Idem*, VI, 210. Centenary ed., V, 218.

[49] *Past and Present*, Bk. III, chap. XI, X, 197 f.

[50] *Sartor Resartus*, Bk. II, chap. IX, I, 157.

[51] See Goethe, *West-Oestlicher Divan*, "Buch der Sprüche":

> Noch ist es Tag, da rühre sich der Mann!
> Die Nacht tritt ein, wo niemand wirken kann.

[52] Cf. Carlyle's letter to Goethe of April 15, 1827: "If I have been delivered from darkness into any measure of light, if I know aught of myself and my duties and destination, it is to the study of your writings more than to any other circumstance that I owe this." *Correspondence between Goethe and Carlyle*, ed. Charles E. Norton (London, Macmillan & Co., 1887), p. 7.

[53] "Goethe's Works," *Essays*, II, 434.

[54] Goethe, *Maximen und Reflexionen*, herausgegeben von Max Hecker, "Schriften der Goethe-Gesellschaft," Band XXI, Nos. 442, 443 (Weimar, Verlag der Goethe-Gesellschaft, 1907), 93. ("How can we come to know ourselves? Never by speculation, but by action. Try to do your duty and you will know at once what you are worth." "But what is your duty? The demand of the day.")

[55] "Characteristics," *Essays*, III, 7 f.

[56] *Sartor Resartus*, Bk. II, chap. X, I, 156.

[57] *Idem*, Bk. II, chap. VIII, I, 132.

[58] "Goethe's Helena," *Essays*, I, 157.

[59] *Sartor Resartus*, Bk. III, chap. VIII, I, 205 f.

[60] *On Heroes*, Lect. III, p. 78. Centenary ed., V, 80. See Goethe, *Gedichte* (Weimar ed.), III, 88.

> Müsset im Naturbetrachten
> Immer eins wie alles achten;
> Nichts ist drinnen, nichts ist draussen:
> Denn was innen: das ist aussen.
> So ergreifet ohne Säumnis
> Heilig öffentlich Geheimnis.

[61] "Novalis," *Essays*, II, 33; cf. Novalis, *Lehrlinge zu Sais*.

[62] *On Heroes*, Lect. I, p. 21. Centenary ed., V, 22.

[63] Goethe, *Winckelmann und sein Jahrhundert* (Weimar ed.), XLVI, 25 ff.

[64] *On Heroes*, Lect. I.

[65] Eckermann, *Conversations with Goethe*, March 11, 1832. English trans. by John Oxenford (Everyman's Library, London, J. M. Dent & Sons; New York, E. P. Dutton & Co., 1930), p. 422.

[66] Goethe, *Maximen und Reflexionen*, No. 809, p. 179.

[67] *Idem*, No. 807, p. 179.

[68] Goethe, "Künstler-Lied," Aus den *Wanderjahren*. Carlyle's trans., XXIV, 329:

> As all Nature's thousand changes
> But one changeless God proclaim;
> So in Art's wide kingdom ranges
> One sole meaning still the same:
> This is Truth, eternal Reason,
> Which from Beauty takes its dress,
> And serene through time and season
> Stands for aye in loveliness.

[69] *Maximen und Reflexionen*, No. 512, p. 111.

[70] For further details see E. Cassirer, *Goethe und die geschichtliche Welt* (Berlin, B. Cassirer, 1932).

[71] *Sartor Resartus*, Bk. II, chap. VIII, Centenary ed., I, 142.

[72] See "Schiller," *Essays*, II, 167.

[73] "State of German Literature," *Essays*, I, 77.

[74] See Fichte, *Grundzüge des gegenwärtigen Zeitalters.* English trans. by W. Smith, *The Popular Works of Johann Gottlieb Fichte* (4th ed. London, Trübner & Co., 1889), II, 17. Lect, II.

[75] See *Correspondence with Goethe*, April 15, 1827.

[76] Fichte, *Bestimmung des Menschen*, "Sämtliche Werke," ed. J. H. Fichte, II, 246 ff. *Popular Works*, I, 404-406.

[77] *Sartor Resartus*, Bk. II, chap. IV, I, 96.

[78] *Past and Present*, Bk. III, chap. XI, X, 198.

[79] "Jean Paul Friedrich Richter Again," *Essays*, II, 111.

[80] *Sartor Resartus*, Bk. I, chap. VIII, I, 41.

[81] Fichte, *Über das Wesen des Gelehrten*, "Sämtliche Werke," VI, 363 f. *Popular Works*, I, 224 f.

[82] For a closer analysis of Fichte's *Wissenschaftslehre* see E. Cassirer, *Das Erkenntnisproblem* (Berlin, B. Cassirer, 1920), Vol. III.

[83] Fichte, *Über den Grund unseres Glaubens an eine göttliche Weltregierung*, "Sämtliche Werke," V, 185.

[84] See Fichte, *Erste Einleitung in die Wissenschaftslehre*, "Sämtliche Werke," I, 434 f. "Was für eine Philosophie man wähle, hängt sonach davon ab, was man für ein Mensch ist . . . Ein von Natur schlaffer . . . Charakter wird sich nie zum Idealismus erheben."

[85] Fichte, *Grundzüge des gegenwärtigen Zeitalters.* See *Popular Works*, II, 47 f. Lect. III.

[86] Cf. *Sartor Resartus*, Bk. I, chap. X, I, 54.

[87] *On Heroes*, Lect. VI, p. 189. Centenary ed., V, 196.

[88] See above, p. 190, n. 5.

[89] *On Heroes*, Lect. VI, p. 230. Centenary ed., V. 238.

[90] *Idem*, Lect. VI, p. 203 f. Centenary ed., V, 211.

[91] *Idem*, Lect. II, p. 43. Centenary ed., V, 44.

[92] *Idem*, Lect. II, p. 53. Centenary ed., V, 55; Lect. IV, 125, Centenary ed., V, 128.

[93] *Idem*, Lect. I, p. 21. Centenary ed., V, 21.

[94] *Sartor Resartus*, Bk. II, chap. IV, I, 95 f.

[95] *On Heroes*, Lect. III, p. 102. Centenary ed., V, 105.

[96] Goethe, *Dichtung und Wahrheit*, Buch XIV. English trans. by John Oxenford (Boston, S. E. Cassino, 1882), II, 190.

[97] *On Heroes*, Lect. III, p. 90. Centenary ed., V, 92.

[98] *Idem*, Lect. VI, p. 197. Centenary ed., V, 204.

[99] Goethe, *Noten und Abhandlungen zu besserem Verständnis des West-Oestlichen Divan*, "Werke" (Weimar ed.), VII, 157.

[100] *Essays*, III, 248.

[101] Goethe, *Dichtung und Wahrheit*, Bk. XI. English trans., *op. cit.*, II, 82.

[102] "Werke" (Weimar ed.), XLV, 1-322. For further details see E. Cassirer, "Goethe und das achtzehnte Jahrhundert," *Goethe und die geschichtliche Welt* (Berlin, B. Cassirer, 1932).

[103] *On Heroes*, Lect. IV, p. 117. Centenary ed., V, 120.

[104] See Eckermann, *Conversations with Goethe*, December 16, 1828; English trans. by John Oxenford (see above, . . . , n. 65), p. 286.

[105] "Voltaire," *Essays*, I, 464 f.

[106] "Diderot," *idem*, III, 177.

[107] See the books of Mrs. L. Mervin Young, *Thomas Carlyle and the Art of History* (Philadelphia, University of Pennsylvania Press, 1939), and Hill Shine, *Carlyle and the Saint-Simonians* (Baltimore, The Johns Hopkins Press, 1941). For a criticism of these books see René Wellek, "Carlyle and the Philosophy of History," *Philological Quarterly*, XXIII, No. 1 (January, 1944).

[108] See Ernest Seillière, *La philosophie de l'impérialisme* (Paris, Plon-Nourrit et Cie., 1903-6). 4 vols.

[109] See G. von Schulze-Gaevernitz, *Britischer Imperialismus und englischer Freihandel* (Leipzig, Duncker & Humblot, 1906); Gazeau, *L'impérialisme anglais*. That this description is incorrect has been shown by C. A. Bodelsen, *Studies in Mid-Victorian Imperialism* (Copenhagen and London, Gyldendalske Boghandel, 1924), pp. 22-32.

[110] On this point see Bodelsen, *op. cit.*

[111] *On Heroes*, Lect. III, p. 109 f. Centenary ed., V, 113.

[112] "Characteristics," *Essays*, III, 12.

Francis X. Roellinger, Jr. (essay date 1957)

SOURCE: "The Early Development of Carlyle's Style," in *PMLA*, Vol. LXXII, No. 5, December, 1957, pp. 936-51.

[*In the following essay, Roellinger asserts that the eccentric style of Carlyle's* Sartor Resartus *is absent from Carlyle's earlier writings. Roellinger maintains that a review of Carlyle's early writings shows that Carlyle "first mastered a rather conventional style," patterns of which remain largely unbroken until the late 1820s.*]

In his admirable lectures, *The Problem of Style,* J. Middleton Murry illustrates one of the most common meanings of the word "style" by this remark: "I know who wrote the article in last week's *Saturday Review*—Mr. Saintsbury. You couldn't mistake his style." Here, according to Mr. Murry, "'style' means that personal idiosyncrasy of expression by which we recognize a writer."[1] This is a limited conception of style, but it is useful in studying the style of certain writers. Murry mentions Dr. Johnson, Gibbon, Meredith, and Henry James as appropriate subjects for this approach. We may add, with the authority of precedent, Thomas Carlyle.

For it is in this sense of "style" as a characteristic mode of expression, a highly individualized and frequently eccentric idiom, that critics have spoken of the style of *Sartor Resartus* and the later works. Some have gone so far as to call it, with or without disparagement, "Carlylese." Its more obvious elements—syntactical aberrations in imitation of German idiom, arresting interrogations, remote allusions, picturesque metaphors, typographical eccentricities, and so on—have been inventoried and discussed many times. Moreover, the sources of this style are by now generally agreed upon, and the view, first set forth by Thoreau, and after him by Lowell, that Carlyle was an imitator of Richter, has been superseded by the theory, of which Charles Harrold's account is representative, that Richter was only one of several sources of inspiration to an otherwise original stylist.[2]

The defense of Carlyle against the charge of imitating Richter has led into another question of equal interest. In their eagerness to demonstrate the extent and depth of Carlyle's originality, his advocates have argued that the style of *Sartor* is present in his earliest writing. Archibald MacMechan, for example, discovers intimations of Teufelsdröckh in an early letter, from which he infers that the idiom of *Sartor* is Carlyle's "habitual method of expressing himself."[3] And Harrold agrees that it appears "as early as 1814, when his friend Thomas Murray prophetically remarked on Carlyle's 'Shandean turn of expression'" (p. ix). But James Froude, despite his denial of the importance of Richter's influence, thought that Carlyle's style "remained undistinguished by its special characteristics till he had ceased to occupy himself with the German poets."[4] A priori, Froude's generalization would seem more reasonable than the MacMechan-Harrold view, which is based on the doubtful assumption that Carlyle was capable of the style long before he was possessed of the ideas and attitudes of *Sartor.* Such a bifurcation of content and expression over a substantial period of a writer's career might plausibly be assumed of, say, Macaulay, whose

views did not undergo crucial change. But Carlyle suffered through years of spiritual and physical affliction, and, after a long ordeal of religious and philosophical despair, underwent a conversion to the convictions set forth in *Sartor.* Meanwhile he had undertaken an apprenticeship in several kinds of writing, including fiction, translation, biography, and critical essays. And when, after a decade of such writing, most of it in the form of comment on the work of others, he attempted *Sartor,* it was clearly in the nature of an experiment, radically different in kind from the rest, "a *Kunstwerk* of my own!" he called it in reference to his earliest meditations upon it. To imply, as MacMechan and Harrold do, that the effect of all this was merely to heighten and mature a style already present in letters written when Carlyle was nineteen, is to press to an unlikely extreme the *sui generis* notion of style.

A study of the style of the early writings will, I think, justify Froude's view. It will show that Carlyle first mastered a rather conventional style, a mildly Johnsonian mode, as typical of the prose of the late eighteenth and early nineteenth centuries as the heroic couplet is of the poetry of the same time; that, although there are some departures from this style, its patterns are not often broken through until the late 1820's, when the essays become less expository and more hortatory, as in the articles on Burns and Voltaire; and that, despite a gradual emergence of some of the traits of *Sartor,* there is a break between *Sartor* and the precedent works, a break too radical to admit the description of its style as mere exaggeration of a former manner, or a "development of tendencies apparent in Carlyle's earliest writings."

I

The reader who approaches the early letters with his expectations aroused by the remarks of MacMechan and Harrold will be disappointed. Instead of frequent foreshadowings of the later style, he will find, again and again, a prose of which the following, from a letter to a friend in 1815, is a fair example:

> I am highly indebted to you for Hume. I like his essays better than anything I have read these many days. He has prejudices, he does maintain errors,—but he defends his positions with so much ingenuity, that one would be almost sorry to see him dislodged. His essays on "Superstition and Enthusiasm," on "The Dignity and Meanness of Human Nature," and several others, are in my opinion admirable both in matter and manner, particularly the first, where his conclusions might be verified by instances with which we are all acquainted. . . . But many of his opinions are not to be adopted. How odd does it look, for instance, to refer *all* the modifications of "national character" to the influence of moral causes. Might it not be asserted with some plausibility, that, even those which he denominates moral causes, originate from physical circumstances?[5]

To anyone looking back from *Sartor,* the style of this

passage is as unrecognizable as its argument for the importance of physical causes. It is as strange to hear Carlyle say that he would be "almost sorry" to see Hume dislodged from positions defended "with so much ingenuity," as it is to find him carefully qualifying a favorable judgment with an exception, and using a conventional turn like "verified by instances with which we are all acquainted." The polite, impersonal tone, the smooth sequence of thought from one sentence to another, the low pitch and mildness of manner—all are features that oppose this style to that of *Sartor.*

But perhaps the individual, the characteristic note is to be found in the vein of personal reflection. Not so: as the youthful hopes of the early Annandale years become dimmed by illness, intellectual frustration, and the drudgery of teaching at Kirkcaldy, the style of Carlyle's letters remains subdued and remarkably unprophetic of the later manner:

> I have thought much and long of the irksome drudgery— the solitude—the gloom of my condition. I reasoned thus: These things must be endured, if not with a peaceful heart, at least with a serene countenance; but it is worth while to inquire whether the profit will repay the pain of enduring them. A scanty and precarious livelihood constitutes the profit; you know me, and can form some judgment of the pain. But there is loss as well as pain. I speak not of the loss of health: but the destruction of benevolent feeling, that searing of the heart, which misery, especially of a petty kind, sooner or later, will never fail to effect—is a more frightful thing. (p. 85)

But it is not too frightful to find expression in carefully patterned sentences, so closely related that it is impossible to break the series without omitting an essential linking reference, or disturbing the balanced consideration of "profit" and "pain," or destroying the climactic effect of the final sentence.

Later he would be scornful of commiseration over the state of one's feelings, and the opposing attitude would generate a very different style. Meanwhile it was characteristic of him to set forth his gloomiest reflections in a manner most un-Teufelsdröckhian, and intensification of his gloom served only to heighten the conventional rhetoric of his habitual mode rather than to break it down:

> Had I lived at Athens, in the plastic days of that brilliant commonwealth, I might have purchased "a narrow paltry tub," and pleased myself with uttering gall among them of Cynosarges. But in these times— when political institutions and increased civilization have fixed the texture of society—when Religion has the privilege of prescribing principles of conduct, from which it is a crime to dissent—when, therefore, the aberrations of philosophical enthusiasm are regarded not with admiration but contempt—when Plato would be dissected in the *Edinburgh Review,* and Diogenes laid hold of by "a society for the Suppression of Beggars"—in these times—it may not be. (p. 86)

The reference to Diogenes and his tub is prophetic of *Sartor,* as is the satiric invention of the "Society for the Suppression of Beggars." But the ideals—"Athens, in the plastic days of that brilliant commonwealth," dissent from religiously prescribed principles of conduct, tolerance of philosophical aberrations—and the form in which these ideals are expressed—the long periodic sentence with its careful array of parallel "when" clauses—might deceive a student of nineteenth-century prose into concluding that this is a passage from John Stuart Mill.

Even so, the style of these early letters seems informal when compared to the manner of the articles contributed to Brewster's *Edinburgh Encyclopaedia.* A single passage will suffice to show the style of Carlyle's apprenticeship to his newly chosen profession. Here is a typical passage from the article on Montesquieu:

> But although the *Esprit des Lois* cannot be regarded as a full and correct solution, it is at least a splendid theory; and the labor of twenty years devoted to produce it, the enthusiasm required for sustaining such an effort, were by no means misapplied. The abundance of curious, and generally authentic, information, with which the work is sprinkled, renders it instructive even to a superficial reader; while the vigorous and original ideas to be found on every page of it, by an attentive one, never fail to delight and astonish where they convince, and to improve even where the truth of them seems doubtful.[6]

This is a fair example of the style of the early nineteenth-century formal essay, of the Ciceronian mode adapted to English and made popular chiefly through the influence of its greatest exponent, Dr. Johnson. It was the style that every young professional essayist had to learn if he wished to see his work in print. In some ways it is the prose counterpart of the heroic verse of the period: it sacrifices particularity to generalization tightly governed by a texture of parallel structure frequently in the form of balance and antithesis, even at the risk of being stilted and at times orotund, or doubtful in sense. In the last clause of the above passage, for example, "to *improve* even where the truth of them seems doubtful" does not seem to be a very satisfactory counter to the foregoing clause. It is nonsense to say, as MacMechan does, that Carlyle wrote these early articles "in manacles," for their style was as "natural" and appropriate to their purpose as that of *Sartor* and the later works to their very different one. It would be as reasonable to say that *The Comedy of Errors,* or "L'Allegro," or *Dubliners,* or the early work of any writer whose thought and style underwent significant change, was written "in manacles." Like Shakespeare, Milton, Joyce, and many other great stylists, Carlyle served an apprenticeship in which he mastered a traditional medium before experimenting and finally hewing out a style of his own.

II

Was Carlyle's departure from this traditional style gradual or abrupt? Froude's remark, to the effect that the style "remained undistinguished by its special characteristics till he had ceased to occupy himself with the German poets," is indeterminate. *Sartor* was begun in September 1830 and finished in July 1831. The second essay on Richter appeared in January 1830. Perhaps Froude had in mind the years 1827-29, which embrace the publication of the essays on Richter, German literature, Werner, Goethe, Heine, and Novalis. At any rate, the period implied by Froude is short. The other possibility, that of a gradual emergence of the style in the intervening works, between, say, the *Life of Schiller* and *Sartor,* is suggested by Emery Neff, who regards the style of *Sartor* as a culmination of tendencies that appear in those works. Some support for this view comes from D. L. Maulsby's study, *The Growth of Sartor Resartus,* published in 1899.[7] Although Maulsby was chiefly interested in the development of Carlyle's thought, his essay has inevitable implications regarding style, for its purpose is "to show that the leading ideas of *Sartor Resartus,* the principal devices of its method, and even the equivalents of many of its phrases, are anticipated in Carlyle's earlier essays." Maulsby has done a remarkably thorough job of searching out innumerable repetitions in *Sartor* of ideas from the foregoing articles, frequently in the form of metaphors and rhetorical patterns. Unfortunately, he includes among the earlier essays about ten written after August 1831 and before August 1834; that is to say, after the completion of the final version of *Sartor* and before the publication of the last installment in *Fraser's Magazine.* These comprise about a third of all the essays considered, and the result is that Maulsby's compilation of repetitions of idea and phrase is considerably expanded by examples from essays written after the style of *Sartor* had crystallized. But even when these essays are included, an interesting fact remains, one that Maulsby, who calls attention to it, is unable to explain. *Sartor* was, of course, published anonymously, and Maulsby remarks: "It is difficult to understand how, even at that early period of his career, some of [Carlyle's] previous writing had not exposed him at once, on the appearance of *Sartor,* as himself the veritable Teufelsdröckh, instead of leaving the secret of his mystification only gradually to struggle into light" (pp. 22-23). But is it so difficult to understand? The first readers of *Sartor* did not have the benefit of Maulsby's hindsight. Maulsby has read Carlyle backwards, searching diligently for the ideas and idiom of Teufelsdröckh in the precedent essays; he is, naturally, impressed by the number of anticipations he has found, but he seems to forget that these are scattered over more than a thousand pages. And even though the important ideas are there, the style of *Sartor* was perhaps different enough to disguise them.

Here and there in the early letters and articles are hints of what is to come, and in the writings of the middle and late 1820's there are departures from the norm of the traditional style described above. But there is no such pattern of gradual emergence as would justify speaking of *Sartor* as a culmination. Until the philosophy of *Sartor* begins to be formulated, the resemblances are superficial, but interesting enough to merit notice.

Among the earliest passages, we may put beside the one cited by MacMechan an inscription from a book of Greek prose that evidently belonged to "Thomas Carlyle, student, 1814":

> Oh, Fortune! thou that parcellest out to man his lot of pleasure or of pain, that givest to one to feast upon fat things, and dash through life in a coach and six,—and to another to starve on his salted herring, and drive through life his Cutler's Wheel,—Bestow (if it please thee) crowns and kingdoms and principalities and purses and puddings and power, upon the great and the noble and the fat ones of the earth: Grant me that with a heart of independence, unseduced by the world's smiles, and unbending to its frowns, I may attain to literary fame.
>
> And though starvation be my lot I will smile that I have not been born a king!!![8]

The thought is uncharacteristic of Carlyle and is said to have surprised David Masson. There can be no doubt of its authenticity, however, for the passage appears, with some alterations, in a letter to Murray of August 1814 (see Froude, I, 38). A reader of *Sartor* might reasonably ascribe it to Carlyle because of the declamatory apostrophe, the Biblical tags, the ironic contrast, and the metaphors of "feast upon fat things, and dash through life in a coach and six" and "starve on his salted herring, and drive through life his Cutler's Wheel," the humorous interpolations of "purses and puddings" and "the fat ones of the earth," the capitalization and punctuation. The whole passage is a parody of prayer not too unworthy of the wit of Teufelsdröckh.

And then there are a few satirical observations on the rejected professions of ministry and law that provide a mild foretaste of the denunciatory vein of *Sartor.* To a friend in 1818, he writes contemptuously of the conversation of preachers and divinity students as "nearly confined to the church or rather kirk-session politics of the place . . . the vacant parishes and their presentees, with patrons, tutors, and all other appurtenances of the tythe-pigtail." In like manner, he ridicules David Hume's lectures on law as being too full of "long-winded, dry details . . . uncounted cases of blockhead A *versus* blockhead B, with what Stair thought upon them, what Bankton, what the poor doubting Dirleton; and then the nature of actions of—*O infandum!*" (pp. 67, 144).

Whenever he has occasion to give vent to the pet notions and prejudices that became the obsessions of later years, his early prose takes on some of the coloring of *Sartor.* In a letter to his brother Alexander, in 1821, the contrast between city and country life is expressed in the symbols of the dandy and the peasant. If, he says, Alec could see the dandies "hunting and drinking and debauching all ways; dancing, dressing, strutting," then he would gladly forsake "the switch and quizzer and other *plaiks* [playthings] invented by French barbers and the like, for the venerable plough—invented by Father Adam himself, and dignified by the usage of patriarchs and heroes, and still better dignified as the Upholder of the human race" (p. 167).

But such passages are brief, being the exception rather than the rule, and they might be easily missed by someone not on the lookout for them. One has to look hard and long in the early letters for one of the most conspicuous hall marks of the diction of *Sartor,* jingling pairs of words, before coming at last upon "this is a wild, fighting, loving, praying, blaspheming, weeping, laughing sort of world! The *literati* and *literatuli* with us are wrangling and scribbling; but effecting nothing, except to 'make the day and way alike long'" (pp. 252-253). Sustained Carlylese is not to be found in the letters before March 1831, when Carlyle was in the midst of rewriting the rejected version of *Sartor* and was at last confident that he had a message of his own to deliver. In a letter to his brother John, he announces that he might go to London in the following winter to lecture:

> Does there seem to thee any propriety in a man that has organs of speech and even some semblance of understanding and sincerity, sitting forever, mute as milestone, while Quacks of every color are quacking as with lungs of brass? True, I have no Pulpit: but as I once said, cannot any man *make* him a pulpit, simply by inverting the nearest Tub? And what are your Whigs, and Lord Advocates, and Lord Chancellors, and the whole host of unspeakably gabbling Parliamenteers and Pulpiteers and Pamphleteers,—if a man suspect that "there is fire enough in his belly to burn up" the entire creation of such! These all build on Mechanism: one spark of Dynamism, of Inspiration, were it in the poorest soul, is stronger than they all . . . [9]

That is unmistakably the rhetoric of *Sartor,* and it shows how inseparable that rhetoric is from the thought and attitude of the work. Here we have, expressed or implied, the most important social ideas of *Sartor:* that the age is in need of spiritual deliverance, that liberal reform is futile because it regards society as a mechanism, and that society, as a spiritual whole, will respond only to spiritual forces. The vehicle of these ideas resembles *Sartor* in its staccato phrasing, rhetorical interrogations, reference to quackery, jeering neologisms—"Parliamenteers and Pulpiteers and Pamphleteers," alliteration—"mute as milestone," use of the subjunctive inversion "were it" instead of the more common "if it were," and capitalization of important nouns, not only for emphasis, but in one instance, "Tub," to designate metaphor.

III

As illustrations of the persistence of the traditional style and of occasional aberrations, more interesting than the letters of this period are the articles written after the

Life of Schiller but before the first version of *Sartor.* There are thirteen of these, from the first essay on Jean Paul in 1827 to the essay **"On History"** in 1830, and they include the well known essays on Burns and Voltaire and **"Signs of the Times."**

Although it contains the description of Richter's style often quoted as an apt characterization of the manner of *Sartor,* the first essay on Jean Paul is not remarkable for departures from the norm of earlier essays. It was Carlyle's first contribution to the *Edinburgh Review,* and it seems to have been accepted by Jeffrey without requests for revisions, a fact of some significance regarding its style, suggesting that it could not have been much at odds with Jeffrey's expectations. It has some of the grandiloquence of the *Life of Schiller,* but the parallel phrases are now set off by semicolons, making for the interrupted effect typical of the later style:

> [Richter] has an intellect vehement, rugged, irresistible; crushing in pieces the hardest problems; piercing into the most hidden combinations of things, and grasping the most distant: an imagination vague, sombre, splendid, or appalling; brooding over the abysses of Being; wandering through Infinitude, and summoning before us, in its dim religious light, shapes of brilliancy, solemnity, or terror: a fancy of exuberance literally unexampled; for it pours its treasures with a lavishness which knows no limit, hanging, like the sun, a jewel on every grass-blade, and sowing the earth at large with orient pearl. (XXVI, 14)

One can see here the beginning of the disintegration of the closely knit, precisely patterned sentence of the articles written for Brewster. Parallelism is sustained, but without much balance, so that punctuation, the colon, rather than structure, signals the threefold division of "intellect," "imagination," and "fancy." The climactic design is less evident, less mechanical. The diction is still rather abstract—"brooding over the abysses of Being; wandering through Infinitude"—and the imagery is conventional and flowery.

"The State of German Literature," the essay that followed in the same year and in the pages of the same periodical, was unrecognizable to Goethe, with whom Carlyle was now in correspondence. "Can you tell me," Goethe asked, "who has written the paper on the state of German literature in the *Edinburgh Review?* It is believed here to be by Mr. Lockhart, Sir Walter Scott's stepson" (Froude, I, 407). Goethe and his friends could not have been too well informed, for in 1827 Lockhart was editor of the Tory *Quarterly Review* and an unlikely contributor to its Whig rival. The remark is evidence, however, that to Goethe, who was familiar with Carlyle's previous writing, his style was not yet obviously recognizable. To mistake Carlyle for Lockhart was not then so imperceptive as it seems now, so far as style is concerned, for the bulk of the essay is expository in a manner that would be difficult to distinguish from the prose staple of a host of anonymous reviewers and essayists of the day. But with the advantage of hindsight it is easy to recognize Carlyle in this passage:

> We confess, the present aspect of spiritual Europe might fill a melancholic observer with doubt and foreboding. It is mournful to see so many noble, tender and high-aspiring minds deserted of that religious light which once guided all such: standing sorrowful on the scene of past convulsions and controversies, as on a scene blackened and burnt up with fire . . . pitching tents among the ashes, and kindling weak earthly lamps which we are to take for stars. The darkness is but transitory obscuration: these ashes are the soil of future herbage and richer harvests. . . . In any point of Space, in any section of Time, let there be a living Man; and there is an Infinitude above him and beneath him, and an Eternity encompasses him on this hand and on that; and tones of Sphere-music, and tidings from loftier worlds, will flit round him, if he can but listen . . . Happy the man . . . that can hear these tidings; that has them written in fit characters, legible to every eye, and the solemn import of them present at all moments to every heart! (XXVI, 85-86)

That is the unique vision of Carlyle, set forth in several images familiar to the reader of *Sartor* and the later works: the fire-image, symbol of the destruction of traditional institutions, and ashes, symbol of the source of reincarnation; sphere-music, an allusion to the Pythagorean notion of the sound made by the movement of the planets, symbol of eternity; hieroglyphic characters, representative of appearance, through which man interprets reality. In this passage, part of a concluding paragraph, the expository vein of the essay is abandoned for a flight into poetic prose that employs some of the images but none of the violent, grotesque, and broken utterance of *Sartor.* The passage is transitional and seems to show that the imagery of the later style preceded departures in syntax.

The most conspicuous development in the direction of *Sartor* appears in the essay on Burns, also published in the *Edinburgh Review,* but only after an altercation with Jeffrey over the manuscript. As long as Carlyle was content to be a mere expositor of German literature, as in his first two essays for the *Edinburgh,* and as long as his style did not violate the preconceptions of its readers, Jeffrey seems to have accepted his work without requests for revisions, but when Carlyle received the proof sheets of the article on Burns, he found that Jeffrey had deleted several important passages. After restoring these, he returned the sheets to Jeffrey with a note to the effect that the article might be rejected but not mutilated. Jeffrey acquiesced, but not until he had scolded Carlyle for his "delusive hope of converting our English intellects to the creed of Germany and being the apostle of another Reformation." As for the effect of "this *foeda superstitio*" on Carlyle's style, Jeffrey added: "The only harm it has yet done you is to make you a little verbose and prone to exaggeration. There are strong symptoms of both in your

Burns. I have tried to staunch the first, but the latter is in the grain, and we must just risk the wonder and ridicule it may bring upon us" (Froude, II, 38-40).

Jeffrey was right in perceiving that Carlyle had forsaken the role of expositor for that of apostle, and several passages in the essay justify his remarks on the effects of the transformation upon style. Instead of writing the usual judicious and informative review of Lockhart's *Life of Burns,* Carlyle exploited the occasion to express his own views on many subjects— biography, aristocracy, poverty, genius, necessity, obedience, patronage, wisdom, religion, and the true happiness of man. In Burns, Carlyle saw the tragic pattern of the writer of near-heroic virtue driven to destitution and degradation by a pleasure-loving faithless age. The heightened strain that distressed Jeffrey is sounded whenever Carlyle touches upon his favorite themes of pity and admiration for Burns and scorn for the age that failed to realize his true worth. In a disarming aside that might well have been inserted after Jeffrey's criticism, Carlyle says: "We are anxious not to exaggerate; for it is exposition rather than admiration that our readers require of us here; and yet to avoid some tendency to that side is no easy matter. We love Burns, and we pity him; and love and pity are prone to magnify" (XXVI, 263-264). A rhapsodic passage that follows this remark seems to justify it:

> How his heart flows out in sympathy over universal nature; and in her bleakest provinces discerns a beauty and a meaning! The "Daisy" falls not unheeded under his ploughshare; nor the ruined nest of that "wee, cowering, timorous beastie," cast forth, after all its provident pains, "to thole the sleety dribble and cranreuch cauld." The "hoar visage" of Winter delights him; he dwells with a sad and oft-returning fondness in these scenes of solemn desolation; but the voice of the tempest becomes an anthem to his ears; he loves to walk in the sounding woods, for "it raises his thoughts to *Him that walketh on the wings of the wind.*" (XXVI, 265)

At the risk of bathos, this strain must be forced still higher in praise of Burns's sympathy for human nature: "What warm, all-comprehending fellow-feeling; what trustful, boundless love; what generous exaggeration of the object loved! His rustic friend, his nut-brown maiden, are no longer mean and homely, but a hero and queen, whom he prizes as the paragons of Earth." That is certainly more extravagant than anything in the preceding essays, and it is recognizably Carlyle. But as an attempt to rise to an *O Altitudo* it seems forcible-feeble compared to the eloquence of, say, the famous passage in *Sartor,* "Two men I honor and no third. . . ."

More effective, as well as more prophetic of the style of *Sartor,* are satirical passages in which Carlyle denounces the society he held partly responsible for Burns's failure to live up to his youthful promise. Here the reference is to the present as well as the past, however generalized, and the theme is typical of *Sartor.* In a passage that must have been especially offensive to Jeffrey, Carlyle compares the false impressions of Burns given by some of Lockhart's authorities with a biography of Shakespeare written by "a dining acquaintance of Sir Thomas Lucey's," and after suggesting its absurd inadequacies, he adds:

> In like manner, we believe, with respect to Burns, that till the companions of his pilgrimage, the Honorable Excise Commissioners, and the Gentlemen of the Caledonian Hunt, and the Dumfries Aristocracy, and all the Squires and Earls, equally with the Ayr Writers, and the New and Old Light Clergy, whom he had to do with, shall have become invisible in the darkness of the Past, or visible only by light borrowed from *his* juxtaposition, it will be difficult to measure him by any true standard, or to estimate what he really was and did, in the eighteenth century, for his country and the world. (XXVI, 259)

Carlyle has omitted his favorite epithet in this strain— "game preserving"—but otherwise this passage shows that he had mastered the art of name-calling characteristic of his later satirical rhetoric. "The New and Old Light Clergy" is a palpable hit worthy of the mature Carlyle at his best—or worst, depending on the reader's point of view.

IV

The style of the essay on Burns is transitional and experimental: Carlyle seems to be striving for an idiom of his own, and in so doing hits upon some of the features of the later manner and achieves a recognizable style, but it is uneven and sometimes forced. In the remaining articles written before the first version of *Sartor,* he consolidates this style somewhat short of the reach attempted in the Burns; it is as if he were content with the means in hand until a new end, that of a "Kunstwerk" of his own, declared itself, and new means had to be found.

The recognizable style of the articles written after the Burns is not easy to describe. The occasional characteristic metaphor, apostrophe, rhetorical question, and odd turn of phrase tell only part of the story. These can be found by the diligent searcher, who is inevitably more impressed by their presence than by their absence. In the essay on Heine, for example, he will find this typical figure: "It is curious . . . to see with how little of a purely humane interest he looks back to his childhood; how Heine the man has almost grown into a sort of teaching machine, and sees in Heine the boy little else than an incipient Gerundgrinder, and tells us little else but how this wheel after the other was developed in him, and he came at last to grind in complete perfection" (XXVI, 325). Nor will he miss the oratorical interrogation at the bottom of a page of the essay on Voltaire: "What Plough or Printing-press, what Chivalry or Christianity, nay, what Steam-engine, or Quakerism, or Trial by Jury, did these Encyclopedists invent for mankind?" The search for jin-

gling pairs of alliterative words will be even more rewarding: "theogony, theology," "pudding, praise," "vibrations, vibratiuncles," "Dapperism and Dilletantism and rickety Debility." Looking for another hallmark of Carlyle's diction, the pluralizing of proper nouns, he will come up with: "our Knowleses, Maturins, Shiels, and Shees," "Lord Mayor Shows and Guildhall dinners," "Royal and Imperial Societies, the Bibliothèques, Glyphothèques, Technothèques."

But the main current of the style of these essays is seldom recognizable, for despite occasional intrusions of reflective and hortatory passages, the narrative and expository burden is still formidable, and it offers few occasions for stylistic fireworks. The prevailing tone is still that of the polite, impersonal, and anonymous reviewer: "So much, in the province to which he devoted his activity, is Heine allowed to have accomplished. Nevertheless, we must not assert that, in point of understanding and spiritual endowment, he can be called a great, or even, in strict speech, a complete man" (XXVI, 351). What happens to this manner when occasion offers illumination of the apostolic message is well illustrated in the following, on Voltaire's last visit to Paris:

> Considered with reference to the world at large, this journey is further remarkable. It is the most splendid triumph of that nature recorded in these ages; the loudest and showiest homage ever paid to what we moderns call literature; to a man that had merely thought, and published his thoughts. Much false tumult, no doubt, there was in it; yet also a certain deeper significance. It is interesting to see how universal and eternal in man is love of wisdom; how the highest and the lowest, how supercilious princes, and rude peasants, and all men must alike show honor to Wisdom, or the appearance of Wisdom; nay, properly speaking, can show honor to nothing else. (XXVI, 437)

If this is one of the earliest, it is also one of the most restrained statements of Carlyle's idea of worship of the hero as man of letters. Departures from conventional expression are slight but recognizable. The first sentence is commonplace, and the second is remarkable only for the use of the semicolon where conventional practice would suggest the comma. The fuller stop emphasizes each phrase or clause and interrupts the flow of thought. The third sentence shows what is happening to the usual balance and antithesis: instead of "there was not only much false tumult but also a certain deeper significance," we have an inversion: "Much false tumult, no doubt, there was in it; yet also a certain deeper significance." The inversion places the balanced elements at opposite ends of the sentence instead of within the conjunctive frame. The last sentence is most prophetic of the later style, not only in its interrupted, staccato parallel phrasing and unusual number of monosyllabic words, but in its use as climax of what Bonamy Dobrée has called the "door-banged" effect: "Nay, properly speaking, can show honor to nothing else."

A comparison of this passage with a brief paragraph on the same subject in *Sartor* shows how far the style of *Sartor* goes beyond the most recognizable manner of the precedent essays. Despite its "door-banged" conclusion, the passage from the Voltaire is almost urbane: Carlyle is as gentle and tolerant as he could be to an unsympathetic subject. Voltaire's journey is admittedly "the most splendid triumph of that nature recorded in these ages," and the qualification, "much false tumult, no doubt," is a mild concession. The writer is above the reader, as he is in most reviews of the day, but his attitude is polite and courteous: if the reader will but look and consider, he will "see how universal and eternal in man is love of wisdom." This attitude to subject and reader reflects in part the truth of Louis Cazamian's observation: "Carlyle's mind was never again so liberal as when he wrote these essays; at this happy period, allied with his rugged independence was a plasticity of mind, a tolerance, that age and fame gravely weakened."[10] The style of the passage from *Sartor* might show the weakening; certainly it shows how the whole form and purpose of that work demanded and received a radical change in style. In it Teufelsdröckh cites Voltaire's last journey to Paris as an instance of hero-worship, which he calls "the corner-stone of living rock, whereon all Polities for the remotest time may stand secure": "Do our readers discern any such corner-stone, or even so much as what Teufelsdröckh is looking at? He exclaims, 'Or hast thou forgotten Paris and Voltaire? How the aged, withered man, though but a Sceptic, Mocker, and millinery Court-poet, yet because he seemed the Wisest, Best, could drag mankind at his chariot-wheels, so that the princes coveted a smile from him, and the loveliest of France would have laid their hair beneath his feet! All Paris was one vast Temple of Hero-worship; though their Divinity, moreover, was of feature too apish.'"[11]

In place of the polite reviewer patiently pointing out the moral to his gentle reader, we have Teufelsdröckh on his inverted tub, scolding and haranguing the multitude. He is introduced by a question from his supposititious editor, whose attitude to the reader is hardly distinguishable from that of Teufelsdröckh himself, for the implication is that the reader is a dolt because he will *not* "discern any such corner-stone." He will not only fail to see what Teufelsdröckh sees: he will even fail to see a great deal less. This scornful attitude to the reader is, of course, a rhetorical device of deliberate provocation; throughout the work he is frequently addressed as "Fool!" Nevertheless he is apparently expected to know what is alluded to in the question, "Or hast thou forgotten Paris and Voltaire?" No previous mention is made of the incident, nor is the reference self-explanatory; like many other obscure allusions in *Sartor,* it requires a note.

Scorn for the reader is more than matched by contempt for Voltaire, caricatured as "the aged, withered man," called names, "Sceptic, Mocker, and millinery Court-poet," and referred to in the coarse anti-climax of the passage as a "Divinity . . . of feature too apish." In the review, by the way, he is the "lean, tottering, lonely old man," to whom "we feel drawn . . . by some tie of affection, of kindly sympathy." The scornful exaggeration of the description, including the princes coveting Voltaire's smile, and "the loveliest of France" laying their hair beneath his feet makes something of a paradox of the "vast Temple of Hero-worship." In general, the two passages employ opposed strategies: the strategy of the review is the sympathetic approach; that of *Sartor* might be called the shock treatment.

The truth is that Carlyle mastered at least two styles, the first based on the traditional prose required of the periodical reviewer, the second an unconventional, eccentric idiom designed to meet the requirements of the fiction of Teufelsdröckh and his book on clothes. Perhaps neither was his "natural voice," whatever that may mean; both betray signs of deliberate and painstaking construction. W. C. Brownell has shrewdly suggested that Carlyle's praise of unconsciousness was "a reaction from the discomfort and often the misery with which his extremely conscious composition was attended. No writer ever thought more of *how* he was to do whatever he did. His journal records that he sat three days before the sheet of paper at the top of which the word 'Voltaire' was written before writing a line of his famous essay. Certainly, during that time, he was not thinking what to say."[12]

As a final piece of evidence in favor of Brownell's suggestion and in support of the conclusion of this essay, two more passages might be cited without much comment, for they speak for themselves. The first is from **"Characteristics,"** written after the first version of *Sartor,* and possibly while Carlyle was in the midst of revising and enlarging it. At the time when he had already mastered the idiom of Teufelsdröckh, Carlyle could still, on occasion, write a whole essay in this vein:

> If Society, in such ages, had its difficulty, it also had its strength; if sorrowful masses of rubbish so encumbered it, the tough sinews to hurl them aside, with indomitable heart, were not wanting. Society went along without complaint; did not stop to scrutinize itself, to say, How well I perform!, or, Alas, how ill! Men did not yet feel themselves to be "the envy of surrounding nations"; and were enviable on that very account. Society was what we can call *whole,* in both senses of the word. The individual man was in himself a whole, or complete union; and could combine with his fellows as the living member of a greater whole. For all men, through their life, were animated by one great Idea; thus all efforts pointed one way, everywhere there was wholeness. (XXVIII, 15)

The second passage, on the same subject, is from *Sartor:*

> "Call ye that a Society," cries he again, "where there is no longer any Social Idea extant; not so much as the Idea of a common Home, but only of a common over-crowded Lodging-house? Where each, isolated,

regardless of his neighbor, clutches what he can get, and cries 'Mine!' and calls it Peace, because in the cut-purse and cut-throat Scramble, no steel knives, but only a far cunninger sort, can be employed? Where Friendship, Communion, has become an incredible tradition; and your holiest Sacramental Supper is a smoking Tavern Dinner, with Cook for Evangelist? Where your priest has no tongue but for plate-licking? and your high Guides and Governors cannot guide; but on all hands hear it passionately proclaimed: *Laissez faire:* Leave us alone of *your* guidance, such light is darker than darkness; eat your wages, and sleep!" (p. 232)

"**Characteristics**" was not only accepted by Jeffrey's successor, Macvey Napier, and published in the *Edinburgh Review;* it was, according to Froude, "received with the warmest admiration from the increasing circle of young intellectual men who were looking up to [Carlyle] as their teacher, and with wonder and applause from the reading London world" (II, 266). But when **Sartor,** having failed of publication in book form, finally began to appear in *Fraser's Magazine,* which, we are told, "had a reputation for audacity, exuberance, and boisterous humor and satire" (**Sartor,** p. 11, n.), no one could tell what to make of it, and Froude informs us that "the writer was considered a literary maniac, and the unlucky editor was dreading the ruin of his magazine" (II, 363). History does not record that any of the "young intellectual men" or of the "reading London world" was heard to remark, "I know who wrote the article in the last month's *Fraser's*—Mr. Carlyle. You couldn't mistake his style."

Notes

[1] New York and London, 1922, p. 4.

[2] Ed. *Sartor Resartus* (New York, 1937), Introd., pp. lix-lx.

[3] Ed. *Sartor Resartus* (Boston and London, 1900), Introd., pp. xlvii-xlviii.

[4] *Thomas Carlyle: A History of the First Forty Years of His Life,* 1795-1835 (London, 1882), I, 396.

[5] *Early Letters of Thomas Carlyle,* ed. Charles E. Norton (New York and London, 1886), pp. 20-21. Subsequent references to the early letters are to this edition and are in the text.

[6] *The Works of Thomas Carlyle,* ed. H. D. Traill, Centenary ed. (New York, n.d.), xxx, 83. Subsequent references to Carlyle's essays are to this edition and are in the text.

[7] Tufts Coll. Stud., 2nd Ser., No. 1 (Malden, Mass.).

[8] David A. Wilson, *Carlyle Till Marriage, 1795-1826* (London, 1923), p. 93.

[9] *Letters of Thomas Carlyle, 1826-1836,* ed. Charles E. Norton (New York and London, 1899), pp. 197-198.

[10] *Carlyle,* trans. E. K. Brown (New York, 1932), p. 91.

[11] Harrold's edition, pp. 251-252. Subsequent references to *Sartor* are to this edition.

[12] *Victorian Prose Masters* (New York, 1928), p. 78.

David J. Delaura (essay date 1969)

SOURCE: "Ishmael as Prophet: Heroes and Hero-Worship and the Self-Expressive Basis of Carlyle's Art," in *Texas Studies in Literature and Language,* Vol. XI, No. 1, Spring, 1969, pp. 705-32.

[*In the following essay, Delaura argues that the unity of Carlyle's lectures on heroes and hero-worship is based in Carlyle's attempt to identify the personal characteristics, message, and role of the prophet. Furthermore, Delaura suggest that at times Carlyle presented himself as a prophet.*]

No reader of Thomas Carlyle's lectures **On Heroes, Hero-Worship and the Heroic in History,** delivered in May 1840, has missed the crucial unifying theme of the possibility of "Prophecy" in the nineteenth century. Carlyle is guardedly optimistic as he glances at the achievement of Goethe, about whom he had written for two decades. If the prime quality of the prophet is his "vision of the inward divine mystery," then Goethe eminently qualifies; for under Goethe's "guise of a most modern, high-bred, high-cultivated Man of Letters," Carlyle discerns that his works are "really a Prophecy in these most unprophetic times."[1] Writing to Mill the following February, Carlyle notes that the message of *Heroes*—"a stranger kind of Book than I thought it would [be]"—already lay, for the perceptive reader, "mostly legible in what I had long since written" (*LCM,* p. 174). And indeed, the theme of prophecy, especially in its relation to modern times, was a chief concern of Carlyle's early essays, above all in "**Characteristics,**" where he had suggestively invoked the metaphysics and "higher Literature" of modern Germany to support his view that "This age also is not wholly without its Prophets" (XXVIII, 41).

The present paper explores the implications of the idea that the unity of *Heroes,* and with it much of Carlyle's early thought, is to be found in the deeply personal character of his painstaking attempt to define the characteristics, the message, and the social role of the prophet, especially in the nineteenth century. The pervasiveness of this theme, and the intensity of personal involvement with which it is pursued, suggest that in it we touch a central and vital source of Carlyle's literary dynamism, a key to the intentions of his career as well as to its substantive content. The mingled literary and biographical problems which this theme brings up are nearly unique; rarely has a developed literary art occupied so large a tract of the frontier between personal experience and objective artistry. Carlyle's favorite heroes and prophets are presented as figures who struggle for insight and for public recognition. His own parallel struggle is twofold: at the personal level, the search for a public and for literary distinction; in a larger context, the search for a "message" and the question of whether he could really affect the mind and sensibility of his times. As we shall see, the problem of "voice"—already recognized as crucial in a work like *Sartor Resartus*—is at issue here. For it seems clear that the youthful generation of the 1840's which was so strongly attracted to Carlyle—the generation of Matthew Arnold and Arthur Hugh Clough[2]—was responding not only to the prophetic strain in Carlyle (a point long recognized) but also to the uniquely authentic and authoritative presence of Carlyle in his own prophecy. Through the variety of roles and attitudes he assumes in a work, Carlyle convinces us of the integrity of his own embodied personality, sensed as a single energizing force behind all particular statements. This constantly expanding and controlling "virtual" personality is the basis of the integrity of the work as a whole. The theme of prophecy thus goes some distance toward clarifying the precise power and effect of Carlyle's complex art.

I

The familiar story of Carlyle's intense struggle and bitter frustration of the 1820's, reflected in the unfinished *Wotton Reinfred* and in *Sartor Resartus,* is the backdrop for Carlyle's early concern for prophecy. Though *Sartor* finally represented a style and literary form adequate to Carlyle's slowly maturing philosophy of dynamic idealism,[3] the work on its appearance in *Fraser's* in 1833-1834 was greeted with almost universal disapproval. Only with the publication of *The French Revolution* in 1837 can Carlyle be said to have begun to find the public he sought. But even in the first essay in which Carlyle discovered his authentic tone and manner, **"Signs of the Times"** (1829), he had fulfilled three traditional functions of the inspired prophet: the analysis and denunciation of the present as somehow falling below a divine standard; the announcement of a direct "message" from, or "insight" into, truth; and a literal prophecy or prediction of man's future or at least of his potentialities. **"Characteristics"** (1831), however, was to prove even more important in the humanist struggles of the nineteenth century, in its definition of "the region of meditation" as superior to "the region of argument and conscious discourse" (XXVIII, 4-5). A generation of younger readers responded to the assertion that, in the contemporary rupture of the natural tie between religion and this meditative mode, "the Thinker must, in all senses, wander homeless, too often aimless, looking up to a Heaven which is dead for him, round to an Earth which is deaf" (XXVIII, 29-30). Carlyle must have seemed close to the surface as he announced that the noblest now are those who do not

fall back on a "worn-out" creed or end in scepticism or hedonism, but who "have dared to say No and cannot yet say Yea, but feel that in the No they dwell as in a Golgotha, where life enters not, where peace is not appointed them" (XXVIII, 31). The nobler such men, the harder their fate:

> In dim forecastings, wrestles within them the 'Divine Idea of the World,' yet will nowhere visibly reveal itself. They have to realise a Worship for themselves, or live unworshipping. The Godlike has vanished from the world; and they, by the strong cry of their soul's agony, like true wonder-workers, must again evoke its presence. (XXVIII, 31)

The struggle of the nobly prophetic spirit, seeking in vain the revelation of the divine but compelled nevertheless to evoke its presence, is plainly a program for Carlyle's career, now that through *Sartor* and the essays of this period he had found his special voice and métier. The sketch Carlyle provides of the approved prophet—alone and wandering, detached from institutions and lacking a sympathetic audience, but always struggling both for insight into the divine and for means adequate to express it—is very much the pattern he was to find for the most sympathetic of his great men in *Heroes.* The personal force suffusing his elaborate discussion of the possibilities of prophecy in the nineteenth century becomes even clearer near the end of **"Characteristics"** when he announces, as we have seen, "This age also is not wholly without its Prophets"; the reader is thoroughly prepared, even if not wholly conscious of the effect, to apply the remark—made in the first place with reference to German philosophy and literature—to Carlyle himself. Evidently the Carlyle who ended by predicting that "The genius of Mechanism . . . will not always sit like a choking incubus on our soul; but at length, when by a new magic Word the old spell is broken, become our slave, and as familiar spirit do all our bidding" (XXVIII, 42-43), felt, increasingly, that *he,* above all others of his generation in England, was in possession of that "new magic Word."

Carlyle's discovery of himself and of his role through his definition of the prophet in *Sartor* and the essays of 1829-1831 is the prelude to a larger cluster of concerns in the thirties which reveal his growing insight into the relationship of artistry to self-knowledge—though generally overlooked, this is one of the richest bodies of reflection on the creative process in the nineteenth century. Froude, praising the *French Revolution* as Carlyle's "most perfect" work, speaks of his defective sense of form in the others: "He throws out brilliant and detached pictures, and large masses of thought. . . . There is everywhere unity of purpose. . . . But events are left to tell their own story. He appears continually in his own person, instructing, commenting, informing the reader at every step of his own opinion. His method of composition is so original that it cannot be tried by common rules"

(*LL*, p. 87). What has not been studied is how Carlyle's "unity of purpose" is largely secured precisely by his various modes of self-presentation.

As early as 1827, in his first two essays on Jean Paul, Carlyle had added to the familiar Romantic view that Jean Paul's works are "emblems . . . of the singular mind where they originated" (XXII, 127) the more fruitful perception that in his works, whether fictional or not, the author "generally becomes a person in the drama himself" (XXVI, 12).[4] But only in 1833, with the writing of the ***Diamond Necklace,*** had Carlyle achieved considerable freedom in handling his own "presence" in his writing. As Carlisle Moore has showed, Carlyle in this work not only indulges in his familiar didactic "tendency to moralize, to philosophize, to judge the significance of things," but he also steps into the narrative "as a person of as many moods as ideas." Though Carlyle continually reveals his ignorance of the reader's personality, he becomes a kind of stage director who also repeatedly addresses the reader, warning, commanding, conversing, and persuading.[5] But this same year, 1833, is also important because it was then that Carlyle seems first to have seen the convergence in himself of the various burdens of the nineteenth-century prophet. Two remarkable journal entries reveal that Carlyle's still unresolved religious crisis is at the center. He writes on March 31: "Wonderful, and alas! most pitiful alternations of belief and unbelief in me. . . . Meanwhile, continue to believe in *thyself*. . . . Neither fear thou that this thy great message of the Natural *being* the Supernatural will wholly perish unuttered."[6] The message is even less secure in an entry dated August 24, where his acknowledgment that "For the last year my faith has lain under a most sad eclipse" preludes his plaintive insistence: "In *all* times there is a word which, spoken to men, to the actual generation of men, would thrill their inmost soul. But the way to find that word? The way to speak it when found?"[7] Obviously, "faith" or "belief," in startlingly traditional senses of those terms, precedes belief in oneself, the external "word" or message of the Natural Supernatural, the style of its expression, and the hoped-for soul-shaking effect on the present generation.

The only element lacking in this self-analysis, the cultural crisis of the age, was supplied on one of Carlyle's most penetrating letters to Emerson, dated August 12, 1834. Far from defending himself against Emerson's "saucy" objection that his idiosyncratic style results from his not knowing his public, Carlyle agrees and calls it "questionable, tentative, and only the best that I in these mad times could conveniently hit upon." For he has a strikingly modern sense "that now at least we have lived to see all manner of Poetics and Rhetorics and Sermonics, and one may say generally all manner of *Pulpits* for addressing mankind from, as good as broken and abolished." He sees the modern prophet's problem as the fact that, though "pasteboard coulisses, and three unities, and Blairs lectures" are now

gone, even perennially sacred "inspired utterance" will remain "inconceivable, misconceivable to the million; questionable (not of *ascertained* significance) even to the few." He pictures himself as trying new methods, and getting "nearer the truth, as I honestly strive for it." But he ends, more guardedly than in his journal, with a weak and bleakly voluntaristic version of his contentless religious "faith": "Meanwhile I know no method of much consequence, except that of *believing,* of being sincere . . ." (*CE*, pp. 103-104). This line of thought is renewed a year later, in June 1835, when he argues against Sterling that "purism of style" cannot be his concern: "With whole ragged battalions of Scott's novel Scotch, with Irish, German, French and even newspaper Cockney (where literature is little more than a newspaper) storming in on us, and the whole structure of our Johnsonian English breaking up from its foundations, revolution *there* is visible as everywhere else" (*LL*, p. 41).

These concerns are refocused and clarified in a later stage of self-awarness, during and after the writing of the ***French Revolution.*** As early as June 1831, Carlyle had told Goethe that in ***Sartor*** "It is . . . not a picture that I am painting . . . but a half-reckless casting of the brush, with its frustrated colours, against the canvas."[8] In July 1836, near to finishing the ***French Revolution,*** he repeats the image, saying that he will "splash down what I know, in large masses of colour; that it may look like a smoke-and-flame Conflagration in the distance, which it is."[9] And Carlyle is aware that even his relatively objective history reflects his special temperament and situation. He is excessively self-depreciating to Emerson in November 1836—"it is a wild savage ruleless very bad Book; which even you will not be able to like"; but revealingly, he insists that these qualities are the very sign of its authenticity: "Yet it contains strange things; sincerities drawn out of the heart of a man very strangely situated" (*CE*, p. 152). This is amplified in a letter to his brother John the following February: "It is a book written by a *wild man,* a man disunited from the fellowship of the world he lives in, looking king and beggar in the face with an indifference of brotherhood and an indifference of contempt" (*LL*, p. 81).

Carlyle, then, shows a developing consciousness of his complex, perhaps unique, artistry, a development which draws on his experience and on his insight into his experience as *both* (in Eliot's phrase) the man who suffers and the mind which creates. His scattered formulation by 1837 of the personal basis of his style, for which there can be no premeditated "Art," involves the convergence of his insights into the profound cultural crisis of the age; the consequent breakdown of traditional categories of truth; a corresponding disablement of traditional modes of utterance; the difficulty which even divine truth has in finding a fit audience; and most important, the fact that he is one of a special class of individuals with an historic mission, marked to suffer in the self-annihilating task of apprehending essential moral and social truth. These, then, are the awarenesses and burdens of what we may call the "pilgrim" prophet, the only adequate prophet for the nineteenth century. His oracles are emphatic enough, but they inevitably reflect, and are the product of, his own vanguard position, pushing on into truth a few steps ahead of his fellows. He will proclaim a new truth, at least to the extent that Natural Supernaturalism has never before been preached in England; his is a new mode of discovery, drawing on the prophet's own personal quest, suffering, and sincerity; his is a uniquely "personal" mode of disjointed utterance, a hectic "splashing" down; and finally, his discovery of his unknown audience, even his creation of that audience, is part of the truth-seeking process. The splashing-down images suggest that truth is not objective, pre-existent, waiting for its recorder; instead, it is found as part of the act or process of artistic creation itself: prophecy discovers and perhaps even creates truth.

Here is the complex heart of the usual simplicity attributed to Carlyle, that the great artist is simply the great-souled man.[10] To employ his tentative and heuristic method, to "speak" sincerely, is to educe "strange," even frightening, aspects of truth. This is Carlyle's central, and modern, insight that truth is, in a fundamental sense, correlative to personal quest, very nearly a function of personality and moral disposition. We are not far here from some of the later insights into the "personal" quality of truth in Newman, especially in the *Grammar of Assent.* Thus Carlyle in effect sees that his not easily described method develops certain premises of Romantic egoism—above all, the efficacy of the suffering self—for their "expressive" power. In *Heroes and Hero-Worship,* as we shall see, it even becomes a quasi-structural principle and a source of "meaning" as the narrative pattern of the hero's struggles emerges as representative of the experience of the age. It predicts a Victorian mode, too, in being a kind of extended monologue or a series of interlocking monologues.

II

By the time he came to compose **"Chartism"** in the second half of 1839, Carlyle was far more confidently the prophet than he had been when he composed *Sartor* in obscurity. The peculiar personal pressure discernible in his early discussion of the prophet's mission had by 1839 become the fully developed manner of the assured sage. To attempt to describe the prophet's message and manner was indeed increasingly to *act* the prophet, to *adopt* his message and manner.[11] Though Carlyle could depreciate his lectures of 1838 as "a mixture of prophecy and play-acting" (*LL,* pp. 136), the phrase is suggestive in clarifying the nature of Carlyle's art in this period. For the four series of lectures (1837-1840) not only mark the culmination of his fame and influence, the reward of his years of suffering; they also bring out a new and intensified awareness of the basis of his art in a special apprehension of "self." In **"Chartism,"** and in some of the most striking passages of *Heroes* and *Past and Present,* Carlyle is able to present *himself* far more directly as teacher and seer—and for the most part without the disguise of a Teufelsdröckh or even a Sauerteig—than he had in *Sartor* or the early essays. The question of "voice" becomes crucial here.

I point especially to a mechanism at work in a passage quoted at length for its special and elaborate use of the first-person pronoun. Carlyle retorts against "the British reader" who would limit the function of society to that of protecting property:

> And now what is thy property? That parchment title-deed, that purse thou buttonest in thy breeches-pocket? Is that thy valuable property? Unhappy brother, most poor insolvent brother, I without parchment at all, with purse oftenest in the flaccid state, imponderous, which will not fling against the wind, have quite other property than that! I have the miraculous breath of life in me, breathed into my nostrils by Almighty God. I have affections, thoughts, a god-given *capability* to be and do; rights, therefore,—the right for instance to thy love if I love thee, to thy guidance if I obey thee: the strangest rights, whereof in church-pulpits one still hears something, though almost unintelligible now; rights stretching high into Immensity, far into Eternity! Fifteen-pence a-day; three-and-sixpence a-day; eight hundred pounds and odd a-day, dost thou call that my property? I value that little; little all I could purchase with that. For truly, as is said, what matters it? In torn boots, in soft-hung carriages-and-four, a man gets always to his journey's end. Socrates walked barefoot, or in wooden shoes, and yet arrived happily. They never asked him, *What* shoes of conveyance? never What wages hadst thou? but simply, What work didst thou?—Property, O brother? 'Of my very body I have but a life-rent.' As for this flaccid purse of mine, 'tis something, nothing; has been the slave of pickpockets, cutthroats, Jew-brokers, gold-dust robbers; 'twas his, 'tis mine;—'tis thin, if thou care much to steal it. But my soul, breathed into me by God, my *Me* and what capability is there; that is mine, and I will resist the stealing of it. I call that mine and not thine; I will keep that, and do what work I can with it: God has given it me, the Devil shall not take it away: Alas, my friends, Society exists and has existed for a great many purposes, not so easy to specify! (XXIX, 163-164)

The "I" here rises to an altogether more elevated and intense note of personal involvement than in the rather conventional "we" and "us" which is the sustained usage of **"Chartism."** Carlyle presents himself, first, as directly testifying to the special quality of his own prophetic mission. This openly "stagy" performance (the Shakespearean echoes would not be missed by an educated reader) becomes a dramatized authentication of that mission, working by the true prophet's heightening, repetition, and intensity. Second, the "I" is representative: Carlyle presents himself as a divinely commissioned, archetypal human being. "Brother" and "friends" are not the usual lecturer's amenities here, for Carlyle is acting out a higher, quasi-religious sense of community, his very topic being "Society" in a transcendent sense. In both of these uses of the first-person pronoun, Carlyle speaks directly, without the most usual mask, and with the special accent of one "inspired" and the bearer of a divine message.

The evidence so far presented goes to support the contention that Carlyle's continuing concern with prophecy in his writings through **"Chartism"** is a function of his personal quest to define his own prophetic mission and message, to achieve an adequate style, and to find an audience. The letters of the period of **"Chartism"** and *Heroes* are even more explicit on Carlyle's conception of himself as prophet. For Carlyle's own struggles of these years, especially as he is vindicated in his emergence from obscurity, strikingly parallel the full pattern of experience which he discovers in his favorite prophets of the *Heroes* lectures. In the spring of 1839 Carlyle delivered a lecture series called **"On Modern Revolutions."** He writes Emerson on April 13, concerned quite literally with prophetic inspiration: "How true is that of the old Prophets, 'The *word of the Lord* came unto' such and such a one! When it does not come, both Prophet and Prosaist ought to be thankful (after a sort), and rigorously hold their tongue" (*CE,* p. 222). Four days later, he writes of the agony of composition: "My Lectures come on, this day two weeks: O Heaven! *I* cannot 'speak'; I can only gasp and writhe and stutter, a spectacle to gods and fashionables,—being forced to it by want of money" (*CE,* p. 226). But on May 29, the lectures now over, he is eager to master the art of public speaking: "I found . . . that extempore speaking . . . is an *art* or craft, and requires an apprenticeship, which I have neve[r] served. Repeatedly it has come into my head that I should go to America, [this] very Fall, and belecture you from North to South till I learn it!" (*CE,* p. 236). Obviously, Carlyle does in some sense conceive of himself as a prophet, and "inspired," and he wishes to conquer a broad public on both sides of the Atlantic. Even his complaint about finding the proper mode in which to "speak" is, we perceive, part of the prophet's role; for, as *Heroes* was to make clear, a gasping, writhing, stuttering speech is a common sign of the divinely given power whelming up in the authentic prophet. Carlyle again and again suggests that *smoothness* of speech and of mental process indicates superficiality; the "open secret" of Nature is essentially simple, but it can be captured only by intuition, which resists easy formulation.

Although Carlyle regularly speaks of lecturing as "intensely disagreeable" (*CE,* pp. 249, 259; *NL,* pp. 193, 194), he is much concerned about his influence upon the British public. A letter to his brother, June 20, 1839, indicates his satisfaction that his opinions, "pretty well uttered now," are "making their way with unexpected undeserved rapidity in my generation" (*NL,* p. 166). This was not, it is important to note, a conventional search for "fame," about which Carlyle could be impressively scornful. But a crucial letter to his mother of October 24, 1839, makes clear that this year of marvels—signalized by the publication of the *Critical*

and Miscellaneous Essays and Sterling's laudatory article in the *Westminster*—marked the end of his period of obscurity and heroic struggle.

> What reason have I to thank a kind Providence that has led me so mercifully thus far! It is a changed time with me from what it was but a few years back; from what it had been all my life. My sore sufferings, poverty, sickness, obstructions, disappointment were sent me in kindness; angrily as I rebelled against them, they were all kind and good. My poor painful existence was not altogether in vain. (*NL,* p. 171)[12]

This sentiment is to be distinguished from self-pity by the fact that Carlyle's personal vindication after his years of struggle exactly parallels his heroes' path of suffering, poverty, and obstruction leading to triumph. This new conviction did not, of course, imply that the newly recognized prophet had been exempted from the struggle of *expressing* his vision, any more than the writing of *Sartor* eight years before had meant the achievement of perfect clarity of vision.[13] He wrote Emerson on December 8, 1839, distressed that he can find no publisher for **"Chartism"**: "nevertheless I had to persist writing; writing and burning, and cursing my destiny, and then again writing." Moreover, though the "thoughts were familiar to me, old, many years old," the problem remained that of "the utterance of them, in what spoken dialect to utter them!" (*CE,* p. 250). By "dialect," a favorite word of Carlyle's, he seems to mean something more than "style," almost what we would today call "dramatic voice" or rhetorical posture.

Certainly the tone and content of **"Chartism"** in no sense represent a conscious attempt to meet the tastes or the expectations of the English public. The great essay he had written "cursing" was done in obedience to some higher impulse: "I do not care very much," he writes on December 30, 1839, "*what* the world say or forbear to say or do in regard to the thing: it was a thing I *had* to write." At the same time, he is a mixture of pride and self-depreciation about the favorable reception of the *Essays:* "It rather seems the people like them in spite of all their crabbedness." Perhaps it is this matter of "crabbedness" which makes him reflect wistfully that "ten years of my life lie strangely written there; it is I, and it is not I, that wrote all that!" (*NL,* p. 178). Carlyle was concerned, then, about his perhaps forbidding style (along with the problem of what "I" it could be said to represent), about the essential integrity of his witness before his generation, and, in a complex way, about his effect upon the public consciousness. He shows some apprehension concerning what *public* he was in fact addressing. His references to the "fashionables" and the "beautiful people" who attended his lectures are a mixture of scorn and flattered vanity. At times he seemed to imagine—perhaps sentimentally and, surprisingly, in the vein of Matthew Arnold—that he had access to a body of "rational and just" readers freed from class and party thinking. In January 1840 he has no hope of affecting "the present Radical Members and Agitators": "for the cause of the Poor, one must leave them [the Radicals] and their battles out of view, and address rather the great solid *heart* of England, the rational and just men of England, and avoiding all outposts and their inconclusive tumult, go right to the heart of the matter" (*NL,* p. 181).

The intermingled concerns with style, "audience," and prophetic message were intensified during the months of the composition, delivery, and revision of the lectures on *Heroes.* Carlyle was pleased with his increasing audience during the lecture series in May, and in mid-June he describes his intention in rewriting: "I am endeavouring to write down my Lectures somewhat in the style of *speech*" (*NL,* pp. 195, 196). This new emphasis on *speech* marks what is very likely the high point of Carlyle's personal enthusiasm for the prophetic office; for impassioned speech, as an indicator of sincerity and authenticity, was, he evidently felt, the appropriate mode for what he explicitly called his "preaching," a preaching done "in the name of God." As he explained in May, *Heroes* occupied a special position among his lecture series, since "I am telling the people matters that belong much more to *myself* this year, which is far more interesting to me" (*LL,* p. 182; my emphasis). Some of this relation to himself is revealed in an extraordinary letter to Emerson of July 2, where Carlyle is found, in a mood of mingled exuberance and conviction, bursting forth in the high-prophetic tone in which he would *like* to preach the otherwise familiar message of *Heroes:*

> The misery of it was hardly equal to that of former years, yet still was very hateful. I had got to a certain feeling of superiority over my audience; as if I had something to tell them, and would tell it them. At times I felt as if I could, in the end, learn to speak. The beautiful people listened with boundless tolerance, eager attention. I meant to tell them, among other things, that man was still alive, Nature not dead or like to die; that all true men continued true to this hour. . . . On the whole, I fear I did little but confuse my esteemed audience: I was amazed, after all their reading of me, to be understood so ill;—gratified nevertheless to see how the rudest *speech* of a man's heart goes into men's hearts, and is the welcomest thing there. Withal I regretted that I had not six months of preaching, whereby to learn to preach, and explain things fully! In the fire of the moment I had all but decided on setting out for America this autumn, and preaching far and wide like a very lion there. Quit your paper formulas, my brethren,—equivalent to old wooden idols, *un*divine as they: in the name of God, understand that you are alive, and that God is alive! Did the Upholsterer make this Universe? Were you created by the Tailor? I tell you, and conjure you to believe me literally, No, a thousand times No! Thus did I mean to preach, on "Heroes, Hero-worship and the Heroic," in America too. (*CE,* pp. 274-275)

The fire dwindled, the mood of the lion passed; still, he resolves to publish the lectures, "and in *some* way promulgate them farther." The urgency persists: he writes

his brother on July 15 that the message, "in some way or other, must not be lost. It is not a new story to *me;* but the world seemed greatly astonished at it; the world cannot too soon get acquainted with it" (*NL,* p. 201). But by August 1 the lectures looked to Carlyle "absolutely worth nothing at all," precisely because, "wanting all the unction of personal sincerity expressed by voice and face, they look entirely dull and tame on paper" (*NL,* p. 201). "Nothing which I have ever written pleases me so ill," he continues later in the same month, as he strives to make the lectures "low-pitched, as like talk as possible" (*LL,* p. 195).

The printed lectures also evoked in Carlyle a familiar but suggestively intense ambivalence. On the one hand, fretting over proofsheets, he sees the completed book with a kind of wondering incomprehension: "This thing on Heroes [he writes Mill on February 24, 1841] proves to be a stranger book than I thought it would. Since men do read without reflection, this too was worth writing" (*LCM,* p. 174). It was even "a *goustrous* [strong, boisterous] determined speaking out of the truth about several things. The people will be no worse for it at present" (*LL,* p. 207). And yet within a month he writes Mill again, in an almost suspicious fit of revulsion: "now that it all lies there, little is visible but triviality, contemptibility,—and the happy prospect of washing one's hands of it forever and a day. No Book of mine ever looked more insignificant to me" (*LCM,* p. 176). But the prophet in Carlyle, however much dismayed by his own most "prophetic" book, was not to be put down. Less than two months later—on May 13—we find him struggling over Cromwell's life, fearful, as he tells Sterling, that "the man to write it will probably never be born." But he all at once changes subject and exclaims: "Or leaving History altogether, what do you say of Prophecy? Is not *Prophecy* the grand thing? The volcanic *terra da lavoro* of Yorkshire and Lancashire: within that too lies a prophecy grander than Ezekiel's . . . !" (*NL,* p. 230). To the end the Carlyle who doubted whether it was "the duty of a citizen to be silent, to paint mere Heroisms, Cromwells, &c." (*LL,* p. 222) admitted only one "secret of *Kunst*" in his method, that of the chosen sufferer for truth who must yet struggle heroically to express it, part sublime prophet and part impromptu play actor. The *"intelligence* of the *fact,"* as he writes Sterling early in 1842, "once blazing within me, if it will ever get to blaze, and bursting to be out, one has to take the whole dexterity of adaptation one is master of, and with tremendous struggling, really frightful struggling, continue to exhibit it, one way or the other" (*LL,* p. 231).

III

"Is not *Prophecy* the grand thing?" The evidence of the letters, along with an internal analysis of *Heroes,* suggests that much of the "strange" quality of the lectures was due precisely to its "prophetic" character, as an intense focusing of Carlyle's deepest desire to be recognized in his own generation as seer and sage and, to a degree difficult to gauge, as a leader. The subject chosen for the lectures, the lecture form itself, as well as the precise moment of Carlyle's critical engagement with the English public—all these conjoined to evoke from him his profoundest exploration of the prophet's mission: the prophet's credentials, his message, and his special mode of utterance. In doing so he rather wonderfully revealed his fundamental conception of himself, of his own role, and of the titanic stance he had adopted in this most "unheroic" and "unprophetic" time. The ultimate hero of the *Heroes* lectures, as well as the source of its unity, is Thomas Carlyle: he is implicitly the chief character, and the work is nearly as autobiographical as Book II of *Sartor.*

Heroes is so staged as to throw Carlyle's own role in his generation into the strongest light, and to give it the greatest significance. The series of historic figures brought forward for description and moralizing are so many cases which bear upon the regularly recurring theme of the Prophetic Office in the nineteenth century. Implicitly, the man with special insight into Heroes and Heroism is inevitably a hero himself: this impression is conveyed both in Carlyle's own prophetic assertions, which simply duplicate the rather restricted range of his heroes' perceptions, and his own special style or mode of utterance, which exhibits their "rude" and "rugged" character. Moreover, Carlyle's conception of himself, as well as his personal and literary problems, which we have seen revealed in the correspondence of this period, are worked into the pattern which he more or less arbitrarily imposes upon his most congenial heroes—Mahomet, Dante, Luther, Knox, Johnson, Cromwell. The final evidence of the autobiographical pressure in *Heroes* is the frequent approximation to the pattern of experience elaborated much more fully in *Sartor,* a book which has long been recognized to be autobiographical in important respects. Without great exaggeration, then, *Heroes* can be read as an extended essay, in the artistic guise of a series of biographical studies, on Carlyle's talent and vocation.

Carlyle is continually at pains, first of all, to point out the contemporary relevance of his reflections on heroism. Again and again—through the repeated use of expressions like "still," "yet," "to this hour"—he insists that the Poet, the Prophet, or the Priest, even in "such a time as ours," is "a voice from the unseen Heaven": "So in old times; so in these, and in all times" (pp. 9, 11-12, 28, 24, 80, 115). The climax of this constant pointing forward to the nineteenth century comes in Lecture V, on The Hero as Man of Letters, who, though "altogether a product of these new ages," speaks forth his inspiration as did the Gods, Prophets, and Priests of past times. In "uttering-forth . . . the inspired soul of him," the Man of Letters becomes "our most important modern person," "the soul of all." His exalted function—to proclaim Carlyle's familiar message that "the True, Divine and Eternal . . . exists always, unseen to most, under the Temporary, Trivial"—is exactly what

all heroes "are sent into the world to do" (pp. 154-156). Carlyle repeats an idea of Fichte's he had first approved in the 1820's, that the Man of Letters, preaching the "Divine Idea of the World," in fact *guides* the world, "like a sacred Pillar of Fire, in its dark pilgrimage through the waste of Time" (p. 157). This attempt to enhance the importance of the modern Man of Letters is bolstered by a recurrent theme: that "at bottom the Great Man, as he comes from the hand of Nature, is ever the same kind of thing: Odin, Luther, Johnson, Burns; . . . these are all originally of one stuff" (p. 43). Differentiated only by "the different *sphere*" in which he works and by "the kind of world he finds himself born into" (p. 78; see p. 115), the hero, even of modern times, retains an amazing omnicompetence: "A Hero is a Hero at all points" (p. 28).

The climactic ordering of the lectures toward the apotheosis of the Man of Letters is aided by Carlyle's frequently reiterated definition of the Hero as essentially a *Prophet,* the *speaker* of the "revelation" of the open secret of the universe: the "word" is his province. The prophet is of course "inspired," and he is everywhere marked by *insight* and *sincerity:* as Seer and Thinker he *sees* the truth, and as Prophet he *utters* it, with whatever difficulty. The great man's "word is the wise healing word which all can believe in" (p. 13). The "shaped spoken Thought" of "the great Thinker, . . . the *original* man, the Seer," articulates what "all men were not far from saying, were longing to say" (p. 21). The image Carlyle presents of the prophet is that of the "earnest man, speaking to his brother men" (p. 26). As a "messenger . . . sent from the Infinite Unknown with tidings to us," we all feel of the Prophet that "the words he utters are as no other man's words." If the Prophet is always "a voice from the unseen Heaven" (p. 115), the Man of Letters is the key modern figure "endeavouring to speak forth the inspiration" in him through printed books (p. 154). For such men are above all "Prophets" and "speakers . . . of the everlasting truth" (p. 178).

But the peculiarly personal concern which unifies Carlyle's reflections is most evident in the pattern of experience he assigns to his heroes, and in their special qualities of style. The personal qualities of the hero are fairly uniform: these are rendered by recurrent epithets like "rude," "rugged," "earnest," "fervent." Some—for example, Shakespeare and Johnson—are presented as "unconscious," apparently as a consequence of the very inexpressibility of their intuitive apprehension of the divine. Frequently, too, these favorite heroes are melancholic by temperament; certainly they are compelled to accept a full share of sorrow and sadness in life. These "rude" figures are almost always presented as titanic, struggling, even "wild" and "savage" ("there is something of the savage in all great men" [p. 193]). Above all, they are uniformly men of *sincerity* ("rude sincerity," "Wild sincere heart") and *insight* ("the clear, deep-seeing eye," "depth of vision"). The fundamental double image of *Heroes,* in fact, is one of *depth* and *penetration,* repeated in literally dozens of forms.

The hero is thus a man of what we might call down-and-in-sight, suggested by what is in effect a series of highly kinetic images of plunging and piercing.[14] Of course the man who can penetrate to the depth in each of these heroes is himself a man of insight and depth. But the effect is incalculably strengthened by a seemingly innocent device, Carlyle's constant repetition of "at bottom," a simple adverbial expression which becomes part both of the prophetic message and of Carlyle's credentials as a prophet in his own right.

Coming even closer to Carlyle himself, his rugged, earnest hero is presented as undergoing a special pattern of experience. Hampered usually by disadvantageous origins, he is literally or figuratively at some time outcast, wandering, solitary, in exile; but he valiantly struggles forward under the burden of suffering, sorrow, and darkness and eventually wins through to clarity, triumph, vindication. One is frequently struck by the similarity of this heroic course to that undergone by the autobiographical figure of Teufelsdröckh in *Sartor*.[15] Even more pertinent, only six months before he composed *Heroes* we saw Carlyle speaking of the "changed time" a merciful Providence had suddenly brought him: "My sore sufferings, poverty, sickness, obstruction, disappointment were sent me in kindness; angrily as I rebelled against them, they were all kind and good. My poor painful existence was not altogether in vain" (*NL*, p. 171). At this period, it seems clear, Carlyle saw himself and his struggles in the lives of his chief heroes, and this fact was conveyed to his audience, including even the residue of self-pity latent in "my poor painful existence." He, like them, had run the full harrowing gauntlet of the heroes' course and had at length emerged into the daylight of recognition and full articulateness.

The plausibility of this view of the autobiographical basis of *Heroes* is strengthened by Carlyle's open avowal of personal affinity with several of his struggling heroes. Mahomet, for example, is displayed as an exile, "driven foully out of his native country, since unjust men had not only given no ear to his earnest Heaven's-message, the deep cry of his heart, but would not even let him live if he kept speaking it" (p. 60). Later, Carlyle's tone regarding the portrait of Dante takes on a very personal urgency: "To me it is a most touching face; perhaps of all faces that I know, the most so"; "lonely," bespeaking "deathless sorrow and pain" as well as "the known victory which is also deathless," this "mournfulest face" is "altogether tragic, heart-affecting." Clearly Carlyle felt a special affinity with the Dantean temperament, its mature softness and tenderness "congealed into sharp contradiction, into abnegation, isolation, proud hopeless pain." Of special interest is the fact that Carlyle—whom R. H. Hutton once described as spending "all his energies in a sort of vivid passion of scorn"[16]—is deeply affected by Dante's "silent scornful" pain, his "godlike disdain," his "implacable indignation" against the world (p. 86). But Dante had a "nobler destiny" appointed him "and he, struggling like a man led towards death and crucifixion, could

not help fulfilling it." For Dante, "poor and banished," "there was now no home in this world. He wandered from patron to patron, from place to place" (p. 88). He realized "that he had no longer any resting-place, or hope of benefit, in this earth. The earthly world had cast him forth, to wander, wander; no living heart to love him now" (p. 89).

These two literal wanderers provide the pattern of more metaphorical struggle, exile, and triumph for Carlyle's latter-day heroes. We hear of Luther, "born poor, and brought-up poor," plagued by "all manner of black scruples, dubitations": "He fell into the blackest wretchedness: had to wander staggering as on the verge of bottomless Despair" (pp. 128-130). The pattern is found in Knox, too, with an added fillip of personal concern: "This Prophet of the Scotch is to me no hateful man!— He had a sore fight of an existence: wrestling with Popes and Principalities; in defeat, contention, life-long struggle; rowing as a galley-slave, wandering as an exile. A sore fight: but he won it" (p. 151). The climax and clarification of the pattern comes with Carlyle's prediction that "Men of Letters will not always wander like unrecognised unregulated Ishmaelites among us!" (p. 165). For we must be brought to see that even a Burns fits the titanic role: "He must pass through the ordeal, and prove himself. *This* ordeal; this wild welter of a chaos which is called Literary Life; this too is a kind of ordeal!" (p. 167). Carlyle's intention becomes explicit finally in the assertion that the literary man must accept "the common lot of Heroes": "our Hero as Man of Letters had to travel without highway, companionless, through an inorganic chaos,—and to leave his own life and faculty lying there, as a partial contribution towards *pushing* some highway through it." We suddenly realize that Carlyle's ultimate hero is the literary man after the pattern earlier presented in *Sartor*. If Luther's "blackest wretchedness," as he wandered "staggering as on the verge of bottomless Despair," sounded remarkably like the struggles of Teufelsdröckh in his Baphometic Fire-Baptism, our suspicions are confirmed by the fact that Carlyle's modern literary hero has the "fatal misery" of "the *spiritual paralysis*" of the sceptical eighteenth century, involving both intellectual and moral doubt. Indeed, rarely in history has a life of heroism been more difficult than in modern times, for the last age was "a godless world," without wonder or greatness (pp. 170-171). Thus Carlyle's supreme heroes, especially the men of letters, undergo struggles very similar to those of the earnest nineteenth-century agnostic, struggling for intellectual clarification and moral certitudes; these were the struggles also embodied semifictionally, in *Sartor;* they are, finally, the struggles of Carlyle's career.

If the hero is fundamentally a prophet, or *speaker* of truth, the quality of his utterance will be unique, especially since the truth he expresses, though simple, resists rational formulation. The struggle for expression, indeed, becomes a chief mark of the prophet's authenticity, the chief arena of the titanic hero's agony. The pattern is established in Carlyle's discussion of the Koran as a "wearisome confused jumble, crude, incondite; endless iterations, long-windedness, entanglement" (pp. 64-66):

> It is the confused ferment of a great rude human soul; rude, untutored, that cannot even read; but fervent, earnest, struggling vehemently to utter itself in words. With a kind of breathless intensity he strives to utter himself; the thoughts crowd on him pellmell: for very multitude of things to say, he can get nothing said. The meaning that is in him shapes itself into no form of composition, is stated in no sequence, method, or coherence;—they are not *shaped* at all, these thoughts of his; flung-out unshaped, as they struggle and tumble there, in their chaotic inarticulate state.... The panting breathless haste and vehemence of a man struggling in the thick of battle for life and salvation; this is the mood he is in! A headlong haste; for very magnitude of meaning, he cannot get himself articulated into words. (p. 66)

Now, this elaborate passage (which partially imitates what it is describing) far exceeds any possible knowledge Carlyle might have had of Mahomet's habits of composition. What this discussion of the "prophetic" manner, which in varying proportions he attributes to all his heroes, seems above all to embody is Carlyle's sense of his own creative habits. We recall his description of the *Heroes* lectures as "the rudest *speech* of a man's heart" going direct to other men's hearts. Where Mahomet's thoughts were "flung-out unshaped as they struggle and tumble there," we found Carlyle writing: "I there *splash* down (literally as fast as my pen will go) some kind of paragraph on some point or other.... I shall be the better able to *speak* of the things written of even in this way." And in revising he tries to write "in the style of *speech.*"

This struggle is repeated throughout the book. We sense a personal note behind Carlyle's description of Dante's *Comedy:* "His Book, as indeed most good Books are, has been written, in many senses, with his heart's blood. It is his whole history, this Book" (p. 90)—and we inevitably think of *Sartor.* We are not surprised that Luther, with his personal "rugged honesty" and "rugged sterling sense and strength," "flashes-out illumination" in his "smiting idiomatic phrases," that his common speech "has a rugged nobleness, dramatic, expressive, genuine" (pp. 139, 141). But it is in his extended discussion of Cromwell's "inarticulate" eloquence that Carlyle reveals the intensity of his personal concern. For in it, I would argue, we have something like a rationale of Carlyle's struggle to create a "dialect" of his own (what Sterling called "Carlylism" and Matthew Arnold, less sympathetically, "Carlylese"), the struggle which in the years before *Sartor* meant the rejection of the eighteenth-century style-of-all-work in which his earliest essays were written.[17] Carlyle heaps scorn on that "respectable" style of speech and conduct "which can plead for itself in a handsome articulate manner" (p. 208). The eighteenth century could not recognize the greatness of Cromwell, a "King coming to them in the rugged *un*formulistic state": "their measured euphemisms, philosophies, parliamentary eloquences" leave the heart cold (pp. 208-209). Thus "Poor Cromwell,—great Cromwell! The inarticulate Prophet; Prophet who could not *speak*. Rude, confused, struggling to utter himself, with his savage depth, with his wild sincerity"—Cromwell is made, in Carlyle's theory of inspired utterance, the archetypal prophet. Such struggling for speech, like his and Samuel Johnson's, under the weight of misery, sorrow, and hypochondria, "is the character of a prophetic man; a man with his whole soul *seeing,* and struggling to see" (pp. 217-218). Significantly, though Cromwell could not speak, he could *preach:* his "rhapsodic preaching" relied on no method, simply "warmth, depth, sincerity" (p. 218). "He disregarded eloquence, nay despised and disliked it; spoke always without premeditation" (p. 219). We recall Carlyle's attempt, in revising *Heroes,* to retain the spontaneous quality of *speech,* "all the unction of personal sincerity expressed by voice and face."

But Carlyle himself makes almost explicit the apologetic relevance of his discussion of Cromwell's "rugged bursts of earnestness," his "helplessness of utterance, in such bursting fulness of meaning" (pp. 226, 233-234). He had discerned in Cromwell "a real *speech* lying imprisoned in these broken rude tortuous utterances; a meaning in the great heart of this inarticulate man!" (p. 235). Now, when he comes to end his own final lecture, Carlyle turns directly to his auditors:

> there was pleasure for me in this business, if also much pain. It is a great subject.... It enters deeply, as I think, into the secret of Mankind's ways and vitalest interests in this world, and is well worth explaining at present.... I have had to tear it up in the rudest manner in order to get into it at all. Often enough, with these abrupt utterances thrown-out isolated, unexplored, has your tolerance been put to the trial.... The accomplished and distinguished, the beautiful, the wise, something of what is best in England, have listened patiently to my words. (pp. 243-244)

In the very act of ostensibly asking for indulgence, Carlyle is, first, attributing to himself the rude, abrupt, ejaculatory mode proper to his highest heroes; second, acknowledging that he has at last gained the ear of the "accomplished" audience he had sought; and third, claiming to have special access to "the secret" of Mankind's most vital interests—the very sphere of the prophet.

The theme of hero worship, as it recurs throughout the lectures, suggests the complexity of Carlyle's relation to his "audience." The letters reveal Carlyle to have been quite extraordinarily indifferent to easy popular success, with its attendant celebrity and money. On the other hand, we have noted his insistence that "the world cannot too soon get acquainted" with the "story" he had to tell it. The explanation evidently is that, though by no means unflattered by the tolerance and attention of the "beautiful people," Carlyle conceived himself as standing in a relationship to his age unlike that of the literary man to his "public." The theme of the reception of heroes in their own time provides a clue; and again, it is developed with noticeable personal intensity, and with almost unvarying attention to the contemporary situation. Carlyle announces in his first lecture, "To me there is something very touching" in primitive Scandinavian hero-worship, "in such artless, helpless, but hearty entire reception of a Hero by his fellow-men. . . . If I could show in any measure, what I feel deeply for a long time now, That it is the vital element of mankind, the soul of man's history here in our world,—it would be the chief use of this discoursing at present" (p. 29). We sense the nineteenth-century relevance in the assertion, "The most significant feature in the history of an epoch is the manner it has of welcoming a Great Man" (p. 42), as well as in the rather nervous exhortation concerning the Poet and Prophet: "we must listen before all to him" (p. 46). As usual, the status of the man of letters and the needs of the present age are uniquely intertwined: "the world knows not well at any time what to do with him, so foreign is his aspect in the world," says Carlyle of the man of letters, observing, perhaps with a trace of self-pity, that he rules "from his grave, after death, whole nations and generations who would, or would not, give him bread while living" (pp. 154-155). Carlyle's own perplexities appear when he says of the Hero-King: "That we knew in some tolerable measure how to find him, and that all men were ready to acknowledge his divine right when found: this is precisely the healing which a sick world is everywhere, in these ages, seeking after!" (pp. 199). But Carlyle's perhaps more realistic, if pathetic, assessment of the relation between the hero and the age is evident in the remark, "Not a Hero only is needed, but a world fit for him; a world not of *Valets;*—the Hero comes almost in vain to it otherwise!" (p. 216). The tragedy of Carlyle's life can be measured in the distance between this scornful judgment of his age and the figure he employed to express what heroes, implicitly including Carlyle, should be able to expect: "the Great Man was always as lightning out of Heaven; the rest of men waited for him like fuel, and then they too would flame" (p. 77). Instead, the beautiful people applauded and bought his books, and young men wrote letters in playful mock-Carlylese.[18]

Perhaps most important of all, Carlyle himself repeatedly acts the prophet in the course of the lectures. The prophetic message is simple enough, so simple and so often repeated with little variation, that one suspects that therein lies at least part of the cause for the intense revulsion Carlyle later felt for the book. The Goethean "open secret of the Universe" is almost totally exhausted in the announcement that both the world and man's life are miraculous, mysterious, living, and divine—the revelation of the workings of God, an awful Fact and Reality, full of Divine Significance. But there is also a considerable amount of literal "prediction" in

Heroes; despite the gloomy fate of prophets and the traces of his own temperamental melancholy, Carlyle exerts himself almost galvanically to a series of optimistic statements regarding the future of modern society. His imagination has a natural affinity for crisis and violent incendiary disaster; for him, the Prophet becomes the sponsor of a new Revolution and a new Reformation. The Great Man, we saw, is "the lightning out of Heaven" who will kindle the dry dead fuel. That fuel is "common languid Times, with their unbelief, distress, perplexity, with their languid doubting characters and embarrassed circumstances, impotently crumbling-down into ever worse distress towards final ruin" (p. 13): the reference is clearly to his own age. But scepticism itself has a hopeful prognostic: it is "not an end but a beginning." "Let us have the crisis; we shall either have death or the cure"; Ultilitarianism is only "an approach towards new Faith" (p. 172). Protestantism likewise is but the first of a series of honest demolitions, for beyond even the present confusion we look "afar off to a new thing, which shall be true, and authentically divine!" (p. 123). This world in preparation will be a "world all sincere, a believing world: the like has been; the like will again be,—cannot help being" (p. 127). The tone rises ringingly once or twice: "I prophesy that the world will once more become *sincere;* a believing world: with *many* Heroes in it, a heroic world!" (p. 176). But of course he does not spell out the details of this new "union," beyond stating that it will be a "Theocracy," making "a God's Kingdom of this Earth" (p. 153). These hopes that "Dilettantism, Scepticism, Triviality" will be cast out—"as, by God's blessing, they shall one day be" (p. 85)—are at once distantly visionary and no doubt somehow futile and peevish, a product of wish fulfillment; though sometimes Carlyle more cautiously reminds us that in times of inevitable revolution "there are long troublous periods before matters come to a settlement again," and that this is a time of "*transition* from false to true" (pp. 119, 203).

Carlyle's prophecies are not convincingly managed for the twentieth-century reader and very likely were not always fully satisfying even to the Victorian public, who sought and sometimes found in him an ethical and metaphysical assurance he himself did not firmly possess. But we are concerned here with the manner and tone which Carlyle adopts in *Heroes,* and the inferences his auditors and readers would draw from them. As the weight of the evidence presented here suggests, Carlyle (perhaps with less than the fullest self-consciousness) was presenting himself as the prophet and leader to his times; in the England of 1840, there was scarcely any other candidate for the role as Carlyle had defined it. It should not be impossible for the modern reader to imagine that a nineteenth-century reader of *Heroes,* and much more an auditor of the lectures, would have been able to *believe,* even if only for the moment, that here was indeed the great man whose "wise healing word" would enkindle the dry fuel of contemporary unbelief and perplexity. Convinced that men of letters were "incalculably influential," Carlyle seems in 1840 to have believed that his own prediction concerning them—that they "will not always wander like unrecognised unregulated Ishmaelites among us!"—had been fulfilled in himself. The exuberance of the letter of July 2 to Emerson, in which in "the fire of the moment" he planned to preach "like a very lion" throughout America, and the immediately following collapse of his plans; the "strange" quality he musingly detected in the completed work, and the almost immediate extreme depreciation of the book: these oscillations suggest that Carlyle himself may have detected there more of one side of himself, unprotected by irony and masks, than he was customarily willing to reveal.

An important device helps indicate finally the extent of Carlyle's unique omnipresence in *Heroes*. It is that of "voice," of the assumed stance and authority of the first-person speaker. Perhaps three or four modes of self-presentation can be distinguished. There is, pervasively, the "I" of the reasonable, ingratiating nineteenth-century lecturer. The opening pages of the first lecture are thickly strewn with phrases like "as I say," "as I take it," "what I call Hero-worship," "could I . . . make manifest to you," "I must make the attempt," "it seems to me," "I find," "I cannot yet call." These are intermingled with a tissue of plurals designed conventionally to draw in his benevolently disposed audience: "We cannot look, however," "we see men of all kinds," "a thing that fills us," "we may pause," "We shall not see," "if we do not reject," "Let us consider," "we may say," "Let us try," etc. But a second, more authoritative tone is detectable in the accumulation of slightly more emphatic versions of the same terms. We sense the personal authority assumed in the following phrases, rather reminiscent of John Henry Newman's manner, all from two successive paragraphs: "I do say," "I will not," "I say," "I define," "truly" (pp. 173-174). Even more emphatic, if hard to classify, are those memorable moments when Carlyle steps forward to evince special interest in his favorite heroes. "This Prophet of the Scotch," he says of Knox, "is to me no hateful man!" (p. 151). "To me," he says of Dante, "it is a most touching face; perhaps of all faces that I know, the most so" (p. 86). Perhaps most remarkable, however, is a passage in which Carlyle shifts, without benefit of quotation marks, from his own intensely personal mode to the putative words of Luther:

> I, for one, pardon Luther for now altogether revolting against the Pope. The elegant Pagan, by this fire-decree of his, had kindled into noble just wrath the bravest heart then living in this world. The bravest, if also one of the humblest, peaceablest; it was now kindled. These words of mine, words of truth and soberness aiming faithfully, as human inability would allow, to promote God's truth on earth, and save men's souls, you God's vicegerent on earth, answer them by the hangman and fire. You will burn me and them. . . . (p. 133)

And so on: the result being that the final assertion of the paragraph—"that Life was a truth, and not a lie!"—though actually the words of Carlyle, hovers suggestively between the two dramatic voices, and adds to Carlyle's personal sincerity the thundering authority of Luther. The effect is comparable, in its heightened prophetic tone and its note of intense personal conviction, to the long passage cited above from **"Chartism."**

IV

I have argued that the fundamental unity of *Heroes* derives from Carlyle's varied but continuous forms of self-presentation, the totality conveying the impression that Carlyle is indeed a prophet, at times *the* prophet whose wise and healing word the age looked for.[19] This is not to deny that he does not always speak in his own person; John Holloway has authoritatively studied Carlyle's "dramatization of discussions."[20] Nevertheless, *Heroes* is admittedly freer of dramatization, of mask and irony, than *Sartor* and even than the relatively more "objective" early essays. Nor is this to fall, in any simple way, into the intentional fallacy, though Carlyle's works defy many of our usual and valid canons of critical separation between the art work and its biographical and historical origins. For if *Heroes* is a peculiarly personal statement of Carlyle's, the letters of the period only corroborate and clarify what is evident in the work itself.[21] Nor would I deny, finally, that the prophet's role assumed in *Heroes* is *itself* a "mask," a necessary pose. Carlyle's "sincerity" and personal conviction are evident, but the letters, as well as a frequent uncertainty of tone in the lectures, reveal that the prophetic afflatus was at best intermittent with him and that the manner had to be wilfully maintained and at times forced. Moreover, at bottom Carlyle very likely harbored a contempt for—or at least a strong reservation regarding—the "mere" man of letters: his instinctive sympathies always (and increasingly as he grew older) lay with the man of decisive *action*.[22]

There was, indeed, one further cause of Carlyle's special willingness in the spring of 1840 to adopt the prophet's tone, a cause which throws light on the intentions of the lectures. For *Heroes* represents a decided heightening of the style of the *Lectures on the History of Literature,* delivered two years earlier, in which Carlyle dealt with four of the major figures of *Heroes* (Dante, Shakespeare, Knox, Johnson) and some of its major themes (sincerity, earnestness, unconsciousness, humor) in an altogether flatter manner. If there is any single major cause for the newfound confidence which is evident in the adoption of the prophet's tone, it is to be found in John Sterling's long, adulatory review of "Carlyle's Work" in the *Westminster* of the preceding autumn. Sterling, though he had known Carlyle well since 1835, did not blush to refer to him as "among . . . the immortals of history," "the most resolute and mighty preacher in our day," the man of "the most fervid, sincere, far-reaching genius" to have arisen in England in twenty years.[23] Sterling, who had a capacity for hero-worship, had found a hero:

> clear, swift, far-sounding as a torrent his words spread forth, and will stream into many hearts. The heavy lamentation will come as a voice of hope. . . . Amid the clamorous snarl and gossip of literature, and the dead formulas of superficial science, here sounds a true prophetic voice. . . . Nor will it be without fit audience among us. . . . (p. 38)

Sterling's review was a decisive event in Carlyle's career, because he had at last found an adequate disciple. He saw the review late in September and wrote Sterling: "there has no man in these Islands been so reviewed in my time; it is the most magnanimous eulogy I ever knew one man utter of another man whom he knew face to face. . . . incredible to all men, incrediblest of all to me; yet sweet in the highest degree, for very obvious reasons, notwithstanding" (*LCM,* p. 224). That this was a turning point in Carlyle's life is evident when we note that the letter in which he told his mother of the "changed time" in his fortunes was dated October 24. In fact, a reading of Sterling's review suggests that it provided the germinal conception of the **Heroes** lectures—not simply the "doctrine" of heroes, which had been adumbrated much earlier, but the peculiarly personal intensity of its presentation. For Sterling saw not only that Carlyle was a hero-worshiper, prophet, and hero himself, but that Carlyle's art had a specially autobiographical basis. Sterling spoke of Carlyle's "fervid worship of many a ragged, outcast heroism" (p. 22): "to Mr. Carlyle the objects of chief interest are memorable persons—men who have fought strongly the good fight. . . . especially . . . those living nearest to our own time and circumstances, in whom we may find monumental examples of the mode in which our difficulties are to be conquered" (pp. 12-13). Carlyle studied the "hindrances such a man had to overcome, the energies by which he vanquished them, and the work, whatever it may have been, which he thus accomplished for mankind" (p. 13).

More important, Sterling again and again detected in Carlyle the qualities of Carlyle's heroes. He speaks of Carlyle's "apparent rudeness, harshness, lawless capriciousness of style; full of meanings and images, but these looking incoherent, or at least as yet unreconciled" (pp. 9-10). Carlyle is like Jean Paul in being one of the "inspired painters of symbols for the fundamental realities of our existence" (pp. 10-11); but he goes beyond him in that "he lives to fight, breathes war-flames of disdain and zeal, and moves only to wrestle and trample forward." The requirements of the hero are one by one applied to Carlyle as we hear that his "tumultuous abruptness" and "gloomy spectral fervour," his "rugged" sentences and his "short, sharp, instantaneous mode of expression," are explained by the fact that "he is not naturally fluent" and is unable "to use with smooth dexterity a conventional mechanism of discourse" (pp. 21-22). He paints Carlyle as "large of bone, . . . sturdy, and

with a look of combat, and of high crusader-enthusiasm," "resembling, perhaps, a great Christianized giant of romance, a legendary Christopher" (p. 24). Even more suggestive, perhaps, is Sterling's elaborate comparison with Luther, whom Carlyle most resembles "in the essentials of his character." There is a likeness "in the type and scale of their tendencies and faculties" (p. 64); in both there is "sincerity, largeness, fervour, . . . sudden and robust eloquence, and broad and unshackled views of all things; a flowing cordiality based on deep and severe, often almost dismal and sepulchral conscientiousness" (pp. 64-65). In each man there is "fierce and scornful prejudice" and great exaggeration: "Their fundamental unity of conception lives in a religious awe of the Divine" (p. 65).

These reflections had been adumbrated in Sterling's well-known letter of May 29, 1835, which was in effect the first serious literary criticism Carlyle had received. In discussing the "form" of *Sartor,* Sterling had aligned Carlyle with the "subjective" masters of modern literature—and put him in the company of Rabelais and Montaigne, Sterne and Swift, Cervantes and Jeremy Taylor. Most important, he noted that the "multitude of peculiar associations and relations" in such writers, which open them to charges of lawlessness and capriciousness, cannot be defended aesthetically by "any one *external* principle" but are in fact "connected by the bond of our own personality" (XI, 109-110). This line of thought, culminating in the review of 1839, must have had an important influence on Carlyle as his own reflections on the personal basis of his art gathered to a focus. That the review in the *Westminster* marked an epoch in Carlyle's conception of himself is evident, not only in the letter of October 24 to his mother, but in a passage in the **Life of John Sterling,** published more than a decade later. Carlyle remembers

> the deep silent joy, not of a weak or ignoble nature, which it gave to myself in my then mood and situation; as it well might. The first generous human recognition, expressed with heroic emphasis, and clear conviction visible amid its fiery exaggeration, that one's poor battle in this world is not quite a mad and futile, that it is perhaps a worthy and manful one, which will come to something yet. . . . The thought burnt in me like a lamp, for several days; lighting-up into a kind of heroic splendour the sad volcanic wrecks, abysses, and convulsions of said poor battle, and secretly I was very grateful to my daring friend, and am still, and ought to be. (XI, 191-192)

The role of "heroic splendour" in which Sterling had cast his friend carried Carlyle through the composition of **Heroes and Hero-Worship,** and contributed to the temporary identity—some would say confusion—of Carlyle with his own heroes.

I submit that in the pages of Sterling's review we find the germs, not merely of the substance of **Heroes,** but of that peculiar implicit presentation of himself which unifies and vivifies Carlyle's lectures, a unique and not easily formulated unity in Carlyle's writings, resting on the deepest ground of his experience and personality. Sterling's review conjoined with the other favoring circumstances of Carlyle's life to produce the euphoria of 1839 and 1840; it also, by suggesting the unstated personal basis of the hero doctrine, goes some distance in explaining the unique tone and rhetorical stance of **Heroes.** In the review, no doubt to some extent unconsciously, Carlyle had discovered a series of formulas which led him to the precise point where his fundamental doctrine and his personal quest for self-definition met, enabling him to write what is perhaps the most openly "prophetic" book of the nineteenth century in England and a masterpiece of Romantic art.

Notes

1 *On Heroes, Hero-Worship and the Heroic in History,* ed. H. D. Traill (Centenary Edition; New York, 1897-1901), V, 157. All later references to *Heroes* are to this edition, as are references to the *Essays* and *Past and Present;* volume and page numbers are given parenthetically. Other abbreviations:

CE: The Correspondence of Emerson and Carlyle. Ed. Joseph Slater. New York, 1964.

LL: James Anthony Froude, *Thomas Carlyle: A History of His Life in London, 1834-1881.* 4th ed.; vol. I. London, 1885.

NL: New Letters of Thomas Carlyle. Ed. Alexander Carlyle. London and New York, 1904.

LCM: Letters of Thomas Carlyle to John Stuart Mill, John Sterling and Robert Browning. Ed. Alexander Carlyle. London, 1923.

SR: Sartor Resartus. Ed. Charles Frederick Harrold. New York, 1937.

2 On Carlyle's strong and widespread influence on the youthful generation of the 1840's, see Kathleen Tillotson, "Matthew Arnold and Carlyle" (Warton Lecture on English Poetry), *Proceedings of the British Academy,* XLII (1956), 135-138.

3 The two best studies of "form" in *Sartor* are Leonard Deen's "Irrational Form in *Sartor Resartus," Texas Studies in Literature and Language,* V (Autumn 1963), 438-451, and Chap. IV, "The Structure of *Sartor Resartus,"* in G. B. Tennyson's *"Sartor" Called "Resartus"* (Pinceton, 1965). See also Daniel P. Deneau, "Relationship of Style and Device in *Sartor Resartus," Victorian News-letter,* No. 17 (Spring 1960), pp. 17-20; and John Lindberg, "The Artistic Unity of *Sartor Resartus," ibid.,* pp. 20-23.

4 Equally important is the fact that, in both essays, Jean Paul becomes one of the major prototypes, not only of Teufelsdröckh and his style, but of the "vehement" and "rugged" heroes of the *Heroes* lectures.

5 Carlisle Moore, "Carlyle's 'Diamond Necklace' and Poetic History," *PMLA,* LVIII (June 1943), 537-557, especially 544 ff.

6 James Anthony Froude, *Thomas Carlyle: A History of the First Forty Years of His Life, 1795-1835* (London, 1882), II, 345.

7 *Ibid.,* p. 354.

8 *Correspondence between Goethe and Carlyle,* ed. Charles Eliot Norton (London, 1887), p. 285.

9 Thomas Carlyle, *Letters to His Wife,* ed. Trudy Bliss (London, 1953), p. 114.

10 See F. W. Roe, *Thomas Carlyle as a Critic of Literature* (New York, 1910), pp. 148-149, for the principles of Carlyle's historical and biographical method of criticism.

11 The discussion in John Holloway's *The Victorian Sage* (London, 1953), pp. 21-85, is easily the best we have of the identity of "expression" and "confirmation" in Carlyle's work, of his "modifying the reader's perceptiveness" as opposed to "persuasion" in the classical sense. Holloway's concern, however, is largely atomic, and he does not, except for the histories, apply his insights to the unity of a whole work.

12 Carlyle had told his brother in May 1837 that his "new profession'" was his way to "get delivered out of this awful quagmire of difficulties in which you have so long seen me struggle and wriggle," since his three years in London have been "sore and stern, almost frightful" (*LL,* pp. 104-105). Even with the success of the *French Revolution,* Carlyle pictured himself, late in 1837, as "a half-dead enchanted spectre-haunted nondescript," disgusted with the literary profession (*LL,* p. 120; and see p. 130, February 19, 1838). Only in early 1838 does he first admit that "these long years of martyrdom and misery . . . were not utterly in vain" (*LL,* p. 128), though his "remorse" over his "conceit" and "ambition" in his new success—not to speak of his evident inability to allow any feeling of "happiness"—continue through the delivery of the *Heroes* lectures to fill the letters and journals.

13 See Carlisle Moore, "The Persistence of Carlyle's 'Everlasting Yea,'" *Modern Philology,* LIV (February 1957), 187-196.

14 The continuous use of "deep," "deep-hearted," "deep-feeling," "deep-seeing," "the perennial Deeps," "depth," etc., is supported by a multitude of suggestive phrases using words like "kernel," "heart," "inner," "inmost," "unfathomable," "central essence," "roots," "underground"—not to speak of numerous sea images.

15 Teufelsdröckh is presented as "our young Ishmael,"

"'the Wanderer,'" and is twice compared to the Wandering Jew (*SR,* pp. 113-114, 78, 17, 156). Carlyle even once referred to himself as "a Bedouin, . . . a rough child of the desert" (*LL,* p. 288).

[16] *Essays on Some of the Modern Guides to English Thought in Matters of Faith* (London, 1888), p. 38.

[17] See F. X. Roellinger, Jr., "The Early Development of Carlyle's Style," *PMLA,* LXXII (December 1957), 936-951.

[18] See letter of March 1845, in *Letters of Matthew Arnold to Arthur Hugh Clough,* ed. Howard Foster Lowry (London and New York, 1932), pp. 55-57; and one of May 1848, in *The Correspondence of Arthur Hugh Clough,* ed. Frederick L. Mulhauser (Oxford, 1957), I, 207.

[19] John Lindberg, in "The Decadence of Style: Symbolic Structure in Carlyle's Later Prose," *Studies in Scottish Literature,* I (January 1964), 183-195, makes several comments on Carlyle as prophet and as "sympathetic suffering hero," but from a point of view somewhat different from my own.

Albert J. LaValley, in *Carlyle and the Idea of the Modern* (New Haven and London, 1968), which appeared after the present essay was completed, declares (p. 248)) that the heroes Carlyle "really admires are images of himself or a wishfulfilled self." LaValley fascinatingly presents *Heroes* (pp. 236-252) as an example of retreat, confusion, distortion, failure, and rationalization; still, in my opinion he fails to see the positive importance of the book in Carlyle's personal development up to 1840.

[20] *Victorian Sage,* p. 27.

[21] B. H. Lehman, in *Carlyle's Theory of the Hero* (Durham, N.C., 1928), pp. 196 ff., reverses the process and looks for the ways in which Carlyle the man attempted to conduct himself in accordance with the hero theory. George Levine, in "'Sartor Resartus' and the Balance of Fiction," *Victorian Studies,* VIII (December 1964), 131-160, using what I believe is a method somewhat similar to my own, explains that the "form" of *Sartor,* as well as the hitherto unsolved problem of the relation of the Editor to Teufelsdröckh, can only be understood as Carlyle's "deeply personal affirmation and discovery of his identity" and as the expression of his "self-awareness" of his complex relation to his audience (pp. 154, 146). I agree that *Sartor,* through its fictional devices, represents the high point of Carlyle's "flexibility and openness to experience"; but I would argue that as late as 1840 Carlyle still maintained a considerable complexity and "uncertainty" and a quasi-fictional set of "masks."

[22] Froude comments that Carlyle "was conscious of possessing considerable powers, but he would have preferred at all times to have found a use for them in action" (*LL,* p. 48). For Froude's own startling comments on literature as "but the shadow of action; the action the reality, the poetry the echo," see *LL,* pp. 130-131.

[23] *London and Westminster Review,* XXXIII (October 1839), 10,37,52. Hereafter cited parenthetically by page number alone.

Robert W. Kusch (essay date 1971)

SOURCE: "The Eighteenth Century as 'Decaying Organism' in Carlyle's *The French Revolution,*" in *Anglia,* Vol. LXXXIX, No. 4, 1971, pp. 456-70.

[*In the following essay, Kusch examines the interplay between metaphor of the eighteenth century as a "decaying organism" and theme of decay advancing toward "spontaneous combustion" in Carlyle's* The French Revolution.]

If a poet is a man who sees in metaphor a primary way of knowing and uses language for evocation as well as description, then Carlyle was one of the great poets of the nineteenth century. Other scholars have said as much, and John Holloway, in *The Victorian Sage,* has classified some lines of metaphor as they appear in work after work.[1] We know that certain images recur in Carlyle's mind, and they may become so powerful, I believe, that the arc of his metaphoric flight defines the horizon of his awareness. Carlyle was aware that the energy of metaphor might do this. In *Sartor,* he sees the "symbol" as a technique of revelation and concealment, a power whose light inheres in its darkness[2]. In ***The French Revolution,*** he illustrates a similar point about metaphor with his extended interplays between tenor and vehicle. A single idea in ***The French Revolution***—his view of the eighteenth century—may show how the whole process works. Carlyle focuses his view of the eighteenth century through the "decaying organism" that leads to "spontaneous combustion". Metaphor and theme generate a vitality neither could manage alone, and this vitality, I think, is his artistry at its best.

By 1833, in conquering his doubt through the Leith Walk experience and the writing of *Sartor,* Carlyle had begun to change his perspective on the eighteenth century. Through *Sartor* he saw it as a kind of moral landscape, a wasteland of unbelief that various questers such as Goethe and Burns must cross. "A black, chill, ashy swamp . . . where the Tree of Life once bloomed and brought forth fruit of goodliest savor, there was only barrenness and desolation"[3]. Goethe's battles, as Carlyle traced them through *Werther, Faust,* and *Wilhelm Meister,* were not only battles for a kind of personal survival, but the symbolic plight of a "modern" man in a skeptical and destructive age. For Carlyle, Burns succumbed to a whole century of deceit only when he left the natural sources of his inspiration for Edinburgh society. Teufelsdröckh's wanderings through doubt and indifference are set in the reign of Frederick the Great, and the interior journey, when given external form, winds across "a grim Desert . . . wherein is heard only the howling of wild beasts, or the shrieks of despairing, hate-filled men; and no Pillar of Cloud and no Pillar of fire by night, any longer guides the Pilgrim"[4]. As Carlyle slowly came to terms with doubt and gained perspective on the century, however, the image of the landscape faded and another began to emerge. He now saw it as a kind of "decaying organism", the final phase of a thousand year cycle of growth and decay. Like the death of the Roman empire, which closed another stage in human history, this death would not be easy. From Carlyle's point of view, if the ideal Zeitgeist is an organism moving in noiseless, consistent self-regulation, then the destruction of that organism will necessarily be violent. In **"Characteristics"**, his first essay after *Sartor,* his change in perspective on the century is already apparent. The "wasteland" has disappeared and in its place is a "condition" that must be continuously diagnosed. "The healthy know not of their health, but only the sick"[5] indicates the whole tone and style of Carlyle's later thinking about the time. When philosophers are compelled to dissect the assumptions by which men live, then the end of a "spirit" is already in sight. Two years after **"Characteristics"**, in **"Diderot"**, he could encompass all of these ideas by showing that, of necessity, men will destroy the institution that houses an idea when they can no longer confirm the idea in their daily lives. "There comes a time when the mouldering changes into a rushing; active hands drive in their wedges"[6]. This view of history, essentially poetic and religious, is the starting point for *The French Revolution.*

II

In *The Philosophy of Literary Form,* Kenneth Burke has suggested a challenging method of analysis for any author as complex and dramatically inclined as Carlyle. The essential mind of the artist will show itself, he suggests, in a series of "watershed moments" or critical points in the work of art, and the language the artist uses at these moments, in concert with the reality he is trying to represent, is especially significant:

> First: We should watch for the dramatic alignment. What is vs. what. As per Odets: violin vs. prizefight . . . (then) . . . we should watch for "critical points" within the work as well as the beginnings and endings. These are often "watershed moments," changes of slope when some new quality enters . . . Also, since works embody an agon, we may be admonished to look for some underlying imagery (or groupings of imagery) through which the agonistic trial takes place . . . [7]

The relation of the "critical points" to the "dramatic alignment" may very well be a means-end relation. As it is possible to determine a man's strategy for living by examining his responses to critical situations, so it is also possible, by analyzing the images and themes occurring at critical points of a work of art, to determine its alignment and shaping principle. This is particularly true with a historical work, where the critical turns cannot be invented, only heightened or toned down. If the same images and themes recur, then an inclusive generalization may be drawn about the whole work.

What are the critical points? Carlyle has not outlined them, but the occasions he describes with eloquence are those that involve men and action, not social analysis and political implication. No major historian of the Revolution has written a more vivid account of the fall of the Bastille; but his account of the making of the August Constitution is vague. His passion for "all those sectionary tumults, convention-harangues, guillotine-holocausts, Brunswick discomfitures", for "flaming Reality"[8], never abates. The occasions he would naturally stress are those that show clusters of men in violent activity, personal achievements or failures in high office, or revelatory acts that presage success or failure on a larger stage. The storming of the Bastille; the insurrection of women; Louis' transfer to Paris, his attempted flight, condemnation, imprisonment and death; the varieties of terror—all, in one way or another, are occasions for Carlyle's intensity.

Several of these occasions show, I believe, a theme occurring again and again. The first does not come from a significant point in the revolution itself; it does, however, occur at a consequential point in the artistic structure of the book. After Carlyle has opened the first chapter with a description of Louis XV's fatal illness, he generalizes the whole idea of decay by locating it in the complex that is the age:

> In such a decadent age, or one fast verging that way, had our poor Louis been born. Grant also that if the French Kingship had not, by course of Nature, long to live, he of all men was the man to accelerate Nature. The blossom of French Royalty, cactus-like, has accordingly made an astonishing progress. In those Metz days, it was still standing with all its petals, though bedimmed by Orleans Regents and *Roué* Ministers and Cardinals; but now, in 1774, we behold it bald, and the virtue nigh gone out of it.[9]

The placement of the idea in the context of Louis' illness is of some importance in itself, but, for the purpose of determining the overall strategy of the book, only the theme and images will be discussed here. "Decadent" and "bald" establish that theme. Louis' illness stands for something more; from Carlyle's point of view, blight and death seem to be everywhere. The responsibility of kingship and a mature and creative religious belief, the political and philosophical centers of society, have been lost. A new well-intentioned king and queen bring some hope, but their intent cannot guarantee the vision needed to restore direction and belief. The slow processes of decay go on. Thus, after describing the high hopes appearing in the first days of Louis XVI's rule, Carlyle introduces the ominous theme again: "As indeed, evils of all sorts are more or less kin, and do usually go together: especially it is an old truth, that wherever huge physical evil is, there, as the parent and origin of it, has moral evil to a proportionate extent been"[10].

The capture of the Bastille is of little political importance in itself, but it is symbolically important: it is the first open defiance of authority and it begins the long course of revolution. Carlyle does not comment directly on the ineffective leadership that allows the people's dissatisfaction to congeal, but, in biting detail, he focuses on a bust of Louis XIV in the Rue de la Vannerie:

> Thou thyself, O Reader, when thou turnest that corner of the Rue de la Vannerie, and discernest still that same grim Bracket of old Iron, wilt not want for reflections. "Over a grocer's shop", or otherwise; with "a bust of Louis XIV in the niche under it", now no longer in the niche,—*it* still sticks there; still holding out an ineffectual light, of fish-oil; and has seen worlds wrecked, and says nothing[11].

The next two quotations come from phases in the downfall of the French monarchy. From Carlyle's point of view, however, more than the monarchy itself is involved. The existence of kingship through eight centuries in France demands not only a particular social structure; it also implies a philosophie perspective that recognizes the importance of a king. Decay and death of monarchy are also the end of a traditional perspective—and hence the end of an important ideal making up the Zeitgeist. Just after Louis is forced to leave Versailles, Carlyle comments again:

> And thus has Sansculottism made prisoner its King; *revoking* his parole. The Monarchy has fallen; and not so much as honourably: no, ignominiously; with struggle, indeed, oft-repeated; but then with unwise struggle; wasting its strength in fits and paroxysms; at every new paroxysm foiled more pitifully than before[12].

After the king and queen have attempted to flee, have been captured, returned, and Louis has been condemned, Carlyle comments again:

> To this conclusion, then, has thou come, O hapless Louis! The Son of Sixty Kings is to die on the Seaffold by form of Law. Under Sixty Kings this same form of Law, form of Society, has been fashioning itself together, these thousand years; and has become, one way and other, a most strange Machine. Surely, if needful, it is also frightful, this Machine; dead, blind; not what it should be; which, with swift stroke, or by cold slow torture, has wasted the lives and souls of innumerable men . . . [13]

Even though the monarchy continually stands for something more than itself, the death of Louis XVI is not the climax of Carlyle's vision of decay and death. In two more books, he details the "Reign of Terror" and continues the theme. That the theme is continued at this point suggests how thoroughly it forms the center of the book. Not monarchy alone, nor even the symbolic implications of monarchy, but the whole complex of lies Carlyle identifies with the Zeitgeist is being torn down. Carlyle's last paragraphs recapitulate:

> On the whole, therefore, has it not been fulfilled what was prophesied, *ex-post facto* indeed, by the Arch-quack Cagliostro, or another? He, as he looked in rapt vision and amazement into these things, thus spake: 'Ha! What is *this?* Angels, Uriel, Anachiel, and ye other Five; Pentagon of Rejuvenescence; Power that destroyedst Original Sin; Earth, Heaven, and thou Outer Limbo, which men name Hell! Does the EMPIRE OF IMPOSTURE waver! Burst there, in starry sheen updarting, Light-rays from out of *its* dark foundation; as it rocks and heaves, not in travailthroes but in deaththroes? Yea, Light-rays, piercing clear, that salute the Heavens,—lo, they *kindle* it; their starry clearness becomes as red Hellfire![14]

Gomorrah was not destroyed with a more righteous anger.

It is certainly true that, from another point of view, disintegration need not end in violent death. Carlyle was always fond of quoting Schiller's famous dictum about truth— *"immer wird, nie ist"*—and his view of truth emphasizes process, becoming and metaphoric contour. By 1837, as I have already suggested, he had joined decay to violent death through the image of the "falling structure" and had emphasized that destruction quickens in intensity as decay progresses. The "falling structure" is only one of several possibilities for joining the two, however. In *Sartor* and elsewhere, he uses the "phoenix" as an interpretive metaphor of death and rebirth. As the story goes, the phoenix anticipates its own death, builds its pyre, starts the flame by fanning its wings, is consumed, and is reborn out of its own ashes. Even in its destructive aspect, however, the story does not seem to integrate the design of *The French Revolution.* Carlyle sees the Revolution as a series of violent outbursts caused by the decay of the Zeitgeist and the end is morally "accretive"; whereas the "phoenix" presents death as an amoral occasion, the effect of age alone.

Perhaps no myth or metaphor can explain the design of *The French Revolution.* But another comes much closer. Carlyle was certainly aware of the old folk belief in "spontaneous combustion". In one form, the story is nothing more than that an explosion occurs if a certain point of decay is reached. In the folk imagination, however, the story had taken on a moralistic cast so that such vices as profligacy and drunkenness were thought to have their consequence in a bodily explosion. In an early essay, Carlyle had alluded to this idea when he said that Werner was "a man dissolute; that is, by a long course of vicious indulgences, enervated and *loosened asunder*"[15]. Werner's death is not explosive, but the description carries its own portent of disaster. In *The French Revolution,* Carlyle alludes to the idea once when he talks about the "inward decomposition, of decay that has become self-combustion:—as when, according to Neptuno-Plutonic Geology, the World is all decayed down into due attritus of this sort; and shall now be *exploded* and new made!"[16] In Victorian literature, no better example occurs than the death of Mr. Krook in *Bleak House,* however. Dickens does not focus upon his death directly, but it is apparent that moral disintegration ends in physical catastrophe, because only "a smouldering suffocating vapour in the room, and a dark greasy coating on the walls and ceiling"[17] remain. Krook's death and Carlyle's view of the death of the eighteenth century have striking parallels. Both occur to organisms after long processes of decay that are specifically named as moral, a cause and effect relation between decay and violence exists, and the end itself is explosive, final. If the metaphor did no more than explain the process of decay and explosion, it would be worth serious consideration, but it also aligns several of the major images in *The French Revolution*—images of age, disease, explosion and death-by-fire.

The various ways in which Carlyle projects decay and violence through the book suggest, I think, how extensive and unified theme and metaphor are. To make the book, he could have written an account of the inability of the established economic system to meet current demands, or a political narrative about the lack of real options, or a philosophic account of the change of belief in the importance of the individual. All of these would have been valid, but his imagination sees the symbolic-in-the-particular far more than the design of any of them would have allowed. Without effort, he begins with the concrete and the particular. When he shows a conglomerate of persons, he often draws the scene together by looking at the dominant figure. Necker, Mirabeau, Danton, Marat and Robespierre appear through scenes of conflict or harmony, but always as physical forces, bodying forth influential opinion. Even when the diversity of a situation seems to lead away from the emergence of one figure, Carlyle splits it into a series of occasions, each one dominated by a different man. The capture of the Bastille, for example, can easily be conceived as a leaderless movement held together by the energy of mass hatred. But Carlyle divides it into a series of explosive harangues leading to action (Camille Desmoulins and others) and desperation on the part of the defenders (Besenval and De Launay). With only a few descriptive breaks, the action is focused from man to man, each one the center where violence or frustration clusters.

As he often particularizes a scene by drawing on one man, so he also particularizes a sequence of actions by drawing out the critical point. Hundreds of decisions are made throughout the course of *The French Revolution,*

and Carlyle often slows the pace of the narration to catch the particular man in the moment of immediate contact with history. Besenval's confusion during the storming of the Bastille, Louis' decision to attempt escape across the border, various Girondins balloting at Louis' death, Robespierre's choice to stand before the Assembly—all, for Carlyle, are collocations of men and temporal moments that turn the Revolution into decisive courses.

It would be too much to say that every death in *The French Revolution* symbolizes the death of the century, but, in their totality, these deaths add up to the death of a way of life. Whatever continuing force the Zeitgeist may have in other lands, its existence, for Carlyle, ends in France through the execution of so many members of the aristocracy. The following are consecutive incidents in "Terror the Order of the Day". The first is the execution of Madame Roland; the second of Bailly, former First Mayor of Paris:

> There went with her (Madame Roland) a certain Lamarche, 'Director of Assignat-Printing'; whose dejection she endeavoured to cheer. Arrived at the foot of the scaffold, she asked for pen and paper, 'to write the strange thoughts that were rising in her': remarkable request; which was refused . . . For Lamarche's sake, she will die first; show him how easy it is to die: 'Contrary to the order', said Samson.—'P'shaw, you cannot refuse the last request of a Lady'; and Samson yielded . . . Like a white Grecian Statue, serenely complete, she shines in that black wreck of things;—long memorable. Honour to great Nature who, in Paris City, in the Era of Noble-Sentiment and Pompadourism, can make a Jeanne Philipon, and nourish her to clear perennial Womanhood, though but on Logics, *Encyclopédies,* and the Gospel according to Jean-Jacques![18]

> Still crueller was the fate of poor Bailly, First National President, First Mayor of Paris: doomed now for Royalism, Fayettism; for that Red-Flag Business of the Champ-de-Mars;—one may say in general, for leaving his Astronomy to meddle with the Revolution. It is the 10th of November 1793, a cold bitter drizzling rain, as poor Bailly is led through the streets; howling Populace covering him with curses, with mud . . . pulse after pulse still counting itself out in the old man's weary heart. For hours long; amid curses and bitter frost-rain! 'Bailly, thou tremblest', said one. '*Mon ami,* it is for cold', said Bailly, *'c'est de froid'.* Crueller end had no mortal[19].

For Carlyle, every human act exists in its radical individuality, but, at the core of that individuality, every act also has symbolic possibilities. Madame Roland's death is very different from Bailly's, but each, in its own way, concretely reflects something of the death of the Zeitgeist. Madame Roland's admirable qualities are cut off by the violence of the mob and Carlyle's comment on her death suggests the whole force of indiscriminate destruction. Though he writes with sympathy about Bailly's death, Carlyle still sees him as one of the ineffective old order—he "left Astronomy to meddle with the Revolution"—and his death is also the partial death of "Noble Sentiment and Pompadourism"[20]. By reiteration, by accumulation of particulars and symbolic extension, Carlyle plots the death of the Zeitgeist until, at the end, when he says that "Imposture is burnt up"[21], it is clear that much of the eighteenth century system of values has been simultaneously destroyed.

One death in *The French Revolution* is so significant in placement, structure, and thematic implication that it ought to be examined in detail. Carlyle selects the "Death of Louis XV" as his opening episode, and, at first glance, his selection of this particular detail for so important a place seems awkward. For the death of a king in 1774 appears unrelated to the immediacy of the Revolution. He might have begun with the ascension of Louis XVI, which would have provided the dramatic continuity of the decline and fall of one major character. Or with the opening of the Parliament of Paris, the first concession to the people's representation in government. Or the fall of the Bastille, the beginning of active revolution. But apparently no one of these incidents provided the multiplicity of moral and thematic possibilities that the death of a once-admired king offered. And it is an extraordinary choice. It is a particular incident that contains all the characters of intrigue and byways of depravity that lead Carlyle to an examination of the state of the time. The cast around the king is as interesting as the king himself. As persons who fear his death—and consequent loss of their own positions—in very particular ways, Dubarry, the Duke D'Aiguillon, and Abbé Terray worry the bedside with problems and questions. Representing prostitution, self-seeking aristocracy and economic corruption, however, they illustrate the inclusiveness and penetration of decay. Carlyle follows the symbolic line from personal detail to general characteristic until, by the end of the first book, he has delineated many different areas of the "Armida Palace", "D'Aiguillon and Company", and "Dubarrydom"[22]. The death of Louis also gives Carlyle scope to exercise his bent for seeing moral contrasts in the life of a single character, and to provide a large historical contrast between the medieval ideal of kingship and its debility in the eighteenth century. And, for Carlyle, the life of Louis provides a host of moral contrasts. Once admired and served with pride, Louis, on his deathbed, is forgotten or cursed for irresponsibility. His original concern for the people has been shaped by courtiers and the "Scarlett Woman"[23] until he himself sees no further than their wishes. Carlyle sharpens the contrast by ironic chapter titles and incidents. In "Louis the Well-Beloved", he shows the people's concern for the king in his supposed fatal illness at Metz in 1744; but in "Louis the Unforgotten", at the king's death, he illustrates how "the vaults of St. Denis receive their own, unwept . . ."[24] "Him they crush down, and huddle underground him and his era of sin and tyranny and shame; for behold a New Era is come"[25]. The promise of Louis' reign has not matured into

achievement, and Carlyle expands the signature of failure by contrasting, in "Realized Ideals", the confident and vigorous success of "Charles the Hammer, Pepin Bowlegged" "Clovis"[26] and even "Louis the Grand"[27]. Political failure and moral rootlessness united with fatal illness is thus the theme of the whole episode, and the selection of the detail is brilliantly appropriate for introducing the theme of the work. From here, the ephemeral celebration of a new king and queen in "The Paper Age" (analogous to the time when Louis XV was "Well-Beloved") declines into a general recognition of irresponsibility and, finally, revolutionary outbursts. Louis' death foreshadows the whole theme of decay in just those areas Carlyle wants to emphasize: politics and morality leading to physical collapse.

Carlyle's commentary contributes to this design. Charles Frederick Harrold has estimated that of the 1700 or so paragraphs in *The French Revolution,* "more than 500 contain no historical material whatsoever, but express Carlyle's reactions to events and ideas of the Revolution"[28]. The spectrum of themes in these paragraphs of commentary is not wide. His feeling at the deaths of Madame Roland and Bailly show his sympathy, but, as his statements at the critical points already indicate, he is continually preoccupied with prophecies of impending doom and the excoriation of evil. One chapter may illustrate. "Astrea Redux" is a survey of the years 1774-84, the opening years of Louis XVI's reign and, for Carlyle, the beginning of "The Paper Age". It covers a relatively quiet and prosperous time. Carlyle's intent, just after shaping the sickness of Louis XV into the symbol of a sick society, is not to show the further penetration of decay. Rather he is interested in showing the apparent release from corruption: Louis XV, Dubarry and D'Aiguillon are gone. They have been replaced by a new king's good will. Carlyle's irony, however, circles the future, and between descriptions of the serenity of the palace, he centers on the destruction to come. Quoted in order, the first sentence of each paragraph in the chapter shows how description is balanced with prophecy:

> A paradoxical philosopher, carrying to the uttermost length that aphorism of Montesquieu's, "Happy the people whose annals are tiresome", has said, "Happy the people whose annals are vacant".

> The oak grows silently, in the forest, a thousand years; only in the thousandth year, when the woodman arrives with his axe, is there heard an echoing through the solitudes; and the oak announces itself when, with far-sounding crash, it *falls.*

> It is thus everywhere that foolish Rumour babbles not of what was done, but of what was misdone or undone; and foolish History (ever, more or less, the written epitomized synopsis of Rumour) knows so little that were not as well unknown.

Is it the healthy peace, or the ominous unhealthy, that rests on France, for these next Ten Years?

Dubarrydom and its D'Aiguillons are gone for ever. There is a young, still docile, well-intentioned King; a young, beautiful and bountiful, well-intentioned Queen; and with them all France, as it were, become young.

Then how "sweet" are the manners; vice "losing all its deformity"; becoming *decent* (as established things, making regulation for themselves, do); becoming almost a kind of "sweet" virtue!

The prophetic song of Paris and its Philosophes is audible enough in the Versailles Oeil-de-Boeuf, and the Oeil-de-Boeuf, intent chiefly on nearer blessedness, can answer, at worst, with a polite "Why not?"

Events? The grand events are but charitable Feasts of Morals (Fêtes des moeurs), with their Prizes and Speeches; Poissarde Processions to the Dauphin's cradle; above all Flirtations, their rise, progress, decline and fall.

Meanwhile the fair young Queen, in her halls of state, walks like a goddess of Beauty, the cynosure of all eyes; as yet mingles not with affairs, heeds not the future, least of all dreads it.

Monsieur, the King's elder Brother, has set up for a kind of wit; and leans toward the Philosophe side[29].

In the context of the drama, Carlyle's dire portent is to the life of Louis as the oracle is to Oedipus: equivocal and seemingly unimportant at first, its meanings are fixed with a terrible reality. While it is possible for the reader to be unimpressed with the omniscience of Carlyle's commentary because it is the omniscience of hindsight, Carlyle's artistic integrity is impressive and *The French Revolution* is a remarkable whole.

Carlyle's high achievement in *The French Revolution* soon issued in tragedy. A few weeks after he finished it, the only draft of the first volume was mistakenly burnt in the home of Mrs. Harriet Taylor[30]. It is not as if individual notes, sources and quotations were lost. Carlyle kept his library and his memory. He was no specialist in paste and patch, however, and all those intuitions that had alchemized structure and nuance were lost altogether. Carlyle's courage has been often praised—and it ought to be praised—but if the first *French Revolution* was at all like the second, it seems as if he was finally saved by the strength of his perspective on the death of an epoch.

In his imagination, the eighteenth century itself has now assumed a unique place among ages. Its interest for him shows in his continual desire to set it off, to show how it is cursed, and, at the same time to articulate its workings with his finest diction and syntax. No other century holds him with such fascination. He describes the seventeenth century as an age of faith, an age that produced a Milton, but he never traces Milton's complexity back to the age, which must be done if the age is truly to sustain a Carlylean Milton. How different are the elaborate relationships Carlyle establishes between Diderot or Louis XVI and the eighteenth century. Each one is individual and, at the same time, a product of his time. Again, Carlyle sees great creative potential in the nineteenth century, and he proclaims Goethe and Schiller founders of this new age, but he never relates Goethe to the nineteenth century in the complex way that he relates Voltaire to the eighteenth. Goethe is only prophet of his age, while Voltaire is the child, priest and symbol of his. The "decaying organism" is the organizing center of Carlyle's thought, but the scope and complexity of his view can be seen by a comparison with what he sees as another age of decay. In specific terms, he speaks of only one other. At the conclusion of **"Voltaire",** he compares the eighteenth century with that of the "Roman Emperors":

> . . . this era considerably resembles that of the Roman Emperors. There too was external splendor and internal squalor; the highest completeness in all sensual arts, including among these not cookery and its adjuncts alone, but even "effect-painting" and "effect-writing"; only the art of virtuous living was a lost one. Instead of Love of Poetry, there was "taste" for it; refinement in manners, with utmost coarseness in morals: in a word, the strange spectacle of a Social System, embracing large cultivated portions of the human species, and founded only on Atheism. With the Romans, things went what we should call their natural course: Liberty, public spirit quietly declined into caput-mortuum; Self-love, Materialism Baseness even to the disbelief in all possibility of Virtue, stalked more and more imperiously abroad; till the body-politic, long since deprived of its vital circulating fluids, had now become a putrid carcass, fell in pieces to be the prey of ravenous wolves[31].

Carlyle's view of the "era . . . of the Roman Emperors" is not elaborate and complex. There are some generalizations on splendor and squalor, personifications of "Self-Love", "Materialism", and "Baseness", reference to the decaying organism, and the implicit conclusion that immorality results in violent destruction. No consideration of all the factors that might be relevant occurs; no representative persons or episodes are there. The whole characterization can be reduced to a statement of simple moral cause and effect. Carlyle can hardly be blamed: his intent is to use the "era . . . of the Roman Emperors" for comparison—no more. But the point remains that the eighteenth century, for him, is unique in its intricacy, its fully developed cast of characters, its magnificence and doom.

Notes

[1] John Holloway, *The Victorian Sage* (London, 1962), pp. 21-50.

[2] Carlyle, *Sartor Resartus.* ed. Charles Frederick Harrold (New York, 1937), p. 216.

[3] Carlyle, *Essays* in Centenary Edition of *Works,* ed., H. D. Traill (London, 1898), I, 211, 212.

[4] Carlyle, *Sartor,* 161.

[5] *Essays,* II, 344.

[6] *Essays,* III, 85.

[7] Kenneth Burke, *The Philosophy of Literary Form* (New York, 1957), pp. 58, 66, 70.

[8] Carlyle, *Letters of Thomas Carlyle to John Stuart Mill, John Sterling, and Robert Browning,* ed., Alexander Carlyle (London, 1923), p. 70.

[9] Carlyle, *The French Rerolution, a History* (London, 1898), I, 13.

[10] *Ibid.,* 36, 37.

[11] *Ibid.,* 202.

[12] *Ibid.,* II, 3.

[13] *Ibid.,* 115.

[14] *Ibid.,* III, 205.

[15] *Essays,* I, 139.

[16] *The French Revolution,* I, 79. In 1864, when he observed the Revolution from the last pages of *Frederick,* Carlyle defined it as "the breaking out of universal mankind into Anarchy, into the faith and practice of No-Government,—that is to say (if you will be candid), into unappeasable Revolt against Sham Governors and Sham Teachers,—which I do charitably define to be a Search, most unconscious, yet in deadly earnest, for true Governors and Teachers . . . Nor is the progress of a French or European world, all silently ripening and rotting towards such an issue, a thing one wishes to dwell on. Only when Spontaneous Combustion breaks out; and many-colored, with loud noises, envelopes the whole world in anarchic flame for long hundreds of years: then has the Event come; there is the thing for all men to mark, and to study and scrutinize as the strangest thing they ever saw". (*Frederick* in Centenary Edition of *Works,* VII, 181.)

[17] Charles Dickens, *Bleak House* (London, 1933), p. 421.

[18] *The French Revolution,* III, 213.

[19] *Ibid.,* 214.

[20] *Ibid.,* 213.

[21] *Ibid.,* 318.

[22] *Ibid.,* I, 17.

[23] *Ibid.,* 5.

[24] *Ibid.,* 27.

[25] *Ibid.*

[26] *Ibid.,* 9.

[27] *Ibid.,* 12.

[28] Charles Frederick Harrold "Carlyle's General Method in *The French Revolution,*" *PMLA,* 43 (1928), 1150n.

[29] *The French Revolution,* I, 28-34.

[30] David Alex Wilson, *Carlyle to "The French Revolution"* (London, 1924), p. 379.

[31] *Essays,* I, 453.

Lee C. R. Baker (essay date 1986)

SOURCE: "The Open Secret of *Sartor Resartus*: Carlyle's Method of Converting His Reader," in *Studies in Philology*, Vol. LXXXIII, No. 2, Spring, 1986, pp. 218-35.

[*In the following essay, Baker attempts to identify the questionable function of the British Editor in* Sartor Resartus. *Baker argues that the Editor's apparent skepticism, which seems to undermine Carlyle's goal of converting readers to the "Clothes Philosophy," is actually irony needed to help the reader understand Carlyle's philosophy.*]

I

Carlyle's purpose in writing **Sartor Resartus** is to convert British readers to the Clothes Philosophy. He indicates his intention quite clearly when he writes to Jane that his "persuasion that Teuf*k* is in his place and his time here grows stronger the more I see of London and its philosophy: the Doctrine of the *Phoenix,* of *Nat. Supernaturalism* and the whole Clothes Philosophy (be it but well stated) is exactly what all intelligent men are wanting."[1] However, the means Carlyle uses to present this philosophy seem to subvert rather than achieve his goal. He does not choose a familiar, explicit and didactic method of persuasion. Rather, he creates as his spokesman an eccentric German Professor, a figure who doubtless puzzles many of his readers. To compound the confusion, he conveys Teufelsdröckh's philosophy through the mediation of a British Editor whose scepticism about the Professor's views never seems to allow him to commit himself fully to the Clothes Philosophy. Quite early the Editor complains that "It were a piece of vain flattery to pretend that this work on Clothes entirely contents us."[2]

The function of the Editor has consequently puzzled more than one commentator, for the interpreters of the Editor's function have consistently stumbled on the apparent contradiction between Carlyle's stated intention and the evidence of *Sartor* itself. The oldest and still widely accepted view of the Editor's role gives priority to Carlyle's intention by claiming that the Editor is converted to the Clothes Philosophy sometime during the course of *Sartor*.[3] Since the late 1950s, however, more and more critics have acknowledged the reductiveness of this interpretation since it disregards the reasons for and nature of the Editor's conflict with the Professor. According to this later theory, the disagreement between the Professor and the Editor is evidence of Carlyle's own divided consciousness, of his simultaneous enthusiasm and scepticism for the Clothes Philosophy.[4]

As tempting as the divided-consciousness theory is, some of the most influential and perceptive critics, heeding Carlyle's own explicitly stated intention, have begun once again to emphasize his endorsement of Teufelsdröckh's philosophy. But they nonetheless, like the divided-consciousness theorists, affirm that the Editor reflects some kind of hesitation in Carlyle.[5] As a consequence, these well-intentioned critics end in a more hopeless contradiction than the divided-consciousness camp since they inconsistently assert that the Editor is both for and against the Clothes Philosophy.

What then is the proper function of the Editor in *Sartor Resartus*? Is his role stable, or is he so ambiguously and variously drawn that we cannot determine how he is supposed to work? Can it be that *Sartor* does not adequately body forth Carlyle's intention to further the ideas of the Clothes Philosophy? Is *Sartor* a bungled text which does not show any artistic integrity?

The solution to this problem lies in an understanding of the nature of the romantic irony which permeates the whole of *Sartor Resartus*. Whenever there is an apparent contradiction between the Editor and the Professor, the Editor is being ironic; in fact, he openly indicates his irony. But this understanding necessarily involves the reader in another important, unresolved question. If the Editor agrees with the Clothes Philosophy, why is he not more obvious in his assent? Why must he resort to irony? This question suggests that Carlyle was attempting to express a meaning so subtle and fugitive that more direct means of explaining his message were inadequate. His depiction of the Editor cannot therefore be regarded as a rhetorical strategy in the usual sense, but as a maieutic one, that is, as one which acts as a mid-wife to help bring forth the reader's

own understanding of the Clothes Philosophy. To see through the ironies is to reveal the Open Secret of Carlyle's new rhetorical method or, what amounts to the same thing, to follow the intricacies of Carlyle's play with illusion. This procedure perfectly accords with Carlyle's larger intention, for his new method allows the reader to see the symbolic and divine significance of the world around him. But before we examine the appropriateness of Carlyle's method to his message, we should more specifically observe his statements which contrast his method to conventional forms of rhetoric.

II

Sartor's message is not revealed through the conventional methods of persuasive rhetoric which work according to Aristotelian tenets.[6] *Sartor* is not intended to persuade logically. "The grand difficulty . . . with us all," Carlyle writes J. S. Mill in 1833, "is to see somewhat, to believe somewhat; a quite mystic operation, to which Logic helps little" (*CL*, 6.413). Carlyle's antagonism to logic is well known and is related to his distaste for the excesses of the Enlightenment's focus upon reason. As the Professor says, "not our Logical, Mensurative faculty, but our Imaginative one is King over us" (*SR*, 222). John Holloway recognizes the inadequacy of typical rhetorical devices to describe what Carlyle is doing when he says that "we are not studying techniques of persuasion; not at least in one common sense of that phrase. . . . [T]he methods traced here [in *Sartor*] persuade because they . . . are organic to a view presented not by one thread of logical argument alone, but by the whole weave of a book."[7]

In the main, Holloway's emphasis is well taken, for *Sartor* manifests a new form of persuasion—a form required because traditional rhetoric is inappropriate and inadequate for Carlyle's purposes. During that humiliating Autumn in 1831 while in London looking for publishers for *Sartor*, Carlyle wrote: "What an advantage has the Pulpit, where you address men already arranged to hear you, and in a vehicle which long use has rendered easy: how infinitely harder when you have all to create, not the ideas only and the sentiments, but the symbols and the mood of mind!"[8] The situation in which Carlyle found himself is clarified by a passage from his essay **"The State of German Literature,"** written some four years earlier in 1827. Carlyle there distinguishes two types of explanation, one in which "whoever has a material and visible object to treat . . . may reason of it, and discuss it, with the clearness . . . of geometry itself."

> Another matter it is, however, when the object to be treated of belongs to the invisible and immaterial class; cannot be pictured out even by the writer himself, much less, in ordinary symbols, set before the reader. . . . He must devise new means in which this invisible idea arises, the false persuasions that eclipse it, the false shows that may be mistaken for it, the glimpses of it that appear elsewhere; in short, to guide his reader up to the perception of it; in all which,

moreover, the reader must faithfully and toilsomely co-operate with him, if any fruit is to come of their mutual endeavour.[9]

Carlyle clearly realizes that he must devise a new persuasive method if his readers are to learn how to perceive their surroundings in a new way. He would like to show others how they, like Teufelsdröckh, can see nature as the "Garment of God," how they can view the world as symbolic of the Divine. He wants his audience to recognize the Divine Idea of the World, which, as G. B. Tennyson observes, is synonymous with the Open Secret, a phrase which Carlyle took from Goethe and which he uses to explain the poet's special task.[10] "The true Poet is ever, as of old, the Seer; whose eye has been gifted to discern the godlike Mystery of God's Universe, and decipher some new lines of its celestial writing; . . . he sees into this greatest of secrets, 'the open secret'; hidden things become clear" (*Works,* 27.377). Carlyle's reader, then, must not learn to see different things, but to see things differently. And so Carlyle must create a situation by or through which the reader "sees the changes of many-coloured existence, . . . sees the loveliness and deep purport which lies hidden under the very meanest of them" (*Works,* 26.225).

But how does an author get a reader to see the Open Secret for himself? Not only is conventional rhetoric unfairly manipulative; it is also completely inadequate to express Carlyle's meaning. Typical rhetoric is logical and linear; Carlyle's message is complex and multi-dimensional. In addition, the kind of persuasion Carlyle wants does not force the reader, does not conquer or convince him. Instead, he wants the reader to be allowed to discover the Open Secret of the Clothes Philosophy for himself. To this purpose Carlyle creates the multi-form ironies which play with the illusion of the surface appearance of the world about him. He does not tell us exactly what we should see. Instead, his pervasive ironic play with the meaning of symbols "guides" the reader, as Carlyle says, to a stage of enlightenment whereby he begins to see the Open Secret of the Clothes Philosophy. Carlyle's method, then, is best termed maieutic rather than rhetorical, for he acts as a midwife to bring forth this realization which the reader himself achieves.[11] To involve oneself with the maieutic method is to perceive the Open Secret of Carlyle's new method of persuasion.

III

The first step in this process of maieutic enlightenment is to throw the reader into the disassociation embodied in the apparent chaos of *Sartor Resartus'* anatomy of miscellaneous, eccentric knowledge. This shattering of the reader's conventional view involves both the Professor's and the Editor's ironic play with the questionable nature of the world. Do men and in-stitutions really manifest what they were intended to or not? Are they truly symbolic of the Divine Idea of the World, or are they shams?

One such excursion into the dismantling of symbols involves the Professor's assertion that "Aprons are Defences" (*SR,* 43). The builder's "thick-tanned hide" and the blacksmith's "sheet-iron" coverings are literal examples of the apron. The nature of the object in question becomes problematic, however, when the Professor calls our attention to "the thin slip of notched silk (as it were, the emblem and beatified ghost of an Apron), which some highest-bred housewife . . . has gracefully fastened on" (*SR,* 44). In this instance, the literal object has lost its original meaning and instead manifests only the frivolous status of a woman who pretends to housewifery.

The Professor next turns his attention to the clergy: "But of all Aprons the most puzzling to me hitherto has been the Episcopal or Cassock. Wherein consists the usefulness of this Apron? The Overseer (Episcopus) of Souls, I notice, has tucked in the corner of it, as if his day's work were done: what does he shadow forth thereby?" (*SR,* 44). There are two ironies in this passage: one questions the utilitarian view of religion by asking about the clergy's usefulness; the other questions the actual practice of the clergy by asking what the present-day examples really symbolize. It is not that Carlyle finds religious men superfluous; rather, Carlyle doubts that the religious principle is being bodied-forth adequately. He suggests that the clergy are a sham since they neglect their true duties.

Examples of the kind of irony which renders the world into its original chaos are found throughout *Sartor* and are meant to move the reader himself to determine whether something is authentic or whether it is a sham. But this procedure has often been confused with hoax. Carlyle's indirection and irony has been mistaken for inappropriate mystification or deception, that is, for a kind of hoax foisted upon the reader.[12] According to this view, play with illusion strongly suggests mendacity wherein the Professor has a joke at the reader's expense. But the function of Teufelsdröckh's irony is quite the opposite.

Of course Carlyle does refer to the procedure in *Sartor* as a kind of hoax. But he is being ironic. And so, in order to understand how he intends this "hoax," it is necessary to distinguish between two different audiences for *Sartor.* As in any ironic strategy, there will be those who fail (hopefully for only a short time) to see the ironic play with symbols; but there are others who are not victims of the irony. No matter that they may have initially been confused by the Professor's capricious play; they finally see through the ironic mask and enjoy the clever performance of the illusionary tricks as the Professor pretends to puzzle over whether something is real or a sham. These readers will have seen the Divine Idea of the World—they will have seen the Open Secret of Carlyle's maieutic method.

The confusion into which **Sartor** throws its audience is testified to by the reactions of its contemporary readers. The shocked reaction of the subscribers to *Fraser's Magazine's* publication of **Sartor** is notorious for its vituperation. Even Leigh Hunt, after reading **Sartor** in *Fraser's,* confessed that he "was mystified enough when your **Sartor Resartus** first appeared, to take it for a satire on 'Germanick[?ism]'."[13] But perhaps the most revealing response to **Sartor** is John Stuart Mill's. Also writing soon after **Sartor** had appeared in *Fraser's,* Mill tells Carlyle that "It is true the prejudices of our Utilitarians are at least as strong against some of your writings as those of any other persons whatever, & though the individual signature would smooth many difficulties, even *that* would hardly, with them, have covered your 'Characteristics' or 'Teufelsdröckh'." As sympathetic a reader as Mill was, he finally could not overcome the eccentricities of **Sartor.** "About that Cagliostro and that Teufelsdreck," Mill elaborates, "it has frequently occurred to me of late to ask of myself and also of you, whether that mode of writing between sarcasm or irony and earnest, be really deserving of so much honour as you give to it by making use of it so frequently; . . . are there many things, worth saying, and capable of being said in that manner which cannot be as well or better said in a more direct way"[14]

In short, **Sartor** found a bewildered reception with the audience of its day; neither Tories, Utilitarians, nor Whigs really understood it. And this confusion was due to Carlyle's intentional disruption of the expectations of his British audience's naive realism. Judging by some of the criticism still being written on **Sartor,** present-day commentators are liable to the same confusions and difficulties which the best minds of Carlyle's day incurred. In this instance, at least, we should not feel too superior to past ages. And even so, those modern critics who have understood Carlyle's irony should nonetheless recognize that Carlyle set his strategy for those who had not yet seen the significance of the symbolism of the Clothes Philosophy.

Another procedure for confusing the audience is the Professor's indirection. He never openly tells us his own opinions. Instead he asks questions, just as Socrates would when trying to get his interlocutors to discover the truth of the matter along with him. "What does he shadow forth thereby?" asks Teufelsdröckh (**SR,** 44). The correct response may be implied by the slightly derogatory "shadow forth" instead of the more positive "body forth," but the answer is really left up to the reader; he must decide. These are maieutic questions designed to act as gad-flies in order to get the reader to speculate on his own, to act as a midwife for his own discovery of knowledge.[15]

Although Carlyle's maieutic method makes many demands on the reader, it is ultimately designed to help him. This paradoxical process is described by Stanley Fish, who sees that the relationship of a dialectician or, to be consistent, of a *maieutikos* to his audience is like that of a good physician to a patient for whom a strong and unpleasant medicine is prescribed.[16] The *maieutikos* as midwife signifies much of Teufelsdröckh's function as a good physician. To this purpose, the Professor's writings are likened to a kind of remedy for Hofrath Heuschrecke, "to whom no doughpill [the Professor] could knead and publish was other than medicinal and sacred" (**SR,** 26). And of course the well-known association of Teufelsdröckh with the aloetic drug, asafoetida, coincides with the maieutic nature of the Professor as he provides the medicine to cure "the pudding stomach of England."[17] It may seem peculiar to associate the dissimilar functions of birth and purgation, but they are both appropriately applied to the Professor's healing character since he rids his readers of their old, diseased beliefs and helps them create new and more curative ones.

There is, moreover, another significance to the name Teufelsdröckh which connects the Phoenix-process with maieutics. E. M. Vida claims that the name Teufelsdröckh was probably suggested by Jean Paul Richter's term "Teufelsferment," an agent which destroys the whole world.[18] This genesis seems reasonable since Carlyle associated fermenting not only with the creation and destruction of the Phoenix-cycle, but also with the Professor's function. The name of another of Carlyle's eccentric German commentators refers to this same process. Herr Sauerteig is a man who forever questions conventional meanings as he destroys old associations in order to create new ones. Similarly, from his tower-apartment the Professor looks down upon Weissnichtwo and wonders: "under that hideous coverlet of vapours, and putrefactions, and unimaginable gases, what a Fermenting-vat lies simmering and hid!" (**SR,** 22). The Professor leads a life which the Editor sees as "a mad Fermentation; wherefrom, the fiercer it is, the clearer product will one day evolve itself" (**SR,** 158). And even the Professor's first name, Diogenes, with its connotation of God-born or, as Carlyle translates the term (*SR,* 114), "newborn of Heaven," also implies one who passes through the Phoenix-cycle. The Professor hopes for a similar metamorphosis in society, for he has faith "that a new heaven-born young one will rise out of her ashes!" (**SR,** 237).

Acting as a Phoenix-fermenting agent upon the reader's mind, the Professor's ironic play with the meaning of symbols destroys old, utilitarian views by helping the reader create new ones which better symbolize or body-forth the Divine Idea of the World. The Professor's irony is then as related to hoax as the good physician is to the false medicine man. The latter wants us to believe his elixir is efficacious when what we really learn

SARTOR RESARTUS.

IN THREE BOOKS.

Thomas Carlyle

Mein Vermächtniß, wie herrlich weit und breit!
Die Zeit ist mein Vermächtniß, mein Acker ist die Zeit.

BOSTON:

JAMES MUNROE AND COMPANY.

M DCCC XXXVI.

firm arch, . . . only, as was said, some zigzag series of rafts floating tumultuously thereon. Alas, and the leaps from raft to raft, were too often of a breakneck character" (*SR,* 268). The reader must, in other words, make his own leaps of imagination from the fragmented, raft-like guidance which the Editor has provided him. That the Editor, as English and unfamiliar as he is with Teufelsdröckh's method, has nonetheless been able to master it, is a sign that other Englishmen can do likewise. The Editor's dissimulation is consequently as socratic as Teufelsdröckh's when he pretends that he knows nothing.

The Editor indicates his awareness of the Professor's play with the appearance of symbols when he makes the following commentary on Teufelsdröckh's method:

> may we not say that Teufelsdröckh's Biography, allowing it even, as suspected, only a hieroglyphical truth, exhibits a man, as it were preappointed for Clothes-Philosophy? To look through the Shows of things into Things themselves he is led and compelled; . . . only by victoriously penetrating into Things themselves can he find peace and a stronghold. But is not this same looking-through the Shows, or Vestures, into the Things, even the first preliminary to a Philosophy of Clothes? Do we not, in all this, discern some beckonings towards the true higher purport of such a Philosophy; and what shape it must assume with such a man, in such an era? (*SR,* 205-06)

Not only is the Editor aware of the Professor's method, but he makes it his own. His pretense of disagreeing with the Professor is designed to shock his naive audience into rethinking its views. Of course, those who are participants in the irony will enjoy the dry tone of the Editor's play with illusion: is the German Professor insane, or is there something to what he is trying to say? Thus the Editor refers to a purged and re-created audience when he confesses that, "if through this unpromising Horn-gate, Teufelsdröckh, and we by means of him, have led thee into the true Land of Dreams . . . then art thou profited beyond money's worth" (*SR,* 269-70). But on the way to re-making his audience, the Editor uses those same "tricksy turns" which he sees in the Professor (*SR,* 31). He may claim to be unsure of the Professor's meaning, but the fact that the Editor knows what terms to use to delimit the Professor's character shows that he is aware of Teufelsdröckh's true purport.

The Editor is a participant in the irony; his appearance of ignorance is just as openly deceptive as the Professor's, for, in keeping with the standard of open confession in Schlegel's *Lyceum* Fragment 108, the Editor tells us he is in on the dissimulation.[19] This simultaneous openness and concealment further defines the significance of Carlyle's Open Secret. For example, after the Professor has explored the meaning of clothes as a covering of the spirit of man, the Editor initially seems to criticize the good Diogenes: "Let no courteous reader take offence at the opinions broached in the conclusion of ["The World Out of Clothes"]. The Editor himself, on first glancing over

is that his medicine works superficially, if at all, or only for a short time and ultimately leaves us no better than we were. Often it leaves us much worse. The strong medicine of the *maieutikos,* or good physician, is in contrast painful at first, but eventually effects a cure. Although the Professor's method is often puzzling, often because of its lightness of tone, it has serious implications and is ultimately meant to help us.

But even though confusion and destruction are a necessary first step in Carlyle's maieutic strategy, we must go forward, as the Editor urges us, and make an order out of this apparent chaos. The metaphor of the Editor's task as a bridge for the reader thus signifies his role as guide through this confusion.

> For in this Arch . . . the materials are to be fished-up from the weltering deep, and down from the simmering air, here one mass, there another, and cunningly cemented, while the elements boil beneath: nor is there any supernatural force to do it with; but simply the Diligence and feeble thinking Faculty of an English Editor, endeavoring to evolve printed Creation out of a German printed and written Chaos. (*SR,* 80)

At the end of the book, the Editor admits that he has built "No that singular passage, was inclined to exclaim: What, have we got not only a Sansculottist, but an enemy to Clothes in the abstract?" The Editor playfully takes on the persona of a utilitarian British reader (perhaps referring to his own initial confusion) and apparently upbraids the Professor:

> Consider, thou foolish Teufelsdröckh, what benefits unspeakable all ages and sexes derive from Clothes.... Nay, ... hast thou always worn them perforce, and as a consequence of Man's Fall; never rejoiced in them as in a warm movable House, a Body round thy Body, wherein that strange Thee of thine sat snug, defying all variations of Climate? ... Or, cries the courteous reader, ... would he ... betake ourselves again to the 'matted cloak,' and go sheeted in a 'thick natural fell'? (*SR*, 57-59)

All the Editor's questions seem to indicate that he agrees with the conservative British audience, but he is having fun playing with the possible literal and utilitarian meanings of the Professor's caprice regarding the stripping of man's surface significance in order to get to his spiritual nature. Finally, he confesses:

> Nowise, courteous reader! The Professor knows full well what he is saying; and both thou and we, in our haste, do him wrong. The truth is, Teufelsdröckh, though a Sansculottist, is no Adamite; and much perhaps as he might wish to go forth before this degenerate age as 'a Sign,' would nowise wish to do it, as those old Adamites did, in a state of Nakedness. The utility of Clothes is altogether apparent to him: nay perhaps he has an insight into their more recondite, and almost mystic qualities, what we might call the omnipotent virtue of Clothes, such as was never before vouchsafed to any man. (*SR*, 59-60)

The candidness of the Editor's confession makes the Open Secret of Carlyle's method even more transparent.

Still yet another example of the Editor's participation in confusing the reader is shown in his sportful use of the Professor's discussion of George Fox. The Editor here plays with the Professor's capricious discussion of the founding of Quakerism, which is symbolized by Fox's manufacture of a "perennial suit" of leather. "For us," the Editor announces, "aware of his deep Sansculotism, there is more meant in this passage than meets the ear.... Does Teufelsdröckh anticipate that, in this age of refinement, any considerable class of the community ... will sheathe themselves in closefitting cases of Leather? The idea is ridiculous in the extreme" (*SR*, 212). The Editor has literalized the symbolic meaning of the Professor's example. He has temporarily made the Professor appear foolish by ironically misinterpreting Diogenes to mean that the reader should follow Fox's example by simply wearing the same clothing he wore. But the Editor eventually corrects the misunderstanding and elucidates the Professor's true meaning by taking the falsely literal significance of the symbol to its logical absurdity: "Would not the rich man purchase a water-proof suit of Russia

Leather; and the high-born Belle step-forth in red or azure morocco, lined with shamoy: the black cowhide being left to the Drudges and Gibeonites of the world; and so all the old Distinctions be re-established?" (*SR*, 213). Would, that is, the original religious intention of observing the ultimate equality of all before God be circumvented by the literal interpretation of Fox's meaning? But the Editor lets the reader into the Open Secret through still yet another question: "Or has the Professor his own deeper intention; and laughs in his sleeve at our strictures and glosses, which indeed are but a part thereof?" (*SR*, 213). The Editor openly admits that his method is part of the Professor's, and his confession helps the reader see that the Professor would laugh at those who so literally interpret his discussion of George Fox. The Editor's playfulness coincides with the Professor's "deeper intention" to get us to discover the true, symbolic meaning of Fox's creation of a new religion. The reader is not supposed to form a religion exactly the same as Fox's; he is to take Fox's example only insofar as he seeks to find an authentic connection with the Divine Idea of the World and to create a new symbolic manifestation of the religious impulse.

A summary of the Editor's function can best be given in the following analogy: if the Professor plays with the nature of the appearance of things, the Editor plays with the nature of the Professor's ironic appearance. Even though the maieutic procedure is meant to enlighten the reader, it is this layering of irony upon irony which is the barrier to a consistent interpretation of *Sartor Resartus.* If the reader is not careful to sort out the strands of the Editor's ironies from the Professor's, he will become dizzy and lose his way. But ultimately, the Editor, like the Professor, is interested in helping him gain a working knowledge of the Clothes Philosophy. Moreover, through the ironies of *Sartor,* Carlyle teaches his audience how to see, for he involves them in discriminating between real and sham symbols. Simply to tell the reader what is real or sham would be impossible, partly because the meaning is ineffable and partly because knowledge is only won by hard work and mistakes. It is more appropriate to test the reader's understanding of the Clothes Philosophy by subjecting him to the many complicated ironies in *Sartor.* By these means, Carlyle plays the role of midwife as he helps the reader discriminate true symbols from false ones on his own.

Another way of seeing why Carlyle's method is maieutic rather than conventionally rhetorical is to note that he does not tell us *what* to see, as the rhetorician would; he shows us *how* to see. He offers no particular solutions, but allows us to see what needs to be done. As the Editor recognizes,

> Yes, long ago has many a British Reader been, as now, demanding with something like a snarl: Whereto does all this lead; or what use is in it? In the way of replenishing thy purse, or otherwise aiding thy digestive

faculty, O British Reader, it leads to nothing, and there is no use in it; but rather the reverse, for it costs thee somewhat. (*SR,* 269)

Rather than lead us to utilitarian goals, the maieutic method gives the readers an experience of a process or state of mind. "We are to guide our British Friends into the new Gold-country, and show them the mines," the Editor says; "nowise to dig-out and exhaust its wealth, which indeed remains for all time inexhaustible. Once there, let each dig for his own behoof, and enrich himself" (*SR,* 208). The Editor, like the Professor, is not interested in immediate practical results, but in a vision which will lead eventually to results which are beyond conventional practicality, but which are equally efficacious nonetheless.

IV

Carlyle's method is related to romantic irony, for his aggressive questioning of the meaning of symbols closely resembles Schlegel's views about system-making. It is true that Carlyle's irony is not as capricious as Schlegel's, but it is equally as radical for it works on the same assumptions. In *Athenaeum* Fragment 53, for example, Schlegel paradoxically asserts that "It is equally deadly for the spirit to have and not to have a system." This key romantic statement establishes an abyss between the bewilderingly complex chaos of the universe and man's attempts to give an adequate expression to that chaos. Romantic irony posits as a referent an ideal towards which the romantic is always infinitely striving, but which he realizes he can never reach nor sufficiently embody. Thus, it is wrong to have a system because it can never do justice to the infinite variety of the universe and of experience. But it is equally wrong not to have some kind of theoretical construct since it is important to try to make sense of the universe and of man's relation to it. Even though there is, in other words, an unbridgeable gap between expression as system-making and that towards which the system points, there should nonetheless be an attempt to account for the chaos of the universe. This incommensurability is precisely what Carlyle refers to when he has the Editor talk about the incomplete, raft-like character of his bridge between the Professor and the British audience. And since the romantic ironist understands that there can be no easy expression of the ineffable, he, unlike Mill with his demand for a more direct expression of meaning, will recognize that there is no one-to-one concurrence between referent and referee. This conception is essential to understanding why Carlyle has the Professor and the Editor constantly worry about the meaning of symbols.

It would be difficult enough to describe the Professor's experience if it were amenable to empirical explanation. But since the Professor's view of his relationship to the world about him is complicated by its symbolic mediation, it is even more impossible to describe that experience. Besides, immediate experience can never be given in a poetic statement. No matter how evocative or full the poetic attempt at recreating immediate experience, the text will always stand between the reader and the author as experiencer; this is the mediation of poetry. The very mediational function of the Editor symbolizes Carlyle's awareness of the ineffability of the Professor's Clothes Philosophy. The poetic statement, in other words, is not the poet's experience. The middle, biographical chapters in *Sartor* give only a shadow of Teufelsdröckh's life. And *Sartor Resartus* is not the Professor's *Die Kleider,* even though that is one of its essential referents. The text can never be anything more than a means to elicit another experience for the reader. As a consequence, those who seek only ideas from Carlyle's novel will forever miss the experience of *Sartor.*

In addition, the Professor wants the reader to see more precisely what a phenomenon truly symbolizes. This intention is shown by the clever persiflage about what sorts of aprons housewives and members of the clergy wear, as well as the humor about the kind of leather in which the sophisticated woman of fashion will dress herself. In a corrupt age, the surface meaning of a phenomenon will be taken as the true one. But the Professor wants us to question this naive assumption. It is essential to Carlyle's radical vision to create an environment in which a person compares and contrasts the surface meaning of an actual phenomenon with its ideal. This romantic vision ironically sees the inadequacy of finite existence as an expression of God's infinity. It does not deny the validity of the ideal, but laughs at the ridiculousness of the actual formulations to embody that ideal. Thus the irony of *Sartor Resartus* is evident in the perspective of both the Professor and the Editor. The Professor questions whether symbols body forth the infinite ideal and the Editor pokes good-natured fun at the Professor's eccentric and often ridiculous attempts to explain his religious view in terms of the clothes metaphor. It is not that the Editor fails to value the Professor's vision or his procedure. Instead he recognizes the Professor's own inability to manifest the ideal in the actual, that is, to give an adequate expression to his symbolic vision. The Editor's quibbles are not a rejection of the Professor's message. His doubts are, on the contrary, completely in accord with those of the Professor, for they recognize that even the Professor's tentative explanations are inadequate and must be displaced by future systems, themselves to be similarly displaced by better and better approximations of the divine ideal in the actual world. In this regard, the Editor's own disclaimers show his humble recognition of his inadequacy to explain the Professor's true meaning and purport as well.

Of course, the most sophisticated way by which *Sartor* demonstrates the disjunctures between system and referent involves the reader in an experience of romantic irony which can be mistaken for an imitative fallacy. Put as simply as possible, Carlyle attempts to give the reader an experience of his vision by imitating its essential procedures. This process is not the usual kind of imitative fallacy whereby one demonstrates confusion by being confused or by writing a confusing text. Imitative fallacy in this sense is a kind of pun. In Carlyle's method, the emphasis is on recreating a simulacrum of the original experience of seeing the world as incomplete symbol. In addition, the relationship which a pun hints at can be stated in direct terms. This is probably why puns cause groans; their solution is too simple. But in the case of the procedure in *Sartor,* there is no possibility of a direct statement. This essential experience is best described by Friedrich Schlegel's *Lyceum* Fragment 108, which says that romantic irony "arouses the feeling of the indissoluble antagonism between the unlimited and the conditioned, between the impossibility and necessity of complete communication." Carlyle thus immerses the reader in an ironic environment in which symbols are destroyed and recreated; they are scrutinized for their concurrence with an unlimited ideal and, if found wanting, are identified as shams which must be replaced by closer approximations to the ideal, by the new vision of what is adequate to the ideal.

Insofar as *Sartor* destroys and recreates the reader's experience of its own textual world in much the same manner as Teufelsdröckh destroys and recreates symbols, then it strives to make him a romantic ironist. In other words, if a work of art attempts to call the reader's attention to the distance between the unlimited as represented and the symbol as limited representer by ironically displaying the contrast between the infinite and the concrete actual, then it acts as a midwife for the birth of the romantically ironic vision. The reader must always keep the ideal in mind while he considers whether or not the author is ironizing the actual. He must, as Virginia Woolf says, have a vast memory, for he will be expected to enter a hermeneutic circle in which he will constantly be testing the individual details of the work against the whole, as well as the limited symbols against the infinite ideal. When he has succeeded in making these contrasts without completely denying the validity of the actual manifestations, he will have established the proper perspective. He will have become a romantic ironist.

Some would say that the maieutic process deals with the reader in an unfair fashion. In fact, the reason why so many have thought of *Sartor* as a kind of hoax which makes fun of the reader is probably owing to the difficulty of detecting the stable source of its ironies. If the reader shares in the irony, he will have succeeded in discovering a new vision and will enjoy Carlyle's play with the illusion of symbols and *Sartor*'s main characters. But if he fails to see this sport, he will then become a victim of the irony, and, like the bungler described in Schlegel's *Lyceum* Fragment 108, may take offense when he senses he has missed the Open Secret of Carlyle's maieutic method. As Schlegel explains, the socratic function of romantic irony "is meant to deceive no one except those

who consider it a deception. . . . In this sort of irony, everything should be playful and serious, guilelessly open and deeply hidden." Even if we grant that Carlyle is having a little fun at the reader's expense, he does so for properly ulterior reasons. There is nothing like the realization that one might be a fool to jar him into a state of revaluation. But when the reader begins to see the difference between the symbol and the ideal, when he perceives that both the Professor and the Editor are gadflies urging him to attain this perception, then the reader has a vision of Carlyle's deceptively candid method. Just as the Open Secret of the world is plainly visible to the Editor before he understands the Clothes Philosophy, so too is the message of *Sartor* clearly before the reader if he will only see it. This romantically ironic vision is the experience which Carlyle wants to recreate for his reader.

Notes

[1] *The Collected Letters of Thomas and Jane Welsh Carlyle,* Duke-Edinburgh Edition, ed. C. R. Sanders, Kenneth J. Fielding, et al. (Durham, 1970-), V, 354; see also VI, 396. Hereafter cited as *CL.*

[2] *Sartor Resartus,* ed. C. F. Harrold (New York, 1937), p. 28; see also p. 292. Hereafter cited as *SR.*

[3] Cf. Paul Hensel, *Thomas Carlyle* (Stuttgart, 1922), pp. 84-85; Theodor Geissendoerfer, "Carlyle and Jean Paul Friedrich Richter," *JEGP,* 25 (1926), 545; Albert J. LaValley, *Carlyle and the Idea of the Modern* (New Haven, 1968), p. 34; Janet Ray Edwards, "Carlyle and the Fictions of Belief: *Sartor Resartus* to *Past and Present,*" *Carlyle and His Contemporaries: Essays in Honor of Charles Richard Sanders,* ed. John Clubbe (Durham, 1976), p. 107; and Gerald L. Bruns, "The Formal Nature of Victorian Thinking," *PMLA,* 90 (1975), 907.

[4] Cf. Morton L. Gurewitch, "European Romantic Irony," Diss. Columbia University 1957, p. 226; John Lindberg, "The Artistic Unity of *Sartor Resartus,*" *Victorian Newsletter,* No. 17 (1960), 21-2; Leonard W. Deen, "Irrational Form in *Sartor Resartus,*" *Texas Studies in Language and Literature,* 5 (1963), 438, 444-6; Masao Miyoshi, *The Divided Self* (New York, 1969), pp. 143-5; Philip Rosenberg, *The Seventh Hero* (Cambridge, 1974), pp. 45-6. Most recently some critics have identified Carlyle's alleged divided consciousness with romantic irony. Cf. Gurewitch, passim, but esp. p. 226; Janice L. Haney, "'Shadow-Hunting': Romantic Irony, *Sartor Resartus,* and Victorian Romanticism," *Studies in Romanticism,* 17 (1978), 319-20, 325-6, 328-9; and Anne K. Mellor, *English Romantic Irony* (Cambridge, 1980), pp. 113, 120-1.

[5] Cf. George Levine, *The Boundaries of Fiction* (Princeton, 1968), pp. 55-7, 30, 64-5, and G. B. Tennyson, *Sartor Called Resartus* (Princeton, 1965), pp. 180, 178, 183; 175. See also M. H. Abrams, *Natural Supernaturalism*

(New York: Norton, 1971), p. 130. Elsewhere, p. 133, Abrams suggests that the Editor and the Professor are the same person. Mellor's argument has some of the same problems as Levine's and Tennyson's since she believes that the Editor voices Teufelsdrökh's philosophy, and yet cannot explain why the Editor criticizes the Professor.

[6] The best examples of the rhetorical method are Gerry H. Brookes' *The Rhetorical Form of Carlyle's 'Sartor Resartus'* (Berkeley, 1972), pp. 28-9, 74-5, 124, and Jerry A. Dibble's *The Pythia's Drunken Song* (The Hague, 1978), pp. 5, 36, and 51-3.

[7] John Holloway, *The Victorian Sage* (New York, 1965), p. 11.

[8] *Two Note Books of Thomas Carlyle,* ed. Charles Eliot Norton (1889; rpt. Mamaroneck, New York, 1972), p. 215.

[9] *The Works of Thomas Carlyle,* Edinburgh Edition, ed. H. D. Traill (New York: Scribner's, 1903-04), XXVI, 71-2. Hereafter cited as *Works.*

[10] Tennyson, pp. 90-1.

[11] This procedure is surely what Holloway means when he talks of the way Carlyle's nodal propositions work on the reader; see pp. 51; 9-10.

[12] See Carlisle Moore, "Thomas Carlyle and Fiction: 1822-1834," *Nineteenth Century Studies,* ed. H. J. Davies et al. (Ithaca, 1940), pp. 149-152; and Levine, pp. 60, 64.

[13] Quoted from Charles Richard Sanders, "The Correspondence and Friendship of Thomas Carlyle and Leigh Hunt: The Early Years," *Bulletin of the John Rylands Library* (Manchester), vol. 45, No. 2 (March 1963), 464.

[14] *The Earlier Letters of John Stuart Mill: 1812-1848,* ed. Francis E. Mineka (Toronto, 1963), I, 202, 176.

[15] As G. B. Tennyson, p. 256, has observed, the whole of *Sartor* is filled with questions: "Teufelsdröckh seems always to be either exclaiming or questioning."

[16] Stanley E. Fish, *Self-Consuming Artifacts* (Berkeley, 1972), pp. 2-3.

[17] Tennyson, pp. 220-2.

[18] E. M. Vida, "The Influence of German Romanticism on Thomas Carlyle: A Reinterpretation of His Early Works," Diss. Univ. of Toronto 1969, p. 64. The term comes from one of the stories which Carlyle translated: "Schmelzle's Journey to Flaetz," *Works,* 22.189-91.

[19] *Lucinde and the Fragments,* trans. Peter Firchow (Minneapolis, 1971), pp. 156-7. Hereafter cited by fragment number.

Roderick Watson (essay date 1988)

SOURCE: "Carlyle: The World as Text and the Text as Voice," in *The History of Scottish Literature*, Volume 3, edited by Douglas Gifford, Aberdeen University Press, 1988, pp. 153-68.

[*In the following essay, Watson examines the events in Carlyle's life which led him to the philosophy presented in* Sartor Resartus. *Watson then studies that philosophy as Carlyle reveals it through the course of* Sartor, *noting that Carlyle's vision is a religious one, without the concept of a personal God, a vision in which it becomes essential to recognize the power of symbols and to be able to see through them.*]

Carlyle occupies a unique place in British cultural history. As a social historian, he was possessed by a vision of human fate which was essentially poetic. As a nineteenth-century intellectual, his impatient and iconoclastic mind created nothing less than an early version of modern semiotic study which claimed a role of crucial intellectual and social importance for what had hitherto been the rather less urgent avocation of essayist or 'man of letters'. As a 'Victorian sage', Carlyle speaks with Dostoevsky, Turner, Whitman, Nietzsche and Yeats as among the first of the Modernists, and indeed, many of the strengths—and the failings—of his vision were to become those of modernism itself. No doubt it was this potential that Walt Whitman glimpsed when his obituary for the old and 'altogether Gothic' Scotsman maintained that 'as a representative author, a literary figure, no man else will bequeath to the future more significant hints of our stormy era, its fierce paradoxes, its din and its struggling parturition periods . . .'[1]

It was **Sartor Resartus** which brought Carlyle to the stage of such potential and to his mature fame. Undoubtedly **The French Revolution** confirmed his public stature as spokesperson for the universe as a place of unseen forces—driven by ideas, and not by steam—a place newly revealed as the ever-changing locus of threat and excitement and dynamic change; but the special force of Carlyle's peculiar genius belongs to the earlier book. It is a difficult text to define, unique in its day for conflating philosophy, social satire, poetic insight and deeper truth-telling, all through the odd convention of a tongue-in-cheek fictionalised critical biography. Such an approach may be more familiar to post-modernist readers—in the spirit of Borges or Umberto Eco, perhaps—but even today it seems a rare and taxing book.

The title itself speaks for a certain wayward opacity: **Sartor Resartus,** (the tailor re-tailored, or, more properly, the old-clothes mender patched-up again) purports to be a nameless editor's summary, with the help of a German colleague, of the life and theories of Herr Dr Diogenes Teufelsdröckh (devil's dung), Professor of 'Things-in-General' at the University of Weissnichtwo.

Teufelsdröckh's philosophy proposes that all human structures are merely 'clothes', or vestments of our animating minds, and like clothes, our ideas and symbols and institutions go out of fashion, or lose their usefulness, and must be remade. We need to 'see through' such conventions until they become 'transparent'. The main burden of Carlyle's argument is often taken to be an insistence—derived from German Idealism—that everything is fundamentally the product of mind or spirit; but in fact the intellectual wit and the social focus of his argument throws as much or more light on the nature of our dependence on 'clothes'. Our social and political conventions and symbols have no intrinsic value at all, he argues, for everything is extrinsic, acquired or constructed ('tailored') by us. In the early nineteenth century, in the pride of materialism, utilitarianism, imperial confidence and the 'railway age', such views were potentially upsetting, to say the least.

At least one early reviewer was sufficiently caught-up by the narrative's intellectual conviction and its various 'editorial' devices to spend some effort in doubting the literal existence of its scholarly hero. In fact such combinations of literary mystification and—apparent—facticity (Teufelsdrockh's autobiographical writings turn out to be six large paper bags filled with random jottings, philosophical memos and laundry lists), were a not uncommon device among Romantic writers at the time. (Carlyle admired Laurence Sterne's *Tristram Shandy,* while Henry Mackenzie's *The Man of Feeling* purported to be scattered fragments reclaimed by a rather reluctant editor. The German author E T A Hoffmann played similarly teasing games in the presentation of his tales of mystery and the supernatural,[2] while James Hogg set his *Confessions of a Justified Sinner,* 1824, within a similar framework of editorial comment and parallel 'documentary' narratives, just as R L Stevenson was to do for *Jekyll and Hyde* over sixty years later.) What *is* striking about Carlyle's book is that such a mock-ponderous fictive device should have been chosen as the vehicle for a passionately serious critical thesis, not to mention a thinly-veiled account of the author's own deepest and most painful moments of spiritual crisis. *Sartor Resartus* encompasses and prefigures so much of Carlyle's unique intellectual force that it makes the most appropriate focus for this chapter on one of the most original and controversial minds of the nineteenth century.

Widely famous in his own lifetime, Carlyle's popular reputation has wavered ever since between over-reverent accounts of him as 'the Sage of Chelsea' and denunciations of his work as wilfully iconoclastic or cryptofascist. It is not our purpose to follow every trial and detail of this stormy career, and a brief summary will have to suffice. He had great difficulty, for example, in placing *Sartor,* which was completed in 1831, but *Fraser's Magazine* in London eventually published it in three parts, between 1833 and 1834. An American edition prefaced by Emerson (who had visited the Carlyles in Scotland)

was published two years later, but the first British edition did not appear until 1838, a year after the success of *The French Revolution* on both sides of the Atlantic had made its author well known at last, and financially secure for the first time, at the age of 42. *The French Revolution* was written in Chelsea—then an unfashionable part of London—where Carlyle and his wife had moved in 1834. Public lectures were undertaken on a variety of subjects, and the publication of 'Chartism' (1839), *On Heroes and Hero-Worship* (1841), and *Past and Present* (1843) soon followed. Carlyle became internationally known, and his many new friends and contacts included Emerson, J S Mill, Lockhart, Dickens, Tennyson, Arthur Clough, Thomas Arnold and Sir Robert Peel.

J A Froude (Carlyle's contemporary and first biographer) summarised his friend's reputation at this time, and also something of his notoriety:

> *Past and Present* completes the cycle of writings which were in his first style, and by which he most influenced the thought of his time. He was a Bedouin, as he said of himself, a rough child of the desert. His hand had been against every man, and every man's hand against him. He had offended men of all political parties, and every professor of a recognised form of religion. He had offended Tories by his Radicalism, and Radicals by his scorn of their formulas. He had offended High Churchmen by his Protestantism, and Low Churchmen by his evident unorthodoxy. No sect or following could claim him as belonging to them; if they did some rough utterance would soon undeceive them. Yet all acknowledged that here was a man of extraordinary intellectual gifts and of inflexible veracity. If his style was anomalous, it was brilliant. No such humourist had been known in England since Swift . . .'[3]

The analogy with Swift is a fitting one, for in *Sartor Resartus* Carlyle had described the absurdities of war with his most savage ridicule:

> Straightway the world 'Fire!' is given: and they blow the souls out of one another; and in place of sixty brisk useful craftsmen, the world has sixty dead carcasses, which it must bury, and anew shed tears for. Had these men any quarrel? . . . not the smallest! . . . How then? Simpleton! Their Governors had fallen-out; and, instead of shooting one another, had the cunning to make these poor blockheads shoot. (*Sartor Resartus,* 'Centre of Indifference')

In 'Chartism' and *Past and Present* he had used an even darker Swiftean irony to expose contemporary complacencies about the freedom of the individual in a society where the labouring classes are condemned to work or not to work (to eat or not to eat) according to capitalist laws of 'free' supply and demand. By the 1850s, however, Carlyle's Calvinist penchant for excoriating the worldly failings of his time had slipped into a harsher and narrower preaching of the most misanthropic sort. Thus the would-be ironical tone of many of the *Latter-Day Pamphlets* (1850) is in fact wildly unstable, as is his notoriously racist defence of slavery as both a philosophical and an economic concept in **'Occasional Discourse on the Nigger Question'** from the previous year.

It is as if Carlyle could no longer cope with his earlier and essentially Romantic vision of the universe as a place in constant flux, redefining its truths with every generation, and all under the final existential absurdity implied by the surrounding infinitudes of space, time and extinction. Constant striving, individual freedom of the most radically scathing sort and the passionate conviction of 'heroic' lives, had seemed to be the most valid response to such a condition, and indeed his own stoutly puritan roots had early led him to admire the unrelenting drive behind such figures as Mahomet, Luther, Knox and Cromwell—unlikely heroes for sophisticated London. In later years, however, the arc described by such exceptional careers led Carlyle to conclusions about the rule of the fittest and the exercise of individual authority for its own sake, while the initial intensities of his visionary assurance slipped into a strained and raucous intolerance instead.

The Calvinistic elements in such a progression are not far to seek, and it will be necessary to return to Carlyle's early years in order to show how much both the genius and the failings of the vision behind *Sartor Resartus* can be derived from his particular Scottish roots.

Carlyle was brought up in Ecclefechan as a member of the 'New Licht' Burghers a long standing sub-branch of the Seceders who had parted from the established Church of Scotland on the grounds that it was too little committed to the finely legalistic details of the old Covenant against patronage and state interference in matters religious. His father, James Carlyle, was a taciturn, irascible man, little read but given to absolute faith in the Bible and the virtues of manual labour at his trade as a stonemascn, and later as a small farmer. Carlyle admired him greatly, and honoured his memory in the papers which were collected posthumously as his *Reminiscences.* But he confessed, too, that he 'was ever more or less awed or chilled before him', and that 'my heart and tongue played freely only with my mother.'[4] Like so many of their following, the family had hopes that Thomas would enter the Church, and indeed this was considered to be the ultimate aim when he left home in his fourteenth year (not unusual at the time) to study at Edinburgh University.

The son of a peasant, hard-up, shy and socially awkward, the young Carlyle was never to meet or mix in the literary circles of Burns and Scott. Despising all affectation, he was noted among fellow students for his impatient, impassioned seriousness and they learned to be wary of his caustic tongue. His best subject was mathematics, a field properly fitted for the total certainties which he seemed to crave. Having finished his course in the Arts,

Carlyle had to support himself for the further years required of a student in Divinity. He took various teaching posts in mathematics, though he came to hate teaching, and busied himself, like his *alter ego* Teufelsdröckh, with intensive reading in a wide range of subjects.

Carlyle continued his studies in law, but by now a career in the Church did not appeal. He was entering 'the three most miserable years of my life'. Solitary, depressed, a martyr to dyspepsia and his own hypochondriac fears, he was suffering a crisis of faith in the religion of his childhood, and a crisis of self-confidence about his own vocation. Having early confessed to 'the wish of being known', he had yet to find a professional calling which seemed worthy of such an intensely cerebral nature. By the early 1820s, Carlyle seems to have come to something like the existential crux he later described in *Sartor Resartus:*

> . . . the net-result of my Workings amounted as yet to—Nothing. How then could I believe in my Strength, when there was as yet no mirror to see it in? . . . Invisible yet impenetrable walls, as of Enchantment, divided me from all living . . . To me the Universe was all void of Life, of Purpose, of Volition, even of Hostility: it was one huge, dead, immeasurable Steam-engine, rolling on, in its dead indifference, to grind me limb from limb. (*Sartor,* 'The Everlasting No')

For eighteenth-century thinkers the universe as a well-made clock had seemed a cheerful argument for the existence of some divine Maker. On the other side of the industrial revolution, however, the metaphor has become a steam engine, and for Carlyle, like Dickens later,[5] that meant a 'Mill of Death'—powerful, mindless, insensate and automatic. The solution was to redefine the primacy of spirit and the power of mind, and that meant for him (as it was for Teufelsdröckh) a new conception of what his vocation was to be.

Carlyle described *Sartor* as 'symbolical *myth*', but he did attest to the personal authenticity, at least in essence, of the crisis he gave to Teufelsdrockh. This response was somewhere between a religious conversion to 'the light', and an existential leap of faith. Faced with universal nullity, he asserted a fundamental sense of individual freedom:

The Everlasting No had said: 'Behold, thou are fatherless, outcast, and the Universe is mine (the Devil's)'; to which my whole Me now made answer: '*I* am not thine, but Free, and forever hate thee!'

Where before the world had seemed to be the grimmest of places, alien to the very possibility of any Ideal, now it could be a realm of endless potential, for eyes that could see it thus:

> . . . here in this poor, miserable, hampered, despicable

Actual, wherein even now thou standest, here or nowhere is thy Ideal . . . Fool! the Ideal is in thyself, the impediment too is in thyself . . . O thou that pinest in the imprisonment of the Actual, and criest bitterly to the gods for a kingdom wherein to rule and create, know this of a truth: the thing thou seekest is already with thee, 'here or nowhere,' couldst thou only see! (*Sartor,* 'The Everlasting Yea')

What Carlyle saw was his vocation—a vocation which would allow his critical eye to decode the world itself, to read the text of the Actual now that he had turned from both the Bible and his books of law.

There are other factors in this renewal of confidence, of course, as there always are. He had begun courting Jane Welsh Carlyle, who was to become his devoted and life-long companion after their marriage in 1826; his finances were improving; and his studies in German had led to translations of Goethe and Schiller, and various critical articles and the beginnings of a reputation in literary circles.[6] Even so, Carlyle was still his father's son, and a modest literary fame was not quite enough for one brought up to believe 'that man was created to work, not to speculate, or feel, or dream'.[7] There had to be a further calling, more worthy perhaps of James Carlyle's Spartan ideal of meaningful labour and his horror of redundant words.

That labour took Carlyle out of Edinburgh to Craigenputtoch, an isolated farm-house from his wife's inheritance, where the couple managed a frugal life together for the six years before their move to London. Here Carlyle assembled his library and, surrounded by the bleakest of moors, did more than any individual in his day to introduce German literature to British readers. Key essays for his intellectual development also stem from this period, most especially **'Signs of the Times'** (1829) and **'On History'** (1830). Here too, wrestling with his health and his peace of mind, he set about the writing of *Sartor Resartus,* determined to 'speak out what is in me . . . I have no other trade, no other strength, or portion in this Earth.'[8]

In the 'symbolic myth' of *Sartor,* Teufelsdröckh's commitment to the Actual provides us with the model for his creator's discovery, or rather for his *invention* of his own vocation. Carlyle may have lost faith in the form of his father's Christianity, but, against the nullity of that 'Everlasting No', he had never doubted the *need* for faith nor the crucial importance to himself of a more than merely materialistic vision of the world. No Scottish Presbyterian divine would have quarrelled with the German professor's strictures on the need for work—existentially derived, perhaps—but also taken directly from Ecclesiastes:

Up! Up! Whatsoever thy hand findeth to do, do it with thy whole might. Work while it is called Today; for the Night cometh, wherein no man can work. (*Sartor,* 'The Everlasting Yea')

Whatsoever thy hand findeth to do, do it with thy

might; for there is work, nor device, nor knowledge, nor wisdom, in the grave, whither thou goest. (Ecclesiastes 9:10)

Carlyle's philosophy has been called 'Calvinism without theology', and his friend and early admirer John Sterling was one of the first to note that although Teufelsdröckh retained an essentially religious vision of the universe, he lacked any conception of a personal God.[9] Even so, an Old Testament spirit abounds in *Sartor,* and this is more than just a matter of Carlyle's habitual use of Biblical allusions, or his rough but vividly oral style of writing, as if he truly were speaking from some pulpit. In fact the echoes from Ecclesiastes are revealing, for as a favoured text in the Scottish canon it is much given to reflections on the vanity of human affairs, with little to say about a personal God. Equally telling is its awareness of the endless cycle of life and the ever-present certainty of death, which is a vision very close to Carlyle's own, as is its account of a crisis of faith such as Teufelsdrockh had to undergo:

Then I looked on all the works that my hands had wrought, and on the labour that I had laboured to do: and behold, all was vanity and vexation of spirit, and there was no profit under the sun. (Ecclesiastes 2:11)

The parallels can be taken much further, for the very spirit of **'Chartism'** is to be found in lines such as:

The sleep of a labouring man is sweet, whether he eat little or much: but the abundance of the rich will not suffer him to sleep. There is a sore evil which I have seen under the sun, namely, riches kept for the owners thereof to their hurt. (Ecclesiastes 5: 12 and 13)

Teufelsdröckh knows that man is a prey to death when he reminds us that 'TIME, devours all his Children: only by incessant Running, by incessant Working, may you (for some threescore-and-ten years) escape him; and you too he devours at last' (*Sartor,* 'Getting Under Way'); and the Preacher, too, has much the same to say on the same theme:

I returned, and saw under the sun, that the race is not to the swift, nor the battle to the strong, neither yet bread to the wise, nor yet riches to men of understanding, nor yet favour to men of skill; but time and chance happeneth to them all. (Ecclesiastes 9: 11)

Faced with such certainty, what can we hope for? The universe is a 'Sphinx-riddle' for Teufelsdröckh, and although Ecclesiastes believes that wisdom is good, he has to admit that we will never know the work of God under the sun 'because though a man labour to seek it out, yet he shall not find it.' (8: 17). Yet neither accept despair, and if their predicament cannot be escaped, at least it can be greatly eased by a clear-sighted recognition of it.

Hence both the German professor and the Old Testament preacher accept 'light' as their salvation in the end, even if so few get the chance to see it, and its only achievement is to assure them of the ever-present darkness:

> Truly the light is sweet, and a pleasant thing it is for the eyes to behold the sun: But if a man live many years, and rejoice in them all; yet let him remember the days of darkness; for they shall be many. All that cometh is vanity. (Ecclesiastes 11: 7 and 8)

> . . . the thing thou seekest is already with thee, 'here or nowhere,' couldst thou only see! But it is with man's soul as it was with Nature: the beginning of Creation is—Light. Till the eye have vision, the whole members are in bonds. (*Sartor*, 'The Everlasting Yea')

> It is not because of his toils that I lament for the poor: we must all toil, or steal (howsoever we name our stealing) . . . But what I do mourn over is, that the lamp of his soul should go out; that no ray of heavenly, or even of earthly knowledge, should visit him . . . That there should one Man die ignorant who had capacity for Knowledge, this I call a tragedy . . . (*Sartor*, 'Helotage')

> Then said I, Wisdom is better than strength: nevertheless the poor man's wisdom is despised, and his words are not heard. (Ecclesiastes 9: 16)

Ecclesiastes' 'light' revealed the vanity of the world and the coming judgement of God; what it showed to Teufelsdröckh was a much more complex and sophisticated thing, fully illustrative of the originality and the striking modernity of Carlyle's thinking.

In **'Signs of the Times',** the very first of his social essays, Carlyle had set out to chastise the Victorian world for its complacent materialism and the mechanistic implications of its love affairs with Utilitarianism. He believed that 'the great truth' is 'that our happiness depends on the mind which is within us, and not on the circumstances which are without us.' As opposed to this, he felt that thinkers such as Adam Smith and Jeremy Bentham were set on redefining human nature along the materialistic (and hence mechanically applicable) principles of enlightened self-interest. Thirty-five years later, Dostoevsky was to make an identical attack on the 'mathematical certainties' and 'the laws of nature' to which all such systems pretended, noting that

> . . . a man, whoever he is, always and everywhere likes to act as he chooses, and not at all according to the dictates of reason and self-interest . . . where did all the sages get the idea that a man's desires must be normal and virtuous? Why did they imagine that he must inevitably will what is reasonable and profitable? What a man needs is simply and solely *independent* volition, whatever that independence may cost and wherever it may lead.[10]

Notes from Underground championed the freedom of the spirit against all would-be rational social controls and the limitations of easy definition, and, as with Carlyle, Dostoevsky's creed leads to an essentially modernist account of the universe as a place of restless and dynamic change. (In this respect Carlyle's vision also prefigured much in the work of Hugh MacDiarmid.)

The Russian argued from the psychological standpoint of a perverse but convincing individual, but Carlyle's essay takes a more abstract line based on a subtle understanding of the importance of language. Thus in opposition to the new fashion for speaking of society as a 'machine', the Scot sets up the deliberately insubstantial metaphors of 'foam' and 'fire' and 'light' and 'sparks', (the very stuff of Turner's paintings—another great Romantic precursor of the modern sensibility), pointing out that 'man is not the creature and product of Mechanism; but, in a far truer sense, its creator and producer.' Well versed in German Idealism, Carlyle insists that mind and spirit are primary: which is all the more reason to choose our social metaphors with care, for if we speak too carelessly of 'the Machine of Society', then all too easily '"foam hardens itself into a shell" and the shadow we have wantonly evoked stands terrible before us and will not depart at our bidding.' (**'Signs of the Times'**). This is not highflown idealism, but a real and subtle understanding of how human perception is controlled by the terms within which we choose to frame it.

For Carlyle, these terms are all we have. He needs no abstruse argument to prove that all is spirit, for *sub specie aeternitatis,* as he sees it, nothing else remains:

> . . . sweep away the illusion of Time; compress the threescore years into three minutes: what else was he, what else are we? Are we not Spirits, that are shaped into a body, into an Appearance; and that fade-away again into air and Invisibility? That is no metaphor, it is a simple scientific *fact*. . . . (*Sartor*, 'Natural Supernaturalism')

So history is the record of how that spirit passed, but like Ecclesiastes's works of God under the sun, it may never be possible to see it fully. This is what Carlyle understood in his essay 'On History', when he noted that 'Narrative is *linear*', but

> . . . actual events are nowise so simply related to each other . . . every single event is the offspring not of one, but of all other events, prior or contemporaneous, and will in its turn combine with all others to give birth to new: it is an everliving, everworking Chaos of Being, wherein shape after shape bodies itself forth from innumerable elements. And this Chaos, boundless as the habitation and duration of man, unfathomable as the soul and destiny of man, is what the historian will depict, and scientifically gauge, we may say, by threading it with single lines of a few ells in length!

Hence Carlyle concludes that 'History is a real Prophetic

manuscript, and can be fully interpreted by no man.' Such a vision of simultaneity and flux places Carlyle once again among the precursors of modernism, as does his understanding of the relativity and the transience of all established opinion—'Thus all things wax, and roll onwards; Arts, Establishments, Opinions, nothing is completed, but ever completing.' (*Sartor,* 'Organic Filaments'.)

Thus it follows that each age must recreate its own version of the truth, for systems and sacred texts and symbols, 'like all terrestrial Garments, wax old,' and 'the Solution of the last era has become obsolete, and is found unserviceable.' (*Sartor,* 'The Everlasting Yea'.) Such a point of view must have been a considerable comfort to Carlyle, as a young intellectual who had lost faith in his father's church, but had not lost the desire to put himself to some worthy and needful task. Thus was born the Professor of 'Things in General' and his Clothes-philosophy. Behind the droll facade of Diogenes Teufelsdröckh, we can see Carlyle struggling to define a valid role for himself—very much like Milton's search to find 'some graver subject'. Literature and literary criticism do not impinge enough on the world of affairs (and we recall that the elder Carlyle held a very low opinion of fiction and poetry—even the verse of Burns), while the conventions of university philosophy could scarcely satisfy the Romantic drive of Carlyle's poetic vision of the instability of the universe. What he did was to define the world itself as a text, and to appoint himself the critic (or prophet) uniquely suited to decode the 'celestial hieroglyphs', even if they can be discerned in only a line or two here and there.

The model is not exclusively literary, of course, for Biblical exegesis is the true forerunner of all such practice. Indeed, one of Carlyle's favourite metaphors is that history is a text 'whose Author and Writer is God . . . With its Words, Sentences, and grand descriptive Pages . . . spread out through Solar Systems and Thousands of Years . . .'[11] It was just this sense of scale which Carlyle found in his readings in German Idealism, along with his belief in an ultimate cosmic unity in which spirit is the only reality.

> . . . this so solid-seeming World, after all, were but an air-image, our ME the only reality: and Nature, with its thousand fold production and destruction, but the reflex of our own inward Force, the 'phantasy of our Dream' . . . *the living visible Garment of God.* (*Sartor,* 'The World Out of Clothes')

He did *not* believe, however, that man was created to 'dream' alone, and the key concept in his idealism lies in that phrase about the world also being 'the reflex of our own inward Force'. For him the spirit expresses itself through *work* and the world is no less than the fruits of our labour (spirit) made manifest. If the world

is ultimately God's book, we too can still make books, we too can make history and create reality, we too can become critics or little Creators:

> So spiritual [*geistig*] is our whole daily life: all that we do springs out of Mystery, Spirit, invisible Force . . . Visible and tangible products of the Past, again, I reckon up to the extent of three: Cities, with their Cabinets and Arsenals; then tilled Fields . . . and thirdly—Books. (*Sartor,* 'Centre of Indifference')

Carlyle's insight can be compressed and summarised as follows: everything is spirit: the spirit manifests itself in mind and the mind expresses itself through work: work can be seen all around us: truly nothing is insignificant. Cities may crumble, but books—because they are the expression of mind—can last much longer, each with a different 'produce of leaves (Commentaries, Deductions, Philosophical, Political Systems; or were it only Sermons, Pamphlets, Journalistic Essays)' for each of the ages they pass through. Thus for Carlyle, thought never dies (though it may evolve) and the scholar can achieve a kind of immortality. Indeed 'the Wise man stands ever encompassed, and spiritually embraced, by a cloud of witnesses and brothers; and there is a living, literal *Communion of the Saints,* wide as the World itself, and as the History of the World.' (*Sartor,* 'Organic Filaments'.) The use of words such as 'witness' and 'communion', reveals how fully Carlyle has remodelled the calling of his father's faith to fit his vocation as a culture critic, a new kind of intellectual hero, a reader of the world and all its symbols—the first semiotician of Victorian Britain.

For such a man everything is symbolic, and nothing, however mean, is without illumination: 'Rightly viewed no meanest object is insignificant; all objects are as windows, through which the philosophic eye looks into Infinitude itself.' (*Sartor,* 'Prospective'.) Teufelsdröckh's task is to show that if the final reality is spirit and spirit alone, then everything else in this world is merely a matter of 'garments'. In the last analysis our clothes, houses and political institutions are merely how we 'dress' ourselves, and our bodies and our senses and even language itself are merely 'garments' of flesh and thought.[12] Yet this is not to dismiss such garments as trivial or beneath serious attention. On the contrary, the burden of Teufelsdröckh's whole philosophy—presented to us through an eccentric *persona,* and qualified by his 'biographer' as it may be—is to take the analysis of surface symbols very seriously indeed, and to use such subtle practice towards a cultural and political critique in an age otherwise wholly dedicated to stoutly practical, 'mechanistic', and materialistic ends. In other words, to invent semiotics.

This is not to say that Carlyle does not enjoy the fun of upsetting established priorities, and many of his propositions are as intellectually playful as anything written by Roland Barthes or Umberto Eco:

'Perhaps the most remarkable incident in Modern History,' says Teufelsdröckh, 'is not the Diet of Worms, still less the Battle of Austerlitz, Waterloo, Peterloo, or any other Battle; but an incident passed carelessly over by most Historians, and treated with some degree of ridicule by others: namely, George Fox's making to himself of a suit of Leather.' (*Sartor,* 'Incident in Modern History')

Teufelsdröckh's name and his strange origin, the autobiography in six paper bags, his Romantic 'Sorrows', and his 'editor's' asides and doubts about his 'sansculottism', all these speak for textual playfulness and perhaps a certain defensive irony in Carlyle's case. But there is no mistaking the intent behind his deconstruction of the nature of war, (in 'Centre of Indifference'); the passionate indignation behind his attack on the values of the landed classes (in 'Helotage'); nor the pointed satire of his vision of a naked House of Lords (in 'Adamitism'); nor his hatred for all the outworn ideas and dead symbols which continue to rule our lives—the 'old clothes' of an unexamined existence, ' . . . with its wail and jubilee, mad loves and mad hatreds, church-bells and gallows-ropes, farce-tragedy, beast-godhood,—the Bedlam of Creation!' (in 'The Phoenix' and 'Old Clothes').

Carlyle's understanding of the power of symbols and how important it is to see through them, 'to look fixedly on Clothes . . . till they become *transparent*', goes further still, for he recognises the arbitrary nature of perception and even language itself—how we are governed by how we choose to see and to say things. If symbols 'have no intrinsic, necessary divineness, or even worth; but have acquired an extrinsic one', it follows that we should choose them with care, or look closely at those we have inherited to be sure that they are worthy of us. This is the first task of the culture-critic, for 'are not the tatters and rags of superannuated worn-out symbols (in this Rag-fair of a world) dropping off everywhere, to hoodwink, to halter, to tether you; nay if you shake them not aside, threatening to accumulate, and perhaps produce suffocation?' (*Sartor,* 'Symbols'.) The culture-critic's second task is to be alert to the emergence of *new* symbols, and these two terms go far towards defining Carlyle's approach to history, and most especially to his treatment of the French Revolution.

The point about the world of clothes is that fashions change and styles of dress go in and out of favour with great regularity. We have seen that this metaphor holds true for Carlyle's vision of the Universe as a place of constant flux, and of society, too, as a structure in 'perpetual metamorphosis'—phoenix-like—as new forces and new symbols within it rise and fall and rise again. Such is the text of the world which Teufelsdröckh has set himself to decipher for us. It is entirely fitting, then, that his own text should show something of that dynamic energy too, and it is here that the presumed identity between Carlyle and his German professor is most clearly demonstrated. *Le style c'est l'homme',* and Carlyle's prose is unique.

He was much criticised, even by admirers, for the self-assertive roughnesses, the repetitive insistence, the odd allusions, constant exclamations, and the generally unclassical lawlessness of his writing. But Carlyle defended himself, for surely this was not the time for 'Purism of Style', and after all, style is a product of 'all that lies under it . . . *not* to be plucked off without flaying and death.'[13]

Indeed, Carlyle's style is very much the mirror of the raw energy and the dynamic tensions within himself, which he identified as the condition of the world all around him. Carlyle had much admired the rough earnestness of his own father's speech, 'flowing free from the untutored Soul' (*Reminiscences*), and this *oral* insistence is central to his own written prose. True to his earliest experiences of exposition in the Burgher Church, Carlyle stands before the text of God (except that in his case the book is not the Bible, but History itself) and preaches the word.

Of course Carlyle's prose has long been recognised as an essentially (and sometimes exhausting) form of rhetorical address—full of sermon-like locutions, exclamations, and asides to the reader—while his punctuation and sentence structures make full use of dashes and sudden associative digressions.[14] Nevertheless, this is not simply the style of a self-appointed demagogue, despite its later decay into intolerance and insistence, for Carlyle was right to maintain that the mental set behind Johnsonian English was collapsing under the new apprehensions of the Romantic age, and right, too, in his conviction that his style, like the skin of an animal, is integral to 'the exact type of the nature of the beast'.[15]

Thus it is in his choice of metaphors, ('foam', 'fountains', 'sparks'), and in the very structure of his sentences, that Carlyle seeks to demonstrate his passionate apprehension of life as a fully dynamic state. Hence the turmoil of history is evoked at great length and by an extraordinary effort of the imagination in the recurring historical present tense of the prose in *The French Revolution*—a book that cost him the most desperate effort to write. It is fitting, too, that most of his sources were drawn from the memoirs of participants themselves, another recognition of Carlyle's commitment to the importance of lived experience and point of view in history. Again and again Carlyle's prose seeks to engage us in the whirl of events as they evolve from the experience, the plans and the half-formed apprehensions of his protagonists:

> Still crueller was the fate of poor Bailly, First National President, First Mayor of Paris: doomed now for Royalism, Fayettism; for that Red-Flag Business of the Champ-de-Mars;—one may say in general, for leaving his Astronomy to meddle with Revolution. It is the 10th of November 1793, a cold bitter drizzling rain, as poor Bailly is led through the streets; howling Populace covering him with curses, with mud; waving over his face a burning or smoking mockery of a red Flag. Silent, unpitied, sits the innocent old man. Slow

faring through the sleety drizzle, they have got to the Champ-de-Mars: Not there! vociferates the cursing Populace; such blood ought not to stain an Altar of the Fatherland: not there; but on that dung-heap by the River-side! So vociferates the cursing Populace; Officiality gives ear to them. The Guillotine is taken down, though with hands numbed by the sleety drizzle; is carried to the River-side; is there set up again, with slow numbness; pulse after pulse still counting itself out in the old man's weary heart. For hours long; amid curses and bitter frost-rain! 'Bailly, thou tremblest,' said one. '*Mon ami*, it is for cold,' said Bailly, *'c'est de froid.'* Crueller end had no mortal. (***The French Revolution,*** Part III, Book V, 'Death')

Despite Carlyle's talent for dramatic recreation and his dependence on contemporary memoirs, later historians have verified the accuracy of much of this work. Furthermore, his sources have a different and more theoretical kind of validity as well, for however fallible and biased they may be, in their own way they are fully part of the flux of their times—immediate and, in a sense, oral too.

Carlyle's conviction about the spontaneity, the fluidity, and the power of human impulse as it operates, evolves and clothes itself in different ways within the flux of history, meets its proper correlative in his style. In so far as this prose is a 'voice' he can recognise the uniqueness and the relativity of all opinion, and yet at the same time he can also demonstrate its living, persuasive power across the centuries in that 'communion of saints' he longed to join. Carlyle's voice may be speaking to us from another century, yet, with all the force of literature—grammatically, rhetorically, ironically—his vision of lost times and the never-ending turbulence of human experience becomes immediately and palpably present. The closing lines of ***The French Revolution*** speak openly for the poignancy of this condition, but they also note its potential for endless growth and renewal:

> And so here, O Reader, has the time come for us two to part. Toilsome was our journeying together; not without offence, but it is done. To me thou wert as a beloved shade, the disembodied or not yet embodied spirit of a Brother. To thee I was but as a Voice. Yet was our relation a kind of sacred one; doubt not that! For whatsoever once sacred things become hollow jargons, yet while the Voice of Man speaks with Man, hast thou not there the living fountain out of which all sacredness sprang, and will yet spring? Man, by the nature of him, is definable as 'an incarnated Word.' Ill stands it with me if I have spoken falsely: thine also it was to hear truly. Farewell.

These words do not speak for the historian alone, for they recognise the fragility, and the intimacy, and the crucial importance of all discourse between all readers and all writers, when the world becomes text and the text becomes a voice.

Notes

[1] Walt Whitman, 'Death of Thomas Carlyle' (1881), in *Thomas Carlyle: The Critical Heritage,* J P Seigel (ed) (London, 1971), p. 456.

[2] Hoffmann was among a number of writers translated by Carlyle for his four volume book *Specimens of German Romance,* 1827.

[3] *Froude's Life of Carlyle,* abridged and edited by J Clubbe (London, 1979), p 417.

[4] From 'James Carlyle', in *Reminiscences* (1881).

[5] *Hard Times* (1854), was dedicated to Carlyle.

[6] His reading of Goethe had been very influential, especially *Wilhelm Meister's Lehrjahre,* as a semi-autobiographical development novel about a similarly ardent young spirit at large in banal society. (Carlyle's translation of it appeared in 1824.)

[7] From 'James Carlyle', in *Reminiscences.*

[8] Letter from Carlyle to his brother John, 17 July 1831.

[9] John Sterling, letter to Carlyle, 29 May 1835, *The Critical Heritage,* pp 31-3.

[10] Dostoevsky, *Notes from Underground* (1864), Chapter One. 'The Underground'.

[11] *Sartor Resartus.* 'Natural Supernaturalism'; *see also* ' . . . all history is a Bible . . .' a rejected MS quoted in *Froude's Life,* pp 224-6.

[12] *Sartor,* 'The World out of Clothes' and 'Pure Reason'.

[13] This debate is touched on in *Froude's Life,* pp 339-41; *see also Critical Heritage,* pp 26-33.

[14] Recent research has shown that Carlyle's editors set out to regularise his punctuation in subsequent editions of his work. It is worth noting that the rather diffident delivery of his early lectures was much at odds with the considerable force of his written prose.

[15] Letter to John Sterling, 9 June 1837.

Wendell V. Harris (essay date 1990)

SOURCE: "Interpretive Historicism: 'Signs of the Times' and *Culture and Anarchy* in Their Contexts," in *Nineteenth-Century Literature*, Vol. 44, No. 4, March, 1990, pp. 441-64.

[*In the following essay, Harris examines the rhetorical*

strategies used by Carlyle in "Signs of the Times," and argues that while the essay may appear to be controversial and "extravagant," when seen within the context of the time and culture in which the essay was written, "Signs of the Times" is actually rather mild and not as revolutionary as it may seem.]

To adapt Northrop Frye's metaphor, Carlyle's stock has been steadily falling. To the contemporary reader his works are likely to look like mere rhetorical steam—at high pressure, but vaporous nonetheless—becoming substantial only when politically ominous. That Carlyle created the role of the Victorian sage is generally acknowledged, but the attribution can seem an indictment as well as a tribute. At the same time, while Matthew Arnold seems as much in the critical eye as ever, he has become a name for masked social elitism and political conservatism. The argument I want to make is that, when viewed against the interpretive context or cultural "horizon" of its time, Carlyle's rhetorical strategies show themselves to be a great deal less extravagant, and that, similarly examined, Arnold's social prescriptions in *Culture and Anarchy* prove a great deal less conservative.[1] That is hardly a novel thesis, but I think it a timely one now that the question of the proper relation between literary texts and their historical contexts has been actively reopened.

The essay that stands at the head of what became a torrent of prose on the "condition of the culture" is **"Signs of the Times,"** originally published in the *Edinburgh Review* for June 1829. It can also make a strong claim to have initiated the quintessential Carlylean stance; as W. S. Johnson wrote, "From some points of view this is the most important of the early essays. . . . It contains the germinal thought of all his later work. . . ."[2] Carlyle's basic meaning can hardly be said to be in doubt. From Johnson's five-sentence summary (1911) through Augustus Ralli's two-page precis (1920), Emery Neff's long paragraph (1932), Julian Symons's half-page (1952) and Albert LaValley's two-page comment (1968), the same major points receive paraphrase.[3] After an initial warning of the dangers of indulging too much in forecasting the future from present omens, Carlyle adverts to what many regarded as signs of imminent crisis—the repeal of the Test Acts and Catholic emancipation. Agreeing that the present is important because "the poorest Day that passes over us is the conflux of two Eternities," Carlyle announces that he will attempt to "discern truly the signs of our own time."[4] The overriding characteristic to which he then points is the "mechanical" nature of the age: machines are changing the nature of work and life, but more importantly, men have come to put their faith in social machinery. Human relationships and the universe have both come to be conceived on a mechanical model—the calculation of profit and loss—that overlooks man's dynamical characteristics: "the mysterious springs of Love, and Fear, and Wonder, of Enthusiasm, Poetry, Religion" (p. 68). These the individual must cultivate in himself: the wise man knows that the only "solid" reformation "is what each begins and perfects on *himself*" (p. 82).

No great effort is required to fault this Carlylean construction. Biographical critics can point to extra-textual comment as evidence that Carlyle himself was dissatisfied with this essay, whose origin lay in Francis Jeffrey's request for something controversial from Carlyle for the last volume of the *Edinburgh Review* he would edit.[5] Carlyle's entry in his Craigenputtock diary reads: "Also just finished an article on the 'Signs of the Times' for the 'Edinburgh Review,' as Jeffrey's last speech. Bad in general, but the best I could make it under such incubus influences."[6] A "New Historicist" of Marxist orientation can easily argue that though Carlyle had recognized the dehumanizing tendencies of profit-and-loss capitalism governed by mechanistic principles, he had been unable to envision or face the implications of a noncapitalist system and so escaped from the socioeconomic realm altogether by calling for self-cultivation rather than socialism. A phrase like "signs of the times" offers an attractive target for critics with structuralist preoccupations: if the relations between signs change between the slices that make up the synchronic axis of language, the potential meanings of a sign are a function of time. Times then reveal signs, not signs time. Finally, the ordinary, minimally ideologically conscious or theory-oriented present-day reader may well simply find **"Signs of the Times"** vague and pretentious.

That readers who want to understand Carlyle's originally intended meaning must place **"Signs of the Times"** in its 1829 context seems a truism, but present-day speech-act theory allows us to state that point somewhat more exactly. What is to be recovered are the "implicatures" generated by the interaction of the text and the information and attitudes current at the time.

For instance, it is worthwhile to investigate what would have been the contemporary awareness of the phrase "signs of the times." One assumes that Carlyle expected his readers to recognize the source of his title in Matthew 16: 1-4:

> 1 The Pharisees also with the Sadducees came, and tempting desired him that he would shew them a sign from heaven.
>
> 2 He answered and said unto them, When it is evening, ye say, It will be fair weather: for the sky is red.
>
> 3 And in the morning, It will be foul weather to day: for the sky is red and lowring. O ye hypocrites, ye can discern the face of the sky; but can ye not discern the signs of the times?
>
> 4 A wicked and adulterous generation seeketh after a sign; and there shall no sign be given unto it, but the sign of the prophet Jonas. And he left them, and departed.

The allusion suggests that Carlyle's readers can expect

no sign from heaven; that the times must therefore be interpreted directly; that at present, just as when the Pharisees and Sadducees asked, evil abounds; and (more indirectly) that defense against such evil requires personal transformation.

But reading about in the major periodicals of the time, one discovers that readers in the 1820s and 1830s would have responded to the unusual topical currency of that phrase as well as to its biblical origin. "Signs of the times" has done duty in both sacred and secular writing since the King James translation (the earliest uses as a title appearing in the British Library catalogue are dated 1681 and 1742), but the phrase appears with such frequency in early nineteenth-century essays that it seems to sum up an almost obsessive preoccupation with the state and prospects of the nation. As a title it was of course relevant to the publications Carlyle was ostensibly reviewing (one remembers that the essay belongs to that now curious genre, the early nineteenth-century review-essay). The works listed at the head of the *Edinburgh* essay were:

> 1. *Anticipation; or, an Hundred Years Hence.* 8vo. London: 1829.
>
> 2. *The Rise, Progress, and Present State of Public Opinion in Great Britain.* 8vo. London: 1829.
>
> 3. *The Last Days; or Discoveries on These Our Times, &c. &c.* 8vo. London: 1829. By the Rev. Edward Irving.

I have not been able to locate a copy or identify the author of the first work, though its title suggests that it belongs to the prophetic, probably cautionary, kind. The author of the second, identified in a contemporary review in the *Quarterly* as William Alexander Mackinnon, laboriously argued that the increase in the powers of machinery was rapidly augmenting the middle class, which was the source of sound public opinion, which in turn was the force behind increasing liberalization of government. The Reverend Irving's message was simply that the second coming was at hand, and since Irving himself published a pamphlet with the title "Signs of the Times" in 1829, the relevance of Carlyle's title could have been all the clearer to certain readers.

The title was, however, equally relevant to a general uneasiness about the future of England of which the three volumes under review represent only marginal aspects. The fact is that when Carlyle was asked to contribute to this volume of the *Edinburgh* the work he would have liked to review was the most prominent essay on this subject, Southey's *Sir Thomas More: Or, Colloquies on the Progress and Prospects of Society,* published in April 1829.[7] Conducted as a pretentiously formal dialogue between Montesinos (Southey) and Sir Thomas More, its mode of arguing for a return to the pieties and

uses of a much older day now seems ludicrous. But the Poet Laureate was taken seriously enough to be treated at length in reviews in each of the great journals of the time. Since the review of the *Colloquies* had already been assigned to Macaulay, Carlyle in essence responded to what he regarded as Southey's failure to see the real problems of England by taking three marginally related books as his ostensible subject.

Exemplary of the many contemporary attempts to gain perspective on the time was an article in the *Quarterly* for April 1829 (the same month that saw the publication of the *Colloquies*) entitled "The State and Prospects of the Country"—which may also have been written by Southey. This essay begins its survey of history in the fifteenth century, tracing general improvement up to the present, but finds "that the burden of the rich and misery of the poor, are at this hour generally and rapidly advancing" (39:509).[8] It is a flaccid enough performance, but it nevertheless attracted notice. An unidentified writer in the June *New Monthly,* responding with partial agreement in "The Present Times, with Remarks on a Late Article in the *Quarterly,*" states that the *Quarterly* article has "made a deep impression on the country" (25:573). The point is that politically motivated as were such articles, again and again the whole direction of English society was being brought into question. Thus the July *Blackwood's* included David Robinson's "The Condition of the Empire," an attack on the doctrines set forth in the *Quarterly* article, while the September number brought a less partisan essay by William Johnstone repeating the title "State and Prospects of the Country."

The phrase "Signs of the Times" was as ubiquitous as the topic. The *New Monthly*'s T. C. Morgan, opening the January issue with "Opinions for 1829," refers to changes in the ministry and policies since the death of Canning as "unequivocal signs of the times" (25:2); the author of "The Present Times" in the June issue of that journal protests that the author of the *Quarterly* essay looked in the wrong places for "the signs of the times" (25:575). In Southey's *Colloquies* Sir Thomas More is made to ask "Is there a considerate man who can look at the signs of the times without apprehension, or a scoundrel connected with what is called the public press, who does not speculate upon them, and join with the anarchists as the strongest party?"[9] Southey's reviewer in the *Quarterly* writes, "In many of the apprehensions here entertained, we confess that we ourselves participate; nor can we see how any man who watches the signs of the times can prophesy smooth things only" (41:1).

What and how dire were the signs that solicited so much interest? Southey makes More's apparition speak of "these portentous and monster-breeding times; for it is your lot, as it was mine, to live during one of the grand climacterics of the world."[10] The *New Monthly*'s writer on "The Present Time" warns "Great Britain has now reached a crisis in which she must make efforts, that to many persons may appear appalling, to maintain her station among the dynasties of Europe . . ." (25:574). William Johnstone's "State and Prospects of the Country" in *Blackwood's* asserts: "In the present time, let us go where we will, in any place from Caithness to Cornwall, wherever men speak seriously respecting their own condition, and that of those around them, there seems to be an unanimous consent to this proposition, 'that there is a necessity for some great change'" (26:464).

Such fears, as powerful as indefinite, haunted writers despite the surprising ease with which the nation had negotiated the specific crises to which Carlyle alludes early in his essay. The repeal of the Test and Corporation Act, removing the political disabilities of dissenters, was accomplished on Lord John Russell's motion of 1828, which easily carried over rear-guard Tory opposition. The second issue, Catholic emancipation, had seemed much more threatening: the historian George C. Brodrick writes that "the whole interval between July, 1828, and April, 1829, was occupied by the discussion of this question, or circumstances arising out of it, and it may truly be said to have filled the whole horizon of domestic politics."[11] George IV opposed emancipation almost to the last, 900 anti-Catholic petitions were sent to the House of Commons, and the heat of controversy had brought Wellington into a duel with Lord Winchilsea. *Blackwood's* vehemently opposed emancipation, calling upon parliament to "fly to the defense of its Throne and Altar" (25:287). The *Westminster Review* gave thirty-six pages to replying to fifty-four different statements against Catholic emancipation, concluding, "men want now to make trial of mercy instead of sacrifice, and to give up the dark glass of prophecy, for what it has pleased God to make the broad day-light of justice and common sense" (10:36). The summer of 1829 was an uncomfortable time for all parties—Whigs, Tories, and Liberals—for another reason. The next generation of leaders was not yet evident: since early 1827 Lord Liverpool's government had been followed by Canning's, which had been replaced by Lord Goderich's, which had been succeeded by that headed by Wellington.

The more general intellectual context is of course closely connected with the political. Annotations to twentieth-century editions of **"Signs of the Times"** generally insure that their readers will understand that the references to "mechanical" philosophy specifically challenge the Utilitarians. However, it is necessary to realize just how strong an influence the Utilitarian tide in philosophy, morals, economics, and social theory was exerting at the end of the 1820s. While Bentham's *Introduction to the Principles of Morals and Legislation* had been published as long before as 1789 and David Ricardo's *Principles of Political Economy and Taxation* in 1817, James Mill's *Elements of Political Economy* had appeared in 1821. Of especial value to the Utilitarian cause was the Supplement to the fourth, fifth, and sixth editions of

the *Encyclopaedia Brittanica,* published between 1820 and 1824. The Supplement was in many ways a manifesto of the Utilitarians and "Philosophical Radicals" generally: James Mill contributed eleven articles, including the subsequently famous ones on "Government," "Jurisprudence," and "Liberty of the Press"; even the one on "Beggars" gave him the opportunity to present Utilitarian doctrines. John McCulloch, a disciple of Ricardo's, contributed not only "Political Economy," but "Interest," "Money," and "Taxation."

The private reprinting of Mill's "Government" in 1824 (and subsequently other of his encyclopaedia articles in 1828) gave the entire issue of representative government a special prominence that was much increased by Macaulay's celebrated attack on Mill's "Government" in the March 1829 *Edinburgh Review:* "We have here an elaborate treatise on Government, from which, but for two or three passing allusions, it would not appear that the author was aware that any governments actually existed among men" (49:161-62). The *Westminster Review* replied in its July issue (in an article by Thompson incorporating notes from Bentham); Macaulay responded in the June *Edinburgh,* the *Westminster* in its October issue, and Macaulay in the October *Edinburgh.*[12]

Political economy, the special preserve of the Philosophical Radicals, was steadily gaining respectability, though against spirited opposition that kept it before the eye of the educated public. In May 1824, the year the Supplement to the *Britannica* was completed, *Blackwood's* began publishing a series of five articles by William Stevenson presenting a conservative, traditional view of political economy.[13] A reviewer in the July 1827 *Westminster* and Richard Whately in the September 1828 *Edinburgh* congratulated Oxford on its new Chair of Political Economy. In September 1829 David Robinson, signing himself "One of the Old School," would launch a series of four *Blackwood's* articles addressed "To the Heads of the University of Oxford" designed to prove that political economy could *not* be a science; it was "essentially fallacious," "a mass of fictions"; and the heads would be scolded for allowing it to be taught and thus "deeply disgracing your University, and destroying your own reputation as men of science" (26:510). To which the *Westminster* would reply: "But the day, or rather the night, of the old school is passing away. All that now remains in doubt is, whether the morning that is to succeed it will open in storm or in sunshine. The oppressions and the follies of feudalism will be swept off, but will it be by a reform or by a revolution?" (11:514).

Now it is hardly news to a moderately informed present-day reader of Carlyle that he was writing at a time when the government appeared more than usually unstable and unpredictable or that the great debates over theories of government and political economy were fully joined in 1829 and underlay many other issues. Moreover, readers of Carlyle know that **"Signs of the Times"** is unusually free from "Carlylese." However, only if one is aware of the hyperbolic declarations of political and religious writers all around him can Carlyle's remarkable control be adequately recognized. Carlyle's restraint, and the limits he sets to what he evidently already sees as his prophetic office are especially remarkable in the midst of social and political alarm. It seemed to many a time for dire warnings of the "hearken ere it is too late" variety, but for all his stylistic eccentricity Carlyle is more the counselor than the doomster here. His surprisingly mild tone constituted an "implicature" in itself when seen against the genre to which it belonged. That Carlyle does not really discuss any of the three books he proposes to review is of course a reflection of the tenuous relationship of many an essay in the quarterlies to their putative occasion. But, given Irving's contemporary fame, the fact that Carlyle never directly mentions his book, whose dire warnings could so easily have been satirized, implied to his contemporaries that his book was of no substantive interest in itself.[14] He equally contented himself with passing dismissal of Mackinnon, whose tediously recapitulated and largely superficial analyses and bubbling optimism must have made him a tempting target.

It requires some effort to recall how marked the contrast would have been between Carlyle's avoidance of political partisanship and typical articles in *Blackwood's,* the *Quarterly,* the *Westminster,* the *New Monthly,* and the *Edinburgh* itself that focused tenaciously on the details of parliamentary bills, party alignments, and cabinet power struggles. In the midst of these clashes Carlyle's very tone not-so-obliquely announced that the questions at issue had been misconceived and the sense of crisis had been artificially created. The mechanism of government was a secondary matter; the spiritual condition of those in a position to act was all-important. Though he is briefly ironic in referring to the embarrassment of those who had sheltered under the "slumbering Leviathan" Intolerance until it "suddenly dived under," his avoidance of questions of party and of denunciatory language directed at individuals would have suggested to readers that he was attempting something quite different from most articles analyzing "the current state" of English society. Dispassionate assessment was in order. Readers would have recognized clearly that the repeal of the Test and Corporation Act and removal of Catholic disabilities were apt demonstrations of Carlyle's calm dismissal of such portents: "The 'State in Danger' is a condition of things, which we have witnessed a hundred times; and as for the Church, it has seldom been out of 'danger' since we can remember it" (p. 57).

As a touchstone of the accepted style of article writing in the 1820s we may take the opening of William Johnstone's "The Rise and Fall of the Liberals" from the July 1828 issue of *Blackwood's:*

> We have this month to congratulate our readers, that is to say, all the good men and true who live under the British flag in every quarter of the world, upon a most important

change which has taken place in the constitution of his Majesty's Ministry. We have at last, thank God, got rid of the Liberals, and once more have the happiness to live under a pure Tory government. Not a remnant, we rejoice to say, of that bastard political sect, that cunning, cowardly, compromising, conciliatory school, has been left to divide and weaken the measures of the Cabinet. (24:96)

Pointing the way for Ruskin, Arnold, and Morris, Carlyle must quite consciously have wished to lift the argument of **"Signs of the Times"** clear of the swamps of specific party allegiances, parliamentary motions, and debates between individuals. The contrast with the fate of Southey's *Colloquies* is instructive. Though Southey's elaborate structure was evidently meant to project a facade of historical objectivity, the book fueled all sorts of party prejudices, and was reviewed almost purely on the basis of party principles. The *Quarterly*'s lead article for July 1829 began "This is a beautiful book, full of wisdom and devotion—of poetry and feeling" (41:1) and gave twenty-seven pages to seconding Southey's desire to make an enforced Christian education the great means of improving society. The review in the October *Blackwood's* reflects a similar Toryism:

> "A good man, out of the abundance of his heart, bringeth forth good things." Never was this sacred truth better illustrated than by the work before us. It is all good: very good. Excellent in conception; unexceptionable for the matter which it contains; and admirable for the spirit by which it is pervaded. (26:611)

On the other hand, the *Westminster* of the same month spoke for the Philosophical Radicals (Utilitarians):

> This sickly and splenetic denial of manifest improvement— these wretched attempts to exalt ages of darkness, ignorance, and barbarity, into equality, or preference, simply because a larger portion of the mass of humanity lay mentally prostrate before power and priestcraft, would be truly disgusting, if the astonishing complacency with which the nonsense is submitted to the world did not merge anger at the sophistry, into amazement at the self-delusion. (11:199-200)

The first paragraph of Macaulay's famous review, which did not appear in the essentially Whig *Edinburgh* until January 1830, includes:

> We have, for some time past, observed with great regret the strange infatuation which leads the Poet-laureate to abandon those departments of literature in which he might excel, and to lecture the public on sciences of which he has still the very alphabet to learn. He has now, we think, done his worst. (50:528)

Further:

> Wherever the thickest shadow of the night may at any moment chance to fall, there is Mr Southey. It is not

every body who could have so dexterously avoided blundering on the daylight in the course of a journey to the Antipodes. (534)

Macaulay himself, the clarity and vigor of whose writing made him a model of controversial tactics, nevertheless bound himself to almost wholly partisan interest. His review of Mill's "On Government" led to a series of responses and counterresponses extending over months. In contrast, Carlyle, who paralleled Macaulay in distrust for the Utilitarians (though of course differing from him greatly in the assessment of other signs of the times), contrived to suggest a disabling shallowness in Utilitarian thought while avoiding either attacking personalities or becoming enmeshed in debates over specifically stated Utilitarian principles: "For the wise men, who now appear as Political Philosophers, deal exclusively with the Mechanical province; and occupying themselves in counting-up and estimating men's motives, strive by curious checking and balancing, and other adjustments of Profit and Loss, to guide them to their true advantage: while, unfortunately, those same 'motives' are so innumerable, and so variable in every individual, that no really useful conclusion can ever be drawn from their enumeration" (p. 69). That sentence of Carlyle's carries the gist of Macaulay's argument against Mill's a priori construction of the principle of government, but then shears off without leading the reader into the intricacies of political economy.

Sweeping in its judgments, **"Signs of the Times"** is moderate in tone, avoiding personalities, making no hostile sorties, counseling the long view rather than immediate action, dissolving party prejudice in broad principles. The result was the transformation of the review-essay into that essentially new and especially Victorian genre, the philosophical commentary on culture. Carlyle's reputation for cantankerousness and angry rhetoric in later essays like those of *Latter-Day Pamphlets* has caused many readers to think him ever disputatious. But it was by finding a way to give essays like **"Signs of the Times"** a profound seriousness without contentiousness that Carlyle pointed the way for the coming age of sages. He avoids equally Southey's appeal to old-fashioned conservative values and institutions and the Utilitarian calculus as remedies for the evils he insists upon. One is not accustomed to think of Carlyle occupying the middle of the road, but that is precisely where he takes his stand in this essay.

If Carlyle's **"Signs of the Times"** turns out to be an example of calm reasonableness against the background of the time itself, portions at least of *Culture and Anarchy* prove far more radical than our usual view of Arnold would allow. *Culture and Anarchy* has come to be the central document in contemporary indictments of Arnold's conservatism while the chapter "Our Liberal Practitioners" has seemed the epitome of his intransigent allegiance to the status quo and invincible opposition to political action.

Arnold's choices of political issues in that chapter, which appear strange enough to most readers, are a clue to what he is about. They are, one recalls: the disestablishment of the Irish Church; the Real Estate Intestacy Bill; the bill to enable a man to marry his deceased wife's sister; and the free-trade policy. The selection is oddly uneven. Disestablishment of the Anglican Church in Ireland was being fiercely contested—it was to prove the primary issue in the election of 1868. While the Bill to Render Legal Marriage with a Deceased Wife's Sister is likely to seem to the present-day reader to have been chosen to illustrate the triviality of certain political questions, that was not in fact the case. As late as 1882 Lord Forbes, addressing a "Meeting of Scottish Churchmen in Edinburgh," declared the question to be "of the deepest ecclesiastical importance to the whole Church, and as regards Great Britain in particular, one of the gravest concern."[15] It was certainly well ventilated in pamphlet after pamphlet from 1849 on. In contrast the Real Estate Intestacy Bill, though it had been raised several times previously to 1868, was hardly a burning question—it was certainly not perceived to be an attack on the landed wealth of the great families. And the question of free trade had been settled twenty-five years before by Peel—it would not again become an important issue until the 1890s.

The fact is that the more one knows about these issues, the clearer it is that the contemporary state of none of them really interested Arnold. While to us, looking back over a hundred years, it seems that Arnold is merely criticizing the grounds on which the Liberals were proceeding without offering alternatives, in effect he was cutting each issue away from the arguments to which his readers were accustomed. Readers of his own time would have been keenly aware that he was ignoring the constant unrest in Ireland that had occupied so much parliamentary debate for decades and that the bill for Disestablishment of the Irish Church was intended to help calm. Rather, Arnold satirized the bill's embodiment of the "Nonconformists' antipathy to establishments."[16] He similarly ignored the substance of the parliamentary debate on the Real Estate Intestacy Bill. Laws of inheritance at the time made a distinction between personal property and the real estate of a person dying intestate: the first was subject to division among the survivors while the second went as a whole to the eldest son, if any. The question at issue was whether real estate should be treated the same as personal property. The report of the debates in Hansard's makes clear that no one much feared that those of rank and wealth would neglect to provide for the integrity of their estates (which were ordinarily severely entailed in any case). The question was the effect on small landowners: would the death of the owner of a few acres without a will mean the subdividing of land into portions too small to support a family, or alternatively, force its immediate sale to an adjacent squire, thus increasing the lands of the wealthy and decreasing the number of small freeholders? Arnold wholly dodges such questions, transmogrifying the issue by pointing out the absurdity of the existence of the Barbarian class itself.

In looking toward the Liberals' free-trade policy (which was hardly assailable on the ground of its success in expanding wealth and commerce), he again quickly modulates into a different topic: "The untaxing of the poor man's bread has . . . been used not so much to make the existing poor man's bread cheaper or more abundant, but rather to create more poor men to eat it" (p. 210). How has free trade done this? Arnold doesn't say—though presumably the mercantile class that has directly benefited from free trade had not passed on those benefits to the working class—because his real topic is not free trade but overpopulation.

Arnold's treatment of marriage with a deceased wife's sister is especially revealing of the way he lifted issues away from the arguments and history that had long surrounded them.[17] The extensive background of the situation will repay a somewhat detailed look. Henry VIII's marriage to Catherine of Aragon had required Papal approval because Catherine had married Henry's brother Arthur five months before Arthur's death and canon law forbade marriages between near kin through the fourth degree whether the kinship was one of consanguinity or affinity (by marriage). When Henry wished to divorce Catherine in order to marry Anne Boleyn, he argued that despite the Papal dispensation he had received, the marriage to Catherine was invalid since it fell within the prohibited degrees. After the failure to achieve Papal approval had fueled his disavowal of Papal authority, the divorce was achieved in 1533 through a bill that not only declared marriage between certain prohibited degrees of kinship improper, but provided that previous such marriages were revoked and all future ones prohibited.[18] A table drawn up in 1563 by Archbishop Parker set forth more clearly the prohibited degrees of kinship (both of blood and affinity) relying primarily on Roman law and Leviticus 18:5-18. The ninety-ninth of the Canons of the Church of England as laid down in 1603 forbade marriage between near kin as set forth in that Table of Prohibited Degrees, which table came to be incorporated in the Book of Common Prayer. In 1835, a full two centuries later, an act was introduced presumably for the purpose of putting the legitimacy of the marriage of the Duke of Beaufort beyond all doubt. In its final form, after various amendments, this made all previous marriages between a man and his deceased wife's sister valid while at the same time making all such future marriages void. Efforts to lift this prohibition began in 1841 and a Royal Commission was appointed to investigate whether such marriages violated God's commandments (though the Commission reported that marriages with a deceased wife's sister were not indeed prohibited by Scripture, parliament refused to sanction them until 1907).

The question was fought out on both religious and moral grounds, the arguments regarding which seem as quaint as any scholastic controversy. When marriage is said to make husband and wife "one flesh," does that mean that the husband becomes of one flesh with the wife's sister, thus in effect transforming the relationship from one of affinity to one of consanguinity? Does Leviticus 18:18 ("Neither shalt thou take a wife to her sister, to vex her, to uncover her nakedness, beside the other in her life time") tell for or against the prohibition? Does Deuteronomy 25:5 ("If brethren dwell together, and one of them die, and have no child, the wife of the dead shall not marry without unto a stranger: her husband's brother shall go in unto her, and take her to him to wife, and perform the duty of an husband's brother unto her") bear *mutatis mutandis* on the question? To what extent are laws given by God to the Jews binding on Christians? Did the whole issue of marriage to a deceased wife's sister arise in such vexed form simply because Henry VIII wanted to divorce Catherine of Aragon? Was the whole purpose of the bill to legalize marriage with a deceased wife's sister to give freedom to certain noble members of the realm who wished to marry wealthy deceased wives' sisters, or would its primary benefit be to the poor? (The sisters of deceased wives of poor men frequently and fittingly—or not, depending on one's point of view—took over the care of the children. They also frequently—or occasionally, depending on whose evidence one accepted—entered into all the other relations of a wife. The advantage of regulating such arrangements among the poor was the major argument put forward in a set of five letters by well-known churchmen in 1849, supported by a petition signed "by Many Hundreds of Parochial Clergy.")[19] Would the passage of such a bill wholly change the relation of men to their sisters-in-law, causing wives to be jealous of their sisters and making it indelicate for the sister to be a member of the household even during the wife's lifetime?

This last question was almost as perennial a part of the controversy as the proper interpretation of Leviticus 18. To better realize the passionate feelings of the controversialists we may look beyond the 1859 discussion to an especially succinct statement made by the Reverend Canon Knox Little in 1883:

> I declare that on the marriage morning, when a young man is looking with loving earnestness to be united to the sweetheart who has been dear to him, and whom he is about to make his wife—if on the morning it should be thought possible by those who gather round the bride that the sister who stands behind her as her bridesmaid, and who has accepted the man as her brother, confiding and trusting in him with sisterly love, would ever take the place of that wife beside him, it would cast over the marriage morning a gloom of darkness, just as this Bill, if it is carried, will cast a cloud of darkness over the whole sentiment of England, and the great tradition of her love of the marriage state, her devotion to home, her recognition of all that is best and dearest to honest-hearted loving men.[20]

Now the complexity of the history and the bearing of the many corollary issues could have been kept in mind only by those actively engaged in the debate, but so many pamphlets poured forth, and so full and frequently was the question debated in parliament, that Arnold's readers would have been conversant with many of the arguments on each side. Arnold enters on none of the usual arguments, but rather addresses himself to the assertion made by one of the bill's proponents that liberty is the law of life, and calls for the development of greater delicacy and finer shades of feeling in its Philistine sponsors. Primarily he is attempting to float the issue free of conflicting arguments about social utility and scriptural interpretation so that cultural tact can address it. Nevertheless, readers of the time would have been aware that Arnold was adverting to several of the stock arguments in a somewhat eccentric way. Consider:

> And his [the Philistine's] true humanity, and therefore his happiness, appears to lie much more, so far as the relations of love and marriage are concerned, in becoming alive to the finer shades of feeling which arise within these relations, in being able to enter with tact and sympathy into the subtle instinctive propensions and repugnances of the person with whose life his own life is bound up, to make them his own, to direct and govern in harmony with them the arbitrary range of his personal action, and thus to enlarge his spiritual and intellectual life and liberty, than in remaining insensible to these finer shades of feeling and this delicate sympathy, in giving unchecked range, so far as he can, to his mere personal action, in allowing no limits or government to this except such as a mechanical external law imposes, and in thus really narrowing, for the satisfaction of his ordinary self, his spiritual and intellectual life and liberty. (p. 207)

Now, in the midst of that long and seemingly general proposition, the words "the subtle instinctive propensions and repugnances of the person with whose life his own is bound up" and "these finer shades of feeling" would have been understood as an oblique reference to the view that wives might feel jealousy toward a sister.

An equally oblique allusion resides in Arnold's question (sometimes cited as evidence of his bigotry), "who, that is not manacled and hoodwinked by his Hebraism, can believe that, as to love and marriage, our reason and the necessities of our humanity have their true, sufficient, and divine law expressed for them by the voice of any Oriental and polygamous nation like the Hebrews?" (p. 208). That would have been understood by careful readers not only to refer to the argument that commandments given to the Jews were not necessarily applicable to Christians but also to cast a shadow on both Leviticus 18 and Deuteronomy 25. Arnold is suggesting a less legalistic mode of reading the Bible that will be developed in *St. Paul and Protestantism* and *God and the Bible*. Again:

> All these discoveries [of the Philistines] are favourable to liberty, and in this way is satisfied that double craving so characteristic of our Philistine, and so eminently exemplified in that crowned Philistine, Henry the Eighth,— the craving for forbidden fruit and the craving for legality. (p. 206)

Here the usual argument that the prohibition against marriage with a deceased wife's sister would not have entered the Table of Prohibited Degrees had not Henry wished to rid himself of Catherine of Aragon is transformed so that Henry VIII becomes a cautionary example of the desire to interpret God's laws for one's own purposes. Arnold is thus able to state his own lack of sympathy with the bill while shifting the question in order to challenge the principle that "Liberty is the law of human life" and that the Old Testament should be our guide in such matters. It is not surprising that Arnold exasperated the Liberals of the 1860s. After all, when one is bending all one's forces to remodel an offending niche in the castle of polity, the fellow who stands leaning against a wall refusing to take a hand, while arguing that the whole wing must come down, is hardly regarded as an ally. Nor is it surprising that his animadversions on specific arguments at the time were too quiet and too topical to be noted by later readers.

As several critics have noted, given his advocacy of the free play of the mind about an issue, Arnold was barred both from offering a practical solution or endorsing either side of any of these controversies. Culture had to be seen as a means of suggesting new, and presumably higher, points of view rather than as a means of deciding between already defined positions. Arnold's concept of culture could "float" an idea, but could neither construct a policy nor argue it. If judgments about the fitness of a thing or the best of several alternative courses of action depend on "tact," a developed sense of sweetness and light, and a comparison with carefully chosen touchstones, then not even rhetorical enthymemic argument will be suitable. Any argument attempting to establish the "best" would be swamped in factual detail. The light of Hellenism would lose its clarity amid the murk of practicality. Arnold himself, after suggesting that the Irish endowment might be apportioned among the various churches, adds:

> But the apportionment should be made with due regard to circumstances, taking account only of great differences . . . and of considerable communions. . . . It should overlook petty differences, which have no serious reason for lasting, and inconsiderable communions, which can hardly be taken to express any broad and necessary religious lineaments of our common nature. (p. 193)

The amount of analysis necessary to make such distinctions, the amount of argument necessary to support them, and the difficulty of stating them statutorily is daunting. Or, if one wishes not merely to point as does Arnold to the high birth rate among the poor, but to propose remedies, one would have to consider the technicalities of developing an economic program that would replace the great incentive for having many children: the hope of receiving support from at least some of them in old age. More vexed yet is the question of the control of birth itself: what methods should one advocate, especially at a time when the effectiveness of various modes of contraception was moot and the immorality of contraception generally assumed. One can imagine Bradlaugh entering such an arena (he in fact did), but hardly Arnold. For all his willingness to do battle, Arnold had to keep his distance from practice.

Nevertheless, twentieth-century readers who allow their minds to play freely about the historical context will discover that Arnold was no mere trimmer, but just what he called himself, a "Liberal of the Future."[21] His strategies in *Culture and Anarchy* imply goals that he evidently did not yet think it useful to state directly, but if his strategies were conservative, his goals were radical enough. His "floatings" are particularly subversive of orthodox religious beliefs, whether of church or chapel; *God and the Bible* and *St. Paul and Protestantism* are both here latent. His entire discussion of the disestablishment of the Irish Church implies that doctrines are less important than the fact of worship. Indeed, Arnold's belief that the greater grace and beauty of Anglican worship gives it an advantage (however biased his assessment may be) was an argument against the importance of dogma and speculative theology. *Culture and Anarchy* proclaims religious liberalism with a vengeance. Arnold's comments on marriage with a deceased wife's sister in effect deny that the Bible is to be read literally, and deny specific inspiration. The especially caustic attack on those who applaud the "swarming" of men and women challenges the orthodox view of the benevolent harmony of the natural forces set in motion by God's design. Though he urges no direct assault on the wealth and privilege of the Barbarian class, his metamorphosis of the issues in the Real Estate Intestacy Bill leaves no doubt that in the long view Arnold was a socioeconomic leveler.

In such matters Arnold's prophetic position has been vindicated. His views of the place of dogma, of a poetic approach to the Bible, of the necessity of controlling population growth, and of the necessity of reducing the wealth and power of the aristocracy are those toward which the world has for good or ill been marching.

In one of the earliest of the manifestos of "The New Historicism" Stephen Greenblatt distinguishes that theoretical/critical/political movement from "the dominant historical scholarship of the past and the formalist criticism that partially displaced this scholarship in the decades after World War Two." The first, we are told, "is concerned with discovering a single political vision, usually identical to that said to be held by the entire literate class or indeed the entire population."[22] The favorite example among New Historicists is Tillyard's *The Elizabethan World Picture.* In contrast, the New Historicism (generally drawing on Marxist assumptions) investigates the conflicts between political forces or ideologies at the time the text was written and/or between those of readers at different historical moments.

Perceptive as such analyses may be, Greenblatt's is a programmatically reductive model, one that excludes, among many other useful literary-critical approaches, quite another "old historicism": the investigation not of a "single political vision," but of the complexly shared context of cultural knowledge assumed by both author and reader. This has been so obvious an activity for centuries that it has had no separate name; it has simply been part of "scholarship." Its object is to discover the shared background of knowledge and beliefs on the basis of which authors constructed and readers interpreted literary texts, but until the recent work of discourse analysts and speech-act theorists there has been no framework through which to give it theoretical justification. One finds with surprise that such old-fashioned historical research, though assumed by the authors of the standard work on literary theory of the 1940s and 1950s, falls between the central "intrinsic" and "extrinsic" classifications of Wellek and Warren's *Theory of Literature* as completely as it falls between Greenblatt's categories. One might call this kind of "historicism" or historical scholarship "contextualism" if that term were not already going the way of "historicism" and becoming identified with Marxist criticism.[23] Perhaps Jauss's term "horizon of expectation" comes closest to describing the object of such study, so long as it is evident that the original horizon, the context of knowledge and belief in which an author understood himself to be writing, is privileged insofar as the author's intended meaning is the reader's object. In an attempt to find an alternative word I have elsewhere called the emphasis on the elucidation of the contexts shared by author and anticipated reader "ecological."[24] I have not intended here to defend the assumptions of this very traditional kind of literary commentary, but rather to practice openly what has always been the major effort of literary historicism (as opposed to literary history): the preservation of the role and place of the author in his own time alongside the significances that preoccupy a later period.[25]

Notes

[1] "Context" has a wide range of meanings; by "interpretive context" I mean the knowledge and attitudes the author could assume the anticipated audience shared and would use in interpreting the text. An example of "context" used quite differently is the excellent essay by Lawrence Poston titled "Millites and Millenarians: The Context of Carlyle's 'Signs of the Times'" (*Victorian Studies,* 26 [1983], 381-406). The contexts Poston is interested in are primarily the relation between Carlyle's earlier and later works, and between his particular interests at the time of writing and the books "reviewed" in the essay.

2 William Savage Johnson, *Thomas Carlyle: A Study of His Literary Apprenticeship, 1814-1831* (New Haven: Yale Univ. Press, 1911), p. 85.

3 Johnson, pp. 85-86; Ralli, *Guide to Carlyle,* 2 vols. (London: Allen Unwin, 1920), 1:88-90; Neff, *Carlyle* (London: Allen and Unwin, 1932), pp. 105-6; Symons, *Thomas Carlyle: The Life and Ideas of a Prophet* (New York: Oxford Univ. Press, 1952), p. 125; Albert J. LaValley, *Carlyle and the Idea of the Modern: Studies in Carlyle's Prophetic Literature and Its Relation to Blake, Nietzsche, Marx, and Others* (New Haven: Yale Univ. Press, 1968), pp. 60-62.

4 Carlyle, "Signs of the Times," in *Critical and Miscellaneous Essays, Volume II,* vol. 27 of *The Works of Thomas Carlyle,* ed. H. D. Traill, Centenary Edition (London: Chapman and Hall, 1896-99), p. 59. Parenthetical citations in the text are to this volume. The essay was originally published in the *Edinburgh Review* in June 1829.

5 See James Anthony Froude, *Thomas Carlyle: A History of the First Forty Years of His Life, 1795-1835,* 2 vols. (London: Longmans, Green, 1903), 2:59.

6 Froude, 2:77.

7 See Froude, 2:59.

8 In the interest of convenience, I have included parenthetical volume and page numbers in the text for quotations from periodical articles. Full bibliographical information for the contemporary periodical articles mentioned in the text will be found in the list in the final footnote. I have relied on Walter Houghton's now-too-often-taken-for-granted *Wellesley Index of Victorian Periodicals* for identification of authors.

9 Robert Southey, *Sir Thomas More: Or, Colloquies on the Progress and Prospects of Society,* 2 vols. (London: John Murray, 1829), 1:30-31.

10 *Colloquies,* 1:18.

11 George C. Brodrick, *The History of England From Addington's Administration to the Close of William IV's Reign (1801-1837),* Completed and Revised by J. K. Fotheringham (London: Longmans, Green, 1928), p. 237 (Volume 11 of *The Political History of England,* ed. William Hunt and Reginald L. Poole).

12 A glance at the order of the above responses reminds us to be wary of the putative dates of journal issues: the *Westminster*'s rejoinder in its July issue was answered by Macaulay in the *June* issue of the *Edinburgh,* which, if we can trust the 5 August date of Carlyle's diary entry recording completion of "Signs of the Times," could not have appeared before the middle of August. In any case, Carlyle's review article appeared in the same issue with Macaulay's rejoinder to the *Westminster*'s first response, so that the debate was well under way by that time.

13 The subject is indeed worthy of study, writes Stevenson, but he proposes to show that "Ricardo, Malthus, &c. have perplexed the subject, and exposed it to unmerited prejudice . . . and that Political Economy has been little, if at all, advanced by them, beyond the confessedly imperfect state in which it was left by Adam Smith" (15:526).

14 Irving's beliefs would have been widely known even by those who had not seen *The Last Days,* his reputation as a preacher having quickly spread from the time of his 1822 arrival in London as minister of a Hatton Garden church. By 1829 his fixed belief was being vigorously promulgated. Given Carlyle's long-standing but increasingly strained friendship with Irving, inclusion of Irving's book among those he was "reviewing," as well as his abstention from actual comment on it, have interesting biographical implications, but this is a matter outside the meanings intended for his general audience.

15 Lord Forbes (Horace Courtenay Gammel, Twentieth Baron Forbes), *Marriage with a Deceased Wife's Sister. An Address Delivered to a Meeting of Scottish Churchmen in Edinburgh . . . November 28, 1882* (Aberdeen: A. Brown & Co., 1883).

16 Arnold, *Culture and Anarchy,* vol. 5 of *The Complete Prose Works of Matthew Arnold,* ed. R. H. Super (Ann Arbor: Univ. of Michigan Press, 1960-1977), p. 210. Subsequent parenthetical citations in the text are to this volume.

17 A useful history with somewhat different emphases from the brief summary I give here is Cynthia Fansler Behrman's "The Annual Blister: A Sidelight on Victorian Social and Parliamentary History," *Victorian Studies,* 11 (1968), 483-502.

18 25 Henry VIII, Cap. 22.

19 *Marriage with a Deceased Wife's Sister: Letters in Favour of A Repeal of the Law which Prohibits Marriage with the Sister of a Deceased Wife;* by The Rev. W. W. Champneys, The Rev. Thos Dale, The Rev. J. H. Gurney, The Hon. and Rev. H. Montagu Villiers, and The Rev. Walter Farquhar Hook, D. D. To which Is Added the Form of a Petition Signed by Many Hundreds of the Parochial Clergy (London: Seeley's, 1849).

20 Knox Little, in *Report of the Proceedings of a Meeting in Opposition to the Deceased Wife's Sister's Bill,* held in Freeman's Hall, Lincoln's Inn Fields, June 7, 1883, pp. 27-28 (London: The Church Printing Co., 1883).

21 Arnold, "The Future of Liberalism," in *English Lit-

erature and Irish Politics, vol. 9 of *The Complete Prose Works of Matthew Arnold,* p. 138. Originally published in the *Nineteenth Century,* July 1880.

[22] Introduction, *The Power of Forms in the English Renaissance,* edited and with an Introduction by Stephen Greenblatt (Norman, Okla.: Pilgrim Books, 1982), p. 5.

[23] For instance, it is so used by Howard Felperin in *Beyond Deconstruction: The Uses and Abuses of Literary Theory* (Oxford: Clarendon Press, 1985), pp. 16-17.

[24] See my *Interpretive Acts: In Search of Meaning* (Oxford: Clarendon Press, 1988).

[25] Following are the relevant articles contemporary with "Signs of the Times":

BLACKWOOD'S

William Stevenson, "The Political Economist," 15 (May, 1824), 522-31; 15 (June, 1824), 643-55; 16 (July, 1824), 34-45; 16 (August, 1824), 202-14; 17 (February, 1825), 207-20.

William Johnstone, "The Rise and Fall of the Liberals," 24 (July, 1828), 96-101.

David Robinson, "The Assembling of Parliament," 25 (March, 1829), 271-87.

———, "Political Economy, No. 1: To the Heads of the University of Oxford," 26 (September, 1829), 510-23.

———, "The Condition of the Empire," 26 (July, 1829), 97-119.

William Johnstone, "The State and Prospects of the Country," 26 (September, 1829), 464-73.

Samuel O'Sullivan, "*Colloquies on the Progress and Prospects of Society,* by Robert Southey," 26 (October, 1829), 611-30.

THE EDINBURGH REVIEW

Richard Whately, "Oxford Lectures on Political Economy," 48 (September, 1828), 170-84.

Thomas Babington Macaulay, "Utilitarian Logic and Politics," 49 (March, 1829), 159-89.

———, "Bentham's Defence of Mill: Utilitarian System of Philosophy," 49 (June, 1829), 273-99.

———, "Southey's *Colloquies on Society,*" 50 (January, 1830), 528-65.

———, "Utilitarian Theory of Government, and the 'Great-

est Happiness Principle,'" 50 (October, 1829), 99-125.

THE NEW MONTHLY MAGAZINE

T. C. Morgan, "Opinions for 1829," 25 (January, 1829), 1-9.

"The Present Times, with Remarks on a Late Article in the *Quarterly,*" 25 (June, 1829), 573-821.

THE QUARTERLY REVIEW

"Southey's State and Prospects of the Country," 39 (April, 1829), 475-520.

J. J. Blunt, "*Colloquies on the Progress and Prospects of Society,* by Robert Southey," 41 (July, 1829), 1-27.

THE WESTMINSTER REVIEW

"An Introductory Lecture on *Political Economy*" (review), 8 (July, 1827), 177-89.

T. P. Thompson, "The Catholic Question," 10 (January, 1829), 1-36.

——— (with Jeremy Bentham), "Greatest Happiness Principle," 11 (July, 1829), 254-68.

"Dr. Southey's *Sir Thomas More,*" 11 (July, 1829), 193-211.

"Letter to the Heads of the University of Oxford By One of the Old School" 11 (October, 1829), 510-14.

T. P. Thompson, "The *Edinburgh Review* and the 'Greatest Happiness Principle,'" 11 (October, 1829), 526-36.

Michael Cotsell (essay date 1990)

SOURCE: "Carlyle, Travel, and the Enlargements of History," in *Creditable Warriors, Vol. 3, 1830-1876,* edited by Michael Cotsell, The Ashfield Press, 1990, pp. 83-96.

[*In the following essay, Cotsell investigates the impact of Carlyle's travels upon his writing and concludes that Carlyle's "sense of the world, as it reveals itself in his travel and other writings," is larger than the "single vision of imperial rule" which he applauds and advocates in much of his writing.*]

It is indeed an "extensive Volume", of boundless, almost formless contents, a very Sea of Thought; neither calm nor clear, if you will; yet wherein the toughest pearl-diver may dive to his utmost depth, and return not only with sea-wreck but with true orients. (*Sartor Resartus* 10; bk. 1, ch. 2)

Sartor Resartus (1833-34) humorously enacts Thomas Carlyle's imaginative relation to England: an incomprehensible and fragmentary German philosophy and life delivered, by "the kindness of a Scottish Hamburg Merchant, whose name, known to the whole mercantile world, he must not mention" (74; bk. 1, ch. 22), to a confused English editor who has the task of getting the thing into some sort of order for the English reader. Carlyle, of course, had not traveled to Germany, preferring at the time to keep it a "country of the mind." Travel, though, is a major part of Teufelsdröckh's experience. His sorrows become his travels, "a perambulation and circumambulation of the terraqueous Globe" (47; bk. 2, ch. 6), beginning with an evocation of mountain grandeur, though, typically, Carlyle disabuses his hero of a taste for the picturesque, that "epidemic, now endemical, of View-hunting" (151; bk. 2, ch. 6). Teufelsdröckh becomes a wanderer seeking to escape from his own shadow, and in that Byronic, but his wanderings provide the dimension of his experience:

> My breakfast of tea has been cooked by a Tartar woman, with water of the Amur, who wiped her earthen kettle with a horse-tail. I have roasted wild-eggs in the sand of Sahara; I have awakened in Paris *Estrapades* and Vienna *Malzleins,* with no prospect of breakfast beyond elemental liquid. (155-56; bk. 2, ch. 6)

The "bewildered Wanderer," interrogating the world for meaning, traverses it to its Mediterranean origins: the "Sybil-cave of Destiny," a "grim Desert" with "no Pillar of Cloud by day, and no Pillar of Fire by Night" (161; bk. 2, ch. 7). After his experience in the Rue Saint-Thomas de l'Enfer, Teufelsdröckh continues his "Pilgrimings" in a different spirit, open to the world, rather than demanding of it. He now concerns himself with the varieties of human activity that travel reveals, the building of cities, battlefields, "great Scenes"—the "Palm-trees of Tadmor," the "ruins of Babylon," the "great Wall of China"—and "Great Events"—"the World well won, and the World well lost," and the "birth-pangs of Democracy." He attends Schiller and Goethe at Jena, meets Nepoleon and compares him to an American backwoodsman, and encounters a Russian smuggler at midnight in "Arctic latitudes" (176-77; bk. 2, ch. 8). At the work's end he is inspired by the July Revolution of 1830 in Paris—*"Es ghet an"* (It is beginning) (296; bk. 3, ch. 12)—though he may be in London. Travel is an essential of the narrative mode of *Sartor Resartus.* It also informs the work's thought: the philosophy of clothes depends on the estrangement of the traveler's eye, and the vision of "Natural Supernaturalism" is filled with the wonderous reports of scientific travelers: "The Ocean Tides and periodic currents, the Trade winds, and Monsoons"; "the *infernal* boiling-up of the Nether Chaotic Deep"; "the Giddy Alpine heights of Science" (258, 266; bk. 3, ch. 8).[1]

The form of *Sartor Resartus* suggests something about the relations of Carlyle's imagination to the England he wished to influence. He sought to defamiliarize English society, to reveal its spiritual lineaments, and to expand and mobilize its thought and energies. He also strove to present history to the English as though contemporary England was poised at a crisis, and contemporary England refused to be that. His imagination was filled with images of men of great faith wrestling with societies in the making, with fierce militarists and violent revolution—with, in fact, history that is not English. Even the great undeniable fact of poverty did not stir the English system as it stirred him. English history never quite rises to the scenario Carlyle demands. In the end this gap, which gradually widened through his career, produced in him a fury and, as regards England, a corresponding unreality.

It is as though England could never fulfill the imaginative demand of this intensely earnest Scot, and, correspondingly, as though Carlyle could never finally *imagine England* as he wished. Perhaps the most significant instance of this is his failure to activate his project of a major work on Cromwell, to tell the heroic English story that, in his view, most closely matched the great events of modern European times. It was partly a matter of historical distance, partly also a sense of the tedium of tracing complicated constitutional issues. At any rate, it is Cromwell abroad, terrorizing Ireland, who most comes to life in Carlyle's imagination. Indeed, Carlyle may be said to imaginatively circle English history, seeking to inspire it to a sense of crisis and potential grandeur. His imaginative bearing is very often from abroad. He is the great interpreter of Germany, the historian of the French Revolution. His home in Chelsea was habituated by European dissidents of one order or another—Mazzini and his followers, Alexis de Rio, Cavaignac, Duffy and other Young Irelanders—whatever he thought of them. In 1849, at the time of the Irish famine, he wrote:

> Ireland really *is* my problem; the breaking point of the huge suppuration which all British and all European society now is. Set down in Ireland, one might at least feel, *"Here* is thy problem: In God's name what wilt thou do with it?"[2]

No English writer of the period felt like that about Ireland. Even Carlyle's linking of "all British and all European society" in a common problem is uncharacteristic of English political thought.

It is not surprising, then, either that Carlyle traveled, or that his travels had important consequences for his writings. Admittedly, he was a reluctant and unhappy traveler and he mistrusted the cult of tourism—seeking after the picturesque, dawdling around art galleries. Nor was he, by Victorian standards, a great traveler, though he thought of going further than he went; he did not see the Alps or visit Italy (and then he only crossed the border) until very late in life. But, after the early and brief visit to Paris made in 1824, Carlyle wrote extended accounts of four of the seven further visits he was to make abroad (the exceptions are his first brief visit to Ireland in 1846, his similarly brief trip to Germany in 1852, and the Italian trip, which are reported in letters). Composed directly on his return with an evident imaginative fluency, each of these accounts has a distinct mood and theme, and three of them inform to an important degree a subsequent major work.

Carlyle's vivid impressionistic mode of seeing is evident in his letters from Paris in 1824. He seeks for images of a state of society; he eliminates causation other than in moral terms. The result is an impression at once perceptive and prejudiced, penetrating and idiosyncratic; a sharp confrontation between the will to significance and the immediate facts. This gives the travel writings their literary quality; if they are insufficient as historical analysis, they become history: testaments of a man alive in his times. In Paris, Carlyle juxtaposes details of the life of the city so as to provide a moral commentary on the state of society:

> Their shops and houses are like toyboxes; every apartment is tricked out with mirrors and expanded into infinitude by their illusion. . . . The people's character seems like their shops and faces; gilding and rouge without; hollowness and rottenness within. . . . Oh the hateful contrast between physical perfection and moral nothingness! Between this extreme of luxury and the extreme of wretchedness unrelieved by hope or principle! Yesterday I walked along the *Pont Neuf;* jugglers and quacks and cooks and barbers and dandies and gulls and sharpers were racketting away with a deafening hum at their manifold pursuits; I turned aside into a small mansion with the name of *Morgue* upon it; there lay the naked body of an old grey-headed artisan whom misery had driven to drown himself in the river! His face wore the grim fixed scowl of despair; his lean horny hands with their long ragged nails were lying by his sides; his patched and soiled apparel with his apron and *sabots* were hanging at his head; and there lay fixed in his iron slumber, heedless of the vain din that rolled around him on every side, was this poor outcast stretched in silence and darkness forever.[3]

Although it would be exaggerated to read this as the germ of the early chapters of *The French Revolution* (1837), it would seem equally unlikely that this personal experience failed to provide some stimulus to Carlyle's subsequent studies.

A more substantial claim can be made for the first of his extended travel writings, his **"Notes of a Three-Days' Tour to the Netherlands"** of 1842. Again, it is a sense of a society that Carlyle establishes, though a very different society. All travelers, of course, remark on the societies they encounter, and contrast them with their own. But certain Victorian writers, acutely conscious of their own society as a precarious organization, in a way that previous generations were not, sought for and found in foreign scenes images of a society that had a quality of life and spirituality absent from contemporary England.

Carlyle's **"Three-Days' Tour"** is a concentrated and unified piece, which, from the moment of parting company with the motley assemblage of English travelers on the down-river steamer and the dubious vivacities of the ballroom at Margate, continuously celebrates images of right society, right ways of life: the neat little cutter, the *Vigilant,* a "model; clean all as a lady's work box" (498); the admirable crew and "little Captain" (501); clean, orderly, and Protestant Ostend. At the center of the experience, though, are the cities of Bruges and Ghent, which for Carlyle provide images of the continuity of civic order and efficiency:

> This city of the "Bridges", with its winding streets, its broad marketplaces, its fantastic edifices secular and religious very strange to a modern eye. Honour to the long-forgotten generations; they have done *something* in their time: this city, nay this country is a work of theirs. Sand downs and stagnating marshes, producing nothing but heath, but sedges, docks, marsh-mallows, and miasmata: so it lay by nature; but the industry of man, the assiduous, unwearied motion of how many spades, pickaxes, hammers, wheelbarrows, mason-trowels, and ten-thousandfold industrial tools have made it—this! A thing that will grow corn, potherbs, warehouses, Rubens Pictures, churches and cathedrals. Long before Caesar's time of swords, the era of *spades* had ushered itself in, and was busy. "Tools and the man!" "Arms and the man" is but a small song in comparison. (506)

It is the churches that at once draw and challenge Carlyle, not only because of their architectural grandeur, but because they represent both the civic spirit and a traditional Catholicism alive in the present day:

> few things that I have seen were more impressive. Enormous high arched roofs (I suppose not higher than Westminster Abbey, but far more striking to me, for they are actually in *use* here), soaring to a height that dwarfed all else; great high altar-pieces with sculpture, wooden-carvings hanging in mid-air; pillars, balustrades of white marble, edged with black marble . . . above all, actual human creatures bent in devotion there . . . it struck me dumb.(509-10)

The sight of the past and present of Catholic devotion produces in Carlyle a painful oscillation. "You could not say," he believes, that the worshippers "were without devotion," but he feels for their "fat priests" a "kind of hatred." Yet this reaction is checked: "Things are long-lived, and God above appoints their term"; and checked again by the reflection that, "At bottom, one cannot *wish* these men kicked into the canals; for what would follow were they gone? Atheistic Benthamism, French editorial 'Rights of man' and *grande nation,* that is a far worse thing, a far *untruer* thing." (510).

Proceeding to Ghent, Carlyle again develops the sense of living order:

> a good leaden gutter ran round the eaves, our window-rabbets were of white polished stone, all was right and tight, and, in its exotic shape and arrangement, yet perfection of result, a kind of pleasure to contemplate. (629)

Missing his rendezvous with his companions, he is freed to his own response: "I wandered at my own sweet will" (631). It is an unusually open and happy moment in Carlyle's writing. Once again it is a Catholic church that impresses most. Carlyle is led to appreciate that civic values and religious devotion were linked for the church builders; modern times, by comparison, seem devoid of adequate belief. It is a moment which is self-confessedly significant for him:

> An ancient pious burgherhood, looking ever into Eternity out of their busy Time-element, has left here a touching proof of its wealth, devoutness, generous liberality, and *taste*. . . . Good merchant burghers of Ghent—ah me, what a brutal heathenism are our Railway Terminuses, Pantechnicons, Show-bazaars in comparison: *good* so far as they go; yes,—but going no farther than the *beaver* principle in man will carry him; as if man had no *soul* at all, but only a work-faculty. . . . Such thoughts crowded on me in all these places; and their architectural twirls and fantasticalities, steeples like giant pepperboxes, like slated unicorns' horns, three hundred feet in height,—like slated Mandarins, with slate umbrellas, like what slate and stone absurdity you will, were full of beauty and meaning to me.—(632-33)

The playfully fantastic imagery at the conclusion of this passage recognizes that the imagination has been provoked to activity.

There are points of criticism and discontent in what follows, but the concluding paragraph of the piece emphasizes its nature as a vision of social alternative:

> Thus had kind destiny projected us rocket-wise for a little space into the clear blue of Heaven and Freedom: thus again were we swiftly reabsorbed into the great smoky simmering crater, and London's soot volcano had recovered us. (640)

The pitch is forward and hopeful, and the phrase "Heaven and Freedom" suggests the clear vision of a potential modern spirituality.

The place of the **"Three-Days' Tour"** in the compositional history of Carlyle's works at this time is indicated by Jane Carlyle's first unenthusiastic response to it: "Is it not a mere *evading of your destiny* to write

Tours just now! with that unlaid and unlayable ghost of Cromwell beckoning you on!" The Cromwell was faltering. In midsummer of 1842 Carlyle had indeed been thinking of abandoning the task. He traveled to the Netherlands early in August and wrote up the **"Three Days' Tour"** between 12 and 16 August. By August 20 he was again "writing, writing"; according to his recent biographer, Fred Kaplan, it may have been the Cromwell or the beginning of something on the "'condition of England.'"[4] Then in the first week of September, he took horse and made a brief Cromwellian tour, which is doubtless the source of the tourist-like opening of *Past and Present.* By November he had begun writing *Past and Present.* It is thus likely that the tour to the Lowlands played some part in freeing and engaging Carlyle's imagination in a way that the Cromwell project was failing to do. It helped him toward a vision of a Catholic past that was not mere superstition, but which expressed a combination of human enterprise and devoutness that might presage what a future could be. Ghent and Bruges challenged him to look at Europe's past through other than narrow Protestant or even puritan eyes; and to see that the spirit he sought to activate might have inhabited medieval and Catholic Europe. As well, the two cities provided an image of that past alive in the present; the geographical coexistence of that world with modern Britain parallels Carlyle's dramatic juxtaposition of past and present in his great work. It may be that this journey enabled Carlyle's imagination to make this leap. Through travel, he learned to overcome both the distance and the determinations of history. Travel restored his imagination and enabled him to envisage a form in which the imagination restores history.

Carlyle did not travel abroad again until his brief trip to Ireland in 1846, which was connected with the Cromwell project. He had become acquainted with Gavan Duffy and others of the Young Irelanders, and though he could not share their political views, he was, in a measure, sympathetic to the spirit of their enterprise. It was through this connection that he came to visit Ireland again, for a longer visit, in 1849, and to write his longest travel work, *Reminiscences of My Irish Journey in 1849.*

Carlyle's *Irish Journey* is almost totally opposed in spirit to the **"Three-Days' Tour"**: it is a work of hopelessness and anger, envisioning not the promise of society but its complete and desperate failure. The difference between the two works is evident even in a comparison of the two accounts of passage. Instead of the bright images of human capability of the passage to Ostend, the passage in the *Irish Journey* is a kind of horror of desolation. There is an upright ex-sergeant on board, and a "good old Captain," but far more striking is the "lean, angry misguided, entirely worthless looking creature" (15) who quarrels with his captain, gets drunk, and then is lost overboard: "I was struck in general with the air of faculty *misbred,* and gone to waste" (17). Two Irish women, genteel poor, "*mis*venturous," have given up their plan to emigrate to Australia and are "cowering back to Ennis in Clare" (21). There is a sick and paralyzed man on deck.

If the human spirit seems lonely, weak, and defeated, the seascape emphasizes the hopelessness. The coastline provides a desolate geology lesson. "After Wight, Needles &c. (terribly worn, almost dilapidated and ruinous-ugly looking)" (14); the rocks at the Lizzard have "a haggard skeleton character, worn haggard by the wild sea" (28); "sheer and black. . . . angry skeleton rocks in these ever-vexed waters" (29); "like the ruins of a Cathedral" (28); "no motion that was not of the *chaotic* powers" (32). The coast speaks the hostility of nature and the failure of the human dream.

Ireland appears to lowered spirits flat, "rather *bleared*," "feeblish," "out of repair" (35); a "state of ineffectuality," the "afternoon sinking lower," the "genius of vacancy alone possessing it" (36-37). Carlyle is set down in Dublin "in wind and dust, myself a mass of dust and inflamatory ruin" (38). Then, as the account of Ireland proceeds, Carlyle develops the notion of the country's malformation, ill-condition, even idiocy. Kilkenny is an "idle old city; can't well think how they live" (85), Youghal a "dingy town," the houses "dim, half dilapidated," the population "dingy semi-savage" (110-11). Of the countryside around Killarney he remarks:

> Ragged wet hedges, weedy ditches; nasty ragged, spongy-looking flat country hereabouts;—like a *drunk* country fallen down to sleep amid the mud. (135)

There is a sense of Irish life as moronic, deceitful, slovenly.

The Irish landscape, far from being romantically beautiful or stirring, is similarly lowering. A day's outing at Killarney is devoted to the "picturesque," but "*something* of dilapidation, beggary, human fatuity in one or other form, is painfully visible in nearly all" (139). The best that can be said is that there is "a wild beauty looking thro' the squalor of one's thoughts" (140). Carlyle finds nothing attractive about the Irish boglands: "all this region, by nature, execrable, drowned bog" (177). The best efforts Carlyle comes across, those of the benevolent landlord Lord George Hamilton, are insufficient: "'improvements' all are swallowed in the chaos, chaos remains chaotic still" (240). Faced with a "*continent* of haggard crag-and-heather desolation" (241), Carlyle expresses a crisis in confident Victorian improvement.

The Irish landscape bespeaks the failure of man's works and also of his faith. In marked contrast to his experience of Bruges and Ghent, Carlyle now finds the ruins of religious buildings: it is as though the idea of *Past and Present* is cancelled out. At Howth, there is the "big old Abbey over-grown with thistles, nettles, burdocks and the

extremity of squalor" (65); at Kildare, the "old ruin of cathedral . . . poor enough" (69). The early monastic buildings at Glendalough are to him only a "wreck of *grey* antiquity grown *black*" (73).

The problem is, of course, the famine, and the appalling poverty of the Irish peasantry. Carlyle provides in this work some of the most terrible images of poverty in mid-nineteenth-century literature. Kildare is "a harpy-swarm of clamorous mendicants, men, women, children:—a village *winged,* as if a flight of harpies had alighted in it" (70). At Glendalough, "never saw such begging in this world; often get into a rage at it" (76). There he comes across a

> scarecrow boatman, his clothes or rags hung on him like *tapestry,* when the wind blew he expanded like a tulip: *first* of many such conditions of dress. (77)

At Killarney, "beggars, storming round you, like ravenous dogs round carrion; this is Killarney. Swift, O swift, into the car for 'Roche's', for anybody's; and let us off!" (130). As the reaction there suggests, Carlyle is brought to the point where "human *pity* dies away into stony misery and disgust" (137).

In fact, Carlyle escapes the misery by a fury which gives the work a monotony of ugly denouncement. The same qualities of fury and disgust are evident in the writings that immediately follow the *Irish Journey.* Some of the heatedness of the infamous **"The Nigger Question"** (1849) derives from the inflamed contrast between "Blacks sitting there up to the ears in pumpkins, and doleful Whites sitting here without potatoes to eat." Similarly, some of the ferocity of the *Latter-Day Pamphlets* (1850) may also be attributed to the Irish experience: it is noticeable that the imagery of dung-heaps and human swinery in *Latter-Day Pamphlets* runs through the travel work: the famine workhouses had in Carlyle's view reduced the Irish to "swine's *destiny.*" It is an image at the point of the failure of both pity and analysis.

The *Latter-Day Pamphlets* was Carlyle's last extended work on the state of contemporary society. By the time he made his next trip abroad he was already contemplating a life of Frederick the Great. He had begun to imaginatively distance himself from the society of his day, and his *Excursion (Futile Enough) to Paris; Autumn 1851* is the only one of his travel writings to bear no relation to a major work. Travel now provides metaphors for the flow of events: "How we come and go in this world!" (150). Carlyle puts himself in the hands of his fellow travelers (the Brownings), representatives of a younger generation. Lack of involvement is the note: "France there and no mistake. If France were of much moment to me!" (155). Everywhere he sees change— "Rue de Rivoli had been mainly built since my former visit"—and the change is uninteresting: "Streets straight as a *line* have long ceased to seem the beautifullest to me" (166). The Place de la Revolution is "*altogether* altered," with "big *gilt* columns, big fountain (its Nereids all silent)" (166-67); the Louvre is "getting itself new-faced" (167). He goes with companions to see a balloon ascent from the Champ de Mars, which is "terribly sunk now; instead of 'thirty feet' hardly eight or ten, without grass" (174). The aging historian of the Revolution sees in busy modern Paris an indifference to what were the milestones of history.

Modern society goes on modernizing and accumulating goods, evidence for Carlyle's conclusion that the future may well belong to those with a "*sincerity* of greed and eagerness" (180). Such people seem to him more real than the politician play-actors or literary men, some of whom are dismissively sketched. Perhaps the most striking passage in the work is Carlyle's description of a bad night's sleep—"The history of the day was done; but upstairs, in my naked noisy room, began a history of the night":

> thoughts enough, looking over the Tuileries garden there, and the gleam of Paris city during the night watches. I could have laughed at myself, but indeed was more disposed to cry. Very strange: I looked down on armed patrols stealthily scouring the streets, saw the gleam of their arms; saw sentries with their lanterns inside the garden; felt as if I could have leapt down among them—preferred turning in again to my disconsolate truckle bed. (164-65)

In this intimation of the coup d'état, it is as though despair leads to the impulse to give up his spirit to the rats in the nightmare alleys of history. The future belongs to them and to the sincerely greedy and eager.

Carlyle's next two journeys abroad were to Germany. The first, made at the end of August 1852, is reported only in letters, the second in his travel journal, *Journey to Germany Autumn 1858.* He was engaged on a great work, an epic of German history; he was visiting the country which had seemed to him to most adequately speak to modern times. The reader might, then, expect an account of a concentrated experience. Instead the work is diffuse and grumblingly good-humored, and there is, oddly, more attention to the picturesque than in any of his other travel writings. Surprisingly, it is the most urbane of those writings. Indeed, the *Journey to Germany* can be seen as a kind of comedy in which the imperative to make history declare meaning is relaxed, and, instead, its diversity is accepted, as though Carlyle were resigned to the passing of the heroic age which he had urged upon his own times.

In prosperous central Germany, Carlyle found a flatland that interested him and presented him with images of intermixed natural beauty and relaxed historical continuity. One of the most striking images he offers is a description of a country house so homely and functional that it reminds him of ancient ways of life:

> Aspect of the House and Establishment was curiously *medieval* to me, brought Ulysees and *his* to mind: mongrel between palace and farmhouse; irregularity, dust and neglect combining with a look of sufficiency and even opulence. (23)

Suggestions of the heroic and medieval ages are combined within a picturesque present that charms by its diversity and by the sense of a mixture of labor and calmness. Things all come together right in such an image: the mind is relieved from the burdens of concern, the demands of history, and expands into a more curious and relaxed appreciation.

This is not without a sense of loss, but the sense of loss is somehow uninsistent and poses no crisis. Carlyle's own imaginative task on this journey can be compared to that of the raiser of monuments, architectures which challenge the complacency of the present, but which can rapidly become mundane. Two such images, which recall the experiences of the 1852 journey, presage this fate. At Prag:

> In a Barber's shop, corner of the *Markt* and big street near hand to our right, are two Blocks with elaborate shining wigs on them, newest fashion: one is an ideal Block of the usual fashion; the other is, recognisably at once,—the Head of Goethe! Such a form of "fame" I had never fallen in with before. (85)

Similarly, a curious comparison to the advocate of Goethe and the author of *Frederick* can be developed from his account of the "monument" of the pamphleteer Fuchs:

> poor old Fuchs he had set his heart on a monument to Mollwitz Battle, and could not get the people to subscribe freely; wrote that distracted Pamphlet, still little subscribing; quarried and hewed and carted hither, at his own expense, from Strehlen Quarries, a big granite Obelisk with proper inscription, built a stone and mortar basis for it and small artificial height; had not cash for the requisite *pulley*—machinery;—assembled all the people to "inaugurate," and bring Obelisk and basis together; discoursed with unction, eloquent rigmarole, amid a crowd of people (perhaps twenty or 30 years ago); and there the Obelisk still lies; cattle have scratched away the masonry a good deal, and poor old Fuchs is dead, leaving a grin of mockery in his fellow-creatures. (64)

A similar feeling is developed in the accounts of the difficulty of finding people who can identify or recognize the features of the scenes of Frederick's battles. Often the locals are vague or useless. People would like to be helpful but are not; views, usually attempted from church steeples, are obtained with difficulty. It is, Carlyle observes, a "rare case" when he ends up seeing what another points out; only a "young gentleman" (63) at Mollwitz and an "intelligent" village schoolmaster (99), who yet cannot read the Latin epitaph on the monument to Marshall Keith, are helpful. He learns that the bones of seven hundred men killed in the churchyard of the latter's village were only discovered "in founding a new cattle-house for our Schoolmaster" (98). Such passages communicate a sense of human relationship neither spiritually and socially integrated, as was imagined in the **"Three Days' Tour,"** nor tragically and miserably separate as in the *Irish Journal.* There is much friendliness and cooperation, but also distance, forgetfulness, indifference, and incomprehension.

It is not so much as heroic scenes, but as theaters of earnest futility, that Frederick's battlefields appear, though even that description is too poignant, for the landscape, at once banal and beautiful, repeatedly distracts the eye from the contemplation of the past. The scenes are pleasantly unevocative: Zorndoff is "a littery but substantial clay village," the "impassable bogs'" of the battle "hard meadow now" (150); another site is "a wide nearly level region, growing lupins, potatoes, scraggy grass, much fir-wood round it" (57); at another, the "'six hills'" of the battle are "trifling swells in the ground" (75). At the beginning of the work, Carlyle complains about being dragged about sightseeing, "the Picturesque all to do" (32). But, despite his complaints, he is genuinely struck by the view at the Stubbenkammer: "a sheer white precipice, sharp-edged [,] hard [,] plunges down 400 feet or so,—awful to look upon;—and lifting your head there is nothing but the shipless immensity of Baltic lying eastward" (38). This distraction from history to the peaceful meaninglessness of the wide natural world is a repeated movement in the work. Germany shows a breadth and continuity of human and natural life that brings a curious quiescence to the urgencies of Carlyle's vision. *Frederick the Great* (1858-65), of course, continued his heroic project, but it is not unaffected by the sense of irony and distraction that the *Journey* displays.

The travel works enable us to reflect on Carlyle as an advocate of expansion and empire. His favorite scenarios of strong men wrestling with undeveloped nature and peoples (see the essay **"Dr. Francia,"** 1843) were very adaptable to imperial purposes, and his influence on advocates of imperialism like Froude and the Kingsleys was as strong as it was on the "socialist" tradition in which Ruskin and Morris figure. An imagery of expansion runs through his works, even when it is not the primary subject as it is in parts of **"Chartism"** (1839) and *Past and Present* (1843). The project of *Sartor Resartus* is characterized in this way:

> How often have we seen some such adventurous . . . wanderer light on some out-lying, neglected, yet vitally-momentous province . . . thereby, in these his seemingly so aimless rambles, planting new standards, finding new habitable colonies. (7; bk. 1, ch. 1)

The frustrated later works can be emphatically imperial, for instance, **"Shooting Niagara"** (1867); in this last attack on the progress toward democracy in Britain he rather ludicrously recommends that the younger sons of the aristocracy each be given a sugar island to bring into order. But Carlyle's sense of the world, as it reveals itself in his travel and other writings, is too large to be accommodated within the single vision of imperial rule. There is an attractive moment in *Past and Present* when, having applauded the epic of British expansion, Carlyle breaks in with a passage beginning, "Or let us give a glance at China." What follows is an urbane and relaxed account of the lucid reasonableness of Chinese religion and society, which concludes with the reflection that:

> These three hundred millions actually make porcelain, souchong tea, with innumerable other things; and fight, under Heaven's flag, against Necessity;—and have fewer Seven-Years Wars, Thirty-Years Wars, French-Revolution Wars, and infernal fightings with each other, than certain millions elsewhere have! (232-33; bk. 3, ch. 15)

A far cry from "Better fifty years of Europe than a cycle of Cathay" (Tennyson, *Locksley Hall*, 1842, 184). Carlyle exceeds his own heroic vision of history, which is to say that he was larger than his will.

Notes

Quotations from the works of Carlyle are from the following editions: *Sartor Resartus,* ed. Charles Frederick Harrold (New York: 1937); *Past and Present* ed. Richard D. Altick (New York: 1977); "The Nigger Question," *Critical and Miscellaneous Essays* Vol. 4, *The Works of Thomas Carlyle,* Centenary Edition, 30 vols (London: 1899); "Notes of a Three-Day's Tour to the Netherlands," ed. Alexander Carlyle, *Cornhill Magazine* 53 (1922): 493-512, 626-40; *Reminiscences of My Irish Journey in 1849,* ed. James Anthony Froude (London: 1882); "Excursion (Futile Enough) to Paris; Autumn 1851: Thrown on Paper, Pen Galloping, From Saturday to Tuesday, October 4-7, 1851," *Last Words* (1892; London: 1971) 149-91; *Journey to Germany Autumn 1858,* ed. R. A. E. Brooks (New Haven: 1940).

[1] As K. J. Fielding has remarked in his "Unpublished Manuscripts I: Carlyle Among the Cannibals" (*Carlyle Newsletter* 1 [1979]: 22-28), "Carlyle was drawn to travel books just because they brought a new revelation about Creation." (23).

[2] Quoted from Carlyle's Journal by Froude, *Irish Journey* v.

[3] *The Collected Letters of Thomas and Jane Welsh Carlyle,* Duke-Edinburgh Edition, ed. C. R. Sanders, K. J. Fielding, Clyde Ryals, et al (Durham, NC: 1970-) 3.178-83.

⁴ See Fred Kaplan, *Thomas Carlyle: A Biography* (Ithaca, NY: 1983) 293; and *Collected Letters* 15.32.

Elizabeth M. Vida (essay date 1993)

SOURCE: An introduction to *Romantic Affinities: German Authors and Carlyle; A Study in the History of Ideas*, University of Toronto Press, 1993, pp. 3-8.

[*In the following essay, Vida surveys the influence of German literature and Romanticism on the views of Carlyle.*]

> In affirming that any vestige, however feeble, of this divine spirit, is discernible in German poetry, we are aware that we place it above the existing poetry of any other nation. (Carlyle, **'State of German Literature'**)

To ascertain Carlyle's approach to his German Romantic sources must be the starting-point for their revaluation. Did Carlyle have a unified view of the essence of German Romanticism, and, if so, what were the tendencies that struck him as new and most noteworthy?

Carlyle saw continuity rather than opposition in the relationship between the German Classics Goethe and Schiller and the evolving Romantic movement.[1] In the preface to his translations from Tieck in **German Romance,** he is quite explicit on the subject. Attempting neither a description nor a judgment regarding the 'New School', he rejects the epithet 'School' altogether and denies that the great change was brought about solely by three young men, living in the little town of Jena: 'The critical principles of Tieck and the Schlegels had already been set forth in the form both of precept and prohibition, and with all the aids of philosophic and epigrammatic emphasis, by the united minds of Goethe and Schiller in the *Horen* and the *Xenien*. The development and practical application of the doctrine is all that pertains to these reputed founders of the sect' (**German Romance I,** 260).

For Carlyle then, German Romanticism issued forth from Goethe's and Schiller's efforts to challenge rationalistic tendencies of the Enlightenment, an undertaking that eventually resulted in the third great period of German literature, 'full of rich prospects of spirituality, faith, reverence, freedom, and fusion of art and religion.'[2] Grouping all poets who followed the new trend under the watchword 'Moderns'—a term Carlyle was familiar with from English literature—he believed writers such as Tieck, E. T. A. Hoffmann, Fouqué, and Zacharias Werner to have built on these solid foundations of the 'German Classics.'

Accordingly, he recommends for a study of the principles of German aesthetics certain treatises by Kant, Schiller, Jean Paul, and the Schlegels—a mixture that would hardly please some German literary critics of today. However, contemporary evaluations of new literary phenomena do not always fall in line with a strict classification into literary periods. That Carlyle, with little critical precedence to go by, arrived at conclusions that differ from those of critics of our own time does not prove his judgment invalid. Justifiably M. Joachimi points out that Classicism and Romanticism are not necessarily to be conceived of as strict opposites but may well complement each other.[3] Goethe, a Shakespeare enthusiast in his Storm and Stress years, found inspiration in Classical aspects of art, before returning to *Faust*; Schiller wrote *Die Braut von Messina,* as well as *Die Jungfrau von Orleans,* subtitled 'a romantic tragedy.'

Carlyle's great admiration for Goethe most likely determined his attitude to German literature as a whole, which he judged in the light of illumination he had received from such works as *Faust* and *Wilhelm Meister*. What he repeatedly stresses in his essays on the subject is Goethe's timelessness or, as Carlyle prefers to call it, his modernity: 'Poetry of our own generation; an ideal world, and yet the world we even now live in.'[4] In *Werther,* otherwise not one of Carlyle's favourites, Goethe is 'deeply important to modern minds,'[5] as a poet who embodies 'the Wisdom which is proper to this time.'[6] Besides, Goethe had proved his relevance for Carlyle himself, by helping him solve his own spiritual problems as a kind of poetic mentor.

Setting aside the complicated matter of the origins of German Romanticism, it must be admitted that, without Goethe's *Wilhelm Meister,* the Romantic Movement in Germany would have lacked a model to illustrate effectively the poetic theories Friedrich Schlegel was in the process of evolving in his periodical *Athenaeum* in the first phase of his critical activity. It was he who, in his review 'On Goethe's *Meister,*' set up this novel as worthy of emulation, indeed as a standard of excellence. Mainly on the basis of its Classical aloofness, which could be taken as a manifestation of Romantic irony, it was hailed as 'a divine growth.'[7] Nor did Friedrich Schlegel's praise abate two years after the initial review, for in his 'Conversations on Poetry' he reiterates his conviction that this work manifested 'the classical spirit in modern form', bringing about 'the harmony of the classical with the romantic.'[8] This repeated emphasis on both the Classical *and* the Romantic features of this epoch-making *Bildungsroman* must be connected with the background peculiar to the Schlegels. Both brothers had taken their starting-point in criticism from a deep appreciation of classical antiquity, its literature and art, before applying their ingenuity to the new Romantic field. If the designated founders of the new movement proclaimed in this manner an inner continuity, Carlyle's doing so can hardly be considered out of tune with developments. He had not only read Friedrich Schlegel's famous *Meister* review, but also knew of the Schlegel's Classical origins in criticism.[9]

In spite of later value judgments Goethe made on the

movement, linking Romanticism to a state of disease, as opposed to the health expressed in Classicism,[10] he never erected insurmountable barriers between Classical and Romantic literature. On the whole he was not displeased by the tribute the younger generation paid him, prior to Novalis's attempt to outdo *Wilhelm Meister* in his own novel *Heinrich von Ofterdingen.* Goethe even believed, rightly or wrongly, that he and Schiller had unwittingly introduced the terms into German literature: 'The concept of classic and romantic poetry, now spread over the whole world and causing much commotion and division, originated from Schiller and myself . . . Schiller even proved to me that I myself was, if unconsciously, romantic . . . The Schlegels took up the idea and carried it further so that it has now spread over the whole world and everybody speaks of Classicism and Romanticism, unheard of fifty years ago.'[11]

In his *Faust,* Goethe had used the Classical-Romantic linkage with great effect for his Helena episode, the first fragmentary continuation of his tragedy, which Carlyle had reviewed.[12] By employing the subtitle 'klassisch-romantische Phantasmagorie,' Goethe suggested a concept Carlyle regarded as valid. Beyond this phrase—the model for Carlyle's several 'phantasmagoria' references in *Sartor*—an interpretative hint lay in the episode itself: the union between Classical form, represented by Helena, and the medieval spirit of the North, in the person of Faust, produces as offspring the new spirit of Poetry, personified in the youthful Euphorion, modelled on Byron. Carlyle interprets the episode along these lines: 'Our readers are aware that this Euphorion, the offspring of Northern Character wedded to Grecian Culture, frisks it here not without reference to Modern Poesy, which had a birth so precisely similar' (*Essays I,* 191).

Jean Paul left just as important a mark as Goethe's on the evolving theories of the day. In his *Vorschule der Ästhetik* (25), he presents Schiller and Goethe as Romantics—especially the latter, in connection with the episodes relating to Mignon and the Harper in *Wilhelm Meister,* which impressed themselves as images with a strong Romantic flavour on the minds of the contemporary reader. F. Schlegel then set another literary precedent by advocating that Jean Paul's own formless novels were a congenial prototype of Romantic fiction. According to his later views, Romanticism consisted in 'sentimental material presented in a fantastic form,'[13] a definition that fitted Jean Paul's arabesque style perfectly. It seems indeed remarkable that German Romantic theory, emerging prior to actual works written in the style, turned to the immediately preceding generation to find suitable literary models in its formative period.

Another critical voice that joined the Schlegel chorus on a lesser level also helped shape Carlyle's judgment on Classical-Romantic relationships. This was Franz Horn, whose opinions Carlyle followed closely in his emphasis on the role of the *Xenien* as being directed primarily against the Enlightenment. Horn names both Schiller's periodical *Die Horen* and the *Xenien* epigrams written in collaboration with Goethe as epoch-making publications, aimed at 'the destruction of irreligious, anti-philosophical and anti-poetical Philistines' who, subscribing to the narrow doctrine of utility, 'did not blush to invest even the Highest Being with mediocre aims.'[14]

Carlyle also shares with Horn the view that the Schlegels' so-called School of Poetry was no school at all, and adds broadening implications, lacking in Horn, when he sees the change as originating 'not in the individuals but in the universal circumstances, belonging not to Germany, but to Europe,'[15] an opinion that proved to be right. As a foreigner he was in a better position to judge literary tendencies from outside the purely national pale.

If a unified view of German literature is basic to Carlyle's approach—and reasons for this view have been suggested—it also applies to the values he found expressed therein. As an expositor of the higher literature of Germany to British readers more or less unacquainted with the field, Carlyle felt inclined to stress unity rather than diversity, particularly as he had to do away with the scarecrow of 'Mysticism'.

What struck Carlyle as unique in all his readings was the spiritual, quasi-religious note: 'In the higher Literature of Germany there lies, for him that can read it, the beginning of a new revelation of the Godlike.'[16] This theme he repeats in several variations, for example, 'Their Literature, alone of all existing Literatures, has still some claim to that ancient 'inspired gift,' which alone is poetry.'[17]

The tribute of having first drawn attention to this characteristic goes to Madame de Staël. Not only did she notice that in Germany at the time a fund of new ideas was being tapped, 'which the other nations of Europe will not for a long time be able to exhaust',[18] but she was also aware of its illuminating qualities in things transcendental: 'When I began to study German literature, it seemed as if I was entering on a new sphere, where the most striking light was thrown on all that I had before merely perceived in a confused manner . . . the peculiar character of German literature is, to refer everything to an interior existence' *Germany,* II, 271-2).

This alliance between religion and genius did not escape Carlyle's own observation. His enthusiastic comments, too well known to have to be cited, confirm the rewarding nature of his search. He states and restates his 'New Evangel,' and shows how it grows from a dual root, the fusion of poetry with philosophy. From here evolves the ideal of the philosophical poet: 'To seize a character in its life and secret mechanism, requires a philosopher; to delineate it with truth and impressiveness, is the work of a poet.'[19]

In view of this insistence on the union of poetry and

thought, it seems evident that the value of German literature was, for Carlyle, never restricted to thought-content alone. This perspective derives, in part, from his notions about the emblematic nature of language, which contributes decidedly to the idea taking shape in the reader's mind. He himself depended for effectiveness in his own writing on this very quality of language.

Thought embedded in poetry or 'the infinite clothed in the finite'—in Friedrich Schlegel's famous phrase—forming a harmonious whole is a particular quality of the writing of Goethe, the epitome of the poet-prophet for Carlyle. Because the linkages of this unity are so closely knit, C. F. Harrold, in *Carlyle and German Thought,* experiences difficulties in trying to extract thought from poetic vision. Carlyle, in contrast, refrains from attempting to tear it apart, but treats it as a significant trait of this new type of literature. Those who followed it were Romantics for him. In all the biographical delineations of the German poets, mainly in **'Goethe'** and **'Jean Paul Richter,'** this ability to combine both faculties is sharply brought into focus. Carlyle considers Goethe to be 'a richly educated Poet . . . a master both of Humanity and of Poetry; one to whom Experience has given true wisdom, and the "Melodies Eternal" a perfect utterance for his wisdom.'[20] Jean Paul, too, is characterized in this manner as 'a moralist and a sage, no less than a poet and a wit.'[21] Novalis and Werner also fall in line with this ideal: 'As a Poet, Novalis is no less Idealistic than as a Philosopher.'[22] Werner strives 'earnestly not only to be a poet, but a prophet.'[23]

Whichever aspect—thought or poetry—is stressed, the uniqueness of German literature consists in this combination and forms, in Carlyle's view, the strongest bond among all German poets.

Notes

[1] Although R. Wellek has, in passing, drawn attention to Carlyle's unified view of German literature, he does not probe into the reasons for his taking this approach; nor does he investigate how it relates to other contemporary opinion (Wellek, *Confrontations,* 50). R. Ashton, in *The German Idea,* where only thirty-two pages are given to a discussion of Carlyle's contribution, avoids the issue. Restricting her comments to Goethe and German philosophy, as far as German influences are concerned, she offers no more than a few generalizations, in a study best classified as being of the historical-survey type. In her brief section on *Sartor Resartus* she concedes that Carlyle, in later years, 'still followed the custom of heading his works and rounding off articles with German phrases,' (p. 99), but offers no evidence.

[2] *Correspondence between Goethe and Carlyle,* 190-1

[3] Jaochimi, *Weltanschauung,* 3: 'Die Romantik und der Klassizismus eines Goethe und Schiller sind deshalb nicht als Gegenteile, sondern als zwei sich ergänzende Seiten zu verstehen.'

[4] Carlyle, *Essays I,* 'State of German Literature,' 65

[5] Ibid., 'Goethe,' 212

[6] Ibid., 'Goethe,' 208

[7] F. Schlegel, *Kritische Ausgabe II,* 'Über Goethes *Meister,*' 133

[8] Ibid., 'Gespräch über die Poesie,' 346

[9] Carlyle, *Essays I,* 'Goethe,' 230

[10] Goethe, *Maximen und Reflexionen,* no. 863 *Werke,* XII, 487

[11] Eckermann, *Gespräche,* 21 March 1830, vol. 2, 31-2: 'Der Begriff von klassischer und romantischer Poesie, der jetzt über die ganze Welt geht und so viel Streit und Spaltungen verursacht . . . ist ursprünglich von mir und Schiller ausgegangen . . . [Schiller] bewies mir, dass ich selber wider Willen romantisch sei . . . Die Schlegel ergriffen die Idee und trieben sie weiter, so dass sie sich denn jetzt über die ganze Welt ausgedehnt hat und nun jedermann von Klassizimus und Romantizismus redet, woran vor fünfzig Jahren niemand dachte.' The English translation is mine, as is the case hereafter unless stated otherwise.

[12] Carlyle, *Essays I,* 'Helena,' 146. Written for the *Foreign Review,* 1828. Carlyle points out the significance of Goethe's subtitle and translates it as 'a classico-romantic Phantasmagoria.'

[13] F. Schlegel, *Kritische Ausgabe* II, 333: ' . . . was uns einen sentimentalen Stoff in einer fantastischen Form darstellt.'

[14] Horn, *Umrisse,* 66: ' . . . die Vernichtung alles irreligiösen, antiphilosophischen und antipoetischen 'Philisterthums' . . . das nicht errötet selbst dem höchsten Wesen mittelmässige Zwecke zu leihen.'

[15] Carlyle, *German Romance I,* 261

[16] Carlyle, *Essay III,* 'Characteristics,' 41

[17] Carlyle, *Unfinished History of German Literature,* 11

[18] De Staël, *Germany,* II, 370

[19] Carlyle, *Essays I,* 'State of German Literature,' 33

[20] Ibid., 'Goethe,' 246

[21] Carlyle, *German Romance II,* 118

²² Carlyle, *Essays II,* 'Novalis,' 28-9

²³ Carlyle, *Essays I,* 'Life and Writings of Werner,' 115

D. Franco Felluga (essay date 1995)

SOURCE: "The Critic's New Clothes: *Sartor Resartus* as 'Cold Carnival'," in *Criticism,* Vol. XXXVII, No. 4, Fall, 1995, pp. 583-99.

[*In the following essay, Felluga maintains that some critics have attempted to "retailor"* Sartor Resartus *by viewing the work as "an ornate and stable system of thought." Felluga states that these reviewers have failed to address "Carlyle's carnivalesque efforts to expose all systems as limiting and false."*]

Hans Christian Andersen's tale, "The Emperor's New Clothes," provides me with a parable for what I find questionable in certain previous treatments of *Sartor Resartus.* As the story goes,

> In the large town where the emperor's palace was, life was gay and happy; and every day new visitors arrived. One day two swindlers came. They told everybody that they were weavers and that they could weave the most marvelous cloth. Not only were the colors and the patterns of their material extraordinarily beautiful, but the cloth had the strange quality of being invisible to anyone who was unfit for his office or unforgivably stupid.¹

Of course, no one in the palace wants to admit that s/he is unsuited to the office s/he holds, least of all the king. When the king finally does go to meet the masses in his new non-existent vesture, he is, as a result, thoroughly ridiculed. Though I do not wish to suggest that previous critics writing on *Sartor Resartus* are swindlers, I would question their efforts to retailor the work into an ornate and stable system of thought despite Carlyle's carnivalesque efforts to expose all systems as limiting and false. Their efforts to convince us of the text's underlying, or should I say underworn, system of thought—its true clothing—nonetheless reflects an essential problematic in the interpretation of *Sartor Resartus* itself. Is Carlyle setting up in this work the authoritarian, dogmatic ideas of his later essays or is he honestly exposing the contingency of all dogmas?

Slavoj Žižek's use of the Hans Christian Andersen tale in *For they know not what they do* illustrates the difficulty of answering this question. As he points out, the boy who is the first one to laugh at the king does not simply deliver us from hypocrisy, forcing us to confront the actual state of things (the king's nudity); he actually undoes "the very community of which we were a member . . . by blurting out what should remain unspoken if the existing intersubjective network is to retain its consistency."² The child exposes the purely formal operation by which the king "'quilts' the social edifice" (19). He does not expose the king's nudity so much as expose the underlying injunction that accompanies kingliness: do not obey because the king is chosen by God or determined by Nature through biological lineage; obey because, if you don't, the political fabric unravels.³ Though you know the king is naked, you must act as if he were clothed with all the trappings of power to prove that you yourself are suited to your office, that you support the formal structure of the existing intersubjective, formal network. It is this action which constitutes ideology and the corresponding stability of the social system, not belief in the legitimacy of the king. As Žižek formulates it, "belief, far from being an 'intimate,' purely mental state, is always *materialized* in our effective social activity: belief supports [in this material, active way] the fantasy which regulates social reality."⁴ By exposing this formal, ideological support for social reality the child in the Andersen story uncovers the self-deception that empowers the system.

Herein too lies the power of *Sartor Resartus:* the text laughs at the social acts that artificially structure ideological fields, uncovering the naked man behind the king's trappings of power. And yet, it is in the uncovering of the vanity of earthly existence that we can also find the principle of Carlyle's increasingly authoritarian stance on many issues: beyond this world (and that which allows us to estrange ourselves from our social existence) is the greater power of God—what Žižek, following Lacan, terms the Ego Ideal or the quilting point.⁵ As Carlyle puts it, "through every star, through every grassblade, and most through every Living Soul, the glory of a present God still beams" (*Sartor,* 307). Once again the question arises: is Carlyle laughing at conventions or affirming a covenant with God? Is he legitimating a dogma or is he dodging legitimation? So far, critics have tended to read *Sartor Resartus* from the standpoint of Carlyle's later work and, therefore, have seen it as the "quilting" of a dogmatic system. Nonetheless, I would argue that Carlyle refrains at this stage in his writing career from using a quilting point (be it God or the transcendent) to knit and bind an authoritarian system of ideology. "The Dandaical Body," the chapter which immediately follows the more commonly quoted "Natural Supernaturalism," appears to parody just this effort by the Editor—and, by extension, the reader—to reduce Professor Teufelsdröckh's own treatise to certain determinate "articles of faith." Carlyle appears to be more willing in *Sartor Resartus* to work through "the 'phantasy of our Dream'" (*Sartor,* 161) in order to see the lack inherent in the symbolic order—in any ideological field. In this way, he appears at times to follow something like Lacan's injunction always to "go through the fantasy."⁶ The true insight for Carlyle at this point is that "In every the wisest Soul lies a whole world of internal madness . . . out of which, indeed, his world of Wisdom has been creatively built together, and now rests there, as on its dark foundations does a habitable flowery Earth-rind" (*Sartor,* 304). Not even his own formulations can escape at this point the need, as Carlyle puts it, to "thatch myself anew" (*Sartor,* 162) from day to day.

In my own examination of Carlyle, I will not attempt to quilt a stable system out of Teufelsdröckh's ramblings because I feel that Carlyle parodically unravels any such efforts (including his own) through the stylistic medium he has chosen to bear his "transcendental philosophy." Instead, I will examine the transformations of that philosophy within the interweavings of Carlyle's style. Using Mikhail Bakhtin's theories of dialogue and of novelistic prose, I will explore the extent to which the radical dialogism of *Sartor Resartus* in fact frustrates our very desire to impose on it a stable, monologic system. Most studies done on Carlyle's text so far have concentrated on his thematics and utterly ignored his prosaics, that is, the actual novelistic and carnivalesque vehicle he employs to convey and inveigh against the tenor of his writing.[7] What much Carlyle criticism lacks is a willingness to examine how the carnivalesque and dialogic exposition of Carlyle's ideas affects the "transcendental" aspects of Carlyle's philosophy. To what extent is Carlyle still laughing "in his sleeve at our strictures and glosses" (*Sartor,* 271), as the Editor suspects of the "Clothes Philosophy"?

Of course, there have been studies that have posited a necessary relationship between Carlyle's style and his content, and I am much indebted to them, particularly work by John Holloway, G. B. Tennyson, George Levine, and Leonard Deen.[8] However, as Chris R. Vanden Bossche suggests, in a superb re-evaluation of Carlyle's "revolutionary" style, "in so far as their approach assumes that the meaning exists apart from and prior to the style, it can be misleading; Carlyle's style does not merely reflect his meaning, it makes his meaning."[9] Steven Helmling makes a similar argument in his book, *The Esoteric Comedies of Carlyle, Newman, and Yeats,* in which he provides the most extensive examination of the comic aspects of *Sartor Resartus:* Carlyle's "parody of verbal styles, generic conventions and decorums of literary address acts to expose the unconscious operation of convention itself to the scrutiny of conscious reflection."[10] My goal in this article will be to pursue the claims of Vanden Bossche and Helmling through the mediating theoretical framework of Bakhtin's theories.

Dominick LaCapra, in an aside, is one of the only critics who has suggested that Bakhtin's theories can apply to *Sartor Resartus.* As he asserts in his critique of M. H. Abrams's desire to systematize Carlyle, "We get little sense [in Abrams's work] of how *Sartor Resartus* is a tremendously critical, remarkably hybridized, and outrageously funny Menippean satire—a stunning example of carnivalized literature or both high and low comedy of ideas in which the very acceptance of certain conventions is put into "deep" play."[11] It is this "deep play" that I hope to foreground in my analysis of Carlyle's text; the "Clothes Philosophy" cannot help but be infected by its carnivalesque surroundings, despite the tendency of literary anthologies

to extract and, thus in essence, to disinfect sections from it. Although we may try to piece together a monological philosophy from the work as a whole, the very fact that we find these "transcendental" statements in the context that we do subverts any pretensions the text may have to high seriousness. As Bakhtin states in reference to Rabelais, "Even the lines which in a different context or taken separately would be completely serious . . . acquire in their context an overtone of laughter," for "the reflexes of surrounding comic images react on them."[12] After all, the Editor himself comes to realize in his translation of Teufelsdröckh's text that, even in the most "Transcendental or ultimate Portion" (274) of the Clothes Philosophy, "the tone, in some parts, has more of riancy, even of levity, than we could have expected!" (253).

I am not saying that Carlyle does not posit a transcendental philosophy. Carnivalesque tendencies in Carlyle do not necessarily belie, as Bakhtin illustrates in Rabelais, a belief in transcendental ideals. They rather attack any pretensions to a static conception of truth. After all, cant was for Carlyle, as it was for Rabelais, "the *materia prima* of the Devil; from which all falsehoods, imbecilities, abominations body themselves; from which no true thing can come."[13] Carlyle does posit such a thing as a God's truth; the point is that no one may know it definitively. His very belief that the power of wonder necessarily combats the deadening effect of custom underlines the carnival assertion that "our very Axioms . . . are oftenest simply such Beliefs as we have never heard questioned" (*Sartor,* 303). We can only understand truth in the eternal death and rebirth of *symbols for* truth, in the endless questioning and reworking of ossified beliefs. For Carlyle, "all theories, were they never so earnest, painfully elaborated, are, and, by the very conditions of them, must be incomplete, questionable, and even false" (*French,* 2:54). This fact must extend to Carlyle's own philosophy, which he presents in a carnivalesque form in order to keep openended his confrontation with questions of truth. To find truth, Carlyle must first, like Socrates in the carnival ambivalences of the early dialogues, level all pretensions to truth, including his own. For Carlyle, as for Socrates, "they only are wise who know that they know nothing" (*Sartor,* 161).

Of course, Carlyle is by no means a sensualist or a libertine even at this stage in his career; G. B. Tennyson in his introduction to *Sartor Resartus* makes clear that, and here he voices the opinion of many readers of Carlyle, "There are times when exhortation becomes harangue, when the deep-toned voice turns strident, or when conviction changes to bigotry."[14] Certainly in his later work, as he adopts a more and more monologic essay form, Carlyle loses the sense of open-endedness that characterizes his earlier explorations into the transcendental and the supernatural.[15] However in *Sartor Resartus,* the recourse to a carnivalesque and dialogic style has the effect of questioning authoritarian convictions, not to mention the authorial voice, by emphasizing the relative and historical nature of all claims to truth. Carlyle always tempers the sometimes "strident" tone of Teufelsdröckh and the "proselytising" tendencies of the Editor (*Sartor*, 129) by not only placing their markedly different world views into conflict, but by incessantly juxtaposing both transcendental and what the Editor terms "descendental" subject matter (169) within a parodic and carnivalesque form.

The very principle behind the "Clothes Philosophy," the effort to see that man "is by nature a *Naked Animal*" (126), to see, as one chapter puts it, "The World Out of Clothes," seems to epitomize what Bakhtin calls "this novelistic spirit" of "popular laughter": "The object is broken apart, laid bare (its hierarchical ornamentation is removed): the naked object is ridiculous; its "empty" clothing stripped and separated from its person, is also ridiculous."[16] In this way, as Bakhtin continues, laughter begins "to investigate man freely and familiarly, to turn him inside out, expose the disparity between his surface and his center, between his potential and his reality" (*Dialogic*, 35). Of course, these comments very closely resemble similar statements by the Professor in his "Clothes Philosophy": "Nevertheless there is something great in the moment when a man first strips himself of adventitious wrappages; and sees indeed that he is naked. . . . yet also a Spirit, and unutterable Mystery of Mysteries" (163). The spirit behind the "Clothes Philosophy" places the work in a carnival tradition which exposes all static power structures as artificial. As the clothes fly off in the Professor's imagination, "the whole fabric of Government, Legislation, Property, Police, and Civilised Society, *are dissolved*, in wails and howls" (166).

I will not go over specific aspects of carnival in Carlyle, however, since this argument seems to be not only the easier one to make but also the most precarious, given recent criticism of Bakhtin's overly optimistic conception of the carnival tradition. As Umberto Eco explains, "Carnival, in order to be enjoyed, requires that rules and rituals be parodied, and that these rules and rituals already be recognized and respected. One must know to what degree certain behaviors are forbidden, and must feel the majesty of the forbidding norm, to appreciate their transgression. Without a valid law to break, carnival is impossible."[17] My argument for Carlyle will be, on the contrary, that *Sartor Resartus* approaches the more radical kind of social critique that Eco has termed "cold carnival."[18] Carlyle does not simply topple the king in an explosion of violence that mirrors in inverse form the radical obedience to the strictures and norms of the king that contain subversion in everyday life. Instead, Carlyle questions the very desire that we feel for strictures and norms, revealing all sciences and all systems as "so many weaving-shops and spinning mills" (*Sartor*, 312). He directs his laughter at the reader in order to expose our very efforts to silence or monologize the dialogic open-endedness of *Sartor Resartus*.

Carlyle therefore examines the very act of interpreting, and thus of entering into dialogue with, a text's otherness. Indeed, Carlyle dramatizes in various ways Bakhtin's very definition of the novelist's main activity:

> In a word, the novelistic plot serves to represent speaking persons and their ideological worlds. What is realized in the novel is the process of coming to know one's own language as it is perceived in someone else's language, coming to know one's own belief system in someone else's system. There takes place within the novel an ideological translation of another's language, and an overcoming of its otherness. (*Dialogic*, 365)

In Carlyle, a self-conscious sense of "ideological translation" (represented as "polyglossia") in fact enters the very heart of the work in the clash between the Editor's English and the Professor's German cultures.[19] The question becomes: "how could the philosophy of Clothes, and the Author of such Philosophy, be brought home, in any measure, to the business and bosoms of our own English Nation?" (*Sartor*, 129). The act of reading is thus explicitly aligned with the act of translation; the Editor, who at times stands in for the reader, must come to recognize his own belief system in the very diverse belief system of Herr Teufelsdröckh. Carlyle thus points to the fact that all interpretation resembles a dialogue between the surplus of meanings in a text and the political intentions a reader brings to his or her own reading of the work. By alerting the reader to this fact, Carlyle foregoes any simple notion of authorial voice in favor of the dialogic confrontation of different ways of perceiving. Carlyle almost does away with plot altogether so that the real story in *Sartor Resartus* becomes the very dialogue that occurs between the "Clothes Philosophy," a "writerly text" in Roland Barthes's full sense of the term, and the Editor's very active "reading" of this work.[20] At least in this way, Carlyle anticipates the fictions of Dostoevsky, which Bakhtin characterizes in *Problems of Dostoevsky's Poetics* as the first and best examples of the polyphonic novel.[21] As Gary Saul Morson and Caryl Emerson write of Dostoevsky, "One must read not for plot, but for the dialogue and to read for the dialogues is to participate in them."[22]

The confrontation with foreign ways of perceiving is for Carlyle regenerative, for his distrust of systems extends to a distrust of any effort to systematize the creative potentials of a medium as fluid as language. As the editor asks at one point, "what work nobler than transplanting foreign thought into the barren domestic soil" (179)? Carlyle, by foregrounding the act of translation, thus incorporates in *Sartor Resartus* what Bakhtin terms "extranational multi-languagedness," a participation in different languages that underlines "the disassociation" that exists "between language and intentions, language and thought, language and expression" (*Dialogic*, 369). The linguistic medium of *Sartor Resartus* is, therefore, made problematic by Carlyle; he addresses its artificiality, undressing it as "the Flesh-Garment, the Body, of Thought" (*Sartor*, 174), since any static form for Carlyle's transcendental content or meaning risks solidifying into "the tatters and rags of superannuated worn-out Symbols . . . dropping off everywhere, to hoodwink, to halter, to tether you" (*Sartor,* 280). Even in the Professor's "piebald, entangled, hypermetaphorical style of writing, not to say of thinking" (*Sartor,* 327), Carlyle moves from metaphor to metaphor, unwilling to rest his meaning, his authorial intention, in any one set of symbols.[23] Carlyle instead turns to the dynamic medium of parody and "multi-languagedness" to make the reader more aware of the disassociation that necessarily exists between language and "reality," form and content.

Carlyle's style also opens up his text to the forces in society which undermine a static, Johnsonian conception of language. We can see Teufelsdröckh's text as the epitome of Bakhtin's notion of "heteroglossia," with its disregard for grammatical rules, the inclusion of German words and stylistic variations, and its metaphorical neologisms. Indeed, as Carlyle asks in response to John Sterling's criticism of his style,

> But finally, do you reckon this really a time for Purism of Style; or that Style (mere dictionary Style) has much to do with the worth or unworth of a Book? I do not: with whole ragged battalions of Scott's-Novel Scotch, with Irish, German, French, and even Newspaper Cockney (when "Literature" is little other than a newspaper) storming in on us, and the whole structure of our Johnsonian English breaking up from its foundations,—revolution *there* as visible as anywhere else![24]

Carlyle is always sensitive to the forces of revolution and stasis which pervade all levels of existence. Indeed, for Carlyle, Matthew Arnold's forces of concentration and expansion, which govern the rise and fall of civilizations, exist together at any given moment and find a parallel in the constructive and deconstructive forces which operate in language. The two processes, social and linguistic, are tied together, and in either sphere constructive and destructive forces impinge on every effort to fix either a social system or a coherent text. As in the vision of the "World-Phoenix," "Creation and Destruction proceed together" (*Sartor,* 293) at any given moment in language or society. Carlyle goes so far as to dramatize this ongoing struggle in the very confrontation that occurs between the Editor and the Professor's chaotic text.

Teufelsdröckh and his writings align themselves, on the one hand, with subversive elements in both language and society, questioning what Bakhtin calls *"the forces that serve to unify and centralize the verbal-ideological world"* (*Dialogic,* 270). Through the medium used to express his transcendental philosophy, the Professor seriously strains our ability to extract one consistent, philosophical system or even one determinate biographical narrative from his linguistic "farrago" (*Sartor,* 258).[25] Indeed, because of Teufelsdröckh's parodic inclusion of so many generic, national, and social "languages," *Sartor Resartus* goes beyond any label to become, as Paul Jay puts it, "a patchwork parody that subverts any attempt to create for it a generic pigeon-hole large enough to hold any other work."[26] We find ourselves confronted here with a wild, parodic conglomeration of various genres, including biography, autobiography, *Bildungsroman, Künstlerroman,* sentimental novel (II, chapter 5), adventure novel (II, chapter 8), and so on. Carlyle enters various narrative forms into a forum of dialogue so that each necessarily questions in its impurity and juxtaposition with other kinds of literature the principles that underlie each individual style.[27] As Albert LaValley has it, for Carlyle, "the infinite possibilities of an open and organic universe militated against the stability of meaning and of self . . . rendered the possibility of artistic form itself questionable" (100).

The Editor, presenting himself as a unifying force who is trying to create an ordered plot structure out of Professor Teufelsdröckh's chaotic fragments, attempts, on the other hand, "to evolve printed Creation out of a German printed and written Chaos" (*Sartor,* 179). In other words, he attempts to complete the act of authoring. The Professor's text is altered as a result not simply because of the ensuing translation but because of the Editor's desire to "defend" the "Institutions of our Ancestors . . . according to ability, at all hazards" (132). The Editor does not, however, arrive at an authoritative text; instead, he enters into a profound struggle with the ur-text, feeling it resist his translation and imagining the Professor laughing "in his sleeve at our strictures and glosses" (271).

The extent to which Carlyle allows the dialogue to influence his own authoritative voice—if we wish to accept Teufelsdröckh's words as those of Carlyle—may of course be questioned. In some ways, after all, Carlyle's work does not conform to Bakhtin's conception of a truly dialogic, novelistic text. The Professor's words, for example, remain pure insofar as their boundaries are demarcated for the most part by the Editor's quotation marks; however, we are not presented with a purely "authoritative discourse" either. Indeed, Bakhtin asserts, "One cannot divide [an authoritative discourse] up—agree with one part, accept but not completely another part, reject utterly a third" (*Dialogic,* 343). In actual fact, the Editor does just this, actively opposing and questioning the words of the ur-text, which must struggle against his ordering consciousness. At the same time, although the Editor finds himself in an authoritative position and although Teufelsdröckh's text cannot respond to the Editor as in an actual dialogue between individuals, that text still manages to defy the Editor's ordering consciousness.

Indeed, the text has quite a profound effect on the Editor; he must acknowledge by the end that "this remarkable Treatise, with its Doctrines, whether as judicially acceded to, or judicially denied, has not remained without effect" in "the present Editor's way of thought"

(128). The Professor even succeeds in transforming the editor's Johnsonian English: "has not the Editor himself, working over Teufelsdröckh's German, lost much of his own English purity?" (327-28). One cannot enter a foreign mode of utterance without having it affect one's conception of the rules and conventions that govern one's own linguistic purview. Perhaps we should therefore speak not of translation (*trans-ferre/ trans-latus:* to bear across) when referring to the Editor's efforts but of "interlation," for we are dealing here not only with the bearing of meaning from one culture to another but with the very active interaction that can occur between languages, not to mention the foregrounding of the linguistic problems that translation entails. Perhaps we should read *Sartor Resartus,* then, not as it has been in the past—as a monologic doctrinal treatise—but as a manifestation of what Bakhtin would come to theorize as the dialogic imagination. We are presented, after all, with the dynamic interaction that occurs between the two posited languages and purviews of the Editor and the Professor.[28] In addition, Carlyle dramatizes the endless confrontation which Bakhtin theorizes between centrifugal and centripetal forces in language by personifying these two tendencies in the two sides of the enacted dialogue. The Professor decenters language while the Editor works to centralize and stabilize language through the imposition of logical, narrative, and thematic order onto Teufelsdröckh's work. Carlyle is interested in underscoring the act of translation and mediation that occurs whenever a reader engages an unfamiliar text. Any authorial text is ordered in a centripetal manner according to the reader's own world view, not to mention the reader's need to impose semantic order on the potential indeterminacy of textual language; on the other hand, the reader experiences an "impurification" because of the text's influence and the threatening incursion of language's heteroglot, centrifugal foundation. Carlyle dramatizes how meaning is constructed and deconstructed in any reading of a text, in the everyday linguistic mediation inherent in dialogue.

Professor Teufelsdröckh's text therefore represents, as Gerald Bruns suggests, "a problem of meaning."[29] By pointing out the unstable nature of meaning to the reader, Carlyle manages to escape the limitations of simple carnival inversion by making the reader aware of the linguistic conventions which serve to artificially stabilize the socioideological world. The text forces us to question the various linguistically authoritative ways of communicating one's intention to the reader; indeed, it explicitly includes the reader in the process of interpreting and answering the text, which is then seen rather as a rejoinder in a greater dialogue, as the initiation of an endless process of interpretation. The Editor's metaphor for the act of interpretation as the construction of a "Hell-gate Bridge over Chaos" (266) is apt, for the writing of the author's "autobiography," like the writing of *Sartor Resartus* itself, becomes partially that of the reader: "Biography or Autobiography of Teufelsdröckh there is, clearly enough, none to be gleaned here: at most some sketchy, shadowy fugi-

tive likeness of him may, by unheard-of efforts, partly of intellect, partly of imagination, on the side of Editor and of Reader, rise up between them" (*Sartor,* 178). The Editor's metaphor of the "Hell-gate Bridge," which he imagines being constructed between the Editor and the reader, in fact anticipates a similar bridge metaphor used by Valentin Voloshinov, a member of Bakhtin's circle of friends in the 1920s: " . . . *word is a two-sided act. . . .* [It] is a bridge thrown between myself and another. If one end of the bridge depends on me, then the other depends on my addressee. A word is territory shared by both addresser and addressee, by the speaker and his interlocutor."[30] Communication does not occur as a speech act directed to a passive listener but rather in the very active response of a listener's interpretation. As a result, the construction of the bridge is the responsibility of both Editor and reader: "Forward with us, courageous reader; be it towards failure, or towards success! The latter thou sharest with us; the former also is not all our own" (*Sartor,* 179). As Carlyle writes of the reader's role in interpreting Goethe's style, "The reader is kept on the alert, ever conscious of his own active coöperation [sic]."[31]

The act of authorship thus never ends since "interpretation" should include, Carlyle suggests in *Sartor Resartus,* not only the synchronic play of the text's rhetorical structures, but also diachronic relations among all periods included in the given text's reception. For this reason, the Editor must admit failure in the end and allow the reader, whose voice has been heard throughout the text, to continue the dialogue. As the Editor confesses, "No firm arch, overspanning the Impassable with paved highway, could the editor construct; only, as was said, some zigzag series of rafts floating tumultuously thereon" (310). As in "the actual life of speech," here "Understanding comes to fruition only in the response" (Bakhtin, *Dialogic,* 282). The dialogue with the Editor's text never ends; it is merely continued by "New labourers," for, the Editor explains, "it is in this grand and indeed highest work of Palingenesia that ye shall labour each according to ability" (310).

The imposition of the bridge is the necessary transgression against the other which allows for communication; however, the bridge remains unstable, just as the relationship between text and reader must remain open. There always exists an aporia between the author's expression and the reader's understanding, just as there always exists a gap between the transcendental tenor and the chaotic vehicle which allows for further interpretation.

The question I wish finally to ask is: to what extend does the carnivalesque form of *Sartor Resartus* affect its content? For one, the reader assumes a more active role in interpreting Carlyle's text and comes to understand the very process of trying, and inevitably failing, to constitute one static system of meaning.[32] In addition, the form puts into question the efforts of previous critics to pinpoint a "virtual personality" or an "implied orator" within *Sartor Resartus.*[33] Carlyle of all writers does not stand behind the text as the master puppeteer who manipulates the reader to accept the validity of his ideas, but rather points to the entrenched conventions and reductionist tendencies which lead the reader him or herself to posit authorial intention in order to legitimate his or her particular reading of the work.

Carlyle makes clear in a letter to John Sterling his own "decided contempt for all manner of Systembuilders and Sectfounders."[34] In the parodic medium of *Sartor Resartus,* Carlyle tries to anticipate the desire of future readers to reduce his work to an easily understandable system. Carlyle's humor, at least in *Sartor Resartus,* attempts to affect and infect future efforts by critics to inoculate themselves against the works' contagious self-parody. The text also interferes with our own desire to shut down the interlocutory space of indeterminacy, that inescapable gap between content and form. There is, I think, a certain danger in suggesting, as some critics have tried to do, that there is an "Open Secret" to *Sartor Resartus,* that the reader must try to "see through the ironic mask and enjoy the clever performance of the illusionary tricks as the Professor pretends to puzzle over whether something is real or a sham."[35] To do so is to transpose polyphony into monody. Though the editor and Teufelsdröckh may be "reflexes of the same mind," as another critic suggests, they represent two very different and contradictory tendencies in Carlyle's thinking which he wishes to dramatize by placing into conflict.[36] We should perhaps not transcend the style to discover the real meaning so much as discover through the style our own desire to foreclose prematurely the creative act of re-interpretation. Rather than trying to present a particular ideology, Carlyle instead involves the reader in the process of categorically unclothing all static conventions to expose the very act of trying to achieve understanding. In this "cold carnival" and as in "The Emperor's New Clothes," we come to understand our desire to create clothes, though we never succeed in eliminating the need either to wear them or to bare ourselves now and again.

Notes

I would like to thank Garrett Stewart, Robert Newsom, John Matthews, and Clive Thomson for their invaluable comments on earlier drafts of this essay. I would also like to thank the Calgary Institute for the Humanities and the Social Sciences and Humanities Research Council of Canada for funding this work.

[1] Hans Christian Andersen, *The Complete Fairy Tales and Stories,* trans. Erik Christian Haugaard (New York: Doubleday, 1974), 77.

[2] Slavoj Žižek, *For they know not what they do: Enjoyment as a Political Factor* (London: Verso, 1991), 12. Further references to this work appear in the text.

[3] Carlyle in fact comes to the same conclusion when he imagines "Majesty" suddenly naked: "How each skulks into the nearest hiding-place; their high State Tragedy (*Haupt- und Staats-Action*) becomes a Pickleherring-Farce to weep at" and "the whole fabric of Government, Legislation, Property, Police, and Civilised Society, *are dissolved,* in wails and howls" (*Sartor Resartus,* in *A Carlyle Reader: Selections from the Writings of Thomas Carlyle,* ed. G. B. Tennyson [Cambridge: Cambridge University Press, 1984], 166. All further references to this work are from this edition and will appear in the text).

[4] *The Sublime Object of Ideology* (London: Verso, 1989), 36.

[5] Žižek explains these terms as follows: "What we have here is an inversion by means of which what is effectively an *immanent,* purely textual operation—the 'quilting' of the heterogeneous material into a unified ideological field—is perceived and experienced as an unfathomable, *transcendent,* stable point of reference concealed behind the flow of appearances and acting as its hidden cause" (*For they,* 18).

[6] Again, Žižek: "the final moment of the analysis is defined as 'going through the fantasy [*la traversée du fantasme*]': not its symbolic interpretation but the experience of the fact that the fantasy-object . . . is merely filling out a lack" (Ibid. 133).

[7] For an exploration of the concept of "prosaics" in terms of Bakhtin's theories, see Gary Saul Morson and Caryl Emerson, *Mikhail Bakhtin: Creation of a Prosaics* (Stanford: Stanford University Press, 1990).

[8] John Holloway, *The Victorian Sage* (Hamden: Archon, 1962), 23-47; G. B. Tennyson, *Sartor Called Resartus: The Genesis, Structure, and Style of Thomas Carlyle's First Major Work* (Princeton: Princeton University Press, 1965), especially pages 259-73 for an analysis of Carlyle's style and pages 273-83 for an examination of Carlyle's humor; George Levine, "The Use and Abuse of Carlylese," in *The Art of Victorian Prose,* ed. George Levine and William Madden (Oxford: Oxford University Press, 1966), 104-11; George Levine, *The Boundaries of Fiction* (Princeton: Princeton University Press, 1966), 42-51; and Leonard W. Deen, "Irrational Form in *Sartor Resartus,"* *Texas Studies in Literature and Language* 5 [1964]: 438-51. See also Jerry A. Dibble's *The Pythia's Drunken Song: Thomas Carlyle's* Sartor Resartus *and the Style Problem in German Idealist Philosophy,* International Archives of the History of Ideas 19 (Boston: Martinus Nijhoff, 1978), 37-43.

[9] Chris R. Vanden Bossche, "Revolution and Authority: The Metaphors of Language and Carlyle's Style," *Prose Studies* 6 (1983): 274. Vanden Bossche is discussing Holloway, Tennyson, and Levine in this quote, not Deen, although Vanden Bossche's comment also applies to Deen's article.

[10] Steven Helmling, *The Esoteric Comedies of Carlyle, Newman, and Yeats* (Cambridge: Cambridge University Press, 1988), 15. Although our conclusions are often similar, my use of Bakhtin nonetheless leads me to certain interpretations that differ from those of Helmling, particularly my interpretation of the Editor's "dialogic" function in Carlyle's work. See also Albert J. LaValley, who presents Carlyle as a precursor to various modern writers (*Carlyle and the Idea of the Modern* [New York: Yale University Press, 1968], 69-118). Another critic who has explored the comic side of Carlyle is Richard J. Dunn in his article, "'Inverse Sublimity': Carlyle's Theory of Humour," *University of Toronto Quarterly* 40 (1970): 41-57. See also Jacques Cabau for an examination of the revolutionary aspects of Carlyle's style (*Thomas Carlyle ou le Promethée enchaînée: essai sur la genèse de l'oeuvre de 1795-1834* [Paris: Presses Universitaires, 1968]).

[11] Dominick LaCapra, *Soundings in Critical Theory* (Ithaca: Cornell University Press, 1989), 99. Note, however, that Northrop Frye, back in 1957, defined *Sartor Resartus* as a Menippean satire, although he gave the generic term a new designation, the "anatomy" (*Anatomy of Criticism: Four Essays* [Princeton: Princeton University Press, 1957], 313). Frye thus aligns Carlyle's text with such carnivalesque authors as Petronius, Apuleius, Rabelais, and Swift. Steven Helmling explores the viability of this designation and suggests an even more specific label of "esoteric comedy" for Carlyle in his book, *The Esoteric Comedies of Carlyle, Newman, and Yeats;* see, in particular, pages 4-29, 35-47, and 75-78. Outside of LaCapra, only Murray Baumgarten has tied Carlyle to Bakhtin, specifically to Bakhtin's concept of dialogism ("The Mind is a Muscle: Carlyle, Literary Revolution, and Linguistic Nationalism," in *Nationalism in Literature: Literature, Language and National Identity,* ed. Horst W. Drescher and Hermann Volkel [Frankfurt am Main: Verlag, Peter, Lang, 1989], 45, 55). Vanden Bossche, in his article on Carlyle, has an endnote in which he implicitly ties Bakhtin to Carlyle, but he does so in a passage that is explicitly discussing Browning (289n).

[12] Mikhail Bakhtin, *Rabelais and His World,* trans. Hélène Iswolsky (Bloomington: Indiana University Press, 1984), 135.

[13] *The French Revolution,* vols. 2-4 of *The Works of Thomas Carlyle,* 30 vols. (New York: Scribner's, 1896-1901), 2:55. All further references to this work are from this edition and will appear in the text.

[14] This introduction appears in the *Sartor* edition that I quote throughout the essay. This particular citation is on page xxxvii.

[15] Richard Dunn explores this progression in Carlyle's career from the "inverse sublimity" of *Sartor Resartus* to the "true sublimity" of his later work: Carlyle's "growth of faith in the hero and in the hero-worshipper's loyalty," especially after his move to London in 1834, "severely restricted Carlyle's opportunity for humorous writing," for "The hero has little to do with the truly humorous viewpoint; he perceives and represents not inverse but true sublimity" (54). In *Sartor Resartus* on the other hand, as Leonard Deen suggests, "Teufelsdröckh is to some extent a parody of the prophetic 'voice' (as he is of the romantic rebel and the anatomist), and this fact helps to account for the editor's ambiguous attitude towards him" (444).

[16] Mikhail Bakhtin, *The Dialogic Imagination,* trans. Caryl Emerson and Michael Holquist (Texas: University of Texas Press, 1981), 22-23, 23-24. Further references to this work will appear in the text.

[17] Umberto Eco, "The Frames of Comic 'Freedom,'" in *Carnival!,* ed. Thomas A. Sebeok, Approaches to Semiotics 64 (Berlin: Mouton, 1984), 6. Perhaps not surprisingly, then, one of the loci for carnival upheaval in eighteenth-century France, according to Michel Foucault, is precisely the site of capital punishment: "The public execution allowed the luxury of these momentary saturnalia, when nothing remained to prohibit or punish. Under the protection of imminent death, the criminal could say everything and the crowd cheered" (*Discipline and Punish: The Birth of the Prison,* trans. Alan Sheridan [New York: Vintage, 1979], 60).

[18] Richard Dunn, in an examination of Carlyle's own theories of humor, suggests that Carlyle himself made a distinction between a "lower comedy" that depends for effect on simple distortion and reversal and "true humour," which "sympathetically transcends derision" and "evinces a most humane and often liberating form of laughter" (43).

[19] Bakhtin uses the term "polyglossia" to distinguish this intermingling of national languages from his other more famous term, "heteroglossia." The former term, as Caryl Emerson and Michael Holquist define it in their glossary to Bakhtin's *The Dialogic Imagination,* refers to "the simultaneous presence of two or more national languages interacting within a single cultural system" (431), whereas the latter term refers to the co-existence of different "dialects" within a single national language. As Bakhtin explains, the dialects that make up heteroglossia reflect "contradictions . . . between differing epochs of the past, between different socio-ideological groups in the present, between tendencies, schools, circles, and so forth" (*Dialogic,* 291).

[20] For Barthes's definition of "writerly" and "readerly," see his *S/Z: An Essay,* trans. Richard Miller (New York: Noonday, 1974), 4-6: "the writerly text is *ourselves writing,* before the infinite play of the world . . . is traversed, intersected, stopped, plasticized by some singular system (Ideology, Genus, Criticism)" (5). The reader

of a "readerly text" on the other hand "is intransitive . . . instead of functioning himself, . . . he is left with no more than the poor freedom either to accept or reject the text: reading is nothing more than a *referendum*" (4).

[21] See Mikhail Bakhtin, *Problems of Dostoevsky's Poetics,* trans. Caryl Emerson, ed. Caryl Emerson (Minneapolis: University of Minnesota Press, 1984). A polyphonic novel is one that is, literally, "many-voiced," in which characters approach the level of "autonomous subjects," independent from the ideological purview of the author. Also, in such a novel, "Every experience, every thought of a character is internally dialogic, adorned with polemic, filled with struggle, or is on the contrary open to inspiration from outside itself—but it is not in any case concentrated simply on its own object; it is accompanied by a continual sideways glance at another person" (*Problems,* 32).

[22] Morson and Emerson, 249.

[23] In his conception of metaphor, Carlyle could even be said to anticipate Paul Ricoeur's contention that "Symbolism in general is not a secondary effect of social life; it constitutes real life as socially meaningful" ("Can There Be a Scientific Concept of Ideology?" in *Phenomenology and the Social Sciences: A Dialogue,* ed. Joseph Bien [Boston: M. Nijhoff, 1978], 51). Ricoeur, after realizing in *The Rule of Metaphor* Carlyle's belief that "A truly useful and philosophical work would be a good *Essay on Metaphors*" (*Two Note Books of Thomas Carlyle,* ed. Charles Eliot Norton [New York: Grolier Club, 1898], 142), concludes in the later *Ideology and Utopia* that we can only critique ideology when we "destroy a metaphor by the use of a contrary metaphor; we therefore proceed from metaphor to metaphor" (*Lectures on Ideology and Utopia,* ed. George H. Taylor [New York: Columbia University Press, 1986], 154). Carlyle too moves from metaphor to metaphor precisely for the purpose of, as Vanden Bossche has it, "prying us out of literal apprehension and forcing us to recognize the metaphors through which we perceive the world" (283).

[24] Letter to John Sterling, 4 June 1835, in *A Carlyle Reader,* 340-41.

[25] This fact led early critics to disparage Carlyle's abilities as a writer. Michael St. John Packe dismisses *Sartor Resartus* as "absolutely without form, devoid of coherent exposition, and couched in a quite unprecedented jargon" (*The Life of John Stuart Mill* [London: Secker and Packe, 1954], 167). John H. Muirhead similarly states that "no literary brilliancy could make up for the want of firmly drawn, consistently developed philosophical principles" (*The Platonic Tradition in Anglo-Saxon Philosophy* [London: Allen and Unwin, 1931], 141). Bakhtin, I would argue, offers us not only a way of interpreting the vagaries of Carlyle's style but of valorizing them.

[26] Paul Jay, *Being in the Text: Self-Representation from Wordsworth to Roland Barthes* (Ithaca: Cornell University Press, 1984), 2.

[27] Bakhtin makes a similar suggestion in "The Problem of the Text": "When there is a deliberate (conscious) multiplicity of styles, there are always dialogic relations among the styles" (*Speech Genres and Other Late Essays,* trans. Vern W. McGee, ed. Caryl Emerson and Michael Holquist [Austin: University of Texas Press, 1986], 112).

[28] I am indebted to those previous critics who have insisted on the importance of the Editor's role in Carlyle's text, particularly G. B. Tennyson's examination of the Editor in Tennyson's book, *Sartor Called Resartus:* "we must not overlook the way the material is presented and . . . we must not forget that Teufelsdröckh is, until the end, surrounded by the Editor" (182). See also LaValley, 90-94, and Dibble, 36-7, 43, 49.

[29] Gerald Bruns, "The Formal Nature of Victorian Thinking," *PMLA* 90 (1975): 906.

[30] Valentin N. Voloshinov, *Marxism and the Philosophy of Language,* trans. Ladislav Matejka and I. R. Titunik (Cambridge: Harvard University Press, 1973), 86.

[31] Carlyle, "Goethe's Helena," in *The Works of Thomas Carlyle,* 26:149. See also Helmling's argument for the "active" role of the reader in *Sartor Resartus* (37-41).

[32] Helmling makes a similar point about *Sartor Resartus:* "the whole activity of reading, of interpreting, of making sense and order out of difficult materials is one to which the reader is made both witness and self-conscious participant" (42).

[33] The former phrase is from David DeLaura, "Ishmael as Prophet: *Heroes and Hero-Worship* and the Self-Expressive Basis of Carlyle's Art," *Texas Studies in Literature and Language* 11 (1969): 708; for the latter term, see Gerry H. Brookes, *The Rhetorical Form of Carlyle's* Sartor Resartus (Berkeley: University of California Press, 1972), 63-78.

[34] Letter to John Sterling, 4 June 1835, in *A Carlyle Reader,* 342.

[35] Lee C. R. Baker, "The Open Secret of *Sartor Resartus:* Carlyle's Method of Converting His Reader," *Studies in Philology* 83 (1986): 224.

[36] See Brookes, 67.

John B. Lamb (essay date 1995)

SOURCE: "Carlyle's 'Chartism,' the Rhetoric of Revolution, and the Dream of Empire," in *Victorians Institute Journal,* Vol. 23, 1995, pp. 129-50.

[*In the following essay, Lamb contends that Carlyle, in*

his essay "Chartism," exploited what had become the "myth of the French revolution," in order to paint the Chartism movement in revolutionary terms and to thereby highlight its significance. Carlyle sought, Lamb argues, to advocate British imperialism as a cure for the country's social and economic distress, of which Chartism was a manifestation.]

Thomas Carlyle's **"Chartism"** first appeared in December 1839, a crucial moment in the debate over Parliamentary reform and the "Condition-of-England Question." The year 1839 was an extremely important period in the development and shaping of the Chartist movement and in the evolving strategies aimed at pressuring the government into again extending the franchise. Throughout that year, Victorians were either excited or alarmed by numerous and occasionally hysterical accounts in the periodical press of Chartist activities. In addition to extensive coverage of Chartist proceedings in radical publications like the *Northern Star* or the more virulent *London Democrat,* frequent reports of working-class agitation could be found in the *Examiner,* the *Spectator,* and the *Times,* all of which informed the public of mass meetings, riots, the discovery of arms caches, and the use of seditious language by Chartist orators.[1] For almost a week in July readers were treated to rumors of Birmingham in flames following the Bullring Riots, and in November reports of the Newport Rising in Wales received national attention. "Revolt" and "Insurrection" became watchwords of the day, and from Parliament to public platforms, from radical pamphlets to Tory journals, the rhetoric of revolution abounded. Coupled with accounts of a call to arms by some Chartist agitators, this rhetoric of violent revolt once again conjured up images of the French Revolution in the Victorian political imagination.

As David Lodge suggests, while responding to real historical events, the public impression of the Revolution was part of a "highly imaginative, quasi-fictional interpretation of that history" (127). By 1839 the French Revolution was a popular political myth, and Carlyle was apparently quite prepared to exploit this historical analogue himself in order to advocate his own solution to working-class unrest. Nor was it particularly unusual that he should do so. Nearly three years earlier, he had published his own contribution to the popular conception of French history,[2] and in May 1839 he had given two lectures on the French Revolution, one on "Girondism" and another on "Sansculottism." A month later, when Carlyle began contemplating his essay in earnest, he was apparently finishing up corrections for the second edition of *The French Revolution*[3]; so it is no wonder that event found its way into the pages of "Chartism." As Chris Vanden Bossche suggests, "Carlyle considered Chartism the latest rebirth of revolution" (92), and he was acutely concerned that it be correctly defined. "Chartism," Carlyle declares, "means the bitter discontent grown fierce and mad, the wrong condition therefore or the wrong disposition, of the Working Classes of England. It is a new name for a thing which has many names, which will have many" (119); and he intended that his designation of it should differ from that of "Girondin Radicals, Donothing Aristocrat-Conservatives, and Unbelieving Dilettante Whigs" (*Letters* 11: 218). It seems somewhat ironic, then, that given this intention, he should depend in his description of Chartism on a popular concept of the French Revolution that had been employed by British politicians since the fall of the Bastille and which was currently being exploited by the very Radicals, Whigs, and Tories he set himself to instruct. In fact, allusions to the French Revolution were a staple element in Chartist rhetoric itself, and by 1839 the invocation of the French Revolution was fast becoming a political cliché.

Perhaps it was not in the *use* of this particular historical myth that Carlyle saw himself diverging from his contemporaries, but in the *uses* to which such a myth could be put. As he claimed in *The French Revolution,* "Any approximation to the right name has value; were the right Name itself once here, the Thing is known henceforth, the Thing then is ours, and can be dealt with" (4: 204). To "name" the Chartist movement rightly was first to know it, and by comparing working-class agitation in 1839 to the French Revolution, Carlyle hoped to invoke his own history of that event and to suggest three things: that working-class distress is a direct result of "Aristocracies that do not govern, Priesthoods that do not teach" (161), that the Chartist movement itself is a revolt against the Utilitarian formulas, like the New Poor Law, by which the working classes were governed, and that like all revolutions, the chaos of Chartism is evidence of what he called in *The French Revolution* "a new Order shaping itself free" (3: 97). But more important, "right-Naming" is a form of political and ideological control, a way to order the anarchy of working-class discontent and channel its energies. The questions surrounding the insurrectionary fervor of working-class agitation in 1839 were the same as those Carlyle believed confronted the French in 1793, "What will it do; how will it henceforth shape itself?" (4: 114) For revolutions like Chartism, revolts of what Carlyle called the Sansculottic-kind, were self-consuming, leaving behind a moral and political "vacancy" and silence out of which the "new Order" and the rhetoric, the "right-Naming," that defined it would emerge.

Revolution, Carlyle declares in *The French Revolution,* means:

> the open violent Rebellion, and Victory of disimprisoned Anarchy against corrupt worn-out Authority: how Anarchy breaks prison; bursts up from the infinite Deep, and rages uncontrollable, immeasurable, enveloping a world; in phases after phases of fever-frenzy;—till the frenzy burning itself out, and what elements of new Order it held . . . developing themselves, the Uncontrollable be got, if not reimprisoned, yet harnessed, and its mad forces made to work towards their object as same regulated ones. (2: 211-12)

It was not revolution Carlyle feared; it was the power vacuum that inevitably came in its wake, before the "Uncontrollable" of contemporary working-class dissatisfaction could be harnessed. If the Chartist Movement was Victorian England's French Revolution, then Carlyle hoped it was a revolt that could be transacted "by argument alone" (150). In **"Chartism"** Carlyle seeks to fill the political silence that must inevitably follow this current manifestation of revolution by transforming the horror and nightmare of revolution and the "dumb deep want of the people" (121) into a new discourse, into a dream of empire.[4]

I

"Chartism," therefore, emerged on the eve of the "Hungry Forties" against a political backdrop of impending revolution and of revolutionary rhetoric, and that rhetoric had a long and illustrious history. The French Revolution had, as Clive Emsley suggests, a double impact in Britain. It not only produced a conservative backlash which hampered political reform, but it also revived reformers' hopes, and conservatives and radicals alike energized their propaganda with frequent allusions to events in France (54). During the first third of the nineteenth century, particularly in times of social unrest, the French Revolution became a popular historical analogue and served to remind the British of the anarchy that could ensue if, depending on one's political persuasion, reform measures either were or were not carried out. Between 1827 and the passage of the Great Reform Act of 1832, the French Revolution supplied Victorian politicians, like Macaulay, with a "ready-made armory of helpful warnings, contrasts, and analogies" which could be applied to current situations (Clive 103). In an 1831 speech delivered before the House of Commons, Macaulay used the French Revolution to underscore the necessity for reform: "It is because the French aristocracy resisted reform in 1783, that they were unable to resist revolution in 1789. It was because they clung too long to odious exemptions and distinctions, that they were at last unable to save their lands, their mansions, their heads" (443).

By 1833 it was clear to many Radical reformers that the Great Reform Act had done nothing to redress the grievances of the working classes, and extended or "Universal" suffrage was seen as the only way to avoid revolution. The passage of the New Poor Law in 1834 served only to increase the use of the rhetoric of revolt and allusions to the French Revolution, particularly by future Chartist leaders. Workhouses were termed "Bastilles," and books like G. R. Wythen Baxter's *The Book of the Bastile* continued the tradition of employing the French Revolution as a warning of what was to come:

> Had there been no *lettre de cachet*, the revolutionary *Marseillaise* would never have been turned in retribution, and Louis XVI would have died in his bed, and not on the block. Had there been no New Poor-Law, the name of Chartist would never have been heard; nor would

Birmingham have been heated in fire and fury, or Newport have run red with the gore of Britons from the hills. (quoted in Cole 341)

By 1837 agitation against the New Poor Law contributed to the creation of a "disturbed and anxious population in the manufacturing districts," and out of this agitation and anxiety Chartism was born (Thompson 57).

From the beginning, "physical force" Chartists like George Julian Harney, Dr. John Taylor, and Peter Bussey advocated open and violent resistance and attempted to intimidate the government by employing the menacing and often seditious rhetoric of revolt and by creating a kind of revolutionary theater at their mass meetings. Of the physical force Chartists, no one was more adroit at capitalizing on the rhetoric and symbology of the French Revolution than Harney, the leader of the London Democratic Association, one of the most militant political organizations to come to prominence in the 1830s. Harney took as his prototype Marat, and he and his fellow Democrats often arrived at meetings wearing tricolored sashes and carrying placards announcing their avowed Jacobin principles. The address to "The Enslaved, Oppressed, and Suffering Classes of Great Britain and Ireland," published in the *London Democrat,* is vintage Harney and is typical of the way in which Chartist orators exploited the Radical myth of the French Revolution to incite their working-class audiences to action and to frighten the general public into reform. Harney begins his remarks by declaring that the fate of the oppressed classes in past history has been to be the "eternal prey of blood-stained kings and conquerors." The French Revolution, however, overthrew "strongholds of tyranny"; and even if the Revolution failed, the principles of equality on which it was based are "immortal." Furthermore, Harney maintains,

> Those principles transplanted into "Church-and-King"-ridden England, are marching onward in triumph and glory in the *Democratic Association,* the *Jacobin Club* again lives and flourishes, and the villainous tyrants shall find to their cost, that England too has her *Marats, St. Justs,* and *Robespierres.* (332)

As Martha Vicinus points out, however, the inheritance of the French Revolution, used as part of a rhetorical strategy to force a hostile government to grant the working classes political rights, was an ambiguous one (481-82). It could clearly backfire. Although the government's response to Chartist agitation was on the whole rather even-tempered and cautious, in March of 1839 Lord John Russell, the Home Secretary, announced in a letter on the "Disturbed Districts" the government's willingness to accept the services of local militia formed for "the protection of life and property" should rioting seem imminent ("Disturbed Districts"). Towards the end of April the Home Office called up three regiments of regular troops from Ireland. While these measures were in large part due to the storing and selling of arms by alleged Chartists, the violent rhetoric used by physical force advocates could only have added to the government's wariness and fueled the public's perception that the Chartists were, indeed, planning an insurrection.

But more important, the rhetoric of revolution was not the privileged discourse of the Chartists alone. Comparisons of working-class unrest to the French Revolution appeared in the speeches and essays of politicians and writers of very different political persuasions, and Conservatives and Radicals alike vied for the authority to interpret history and use it as an analogue for the present day crisis. Thus, when Thomas Attwood, one of the few Chartist leaders who was a member of Parliament, presented the National Petition to the House of Commons on July 12, 1839, "he could not avoid calling to their [the members of the House of Commons] recollection the situation of Louis 16th in 1787 and 1789. When Louis was asleep ruin was stalking through the land." As part of his reply to Attwood, Lord Russell could claim "that those persons . . . who have promoted this petition, have been found going through the country, from town to town and from place to place, exhorting the people in the most violent and revolutionary language—language not exceeded in the worst times of the French Revolution—to subvert the laws by force of arms" (*Hansard* cols. 230-31, 236). In both cases, allusions to the French Revolution appeared to warn the people of a coming insurrection and were used in the propaganda war either to encourage or to sabotage reform. The debate surrounding the National Petition and working-class discontent, then, clearly involved the use of the myth of the French Revolution, and history in general, for quite different political ends.

When Parliament rejected the National Petition, the political climate became more and more heated and revolutionary rhetoric took on a decided edge. By August, the *Monthly Magazine* was declaring that "the highest Institution—the monarchy itself is in peril. The Queen needs protection" ("Progress" 236), and in September the Tory journal *Blackwood's* was asking how the British people were "to be saved from the horrors of a convulsion similar to that which, fifty years ago, spread desolation and misery through the whole of France" ("The Chartists" 289). When armed Chartists tried to take Newport by force, it seemed as if it was already too late; the revolution had arrived.

II

It is against such a backdrop that **"Chartism"** needs to be read, because Carlyle clearly capitalizes on the political climate in late 1839 and on the rhetoric of revolt. As I suggested earlier, Carlyle made a significant contribution to the popular myth of the French Revolution with the publication of his history in 1837; and clearly for many of his readers *The French Revolution* was both

a history of events in France and a tract for the times, a powerful parable of the contemporary political situation in Victorian England. This was Thackeray's view, and in an unsigned review of *The French Revolution* in the *Times,* he commends the book to his readers for its cautionary moral:

> The hottest Radical in England may learn by it that there is something more necessary for him even than his mad liberty—the authority, namely by which he retains his head on his shoulders and his money in his pocket. . . . It teaches . . . to rulers and ruled alike moderation, and yet there are many who would react the same dire tragedy, and repeat the experiment tried in France so fatally. (Siegel 74)

Carlyle himself saw his history as offering a warning to the British people as well, and toward the close of *The French Revolution* he offers his readers this advice: "That there be no second Sansculottism in our Earth for a thousand years, let us understand well what the first was; and let Rich and Poor of us go and do *otherwise*" (4: 313). But by the end of 1839, it was clear to Carlyle and others that the English people—"Rich and Poor"—had not done otherwise and that chaos and Sansculottism had come again.

Sansculottism, Carlyle claimed in *The French Revolution,* was not a thing to be feared, but it did need to be known for what it was: "the portentous inevitable end of much, the miraculous beginning of much." But he warned against reducing the phenomenon "to a dead-logic formula" (2: 214). In **"Chartism"** Carlyle reacted to attempts by others to measure the discontent of the working class in England, to turn the poor and their grievances into statistics. This, to Carlyle, was not only wrong; it was absolutely foolhardy, because in its attempt to account for the symptoms, it ignored the disease: "Chartist torch-meetings; Birmingham riots, Swing conflagrations, are so many symptoms on the surface; you abolish the symptom to no purpose if the disease is left untouched" (120). Carlyle, then, set out in his essay to suggest a cure for the infection of the body politic known as **"Chartism."** But, before he could do so, he had to diagnose correctly the essence of the illness; for such an interpretation of working-class distress, he claimed, "were equivalent to remedy of it" (122). But to make such a diagnosis, he needed to reclaim the French Revolution from the political rhetoric of the day. If Chartism was a "second Sansculottism," then Carlyle wanted to claim the right to interpret such a "great Phenomenon," to make history and employ it in the fashioning of a "new Order." He wanted to transform the popular myth of the French Revolution into a "genealogic Mythus" of imperial conquest.

The idea of mythus is central to Carlyle's project in **"Chartism,"** because it is in this essay that he seeks to find a credible replacement for the idea of revolution he proposed in the *French Revolution.* Carlyle defines mythus in *Sartor Resartus* as a "new vehicle and vesture" (144) that, as Chris Vanden Bossch points out, is aimed at engendering a rebirth of society (62). But in **"Chartism,"** Carlyle's new mythus of empire partakes of the order of *märchen,* those popular traditional tales that are, in part, the subject of *German Romance* first published in 1827. Like *märchen,* Carlyle's "history" of the British race in **"Chartism"** images forth "in shadowy emblems the universal tendencies and destinies of man" (*German Romance,* II: 266). As Albert J. LaValley notes, Carlyle's invocation of a new mythus in works like *Sartor Resartus, The French Revolution,* and **"Chartism"** is both a return to a "primitive ground that is ultimately all-powerful" and the promise of a new social and political order that is based upon that ground (143). Carlyle's new "genealogic Mythus," and the "Epic Poem" that the historical manifestation of such a mythus creates, provides the imaginary structure and vehicle for imperial conquest as a national ideal. As LaValley further notes, the new society which emerges from out of the practices inherent in this mythus "promises to be consonant with man's economic and instinctual necessities" (144). "Mythus" is, therefore, the rhetorical vesture of Carlyle's emerging politics, one of the many forms of "right-Naming" his works set out to achieve.

In *The French Revolution,* the new "vehicle and vesture" was what Carlyle called "vital Chaos" or "a new Order shaping itself free." But the moral that ends his history, "let us do *otherwise,*" suggests in the end a less than enthusiastic endorsement of the mythus of revolution.[5] The mythus of empire that Carlyle inaugurates in **"Chartism"** was aimed at controlling the chaos and destruction of revolution itself while addressing the economic uncertainties of the times, particularly over-population. By discovering in England's history a genealogy of conquest, Carlyle hoped to "articulate correctly" (176) the hereditary might of British people and supplant the rhetoric of reform with a rhetoric of imperialism.

Reform rhetoric with its ghastly portents of revolution inextricably linked Chartism and the "Condition-of-England Question" with the issue of Parliamentary representation, with democracy. As Carlyle notes in **"Chartism,"** "Democracy, we are well aware, what is called 'self government' of the multitude by the multitude, is in words the thing everywhere passionately clamoured for at present" (158). For Radicals, democracy was the great panacea for working-class distress; for Conservatives democracy was not the cure but the cause of civil unrest. In "Chartism" it is interesting to note what little attention Carlyle actually gives to what was the most important demand in the National Petition, Universal Suffrage. For Carlyle, democracy is neither the cause of nor the cure for working-class discontent. Merely another symptom of that discontent, it is, Carlyle claims, ultimately the "consummation of No-government and *Laissez-faire*" (159). Democracy, like revolution itself, is a "self-canceling business" (158): it is "found but as a regulated method of rebellion

and abrogation; it abrogates the old arrangement of things; and leaves, as we say, *zero* and vacuity for the institution of a new arrangement" (159). Carlyle, thus, equates revolution with reform itself, democracy with the very working-class discontent it sets out to cure, and all, he insists, create a political vacuum in which there is no center of authority. Democracy, reform, and revolution are forms of chaos that destroy but do not necessarily create.

The failure and absence of authority is one of the lessons that the history of the French Revolution can teach, and for Carlyle the Chartist Movement is a historical palimpsest beneath which lie the terror and horror of the French Revolution. The truth that it images forth is "as Hierarchies and Dynasties of all kinds . . . have ruled the world; so it was appointed, in the decree of Providence, that . . . Victorious Anarchy, Jacobinism, Sanculottism, French Revolution, Horrors of French Revolution, or what ever mortals name it, should have its turn" (2: 212) As Carlyle makes quite clear in his essay, one of the new names for this recurrent anarchy is "Chartism" itself: "These Chartisms, Radicalisms, Reform Bill, Tithe Bill, and infinite other discrepancy, and acrid argument and jargon that there is yet to be, are *our* French Revolution" (149-50). Hence, like the French Revolution, Chartism represents the struggle against the world of political and social formulas which fail to address the realities of working-class dissatisfaction. At least one important inference, Carlyle believes, can be drawn from the Chartist agitation of 1839, "that in brief, a government of the under classes by the upper on the principle of *Let-alone* is no longer possible in England in these days" (155). The Chartist Movement, with its torchlight meetings, announces the failure, and indeed, the extinction, of a utilitarian form of government and "As good as announces an *abdication* on the part of governors" (156).

Like other writers who addressed the "Condition-of-England Question," Carlyle sees the problems of the working classes as stemming from such a failure of government and the loss of an effective center of authority. But while, like others, he sees little hope to be found in the Tory aristocracy or the Whig government,[6] he is no advocate of what he calls "Paralytic Radicalism" (191), for the Parliamentary Radicals who call for universal suffrage simply seek to continue the tradition of "No government" and have failed to procure for the working classes anything of lasting value.

What *The French Revolution* makes clear to Victorians is that all formulas—Tory, Whig, and Radical alike—are solecisms, failures in discourse, and deviations from the natural order of things; and such solecisms, Carlyle maintains in his history, are liable "to such abysmal overturns and frightful instantaneous inversions of the center-of-gravity" (2: 207). But, Carlyle also insists, "man lives not except with formulas; with customs, *ways* of doing and living. . . . There are modes wherever there are men. It is the deepest law of man's nature; whereby man is a craftsman and 'tool-using animal'; not the slave of Impulse, Chance and brute Nature" (4: 168). If Chartism represented a revolt by the working classes against the formulas by which they were governed and if it signalled an equal failure in the political discourse of the day to avert such a revolution "by argument alone," then clearly what was needed was a new formula, a new way of doing for the "'tool-using'" Englishman. For Carlyle the elements of that new formula and the "new Order" it would engender were work, manifest destiny, and imperialist enterprise, and these were the elements of a new political rhetoric or "mythus" as well.

III

"Work," Carlyle declares in **"Chartism,"** "is the mission of man in this Earth" (133), as well as the first law of nature, and as such, work partakes not of chaos but of order. But for the working classes in Victorian England that "mission" had been complicated by the rise of capitalism and "Cash Payment": "English Commerce with its world-wide convulsive fluctuations, with its immeasurable Proteus-Steam-demon, makes all paths uncertain for [the working classes], all life a bewilderment" (143). In the face of such economic uncertainties, the working classes could not "any longer go without government; without being *actually* guided and governed" (155), and the utilitarian formulas, like the New Poor Law, by which they were now led only crippled them. The Poor Law Amendment Act, Carlyle declares,

> was a broken reed to lean on, if there ever was one; and did but lame [the working man's] right-hand. Let him cast it far from him, that broken reed, and look to the opposite point of the heavens for help. His unlamed right-hand, with the cunning industry that lies in it, is not this defined to be 'the scepter of our Planet'? He that can work is born a king of something; is in communion with Nature, is master of thing or things. (134-35)

For Carlyle, every worker, even the Irish "Sanspotato," was at heart an imperialist, with "desires illimitable as the Autocrat of all the Russias!" (136). But, if work bestowed sovereignty upon the working classes, it still left them without a kingdom to rule, and neither the Tories nor the Whigs were prepared to share their property. For the workers to be masters and not slaves, to have their sense of injustice mollified and their "illimitable" imperial desires sated, then there had to be "kingdoms" for them to conquer.

Carlyle introduces his vision of an imperial work force in a "Chapter on the Eras of England," written by Carlyle's alter-ego, Herr Professor Sauerteig. The shift from the history of the French Revolution to the history of England since the days of "Hengst and Horsa" is central to the transition from the theme of revolt to the theme of empire in "Chartism." In 1839 popular po-

litical sentiment was apt to view current disturbances on the Continent as an ongoing result of the French Revolution, and while Carlyle clearly wanted to invoke the horrors of that event in his essay and to define its causes, he did not want to imply that England's fate would be the same as France's. For England's history told of a different and, indeed, manifest destiny:

> Of a truth, whosoever had, with the bodily eye, seen Hengst and Horsa mooring on the mud-beach of Thanet, on that spring morning of the Year 449; and then, with the spiritual eye, looked forward to New York, Calcutta, Sidney Cove, across the ages and oceans; and thought what Wellingtons, Washingtons, Shakespears, Miltons, Watts, Arkwrights, William Pitts and Davie Crocketts had to issue from that business, and do their several taskwork so, *he* would have said, those leather-boats of Hengst's had a kind of cargo in them! A genealogic Mythus superior of any in the old Greek, to almost any in the old Hebrew itself; and not a Mythus either, but every fibre of it fact. (172)

In **"Chartism"** the epic poem of the French Revolution metamorphoses into a new "Epic Poem" (172), the epic of empire, as England becomes a second Rome and Carlyle pays homage to the universal law of might: "By the same great law do Roman Empires establish themselves, Christian Religions promulgate themselves, and all extant Powers bear rule. The strong thing is the just thing" (174). The new "Mythus" that comes in answer to the new era with its seething working-class discontent will be a mythus of conquest, and like "any in the old Hebrew itself," it will prophesy the triumph of a chosen people.

That prophecy comes in the answer to the question with which Sauerteig's history commences, "Who shall say what work and works England has yet to?" (171):

> To this English People in World-History, there have been, shall I say, two grand tasks assigned? Huge-looming through the dim tumult of the always incommensurate Present Time, outlines of two tasks disclose themselves: the grand Industrial task of conquering some half or more of this Terraqueous Planet for the use of man; then secondly the grand Constitutional task of sharing, in some pacific, endurable manner, the fruit of said conquest, and showing all people how it might be done. (175)

The note of pacifism fails to disguise the fact that here is a nascent imperial dream. England, led by latter-day "Watts, Arkwrights, Brindleys" will, like an industrialist Prospero, take "captive the world," and with iron as its "missionary," preach "*its* evangel to the brute Primeval Powers, which listen and obey" (181).

For England to conquer the planet and build a brave new world, the gospel of work must now become the gospel of empire and announce the coming of "New Men." If the country is over-populated and plagued with the contagion of working-class distemper, Carlyle exclaims, "does not everywhere else a whole vacant Earth, as it were, call to us, Come and till me, come and reap me!" (200). The disease known as Chartism, the revolution come again with its "swelling" and "simmering" unrest, is but a case of toxemia infecting the body politic, and therefore, Carlyle insists at the close of this essay, as a disease it is "the noblest of all—as of her who is in pain and sore travail, but travails that she may be a mother, and say, Behold, there is a new Man born!" (203). Mother England, it seems, will give birth to Victoria's imperialists.

But at the end of **"Chartism"** the question remains, now that the evangel of imperialism has been written, who will lead these "new Men" in their conquest of the world? Although Carlyle laments the lack of contemporary "Hengsts and Alarics" (204), of an empire-building aristocracy, his use of his own history of the French Revolution in his description of the causes and symptoms of working-class unrest suggests that he did have a particular type of leader in mind, a new hero to lead the "new Man," even though he fails to find him in 1839. Chartism, like the French Revolution, is "a thing *without* order," and it must "work and welter, not as a Regularity but as a Chaos; destructive and self-destructive, always till something that *has* order arise, strong enough to bind it into subjection again." Further, Carlyle suggests, what the "something" is "will not be a Formula, with philosophical propositions and forensic eloquence, but a Reality, probably with a sword in hand!" (4: 114).

Carlyle delineates the image of that leader, "sword in hand," five months later, in the sixth of his lectures on hero-worship, "The Hero as King," and that leader is Napoleon Bonaparte. Although Carlyle's opinion of Napoleon is mixed, for Napoleon the Revolution-tamer he reserves unstinting praise. What Napoleon succeeded in was bringing order to the Revolution, harnessing the destructive energies of the people and turning them toward the building of an empire. His destiny was "To bridle-in that great devouring, self-devouring French Revolution; to *tame* it, so that its intrinsic purpose can be made good, that it may become *organic,* and be able to live among other organisms and *formed* things, not as a wasting destruction alone" (240).

Napoleon entered the history of the French Revolution precisely at the moment when Sanscullotism had devoured itself, and Carlyle feels that in 1839 England is facing a similar moment. As Carlyle makes clear in **"Chartism,"** the "intrinsic purpose" of a country beset by revolution can only be realized in a "change of practice" (170). If England's "intrinsic purpose" is to conquer the world, then the new "practice" would be empire building, and what England needs is another Napoleon. The "wish and prayer" of the working class is "Give me a leader; a true leader, not a false sham-leader; a true leader, that he may guide me on the way" (159), and the only viable answer to that prayer, Carlyle insists, is an "Iron Missionary," sword in hand. The "true way," therefore, leads not towards democracy or continued reform, but rather towards the brave new world of the British Empire.

IV

In *The Origins of Totalitarianism,* Hannah Arendt claims that imperialism was "an entirely new concept in the long history of political thought and action" (125), and when the imperialist idea found favor following the economic crisis in England in the late 1860s, it "seemed to offer a permanent remedy for a permanent evil": "superfluous capital and superfluous working power" (150). For politicians like Gladstone, who were sensitive to working-class distress and who shared the popular conviction that class struggle was so endemic to modern politics that it threatened the very stability of the state, "Expansion again appeared as a lifesaver, if and insofar as it could provide a common interest for the nation as a whole" (152). But Gladstone did not become Prime Minister until 1868, nearly thirty years after the publication of **"Chartism."** Considering the fact that "by 1840 there was an aggressive and decidedly vocal body of anti-imperial opinion in England" (Schuyler 77), Carlyle's essay appears to be an anomaly in early Victorian political thought and an uncanny bit of prophecy. Indeed, to a degree, it is. Granted, the idea of emigration and colonization as a solution to over-population and working-class distress was not new.[7] But there was little discussion of emigration during the early years of Chartist agitation. It was not until 1847-48, when the energy of the Chartist movement had all but dissipated, that emigration become a recurrent topic in the periodical press, and it was never seen as a way to avoid directly the threat of revolution.[8]

Despite the mixed reception and overall critical neglect that **"Chartism"** has received since its publication in 1839, it is a crucial work in Carlyle's oeuvre and an important political document of its time. It is perhaps the best example of the ideological control inherent in Carlyle's concept of "right-Naming," for "right-Naming" is not just a form of knowledge; it is a form of power. Neither Carlyle's comparison of the Chartist Movement to the French Revolution nor his advocacy of emigration was novel. As I have shown, such a comparison was a staple element in the political rhetoric of the day, and it allowed Carlyle the opportunity to exploit the worst fears of his largely middle-class audience, an audience that was not eager to extend its new-found political power any further. But **"Chartism"** is not just a jeremiad, since it goes beyond a lamentation for the present times in its vision of a nation of happy, hero-worshipping empire builders. Carlyle presents that vision, that imperialist dream, as the cure for the disease of economic and political distress, and it is one which can be accomplished without Universal Suffrage. Carlyle's essay attempts to elide the rhetoric of working-class revolt and its Parliamentary counterpart by suppressing the question of Universal Suffrage almost altogether. Revolution, although an inevitable aspect of political growth, raised the question not of the right of representation, which is to Carlyle's way of thinking simply another manifestation of revolt itself, but of national destiny. Reform rhetoric is solecistic, and he wishes to supplant it in the political rhetoric of the day with one more "proper" for the descendants of Hengst and Horsa, with the discourse of empire. While C. A. Bodelsen may be correct in asserting that "on the whole Carlyle's influence on Imperialist thought and the growth of the Imperial movement is not striking" (24), given his growing stature and influence as a writer, his participation in this shift in political discourse from the rhetoric of revolution to the rhetoric of empire is significant.

In 1841 Henry Chapman commenced an essay on "Emigration" in the *Westminster Review* with language that is reminiscent of **"Chartism"**:

> The great activity of the spirit of colonization is among the most conspicuous features of the times. From the earliest period of history, the English people have been essentially restless and migratory. Themselves a colony, they seem never to have lost the habits of their Saxon ancestry; and when the discovery of a New World opened a more extended field for the exercise of that migratory disposition, it is not at all surprising that the British nation took a lead in what Bacon called the "heroic work" of planting new colonies. (132)

While Chapman is no Sauerteig, his essay announces a "new Era" in the building of the British empire and proclaims the return of the "spirit of colonization." In fact, Chapman argues that "A complete revolution in the state of opinion respecting emigration . . . has taken place" (132). Although Chapman's claims are certainly exaggerated, an imperialist revolution was slowly beginning to take shape; and Carlyle's **"Chartism"** must be seen as a formative document in that transformation of Victorian political thought. For out of the rhetoric of revolution, Carlyle had helped to fashion a new discourse on which a "new" Imperial "Order" could be founded.

One of the most interesting motifs in ***The French Revolution*** depicts the frenzied inarticulateness of the revolutionary classes. By September 1792, Carlyle declares, "All France . . . moans and rages, inarticulately shrieking" (4: 46). He repeats this theme in **"Chartism,"** describing the working classes as "struggling . . . with inarticulate uproar, like dumb creatures in pain, unable to speak what is in them!" (122). Revolution brings anarchy to language, as well as to the state. Revolution *dis*orders language, deconstructs it and the hierarchies—the "*ways* of doing and living"—that language encodes. The French Revolution exhausted itself, Carlyle suggests, with the final shriek of Robespierre, when the executioner "wrenched the dirty linen" from his broken jaw (4: 285); and then for a time came silence. The Chartist Movement, that manifestation of the fierce discontent of the "great dumb toiling class which cannot speak" (121), Carlyle implies in his essay, will fall into silence too; and out of the speech that follows, if it be heard, a "new Order" and a "new Era" will be born. In **"Chartism,"** perhaps for the only time in his life, Carlyle preaches an evangel that comes true.

Notes

[1] For example, on 7 July 1839, the *Examiner,* reporting on a Chartist meeting in Stockport, claimed, "Last night another inflammatory gathering of Chartists was held, at which upwards of 10,000 persons attended, and the language was, if possible, more direct and daring than any preceding meeting. The people were exhorted immediately to procure fire-arms, swords, daggers, &c., of every description."

[2] It is important to make a distinction here between the myth of the French Revolution as it existed in the popular political imagination and Carlyle's use of mythic patterns and allusions to literary mythologies in his own history. While much recent work has been done on myth in the *French Revolution,* little has been done on Carlyle's participation in and shaping of the larger "quasi-fictional" public interpretation of the Revolution that Lodge speaks of. See, especially, Mark Cumming 73-91; Chris R. Vanden Bossche 40-89; John D. Rosenberg 29-114; and Albert J. LaValley 121-182.

[3] See Carlyle's letter to his mother, dated 7 June 1839; in *Collected Letters* 11:124.

[4] Carlyle's use of parallels to the French Revolution in "Chartism" and his "imperialist" tendencies have been the subject of earlier study, although the relationship between the two has never been drawn. See, especially, Patrick Brantlinger 81-83, and C. A. Bodelsen.

[5] John Rosenberg suggests that Carlyle's response to the French Revolution combined "elements of admiration and fear," and that while Carlyle found all forms of civil disorder abhorrent, he "was also fascinated by violence in all of its manifestations." Hence, Rosenberg argues, Carlyle's "let us go and do *otherwise*" is more ambivalent than it appears (95).

[6] It is interesting to note that Carlyle originally intended his essay to appear in the Conservative *Quarterly Review,* and told its editor, John Gibson Lockhart, "It seems to me the better class of Conservatives were on the whole the persons to whom it were hopefullest and in many ways fittest to address myself" (*Letters* 11: 101). Lockhart, however, eventually rejected the essay, and Carlyle came to feel that it would find no safe harbor in any of the party journals.

[7] C. C. Eldridge notes that "During the years of periodic unemployment and trade depression after the Napoleonic wars, when much talk was heard of the danger of social revolution, colonization was advocated as a means of alleviating the widespread pauperism, the abject poverty and distress in the English agricultural counties, as well as overpopulation in Ireland" (28). And as P. J. Cain and A. G. Hopkins point out, despite such anti-imperialist sentiment, "The period 1837-42, when domestic depression was acute and Chartism reached its climax, also saw more frequent use of the 'political arm' of overseas expansion" (480).

[8] E. M. Palmegiano lists only a handful of articles on emigration in the late 1830s and early 1840s in *The British Empire in the Victorian Press, 1832-1867: A Bibliography.*

Works Cited

Arendt, Hannah. *The Origins of Totalitarianism.* New York: Harcourt Brace, 1973.

Bodelsen, C. A. *Studies in Mid-Victorian Imperialism.* New York: Knopf, 1925.

Brantlinger, Patrick. *The Spirit of Reform.* Cambridge: Harvard UP, 1977.

Cain, P. J., and A. G. Hopkins, "The Political Economy of British Overseas Expansion." *Economic History Review* 33 (1980): 463-90.

Carlyle, Thomas. "Chartism." Vol. 29 of *The Works of Thomas Carlyle.* Ed. H. D. Traill. 30 vols. London: 1899.

———. *The Collected Letters of Thomas and Jane Welsh Carlyle.* Eds. Charles L. Sanders and K. J. Fielding. 24 vols. Durham: Duke UP, 1970-1995.

———. *The French Revolution.* Vols. 2-4 of *Works.*

———. *German Romance.* Vols. 21-22 of *Works.*

———. *On Heroes and Hero-Worship.* Vol. 24 of *Works.*

———. *Sartor Resartus.* Ed. C. F. Harrold. Indianapolis: Odyssey, 1937.

Chapman, Henry. "Emigration: Comparative Prospects of Our New Colonies." *Westminster Review* 35 (1841): 131-87.

"The Chartists and Universal Suffrage." *Blackwood's Edinburgh Magazine* 96 (1839): 289-302.

Clive, John. "Macaulay and the French Revolution." Crossly and Small. Oxford: Oxford UP, 1989. 103-22.

Cole, G. D. H., and A. W. Filson. *British Working-Class Movements, Select Documents, 1789-1875.* London: Macmillan, 1951.

Crossly, Ceri, and Ian Small, eds. *The French Revolution and British Culture.* Oxford, Oxford UP, 1989.
Cumming, Mark. *A Disimprisoned Epic: Form and Vision in Carlyle's "French Revolution."* Philadelphia: U of Pennsylvania, 1988.

"Disturbed Districts. Letter from the Secretary of State for the Home Department to the Lords Lieutenant of Certain Counties." *Parliamentary Papers* 38 (1939): 299.

Eldridge, C. C. *England's Mission: The Imperial Idea in the Age of Gladstone and Disraeli 1868-1900.* Chapel Hill: U of North Carolina 1973.

Emsley, Clive. "The Impact of the French Revolution on Brit-

ish Politics and Society." Crossly and Small. 31-62.

Hansard, Third Series. 99 (12 July 1939): cols. 219-77.

Harney, George Julian. "Address to the Enslaved, Oppressed, and Suffering Classes of Great Britain and Ireland." *An Anthology of Chartist Literature.* Ed. Y. V. Kovalev. Moscow: 1956.

Hollis, Patricia, ed. *Class Conflict in Nineteenth-Century Britain.* Boston: Routledge, 1973.

LaValley, Albert J. *Carlyle and the Idea of the Modern.* New Haven: Yale UP, 1968.

Lodge, David. "The French Revolution and the Condition of England: Crowds and Power in the Early Victorian Novel." Crossly and Small. 123-50.

Macaulay, Thomas Babington. *The Works of Lord Macaulay.* Vol 11. London: 1914.

Palmegiano, E. M. *The British Empire in the Victorian Press, 1832-1867: A Bibliography.* New York: Garland, 1987.

"Progress of Insurrection." *Monthly Magazine* 98 (1839): 232-36.

Rosenberg, John. *Carlyle and the Burden of History.* Cambridge: Harvard UP, 1985.

Schuyler, Robert Livingston. *The Fall of the Old Colonial System.* Hamden, Connecticut: Archon Books, 1966.

Siegel, Jules Paul, ed. *Thomas Carlyle: The Critical Heritage.* New York: Barnes and Noble, 1971.

Thompson, Dorothy. *The Chartists.* New York: Pantheon Books, 1984.

Vanden Bossche, Chris R. *Carlyle and the Search for Authority.* Columbus: Ohio State UP, 1991.

Vicinus, Martha. "'To Live Free or Die': The Relationship between Strategy and Style in Chartist Speeches, 1838-39." *Style* 10 (1976): 481-500.

FURTHER READING

Criticism

Adrian, Arthur A., and Vonna H. Adrian. "Frederick the Great: 'That Unutterable Horror of a Prussian Book.'" In *Carlyle Past and Present: A Collection of New Essays,* edited by K. J. Fielding and Rodger L. Tarr, pp. 177-97. New York: Barnes and Noble Books, 1976.

Examines Carlyle's attraction to the Prussian emperor Frederick the Great as a subject of biography, and argues that, while Frederick's forceful ruling style appealed to Carlyle's political convictions, it was the emperor's "personal circumstances and qualities" (which Carlyle felt he shared with his hero) that drew Carlyle to Frederick.

Annan, Noel. "Historians Reconsidered: IX: Carlyle." *History Today* II, No. 10 (October 1952): 659-65.

Studies the apparent contradictions in Carlyle's beliefs and asserts that "the clue to these contradictions" may be found by examining Carlyle's interpretations of history rather than his personal experiences.

Behnken, Eloise M. *Thomas Carlyle: "Calvinist Without the Theology."* Columbia, Mo.: University of Missouri Press, 1978, 149p.

Explores "the writings of Carlyle as contributions to the Victorian quest for belief."

Beimard, Charles A. "Rebelling from the Right Side: Thomas Carlyle's Struggle against the Dominant Nineteenth-Century Rhetoric." *Studies in Scottish Literature* 22 (1987): 142-56.

Examines Carlyle's break from the "rhetorical paradigm of his age" as significant in its rejection of the theories of the eighteenth century.

Brookes, Gerry H. *The Rhetorical Form of Carlyle's* Sartor Resartus. Berkeley: University of California Press, 1972, 201p.

Studies the rhetorical devices of *Sartor Resartus*, including the problems related to the form of the book and the role of the Editor as the "controlling voice."

Dibble, Jerry Allen. "Carlyle's 'British Reader' and the Structure of *Sartor Resartus*." *Texas Studies in Literature and Language* XVI, No. 2 (Summer 1974): 293-304.

Analyzes the role of the Reader in *Sartor Resartus*, arguing that the reader undergoes "a course of instruction" throughout the book, and that the organization of the book reflects the progress and changes in attitude of the Reader.

Goldberg, Michael. "A Universal 'howl of execration': Carlyle's *Latter-Day Pamphlets* and Their Critical Reception." In *Carlyle and His Contemporaries*, pp. 129-47. Durham, N.C.: Duke University Press, 1976.

Reviews the overwhelmingly negative reaction to *Latter-Day Pamphlets* and argues that this negative response reflected a major shift in the public's opinion of Carlyle.

Ikeler, Abbott A. "Carlyle on Literature: Conflicting Views." In *Puritan Temper and Transcendental Faith: Carlyle's Literary Vision*, pp. 3-38. Columbus, Ohio: Ohio State University Press, 1972.

Studies Carlyle's "declining opinion" of literature that seems to occur between the publication of *Sartor Resartus* and *Latter-Day Pamphlets*, and concludes that this shift is not strictly due to Carlyle's age because similar views are found in Carlyle's earlier works.

John, Brian. "The Fictive World of Thomas Carlyle." In *Supreme Fictions: Studies in the Work of William Blake, Thomas Carlyle, W. B. Yeats, and D. H. Lawrence*, pp. 75-147. Montreal: McGill-Queen's University Press, 1974.

Argues for the "distinctively *fictive* character of Carlyle's work" as seen in his portrayal of the forces of darkness and light and in his stylistic and technical achievements.

Levine, George. "*Sartor Resartus* and the Balance of Fiction." In *The Boundaries of Fiction: Carlyle, Macaulay, Newman*, pp. 19-78. Princeton: Princeton University Press, 1968.

Uses Carlyle's *Sartor Resartus* in exploring how fiction affected Victorian society.

Morrow, John. "Heroes and Constitutionalists: The Ideological Significance of Thomas Carlyle's Treatment of the English Revolution." *History of Political Thought* XIV, No. 2 (Summer 1993): 205-23.

Maintains that Carlyle's historical writings grew out of his belief that a figure was needed "who would do for modern government and society what Cromwell had done for mid-seventeenth-century England," and that these writings were integral to Carlyle's efforts to convince his contemporaries of the need for "a new form of leadership and organization."

Tennyson, G. B. "Carlyle: Beginning with the Word." In *The Victorian Experience: The Prose Writers*, edited by Richard A. Levine, pp. 1-21. Athens, Ohio: Ohio University Press, 1982.

Provides a general review of the ways in which Carlyle has been read and studied from his time to the present.

Tillotson, Geoffrey. "Carlyle." In *A View of Victorian Literature*, pp. 55-111. Oxford: Clarendon Press, 1978.

Offers a general discussion of Carlyle, focusing on the author's essential sympathy for humanity and on his influence upon other Victorian writers.

Elizabeth Cleghorn Gaskell

1810-1865

(Born Elizabeth Cleghorn Stevenson; used the pseudonym Cotton Mather Mills) English novelist, biographer, short story writer, and poet.

For additional information on Gaskell's life and works, see *NCLC,* Volume 5.

INTRODUCTION

A figure of the "golden age" of nineteenth-century English literature, Gaskell is best known for her novels of social reform and psychological realism, notably *Ruth* (1853) and *North and South* (1854). Her treatment of issues ranging from prostitution to mother-daughter relations both captured the public imagination and caused a great deal of controversy during Gaskell's own lifetime and has attracted the attention of more recent critics interested in problems of authorship and social responsibility. Gaskell's refined and compassionate portrayals of her central characters—often young, unmarried women who suffer misfortune—and her skillful use of detail have established an enduring popularity for and interest in her work.

Biographical Information

Born in London in 1810, Gaskell was the daughter of an occasional minister of the Unitarian Church in England. Gaskell's mother died when Elizabeth was a year old, and Elizabeth was sent to live with her maternal aunt in rural Cheshire, where she attended a school for girls. Educated in fine arts and languages, Gaskell began to read extensively, particularly novels, developing a love for books that would be sustained throughout her life. In 1831, she travelled to Newcastle, Edinburgh, and Manchester to visit prominent Unitarian ministers. In Manchester, she met William Gaskell, a young Unitarian clergyman; they were married in 1832 and lived in Manchester. Of her six children, four daughters survived infancy, and Gaskell maintained close relationships with all of them. It was in response to the death of her second child, William, from scarlet fever in 1845 that her husband suggested Gaskell begin writing as a form of distraction from mourning. The resulting novel, *Mary Barton* (1848), reflected Gaskell's interest in the plight of families, and particularly of women, affected by the industrialization of England. After the popular success of *Mary Barton*, Gaskell produced a prolific number of short stories and novels over the remaining years of her life.

Because William Gaskell was a professor of history and literature at Manchester New College, the family was relatively wealthy, and Gaskell became deeply occupied with charitable endeavors as well as with her now-successful writing career, while also finding time to travel in Europe. Additionally, she developed friendships, often sustained primarily through letters, with a number of prominent persons of literary or charitable circles, such as George Eliot, Mary Howitt, Charlotte Brontë, and Florence Nightingale. Gaskell published many of her short stories and serialized novels in *Household Words*, a popular journal that Charles Dickens edited. Gaskell was known in Manchester to be a gracious hostess and a very private celebrity, and she clearly struggled to negotiate the demands of private and public life, as many of her central characters do. At the height of her career, Gaskell was asked by the Reverend Patrick Brontë to write a biography of his daughter Charlotte, who had recently died. This work was published in 1857 as *The Life of Charlotte Brontë* and raised some controversy regarding the accuracy of the account. For many critics, Gaskell's friendship with

Brontë had resulted in an overly sympathetic and sentimental tendency in the work, which, according to reviewers and the Brontë family alike, produced major misrepresentations of the subject. Disappointed at the reception of the Brontë biography, Gaskell returned to writing fiction, completing several full-length works. She died in Manchester in 1865, leaving her last novel, *Wives and Daughters* (1864-66), unfinished.

Major Works

Gaskell's novels are often characterized as simultaneously industrial and domestic. As a group, they are novels of social reform that focus on deeply personal injustices. Beginning with *Mary Barton*, Gaskell was preoccupied with the role and status of women and specifically of women before marriage. The narratives reveal characters who are struggling to flourish in a strictly contained and frequently irrational world, such as the title characters of *Ruth* and *Sylvia's Lovers* (1863). True to her Unitarian faith, Gaskell wrote with a serious concern for the rational responsibility proper to human beings; yet she also recognized the overwhelming forces of public opinion, economic desperation, and misfortune. Her novels thus reflect a tension between the operations of freedom and destiny. *Mary Barton*, for instance, has tragic elements, but the moral responsibility of the central characters takes precedence. In this way, Gaskell used the interplay of the melodramatic and the ordinary to focus on forms of social injustice. Also, the moral seriousness of Gaskell's novels reflects the concerns of the Victorian era in questioning the legitimacy of authority: the characters with the most political or social power are often the least trustworthy (for Gaskell), and those with little or no power to fashion their own destiny, notably single women, servants, and the poor (such as the heroines of "Lizzie Leigh" [1850] and *Ruth*) are the central or more sympathetic figures. Her writing also reveals an ear highly attuned to dialect and natural conversation. Gaskell's last two novels, *Sylvia's Lovers* and the unfinished *Wives and Daughters*, were praised for the vividness of the characterizations and the portrayals of ordinary life. Her letters, which span her entire writing career, contain both personal communications and comments upon her own writing and other works of literature.

Critical Reception

Gaskell is best known for her insightful understanding and delicate expression of emotional and psychological suffering. W. A. Craik characterizes her as a "primitive"—one whose voice as an author developed not out of the study of classical technique but out of her own keen observational powers and compassion. What is most consistently praised in Gaskell's writing is the realism of plot, setting, and character (in spite of the fact that several stories give a prominent place to the supernatural); attention to detail and to the intimate dynamics of domestic life are also central features of her narratives. According to critical consensus, Gaskell generally avoided a didactic or self-righteous tone by letting the wealth of realistic details of domestic life and the vividness of the characters absorb the political message. The hesitancy that marks Gaskell's early novels evolves into a subtle and "unobtrusive" presence of the author. Very well received during and immediately after her lifetime, Gaskell was dismissed throughout much of the twentieth century as a writer who reflected the conventionality of the Victorian era and was considered a social conservative and a sentimental novelist. Early feminists criticized the "nostalgia" of her resolutions: marriage remained the goal for most of the heroines, and, like Dickens, Gaskell tended to romanticize the natural and the pastoral over and against the industrialized clamor of the urban. More recent critics have instead emphasized the tensions that animate Gaskell's novels and foreshadow major social reforms—tensions between the working and middle classes, between traditional authority and young women, and between the responsibilities of the public and the responsibilities of the individual.

PRINCIPAL WORKS

Mary Barton (novel) 1848
"Lizzie Leigh" (short story) 1850
Cranford (novel) 1851-53
"The Old Nurse's Story" (short story) 1852
Ruth (novel) 1853
North and South (novel) 1854
"The Poor Clare" (short story) 1856
The Life of Charlotte Brontë (biography) 1857
My Lady Ludlow (novella) 1858
Cousin Phillis (novella) 1863
Sylvia's Lovers (novel) 1863
Wives and Daughters (unfinished novel) 1864-66
The Letters of Mrs. Gaskell (letters) 1966

CRITICISM

J. A. V. Chapple and Arthur Pollard (essay date 1966)

SOURCE: An introduction to *The Letters of Mrs. Gaskell*, edited by J. A. V. Chapple and Arthur Pollard, Manchester University Press, 1966, pp. xi-xxix.

[*In the following introduction to Gaskell's collected*

letters, Chapple and Pollard discuss the significance of the letters as reflections and commentaries on her experience and writing.]

I

'Don't you like reading letters? I do, so much. Not grand formal letters; but such as Mme Mohl's, I mean' (195).[1] Mrs Gaskell knew the fascination of other people's letters. Writing to her sister-in-law, Mrs Charles Holland (née Elizabeth Gaskell), she wondered 'if odd bundles of old letters would amuse you in your confinement' (145). She also recognised the importance of letters written by famous people. Her own biography of Charlotte Brontë relies substantially upon its subject's correspondence. It does so, because Mrs Gaskell realised the supreme value of letting Charlotte speak for herself. In this way, she knew, her readers would gain a better idea of Charlotte Brontë than from anything she might herself say. The unique revelation which letters provide and the intrinsic attractiveness of Mrs Gaskell's own writings in this mode will serve, it is hoped, sufficiently to justify the publication of this work.

At the same time the editors are conscious of what might have been Mrs Gaskell's own feelings on the subject. She had set her face against any biography in her lifetime (570, 571) and two of her daughters sought assiduously to prevent any being written after her death. G. A. Payne, presumably repeating an oral tradition, ascribed this to a desire on Mrs Gaskell's part expressed after hearing that Thackeray had stated a similar wish to his daughters (*Mrs Gaskell, A Brief Biography*, 1929, p. 14). It may also be that Mrs Gaskell remembered the troubles that surround the writing of biography from her own unhappy experience with the **Life of Charlotte Brontë:** 'Oh! if once I have finished this biography, catch me writing another!' (318). She appears to have been opposed not only to a biography, but even to the preservation of some at least of her letters. She bade her eldest daughter Marianne to burn those she received (185), and she tried carefully to separate those to her publisher George Smith which he might keep from those she wanted destroyed: '*Don't* send them to the terrible warehouse where the 20,000 letters a year are kept' (324). Fortunately for posterity some of her correspondents did not take her at her word. Chief among these was Marianne, and it is through the very great kindness of Marianne's granddaughter, Mrs Trevor Jones, that it has been possible to publish this work. Appropriately at Knutsford she showed to one of the editors, Mr Pollard, the substantial collection of letters in her possession and hitherto not known to scholars. This volume took its origin from that occasion, and the encouragement of Mrs Trevor Jones played an essential part in the inception of the task. Nevertheless, we still recognise that it is possible that this edition would not have pleased Mrs Gaskell herself. We also feel that a public figure by the very act of becoming so forfeits much of his or her right to privacy. When that public figure takes on historical importance, we think that later generations should feel even less inhibited in their investigations. It might be claimed that only those aspects of the subject's career which influenced the public role should be matter for enquiry. If that is admitted, there follows the immediate difficulty of deciding what is relevant and what is not. The case of the author is here most difficult of all, for out of the inmost thoughts and feelings and out of the intimate and even apparently insignificant experiences the stuff of the writings takes its birth. Whatever be the ultimate judgement of this question, the letters discovered and printed here have more than justified the belief with which the editors set out, namely, that they would be worth collecting and that together they would enhance the reputation which Mrs Gaskell already so deservedly enjoys as a woman of character and a considerable writer.

The six hundred and fifty odd letters in this edition are the fruits of a search which found a ready and heartening response from owners, both individuals and institutions, in this country and America. The principal collections are in the possession of Mrs Trevor Jones, Sir John Murray, the Universities of Leeds (Brotherton Collection), Harvard, Princeton and Yale, and the Pierpont Morgan Library. A complete list of owners and locations is set out in Appendix B, and the editors are grateful for the kindness and generosity they almost everywhere encountered. Mrs Gaskell's principal correspondents were Marianne, her friend Eliza ('Tottie') Fox, her publisher George Smith and the young American friend of her later years, Charles Eliot Norton. There are also smaller groups of letters to her sister-in-law Elizabeth Gaskell, later Mrs Charles Holland, to her first publisher Chapman, to Lady Kay-Shuttleworth and to Catherine Winkworth. It is difficult to believe that only those letters have survived which are here printed to a friend so close as Miss Winkworth. The doubt is accentuated by the fact that Elizabeth Haldane (*Mrs Gaskell and Her Friends*, 1931) knew of and had access to letters which have eluded our enquiries in spite of repeated attempts to find them. This is but one instance of our disappointment.[2] After what Mrs Gaskell said of Madame Mohl's letters, it is sad to have none of Mrs Gaskell's missives to that remarkable Englishwoman in Paris, with whom she shared such an intimate friendship. The search for these letters involved enquiries in Paris, Basle, Grenoble, Munich and Berlin, only for us to discover that it is presumed that any letters there may have been were destroyed in the bombing of the last-named city in 1944. On the same day as this information was received the editors were also told that any Gaskell papers which the family's solicitors in Manchester may have held (and there was reason for thinking there were some) must have perished when an incendiary bomb hit the office during the war. Besides the paucity of letters to Catherine Winkworth and the absence of those to Madame Mohl there is a still greater omission. There are no letters to Mrs Gaskell's husband, William, and only a few to the other daughters apart from Marianne. Mrs Gaskell was often away from home, and both she and her husband were given to journeying apart. She must have written to him often; and the intimacy of later years between herself and her second daughter Meta (Margaret Emily) must have produced its own considerable correspondence. The disappearance of these letters is explicable. It is quite unlikely that they would have been found among any family papers which survived. In the last months of her life, report has it that Meta (doubtless as she felt in pursuance of her mother's wish not to be written about) held a series of bonfires in which she systematically destroyed a large quantity of family papers. What and how much then perished we shall never know.

II

The letters in this volume cover the whole period of Mrs Gaskell's life, from just before her marriage to the last dated letter which was written in the week of her death and is appropriately concerned with business about the house she had bought for her husband's retirement. It is easy to argue, as Aina Rubenius has done (*The Woman Question in Mrs. Gaskell's Life and Works,* 1950), that there was a strain between husband and wife, but it seems wrong to do so. William Gaskell went his own way, spent his holidays apart from his family, was active in the many pursuits in which his work as a Unitarian minister involved him (570); and altogether he seems to have been a singularly self-sufficient person. It is also evident from the letters that his wife occasionally became irritated by some of his ways. To this it is perhaps sufficient to remark that it would have been an unusual marriage indeed if she had not. Against any annoyance must be set her tireless efforts for his welfare. The purchase of the house at Alton is one instance; her negotiations to free him from his duties for a holiday in Italy are another (531). These examples come from the last years of Mrs Gaskell's life, but there is nothing to suggest that they represented a growing together after a growing apart. The marriage may not have had much of the nature of a passionate alliance, but it seems to have been firmly based upon deep mutual respect and affection. In any event, the evidence is by no means enough to be conclusive.

This is not the case with Mrs Gaskell's relationship with her daughters and especially with Marianne. Here there is plenty of evidence. There was a tremendous vitality of passion in her; this can be traced especially in the honeymoon letter (2). She was certainly attracted by and attractive to men (633), and William may have been rather remote and reserved. The result may, to some extent, have been to direct Mrs Gaskell's passion even more strongly than it would normally have been towards her children. The marriage took place in Sep-

tember 1832, and there were six children, of whom four survived. The first was still-born and a son, 'little Willie', died at the age of ten months. The loss of this child was a terrible blow (25a, 70). Marianne was born on 12 September 1834, Meta on 5 February 1837, Florence Elizabeth on 7 October 1842 and Julia Bradford on 3 September 1846. When Marianne was born, Mrs Gaskell began to write a Diary (privately published by Clement Shorter, 1923), the opening lines of which read: 'To my dear little Marianne I shall "dedicate" this book, which, if I should not live to give it to her myself, will I trust be reserved for her as a token of her mother's love and extreme anxiety in the formation of her little daughter's character.' There was extreme anxiety on more accounts than this. MA, as Marianne was called (she is also Polly and Minnie and even on one occasion Molly), was a delicate child; and Mrs Gaskell at times feared as well for her own survival. There is a moving letter (16) to her sister-in-law Nancy Robson, in which Mrs Gaskell begs her to care for the children in the event of her own death. But besides the anxiety there was also the intense joy of the young mother, as in the description she gave to her other sister-in-law Elizabeth Gaskell: 'Baby is at the very tip-top of bliss . . . oh! you would laugh to see her going about, with a great big nosegay in each hand, & wanting to be *bathed* in the golden bushes of wallflowers' (4). Such was Mrs Gaskell's pride in and anxiety for Marianne. The intimacy of mother and eldest daughter remained throughout life, and the solicitude of early years is matched by that of the final months when Mrs Gaskell wrote to Marianne's future husband, Edward Thurstan Holland, about her daughter's state of health (581). There is no doubt that in an especial sense Marianne was, as her mother at the last addressed her, 'my own darling' (585, 588).

Mrs Gaskell knew her children. In a letter to Nancy Robson (101) who seems to have been her confidante in family affairs (see 570) she gives a shrewd analysis of the salient character-traits and attitudes of all four— Marianne, 'a "law unto herself" now, such a sense of duty, and *obeys* her sense . . . looks at nothing from an intellectual point of view; Meta is untidy, dreamy and absent; but so brimfull of . . . something deeper, & less showy than talent . . . Florence has no talents under the sun; and is very nervous, & anxious . . . Julia is witty, & wild, & clever'. It was this five-year-old youngest child that won the heart of Charlotte Brontë when she stayed with Mrs Gaskell, two months before the lines above were written (*The Shakespeare Head Brontë,* ed. T. J. Wise and J. A. Symington, Vol. III, pp. 269, 278). Even at this time Meta at fourteen was '*quite* able to appreciate any book I am reading', and not surprisingly it was with her that her mother found her closest intellectual companionship in later years. This bond was probably strengthened by Mrs Gaskell's increased care and their travels together after Meta's brief engagement in 1857 and 1858 was broken off.

We must return to Marianne, however, for an insight into Mrs Gaskell's close and sustained parental care. Marianne's 'law unto herself' comprised not only a sense of duty but also other and less attractive qualities including simultaneously both a too easy compliance and a perverse obstinacy. During her schooldays she received a sharp rebuke about her apparently facile espousal of Free Trade views: 'Do not again give a decided opinion on a subject on which you can at present know nothing' (93). In later years her mother was worried about 'her proclivities to R.C.-ism' and of her being driven further towards it by her father's hostility to it (507): 'Marianne has all her life been influenced by people, *out of her own family*—& seldom by members of it, in anything like the same degree.'

It would be wrong, however, to conclude on this note and better to end on one less serious with some of the humorous 'Precepts for the guidance of a Daughter' (MS. in the possession of Mrs Trevor Jones):

2. Wash your hands.

3. *When* you have washed them, hold a book in them.

8. Talk German so fast that no one can ascertain whether you speak grammatically or not.

9. Don't gobble; it turns maidens and turkey-cocks purple.

11. Don't talk like Scott & Adsheads' about young men's dress.

14. Assume the power of reading if you have it not.

15. Hold your book right way up. . . .

Altogether to conduct yourself as becomes the daughter of E. C. Gaskell.

The charm, vitality and good-humour here displayed had much to do with Mrs Gaskell's social success both as a hostess and as a guest. All three Manchester homes at Dover Street, Upper Rumford Street and especially Plymouth Grove were the resorts of innumerable friends, both famous and otherwise. There were such early acquaintances as the Bradfords, the glitter of whose wealth seems both to have dazzled and embarrassed Mrs Gaskell (9); there were the Darbishires, at one time so close and then as a result of a misunderstanding so distant; above all, among the Manchester friends there were the ever-welcome Winkworth sisters who seem—or Susanna at least—to have broken down even William Gaskell's reserve. There were also less interesting characters, people on whom the narrowness of provincial and nonconformist society had such an effect that Mrs Gaskell could not help satirising them. One such was another Unitarian minister's wife, Mrs J. J. Tayler, who objected to five minutes' talk that Mrs Gaskell had had with one or two girls about Scott's *Kenilworth*—on a Sunday! (32). When this lady 'got an impromptu baby at Blackpool', Mrs Gaskell could not avoid remarking that 'Bathing places do so much good. Susan & Mary went to Blackpool last year, but did not derive the same benefit' (9). Besides narrowness there was also vulgarity and pretentiousness in Manchester society of the early and mid-Victorian age, seen in parties such as that at the Ewarts 'large, vulgar & overdressed' (175) and in the taste which rejected a cameo as 'not "large" enough for them, & cutting & execution is nothing to size' (255).

Crude though in many ways it was, based upon first-generation wealth from rapidly expanding industry, Manchester society, nevertheless, was intellectually alive. It tended to lionise its heroes, but at any rate it knew how to identify, and in some measure to appreciate, them. Some of the intellectual and cultural interest of the city must undoubtedly be ascribed to the small German colony, members of which often subscribed to the Unitarian faith as being nearest to the views of men who came from a country in which biblical criticism had originated and made most ready progress. The Schwabes and the Schuncks, to name no others, are found among the Gaskells' friends. Nor should we forget another foreigner, Charles Hallé. His name is a reminder of what is probably Manchester's greatest claim to cultural importance. His concerts began in the Manchester of Mrs Gaskell's time. In that time also Owens College was founded, later to become the first and largest of the civic universities. Its professors were among the Gaskells' friends, and William lectured there from its inception for many years (see 570). In 1857 the city staged its great Art Exhibition; and the British Association for the Advancement of Science, of which William Gaskell was an active member, met in Manchester in 1842 and 1861, on the latter occasion under the presidency of the Gaskells' friend, Sir William Fairbairn. The Art Exhibition in special buildings at Old Trafford was guaranteed by a hundred subscribers to the extent of £74,000. It included 2,000 paintings by old and modern masters, nearly a thousand water-colours and some 13,000 examples of other arts ranging from sculptures through furniture and ceramics to ivories and enamels. In five and a half months it was visited by 1,300,000 people, and the daily concert was, in fact, the means of inaugurating the Hallé Orchestra.

Manchester was an exciting place to live in and to visit. Besides these musical and artistic activities there were lectures and meetings in plenty. Mrs Gaskell describes some of these such as the meeting in support of Florence Nightingale (279) and mentions others such as Thackeray's lectures (134) and the banquet of the

Guild of Literature and Art (131). On this last occasion the Dickens were in Manchester and visited the Gaskells. 42 Plymouth Grove was a house of hospitality and culture, and over the years its visitors included, among others, Charlotte Brontë, Harriet Beecher Stowe, and Richard Monckton Milnes. In her turn Mrs Gaskell visited the homes of many of the famous. She stayed at Haworth; in the Lake District she lodged with the Kay-Shuttleworths, met the Arnolds and Mrs Wordsworth and narrowly missed meeting Tennyson; in London she took part in one of the last of Rogers' famous breakfasts, met the ageing Leigh Hunt, the Carlyles and many others. Trollope she did not know, but she met his brother in Italy, where she established friendships with the Americans, the sculptor William Wetmore Story and the young Charles Eliot Norton. Her genius for friendship enabled her to create close relationships with young people. Norton is one example, Charles Bosanquet was another, and John Addington Symonds was a third. Her genius seems to have failed with only one author, Thackeray, whom she does not appear to have liked overmuch. Of others it is perhaps sufficient to mention her friendship with Ruskin, about whose marital difficulties she has left an important letter (195). Non-literary friendships of interest and significance included those with the beautiful and cultured Mrs Davenport of Capesthorne (later Lady Hatherton of Teddesley) and the Nightingale family.

Mrs Gaskell's travels provided her with much material for her letters. Amongst the most interesting are those in which she describes an unexpected visit to Chatsworth and a German holiday in the Rhineland. At Chatsworth there was a tour of the estate concluding with a drive through the conservatory, a large dinner-party followed by a concert given by the duke's private band, during which the duke, partially paralysed and very deaf but 'he can hear talking whenever music is going on', sat next to Mrs Gaskell and 'talked pretty incessantly' (372). Reputation could not awe Mrs Gaskell into respect. She found the Rhine a disappointment and Cologne, she thought, smelt of the bones of the three thousand virgins. Heidelberg, on the other hand, she found surprisingly beautiful, 'splendid scenery, dark pine woods[,] rocks, & the picturesque town, and noble castle to complete it' (15). She cherished the recollection of the places she enjoyed. Her long correspondence with Norton is full of happy reminiscences of her visit to Rome in 1857. Paris, too, was a city of pleasant associations. She stayed there on a number of occasions with Madame Mohl at her house in the Rue du Bac. She showed Meta many of the important places in the city, she met various notable figures of the time, and a *soirée* was given in her honour (see 230).

It will by now be sufficiently evident that Mrs Gaskell's life impinged upon that of some of the most interesting people of the period. None, however, was more interesting than Florence Nightingale. Mrs Gaskell made her acquaintance a few months before the Crimean War. She was in close touch with the family at this most important period of Florence's life. She stayed with them at Lea Hurst near Matlock, and it was there that she wrote a considerable part of *North and South.* From there on 20 October 1854 she told Catherine Winkworth of the noble work which Florence was doing at the Middlesex Hospital, coping with the cholera epidemic then raging (211). In later letters she spoke of the popular heroine-worship of Florence during the Crimean War, of 'babies ad libitum . . . being christened Florence here; poor little factory-babies, whose grimed stunted parents brighten up at the name' (255) and of a workman's rebuke of '*you* benevolent ladies [who] play at benevolence—Look at Florence Nightingale—there's a woman for you' (279). It is such details as these that give Mrs Gaskell's letters an importance as social report and commentary. Another such sidelight may be mentioned in passing: she gives a touching account of the sad Christmas of 1861 with the deep national sorrow that affected all ranks of society following the death of the Prince Consort (496).

It is, however, for their comment upon literature and Mrs Gaskell's own work, in particular, that the letters possess an especial value. The letters to her publishers tell us much about the business negotiations connected with her writing, and the series to George Smith gives us an almost stage-by-stage account of the progress and problems of the *Life of Charlotte Bronte.* There are also a number of letters which quite vividly indicate her difficulties with *North and South* and especially her troubles with Dickens arising from the serial publication of this novel (220, 225).[3] It is interesting also to compare her attitude towards her work at different periods of her life, to note her increasing assurance about its worth whilst all the time remaining deeply conscious of its defects. She chose to ignore reviews whenever she could (38), but she nevertheless feared them (326, 344) and at least once, with the publication of the *Life of Charlotte Brontë,* public reaction caused her acute suffering: 'I have cried more since I came home than I ever did in the same space of time before' (352). The sense of injury was the greater in proportion to what she thought to be the nobility of the task and the extent of her achievement. The *Life* derives its greatness as biography not least from the passion with which its author regarded its subject. It was not the first time Mrs Gaskell had had to suffer. *Mary Barton* had quickly stirred up a storm of protest (35 et seq.), and *Ruth* provoked a similar reaction (148, 154). *Cranford,* however, one is happy to discover, was a constant source of joy, and Mrs. Gaskell once wrote in reply to an admiring letter from Ruskin that she could still pick it up when she was feeling low and 'laugh over it afresh' (562).

It is not only reactions to her work that the letters so vividly reveal. We are able also to see something of the process of composition. The research for the biography of Charlotte Brontë is particularly well documented. We read of her quest for letters and papers, of her visits to Haworth, to Birstall and even to Brussels, of her queries to George Smith about publication dates and of a host of other details, some of which can be quite startling: 'Do you mind the law of libel.—I have three people I want to libel . . .'! (314). Many of her novels are set in places she knew well. She relied much upon her own experience. The Ruskin letter contains a humorous tale of real life, 'a bit of "Cranford" that I did not dare to put in, because I thought people would say it was ridiculous, and yet which really happened in Knutsford' (562). Even in *Sylvia's Lovers* she used her ten-day visit to Whitby in 1859 to give her the setting for her work (537). With this book also, placed as it was in an earlier era than her own, she appears to have engaged in some minute historical research (457). Besides the preparatory work we read also of the progress of her writing. She seems to have been able to write swiftly and continuously, given the opportunity. There was the Lea Hurst visit when she was shut up alone with her manuscript (211) and the so-called holidays at Dumbleton and Boughton when she wrote so much on Charlotte Brontë (308). The first of the letters referred to in the last sentence also shows something of the author's problems with *North and South.* More than once we can see her pondering as to how she should proceed with events in her tale (211, 217). The progress of her last novel, *Wives and Daughters,* is illustrated in another and pathetic way as we read of her struggle to write, of the battle between the need to complete the story and the failing physical health and strength that constantly impeded the effort (570).

It may be apposite to mention one other way in which these letters are interesting from a literary point of view. It is to be regretted that only so small a portion of Mrs Gaskell's correspondence with her fellow-writers has survived, for there must have been much more than we have found; but even in what remains and especially in what she says to her publisher George Smith we notice her deep interest in and shrewd judgement of literature. There is, for instance, the succinct summary of the first two chapters of *Little Dorrit* read over someone else's shoulder! (273). There is the sensitive appraisal of *Villette,* based on her knowledge of the author (154). Again, there is her immediate recognition of the greatness of *Adam Bede.* It is worthy of note that, strive as she had to do, Mrs Gaskell did not allow herself to be led into condemning the book, even though she deplored the author's manner of life (438, 451). Indeed, she wrote to George Eliot in praise of the novel (449). Another novel to which she gave unstinting approbation was Trollope's *Framley Parsonage;* she wished that it would go on for ever (456).

Most interesting of all her comments, however, is a letter of advice which she gave about *The Three Paths,*

a work submitted by a would-be author, 'Herbert Grey' (420). She insisted that a novel must be a novel and not an essay, that it must be more than a set of opinions, that there must be a good plot, that this is more likely to come from observation and experience than from introspection, that the plot is the necessary ground-structure of the whole, that the author must so imagine events as to see them happening, that not a character must appear who is other than essential, and that the expression must be as economical as possible. The whole letter is a model brief guide to novel-writing, although we must admit that explicit comments on more subtle literary matters are lacking in this letter to a beginner. Indeed, comments such as the one about *Mary Barton* as Mrs Gaskell's 'idea of a tragic poem' (37, 42) are comparatively rare in the surviving letters, considering the quality and maturity of her actual practice as a novelist.

More important than what these letters have to tell us of Mrs Gaskell's views on either literature or anything else, more important than what they show of what she did is the evidence they reveal of what she was. They come from the pen of a ready writer, and thus in their spontaneity they give us a fine impression of the woman as she really was. She was not writing for effect. As a result, we are able to appreciate her supremely human qualities. Because she was so human, so aware of her own humanity, she was so interested in other people, in their humanity. One feels her regard for her reader; she is always writing *to* the particular correspondent she is addressing. This is one aspect of her general kindliness. The letters also appeal in their revelation of another aspect of this quality. She was the minister's wife and she ably seconded her husband in his work, but there was no hint of 'professionalism' about her benevolence. It sprang from her character, from what she was. In her work for the needy mill-workers during the 'Cotton Famine' of the American Civil War years, in her efforts for factory girls and women prisoners, we notice a genuine human concern. This was surely an extension of that love and affection which she showed as a mother and so movingly in her young womanhood as a foster-daughter to Aunt Lumb.

Next of her great qualities we must note Mrs Gaskell's moral seriousness. Mrs Carlyle indeed thought her dull and strait-laced in a peculiarly Unitarian fashion. She may have seemed so in 1848 to one so much more sophisticated than herself, but if the evidence of the letters is any guide, it would be difficult to argue that this was the kind of impression she gave in subsequent years. She could not have appealed to so many as she did if Mrs Carlyle had accurately expressed her attitude. There is a serene assurance about Mrs Gaskell's moral position. She knew generally where she stood, but rarely felt that she had need explicitly to indicate her situation. When it was necessary, however, she did so. This is seen in the candour with which she showed what she thought of George Eliot's liaison with Lewes. Yet she was no walking exemplar. Indeed, some of the most endearing of her letters are those in which she confesses her frailties and occasional uncharitableness about people. She was not without a light, attractive malice, which she deployed effectively at times. Witness Mrs J. J. Tayler, or the Darbishire family hypnotised by Froude (49) or her repetition of the story about Martin Tupper's extravagant salutation to Nathaniel Hawthorne (292). On occasion, her sharpness sprang from concern for others, as when she wrote of Mrs Wordsworth, 'It is curious the loving reverence she retains for Coleridge, in spite of his rousing the house about one in the morning, after her confinement, when quiet was particularly enjoyed, to ask for eggs and bacon! and similar vagaries' (139)—a very slight echo of the note she struck so firmly in her 'social novels'.

Her impulsive reactions remind us of yet another of her endowments as a person—her vitality. At some times this expressed itself in a piquant humour at the expense of pretension; at others it showed in the vivacity which marked her participation in events and her appreciation of people. She was so interested in everything that was going on around her—her children's dress, the latest batch of eggs for sitting, the last Hallé concert, the most recent books; everything from a cook's illness to abstruse political economy engaged her full attention and considerable powers. She never knew when to stop, and often, especially with her literary work, she drove herself into headaches, breakdown and enforced rest. It is this sense of her vitality, of life lived to the full, that in retrospect gives to the last letters much of their pathos. She was so tired. She who had done so much, who yet felt that within her there remained so much still to do, was moving swiftly to that sad day when literally in a moment she was cut off in the fullness of her powers. Only a few days before her own death she was lamenting that she would never see Florence's father-in-law, Judge Crompton, again. The lament assumes an ironic tinge as we contemplate the fact that the day approached in which those around her—and many in a wider circle—would have yet greater cause for lamentation. Though she died with much apparently still to give, there was (and is) the consolation that the life she lived was such as to leave behind the memory of a noble woman and a distinguished novelist.

Her letters strengthen this impression. Only a few are long, deliberately composed epistles. Most are hastily written, *calamo currente*. All, however, show her to have been a woman of intelligence, integrity and grace, gifted with an insatiable curiosity about life, a ready understanding of things and people, a deep regard for truth and a boundless sympathy for others. It is not surprising that Mrs Gaskell had so many friends. The letters reveal what a privilege it must have been to have been counted amongst them.

Notes

[1] References to letters will be given by the number assigned to them in the main text below.

[2] See, for example, the fragmentary letter 149 below. If the rest of the letter is as lively as the brief portion we print from Haldane, our failure to find the original is doubly disappointing.

[3] The former letter, hitherto unknown, is the only one surviving of Mrs Gaskell's side of the correspondence. (Cf. A. B. Hopkins, *Elizabeth Gaskell, Her Life and Work,* 1952, p. 135).

W. A. Craik (essay date 1975)

SOURCE: "*Mary Barton,*" in *Elizabeth Gaskell and the English Provincial Novel*, Methuen & Co Ltd., 1975, pp. 1-46.

[*In the essay that follows, Craik contends that although Gaskell's* Mary Barton *is concerned with issues of social reform, it avoids a didactic tone in order to emphasize realistic situations and characters.*]

Mary Barton in 1848 is new ground for the English novel. It has new materials, presents new ways of seeing and handling both its own materials, the world in which any writer finds himself, and the human nature which it is an essential part of most writers' task to reveal. Elizabeth Gaskell, by beginning her writing career in other forms than the novel, and by not seeing herself at first as a professional novelist—or even a professional writer—makes as nearly as can be a fresh beginning to the novel as a form. Like the primitive in other arts, she virtually unconsciously creates an unobtrusive, wholly invigorating and wholly beneficial revolution. That she is not aware she is an innovator is a great advantage both to herself and to the later novelists who in their own ways derive from and extend beyond her. She leaves herself always free to grow and to extend her powers; each of her novels is different in subject from the previous one, wider in range and more assured in its achievement. She never develops a mere formula for success, so, consequently, her influence is never that of a formula or doctrine. She points ways, and reveals means, so that novelists as widely different as Anthony Trollope, George Eliot and Thomas Hardy have the way to their own different kinds of greatness charted for them by the writer who began seven years before Trollope (*The Warden,* 1855), ten years before George Eliot (*Scenes of Clerical Life,* 1858), and twenty-three years before Hardy (*Desperate Remedies,* 1871). All these writers, like Elizabeth Gaskell herself, begin somewhat tentatively and develop rapidly. All, having discovered and established what it is in them to create, reveal her aid in their most mature, greatest, and most original novels. This is not to say they deliberately imitate her, or that they consciously model themselves on her; hers is the most vital and fruitful sort of help to those who come after her, in that the new areas and skills she herself develops offer further areas, and exploitable and extensible techniques, to those who, coming after her, explore the areas further, and develop and extend the techniques, not only for the purposes she herself has, but for other, sometimes more profound, ends of their own. Elizabeth Gaskell not only touches greatness herself; she enables others to reach their own kinds of greatness.

Elizabeth Gaskell is obviously well placed to write 'A Tale of Manchester Life' as she subtitles *Mary Barton.* She had been, when she wrote it, for fourteen years absorbed within that life in her role as the active wife of a Unitarian minister. Her childhood and upbringing were close to it, only a few miles away at Knutsford in Cheshire. She saw and experienced and was part of what she writes.

But situation cannot account for success. One needs only to recollect the innumerable other similar but unsubstantial 'tales' turned out in the course of the age—all too often by women—which faded and left not a rack behind. First-hand experience is *per se* very useful to a writer. So, also, is detachment. Elizabeth Gaskell has both. *Mary Barton,* her first novel, stands apart from her others in being, professedly, a novel of social reform, exploring injustice, abuse and inequity. Like Disraeli's and Kingsley's novels, it deals with industrial and poor provincial workers and their plights; like theirs, it is factually accurate in its account; like theirs, its author cares passionately about the conditions she reveals. As a novelist of social reform, Elizabeth Gaskell has the advantage over them of personal experience and personal contact, of having not only observed, but known, visited, and helped men like John Barton and the other mill-workers, or households like that of the Wilsons; as well as having visited and known socially mill-owners and industrialists like the *nouveau riche* Carsons. Elizabeth Gaskell has also the asset of being provided by circumstance with the right degree of dissociation. Her Knutsford background—the place she knew and loved and balanced against her feelings of commitment to and distaste for Manchester—gives her the detachment that even her own characters could achieve from their imprisoning circumstances, as they do in the opening of *Mary Barton,* where the Barton and Wilson families, parents and children together, can have a brief and idyllic walk in the modest south Lancashire countryside. Just as that idyll proportions and intensifies the troubles their town life inflicts upon them, so Elizabeth Gaskell's own detaching awareness enables her to do justice to their miseries, never underestimating them, but never exaggerating with excessive pathos or melodramatizing past belief, as did, on occasion, the city-based Disraeli before her or the invincible Londoner Dickens after her. At intervals in her story—even at times of greatest misery, the urban cloud lifts for a while. Mary, desperately pursuing the sailor Will Wilson, whose evidence is to save Jem from being hanged for murder, goes by train from Manchester to Liverpool, and sees from her back seat 'the cloud of smoke which hovers over Manchester' and looks with unseeing eyes at 'the cloud-shadows which give beauty to Chat-Moss, the picturesque old houses of Newton'; and then, being rowed down the Mersey in pursuit of Will Wilson's ship, she sees Liverpool too become something distant and detached, from the 'glassy and motionless [river], reflecting tint by tint of the Indian-ink sky above' (XXVI).

These advantages of personal situation are perhaps even less important than her approach as a writer. Her first steps in writing were not novels. She began[1] with a poem in the manner of Crabbe called 'Sketches Among the Poor',[2] written jointly with her husband; next came a little descriptive essay, an account of a visit to Clopton Hall in Warwickshire;[3] then 'Libbie Marsh's Three Eras'[4] (a short tale of a lonely young sewing woman's

MARY BARTON BY MRS. GASKELL

EVERY MAN I WILL GO WITH THEE & BE THY GVIDE

IN THY MOST NEED TO GO BY THY SIDE

LONDON: PUBLISHED by J. M. DENT & SONS L^{TD} AND IN NEW YORK BY E. P. DUTTON & CO brief friendship with a crippled boy, and her final coming together with the boy's mother when he dies), published in *Howitt's Journal* along with another short tale 'The Sexton's Hero', which in the following year brought out her 'Christmas Storms and Sunshine'.

Mary Barton however is both more than the customary novel of social reform, and different from it. Though its overt aim may be didactic, its fundamental ones are neither didactic nor reformatory; its author is not a clergyman or political figure who elects to use the novel to further his beliefs. She is a novelist first, an artist whose aims are wider than those of the reformer. She is concerned with one of the ultimate subjects of all literature—the predicament of men within their mortal span of life. So her novel has not 'dated' as social reformers' novels do, losing all but their historical interest when the conditions they deal with no longer survive. She is paradoxically less cynical, artistically speaking, than the novelist with a purpose, who exploits the medium as a means to non-artistic ends. She is, naturally, not a mere documenter of facts. Her religion is at the heart of her and of all she writes, and her social concern for those of whom she writes is a practical manifestation of that religion. In this way she is a novelist with a moral purpose in the same sense that Jane Austen is, and in this way is perhaps the last voice speaking from that position of securely-held belief that ends somewhere in the mid-nineteenth century. The fact is perhaps not so evident in *Mary Barton* as in *Ruth, North and South* or *Sylvia's Lovers,* whose themes and characters question orthodox belief, but its truth is proved by the absence of doubt, contrasted with later writers. George Eliot in *Adam Bede* (1859), writing of an age and society in which Christian belief is secure, is neither secure herself, nor depends on that security in her readers. She is detached not only from the extreme Wesleyanism of Dinah, but from the orthodox inert Christianity of the clergyman Mr Irvine. Trollope, who would seem committed to handling creed by choosing to write of clerics, avoids in his Barchester novels all but the most rudimentary morality, and has virtually no dealings with Christian belief.

When Elizabeth Gaskell does have a specific social aim in writing, as here and in *Ruth* (and somewhat in *North and South*), it is rather to inform than to reform. She acts on the faith that if facts are known, then improvement may follow, and so feels no obligation to exaggerate, or dramatize or heighten. One can often feel indeed that Elizabeth Gaskell needs the social aim only to justify writing at all; that it arises as much from personal diffidence as from social zeal. Her turning away from vexed social questions in her later novels reinforces the feeling.

Elizabeth Gaskell is apart from novelists of her time, as well as social reformers. She is a 'primitive', working out her own art and craft of the novel for herself, enlarging and perfecting it in the course of her career, very much independently of novelists before her, and those around her. Naturally, therefore, she blunders, she sometimes lacks assurance, she sometimes over-emphasizes. These faults of a beginner are most visible in *Mary Barton,* as is another fault of a very interesting kind. Elizabeth Gaskell shows she is aware that she is learning her craft, by the way that in some parts of this novel she depends on and uses the traditional material of the novel, such as the love story of a young heroine, the subject of seduction, sensational and improbable happenings, and a test of heroism for her central characters. *Mary Barton* suffers from being an amalgam of what can be seen as two distinct novels, one of them a quite original tragic novel, the other a much more conventional one which, though in many ways congenial and suited to her, is yet a sign of her depending on what she knows will be acceptable to a novel-reading public. The tragic novel concerns John Barton, driven by his sense of justice, his loyalties to his fellow mill-workers and to his Trade Union, into the extreme act of murdering his employer's son; through it Elizabeth Gaskell explores his social problem of the struggles between masters and men. It has its end in the superb reconciliation between the broken and dying Barton, and the father of the murdered man. The theme is great enough for a novel and gives enough scope on its own, as the wiser Elizabeth Gaskell of *Sylvia's Lovers*—her great and achieved tragic novel—would have known. Her second story is that of John's daughter Mary, the much more orthodox heroine, who hesitates between her real love, the workman Jem Wilson, and the dazzling wealthy lover Harry Carson; who, rejecting the one, on the murder of the other suffers the terrible dilemma of having to save Jem from being hanged, without revealing her father's guilt. This exciting plot, with the capacity for a (qualified) happy ending, is both more conventional and more sensational. Providing a study of the moral and spiritual growth of a young girl, it suits its author, and it provides some of the novel's finest scenes. Yet undoubtedly the two stories are too much for a single work, and account for many of its incidental failures in emphasis and proportion. Yet *Mary Barton* is an exciting whole, for its originality of subject matter, of character, and of methods, and impressive for the unobtrusive assurance of its writer, not least when she appears quite unaware that what she is doing is wholly new.

In discussing this novel, like *Ruth,* and unlike her other three full-length works—*North and South, Sylvia's Lovers* and *Wives and Daughters*—one must examine, account for, and assess the signs of unsureness, as well as the originality, initiative and success. One must look backwards to the novel as it existed as a tradition and a model before her, as well as forwards to the novelists after her, who developed in their own ways and for their own purposes the new ground she opened up for them and herself, and the new means she created of handling it.

Manchester is not only the setting for **Mary Barton,** it is its world. Elizabeth Gaskell herself, all her characters, the experiences that shape them and rule their lives, the present world from which they view life, religion, eternity, are within it. It is the life and time from which they view the rest of the universe, and from which we, the readers, view it during our reading. This is its great strength and its main originality. Earlier novels had often taken regional settings; Maria Edgeworth wrote of Ireland, Disraeli and Kingsley had deliberately chosen their areas of the English provinces; but with all these there is the authorial remoteness that comes from writing with the feeling of a metropolitan audience, and from a standpoint that accepts metropolitan standards as a norm, from which those of the novel are departures and regional aberrations.[5] Almost all of Elizabeth Gaskell's innovations as a provincial novelist rise from her unconscious acceptance of the world she chooses as a valid norm in itself, from which to understand and interpret the great issues of human life. She ignores social and geographical detachment, recognizing and revealing, not the 'otherness' of Manchester compared with London, but of London and elsewhere compared with Manchester; and feeling the present time of 'ten or a dozen years ago' (1838) of the opening of **Mary Barton,** from which all other times—even the 1848 of its publication—are past or future. She is not, naturally, devoid of artistic or moral detachment, but her judgements rise from and get their worth from her ability to participate, at the same time as she assesses. This stance in relation to her setting and subject is the most obvious gift she bestows on the nineteenth-century novelist—bestowed in the way of most such gifts, so that the beneficiaries are unaware of receiving it. George Eliot, writing her first fiction, *Scenes of Clerical Life,* ten years later, is in no sense an imitator of Elizabeth Gaskell; nor is Trollope in his first Barchester novel *The Warden* in 1854; Thomas Hardy creating Wessex still later, is even less so; but all three have the way to their own separate, and original, areas of greatness made smooth by her opening of the road. Charlotte Brontë, bringing out *Shirley* only a year later, was aware of the similarity between her own subject and her friend's, but the two novels are separated by their different aims: Charlotte's, despite its Yorkshire West Riding cotton-mill milieu, is, like all her novels, more a progress of the soul of its main character than a view of the world, quite apart from being also a study of the Napoleonic period.

Elizabeth Gaskell's assumptions about the novel are clear from the beginning, her main one being that its material must be the actual present world of everyday observation. Hence, though in later novels she may move in time (*Sylvia's Lovers* is historical) or disguise place (Milton instead of Manchester, or Cranford or Hollingford instead of Knutsford), no conventionalizing to fit a literary mode takes place. Hence, naturally, she presents herself enormous problems. Her method must be one rather of comprehensiveness than selection, of total understanding rather than detachment, allowing judgements to emerge by a multitude of juxtapositions and comparisons, rather than by heightenings, or sharp changes of tone and mood.

Therefore, she is closest among her great precursors to Scott at his best, who can in *Old Mortality* present with equal fairness the fanatical Balfour of Burley and the aristocratic cavalier Marquis of Claverhouse; and range socially, in *Heart of Midlothian,* from the humble Deans family to the illustrious Duke of Argyll. Elizabeth Gaskell's range in **Mary Barton** is less great, because Manchester offers less spread: the factory-owning Carsons are her highest; Alice Wilson, living by dispensing herb-medicines from her one-room damp cellar, and the prostitute Esther, who lives nowhere at all, are her lowest. But Elizabeth Gaskell's richness and fullness of creation is accordingly much greater. Resembling Scott, however, does not mean literary influence by Scott. It is as hard to detect any definite literary borrowing or learning from him as it is from any other previous novelist. The very signs of insecurity in this first novels are signs of her courage, and reveal her lack of dependence on those before and around her.

The relation between author and reader is one of any novelist's most powerful assets, and most personal traits, as well as perhaps one of his greatest problems. It is a great source of Elizabeth Gaskell's power and distinction, and causes her apparently few uneasinesses. She once wrote that the idea of a reader caused her uneasiness and distress, yet she shows few signs of having, even in her first full-length work, to grapple with the problem. At her best, she is assured, candid, unassuming, engaging to her reader in assuming their complete equality and communion of intellect and beliefs, and in having no reserves from him. She never hectors a public, as Dickens sometimes does; has no suspicions, such as Thackeray has, as to the reader's good nature or goodwill; nor any detaching irony such as George Eliot can show. At first reading, in her opening, her tone is so transparent as to seem, deceptively, almost naïve, as when she speaks thus of Green Heys Fields, outside Manchester:

> Here in their seasons may be seen the country business of hay-making, ploughing, etc., which are such pleasant mysteries for townspeople to watch: and here the artisan, deafened with the noise of tongues and engines, may come to listen awhile to the delicious sounds of rural life; the lowing of cattle, the milkmaid's call, the clatter and cackle of poultry in the old farmyards. You cannot wonder, then, that those fields are popular places of resort at every holiday time; and you would not wonder, if you could see, or I properly describe, the charm of one particular stile, that it should be, on such occasions, a crowded halting-place. (I)

She goes on to describe it delightfully. Such a tone immediately establishes trust in the speaker, faith in her accuracy, and willingness to go where she leads. She can then lead to strange, new, even repellent places, scenes, events, opinions and conclusions. She can describe the Davenports' cellar, for instance, without arousing disbelief.

> Never was the old Edinburgh cry of *Gardez l'eau!* more necessary than in this street. As they passed, women from their doors tossed household slops of every description into the gutter; they ran into the next pool, which overflowed and stagnated. Heaps of ashes were the stepping-stones, on which the passer-by, who cared in the least for cleanliness, took care not to put his foot. Our friends [Barton and Wilson] were not dainty, but even they picked their way, till they got to some steps leading down to a small area, where a person standing would have his head about one foot below the level of the street, and might at the same time, without the least motion of his body, touch the window of the cellar and the damp muddy wall right opposite. You went down one step even from the foul area into the cellar in which a family of human beings lived. It was very dark inside. The window-panes, many of them, were stuffed with rags, which was reason enough for the dusky light which pervaded the place even at mid-day. After the account I have given of the state of the street, no-one can be surprised that on going into the cellar inhabited by Davenport, the smell was so foetid as almost to knock two men down . . . [Barton] had opened a door, but only for a minute; it led into a back cellar, with a grating instead of a window down which dropped the moisture from pig-sties, and worse abominations. It was not paved; the floor was one mass of bad smelling mud. It had never been used, for there was not an article of furniture in it; nor could a human being, much less a pig, have lived there many days. Yet the 'back apartment' made a difference in the rent. (VI)

She can cope with Mrs Barton's death in childbirth in her second chapter without seeming sensational or morbid; by the same simple, candid manner she can unobtrusively suggest all the young singer Margaret's terrors as she gradually goes blind, the conflicts of loyalties of the striker committed to his course for his fellow-workers' good, yet agonized by seeing his friend starve, and his friend's children die. She can go on finally to present a reconciliation between a murderer and the father of his victim, which falls into neither melodrama, nor sentimentality, nor religious transport; and she can make all these as much the stuff of every-day life as the hesitations of the inarticulate young workman Jem in love with an indifferent girl, the humours of the scientifically-minded old Job Legh with a mania for biological specimens, or the pathetic child-like ramblings of the dying old woman Alice Wilson.

Naturally she does have some difficulties with her relations with her reader. They arise from the nature of her subject, more than from being unsure of her own narrative personality. She realizes that in Manchester she is writing of a place unfamiliar to most: the mill-workers and their families, a new class in 1848, confined to the Northern English region, are a social class every detail of whose way of life may be new. Hence the rather frequent and often unnecessary footnotes of the earlier chapters, explaining the meaning and origins of dialect words. Plainly she is anxious not only that they be understood, but also that the reader shall not see them as signs of uncouth speakers; by the dignity of the derivation from Lydgate, Chaucer or Skelton, for instance, she wishes to establish the dignity of those who use them. She realizes that their springs of conduct, their religion, their morality and, still more, their view of society may be unknown and surprising. And, finally, she knows that with them she is on dangerous ground: that the troubles of factory workers, strikes, the relation between management and labour (or 'masters and men' as Elizabeth Gaskell prefers to term them) and the rising Trades Unions, are the subject of economists' and reformers' debates, of public disapproval, anxiety, and even panic, and that the novel has already been made to treat of them, notably in Disraeli's *Coningsby* (1844) and *Sybil* (1845).

Being conscious of these difficulties, she sometimes over-exerts herself to make the way plain for the reader. She intrudes as speaker when the action and characters can be left to speak for themselves. Occasionally descriptions of physical conditions can go on too long, or she makes a character the vehicle for too much or too detailed a set of moral or religious musings, and sometimes she feels compelled to state her position—a dispassionate one—on the subject of employers and employed, with unneeded emphasis:

> At all times it is a bewildering thing to the poor weaver to see his employer removing from house to house, each one grander than the last, till he ends in building one more magnificent than all, or withdraws his money from the concern, or sells his mill, to buy an estate in the country, while all the time the weaver, who thinks he and his fellows are the real makers of this wealth, is struggling for bread for his children, through the vicissitudes of lowered wages, short hours, fewer hands employed, etc. And when he knows trade is bad, and could understand (at least partially) that there are not buyers enough in the market to purchase goods already made, and consequently that there is no demand for more; when he would bear much without complaining, could he also see that his employers were bearing their share, he is, I say, bewildered and (to use his own word) 'aggravated'. . . . The contrast is too great. Why should he alone suffer from bad times?

> I know this is not really the case; and I know what is the truth in such matters; but what I wish to impress is what the workman feels and thinks. (III)

Though these are times at which she uses political terms of her day, such as Chartist, Communist, or radical, the general absence of jargon is another small but significant reason why her work does not date, compared with other writers with a social purpose, whose free use of such terms—now no longer meaningful except in their historical context—impedes and alienates the reader of a later age. It is not surprising that such insecurities happen: it is surprising that they happen so rarely.

Yet she is, for her time and with her aims, very sparing of addresses to her reader. She seems consciously to avoid haranguing him, even when she addresses him. She was known to her friends as a brilliant and exciting teller of tales orally, and the voice of the oral story-teller is her voice as narrator, essentially simple in expression, and with the inner eye entirely on the matter of the story. When she does intervene, it is because of the feelings her story arouses, and these are always legitimate, powerful ones. When Mary agonizes over realizing that her own father has, in fact, done the murder of which her lover Jem is accused, Elizabeth Gaskell perceives that

> in the desert of misery with which these thoughts surrounded her, the arid depths of whose gloom she dared not venture to contemplate, a little spring of comfort was gushing up at her feet, unnoticed at first, but soon to give her strength and hope.

> And *that* was the necessity for exertion on her part . . . It is the woes that cannot in any earthly way be escaped that admit least earthly comforting. Of all the trite, worn-out, hollow mockeries of comfort that were ever uttered by people who will not take the trouble of sympathising with others, the one I dislike the most is the exhortation not to grieve over an event, 'for it cannot be helped'. Do you think if I could help it, I would sit still with folded hands, content to mourn? Do you not believe that as long as hope remained I would be up and doing? I mourn because what has occurred cannot be helped. (XXII)

Whether we choose to remember or not at this point that Elizabeth Gaskell began to write as an escape from her own grief that 'could not be helped'—her baby son's death—we realize the robust unsentimental attitude that recognizes the comfort of action, and demands it of her characters even in the most desperate of crises. Elizabeth Gaskell may be gentle with her characters, but she is also uncompromisingly tough. Heaven in her novels never tempers the wind to the shorn lamb; her own and the reader's pity never induce her to falsify events, nor minimize distress, any more than moral indignation induces her to exaggerate suffering.

The author's relations with his reader are closely bound

to his relation to his subject. Here again Elizabeth Gaskell is clearly working her way towards her own original method. Her previous writings have plainly helped her. She began with descriptive writing and sketches,[6] which are simple, unpolemic, faithful documentary accounts with a mere outline of story. She gradually introduces plot, attaching this precise noting of situation and detail to a developing narrative. Her habit of letting facts as she sees them speak for themselves is her natural and most precious power when she comes to a full-length work in **Mary Barton.**

Her powers are perhaps best defined by a negative: she has the ability of *not* passing judgement, or condemning. She simply selects and presents events and characters so that the reader understands them. This is one of the great powers of the nineteenth-century novel, and one for which George Eliot, not to mention the greater later Russians, is rightly admired. Elizabeth Gaskell's power here is akin to Charlotte Brontë's, who writes alongside her; but they differ in that Charlotte Brontë, in her social novel, *Shirley,* does rigid justice, despite her dislike, to uncongenial facts and characters, whereas Elizabeth Gaskell's charity does not permit us even to give way to dislike. Like George Eliot she requires and supplies justice and understanding for the admitted wrongdoer, felon or even criminal, like John Barton himself, or the minor character, the intriguing scandal-mongering Sally Leadbitter. But unlike George Eliot she presents them from a Christian as well as a moral position. Her characters are assessed finally for their whole life and ideas, not for a single act: John Barton is so assessed, not condemned, because he has killed a man; he is judged as sinner, not criminal. The murdered man's father, Carson, is revealed as just as faulty, not only because he nearly causes the wrong man, Jem, to be hanged for the crime, but because he has given his whole being up to the thirst for vengeance. By contrast George Eliot can seem naïvely orthodox, when for instance in *Adam Bede* she does not bring Arthur Donnithorne forward for judgement until he has actually committed his offence against Hetty, and, when he has done so, condemns him extremely harshly. There is a flavour of poetic rather than real justice when Arthur gives up the estate so dear to him, to go into the army, as though George Eliot contrives against probability that his punishment shall in some way equal Hetty's. She has neither Elizabeth Gaskell's generosity, nor the eighteenth-century honesty that enables Jane Austen to say:

> That punishment, the public punishment of disgrace should in a just measure attend *his* share of the offence is, we know, not one of the barriers, which society gives to virtue. In this world, the penalty is less equal than could be wished. (*Mansfield Park,* XLVIII)

Admittedly George Eliot matured, and handles sin and

eventual inevitable retribution very much more surely when she comes to Mrs Transome, in *Felix Holt,* but it is fair to compare George Eliot's first full-length novel with Elizabeth Gaskell's.

Just as she will not rigidly judge or condemn, Elizabeth Gaskell will not impose any of the usual kinds of novelist's order on her material by her attitude to it. She uses her characters themselves, their eyes and thoughts, to reveal what happens. She does not use a narrator's personality as a lens, as Thackeray does, to impose unity and provide interpretation; she does not use the consciousness of one leading character, like Jane Austen or Henry James; nor does she adopt George Eliot's position of standing back and seeing more, and more wisely, than her characters. To the reader expecting a visible guide and shaping hand, such a narrator is disconcerting; and the consequence a sense of formlessness. As will be seen later, her novels are far from formless and her sense of form grows rapidly; they work by cumulation and juxtaposition. But the method, like all new methods, can be exhausting, when there are no easy distinctions between major and minor characters, and when any incident is required to be seen from many different views. Before Jem's trial for instance (XXXII)—one of the novel's greatest scenes—we are made to feel innumerable emotions in succession and at the same time: we feel pity for Mary and intense excitement under the suspense of wondering what will be the verdict; we feel irritation with Job for thinking Jem may be guilty, yet must realize that he (and Margaret) have just as good reasons as Mary for what they think:

> 'Who is to believe me—who is to think him innocent, if you, who know'd him so well, stick to it he's guilty?'

> 'I'm loth enough to do it, lass,' replied Job; 'but I think he's been ill-used, and—jilted (that's plain truth, Mary, bare as it may seem), and his blood has been up—many a man has done the like afore, from like causes.'

> 'O God! Then you won't help me, Job, to prove him innocent? O Job, Job; believe me, Jem never did harm to no one.'

> 'Not afore;—and mind, wench! I don't over-blame him for this. (XXII)

But we realize that on the evidence—that Jem had actually quarrelled with and struck the murdered man, his rival with Mary, who was found shot with Jem's gun—Job has grounds for his belief, and to think otherwise than he does would be worse than sentimental, it would be soft-headed. Such assessments from the points of views of different characters are not primarily to intensify the heroine's plight—though they do

that—but to give the wholeness of the situation. Later, during the trial itself, Elizabeth Gaskell gives scrupulous attention to everyone concerned: to Mary and Jem, the key figures; to Jem's mother Mrs Wilson, miserably and inadvertently giving evidence against him while yet 'trying to check her sobs into composure, and (unconsciously) striving to behave as she thought would best please her poor boy, whom she knew she had often grieved by her uncontrolled impatience' (XXXII); to the murdered man's father, Mr Carson, who, seeing Mary, feels 'a kind of interest yet repugnance, for was she not the beloved of the dead' (XXXII):

> It never shook his belief in Jem's guilt in the least, that attempt at *alibi;* his hatred, his longing for vengeance, having once defined an object to itself, could no more bear to be frustrated and disappointed, than a beast of prey can submit to have his victim from his hungry jaws . . . he seemed to *know,* even before the jury retired to consult, that by some trick, some negligence, some miserable hocus-pocus, the murderer of his child, his darling, his Absalom, who had never rebelled,—the slayer of his unburied boy would slip through the fangs of justice, and walk free and unscathed over that earth where his son would never more be seen. (ibid.)

She can even register the reactions of the defence lawyer who puts Will on the witness stand,

> not so much out of earnestness to save the prisoner, of whose innocence he was still doubtful, as because he saw the opportunity for the display of forensic eloquence. (ibid.)

and of the jury,

> shaken and disturbed in a very uncomfortable and perplexing way, and almost grateful to the prosecution [for trying to demolish] evidence, which was so bewildering when taken in connection with everything previously adduced. (ibid.)

The proof of Elizabeth Gaskell's triumph here is to be seen in comparison. The scene has often been admired by readers, who respond to the excitement it generates. Any reader juxtaposing it with comparable episodes, like the trial of Felix Holt for the accidental killing of a rioter, or the trial of Sidney Carton in Dickens's *Tale of Two Cities,* will feel a fullness of response in Elizabeth Gaskell, a sense of a whole world involved, and of ultimate and universal values at stake. Yet this is merely the trial of a local engineer for a small-town manufacturer's son's death. Like Jane Austen, though not by Austenian methods, Elizabeth Gaskell reveals the universal significance of the apparently minor.

Towards her characters, Elizabeth Gaskell is very unlike most novelists before her. She readily treats all her characters by all the means she possesses: seriously, humorously, by speech, account of their actions or thoughts, favourably or with reservations; and she will use any of them at various points as a means of narration or focus. So it is difficult, even irrelevant, to classify them in the usual ways, as major or minor, 'flat' or 'rounded', comic, satiric, caricatured, grotesque, or heroic. From a single incident, it would often be impossible to say from the way Elizabeth Gaskell treats and regards him whether any character concerned were a leading or a secondary one. Major is distinct from minor not through the author's attitude, but through the material: the complexity of the character itself, or the circumstances which he undergoes or creates. The value of her method is one that novelists only gradually realize, for the enormous enrichment it permits. Trollope can be like her in recognizing that a stupid or even ludicrous person can respond and experience as intensely as a hero or heroine. In *Barchester Towers,* for instance, he can pause to perceive and analyse the conflicts and concerns of the feckless Stanhopes, who are at other times his butt. But Trollope is at all times a more leisurely teller of tales than Elizabeth Gaskell, without her driving moral impulse or overriding seriousness of intention. George Eliot develops the method, most notably in *Middlemarch,* where she can devote serious care to faulty, limited characters, and to apparently not very 'deep' ones, like the well-known example of Bulstrode, or the easy-going bachelor cleric Farebrother. Or, to compare her earlier work with Elizabeth Gaskell's, there is the clergyman Mr Irvine in *Adam Bede,* rector of Hayslope, a *bon-vivant* and an indifferent preacher:

> if that handsome, generous blooded clergyman had not had these two hopelessly-maiden sisters, his lot would have been shaped quite differently: he would very likely have taken a comely wife in his youth, and now, when his hair was getting gray, would have had tall sons and blooming daughters. . . . As it was, having with all his three livings no more than seven hundred a-year, and seeing no way of keeping his splendid mother and his sickly sister, not to reckon a second sister, who was usually spoken of without any adjective, in such ladylike ease as became their birth and habits, and at the same time providing for a family of his own—he remained, you see, at the age of eight-and-forty, a bachelor, not making any merit of that renunciation, but saying laughingly, if any one alluded to it, that he made it an excuse for many little indulgences which a wife would never have allowed him. (*Adam Bede,* V)

George Eliot preserves also at first the more usual attitudes to character, and so her excursions of this sort into secondary characters are generally, like this, author's analyses for which the action pauses; when it resumes, the character behaves in his usual way as a secondary character, coloured for the reader by the extra knowledge he has been given. In her later, larger novels too, she has problems of perspective larger than Elizabeth Gaskell undertakes, which demand some simplifying of the way characters and situations can be handled. She preserves too her narrative detachment from the situations in which her characters are placed, and so, as a wiser and often ironic and slightly wry commentator, she does not depend so fully as Elizabeth Gaskell on the method Elizabeth Gaskell pioneers. As is to be expected of one who is not an imitator but an original developer, she takes over what is useful to her, and amalgamates it with her own new and original forms. When she in her turn undertakes the trial for life— Hetty's for child-murder in *Adam Bede*—at a parallel stage in her development as a novelist, she concentrates her forces on Adam's response, and on the simple accounts of the witnesses, saving the fluctuations of Hetty's agony for the later scene of confession to Dinah. George Eliot's method is a simpler, more orthodox one, linked to Elizabeth Gaskell's by its aim at avoiding theatricality and melodrama, and by its wish to present the helplessness of the ordinary humble man caught up by the inexorable operation of social forces and laws upon him.

As a narrator Elizabeth Gaskell only gradually develops ironic detachment, as will be seen later in *Sylvia's Lovers* and *Wives and Daughters,* of her own original kind. Her strengths as a beginner are with the poignant and pathetic; what irony there is, contributes to them, and arises naturally out of the material itself rather than out of the way the author presents or views it. When, for instance, the prostitute Esther visits her niece Mary, with the paper in Jem's handwriting found on the scene of the crime, the irony of situation springs from Esther's unawareness that Mary loves, not the dead Harry Carson, but Jem, and wishes to save him; and the irony of relationships comes from Esther's pathetically pretending to be a respectable and prosperous married woman:

> Her words shot a strange pang through Mary's heart. She had always remembered her aunt's loving and unselfish disposition; how was it changed, if, living in plenty, she had never thought it worth while to ask after her relations who were all but starving! She shut up her heart instinctively against her aunt. (XXI)

This irony offers no surprises with new facts, only of new ways of seeing facts already known, like Job's remark that, to prove Jem's innocence,

> 'Best way, if you know'd him innocent, would be to find out the real murderer. Some one did it, that's clear enough. If it wasn't Jem, who was it?' (XXII, p. 288)

The reader knows it was Mary's own father; Job's

question reveals both Mary's 'agony of terror' and the poignant irony of Job's own position, unaware of his own friend's guilt. This kind of pain of ironic circumstances looks forward to Thomas Hardy, who, without Elizabeth Gaskell's religious faith, is far more troubled than she by the helplessness of men in the grip of fates created by themselves, yet beyond their knowledge or control. Elizabeth Gaskell, unlike Hardy, saw this consequence not as her end, but as her fault. Hardy ends his novelist's career with his darkest work, *Jude the Obscure;* Elizabeth Gaskell, writing of Mary Barton, said 'I acknowledge the fault of there being too heavy a shadow over the book',[7] and ended her writing life with her wisest and most generous work, ***Wives and Daughters.*** Even so, Elizabeth Gaskell is always serious, and can be sombre. ***Wives and Daughters*** is no more a gay book than ***Mary Barton*** or the tragic ***Sylvia's Lovers.*** As her understanding deepens, she realizes that the seriousness of life does not involve sensational events, but is the very substance of everyday living, that though cheerfulness keeps breaking in, and though comedy is of the stuff of life, so also are distress, anxiety, frustration, sorrow, and the temptation to despair.

With such an attitude both to her readers and her material, Elizabeth Gaskell does not run into the difficulties that face other novelists who, like her, document a social reality, reveal a contemporary situation and intermingle historical and fictional material. Her fidelity to the actual, and her wish for complete and fair comprehensiveness, make it easy for her. Though her characters and their predicaments may be invented, she feels that they are also close to the actual, because they are representative of so much that happened historically. The circumstances and settings and details that attend them are vividly actual because they are those common to their kind. Her success in combining historical fact and documentary detail with her invented story is virtually complete, on both the greatest and most trivial levels. Probably the most important single incident she employs is the mill-workers' march and petition to Parliament of 1839. It is so completely worked into the fabric of the novel that the reader feels he would not know, from the texture of the narrative, that this event is of a different kind from the invented material. In a sense, it is not, for the hunger that gradually oppresses the Bartons, the fever that attacks the Davenports, the accident that years before crippled Mrs Wilson when she 'cotched her side' in the spinning machine, are all actual happenings to many actual people of their time. On the other hand, the reader's awareness that the Chartist petition was a historical event gives substance to the fictional events because of the identical artistic effect made by it, and by what Elizabeth Gaskell invents elsewhere.

The petition is presented wholly through the participant's eyes, which are wholly adequate for the aspects of the political situation that Elizabeth Gaskell explores, since she has already created them as thinking, intelligent men hampered only by ignorance and the limited views their position has forced upon them.

> An idea was now springing up among the operatives, that originated with the Chartists, but which came at last to be cherished as a darling child by many and many a one. They could not believe that Government knew of their misery: they rather chose to think it possible that men could voluntarily assume the office of legislators for a nation who were ignorant of its real state. . . . So a petition was framed, and signed by thousands in the bright spring days of 1839, imploring Parliament to hear witnesses who could testify to the unparalleled destitution of the manufacturing districts. Nottingham, Sheffield, Glasgow, Manchester, and many other towns, were busy appointing delegates to convey this petition, who might speak, not merely of what they had seen and had heard, but from what they had borne and suffered. Life-worn, gaunt, anxious, hunger-stamped men were those delegates.

One of them was John Barton. (VIII)

Elsewhere she presents, just as fairly, how the recession in trade affects the employers also, forcing them to lay off workmen and lower wages, even though in this novel she is not as anxious as she is in ***North and South*** to present the whole of the economic conflict. Her facts once stated, she has no need to go again further than her characters can see: the petition, its reception in London, and the consequences, form the substance of John Barton's magnificent and poignantly comic account in Chapter IX. The whole episode gains power by being intermingled with and juxtaposed to other happenings: George Wilson's sudden death, Mary's relations with her would-be seducer Harry Carson and his go-between Sally Leadbitter, and Job Legh's tale—a wonderful short story in its own right—of his own journey to London a generation before.

She copes equally with documentary fact. She knows and avoids the heavy thud usually made by statistical details in a story, for instance, when John Barton reports his discovery that, in factories and mills, 'by far th' greater part o' th' accidents as comed in [to the infirmary] happened in th' last two hours o' work' (VIII); the context is delightfully comic, for his only audience is Jem, who, since he came to court the unwilling Mary (who has coyly escaped to her bedroom), is not listening to him at all. She copes as equally with necessary horror, when her subject demands, for example, that she shall deal with the physically unpleasant. Her method neither minimizes nor melodramatically heightens. When (XVI) a brought-in workman is the victim of vitriol thrown at him by a striker, she wisely subsumes the incident by presenting it through one of the characters' own reactions. The sheer physical horror is minimized, so that the reader is able to respond with pity and judgement, rather than merely be sickened.

Her complete familiarity produces complete confidence, without any of the sense of strain or overwriting of Dickens's nightmare evocation of the steelworks in *Old Curiosity Shop,* and without resorting to imagery and symbolism as he does in *Hard Times* or, also in that novel, embarrassingly idealizing the virtuous workman bodied forth in Stephen Blackpool, whose reflections on his plight never get beyond the catchphrase 'It's aw a muddle'; and equally without any undigested sections like Disraeli's near-farcical account of a Union initiation[8] or of the iron-working community of Wodgate.[9]

Such use of contemporary or near-contemporary history is a necessary and fast-growing part of the nineteenth-century novelist's subject and, much more, of those who write from outside London. Though Dickens uses social conditions, he rarely uses events; but both Trollope and George Eliot, different as they are, follow Elizabeth Gaskell's lead in absorbing the historical and embodying it in the fictional. Though neither ventures to use an actual place as Mrs Gaskell uses Manchester, Trollope bases the Barchester controversy over the finances of the almshouses in *The Warden* on those of St Cross, Winchester; and George Eliot uses the Chartist riots and the 1832 Reform Bill, in *Felix Holt* and *Middlemarch.*

Just as confidently as she incorporates history into fiction Elizabeth Gaskell incorporates those parts of human existence which reach out towards the eternal: death, and religious belief. Both are essential elements in the world of **Mary Barton,** as they are, in even deeper and greater degrees, in the novels that follow. Generally speaking, before her, death is something extra, and strange to, the existence of characters and action in novels. Minor characters can die, for thematic reasons, or simply as a means of being got rid of; heroes and heroines are immortal, unless their dying is, like Little Nell's, the culminating excitement and climax for the reader. Death, for the novelist before Elizabeth Gaskell, is either a casual accident, or of momentous significance. Jane Austen notoriously avoids it; Scott's great characters die, in ways befitting themselves, and as emblematic as the characters themselves: like Fergus McIvor in *Waverley,* that embodiment of a lost cause and forsaken belief, whose execution is as brutal as the reality which crushes his Jacobite cause and the clan system, and as magnificent as the devotion and loyalty he both gave and inspired. Charlotte Brontë, whose *Jane Eyre* is but a year before **Mary Barton,** recognizes death as a part of life, but her characters' deaths—Helen Burns's and Mrs Reed's—though natural accidents of time and chance, are momentous and significant landmarks in the heroine's spiritual and moral voyage. Only rarely before Elizabeth Gaskell's

novels is death a necessary inescapable eventuality within life and society as a whole. For her, sad and solemn though it invariably is, it is no subject for hysteria, for melodrama, for sentimentality, or for terror; it may even be recognized as a mysterious blessing or a welcome release; it is always accepted as the one inevitable fact of life.

More of the people who die in Elizabeth Gaskell's novels are in no way exceptional for doing so than is the case in most other nineteenth-century writers' works. Their deaths may be of the conventional novelist's sort, crucial to the plot, like Henry Carson's murder by John Barton; they may be the necessary thematic and moral end for a character who has no more life to live, like Barton's own; they may embody the social message, like the death of John Davenport, from starvation and disease, lack of work and vile living conditions. But these deaths never seem consciously contrived, or rigged to point a moral, still less adorn the tale. Besides these are other characters, whose deaths are much more an embodiment and acceptance of death as an inescapable element in life. Of this kind are most notably the Wilson twins, Mary Barton's mother, and Alice. The twins are ailing children—'Who like many a pair of twins, seemed to have but one life divided between them' (VIII)—frail from their birth to a crippled mother 'a cranky sort of body at the best of times' (I), 'little feeble twins inheriting the frail appearance of the mother' (VII), who, since their brother Jem is adult, obviously had them late in life. It is no surprise to the reader then that, when typhus fever breaks out in undernourished, unemployed Manchester, 'the twins, after ailing many days and caring little for their meat, fell sick on the same afternoon, with the same heavy stupor of suffering' (VII). It is physiologically probable that they should die, and psychologically right that their death should be both sad and yet secondary to the main course of events. Elizabeth Gaskell recognizes the genuine sorrow of their dying, but sees it entirely without sentimentality. It is thus reported to their brother Jem:

> He would make his aunt speak: he would not understand her shake of the head and fast coursing tears.
>
> 'They're both gone,' said she.
>
> 'Dead!'
>
> 'Aye, poor fellows. They took worse about two o'clock. Joe went first, as easy as a lamb, and Will died harder like.'
>
> 'Both!'
>
> 'Aye, lad! both. The Lord has ta'en them from some evil to come or he would na ha' made choice o' them. Ye may rest sure o' that.' (VII)

The religious message, which comes in appropriately from Alice, the character with the most simple faith in the ways of God, is not the 'message' of the scene, but simply an essential of its context. Elizabeth Gaskell does with assurance what other novelists touch at their peril; and in thus removing death from an aura of sentiment and sanctity, begins to lay the way clear for Hardy's *Tess of the d'Urbervilles,* forty-three years later. Tess's child is like the Wilson twins, a natural element in his world, and a minor one, whose going is as arbitrary, or as inevitable, as his birth. Though Hardy's infant has a symbolic force in the novel as a whole quite different from that of Elizabeth Gaskell's Wilson twins, the actual handling of the children within the fabric of the novels, and the recognizable human world at the basis of both, is very closely akin, and lies in a different area, and a more realistic one, from any similar material in, say, Dickens, who can never lose a child to death with such balanced and robust equanimity.

Elizabeth Gaskell is equally secure with the mature and the old. Mrs Barton, Mary's mother, dies in childbed in the novel's third chapter. One can see the death is useful, in leaving the heroine alone in her future trials; one sees also that the novel could have begun with Mrs Barton already dead, without any loss to the story [as does *Heart of Midlothian,* or *Emma,* or *Middlemarch,* or *The Warden*]. Mrs Barton's death, faced as unflinchingly, and as briefly, as the twins',[10] establishes that mortality and the chances of life are contingencies as inescapable for characters in the novel as for men and women in real life. Such events impress upon the reader that though Elizabeth Gaskell will adhere to the basic conventions of the novel, and will produce an artistic whole, she will not only not leave us before a conventional plot has been concluded, but she will adhere to natural probability and consciously and deliberately enforce it.

Alice's death is both more central, and more functional. Hers is neither sudden, unexpected, nor cruel. It does not need to be acknowledged as the workings of a providence the characters cannot comprehend, nor is it a necessary adjunct to the working out of the plot. To the modern reader, it may seem only too obviously functional, in reinforcing her life's simple Christian messages of faith and trust in the beneficence of God's will. But, apart from the fact that what a character believes is not necessarily what its author believes, Alice's own circumstances both in life and death are neither happy nor fulfilled. She lives on the edge of poverty, gradually loses her hearing and her sight, and dies after a stroke, in second childishness and mere oblivion, having never had her one wish, to go back to the Cumberland home she left as a girl. But Alice herself tries always to see her life as shaped by the hand of a kindly God:

'Yo're mourning for me, my dear! and there's no need, Mary. I'm as happy as a child. I sometimes think I am a child whom the Lord is hushabying to my long sleep. For when I were a mere girl, my missis always told me to speak very soft and low and to darken the room that her little one might go to sleep, and now all noises are hushed and still to me, and I know it's my Father lulling me away to my long sleep. I'm very well content, and yo mustn't fret for me. I've had well-nigh every blessing in life I could desire.' (XIII)

And in her dying ramblings she indeed believes herself back in her home and her childhood. However, though the characters recognize that her death is a happy one, Elizabeth Gaskell does not expect her readers to swallow this draught of undiluted sweetness. The contrasts between Alice's resignation and her circumstances are ironically astringent, make the reader appreciate the cruel limitations of a life so restricted that she can never return the few miles from Manchester to her home, the rigours of a service that prevented her reaching a dying mother, the physical ills that prevent her seeing or hearing properly her beloved sailor nephew Will Wilson, and the ironically poignant comfort of her fancied return in her dying imaginings. Alice's life as seen in the novel is in effect a long dying, contrasting, by being the inevitable conclusion of old age, with the other deaths from age, agues, tyrannies, despair, law, chance, which threaten or occur. In this, her first full-length work, Elizabeth Gaskell shows herself able to see not only life but death steadily and see it whole, as few English writers before or since have done. She looks forward, though her scale is so much smaller, more to the Tolstoy of *War and Peace* than to any English writer, and is fortunate perhaps in her historical position, living at a time when death was so much more an inescapable fact and event of life, when a man must face the possible loss of a wife in childbirth, and of a child in infancy, and when death was not to take place concealed within a hospital, or shuffled off without any religious assurance. Though she handles death in all her novels, and, with increasing artistic power, she is assured from the first.

Alice is also the clearest voice in the novel of Christian moral precepts. Her voice runs through the novel with its gentle reflections on personal submission and duties, alongside that other afflicted character, the blind singer Margaret Legh. But though these two voices may be the clearest, they are not alone, nor to be taken as speaking for their author. Christianity pervades **Mary Barton,** but there are varieties within it, and Christian ethics can be and are challenged.

It is no more a didactic religious novel than it is a novel of social reform. It is untheological and unsectarian. From reading, it would be impossible to deduce that it is the work of a Unitarian by upbringing, who was the wife of a Unitarian minister. The beliefs are embodied, enacted, and voiced by the characters rather than the author, with comments that are almost always on the separate situation, not on life in general. It is nevertheless always clear—even though no character goes to church, and many do not read the Bible—that Elizabeth Gaskell is writing of and in a world where ethical and moral principles are *ipso facto* Christian ones; that faith, hope, and charity are vital springs of action; that love to one's neighbour is the equivalent of love of God, and that life after death and reunion with loved ones are the compensations for a harsh and unjust world. Elizabeth Gaskell is perhaps the last novelist of real stature who not only possesses this security, but can, for her purposes as a novelist, assume it in her readers. The advantages to her of so doing are as great as, contrarily, are those to later writers, like George Eliot and Hardy, who neither have the faith themselves, nor can depend on any kind of faith or similarity in their readers, and so have to establish moral standards by re-examining conventional positions and beliefs. Elizabeth Gaskell shares her security with the eighteenth century, though in her questioning she is unmistakably nineteenth century. The personal questionings are mainly part of Mary Barton's story, who has the traditional dilemma in her own great crisis, of having to prove the innocence of one person, without committing a sin herself, in betraying her father; her dilemma recalls that of Jeannie Deans who, in Scott's *Heart of Midlothian,* has to save *her* sister's life without the sin of a lie; as with other moral tests in the novel generally, the later writer's is more severe and complex than the earlier. Elizabeth Gaskell herself is not so much concerned here with personal morals as in her later work; the ethical dilemma facing Mary is very simple compared with those in *Sylvia's Lovers;* nor is Mary so much in the grip of forces she cannot control, imposed by society and other personalities, as is Molly in *Wives and Daughters.* The public questionings, on the ordering of society, are less clearly put, but more germane, and though brief, far more startling and revolutionary.

> ' . . . God being our Father, we mun bear patiently what'er he sends.'

> 'Don' ye think he's th' master's Father, too? I'd be loth to have'em for brothers.' (VI)

As with her social problems, Elizabeth Gaskell does not see it as her duty as a novelist to provide revolutionary answers—she neither expects nor desires revolution. Her answer—the reconciliation in mutual goodwill, recognizing of wrongdoing, and attempts to amend—is virtually 'Go and sin no more'. As an answer, it means less to modern readers than to contemporary ones; since Elizabeth Gaskell's day, more revolutionary answers have been given, and tried. One must not, even so, dismiss Elizabeth Gaskell's. If it is both naïve and a cliché, it has the power of clear sight that *naïveté* can have, and the power (that has made clichés what they are) of universal truth. . . .

Elizabeth Gaskell is a master of detail. Her wise use of it in the whole world she creates is extraordinarily vivid and precise. It extends to her means as well as her material—to dialogue, and all the varieties of her settings of scenes, in natural scenery, weather, and sense-impressions. Through such detail and its juxtapositions and accumulations, she shapes the larger sections of her work, and builds up her climaxes. Her structure is thus cumulative rather than episodic. There are rarely any sharp breaks, or dramatic changes of scene or mood. It is hard to say where scenes or events begin or end. Her work has thus the ebb and flow of life rather than the sharp division of drama—which has always indirectly influenced the structure of the novel. Such structuring accounts in large measure for the difficulty of demonstrating Elizabeth Gaskell's unobtrusive art; it is even harder to catch her in the act of greatness than it is Jane Austen: we feel the consequences, but cannot promptly pick out the components.

Her use of speech is one of the more accessible. In **Mary Barton** she commits herself to one of its most difficult kinds, with characters who speak a dialect. She solves from the start the difficulties of representing sound without making phonetic transcript a formidable barrier for the reader, by representing only the more pronounced discrepancies from received English, and depending for the rest on her perfect ear for idiom.[12] After her faintly uneasy start, in which she feels she must justify dialectal forms by footnoted literary precedents, she proceeds with ever-increasing power and originality. The un-self-conscious and dignified Lancashire she writes is still easy on the tongue of a Lancashire speaker. Almost any example will show its power:

> So, one day, th' butcher he brings us a letter fra George, to say he'd heard on a place—and I was all agog to go, and father was pleased like; but mother said little, and that little was very quiet. I've often thought she was a bit hurt to see me so ready to go—God forgive me! But she packed up my clothes, and some of the better end of her own as would fit me, in yon little paper box up there—it's good for nought now, but I would liefer live without fire than break it up to be burnt; and yet it's going on for eighty years old, for she had it when she was a girl, and brought all her clothes in it to father's when they were married. (IV)

Alice, quoted here, is one of the broadest speakers; but even with more articulate and thoughtful characters Elizabeth Gaskell has no truck with the well-established convention (akin to that whereby Shakespeare's secondary prose-speaking characters change to verse at moments of crisis or heightened mood) that major characters speak more correctly than minor, or speak without accent at climaxes and crises. Her naturalistic honesty is a literary virtue; the power of language is at its most intense at the points of intensest emotion. The dying John Barton confesses to Jem,

'Lad, thou hast borne a deal for me. It's the meanest thing I ever did to leave thee to bear the brunt. Thou, who wert as innocent of any knowledge of it as a babe unborn.' (XXXV)

The homely idiom of this makes it as impressive as the 'standard' speech of Mr Carson's terrible utterance:

'Let my sins be unforgiven, so that I may have vengeance for my son's murder.' (XXXII)

Both utterances gain by the contrast.

But there are lapses in *Mary Barton,* where her hold on her material is insecure, where the author gives way to conventional moral utterances, or presents situations not fully realized or apprehended. The most striking instance is in the prostitute Esther, who, as Mary's mother's sister, should speak like the rest of her family. Though decent and restrained compared with many of her kind in the novel, hers is nevertheless the standard English and stereotyped rhetoric of the fictional 'fallen woman':

'And do you think one sunk so low as I am has a home? Decent, good people have homes. We have none. No: if you want me, come at night and look at the corners of the streets about here. The colder, the bleaker, the more stormy the night, the more certain you will be to find me. For then . . . it is so cold sleeping in entries, and on doorsteps, and I want a dram more than ever.' (XIV)

Such lapses do not occur in her later work; she goes on to more assured gradations of language in *North and South,* and to her greatest achievement in speech, the rendering of what was not even native or familiar to her, the north-east Yorkshire of *Sylvia's Lovers.*

Elizabeth Gaskell does for dialect in the English novel what Scott had done for Scotland and its language. There can be no sense, however, in which she can be said to have imitated him. She learned from him ways in which local speech can be presented and employed in the novel, and she transmits these means for other provincial writers to develop therefrom their own opportunities. But she does not establish a 'type'—as Scott's Lowland Scots became a type, or as London Cockney was—which later writers go on using even after it has ceased to represent current idiom. George Eliot afterwards can employ the Midland English of Warwickshire for her own purposes, realizing its possibilities because Elizabeth Gaskell had seen those of Lancashire; and the new ground of local speech is plain and open by the time Hardy creates Wessex. Neither of these, however, uses local language so comprehensively as Elizabeth Gaskell in *Mary Barton* and *Sylvia's Lovers* but, as will be seen later, on principles closer to those of *North and South.*

Elizabeth Gaskell's own narrative is deceptively simple and never obtrusive. Yet details of setting, scenery, weather, and the sensuous apprehensions they convey to the reader, and reveal in the characters, are powerful elements. Much of the mood, and quality and depth of feeling, is conveyed through them. It is always with such matters of content, rather than questions of style, that Elizabeth Gaskell's genius can be defined.

Her descriptive detail creates delight as well as horror; there are perhaps more passages revealing the small pleasures and comforts of the characters than their distresses; such passages bring out clearly the degrees of prosperity among those whose wealth is never more than modest. The comforts of the Barton family are vividly defined by their house: 'the place seemed almost crammed with furniture (sure sign of good times among the mills)'; prosperity is witnessed by 'geraniums, unpruned and leafy' on the window-sill, and by

a cupboard apparently full of plates and dishes, cups and saucers, and some more non-descript articles, for which one would have fancied their possessors could find no use—such as triangular pieces of glass to save carving knives and forks from dirtying table cloths. However, it was evident Mrs Barton was proud of her crockery and glass, for she left her cupboard door open. (I)

Elizabeth Gaskell never lets an artificial taste or the fastidiousness of another class intrude: she shares and lets the reader share her characters' delight:

On [the table] resting against the wall, was a bright green japanned tea-tray, having a couple of scarlet lovers embracing in the middle. The firelight danced merrily on this, and really (setting all taste but that of a child's aside) it gave a richness of colouring to that side of the room. It was also in some measure propped up by a crimson tea-caddy, also of japan ware. (I)

Such details are not idle; they contrast within a few pages with Alice's much humbler one-room cellar:

Two chairs drawn out for visitors, and duly swept and dusted; an old board arranged with some skill, two old candle boxes set on end (rather rickety, to be sure, but she knew the seat of old, and when to sit lightly; indeed the whole affair was more for apparent dignity of position than for any real ease); a little, a very little round table, put just before the fire, which by this time was blazing merrily; her unlacquered, ancient, third-hand tea-tray arranged with a black tea-pot, two cups with a red and white pattern, and one with the old friendly willow pattern, and saucers, not to match (on one of the extra supply the lump of butter flourished away); all these preparations complete, Alice began to look about her with satisfaction, and a sort of wonder what more could be done to add to the comfort of the evening. (IV)

The comfort takes the form of Cumberland oat-cake as an addition to the half-ounce of tea, quarter of a pound of butter and common loaf which have 'gone far to absorb her morning's wages' (ibid.). The Bartons by contrast provided for their tea for the Wilsons (seven people altogether) two pounds of Cumberland ham, an egg apiece, a penny-worth of milk, bread, butter, tea, and 'sixpenny worth of rum, to warm the tea' (I). As hardship overtakes John Barton, its growth is charted by the gradual disappearance of the tea-tray and caddy, and the selling of the furniture. After such an opening, the reader feels the pain, as well as the penury, involved in the loss of these treasures.

Elizabeth Gaskell is continually aware of the power of physical sensation over mood and personality.

> There came a long period of bodily privation; of daily hunger after food; and though he tried to persuade himself he could bear want himself with stoical indifference, and did care as little about it as most men, yet the body took its revenge for its uneasy feelings. The mind became soured and morose, and lost much of its equipoise. It was no longer elastic, as in the days of youth, or in times of comparative happiness; it ceased to hope. And it is hard to live on when one has ceased to hope. (XV)

John Barton's feelings for his fellow-workers and against the masters are thus intensified by his hunger, and his moral desperation by his resorting to opium, the common cheap remedy for the pangs of hunger. Similarly Mary is weakened and her moral crises made more dangerous by sleepless nights, spent helping Margaret sew mourning clothes, and by sitting up with the prostrated Mrs Wilson and the dying Alice. Physical as well as mental exhaustion thus causes her breakdown after the trial.

The relative importance of events can be registered by similar detail: when John Barton is about to leave with the Chartist petition to London, Mary's occupation was

> the same as that of Beau Tibbs' wife 'just washing her father's two shirts', in the pantry back-kitchen; for she was anxious about his appearance in London (the coat had been redeemed [from the pawn-broker's] though the silk handkerchief was forfeited). (VIII)

Climaxes are built up, and the novel's highest moments of intensity created, by constant use of such minutiae, and by the juxtaposition and accumulation of small events and smaller detail. This is Elizabeth Gaskell's most original and finest skill. It is also what makes her difficult to reveal in extract, or by quotation. The novel's

most moving moments, like some of Shakespeare's most moving lines, are apt to look rather flat out of context. She has no power like Dickens's of creating the quotable or unforgettable moment in isolation. Nothing in her corresponds to Oliver's asking for more, or Sidney Carton's last speech, or Bill Sikes's death. But she has no need of them. No one can fault Jane Austen because there is no single memorable utterance in Wentworth's proposal to Anne Elliot in *Persuasion,* or Scott because there is none in Fergus McIvor's farewell to Waverley. Nor should one so fault Elizabeth Gaskell. The sequence from Jem's arrest to his acquittal is a superb piece of writing, taking its effect from the vast number of its elements, rather than from the heightening of individual ones. Alice's death, Mrs Wilson's despair, Margaret's disapproval, Job's interview with the lawyer, the various sensations of Mary's journey, the jarring contact with uncomprehending strangers—Mrs Jones, Will's landlady, who tells Mary she is too late to catch him before he sails, and her wild young son who guides Mary to the rough boatmen who take her on her nightmare sail down the Mersey, the boatman himself who gives her a roof over her head—all these, together with Job's interpolated comico-pathetic wait for Will and Mary in the Liverpool lawyer's office, build up by their very variety the extreme tension before the trial itself. Elizabeth Gaskell concentrates on no single mood or emotion, but works by contrast and by cumulation of small tensions and abrupt changes. Mary reaches exhaustion and despair when she has seen Will sail away over the bar, despite his promise to return on the pilot-boat:

> She sat down quietly on the top step of the landing, and gazed down into the dark, dark water below. Once or twice a spectral thought loomed among the shadows of her brain, a wonder whether beneath that cold dismal surface there would not be a rest from the troubles of earth. (XXVIII)

Rescued by the boatman, with '"Come with me and be d——d to you!" replied he, clutching her arm to pull her up' (XXVIII), Mary is abandoned by her author, who moves to Job awaiting her, fidgeting in the lawyer's office, then enquiring for her at Mrs Jones's, then back to the lawyer, and back to Mrs Jones, then, finally, reaching his own little climax of despair, when he lies to Mrs Wilson that Mary and Will are safe and ready to prove Jem's alibi at the trial on the morrow. Then comes the return to Mary, roughly cared for by the boatman's wife, and sitting alone all night waiting for the wind to change:

> And quietly, noiselessly, Mary watched the unchanging weathercock through the night. She sat on the little window-seat, her hand holding back the curtain which shaded the room from the bright moonlight without; her head resting its weariness against the corner of the window-frame; her eyes burning, and stiff with the intensity of her gaze.

The ruddy morning stole up the horizon, casting a ruddy glow into the watcher's room.

It was the morning of the day of trial! (XXXI)

So the chapter ends. The next brings its own shock, for Elizabeth Gaskell turns our gaze upon one we had almost forgotten, 'the father of the murdered man', Carson, and adds his burden of pain to that of 'all the restless people who found that night's hours agonising from excess of anxiety' (XXXII); and so she plunges into the trial itself, with the cumulative intensities of Mrs Wilson's evidence and Mary's, finally ended with Will's dramatic arrival. But even so there is no melodramatic collapse of opposition, or improbable paean of triumph. Will's evidence is doubted by the prosecution—'Will you have the kindness to inform the gentlemen of the jury what has been your charge for repeating this very plausible story?' (XXXII)—and the verdict is, in essence, rather 'Not proven' than 'Not guilty'.

One can hardly fault Elizabeth Gaskell's art in this closing section, but one suspects that it is not only new to her, but her first discovery of it, for *Mary Barton* contains one other sensational scene of a quite different kind. This is the fire at Carson's mill. While it is the traditional material of heroism and hairbreadth 'scapes (Jem's rescue of his father and another man), and the all-too-traditional fainting heroine, though it advances the action by putting men out of work, and though it reveals the cynicism of the employer who would rather have insurance money than old outdated machinery, it serves very little structural purpose beyond its intrinsic excitement. As a first essay at a scene of violent action and men in the mass (the crowd is well handled) it serves Elizabeth Gaskell in good stead when she comes to write the attack on Thornton's mill in *North and South* and shows that her handling owes nothing there to Charlotte Brontë's mill-riot in *Shirley*.

In a final estimate, it has been generally agreed that *Mary Barton* is both a good and an important novel. It has always been considered so for its new subject matter, for revealing the industrial working-class of Manchester, for its penetrating and vividly realistic picture of social conflict, and for its deep understanding of the life and personal distresses of those caught up in strife and change. But these are as much the virtues of the social document as of the work of art. *Mary Barton* is undeniably valuable for these things; it is even more valuable for the qualities in it that are not of an age, that make it rewarding for those who care nothing for history or politics, which make it literature. It stands forth as the early, secondary work of a great writer, like *Northanger Abbey,* or *Guy Mannering,* or (to come into her own time) *Nicholas Nickleby, The Luck of Barry Lyndon,* or *Silas Marner.* It is not an ambitious work: the plot is not complicated, it does not have an unduly large number of characters (about twenty

of any stature) nor a wide range of scene. It is the more a success because its reach does not exceed its grasp. It establishes its writer as a novelist of stature, though anonymously. It was reviewed by the influential and established organs, and read by the illustrious and influential, who thought enough of it to record their reactions. Through *Mary Barton* Elizabeth Gaskell becomes professional; she learns her strength, and advances on her way towards her greater work.

Notes

[1] Though one could mention that her writing might be considered to begin with 'My Diary: The Early Years of my Daughter Marianne', begun in 1835 (privately printed, Clement Shorter, 1923), it would be even less fair to take this as her first literary composition than it would be to consider her letters in the same light. It was an entirely private piece of writing, not even intended for friends' eyes, still less the public's.

[2] *Blackwood's Magazine,* XLI (January 1837), pp. 48-51.

[3] Introduced by W. Howitt into his *Visits to Remarkable Places* (1840), pp. 130-46.

[4] 'Libbie Marsh's Three Eras: A Lancashire Tale', *Howitt's Journal,* I (1847).

[5] Scott is a different case, since he wrote of Scotland for the Scots, aware more of a universal than an English set of values. A fairer parallel with Maria Edgeworth, on the Scottish scene, would be Galt, who writes his provincial topics from a standpoint which like the others' is aware of a norm from which his characters are aberrations.

[6] Her first published work was 'Sketches Among the Poor', *Blackwood's Magazine,* XLI (January 1837).

[7] Letter to Mrs Greg, undated, written early 1849, letter 42 in *The Letters of Mrs Gaskell,* ed. J. A. V. Chapple and Arthur Pollard (Manchester, 1966).

[8] *Sybil,* Book IV, 14.

[9] *Sybil,* Book III, 4.

[10] Mrs Barton's death takes two pages, the twins', four.

[12] An example of a writer with an equally perfect ear who almost ruins one of her richest creations is Emily Brontë, whose Joseph in *Wuthering Heights* is virtually unreadable on the page: most readers lose his humour through sheer exhaustion with deciphering it.

Works Cited

[E. C. Gaskell.] *The Works of Mrs Gaskell,* Smith, Elder & Co., 1906 (The Knutsford Edition), 8 vols.

[————.] *The Life of Charlotte Brontë,* Smith, Elder & Co., 1914 (Haworth Edition).

[————.] *The Letters of Mrs Gaskell,* ed. J. A. V. Chapple and Arthur Pollard, Manchester U.P., 1966.

[George Eliot. Mill on the Floss, Blackwood & Sons, 1860.]

Rosemarie Bodenheimer (essay date 1981)

SOURCE: "Private Grief and Public Acts in *Mary Barton,*" in *Dickens Studies Annual: Essays on Victorian Fiction,* Volume 9, edited by Michael Timko, Fred Kaplan, and Edward Guiliano, AMS Press, Inc., 1981, pp. 195-216.

[*In the following essay, Bodenheimer contends that* Mary Barton *can be read as a novel of mourning—one which deals with two primary issues: what to do in response to injustice, and how such responses might traverse the divide between the private and public spheres.*]

Mary Barton is a novel about responding to the grief of loss or disappointment. Its pages are filled with domestic disaster; the sheer accumulation of one misfortune after another is the organizing principle of the first half of the narrative. The story begins with Mrs. Barton's grief about the disappearance of her sister, and the Barton-Wilson tea party that is organized to help comfort her ends with the social awkwardness of her returning tears. The contrasting characterizations of immediate responses to deaths in the family—John Barton's stunned and silent dignity, Jane Wilson's garrulous hysteria, Jem Wilson's quiet stance when his little brothers die—elicit much of the best writing in the novel. The pretentious Ogden funeral, for which Margaret Legh strains her eyes to stitch mourning gowns, is set against the simple feeling of the Davenport pauper's burial. And the novel's middle-class centerpiece, the Carson family portrait, is taken at the moment when each member reacts characteristically to the news of Harry Carson's murder. When we hear, in the little Canadian epilogue, that Margaret Legh has regained her sight, the news comes with a sense of violated tone, for it is the only piece of simple "good tidings" in the book.[1]

If steadily widening and worsening doses of bad news and hard times form the main substance of the narrative, the question of what to do about them is at its core, the source of the novel's deepest energy, and division. *Mary Barton,* itself a response to devastating personal grief, was its author's first assumption of a public voice, raised on behalf of other private grieving voices. The careers of both major characters, John and Mary Barton, are shaped in some image of their creator's: both father

and daughter, out of their personal woe, fare forth on journeys that render them momentarily public figures, voices raised in middle-class forums of judgment in the name of working-class victims of social or legal injustice. Yet the narrative presentations of those actions and the other responses to misfortune that are explored are riddled with ambivalence, shifts of class perspective, and frustrating revisions of moral terminology. Meanwhile, an astonishing and hitherto unemphasized proportion of the novel is devoted to the depiction of domestic scenes: family life, neighborly help, and the apparently irrelevant small talk that humanizes private and daily life.

What, then, are the real animating divisions, the structures of conflict that shape the movement of this narrative? *Mary Barton* has always been seen as a "split" novel. Its well-deserved status as the best of the industrial novels to come out of the 1840s[2] has led almost all of Gaskell's critics to notice the problematical split between her sympathy for the poor and her occasional retreats to middle-class liberal platitude.[3] Moreover, the novel has conventionally been seen to fall into two unequally serious parts: the "tragic" story of John Barton's vision of social injustice, with its consequent action and suffering, and the "conventionally romantic" story of his daughter Mary's love triangle, with her exciting mission to save her working-class lover from conviction for a crime committed by her father against her would-be seducer. It has been assumed almost universally that these plots are only circumstantially connected, that the important contribution of the novel is the portrait of John Barton, and that the story of Mary relies directly on romantic patterns and is designed to entertain the reading public.[4]

In the face of such readings, I want to argue for an essential consistency in the novel's internal conflicts, and for the ways that its troubling issues cut across both plots, and even shape the fluctuations of the narrative voice. The issues might best be posed, at the outset, in the form of two questions: Should the response to misfortune or injustice be active or passive?; and, What is the relation between public actions and domestic virtues? These questions are knotty ones, ones that remain unresolved; and they pertain not only to Gaskell's uneven presentation of social problems, but also to her wavering performance as a narrator in this first of her public appearances. They are also responsible, however, for what I would call the genuine seriousness of the novel: its concrete account of the dignity, and the historical integrity, of working-class family life.

Of all the important nineteenth-century novelists, Gaskell is the one whose themes most consistently emerge implicitly, from juxtaposition without explicit narrative direction, and in apparently artless repetition, without the glue of narrative metaphor. *Mary Barton* works like this, but ***Mary Barton*** is also, noticeably, an apprentice novel. Because its technical discontinuities are significantly related to its political ones, I begin with some attention to the important virtues and failures of Gaskell's first sustained piece of narrative.

Technical difficulties are most prominent in the first half, which juggles multiple story-lines and covers a period of several years. Here the transitions from dramatized scene to narrative summary are awkward and abrupt. Many chapters seem at first to be collections of disparate material, giving us what would seem to be thematically unimportant scenes, while crucial movements of mind are left to be generally accounted for in narrative summary. It is surprising, for example, to discover how rarely John Barton appears as an actor in dramatized scenes, and how often he is "one of those" men about whom we get, in several installments, an historical account centering on the failure of Chartism and the growth of trade unionism. Although the narrator tells us feelingly of Barton's increasing depression and its causes, there is little sense of an inevitable dramatic set of choices determined by defined complexities in his character. A similar failure to develop character can be seen in other cases as well; many scenes offer new introductions to a character's dominant traits, rather then developments of previously demonstrated conflicts.

Such apparent weaknesses of direction suggest that we must look at the content of the dramatized scenes for the material that most engaged Gaskell's novelistic skills. These prove to be predominantly scenes of familial or neighborly mutual help, grief-sharing, story-telling, or opinion-giving; they are the activities that provide the novel's true tone and texture. Next to them some of the "plot actions", like Barton's and Jem's interviews with the prostitute Esther, or Jem's confrontation with his rival Harry Carson, stick out as contrivances of a different kind. "It's the poor, and the poor only, as does such things for the poor." Barton says in the first chapter,[5] and Gaskell's series of domestic tableaux show just how well, how graciously, how sensitively, how courageously and good-humouredly, the poor do such things.

While she often has been praised for her inventories of domestic interiors,[6] Gaskell may be even better at noting details of manners in close quarters: how the Wilsons pretend not to hear the Bartons' negotiations about buying food for their tea-party; how Margaret Legh can tell from the sounds in the apartment below, when it would be appropriate to knock at Alice Wilson's door. In a similar way, whole scenes that may appear to be distractions insist quietly upon the resources indigenous to working-class culture. Story-telling, for example, is an important source of entertainment and hospitality in ***Mary Barton,*** and the skill of the tellers forms part of our sense that Gaskell's working-class world is full of hidden talent. Margaret's kitchen comedy of the scorpion loose in the house, Will Wilson's tall tales, Barton's account of London folk, Job Legh's story of Margaret's birth, even Jane Wilson's story about the first time she cooked potatoes for her new husband, amuse or move their audiences as fully as do the verses that Gaskell writes into her text. While the narrator makes no summary comment about her subjects' ability and inclination to transform their own painful experience into art, her decision to give us so many instances constitutes just such a point, and effectively identifies the storyteller herself with the activites of her fictional working-class characters.

Gaskell's most persuasive holds upon her readers' sympathies come from the recording of such family talents, dignities, and traditions; and there is a wide gap between the particular accounts of daily life and the more general attempts at social explanation and apology undertaken in some of the narrative summaries. The gap results both from the awkward melding of scene and summary, and from an unacknowledged shift in narrative role, from domestic observer to social historian. The uneasiness of the fit between the domestic and the political activities of the narrative is audible in the sometimes disconcerting shifts of language and tone in the storytelling voice.

While Gaskell assumes an unusually direct stance in relation to the "you" she often addresses, she is not always certain about who the "you" is, or what it might be assumed to believe. Characterized most generally, the narrative is astonishingly informal; it sounds like the spoken voice of a habitual story-teller, perhaps improvising out loud to her children about the hearth.[7] To take a short "clip" from the account of Mary's apprenticeship:

> Besides, trust a girl of sixteen for knowing well if she is pretty; concerning her plainness she may be ignorant. So with this consciousness she had early determined that her beauty should make her a lady; the rank she coveted the more for her father's abuse; the rank to which she firmly believed her lost Aunt Esther had arrived. Now, while a servant must often drudge and be dirty, must be known as her servant by all who visited at her master's house, a dressmaker's apprentice must (or so Mary thought) be always dressed with a certain regard to appearance; must never soil her hands, and need never redden or dirty her face with hard labour. Before my telling you so truly what folly Mary felt or thought injures her without redemption in your opinion, think what are the silly fancies of sixteen years of age in every class, and under all circumstances. The end of all the thoughts of father and daughter was, as I said before, Mary was to be a dressmaker; and her ambition prompted her unwilling father to apply at all the first establishments, to know on what terms of pains-taking and zeal his daughter might be admitted into ever so humble a workwoman's situation. But high premiums were

asked at all; poor man! he might have known that without giving up a day's work to ascertain the fact. (Ch. 3)

This charming mixture of neighborly gossip, social irony, general psychologizing, and spontaneous exclamation is typical of the almost "unwritten" quality of the narrative throughout. The "you" seems to be a friendly audience which may have a tendency to jump too quickly to negative judgments; and the job of the story-teller is to get this audience to sympathize with even the more dangerous fantasies of her characters, and to share the concrete considerations that her practical intelligence notices—Barton's sacrifice of a day's work for nothing is a strong touch.

When it comes to the passages in which Gaskell feels compelled to present Barton as a piece of social history, however, her sympathetic imagination can turn defensive. It is as though her "you" then becomes a public audience, better-informed and more articulate than she is; and when that audience enters her head, she bows to the teachings of its liberal-economic members. Her disturbing leaps to middle-class platitudes have been well-discussed elsewhere, and her unwillingness to challenge such dicta has been variously described.[8] What seems especially interesting about those leaps is, however, a matter of language: when Gaskell turns to placate her middle-class audience, she sounds like a novelist who has dropped momentarily into sociologese. There is simply no continuity of imagination between her concrete presentation of the visible evidence affecting John Barton and sentences like " . . . what I wish to impress is what the workman thinks and feels. True, that with childlike improvidence, good times will often dissipate his grumbling, and make him forget all prudence and foresight" (Ch. 3). That generic "him," the workman as a species of child, is the creation of social essayists and religious moralists; and when Gaskell turns to such talk, she herself sounds like a child reciting its lessons. The defensiveness suggests, I think, her fear of drawing social conclusions from the evidence she records, and some distrust of her own powers of generalization that leads her to shy away—at least in this first novel—from extending a position for public judgment.

Gaskell's finest imaginative energy is directed toward the project of uncovering hidden histories; of taking us into minds, and cellars, through descriptions that quite consciously defy the middle-class instinct to categorize and distance. There is a palpable narrative identification with the "hidden power" (Ch. 4) of Margaret Legh's voice singing working-class ballads; and with the Chartist belief that "their misery had still to be revealed in all its depths, and then some remedy would be found" (Ch. 8). And Gaskell's primary technique of "discovery" is to get us to see her characters in the context of their whole lives, with family histories, pet stories, favorite objects, and generational continuities. By creating a set of interlocking families, she succeeds in avoiding the contemporary rhetorical tendencies to create images of an ahistorical, rootless mass, on the one hand, and dispossessed middle-class "working-class heroes," on the other. Yet this apparently unrhetorical and domestic activity exists in a perpetual state of tension with the essay-like social commentary. And the dichotomizing impulse that creates those uneven levels of diction in the narrative voice may also be found in the structures that organize Gaskell's invention of characters, families, and plot actions.

The Barton and Wilson families are carefully distinguished in ways that focus the conflict between active social thought and passive domestic response, and the differences are grounded in the social histories of the families. John Barton is the son of Manchester manufacturing folk; even that simple fact gives an immediate historical depth of tradition to the town that figures so often as a visual symbol in contemporary accounts of industrial culture. George Wilson and his sister Alice have, by contrast, come to Manchester from an impoverished rural family; George has successfully found work and fathered a son who has risen to foundry work, and who becomes responsible for a technical invention. But if Jem Wilson is a technological as well as a moral hero, he nonetheless shares the indifference to class politics, and the lack of intellectual curiosity, that characterizes his countrybred family. Preoccupied with his love for Mary, Jem is immune to John Barton's attempt to involve him in the "short hours" issue. His inability to listen to talk that actually draws conclusions from social observation is like his father's; George Wilson's part in his dialogues with Barton is to take the personal line, or one sympathetic to the masters' accounts of themselves. Gaskell suggests, both in this pair of characters and through incidental narrative comments, that town life breeds admirably independent intelligences while rural life is conducive to mental passivity. Mrs. Barton, for example, has "somewhat of the deficiency of sense in her countenance, which is likewise characteristic of the rural inhabitants in comparison with the natives of the manufacturing towns" (Ch. 1).

The richest episode in the Barton-Wilson contrast is the finely organized sixth chapter, in which the two men nurse and feed the family of the dying Davenport. It is one of the few chapters in the novel that juxtaposes scenes of rich and poor for ironic effect: we see the brilliantly lighted shops in the London Road, "within five minutes' walk" of the Davenport's cellar; and we hear the Carson servants and children discuss the high prices of salmon and hothouse flowers while Wilson quietly sickens from hunger in their kitchen. But the two men, both heroically generous in domestic action, bring very different minds to these contrasts, as each goes forth on an errand for medical help. Barton "felt the contrast between the well-filled, well-lighted shops and the dim gloomy cellar, and it made him moody that such contrasts should exist." His bitterness is dutifully chastised by the same voice that calls our attention to the contrast; it is said to be caused by Barton's ignorance of the hearts of the passers-by in the streets, and his quite natural thoughts are condemned in religious terms: "the thoughts of his heart were touched by sin, by bitter hatred of the happy, whom he, for the time, confounded with the selfish." Although the narrator here seems to align herself with the "Methodee" sentiments of Davenport, "that we mun bear patiently whate'er he sends," her intelligent distinction between the happy and the selfish softens her judgment; and she goes on to dramatize, in the Carson section, more and more actual reasons for bitterness. In that section, however, Wilson becomes the witness; and this narrative choice increases the discomfiting ironies in the portrayal even as it mutes the possibility of drawing inferences from it.

Wilson brings to the factory owner's house an essentially feudal spirit. He is tempted to stop and admire the pictures and gilding, "but then he thought it would not be respectful." Let into the comfortable kitchen, he amuses himself by guessing at the nature and use of the familiar utensils hanging about, as though he had not just come from a painfully different place. Surrounded by odors of cooking food, he starves in silence, and it is only a piece of good luck, the cook's second thoughts, that sends him away with a handful of bread and meat. As he emerges with an inadequate out-patient's order and a casually bestowed five shillings, Wilson's conclusions are muddy, to say the least: "Wilson left the house, not knowing whether to be pleased or grieved. It was long to Monday, but they had all spoken kindly to him, and who could tell if they might not remember this, and do something before Monday." These are clearly naive and child-like responses; as alternatives to Barton's "sinful thoughts" they are hardly acceptable. Yet it seems that Gaskell can fully dramatize the contrast between rich and poor only in the presence of a political innocent: *we* get the point, but Wilson retains a sort of unfallen virtue which is the legacy of his rural origin, while the narrator remains free not to draw conclusions.

This troubled contrast between Wilson and Barton[9] represents an impasse that is related to Gaskell's position as a narrator. Wilson is incapable of generalization or intellectual connection; he is a good character because he functions generously in family and neighborly spheres. Barton's ability to connect renders him dangerous, even sinful; his self-consciousness is that of the fallen man, the creature of industry. When Gaskell demurs at Barton's intelligence, she is simultaneously retreating from her own: she allows neither her narrator nor her character to challenge the authority that describes the world in middle-class terms. Yet

at the same time as she fears the arrogance of critical generalization, Gaskell dramatizes, with admiration, the superior powers of intelligence that would inevitably reach for it.

In the portrait of old Alice Wilson, Gaskell's mixed feelings about domestic tranquillity—and rural ignorance—are stabilized through the creation of a recognizably literary figure. If her brother is naive, Alice is regressive: she has made a seamless transition from childhood to old-maidenhood. Her history brings the pastoral world into the novel, but not as an alternative to Manchester life: there is no pastoral sentimentality even in the presentation of Alice's unfulfilled longing to return to her childhood home, as there is no trace of retreatist rural nostalgia in the novel.[10] Rather, Gaskell pays homage to Alice's "prelapsarian" virtue by imagining her as a genre character, a "tale from humble life."[11]

The rocky terrain of Alice's childhood, the heather-gathering children, and the fatalism suggest above all a Wordsworthian figure—a version of an idiot boy, perhaps, or one of those who tell tales of loss with bleak pleasure. And Alice's function in the moral terrain of the novel is akin to that of Wordsworth's Cumberland Beggar: she is there to be revered and cared for, despite her social blunders and in the midst of other woes; for she is a precious link with the past, a test of the virtue of others. A good deal of narrative attention is paid, for example, to the arrangements for nursing Alice during the period when Mary's plot is at its most frantic. Alice is there to provide the domestic grounding, the reality of slow mortality, against which the fast-moving excitement of Mary's brief adventure is deliberately set. Mary passes the moral test when she pays emotional attention to the dying old woman as well as to her falsely accused lover. The case of Old Alice thus treats and rejects the pastoral "solution," but at the same time it brings up an alternative locus for virtue and stability in the idea of family life and domestic affection.

The family is the novel's base of activity as well as its source of consolation; and the successful "heroic" actions are essentially domestic ones. This point might best be made, as Gaskell makes it, through the juxtaposition of the two London stories in Chapter Nine: Barton's experiences as a participant in the Chartist march and petition, and Job Legh's moving account of his rescue of the infant Margaret after the deaths of her parents. Job's journey, a private family rescue mission, is a success; John's public and political one, a failure. Job's story is full of anonymous people who help the men in their comic and pathetic attempts to feed the infant; Barton's of pretentious coachmen and insulting policemen. It is not that Job's story is "better" than Barton's—as a satirist, John has good eyes and ears—but that he tells it in order to move his audience's minds away from Barton's deep sense of political failure, as a consolatory tale of domestic affection. It is possible to save lives in **Mary Barton:** Jem saves his father from the fire at Carson's mill; Job saves his granddaughter; Mary saves Jem, the man she wants to marry. The implicit pattern is an apolitical one, suggesting that one is responsible to the lives of family members, to save or to grieve. Such displacements of attention from political issues to individual acts are basic impulses in the novel, as, indeed they prove to be in most fictions about industrial stress. But Gaskell's version of the shift is bound in a special way to the subject of family integrity.

All of the major threats in the novel are rendered in terms of their potential to destroy family life. Factory work for women, a subject discussed at several points, is just such a threat. Esther's gradual spin out of the family orbit leads to a life on the streets, while Barton's fear of that sexual availability leads him to insist that Mary avoid factory work. After the death of Mrs. Barton, the Barton household is composed of two workers—not quite a family; in the absence of that ballast, John begins to swerve toward the union, Mary toward her flirtation with Harry Carson. Turning to the structures of those two main stories, it is especially interesting to observe how consistently Gaskell denies the outer world its full reality by treating such "lapses" from domesticity as the stuff of melodrama and romance.

John Barton comes most fully alive as a particular, internally realized character in the scene describing his reactions and memories at the moment of his wife's death (Ch. 3). It is the single situation in which Gaskell's concrete imaginative energy flows into his character, unimpeded by the ideas that disturb her when she speaks of Barton as a political example. For the rest, Barton's "domination" of the novel's first half may be as much due to the problematical character of the narrative presentation as to his centrality as a character. His story appears in only ten of the first eighteen chapters, after which he disappears from the narrative until the end; and he does rather little on stage. After the opening chapters, he helps the Davenports, leaves and returns from London, rejects his sister-in-law, and turns the anger of his union colleagues from the scabs to the masters. This last scene, done up in the gas-lit melodramatic style conventional in the depiction of unions,[12] is the only one in which we see Barton in a public situation, despite the fact that we hear of his leadership in the movement.

The absence of other public scenes is important, for it is one of the ways that Gaskell blurs Barton's status as a political personage. Most of the time he is present as a sitting, brooding household presence, often registered through the worried consciousness of Mary. The union's impact on the Barton household is described through Mary's nightmare images: "Strange faces of pale men, with dark glaring eyes, peered into the inner darkness, and seemed desirous to ascertain if her father were at home. Or a hand and arm (the body hidden) was put within the door, and beckoned him away" (Ch. 10). This is remarkably effective writing, despite the immediate conventional melodrama of "dark glaring eyes"; those truncated pieces of bodies are dangerous because they intrude insidiously into the safe space of home, threatening to beckon the father away both physically and psychologically. The dehumanization of the union suggested by those images is extended in the depiction of its effect on Barton: he becomes more isolated as he becomes more involved, as though a union could not provide the companionship that it might naturally foster. I am not interested in these matters primarily for the sake of berating Gaskell yet again for her failure to transcend the stereotypes she had absorbed from her own culture, but because of the way the union is placed in relation to the kinds of communal activity that *can* be imagined and dramatized in this novel: the nuclear or extended family and the neighborhood.

Even Barton's political animus is reducible to family sentiment, for it is grounded in his personal desire to revenge the death of his only son. The description of that moment of conversion reveals some of Gaskell's most frightened political leaps:

> Hungry himself, almost to an animal pitch of ravenousness, but with the bodily pain swallowed up in anxiety for his little sinking lad, he stood at one of the shop windows where all edible luxuries are displayed; haunches of venison, Stilton cheeses, moulds of jelly—all appetising sights to the common passer-by. And out of this shop came Mrs. Hunter! She crossed to her carriage, followed by the shopman loaded with purchases for a party. The door was quickly slammed to, and she drove away; and Barton returned home with a bitter spirit of wrath in his heart, to see his only boy a corpse!

> You can fancy, now, the hoards of vengeance in his heart against the employers. For there are never wanting those who, either in speech or in print, find it in their interest to cherish such feelings in the working classes; who know how and when to rouse the dangerous power at their command; and who use their knowledge with unrelenting purpose to either party. (Ch. 3)

Those exclamation points, creating melodrama as in a child's story, are the first clue to what is wrong here: the scene is less realized than insisted upon. And the second paragraph transforms Barton—now again a representative of the distant mass—into someone with strong feelings, but incapable of commanding a political intelligence. His feelings become mindless stores of gunpowder in the arsenals of "outside agitators." And yet the ostensible point of this passage is to make us sympathetic with Barton's union activities through engaging us with the power of his domestic grief. Barton's reality lies in those feelings; what happens to them is abstract, someone else's responsibility. The evil of unions lies, it is implied, in the fact that they extend impulses of feeling into the inappropriate sphere of political action. And that analysis is borne out by the events that precede and explain the murder.

Gaskell's strength in this part of the book lies in her depiction of tempers wearing down under the stress of loss and poverty: Jane Wilson's temper provides a domestic parallel with Barton's in the development of the theme. Barton's first act of violence is a domestic one: he strikes Mary, then quickly repents and apologizes. His second mistake, also set up in parallel with his political behavior, is to reject Esther, whom he blames for his wife's death; again the pattern of action followed by repentance prefigures the end of the story. The decision to kill Harry Carson, set off by the casual cruelty of his caricature, is depicted as a "last straw" move, an attempt to maintain some vestige of manhood under unendurable circumstances. During the union meeting that follows the failure of the negotiation with the masters, Barton demonstrates his humanity by arguing against violence to scabs, and then defends himself against an accusation of cowardice by redirecting the men's violence at the masters. The necessity to do something is made palpable, but it is represented as a form of action necessary to relieve feelings, not as a strategic decision in a political program.

The crime itself is often said to be the act that places Barton beyond our political sympathies.[13] It does have the effect of dealing the final blow to the image of unionization, turning the union into a criminal bond. But in fact it seems to me that the murder works to strengthen our personal sympathies, both toward the murderer and his victim's family. Through killing Harry, Barton creates in the elder Carson a master who is capable of becoming a "brother" in suffering: the reconciliation of Barton and Carson depends on their shared, or parallel, griefs at the loss of an only son. The murder is "successful" in the sense that it is responsible for both Barton's redemption and Carson's; and their similarities of character—revenging and then relenting—effect the temperamental brotherhood that would seem to overleap the social gap. Thus when the possibility of sharing information with workers emerges as a shadow of a solution at the end, we are apt to feel that the industrial relation is really a severed family tie that ought to be repaired rather than a radical change in the nature of industrial social arrangements.[14]

The peculiarity of the murder's function in the plot does not end with the social reconciliation that it engenders. John Barton "ought" to be murdering Harry Carson because Carson has sexual designs upon his

daughter; and Barton's sensitivity to that issue has been carefully created through his antipathy to factory work for women. But the plot is divided in such a way that he does not know the sexual sins of his victim; this knowledge, and its attendant anger, is left for Jem Wilson, who has the interview with Esther that John Barton refuses. Thus Barton and the falsely accused Jem become split doubles in the murder plot. Jem provides the public cover for John's political murder; the cover is a personal and sexual revenge story, not an industrial one.

This splitting does some other work to soften the novel's analysis of the middle-class and its institutions. First and most simply, the false accusation plot deflects our judgment of John Barton as a criminal, turning our "legal" interest to the wish to have Jem legally absolved. The outcome of the trial allows "justice to be done" by the legal machinery in a way that upholds the character of the assizes and shows working-class characters winning a court case against an employer, at the same time as it retains our sympathy for the actual murderer. For we are absorbed into the imaginations of Jem and Mary, each going to the brink in an attempt to keep the guilty one from suspicion; Barton's presence in their anguish keeps him firmly within the circle of our assent. Thus the difficult opposition of justice and legality—which has haunted John Barton—is happily reconciled in two ways at once. Mary's faith in the law as an impartial instrument of justice is upheld when her production of an "alibi" for Jem proves successful. At the same time a combination of natural and divine justice governs the repentance and end of John Barton, beyond the system of law. While the law—demonstrably an instrument of the middle class—retains its technical authority, the higher law prevails as well.

The plot provides a similar muffling of the connection between industrial and sexual exploitation.[15] Harry Carson is a seducer; but Mary is not his employee, and he has no direct economic hold over her. He remains a threat only so long as Mary is willing to entertain the idea of a class romance. Neither Jem nor John is a Carson employee; again the personal and economic connections are of the loosest kind. Even Esther, an example of "the seduced and abandoned," has been betrayed not by a factory owner but by that traditional literary seducer, an army officer. And, because the stories of sexual harassment and economic exploitation are split between Harry Carson and his father, on the one hand, John and Jem on the other, we are not required by the novel's structure to put them back together into a systematic analysis of industrial oppression.

The intertwinings of the two main plots are thus arranged to defuse political issues, but these reflections must also suggest the interdependence of the stories.

The structure of Mary's experience has a good deal in common with that of her father. Neither Barton is resigned; both are pulled away from domestic activities by imaginations of a better life. John is beckoned forth by the ghostly hands of the union; Mary is temporarily drawn toward a chimera depicted with equal unreality, the dream of a middle-class marriage. Both father and daughter go out of Manchester on missions to save their people by telling the truth in a public forum. Mary, focused on a single and personal situation within a legal context, is allowed to be successful. Her story offers a vision of action immersed in loyalty to domestic ties that serves as an antidote and a release of the tensions established in her father's.

Mary's story is often written off as a conventional romance: a young girl chooses between the rich, handsome, dangerous fantasy prince and her true working-class childhood love. This view requires some important amendments. First, Gaskell is almost completely uninterested in the relationship between Mary and Harry Carson. She dramatizes it once, in their final interview; and Mary fends him off during every dialogue we hear between her and the go-between Sally Leadbitter. It is Sally who interests Gaskell, because Sally wants to make Mary into the kind of romantic heroine that Gaskell has been made responsible for in some critical accounts. Secondly, the real issue of heroism in Mary's life lies not in her choice of lovers, but in the question of whether or how to act, once she has recognized her love for Jem. When the murder plot allows her to act, she becomes, though only briefly and ambiguously, a heroine of stature.[16] Two pairs of friends and lovers press on either side of Mary's character, organizing the opposition of domestic tranquillity and romance: Sally Leadbitter and Harry Carson on the false romantic side; Margaret Legh and Jem Wilson on the other.

Mary's flirtation with Carson is introduced with an almost incredible casualness, subordinated to a description of Mary's growing confidential friendship with Margaret Legh (Ch. 5). This nearly parenthetical treatment is in keeping with the general portrayal of Carson: he is important primarily because he is a secret that divides Mary from her loyal, familial friends. Carson is minimally realized, and even Mary is said to know that she is in love, not with him, but with the possibility of wealth and status that her reading of cheap romances has taught her to covet. That by-the-way introduction is also consistent with the most painful results of the public revelation of Mary's relationship with Carson: Margaret's withdrawal at the discovery of her friend's deception, and the tongue-lashing Mary gets from her future mother-in-law.

Margaret and Sally are Mary's good and bad angels; each, in her way, is devoted to art. Margaret makes a gold mine of her blindness by becoming a professional singer of working-class ballads; this, of course, is the proper use of art, to transmute the grief of living into song that moves the hearts of its listeners. Sally wants to create in life the kind of spurious escapist romance celebrated in the novels that form the staple of discussion at Miss Simmons' millinery workroom. Gaskell's diction about Sally is directly reminiscent of Jane Austen:

> She had just talent enough to corrupt others. Her very good nature was an evil influence. They could not hate one who was so kind; they could not avoid one who was so willing to shield them from scrapes by any exertion of her own; whose ready fingers would at any time make up for their deficiencies, and whose still more convenient tongue would at any time invent for them. (Ch. 8)

Playing Isabella Thorpe to Mary's Catherine Morland, Sally's vulgar imagination thrills to the plot that she sustains between Mary and Carson, with no thought for the implications of the seduction she knows to be its only possible fulfillment. The witty, markedly literary, self-consciousness in the treatment of Sally is sustained throughout the novel, making it very clear that Gaskell is offering, by way of contrast, a very different kind of woman's heroism.

Sally's inability "to become a heroine on her own account" (Ch. 8) renders her eager to play a supporting role even when Mary bows out of the Carson fantasy. When Mary becomes a public character, about to set off for the Liverpool Assizes, Sally's value as a source of sheer comic relief is proven in a witty scene. Memorizing Mary's clothes and looks like a fashion reporter, Sally prepares herself to be "a Gazette Extraordinary the next morning at the work-room" (Ch. 25), and she urges Mary to return there after the trial so that her status as heroine will help pick up trade. Once Mary has returned, Sally's mixture of failure, admiration, and envy are expressed in the line "You've set up heroine on your own account, Mary Barton" (Ch. 34). By this time Mary has indeed been set up as heroine, on Gaskell's account—in ways that show her creator in yet another struggle with Victorian conventions.

The positive portrait of Mary has two distinct parts that co-exist rather uncomfortably, corresponding to the opposition of domestic passivity and political action in the John Barton sections. As a heroine of the domestic life celebrated in so much of the narrative, Mary is shown as the impulsive comforter of Jem in trouble, daughter solicitous of her father, neighborly nurse of old Alice Wilson, and maker of the resolve to abstain from telling Jem of her love—even after refusing his proposal—in the name of shrinking from "unmaidenly action" (Ch. 15). As a heroine of rescue, on the other hand, Mary persuades Job and Margaret to support her, travels alone to Liverpool, chases the steamer on which Will Wilson is about to sail away, survives being lost in a strange place, and testifies in a public courtroom to those feelings which would have been "unmaidenly" to reveal in private to her lover. These two portraits are clearly not compatible, and Gaskell does her best to blur the more active one by presenting Mary in a state of near-collapse and then delirious illness during her stay in Liverpool. Still, at the moment she is brought into being, that heroine of rescue touches some of her author's fiercest feelings on the question of action and resignation.

Mary's decision to wait in womanly passivity for Jem to return to his courtship is apparently supported in the narrative: the good angel Margaret counsels patience, and Gaskell gives us a little chapter (Ch. 12) devoted explicitly to the theme of waiting and reward, in which old Alice's desire for Will Wilson's return is set next to Mary's own ordeal of waiting. Yet the action during this period is designed so that Mary misses every opportunity of seeing Jem, even in those sickroom scenes which provide the primary settings for their familial courtship throughout the novel. This Victorian modesty strains against the energy of Mary's character, and the tension produces a small narrative explosion when it comes time for Mary to act.

After Mary deduces that her father is the murderer of Carson (Ch. 22), she discovers "a little spring of comfort" in "the desert of misery": "And that was the necessity for exertion on her part which this discovery enforced." With that, Gaskell goes off into the novel's most personal aside: "Oh! I do think that the necessity for exertion, for some kind of action (bodily or mentally) in time of distress, is a most infinite blessing, although the first efforts at such seasons are painful," she exclaims; and she goes on to have a little fit of anger at those who counsel against grief in situations where no help can be given. This highly charged state of feeling extends into the few sentences that do the work of transforming Mary into an active heroine:

> But with the call upon her exertions, and her various qualities of judgment and discretion, came the answering consciousness of innate power to meet the emergency . . . And you must remember, too, that never was so young a girl so friendless, or so penniless, as Mary was at this time. But the lion accompanied Una through the wilderness and the danger; and so will a high, resolved purpose of right-doing ever guard and accompany the helpless.

> But Mary re-entered her home . . . with . . . a still clearer conviction of how much rested upon her unassisted and friendless self, alone with her terrible knowledge, in the hard, cold, populous world. (Ch. 22)

Two images come into play simultaneously: Mary as the noble quester, full of internal strength, and a vision

of the larger world as wilderness, vast and threatening. The combination of admiration for Mary's courage and fear of the public arena is intensified by the exaggerated, melodramatic account of Mary's isolation. When Mary's excitement grows into a vision of herself as heroine, that isolation remains part of the picture: "She longed to do all herself; to be his liberator, his deliverer; to win him life, though she might never regain his lost love by her own exertions" (Ch. 23). This vision of chivalric rescue carries a dynamic force that merges Mary's romantic imagination with her moral one. Yet one must recall the word "enforced" which accompanies the initial discovery of the need for action: Mary is released into an active, responsible, and independent role only because there is an "emergency."

Even before the emergency is over, the determined actor with her "terrible knowledge" is on the verge of dissolving into something very like a heroine of sensibility. During the trial scene itself, Gaskell falls into some disturbingly romantic and pictorial language about Mary:

> The mellow sunlight streamed down that high window on her head, and fell on the rich treasure of her golden hair, stuffed away in masses under her little bonnet-cap. . . . I was not there myself; but one who was, told me that her look, and indeed her whole face, was more like the well-known engraving from Guido's picture of "Beatrice Cenci" than anything else he could give me an idea of. He added, that her countenance haunted him, like the remembrance of some wild sad melody heard in childhood; that it would perpetually recur with its mute imploring agony. (Ch. 32)

This is a shocking break in the normal narrative relationship with Mary and with her beauty; the objectification of the heroine, from a cultured male middle-class point of view, seems symptomatic of Gaskell's distress at having gotten her heroine into so public a fix. Gaskell apparently needs to pretend that she did not place Mary on the witness stand without some factual precedent that has already made Mary into a well-known legendary figure—and, in fact, into a piece of art.

The oddness of this withdrawal from Mary's own experience in the courtroom may be related to the class confrontation of the trial scene itself. Mary is on display before the middle-class world, for the first and only time; and once again, as Gaskell imagines such an audience, she begins to talk its language, as though Mary's power to move the middle-class world lay only in her ability to push those conventional buttons of sentiment that suddenly intrude upon the prose. Or, perhaps, Mary's moment of public soulbearing raises the spectre of female immodesty; lest she become material for Sally's "Gazette Extraordinary," she is transfixed in a more respectable art form. In any case, it immediately becomes possible to measure the difference between this kind of pictorial ballad-making and the success with which Gaskell takes us into the world of the poor when the middle class isn't looking.

The passage is also, however, a prelude to the more general withdrawal of narrative assent to the daring part of Mary's character. Illness purges her, as it does many a middle-class heroine, of all but the most angelic and domestic impulses. Thereafter the predominant images are of Mary's clinging to Jem on the one hand, and protecting her broken father, "as the Innocent should watch over the Guilty" (Ch. 34) on the other. What remains to be resolved returns us to the world of domestic romance that encloses the courtship of Jem and Mary: Mary and her future mother-in-law must struggle for the possession of Jem's affection; Mary, now fully domesticated, must be received into the family, the relation cemented by the shared secret knowledge of John Barton's crime.

A merger of the Bartons and the Wilsons, repairing the decimation of the original families, is the proper resolution in a novel that locates its virtues so firmly in family solidarity and tradition. The domestic management of grief might even be said to triumph in the private extralegal reconciliation of Barton and Carson, which allows Barton's crime to remain forever buried in the family closet. Thus the primacy of the family finally overcomes the impulse to action in the larger world, allowing Gaskell to dissolve the disturbing aspects of Barton's radicalism and Mary's romantic energy in the brew of familial sympathy. The ending puts Barton in Carson's arms; Mary in Jem's; and Gaskell goes on to apply the liberal-economist's pet panacea, voluntary emigration.

To center the novel in this way is, finally, to see its political movements in their proper context. It is easy enough, by focusing on the plot resolutions, to group *Mary Barton* with other industrial novels that portray social injustices while showing working-class political initiative as manipulated action or animal violence. But *Mary Barton* asks its questions of life in rather different ways. Starting and ending always with the personal grief, the novel is only secondarily about politics as such. Politics figures rather like romance, as a form of "bodily or mental action" that might alleviate or muffle the pain of domestic grief and suffering that is represented as the fundamental matter of experience. The public realm appears as a threatening place of resort in the desperation of poverty or injustice. This world, run by the middle-class, may fortuitously remedy a specific injustice, as in the release of Jem, but it is not likely to answer to generalized social accusations. The proper forum for grief is, rather, the familial and neighborly world. And because Gaskell realizes this world so fully and warmly, she offers an image of her subjects that is at once more conservative and more human than the aggregated urban masses or disintegrat-

ing industrial families of Disraeli or Dickens. Her society of the poor is so full of its own dictions and traditions, and so various in its own right, that the middle-class voices we hear at the Carsons' or before the Liverpool Assizes seem genuine intrusions from another linguistic universe.

At the same time, the centrifugal pull out of the domestic orbit is one of the powerful forces at work in the text, in ways that link the characters with Gaskell's own dilemmas of authorship. So many episodes are devoted to the anatomy of grief that it is nearly impossible to forget that *Mary Barton* was part of Gaskell's grieving process; but it is equally touching to watch the assertions and withdrawals which attend upon her first appearance as a public storyteller. The character of John Barton is based on the same troubled relationship between direct social apprehension and general theory that Gaskell's own narrative reveals. Barton arrives at his radical social conclusions about the gulf between classes out of a battered and embittered spirit. Seeing what he sees, Gaskell's ameliorating narrator leaps in the opposite direction, toward middle-class liberal formulae. If Barton is mimicking his union agitators, Gaskell is, no less, imitating her liberal theorists; and what the book most movingly demonstrates is exactly that conceptual impasse, in narrator and character alike.

In Mary's burst of heroism Gaskell imagined an even more direct image of her own situation. For writing *Mary Barton* was her kind of "bodily or mental action in time of distress," and it leads, like Mary's journey, out of the domestic world and into a public one where one's deepest feelings are put on display for a curious crowd. "I am almost frightened at my own action in writing it," Gaskell wrote to Mary Ewart late in 1848;[17] and Mary's story is shaped by that divided and quickly repentant sense of public assertiveness for women. But despite its fits and starts, its bows to imagined audiences, and its retreats to political and feminine stereotypes, the concrete substance of Elizabeth Gaskell's narrative remains, like Mary's truthful testimony, a genuine mission of rescue.

Notes

[1] The almost unrelenting atmosphere of grief that pervades *Mary Barton* can be related to the fact that Gaskell undertook the novel, at her husband's suggestion, to help take her mind from the death of her infant son in 1845. See Winifred Gerin, *Elizabeth Gaskell: A Biography* (Oxford: Clarendon Press 1976), pp. 74-75. Gaskell herself acknowledged the source of the "heavy shadow" over the book in a letter to Mrs. Greg: "The tale was formed, and the greater part of the first volume was written when I was obliged to lie down constantly on the sofa, and when I took refuge in the invention to exclude the memory of painful scenes

which would force themselves on my remembrance." *The Letters of Mrs. Gaskell,* ed. J. A. V. Chapple and Arthur Pollard (Cambridge, Mass.: Harvard University Press, 1967), p. 74.

[2] Raymond Williams, who made the "industrial novels" into a recognized group in literary history, calls *Mary Barton* "the most moving response in literature to the industrial suffering of the 1840s." *Culture and Society 1780-1950* (London: Chatto & Windus, 1958; rpr. New York: Harper & Row, 1966), p. 87.

[3] Almost every critic of *Mary Barton* notices how the narrative commentary retreats to middle-class judgments of Barton's radicalism. The best, most thorough and sympathetic analyses of the inconsistencies of Gaskell's political position may be found in Margaret Ganz, *Elizabeth Gaskell: The Artist in Conflict* (New York: Twayne, 1969) pp. 55-66; and John Lucas, "Mrs. Gaskell and Brotherhood," in *Tradition and Tolerance in Nineteenth-Century Fiction,* ed. David Howard, John Lucas, and John Goode (New York: Barnes and Noble, 1967), pp. 161-174.

[4] Most Gaskell critics follow Williams's lead in calling Mary's part "the familiar and orthodox plot of the Victorian novel of sentiment" p. 89). See, for example, Ganz, p. 69; W. A. Craik, *Elizabeth Gaskell and the English Provincial Novel* (London: Methuen, 1975), pp. 5 and 31; and Lucas, p. 162. Coral Lansbury's discussion in *Elizabeth Gaskell: The Novel of Social Crisis* (New York: Barnes and Noble, 1975), is an exception that emphasizes Mary's central role and her strength of character.

[5] *Mary Barton,* ed. Angus Easson, Oxford English Novels, (London: Oxford University Press, 1973), chapter 1. Subsequent quotations will be indicated by chapter number in the text.

[6] See especially Angus Easson, *Elizabeth Gaskell* (London: Routledge and Kegan Paul, 1979), pp. 74-76.

[7] Gaskell described her narrative stance in a letter to Eliza Fox (May 29, 1849): "I told the story according to a fancy of my own; to really SEE the scenes I tried to describe . . . and then to tell them as nearly as I could as if I were speaking to a friend over the fire on a winter's night and describing real occurences." *Letters,* p. 82.

[8] See Ganz, pp. 55-66, and Lucas, pp. 161-174. For the remarkable view that Gaskell deliberately lets her characters speak for themselves, while presenting the narrative stance as a strategic sop to her middle-class readers, see Lansbury, pp. 9, 25. Lansbury's analysis is a compelling view of the effect, but Gaskell seems to be so consistently double-visioned in every aspect of the novel that I cannot accept a description of effect as an accurate account of intent.

[9] Ganz identifies a related thematic opposition of resignation and rebellion, primarily in terms of the contrast between Barton and Alice Wilson (pp. 66-67). David Smith, who reads Mary Barton as a straightforward plea for Christian resignation, seems to take certain narrative statements as more definitive moral postures than others. See "*Mary Barton* and *Hard Times:* Their Social Insights," *MOSAIC,* 2(1971-1972), 97-112.

[10] To see Alice Wilson's yearning for the country as a rural-industrial contrast is to oversimplify. See, for example, Arthur Pollard, *Mrs. Gaskell: Novelist and Biographer* (Cambridge, Mass.: Harvard University Press, 1966), pp. 44-45. Lansbury gives a fine account of all the ways that Gaskell works against stereotypical town-country and pastoral-industrial contrasts, especially through the treatment of Old Alice (pp. 25-28 and 33-35).

[11] Old Alice may well be a holdover figure from the rural tale that Gaskell first intended to write. (See her "Perface" to *Mary Barton*); and that she might have seen as a prose version of the "sketches among the poor, *rather* in the manner of Crabbe" that she and William Gaskell had discussed earlier. She describes this unfullfilled plan, quoting a passage from "The Cumberland Beggar," in a letter to Mary Howitt of August 8, 1838. *Letters,* p. 33.

[12] Patrick Brantlinger has shown how the images of unionization prevalent among middle class writers developed from reports of the Glasgow cotton spinner's strikes and violence in 1837. See "The Case Against Trade Unions in Early Victorian Fiction," *Victorian Studies,* 13 (1969), pp. 37-52.

[13] See Raymond Williams, pp. 89 and 90. John Lucas amends Williams's analysis in an interesting way, asserting that the murder plot simplifies the political situation enough so that a moral pattern can be made from "a muddle so colossal that it defeats the explanations of her social creeds" (p. 173).

[14] I have described Gaskell's very different embrace of social change in *North and South* in "*North and South:* A Permanent State of Change," *Nineteenth-Century Fiction,* 34 (1979), 281-301.

[15] I take issue here with Ivan Melada's argument in *The Captain of Industry in English Fiction 1821-1871* (Albuquerque: University of New Mexico Press, 1970), pp. 73-86. Melada calls *Mary Barton* "the novel that consistently criticizes the employer according to assumptions about factory owners common among the working classes . . ." (p. 86). Melada identifies these with a set of accusations made by radical factions against the self-serving legal system, sexual exploitation of women factory workers, and the arrogant pride of class.

[16] Mary's character and plot are given some positive critical attention by W. A. Craik, who also emphasizes Mary's public acting (pp. 35-38), and by Lansbury, who stresses her independence and activity, though without notice to the parts of the narrative that pull Mary in more passive and conventional directions (pp. 23, 29-30, and 31).

[17] *Letters,* p. 67.

Sally Mitchell (essay date 1981)

SOURCE: "The Social Problem," in *The Fallen Angel: Chastity, Class and Women's Reading, 1835-1900,* Bowling Green University Popular Press, 1981, pp. 22-43.

[*In the essay that follows, Mitchell discusses Gaskell's* Ruth *as a novel that attempts to respond to the problem of prostitution, in part by criticizing the presupposition that "fallen women" should be ostracized from society and by suggesting that the general public has a certain responsibility for this problem.*]

During the 1840s there was a sudden proliferation of books and articles about prostitution. It seems an odd opening for the Victorian era until we realize that the interest was a sign of increased public decency rather than the reverse. Though authors treated the great social evil with sometimes surprising frankness, they did so because they were coming to see the prostitute as a problem instead of an inevitable part of the social order.

Most of this writing was intended for men. Women were not expected to read medical treatises. Relatively few would see articles in the quarterly reviews that were read by intellectuals among the upper middle class. Even newspapers were still, before the stamp tax was abolished, expensive enough that men were likely to read them at their clubs or offices instead of subscribing at home. Despite their audience, however, the books and articles and medical essays spoke at length about the prostitute and said little of her clients. The double standard ensured that the social problem was, actually, a problem primarily affecting the sex which was not supposed to know of its existence.

In this new climate, some women writers used fiction to deal seriously with those special aspects of the social problem that they believed were important to women. They wrote both to inform and to reform. These writers inherited from the early nineteenth century evangelical movement a tradition that charity was a natural extension of the feminine role; women were expected to serve others and to provide an influence for moral improvement. Traditionally, women exercised charity by personal contact rather than organized philanthropy. Fiction extends the personal; it turns problems into people. And fiction was read, they knew, by women who would not see medical books or articles in the *Westminster Review* or parliamentary investigations—or even reports of them in the daily newspaper.

The writers discussed in this chapter all wanted women readers to be informed about sexual relations outside of marriage. They all sought to use the emotional power of fiction in order to affect readers' actions. Their immediate moral purposes, however, were not identical. Some emphasized religion; others dwelt on legal and economic questions. Several were influenced by the problems and concepts that would lead, later in the decade, to the first stirrings of organized feminism. And they wrote for different audiences—because of the economics of the publishing trade a writer could know, with some assurance, whether her reader would be Meg in the kitchen or Miss Margaret in the parlor. The style and content of fiction on the social problem was shaped by each author's moral intent and by the audience she wanted to reach. . . .

The only story of this category (i.e., written by a woman for women with the direct intention to do good) that has survived the restrictions of its time, audience and immediate moral is Elizabeth Cleghorn Gaskell's *Ruth* (3 vols. 1853). Mrs. Gaskell has the same literary origins as the women we have been considering. Her first published stories appeared in *Howitt's Journal,* one of them in the same issue as Eliza Meteyard's "Comments on Mr. Spooner's Bill."[23] She and Meteyard spent the evening with the Howitts on Christmas Day, 1850. (Everyone told ghost stories.)[24] Eliza Cook asked Mrs. Gaskell to contribute to her magazine;[25] William Howitt was the agent who placed *Mary Barton* (2 vols. 1848) with its publishers.

With that novel Mrs. Gaskell moved away from the Howitt-Cook school of economic tract into the social problem novel. In the same manner, *Ruth* considers issues raised by other writers of the period—sexual virtue, motherhood, social regeneration through womanly service—but the novel's pace and scope strip the ethical problems of their deceptive simplicity. Ruth's victory is therefore more significant: she is regenerated not in isolation, nor in the altered society of a utopian outback, but within a conventional and recognizable contemporary world.

Ruth Hilton, a fifteen-year-old orphan apprenticed to a dressmaker, is pleased and flattered by the attention of a young rake named Bellingham. She loses her job because she has been seen walking out with him and before long is pregnant and abandoned in a holiday town in Wales. She is rescued by a dissenting minister, Rev. Thurstan Benson, and his sister Faith; they protect her physically by offering her a place to live and socially by pretending that she is a widow. After her

R U T H.

A Novel.

BY THE AUTHOR OF "MARY BARTON."

> Drop, drop slow tears!
>   And bathe those beauteous feet,
> Which brought from heaven
>   The news and Prince of peace.
> Cease not, wet eyes,
>   For mercy to entreat:
> To cry for vengeance
>   Sin doth never cease.
> In your deep floods
>   Drown all my faults and fears;
> Nor let His eye
>   See sin, but through my tears.
>   *Phineas Fletcher.*

IN THREE VOLUMES.

VOL. I.

LONDON:

CHAPMAN AND HALL, 193, PICCADILLY.

1853.

NOTICE.—*The Author of this work reserves the right of publishing a
Translation in France.*

son is old enough to go to school, Ruth becomes governess for the daughters of Mr. Bradshaw, the wealthiest man in Benson's congregation. Then her secret comes out; she is dismissed in disgrace. Meanwhile, Bellingham reappears under a different name as M.P. for the constituency and offers to marry Ruth. She refuses. No longer able to work as a governess, she turns to nursing and ultimately becomes director of the fever hospital during an epidemic. Her honor in the world is wholly regained; the doctor and the clergyman publish her praises. Everyone in Eccleston knows of her past but, as a friend says, "the remembrance of those days is swept away" (Ch 34). Then Bellingham falls ill and Ruth, nursing him, takes the fever and dies amid her honors.

Mrs. Gaskell's immediate aim was to make readers think about their unexamined assumption that a woman who lost her chastity had to be totally cut off from society so that she would not contaminate decent people. "I think I have put the small edge of the wedge in," she wrote, "if only I have made people talk & discuss the subject a little more than they did."[26] Thus the social idea of "respectability" is the initial villain. The dressmaker does not care what her apprentices actually do in their free time—she never advises them about their behavior or asks if they are alone with men—but she instantly dismisses any who are seen in possibly compromising circumstances; her justification is that she must "[keep] up the character of her establishment" (Ch. 4). In Ruth's case, loss of reputation causes loss of chastity, rather than vice versa; Bellingham rises to the occasion and offers his protection and, because Ruth is a totally innocent girl with no job and no money, she accepts.

Later in the book Mr Bradshaw serves as another personification of unjust moral conventionality. He is appalled that his daughters have been "exposed to corruption" by having Ruth as their governess, even though nothing in her character or behavior ever gave him any reason to suspect her past, and even though he admired Ruth's accomplishments and refinement so much that he wanted her to teach his daughters. Bradshaw brushes aside the Reverend Benson's suggestion that Christianity requires him to forgive sinners: "'The world has decided how such women are to be treated; and, you may depend upon it, there is so much practical wisdom in the world, that its way of acting is right in the long-run . . .'" (Ch. 27). Mrs. Gaskell intends the reader to see Mr. Bradshaw in an unpleasant light; he is ostentatious, harsh to his own children, and has an overbearing manner and a tasteless house.

It is also the influence of conventional opinion that leads Benson and Faith to pretend Ruth is a widow. In her treatment of the parallel case of Richard Bradshaw's forgery, Mrs. Gaskell foreshadows the presumption underlying modern juvenile courts; she argues that public censure may harden the beginner into a criminal, and that he will have the best chance for rehabilitation if he is allowed to start over again with an unimpaired reputation. Yet it is wrong to lie. Benson suffers because he acted a lie in order to give Ruth a chance. If the lie was necessary because society required it, there is only one logical conclusion: society should be changed so that lies are no longer needed.

Logic, however, is not the novelist's most effective tool. Mrs. Gaskell achieved her important effects by skillfully manipulating conventions familiar to her audience. In the scene where Ruth's pregnancy is revealed, Mrs. Gaskell presents the typical reaction to an illegitimate child—Faith Benson says that the child is a punishment: a badge of sin—and then replaces it with another convention of greater emotional power. Ruth sees the baby as a blessing: "'Oh my God, I thank thee! Oh! I will be so good!'" (Ch. 11) Motherhood—even illicit motherhood—is woman's highest calling; because she is responsible for another human life Ruth seeks religious redemption, gains both the desire and the means to achieve a place in society, and develops the special feminine virtues.

The same technique of substituting one convention for another is used with greater complexity in the matter of Ruth's innocence. Contemporary critics objected that the opening was unbelievable; both the *Literary Gazette* and the *Spectator* complained that a girl who had worked even three months in a milliners' shop was unlikely to be totally ignorant about the facts of life.[27] Others—including G. H. Lewes—felt that Mrs. Gaskell was herself too conventionally moral; if Ruth was, indeed, so thoroughly exonerated by her total unknowingness, the novelist made her pay too high a price for her fault.[28]

Ruth's innocence, however, has both a practical and a theological function, each with a social moral. Mrs. Gaskell, like Mrs. Trollope, echoes the sentiment Mary Wollstonecraft had expressed in *A Vindication of the Rights of Woman:* "many innocent girls become the dupes of a sincere, affectionate heart, and still more are . . . *ruined* before they know the difference between virtue and vice."[29] She makes this innocence convincing by showing that Ruth knows as little about the ordinary mechanics of living as she does about sexual mores; she is perplexed, for example, about paying for the cup of tea she has at an inn. The sheltered life provided for middle-class girls made them unfit to exist without protection, but in a world where a fifteen-year-old can suddenly be thrown on her own resources, young women should not be allowed to remain helpless children.

And if innocence is not practical, neither is it desirable. One must attain the knowledge of good and evil before one is capable of choosing good. The theological question, wholly avoided by contemporary reviewers, is that of the fortunate fall. Ruth is a faintly Wordsworthian child in the opening chapters; she lives in a dreamy, indistinct haphazardness, vaguely responsive to feelings of pleasure and spiritually moved by the winter sky at night or the pattern of flowers against a wall. Ruth's innocence is so profound that she is quite happy for a time after her fall; there is no natural revulsion at the instant chastity is lost nor are there any immediate moral or psychological penalties. Social reaction opens her eyes; a child refuses to let her kiss his baby sister because he had heard his mother say that Ruth was a "bad, naughty girl" (Ch. 6).

Her first reaction when she is admitted to the knowledge of evil is an overwhelming desire to return to childish innocence. Since there is no return, her second—at the opposite extreme—is to finish her self-destruction by jumping over a cliff. But because God and nature give her good for evil—give her the child as a result of her sin—she develops the desire and the ability to choose good.

These two transmutations and enrichments of convention—the negative value of innocence, the positive value of motherhood—interweave to provide the thematic content of the novel. The primary subject is woman's individual development through her own conscious, informed, responsible choice. In practical terms motherhood is the source, and in figurative terms the metaphor, for the particular strengths that mark woman's special nature.

Ruth begins to educate herself so she can teach her son Leonard. After living for some time in the Benson household she is an altered person: "six or seven years ago, you would have perceived that she was not altogether a lady by birth and education, yet now she might have been placed among the highest in the land, and would have been taken by the most critical judge for their equal" (Ch. 19). Both psychologically—for the sake of the novel's realism—and theologically, for Mrs. Gaskell, conversion does not come in an instant. At first Ruth allows herself to be saved, placing herself under Benson's protection and passively following his suggestions. Much later, after Ruth has been for years a student, a mother, and a governess for the Bradshaw girls, we realize how important her initial pliability was as a contrast to the strong and womanly woman she makes of herself.

The pretense of widowed motherhood is a social parallel to childhood's moral innocence; it may be needed for a time but it should not persist. Long after Ruth is religiously redeemed she suffers her social fall: her sin is made known to the world. Again she rises stronger than before. Her heroic nursing is not a part of her religious penance but rather the means of her social rehabilitation; after the epidemic her son is able to walk "erect in the streets of Eccleston, where 'Many arose and called her blessed'" (Ch. 33). If the lie had not been found out, if Ruth had remained merely a governess, her life would have been less significant. Mrs. Gaskell, like Eliza Meteyard, believed that woman's most special trait was her consideration for the weak, the helpless and the suffering. Ruth had never lost it even in her most fallen state: her headlong rush towards suicide was stopped by a cry of pain from Benson.

The practical caring virtue is at the core of the difference between the sexes. Man considers the verities, woman the humanities. When the lie is out, Benson says:

> "I did very wrong in making that false statement at first."

> "No! I am sure you did not," said Miss Faith. "Ruth has had some years of peace, in which to grow stronger and wiser, so that she can bear her shame now in a way she never could have done at first."

> "All the same it was wrong in me to do what I did."

"I did it too, as much or more than you. And I don't think it wrong. I'm certain it was quite right, and I would do just the same again."

"Perhaps it has not done you the harm it has done me."

"Nonsense! Thurstan. Don't be morbid. I'm sure you are as good—and better than ever you were."

"No, I am not. I have got what you call morbid, just in consequence of the sophistry by which I persuaded myself that wrong could be right. I torment myself. I have lost my clear instincts of conscience. . . . Oh, Faith! it is such a relief to have the truth known, that I am afraid I have not been sufficiently sympathising with Ruth."

"Poor Ruth!" said Miss Benson. "But at any rate our telling a lie has been the saving of her. There is no fear of her going wrong now." (Ch. 27)

They are both right, of course, which is why social attitudes needed to be changed. Yet the sexual difference stands out. In this scene, Benson is thinking of abstract morality and himself, while Faith considers practical results and the other person, Ruth.

The feminine virtues are developed through motherhood. The mother of a nursing infant has to place her body and time at the service of another and learn to sense needs which cannot be communicated in words. Furthermore, the child ties her to practicality, to human society, and to the future. Ruth fears exposure only for its effect on Leonard and wants to earn a reputable place in society primarily so that his chances in life will not be hindered because of who his mother was.

And finally, in the climactic scene of the book, the good of the child gives Ruth courage to rise above society. When Bellingham (now called Donne) proposes marriage to Ruth, society would say that he was offering to make her an honest woman. She refuses. The action is wholly her own, taken without advice, without consultation, and contrary to social expectation. It is also a conscious and active decision, unlike the fact of her motherhood, which had simply been an acquiescence to nature's law. Even some of the most sympathetic reviewers thought that Ruth was wrong:

Is he not the father? . . . Has she such complete dominion over Leonard that she dares, of her own choice, deprive him of his father? . . .

We do not deny that Ruth's rejection of Mr. Donne is natural, and we acknowledge it just. We doubt whether it be Christian, whether, in God's eye, she be not his wife, and forbidden to turn from him when he turns to her; whether, in fact, her refusal of him be not simply the sign that she has not self-sacrifice enough in her to devote her life to the man who has wronged her . . . [10]

But Ruth knows that some things damage a child more than illegitimacy. Her decision is based on mother-right: "'If there were no other reason to prevent our marriage but the one fact that it would bring Leonard into contact with you,'" she says, "'that would be enough'" (Ch. 24).

Caroline Norton's troubles were again in the newspapers in the summer of 1853. Contemporary readers were fully aware that Leonard was over seven and that Ruth, if married, could not have protected him from the influence of an immoral father. As a single woman, she can be a better mother than if she were bound by a promise to obey. At this point in the story it is inescapably evident that in morals, character and possibilities for action, Ruth is a finer and stronger person than she would have been if she had married Bellingham instead of running away with him, and a far different person than if she had never borne a child.

The feminine virtues developed through motherhood lead Ruth to take up nursing. (The novel was written before the Crimea had made nursing a respectable occupation, though Mrs. Gaskell had been for some time acquainted with the Nightingale family. Florence Nightingale admired *Ruth* and was particularly pleased that Mrs. Gaskell "had not made Ruth start at once as a hospital nurse, but arrive at it after much *other* nursing that came first.")[31] At the novel's end, the same womanly virtue leads her to nurse Bellingham/Donne: "'I don't think I should love him, if he were well and happy—but you said he was ill—and alone—how can I help caring for him?'" (Ch. 34) It may be true, as J. M. Ludlow suggested in his review, that Mrs. Gaskell wrote a sad ending so that girls would not admire Ruth so much they wanted to imitate her.[32] However, Ruth's death is clearly not a punishment, but rather a heroic expression of woman's most noble trait.

Ruth is not, as it has sometimes been called, the first English novel to take as its main theme the redemption of the unchaste woman but it is the first to deal fully and realistically with her social rehabilitation. And because a good deal of evidence survives about the work of a major author, we can trace in *Ruth* some of the ways that literature and life influence one another. The book was inspired both by personal experience and by contemporary discussion of the social evil, and it was intended to affect social opinion.

Esther, in Mrs. Gaskell's first novel, *Mary Barton* (1848), was a conventional whore on a downward path, though she had enough human decency to steer her niece Mary away from the same error. Late in the following year, Mrs. Gaskell became personally involved with a young prostitute who wanted to reform. She wrote to Charles Dickens for advice about helping the girl to emigrate; she turned to Dickens not because he was an author but because he was associated with Urania Cottage, a refuge that Angela Burdett-Coutts established in 1847 to teach repentant women household skills and then send them out to the colonies.[33] Soon after Dickens had sent Mrs. Gaskell the advice she wanted he asked her to write something for the magazine he was about to start. She responded with **"Lizzie Leigh,"** which became the leading story in the first issue of *Household Words* on 30 March 1850.[34]

"Lizzie Leigh" tells of a rural mother's search through the streets of Manchester for her daughter who has gone wrong. The daughter, Lizzie, is traced through her child, who she has abandoned but sometimes visits. The child falls downstairs and dies; Lizzie vows to redeem herself so that she may see her baby again in heaven. She goes to live in a secluded cottage, where "every sound of sorrow in the whole upland is heard . . . every call of suffering and sickness for help is listened to, by a sad, gentle-looking woman who rarely smiles . . . but who comes out of her seclusion whenever there's a shadow in any household. Many hearts bless Lizzie Leigh."[35]

The story is about the search; Lizzie's redemption occupies only the last few paragraphs. But two key ideas of *Ruth* are there: religious redemption comes through the child and social rehabilitation through caritative service to others. Nathaniel Hawthorne used similar material in *The Scarlet Letter,* but although Mrs. Gaskell probably read Hawthorne's novel at about the time she began writing *Ruth,*[36] her use of the same themes in the story of **"Lizzie Leigh"**—who also lives like Hester in a lonely cottage on the edge of the wild—makes it coincidence rather than direct influence. **"Lizzie Leigh"** was in Dickens' hands by 14 March 1850 and *The Scarlet Letter* was published in Boston on the sixteenth of the same month.

Mrs. Gaskell used some of the twenty pounds that Dickens paid her for **"Lizzie Leigh"** in the cause that inspired the story. She provided an outfit for the girl who wanted to reform, visited her in prison, and arranged for the master of the ragged school to take her to London and put her on board a ship for the Cape. Even though Pasley had voluntarily entered a refuge and repeatedly said she wanted to reform, Mrs. Gaskell could see that the girl would not succeed unless she had "as free and unbranded a character" as possible.[37] Also, in the meantime, she needed to be physically protected from bad companions. Like Ruth at the outset of the novel, Pasley's pliable nature absolutely demanded supervision.

Other religious and social writers whose work preceded Mrs. Gaskell's had said that girls often fell in ignorance and that a baby could give them a motive to reform. The *Westminster Review* article on prostitution, which appeared in 1850 when Mrs. Gaskell was planning **Ruth** and which she probably saw, since it included a long quotation from *Mary Barton,* dwells on the irony of calling a seduced girl honest only if she is foolish enough to marry the man who had proved his bad character by taking advantage of her; it could well have contributed to Ruth's rejection of Bellingham.[38] There is little, then, in **Ruth** that was new or unique—except for the emphasis that gave the book its total effect. Mrs. Gaskell devoted a whole novel to the unchaste woman and made her a heroine. She showed that motherhood leads to social as well as religious redemption, that the unchaste woman does not differ essentially from the woman who has not sinned except in the strength she develops by taking personal responsibility for her life, and that a woman can, by her exercise of womanly virtues, compel society to respect her.

Mrs. Gaskell's book was not written as a warning to young girls; she did not allow her own daughters to see it, though she intended to read it with the eldest, then eighteen, "some quiet time or other."[39] Nor was it intended to comfort the fallen, though that seems to have been Charlotte Bronte's assumption when she wrote that the book might "restore hope and energy to many who thought they had forfeited their right to both."[40] Mrs. Gaskell knew enough about the economics of publishing and the facts of life among the outcast to realize who would read the book. *Eliza Cook's Journal* praised **Ruth** in a review that proceeded—for nearly eight columns—to retell the story in short declarative sentences, but even this simplified version was not primarily intended for the fallen, for the moral enunciated in the closing paragraph is that the book teaches "charity for sinners . . . love for truth . . . respect for suffering . . . and honour to those who pass through it patiently and humbly."[41] Mrs. Gaskell wrote for ordinary, middle class, feminine novel-readers, and it was for them that she sweetened the dose. Ruth did not spend any time as a prostitute; Mrs. Gaskell kept her the sort of untainted girl who appealed to readers' sympathies.

Nevertheless, Mrs. Gaskell was extremely upset by the immediate responses to the book:

> in several instances I have *forbidden* people to write, for their expressions of disapproval (although I have known that the feeling would exist in them,) would be very painful and stinging at the time. "An unfit subject for fiction" is *the* thing to say about it . . . "Deep regret" is what my friends here . . . feel and express.[42]

These reactions were no doubt colored by Mrs. Gaskell's public position as the wife of a clergyman. Two men in

William Gaskell's congregation burned one volume of the book and another forbade his wife to read it.[43] Reviewers, by and large, were not nearly so hard on the book as Mrs. Gaskell's friends. Only *Sharpe's London Magazine* (edited in that year by Mrs. S. C. Hall) registered an outright moral objection—and at the same time, the review virtually made Mrs. Gaskell's point for her by demanding that novelists be hypocrites. The reviewer defends Mr. Bradshaw's stringent moral standards and criticizes Benson for letting Ruth teach young girls, and yet says the book should not end so sadly, since fallen women do marry and raise families, even when their past is known. The novelist, however, should remain silent about that reality; fiction, says the reviewer, should paint ideals in action instead of setting forth facts.[44] *Ruth* upset that kind of superficial literary and moral taste. One other journal that disliked it called *Nelly Armstrong,* a few months later, "the best book that we have read in some time."[45] *Nelly Armstrong* was a traditional terrible warning; it has scenes far more sordid than any in *Ruth* and for that very reason it was more acceptable.

The reviews in the quarterlies were far more sympathetic. It is significant that the book was reviewed in nearly every major periodical, and often at great length. *Ruth* was read and discussed. Mudie's did not ban it, though another library, Bell's, decided it was "unfit for family reading."[46] It was reprinted. The Parlour Library put out a cheap edition. Celebrated contemporaries who were not personally acquainted with Mrs. Gaskell sent her letters of praise. Elizabeth Barrett Browning wrote from Italy, "I am grateful to you as a woman for having so treated such a subject."[47]

Ruth evidently set people thinking in a way that previous books on the subject had not. Blanche Smith sent a copy to her fiance, Arthur Hugh Clough, who was living in Massachusetts, with, apparently, a challenging list of questions, for he concluded his answer by saying "I am rather sorry you have read it—I think it must have dwelt on your mind—I hope it's all gone away."[48] Mrs. Stanley, wife of the Bishop of Norwich, reported to Mrs. Gaskell that the young men she knew found it "the most virtue-stirring book they ever read."[49]

The most striking reaction is in a memoir by Josephine Butler:

> A book was published at that time by Mrs. Gaskell and was much discussed. This led to expressions of judgment which seemed to me false—fatally false. . . . A pure woman, it was reiterated, should be absolutely ignorant of a certain class of evils in the world, albeit those evils bore with murderous cruelty on other women. One young man seriously declared that he would not allow his own mother to read such a book as that under discussion. . . . Silence was thought to be the great duty on all such subjects.[50]

Soon afterwards Josephine Butler took a young woman who had served a sentence in Newgate for infanticide into her house as servant. She was the first of many that Josephine Butler was to help, first as individuals and later, through her campaign for repeal of the Contagious Diseases Acts, as a class.

Certainly *Ruth* was only one factor setting in motion Josephine Butler's work among prostitutes. She had already been thinking about women's victimization. Mrs. Gaskell's book pointed the finger at society, and the social response impressed Josephine Butler more than the book itself, because it revealed the sexist basis of protectionism. The sentimental idea of the "woman's kingdom"—the immense moral power mothers have because they form the thoughts and characters of men—is revealed as cant when a young man presumes to judge what his mother may be "allowed" to know.

Notes

[23] "Life in Manchester: Libbie Marsh's Three Eras," by "Cotton Mather Mills, Esq.," *Howitt's Journal,* 1 (5-19 June 1847), 310-47.

[24] Margaret Howitt, ed., *Mary Howitt, An Autobiography* (London: Isbister, 1889), II, 65-66.

[25] Ross D. Waller, ed., *Letters Addressed to Mrs. Gaskell by Celebrated Contemporaries Now in the Possession of the John Rylands Library* (Manchester: Manchester Univ. Press, 1935), pp. 48-49.

[26] *The Letters of Mrs. Gaskell,* ed. J. A. V. Chapple and Arthur Pollard (Manchester: Manchester Univ. Press, 1966), p. 226.

[27] *Literary Gazette,* 22 Jan. 1853, pp. 79-80; *Spectator,* 15 Jan. 1853, pp. 61-62.

[28] See G. H. Lewes, "Ruth and Villette," *Westminster Review,* NS 3 (1853), 474-91 and W. R. Greg, "False Morality of Lady Novelists," *National Review,* 8 (1859), 144-76.

[29] Mary Wollstonecraft, *A Vindication of the Rights of Woman,* ed. Charles W. Hegelman, Jr. (New York: Norton, 1967), p. 119.

[30] "Ruth: A Novel," *North British Review,* 19 (1853), 163. Mrs. Gaskell called the review *"delicious"* and asked "Who the deuce could have written it? It is so truly religious, it makes me swear with delight. I think

it is one of the Christian Socialists, but I can't make out which." *(Letters of Mrs. Gaskell,* p. 222.) *The Wellesley Index to Victorian Periodicals, 1824-1890,* ed. Walter E. Houghton (Toronto: University Press, 1966-72), identifies the author as J. M. Ludlow, barrister, Christian Socialist, and known to Mrs. Gaskell (at least by name) as a co-founder with Kingsley, Maurice and others of a cooperative tailors' shop; see *Letters of Mrs. Gaskell,* p. 90. Other reviewers worried about the same point. The writer in *Prospective Review* thinks Ruth's decision is allowable, but finds it necessary to support his opinion with a long legal argument; see *Prospective Review,* 9 (1853), 244-45.

[31] Quoted in A. W. Ward, Introd., *Ruth and Other Tales,* by Elizabeth Gaskell (London: Smith and Elder, 1906), p. xv.

[32] "Ruth: A Novel," *North British Review,* 19 (1853), 162.

[33] *Letters of Mrs. Gaskell,* pp. 98-100.

[34] Elizabeth Gaskell, "Lizzie Leigh," *Household Words,* 1 (30 Mar.-13 Apr. 1850), 2-65.

[35] *Household Words,* 1 (13 Apr. 1850), 65.

[36] She was having *The Scarlet Letter* bound on 14 Jan. 1851 *(Letters of Mrs. Gaskell,* p. 142) and by 25 March 1851 was talking over *Ruth* with her friends; see John G. Sharps, *Mrs. Gaskell's Observation and Invention: A Study of Her Non-Biographic Works* (Fontwell, Sussex: Linden Press, 1970), p. 160.

[37] *Letters of Mrs. Gaskell,* p. 99.

[38] Parallels between the article by W. R. Greg in *Westminster Review,* 53 (1850), 448-506, and Mrs. Gaskell's novel are discussed in Aina Rubenius, *The Woman Question in Mrs. Gaskell's Life and Works,* Essays and Studies on English Lang. and Lit., No. 5 (Upsala: A.-B. Ludenquistka Bokhendeln, 1950), pp. 207 ff.

[39] *Letters of Mrs. Gaskell,* p. 221.

[40] Elizabeth Gaskell, *The Life of Charlotte Bronte* (London: Dent, 1971); p. 358.

[41] *Eliza Cook's Journal,* 8 (26 Feb. 1853), 280.

[42] *Letters of Mrs. Gaskell,* p. 220.

[43] Ibid., p. 223.

[44] *Sharpe's London Magazine,* NS 2 (1853), p. 352.

[45] *Literary Gazette,* 9 Apr. 1853, p. 352.

[46] *Letters of Mrs. Gaskell,* p. 223.

[47] Waller, *Letters Addressed to Mrs. Gaskell,* p. 42.

[48] *The Correspondence of Arthur Hugh Clough,* ed. Frederick Ludwig Mulhauser (Oxford: Clarendon, 1957), II, 418.

[49] Ward, p. xv.

[50] *Josephine E. Butler; An Autobiographical Memoir,* ed. George W. and Lucy A. Johnson (Bristol: Arrowsmith, 1909), p. 31.

Raymond Williams (essay date 1983)

SOURCE: "The Industrial Novels," in *Culture and Society, 1780-1950,* Columbia University Press, 1983, pp. 87-92, 109.

[*In the following essay, Williams argues that* Mary Barton *and* North and South *belong to a tradition of literature that he calls "industrial," given their attempt to portray in careful and sympathetic detail the suffering engendered by Britain's self-transformation into a modern power.*]

Our understanding of the response to industrialism would be incomplete without reference to an interesting group of novels, written at the middle of the century, which not only provide some of the most vivid descriptions of life in an unsettled industrial society, but also illustrate certain common assumptions within which the direct response was undertaken. There are the facts of the new society, and there is this structure of feeling, which I will try to illustrate from *Mary Barton, North and South,* Hard Times, Sybil, Alton Locke, and *Felix Holt.*

Mary Barton (1848)

Mary Barton, particularly in its early chapters, is the most moving response in literature to the industrial suffering of the 1840s. The really impressive thing about the book is the intensity of the effort to record, in its own terms, the feel of everyday life in the working-class homes. The method, in part, is that of documentary record, as may be seen in such details as the carefully annotated reproduction of dialect, the carefully included details of food prices in the account of the tea-party, the itemized description of the furniture of the Bartons' living-room, and the writing-out of the ballad (again annotated) of *The Oldham Weaver.* The interest of this record is considerable, but the method has, nevertheless, a slightly distancing effect. Mrs Gaskell could hardly help coming to this life as an observer, a reporter, and we are always to some extent conscious of this. But there is genuine imaginative recreation in her accounts of the walk in Green Heys Fields, and of tea at the Bartons' house, and again, notably, in the chapter *Poverty and Death* where John Barton and his friend find the starving family in the cellar. For so convincing a creation of the characteristic feelings and responses of families of this kind (matters more determining than the material details on which the reporter is apt to concentrate) the English novel had to wait, indeed, for the early writing of D. H. Lawrence. If Mrs Gaskell never quite manages the sense of full participation which would finally authenticate this, she yet brings to these scenes an intuitive recognition of feelings which has its own sufficient conviction. The chapter *Old Alice's History* brilliantly dramatizes the situation of that early generation brought from the villages and the countryside to the streets and cellars of the industrial towns. The account of Job Legh, the weaver and naturalist, vividly embodies that other kind of response to an urban industrial environment: the devoted, lifelong study of living creatures—a piece of amateur scientific work, and at the same time an instinct for living creatures which hardens, by its very contrast with its environment, into a kind of crankiness. In the factory workers walking out in spring into Green Heys Fields; in Alice Wilson, remembering in her cellar the ling-gathering for besoms in the native village that she will never again see; in Job Legh, intent on his impaled insects—these early chapters embody the characteristic response of a generation to the new and crushing experience of industrialism. The other early chapters movingly embody the continuity and development of the sympathy and cooperative instinct which were already establishing a main working-class tradition.

The structure of feeling from which **Mary Barton** begins is, then, a combination of sympathetic observation and of a largely successful attempt at imaginative identification. If it had continued in this way, it might have been a great novel of its kind. But the emphasis of the method changes, and there are several reasons for this. One reason can be studied in a curious aspect of the history of the writing of the book. It was originally to be called *John Barton*. As Mrs Gaskell wrote later:

> Round the character of John Barton all the others formed themselves; he was my hero, *the* person with whom all my sympathies went.[1]

And she added:

> The character, and some of the speeches, are exactly a poor man I know.[1]

The change of emphasis which the book subsequently underwent, and the consequent change of title to **Mary Barton,** seem to have been made at the instance of her publishers, Chapman and Hall. The details of this matter are still obscure, but we must evidently allow something for this external influence on the shape of the novel. Certainly the John Barton of the later parts of the book is a very shadowy figure. In committing the murder, he seems to put himself not only beyond the range of Mrs Gaskell's sympathy (which is understandable), but, more essentially, beyond the range of her powers. The agony of conscience is there, as a thing told and sketched, but, as the crisis of 'my hero; *the* person with whom all my sympathies went', it is weak and almost incidental. This is because the novel as published is centred on the daughter—her indecision between Jem Wilson and 'her gay lover, Harry Carson'; her agony in Wilson's trial; her pursuit and last-minute rescue of the vital witness; the realization of her love for Wilson: all this, the familiar and orthodox plot of the Victorian novel of sentiment, but of little lasting interest. And it now seems incredible that the novel should ever have been planned in any other way. If Mrs Gaskell had written 'round the character of Mary Barton all the others formed themselves', she would have confirmed our actual impression of the finished book.

Something must be allowed for the influence of her publishers, but John Barton must always have been cast as the murderer, with the intention perhaps of showing an essentially good man driven to an appalling crime by loss, suffering and despair. One can still see the elements of this in the novel as we have it, but there was evidently a point, in its writing, at which the flow of sympathy with which she began was arrested, and then, by the change of emphasis which the change of title records, diverted to the less compromising figure of the daughter. The point would be less important if it were not characteristic of the structure of feeling within which she was working. It is not only that she recoils from the violence of the murder, to the extent of being unable even to enter it as the experience of the man conceived as her hero. It is also that, as compared with the carefully representative character of the early chapters, the murder itself is exceptional. It is true that in 1831 a Thomas Ashton, of Pole Bank, Werneth, was murdered under somewhat similar circumstances, and that the Ashton family appear to have taken the murder of Carson as referring to this. Mrs Gaskell, disclaiming the reference in a letter to them, turned up some similar incidents in Glasgow at about the same time. But in fact, taking the period as a whole, the response of political assassination is so uncharacteristic as to be an obvious distortion. The few recorded cases only emphasize this. Even when one adds the cases of intimidation, and the occasional vitriol-throwing during the deliberate breaking of strikes, it remains true, and was at the time a subject of surprised comment by foreign observers, that the characteristic response of the English working people, even in times of grave suffering, was not one of personal violence. Mrs Gaskell was under no obligation to write a representative novel; she might legitimately have taken a special case. But the tone elsewhere is deliberately representative, and she is even, as she says, modelling John Barton on 'a poor man I know'. The real explanation, surely, is that John Barton, a political murderer appointed by a trade union, is a dramatization of the *fear of violence* which was widespread among the upper and middle classes at the time, and which penetrated, as an arresting and controlling factor, even into the deep imaginative sympathy of a Mrs Gaskell. This fear that the working people might take matters into their own hands was widespread and characteristic, and the murder of Harry Carson is an imaginative working-out of this fear, and of reactions to it, rather than any kind of observed and considered experience.

The point is made clearer when it is remembered that Mrs Gaskell planned the murder herself, and chose, for the murderer, 'my hero, *the* person with whom all my sympathies went'. In this respect the act of violence, a sudden aggression against a man contemptuous of the sufferings of the poor, looks very much like a projection, with which, in the end, she was unable to come to terms. The imaginative choice of the act of murder and then the imaginative recoil from it have the effect of ruining the necessary integration of feeling in the whole theme. The diversion to Mary Barton, even allowing for the publishers' influence, must in fact have been welcome.

Few persons felt more deeply than Elizabeth Gaskell the sufferings of the industrial poor. As a minister's wife in Manchester, she actually saw this, and did not, like many other novelists, merely know it by report or occasional visit. Her response to the suffering is deep and genuine, but pity cannot stand alone in such a structure of feeling. It is joined, in **Mary Barton,** by the confusing violence and fear of violence, and is supported, finally, by a kind of writing-off, when the misery of the actual situation can no longer be endured. John Barton dies penitent, and the elder Carson repents of his vengeance and turns, as the sympathetic observer wanted the employers to turn, to efforts at improvement and mutual understanding. This was the characteristic humanitarian conclusion, and it must certainly be respected. But it was not enough, we notice, for the persons with whom Mrs Gaskell's sympathies were engaged. Mary Barton, Jem Wilson, Mrs Wilson, Margaret, Will, Job Legh—all the objects of her real sympathy—end the book far removed from the situation which she had set out to examine. All are going to Canada; there could be no more devastating conclusion. A solution within the actual situation might be hoped for, but the solution with which the heart went was a cancelling of the actual difficulties and the removal of the persons pitied to the uncompromised New World.

North and South (1855)

Mrs Gaskell's second industrial novel, **North and South,** is less interesting, because the tension is less. She takes

up here her actual position, as a sympathetic observer. Margaret Hale, with the feelings and upbringing of the daughter of a Southern clergyman, moves with her father to industrial Lancashire, and we follow her reactions, her observations and her attempts to do what good she can. Because this is largely Mrs Gaskell's own situation, the integration of the book is markedly superior. Margaret's arguments with the mill-owner Thornton are interesting and honest, within the political and economic conceptions of the period. But the emphasis of the novel, as the lengthy inclusion of such arguments suggests, is almost entirely now on attitudes *to* the working people, rather than on the attempt to reach, imaginatively, their feelings about their lives. It is interesting, again, to note the manner of the working-out. The relationship of Margaret and Thornton and their eventual marriage serve as a unification of the practical energy of the Northern manufacturer with the developed sensibility of the Southern girl: this is stated almost explicitly, and is seen as a solution. Thornton goes back to the North

> to have the opportunity of cultivating some intercourse with the hands beyond the mere 'cash nexus'.[2]

Humanized by Margaret, he will work at what we now call 'the improvement of human relations in industry'. The conclusion deserves respect, but it is worth noticing that it is not only under Margaret's influence that Thornton will attempt this, but under her patronage. The other manufacturers, as Thornton says, 'will shake their heads and look grave' at it. This may be characteristic, but Thornton, though bankrupt, can be the exception, by availing himself of Margaret's unexpected legacy. Money from elsewhere, in fact—by that device of the legacy which solved so many otherwise insoluble problems in the world of the Victorian novel—will enable Thornton, already affected by the superior gentleness and humanity of the South, to make his humanitarian experiment. Once again Mrs Gaskell works out her reaction to the insupportable situation by going—in part adventitiously—outside it. . . .

These novels, when read together [with Dickens's *Hard Times*], seem to illustrate clearly enough not only the common criticism of industrialism, which the tradition was establishing, but also the general structure of feeling which was equally determining. Recognition of evil was balanced by fear of becoming involved. Sympathy was transformed, not into action, but into withdrawal. We can all observe the extent to which this structure of feeling has persisted, into both the literature and the social thinking of our own time.

Notes

[1] Cit. *Elizabeth Gaskell: her life and work;* A. B. Hopkins; 1952; p.77.

[2] *North and South;* E. Gaskell (1889 edn.); Ch. li, p. 459.

Catherine Gallagher (essay date 1985)

SOURCE: "Causality versus Conscience: The Problem of Form in *Mary Barton*," in *The Industrial Reformation of English Fiction: Social Discourse and Narrative Form 1832-1867*, The University of Chicago Press, 1985, pp. 62-87.

[*In the essay that follows, Gallagher studies the influence of Gaskell's Unitarian understanding of moral freedom and responsibility on the writing of* Mary Barton.]

> As in the *Religion of Causation,* Man seemed to be crushed into a mere creature, so was it on his behalf that remonstrance broke forth, and, at the bidding of Channing, the *Religion of Conscience* sprang to its feet. However fascinating the precision and simplicity of the Necessarian theory in its advance through the fields of physical and biological law, it meets with vehement resistence in its attempt to annex human nature, and put it under the same code with the tides and trees and reptiles. Our personality . . . is sure to recover from the most ingenious philosophy, and to re-assert its power over the alternatives before it . . . ; and the second period of our theology is marked by this recovered sense of Moral Freedom.
>
>> James Martineau, "Three Stages of Unitarian Theology"

> No one seems to see my idea of a tragic poem; so I, in reality, mourn over my failure.
>
>> Elizabeth Gaskell, Letter to Edward Chapman

When Elizabeth Gaskell wrote **Mary Barton** (1845-47), many Unitarians were revising their theories about free will. In those years James Martineau was trying to start what he later called the "second period of Unitarian theology," the period in which "moral freedom" was emphasized. James Martineau, Harriet's younger brother, was the most influential English Unitarian theologian of the nineteenth century.[1] In their early childhood he and his sister Harriet established a profound emotional and intellectual bond that remained unbroken throughout their youth.

It was James who suggested she read Priestley, but once Harriet had arrived at her "grand conviction"[2] of Necessarianism, she took every possible opportunity to impress the doctrine on her brother. According to James, Harriet dominated him intellectually throughout their adolescence and early adulthood. Describing their conversation while on a walking tour of Scotland in 1824, he reminisced:

> My sister's acute, rapid, and incisive advance to a conclusion upon every point pleasantly relieved my slower judgement and gave me courage to dismiss suspense. I was at that time, and for several years after, an enthusiastic disciple of the determinist philosophy . . . yet not without such inward reserves and misgivings as to render welcome my sister's more firm and ready verdict.[3]

Harriet managed to suppress James's "inward reservations and misgivings" until after she had become a well-known writer. R. K. Webb reports that in 1832 James still shared her views, and Harriet expressed the hope that James might also share her work of improving mankind: he by "lofty appeals to the guides of [Society], I by being the annalist of the poor."[4]

As this proposed division of labor indicates, Harriet was conscious of certain intellectual and temperamental differences between herself and her brother, even while they espoused the same philosophy. She thought her own talent lay in logical cause-and-effect analysis, while his consisted of eloquence and intuition. In time the differences Harriet perceived in their modes of thinking developed into a philosophical disagreement that separated the intellectually intense siblings for life. As James recalled:

> While she remained faithful through life to that early mode of thought, with me those "reserves and misgivings," suppressed for a while, recovered from the shock and gained the ascendancy. The divergence led to this result,—that while my sister changed her conclusions, and I my basis, we both cleared ourselves from incompatible admixtures, and paid the deference due to logical consistency and completeness.[5]

Harriet's Necessarianism finally led her to accept "free thought"; all organized religious practice came to seem incompatible with the logic of her determinism. James, on the other hand, rejected Harriet's basis, her "Religion of Causality," and reached down to "the springs of a sleeping enthusiasm" for a religion that could carry him "from the outer temple of devout science" to an inner conviction of the "greatness of human capacity, not so much for intellectual training, as for voluntary righteousness, for victory over temptation."[6]

The change in James both symbolized and helped to bring about a vast transformation in the Unitarian Church. William Ellery Channing, the American Transcendentalist, converted James to the doctrine of a "free ideal life . . . which we know is in subjection to nothing inflexible."[7] Channing's idea of the human will had been inspired by the writings of Coleridge,[8] and James, in his turn, set about transforming English Unitarianism from a "Religion of Causality" to a "Religion of Conscience," emphasizing voluntary righteousness. He was not the first English Unitarian to believe in free will; Priestley's determinism had been modified and even opposed by many Unitarian theologians of the early nineteenth century. Indeed, Harriet Martineau's extreme Necessarianism was somewhat anachronistic in the 1830's, for by that decade most Unitarians either ignored the issue or settled for a moderate determinism. James Martineau's version of Transcendentalism, however, strongly insisted on the idea of free will, giving it a new emphasis within Unitarianism. Although James was not the acknowledged leader of English Unitarians until later in the century, during the 1840s and 1850s his thought was a powerful intellectual stimulus that led to the de-emphasis of "scientific" explanations of behavior and a new stress on the other side of Unitarianism—its exhortations to moral exertion.

Although Elizabeth Gaskell and her husband, William, stayed within the old school of Unitarianism on most issues and made no decided moves toward Transcendentalism,[9] they were well acquainted with James Martineau. William Gaskell was a Unitarian minister and a colleague of Martineau's at Manchester New College in the 1840s, and their exposure to Martineau's brand of Unitarianism might easily have served to strengthen Elizabeth Gaskell's interest in the issue of moral responsibility.[10] Moreover, in 1845, at the very time when she first began writing *Mary Barton,* she was deeply influenced by a close friend of Martineau's. Although not himself a Unitarian, Francis Newman, brother of John Henry Newman, associated almost exclusively with Unitarians in the 1840s, and on many issues his thinking closely resembled James Martineau's. Like James Martineau, Newman made much of man's "higher nature," his free moral life. Rejecting the psychological materialism of Priestley and Harriet Martineau, he argued that "human intelligence is a result of other intelligence higher than itself—is not a source, or a result, of what is unintelligent."[11]

To Elizabeth Gaskell in the mid-1840s, Francis Newman seemed a living saint. She claimed to have hung on his every word,[12] and it is quite probable that an 1844 booklet of his, *Catholic Union,* was an important source of inspiration for *Mary Barton.* This booklet, together with a series of lectures given in 1846, clearly reveals Newman's belief in a transcendent "moral energy."[13] These works also, however, contain reminders of Unitarianism's earlier determinism, for in them Newman paradoxically insisted that morality does not exist in a realm apart from social and economic necessity. Thus he believed economic and spiritual issues interpenetrated one another, and like Gaskell in *Mary Barton,* he treated radical working-class movements sympathetically: Communism is called "one mode in which human nature is crying out for a new and better union than has yet been achieved."[14] Although he strove to affirm the independence of the human spirit, he continually reversed himself and implied that spirit is chained to matter, that it does not exist in a separate realm of freedom: "to the support of moral energies," he wrote, "certain material conditions are required."[15]

Elizabeth Gaskell absorbed this ambivalence about moral freedom not only from the works and conversation of Francis Newman, but also from the whole context of Unitarian intellectualism that surrounded her. The Unitarianism that shaped her perceptions was thus a different religion in several important respects from that which nurtured Harriet Martineau. Of course, because Gaskell's social experience also differed markedly from Martineau's, the dissimilarities in the two women's outlooks cannot be attributed solely to their religious beliefs. Nevertheless, important differences in their fiction can be traced to their disparate attitudes toward causality and free will. Martineau believed that Providence worked through natural laws that precluded human free will, whereas Gaskell, without abandoning the idea of Providence, tried to make room in her fiction for moral freedom. Gaskell's use of causality, like that of many other thoughtful Unitarians of the 1840s, was less consistent than Martineau's. It was, however, her very inconsistency, her refusal to be tied down to a single explanatory mode, that marked Elizabeth Gaskell's advance over Harriet Martineau in the craft of novel writing.

To move from the *Illustrations* to *Mary Barton* is to leave behind the narrowness of a unicausal interpretive scheme. The wider range of explanations available to Gaskell partly accounts for our sense that she is a more realistic novelist than Harriet Martineau. As James Martineau wrote, breaking away from the Necessarian doctrine constituted "an escape from a logical cage into the open air."[16] And as he further pointed out, the escape entailed perceptual and stylistic changes: "I could mingle with the world and believe in what I saw and felt, without refracting it through a glass, which construed it into something else. I could use the language of men—of their love and hate, of remorse and resolve, of repentance and prayer—in its simplicity."[17] The firm reliance on what is vividly seen and felt and an expanded use of the simple "language of men" are the hallmarks of Gaskell's realism. The "real" reality for her does not lie behind human behavior in a set of scientific laws; it is on the very surface of life, and although it is often obscured by conventional modes of perception, it can be adequately represented in common language. Indeed, Gaskell specifically objected to the kind of abstract language used by Harriet Martineau: she believed that presenting people as embodiments of labor and capital could only hide their true natures and the underlying motives of their actions.[18]

In one important respect, however, Elizabeth Gaskell must be considered Harriet Martineau's heir: she intended John Barton's story, the story of a working man, to be a tragedy. "I had so long felt," she wrote in a letter, "that the bewildered life of an ignorant thoughtful man of strong power of sympathy, dwelling in a town so full of striking contrasts as this is, was a tragic poem, that in writing he was my 'hero.'"[19] In several ways John Barton is a more successful working-class character than Martineau's William Allen, for many of Allen's characteristics seem inappropriate to a worker. His heroism relies, for example, on an elevated style of speaking, while Barton's tragic heroism gains poignancy from his working-class dialect. Adhering closely to classical models, Martineau presents Allen as far superior to other members of his class: she stresses how unusual his forbearance and intelligence are, and even makes him the victim of the striking workers. Barton, on the other hand, is presented as a typical worker. Indeed, his typicality is precisely what makes his story an important one to tell: "There are many such whose lives are tragic poems," Gaskell wrote, "which cannot take formal language."[20] Moreover, Gaskell did not adopt the reversed chronology of Martineau's fiction, her tendency to reveal the ending at the beginning of the story, destroying suspense and precluding catharsis. In fact, Gaskell believed that the ordering of events was a major flaw in Martineau's work; she complained about one of Martineau's books that "The *story* is too like a history—one knows all along how it must end."[21] Gaskell's own story, although it makes John Barton's decline seem inevitable, is not "like a history": she maintains suspense and seeks an intense emotional reaction from the reader. Barton has neither of Allen's defenses against suffering; he lacks both foreknowledge and stoicism. Barton thus seems more unequivocally victimized than did Allen.

Yet when the book came out, Gaskell complained that no one seemed to see her idea of a tragedy.[22] She concluded that she had failed but could not identify the source of her failure. Her confusion is not surprising, for there are many ways in which Gaskell undercut her own intended tragic effects. One of these, a relatively minor one, reminds us again of the religious kinship between Gaskell and Harriet Martineau: the providential resolution of John Barton's story partly mitigates his tragedy. Although moral freedom was an increasingly important idea in Unitarian theology in the 1840s, Gaskell was still writing within a teleological tradition. John Barton feels responsible for his crime, but in the end the very intensity of his remorse leads to both his own and his enemy's spiritual regeneration.[23] There is not even a hint of possible damnation in the novel; evil is eventually self-effacing and productive of good, although sin is not explicitly ordained by God.[24] The close of Barton's life, therefore, hardly appears to be tragic; his life veers from its tragic course in the final episode, and readers are apt to agree with an early reviewer who complained that the ending was a religious homily, "twisted out of shape, to serve the didactic purpose of the author."[25]

Long before the story's close, however, Gaskell's ambivalence about the tragedy she was writing manifests itself in the book's formal eclecticism,[26] an eclecticism that cannot be traced simply to the contradiction between tragic and providential perspectives. For tragedy and theodicy both contain explanatory systems; both trace cause and effect. A dominant impulse in *Mary Barton,* however, is to escape altogether from causality, to transcend explanation. *Mary Barton* expresses both stages of the Unitarianism of the 1840s; it was inspired by both the "Religion of Causality" that Harriet Martineau advocated and the "Religion of Conscience" that her brother eloquently preached. It contains, therefore, an ambivalence about causality that finds its way into Gaskell's tragedy and creates an irresolvable paradox there: Barton's political radicalism is presented both as proof that he is incapable of making moral choices and as an emblem of his moral responsibility. The author consequently seeks refuge from the contradictions of her tragedy in other narrative forms, primarily melodrama and domestic fiction. The resulting formal multiplicity is most apparent in the first half of the book. Only in the second half, after the tragic action is complete, does she temporarily achieve a kind of generic consistency by retreating into the domestic mentality of her heroine. However, because the major action of these chapters is the suppression of the tragic narrative, the book seems to divide into not merely separate but mutually exclusive stories. In the conclusion, when the narrator must return to the subject of John Barton, she seems to have abandoned any attempt to give a consistent explanation of his development. Instead, we are given several stories that mix social criticism with religious homily, and we are then assured that, after all, causal interpretations are irrelevant to the story's meaning.

Gaskell's inability to commit herself to a causal scheme leads, therefore, to formal inconsistencies, but it also leads to a high degree of formal self-consciousness. Although she does not find a narrative form that satisfactorily reveals the reality of working-class life, she does identify several conventional genres that hide the reality. Her attempt to render the truth is beset by irresolvable difficulties, but some relief, some certainty, is secured in attacking what is obviously false. Thus *Mary Barton* is partly about the ways in which narrative conventions mask and distort reality; form becomes content by this process. But the criticism of false conventions does not succeed in deflecting attention from the absence of a stable, self-assured narrative posture. Rather, it makes us more acutely aware of that absence simply by emphasizing the issue of genre. Thus, in the very act of trying to evade certain narrative responsibilities, the book becomes peculiarly self-regarding.

Gaskell's use of contrasting narrative forms is one of the most interesting and overlooked features of *Mary Barton.* In a sense, the first half of the novel is about the dangers inherent in various conventional ways of organizing reality. The two most obviously false and destructive conventional perspectives on the novel's action are the sentimentally romantic and the farcical. The narrator herself never adopts these modes; rather, they enter the narrative as the distorted literary viewpoints of a few characters. Esther and young Mary hold the sentimental perspective; Sally Leadbitter and Harry Carson hold the complementary viewpoint of farce. Gaskell is careful to point out that the sentimental perspective originates in literature; Mary's "foolish, unworldly ideas" come not only from her Aunt Esther's talk about "making a lady" of her, but also from "the romances which Miss Simmonds' young ladies were in the habit of recommending to each other."[27] And although the narrator excuses both Esther and Mary on the grounds of their youth, she indicates that their conventional literary delusions are truly pernicious. Esther's elopement ruins her and apparently also contributes to the death of Mary's mother, and Mary's desire to marry a gentleman brings her and almost all of the other characters in the book "bitter woe" (p. 80).

The complement to these sentimental notions, the convention that they play into and that makes them dangerous, is farce. Both Sally Leadbitter and Harry Carson see their lives and the lives of others as farce. Sally becomes a *farceuse* because she cannot be a sentimental heroine. Being "but a plain, red-haired, freckled, girl," she tries to make up for her lack of beauty "by a kind of witty boldness, which gave her, what her betters would have called piquancy" (p. 132). Sally is a working-class version of the witty female rogue: "Considerations of modesty or propriety never checked her utterance of a good thing" (p. 132). Her vision is entirely comic; it excludes any serious thought about the consequences of Mary's flirtation with young Carson at the same time that it denies the very possibility that Mary's romantic fantasies might be sincerely held: "Sally Leadbitter laughed in her sleeve at them both, and wondered how it would all end,—whether Mary would gain her point of marriage, with her sly affectation of believing such to be Mr. Carson's intention in courting her" (p. 180). Harry Carson, of course, shares this farcical perspective on Mary's actions. Both he and Sally imagine her to be a character in their own farcical world—a "sweet little coquette" (p. 181), "a darling little rascal" (p. 181) with an "ambitious heart" (p. 183). For Sally and Harry Carson, this characterization gives a conventional authorization, indeed a conventional imperative, to Mary's seduction.

Moreover, Mary's is not the only reality that the farcical perspective distorts: everything that enters Sally's or young Carson's purview becomes comic material. Sally is always "ready to recount the events of the day, to turn them into ridicule, and to mimic, with admirable fidelity, any person gifted with an absurdity who had fallen under her keen eye" (p. 133). The ability to

mimic "with admirable fidelity" is also a talent, indeed a fatal talent, of Harry Carson. Young Carson's farcical vision leads him to caricature not only Mary, but the whole of the working class as well, and as Gaskell points out, these comic caricatures both mask and perpetuate working-class suffering. In her exposition of the dangers inherent in farcical distortions, the author brings together the sexual and social themes of the novel: both Mary and the delegation of striking workers are victimized by Harry Carson's conventional blindness.

If working-class women are seducible "little rascals" for Harry Carson, working-class men are clowns. Young Carson exhibits his blindness to the human reality of working-class men on several occasions (for instance, in his treatment of Mr. Wilson, in his interview with Jem, and in his obstinate behavior at the negotiating table), but the conventional attitude that motivates his behavior is most clearly expressed in the action that precipitates his murder. He is killed for making a joke, for attempting to transform a workers' delegation into a troop of Shakespearean clowns:

> Mr. Harry Carson had taken out his silver pencil, and had drawn an admirable caricature of them—lank, ragged, dispirited, and famine-stricken. Underneath he wrote a hasty quotation from the fat knight's well-known speech in Henry IV. He passed it to one of his neighbours, who acknowledged the likeness instantly, and by him it was set round to others, who all smiled and nodded their heads. (P. 235)

The caricature, tossed away by Carson but retrieved by a curious member of the workers' delegation, so enrages John Barton that he conspires with the ridiculed workers to kill the caricaturist. It is significant that the fatal joke is as much Shakespeare's as it is Carson's: that fact emphasizes the unreal, literary nature of Carson's perception. It also stresses how deeply entrenched the farcical distortion of working-class life is in English culture. Carson's destructive use of Shakespeare reminds Gaskell's readers that although they have the best precedents for laughing at rags and tatters, they must now free themselves from the conventional association between "low" characters and comedy.

But the whole incident raises another question: what new associations should replace the old? It is quite clear that Gaskell intends to expose the dangerous falseness of both sentimental romance and farce; but the ground of her exposition, the narrative mode that she adopted because she believed that it did reflect working-class reality, is difficult to identify. Most literary practices calling themselves realistic rely on contrasts with other, presumably false and outdated narrative perspectives.[28] In *Mary Barton* Gaskell purposely sets up false conventions for contrast, thereby calling attention to her own narrative method as the "true" perspective. The problem is that she then has trouble fixing on any one narrative mode; the ground of the contrast continually shifts in the first half of the book while the author searches for a mode of realism adequate to her subject matter. Thus, in her attempt to juxtapose reality and these false conventions, Gaskell employs several alternative narrative modes: tragedy, melodrama, domestic fiction, and finally religious homily.

The most obvious realistic contrast to both the sentimentality of Esther and Mary and the farce of Sally Leadbitter and Harry Carson is the tragedy of John Barton. Barton is the most active and outspoken adversary of both of these false conventions. It is from his perspective that we first see Esther's romantic folly; the story of the girl's elopement is completely contained within John Barton's gloomy interpretation of it: "bad's come over her, one way or another" (p. 46), he tells his friend Wilson. And his interpretation, of course, immediately undercuts all the story's romance. Moreover, his version of Esther's story makes it merely a part of a larger social tragedy. It includes the girl's social determinism: factory work, he is convinced, led to Esther's downfall by making her recklessly independent and giving her the means to buy finery. As Barton tells Esther's story, he reveals his perspective on the relationship between the classes, a perspective that is itself tragic and productive of tragedy. He opposes Esther's romantic dreams not only because they are dangerous, but also because he hates the class she wishes to join. Barton's is a completely polarized view of social reality: only rich and poor seem to exist, and the rich are the constant oppressors of the poor. The ubiquitous slavery metaphor makes its appearance here, attesting to Barton's radicalism, his polarized social vision, and the determinism that informs his thinking.

> "We are their slaves as long as we can work; we pile up their fortunes with the sweat of our brows; and yet we are to live as separate as if we were in two worlds; ay, as separate as Dives and Lazarus, with a great gulf betwixt us: but I know who was best off then," and he wound up his speech with a low chuckle that had no mirth in it. (P. 45)

Even this closing reference to heavenly justice is a gloomy prophecy of revenge, not a joyful anticipation of saintly rewards.

Barton's tragic perspective, therefore, contrasts sharply with Esther's and, later, with Mary's romantic fantasies. Moreover, his interpretation is corroborated by the plot itself; he is correct to note that Esther's romantic dreamworld is really a disguised stage for tragedy. Barton's relationship to the farcical viewpoint is similar: again he opposes it energetically, and again in his opposition he speaks the truth. In fact, in the most decisive moment of his own tragedy, Barton contrasts

Harry Carson's caricature, his fixed, farcical representation, with the tragic reality that lies behind the conventionally ludicrous appearance:

> "it makes my heart burn within me, to see that folk can make a jest of earnest men; of chaps, who comed to ask for a bit o' fire for th' old granny, as shivers in the cold; for a bit o' bedding, and some warm clothing to the poor wife as lies in labour on th' damp flags; and for victuals for the childer, whose little voices are getting too faint and weak to cry aloud wi' hunger." (P. 238)

Through Barton's eyes we see behind the cartoon images of the ragged men to the suffering of thousands of helpless people. The delegates caricatured by Harry Carson are tragic; they are compelled to strike by their noblest characteristics: their sympathy with and sense of responsibility to their hungry dependents. But Carson's Shakespearean joke attempts to freeze the imagination at the level of appearances, where the workmen become a troop of clowns. In Falstaff's speech, alluded to but not quoted, they are "good enough to toss; food for powder, food for powder; they'll fill a pit as well as better. Tush, man, mortal men, mortal men."[29] Such dehumanization obscures the tragedy, making it perfectly appropriate that the story's central tragic action should be the destruction of this *farceur,* the murder of Harry Carson. Thus farce, the mask of tragedy, becomes its stuff, just as Falstaff's callous speech trails off into a sad and even leveling refrain: "Tush, man, mortal men, mortal men."

Tragedy, then, is the immediate realistic ground against which both romance and farce are contrasted. But the narrative method of this novel cannot be called tragic. As we will see, tragedy is forced to compete with other realistic forms in the book's first half, and in the last half it is present only as a suppressed reality. By examining the part of the story that Gaskell specifically intended as tragic—John Barton's own story—we can see why the author continually shifted to other modes of narration. For John Barton's tragedy is self-contradictory. Because she draws both on traditional ideas of heroic character and on determinist, Owenite ideas of character formation, the author encounters a paradox as she attempts to trace a continuous line of tragic development.

The causality Gaskell attempts to trace follows a traditional tragic pattern; it is the result of the interaction between the character's heroic qualities and external circumstances. As Gaskell told a correspondent after the book's publication, her original intention was to show the operations of inner and outer causes in the destiny of a Manchester weaver:

> I can remember now that the prevailing thought in my mind at the time . . . was the seeming injustice

of the inequalities of fortune. Now, if they occasionally appeared unjust to the more fortunate, they must bewilder an ignorant man full of rude, illogical thought, and full also of sympathy for suffering which appealed to him through his senses. I fancied I saw how all this might lead to a course of action which might appear right for a time to the bewildered mind of such a one.[30]

This was, she said, her original "design": the very qualities that made Barton a hero, his thoughtfulness and sympathy, were to combine with external circumstances to produce a tragic action.

This tragic design is certainly apparent in John Barton's story. We are often reminded by both Barton's speeches and the narrator's characterizations of him that his love for his family and his sympathy for the suffering poor cause his hatred of the rich. His unselfishness is emphasized repeatedly; he feels angry not on his own behalf, but on behalf of those who are weaker and poorer. The need to stress Barton's heroic unselfishness determines many of the plot's details; it is significant, for example, that he is not one of the workers caricatured by Harry Carson. His rude thoughtfulness, his desire to understand the suffering he sees, is a second admirable trait contributing to his downfall. Barton is the only character who consistently seeks causes for the world's phenomena, but his analyses are marred by his ignorance, by the fact that his understanding is circumscribed by his limited experience.

Gaskell carefully shows how these qualities of mind are impressed with a tragic stamp by external circumstances, by what comes to Barton "through his senses." The links in the tragic chain are clearly identified and labeled: his parents' poverty, his son's death, his wife's death, the trade depression and the consequent suffering of neighbors, his trip to London, his hunger, his opium addiction. Each of these incidents or circumstances is noted by the narrator as yet another cause of Barton's bitterness. The account of his wife's death, for example, concludes with the gloss: "One of the good influences over John Barton's life had departed that night. One of the ties which bound him down to the gentle humanities of earth was loosened, and henceforward the neighbors all remarked he was a changed man" (p. 58). The story of his son's illness and death also ends with emphasis on its consequences: "You can fancy, now, the hoards of vengeance in his heart against the employers" (p. 61).

Even the narrator's disavowals of Barton's ideas and feelings are intended to contribute to his story's tragedy. Remarks such as "I know that this is not really the case [that the workers alone suffer from trade depressions]; and I know what is the truth in such matters: but what I wish to impress is what the workman feels and thinks" (p. 60) may seem annoying intrusions to twentieth-century readers, but they were designed to keep the nineteenth-century readers' own opinions from interfering with their ability to follow Barton's tragedy. The disavowals are there to prevent the reader from becoming distracted by the issue of whether or not Barton's ideas are objectively true; Barton, we are told in these asides, reached the wrong conclusions, but the circumstances of his life did not allow him to reach any other.

Their very inevitability, however, creates a problem for the author. Unlike Harriet Martineau, Gaskell is not able to rest comfortably with the determinism she traces. Two obstacles present themselves: first, her idea of heroism entails moral freedom; and second, Gaskell's and Martineau's determinisms are of very different kinds. Martineau's does not explain the development of the protagonist's character. William Allen is a fully formed hero at the story's outset; the development of his character is unexplored and irrelevant to the story. He is a heroic, working-class *homo economicus* whose actions may be explained by his character, but whose character is not itself tragically determined. Gaskell's tragic vision, on the other hand, encompasses the formation and deformation of John Barton's character. Her social determinism is, in this sense, closer to Charlotte Elizabeth Tonna's than to Harriet Martineau's. Both use Robert Owen's brand of social theory, showing how the worker's environment and experiences shape his moral being. But unlike Tonna, Gaskell wishes to show us a worker who is a hero, not a monster; she wishes to give us a tragedy, not a freak show. As she traces Barton's inescapable decline, a decline that entails moral degeneration, she risks reducing him to a character without a will. In the words James Martineau used to describe the effects of Necessarianism, she almost "crushes" him "into a mere creature"[31] with her causation.

Gaskell, then, was writing partly in the determinist tradition as it had been adapted by critics of industrialism, but her writing was also infused with the new Unitarian emphasis on free will. Consequently, a tension developed in her portrayal of John Barton, a tension between his social determinism and his tragic heroism. This tension increases as his crisis approaches until it finally emerges as an observable contradiction when the narrator directly confronts the political model of freedom Barton has come to advocate. His radical ambition to become a shaper of society, to cast off the role of a passive creature, acts as a magnet that draws both poles of the author's ambivalence about freedom toward one paradoxical center. The paradox is most clearly visible in the narrator's very last expository attempt to explain the causality of John Barton's story:

No education had given him wisdom; and without wisdom, even love, with all its effects, too often works but harm. He acted to the best of his judgment but it was a widely-erring judgement.

The actions of the uneducated seem to me typified in those of Frankenstein, that monster of many human qualities, ungifted with a soul, a knowledge of the difference between good and evil.

The people rise up to life; they irritate us, they terrify us, and we become their enemies. Then, in the sorrowful moment of our triumphant power, their eyes gaze on us with a mute reproach. Why have we made them what they are; a powerful monster, yet without the inner means for peace and happiness?

John Barton became a Chartist, a Communist, all that is commonly called wild and visionary. Ay! but being visionary is something. It shows a soul, a being not altogether sensual; a creature who looks forward for others, if not for himself. (Pp. 219-20)

All the elements of the tragedy are present in these metaphoric exchanges. Barton represents the uneducated, who are collected into the image of Frankenstein's tragically determined, larger-than-life monster. Then the monster, defeated and gazing at us, shrinks back to the dimensions of John Barton, the unselfish visionary. But these smooth metaphoric transitions do not quite cover the passage's central paradox: the "actions of the uneducated" grow out of their soullessness, their incapacity to make moral choices. Barton became a "Chartist, a Communist," a visionary in consequence of this soullessness. But the metaphor is too harsh, too denigrating to the hero, and the narrator pulls back and reverses herself: "But being visionary is something. It shows a soul." Suddenly John Barton's rebellious actions, instead of showing him to be a creature "ungifted with a soul," become the proof that he has a soul, the emblem of his humanity and this moral freedom. His heroism is saved, but only at the expense of the causality implied by the Frankenstein metaphor, a causality that traces Barton's crime to "us."

We can argue, therefore, that the paradoxical nature of Gaskell's tragic vision forces her to abandon it in the novel's second half. Even in the first half of the book, though, the narrator never confines her own view to this tragic dynamic, dangerous as it was to the very idea of moral freedom. Instead, she juxtaposes three "realistic" narrative modes in the book's early chapters: tragedy, melodrama, and a working-class domestic tale. The presence, indeed the competition, of the melodrama and the domestic tale allows two things. First, the author is able to avoid her tragic responsibilities, which are too contradictory to fulfill successfully; these other modes distract attention from and obscure the problematic causality of John Barton's story. Second, the presence of the melodrama, in particular, allows Gaskell to extend her critical exploration of conventional ways of interpreting reality.

Gaskell's use of melodrama is skillful: she first invites us into a melodramatic narrative, sets up melodramatic expectations, and then reveals that melodrama is a mere conventional distortion, a genre inappropriate to modern reality. Critics have claimed that *Mary Barton* becomes melodramatic with the murder of Harry Carson,[32] but this formulation is backwards. The first half of the book is much more seriously melodramatic than the second because in the first half there is a melodrama just off-stage, in the wings, as it were, which threatens to take over the drama entirely. Indeed, the reader cannot initially tell whether the early chapters are part of a melodrama or of some other kind of narrative. They contain many melodramatic characteristics.[33] We view Esther's elopement not only from Barton's tragic perspective, but also through the unarticulated, excessive grief of her sister Mary, young Mary's mother. Her grief is so excessive that it kills her, suddenly and surprisingly. It is the kind of parabolical death that abounded in nineteenth-century melodramas, and it leads into young Mary's potential melodrama—the threat of her seduction by the rakish Harry Carson. The narrator, in true melodramatic manner, continually suspends any resolution of Mary's fate and makes dark prognostications about it: "Mary hoped to meet him every day in her walks, blushed when she heard his name, and tried to think of him as her future husband, and above all, tried to think of herself as his future wife. Alas! poor Mary! Bitter woe did thy weakness work thee" (p. 80). The wholly conventional language here ("Alas! poor Mary!") leads us to expect, mistakenly, that Mary's "bitter woe" will also be of the conventional melodramatic kind.

Although romance and farce finally do turn into tragedy in *Mary Barton,* they threaten repeatedly in the first half to turn into melodrama. Mary's renunciation of Harry Carson, her abandonment of romance, brings the melodrama even closer; for it is after his rejection that Harry Carson becomes truly villainous, indeed a potential rapist: "From blandishments he had even gone to threats— threats that whether she would or not she should be his" (p. 224). It is only after she has awakened from her romantic dream that Mary is in danger of becoming a true melodramatic heroine: an innocent girl sexually persecuted by a villain. Indeed, Mary registers the change linguistically. As soon as she understands her true position she declares: "if I had loved you before, I don't think I should have loved you now you have told me you meant to ruin me; for that's the plain English of not meaning to marry me till just this minute. . . . Now I scorn you, sir, for plotting to ruin a poor girl" (pp. 183-84). This is not "plain English," the language Mary usually speaks. It is popular stage English,[34] and it temporarily throws a melodramatic light across Mary's features. Harry Carson's murder, instead of beginning the novel's melodrama, effectively terminates it. In fact, as we will see, in the second half of the book melodrama joins romance and farce as an overtly discredited convention.

In the first half, however, Mary's potential melodrama competes for our attention with her father's tragedy. Through the melodramatic mode of presentation, our concern is solicited for Mary in a way that it never is for John. Indeed, Gaskell so arranges her narrative that we end up looking for the catastrophic event in the wrong plot. The melodrama of Mary's story, therefore, makes us inattentive to the threatening nature of John's career. The careful tracing of his decline does not have the interest of Mary's melodrama because we are not expecting John's story to culminate in some disastrous event. Our sense of impending catastrophe, which is essential to a tragic narrative, is misplaced in **Mary Barton.** It is attached not only to the wrong plot but also to the wrong set of narrative conventions. We mistakenly expect a melodramatic catastrophe, one arising from a simple confrontation between good and evil, but we are given a tragic catastrophe, a complexly and carefully motivated revenge murder, the outcome of an inner as well as an outer struggle. The presence of the melodrama in the book's first half, therefore, prevents us from clearly seeing John Barton's decline as the successive complications of a tragedy, and his story, with its unresolved contradictions, tends to fade into the background.

In the book's second half, most of the characters repeat our mistake. They continue to interpret the plot according to a preconceived melodramatic pattern, assuming that Jem killed Harry Carson. It then becomes Mary's job to discredit their conventional assumptions. To save Jem is to disprove the melodramatic interpretation of the murder. Melodrama is, therefore, explicitly consigned to the category of false conventions. It is associated with other kinds of sensation-seeking, and Sally Leadbitter is its most determined spokeswoman. Because her cliché-ridden mind is only able to perceive situations in terms of popular stage conventions, after Carson's murder she moves with ease from a farcical to a melodramatic interpretation of the plot. She holds to her melodramatic version of the story even after Jem's acquittal. In explaining why Jem was dismissed from his job, she reveals the source of her opinions: "Decent men were not going to work with a—no! I suppose I musn't say it, seeing you went to such trouble to get up an *alibi;* not that I should think much the worse of a spirited young fellow for falling foul of a rival,—they always do *at the theatre*" (p. 427; latter emphasis added). Mary, who is concerned for Jem, gasps, "Tell me all about it," and Sally continues, "Why, you see, they've always swords quite handy at them plays" (p. 427).

At this point in the story, Sally's melodramatic viewpoint is relatively harmless—the basis of a joke. But the same viewpoint predominates among the spectators at Jem's trial, almost costing him his life. It is Mary's hard task to disabuse the court of the notion that Jem was a "young fellow" who had "fallen foul of

a rival." However, the courtroom, like Sally Leadbitter, seems receptive only to melodrama; even Mary's struggle to save Jem must be rendered melodramatically before it can be admitted: "The barrister, who defended Jem, took new heart when he was put in possession of these striking points to be adduced . . . because he saw the opportunities for a display of forensic eloquence which were presented by the facts; 'a gallant tar brought back from the pathless ocean by a girl's noble daring'" (p. 395). This bit of parody points up the difference between the narrative we have just read and the same facts couched in melodramatic language.

Far from being melodramatic, therefore, the last half of the book takes melodrama as its specific point of contrast. The fact that we ourselves formerly shared the melodramatic assumption, however, allows us to understand what a natural reading of the events it is and how difficult it will be to overcome. Because Mary must overthrow the assumptions not only of the other characters, but also of one of the major narrative conventions of the book's first half, we feel that her task is almost overwhelming. The drama of Mary's plight, therefore, is heightened by the narrative reversal, and the reader's interest in Mary's story intensifies.

By discrediting melodrama however, the later chapters raise the question of realistic narrative form even more insistently than do the earlier chapters. For the narrator's reversed attitude toward melodrama broadens her criticism of the conventional, a criticism that depends on a contrastingly realistic narrative ground. Again, the obvious candidate for such a ground is tragedy; the tragic interpretation of the murder is, after all, the truth that the melodramatic interpretation hides. But the tragic reality is precisely what all the actions of the book's second half are designed to conceal. The very causality that the narrator meticulously traced through the first half is hidden in the second. The events of the second half are more than an escape, an avoidance, of the tragic problem; they represent the problem's deliberate suppression.

In the second half of the book, Mary knows the truth, but she refuses to probe it, to ascertain its meaning. Instead, all her energies go into suppressing both public knowledge of her father's crime and her own consciousness of it. The "why" of the crime, the very substance of the tragedy is not even a subject for speculation in the later chapters: "[Mary] felt it was of no use to conjecture his motives. His actions had become so wild and irregular of late, that she could not reason upon them" (p. 301). In the chapters that are largely confined to Mary's consciousness, therefore, those that take place between the murder and Mary's return to Manchester after the trial, the narrator imposes a moratorium on reasoning about John Barton's life, on thinking about tragic causation. Mary's truth-concealing action takes the place of reason; finding an alibi substitutes for seeking the truth. Tragedy is still present as a narrative ground, but is increasingly shadowy; like melodrama, it is a genre Mary struggles against inhabiting. Thus, at precisely the moment when a stable, realistic narrative form is most needed, tragedy becomes unavailable and another genre emerges into prominence as Mary's special domain. Restricted almost entirely to Mary's viewpoint, the narrative becomes a working-class domestic tale that formally authorizes the suppression of tragic causality.

Elizabeth Gaskell was a pioneer of the working-class domestic tale. In 1837 she and her husband published a sketch of working-class life, "*rather* in the manner of Crabbe,"[35] which tried to illustrate that the "poetry of humble life" exists "even in a town."[36] Three short stories she published in *Howitt's Journal* share the intention of the sketch and are characterized by a wealth of domestic detail, illustrations of the charitable affection that the poor have for one another, and an emphasis on the trials and learning experiences of young women. All the women learn one thing: to do their duty, the duty obviously and immediately before them. These stories are also marked by some conspicuous absences: factories and other workplaces are alluded to but never shown, and people from other classes are almost entirely missing. The working-class domestic tales written by Gaskell combined the genres of homily and urban idyll; they were both exclusively domestic and exclusively working-class.

Much of *Mary Barton* is written in this same genre. The documentary realism for which Gaskell is often praised grows out of the impulse to compile domestic details. Thus she gives us elaborate and affectionate descriptions of working-class homes, clothes, and traditions, as well as careful transcriptions of working-class Lancashire dialect. Domesticity dominates the narratives told by old Alice and Job Leigh, narratives that are moving in the matter-of-fact spareness of their language and in the unobtrusiveness of their message: friends and family are all; duty is clear. Even Sally Leadbitter's farcical outlook is inspired by filial affection (pp. 132-33). Most of the working-class characters in the book share this domestic mentality: they think very little about the masters, they endure bad times, and they seek their satisfaction in the love of family and close friends. Margaret, Job Leigh, the Wilsons, and old Alice all belong to the domestic mode. This is the circle of duty and affection that Mary struggles to maintain.

But Mary is firmly established as a domestic heroine only after her interview with Esther, which reveals the truth about Harry Carson's murder, disabusing Mary of her melodramatic ideas. While the heroine glimpses the tragic abyss (a glimpse that speeds her on to the mental reality of a thoroughly domestic character), the narrator contrasts Mary's lot with Esther's. The contrast is explicitly between the domestic nature of Mary's working-class world and the territories of melodrama and tragedy that Esther inhabits. Just moments before, Mary believed she had driven Jem to murder; she is turned out of the Wilsons' home into the "busy, desolate, crowded street," and her own home seems to her "only the hiding place of four walls . . . where no welcome, no love, no sympathising tears awaited her" (p. 284). She thinks of herself melodramatically as an abandoned waif and longs for her mother, the absent center of a lost domestic idyll. She remembers "long-past times . . . when her father was a cheery-hearted man, rich in the love of his wife, and the companionship of his friend;—when (for it still worked round to that), when mother was alive" (p. 286). And while Mary longs, her mother actually seems to appear in the form of Esther, who had hidden her own melodrama *cum* tragedy behind the costume of a working-class wife. From Esther we get an entirely different perspective on Mary's reality: Mary, who a minute before fancied herself a pathetic creature in a comfortless room, is seen by Esther as the lucky inhabitant of "that home of her early innocence" (p. 293). The house is Esther's "old dwelling-place, whose very walls, and flags, dingy and sordid as they were, had a charm for her" (p. 297), and Mary now seems to be a potential mother, the woman with power to heal: "For [Esther] longed to open her wretched, wretched heart, so hopeless, so abandoned by all living things, to one who had loved her once; and yet she refrained, from dread of the averted eye, the altered voice, the internal loathing, which she feared such disclosure might create" (pp. 294-95). The poignant and ironic contrast firmly situates Mary in the narrative space between the distortions of melodrama and the abyss of tragedy. It identifies her as a domestic heroine, one still capable of becoming "the wife of a working-man" and thereby joining "that happy class to which [Esther] could never, never more belong" (p. 292).

The interview makes Mary a domestic heroine at the same time that it reveals the extent to which both her future and her present domestic worlds are threatened by the novel's other forms: the melodramatic lie that might condemn Jem and the tragic truth that might condemn her father. She emerges as a domestic heroine just in time to lock up her little house and embark on her mission to save these two men and rescue her personal life. For this reason, the events and settings of the book's second half are neither particularly domestic nor particularly working-class. We should not, however, let the public and adventurous events obscure the narrative mentality that pervades this part of the novel. As Kathleen Tillotsen has pointed out, the thickness of domestic detail in *Mary Barton* makes its "'big scenes'—the chase down the Mersey, the murder trial . . . seem simply emergencies that must occasionally arise in ordinary life."[37]

Mary's existence is "ordinary," but it is also seriously threatened by the emergency she faces. A flawed social order has allowed melodrama and tragedy to break into Mary's world, and she must reestablish its domestic boundaries. Her task involves travel, public notoriety, and extraordinary events of all kinds, but these are necessary to combat melodrama, suppress tragedy, and save what little remains of her family. Mary's homelessness in the later chapters is symptomatic of the social evils the author is trying to illustrate. Mary's struggle to remain a domestic heroine is itself a social criticism with an ideal image of family life at its center. The domestic keynote of these later chapters sounds again and again: in Mary's relationship to Mrs. Wilson; in the minute but emotionally constrained accounts of Mary's tentative and fearful actions and reactions; in the descriptions of the lives and homes she encounters in Liverpool; and in the idyllic, domestic dreamworld that old Alice inhabits throughout the book's second half. Alice's reverie is both a vision of her own past and of Mary's future; Alice imagines the domestic world Mary's actions are retrieving.

For most of the book's second half, then, the domestic tale predominates and suppresses the tragedy, although the two genres are complexly interrelated throughout the novel. Barton's tragedy is itself fundamentally domestic. The loss of his son is the most decisive blow against him. Domestic also is the tragic reality behind the clownish appearance of the workers' delegation, the barren rooms and the sickly wives and children that *Mary Barton* tries to expose. The book was inspired by scenes of blighted domestic life in the working class,[38] and John Barton's narrative sketches the disastrous course that such suffering might initiate.

Although reality is always domestic in *Mary Barton,* it is by no means always tragic. Tragedy may grow out of working-class domestic life, but it ultimately excludes that life. For the most part, *Mary Barton* is a domestic tale, not a domestic tragedy, and the two genres present mutually exclusive kinds of reality in this novel.[39] Barton's tragic career, we are repeatedly told, increasingly takes him away from home; furthermore, most of the working-class characters, drawn in the domestic mode, are uninterested in Barton's talk about social injustice. In fact, the book's first dialogue, between Barton and Wilson, typifies the interaction between the hero and most of the working-class characters. Barton rails on for half a page against the "gentlefolk," but Wilson cuts him short: "Well, neighbour, . . . all that may be very true, but what I want to know now is about Esther" (p. 45). This kind of exchange is repeated on other occasions with Jem Wilson and with Job Leigh; the other men all express the assumptions that are built into Gaskell's domestic convention: being too aware of social injustice only distracts one from the principal realities of

family and home; conversely, home and family can protect one from the tragedy that attends class conflict.

His respondents never try to refute Barton's social analyses in these exchanges. Rather, the other men quietly recur to their private preoccupations. Thus, after John Barton tells the sad story of his London journey and concludes that "as long as I live I shall curse them as so cruelly refused to hear us" (p. 145), Job Leigh tells his own London story, which includes his daughter's death and his retrieval of his granddaughter Margaret.[40] The narrator confides that Job chose the domestic subject matter because it was "neither sufficiently dissonant from the last to jar on the full heart, nor too much the same to cherish the continuance of the gloomy train of thought" (p. 145). The domestic tale suppresses the tragedy not by explicitly denying it, but rather by eluding its causality. John Barton's tragedy, as we have seen, is primarily concerned with cause and effect, with showing how and why the hero became "a Chartist, a Communist, all that is commonly called wild and visionary." Gaskell's domestic tales, on the other hand, aim at showing how to circumvent tragic cause-and-effect logic by simply acting, doing one's immediate duty, without stopping to ponder all of the consequences.

Inevitability, the solemn basis of tragedy, is thus obscured by a flurry of activity. On learning of her father's guilt, Mary first determines not to speculate about his motives and then wades into the myriad activities of the book's second half. The causal logic of this part of the book is explicitly and enthusiastically stated by the narrator in the first person:

> Oh! I do think that the necessity for exertion, for some kind of action . . . in time of distress, is a most infinite blessing. . . . Something to be done implies that there is yet hope of some good thing to be accomplished, or some additional evil that may be avoided; and by degrees the hope absorbs much of the sorrow. (P. 301)

Thus action itself disproves inevitability: it gradually absorbs the tragic causality at the same time that it keeps that causality from emerging into conscious, public view. John Barton dies, but he dies, as Mary wished, at home.

The domestic tale, therefore, is to tragedy in *Mary Barton* as the "Religion of Moral Freedom" was to the "Religion of Causality" in Unitarian theology in the 1840s. Gaskell could not sustain Barton's tragedy, because in doing so she risked denying his freedom, his heroism, even his humanity. But, as the narrator points out, action implies freedom without overtly denying the tragic causality, without providing an alternate interpretation. The action in the book's second half is specifically anti-interpretative; it is designed to establish an alibi for Jem, not to set up a competing version of the truth. Similarly, the transcendental element in Unitarianism was not so much a competing causality as it was a suspension of the older deterministic causality.

Throughout the Liverpool chapters, however, the narrator reminds us that the suspension is merely temporary, that John Barton's terrible guilt is in no way affected by Mary's adventures. We know that once the alibi is established, there will be nothing left to do but confront the awful truth. Thus Will Wilson's arrival in the courtroom produces Mary's collapse. She breaks under the pressure of the suppressed truth, the truth to which the novel must recur once the melodramatic lie is overthrown. Mary's illness gives some reprieve from the inevitable confrontation with John Barton, as do old Alice's death and the settlements of numerous domestic details between Mary and the Wilsons. Each of these in its own way, however, conjures up the "phantom likeness of John Barton" (p. 414) and the problematic causality that attends his story.

Causation once again becomes an explicit theme in the book, one that haunts and perplexes the narrator. Indeed, at one point she attacks the reader for demanding causal explanations. After giving a somewhat unconvincing account of Jem's reasons for prolonging Mary's (and by extension, the novel's) separation from John Barton, she impatiently asserts that reality is not always amenable to clear cause-and-effect analysis: "If you think this account of mine confused, of the half-feelings, half-reasons, which passed through Jem's mind, . . . if you are perplexed to disentangle the real motives, I do assure you it was from such an involved set of thoughts that Jem drew the resolution to act" (pp. 413-14). It is not, however, the reader, the threatening, skeptical, and ultimately guilty "you" of the novel, who demands cause-and-effect logic; it is the narrative itself. In the sentence quoted above, the narrator turns the novel inward by addressing the expectations that the book itself created and declaring both her inability and her unwillingness to meet them. It is a prominently placed sentence, standing at the end of the chapter between the courtroom scene and Mary's return to Manchester; it is an expression of failure, of liberation, and of formal self-consciousness that might well be taken as a motto for the chapters that follow.

The concluding chapters of *Mary Barton* return us to the story of John; Mary continues in the domestic mode, specifically refusing to think about causes. Indeed, where her father's story should be, there is nothing but a blank in Mary's mind: "He was her father! her own dear father! and in his sufferings, whatever their cause, more dearly loved than ever before. His crime was a thing apart, never more to be considered by her" (p. 422). The narrator, however, cannot so easily refuse to

consider the causes of John Barton's suffering. Having returned to the subject, she must try to conclude it, but she faces the same bind she encountered earlier: she must indict society as the source of Barton's crime and still grant Barton his free will. Whereas her strategy in the Liverpool chapters was to suppress John Barton's story, her strategy in the concluding chapters is to tell different versions of the story. Since she has declared herself free from the necessity to "disentangle the real motives," she allows herself the luxury of presenting an "involved set" of interpretations without really striving after consistency. Thus the recapitulations contain elements of both social determinism and voluntarism. Finally, however, salvation comes in this novel not through retelling John Barton's story, but through making it irrelevant. All John Barton's and the narrator's explanations are for naught; his story is redeemed through the intervention of another story that makes all talk of causality superfluous.

In the terms of James Martineau's dichotomy, "conscience" is the key word in John Barton's development after the murder, just as "causality" had been before. The issue of John Barton's moral responsibility is partly settled by the mere description of the state in which Mary finds him on her return home: "He had taken the accustomed seat from mere force of habit, which ruled his automaton-body. For all energy, both physical and mental, seemed to have retreated inwards to some of the great citadels of life, there to do battle against the Destroyer, Conscience" (p. 422). John Barton now has no will; he acts from "mere force of habit." But the intensity of his remorse implies that in the past he was free. He takes full responsibility for his crime during his interview with Henry Carson, and his remorse intensifies in the course of conversation. So that remorse might appear a completely appropriate emotion, the narrator gives an account of the murder that makes it seem almost a voluntary political act rather than a desperate crime forced by the convergence of uncontrollable indignation and intolerable suffering. The version of Barton's crime given during his interview with Carson contains a causality compatible with freedom. It contains nothing of the intense suffering of the strikers or of Harry Carson's maddening arrogance: "To intimidate a class of men, known only to those below them as desirous to obtain the greatest quantity of work for the lowest wages,—at most to remove an overbearing partner from an obnoxious firm . . . this was the light in which John Barton had viewed his deed" (pp. 435-36). The very word "cause" takes on a new meaning in this account of Barton's story: instead of implying a set of circumstances that led up to the fatal action, it comes to denote the partisan purpose of the trade unionists, the "cause he had so blindly espoused" (p. 436).

This description of the murder as a wholly political, indeed almost unemotional, act contains a social criticism, but one that increases our sense of Barton's guilty freedom. The account allows the narrator once again to argue that domesticity is the ultimate ground of reality. John Barton's reasoning had produced the distortion of human reality that always occurs when men are severed from their domestic contexts: "he had no more imagined to himself the blighted home, and the miserable parents, than does the soldier, who discharges his musket, picture to himself the desolation of the wife, and the pitiful cries of the helpless little ones, who are in an instant to be made widowed, and fatherless" (p. 435). The analogy links Barton's failing to Harry Carson's insensitivity: each in his own way was deaf to "the pitiful cries" of helpless relations. This plea for a more highly developed domestic consciousness is itself a species of social criticism, albeit a vague one. Barton's sin of abstracting Harry Carson from his domestic context is presented as the characteristic error of industrial society. By substituting this kind of broad criticism of an abstract and abstracting mentality for the careful descriptions of social relationships and experiences contained in earlier chapters, the author unites the classes on the basis of a shared human reality, the universal reality of family life. The account of Barton's story that emerges from the interview with Mr. Carson, therefore, makes a critical point, but the point does not relieve the hero of any guilt. Indeed, it increases Barton's crimes by adding to his faults of resentment and murder the crime of insensitivity to human suffering, which was previously attributed to the masters. In this account, the murder is no longer the result but the cause of suffering:

> The sympathy for suffering, formerly so prevalent a feeling with him, again filled John Barton's heart, and almost impelled him to speak . . . some earnest, tender words to the stern man, shaking in his agony.
>
> But who was he, that he should utter sympathy, or consolation? The cause of all this woe. (P. 435)

This version of Barton's story is concerned with causation, but not the kind of causation that the earlier chapters traced. In this retelling, "cause" comes to mean political purpose, and Barton himself becomes the cause of another's suffering. Causation in this version, therefore, is compatible with conscience and its corollary, free will.

Those circumstances formerly presented as the sources of Barton's action, however, are not completely ignored in the resolution of his story. After the unforgiving Mr. Carson leaves him, Barton gives an account of his own tragedy, an account which contains a heavy dose of the social determinism of earlier chapters. From him we hear once more about the moral effects of poverty and ignorance: "You see I've so often been hankering after the right way; and it's a hard one for a poor man to find. . . . No one learned me, and no

one told me" (p. 440). Ignorance and poverty are two determining circumstances, and the hypocrisy of the upper classes is a third: "I would fain have gone after the Bible rules if I'd seen folk credit it; they all spoke up for it, and went and did clean contrary" (p. 440). And we hear again about the hatred inspired by his son's death from want of medicine and proper food: "wife, and children never spoke, but their helplessness cried aloud, and I was driven to do as others did,—and then Tom died" (p. 440).

The image of Barton as a driven man, however, competes in this deathbed account with yet another characterization, one quite new to the novel. Barton acknowledges that he is creating a new self in his storytelling; he describes the act of narration as "wrestling with my soul for a character to take into the other world" (p. 434). Although Barton's characterization of himself has elements of social determinism, it is not completely dominated by that model of causation. Even as he recapitulates the familiar circumstances, he subtly undermines their explanatory power by prefacing them: "It's not much I can say for myself in t'other world. God forgive me: but I can say this . . ." (p. 440). This preface reminds us that John Barton's acknowledged guilt, his full moral responsibility, is the given context of his narrative; he is not rehearsing his story as a defense, as a proof of innocence. Instead, he is describing, somewhat inconsistently, the extenuating circumstances of a crime to which he has already pleaded guilty.

Accordingly, the focus of his narrative is not on the familiar circumstances of his decline, but on a new set of facts about his life, facts implying that he could have avoided his tragic course. We learn for the first time that the hero was once very devout, that he studied the Bible and tried to follow its precepts, that he even had a special comradeship with old Alice, who had tried to "strengthen" him. His faith, however, was not strong enough to survive the corrosive bitterness of his experience; the loss of his faith, we are told, was the turning point of his career: "At last I gave it up in despair, trying to make folks' actions square wi' th' Bible; and I thought I'd no longer labour at following th' Bible myself. I've said all this afore; may be. But from that time I've dropped down, down,—down" (p. 441). Despair, itself a sin, becomes the decisive factor in this religious account of Barton's life. The character that Barton creates "to take into the other world" is thus a cross between the tragically determined John Barton we know and a John Barton we have never seen before, the free but erring subject of a religious homily.

The writer seems to have felt some uneasiness about introducing a completely new version of the story at such a late hour, especially one that fits imperfectly with the older deterministic version, for she has Barton suggest that "I've said all this afore; may be." If the sentence is meant to make the new facts seem less strange, it defeats its own purpose, for it conveys the self-conscious uneasiness of the writer by reminding us that in fact *no one* has "said all this afore," that we are being given a new story, one that is not easy to reconcile with the old. The sentence therefore increases our awareness of the discontinuities of these last chapters.

The issues tangled in the summaries of Barton's life and crime (whether he is fully responsible or not, free or determined) are never finally sorted out. We must accept this "involved set" of accounts, but we are also reassured that ultimately it does not matter how we interpret Barton's story. For the novel we have been reading is finally resolved by the introduction of a different book, the Bible. The narrator finds relief from the multiple reinterpretations of John Barton's story by superimposing the ending as well as the meaning of the Gospel onto her novel, and the meaning of the Gospel is that we need not choose among the several versions of John Barton's story.

While John Barton is recounting his failure to live "Gospel-wise," Henry J. Carson recreates himself (in both senses of the phrase) through the other story: "He fell to the narrative now, afresh, with all the interest of a little child. He began at the beginning, and read on almost greedily, understanding for the first time the full meaning of the story" (pp. 439-40). The "full meaning" of the story turns out to be that John Barton should be forgiven, no matter what the sources or consequences of his crime. Henry Carson comes to forgive John Barton not because he has been told the hero's own story, but because Barton's words "I did not know what I was doing" (p. 435) referred him to the Gospel story.[41] Forgiveness is mandated by the other narrative, and all versions of John Barton's life thus become irrelevant to the novel's concluding and redeeming action: Carson's forgiveness, which is a foretaste of the Christian spirit that the narrator assures us will allow Carson to effect industrial social change.

Thus the conclusion of John Barton's story points to narrative as an instrument of God's Providence without having to sort out the tangle of its own narrative threads. In the few episodes that remain, the characters settle in Canada, and the domestic tale is finally protected by distance from the tragedy caused by industrial vicissitudes. But the final episodes fail to settle the question that the novel repeatedly raises: the question of an appropriate narrative form. It is not surprising that, in Gaskell's words, no one "saw" her "idea of a tragic poem," for the tragedy is even more obscured by antagonistic interpretations at the end of the novel than in the early chapters. We must therefore agree with the author's judgment that she failed to express perfectly her tragic intentions. But we must also re-

member that her tragic purpose contained its own contradiction, which had definite historical roots in the Unitarianism of the 1840s and in certain features of the tradition of industrial social criticism that Gaskell inherited. We should also remember that her failure is the foundation of the book's formal significance, for its very generic eclecticism points toward the formal self-consciousness of later British realism.

Notes

[1] George Rowell, *Hell and the Victorians,* pp. 49-57, gives a succinct account of the sources and impact of James Martineau's thought. See also James Drummond, *The Life and Letters of James Martineau* (New York, 1902), vol. 1, passim.

[2] *Harriet Martineau's Autobiography,* ed. Marie Weston (Boston, 1877), 1:83.

[3] Quoted in Drummond, *Life and Letters of James Martineau,* 2:262-63.

[4] Quoted in Webb, *Harriet Martineau,* p. 96.

[5] Drummond, *Life and Letters of James Martineau,* 2:262.

[6] James Martineau, "Three States of Unitarian Theology," in *Essays, Reviews, and Addresses,* (London, 1891), 4:574.

[7] Ibid.

[8] Rowell, *Hell and the Victorians,* p. 52.

[9] W. Arthur Boggs, "Reflections of Unitarians in Mrs. Gaskell's Novels" (Dissertation, University of California, Berkeley, 1950), p. 23.

[10] Two of Elizabeth Gaskell's letters indicate that she rather disliked James Martineau and was probably not strongly influenced by him personally. See *The Letters of Mrs. Gaskell,* ed. J. A. V. Chapple and Arthur Pollard (Manchester, 1966), pp. 177, 239. One as deeply immersed in Unitarianism as Gaskell was, however, could hardly have escaped being influenced by the emphasis he gave to man's "capacity . . . for voluntary righteousness" (see note 1). *Mary Barton* itself provides sufficient evidence that Gaskell had entered "the second stage of Unitarian theology."

[11] Quoted in William Robbins, *The Newman Brothers: An Essay in Comparative Intellectual Biography* (Cambridge, Mass., 1966), p. 152.

[12] Gaskell's admiration for Francis Newman and her attention to his thought are evident in this description: "We first knew Mr. Newman from his coming here to

be a professor at the Manchester College—and the face and voice at first sight told 'He had been with Christ.' . . . Oh dear! I long for the days back again when he came dropping in in the dusk and lost no time in pouring out what his heart was full of, (thats [sic] the secret of eloquence) whether it was a derivation of a word, a joke or a burst of indignation or a holy thought" (*Letters*, pp. 87-88).

[13] From Francis Newman, *Four Lectures on the Contrasts of Ancient and Modern History* (1846), quoted in Robbins, *Newman Brothers*, p. 93.

[14] *Catholic Union, Essays towards a Church of the Future as the Organization of Philanthropy* (London, 1854), p. 13; first published in 1844.

[15] *Four Lectures*, p. 93.

[16] From *Biographical Memoranda*, by James Martineau, quoted in Drummond, *Life and Letters of James Martineau*, 2:273.

[17] Ibid.

[18] In one of her explanations of John Barton's crime, Gaskell traces it to his reification of the masters. Barton only understands the true nature of his error after Carson ceases to be a capitalist in Barton's eyes and becomes a mere man: "The mourner before him was no longer the employer; a being of another race, eternally placed in antagonistic attitude . . . but a very poor and desolate old man" (p. 435).

[19] *Letters of Mrs. Gaskell*, p. 70.

[20] Ibid., p. 74. See Jeannette King, *Tragedy in the Victorian Novel: Theory and Practice in the Novels of George Eliot, Thomas Hardy, and Henry James* (New York, 1978) for a discussion of the ways in which Victorian writers tried to reconcile their proletarian subject matter and their ideas of social determinism with classical models of tragedy that emphasized the noble status of the hero and the universal, unchanging nature of Fate.

[21] *Letters of Mrs. Gaskell*, p. 47. Gaskell here complains about the narrative structure of Martineau's *Hour and the Man* (1841).

[22] See note 2.

[23] Angus Easson discusses the formal significance of Barton's crime in *Elizabeth Gaskell* (Boston, 1979), pp. 76-77.

[24] The ending of *Mary Barton* strikingly recalls the idea of Providence elucidated in Francis Newman's essay "On the existence of Evil" (1841), in F. W.

Newman, Miscellanies (London, 1888), pp. 1-10. In his essay, Newman argues that the idea of free will reconciles the idea of Providence with the existence of evil. God does not will but merely permits the evil created by man. The evil, he insists, is only temporary because it is self-obliterating: "believe that goodness alone is eternal; and it remains clearly intelligible, how the divine wisdom may have ordained, on the one hand, that man should gain a stable independent holy will, so as to be capable of friendship with his infinite creator; but that, on the other hand, this essentially demanded that he should be left free to sin, and consequently moral evil has abounded and abounds, but only for a time. Sin and its effects, remorse and misery, are to be abolished, and the fruit of holiness shall flourish to everlasting life" (p. 8).

[25] *British Quarterly Review* 9 (1849): 128.

[26] The formal discontinuity of this novel has been remarked by most of its critics. Various sources of the discontinuity have been advanced, and I will mention only three of the most important. In *Culture and Society, 1780-1950* (New York, 1958), pp. 87-91, Raymond Williams divides the novel into halves: the first half is a successful evocation of "everyday life in the working-class"; the second, however, is dominated by the "orthodox plot of the Victorian novel of sentiment." He attributes the split to a shift of emphasis away from John Barton that takes place when "the flow of sympathy with which [Gaskell] began was arrested." The flow of sympathy is arrested, moreover, by a fear of violence, which was part of the middle-class "structure of feeling" that Elizabeth Gaskell inhabited. In "The Early Victorian Social Problem Novel," in *From Dickens to Hardy*, ed. Boris Ford, vol. 6 of *The Pelican Guide to English Literature* (Baltimore, 1958), pp. 169-87, Arnold Kettle also divides the book between the near-tragic story of John Barton (p. 181) and the love story of his daughter. Although Kettle sees connections between the two, he believes the love story was imposed by the demands of the novel form. Stephen Gill, in his introduction to the Penguin edition of *Mary Barton*, agrees with both Kettle and Williams, but he adds a point of his own: Gaskell could not find a solution to the vast social problems she portrayed because her historical perspective was limited by the immediacy of those problems. All of these judgments are sound; all contribute to our understanding of the novel. But they leave certain things out. First, they do not seem to recognize the generic multiplicity within the two halves of the book. Second, they ignore the fact that John Barton's tragedy is more than merely frightening to a middle-class sensibility; it is also unmanageable because it is self-contradicting. Its paradoxical nature is not explicable in terms of a vague "structure of feeling"; it must be traced to the author's precise intellectual context. Third, these three important analyses do not take the author's own formal self-consciousness

into account. For a more recent discussion of the problem, see Angus Easson, for whom the formal ambiguities of *Mary Barton* mark the work of a developing novelist working within a "context of change and debate" in *Elizabeth Gaskell,* p. 58.

[27] *Mary Barton: A Tale of Manchester Life,* ed. Stephen Gill (Baltimore, 1976), p. 121. All subsequent references to *Mary Barton* are to this edition, and page numbers are given in the text.

[28] As Harry Levin has pointed out in *The Gates of Horn: A Study of Five French Realists* (New York, 1966), p. 19, "the movement of realism, technically considered, is an endeavor to emancipate literature from the sway of conventions."

[29] It is Stephen Gill who suggests in footnote 58 of the Penguin edition of *Mary Barton* that this is the quotation, from *Henry IV, Part 1,* 4.3, to which Gaskell alludes. However, my colleague Paul Alpers suggests informally that, although these are his most famous lines in the scene, Falstaff has a much longer speech that yields lines possibly more appropriate to Carson's purpose, such as "ragged as Lazarus in the painted cloth" and "a hundred and fifty tattered prodigals lately come from swine-keeping."

[30] *Letters of Mrs. Gaskell,* p. 74.

[31] See note 6.

[32] Patrick Brantlinger, in "Bluebooks, the Social Organism, and the Victorian Novel," *Criticism* 13 (1972):328-44, contrasts the detailed evocation of working-class life with the "melodrama of the murder plot," and Stephen Gill ("Introduction") also contrasts the realistic sketches of the first half with the conventional "romantic" sensationalism of the second half (p. 22).

[33] My paradigm of melodrama is based primarily on the discussions by Peter Brooks in *The Melodramatic Imagination: Balzac, Henry James, Melodrama, and the Mode of Excess* (New Haven, 1976), pp. 11-20, and by R. B. Heilman, *Tragedy and Melodrama* (Seattle, 1968), passim. Brooks stresses that melodramas portray uncompromising struggles between good and evil. Their mode of action is excessive and parabolical. Heilman discusses the affective difference between tragedy and melodrama, arguing that the former, by portraying an irresolvable internal conflict, produces a complex emotional response, while the latter, by portraying a heroic fight against an external evil force, produces a simpler, self-righteous emotional reaction in the audience.

[34] Kathleen Tillotson, *Novels of the Eighteen-Forties* (London, 1956), p. 214.

[35] Gaskell's description from a letter to Mary Howitt,

Letters of Mrs. Gaskell, p. 33. The sketch was published in *Blackwoods Magazine* 41 (1837):48-51, under the title "Sketches among the Poor, No. 1."

[36] *Letters of Mrs. Gaskell,* p. 74.

[37] Tillotson, *Novels of the Eighteen-Forties,* p. 222.

[38] The often-repeated story is that Gaskell was inspired to write *Mary Barton* while on a mission of mercy to a poor family during the depression of the early 1840s: "She was trying hard to speak comfort, and to allay those bitter feelings against the rich which were so common with the poor, when the head of the family took hold of her arm, and grasping it tightly said, with tears in his eyes, 'Ay, ma'am, but have ye ever seen a child clemmed to death.'" The story is from M. Hompes, "Mrs. E. C. Gaskell," *Gentleman's Magazine* 55 (1895):124.

[39] For a discussion of the various narrative modes in *Mary Barton* as deviations from a dominant domestic mode, see Rosemarie Bodenheimer, "Private Grief and Public Acts in *Mary Barton,*" *Dickens Studies Annual: Essays on Victorian Fiction* 9 (New York, 1981): 195-216.

[40] Tillotson, *Novels of the Eighteen-Forties,* pp. 215-21, contains an excellent discussion of the two London stories.

[41] For a discussion of a possible source for this scene in the work of Caroline Bowles, see Michael D. Wheeler, "The Writer as Reader in *Mary Barton,*" *Durham University Journal* 67 (1974): 92-106.

Works Cited

I. Primary Works: Fiction

Gaskell, Elizabeth. *Mary Barton* (1848). Baltimore, 1976.

II. Other Primary Sources

British Quarterly Review 9 (1849).

Drummond, James. *The Life and Letters of James Martineau.* 2 vols. New York, 1902.

Gaskell, Elizabeth Gleghorn. *The Letters of Mrs. Gaskell.* Edited by J. A. V. Chapple and Arthur Pollard. Manchester, 1966.

———. *The Life of Charlotte Brontë.* London, 1857.

Hompes, M. "Mrs. E. C. Gaskell." *Gentleman's Magazine,* n.s. 55 (1895) 124.

Martineau, James. *Essays, Reviews, and Addresses.* Vol. 4. London, 1891.

Newman, Francis W. *Catholic Union: Essays Towards a Church of the Future as the Organization of Philanthropy* (1844). London, 1854.

————. "On the Existence of Evil." In *Miscellanies,* pp. 1-10. London, 1888.

III. Secondary Works: Literary Studies

Bodenheimer, Rosemarie. "Private Grief and Public Acts in *Mary Barton.*" *Dickens Studies Annual: Essays on Victorian Fiction* 9 (1981): 195-216.

Boggs, W. Arthur. "Reflections of Unitarianism in Mrs. Gaskell's Novels." Dissertation, University of California, Berkeley, 1950.

Brantlinger, Patrick. "Bluebooks, the Social Organism, and the Victorian Novel." *Criticism* 14 (Fall 1972): 328-44.

Brooks, Peter. *The Melodramatic Imagination: Balzac, Henry James, Melodrama, and the Mode of Excess.* New York, 1976.

Easson, Angus. *Elizabeth Gaskell.* Boston, 1979.

Heilman, R. B. *Tragedy and Melodrama.* Seattle, 1968.

Kettle, Arnold. "The Early Victorian Social-Problem Novel." In *From Dickens to Hardy.* Edited by Boris Ford. Vol. 6 of *The Pelican Guide to English Literature.* Baltimore, 1973.

King, Jeanette. *Tragedy in the Victorian Novel: Theory and Practice in the Novels of George Eliot, Thomas Hardy, and Henry James.* New York, 1978.

Levin, Harry. *The Gates of Horn: A Study of Five French Realists.* New York, 1966.

Tillotson, Kathleen. *Novels of the Eighteen Forties.* London, 1956.

Webb, R. K.. *Harriet Martineau: A Radical Victorian.* New York, 1960.

Wheeler, Michael D. "The Writer as Reader in *Mary Barton.*" *Durham University Journal* 67 (1974): 92-106.

Williams, Raymond. *Culture and Society, 1780-1950.* New York, 1960.

IV. Secondary Works: Intellectual, Cultural, and Social History

Robbins, William. *The Newman Brothers: An Essay in Comparative Intellectual Biography.* Cambridge, Mass., 1966.

Rowell, Geoffrey. *Hell and the Victorians: A Study of the Nineteenth-Century Theological Controversies Concerning Eternal Punishment and the Future Life.* Oxford, 1974.

Margaret Homans (essay date 1986)

SOURCE: "Mothers and Daughters I: Gaskell's Stories of the Mother's Word and the Daughter's Fate," in *Bearing the Word: Language and Female Experience in Nineteenth-Century Women's Writing,* The University of Chicago Press, 1986, pp. 223-50.

[*In the following essay, Homans claims that* Mary Barton *and "Lizzie Leigh" are both enactments of a dialogue between mother and daughter, a dialogue that hinges on the transmission of the written word.*]

Central to Gaskell's myth of herself as a writer who put her duties as a woman ahead of her writing is the story of how she began to write seriously. In 1845 her ten-month-old son, William, died of scarlet fever, and "it was to turn her thoughts from the subject of her grief that, by her husband's advice, she attempted to write a work of some length."[1] This work was *Mary Barton,* her first novel, published in 1848 with a preface that encodes her sacred reason for writing: "Three years ago I became anxious (from circumstances that need not be more fully alluded to) to employ myself." Like Mary Shelley in her introduction to *Frankenstein,* Gaskell wishes to demonstrate that her writing begins safely within the bounds of a woman's duty to her family, as behavior that the death of a son might legitimately provoke and of which a protective husband approves. Only when deprived of a woman's proper duties would she consider writing.

Yet the novel also bears an epigraph that encodes a slightly different story of origins:[2]

> Nimm nur, Fährmann, nimm die Miethe,
> Die ich gerne dreifach biete!
> Zween, die mit nur überfuhren,
> Waren geistige Naturen.

Two dead children, not one, thus make their ghostly appearance at the start of this novel. The public myth of her writing would make the death of her son be the pivotal moment of her life, yet the other death, the first death, was that of her first child, a stillborn daughter, in 1833. In 1836 she wrote a sonnet "On Visiting the grave of my stillborn little girl." The poem records, and by doing so enacts, the carrying out of the speaker's "vow" never to forget this child, who was "laid beside my weary heart, / With marks of Death on every tender part," even when another is born. "And thou, my child, from thy bright heaven see / How well I keep my faithful vow to thee."[3] As Gaskell's first self-consciously literary venture, though she never published it, the poem marks a different point of origin for the writer's career from that indicated by the story about the death of her son. Written during the period of the diary about Marianne, the "living infant" who the poem asserts does not supplant the dead one, the sonnet precedes her first published work, the Wordsworthian poem "Sketches Among the Poor" (1837), and her sketch of Clopton Hall published in 1840 in William Howitt's *Visits to Remarkable Places.* Most significantly, the first short story she wrote, in 1838, was **"Lizzie Leigh"** (not published till 1851, after her reputation had already been established by ***Mary Barton***), a story about mothers and daughters that hinges on the death of a little girl. The writing of this story suggests that the poem's vow not to forget the dead daughter continues to provide the impetus to write, even if the child is memorialized by a reenactment of her death. Thus, behind the myth of the writer as mother grieving over her son and directed by her husband's wisdom, who writes novels and publishes them immediately, lies hidden another writer who grieves alone over a daughter and writes a poem and a story she is reticent to publish. It is this second writer I wish to uncover.

When Gaskell's living daughter begins to speak, as Gaskell describes it in the diary, Papa's name and the signs of Papa's arrival make up her earliest language, "leaving poor Mama in the background."[4] With this only partially comic exclusion of the mother from the scene of symbolic language, Gaskell's diary begins making its covert myth about the place of women in language, a myth that in the next diary entry offers as compensation for this exclusion women's traditional role as passive medium for the transmission of men's, or God's, words. Though the diary starts out by uniting mother and daughter as its fused "subject," it also acknowledges the premise of symbolic language, that the text will have meaning only if one or the other of its subjects is dead. In these and other ways, the diary yields up to the predominant myths of language and of writing the primacy and tenacity of a mother's relation with her daughter and of the linguistic possibilities that relation might offer.

Briefly to recapitulate my argument in chapter 1 and its development in intervening chapters, the mother's relegation to the background is the result of her being that against which a male subject and speaker must define his difference, defining her as the difference and absence that constitute symbolic language. But furthermore—and this is what is of particular relevance for our discussion of Gaskell—Nancy Chodorow argues that the daughter's original, preoedipal attachment to her mother outlasts the time of the son's separation from the mother and identification with the father, because unlike the son she is never obliged to renounce the mother. Chodorow argues further that it is the desire to reproduce this early situation that causes daughters, and not sons, to grow up to want not only to bear but to rear—to "mother"—children. Whereas sons seek representations of the mother in later romantic attachments, allowing them to keep the mother at a safe distance (and while daughters seek representations of the father in the same way), daughters seek to reproduce literally the same situation they once lived in, without wanting to distance the mother. As a part of a myth of language, this desire to reproduce the mother-daughter relation, with the non- or presymbolic language that both accompanies it and is modeled on it, is the desire to write in what I have been calling a literal language. This literal language is fleetingly exemplified by the rhythmic, cadenced speech Mrs. Ramsay shares with her daughter in Woolf's *To the Light-house,* a kind of speech that does not matter because it refers to things but rather because it reassures the daughter of her mother's presence, a presence that is not distanced by the law of the father.

However, women writers of the nineteenth century depend too much for the legitimation of their writing on their acceptance of the symbolic order's codes, codes that would exclude them as the silent objects of representation from writing as women, for them to see value in writing in this way as mother or daughter. Or perhaps it would be more accurate to say that those women novelists who have been accepted within the literary canon are those who have accepted these codes and write according to their identification of writing with masculinity. At the same time, the desire to retain and to reproduce something of, or like, this nonsymbolic language may entice women to value a role as bearers of language (and also as bearers of children). This role has the added appeal of offering an alternative way of accommodating paternal codes. Yet situated as it is in a culture that devalues whatever women do, including motherhood, this role becomes a position of subordination, appropriated, as maternity itself is appropriated, to fill the needs of a paternal order. Women are encouraged to define themselves as mothers, yet are permitted only a narrow and subordinate role when writing as mothers. *Frankenstein* articulates a woman writer's protest against this situation perhaps the most clearly, while the Victorian novelists, especially Gaskell and Eliot, who were personally as well as culturally obliged to subscribe to the cultural mythology of woman as mother, both accede to this situation and find ways to accommodate their own writing to it. Eliot is interested in the manipulation of women's given role as bearers of androcentric language—the role that Gaskell sees as available to her as compensation for Mama's relegation to the background—to see how far women's subjection to a masculinist myth of language can yet be made to afford women speech. Gaskell, perhaps more bold in her claims for writing as a woman, is interested in recovering, however fleetingly and however colored by its situation within the confines of the paternal order, that discourse between mothers and daughters that is lost to most women writers before the twentieth century, given up by daughters and mothers alike as the price of any sort of access to the language of fathers. That Gaskell is the least canonical of the novelists considered in this book is directly related to her claiming, however conditionally, that there might be other ways for women to write, beyond the unsatisfactory alternatives either of adopting what her culture perceived as the masculine position or of accepting the narrow definition of the mother as servant to patriliny.

"Lizzie Leigh," the story Gaskell wrote in commemoration of her dead daughter, is the story of mothers' love for their daughters that is, paradoxically, both destroyed by and dependent upon the intrusion into this relationship of paternal authority. Gaskell does not imagine a mother-daughter relation that is not affected by the father; rather she explores the possibility for such a relation as it exists within a patrilineal culture. As a myth of women's relation to the operation of language, the story suggests not so much that a nonsymbolic language shared between mothers and daughters survives from childhood, or that women's linguistic practices are wholly absorbed within the paternal order, but rather that in the interplay between these seemingly contradictory possibilities exists a language that is specific to mothers and daughters and also, importantly, capable of providing pleasure to them. Gaskell celebrates women's difference without losing sight of its cost.

The story contrasts two kinds of relations between generations, which are also two models of language. Patriliny is the inheritance both of the father's property and of his language, by way of women who (like Romola, or like Brontë's Cathy at the end of her life) facilitate inheritance but are excluded from its benefits. Both against and within patriliny, a matrilineal order acknowledges women's marginal place in patriliny and establishes its own separate principles of intergenerational relations that are more fluid and flexible than those of patriliny. The story opens with the death of James Leigh, who for three years has denied the existence of his "fallen" daughter Lizzie, who nonetheless is mourned by her mother, Anne. Anne's first action on hearing the reading of her husband's will, bequeathing to her for life the farm that "had belonged for generations to the Leighs," is to rent it out in order to go to Manchester in search of her lost daughter.[5] In "The Crooked Branch," a later "prodigal son" tale that in turn revises Wordsworth's "Michael," the father, Nathan, similarly liquidates some of his farm's assets to pay his erring son's debts. Yet Anne Leigh's readiness to leave the farm to go in search of her daughter contrasts with

Nathan's reluctance to leave what remains of his country home, and even more strikingly with Michael's refusal to sacrifice any of his land, preferring that his son should go instead:[6]

> Our Luke shall leave us, Isabel; the land Shall not
> go from us, and it shall be free.

Furthermore, Nathan's strict sense of patriliny in "The Crooked Branch" blinds him to his son's real sins, whereas Anne Leigh is perfectly clear-sighted about her daughter's "fall," and the issue is not whether the sin has occurred but how to rescue Lizzie from further misery. As a mother she unequivocally places human life ahead of property, without any of the conflict experienced by Michael or Nathan. This clear vision appears to derive from her inheriting only a life interest in the farm, which is to be passed thereafter to her eldest son. She is quite aware of her marginal place in patriliny.

James Leigh is a perfect patriarch. Gaskell puts it bluntly: "Milton's famous line might have been framed and hung up as the rule of their married life, for he was truly the interpreter, who stood between God and her." Thus both in form and in content, patriarchal authority flows through him. His God is the unforgiving Old Testament God who authorizes the unforgiving condemnation of female sinners. And his son, Will, inherits his stern attitude, along with his eventual inheritance of the ancestral farm. It is above all Lizzie's illegitimate child who is the source of condemnation by her father, whose participation in patriliny ties him to strict notions of legitimacy of birth. Moreover, his attitude toward Lizzie takes a specifically linguistic form: the family learns of her fall through discovering that a letter has not reached her, since, pregnant, she has been sent from her employer's to the work house. Having deviated from the line that patriliny dictates for a daughter's sexuality, no longer in her "place," she ceases to exist, by the patriarch's act of un-naming. Her father "declared that henceforth they would have no daughter; that she should be as one dead, and her name never more be named."

In contrast to this grim portrait, the story also introduces a maternal vision of the inheritance of property and words that both mimics and conflicts with, as well as being defined by its marginal relation to, patriliny and the patrilineal descent of words. Anne's priorities lie neither with the rigid duplication of patriarchal words, and the linear passage of a letter from sender to receiver that comes to stand for this, nor with the equally rigid adherence to patriliny and to the ancestral way of life that her son insists upon as much as her husband did, but with her daughter herself, whose sin Anne sees only as a cause for sorrow and forgiveness. To begin with, as she takes over possession of the moral categories of the story, Anne provides an alternative to James's interpretation of the Bible, preferring the forgiveness that the stories of the prodigal son and Magdalen articulate to the Old Testament harshness of her husband and son. As Lizzie, later in the story, awakes to the awareness of her mother's presence, Anne asserts God's forgiveness: "'I'll tell thee God's promises to them that are penitent.' . . . Mrs. Leigh repeated every tender and merciful text she could remember." She transmits biblical texts, but texts of her own choosing, thus revising and bending to her purposes, but not wholly rejecting, her given place in patriliny.

Further, the mother's recognition—and therefore eventual restoration and consolation—of Lizzie depends upon the only words and property women can bequeath to their daughters, a first name (as opposed to a patronymic) and a dress. While in Manchester with his mother (against his wishes), Will falls in love with Susan Palmer, a beautiful and silent woman who cares for a "niece," Nanny, and who, Will fears, will reject him if she learns the story of his sister. Anne visits Susan to tell her Lizzie's story and thus test her worthiness of Will by her reaction. Susan, recognizing the name of the mistress who turned Lizzie away when she became pregnant, tells Anne that Nanny is not her niece but was, as a baby, dropped in her arms by a sobbing woman, and she brings Anne the baby clothes that came with her. "There was a little packet of clothes—very few—and as if they were made out of its mother's gowns, for they were large patterns to buy for a baby." With the clothes is a letter that says, "Call her Anne." Anne confirms the identity of baby and mother in part through the name—"'Anne,' common though it was, seemed something to build upon"—but mainly through the clothes: "Mrs Leigh recognised one of the frocks instantly, as being made out of a gown that she and her daughter had bought together in Rochdale."

If James Leigh's letter to Lizzie typifies patriliny's view of language, with its assumption that there is only one line a letter may travel and that the letter's failure to reach its destination means Lizzie's nonexistence, this letter that Nanny carries from her mother to Susan and finally to her own grandmother typifies another, a matrilineal language. Although the letter still must travel in a line in order to have meaning, the line is a far more flexible one than James Leigh's. The letter's first recipient, Susan, can read neither the letter nor the message encoded in the clothes; these signs' correct interpretation must wait for the arrival of the original referent both of the name and of the message of the fabric. It is also important to note that these signs would not have existed in the first place had not a harsh paternal law interfered between mother and daughter. Unlike James Leigh's notion of a straight, one-directional line from father to the future by way of marginal women, which also resembles Bardo's view in *Romola,* and equally unlike Tito's horror at becoming one of his own deviant messages delivered back to

his origin, his father, the turning of the line of Nanny's letter back upon itself to reach its source is what constitutes women's pleasure in this story. If a sign signifies only in the presence of what it signifies, especially where that referent is a mother, it undoes and refuses the symbolic economy that stipulates the absence of a referent, especially where the referent is a mother. This kind of sign making suggests that mother and daughter could communicate with one another both as women and within the order of written language. This seeming impossibility contrasts, for example, with the situation in Gaskell's diary in which the words will have meaning only in the absence of one or the other. It also contrasts with the situation of mothers with respect to sons as articulated, for example, in James Leigh's favorite texts, where the mother's absence is said to be the precondition of the son's founding and maintaining of the whole of culture.

This recognition through the dress, bought by the mother, shared with the daughter, made into baby clothes for the granddaughter, takes on another dimension of significance in the light of Victorian critics' assumption that the gender of an anonymous author could be identified by the degree of detailed attention to clothing or other domestic details present in the work.[7] For Gaskell to have Anne recognize Lizzie and the baby by clothing is simultaneously to court recognition of herself—or at least of a woman—as author. Gaskell did not have the powerful motives for anonymity that the Brontës and Eliot had and took no trouble to conceal her identity, yet the story, like *Mary Barton,* was published anonymously as the lead story in the first number of Dickens's *Household Words.* Curiously, though, from its sentimental tone and its honorific position in his magazine, Dickens was commonly assumed to be the author by readers who missed the clue of the clothing, as well as the clue of the intense interest in and positive view of a mother-daughter relationship that distinguishes the story from anything Dickens wrote. The story was as a result first published in the United States under Dickens's name. Despite this accident, Gaskell seems deliberately to have made women's clothing a turning point in the story, to call attention to female authorship by calling attention to the way in which women may send and receive signs in a way that is different from men's and also illegible to men because overlooked by them.[8] A woman's first name and her clothing thus become models for female authorship as matrilineal inheritance, a female word or code to compete with the patrilineal word that dictates, not just the rigid morality within the story, but also the laws of authorship that would prohibit women's writing as women for publication. Yet at the same time that this women's language is in this way distinguished from men's, its existence also clearly depends on the acceptance of women's marginal place in patriliny. In order to signify, this language assumes that first names and clothing are the only things a woman can pass on.

The two major plot-generating events of the story, Lizzie's figurative fall into sin and disgrace and Nanny's literal fall to her death, can be described in exactly the same words: the daughter falls because the love between mother and daughter is in conflict with, and is finally sacrificed to, the father's wishes. In the first case, Anne, speaking to Susan, gives this explicitly as the reason for Lizzie's fall: "I had a daughter once, my heart's darling. Her father thought I made too much on her, and that she'd grow marred staying at home; so he said she mun go among strangers, and learn to rough it. . . . That poor girl were led astray." Anne points out, moreover, that the harm to Lizzie after her fall could have been mitigated if only James had not forbidden Anne to seek her out in Manchester right away. The second case, Nanny's fall, repeats this situation. Susan and Nanny sleep together in an upstairs room. The night of Anne's visit, Susan's unfeeling and bankrupt father comes home late and drunk. Will initially became acquainted with this father "for his father's sake," which suggests a narrative resemblance between the two fathers; also like James Leigh, Susan's father has always objected to Nanny's presence because she draws Susan's attention away from him. Susan, entwined in Nanny's arms, is obliged to "unclose" them to go downstairs to help her stumbling father with the light. Nanny falls to her death because she awakes, misses Susan, sees that she is downstairs, and "dazzled with sleepiness," totters over the edge of the stairs. Thus, like her own mother, Nanny falls into the gap created by the conflict between the mother's love for her daughter and her obligations to the father's authority.

While the two falls stem from the same cause, it is worth noting that the second literalizes the first. While "fall" is a metaphor for Lizzie's illicit sexual behavior, on the model of the fall of Adam and Eve, Nanny literally tumbles downstairs, and while the metaphoric fall brought mortality to humankind, Nanny really dies on the spot. The daughter's literalization of the figure used for her mother recalls most immediately the linguistic situation in Gaskell's account in her diary of the relation between her second daughter's birth and her own foster mother's death, where Gaskell's figurative confinement in childbirth leads, not only to her children's confinement in small rooms, but also, she fears, to her mother's death. The Brontës' novels, as we have seen, explore the association between literalization and the death of a mother because of childbirth, the fear that in a patrilineal culture a child's birth obviates the life of the mother. We have also seen how this process finds linguistic embodiment in the literalization of figures. But in this story, it is not the mother but the child who dies, and indeed her death and replacement by her own mother exactly reverse the wording of the pivotal episode in *Wuthering Heights:* "About twelve o'clock . . . was born the Catherine you saw . . . and two hours after, the mother died" (chap. 16). Susan's call to the doctor, after Nanny falls, brings

Lizzie out of the urban shadows where she lurks, while Susan then fetches Anne to see if Nanny's mother is really Anne's daughter. Within a few lines Susan says to Anne, "Nanny is dead! . . . Her mother is come!" as if Nanny's ceased existence continues in Lizzie.

Lizzie becomes a daughter again through the death of her own daughter. When the doctor arrives intending to help Nanny, Lizzie, overcome by a fit of grief and guilt, has taken her place as the patient. Drugged, she goes to sleep gazing at her dead daughter; she wakes with her eyes fixed on her mother and in a pose—she "lay like one dead"—that duplicates that of her daughter. Lizzie first asks to see her child one more time, but then "she threw her arms round the faithful mother's neck, and wept there as she had done in many a childish sorrow. . . . Her mother hushed her on her breast; and lulled her as if she were a baby." That night, Anne and Lizzie "lay in each other's arms" just as earlier Lizzie goes to sleep holding her dead child and as Susan had used to sleep with Nanny's living arms twined around her. In this part of the story, there is general but not disturbing uncertainty as to who is daughter, who is mother, and of whom. Three mothers contemplate, in grief, the faces of two daughters, one who is dead, one who is "like one dead." After Lizzie falls asleep gazing at and "stroking the little face," Susan too, "gently extricating the dead child from its mother's arms . . . could not resist making her own quiet moan over her darling. She tried to learn off its little, placid face, dumb and pale before her." After this, Anne arrives, recognizes Lizzie, and repeating Lizzie's and Susan's gesture, "stood looking at her with greedy eyes, which seemed as though no gazing could satisfy their longing."

Although the plotting of the story represents a matrilineal inheritance of female experience only insofar as female life is twisted by patriarchal demands, the organizing relations here between mothers and daughters take place notably outside the patriarchal domain. Susan's father, having drunkenly slept through all the commotion, knows only of Nanny's fall; "as yet he was in ignorance of the watcher and the watched, who silently passed away the hours upstairs." Furthermore, the story closes with a telescoped account of their lives afterward, in which mother and daughter continue their stand outside patriarchy and patriliny. Whereas Susan and Will marry and live in the ancestral farm, Nanny is buried on the moor outside the churchyard of the "stern grandfather," and Anne and Lizzie live "in a cottage so secluded that, until you drop into the very hollow where it is placed, you do not see it." Anne, we remember, unnecessary to patriliny once she has borne a son, inherited the farm only for her lifetime, and it is her relative sense of freedom from the obligations of patriliny that allows her to leave the farm to search for Lizzie. The ending confirms her choice in favor of the daughter who was originally excluded by patrilineal property and to live voluntarily outside of it with her. But there is a new "Nanny," Will and Susan's daughter, and the two households love each other, so that exclusion is happily if paradoxically compatible with inclusion.

Indeed, though Anne and Lizzie's happiness was originally ruined by paternal interference, it is now made possible only by the same interference, since Nanny's death, caused by Susan's father's selfishness, was necessary to bring mother and daughter together again. Nanny is the "little, unconscious sacrifice, whose early calling-home had reclaimed her poor, wandering mother." Anne's and Lizzie's happiness, within the scope of the story, depends then, not just on their own love for one another, but emphatically on the situation of that love as something that has been excluded and damaged. The story is thus neither so alarmed by the notion of childbirth and of its consequences for writing as are the Brontës' novels nor so critical of paternal interference in reproduction as is *Frankenstein*. Like Shelley, Gaskell criticizes a father's inappropriate intervention, yet for her the results of such intervention are far from monstrous. At pains to accommodate both a paternal order's view of the proper relations within families and a more gynocentric view of mothers and daughters, the story strangely interweaves these seemingly incompatible strands by making their working out dependent upon each other. The paternal order is satisfied only by excluding Anne and Lizzie, while Anne and Lizzie are satisfied only by the consequences of their exclusion.

A moment we have already looked at typifies this strange interdependence, and also carries it explicitly to the level of language. When Anne Leigh at her suffering daughter's bedside repeats "every tender and merciful text she could remember," she is at once serving as transmitter of biblical words (subordinating her own lovingness to the authority of a higher word), departing from her husband's authority (in choosing these texts over sterner ones), and also speaking in a way of which the distant echo is Mrs. Ramsay's lulling speech at the bedside of her distraught daughter, speech in which sound and presence matter far more than referential meaning. This literal or nonsymbolic speech is very like the fortunate return of Lizzie's letter to its referent, Anne, a situation in which, again, the distancing of the referent in representational language gives way to the presence of the mother. Both the delivery of the letter and Anne's repetitions confirm the literal contact between mother and daughter. At the same time, both the delivery of the letter and Anne's soothing words acknowledge the constitutive presence within them of the exigencies of a paternal order. It is biblical passages that Anne repeats, passages that by preaching the forgiveness of sins define and reify sin in a way that is less forgiving than Anne's own stated wish simply to forget the past. It is Nanny who carries the letter, pinned to her clothes, from her mother to Susan,

and although it is only a coincidence that Anne reads the letter the very day of Nanny's death, the narrative sequence suggests a causal relation between the mother's happily correct decoding of a daughter's letter and the child's death, which results from a father's indifference. Carrying a letter from mother to daughter at once affirms and restores that forbidden relationship and brings paternal authority back to intervene again. Nanny is both the agent of the return of the letter to its maternal referent and the embodiment of women's victimization at the hands of men.

A number of Gaskell's other stories turn on the ambiguous consequences of a female character carrying a letter, an action to which Gaskell always calls attention by making its circumstances peculiarly elaborate. For example, in the search for Carson's murderer in *Mary Barton,* the crucial clue that proves to Mary that her father is the murderer is a valentine sent to her by Jem Wilson, onto a partially blank page of which she copies a poem called "God Help the Poor." Mary gives this paper to her father, who tears it in half and uses part as wadding in the gun with which he shoots Carson, leaving the rest in his pocket. Although the police never find any of this paper, as Michael Wheeler points out, in incorrectly pursuing Jem they are pursuing "the line of reasoning symbolically represented by the valentine greeting" (jealousy), while "the motive of the actual murderer is symbolically represented in the Banford poem written on the 'blank half-sheet'" (vengeance for the poor).[9] In this drama among men about men's passions, Mary is merely an intermediary, receiving and copying onto the letter and passing it on.

Yet it is crucial to the novel that both scraps of the paper once given to her father return to Mary, for it is in this way that she can protect her father as long as she does. The way in which it returns is as elaborately detailed, and as fraught with significance, as its transmission. One half Mary finds in her father's coat pocket, and she takes it back. Mary's Aunt Esther, her mother's sister who has unbeknownst to Mary become a prostitute, finds the other half, the gunwadding, on the road where Carson was shot. Reading a fragment of Mary's name and address and recognizing Jem Wilson's handwriting on the paper, Aunt Esther dresses herself to pretend respectability and visits Mary to return it to her. But the scene of Esther's arrival brings an absent figure back and complicates, by foregrounding female relationships, what has seemed to be a purely masculine drama only mediated by women. When Esther knocks on the door, Mary has been dreaming of "the happy times of long ago, and her mother came to her, and kissed her as she lay, and once more the dead were alive again" (chap. 20). She wakes to hear "the accents of her mother's voice . . . which she had sometimes tried to imitate when alone, with the fond mimicry of affection." She opens the door and "there, against the moonlight, stood a form, so closely resembling her dead mother, that Mary never doubted the identity." She exclaims, "Oh, mother! mother! You are come at last?" and falls into Aunt Esther's arms. For her part, Esther recognizes Mary as "so like [her] little girl" who died (ch. 14), yet she does all she can to keep her distance, not wanting the pure Mary to be "shocked and revolted" by her fall, which is never undone.

What matters here is Gaskell's insistent juxtaposition of Mary's reunion with her lost mother (in however illusory a way, for Mary believes it at the time) with the return of a letter that brings men's dangerous, murderous passions closer to home. Very much as in **"Lizzie Leigh,"** a reunion between daughter and mother is dependent upon the intervention between them of men's demands and violent actions. The return of the letter to its female referent both creates the meaning of a mother-daughter reunion and invokes a dangerous paternal power that threatens it. Moreover, Mary associates her mother with a soothing voice, and her way of trying to recall her in the past has been to imitate her accents, "with the fond mimicry of affection." In this repetition of the mother's sounds remains a trace of the literal or presymbolic language that, in the countermyth we have been tracing, mothers and children share and that daughters do not renounce, a language that is connected with the kind of meaning generated by the return of a letter to its referent. The restoration of the mother is equivalent to a language that does not require the absence of the referent. Both kinds of literal, mother-present language suggest a myth of a female language, a language, however, that is always and inextricably bound up with and interdependent upon paternal power and its determination of women's subordinate linguistic role as transmitters of men's words.

Before turning to examine in depth one final story, **"Lois the Witch,"** which offers a particularly striking version of the myth of the relation between women's linguistic subordination and the specificity of their language, we will pause briefly on Gaskell's *Life of Charlotte Brontë*. In this work, written after **"Lizzie Leigh"** and *Mary Barton* but before **"Lois the Witch,"** a woman's transmission of both men's and women's letters and words is not only one of the major themes but also the organizing principle of the book. The biography contains 350 of Brontë's letters, as well as numerous letters from Brontë's friends Ellen Nussey and Mary Taylor and even from Gaskell herself, together with such authoritative letters as Southey's advice to Brontë on "a woman's proper duties." When not actually transmitting letters, the biography is thematically concerned with transmission as women's duty. A number of people writing on the *Life* have noted Gaskell's way of turning Brontë into a perfect Victorian woman, while at the same time retaining the evidence of Brontë's rebelliousness in her accounts of

how hard it was to be good.[10] The use of the imagination has bad consequences, both selfishness and "coarseness" (the accusation often leveled against *Jane Eyre*), while the transmission of truth is both good and selfless. Writing here as a good woman herself, Gaskell reveals Brontë to be only partially successful at her own passive transmissions of others' words (e.g., at acting on Southey's advice not to write for publication). Yet at the same time, through her very docility as transmitter, through her identification of her goodness with Brontë's, Gaskell covertly suggests the drawbacks for any writer (including herself) in such a role.

One example we might select among many instances of Gaskell's working out her own priorities about writing through Brontë is her treatment of the end of the *Life* in relation to her treatment of Brontë's ending to *Villette*. According to Gaskell, Brontë told her that although "the idea of M. Paul Emanuel's death at sea was stamped on her imagination till it assumed the distinct force of reality," her father, who "disliked novels which left a melancholy impression upon the mind . . . requested her to make her hero and heroine . . . 'marry, and live happily ever after.'" Therefore, unable to alter the ending, "all she could do in compliance with her father's wish was so to veil the fate in oracular words, as to leave it to . . . her readers to interpret her meaning."[11] This startling and improbable revelation—that the ambiguity of *Villette*'s ending arises from the circumstances of her father's whim—may be no more than a little allegory of conflicting impulses within Brontë herself: on the one hand, her deep pessimism about the compatibility for women of work and love, and on the other, the patriarchal voice within, which, by way of the seductive fantasy of romantic love, would seal off the implications, disruptive both to the form of the novel and to the social fabric it emerges from, of leaving the heroine single at the end. Yet what matters here is that Gaskell calls attention to this incident as an example of Brontë's goodness; she does not question but endorses the notion of Brontë's putting her father's wishes on a level with the imperatives of her own imagination.

Gaskell's motives soon become clear. Six pages later, when she comes to the question of the last phase of her own story, the marriage of her heroine, she bends her narrative to another but analogous set of patriarchal wishes. Brontë's marriage, Gaskell writes, "requires delicate handling on my part, lest I intrude too roughly on what is most sacred to memory" (2:12). Again, further into her narrative of the marriage, she writes: "Of course, as I draw nearer to the years so recently closed, it becomes impossible for me to write with the same fulness of detail as I have hitherto not felt it wrong to use" (2:13). Although Gaskell hints at her awareness of Nicholls's inadequacy as a spiritual or intellectual match for Brontë, it is possible to accept at its face value her claim to believe in Brontë's marriage as "that short spell of exceeding happiness" (2:12), so strongly would she wish to believe it. Just as Gaskell earlier writes of Brontë's subordination of her imaginative integrity to her father's wishes, Gaskell herself distorts the imaginative truth of her ending, to meet Nicholls's expectations. Obviously editing from these final chapters anything Nicholls or Patrick Brontë would not have liked to see, anything derogatory to the marriage, Gaskell betrays at least part of the truth of Brontë's experience in order to please patriarchal wishes, exactly as she claims Brontë struggled to do with the ending of *Villette*. She identifies her female predicament with Brontë's on the basis of the identical interference in their work by masculine authority.

Gaskell's transmission of Brontë's letters, as well as obeying paternal authority and cementing an identification between the two women, also brought her a considerable amount of real trouble through the scandal caused by some of her allegations about living people, who protested through both epistolary and legal channels and caused Gaskell to withdraw the first and second editions of the *Life* and replace them with a third, revised, edition. In the first of these cases, Gaskell claimed as facts matters that Brontë protected by the decorum of fiction, the conditions of life at the Clergy Daughters' School at Cowan Bridge, the original of Lowood School in *Jane Eyre*. Yet Gaskell claimed only to be doing what she claimed Brontë had been doing, which was to tell the truth. Striving to find the right balance between two equally crucial feminine virtues, truth on the one hand and polite deference to such authorities as run schools on the other, Gaskell tries in her revisions to claim for Brontë both that "she herself would have been glad of an opportunity to correct the over-strong impression" made by her novel and that she had a "deep belief" in the factuality of her portrayal of the school, both of which claims are probably false.[12]

The other case, the one that actually forced the biography's withdrawal and revision, was a threat of libel that originated, like the Cowan Bridge controversy, in Gaskell's aim both to portray Brontë as a good and proper woman and to portray both herself and Brontë as truthful. Doing research for the *Life,* Gaskell discovered that some of the "coarseness" in Brontë's books originated in an actual experience, her unrequited and illicit love for her teacher in Belgium, M. Héger. She wished to exclude it entirely from the *Life,* on the grounds both of sparing Mr. Nicholls and of protecting Brontë's reputation, and therefore she shifted the blame for Charlotte's depression on returning from Brussels onto the dissolute behavior of Branwell Brontë. Branwell's behavior could in turn be blamed on his employer's wife (now the "depraved" Lady Scott), who, "bold and hardened," seduced him "in the very presence of her children" (1:13) and then, when her husband died, refused to keep her promise to

marry him. The sexual excesses of another woman thus fill the gap left by suppressing Charlotte's, yet eventually Gaskell's efforts to rectify Brontë's impropriety produce accusations against her own impropriety. The lustful Brontë becomes the adulterous Mrs. Robinson who in turn shifts the burden onto the slanderous Gaskell. Gaskell's efforts to make Brontë over into her own image as a good Victorian woman have the ironic effect of making Gaskell appear to be as "coarse" as Brontë. As in the stories, this identification between two women (although here not mother and daughter) exists in the transmission by one of the other's letters, and yet it also depends upon the appropriation of that transmission by official morality and the interference in that transmission by the law.

I would not argue that the plot of the myth of language is identical in the *Life,* "Lizzie Leigh," and *Mary Barton,* but only that Gaskell repeats a similar scenario often enough to suggest that it represents an important concern. If the sequence of these texts' presentations of this scenario can be read as a progression, it is that of a diminishment of the pleasure to be taken in the reunion of mother and daughter (or identification between two women that I have suggested forms an analogy to this reunion in the *Life*), simultaneous with an increase in the cost of this connection. For example, while **"Lizzie Leigh"** joyously reunites a mother with a "fallen" daughter, whose fall is as a consequence mitigated, *Mary Barton* embraces only the illusion of her mother and the fallen woman who enables this illusion is never recovered, and Brontë and Gaskell share an identity only at the expense of the tarnishing of that identity. **"Lois the Witch,"** written shortly after the *Life* and its attendant sorrows, restages the earlier stories' peculiar interdependence between the language shared between mother and daughter and the paternal, symbolic order from which it is excluded and by which it is threatened and appropriated. **"Lois the Witch,"** however, in keeping with the gradual darkening of Gaskell's vision, restages the earlier stories only from the point of view of what is lost. That is, rather than being resolved by a reunion of mother and daughter, this story begins with their irrevocable separation and traces the consequences of that separation both for life and for letters. The daughter, still acting on the terms defining her relation to her mother, yet abandoned by her mother's death to unmitigated patriarchal appropriation and interference, experiences as catastrophic the collision between these two orders, the mother's nonsymbolic discourse and the patriarchal law to which she is obliged to submit.

Lois, whose parents die as the story opens, leaves England for Salem in the late seventeenth century and is hanged there as a witch. She travels to Salem by her mother's "dying wish" for her to live with her mother's brother and his family. In this gloomy story, each of several episodes of letter carrying is both unnecessary and peculiarly highlighted by details, so that these episodes stand out as requiring more explanation than is offered by the simple demands of plot and character development. The first of these letters is the letter Lois's mother dictates on her deathbed to her brother, and as she starts her trip, Lois carries not only this letter but also a letter from her dead father to the captain who will give her passage to Boston. Framing the scene of the mother's dying words are two assertions of Lois's faithfulness to the letter. First, "Lois swallowed her tears down till the time came for crying, and acted upon her mother's words."[13] The mother dictates the letter and asks Lois to promise that she will go to Salem at once: "'The money our goods will bring—the letter thy father wrote to Captain Holdernesse, his old schoolfellow—thou knowest all I would say—my Lois, God bless thee!' Solemnly did Lois promise; strictly she kept her word." The mother's assumption that "thou knowest all I would say" suggests that when Lois "acted upon her mother's words" and "strictly . . . kept her word," she is not simply taking dictation but translating intentions into words.

The letter Lois writes at dictation follows a circuitous course that appears to be unnecessarily particularized. When Lois arrives in Boston, "the letter of her dying mother was sent off to Salem, meanwhile, by a lad going thither," to prepare her new family for her arrival. When Lois reaches Salem, however, she finds that the lad had made an inefficient letter carrier, and that she herself, replacing representation with its referent, arrives before the letter does. Her aunt receives her very coldly. The captain tries to comfort Lois by telling her "if the letter had but been delivered, thou wouldst have had a different kind of welcome," and he takes some pains to recover the letter and punish the boy. The episode, however, is unnecessary, as it is clear that Lois is unwelcome, with or without the letter, for her aunt is not hostile because she doubts Lois's identity but because she hates what Lois represents. Lois's father was an Anglican minister, and her uncle left England and broke from his family as a Puritan. If the straying of the letter is immaterial to Lois's cold reception, why does Gaskell devote such attention to it, to the extent of giving the letter carrier a peculiarly resonant name, Elias Wellcome?

In arriving before her mother's letter and substituting for it, Lois begins a series of literalizations of women's words that prove disastrous. For much the same reasons that Eliot situates *Romola* in fifteenth-century Florence, because that world takes literally what Victorian England takes figuratively, Gaskell uses Puritan Salem as a literalizing version of England. As Lois crosses from the Anglican to the Puritan country, she also crosses from a world of relatively figurative understanding to a world that takes everything literally. (Her ocean passage even literalizes the figure of metaphor, "carry across.") As Lois puts her mother's inten-

tions into practice and as she carries her letter, she literalizes her mother's words, replacing the figures of the letter with their referent, herself. While in **"Lizzie Leigh,"** or even in *Mary Barton,* this co-presence of the letter and its referent signals the happy reunion of mother and daughter, here it points to the absence of the mother and it also, by virtue of the narrative sequence, is arranged to appear to cause the hostility of a patriarchal culture.

Lois also carries two other sets of women's words across the ocean, and in doing so carries them out literally. On her deathbed, directly after dictating the letter to her brother, Lois's mother also expresses a wish: "'Oh, Lois, would that thou wert dying with me! The thought of thee makes death sore!' Lois comforted her mother more than herself, poor child, by promises to obey her dying wishes to the letter." The mother's wish for Lois to die, very strange if taken literally, is quite clearly figurative in context; that is, her words express her love for Lois, her sorrow at parting from her, but not a real wish for Lois to die. Her words are also like Mrs. Ramsay's words at Cam's bedside, which matter not for what they signify representationally but for the love and presence they guarantee. However, Lois's "promises to obey her dying wishes to the letter" have a distinctly ominous ring. In context, "dying wishes" refers back to the letter for the uncle, but to fulfill a wish "to the letter" is to fulfill it literally, and to obey "dying wishes to the letter" is to obey the wish that she will die, that is, to take literally her mother's figurative "Oh, Lois, would that thou wert dying with me." And this ominous suggestion is reinforced a few sentences later by the echo, "strictly she kept her word."

In addition to her mother's words, Lois bears and will carry out another woman's words, the curse of a witch, and the unambiguous negativity of these words helps to clarify the significance of the mother's dying wishes. At a dinner in Boston before Lois reaches Salem, the subject of witches comes up, and Lois tells a story, from when she was four years old, of her own encounter with a witch. Although Lois withholds judgment, she seems half to understand what the reader assumes (but what none of the Puritans sees at all), that this "witch" was nothing but a poor, old recluse, the scapegoat on whom the town chose to blame a series of local illnesses. Out walking with her nurse, Lois says, she saw a silent crowd by the river; they stop and look,

and I saw old Hannah in the water, her grey hair all streaming down her shoulders, and her face bloody and black with the stones and the mud they had been throwing at her, and her cat tied round her neck. I hid my face, I know, as soon as I saw the fearsome sight, for her eyes met mine as they were glaring with fury—poor, helpless, baited creature!—and she caught the sight of me, and cried out, "Parson's wench, parson's wench, yonder, in thy nurse's arms, thy dad hath never tried for to save me, and none shall save thee when thou art brought up for a witch." Oh! the words rang in my ears, when I was dropping asleep, for years after. I used to dream that I was in that pond, all men hating me with their eyes because I was a witch.

This dream comes true, with the exception that she dies not by drowning but by hanging. Although as a child Lois believed the witch's words and although in England witches were indeed killed, nonetheless, growing up in England, where people understand things relatively figuratively, involves learning that such words deserve pity, not fear or hatred. The curse was effective in frightening the child, but it never to occurs to Lois to believe in it now as a performative that could actually cause her to die as a witch.

Lois's listeners, however, take both the story (the identification of the old woman as a witch) and the curse within it literally, as words that could have literal effects. All such transfers from England to New England involve a similar shift from a relatively figurative understanding of words to a relatively literal one. The New England Puritans, who claim to read the Bible more literally than the "popish" Anglicans, excuse their genocide of the native population by their belief "that these Red Indians are indeed the evil creatures of whom we read in Holy Scripture. . . . Holy Scripture speaks of witches and wizards, and of the power of the Evil One in desert places." One "godly" old man upbraids those who would "speak lightly" of Lois's story and insists, "the hellish witch might have power from Satan to infect her mind, she being yet a child, with the deadly sin."

While the story calls attention to the way in which a woman's words can be taken literally and are literalized, it also calls attention to the distorting presence in these words of patriarchal law. The witch would not be a witch in the first place if a culture fearful of otherness did not brand her peculiarities as crimes, and she would not be cursing Lois in particular if she were not the daughter of the minister of the patriarchal church that excoriates her. Women's words might have power, especially in the relation of presence between mother and daughter, but the intervention of a jealous and disapproving paternal law turns that power into a punishment both of speaker and of listener. The story of the witch makes this intervention explicit and suggests that the same law has intervened as well between Lois and her mother, in the passage from the mother's loving intentions and words to their murderous fulfillment.

After Lois has become a part of her uncle's unfriendly family, she tells her cousin Faith, who grieves over an unrequited love, about another set of supernatural beliefs, the Halloween customs and "innocent ways of divination," such as eating an apple facing a mirror, "by which laughing, trembling English maidens sought to see the form of their future husbands." Telling these stories, Lois is characterized by the narrator as "half believing, half incredulous." That is, she takes these stories at least in part figuratively. But her younger cousin, Prudence, New England born, responds to them as entirely literal compacts with supernatural powers: "Cousin Lois may go out and meet Satan by the brookside, if she will." Pleased with the attention she receives, Prudence works up a fit of imitation terror:

> "Take her away, take her away!" screamed Prudence. "Look over her shoulder—her left shoulder—the Evil One is there now, I see him stretching over for the half-bitten apple. . . . "Faith shall stay by me, not you, wicked English witch!"

It is in this manner that the accusation of witchcraft begins, through New Englanders taking literally what the English girl means at least half figuratively.

It is significant that Lois is first accused of witchcraft in the context of a supposed ability to envision her future husband, for her formal accusation turns on the use of the word "bewitch" to refer both to witchcraft and to ordinary sexual attraction. After Lois has told her story about the witch, unaware of how literally it will be taken, her hostess responds, in an effort to shift the discussion to safer, figurative ground, "'And I don't doubt but what the parson's bonny lass has bewitched many a one since, with her dimples and her pleasant ways. . . .' 'Aye, aye,' said the captain, 'there's one under her charms in Warwickshire who will never get the better of it, I'm thinking.'" While Lois has indeed figuratively bewitched a young man back in England, the case against her develops from two instances in which this figurative kind of bewitching is taken literally, as if she had cast spells on the men who fall in love with her. Two jealous women make use of the witch trial to get rid of Lois as a rival, by enforcing the word's shift to its literal meaning. At a public gathering following the hanging as a witch of an Indian woman servant, Hota, Prudence, jealous of the public attention received by the girls who claim to be bewitched by Hota, stages a convulsive fit that she claims is "caused" by "Witch Lois." But though it is Prudence who thus first formally accuses Lois, she is prompted by her sister Faith, who is jealous of Lois; and the damning fact that their mother, jealous on another score, refuses to speak up for Lois's good character, contributes materially to Lois's condemnation.

Aunt Hickson is jealous because Lois has "bewitched" her son Manasseh, a secretly mad, or possibly visionary, young man who has fallen in love with Lois or, as he puts it, has heard a voice telling him "Marry Lois! Marry Lois!" Aunt Hickson has grander plans for her son, who after the death of Lois's uncle is the head of her prosperous household, and she resents his choice of a poor relation. As Manasseh attempts earnestly but disconnectedly to defend Lois and Aunt Hickson realizes that his madness is now embarrassing public knowledge, she mentally elaborates proofs of Lois's witchcraft, which would excuse his madness, by confusing literal and figurative senses of "bewitch": "How he followed her about, and clung to her, as under some compulsion of affection! And over all reigned the idea that, if he were indeed suffering from being bewitched, he was not mad, and might again assume the honourable position he had held in the congregation and in the town." As a result, Lois is tried for having "bewitched" both Manasseh and Prudence.

Faith's jealousy of Lois's ability to "bewitch" comes from the second of the story's peculiarly foregrounded episodes of letter carrying, this one even more conspicuously fabricated than the first. It is Faith who prompts Prudence to see Lois as "Witch Lois": in the act of purloining Lois's cloak (to attend illicitly the hanging of Hota), Prudence trips and falls, and Faith remarks, "Take care, another time, how you meddle with a witch's things." Faith resents Lois because of a scene she has just witnessed between Lois and the man she unrequitedly loves, Pastor Nolan, a scene, however, that Faith herself inexplicably arranges. The morning of the hanging, Faith has asked Lois to deliver to Nolan a letter that "concerns life and death," implying that the letter contains information that would prove Hota innocent. The story offers no reason why Faith neither delivers the letter herself, nor simply tells Nolan, or why, if Faith can't deliver the letter, Lois must. Lois searches Nolan out, but he, depressed by the sinfulness of the "witch," and infatuated with Lois, is absorbed in his gloom and then in the relief afforded by the sight of her "pure, grave face," and he neglects to open the letter. Just as he is putting his hand on Lois's shoulder, "with an action half paternal," and whispering to her, Faith appears and, furious with jealousy, takes back the unopened letter, with sarcastic allusions to the thematic pun on the word bewitch: "Let [Hota] die, and let all other witches look to themselves; for there be many kinds of witchcraft abroad."

The scene seems almost unnecessary. Though the story does require some occasion for Faith's jealousy, such a need hardly justifies this elaborately plotted and inscrutable scene of letter carrying. It functions in something of the same way as the earlier episode of delivering her mother's letter. Lois herself takes the place of the letter, so that the act of delivering it becomes itself a message, as referent replaces representation. Furthermore, the scene makes clear what we also saw in Romola's transmissions of words, which is that to bear a word is also to be transformed into the object of a man's vision, for bearing a word is a daughter's reproduction of the discourse of her mother, but a re-

production that is appropriated by patriarchal demands and by the androcentric view that any mother is the literal and an object.

What seems to have happened prior to the delivery of this letter is that Faith has been scheming to denounce Pastor Tappan, the rival of Pastor Nolan, whom Tappan has driven out of Salem. Faith and the Hicksons' Indian servant, Nattee, together with Hota, who is Nattee's friend and who works for Tappan, arrange for certain "devilish" accidents, such as crashing dishes, to occur in the Tappan household, presumably in order to pin on Pastor Tappan an accusation of complicity with the devil. The scheme, however, backfires and Hota takes the blame, because Tappan's authority makes it impossible for his community to consider him dangerous, and transformed from potential criminal into victim, he appears even holier than before. Faith's letter to Nolan presumably exonerates Hota in some way, perhaps also placing the blame back on Pastor Tappan. However, when she sees Nolan's interest in Lois, she abandons her interest in discrediting Tappan, because she has lost her case with Nolan anyway. In carrying Faith's letter, Lois is continuing to literalize her mother's and the English witch's "dying wishes," in that her delivery of the letter, when she "bewitches" Nolan, will contribute materially to her eventual execution. She is also literalizing the intentions of the letter's sender, if not in precisely the manner Faith had in mind. Though at first it seems that Faith's intentions (to capture Nolan) are reversed, ultimately she does accomplish her aim of ridding herself of a rival, Lois instead of Tappan.

Lois's transformation into the object of a man's vision is a necessary part of her execution as a witch, for it is precisely the passage from figurative to literal that makes her a witch; and her being an object is inseparable from her being perceived by Salem as an other. It is no accident that the three witches accused and executed in the story are not only all women but also foreigners, outsiders, doubly other with respect to the Puritan majority. That Lois is British-born and popish puts her in the same category with the Indians Nattee and Hota. Lois's ability to "bewitch" young men derives from her otherness, the contrast her pink and white English charm makes to the sober grey tones of New England. Part of the function of witch-hunting as Gaskell depicts it is the removal of anomalies; Pastor Tappan, for example, is constitutively not a witch because he is part of the definition of the community that defines itself in opposition to others.

Ironically, Lois's feminine otherness, with its dangerous charms, derives from her loyalty to patriarchal men. Her loyalty to the king stems from her love for her father, preacher at Barford, and the Hicksons' hatred is properly for that father, who split with Ralph Hickson when he rejected these hereditary loyalties. It is because of the religious differences of two men that Lois's mother led a divided, unhappy life, and Lois inherits her mother's position as the ground on which their dispute is enacted. And the dying English witch curses Lois because of her father's role in her persecution. The syntax of the story seems to equate her being other than patriarchal figures like Tappan with her being other because of a patriarchal figure like her father, because she is merely the medium through which their hatreds work. Though she seems, in dying as a witch, to be literalizing her mother's and the English witch's dying wishes, by carrying their letters and words to a place that takes everything literally, what lies behind these curses, what makes them curses, and what she is really carrying out, is the patriarchal prohibition of female difference that victimizes them as much as it does her. In a culture like that of Salem, a culture in which women's speech is suspect, women's words are constitutively curses. Patriarchal authority lies behind the cursedness of women's words and the tendency of women's words to each other to be distorted into curses. They are not cursing each other so much as trying to speak to each other, yet with a speech that is appropriated to do the work of patriarchal words. And not only are women's words distorted in this way, but even their thoughts. Lois begins to fear, after her accusation, that she may indeed be a witch, because of the chance that her unhappy feelings about her foster family may "have had devilish power given to them by the father of evil, and, all unconsciously to herself, have gone forth as active curses into the world." A woman is made to feel that for her feelings to matter at all, in a culture that views them as illegitimate, would be for them to have satanic powers.

This situation is underscored by the one quotation from romantic poetry in the story, the narrator's words for Nolan's feelings for Lois at the crucial moment of their meeting over Faith's letter, under Faith's gaze. Depressed by his view of Hota's otherness as "pollution" and gazing at Lois's "pure, grave face," "faith in earthly goodness came over his soul in that instant, 'and he blessed her unaware.'" Why, to depict this moment, which combines elements of erotic attraction and religious confirmation, does Gaskell choose these words from Coleridge's "The Rime of the Ancient Mariner"? Nolan's blessing contributes to Lois's curse: the scene leads to Faith's betrayal of Lois. Even more immediately than its effect on Lois's life, Nolan's "bless[ing] her unaware" leads directly to Hota's death, for it is because his attention has shifted from Hota to Lois that Nolan neglects his opportunity to exonerate the Indian. The transformation of a blessing into a curse or curses exactly reverses the process to which the line originally refers in "The Ancient Mariner," where the Mariner's outgoing love for the sea snakes brings about his release from the curse brought on by shooting the albatross.[14] Morally complex as "The Ancient Mariner" is, Gaskell reverses its temporary exoneration of the Mariner in order to condemn covertly what speaks

through the pastor. In the largest sense, the blessings of a patriarchal religion can never be more than curses for women who are outsiders, and in this sense Nolan—kind, innocent, and himself eventually victimized—is no different from the tyrannical Tappan.[15] The beneficial effect of the blessing of the sea snakes depends on the challenge to human sympathy created by an inherent ugliness. Not only are they at first "slimy things" on a "slimy sea," but also the rotting sea in which they swim "like a witch's oils, / Burnt green, and blue and white."[16] These blessed witch's oils are recalled in Nolan's blessing of Gaskell's witch, Lois, and remind us that in the androcentric logic of Coleridge's poem or in that of the Puritan ministers that Gaskell criticizes here, the purpose of the blessing has a beneficial effect, not on what is blessed (with its female associations of witches and sliminess), but on him who blesses. Nolan's blessing, by way of Coleridge, blesses only himself, while it obligates Lois to be a witch.

In the same way, Lois's being the object of Manasseh's half erotic and half divine vision hurts rather than helps her case. Manasseh's divinely inspired vision hurts Lois even more directly than Nolan's "blessing," for his crazed and seemingly blasphemous defense of Lois contributes to turning the congregation against her. His final vision makes blessing and condemnation dependent upon each other. He sees angels carrying an unspecified "her" to the beautiful land of Beulah; the vision closes, "I hear her pleading there for those on earth who consented to her death. O Lois! pray also for me!" (His public defense of her rests on the argument that, if divine visions foretell her execution as a witch, she can't be a witch, because she is part of God's plans.) Like the Coleridge quotation, this divine word, carried into the story, brings with it only Lois's further victimization. Likewise, Lois's own religious utterances bring her only increased trouble. Her understandably pausing slightly over the words, "as we forgive those who trespass against us" in a recitation of the Lord's prayer confirms the proof of her witchcraft. Visited in her jail by Aunt Hickson, who is now firmly convinced of her guilt, Lois prays, "God have mercy on you and yours," but Grace cries out, "Witches' prayers are read backwards. I spit at thee."

Just before the execution, Lois comforts her new cellmate, Nattee, and herself by reciting "the marvellous and sorrowful story" of the crucifixion, but the "blessed words" have only an ironic relation to her situation as victim of an entirely purposeless sacrifice. Indeed, the scene is dark parody of a familiar one. When Nattee is first thrown into her cell, Lois "held her in her arms" and "tended" her, and her recitation of biblical passages recalls Anne Leigh's repetitions to Lizzie, in which the soothing sound of the motherly voice is more important than what is repeated: "As long as she spoke, the Indian woman's terror seemed lulled; but the instant she paused, for weariness, Nattee cried out afresh. . . . And then Lois went on." The next day, at the gallows, when "they took Nattee from her arms" to hang Lois first, "she gazed wildly around, stretched out her arms as if to some person in the distance, who was yet visible to her, and cried out once, . . . 'Mother!'" Like the reunion in **"Lizzie Leigh,"** this reunion of mother and daughter is indeed made possible through the intervention of patriarchal authority. The exorbitant cost, however, suggests that Gaskell now views with pessimism her desire to accommodate that authority as well as women's pleasure. The scene recalls, too, the dedication of Gaskell's diary about her daughter, where she suggests that their earliest and closest relation, marred by the symbolic order's requirement that language have meaning only in the absence of one or the other, can be recovered only in heaven, where "we may meet again to renew the dear and tender tie of Mother and Daughter." If mothers' and daughters' love and the nonsymbolic or literal language it includes and thematizes require this severe intervention by the Law of the Father, their accomplishment holds out little promise to those who read and write as mothers or daughters. As the carrying of the mother's words from figurative to literal, not inherently harmful, becomes distorted into a curse by patriarchal law and by subordination to the task of carrying the letter of men's texts, Gaskell exposes her own discomfort at the habitual subordination, which a Victorian woman cannot help but impose upon herself, of her own word to androcentric ones.

As a part of this criticism, just as she reverses the meaning of Coleridge's line when putting it into her story, she also reverses the usual meaning of the patriarchal "line," that a woman's virtuous behavior is rewarded, a line that many of her other stories and most of her novels apparently promulgate. The most conspicuous feature of **"Lois the Witch"** is that Lois, despite her virtue, is not only not rewarded but is punished. The story makes no sense, morally speaking, and that *is* its sense.

Yet despite Gaskell's anger, or perhaps in keeping with its covertness, the story ends on a conciliatory note, both in terms of its characterization of the patriarchal witch-hunters and in terms of its relation to the female author's duty to transmit others' words. The story ends with long quotations from actual documents, the declarations of confession and regret signed by the Salem witch-hunters many years later. The reader is reminded that, not unlike *Romola* or even, in a way, *The Life of Charlotte Brontë,* this story is historical fiction. Although the protagonists are invented, the events are authentic. Cotton Mather himself appears in the scene of Lois's public accusation, and at least two central characters, the two rival pastors, are "taken" from Gaskell's main historical source.[17] Despite the invention of Lois's story, much of the story is arguably devoted to translating history into terms that make

learning pleasurable. In the manuscript, the long verbatim quotations from historical documents, which themselves include scriptural quotations, were, like some of Brontë's letters in the manuscript of the *Life,* copied out by another writer, probably Marianne or Meta. This situation not only defines the story as a good woman's passive transcription but also suggests that Gaskell trained her own daughters to value copying men's words over speaking for oneself, or with one's mother. Although this ending raises the possibility of many of the same ambiguities we found in Eliot's balancing of the claims of fiction and history and of invention and transmission in *Romola,* it does seem to apologize for the rest of the story's resentment of the consequences of women's transmission of men's words, and it restores the author to a safer position as bearer of a patriarchal word.

The story's ambivalence as to whether the daughter is the father's or the mother's reappears in another story written about the same time, and while this second story does not substantially change our picture of Gaskell, it is worth looking at very briefly, if only to show how pervasive are the issues I have been presenting, and also because it introduces an image central to *Wives and Daughters.* **"The Poor Clare,"** set like **"Lois"** in a day and place of a more literal religious belief than Gaskell's own, also centers on a woman's curse that harms her daughter by way of the interference between them of powerful men. Like **"Lois"** too, in contrast to **"Lizzie Leigh,"** it begins with a daughter's separation from her mother and ends, not with their reunion, but rather with the mother's silence. The central figure of the story is the mother, Bridget Fitzgerald, a respected servant at a manor house in Ireland. Although both Bridget and her daughter Mary are "the ruling spirits of the household," against her mother's will, Mary "not unfrequently rebelled. She and her mother were too much alike to agree. There were wild quarrels between them, and wilder reconciliations."[18] This rebellious daughter finally leaves home for a job abroad, unsure to the last whether she wants to leave her mother. Predictably, Mary's letters stop just at the point when she says she is about to marry a "gentleman" of "superior . . . station and fortune." Bridget devotes her life first sorrowfully to waiting for her daughter's return, then to searching for her in Europe. On her return, alone, to England, she earns "the dreadful reputation of a witch" for her half-crazed manner and for her ability to affect people's fortunes by her words and wishes. Knowing that her "wishes are terrible," she fears that her wish "that [Mary's] voyage might not turn out well," which she meant only as a wish for Mary to return home, has been fulfilled. Of her wishes she says, "their power goes beyond my thought." One day a "gentleman" riding by her home shoots Mary's dog, now Bridget's only companion. She curses him: "Hear me, ye blessed ones! . . . He has killed the only creature that loved me—the dumb beast that I loved. . . . You shall live to see the creature you love best, and who alone loves you . . . become a terror and a loathing to all, for this blood's sake."

At this point, the story shifts to several years later and a different scene. The narrator, a young land agent sent to locate Bridget because of an unexpected inheritance, not only finds Bridget and learns her story, but also, in a nearby town, meets and falls in love with Lucy, a beautiful and melancholy woman who has a terrible secret. Lucy turns out to be Bridget's granddaughter, Mary's daughter, and her father turns out to be the man Bridget cursed. Mary has since died through this man's "wilful usage," and Lucy, the creature her father loves best, has become the victim of the curse. "Pure and holy" as she is, Lucy has a monstrous double who impersonates her to do "wicked" things "such as shame any modest woman." This "loathsome demon," whose relation to Lucy resembles that of Bertha Mason to Jane Eyre, is clearly as sexual as Lucy is "pure," for it has "tried to suggest wicked thoughts and to tempt wicked actions; but she, in her saintly maidenhood, [has] passed on undefiled." And when the narrator sees the double, his "eyes were fascinated" and he finds her expression "mocking and voluptuous." When they visit Bridget to seek a release from the curse, this powerful woman is herself terrified by Lucy's double, for the power of her wishes "goes beyond [her] thought."

The story exemplifies the literal power of a woman's word, a power beneficial when inherent in a mother's and daughter's presymbolic relation, but a power that is twisted to evil ends by the intervention of paternal authority between mother and daughter. Mary leaves Bridget ambivalently seeking relief from the intensity of their identification, a relief promised by marriage, but it is because of the man who holds out this promise to her that Mary dies and that Bridget's powerful words have their devastating effect on her own granddaughter. Her horror when she learns that she has cursed the "flesh of my flesh" is the emotional center of the narrative.

The curse takes the form it does because a doubling, or splitting, of a daughter's self makes concrete her ambivalent view of her parents once she has been invited to leave her mother and enter the father's law, the symbolic order. That Lucy first sees her double in a mirror recalls those frequent occasions in the Brontës' novels when the heroine sees herself in a mirror divided from herself and forshadowing her own death. It is a mother's curse on her daughter to divide her daughter's loyalty between herself and the father, between love of and identification with the mother and the desire to separate and enter the father's law. The figure of the mirror, as the agent through which this division is revealed, suggests the helplessness of the mother, who, in patriarchal culture, has already been frozen into a passive reflector of male selves. (In this story, it is not Bridget but Mary who plays the role of the mother killed by male vanity and therefore helpless to save her daughter.) That the daughter is split, or doubled, along the lines of her present or absent sexuality marks the point at which the daughter responds to the father's appeal: it is through her own desire for difference that the father seduces the daughter to leave her mother and enter his law. It is not so much that Lucy is one parent's child while her sexualized double is the other's, but rather that the splitting itself is determined by the antithetical appeal of mother and father.

But the story is not over: Bridget, seeking to release her granddaughter from the curse, travels to Belgium to enter the penitent order of the Poor Clares, hoping, by piety, self-abasement, and good works, to earn forgiveness for "the sin of witchcraft." All along, Bridget has held the belief that the Virgin Mary helps her. She has a shrine to the Virgin in her home and is seen praying to it first for Mary's return and later for the double's disappearance. But Mary is clearly the goddess only of more docile mothers, mothers who more willingly subordinate their wishes and their motherhood to men's requirements. Although for the narrator, as for the New England Puritans of **"Lois the Witch,"** witchcraft and popery go hand in hand, witchcraft as a form of female power is a sin in Catholicism. For Bridget, the significant feature of the Poor Clares must be the vow of silence they take: only if dying of starvation may these women communicate a need, and then only by ringing a little bell. Yet even after so totally yielding her voice up to the father's law, Bridget cannot save Lucy until she subordinates herself even further, to the man she has most reason to hate, Lucy's father, who is conveniently wounded in a riot in Antwerp and whom Bridget tends in her own dying moments. Only then is the curse lifted.

Notes

[1] A. W. Ward, introduction to *Mary Barton* (1848; reprint, Knutsford Edition, London: Smith and Elder and Co., 1906), 1: xxvii–xxviii. Although I have not been able to trace Ward's source for this story—all Gaskell's letters from the time of William's death to 1847 were destroyed at her wish—it has been accepted as fact by Gaskell's readers. Gaskell's most judicious recent critic, Angus Easson, repeating the story, states that "whatever part the children played in her writing . . . only one seems responsible for starting her writing, and that, tragically, her only son, William" (*Elizabeth Gaskell* [London: Routledge and Kegan Paul, 1979], p. 36). Quotations from *Mary Barton* will be from the Knutsford edition, cited by chapter.

[2] Gaskell gives the epigraph in the original German of J. L. Uhland; the translation is from the Knutsford

edition, p. xlix:

> Take, good ferryman, I pray
> Take a triple fare to-day:
> The twain who with me touched the strand
> Were visitants from spirit-land.

[3] Printed in the introduction to the Knutsford edition, pp. xxvi-xxvii.

[4] Gaskell, *Diary,* p. 19. For detailed discussion of this passage in the context of the diary, see chapter 7.

[5] Elizabeth Gaskell, "Lizzie Leigh" (1850); reprinted in *Cousin Phyllis and Other Tales* (Oxford: Oxford University Press, 1981), pp. 1-32.

[6] "Michael," lines 244-45, in *The Poetical Works of William Wordsworth* 2:88.

[7] See Showalter, [Elaine,] *A Literature of Their Own* [: *British Women Novelists from Brontë to Lessing* (Princeton. Princeton University Press, 1977)], p. 92. The example she gives is the debate over the sex of the author of *Jane Eyre.*

[8] I am indebted to Karen Matthews for her account of this publication history and for her analysis of this issue in "Lizzie Leigh," in a paper written for a seminar at Yale in 1978. Annette Kolodny discusses a woman writer's use of the secret female code of domestic detail in "A Map for Rereading; or, Gender and the Interpretation of Literary Texts," *New Literary History* 11 (1980): 451-67.

[9] Michael Wheeler, *The Art of Allusion in Victorian Fiction* (London: Macmillan, 1979), p. 50.

[10] For example, Inga-Stina Ewbank writes of Gaskell's idealization of Brontë (*Their Proper Sphere: A Study of The Brontë Sisters as Early Victorian Female Novelists* [Cambridge: Harvard University Press, 1966], p. 47). Margaret Ganz writes, "her material would be made subservient to her desire, to present Charlotte's life to the world as a moral exemplum," yet Ganz also points out that by quoting Brontë's letters at such length, Gaskell preserves the evidence of Brontë's less conventional side (*Elizabeth Gaskell: The Artist in Conflict* [New York: Twayne, 1969], pp. 182-97; quotation p. 187). Showalter writes of Gaskell's portrayal of Brontë as a "tragic heroine" (*A Literature of Their Own,* p. 106). [Rachel] Brownstein writes of the "smugness" and "slyness" of the revelation of Brontë's struggles to be good, which reveal a discrepancy between Brontë the perfect woman and Brontë the improper and visionary rebel (*Becoming a Heroine* [: *Reading about Women in Novels* (Harmondsworth: Penguin, 1984)], pp. 160-62).

[11] Gaskell, *Life of Charlotte Brontë* [(London, 1857)] 2:11. Quotations from the *Life* are from this text of the first edition, cited by volume and chapter numbers.

[12] These quotations are from the third edition's revised version of vol. 1, chap. 4, included in the appendix to the Penguin edition.

[13] Elizabeth Gaskell, "Lois the Witch" (1859); reprinted in *Cousin Phyllis and Other Tales,* pp. 105-93. All other quotations will be from this edition.

[14] See Geoffrey Hartman's reading of the interchangeability of blessing and cursing in "The Ancient Mariner," in *Saving the Text* (Baltimore: Johns Hopkins University Press, 1981), pp. 99, 131, 164-65.

[15] In the manuscript from this point on, Gaskell continually mistakes one pastor's name for the other's and has to go back and make corrections. The manuscript is in the Houghton Library at Harvard University. Though the Oxford text prints Tappan's name as Tappau, it is clear from the manuscript that this is a misreading.

[16] "The Rime of the Ancient Mariner," lines 125-26, 129-30, in *The Complete Works of Samuel Taylor Coleridge,* ed. E. H. Coleridge (London: Oxford University Press, 1912), p. 191.

[17] Rev. Charles W. Upham, *Lectures on Witchcraft* (Boston, 1831).

[18] Elizabeth Gaskell, "The Poor Clare," in *Round the Sofa* (1859); Knutsford Edition, London: Smith and Elder and Co., 1906), 5:329-90.

Patsy Stoneman (essay date 1987)

SOURCE: "Two Nations and Separate Spheres: Class and Gender in Elizabeth Gaskell's Work," in *Elizabeth Gaskell,* The Harvester Press, 1987, pp. 45-67.

[*In the following essay, Stoneman argues that Gaskell's writing, rather than reflecting the bifurcation of society along class and gender lines, tends to blur the sharpness of these distinctions through role reversal, the behavior of domestic servants, and the description of the "inhuman possibilities of authority."*]

The society in which Elizabeth Gaskell lived and wrote was intersected horizontally by class and vertically by gender divisions. Critics have created a divided image of her work by focusing on one or other of these axes—'industrial' or 'domestic'—and we can simply, but radically, revise this view by considering their interaction. I want to begin by drawing examples from Elizabeth Gaskell's lesser-known fiction, in which the issues are often very clear, but which critics have less completely labelled and categorised; this discussion will then serve as a context for a rereading of the familiar works in subsequent chapters.

What emerges from her work as a whole is that, at subsistence level, gender divisions are blurred: women exercise responsibility; men give basic nurturance. In the middle class, ideology heightens differentiation, producing infantilised women and authoritarian men.

1 Working Women

Because Elizabeth Gaskell's studies of working-class life are read as 'industrial' novels, criticism has focused on factory-workers like John Barton and Nicholas Higgins. Her work as a whole, however, highlights working women—not just factory workers like Bessy Higgins but seamstresses, milliners, washerwomen, 'chars', a tailor, beekeepers, farmers, housewives and domestic servants. Her very first publication is a verse portrait of an old working woman (**'Sketches Among the Poor'**, *K*1: xxii-xxv). Her first published story, **'Libbie Marsh's Three Eras'** (1847), is about the friendship of an unmarried seamstress and a widowed washerwoman. These stories are remarkable for their focus on the physical detail of working-class life. Her Sunday-school stories, **'Hand and Heart'** (1849) and **'Bessy's Troubles at Home'** (1852), bring home the sheer effort required to produce the simplest results—a cup of tea, for instance—in the working-class homes of the 1840s (*K*3: 548-9, 534).

Yet work is not seen primarily as a hardship in these stories but as a means to self-sufficiency and mutual support. In **'The Well of Pen-Morfa'** (1850) an unmarried mother supports herself by breekeeping; in **'The Manchester Marriage'** (1858) a widow, her mother-in-law and their servant keep themselves by running a boarding-house; in **'The Grey Woman'** (1861) a servant supports her former mistress by working as a tailor. As Anna Walters says in her splendid introduction to the Pandora *Four Short Stories* 'we are left as so often in Gaskell's writing with the impression of what women *can* do rather than the reverse' (*P:* 14).

Perhaps the most impressive example of self-sufficiency is that of Susan Dixon, the Cumbrian 'stateswoman' in **'Half A Lifetime Ago'** (1855). As manager and later owner of the farm where she works alongside the labourers, she seems to epitomise Mary Wollstonecraft's ideal: 'how many women . . . waste life away the prey of discontent, who might have practised as physicians, regulated a farm, managed a shop, and stood erect, supported by their own industry' (*W:* 163). Susan's life, however, is grim and lonely until she takes to live with her the widow and orphans of her former lover; 'and so it fell out', the story succinctly ends, 'that the latter days of Susan Dixon's life were better than the former' (*CP:* 102).

Although three of Elizabeth Gaskell's best-known novels (*Mary Barton, North and South* and *Wives and Daughters*) end with a love-match, most of the short stories, together with *Cranford, Ruth, Sylvia's Lovers* and *Cousin Phillis,* stress the unreliability of sexual love and the durability of female friendships. Libbie Marsh and Margaret Hall agree to live together; Mrs Leigh sets up house with her 'fallen' daughter Lizzie; Nest Gwynne in **'The Well of Pen-Morfa'**, betrayed by her lover, takes in an idiot woman 'on the parish'; in *My Lady Ludlow* (1858) an aristocratic lady 'adopts' half-a-dozen needy young gentlewomen; in **'A Dark Night's Work'** (1863) Ellinor sets up house with her former governess; in **'The Grey Woman'** (1861) a servant disguises herself as a man and lives with her former mistress as her husband.

Female alliances occur naturally in the working-class, where needs are urgent and neighbours close by, but for Elizabeth Gaskell's middle-class women, help comes less from friends than from servants. Like Mary Wollstonecraft, she believed that good sense and heroism were more likely where people were forced to confront real crises. 'With respect to virtue', says Wollstonecraft, 'I have seen most in low life . . . gentlewomen are too indolent to be actively virtuous' (*W:* 84).

The revolutionary function of domestic servants in Elizabeth Gaskell's work has been largely over-looked; critics seem blinkered by the stage convention that servants are comic, colourful 'characters'. Yet they provide practical, moral and psychological decision in situations which are sometimes deadly serious. Adrienne Rich argues that 'because the conditions of life for many poor women demand a fighting spirit for sheer physical survival, such mothers have sometimes been able to give their daughters something to be valued far more highly than full-time mothering' (Rich 1977: 247). Elizabeth Gaskell's middle-aged servants are generally childless, but they function as 'fighting mothers' for the middle-class woman in their care. It is Peggy who sustains Susan Dixon, and Betty Cousin Phillis, after the defection of lovers; it is Sally who teaches Ruth to survive by putting effort into proximate tasks; Miss Monro, the governess in **'A Dark Night's Work'**, not only works for Ellinor but stops her going mad; Norah, in **'The Manchester Marriage'**, takes on the moral dilemma about disclosing a family secret; in *Cranford,* Martha becomes her former mistress's landlady to save her from penury; and Nancy is the moral backbone of the Brown family in **'The Moorland Cottage'** (1862). When Mrs Buxton in that tale tells stories of saints and heroines to the little girls, she includes servants (*K*2: 296).

All these situations blur class boundaries, and although Elizabeth Gaskell herself had a number of servants, her behaviour throughout her life defines their relationship as one of function rather than immutable class distinction. When Marianne was a baby, she wrote, 'we have lost our servant Betsy. . . . But we still keep her as a friend, and she has been to stay with us several weeks this autumn' (*MD:* 28). After all the girls were grown up their governess, Hearn, stayed on as 'a dear good valuable *friend*' (*L* 570). In **'French Life'** Elizabeth Gaskell praises the French habit of living in flats because 'there is the moral advantage of uniting mistresses and maids in a more complete family bond. . . . [a] pleasant kind of familiarity . . . which does not breed contempt, in spite of proverbs' (*K7:* 609). A contemporary conduct-book, declaring it 'highly improper for young people to associate with their servants' (*NFI:* 367), emphasises her unconventionality.

In **'The Old Nurse's Story'** (1852) this theme is given a 'gothic' treatment. A 5-year-old girl, the youngest of a decayed aristocratic family, is poised between the drawing-room, occupied by a silent great-aunt, and the warm life of the kitchen. Tempted to her death by a phantom child, she is rescued by her nurse. Under the supernatural surface we can read the author's resistance to aristocratic values— patrilineal pride of possession, sexual rivalry and the ethic of revenge. Hester the nurse and the other working people provide an alternative pattern for personal relationships, unstructured by kinship but united by common nurturance and co-operation.

The care of children is Elizabeth Gaskell's crucial test of moral values; seen as a communal duty (though undertaken by individuals), it takes precedence over all other responsibilities and is never restricted to biological mothers or conventional households. Servants act as 'fighting mothers' to their charges; widows and unmarried mothers cope alone; Libbie Marsh devotes herself to a neighbour's child; Susan Palmer, in **'Lizzie Leigh'** (1850), brings up a baby thrust at her in the street; Bessy looks after her brothers and sisters; Miss Galindo, in *My Lady Ludlow,* adopts her dead lover's child; Lady Ludlow adopts a houseful of girls; in *Mary Barton,* Alice Wilson brings up her brother's son. Everywhere in Elizabeth Gaskell's work the maternal instinct flourishes, inside and outside marriage, with and without biological ties.

2 Nurturing Men

By stressing woman's common need for economic self-sufficiency, supportive friendships and maternal roles, Elizabeth Gaskell's stories blur distinctions between classes and between married and unmarried women. Even more unexpected is that her close acquaintance with working-class life leads her to represent gender divisions as indistinct. Early in her marriage she writes to Mary Howitt:

As for the Poetry of Humble Life, that, even in a town, is met with on every hand . . . we constantly meet with examples of the beautiful truth in that passage of 'The Cumberland Beggar':

'Man is dear to man; the poorest poor
Long for some moments in a weary life
When they can know and feel that they have been,
Themselves, the fathers and the dealers out
Of some small blessings; have been kind to such
As needed kindness, for this simple cause,
That we have all of us a human heart' [*sic*] (*L* 12)

In the crowded necessities of 'the poorest poor', acts of kindess were performed by whoever was nearest, and every home was 'an essential mutual-aid society' (Weeks 1981: 68). In *Mary Barton* two men visit a family where the husband is delirious and the wife and children starving:

rough, tender nurses as they were, [they] lighted the fire. . . . . [Barton] began, with the useful skill of a working-man, to make some gruel; and . . . forced one or two drops between her clenched teeth. . . . Wilson . . . had soothed, and covered the man many a time; he had fed and hushed the little child, and spoken tenderly to the woman (*MB:* 99-100, 102)

Wilson's first appearance is 'tenderly carrying a baby in arms', and almost the first words Barton speaks are, '"now, Mrs Wilson, give me the baby"' (*MB:* 42). Similarly, Job Legh's account of two elderly men bringing a baby from London to Manchester, though comic, is full of tenderness (*MB:* 147-153).

Elizabeth Gaskell's Sunday-school stories are where we would expect to find most explicit didacticism about social role-playing, and each of them stresses gender-role reversal. Bessy learns 'the difficult arts of family life' from an older brother, and in **'Hand and Heart'**, the 'ministering angel' is a little boy. Tom Fletcher creates the sort of domestic peace we associate with Dickens's child-heroines; when orphaned he derives comfort from nursing his aunt's baby (*K3:* 554), and eventually he reforms the whole rowdy, quarrelsome household:

His uncle sometimes said he was more like a girl than a boy . . . but . . . he really respected him for the very qualities which are most truly 'manly'; for the courage with which he dared to do what was right, and the quiet firmness with which he bore many kinds of pain. (*K3:* 555)

In **'The Half-Brothers'** the slow-witted Godfrey gives his life to save the brother entrusted to him by their dying mother, protecting him from freezing with the warmth of his own body; like Tom Fletcher's, his action is both 'manly' and physically succouring. Elizabeth Gaskell's middle-class heroes are often doctors, who have professionalised the nurturing role.

Gender roles in these tales are not only blurred in general but shift according to circumstances. When the hero in **'Six Weeks at Heppenheim'** is nursed by the servant Thekla, her 'support was as firm as a man's could have been' (*K7*: 367), yet when she is distressed he invites her to '"tell me all about it, as you would to your mother"' (p. 374). Later Thekla, though 'strong as a man', is fed like a baby by Herr Muller, while her hands are busy nursing his little boy (p. 402).

The parental imperative is at the basis of Elizabeth Gaskell's unorthodox treatment of gender roles. Parents, whether mothers or fathers, need to be both responsible and caring. In **Mary Barton** and **Sylvia's Lovers** political activism in both men and women rises directly from thwarted parental love. As a political writer, Elizabeth Gaskell has attracted condescending criticism from critics who see 'loving-kindness' as a lame alternative to political action. Yet Eli Zaretsky, in *Capitalism, the Family and Personal Life,* writes:

> Part of our problem in dealing with these questions is that socialists tend to hold conservative and inadequate psychological conceptions, according to which human beings are essentially thought and labour. But the human need to love and be loved is as fundamental as the need to work. We need a more tentative and experimental attitude toward emotional life. (Zaretsky 1976: 142)

Whereas Zaretsky sees personal life as 'one problem among many' (p. 142), materialist feminists see it as fundamental. Dinnerstein, Chodorow and O'Brien, for instance, argue that the inclusion of men in primary child-care would undermine the aggressive masculinity which perpetuates capitalism (Chodorow 1978: 186; see above, Ch. 1 (2vi). Elizabeth Gaskell's enthusiasm for nurturing men bears the same relationship to this developed theory as early Utopian socialism bears to Marxist analysis of class; as Mary O'Brien puts it, 'Utopians were so innocent of the true nature of class struggle that they even called on the ruling class for help in destroying itself' (O'Brien 1981:22). Elizabeth Gaskell extrapolated, from her observation of men on the edge of subsistence, to a general vision of masculine self-deconstruction which initially included a good deal of wish-fulfilment. The optimistic paternalism of **Mary Barton** gives way to a more guarded attitude to men in **North and South** and a more complete focus on women in **Wives and Daughters.** Despite her uncertainty about the means, however, Elizabeth Gaskell's vision of the caring father remains a valid and vital goal, which modern feminists with sharper analytic tools are just beginning to recognise.

3 The Infantilisation of Girls

While necessity eroded gender division, middle-class leisure elaborately reinforced the doctrine of separate spheres. Role-reversal appears ludicrous:

> a husband who should personally direct the proceedings of the housekeeper and the cook, and intrude into the petty arrangements of daily economy, would appear . . . as ridiculous as if he were to assume to himself the habiliments of his wife, or occupy his mornings with her needles and work-bags. (*NFI*, 1824: 69)

The New Female Instructor, or Young Woman's Guide to Domestic Happiness, Being an Epitome of all the Acquirements Necessary to Form the Female Character . . . went through six editions between 1811 and 1836, the period of Elizabeth Gaskell's girlhood. It begins unequivocally with the doctrine that women's role is to please men: 'In their forms lovely, in their manners soft and engaging, they can infuse . . . a thousand nameless sweets into society, which, without them, would be insipid, and barren of sentiment and feeling' (p. 1).

This stereotype contrasts strongly with Elizabeth Gaskell's working heroines; Libbie Marsh is so plain that she is jokingly advised to get a job scaring birds (*P:* 24); Nest Gwynne is crippled, with eyes 'sunk deep down in their hollow, cavernous sockets' (*P:* 87); Susan Dixon's 'skin was weather-beaten, furrowed, brown, . . . her teeth were gone, and her hair grey and ragged' (*CP:* 99); Thelka's complexion is 'bronzed and reddened by weather (*K7:* 364). Even for middle-class women, Elizabeth Gaskell does not see beauty as an asset; she describes Effie Ruskin as 'very close to a charming character; if she had had the small pox she would have been so' (*L* 195).

Mary Wollstonecraft saw the tradition of educating girls only to please, as responsible for women's narcissism, deviousness, sensuality and irrationality. The conduct-books 'render women more artificial, weak characters, than they would otherwise have been . . . [they] degrade one-half of the human species, and render women pleasing at the expense of every solid virtue' (*W:* 26). Similarly, Elizabeth Gaskell shows that this ideology distorts parental feeling, making parents protect girls rather than educate them. Mr. Wilkins in **'A Dark Night's Work'** is a rich and doting father but tells the governess to teach Ellinor '"only what a lady should know"' (*K7*: 415; see also 430, 501), an attitude repeated by Mr Holman and Mr Gibson (below, Chs. 9 and 10). As Peter Cominos points out, although 'a conscious struggle was waged on behalf of their moral purity by overprotective parents and chaperons', the girls themselves were kept 'innocent' and hence irresponsible (Vicinus 1972: 161). But, as these stories show, daughters cannot be protected from every moral decision. Each heroine acquires the strength and knowledge to cope with adult life, often with the help of servants rather than parents, but at unnecessary emotional cost. Elizabeth Gaskell's own daughter, by contrast, was left at 4 years old 'to judge if such an action be right or not . . . [to] exercise her conscience' (*MD:* 38).

The last part of **'Morton Hall'** is an attack on conduct-book education; three maiden aunts try out different 'systems' on their niece. The eldest models herself on Lord Chesterfield, whose 'unmanly, immoral system' is, according to Wollstonecraft, second only to Rousseau's in perniciousness: 'instead of preparing young people to encounter the evils of life with dignity, and to acquire wisdom and virtue by the exercise of their own faculties, precepts are heaped upon precepts, and blind obedience required when conviction should be brought home to reason' (*W:* 116-7). Accordingly, Cordelia in **'Morton Hall'** is subjected to arbitrary rules; she must eat her meals standing, drink cold water before pudding, and never say 'red' or 'stomach-ache' (*K2:* 483). Although Miss Morton poses as a strong-minded woman who despises mere beauty, she is careful that Cordelia preserves her complexion (p. 477). Wollstonecraft points to similar hypocrisy in Dr Gregory's renowned *Legacy to His Daughters,* where daughters are taught that though it is 'indelicate' *obviously* to want to please men, 'it may govern their conduct' (*W:* 36).

Cordelia's second aunt, who educates her 'sensibilities' (*K2:* 478), is subjected to gentle satire which is nevertheless in line with Wollstonecraft's attack on sensibility, which 'naturally relaxes the other powers of the mind, and prevents intellect from attaining that sovereignty which it ought to attain to render a rational creature useful to others' (*W:* 68).

The third aunt has no system but frightens Cordelia with dogmatic and unpredictable ways. This tale is very light humour, but it shows that Gaskell concurred with the Wollstonecraft thesis that conduct-book education based on obedience or sensibility was debilitating and that the marginalised role of many middle-class women made them into dogmatists, invalids or eccentrics.

4 The Fallibility of Authority

If woman's role was obedience, man's was command. Françoise Basch and Erna Reiss give a staggering account of the legal non-entity of Victorian married women. 'A woman, in law, belonged to the man she married; she was his chattel' (Reiss 1934: 6). In the early part of the period she had no rights over her own body, her children, her earned or inherited income or her place of residence. A husband was even responsible for his wife's debts and crimes. This situation clearly conflicts with Elizabeth Gaskell's Unitarian concept of the rational responsibility of every individual for his or her own conduct.

The facile assumption of much Gaskell criticism has been that she 'looked up to man as her sex's rightful and benevolent master' (Cecil 1934: 198; Duthie 1980: 90). But many of her 'horror' stories depend on the inhuman possibilities of authority. In the early part of **'Morton Hall'** a sane Royalist lady is consigned to a mad-house by her Puritan husband; in **'The Grey Woman'** the heroine is married by a well-intentioned father to a man who proves to be a brigand who tortures victims on a heated iron floor; in **'French Life'** (1864) an aristocratic lady is poisoned, forced from a high window and repeatedly stabbed by her male relatives with the connivance of a priest. In **'Lois The Witch'** (1859) several hundred people, mostly women, are imprisoned and nineteen executed during the Salem witch hunt with the approval of every authority figure from fathers, guardians and ministers of the Church to judges and politicians. Although Basch claims that 'Mrs Gaskell and the majority of feminist reformers . . . blamed husbands abusing their powers and the law rather than accuse the powers and the law themselves' (Basch 1974: 270), Gaskell returns so often to the abuse of authority that her work as a whole does constitute a challenge to patriarchy itself, which confers on one set of people the right to command, and on another the duty to obey.

There are rather few 'orthodox' families, with father, mother and two or more children, in Elizabeth Gaskell's work, but when they do appear, *paterfamilias* is always a source of oppression and misery. Lizzie Leigh is driven into prostitution when her father disowns her; the Rev. Jenkyns, in *Cranford,* banishes his son Peter for half a lifetime; Mr Bradshaw, in *Ruth,* tyrannises his family. In **'The Heart of John Middleton'**, the hero begins life as 'Ishmael', the outcast, and only gradually validates his masculine status in the community by proving his ability to earn his living, fight his rivals and support his wife. But whereas as an outcast he had lived in love of his father and fellowship with other poachers, as a churchgoer and upholder of the law he lives by the ethic of 'an eye for an eye'.

Bourgeois men in Elizabeth Gaskell's works are not only tyrannical but culpable. Edward in **'The Moorland Cottage'** and Richard in *Ruth* both exploit positions of trust to embezzle funds; in **'The Squire's Story'** (1858) the heroine's husband turns out to be a highwayman; Mr Wilkins, a lawyer and the heroine's father in **'A Dark Night's Work'**, kills his clerk in anger.

Not only individuals, however, but the law itself is fallible. In **'The Grey Woman'** the heroine escapes her brigand husband but, as an absconding wife, can claim no protection from the law and spends years in flight and disguise. In both *Mary Barton* and 'A Dark Night's Work' the courts are ready to execute an innocent man. The whole of *Sylvia's Lovers* is a protracted protest against the legal injustice of the press-gang. Frederick Hale's mutiny against unjust naval officers in *North and South* is surely meant as a redeeming analogy for the workers' riot against the threat of the militia. **'An Accursed Race',** dealing with the persecution of the 'Cagots' in France and Spain, shows legalised injustice on the scale of genocide. As Noddings puts it, 'obedience to law is simply not a reliable guide to moral behaviour' (Noddings 1984: 201).

Lady Ludlow exposes the contingent nature of 'the law' when she bursts out '"Bah! Who makes laws? Such as I, in the House of Lords—such as you, in the House of Commons"' (*K5*: 38), and repeatedly the stories endorse the distinction between 'justice' and 'the law'. In **'The Crooked Branch'** (1859) a mother, forced to testify against her son, is seized with a stroke, and her husband tells the court: '"now yo've truth, and a' th' truth, and I'll leave yo' to th' Judgment o' God for th' way yo've getten at it"' (*CP:* 238).

The contrast between justice and the law is most developed in **'Lois the Witch',** where the authority-structures of a whole nation are complicit in cruel persecution. The story ends with a confession of guilt and fallibility by the judge and jury responsible for the executions. Two other stories also deal with supposed witches: **'The Heart of John Middleton'** (1850) is set on Pendle Hill, and **'The Poor Clare'** (1856) in the Trough of Bolland—both districts historically associated with witch hunts—and each concerns an independent old woman whose psychology Elizabeth Gaskell analyses in a realistic way. In **'Lois the Witch',** among various psychological determinants of the mass delusion of Salem, she emphasises the gullibility of people who are used to deferring to authority; a powerful preacher like Cotton Mather could influence thousands, and Lois herself begins to wonder whether she is a witch when authoritative voices tell her so. The Unitarian Charles Upham, whose *Lectures on Witchcraft* (1831) were Elizabeth Gaskell's source, attacks 'the leaders of opinion' who constitute 'the law' in its widest sense:

> a physician gave the first impulse to the awful work . . . the judges and officers of the law did what they could to drive on the delusion . . . the clergy were also instrumental in promoting the proceedings. Nay, it must be acknowledged that they took the lead (Upham 1831: 88-9)

Upham concludes that Salem forces everyone to think about 'the cultivation and government of his own moral and intellectual faculties, and . . . the obligations that press on him as a member of society to do what he may to enlighten, rectify and control public sentiment' (p. vi).

The fallibility of 'the law' requires everyone to take moral responsibility for themselves. This position is vehemently endorsed in William Gaskell's sermon 'Unitarian Christians Called to Bear Witness to the Truth' (1862). If we:

> lock up our higher thoughts till infallibility has set its seal upon them . . . priestcraft and intolerance would have strangled everything like free opinion. . . . The apostle's 'we believe and therefore speak', is applicable to every member of the Church universal who has a mind to think, a heart to feel, and a tongue to utter (W. Gaskell 1862: 5-6)

Emphasis on correctness of creed leads to 'inquisitions, persecutions and miseries without end' (p. 14). The justification for a narrowly defined creed enforced by an authoritarian Church has been the doctrine of original sin, which Gaskell sees as a denial of human reason. Thinking people, told:

> that they sinned in Adam . . . that every new-born infant is responsible for an act committed thousands of years ago . . . feel it no heresy to give this a flat denial. Teach them that it required the blood of his innocent Son to turn aside God's ire and reconcile Him to men, and they say at once then He must be essentially vengeful and unjust. Declare to them that, for the sins of this short life, He consigns myriads of his creatures to everlasting woe, and they call it a mockery to represent this as a Father's mode of dealing with his children. . . . Doctrines like this go right against their natural conscience. Their moral feelings revolt at them (pp. 11-12)

Unitarians believe that every human being has the qualities—reason and love—for self-government and social responsibility. William Gaskell calls for 'a faith which, so far from contradicting, will be in full unison with the best dictates of the heart—which, instead of outraging moral feeling, will "commend itself to every man's conscience . . ."' (p. 19). This doctrine, potentially subversive of the authority not only of the Church but of class and gender, underlies everything Elizabeth Gaskell wrote.

Patriarchal power in Elizabeth Gaskell's tales is shown as superceding even class power. Although Lucas claim that she presents '"old" families . . . in an exclusively favourable light' (Lucas 1977: 3), and Duthie that she 'honoured . . . the patriarchal pattern' (Duthie 1980: 90), the stories dealing with great houses (**'Morton Hall', 'Crowley Castle', 'French Life', 'The Old Nurse's Story'**) are a catalogue of torture, madness and lingering death for their women, whose aristocratic status is no defence against masculine power. Theorists like Rousseau argue that the fallibility of male authority only makes a woman's subjection more necessary: 'formed to obey a being so imperfect as man, often full of vices, and always full of faults, she ought to learn betimes even to suffer injustice, and to bear the insults of a husband without complaint' (quoted in *W:* 92). Rousseau is Wollstonecraft's prime target in *A Vindication of the Rights of Woman,* and although by the 1850s Wollstonecraft had fallen into silent neglect, there was still much public debate about women's defenceless position under the law (see Basch 1974: 16-25). Barbara Bodichon and Caroline Norton both wrote books on women and the law in 1854, and Norton, who was quite a close friend of Elizabeth Gaskell (*L*209, 372, 407, 438, 552), was possibly the link between her and Wollstonecraft. Norton's *English Laws for Women in the Nineteenth Century* (1854), largely based on her own sufferings at the hands of her husband, reads like a documentary rerun of Wollstonecraft's novel *Maria, or the Wrongs of Woman* (1798).

When, however, at Bodichon's request, Elizabeth Gaskell signed the 1856 Petition to protect the property of married women, she did so with reservations, saying 'a husband can coax, wheedle, beat or tyrannize his wife out of something and no law whatever will help this that I see' (*L* 276). This statement has been used to suggest that Elizabeth Gaskell was opposed to the 'women's rights' movement (e.g. Thomspon, quoted in Welch 1977: 38; Duthie 1980: 90; Chapple 1980: xiii), but it surely rises from a radical scepticism about the ability of the law to protect women in a society where patriarchal power is entrenched in the most personal relationships. As well as legal enablement, individual women need to strengthen their sense of autonomy, their power to act and speak.

In the writings of Elizabeth Gaskell, as in those of Norton and Wollstonecraft, the actual injuries of women raise less indignation than their induced submission, which makes them less than human, takes responsibility for their fate out of their own hands and denies them the right claimed by William Gaskell for every Christian to 'bear witness to the truth'. For all these writers, public speech is a claim to participate in the symbolic order; obedience is equated with silence. According to Wollstonecraft, 'the being who patiently endures injustice, and silently bears insults, will soon become unjust, or unable to discern right from wrong' (*W:* 92). To those 'who deem a husband's right so indefeasible, and his title so sacred, that even a wronged wife should keep silence', Caroline Norton replies, 'I resist' (Norton 1854: 2-3).

Similarly, Elizabeth Gaskell's tales often hinge around a change from silent endurance to public speech which changes the status of the speaker from submission to authority. In **'Right at Last'** (originally called 'The Sin of a Father'), a husband endures blackmail rather than suffer the exposure of his father's crime; his wife, finding 'something so weak and poor' in his character, determines 'to rely on herself alone in all cases of emergency' (*K*7: 290). Maggie, in **'The Moorland Cottage',** though brought up to obey her brother, defies him for moral reasons. In **'A Dark Night's Work'** Ellinor spends years in dread of her father's crime being discovered, believing herself bound to silence by '"filial piety"' (*K*7: 478); her father tells her to '"stand alone, and bear the sins of thy father"' (p. 510). Eventually, she speaks to protect a friend. 'Bearing witness to the truth', is never, in these tales, a matter of conforming to law, but of judging the circumstances. In **'Right at Last'** the wife delivers the blackmailer to the law because he tyrannises their lives; in **'The Heart of John Middleton'** the wife argues against handing over their old enemy as a mere act of vengeance.

Elizabeth Gaskell's tales resoundingly reject Mrs Ellis's maxim that 'a woman's highest duty is so often to suffer and be still (Ellis 1845: 126). In **'Lizzie Leigh',** the submissive wife, whose husband 'was truly the interpreter, who stood between God and her' (*P:* 48) is disillusioned by his rejection of Lizzie, and when their son Will seems about to act likewise, she speaks:

> 'I must speak, and you must listen. I am your mother, and I dare to command you, because I know I am in the right and that God is on my side. . . . 'She stood, no longer as the meek, imploring, gentle mother, but firm and dignified, as if the interpreter of God's will. (*P:* 67).

In **'The Well of Pen-Morfa'** Nest Gwynne's mother, similarly bold on her daughter's behalf, speaks to her betrayer: '"You *must* tell me." She stood up and spoke in a tone of command' (*P:* 84). And in *Mary Barton* the outcast prostitute Esther speaks with the authority of experience and the courage of parental concern: '"You must listen to me, Jem Wilson", she said, with almost an accent of command. . . . "You must listen", she said again, authoritatively, "for Mary Barton's sake"' (*MB:* 208). When Mr Bradshaw in *Ruth* threatens his son with prosecution, his hitherto submissive wife is driven '"to speak [her] mind, and say to everybody how cruel he is"' (*R:* 404), and his daughter defies him to defend her friend: '"Father! I will speak, I will not keep silence. I will bear witness to Ruth"' (*R:* 335).

Religion, in Victorian England, could serve the ideology of separate spheres. Sandford, for instance, argues that since women have 'many trials . . . they . . . need a sedative influence, and religion is the anodyne' (Sandford 1831: 37). For Elizabeth Gaskell, however, religion required woman as well as men to 'bear witness to the truth': to act and to speak according to their own convictions. These speaking, acting women, who have been invisible to most Gaskell critics, are 'a species of mole as yet not recognised. When they awaken from among the dead, from among the words, from among the laws . . .' (Cixous, in Marks and de Courtivron: 93).

Coda: Ideology as Doom

A text that was anathema to William and Elizabeth Gaskell was that 'the sins of the fathers shall be visited upon the children'. It conceives God as a vengeful, not nurturing, Father and denies the child's right to self-determination. Many of Elizabeth Gaskell's stories reject the obligation of children to suffer in silence their fathers' crimes. Parents, however, can visit their 'sins' on children without committing crimes; the perpetuation of harmful ideologies is enough. To the Gaskells, who saw reason and love as equally necessary for humanity, the doctrine of 'separate spheres', which assigned reason to men and love to women, was a denial of full humanity to both. This harmful ideology is attacked in all Elizabeth's work, but in two of her supernatural tales it emerges as a curse passing from generation to generation.

In **'The Doom of the Griffiths'** (1858), a Welsh family lives under a curse from the time of Glendower, that the family will end when the 'last male . . . shall slay the father' (*KI;* 238). The last son, Owen, alienated from his father, seeks love in a secret marriage with a low-born woman. In a discovery scene, the Squire kills Owen's baby, Owen kills his father, and Owen, his wife and her father are killed trying to escape. The doom is thus fulfilled. But the psychological crisis comes when the Squire, obsessed with family pride and patrilineal inheritance, confronts Owen, who, with his baby in his arms, is like an emblem of the 'nurturing male' of the working-class stories. The 'doom' of the Griffiths is one which every patriarchal family shares; the doom of perpetuating an ideal of manhood which allows men to be only half human. Owen rises against his father as John Barton against Carson, as representative of an unjust 'law' which prevents him from nurturing his child.

'The Poor Clare' is a more elaborate ghost story. Bridget, a servant, obsessively loves her beautiful daughter, Mary, who angers her mother by leaving home. Bridget, now reputed a witch, transfers her love to a spaniel dog, which is killed by a soldier, Gisborne. Bridget curses Gisborne with the threat that his best-beloved will 'become a terror and a loathing to all' (*K5*: 341). Gisborne, however, has seduced Mary and his best-beloved is their daughter, Lucy. Lucy is demure and virtuous but at puberty she begins to be accompanied by a monstrous double, 'a ghastly resemblance, complete in likeness . . . but with a loathsome demon soul looking out of the grey eyes, that were in turns mocking and voluptuous' (*K5*: 362).

The story is set in the early eighteenth century, and all the characters are Catholics or Puritans—both groups which practise repression of the flesh. Lucy's companion explains the haunting by claiming that '"the sins of the fathers shall be visited upon the children"' (*K5*; 363)—that is, Lucy is suffering for her father's sexual crime against her mother. In psychological terms, however, Lucy's double, which is seen, by everyone, makes visible the repressed sexuality of a whole society. The voluptuous demon is the paraxial image of its obsessive chastity (see Jackson 1981: 19 for the concept of the 'paraxial' in fantasy literature). The Mary that Bridget wanted at home, the demure Lucy approved by her father, are only half human, the product of an ideology which denies female autonomy. Bridget loves a child-Mary but rejects her as an adult, projecting her repressed fear of sexuality as a curse. Gisborne uses the sexual Mary, then 'kills' her like the spaniel and raises Lucy to be a child-woman in her turn, projecting his repressed desire as her voluptuous double. The characters within the story see Bridget's curse as responsible for the haunting and, as in **'The Doom of the Griffiths'**, we can see this curse as the passing on, from generation to generation, of a repressive ideology. Although Bridget and Gisborne seem at odds, they perpetuate the same tradition based on fears that women who are not treated as children will 'fall' into loathsome lechery.

Like much Victorian fantasy, **'The Poor Clare'** is not open-ended but offers an ideological resolution of the 'terrors' it has disclosed. This closure, however, is not a reinscription of the status quo but suggests an alternative social order. In the religious terms of the narrative, the curse is raised when Bridget, as an act of atonement, becomes a nun and devotes herself to public charity. In psychological terms, this represents a breach of her claustrophobic obsession with her daughter's chastity and a move towards adult involvement in the community. It is indicative of the complex and surprising meanings underlying Elizabeth Gaskell's explorations of 'motherhood' that Bridget's conventionally protective stance towards her biological daughter is expressed in a stepmother's or wicked fairy's curse, while her nurturing, fairy-godmother role is performed for strangers as one of a chaste sisterhood. As a 'Poor Clare' she relieves a war- and famine-stricken town, and the story ends with a moving scene in which the whole city unites in turn to relieve the Poor Clares. As women and old men, children and soldiers of both armies sweep through the streets with food for the starving nuns, we have an image of human nurturance, cooperation and communication which transcends both the 'masculine' world of war, which has killed Gisborne, and the enclosed 'feminine' world, which prompted Bridget's curse, whose '"roots . . . lie deeper than she knows. . . . The sins of the fathers are indeed visited upon the children"' (*K5*: 367).

Elizabeth Gaskell's Works

C   *Cranford/Cousin Phillis,* ed. Peter Keating (Penguin: Harmondsworth, 1976).

CP   *Cousin Phillis and Other Tales,* ed. Augus Easson, The World's Classics (Oxford University Press: Oxford and New York, 1981).

K1-8 *The Works of Mrs Gaskell,* [The Knutsford edition] 8 vols., ed. A. W. Ward (John Murray: London, 1906).

L   *The Letters of Mrs Gaskell,* ed. J. A. V. Chapple and Arthur Pollard (Manchester University Press: Manchester, 1966). [Note: numbers refer to Letter no, and not page.]

LCB   *The Life of Charlotte Brontë,* ed. Alan Shelston (Penguin: Harmondsworth, 1975).

MB   *Mary Barton,* ed. Stephen Gill (Penguin: Harmondsworth, 1970).

MD   *My Diary: The Early Years of My Daughter Marianne,* printed privately by Clement Shorter, London, 1923.

NS   *North and South,* ed. Martin Dodsworth (Penguin: Harmondsworth, 1970).

P   *Elizabeth Gaskell: Four Short Stories,* introduced by Anna Walters (Pandora Press, Routledge & Kegan Paul: London and Boston, 1983).

R   *Ruth,* introduced by Margaret Lane, Everyman edition (Dent: London and New York, 1967).

SL   *Sylvia's Lovers,* ed. Andrew Sanders, The World's Classics (Oxford University Press: Oxford and New York, 1982).

WD   *Wives and Daughters,* ed. Frank Glover Smith (Penguin: Harmondsworth, 1969).

Other Works

NFI   [Anon] *The New Female Instructor: or, Young Woman's Guide to Domestic Happiness . . .* (Thomas Kelly: London, 1824).

W   Mary Wollstonecraft, *A Vindication of the Rights of Woman,* Everyman edition (Dent: London, 1929 [first published 1792]); this edition also contains John Stuart Mill's *The Subjection of Women.*

Notes

Elizabeth Gaskell

There are two bibliographies:

Selig, Robert L., *Elizabeth Gaskell: A Reference Guide* (G.K. Hall: Boston, 1977).

Welch, Jeffrey, *Elizabeth Gaskell: An Annotated Bibliography 1929-75* (Garland Publishing: New York and London, 1977).

The most useful biographical and critical works are:

Chapple, J. A. V., *Elizabeth Gaskell: A portrait in letters* (Manchester University Press: Manchester, 1980).

Gérin, Winifred, *Elizabeth Gaskell: A Biography* (Oxford University Press: Oxford and New York, 1980).

Lansbury, Coral, *Elizabeth Gaskell: The Novel of Social Crisis* (Paul Elek: London, 1975).

Rubenius, Aina, *The Woman Question in Mrs Gaskell's Life and Works* (A.-B. Lundequista Bokhandeln: Uppsala, 1950).

Victorian Women and Women Writers

Basch, Françoise, *Relative Creatures: Victorian Women in Society and the Novel 1837-67* (Allen Lane: London, 1974).

Gorham, Deborah, *The Victorian Girl and the Feminine Ideal* (Croom Helm: London, 1982).

Moers, Ellen, *Literary Women* (Women's Press: London, 1978).

Showalter, Elaine, *A Literature of Their Own* (Princeton University Press: Princeton, NJ, 1977; Virago: London, 1978).

Vicinus, Martha (ed.), *Suffer and Be Still: Women in the Victorian Age* (Indiana University Press: Bloomington and London, 1972).

Zaretsky, Eli, *Capitalism, the Family and Personal Life* (Pluto Press: London, 1976).

Feminist Theory and Literary Criticism

Abel, Elizabeth (ed.), *Writing and Sexual Difference* (Harvester Press: Brighton, 1982).

Belsey, Catherine, *Critical Practice* (Methuen: London and New York, 1980).

Chodorow, Nancy, *The Reproduction of Mothering* (University of California Press: Berkeley, Los Angeles and London, 1978).

Gorham, Dorothy, *The Rocking of the Cradle and the Ruling of the World* (Souvenir Press: London 1976); published in New York by Harper & Row as *The Mermaid and the Minotaur; Sexual Arrangements and Human Malaise.*

Eagleton, Terry, *Literary Theory: An Introduction* (Basil Blackwell: Oxford, 1983).

Gilbert, Sandra, and Gubar, Susan, *The Madwoman in the Attic: The Woman Writer and the Nineteenth-Century Literary Imagination* (Yale University Press: New Haven, Conn., and London, 1979).

Gilligan, Carol, *In a Different Voice: Psychological Theory and Women's Development* (Harvard University Press: Cambridge, Mass. and London, 1982).

Jacobus, Mary, *Women Writing and Writing About Women* (Croom Helm: London; Harper & Row, New York, 1979).

Keohane, Nannerl O., Rosaldo, Michelle Z. and Gelpi, Barbara C. (eds.), *Feminist Theory: A Critique of Ideology* (Harvester Press: Brighton, 1982).

O'Brien, Mary, 1981. *The Politics of Reproduction* (Routledge & Kegan Paul: Boston, London and Henley).

Spender, Dale, *Man Made Language* (Routledge & Kegan Paul: London, Boston and Henley, 1980).

Carol A. Martin (essay date 1989)

SOURCE: "Gaskell's Ghosts: Truths in Disguise," in *Studies in the Novel*, Vol. 21, No. 1, Spring, 1989, pp. 27-40.

[*In the following essay, Martin discusses the role of the supernatural in Gaskell's novels and shorter works.*]

"Do you believe in ghosts?" someone is supposed to have asked Madame du Deffand, to which she replied, "No . . . but I am afraid of them."[1]

If that question had been posed to Elizabeth Gaskell a hundred years later, she might have responded similarly: "No, but I write stories about them, I tell tales of them by my friends' firesides, and I have seen them." For Gaskell, not unlike Madame du Deffand and many others before and since, is ambivalent—admittedly superstitious and yet a woman of great common sense and considerable knowledge. A cousin of Charles Darwin and a devout Unitarian, in the mid-century crisis of faith she repudiated neither science nor belief and combined, as a minister's wife working among the poor in Manchester, a practical concern for the present with a strong belief in an afterlife.

A survey of criticism of her work, from the earliest reviews to recent Marxist and feminist studies, might give the impression that the here-and-now was almost exclusively her focus, for criticism has touched only occasionally on her treatment of the supernatural. It has dealt instead with what she saw first as the kind of work she wanted to write: fiction that focused on the social problems of her time and on the ordinary, commonplace lives around her. Her avowed models are Crabbe and Wordsworth. In 1837, she and her husband William published a poem, **"Sketches Among the Poor,"** in *Blackwood's Edinburgh Magazine,* which was evidently planned as the first of a series.[2] In a letter dated August 18, 1838, ten years before *Mary Barton,* one of whose characters this early poem anticipates, she says, "We once thought of *trying* to write sketches among the poor," feeling that "the beauty and poetry of many of the common things and daily events of life in its humblest aspect does not seem to me sufficiently appreciated."[3]

Her depiction of life among the workers of Manchester in *Mary Barton* and *North and South* and of quiet, ordinary life in English villages in *Cranford* and *Wives and Daughters* has appropriated critical attention to the neglect of the many short stories she wrote in the 1850s and 1860s for Charles Dickens' two weeklies, *Household Words* and *All the Year Round.* The readers of these serials looked to their editor and his contributors to provide a wide range of subjects in short articles, from mundane topics such as "Houses to Let" and "Chloroform," to pathetic and moral tales like Gaskell's **"Lizzie Leigh,"** which inaugurated the first number of Volume I of *Household Words* on March 30, 1850. But the tastes of the mid-century reader, particularly the reader of the extra Christmas numbers, made it imperative that no volume be complete without something about ghosts. David Punter says of *All the Year Round* that Dickens used it "partly as a means of commissioning tales of the supernatural, from Wilkie Collins and Elizabeth Gaskell among many others,"[4] so one can observe that he sought such tales for its predecessor, *Household Words.* In its ten-year history, from 1850 to 1859, that periodical contains a curious blend of debunking articles on ghosts and witches which assume an enlightened, modern reader and stories which demand, at the least, the willing suspension of disbelief.[5]

Gaskell's own work is similarly Janus-faced. Her stories include short fragments or anecdotes about ghosts and two rather long tales that offer no explanations at the end for the supernatural phenomena they contain: **"The Old Nurse's Story,"** first published in *Household Words* in the extra Christmas number of 1853, and **"The Poor Clare,"** published in three installments of *Household Words,* December 13, 20, and 27, 1856.[6] Other stories, such as **"The Doom of the Griffiths,"** depict curses fulfilled, but preserve an ambiguity that forces the reader to decide whether supernatural or psychological explanations are called for. Still others, especially **"Lois the Witch,"** exploit the reader's interest in the supernatural, but ultimately see hysteria and sexual disturbance, not witchcraft, as the dominating forces in the community of Salem.

This mixture of the supernatural and the realistic is not, of course, peculiar to Gaskell. One finds it too in the work of her major Victorian contemporaries, Dickens, George Eliot, and Charlotte Brontë. Dickens was not only fond of the Christmas ghost story from his own pen, but he also introduced ghosts into, for instance, *Bleak House,* where the ominous step on the Ghost's Walk at Chesney Wold is heard more and more loudly as Lady Dedlock's doom nears. Likewise, George Eliot, in *Adam Bede,* a novel Gaskell much admired (see Letters 418, 444, and 451, for example), introduces into her otherwise realistic narrative the mysterious tapping of the willow wand that signals the drowning of Thais Bede. And Charlotte Brontë, Gaskell's close friend, makes crucial to her plot the inexplicable midnight calls of Jane Eyre and Rochester, which send Jane back to search for him. In her biography of Brontë, written at her father's request after Brontë's death, Gaskell records Charlotte's remarks "in my presence," regarding that incident: someone having objected to it as impossible, "I do not know what incident was in Miss Brontë's recollection when she replied, in a low voice, drawing in her breath, 'But it is a true thing; it really happened.'"[7]

Gaskell's fascination with ghost stories is well documented. A. W. Ward, in his introduction to Volume 7 of the Knutsford edition of her works, notes that "The supernatural always had a strong attraction for Mrs. Gaskell, and her imagination could not fail to concern itself with those human delusions which are closely connected with the terrors largely fed by an instinctive tendency to which her own mind was no stranger."[8] Her letters touch on this instinctive tendency and even, perhaps half-facetiously, suggest its source. Writing to her publisher George Smith, regarding her attempts at correspondence with Thackeray, especially her wish for him to write to Mr. Brontë after Charlotte's death, she comments, "He [Thackeray] never replied to either of these notes of mine, *nor did he ever write to Mr. Brontë.* Now please understand this is no complaint on my part, only a belief that somehow or another my *luck* is against me in any intercourse with him, & being half-Scotch I have a right to be very superstitious; & I have my lucky & unlucky days, & lucky & unlucky people" (Letter 442). In another letter, about the problems she is having with the house she had bought in hopes of providing herself and her husband with a retirement home, she calls it an *"unlucky"* house and refers to delays with the furniture as "unlucky" (Letter 575a). One can, of course, see these comments as simply figures of speech, and yet even into the twentieth century writers testify to the English belief in unlucky houses. Charles Harper observes, "We all know the 'unlucky house.' Every neighbourhood has such a one, which has brought—or has seemed to bring—ill-fortune to all who have resided therein."[9] And Gaskell's new house may indeed be said to have been unlucky, for it absorbed much of her writing time in the last year of her life and it was there she suffered her fatal seizure.

In three other letters she testifies to her own superstitiousness, though how much is tongue-in-cheek is hard to tell. In a letter to her close friend Eliza Fox, she relates a visit to Shottery, near Stratford-on-Avon, where she and friends told "capital" ghost stories and where, on one long drive "(to a place where I believed the Sleeping Beauty lived, it was so over-grown and hidden up by woods) I SAW a ghost! Yes I did; though in such a matter of fact place as Charlotte St I should not wonder if you are sceptical" (Letter 48). In another to the same correspondent, she discusses her daughter Florence: "Florence is turned so sweet and good she quite frightens me. Did you ever hear of people being 'fey'—MA's [Marianne, her eldest daughter's] influence is capital for her" (Letter 169). And the early letter to Mary Howitt which contains the references to "Sketches Among the Poor," discusses numerous folk customs and superstitions, some of which Gaskell acknowledges that she shares:

> Many poetical beliefs are vanishing with the passing generation. A shooting star is unlucky to see. I have so far a belief in this that I always have a chill in my heart when I see one, for I have often noticed them when watching over a sick-bed and very, very anxious. The dog-rose, that pretty libertine of the hedges with the floating sprays wooing the summer air, its delicate hue and its faint perfume, is unlucky. Never form any plan while sitting near one, for it will never answer. (Letter 12)

Several paragraphs later (the letter runs to six pages in the collected letters), Gaskell's wit emerges as she comments on the failure to continue the sketches: "But I suppose we spoke of our plan near a dog-rose, for it never went any further."

This early fascination with the stories told in the countryside around her led to her first published prose piece, which incorporates a ghost story she heard as a school girl. Her essay appeared without her name [she is referred to only as "a fair lady" and "my fair correspondent"[10]] in William Howitt's *Visits to Remarkable Places;* in it she tells the legend of Charlotte Clopton:

> In the time of some epidemic, the sweating-sickness, or the plague, this young girl had sickened, and to all appearance died. She was buried with fearful haste in the vaults of Clopton chapel, attached to

Stratford church, but the sickness was not stayed. In a few days another of the Cloptons died, and him they bore to the ancestral vault; but as they descended the gloomy stairs, they saw by the torch-light, Charlotte Clopton in her grave-clothes leaning against the wall; and when they looked nearer, she was indeed dead, but not before, in the agonies of despair and hunger, she had bitten a piece from her white round shoulder![11]

One sees Gaskell's interest in the macabre in her details: the torch-light, the grave-clothes, the position, leaning against the wall, and the piece out of her round white shoulder. Gaskell's conclusion is inevitable: "Of course, she had *walked* ever since."

William and Mary Howitt were among several friends with whom Gaskell shared her love of sitting by the fire and telling ghost stories. In her *Autobiography,* Mary Howitt writes for Christmas Eve 1850: "Last night Eliza Fox wrote proposing for them and Mrs. Gaskell to come to us this evening. Meggie suggests that we should not be grand and intellectual—but ghost-stories and capital tales should be told, and that we should even play at blindman's buff. We may be merry and tell tales, but I doubt the playing at blindman's buff."[12] That such telling of ghost tales did indeed occur is affirmed by another friend, Anne Thackeray Ritchie, who praises Gaskell's story-telling ability as something she was born with:

> My sister and I were once under the same roof with her in the house of our friends Mr. and Mrs. George Smith, and the remembrance of *her voice* comes back to me, harmoniously flowing on and on, with spirit and intention, and delightful emphasis, as we all sat indoors one gusty morning listening to her ghost stories. They were Scotch ghosts, historical ghosts, spirited ghosts, with faded uniforms and nice old powdered queues. As I think it over I am suddenly struck by the immense superiority of the ghosts of my youth to the present legion of unclean spirits which surround us, as we are told—wielding teacups, smashing accordions and banjos, breaking furniture in bits. That morning at Hampstead, which I recall, was of a different order of things, spiritual and unseen; mystery was there, romantic feeling, some holy terror and emotion, all combined to keep us gratefully silent and delighted.[13]

In contrast, Charlotte Brontë was so sensitive to such stories that she wished not to hear them. Gaskell records in her *Life* of Brontë that "One night I was on the point of relating some dismal ghost story, just before bed-time. She shrank from hearing it, and confessed that she was superstitious, and prone at all times to the involuntary recurrence of any thoughts of ominous gloom which might have been suggested to her."[14]

Though Meggie Howitt might suggest ghost tales as something for fun on Christmas day and Anne Thackeray

Ritchie remember Gaskell's ghost tales with the fondness of recalling good times in childhood, neither Brontë nor Gaskell saw such stories as simply trivial or childish pursuits for an idle moment. That the ghost story was for adults is clear from one of Gaskell's letters, referring to the possible reissue of some of her "moral and sensible" stories, but not, she says, of "one or two of the H. W. [*Household Words*] stories [which] might not so well do for young people. One is an unexplained ghost story for instance" (Letter 260). This letter is dated July 27 (1855) and the unexplained ghost story, clearly, is "The Old Nurse's Story."

Another instance of the seriousness with which she regarded these tales is recorded by Augustus J. C. Hare; he repeats a story told to him after Gaskell's death by Caroline Cholmondeley Hibbert, the auditor to whom Gaskell told the story: in Hare's six-volume *The Story of My Life,* he relates:

> Mrs. Hibbert told me a very remarkable story [that] had been told her by Mrs. Gaskell the authoress, who said that she felt so greatly the uncertainty of life, that she wished a story which might possibly be of consequence, and which had been intrusted to her, to remain with some one who was certain to record it accurately. Three weeks afterwards, sitting by the fire with her daughter, Mrs. Gaskell died suddenly in her arm-chair.[15]

Who intrusted Gaskell with the tale, or what the consequence was to which she referred is not clear. The story is one that Gaskell seems to have had in mind for many years, for, as recorded by Hare, its general outline is very similar to that of "To Be Read at Dusk," a story that Dickens had published in the early 1850s and to which Gaskell referred in a letter to Eliza Fox, tentatively dated 17 November 1851: "How are the Dickens? wretch that he is to go and write MY story of the lady haunted by the face; I shall have nothing to talk about now at dull parties" (Letter 108a). If she told the story to Mrs. Hibbert in 1865, because it needed to be recorded, as Hare says, she must have had a strange lapse of memory regarding the Dickens' work.

The contrast between Gaskell's handling of this tale and that of Dickens is illustrative of her own affinity for the folk origins of the ghost story and of her close relationship with the people among whom such stories originated. Gaskell preserves the link with the supposed origins of the tale by connecting it with people known to her, whereas Dickens provides a more literary and distant context: his tale is told by a traveler who overhears it from couriers at the St. Bernard's Pass. Again, where Gaskell has the mysterious person whose face haunts the young bride appear but once and then without a name or an identity, almost as a shadow, Dickens calls him by the suggestive appellation Signor Dellombra. Gaskell's denouement is swifter and more ominous; the stranger's single appearance and the husband's brief absence are followed almost immediately by the lady's disappearance. Dickens draws out the whole with the husband's attempts to persuade his wife of the unreasonableness of her fears; his lengthy absence, along with Dellombra's frequent visits, may even hint a possible "rational" explanation. At the least, it raises the question, Was the lady seduced, repenting even as the carriage leaves, à la Isabel Vane in the best-selling *East Lynne* a few years later?

Undoubtedly, Gaskell's life in Lancashire and Cheshire inspired her interest in the people of the area, their folklore and folk tales. In her letter to Mary Howitt, quoted from above (Letter 12), she relates numerous folk customs and one supposed haunting of a house in one of "the old nooks of Lancashire," where one Lord Willoughby, who had had two daughters, is alleged by the country folk to "walk." The story has a superficial resemblance to the walking of old Lord Furnivall, who also had had two daughters, in **"The Old Nurse's Story."** The digressions, the interpolated tales to be found in her longer works may also come from her familiarity with the oral tradition around her. One such tale, in *Sylvia's Lovers,* is a ghost story that has numerous analogues.[16] Such short tales, her fragments of ghost stories found after her death and published by Ward in Volume 7 of the Knutsford edition, and a second ghost tale recorded by Hare[17] are evidence of Gaskell's interest in the type and of her skill as a storyteller. Whatever special consequence she thought they had is not clear today.

However, her longer ghost tales, **"The Old Nurse's Story"** and **"The Poor Clare,"**[18] demonstrate not only her skill as a raconteur, but also her concern with social issues. Like many other Victorians, she saw fiction as a way of leading people to unpalatable truths, of extending their awareness and understanding of those around them. Even though *Ruth* created such controversy, she says in one letter (Letter 154), "it has made [people] talk and think a little on a subject which is so painful that it requires all one's bravery not to hide one's head like an ostrich and try by doing so to forget that the evil exists." Her letters show the tension she felt between her belief in writing the truth as she knew it and her sensitivity to criticism, such as *Mary Barton, Ruth,* and *The Life of Charlotte Brontë* evoked. Reflecting on the burning of *Ruth* by two members of her husband's congregation, Gaskell laments that she "must be an improper woman without knowing it, I do so manage to shock people" (Letter 150). Yet, in another letter from almost the same time, she speaks of the care she took "to make both the story and the writing as quiet as I could, in order that 'people' (my great bugbear) might not say that they could not see what the writer felt to be a very plain and earnest truth, for romantic incidents or exaggerated writing" (Letter 152).

Tensions between propriety and truth, between doing what is expected from a woman, a wife, a mother, and acting and thinking according to her own beliefs run throughout Gaskell's letters. From such tensions come the conflicts and passions in her ghost stories. Like much of her other work, these tales show women of strong will and individual action, but they also delineate the ways in which women's power can be frustrated, turned even to a destructiveness which rebounds on the women themselves. These heroines are more blatantly "improper" women than even Ruth or Margaret Hale, for their challenge to the material world reverberates through another, a spiritual world. In Margaret Hale, Gaskell depicts a woman who challenges the opinions of men, makes changes in a masculine world through careful observation, reasoned argument, and a willingness to grow and change herself. This opportunity comes in part because she is in a changing society that is itself challenging older patriarchal systems and values. *North and South,* which was published in *Household Words* after **"The Old Nurse's Story"** and before **"The Poor Clare,"** is an affirmation of human, of woman's, possibilities in life.

Her ghost stories are something else, almost diametrically opposed. Jack Sullivan suggests that "Ghost stories are deftly in touch with our most exaggerated feelings of powerlessness in a chaotic world" and that "The sense of darkness and chaos [ghost writers] saw in the world could be projected in the most uninhibited way in the ghostly tale."[19] Robert D. Hume connects the ghost story with a writer's "profound discontent with man's condition."[20] Gaskell's two major ghost stories express her own profound discontent with the condition of women in a patriarchal society. *North and South* offers a new industrial world as a place in which a woman like Margaret Hale can literally and figuratively walk alone, a place where she can be free of the genteel accompaniment of the Shaw footman. In the two ghost stories, the old patriarchal social order in which Miss Furnivall and Bridget Fitzgerald must live stifles them, turning their potential for good into a power that destroys them. The two women are like Lilith, "locked into a vengeance . . . which can only bring [them] more suffering."[21]

In **"The Old Nurse's Story,"** nearly all the living characters are women, but their lives are dominated still by the ghost of old Lord Furnivall, whose wild playing on an organ that is "all broken and destroyed inside" is the first hint to Hester, the narrator, that something is amiss in Furnivall Manor House (Ward, 2:430). Though distanced in time (told by Hester when she is an old woman of events that occurred when she was not yet 18) and place (in the wild Cumberland Fells region), the story nonetheless presents problems of marriage and women's relationships that were as real in Gaskell's time as a hundred years before.

The Furnivall sisters are not blameless; they are proud like their autocratic father, who was "eaten up with pride" (Ward, 2:439). But they are also victims, not only to the tyrannical old man who "had broken his poor wife's heart with his cruelty" (Ward, 2:439), but to the unscrupulous musician who makes love to them both and deceives them both, turning, in the process, one sister against the other. This relative innocence of the sisters, in contrast to the wickedness of the old lord and the unnamed musician, is suggested by the attitude of the narrator and by the parallel that exists between the Furnivall sisters on the one hand and the child Rosamond, whose nurse Hester is, and the phantom child, on the other.

Young, female, dependent, the narrator has no power to save Rosamond except through her love for the child. Hester is cowed by even the male servant that the present Lord Furnivall sends to escort the orphan and her nurse to the Manor House; though she thinks him wrong, "I did what he bade me, for fear he should complain of me to my lord" (Ward, 2:425). Later, when she would take the child to her own father's home, humble though it is, to escape the phantom, the housekeeper reminds her that she could not "take Miss Rosamond with me, for that she was my lord's ward, and I had no right over her" (Ward, 2:438). The power of both the living and the dead Lords Furnivall strikes fear not only in Hester, but in the rest of the household as well, all the Lords Furnivall having the reputation of being "stern, proud" men (Ward, 2:424). Hester fears the remaining Miss Furnivall too, and yet "even in my fear, I had a kind of pity for [her], at least" (Ward, 2:442). In the final ghostly tableau, the old man "drove before him, with many a relentless gesture of abhorrence, a stern and beautiful woman, with a little child clinging to her dress" (Ward, 2:444), the former his own eldest daughter who had come to fear him and to hate her own sister. That sister triumphed then, as the elder had earlier in announcing that the musician was "her own husband" (Ward, 2:441), but neither triumphs long. Maude loses her sanity and her child, and Grace is doomed to a long life of hopelessness. The treacherous husband-lover disappears and the old lord returns to his organ, with which he instills fear into his household long after his death.

Sympathy with the remaining Miss Furnivall is evoked not only because of the narrator's pity but also through the parallels between the two sisters and the obviously innocent child-victims, the phantom and Rosamond, who are cousins, Rosamond being the great-grand-daughter of the old lord. Unacknowledged and deserted by her father, then driven out to die in the cold by her grandfather, this phantom child-victim seeks to re-en-act Grace Furnivall's betrayal of her sister by luring the innocent Rosamond out to become another victim. The aged Miss Furnivall's cry, "father! spare the little innocent child" (Ward, 2:445) is a cry for the pitiful-pitiless phantom child, for Rosamond, and for herself who had shown no pity to her sister.

In the community of women that is the Furnivall Manor House, this tragedy of women destroyed by the deceit of a man stands in contrast to the comic and sympathetic treatment of a community of women in *Cranford*, published in *Household Words* sporadically between 1851 and 1853. In *Cranford*, the women "are quite sufficient," finding that "A man . . . is *so* in the way in the house" (Ward, 2:1); in Furnivall Manor House, a man's presence severs the bond that Gaskell saw as so important among women, and especially sisters. The importance of such a bond is evident in her letters about her own four daughters as well as in her handling of the step-sisters' relationship in *Wives and Daughters*. In a letter to her daughter Marianne, for instance, she writes: "I could not bear my life if you & Meta did not love each other most dearly, and it is little *unspoken-of* grievances rankling in the mind that weaken affection, & it is so dreary to see sisters grow old, (as one sometimes does,) not caring for each other, & forgetting all early home-times" (Letter 330). In *Wives and Daughters*, loving the same man produces no rift; rather the (temporarily) unsuccessful Molly remains loyal to her step-sister and even risks her own reputation for that step-sister's happiness. **"The Old Nurse's Story"** expresses the ominous possibilities in a relationship Gaskell was, more often, optimistic about; doing precisely what Julia Briggs suggests of the ghost story, it embodies "fears too deep and too important to be expressed more directly."[22]

In **"The Poor Clare,"** Gaskell confronts the dilemma of the powerful woman who seeks to act in a patriarchal society. Again, this story is removed in time, being narrated in 1747 of events that occurred some 30 years earlier, and in place, mostly north-east Lancashire. According to A. W. Ward, this region

> —and especially that part of it which adjoins the Craven district, the home proper of the Lancashire witches of Elizabethan days, and which includes the so-called Trough of Bolland or Bowland, where lay Starkey Manor-house—is . . . a strangely isolated part of the county. The late William Arnold . . . speaks of it as "the least known district of all England." The gentry hereabouts long comprised . . . a considerable Roman Catholic element . . . No locality could, therefore, have been more appropriately chosen for a story in which faith and superstition, bitter hatred and passionate devotion, are the "antithetically mix'd" ingredients. (Ward, 5:xx.)

The narrator is not a dependent woman as in **"The Old Nurse's Story,"** but a London lawyer, who, like the narrators in many ghost tales, is the reasonable person, the skeptic; when he is convinced of the supernatural powers, the reader too must be convinced.

The principal character, Bridget Fitzgerald, is an extraordinary woman. On first meeting her, the narrator notices "something fine and commanding in the erectness of her figure" (Ward, 5:346). Her countenance is "wild, stern, fierce, indomitable," adjectives used more often of men than of women in Victorian fiction, but it is not "cunning" or "malignant" (Ward, 5:347). Her questions to the narrator "convinced me I had to do with no common intelligence" (Ward, 5:349). In her, "strong nature" and "strong will" strive together (Ward, 5:347). In the beginning she does not seem to have had supernatural powers; instead her power comes through the "magic of a superior mind," to which people yield (Ward, 5:334). Her neighbors, for instance, would break into her cottage in her absence in an attempt to save her goods, but they fear her "masterful spirit, and vehement force of will" (Ward, 5:338). Bridget's power comes partly through her role as maid to Madame Starkey, over whom she had "great influence . . . and, through her, over her husband" and partly because Squire and Madame Starkey shun mundane employments and responsibilities: "hence it was that Bridget could exert such despotic power" (Ward, 5:334). Bridget and her daughter Mary become the "ruling spirits of the household," but theirs is never a malignant or destructive power: "They were not disliked; for though wild and passionate, they were also generous by nature" (Ward, 5:334). But their power relies upon chance circumstances and cannot last.

Bridget's very existence after the death of the Starkeys comes to depend upon the sufferance of the men who inherit and control the estate. It is only because of Sir Philip Tempest's orders that she is not ducked as a witch, or worse, as Sir Philip's servant (Ward, 5:341) and later the Protestant clergyman wish. The latter, in fact, would burn her—would "carry a faggot myself to rid the country of her" (Ward, 5:372). Tempest's visitor Gisborne can shoot her dog with impunity, and Bridget, poor, Irish, female, can only appeal to heaven to punish her oppressor, who "half remorseful, but not one whit afraid," offers her "a crown to buy . . . another dog" (Ward, 5:340), with all the arrogance of an Arthur Donnithorne thinking that "if he should happen to spoil a woman's existence for her, [he] will make it up to her with expensive *bon-bons.*"[23] Though they are both unaware of the connection, Gisborne has spoiled the existence and driven to suicide the being that Bridget loves most, her daughter, for whom the dead dog is a surrogate. The "terrible deceit" which Gisborne practiced upon the daughter is never specified, though the phrase Gaskell uses, that she "was neither to have nor to hold, but rushed off from his very arms, and threw herself into a rapid stream and was drowned" (Ward, 5:366), is perhaps a hint that Mary had been deceived in believing herself Gisborne's wife. This interpretation connects this work with **"The Old Nurse's Story"** and other Gaskell tales in which women are victims sexually. Though she was married to the musi-

cian, Maude Furnival is in the eyes of those around her, it is hinted, no better than seduced: she was left "a deserted wife, whom nobody knew to have been married, with a child she dared not own" (Ward, 2:440). Similar sexual deceptions occur in **Mary Barton,** to Mary's aunt Esther and almost to Mary herself, and of course in **Ruth.** In three other major works, the women are not seduced, but they are deceived by men in whom all decision and power as to marriage reside: **Cousin Phillis, Sylvia's Lovers,** and **A Dark Night's Work.** In all of these, the sympathy is with the woman, as it is with Bridget in **"The Poor Clare,"** even when she turns out to be the very witch that the "coarse and common-minded" parson believes her to be (Ward, 5:372).

Though she performs a great expiation and act of forgiveness of her enemy, paradoxically, she seems blameless in human terms, and the curse's falling upon her own granddaughter, a great injustice. In the spiritual world of the story, however, she has called up the powers of hell to punish her enemy instead of forgiving him. In a sense, Gaskell's propriety and belief in Christian forgiveness are at war with her characterization. Gisborne is wholly unsympathetic, not only in his wanton killing of the dog and his later-revealed treachery to Mary Fitzgerald, but also in driving his daughter from home even though he is aware himself that it was his own act and Bridget's curse that produced the terrible spirit that is Lucy's double. In the concluding scenes, his association with the arrogance of the patriarchy is reinforced and extended by his role as an Austrian officer, one of the foreign "masters" of Antwerp. Even more notably than in **"The Old Nurse's Story,"** Gaskell regulates our sympathy here through the narrator, who goes so far as to join the Antwerp workers in their rebellion against their oppressors, including Gisborne. In contrast, though he is fully aware of the consequences of Bridget's curse, having seen Lucy's terrible Doppelgänger, the narrator nonetheless views Bridget as "rather a wild and savage woman than a malignant witch" (Ward, 5:368-69) and protects her by concealing the facts from the parson who would burn her if he could. This distribution of the narrator's sympathies is especially striking when one remembers that the author is a practical-minded Unitarian, tolerant but with no particular liking for Roman Catholicism (her alarm was great when Marianne Gaskell came under the influence of Cardinal Manning in Rome in the 1860s) or for the Irish, who are not compared favorably with English workers in her industrial novels.

Such ambivalence is not unusual for Gaskell. **North and South** was written to correct the bias in favor of working people that critics perceived in **Mary Barton,** even though after that novel was published, Gaskell maintained that she had spoken the truth. Her views about women's proper roles were similarly ambivalent. On one hand, her own independent spirit and her gift for writing made her chafe against the restrictions imposed on her by her roles as woman, wife, mother in a society that elevated the feminine role almost to the obliteration of any other. Her letters reveal a woman who cares intensely about her family, but is often discouraged by demands her social duties place upon her, leaving her little time to write. Letter after letter speaks of "the distraction of children" (Letter 155), of trying to write *North and South* amidst the pressures of a "full household" (Letter 192), of her problem that people "are volunteering visits, visits that would be most charming and acceptable at any other time, but I so want to get on with my writing" (of the *Life of Charlotte Brontë,* Letter 271a). Sometimes her lament is mixed with a comment on her good fortune: "I wrote twenty pages yesterday because it rained perpetually, and I was uninterrupted; such a good day for writing may not come again for months" (Letter 294).

Regarding other women, Gaskell still subscribed to some of the prevailing ideas. She praises Charlotte Brontë's "womanliness" in contradiction of the common idea that she was "a 'strong-minded emancipated' woman" (Letter 326), and she admires Barbara Bodichon's "noble bravery," even though her being "a strong fighter against the established opinions of the world . . . goes against my—what shall I call it?—*taste*—(that is not the word)" (Letter 461). Yet her letters, like her fiction, are aware of what women can and could do and of the restrictions placed on their action; she signed the first petition advocating changes that led to the Married Women's Property Acts because, she says, "our sex is badly enough used and legislated *against*" (Letter 276).

Feeling, then, both rebellious and submissive, defiant of the world's opinion and yet fearing it, it is no wonder that Gaskell uses the possibilities of the ghost story to depict a powerful woman who dares to defy heaven and earth, but whose power turns back upon herself and makes her, once again, a victim. Bridget Fitzgerald embodies most of the traits of Gaskell's most admirable characters in her realistic novels: Margaret Hale's power to accomplish things that others around her cannot, Cynthia Kirkpatrick's spirited disregard for social proprieties, Mary Barton's daring in venturing to strange and dangerous places for those she loves, Ruth's determination to do right and face consequences. Each of these women is limited, however, by a society in which she must act "womanly." But in the remote time and place and the supernatural context of the ghost story, a special wildness, an uncontrolled power, can be allowed to the women characters without their forfeiting the reader's sympathy. At the same time, the ghost story presents a dark vision of the trap women are in, in a culture like Bridget's that views them as it views her, "either a great sinner or a great saint" (Ward, 5:383), with not much room between.

Though she was undoubtedly intrigued by the ghost story for its own sake, liking the lore of the folk around her as well as, simply, a good story, Gaskell's ghost stories, like her other works, tell important truths; they express her deepest fears of what can happen if women do not have the "esprit de corps" of *Cranford,* the sisterly bonding of *Wives and Daughters,* the dynamic outlet of a changing society that offers them scope to act, as in *North and South.* In these tales she acknowledges the sexual and social power of the patriarchy which poses a threat no mid-century rationalism and optimism can deny.

Notes

[1] Charles G. Harper, *Haunted Houses: Tales of the Supernatural With Some Account of Hereditary Causes and Family Legends,* 3rd ed. (1907; rpt. London: Cecil Palmer, 1927), p. v.

[2] *Blackwood's,* 41 (January 1837), 48-50.

[3] Elizabeth Gaskell, *The Letters of Mrs Gaskell,* ed. J. A. V. Chapple and Arthur Pollard (Cambridge, MA: Harvard Univ. Press, 1967), no. 12. Further references to Gaskell's letters will be to this source and will be in parentheses in the text of this article, by letter number.

[4] David Punter, *The Literature of Terror* (New York: Longman, 1980), p. 216.

[5] *Household Words* also included numerous articles debunking a belief in witchcraft, one of which suggests that this belief, found still in remote parts of the country is not unlike the newly fashionable belief in spirit rappings to be found "In the London drawing-room of the wealthy connoisseur" and the belief of the poor in medicines and mixtures of dubious value: "The Light of Other Days," *Household Words,* 12 (September 29, 1855), 201-03.

[6] The term "ghost story" is used here according to the example of Julia Briggs in *Night Visitors, The Rise and Fall of the English Ghost Story* (London: Faber, 1977): it includes "not only stories about ghosts, but about possession and demonic bargains, spirits other than those of the dead, including ghouls, vampires, werewolves, the 'swarths' of living men and the 'ghost-soul' or *Doppelgänger*" (p. 12).

[7] Elizabeth Gaskell, *The Life of Charlotte Brontë,* ed. Alan Shelston (Baltimore: Penguin, 1975), p. 401.

[8] A. W. Ward, "Introduction," *Cousin Phillis and Other Tales,* Vol. 7 of *The Works of Mrs. Gaskell* (London: Smith, Elder & Co., 1906), p. xxiii. All other citations of Gaskell's work, with the exception of the *Life of Charlotte Brontë* will be to this, the Knutsford edition, and will be given within the text of this article, by volume and page numbers.

[9] Harper, p. 62.

[10] William Howitt, *Visits to Remarkable Places* (London: Longman, Orme, Brown, Green, & Longmans, 1840), pp. 135, 139.

[11] Howitt, pp. 136-37.

[12] Mary Howitt, *An Autobiography,* ed. Margaret Howitt (London: Wm. Isbister, 1889), 2:65.

[13] Anne Thackeray Ritchie, "Preface" to *Cranford* (1898; rpt. London: Macmillan, 1891), p. ix.

[14] Gaskell, *Life of Charlotte Brontë,* p. 501.

[15] Augustus J. C. Hare, *The Story of My Life* (London: George Allen, 1896), 3:117-18.

[16] See Angus Easson, *Elizabeth Gaskell* (London: Routledge & Kegan Paul, 1979), pp. 254-55, n. 1.

[17] Hare, 2:224-27.

[18] "The Old Nurse's Story" contains actual ghosts; in "The Poor Clare," the spirit that accompanies Lucy is her diabolical double.

[19] Jack Sullivan, "Introduction" to *Lost Souls, A Collection of English Ghost Stories* (Athens: Ohio Univ. Press, 1983), pp. 5, 3.

[20] Robert D. Hume, "Exuberant Gloom, Existential Agony, and Heroic Despair: Three Varieties of Negative Romanticism," in *The Gothic Imagination: Essays in Dark Romanticism,* ed. G. R. Thompson (Pullman: Washington State Univ. Press, 1974), p. 111.

[21] Sandra M. Gilbert and Susan Gubar, *The Madwoman in the Attic, The Woman Writer and the Nineteenth-Century Literary Imagination* (New Haven: Yale Univ. Press, 1979). p. 35.

[22] Briggs, p. 23.

[23] George Eliot, *Adam Bede,* ed. John Paterson (Boston: Houghton Mifflin, 1968), ch. 12, p. 107.

Hilary M. Schor (essay date 1992)

SOURCE: "'Filled in with Pretty Writing': Desire, History, and Literacy in *Sylvia's Lovers*," in *Scheherezade in the Marketplace: Elizabeth Gaskell and the Victorian Novel*, Oxford University Press, 1992, pp. 153-81.

[*In the following essay, Schor contends that* Sylvia's Lovers *is a plotting of desire—especially female desire, which "works its own narrative transformations" and gestures towards a history, writing, and identity particular to women.*]

"Desire is always there at the start of a narrative," Peter Brooks has suggested: the desire of the reader for movement, of the text for its own end, of the characters for whatever the desideratum of the plot is to be.[1] In both *Sylvia's Lovers* and *Wives and Daughters,* Gaskell's attention moves from the focusing of desire into the marriage plot to the way desire itself is plotted. Where the earlier novels offered fairly conventional progresses of both characters' and readers' desires, here, there is no such easy progression. In these novels, desire is given a gender and a history; it is placed within history (as revolution or evolution) and within gender (in the gothic plot of female desire). In *Sylvia's Lovers,* desire is self-consuming; it loses its place as the force always already (naturally) there. The heroine's plot and its historical analogue (the revolutionary fervor of the Napoleonic wars) take place within a world of doubling, confusion, and narrative self-reflexivity.

Sylvia's Lovers is Gaskell's first historical novel. Although she had written historical fiction previously (*My Lady Ludlow,* a story about the dangers of teaching servants to read in the time of the French Revolution, was published in 1858; *Lois the Witch,* a novella dealing with the Salem witchcraft trials, in 1859), and although *Ruth* was set thirty years in the past, *Sylvia's Lovers* is her most extended venture into the past—and perhaps the most deliberate. The novel not only examines the questions of change and violence these other historical works posed but manages to rephrase as well the question of the relationship between the heroine and the revolutions around her; between individuals and social change; between male and female plots, in a way unique in Gaskell's work. Like Dickens's *A Tale of Two Cities,* published in 1859, the year Gaskell first proposed her novel to George Smith, *Sylvia's Lovers* wants both to trace the passions of individuals at times of intense social change and to understand the parallels between the desires of men and women and the forces of revolution.

Like *Mary Barton, Sylvia's Lovers* begins with the need to marry off a spirited, willful heroine; with two men who love her; with her angry, impassioned father, and his dangerous political violence. Like the earlier novel, it asks which "force" it is that collapses into the other; where do the public and the private end and begin? And like the earlier novel, this book seems deeply aware of its middle-class readers, and their complacency about historical change. The Yorkshire of the novel is at once the land of the Brontës, in which Gaskell had been immersed in writing the biography of her friend Charlotte, and the home of much of the radical working-class protests of the 1830s and 1840s; in this novel, it is also a comment on the absence of real change in later Victorian England.

The novel seems to take its energy from the wilds of the Yorkshire whaling village; it announces itself as a novel of desire, with characters who speak out fiercely what they want. But *Sylvia's Lovers* presents a world of constant oppositions, confusions, and reversals; after speaking their desires, characters find they want something else. As soon as they make their bold claims to freedom, they are forced to recant, realizing they have made some crucial interpretive error or do not know how to name what they want. Throughout the novel, desire is articulated only to be contradicted, and each character's desire exists as one plot among many, amid a mesh of conflicting wishes, repetitions, negations, and returns, in which choice seems at once free-floating and forever fixed.

Not only is *Sylvia's Lovers* filled with a confusion of desires, it argues a central confusion in the construction of desire itself, and unfixes desire as a concept from the realm of sexuality. Desire here is a way of structuring and forming identity, a plot in which identity is gained through conflict and opposition. The central "plot," one written by and for men, and acted out primarily through their love of women, depends on the registering of difference between men and women, and its essential progress is one in which men fix their identity by desiring each other's women.[2] In that light, Gaskell's novel begins by asking how women can acquire *any* identity in a plot that requires them to be only objects, never fully formed subjects, free to choose for themselves. How, if they are known through their "lovers," are they to come into being themselves?

It is here, with that question of desire and change, that history and narrative come back together. Narrative, as Tzvetan Todorov has argued, depends on the tension between "two formal categories, difference and similarity"; that is, neither absolute difference nor absolute similarity will generate narrative.[3] *Sylvia's Lovers* suggests that the realms of similarity and difference have culturally assigned, gendered roles: men live in the world of difference, conflict, history; women in the realm of similarity, repetition, myth. Narrative depends on the play between them, the play we conventionally enact through the romance plot, in which women stay at home, and men have adventures. But *Sylvia's Lovers* will also suggest that in times of violent social change, plots of all sorts become more complicated, and the tension that seems to guarantee narrative can come to contaminate it instead. In *Sylvia's Lovers,* the plot of female desire unfixes difference, and works its own narrative transformations; in *Sylvia's Lovers,* the woman writer's concern with the literary, indeed, with literacy itself, asks what it would mean if the woman

novelist began to tell a new story; if the density of female desire might, instead, write a new history altogether.

i

At the center of *Sylvia's Lovers* is a very dense romantic triangle. Sylvia Robson, the young, high-spirited only child of Daniel Robson, a sailor-turned-farmer, and Bell, his better-born, educated wife, is adored by her mother's cousin, the earnest, sober Philip Hepburn. But she, barely registering Philip's devotion, loses her heart to the handsome, bold specksioneer Charley Kinraid, who in turn promises his love to her—much to the horror of Philip, who believes Charley to be untrue. The novel seems divided between the passions of these characters, and Gaskell's working titles for the novel suggest her interest in all three. At first the novel was to be called "The Specksioneer," and then it became "Philip's Idol," a title to which she seemed deeply attached. She changed it finally to *Sylvia's Lovers,* the only title of these that includes all three central characters. The fluctuation suggests the focus on character *in relation:* each character seems to take over the novel in turn, not taking it over alone but always as he or she is viewed by or matters to others. Hence, Philip is not "Philip," but "Sylvia's Lover"; Sylvia is important in that she is "Philip's Idol;" even the "Specksioneer," significantly, is noted not for his name but for his representative, "heroic" stature as harpooner. And so, too, within the love relationships of the novel, characters assume charged roles, representative positions; not names but functions.

Further, though the emphasis of the novel, as the final title suggests, is on the two men—what they represent for Sylvia and the ways they represent or imagine her— the novel encloses the relations between the three central characters within larger circles of desire that draw in other characters as well. Philip, obsessed with Sylvia, is the object himself of obsessive love: Hester Rose, the Quaker woman with whose mother he boards, loves him as quietly, as passionately as he loves Sylvia. Hester, in turn, is loved by William Coulson, the other junior partner in the Fosters' shop where Philip works. Coulson, when rejected by Hester, is able to turn to another woman, much as Charley Kinraid, when he discovers that Sylvia has married Philip, marries a rich, beautiful, sheltered girl who has none of the qualities he swore would make him love only Sylvia forever.

Although some of these loves seem not to touch the central relations—Philip does not "learn" from Coulson how to love Hester, for instance—at other times, love seems entirely imitative. When Charley and Sylvia meet, each perceives the other as already desired by or belonging to someone else. Charley is pointed out to Sylvia by Molly Corney, and Molly presents him as already practically engaged to her; when he first sees

Sylvia crying at a dead sailor's funeral, he "conclude[s] that she must have been a sweetheart of the dead man."[4] Each act of desire shimmers with the reflection of someone else's (imagined) desire; people are searching for their own image in someone else's story.

This kind of love is always a blending of public and private relations; the novel thrives on eavesdropping, interruptions, trysts, onlookers, and soliloquies, with only the narrator watching all the observers in turn. Yet in this overlapping world, no event takes place only in one person's "story." Even in the scene when Sylvia first speaks to Charley, who thinks her already spoken for, in the presence of Molly, whom Sylvia assumes to be Charley's fiancée, she has been followed in her progress to the specksioneer by her cousin Philip, who wants to protect her from the crowd and keep her to himself. But the repeated parallels, here and throughout the novel, are ignored by the characters: the irony of the opposing romances is noted only by the quiet narrator, who juxtaposes them by moving directly between them:

> "Yo'll come and be nursed at Moss Brow, Charley," said Molly; and Sylvia dropped her little maidenly curtsey, and said, "Good-by;" and went away, wondering how Molly could talk so freely to such a hero; but then, to be sure, he was a cousin, and probably a sweetheart, and that would make a great deal of difference, of course.

> Meanwhile, her own cousin kept close by her side. (p. 72)

Each character is caught up in several plots at once—with an array of conflicting desires, so there is hardly an "individual" or "private" plot to be named. Philip may be the tradesman in one plot, the "cousin" in the next, the earnest lover in his own, but only the narrative translates between one plot and the other; the characters seem unaware of the jumble in which they move.

Sylvia's Lovers seems to pose *intentionally* complicated problems of plots, but do we, initially, take seriously its overlapping stories, conflicting aims, doubled desires? These seem at first essentially comic elements, plots of romantic reversals, where we can expect a kind of "Midsummer Night's Dream" in which "Jack will have Jill; Naught shall go ill." The task of fiction, after all, is often to shuffle lovers from inappropriate choice to appropriate choice. One way of reading *Sylvia's Lovers* would be as a romance plot whose tragic—morbid—overtones take over, as another of Gaskell's novels where the domestic plot turns to melodrama and an essentially familiar novel is derailed by the novelist's penchant for overly dramatic contrasts.

Critics have raised this question to focus on the generic switch into melodrama at the novel's conclusion, when the two heroes find themselves at the Siege of Acre and—improbably—recognize each other. But this one melodrama of doubling—the moment when the heroes face unexpected similarities where they had previously perceived difference, and finally see each other as trapped by the same plot—is part of a larger pattern of doubling (formal and thematic) throughout the novel: plots that trap, confuse, and narrate their characters; plots that force on characters unexpected "returns." This doubling, what Peter Brooks describes as narrative that appears "to partake of the demonic, as a kind of tantalizing instinctual play, a re-enactment that encounters the magic and the curse of reproduction or 'representation,'"[5] is part of a larger drama, a plot *Sylvia's Lovers* reads through sexual conflict. And here the "comic" ending is displaced, in favor of a deeper disruption, for although in comic plots there is room for female activity, and female desire can be acknowledged and its threat contained, in nineteenth-century fiction, desire can be expressed only by men. In this novel, the "curse" is the disruptive power of female desire, in the world where Sylvia's lovers, not Sylvia herself, are empowered and—culturally—given textual authority. This is the truly disruptive possibility the novel's dense plot wishes to entertain: that women would write stories of difference, rather than "standing for" that crucial difference against which men will write their stories; that women could desire, and speak out that desire.

This might suggest again the danger of reading too narrowly the (female) plots of romantic desire in the novel, of missing what Eve Sedgwick has argued of desire, that it is a "social force, the glue, even when its manifestation is hostility or hatred or something less emotively charged," that it is a "structure."[6] It is easy to misread "love" in a novel; to see only the confusion we know as plot, only the plot we call "love." What Sylvia wants when she "falls in love" with Kinraid—what that love is another name for—need not be limited to the structures of romantic love but can be linked to a wider field of desire, to which she gains access by "falling in love" with him. And again, in reading the intense relations between Kinraid and Hepburn—Sylvia's "lovers"—we can see that their inter-interpretations, as well as their readings of Sylvia and her character, express desires that transcend any notions of romantic love. In Charley's ways of promising his love to Sylvia, in Philip's interpretive battle about Charley and his dilemma over his promise to present Charley's love (his "truth") to Sylvia, and particularly in Philip's confusion over his marriage to Sylvia, we see the way that romantic desire promises to function for these characters: it will provide them with something they lack, something, most often, caught up with their own sexual identity and self-definition, but something which has little to do with the real experience or identity of the beloved object.[7] The quest to fill that emptiness, then, goes by the name of romantic love; it is their own identities that Sylvia's lovers most lack.

Philip loves Sylvia, most simply, because she is resistant: she is charming, wayward, beautiful, and completely indifferent to him. What he recognizes from the first is their difference, but it is a difference that sparks his passion. What he wants from her must be that resistance. When they are finally married, after circumstances—her father's execution, her mother's illness, the loss of her farm—have moved Sylvia into his arms, he can notice only the gap between what he wanted and what he in fact has:

> He wanted the old Sylvia back again; captious, capricious, wilful, haughty, merry, charming. Alas! that Sylvia was gone for ever. (p. 330)

What he has is a woman under his "influence," who "obey(s) his expressed wishes with gentle indifference, as if she had no preference of her own," "out of the spirit of obedience" toward her mother. What he wanted was a woman who would be "wilful" and at the same time under his influence: whose will, in essence, would be to be his.

But Philip's desire, which is on the one hand for possession of Sylvia, is also, on some level, to be possessed. Of all the characters, he is the one most obsessed with his "idol," most completely defined as a "lover." His passion nears masochism, in his repeated return to her side despite her scorn, his over-reading in her polite "good-nights" an encouragment to his hopes. Not only does he blur the lines between possessor and possessed, he seems to blur lines of masculine and feminine plots of desire here. He feels within him "a force of enduring love," which is what marks him as unusual: the "thought of her was bound up with his life; and that once torn out by his own free will, the very roots of his heart must come also" (p. 160). That passivity of "enduring love," the suppressed violence of tearing up "by his own free will" the "very roots of his heart," the connection between thinking of her and "his life," are the most violent—and the most conventionally feminine—statements of desire in the novel. But they suggest, further, that that aspect of Philip—desiring, where he seems content; angry, where he seems meek—can, in what are traditionally feminine terms, get expressed only through love. Philip gets a self, as women customarily do in novels, by being in love.

Charley Kinraid's love for Sylvia takes place equally in terms of desire and possession, though in a more mutual struggle for power. Both he and Sylvia enjoy each other's defiance: "they were like two children defying each other; each determined to conquer" (p. 184). For Charley, Sylvia is a "pretty girl," whom he

claims he will "niver forget," but in fact, she seems to slide in and out of his consciousness. What he enjoys, most clearly, is his power over her; what we never know, exactly, is how much he does think of her when she isn't there.

We do know that the men in the novel think constantly of one another, and are unable to read the other(s) except as projections of—or in opposition to—their own psyches. The novel's critique of Charley's "forgetfulness"—and his love for Sylvia—is most clearly in Philip's terms: when he sees Charley kidnapped by the press-gang, and hears his farewell message to Sylvia promising to return, Philip thinks of writing to Sylvia and "telling her—how much?"

> She might treasure up her lover's words like grains of gold, while they were lighter than dust in their meaning to Philip's mind; words which such as the specksioneer used as counters to beguile and lead astray silly women. It was for him to prove his constancy by action; and the chances of his giving such proof were infinitesimal in Philip's estimation. (p. 224)

Philip sees Charley, here, not as his own person but as a type, "such as the specksioneer," rather than this particular specksioneer. (Here Sylvia, too, becomes a type—one of the "silly women" easily led astray.) But Philip sees Charley through his own lens: Charley does not express "constancy" by action such as Philip would choose. Charley *has* just offered proof, by sending a farewell warning to Sylvia rather than just disappearing, but Philip will not "estimate" that proof. He has, of course, just closed Charley's chance of giving any proof, by deciding not to give the message to Sylvia; clearly, we are to read this as Philip's special pleading, his own desire blurring his judgment. But this pattern of reading one's opposite in terms of one's own predispositions continues throughout the novel: when Sylvia overvalues Hester's courage by imagining what she would do if she loved Philip the way Hester does; when Hester tries to imagine anything Philip could do to alienate her affections, as he has Sylvia's; when Philip assumes that he can read Charley's character as clearly as he does the business information he receives in London, where he feels himself "fully capable of unravelling each clue to information, and deciding on the value of knowledge so gained" (pp. 225-226). Philip "took upon himself to decide that, with such a man as the specksioneer, absence was equivalent to faithless forgetfulness." He is leaping from the stories he has heard of Charley's other betrayals to a notion of character; further, he is leaping from his own desires, what his absence would mean, to what it must mean for Charley.

Charley—and Sylvia—make similar assumptions about Philip based on an inability to read a character unlike their own; with Charley and Philip, competing for Sylvia is as much a battle of character as of wills. Each asserts a way of being in the world through the ability to win—to possess—Sylvia. In a sense, each wants her to mirror his success, his self, back to him, and each wants the other man to register this victory. In a stunning moment, after the Corneys' New Year's party to which Philip escorts Sylvia, and at which she first kisses Charley, the Corney family and Charley himself come into the Fosters' store. Philip watches Charley "perpetually," "with a kind of envy of his bright, courteous manner, the natural gallantry of the sailor."

> If it were but clear that Sylvia took as little thought of him as he did of her, to all appearance, Philip could even have given him praise for manly good looks, and a certain kind of geniality of disposition which made him ready to smile pleasantly at all strangers, from babies upwards. (p. 164)

Charley comes to shake hands with him "over the counter":

> Last night Philip could not have believed it possible that such a demonstration of fellowship should have passed between them; and perhaps there was a slight hesitation of manner on his part, for some idea or remembrance crossed Kinraid's mind which brought a keen searching glance into the eyes which for a moment were fastened on Philip's face. In spite of himself, and during the very action of hand-shaking, Philip felt a cloud come over his face, not altering or moving his features, but taking light and peace out of his countenance. (p. 165)

That moment of recognition—of mutual desire—is the forging of a bond that encourages not understanding but confusion. Soon after that, Molly tells of Charley's dancing all the rest of the evening at the party, and Philip is deeply relieved, for he says that after Sylvia's departure, "yearning after the absent one would have been a weight to his legs," and he cannot imagine anyone being different. But in their consciousness of each other, and their constant measuring of themselves by the existence of the other, the two heroes remain deeply linked—neither has an entirely separate (individual) desire.

But female desire is inscribed differently and Sylvia's love plot must be read equally differently. The difference is social: the sharp contrast between her love for Charley and the love of both men for her becomes clear when one notes the locations of the repeated confrontations between Philip and Charley. When Philip watches Charley being taken by the press-gang, Charley is about to go out to sea; Philip is on his way to London. At this moment, as at the end of the novel, when both men are at the Siege of Acre, Sylvia is at home, waiting; the plot of female desire differs most clearly from that of men in that men get to go on the road. Men are to some extent free to walk out to meet their destinies; women must wait for their plot to come to them. Nowhere more than in this simple difference do we see what links Philip and Charley: neither need choose a wife to gain freedom.

But to complicate this further, we might note that Sylvia's love for Charley resembles Philip's love for her more closely than it does any other in the novel: Sylvia, like Philip, wants through desire to gain access to some other world. Desire, for her, expresses a lack. Unlike Philip, however, she does not perceive the lack as in herself: there is nothing *in* Charley that she wants, as Philip wants her charm, her willfulness, her sexuality, at one point, it almost seems, the overtness of her desire for Charley. What Sylvia wants, most clearly, is adventure; if she were able to go to sea herself, she would not be in love with "the specksioneer." There is no doubt but that she is attracted to the sailor, who is, as Philip notes, courteous, smiling, sophisticated, worldly—but these terms begin to blend into something he *has done* rather than something he *has*. She wants his sophistication, only in that she wants to be able to do things.

Sylvia's story, then, does suggest a quest for "similarity" rather than difference—identity through emulation rather than opposition—but a similarity already linked to the process of narrative. Although Charley initially comes to Sylvia's attention marked as desirable by Molly's interest in him, he is further marked as a figure of drama, the hero who has resisted attack and won commendation, who bravely mourns his lost comrade. When he enters Sylvia's life more directly, coming to her parents' house, his way in is paved by his stories: he and her father tell stories of their adventures, and "all night long Sylvia dreamed of burning volcanoes springing out of icy southern seas." But, significantly, she recounts of her listening:

> As in the specksioneer's tale the flames were peopled with demons, there was no human interest for her in the wondrous scene in which she was no actor, only a spectator. (p. 106)

Sylvia is "no actor, only a spectator," because she is a woman. The closest she can come to his islands, volcanoes, and seas is her geography lessons from her cousin Philip, which she spends largely

> stooping over the outspread map, with her eyes,— could he have seen them,—a good deal fixed on one spot in the map, not Northumberland, where Kinraid was spending the winter, but those wild northern seas about which he had told them such wonders. (p. 114)

Her desire is not so much for where he is (Northumberland) but where the "wonders" he had narrated are. Here already she confuses narrating with acting, at a moment when she is not herself moving but sits captivated in his absence by his earlier presence as narrator. Sylvia wants not to be with—or even to be—Kinraid but to see things for herself, to be a heroine. The best she can hope for is to be in love with his stories; it is through her love for him that she hopes to gain heroic stature.

But in this way women's desire seems most imitative—or, rather, reduced to the realms of imitation by convention and by narrative itself. While the men wander the world, gaining experience and choosing for themselves, Sylvia stays home and works—and listens. Through the rest of the novel, Sylvia seems singularly hemmed in by stories, and narrative tradition seems to gain in power. Her mother tells her of "poor Nancy," a Wordsworthian abandoned woman who goes mad waiting for her cheating fiancé, but in the story Sylvia hears only a parallel of her own love (a parallel that traps her more deeply in it); the Fosters' story of Alice Rose's bounder of a husband and Coulson's story of his betrayed sister, abandoned by Kinraid, both lead Philip to lie to Sylvia about Kinraid's absence; Sylvia's father's story—his own originating myth—about cutting off his thumb to escape the press-gang leads him to defy them at last, to participate in the rebellion that will lead to his arrest, conviction, and execution by the state. Stories—as cultural truths, as personal history—seem part of the constant repetition that freezes desire, and specifically, that shapes female movement. As stories name things, they limit possibilities: Sylvia's rebellion cannot take a form unimagined by her mother's and father's stories.

In the same way, as Gaskell herself was constantly learning, women cannot always write new plots for themselves. In this novel, as elsewhere in her work, literature itself is implicated in women's inscription into culture. In *Sylvia's Lovers,* we see the traces of this inscription in two places: in Sylvia's battle with literacy, and in Gaskell's commentary on other Victorian women's novels of female desire. The abstraction of theories of fiction on which I have been dwelling (the repetitions and desires of this overdetermined narrative) here focus on the question of female difference and *its* gothic plot—and its relation to the "plots" of history.

ii

Sylvia's Lovers begins with the story that *North and South* left out: that of the illiterate heroine, the "Jess MacFarlane" of the ballad Gaskell cites, who cannot read the letter her lover sends.[8] If Sylvia could read a letter from Charley, she might have a different story; as is so often true in Gaskell, questions of language and linguistic power become questions of plot. But questions of language also *stay* questions of language, unmetaphorized, as they often do *not* in her novels; this is a story about Sylvia's illiteracy, her learning to

read, and the relation of what is seen as patriarchal language to patriarchal power. Literacy suggests the larger revolutionary questions of the novel, but the discussion of the literary (of already-told stories) offers an equally powerful critique of state- and gender-systems of authority. It is out of Sylvia's illiteracy (and the cultural disempowerment that represents) that the novel's critique of established plots (and the culturally scripted disappearance of female power) will arise.

It is Sylvia's mother who wants Sylvia to learn to read: Sylvia wishes "the man were farred"—and she is sure it is a man—"who plagues his brain wi' striking out new words" (p. 107). Philip, who wants desperately to teach her to read, both so he can reshape her and so he can be near her, offers her "a pen as'll nearly write of itself," but Sylvia, trying to achieve the right "attitude," bursts out, "What's the use on my writing 'Abednego,' 'Abednego,' 'Abednego,' all down a page?" (p. 93) In that endless repetition of male identity, which Sylvia must copy into a "copy-book wi' t' Tower of London on it, [which] we'll fill . . . wi' as pretty writing as any in t' North Riding" (p. 92), is Sylvia's real "lesson": first, that she cannot speak out against education that she feels to be useless; and second, that the ability of men to make women write out men's names over and over constitutes real, not merely textual, authority. In that drone of patronymics, and in Sylvia's forced participation in the scene of male authorship, Gaskell suggests the text's critique of the constriction of women's lives, and of the endless repetition of male names that makes up history—and of literature's participation in both.

Gaskell will attempt, at the end of the novel, to present a more optimistic vision of women teaching women to read, one that contrasts with Philip's lessons, which are only the repetition of his love for her. She never, in this novel, presents a more optimistic view of women's *writing*. But if one takes up the terms of literary doubling as referring to the text's repetition of other texts, one might locate *Sylvia's Lovers,* and its exploration of female desire and female literacy, in the history of the woman novelist. Gaskell wrote *Sylvia's Lovers* directly after writing *The Life of Charlotte Brontë,* and one can easily see traces in Gaskell's novel of the works of both Emily and Charlotte Brontë, of *Wuthering Heights,* in the ways it rewrites the two-suitors problem, as if imagining an Edgar Linton with passion, and of *Jane Eyre*'s attempt to reconcile passion and both male and female masochism. One might think here also of George Eliot, of whom Gaskell was preternaturally conscious throughout these years, and the problematic passions of Philip Wakem and Maggie Tulliver. Gaskell must have been aware of other women novelists' attempts to give freedom to the sexualized heroine, and it is women writers, rather than men, whom she echoes in this novel. In its insistent use of dialect as well we can see *Sylvia's Lovers* commenting on the works of other women novelists: George Eliot's early realism depends on dialect, and as Charlotte Brontë remarked of her sister's novel, the Yorkshire dialect is what makes the characters in *Wuthering Heights* "graphic"—literally, it makes them signify. The kind of challenge this graphicness represented is suggested, however, by Charlotte's own actions in revising *Wuthering Heights,* for she chose to "modify the orthography of the old servant Joseph's speeches" when publishing the revised edition, out of fear the Yorkshire dialect would be "unintelligible" to southern readers;[9] *Sylvia's Lovers,* as if to force readers to confront the unexpected yet once more, gives even its heroine a "northern" dialect, and the "orthography" to go with it. Gaskell worked to revise the second edition of her novel to be more faithful to the Yorshire accent; and indeed, the revised version looks very different on the page. As frequently happens in Victorian fiction—and particularly, I would argue, for women writers, so often defeated by the conventions of "the real"—the realm of realistic detail becomes almost surreal, pushing at the boundaries of readerly expectation. As is consistent with the naturalized gothicism of the text, too much reality jars the text.

The tension between realism and romance seems particularly to conjure up these other women writers: as in the ghostly interventions of *Wuthering Heights,* the presence of the Great Mother in *Jane Eyre* or in *Shirley,* something supernatural seems always about to rip open the surface of *Sylvia's Lovers.*[10] We might see as well some particular connection of the female novel with the gothic: with the experience of female desire as monstrous, thinking briefly of Mary Shelley's *Frankenstein,* which Gaskell mentions in *Mary Barton;* and of her own gothic stories, with their hauntings, repetitions, and spiritual visitations. Gaskell believed in ghosts (or at least ghost stories), with their invocation of another world, and may have viewed it as a specifically female world, in which the limitations placed on women in the realistic novel did not apply. If a questioning woman is, in Adrienne Rich's phrase, a woman in the shape of a monster,[11] Gaskell's novel might need to include the demonic within it to represent the specter of female passion. But at the least, she can be seen as invoking a literary heritage, that of a world haunted by unspoken female desire.

If Sylvia is a prisoner of the narratives of others, of her "lovers" and of "femininity," she cannot desire without being within a gothic plot, part of the monstrous. What we might read more historically, can also be recast in the terms Luce Irigaray offers:

> One would have to dig down very deep indeed to discover beneath the traces of this civilization, of this history, the vestiges of a more archaic civilization that might give some clue to woman's sexuality. That extremely ancient civilization would undoubtedly have a different alphabet, a different language.[12]

As Irigaray goes on to argue, "Woman's desire would not be expected to speak the same language as man's." Gaskell's deliberate invocation of the "primitive" for Sylvia's story might seem close here to Irigaray's "archaic" civilization, but clearly, this pre-cultural realm cannot be achieved in nineteenth-century fiction—or in eighteenth-century Yorkshire. Once again, historical and fictional constraints meet: Irigaray's "digging" for "a different alphabet, a different language" suggests Sylvia's lessons from Philip—and reiterates the ways they are lessons in femininity, in the postponement of desire. They have nothing to do with Sylvia's boldest statement in the novel: when she stares up at Philip, asking him if Charley is indeed dead, and says, directly, "I thought yo' knowed that I cared a deal for him." This is the kind of statement the novel needs to make room for, what there is rarely a language for.

But literacy extends—here, as in *North and South*—into larger social and economic structure. To borrow again from Irigaray's theoretical restatement of this, "Woman is never anything but the locus of a more or less competitive exchange between two men."[13] Woman, as in this novel of shopkeepers, is "a use-value for man, an exchange-value among men; in other words a commodity . . . whose price will be established . . . by 'subjects': workers, merchants, consumers." Irigaray goes on to suggest that women need to move outside this "marketplace," to move beyond "sexual commerce," to claim "a right to pleasure"; what *Sylvia's Lovers* makes clear is that women do not have the economic power to "own"—acknowledge or possess—anything. Hester Rose, the most competent of the younger people at the Fosters' store, will not be made a partner because she is a woman, and to give her property is to give it to some third person you don't know. In one of the novel's best comic scenes, Alice Rose dictates her will to William Coulson, but she knows nothing of official, legal language and insists more on the rhetorical flourishes than on the fact of money itself. That realm, Gaskell says clearly, is closed to women. Sylvia cannot own and run her father's farm, which would save her from having to marry Philip and move into the store—that is as impossible as her becoming a sailor and traveling to Greenland. She would have to cross as great a divide; it would be just as monstrous for her to be economically independent as to be an explorer.

In that light, the world of male history to which I will turn next is even more fatally closed to Sylvia: the unreality of the scenes of battles, for which characters offer a range of oddly textualized explanations, seems entirely unlike Sylvia's scenes of submissive reading, her fireside lessons with Philip. But they recreate a similar story of male identity, in an alphabet Sylvia cannot read. If this chapter began with the fierceness of individual desire in the novel, we need to turn now to the ferocity of history—and of its melodramatic (and self-consciously literary) inclusion in the gothic (romance) text. We must turn, that is, to the world that belongs only to Sylvia's lovers.

iii

The overarching male realm closed to Sylvia is history, and nothing makes clearer Gaskell's sense of Sylvia's constriction than the interruption of the novel by historical events, the way the novel is, to borrow its terms, "impressed." But for all that, in some ways the novel never seems as interested in "history" as are contemporary works: for all that *Sylvia's Lovers* takes its tone (and some of its urgency) from the French Revolution and its echoes in England, its real urgency is domestic, and its energies seem private. Rather than diminishing romance by placing it in history, as Thackeray does in *Vanity Fair,* Gaskell reduces history to a moment of conflict that can be understood *only* by its role in fictional and sexual doubling.

What the novel does draw on is the interest Gaskell had throughout her career in revolution, mob action, and violent historical change.[14] The novel is carefully set around the events of the French Revolution and the subsequent European wars of conquest: the revolution, the conflict that fuels the press-gangs and the wars in which Philip and Charley fight, remains both a hope and threat of transformation in the novel. It stands behind Sylvia's father's small rebellion against the state, when he stages the riot against the press-gang, and behind his questioning of "representation," in which the government exists to speak only what he believes and "govern me as I judge best" (p. 40), mirroring or reproducing his "vote," and his voice, in a larger sphere. In focusing on English response to revolution, especially the violence of the Treasonable and Seditious Actions Act, Gaskell returns to the link she made in *Mary Barton* between limitations on political and sexual choice. In the execution of Daniel Robson, we see the specter of state repression of all dissent. Nowhere does Gaskell suggest that hanging was the appropriate response to so small a disturbance, and her irony at the expense of contemporary readers ("Will our descendents have a wonder about us, such as we have about the inconsistency of our forefathers? . . . It is well for us that we live at the present time, when everbody is logical and consistent.") suggests some of the progress she has made since *Mary Barton.* The action of the authorities can be justified only "looking back on the affair in cold blood," and the defense of the father made by his daughter ("Why, York Castle's t' place they send a' t' thieves and robbers to, not honest men like feyther") carries the ring of Gaskellian conviction. But where alibis and testimony carried weight in the world of *Mary Barton,* and the heroine could act to save her father and win her lover, this novel offers no relief. The darkness of its political vision and the cold-hearted economics of Philip's shopkeeping—which

presages the mechanical industralization in the decades that followed the revolutionary years—serve only to contain more completely the novel's heroine, for the two plots remain linked: through the repressive action of the state and the death of her radical father, Sylvia is left alone, forced to marry the cousin she does not love. History, then, is in some ways most present in the text as a repression of female sexuality. It is the plot's way of moving Sylvia into marriage, but it is left open to criticism.

What happens when we move into the larger historical realm? For one thing, the scale becomes much larger: the battles of Sir Sidney Smith in capturing a lugger at Havre-de-Grace in 1796; the Siege of Acre, in which the British defended the Turks in 1798—the text suggests both the range of Gaskell's research and the desire to escape the provinciality of the novel at the same time. And yet, what happens in the plot is another collapse of the public into the private; in literary terms, what we see is an exposure of the text's habit of doubling, and in that, the return of the romance. In the overlap between the fading out of history and the repetition of the *technique* of repetition, we see the novel producing the unexpected doubling of Philip and Charley—a doubling *so* unexpected that difference seems close to breaking down. At that moment, history and plot both suggest again that essential similarity of male desire, played out against the suppression of female desire.

For this reason, I would argue, and not for melodramatic purposes alone, the novel introduces its coincidence of Philip and Charley at the Siege of Acre—and introduces it precisely as a violation of realism. After Charley returns and accuses Sylvia of betraying him by marrying Philip, and Philip confesses to having concealed the action of the press-gang from Sylvia, Sylvia vows never to forgive Philip, and both men leave. Sylvia makes a life for herself in a community of women, to which I shall return at greater length later, and Philip makes his way out as a soldier, as "Stephen Freeman." We see Kinraid, thinking of his "newly-made wife in her English home," near death on the battlefield, and suddenly a man picks him up, a man with a face "like one formerly known to the sick senses of Kinraid; yet it was too like a dream too utterly improbable to be real." But what this dream figure, this "sickly"-sensed man, utters is Philip's only statement on his *earlier* action: "I niver thought you'd ha' kept true to her" (p. 431). The world of heroism and battle has contracted, unexpectedly, into the realm of romance: it is love, not historical urgency, that haunts men at war.

This is "the coincidence, [which] while limited in extent, is too farfetched to accept," the "improbable encounter" critics have fastened on as breaking the realism that they loved in the earlier sections of the novel.[15]

But the encounter shadows the novel for reasons other than disunity. We, as modern readers, may not be as surprised as these critics seem to be by Philip's reappearance, and further, the dissonance of the return is registered in the text by the varieties of explanations offered by *other* characters when they hear the story. Characters reach into the realm of folklore, typology, system upon system of doubling to explain the unexpected. But it is not so unexpected as all that: we have been told that Philip has gone to be a soldier, and further, have before us the example of Gaskell's sympathy for him. Readers are already positioned, if not willing, not to be shocked at his actions. Yet the text also wants us to see it as unlikely. For Philip's friends back in Whitby, the appearance of Charley Kinraid's wife with a story of Philip Hepburn's saving her husband's life at the battle of Acre is so unbelievable it can be interpreted only by recourse to another realm. Both Kester and Sylvia explain it as a "spirit" that has come to save Charley—a solution suggestive of the superstitious world of Yorkshire but also of their real failure to understand Philip. The doctor on Charley's ship, when Philip cannot be found, suggests that it was sunstroke and imagination, for "faces once seen, especially in excitement, are apt to return upon the memory in cases of fever." An "attendant sailor" suggests it was a "spirit," and adds "it's not th' first time as I've heard of a spirit coming upon earth to save a man's life i' time o' need." Alice Rose invokes yet another sphere of mystery to refute the evidence of Charley's story:

> I can forgive Sylvia for not being over keen to credit thy news. Her man of peace becoming a man of war; and suffered to enter Jerusalem, which is a heavenly and a typical city at this time; whilst me, as is one of the elect, is obliged to go on dwelling in Monkshaven, just like any other body. (pp. 450-451)

This model of "heavenly" and "typical"—that is, perfect—doubling reminds us, clearly, we are reading a novel not in the realm of the gothic but the world of "just like any other body" "dwelling in Monkshaven."

Or is it "any other body"? Behind Alice's religious invocation of "credit" lies the realm of women, who cannot enter Jerusalem at all. Charley has said he was bewildered, for "we hated each other like poison; and I can't make out why he should be there and putting himself in danger to save me." But despite Charley's puzzlement, the men are in the same realm at this moment: still free to move, still free to fight, still, in some sense, free enough to be not only subject to the forces of history but the subjects of history. As so often in the novel, moments of opposition between men give way to the deeper similarities of their desires: here, both wish to gain glory so as to be remembered by the "wife in her English home." Charley and Philip, in the Siege of Acre, are more like each other than they are like those they have left behind. They are abroad, carving out identities for themselves through conflict and difference, translating that initial difference between them (their rivalry in love for Sylvia) into a cultural difference with the French. Their conflict can be transcended because there is always another sphere in which men can posit themselves as agents. Here, difference is resolved into a similarity, so that larger realms of difference can in turn be posed, an endless "reenactment" of Brooks's (Freud's) "instinctual play," in which (to quote Irigaray's nice summary of international conflict) women are "never anything but the locus of a more or less competitive exchange between two men, including the competition for the possession of mother earth."

If Gaskell here collapses history, undoing the novel's careful placement within the larger conflicts of the French Revolution and Napoleonic conquest, it is only to place the "more or less competitive exchange" in the realm of both self-conscious fictionality and the writing of female desire. The remainder of the novel will be taken up with the reconciliation of Philip and Sylvia, an almost equally improbable reunion, but one that the text will recognize as improbable by locating it within a *literary* context: Philip has read, and imagines himself in, the story of Guy of Warwick in *The Seven Champions of Christendom,* a story in which the hero returns from fighting the Paynim and disguises himself as a hermit, winning, on his deathbed, a reconciliation with his lost wife, the countess. So readers are prepared for the invocation of the "literary" solution—prepared, of course, in a way Sylvia is not. Sylvia cannot have her resolution within history without "a different alphabet, a different language." She works her way to the reconciliation not through heroic stories, heroic conflicts, or these models of historical (national) difference but through a removal from that world of "established commerce" and a movement into a world shared by the other "commodities"—women—in the marketplace. Only by removing herself from this male plot can Sylvia become her own subject, but Gaskell may further be suggesting why women, within this plot and this (male) language, can never achieve anything but a "transaction" value, the value of an object passed from buyer to buyer. Gaskell needs to suggest, finally, her own market of fiction, in which her heroine will have her own story: if, unlike Philip, Sylvia cannot act in history, she also cannot read—or reimagine—her life in any existing storybook.

iv

Sylvia does seem to end this novel in a different kind of story, with its own forms of repetition and difference. If the final encounter between Kinraid and Hepburn works to place them in the same world, the same battle, the same net of historical power, the final setting for

Sylvia—before her husband's return—places her within a very different realm of similarity, one that I think held more power and a deeper appeal for Gaskell herself. The end of the novel finds Sylvia in a world composed entirely of women and feminized men, a world in which she and her daughter find a peace that is missing from the rest of the novel. Its peace is not entirely unlike the sterile, cloistered peace that Philip encounters and rejects at the Bedesman's retreat, but Sylvia's is not the same kind of absence from the world: she remains very much in the world, connected with both the nature she requires and the town life she previously shunned. What her retreat seems to offer is a space apart from the world of competitive desire. Sylvia finds, and the novel plays with temporarily, a oneness that does not seek to possess something from the other, in which, using the term loosely, both subjects get to be subjects, without one's becoming an object.

But as the end of the novel makes clear, in the wider world that *Sylvia's Lovers* represents, Sylvia can become a subject only, paradoxically, through submission: the woman in a world of women is still within a world of objects, unable to articulate herself. In an increasingly dense linguistic play of pronouns that slip, nouns that cannot be fixed in meaning, Gaskell imagines what might happen if women were freed from some field of determinism. The novel experiments with a linguistic rearrangement akin to what Irigiray called for in the "different alphabet . . . different language" of women. What the novel reveals increasingly, however, is that women would still have to abandon sexual desire for that unity (that difference) to take place. The world without conflict is not yet a world where women choose their own lives; nor can this novel believe (in a universe where identity, desire, and possession have been so linked) in so fully realized an individual subject, with the firm boundaries and clear "I" we might, in a less complicated novel, expect.

What Sylvia does find in this world-before-conflict is again that language we might connect to the pre-Oedipal, a world of unity with the mother and the end to fixed ego boundaries:[16] a world apart from the domination of history; a world, for Sylvia, where she is returned to maternal love and freed from herself and her own story. After Philip leaves and Sylvia realizes she has been betrayed, she goes with her baby to live with Hester and Alice Rose, supported and aided by the Foster brothers, visited by old Kester, surrounded by the care she lost with her mother's death. This care represents a mirroring that other kinds of love rarely approximate in the novel. Earlier in the novel, in the pivotal moments of her mother's illness before her father's execution, when each admits to the other that she has avoided discussing Daniel's impending death, Sylvia and Bell seem to be in a relationship in which each exactly mirrors the other's needs and essence. Bell Robson has been weakened, made "incapable of

argument" or understanding, entirely dependent on Sylvia's care. But as each reveals what "I niver breathed . . . to thee,"

> Sylvia choked with crying, and laid her head on her mother's lap, feeling that she was no longer the strong one, and the protector, but the protected. Bell went on, stroking her head,

> "The Lord is like a tender nurse as weans a child to look on and to like what it lothed once." (p. 310)

But the metaphor of the child who learns to "look on . . . what it lothed" suggests the ambiguity of Sylvia's "feeling that she was no longer the strong one, and the protector, but the protected." At first, the ambiguous "she" seems to be Sylvia herself, who, after weeks of care, can abandon the effort to protect her mother. But more deeply, what Sylvia is "choking" on is the knowledge that, in the long run, the "she" who is "no longer the strong one" is her mother.

What Gaskell intensifies here is the lack of boundaries between the mother and her daughter: not just a Dickensian substitution of caring child for caring parent, but Sylvia's—and her mother's—inability to tell one set of needs from the other. Each here is looking, like the child, on what she loathes: Bell on Daniel's impending execution, Sylvia on her mother's readiness to die rather than live through the shame. But at the moment of severance—Bell lapses into irritability and "inability of reason" almost immediately after this scene—the problem of similarity between women, the inability to locate difference, is registered syntactically by Gaskell. Maternal language and the daughter's imitation (as in the murmuring sounds Aunt Esther makes, recalling Mary Barton's dead mother) have a powerful narrative force here; what they also suggest, frighteningly, is the daughter's tenuous hold on her *own* plot, and the novel's further haunting by still more possible doubles.

While this overlapping of mother and daughter creates an anxiety about identity formation, a sliding of boundaries and confusion of the self rather than a fruitful union, a very different sliding of boundaries, a very different abandonment of self, occurs in the conclusion of the novel. In the eerie scenes where Sylvia learns of Hester's love for Philip and holds the crying woman on the floor, we see a bonding through repetition of desire—at exactly the moment when Sylvia has begun to learn to appreciate Philip—which we can pose against Philip and Charley's reconciliation-through-division. Although Philip and Charley can see in each other only Sylvia's ruin—that is, the ruin of their image of her—Sylvia says, seriously, to Hester,

> "Poor Hester—poor, poor Hester! if yo' an' he had but been married together, what a deal o' sorrow would ha' been spared to us all!" (p. 444)

At that moment, Sylvia comes closest to understanding the key idea of the novel. As she listens to Hester's grief, she

> made no reply, only went on stroking Hester's smooth brown hair, off which her cap had fallen. Sylvia was thinking how strange life was, and how love seemed to go all at cross purposes; and was losing herself in bewilderment. . . . (p. 445)

In Sylvia's silence, lie the novel's doubts: exactly as love seems to go at "cross purposes," so do characters seem to lose themselves, but this is at once the blight and the gift of the novel. To "lose oneself" as Philip does, in lies and self-betrayal, is the deepest sin; to "lose oneself" in Christian goodness or, perhaps, in true love of another, may be to get free of the obsessive need to forge identity through destruction of the other. As Sylvia can recognize in Hester's pain her own—and Philip's as well—so she gains from her "bewilderment." In that awful imposition of *self*—setting up oneself as an idol through one's love of some exterior object who will reflect oneself back—is the worst kind of certainty, a certainty that exists at the expense of others, as Jeremiah Foster describes Philip's lie to Sylvia: "a self-seeking lie; putting thee to pain to get his own ends" (p. 413).

The world of women living together offers an abandonment (for better or worse) of one's "own ends." It is the perfect world for Sylvia, who is "sick o' men and their cruel, deceitful ways," one in which she can finally learn to read, can acquire some of the habits that will allow her movement—in imagination, at least—beyond her own life. Although once she wanted to learn to read so as to learn geography, to find on the map where Charley Kinraid has gone, where she wishes she could go, now she is able to learn only to read the Bible, for to Alice Rose, who begins to teach her to read the first chapter of Genesis, "all other reading but the Scriptures was as vanity to her, and she would not condescend to the weakness of other books." But though Sylvia was "now, as ever, slow at book-learning; . . . she was meek and desirous to be taught" (pp. 421-422).

In her meekness, of course, she is growing more like Hester—more like Philip as well, if not more like what Philip wanted her to be. In part, Sylvia's desire to be taught suggests the disturbing model of growing accommodation that one might expect a Victorian novel to enact on its heroine: a variant of the process that makes Bella Wilfer a good wife, after her education at her husband's hands. But two things suggest that this novel intends something different. First, Sylvia's softening occurs not through Philip's intervention, that is, through the sexual play of marriage and difference, but through a world of women: a harkening back to Sylvia's mother and her desire that

her daughter read, write, understand analogically rather than through (her father's) oppositions. Although this might seem a small distinction—after all, Philip was Bell Robson's choice for Sylvia, and he, further, is identified by the text as the "scholar," even more than Bell—still, the change is specifically marked as one that cannot happen in the world of men, in the world in which Sylvia is still commodity, object rather than subject.

But the further distinction between Sylvia's conversion and the "accommodation" plot is that Philip has undergone a similar process of transformation—and that both plots trace these as en-gendered transformations. If Sylvia is to "grow up" in this female world, Philip's experience is as "Stephen Freeman," a nameless, generic soldier whom even Charley Kinraid—a man among men—cannot locate. Philip has what we might call a representative male experience among men: he comes back, literally, a hero. His adventures are precisely those that would make him more suitable for Sylvia: not only has he become more like the adventuring specksioneer but he, like Sylvia, has found a way of undoing past denials of others. He has rescued Charley, in a sense, from the death he himself had imagined for his enemy, and inflicted it on himself, much as Sylvia, in recognizing Hester's loss, has guaranteed that she herself will live to act out her repentance for "poor Hester, whose life she had so crossed and blighted, even by the very blighting of her own" (p. 422).

The last conversation between Philip and Sylvia suggests some possible union, at least through syntactic mergers and elisions of borders, though it cannot work its union through the magic of plot. This is the last of the novel's odd doublings, "crossings," and "blightings," but like these other moments, through linguistic doublings and ambiguities, it leaves the fields of similarity and difference confused. The transformations, the "difference" revealed—Sylvia's ability to live near and visit her husband without recognizing him; his ability to become the hero she had always needed to love—seems somehow less important than some similarity that gets revealed in turn. Or rather, it is what Philip experiences as similarity. He, "forgetful of himself in his desire to comfort her," says:

> "You and me have done wrong to each other; yet we can see now how we were led to it; we can pity and forgive one another. . . . God knows more, and is more forgiving than either you to me, or me to you. I think and do believe as we shall meet together before His face; but then I shall ha' learnt to love thee second to Him; not first, as I have done here upon the earth." (p. 496)

Philip can bridge sexual and romantic differences through a third term in which the key difference of

God's knowledge erases the gap between him and Sylvia. And in his dying, as his thoughts move between the oppositions of his mother's love and the love "wiser," "tenderer" than hers to which he goes, he sees in his and Sylvia's "forgive me" the same phrase, the same yearning after that union that can be expressed only typologically in the text: it will have been all right to have had an idol, if one can transform that earthly idolatry into heavenly, perfect love.

Sylvia's final version of unity seems different: the last moments at Philip's deathbed are a confusion of identity, with none of the "bright" certainty Philip saw ahead "in heaven." In the first of these confusions, Hester comes into the room with Bella, hoping to say farewell to Philip. Hester begins to cry, but Sylvia rebukes her, asking,

> "Why do yo' cry, Hester? . . . Yo' niver said yo' wouldn't forgive him as long as yo' lived. Yo' niver broke the heart of him that loved yo', and let him almost starve at yo'r very door. Oh, Philip! my Philip, tender and true." (p. 501)

Even here, Sylvia seems to see her crime in hurting him that loved her; she never claims to love him but rather to value his love for her. But the confusion about what one loves is doubled by another *textual* confusion of the object of affection: the very next paragraph begins,

> Then Hester came round and closed the sad half-open eyes, kissing the calm brow with a long farewell kiss.

Until the "farewell," Hester could almost be comforting Sylvia who, in her grief, is sad but tearless, staring "as if all sense were gone from her." The "almost unconscious" Sylvia needs that kiss as much as Philip at that moment, and it is she who has made the direct appeal for understanding; the text is effecting a series of substitutions in which "sense" "goes from" more than one character, and *to* more than one character.

In the last sentence of the scene, the last sentence before the novel breaks into historical narrative and the characters stop speaking to us except through reported anecdote, Sylvia again raises the question of difference—here, the difference between God's mediation and the earthly idol Philip had asserted Sylvia *had* been to him when he promised to see her "in heaven." Sylvia's constant fear—what prompted Philip's response, what seems to be prompting her sudden expressions of guilt—has been that "I think I shall go about among them as gnash their teeth for iver, while yo' are wheere all tears are wiped away." Even here, we cannot know if what she fears is punishment or separation, but this distinction is immaterial. What seems clearest, as throughout the novel, is the fear that

the real punishment *is* separation. Without an other, reflecting identity, without the "desire" of others, loving or hostile, directed toward you, you not only are alone but do not exist. To go "about among them as gnash their teeth" without Philip is to be most truly in torment. And this is what Sylvia addresses at the novel's end: as Bella clings to her mother, and "the touch of *his* child loosened the fountain of her tears" (emphasis added), Sylvia says,

> "If I live very long, and try hard to be very good all that time, do yo' think, Hester, as God will let me to him where he is?" (p. 501)

Where Philip saw God and the human as still different, that distinction has blurred for Sylvia: the statement surely ought to be, if she wants forgiveness, and wants it in Philip's—God's—terms, "God will let me to *Him* where *He* is?" To be where *he* is is where Philip is, not God. Sylvia is still uniting her destiny—her story—with love, here a suddenly understood love for Philip, but she has so blurred the pronouns as to keep her real desire unclear. What *does* Sylvia want at this moment? Philip? Redemption? God? Union? Forgiveness? At this moment, she has rewritten her life story to be about her eventual death, without any clear goal in sight; surely, at this moment, she has blurred the lines of her life by conflating Philip's love with resurrection, by erasing Philip's "lie" and replacing it with her "sin," as Philip somehow returned her to the twelve-year-old girl he first met and loved, and called, as he repeatedly calls her in this scene, "my little lassie." Through the transitory power of Philip's death and fear of her own impending death, Sylvia seems able to blend in one sentence, for one moment, heavenly and earthly love, the realm of individual (transient) identity and the realm of transcendental (permanent) things.

But what are we to make of this description of blurred difference when it is put back into the romance—the problem of the desiring heroine—with which we began? Sylvia seems to have located her problem of being—of being "very good all that time"—firmly within a romance plot, merely a deferred plot endorsed by a beneficent God who remains uninterested in the "gnashing of teeth." But questions of how to *be* are still resolved by questions of whom to *love,* and Sylvia (and the novel) seem far away from a plot of autonomous identity. In what way does the novel allow for the "woman who chooses" with which it began? In what way has Sylvia become what we might recognize as a fully recognized subject, with independent desires? If the comic novel (with its heroine's acquiescence in her married fate) in some essential way fails in this novel; if the violent desires of the first half of the novel, and the passionate vows of the second, all suggest a world in which the comic plot is not adequate to explain peoples' action, where can this almost apocalyptic novel end? Gaskell's narrative violence, conjuring up purging fires of destruction, seems to want to leave the world, at the end, ready to begin again. But she also seems to want to begin the novel again, begin it differently, and, most important, to put herself in.

That insertion is what focuses the questions we have been discussing, the tension between difference and similarity, male and female, writing and blurring. In *Sylvia's Lovers* the difference of the woman's story (the narrative poised between these oppositions, questioning the opposition itself) is the (woman writer's) telling not only the story but the story of storytelling, the movement of female desire into myth. The final "plot" of the novel is the accumulation of stories that occurs in the last chapter, where a variety of accounts of the events we have just read come together to suggest the imprecision of all (his)story; the novel's final plot, that is, is Gaskell's plotting of this, her last completed novel, and its displacements, disparities, and disappearances.

v

Sylvia's Lovers ends with a coda, a pulling-back into history unique in Gaskell's work, and particularly unusual in its retreat into gossip, conversation, and anecdote. In a way, the end of the novel forces on us a self-consciousness, if not a skepticism, about storytelling, and the story we have read. It also forces on us, as we might expect, given the double-edged progress we have been reading, both a new beginning (in Bella's move to America) and the endless repetition we have been reading for. The conclusion, which follows a row of asterisks that separates it from the novel "proper," gives us both the "now" of our narrative moment, and the unending pattern of nature and biblical time:

> Monkshaven is altered now into a rising bathing place. Yet, standing near the site of widow Dobson's house on a summer's night, at the ebb of a spring-tide, you may hear the waves come lapping up the shelving shore with the same ceaseless, ever-recurrent sound as that which Philip listened to in the pauses between life and death.

> And so it will be until "there shall be no more sea."

> But the memory of man fades away. (p. 502)

Here, the fading of memory becomes as inevitable—as ever-recurrent—as the sea; the only public memory, which she goes on to recount, is of "Philip Hepburn and the legend of his fate"; "our" narrative is rendered as transient as the sounds the dying man heard.

But in this first of several narratives offered in these concluding pages, we begin to see the failure in the patterned story. The "legend" repeated by "a few old people" describes a man who

> died in a cottage somewhere near about this spot,— died of starvation while his wife lived in hard-hearted plenty not two good stone-throws away.

This, we are told, "is the form into which popular feeling, and ignorance of the real facts," have "moulded the story," though the "bathing woman" did know "an old man when I was a girl" who "could niver abide to hear t' wife blamed." "He would say nothing again' th' husband; he used to say as it were not fit for men to be judging; that she had had her sore trial, as well as Hepburn hisself." But despite this emendation— which comes closer, if not closest, to our sense of the novel—the "legend" of Philip Hepburn is about *Sylvia's* guilt, not Philip's lie. Sylvia, not herself but "a pale, sad woman, allays dressed in black," is said to have died "before her daughter was well grown up," leaving her child to Hester Rose, who founded alms-houses for "poor disabled sailors and soldiers" and named them for "P.H." Philip, in short, gets all the decent epitaphs; Sylvia's story, that of the woman who tried to *have* a story of her own, cannot be told. No wonder critics have neglected to read that story into the novel: the conclusion cannot frame it, for it is a story about stories that cannot get written. How could they, when women like Sylvia cannot write? If women are taught to read by men like Philip, and are not free to write their own narratives, then the stories they leave behind will bear only men's initials.

But what is most striking about the novel's end, and its reflections on female texts, is that it is a female conversation that gets the last word in *Sylvia's Lovers.* The last paragraph of the novel concludes the conversation between an unnamed "lady" who went to the "Public Baths" on the "very site of widow Dobson's cottage" and, "finding all the rooms engaged" sat down to talk to the "bathing woman." That "lady," reminiscent of Kinraid's "lady-wife," asks questions about the women in the "legend". It is she who asked "what became of the wife," then asks, "Miss Rose?" after being told it was she who took the daughter, and finally asks, "And the daughter?" Significantly, it is the daughter's story that breaks the seemingly endless "similarity" of the woman's story. In the closing paragraph, we are told by the "bathing woman" that

> one o' th' Fosters, them as founded t' Old Bank, left her a vast o' money; and she were married to distant cousin of theirs, and went off to settle in America many and many a year ago. (p. 503)

This seems to undo much of the novel's chronology, which began overprecisely with "the end of the last century" and only now invokes the storybook time of "many and many a year ago." Bella's departure further reverses the story of origin told in the book's first paragraph, the "traditions of [Monkshaven's] having been the landing-place of a throneless queen." In the possible reversal we can hear the novelist saying, what if there were a strong woman not empowered by law ("throneless"), and what if she began to move?

Bella's departure does not quite add up to all that; what it suggests is, rather, that even to begin to act freely, a daughter would have to be orphaned, become rich, and reside in another community.[17] We want, I think, to read this as an act of freedom, Bella's movement to the uncharted American continent echoing something of her implied spiritual father (Kinraid) in her voyaging, and perhaps fulfilling her mother's desire to go to sea. But even here, she is able to move only toward marriage: an arranged marriage into the Quaker family of the Fosters. She is perhaps less Sylvia and Charley's child—via Philip—than Philip and Hester's—via Sylvia. Bella cannot fulfill both Philip's and Sylvia's plots—or can she, for she does get to go to sea at last, even if it is only to sail into another ordered plot, and that a plot with an adequate bankbook.

If what is hopeful about Bella's departure is its departure from what we have been reading (that she is leaving *some* old plot, *some* old history, behind her, and opening some new possibilities), what seems even more encouraging is the way the final conversation recounts at least part of the story from Sylvia's (imagined, muted) point of view. It seems, again, to render problematic views of history, while vindicating a different kind of romance. One could read the conclusion as merely tying up the loose ends of plot, while suggesting, à la Billy Budd, the skewed ways that facts make their way into legends. But I choose to read in that last story something about the way legends make their ways into novels. The "lady" who comes down to hear the old woman's story, who keeps asking the next question (and that always a question about women) seems to me a figure for the novelist herself: Gaskell, who, turning from her desperate desire to make Charlotte Brontë's hidden life into a legend, chose the life of an unknown, almost unimaginable, completely silent woman on a quest to make her own life significant; Gaskell, who did as much serious research on *Sylvia's Lovers* as on the *Life of Charlotte Brontë;* Gaskell, who may be asking, where in all these cultural stories, these legends of wronged men, the book of Genesis which Sylvia is taught to read, where are the stories of women, the stories they must learn to tell (for) themselves?

She may be asking that question for herself in new ways as well. Edgar Wright has suggested, somewhat cavalierly, that Gaskell "would have been passing through the 'change of life' at this period, with its accompanying restlessness."[18] But we need not read this as a menopausal novel, hence a "mediocre" work,

betraying fatigue, concentrating on "gloom and morbidity." The gloom, which resembles not so much morbidity as the conscious claustrophobia of *Lois the Witch*'s plot, may reflect Gaskell's restlessness not at the "change of life" but at the inability of Victorian formulations of the novel to take in those "changes" she herself was going through. When Elizabeth Gaskell went to Rome in 1857, she was sought out by a young American, Charles Eliot Norton, who had met her years before and been charmed by her. Their friendship, which was immediate, continued till her death: he named his second daughter after her (he would have so named the first, but Gaskell's written approval reached him after the baby's birth); they corresponded regularly with hopes of meeting again; there seems little doubt that, in an unexpected and indescribable way, they had fallen in love. She wrote to friends on her return to England that

> it was in those charming Roman days that my life, at any rate, culminated. I shall never be so happy again. I don't think I was ever so happy before. My eyes fill with tears when I think of those days, and it is the same with all of us. They were the tip-top point of our lives. The girls may see happier ones— I never shall.[19]

In those years, Gaskell was to worry increasingly about her daughters' marriageability; indeed, two of her daughters never married, which to Gaskell, ever a defender of marriage, was a sad end indeed. But she is facing some end of her own here: "The girls may see happier [days]—I never shall." What Sylvia faces at the end of the novel named after her lovers is the end of her own story: she dies soon after, but the bleakness of what she faces, in the death of her now-dear husband and the defection of her adored Charley, is her own movement out of the only possible female plot. What Gaskell may have been living is the failure of that plot to give to her daughters (or even to her) the richness she could imagine.

Gaskell ends *Sylvia's Lovers* with an image of women alone, women in conversation, women retelling history. None of these women fit easily into a marriage plot, any more than did Charlotte Brontë, whose marriage Gaskell, like most of Brontë's friends, thought a mistake, and whose entrance into the true female plot ("wives and daughters," as Gaskell will call it next) leads to her death of "pregnancy-sickness" at thirty-nine. *Sylvia's Lovers* offers several visions: a world of desire crossed by history, which Gaskell read as primarily a world of men forging identity through sexual conflict; a world of isolated women, learning to read but forced to read the Bible and Eve's fall over and over; a world of understanding found "too late," defensible only if submerged into God's plot. In the last scene, as the women tell each other unfinished stories, we might see something else, but we are not yet offered that other novel: it might be Bella's "American novel," where she "went off to settle in America many and many a year ago," and may have found something better; it might be Hester Rose's world of usefulness, writing the piece of stone that says "this building is erected in memory of P.H.," the only edifice that survives the novel; it might be Sylvia's imagined adventure.

Where that difference may reside in this novel is in the voice of storytelling, in the vibrant direct address that Gaskell uses to begin this epitaph to the novel: "Yet, standing near the site of widow Dobson's house on a summer's night, . . . *you* may hear the waves . . . and so it will be until 'there shall be no more sea'" [emphasis added]. That moment of speaking to "you," reminiscent of the engaged fiction of **Mary Barton,** draws *us* back into the narrative: it is the passionate voice of the characters, and the self-conscious reflections of the novel's coda. In the questioning woman who asks, "What became of the wife?" "And the daughter?" one could imagine a new reader, one ready to take on the generic challenge of the female narrative, ready to continue the questioning of culture, history, and myth implicit in the "story" that Gaskell will take up critically in **Wives and Daughters,** but that she could read only tragically in **Sylvia's Lovers.**

Notes

[1] Peter Brooks, *Reading for the Plot: Design and Intention in Narrative* (New York: Knopf, 1984), p. 38.

[2] The essential reworking of the Freudian Oedipal myth into (literary) mediation is René Girard's account of triangular desire in *Deceit, Desire and the Novel: Self and Other in Literary Structure* (Baltimore: Johns Hopkins University Press, 1965). We might here borrow Lacan's rephrasing of the Freudian problem: "desire becomes bound up with the desire of the Other, but . . . in this loop lies the desire to know" ("The Subversion of the Subject and the Dialectic of Desire in the Freudian Unconscious," in *Écrits* [New York: Norton, 1977], p. 301). Interestingly, Lacan posits that the desire for the "other" is the desire for "a presence in that beyond-the-veil where the whole of Nature can be questioned about its design": the epigraph for *Sylvia's Lovers* is a passage from Tennyson's *In Memoriam,* which reads,

> Oh for thy voice to soothe and bless!
> What hope of answer, or redress?
> Behind the veil! behind the veil!

Like post-Freudians, Gaskell made an essential connection between the desire to possess (identity) and the desire to know (to question)—or, perhaps more accurately, Freud made an essentially *Victorian* connection between the quest for self-knowledge and sexual

happiness. Gaskell, Tennyson, and Freud are, of course, all writing about quests that can end (that are defined by ending) only in death.

[3] Tzvetan Todorov, "Narrative Transformations," in *The Poetics of Prose* (Ithaca: Cornell University Press, 1977), p. 232.

[4] *Sylvia's Lovers,* ed. Andrew Sanders (Oxford: Oxford University Press, 1982), p. 71. All subsequent references are to this edition and are included in the text.

[5] Brooks, p. 100.

[6] Eve Kosofsky Sedgwick, *Between Men: English Literature and Male Homosocial Desire* (New York: Columbia University Press, 1985), p. 2. My sense of the centrality of the relationship between Philip and Charley must be informed by Sedgwick's provocative thesis, which might pick up on the class argument so well laid out by Terry Eagleton in his essay "*Sylvia's Lovers* and Legality," in *Essays in Criticism* (1977) 26: 17-27.

[7] See Kaja Silverman, *The Subject of Semiotics* (Oxford: Oxford University Press, 1983), especially chapters 4 and 5. The discussion of the site of the female gaze (p. 223) to which I refer specifically here, draws on the work of Laura Mulvey in "Visual Pleasure and Narrative Cinema" (Silverman cites its original publication in *Screen* 16, no. 3 [1975]: 6-18), to which I have referred in chapter 2 of this volume, in discussing the relationship of women to aesthetic perception in *Ruth.* My discussion of that novel is in part relevant here; in *Sylvia's Lovers,* I think, we see a more wide-ranging analysis of the workings of desire than we did in *Ruth,* but the concern with the construction of female sexuality (of female desire) remains the same.

[8] Gaskell quotes from this ballad in chapter 8, stating Philip "could almost have echoed the words of the lover of Jess MacFarlane," R. K. Webb has also noted the connection to *North and South* in "The Gaskells as Unitarians," in *Dickens and Other Victorians: Essays in Honour of Philip Collins,* ed. Joanne Shattock (London: Macmillan, 1988), p. 162.

[9] *The Brontës: Their Lives, Friendships and Correspondence,* ed. Thomas J. Wise and J. A. Symington, 4 vols. (Oxford: Oxford University Press, 1932; III, 165), quoted in *Wuthering Heights,* ed. William M. Sale (New York: Norton, 1963, 1972), p. 272.

[10] U. C. Knoepflmacher has made a very similar point in a fine essay, "Genre and the Integration of Gender: From Wordsworth to George Eliot to Virginia Woolf," in *Victorian Literature and Society:*

Essays Presented to Richard D. Altick, ed. James R. Kincaid and Albert J. Kuhn (Columbus: Ohio State University Press, 1984).

[11] Adrienne Rich, "Planetarium" (1968), *The Will to Change* (1971); reprinted in *Poems: Selected and New, 1950-1974* (New York: Norton, 1975), p. 146.

[12] Luce Irigaray, "This Sex Which Is Not One," in *This Sex Which Is Not One,* trans. Catherine Porter with Carolyn Burke (Ithaca: Cornell University Press, 1985), p. 25.

[13] Ibid., pp. 31-32.

[14] The image in *Mary Barton* that suggests the unbridled anger of a revolution is the factory fire in which Jem Wilson proves himself a hero. That scene exists partly to establish Jem as the appropriate choice for Mary (appropriate in that his hidden passion matches hers; that his is the real courage [sexuality] of the novel) and also to deflect the need for a riot. It has the mob hysteria missing even from the strike in *North and South.* That fire scene is a corollary of the fire and destruction at the Randyvowse in *Sylvia's Lovers*—it is a false fire alarm that rouses the men who are subsequently unfairly impressed at the tavern—but Gaskell's use of fire suggests the subtler conservatism of her revolutionary anger: recall Elias Canetti's suggestion in *Crowds and Power* that fire, as a symbol for crowds, is important first because "fire is always the same." Here, Gaskell's interest in change again rehearses the idea of similarity—resemblance—amid difference. (See generally, *Crowds and Power,* trans. Carol Stewart [New York: Continuum, 1973 (1960)] and, for fire, pp. 75-80.) In Canetti's phrase, "The dangerous traits of the crowd are often pointed out and, among them, the most striking is the propensity to incendiarism" (p. 77). The crowd in *North and South*—and hence, the more amorphous threat in that novel of group power—is that of a sea. (See Canetti, 80-81.)

[15] Arthur Pollard, *Mrs Gaskell: Novelist and Biographer* (Cambridge: Harvard University Press, 1966), p. 211; Eagleton, p. 18.

[16] Silverman, pp. 154-158. See my discussion of pre-Oedipal language in chapter 1.

[17] I see in Bella's departure a reference to the end of *The Scarlet Letter,* in which Pearl begins a new life but does so ambiguously, by going back to Europe and—presumably—marrying into the nobility, writing letters with "armorial seals" upon them, though they are seals "unknown to English heraldry." These letters may mark Hester as a love interest, and Pearl may have gone to an untimely "maiden grave," but the clearer suggestion of the novel is that the daughter has found her place by leaving the New World, while the mother makes her life there. In Hester Rose's life of service, we may see another echo of Hester Prynne's—and Bella, like Pearl, is unexpectedly left an heiress.

Gaskell was living near Nathaniel Hawthorne, whom she much admired, while writing *Sylvia's Lovers.* She wrote to George Smith, "Do *you* know what Hawthorne's tale [*The Marble Faun*] is about? *I* do; and I think it will perplex the English public pretty considerably." *GL* 441, 20 September 1859, p. 575.

[18] Edgar Wright, *Mrs Gaskell: The Basis for Reassessment* (Oxford: Oxford University Press, 1963), p. 173. He, too, mentions Charles Eliot Norton, but only as an example of Gaskell's feeling of "anticlimax"; he does not relate the affair to narrative motivation. And, though this barely needs to be said, surely no critic would link narrative structure to a male writer's "change of life." Biology is brought in here to support more critical argument than it rightfully can, and brought in as literary destiny in a way it would not be in discussing anyone but a woman novelist, particularly one habitually relegated to the female realm.

[19] *GL* 375, September 1857, pp. 476-477.

Tim Dolin (essay date 1993)

SOURCE: "Cranford and the Victorian Collection," in *Victorian Studies,* Vol. 36, No. 2, Winter, 1993, pp. 179-206.

[In the excerpt that follows, Dolin examines Gaskell's Cranford *as a paradigm of the Victorian experience, specifically because it is organized as a collection of anecdotes centering around women's lives.]*

The freight of victorian things remaining in our own century has left historians with a plentiful resource, but also with a number of special problems. One has only to pause in a recreated drawing-room, at a genre painting, or over a passage of description in a novel, to sense the abundance and oppressiveness of a famously cluttered age. In *The Victorian Treasure-House,* Peter Conrad elicits something of this ponderousness when he pieces together a composite picture of the Victorian frame of mind by showing how things were implicated in cultural forms, scientific practices, and middle-class domestic ideology. The emphasis he places on materiality is especially evident in both his treatment of detail—the ability to isolate, identify, and position the one thing among the many—and his exploration of the familiar texture of accretion—the jumble of furnishings, the unwieldiness of the Victorian novel, the labor of accumulation. Similarly, in *Victorian Things* Asa Briggs sets himself the difficult task of unearthing the "intelligible universe"—or, more properly, universes, for there was more than one—"of the Victorians" (31). Briggs acknowledges this difficulty and prefaces his study with a prolonged reflection on the procedural problems generated by a history of things. He is concerned not only with artifacts themselves, for instance, but with "crucial aspects of categorization": "What were the things that Victorians listed, and what constituted a laundry list or a shopping list . . . ?" (34). Among the many "category questions" which the subject invites, Briggs asks, "Which were specifically women's things? Which men's?" (34). This interleaved inquiry about gender, however, suggests a further question: can we distinguish not only between the categories of things special to women and men, but between the modes of categorization that were brought to bear upon those things? Gender, I would suggest, while it clearly shapes the design and use of Victorian things, also shapes their definition and description.

One central, if loose, mode of categorization was the Victorian collection. A concern with aggregation—organizing individual things into groups of things—informs the domestic handbook, the emporium, the natural sciences, the public museum, statistics, genre painting, and the Victorian novel. These public forms were also paralleled by the private pastime of collecting. It is therefore worth inquiring whether the very notion of the collection differed between the sexes, as it differed amongst classes and races, and whether this difference becomes apparent in writing about collections, and in the assumptions about collecting that underwrite such cultural forms as painting and prose fiction. Briggs's book, itself as much a collection as a history, articulates in its very structure the tension in Victorian culture between systems of meaning, particularly historical systems, and things. It is a tension that surfaces in the development of realism in the arts, in the concerns and methods of the natural sciences, and in the rise of sociology. Taxonomies, statistics, universal expositions, and multiplot novels attest not only to a passion for order, but also to an obstinate disorderliness of things and an anxiety of agglomeration exemplified in the domestic interiors, dustheaps and curiosity shops, and in the populous and unruly plots, of Charles Dickens.

Elizabeth Gaskell's *Cranford* (1863)—no loose, baggy monster, let us admit it—is not the book that comes to mind when we invoke the Victorian novel. Though it is dominated by things in a way that few novels are, even Victorian novels, it recalls collections of a very particular kind. By this I mean that it is associated with that variety of Victorian objects produced by middle-class feminine work—needlework, decorative crafts, domestic arrangement—and is most often characterized as a female collection: a bunch of flowers, a potpourri, or a "ladies' museum." It is a woman's book about a woman's place, and its universe of things encompasses "bonnets, gowns, caps, and shawls" (169), personal mementos, old letters, muddled memories, and above all, stories.

"Our Society at Cranford" first appeared in *Household Words* on 13 December 1851, some two months after the close of that most celebrated Victorian collection, the Great Exhibition. On the face of it, the two events are scarcely comparable: the Crystal Palace is an enduring emblem of Victorianism, and *Cranford* an enduring article of Victoriana. For the historian of Victorian material culture, the Great Exhibition was a key episode, and to popular history it represents the very image of the age. While it gestured toward a coherent account of culture by placing "everything" under one roof, the effort of categorization necessitated by this inclusiveness was, as Briggs explains, doomed to fail (53-56). But the glass structure itself was the triumphant symbol of a massive simplicity of design capable of containing even the irresistible Victorian machinery of progress. It is perhaps this image of the containment of energy, the bounding of the incoherent, that makes the Crystal Palace so favored by critics in search of a symbol for the massive, complex organism that is the Victorian novel. The Great Exhibition, like the novels of Dickens, may have been an indifferent whole, but it was a whole nonetheless.[1]

The marriage of Paxton's formal simplicity (an architectural gesture toward transparent continuity between collection and world) with the insistent materiality and even gorgeous redundancy of the exhibits struck many visitors with a sense of other-worldliness. A spare transparent structure accommodating an exotic plenitude, while it may now be very suggestive of Victorian experience, was then equally suggestive of its antithesis. Owen Jones's Alhambraic scheme for the decoration of this palace, though it was never fully realized, is an example of the deliberate orientalism of the spectacle, an orientalism also underscored in the comparisons consistently drawn between the Exhibition and the East. Writing to her father, Charlotte Brontë expressed delight and wonder at this "Verdopolitan" spectacle:

> "It is a wonderful place—vast, strange, new, and impossible to describe. Its grandeur does not consist in *one* thing, but in the unique assemblage of *all* things. Whatever human industry has created, you find there. . . . It may be called a bazaar or a fair, but it is such a bazaar or fair as Eastern genii might have created." (qtd. in Wise and Symington 3: 243)[2]

The Exhibition demonstrated to Brontë a magical power which "gathered this mass of wealth from all the ends of the earth" and "arranged it thus" (243), but though the effect was Eastern, the power was not. This "assemblage of all things" was controlled by England, and the Great Exhibition represented to its patrons an emblem of the supremacy of national over international progress. Nowhere is this smugness more evident than in an article written by Charles Dickens and R. H. Horne in *Household Words* on 5 July 1851, "The Great

Exhibition and the Little One" (Stone 1: 319-29). Dickens and Horne sarcastically dismiss the Chinese Gallery in Hyde Park Place and the Chinese Junk at Temple Stairs, both showing simultaneously with the Great Exhibition, as the material testimony of "a people who came to a dead stop" (322). As Stone notes in his preface to the article, this is "a view of East and West that Dickens, along with most of his contemporaries, regarded as self-evident" (319), and it is a view implicitly endorsed by Mr. Holbrook when he recites *Locksley Hall* in **Cranford.** John Stuart Mill, for instance, in *On Liberty,* cites "the warning example" of China (88) in his appeal for a rigorous individuality to contest the tyranny of a uniform, uncritical public opinion in England: the Chinese "have become stationary—have remained so for thousands of years; and if they are ever to be farther improved, it must be by foreigners" (89). Significantly, though, in the light of **Cranford**'s treatment of orientalism, both the view of China "shutting itself up, as far as possible, within itself" (Stone 322) and "the Chinese ideal of making all people alike" (Mill 90) also describe Cranford. The conventional association of men and orientalism in Gaskell's novel is challenged by an association of the feminine and the Eastern that is indicated in the dormancy and homogeneity of the Cranfordians. The conflation of the feminine and the oriental is also, I shall argue, implicated in the idea of the female collection, an idea that is central to **Cranford**'s exploratory form.

Cranford presents an ironic reversal of *Locksley Hall.* The poem's relevance to the town is summarized by Miss Matty's snooze during its recitation: whatever does become of Victorianism, it is not at Cranford. The poet's desire for a renewal of creativity at "the gateways of the day" (where he imagines he will "take some savage woman" to rear his "dusky race") is a longing to step outside the tumult of history, outside the "heavens [filled] with commerce":

> There methinks would be enjoyment more
> than in this march of mind,
> In the steamship, in the railway, in the
> thoughts that shake mankind.

The poet-speaker's Cathay is outside history because Europe is history. As Dickens and Horne complain: "Well may the three Chinese divinities of the Past, the Present, and the Future be represented with the same heavy face" (Stone 322). The Chinese Exhibition, like Tennyson's Cathay, is illegible within the narrative of human progress because its exhibits do not, as in the Victorian museological imperative, stage a comprehensive history of development. Chinese things are merely curious, displaying what Dickens and Horne scorn as the "essential" quality of "always doing the same thing" (328). It is an incoherence that confounds the imperious and coercive narrative inherent in the Great Exhibition.[3]

The image of the Crystal Palace as a bazaar calls to mind not only the Chinese Exhibition nearby, but other bazaars operating in London at that time. Extending the argument of Gary Dyer, who has traced the history of the ladies' bazaar in early nineteenth-century London, I would like to consider a mid-century image of the charity sale. *At the Bazaar* was exhibited at the Royal Academy in 1857 by the onetime Pre-Raphaelite James Collinson. . . .

The ladies' museum, . . . at the center of Collinson's *At the Bazaar,* frustrates our efforts to ascribe public meaning—some convention of narrative, commercial, or scientific order—to its displaced collection of objects. The authority missing from the bazaar and the woman's collection is dramatized by the very absence of a male reference point within Collinson's painting. Of the thousands of modern life pictures painted during the period, many described the private domestic experience of women: there were countless images, by painters of both sexes, showing women preparing to go out, playing music, sewing, talking with sisters and friends, and being with their children. But many of the most powerful images of women present them in relation to a dramatic situation outside the frame, to be inferred by the viewer. These are images of separation and waiting, correspondence and death; and images of women "lost" in thought, memory, or reverie (see Yeldham v.l, Ch.3). In these works, the single figure of the woman most commonly enters into narrative in relation to an absent man. That the image equated the faraway hero and the public world is evident from two examples. In John Byam Shaw's picture *The Boer War, 1900,* a "public" meaning is present only in the explanatory title, and in Joseph Clarke's *The Labourer's Welcome* the reflected figure of the workman returning home appears precisely where the viewer should be. In *At the Bazaar,* though, no such absence can be inferred. The central figure and the objects arrayed around her do not consolidate into the readable plot of a foregrounded heroine and an offstage hero. They tell no story about her and she tells no story about them. She is neither protagonist nor narrator. She is outside the proper context of her identity, her home, and presides over a drama of superfluity.

This suggests that images of waiting women make explicit the impossibility of coherent domestic narratives without men, just as the bazaar and the female collection are commercial and scientific enterprises bankrupted of authority and coherence by the absence of a male point of reference. The presence of a man authenticates a "feminine" domestic drama, but what of the reverse? The woman must impose domesticity on the marketplace if her presence there is to be at all comprehensible (as Bathsheba must in Hardy's *Far from the Madding Crowd*).[10] Images of commerce in which women feature are not common in Victorian contemporary genre painting: when they do appear (as in Hicks's *Dividend Day at the Bank of England* [fig. 6]), it is frequently a scene in which men confer upon them special attention and courtesy, and in which a point is made about the humanizing influence of the feminine visitant. The formal design of domestic fiction must be brought into question when a woman cannot alone constitute her own story. What formal qualities would such a novel display? What does such a book look like? These issues are at the heart of *Cranford.*

My argument, in brief, is that *Cranford*'s narrative form, loosely episodic, is reminiscent less of a conventional Victorian novel than a woman's collection. Two passages in *Cranford* describe two special kinds of "texts" which are also domestic appurtenances, and they might also be describing the novel itself. In Mrs. Jamieson's drawing-room,

> There was another square Pembroke table dedicated to the Fine Arts, on which were a kaleidoscope, conversation-cards, puzzle-cards (tied together to an interminable length with faded pink satin ribbon), and a box painted in fond imitation of the drawings which decorate tea-chests. (122)

Later, Miss Matty recalls how

> "My father once made us . . . keep a diary, in two columns; on one side we were to put down in the morning what we thought would be the course and events of the coming day, and at night we were to put down on the other side what really happened. It would be to some people rather a sad way of telling their lives." (158)

Cranford, as I will explain, is organized like a collection of anecdotes printed on cards and bundled together;[11] its miscellaneous form, however, is also one response to the diary in two columns. The poignancy of passing time is expressed in Matty's sudden recollection of hopeful expectancy; the blank of forgetfulness calls back the blank of a future that day by day is not to eventuate. This fitful history records most faithfully the handing over of the past simultaneously to remembrance and oblivion. (The memorialization and annihilation of each of Matty's ancestors is dramatized in the slow reading through and burning of letters.) There is no bygone voice which answers or accounts for anything; only the charm of a preserved collection, and the shuffling of tales into multiple histories. These histories refuse to affix themselves to anything "public," and are detached from the historical background that is so germane to other more formidable Victorian novels. *Cranford* asks what it means to write imaginative histories of private life and to place them, as Cranford is placed within England, like an enclave within the larger narrative of history. While its form is not entirely discontinuous, it privileges formal discontinuity as part of its experimentation with an appropriate form for this history of private life.[12] Its thematic concern with things and their collection in a world without men is connected with this exploration of stories and their collection in a world without beginnings, middles, and ends.

This is not to say that *Cranford* rejects conventional literary modes, along with men, in a zeal of feminist revisionism. Its sentimental allegiances are to its maiden ladies, but the moral new world promised by its old-world values is severely tested by the keen pathos of its discontents: its poverty, rancor, competitiveness, loneliness. The novel shifts, "vibrates" (like Mary Smith), between a vision of the singularity and the triviality of its subject, and between apotheosis and critique. This alternation is registered textually in shifts between pastoral, social realism and social comedy, and utopianism. Nina Auerbach describes Cranford as "an organic community rooted in the past and containing the future" (89), but its temporality is explained not through historical but through literary modes. The sense of the past is fixed to the pastoral, the present impinges in the form of the realist and the comic, and the future exists only as an expression of the utopian.

What *Cranford* takes from pastoral is that mode's sense of melancholy relinquishment, the poignancy of presiding over a residual world. Gaskell first experimented with the ironical juxtaposition of pastoral and social realism in *Mary Barton*'s holiday opening. This juxtaposition attempts to re-educate the (middle-class) reader's eye, to banish the complacent distance of the picturesque and magnify the laboring classes from pastoral fixtures to fully-realized characters. *Cranford,* however, is more complex. Its mood of reminiscence and regret is tempered but not negated by the penetrating irony of Mary Smith's narration, and the pathos of privation is never entirely demeaned by the magnitude of Cranfordian snobbery. Unlike *Mary Barton, Cranford* does not propose social realism as the necessary corrective aesthetic to an indulgent nostalgia.

The informal title "The Cranford Papers" also places the novel within the Victorian comic tradition of Pierce Egan, Robert Smith Surtees, and Dickens. Like the Pickwickians and the heroes of other sporting novels, the ladies of Cranford are members of a kind of gender-exclusive club. The difference, of course, lies in the fact that the adventures of gentlemen's clubs, almost always of the gallivanting kind, rely upon mobility, whereas the "adventures" of *Cranford* derive their comedy from the almost complete inertia, indeed the very sleepiness, of the spinsters. This comic aspect of the book is critical (especially given Captain Brown's fatal fondness for Dickens) to the dispute over Boz and Dr. Johnson. As Hilary Schor has convincingly argued, the relationship between *Rasselas, Cranford,* and *Pickwick Papers* is as much about female authorship as it is about a precise moment of literary-historical transition. To read the death of Captain Brown as the symbolic submission of the age of Dickens to the age of Johnson and Jane Austen, as Valentine Cunningham does (142), is surely mistaken. Indeed, to read it as anything but Pickwickian is to overlook the debt Captain Brown owes to Sam Weller (see Auerbach 84). Nor does the Captain's demise spell the end of the matter by any means, as the arrival of another Sam and another Brown—Signor Brunoni—makes clear.

Cranford is also nowhere. It is not simply an escapist provincial idyll, but, in the tradition of utopian discourse, a nexus of the social, the political, and the imaginary. The town can hardly be said to provide an exemplary existence, however. Its comic and sentimental elements intercept any genuinely prescriptive utopianism with their emphasis on the town's ineffectualness and indulgence. *Cranford* is an ironical utopia in which the optimism vested in an imaginary future—in fact, futurity itself—is played off against the eternal senility of its inhabitants and the impossibility of procreation. As Miss Pole wryly observes:

> "As most of the ladies of good family in Cranford were elderly spinsters, or widows without children, if we did not relax a little, and become less exclusive, by-and-by we should have no society at all." (109)

Cranford is a fantasy of the social and political empowerment of women alone and it is at the same time a caricature of (comfortable middle-class female) everyday life in Victorian England, devoted to the filling-in of time. It is a utopia of the superfluous. This idealism, problematic at the very least, contributes to an effect of incoherence and open-endedness, and to the impression that such a place cannot be sustained, such a text cannot be satisfactorily concluded. There is no future in Cranford. When in *North and South* (1855) John Thornton confesses to Margaret Hale that commercial ill-fortune has made of his middle age a "starting-point which requires the hopeful energy of youth" (528), Gaskell is providing the convenient stimulus to matrimony without which that novel cannot end. But what is to happen after the end of *Cranford*? There, the future is so empty of promise that it represents only a return to "the old friendly sociability" (218). As Mary Smith notes of her return to the town in Chapter Two, there "had been neither births, deaths, nor marriages since I was there last. Everybody lived in the same house, and wore pretty nearly the same well-preserved, old-fashioned clothes" (52). *Cranford* stands still in Mary's absence, in a state of perfect preservation, like a tourist destination. Indeed, she is something of a tourist narrator (as Hilary Schor notes, "we are reading her holiday self" [299]) and she animates by her narratorial presence the waiting town. Thus, *Cranford* can claim none of the roundedness of the pastoral tale: the spinsters' unfinished sentences and

imperfectly-realized tales suggest a trailing off, and the novel's ending, far from delivering any sort of resolution, simply ends. Gaskell's own long silences during the protracted serial publication, when she was engaged with the writing of *Ruth,* indicate that she, like Mary Smith, was often unavoidably delayed in Drumble on business. If *Cranford* must end, it does so in the service of other weightier matters, of which *North and South* was perhaps the weightiest.

But the concerns of social realism are not entirely absent from *Cranford,* in spite of critics' claims that the "retreat to Cranford is an escape from the city, atheism, Dissent, the age of railways, the present" (Cunningham 142). The novel does not depict a sentimental pre-industrial existence, a golden age. This may be "the last generation of England," but it is placed alongside Victoria's generation, the generation of *North and South.* Pastoral, history, and social realism are all complicated by the geographical propinquity of Cranford and Drumble. The rigorously excluded historical "present" which abuts the present of Cranford represents an entire world of commerce, manufacture, engineering, and imperialism, all of which are gathered under the masculine. This is the muscular Victorianism of Mr. Holbrook's *Locksley Hall* with its conception of the machine of progress fuelled by sexual distrust, class anger, and racial superiority. But fear of the foreignness of men in *Cranford* also finds its way into a kind of sexual xenophobia: the exoticism of the gender, and, by extension, of Victorianism, is registered as orientalism. This oriental exoticism is adumbrated in Captain Brown, acted out by Signor Brunoni (who was "like a being from another sphere" [134]), and literally realized in the brown-skinned Aga Jenkyns ("like dear Captain Brown" [94]) and others of his tribe. The threat of the irruptive, oracular male is constantly posited and deflected.[13] On meeting the major, Matty is reminded of Bluebeard, and on meeting Signor Brunoni, Miss Pole is reminded of the heroes of popular romances: "He spoke such pretty broken English, I could not help thinking of Thaddeus of Warsaw, and the Hungarian Brothers, and Santo Sebastiani" (130). The speech and writing of men, often characterized as "cabbalistic," places them at the furthest remove from occidental Cranford. Inscriptions on tea-chests merge with Signor Brunoni and the Aga Jenkyns to symbolize this inscrutable foreigner. As Miss Matty nervously admits: "They are very incomprehensible, certainly!" (145). The panic (a threat of violent male incursion) subsides without incident, though, and Signor Brunoni turns out to be not a gypsy thief but an ailing Englishman. The colorful orientalism of his imperfect speech merges with the more general menace of men dressed as women, but both dissolve into benign feminine incapacitation. The ineffectual heroism of the male is also enacted in Mr. Holbrook, who looks like Mary Smith's "idea of Don Quixote" (73).

This feminization, a domestication of the foreign, only

further undermines any fixed point of masculine-occidental authority. Additionally, the Cranfordians, with their "love of the marvellous" (155), are equally "oriental" (or Amazonian) to their distant male antagonists: "words that [Matty] would spell quite correctly in her letters to me, became perfect enigmas when she wrote to my father" (186). Moreover, when Peter returns from India with "more wonderful stories than Sinbad the Sailor" (211), he does not realize just how Cranfordian he is. Part Aga and part Amazon, he is a curious embodiment of the ladies' defeated aspirations. His youthful female impersonations are so unnerving because they represent two extremes of the woman who is defined outside the home: the independent bluestocking passing through (94), and the fallen woman. These pantomimes are punished with Peter's expulsion, but it is an expulsion that takes him to the place he belongs. Unlike Ruth Hilton, whom he might also be impersonating, Peter is, one might say, cast in. When he returns to Cranford he assumes control of the novel's story-telling and the town's social diplomacy, earning only Mary's reproach: "he laughed at my curiosity, and told me stories that sounded so very much like Baron Munchausen's, that I was sure he was making fun of me" (208). In his bravura performances, still calculated to give the ladies something to talk about, he becomes only another tale-teller in a novel so notable, as Nina Auerbach has argued, for embellishment and deceit. He divides his stories into the fantastic and the factual strictly along the lines of gender: "when the rector came to call, Mr. Peter talked in a different way about the countries he had been in" (211). His gesture to the Cranford historian—"[d]on't be shocked, prim little Mary, at all my wonderful stories" (217)—is surely ultimately Mary's victory over his autocracy of the tale, for he cannot know the centrality and power of story in the lives of these women.

The double expulsion from Cranford of men and "the world," obscuring as it does distinctions of gender, race, and class, correspondingly obscures the opposition between private and public. Novels, like museums, imply that the materials of privacy can be made publicly available. Yet both also imply certain (clearly or obscurely defined) prohibitions upon that availability. Prohibition, as Lefebvre writes, "is the reverse side and the carapace of property"; and "the symbol of this constitutive repression is an object offered up to the gaze yet barred from any possible use, whether this occurs in a museum or in a shop window" (319). In reversing the spatial prohibition imposed on women which restricts them to the home. *Cranford*'s exclusionary space, and its critique of the usefulness of domestic things, accentuates the hinge between the home and the world which operates in Victorian fiction at large.

The relationship between private lives and historical forces, then, which social realism formally invokes and which Gaskell makes the overt thesis of *North and South,* is under suspension in *Cranford.* The "condition of England" novel is anxious to demonstrate how public issues are susceptible of treatment (and I intend here also the therapeutic sense of that word) by the domestic romance. This is perhaps best exemplified in the most memorable incident in *North and South,* the encounter between Margaret Hale and John Thornton on the steps of his house. Critical to this scene is the heroine's emergence from the house, which puts into dramatic shorthand the function of the street door in any representation of the passage of the woman into public life. The transition from the domestic interior (here literally a sanctuary against chaos and destruction) to the mob outside is a disturbingly immediate transition from the sphere of private relations to the sphere of public experience. As more than one critic has remarked, the confrontation is a problematic one, and its consequences for the fate of the novel's romantic plot are far-reaching (see Harman, esp. 361-70; and Yeazell). Most disturbing is Gaskell's inversion of the relationship between domestic romance and history. Instead of momentous public conflicts finding their way into the parlors of fiction on the boots of the men, as it were, the woman steps out from the parlor into history. It is a bold move on Margaret's part, certainly, but the image of emergence is also fraught with sexual confusion and threat. The threat is to the workers, who respond to her misplacement by protecting her from themselves; and the confusion is experienced by Thornton, who construes Margaret's unconscious motives as personal (that is, as romantic). Yet for all its radicalism, the only real effect of Margaret's actions *is* the advancement of the romantic plot. As Barbara Harman argues, "Margaret's act is particularly acute in light of the fact that on one reading she reverses the conventional understanding of gender relations (in which men take public stands on behalf of women, not women on behalf of men) and on the other she reinstates it (women convert even political events into romantic ones, public events into private ones)" (368).

Compare this incident and the moment when Miss Matty Jenkyns realizes she may have to confront the directors of the lately collapsed Town and County Bank in *Cranford.* This scenario is only entertained for its comic incongruity, of course. Idealizing the notion of shareholding, Miss Matty imagines the corporation as a group of individuals like herself. Yet her duty to honor the stranger's valueless bank note at Mr. Johnson's, while it reveals both her integrity and naivete, also represents her assumption of a public role. Her loss of property in the collapse of the bank is figured as a sentimental loosening of the "bonds" of the world. The decision of the ladies of Cranford to meet and take responsibility for Miss Matty's financial welfare is central to the town's installation of its own versions of the public institutions that violate its borders. Like "the great Cranford parliament," the first annual general meeting of the genteel shareholders and Miss Matty's foray into "trade" are both examples of the Republic of Cranford's appropriation of the notion of "joint stock."

The ambivalence of Margaret Hale's appearance on the stage of industrial relations, which debases public intervention into a masquerade of romance, resurfaces as a central problem in **Cranford**. A man may be "*so in the way in the house*" (39), and Cranford is after all a kind of vast house, that his absence empties the domestic space of all its potential as a point of convergence of public and private. As Mr. Smith's attitude to the tea-shop Miss Matty opens makes clear, hers is only a toy institution:

> my father says, "such simplicity might be very well in Cranford, but would never do in the world." And I fancy the world must be very bad, for with all my father's suspicion of every one with whom he has dealings, and in spite of all his many precautions, he lost upwards of a thousand pounds by roguery only last year. (201)

Likewise, the Cranfordians have their adventures, but they are only pretend adventures, without real villains or heroines. Under the hegemony of the drawing room, a hegemony of privacy, women in the novel play at politics, finance, and trade. Mary Smith's assessment of Mr. Holbrook's inhospitable parlor holds too for Drumble: "It was the smarter place; but, like most smart things, not at all pretty, or pleasant, or home-like" (74). **Cranford**'s "incorporation" of public affairs and commerce by domesticity is simultaneously a drama of their devaluation by the home-like. Cranford's autonomy is finally achieved in its independent economic order, but the sacrifice of an acknowledged hierarchy of public and private (in effect Cranford's sacrifice of its men) reduces its institutions to tea parties and its commodities to trinkets.

Its collection of trinkets, however, is precisely what makes **Cranford** so radical a novel. Far from being limited to the function of setting or local color, objects enter the narrative-historical dimension of the novel in two ways. Each object is described with special attention to its historical moment, so that the history of the town is related to the acquisition, relinquishment, and recollection of material tokens. And secondly, narration and materiality are fundamentally affined in **Cranford**. Mary Smith collects anecdotes and gathers them into the text like the little hanks of string "picked up and twisted together, ready for uses that never come" (83). No article is of so little value that it cannot be saved, or adapted to another use, or refashioned, and everything is precisely and individually accounted for by narration, observation, comment, chatter: "I had often occasion to notice," Mary remarks, "the use that was made of fragments and small opportunities in Cranford" (54). Fragments and small opportunities do not consti-

tute the novel's background, but its very structure. The most valued possession is story itself, exchanged with a reverence for the magic with which it bestows the power of dispensing with event. So little actually happens in Cranford that its most valuable currency is language, and "happenings" become important only in their exchangeable form, as stories. Discourse displaces experience in episodes of reading and writing, talking and listening, recalling and recounting. That property can be vested not in houses but in what is material and potential—bodies, things, and voices—is also made clear in Gaskell's industrial novels. In **Mary Barton,** as Gillian Beer points out, Gaskell "uses individual speech-styles, Manchester songs, life-narratives, in ways that suggest she is trying to make her middle class readers *hear* and pay attention to living working class speech" (243). Writing novels about "these dumb people" (as Gaskell calls them in the author's preface to **Mary Barton**) presented the Victorian reader with something strikingly novel: "things nameless" (Beer 243).

What is unnamed in **Mary Barton**'s Manchester is succeeded by what is unspoken in Cranford. As romantic intimacy is censured in the town, an effect of the tireless maintenance of class barriers, so "smallness" of voice is privileged. Captain Brown's first and most telling transgression is vocal: he speaks "in a voice too large for the room" (43). The distaste of the Cranfordians for personal disclosure, which results in the oppressive ritualization of speech and writing, does not, however, foreclose sympathy. Language, destitute of the power of intimacy, is redirected into communal mythologizing. The reiteration of a common voice, like the individualized voice of the working class or the voice of the fallen woman, transforms personal events into history. By standing in for each other as historians—Miss Pole narrates the history of Matty and Mr. Holbrook, Matty narrates the history of Deborah, and so forth—the ladies of Cranford are able to transcend a notion central to the development of omniscient narration in the novel and in the writing of history: that authentic utterance and private experience are only accessible to the unified self that is implicit in a consistent governing voice. The choice of narrator is crucial to this critique of narrative discourse and private life. The delimiting structure of romance is impugned by Gaskell's installation of a key figure who is able to represent both narrative authority and its revocation. That figure is Mary Smith.

Cranford's narrator, one of the novel's few mobile women, is also conspicuously without property. She lives in her father's house, or stays in any spare accommodation that Cranford can afford. Moving about between rooms, however, enables her to achieve multiple perspectives on the town: "It was impossible to live a month at Cranford, and not know the daily habits of each resident" (49). The fact that Mary alternates between Drumble and Cranford, an outsider and a native, permits Gaskell to cultivate a narrative tone of affection mingled with gentle mockery. "How naturally one falls back into the phraseology of Cranford!" (42). But there are two Mary Smiths, for each of whom a different phraseology is appropriate. We do not have the sense of two selves ironically interleaved into the narrative, as in such first-person *Bildungsromane* as *Jane Eyre* or *Great Expectations*. Mary develops from an unidentified narrator into a poorly-defined character. Her development, it has been argued, is made possible by the benevolent and redemptive atmosphere of Cranford unconsciously presided over by Miss Matty (see Dodsworth). But she is neither omniscient nor properly a character, and the question of what she represents as a narrator returns us to the question of where she belongs in the book (for an excellent discussion of Mary Smith's role in the novel, see Gillooly). There is no sense of an older, more mature Mary, but neither is there a sense of her immaturity; she is young, in that she represents the next generation, but she seems ageless. Finally, she is not "above" the text in the way that an omniscient narrator is, by virtue of superior knowledge of the plot's outcome; yet she can judge, interject, comment, as though she were not herself a part of the narrated world. In both senses of the phrase, she sometimes *looks in on* Cranford.

Yet it can also be argued that Mary does not really fall back into the phraseology of Cranford at all. In a novel notable as much for its female impersonators as for its surrogate male authority figures, Mary is perhaps its most complete male impersonator. Her educated tone and easy habit of allusiveness (most unprovincial, where provincial equals feminine) provide an ironic relief to the sometimes pompous and mostly faltering speech of Cranford. She faintly ridicules Deborah's anachronistic Johnsonian convolutions, but is herself presented with "the handsomest bound and best edition of Dr Johnson's works" (210), a prize befitting Deborah's successor. She never fails to point out Miss Matty's bad spelling (52) or her tendency to begin "many sentences without ending them, running them one into another, in much the same confused sort of way in which written words run together on blotting-paper" (128). Nor do the horizontal and perpendicular tangents of Miss Pole and Mrs. Forrester (163-64) escape her notice. But her own text is both truly Johnsonian *and* Cranfordian. Remembering the announcement of Lady Glenmire's marriage to Mr. Hoggins, she writes: "the contemplation of it, even at this distance of time, has taken away my breath and my grammar, and unless I subdue my emotion, my spelling will go too" (165). The irony here is directed at the spinsters' reception of this "stupendous" news, but also against herself and her makeshift style. This easy compatibility is perhaps her most remarkable quality as a narrator, and it makes her abrogation of narratorial authority seem inevitable. No symptom of self-repression (as in the case of Lucy Snowe in Charlotte Brontë's *Villette*) this ab-

rogation is rather a gesture of community. Mary consistently hands over to the ladies of Cranford their own narration, relinquishing her role as historian and allowing a more radical form of history to be written. Her narrative is like the letter she sends to Peter, "familiar and commonplace," which once out of her hands has adventures of its own: "It was gone from me like life—never to be recalled" (182). As Hilary Schor has shown, the tension between the Johnsonian and the Cranfordian is a tension between an inherited masculine grammar ("My father recommended it to me when I began to write letters,—I have formed my own style upon it" [48]) and the style that Mary Smith clearly indulges, that informed by Cranford's peculiar "leisure for the delights of perplexity" (174).

Critical to the history Gaskell is proposing, finally, is the powerful ubiquity of the narrating present. The moment of recounting, of bringing into voice, imports the past into utterance with an immediacy that is startling and sometimes violent. This is what invests the "old things" of the novel (the very materiality of its story-artefacts) with the keenness of perfect preservation, as in the old Jenkyns letters: "There was in them a vivid and intense sense of the present time, which seemed so strong and full, as if it could never pass away" (85). As James (in *The Turn of the Screw*) and Conrad (in *Heart of Darkness*) were later to do, Gaskell experiments with the tension between utterance and event by exploring ways of clearing a space for narration. Matty prepares to tell the story of Peter's exile by sending Martha away, locking the door, and putting the candle out (95): the tale is told in a darkness that obscures place and time. Matty's sense of the theatricality of narration, her relish of story-telling, is attested to by the very violence of the tale, at once so present and so distant. Stories are adventures.

In summary, then, *Cranford*'s collection of stories and women, curios both, do not belong in the world to which the narration is directed. That commercial world, belonging to the Londoner of Chapter One and the Mr. Smiths of Drumble, ridicules the novel's and the town's seemingly valueless modes of exchange, of which the most important is the exchange of stories. The structure of Gaskell's bazaar draws attention to relationships between men and the imperative of classification and history, narrative order and development: the progress of the tale, like the progress of the hero, is explicable in terms of the related public enterprises of commerce, museology, and history. *Cranford*'s interrogation of gender, materiality, and history is consequently overlooked by those celebrations of its charm which finally debase both its "elegant economy" and its narrative economy. But the novel finally questions the authority of any such critical position. It carries the Victorian orthodoxy of the separate spheres to its logical conclusion by imagining a world in which sexual division is so absolute as to be experienced as geographical segregation. This enables Gaskell to interrogate imaginatively the myth of the parallel existence of the sexes precisely at the point when Victorian middle-class women were undermining it by initiating public debate on these issues. Eschewing polemic, *Cranford*'s nervous sexual apartheid simply explodes the rhetoric of separateness by establishing a kind of omnipotence of the powerless: the town is at once marginal and total, excluded and exclusive. It is a world which relocates "the world" on its outskirts (as the Amazons might phrase it), and allows a radical revision of the formal authority of the masculine and the occidental in the writing of private life. To return to the paradox with which I began: *Cranford* is removed from the central issues of Victorianism yet, almost from the day of its publication, it has occupied a privileged place in representations of the Victorian. It is clearly not entirely an isolated and discontinuous text, but rather highlights the complex negotiations throughout Victorian fiction between private enclosures and public realms, domestic and public spaces. In this lies the significance of those scenes where the narrative lingers at the town's thresholds: Mr. Holbrook's house; the public-house "standing on the high road to London, about three miles from Cranford" (152) where Samuel Brown breaks down; and Mary's long pause at the post-box.

Notes

¹ Martin Tropp, for instance, comments that Dickens's "marvellous construction [*Bleak House*], like Paxton's, both contained and symbolized a world" (68).

² See Briggs on Peter Conrad on the Great Exhibition (54). Briggs also writes how "Dostoievsky found it 'astonishing.' 'You gasp for breath.' 'It is like a Biblical picture, something out of Babylon'" (59). Macaulay, too, thought it "beyond the dreams of the Arabian romances" (qtd. in Priestley 78). Jones's Eastern design is discussed in Sweetman 128-30.

³ Richard Altick discusses the Chinese Exhibition showing in London in 1841-3, and the Junk Keying, which arrived nearly three years after it embarked from Hong Kong (292-97).

⁹ Women were excluded from the anthropological enterprise at least in part because they were (again, like the Chinese) among its principal objects of study. The rise of social anthropology in the mid-century, and the social Darwinism of anthropologists such as Maine, McLennan and Spencer all forwarded the belief that, in Elizabeth Fee's words, "patriarchalism was . . . inextricably linked with the progress of civilization" (38).

¹⁰ Lewis Hyde argues that "boys can still become men, and men become more manly, by entering the marketplace and dealing in commodities. A woman can do the same thing if she wants to, of course, but it will not make her feminine" (105).

¹¹ Andrew Miller calls Gaskell a "narrative *bricoleur*"; as well as *bricolage*, *Cranford*'s form recalls that other Victorian artform practiced by Victorian women, *decoupage*.

¹² "If *Cranford*'s narrative is cohesive, its unifying principles derive more from the circumscribed stasis associated with spinsterhood than from precepts of conventional narrative linearity" (Boone 296). Andrew Miller asserts that "Gaskell carefully interweaves stories of detection and financial failure in two linear plots" which contest what he calls the "'recursive' movement of narratives of everyday life." Eileen Gillooly argues that *Cranford*, "strung and knotted together by the association and repetition of trope and event, loosely *tied* by episodic moments rather than driven by inexorable plot, stands as an attempt to connect with the lost source of nurturance, the preoedipal mother. . . . Put another way, in being preoedipal, non-linear, non-phallocentric, the narrative denies the authority of the Law that has superseded the mother's presence" (903-04).

¹³ Auerbach goes further, claiming Cranford has an "unsettling power to obliterate men" and a "corresponding gift of producing them at need" (81).

Works Cited

Allen, David Elliston. *The Naturalist in Britain: A Social History.* Harmondsworth: Penguin, 1978.

Altick, Richard D. *The Shows of London.* Cambridge: Harvard UP, 1978.

Auerbach, Nina. *Communities of Women: An Idea in Fiction.* Cambridge: Harvard UP, 1978.

Beer, Gillian. "Carlyle and *Mary Barton:* Problems of Utterance." *1848: The Sociology of Literature (Proceedings of the Essex Conference on the Sociology of Literature, 1977).* Ed. Francis Barker, David Musselwhite et al. Colchester: U of Essex, 1978. 242-55.

Boone, Joseph Allen. *Tradition Counter Tradition: Love and the Form of Fiction.* Chicago: Chicago UP, 1987.

Briggs, Asa. *Victorian Things.* London: Penguin, 1990.

Calder, Jenni. *The Victorian Home.* London: Batsford, 1977.

Conrad, Peter. *The Victorian Treasure-House.* London: Collins, 1973.

Cunningham, Valentine. *Everywhere Spoken Against: Dissent in the Victorian Novel.* Oxford: Clarendon,

1975.

Dodsworth, Martin. "Women Without Men at Cranford." *Essays in Criticism* 13 (1963): 132-45.

Dyer, Gary R. "The 'Vanity Fair' of Nineteenth-Century England: Commerce, Women, and the East in the Ladies' Bazaar." *Nineteenth-Century Literature* 46 (1991): 196-222.

Fee, Elizabeth. "The Sexual Politics of Victorian Social Anthropology." *Feminist Studies* 1 (1973): 23-39.

Flower, William Henry. "Boys' Museums." *Essays on Museums and Other Subjects Connected with Natural History.* London: Macmillan, 1898. 63-69.

Gaskell, Elizabeth. *Cranford/ Cousin Phyllis.* Ed. P. J. Keating. Harmondsworth: Penguin, 1976.

————. *North and South.* Ed. Dorothy Collin. Harmondsworth: Penguin, 1970.

Gillooly, Eileen. "Humor as Daughterly Defense in *Cranford.*" *ELH* 59 (1992): 883-910.

Harman, Barbara Leah. "In Promiscuous Company: Female Public Appearance in Elizabeth Gaskell's *North and South.*" *Victorian Studies* 31 (1988): 351-74.

Hollis, Patricia, ed. *Women in Public 1850-1900: Documents of the Victorian Women's Movement.* London: Allen, 1979.

Howell, Sarah. *The Seaside.* London: Studio Vista, 1974.

Hudson, Kenneth. *Museums of Influence.* Cambridge: Cambridge UP, 1987.

Hyde, Lewis. *The Gift: Imagination and the Erotic Life of Property.* New York: Vintage, 1979.

Lefebvre, Henri. *The Production of Space.* Trans. Donald Nicholson-Smith. Oxford: Blackwell, 1991.

Mill, John Stuart. *On Liberty, Representative Government, The Subjection of Women: Three Essays.* London: Oxford UP, 1974.

Miller, Andrew H. "The Fragments and Small Opportunities of *Cranford.*" *Genre,* Forthcoming.

Parkinson, Ronald. "James Collinson." Parris 61-75.

Parris, Leslie, ed. *Pre-Raphaelite Papers.* London: The Tate Gallery, 1984.

Priestley, J. B. *Victoria's Heyday.* Harmondsworth: Penguin, 1974.

Russell, Colin A. *Science and Social Change 1700-1900.* London: Macmillan, 1983.

Schor, Hilary M. "Affairs of the Alphabet: Reading, Writing and Narrating in *Cranford.*" *Novel* 22 (1989): 288-304.

Stewart, Susan. *On Longing: Narratives of the Miniature, the Gigantic, the Souvenir, the Collection.* Baltimore: Johns Hopkins UP, 1984.

Stone, Harry, ed. *The Uncollected Writings of Charles Dickens: Household Words 1850-1859.* 2 vols. London: Lane, 1969.

Sweetman, John. *The Oriental Obsession: Islamic Inspiration in British and American Art and Architecture 1500-1920.* Cambridge: Cambridge UP, 1988.

Tropp, Martin. *Images of Fear: How Horror Stories Helped Shape Modern Culture.* Jefferson, NC: McFarland, 1990.

van Keuren, David K. "Museums and Ideology: Augustus Pitt-Rivers, Anthropological Museums, and Social Change in Later Victorian Britain." *Energy and Entropy: Science and Culture in Victorian Britain.* Ed. Patrick Brantlinger. Bloomington: Indiana UP, 1989. 270-88.

Wise, T. J., and J. A. Symington, eds. *The Brontes: Their Lives, Friendships and Correspondence.* 4 vols. Oxford: Blackwell, 1980.

Yeazell, Ruth Bernard. "Why Political Novels Have Heroines: *Sybil, Mary Barton,* and *Felix Holt.*" *Novel* 18 (1985): 126-44.

Yeldham, Charlotte. *Women Artists in Nineteenth-Century France and England: Their Art Education, Exhibition Opportunities and Membership of Existing Societies and Academies, With an Assessment of the Subject Matter of Their Work and Summary Biographies.* 2 vols. New York and London: Garland, 1984.

Philip Rogers (essay date 1995)

SOURCE: "The Education of Cousin Phillis," in *Nineteenth-Century Literature*, Vol. 50, No. 1, June, 1995, pp. 27-50.

[*In the following essay, Rogers contends that Gaskell's short story "Cousin Phillis" describes the predicament of the well-educated woman in Victorian Britain; his analysis also focuses upon the significance of the title character's name.*]

For Elizabeth Gaskell the story of Phillis Holman's disappointment in her first love in **"Cousin Phillis"**

(1865) is inseparable from the process and content of her unusual education. As both daughter and lover—the only roles open to her as learner—Phillis is inescapably a pupil of men who control her education in ways that serve their interests. Learning from men what men traditionally have taught other men does not make her, as her cousin Paul naively supposes, "more like a man than a woman."[1] On the contrary, the lessons of her reading and the experience of male tuition inculcate contradictory and damaging definitions of womanhood, diminishing her independence and sense of self. Like Gaskell's narrator, most critics of **"Cousin Phillis"** have interpreted Phillis' learning simply as evidence of her superior intelligence and promise rather than as allusive commentary on her predicament and that of educated women generally.[2] Far from liberating her from the conventional constraints of Victorian womanhood, Phillis' readings in Virgil, Dante, and Alessandro Manzoni comprise no less prescriptive guides to woman's behavior than her mother's conduct book, the "Housewife's Complete Manual." The shame-sickness of her breakdown is thus as much a product of her male education as of her loss of Holdsworth.

Learning in **"Cousin Phillis"** is the province of men. Gaskell's representation of teaching and learning among the male characters—a pervasive concern of Paul Manning's frame-narrative—defines the social context in which the nature and ends of Phillis' education are explored. Just as Maggie Tulliver's "yearning for effectual wisdom" in George Eliot's *The Mill on the Floss* (1860)—Maggie is a probable model for Gaskell's heroine[3]—is fully understood only in relation to her brother's education and apprenticeship, Phillis' learning is defined by contrast with that of her cousin and the other men. Relationships among men in **"Cousin Phillis"** all possess a tutelary component. Holdsworth learns about driving wheels from Paul's father; Paul, in turn, is Holdsworth's apprentice. The friendships that form between Paul, Holdsworth, Mr. Manning, and Minister Holman are confirmed in scenes of mutual instruction. In her analysis of male learning Gaskell is especially attentive to issues of authority. The mutual esteem of men depends on their possessing exclusive knowledge and being able to tell others something that they do not know. Their knowledge, like Manning's winch, is patented, a possession exchangeable for the knowledge of others. Thus, in his first visit to Hope Farm, Mr. Manning must display his expertise as inventor; in response, Holman explains the fine points of the cow. Holdsworth teaches Holman "the practical art of surveying and taking a level" (p. 308), and Paul reinflates his Phillis-punctured ego by showing her and the minister that he knows "something worth knowing" about engineering (p. 276). And in the central action that all this teaching activity points toward, the minister teaches Phillis Greek and Latin and Holdsworth instructs her in Italian, providing texts, dictionaries, lessons, and marginal annotation.

Paul represents this round-robin of instruction approvingly. To him the participants are all engaged in wholesome self-improvement, Phillis also evincing "manly" eagerness to expand her intellectual horizons in the realm of male knowledge. However, an important difference is evident, if unremarked by Paul: Phillis' participation in learning, unlike that of the men, is never mutual. Although she is distinguished by her educational attainments and ambition, Phillis holds no patents and remains invariably the pupil. Paul, her only potential student, will not subject himself to the teaching of a younger, taller woman and disparages the utility of her kind of knowledge as "dead-and-gone languages" (p. 276). In subjects that the men view as specifically male concerns, Phillis' status is even less than that of the pupil: when Holdsworth and Manning instruct Holman in surveying and dynamics (pp. 289, 308) Phillis is merely an onlooker, struggling to hear what is said. Her father is "almost unconscious" of her presence as she peers over his shoulder, "sucking in information like her father's own daughter" (p. 289), as Paul aptly notes, unconscious of the irony. Even in Phillis' study of language and literature, Gaskell implies, "her father's own daughter" has been permitted access to male knowledge only by default. The minister's motive in teaching Phillis arises not from a belief in his daughter's unique promise or the desirability of her knowing Latin and Greek but rather from his having made her a son-surrogate. Mr. Manning accounts for Phillis' anomalous education by noting that "she is the only child of a scholar" (p. 292). Paul observes that Phillis becomes more and more "the very apple of her father's eye" as she grows to resemble the little boy who died (p. 327). Had Brother Johnnie lived, Sister Phillis would instead have been the apple of her mother's eye.

A second aspect of male learning against which Gaskell measures Phillis' education is its emphasis on utility. In particular, the engineering-inventing-agricultural institutions to which the men each belong stress concrete outcomes. For them knowledge is the production of driving wheels and turnip cutters, hay and milk. Even the minister's literary studies reflect a utilitarian motive; his Virgil is the *Georgics,* read for its shrewd advice on "rolling and irrigation . . . choice of the best seed . . . keep[ing] the drains clear" (p. 334). Gaskell also stresses the utility of learning for males in its direct connection to social advancement; learning is rising and "manning": promotion, partnership, the boss's daughter, and one's own carriage.

In contrast to the purposes of men's learning, Phillis' studies relate to no apparent institution or end. As Gaskell observed in distinguishing the Brontë family's attitudes toward Branwell and his sisters, men are "expected to act a part in life; to *do* while [women] are only to *be*."[4] The only image in the text of Phillis' reading represents it as an awkward distraction from a more pressing responsibility—paring apples in the kitchen.[5] Her father's pupil, she is more fundamentally her mother's apprentice. In contrast to the tool-equipped men, whose spades, rulers, theodolites, burnt sticks, and pencils (noticeably not ungendered implements) serve as emblems of authoritative, engaged male knowledge, Phillis wields only a paring knife and produces only pies. Gaskell defines the Holmans' social position in order to emphasize the detachment of Phillis' learning from necessary ends. As the only child, she will inherit the family farm; thus she has no need for teaching credentials, the motive for learning for a Jane Eyre or Lucy Snowe. Further, given the limited opportunities of a country town and the personal constraints implied in the Holman family religion, any future application of Phillis' education appears improbable. Indeed, in Mr. Manning's opinion, her being a scholar is worse than pointless, the sole flaw in her eligibility for marrying his son. His prediction defines her problem unsympathetically: "once she's a wife and a mother she'll forget it all" (p. 292). Gaskell resents Manning's glib certainty, yet in the text she nonetheless wonders what difference Greek and Latin can make to a wife and mother in a world harmonized by Minister Holman's spade and propelled by Inventor Manning's driving wheel.

What then does Gaskell imply Phillis' aim to be in seeking to educate herself? Gaskell denies her male characters—and especially her narrator—any insight whatever into the nature or object of Phillis' intellectual ambitions. As Gaskell's title implies, Paul Manning writes about Phillis not as a person in her own right but as his cousin. His narrative (manifestly driven by self-exculpatory motives) defines her in terms of his own indiscretion, the sole unhappy episode in an otherwise successful *Bildung.* He writes to put her behind as well as beneath him. Readers of Gaskell's subtle, ironic text are consequently invited to reshape a Phillis from the evidence of Paul's ignorance and distortions, to recover Phillis' inner life from small revelations that Gaskell permits to leak through the fine filters of male bias and obtuseness.[6]

That Phillis views her education, despite its inutility, as a kind of liberating self-fulfillment, a way to "be," is implied in the intensity of her desire to learn in spite of the frustrations she encounters, always doing "two things at once" (p. 283). That she wishes to escape the limits of her father's tutoring, to reject the intellectual pinafore and achieve an independent sense of self as an adult woman (possibilities unrecognizable by Paul) is especially evident in her attempting to read in Italian, a language unknown to her father. In undertaking the *Inferno* she too, like Dante, seeks a new life. Paul, of course, has not glimpsed her "dark wood" or the leopard blocking the way; he can only make out the

connection of inferno to "infernal" (p. 282), an association sufficient to alert readers to the ominous import of Gaskell's allusion. For Phillis, however, the aim of entering the *Inferno* is to abandon not hope but Hope Farm. She recognizes that in learning Italian the "meaning of the hard words"—her father's knowledge, the parental definition of her—no longer suffices. Her attraction to a new text, a foreign language, and a man with foreign knowledge and experience implies not merely her sexual coming of age but also the desire to escape the limitations of Heathbridge, a "dark wood" indeed for an ambitious, educated woman. The arrival of the railroad bringing Holdsworth to Heathbridge also offers Phillis the means to a way out. Phillis' interest in Holdsworth, as her father immediately recognizes, implies a desire to leave: "you would have left us, left your home, left your father and your mother, and gone away with this stranger, wandering over the world" (p. 346).

But Gaskell implies no liberation for Phillis in her reading; undertaking the new language does not lead her to independent individuality and travel, because dictionaries and passports, like most of the tools in her world, are male possessions. Even Phillis' vocabulary is monitored. Holdsworth's intrusive annotation of the hard words in her text comprises subtle censoring: knowing a range of possible choices, he chooses for her, "writ[ing] down the most accepted meanings" (p. 302). Virgil's presence in the *Inferno* as Dante's guide implies not a successful escape for Phillis into a new text but rather the repetition of Phillis' Latin texts and paternal limits in a less spacious setting; in learning Italian, Phillis merely substitutes a lover-tutor for a father-tutor, a development that appears to deny her education any moment of self-direction or even the privacy expressive of independent womanhood. That Phillis and Holdsworth's love blossoms in their sharing of books, in their reading together of Dante and Manzoni, suggests that Gaskell's allusion to the *Inferno* points in particular to its best-known episode, the tale of Paolo and Francesca[7]—whose illicit love was also mediated by fiction, the tale of Lancelot and Guinevere. Gaskell thus associates Phillis not with Dante, the pilgrim passing through the Inferno on an upward journey, but with the book-betrayed Francesca, a permanent resident.

Yet while learning in "Cousin Phillis" is the province of men, Gaskell shows it to be a realm beyond their mastery: men know less than they suppose. In spite of Paul's talking up the triumphs of engineering and invention, his meeting his cousin emerges as the consequence of an engineering failure: Phillis enters Paul's and Holdworth's lives at that point in the building of the railroad where the engineers are puzzled and brought to a halt. The Heathbridge myrtle bogs, while "very wild and pretty" country, prove to be "shaking, uncertain ground" (pp. 261, 263), lacking a "steady bottom" (p.

275); no sooner is one end of the line weighted down than the other goes up. The Heathbridge myrtle bog may be bridged but not tracked. Gaskell represents engineering to be a visual science; Holdsworth surveys, maps, sketches. But the uncertain depths of the bog are invisible to theodolites, and the engineers are obliged to abandon Heathbridge to lay their track on firmer ground. One need not know (as Virgil notes at the beginning of Holman's favorite text, the *Georgics*) that myrtle is Venus' plant in order to see the failure of the Heathbridge line as emblematic of Phillis' abandonment by the unsuccessful engineer.[8] Yet the tracking-of-the-myrtle bog metaphor suggests a reading of Phillis and Holdsworth's relationship quite different from the narrator's. Paul's narrative—which bridges rather than tracks his cousin—stresses Phillis' failures: she cannot hold Holdsworth, cannot control her feelings for him after he leaves, and cannot, as is implied in the unspecific account of her later years, establish a new life worthy of Paul's mention. In the context of Victorian fictional convention this implies a woman's ultimate failure—to become a wife and mother. The impossibility of laying track in the bog, on the other hand, invites readings that identify the failures in **"Cousin Phillis"** not as Phillis' but as those of men out of their depth.

Paul presents Holdsworth's abandonment of Phillis as merely circumstantial, the consequence of his departure for a new job. Yet the story of Paul's own aborted interest in courting his cousin clearly anticipates and comments on Holdsworth's. Paul's dread of a wife who knows more than he does might appear to be the opposite of Holdsworth's encouragement of Phillis' learning, yet the scenes of Holdsworth's wooing of Phillis similarly prefigure his abandoning her for Lucille Ventadour. Holdsworth's abortive sketching of Phillis exactly parallels the railroad failure; the analogy of his attempt to map her surface to the process of survey and measurement by theodolite (scenes that Gaskell juxtaposes) is evident in his abstracting her as Ceres. Since, like the bog's, Phillis' depths are invisible to him, Holdsworth can deal with Phillis only by defining limits: he marks her off within the boundaries of a mythological parcel; he takes her level in "most accepted meanings." But just as she resists his suggestive whispers in the theodolite episode, Phillis will not return the engineer-portraitist's surveying gaze or submit to his command ("Please look at me for a minute or two, I want to get in the eyes" [p. 311]), nor will she hold the assigned pose.[9] The track cannot be weighted down, the sketch is abandoned. Holdsworth has not succeeded in mapping Phillis' depths. He understands her resistance only in clichés; he would make her an English fertility goddess if she would submit, but she is innocent, passionless, an unawakened sleeping beauty. Thus his sketch of her is incomplete, lacking "shading or colouring" (p. 315). Reading backward from Hardy, we recall Tess' annoyance at Angel Clare's mythologizing her as Artemis and Demeter.[10] Like Angel's, Holdsworth's stereotypes are as inherently contradictory as they are wrong, celebrating Phillis simultaneously as the essences of both chaste innocence and natural sexuality: "What a sweet innocent face it is! and yet so—Oh, dear!" ("Cousin Phillis," p. 315). No sooner is the sweet, innocent-faced end of Holdsworth's track weighted down than it is destabilized by ("Oh, dear!") her "pretty mouth" (pp. 292-93). Holdsworth's failure to recognize qualities in Phillis other than these stereotypes explains his abandoning her. Any other woman can serve such interests as Holdsworth's, and indeed, to him, Lucille Ventadour "is curiously like" Phillis (p. 329).

Minister Holman's learning is no more efficacious than Holdsworth's in tracking Phillis. From the first it is apparent that the coherence of Holman's learning, the system of his knowledge as it relates to his daughter, depends on suppressions: he seeks to deny his daughter's adult sexuality, to keep her in pinafores. Less obvious in Holman's attempts simultaneously to educate and to control Phillis are the contradictory premises of his teaching. Gaskell undermines the validity of Holman's claim of authority over his daughter by showing his knowledge to be not in fact "whole" but rather an unstable pairing of conflicting halves. The two ends of Holman's track are apparent first in his dual roles as minister and farmer. The introduction to Holman in Paul's narrative implies the potential incompatibility of the two. Both before and after Paul's first visit Holdsworth questions the minister-farmer pairing: "It is not often that parsons know how to keep land in order, is it?" (p. 264); "how do preaching and farming seem to get on together?" (p. 268). Gaskell also stresses centripetal tendencies of preaching and farming in the incident of Holman's prayer for his sick cow. In asking a blessing for Bessie, Holman forgets to order her "warm mash," the means to cure her: "here was I asking a blessing and neglecting the means, which is a mockery" (p. 279).

The cover illustration of the 1867 edition of **Cousin Phillis and Other Tales** represents Holman's halves in a memorable emblem. Grouped in the stubble field, Phillis and two workmen sing the psalm "Come all harmonious tongues" as the minister beats time with his spade and Paul looks on (p. 271). The scene's implied harmonizing of the minister's two "tongues"—preaching and farming linked by an act of devotion in the fields—is rendered discordant by its most trenchant detail, the incongruous spade that beats time. This staff, which seeks to harmonize and control by main force the orders of nature and grace, soon bifurcates (like the engineers' unbalanced tracks) into dual, not ungendered staves specific to Holman's halves: the minister's parish rod of discipline and the farmer's parish bull (p. 274)—images expressive of the contrary modes of authority implicit in preaching and procreation, the blessing and the means. The bearing of Holman's unharmonious tongues on the education of Phillis is evident in the texts that voice their respective practices—the Bible (and Holman's religion generally) and Virgil's *Georgics,* which articulates the tongue of agriculture. In making her minister-farmer also a student of the classics, Gaskell accomplishes various purposes.[11] Most obviously, the classical knowledge allows her to explore the implications of Phillis' receiving from her father a man's education. Then, by linking Holman's Latin teaching to Virgil's *Georgics,* his agricultural "Bible," Gaskell extends the thematic implications of the minister-farmer duality to include the opposition of Christian and pagan texts, a conflict especially relevant to Phillis' learning the contradictory lessons that men teach men about women: "the true adornment is a meek and quiet spirit" (p. 285), yet oh, dear!—her pretty mouth. As the Heathbridge community walks to church the minister contemplates his discourse, and the young men, like Holdsworth, "cast admiring looks" on Phillis. The opposition of Virgilian and Christian sexual mores is underscored in Holdsworth's ironic reply to Paul's doubting the minister's willingness to have Phillis read novels: "You don't suppose they take Virgil for gospel?" (p. 304).

Ironically, for Holman the *Georgics is* Gospel. He values Virgil not as poetry but for its present-time accuracy of observation and its practical advice to farmers: "It's wonderful . . . how exactly Virgil has hit the enduring epithets, nearly two thousand years ago, and in Italy; and yet how it describes to a T what is now lying before us in the parish of Heathbridge, county—, England" (p. 273). Undermining Paul's defensive dismissal of Latin as a "dead-and-gone" language, Gaskell quite insistently stresses the relevance of the minister's and Phillis' classical readings to their own present-day lives, especially to Phillis' relationship with Holdsworth. As the minister notes, Holdsworth's talk of Italy "makes Horace and Virgil living, instead of dead, by the stories he tells me of his sojourn in the very countries where they lived, and where to this day, he says—" (p. 305).[12] "Where to this day, he [and Virgil and Horace] says—" what?, the reader is made to wonder. Gaskell's allusions, reinforced by Paul's frequent protests of his ignorance of languages and hymns, plainly direct the reader to consider the relevance to **"Cousin Phillis"** of Virgil, Horace, Dante, and Manzoni, as well as the "profane" but suggestively suppressed subjects of Holdsworth's Italian anecdotes.[13]

Shortly before Phillis' breakdown (and perhaps its proximate cause) the minister reads Virgil aloud as he beats time, now with a ruler. "It [the *Georgics*] is all living truth in these days," he repeats (p. 334). Ironically, the nature gospel of the *Georgics,* its "living truth," that Holman devoutly "chants" and conducts—as earlier he led the singing of the hymn—also "describes to a T" the sexual passions that Holman refuses to acknowledge in his daughter; he is as blind to the

implication of Virgil's "enduring epithets" as he is to his daughter's sexuality, which cannot be measured or contained either by theodolite or the spatial and temporal limits implied by a time-keeping ruler. Preoccupied with blessings and grace, he has neglected nature's means. The *Georgics* exposes the "mockery" of such censorship; Virgil represents sexual passion as Phillis experiences it: maddening, uncontrollable, inescapable—an "uncertain ground" not to be "ruled," a tongue beyond harmonizing:

> Yea, every single race on earth, man and beast, the tribes of the sea, cattle and birds brilliant of hue, rush into fires of passion: all feel the same Love.
>
> (pp. 171-73; III, ll. 242-44)

In specific contrast to Holman's and Holdsworth's view of Phillis as a sleeping beauty who will feel passion only when a parentally approved male has first aroused it with a formal declaration, Virgil represents females, both human and animal, as no less dominated by sexual urges than males. So intense is female desire that it annuls even the maternal instinct (an observation Gaskell would surely have remarked):

> At no other season doth the lioness forget her cubs, or prowl over the plains more fierce.
>
> (p. 173; III, ll. 245-46)

Indeed, the most violent of all creatures in the mating season is female, and her rage, significantly, is no aberration but rather divinely ordained by the myrtle-loving goddess:

> But surely the madness of mares surpasses all. Venus herself inspired their frenzy, when the four Potnian steeds tore with their jaws the limbs of Glaucus. Love leads them over Gargarus and over the roaring Ascanius; they scale mountains, they swim rivers.
>
> (p. 173; III, ll. 267-70)

Especially relevant to **"Cousin Phillis"** is Virgil's comment on the inability of parents to restrain their impassioned children: Leander's "hapless parents" cannot "call him back" from the Hellespont and Hero (III, l. 263).

The *Georgics* also comments on Holman's refusal to accept Phillis' May-first birthday as May Day. The minister, of course, must dissociate his chaste daughter from the grass-staining celebration of fertility rites associated with the English Cerealia. Virgil, however, specifically enjoins the farmer to venerate Ceres:

> Above all, worship the gods, and pay great Ceres her yearly rites, sacrificing on the glad sward, with the setting of winter's last days, when clear springtime is now come. . . . Then let all your country folk worship Ceres . . . while the whole choir of your

comrades follow exulting, and loudly call Ceres into their homes; nor let any put his sickle to the ripe corn, ere for Ceres he crown his brows with oaken wreath, dance artless measures, and chant her hymns.

(p. 105; I, ll. 338-40, 343, 346-50)

In the context of the *Georgics,* Holman's singing hymns in the stubble field may be read as an attempt to christianize Virgil's Cerealia. Adapting Virgil's mode of veneration to the minister's biblically defined prescription of women's place entails, of course, the suppression of Ceres and her "yearly rites," a censoring that reflects Holman's appropriation of all sexual authority (the parish bull) to males and his keeping Phillis unadorned and meekly pinafored.[14] Holdsworth, of course, specifically identifies Phillis as Ceres, but his coercive posing of her for his sketch implies not a veneration of the goddess in opposition to the minister's censorship but rather, like Holman's, an appropriation of authority over Ceres, the analogue of his attempt to track Venus' myrtle bog.

Gaskell's allusions to the *Georgics* illuminate the suppressions entailed in Minister Holman's denying his daughter's sexuality, his viewing Phillis as solely the child of grace. Yet Virgil's texts also represent a censored view of women by limiting them exclusively (in the traditional association) to the order of nature, the opposite end of Holman's track. In this too Virgil "describes to a T" the "living truth" of Holdsworth's reductive view of Phillis as Nature, or Ceres, and his denying her individuality by posing her as the passive object of desire, another marginal imposition of "the most accepted meanings." This too is "mockery." Gaskell's choice of the name Phillis for her heroine, the most significant of the work's numerous allusions, refers directly to this opposite mode of censorship and implies a specific critique of the representation of women in literary texts ancient and modern. Lessons from these texts will not make Phillis like a man.

Phyllis in Virgil's *Eclogues* is the compliant, ardent, and promiscuous country girl. Horace, in his fourth "Ode," urges his parsley-garlanded Phyllis to "cut short far-reaching hopes" of winning a younger man and to respond instead to Horatian ardor.[15] The Phyllis of Ovid's *Heroides,* whose story Dante cites in *Paradiso* (IX, ll. 100-101)[16]—and Jean de Meung, Chaucer, and Gower repeat, respectively, in the *Roman de la Rose* (c. 1280; ll. 13,211-14), *The Legend of Good Women* (c. 1386; ll. 263, 2,394-561), and *Confessio Amantis* (c. 1390; IV, ll. 731-886)—is dominated and destroyed by passion for the man who leaves her; her story so closely parallels Phillis Holman's that Gaskell's allusion is unmistakable. With her companions—Amarillis, Corydon, Thyrsis, etc.—Phillis is also, of course, a stock character of Arcady in Renaissance and eighteenth-century poetry, where, when not busy with sheep,

she prepares bucolic luncheons and seizes the day with literary tourists. Thus Phillis Holman's name compounds the impropriety of her May Day birth.[17] Phillis' being named for her mother provides Gaskell with an excuse for this otherwise improbable choice of name for a minister's daughter, especially a minister familiar with classical texts. Resisting Angel Clare's mythologizing her as a "daughter of Nature" (*Tess,* p. 95), an Artemis or Demeter, Tess exclaims, "Call me Tess" (p. 103). A similar protest by Phillis Holman would be grimly ironic.

In Virgil's *Eclogues* Phyllis is fully and harmoniously a child of nature. As in Ovid, Servius, Hyginus, and (following them) Chaucer and Gower, the etymological association of her name with leaves (*phylla,* Phillis as foliage) links her character with the pastoral setting and the thematics of seasonal temporality. For Thyrsis and Corydon in *Eclogue* VII her presence and preferences are associated with the flourishing of leafy plants:

Thyrsis

The field is parched; the grass is athirst, dying in the tainted air; . . . But at the coming of Phyllis all the woodland will be green, and Jupiter, in his fullness, shall descend in gladsome showers.

Corydon

The poplar is most dear to Alcides, and the vine to Bacchus, the myrtle to lovely Venus, and his own laurel to Phoebus. Phyllis loves hazels, and while Phyllis loves them, neither the myrtle nor laurel of Phoebus shall outvie the hazels.

(p. 53; VII, ll. 57-64)

Gaskell draws extensively from this seasonal greening of the pastoral Phyllis. Phillis Holman's mother was maiden-named (and tinted) Phillis Green. The flowering of Phillis' passion for Holdsworth is set against a sudden rainstorm that relieves sultry summer weather, conditions that Gaskell repeats as the setting for Phillis' breakdown. Most pointedly allusive to Phyllis' *phylla* is Gaskell's description of trees delicately poised on the seasonal brink of exfoliation at the moment Phillis presents the flowers to Holdsworth: "The yellow leaves hung on the trees ready to flutter down at the slightest puff of air" (p. 312). In his commentary on Virgil's *Eclogue* V, Servius explains that the abandoned Phyllis was transformed into an almond tree that dropped its leaves when her lover, returning too late, embraced it.[18] Paul's memory of Phillis' happiest moments juxtapose her against the vernal greening of foliage: "I can see her now, standing under the budding branches of the grey trees, over which a tinge of green seemed to be deepening day after day . . . her hands full of delicate wood-flowers" (p. 327). Gaskell's association of Phillis with both leaves and books invites a reading of her circumstances in terms of the conventional metaphor of leaves as pages (folio/foliage), rendering Holdsworth's annotation of her leaves more obviously an attempt to define her identity as well as the "hard words"—to make her his text, an action parallel in kind to his surveying, sketching, and bog tracking.

Less subtle than its etymological meanings, the traditional associations of Phillis' name are plainly with sexual freedom or excess. Isaac Watts, author of Holman's spade-conducted hymn "Come all harmonious tongues" and like Minister Holman a classically educated dissenting minister, chooses the name Phillis specifically to exemplify the carnal eroticism of pagan literature. In his "Meditation in a Grove" Watts would christianize the pastoral setting by expelling its wanton Phillises: "But hence, ye wanton young and fair, / Mine is a purer flame; / No Phyllis shall infect the air, / With her unhallow'd name."[19]

In choosing to give his representative wanton the name Phillis, Watts may have had in mind the Phillis of Rochester's poems "Song" ("By all Love's soft yet mighty Pow'rs") and "The Mock Song" ("I swive as well as others do"), among the most obscenely air-infecting verses in the English language;[20] yet the Phyllis of the *Eclogues* is herself sufficiently promiscuous to justify expulsion from the groves (and stubble fields) of Dissent. Even within the *Eclogues* her reputation is already traditional; in *Eclogue* V, Menalcas invites Mopsus to sing the song of "Phyllis and her Loves": "Begin first, Mopsus, if you have any strains on your flame Phyllis, or in praise of Alcon, or in raillery at Codrus" (p. 35; V, ll. 10-11).

Just as the song of Phyllis is one possible diversion among many, Phyllis herself is invariably represented as another, a country girl interchangeable with other country girls and herself willing to be pursued by and shared among numerous males.[21] To the love-stricken Gallus in *Eclogue* X she is one of many available to console him:

> And O that I had been one of you, the shepherd of a flock of yours, or the dresser of your ripened grapes! Surely, my darling, whether it were Phyllis or Amyntas, or whoever it were . . . my darling would be lying at my side among the willows, under the creeping vine—Phyllis culling me garlands, Amyntas singing songs.

(pp. 73-75; X, ll. 35-38, 40-41)

In **"Cousin Phillis"** this representation of women as readily available and interchangeable relates to Gaskell's concern with Phillis as an individual and Holdsworth's failure to see her individuality; Phillis or Lucille, or some other love, will pick his garlands. Minister Holman underscores this theme in his deprecation of Holdsworth's love for his daughter as "a love that is ready for any

young woman" (p. 345). The allusive shadow of Virgil's Phyllis falls on Phillis Holman even in moments that appear to reveal an expression of her individual will. Her presenting the flowers to Holdsworth, a token of interest in him that defines her as distinctively an exception to the passive, sleeping beauty stereotype, merely repeats the conventional role of her arcadian namesake, the garland-picking Phyllis of *Eclogue* X. The giving of garlands and flowers cannot distinguish Phillis, who as "phylla"— a leaf among leaves—remains necessarily a feature of the pastoral background, herself a setting.

More demeaning even than the easy interchangeability of Virgil's Phyllis and Amyntas in *Eclogue* X is Damoetas' request to Iollas in *Eclogue* III that he lend Phyllis to him for the day as a birthday gift: "Send Phyllis to me; it is my birthday, Iollas" (p. 23; III, l. 76). She is further degraded when Menalcas offers Damoetas the exclusive use of Phyllis as a prize for cleverness in the singing contest: "Tell me in what land spring up flowers with royal names written thereon—and have Phyllis to yourself!" (p. 29; IV, ll. 106-7).

While Virgil's Phyllis broadly suggests terms governing the relationship of men and women in **"Cousin Phillis,"** it is the Phyllis of Ovid's *Heroides* that most closely comments on the story's action. While the *Heroides*, unlike the *Eclogues*, gives Phyllis a voice, she is again just another woman—this time a complaining, suicidal victim in an anthology of numerous aggrieved, abused women.[22] Ovid's Phyllis is the daughter of Lycurgus, ruler of Thrace. When Demophoon, the son of Theseus, is shipwrecked in Thrace, he and Phyllis fall in love. Before he leaves for Athens he promises to return and marry her. Yet he marries another and does not return; Phyllis is left to contemplate various suicides—drowning, poison, the sword, hanging. (In Chaucer's, Gower's, and de Meung's versions she hangs herself.)

Gaskell's Holdsworth recalls Demophoon in the circumstance, much stressed in both Ovid and Gaskell, of his crossing the stormy sea as he departs. The marriage and the failure to return offer exact parallels. A subtle resemblance suggesting Gaskell's conscious use of the Ovid text is Phyllis' complaint that Demophoon betrayed her while he was her guest. Phyllis' care for the shipwrecked Demophoon parallels Phillis Holman's care for the convalescent Holdsworth. Both Holdsworth and Demophoon betray the obligations of hospitality as well as promises of love.

But has Holdsworth betrayed Phillis at all? Some critics, those who miss the irony of Paul's narration, accept his exculpation of Holdsworth (and thus himself) of serious blame.[23] Gaskell's allusion to Demophoon, however, obviously implies betrayal, and this interpretation of Holdsworth's action also has ample support within **"Cousin Phillis."** Betty's insight into Holdsworth's "beguiling" of Phillis clearly undermines Paul's defensive claim that Holdsworth never spoke a word of love to Phillis. Betty replies, "Aye. aye! but there's eyes, and there's hands, as well as tongues; and a man has two o' th' one and but one o' t'other" (p. 336).

The Betrothed, Holdsworth's chosen text for teaching Italian to Phillis, introduces Gaskell's heroine to yet another abused country girl. Like Virgil's Phyllis in *Eclogue* III, Lucia, the long-suffering heroine of Manzoni's novel, is the object of a group-lust. The novel's action emerges from a chance meeting in which Don Roderigo and his cousin see Lucia for the first time and are taken with her beauty. Roderigo wagers that he can have her and proceeds to block her impending marriage so as to assert his *droit du seigneur*. Holdsworth's choice of *The Betrothed* for Phillis' language lessons is illuminated by Paolo's reading with Francesca of the Lancelot and Guinevere story. Holdsworth's description of *The Betrothed*—"as pretty and innocent a tale as can be met with" (p. 304)—renders all his other uses of "pretty" and "innocent" suspect, especially the "pretty mouth"/"pure innocence" formula that typifies his apprehension of Phillis. If Phillis finishes *The Betrothed* she will discover that Renzo, Lucia's betrothed, is true to their betrothal until the end—in contrast to Holdsworth, whose counterpart in the novel is not the faithful Renzo but the gazing Roderigo.[24]

The reduction of women in Virgil and Manzoni to gifts, prizes, and wagers—objects altogether lacking in volition—provides a context from which to read the treatment of Gaskell's Phillis. Sleeping beauties obviously have no choice of princes, and Holdsworth entertains no anxious doubt that Phillis will be dormant until he returns. Since she is asleep, Holdsworth need not declare himself. Paul's decision not to inform Holdsworth that he has told Phillis about his love arises from the wish to maintain the sleeping beauty fiction, to preserve (intact) for the returning prince "the pleasure of extracting the delicious tender secret from her maidenly lips" (p. 325). Phillis' catastrophe thus results directly from Paul and Holdsworth's commitment to the myth of women's passive availability and their own princely prerogatives as brokers of pretty innocence. Similarly, Mr. Manning proposes the idea of marrying Phillis to Paul with little concern that Phillis might have different plans; the choice is Paul's to make. Discussing Phillis' availability and, however primly, her body, the three are illuminated by the analogue of Manzoni's Don Roderigo and his two bravoes plotting against Lucia. As he gives directions for her abduction, Roderigo insists that no harm come to Lucia: "don't touch a hair of her head; and, above all, treat her with every respect" (p. 87). Roderigo's ability to see himself, the would-be rapist, as Lucia's defender comments on Holdsworth and Paul's idealizing of Phillis' tranquility and innocence and, more broadly,

on the self-flattering teacher-protector role that Phillis' men assume in order to legitimize their control of her sexuality. In spite of his overt observation of Victorian pieties, Mr. Manning's admiration of Phillis and his wish that Paul might marry her plainly arise from his own sexual attraction to her and the subtly illicit memory of "his" Molly, a woman he preferred to Paul's mother. Like Holdsworth, Manning discovers "curious" resemblances in beautiful women. His interest in Phillis focuses on her beautiful eyes (like poor Molly's) and especially on her "pretty mouth," a detail that piques Holdsworth's interest even before he meets Phillis. The fate of Molly subtly parallels that of Phillis: like Holdsworth, Manning left "poor Molly" to earn his bread; he meant to return but before he did so, she died. Another woman assumed to be dormant, Molly never knew how Manning loved her; the possibility of her loving him is not contemplated. Her death is thus implied to arise from a disappointment similar to the one that nearly kills Phillis.[25] The reader is invited as well to read the fate of Lydia Green, Phillis' aunt, as yet another instance of death by disappointment: she "died of a decline" when she was about the same age as Phillis (p. 320).[26] Even within her narrow world Phillis, the daughter of Phillis, is only another; her fate is characteristic rather than distinctive.

Mr. Manning's likeness to Holdsworth as admirer of Phillis' mouth and abandoner of Molly invites a closer look at the burnt stick-pencil with which he draws his turnip cutter. Drawn from the fire in a moment of inspiration, it violates Mrs. Holman's wooden dresser, a domestic shrine she keeps "scoured to the last pitch of whiteness and cleanliness" (p. 289), implying a symbolic violation of women far in excess of the episode's circumstances. Like Gaskell's allusions to the fate of Manzoni's Lucia, Dante's Francesca, and Ovid's Phyllis, the burnt stick points the reader toward overt seduction—even rape—and betrayal, subtextual potentialities from which the parlor decorums of Gaskell's Victorian idyll avert the narrator's consciousness: he cannot read those languages. Considered among the other male gender staves with which it is obviously allied—Holman's spade, parish rods of discipline and procreation, and ruler; Holdsworth's theodolite and sketching and word-defining pencil; and, not least, Paul Manning's pen of narration—the burnt stick implies as well the intrusiveness of respectable males as they impose on Phillis as enforcers of women's roles and discipline. Finally, as a graphic tool, Manning's burnt stick specifically links the violation of whiteness and purity to the printing of books and the annotation of Phillis' *phylla:* in brief, her education.

Paul's celebration of Phillis' recovery—her will, as he interprets it, to "be what she had been before" (p. 353)—attempts, like the rest of his narrative, to suppress discord and ambiguity under a surface of apparent harmony. Like Mrs. Holman, Paul would erase the black marks from the scoured white dresser. His narrative chooses for its curtain line Phillis' assertion that she can and will "go back to the peace of the old days" (p. 354). Yet **"Cousin Phillis"** teaches that such a return—Phillis back in her pinafore, reading Virgil with her father—is both impossible and undesirable. This will not happen and could not bring her peace. The reader groans to think Phillis could wish it.

The resonantly hollow hopefulness of Phillis' closing words, like the other polite suppressions of **"Cousin Phillis,"** implies its opposite: the ineradicability of Phillis' black marks. The rhetoric of Gaskell's critique of education necessarily entails stressing its permanent, damaging consequences. Phillis fully accepted both her texts and tutors; at her lowest point she weeps over Holdsworth's annotations, the identity he sought to impose on her and she embraced (pp. 321-22). The irreversibly blighting effect of Phillis' education is implied in Gaskell's botanical analogue: Holman's prized Ribstone pippin tree, loaded with apples, is killed outright—dropping its *phylla*—when half-wit Timothy (a suitable surrogate for the halved Holman) piles quicklime against its trunk. Timothy and the minister are ultimately reconciled, but the tree, "the apple of his eye," is dead. The minister's own black marks also prove indelible; ironically, the well-meaning sympathy of his changed attitude toward Phillis reveals once again his limitations. Bringing her the blue ribbons, his concession to "feminine vanities," he evinces the same blindness to her inner life as when he sought to keep her in pinafores.

Yet a more hopeful aspect of Gaskell's ending is perhaps implied in Phillis' refusal of the blue ribbons and her Latin and Italian books. Paul is content to read this simply as evidence of sadness over the loss of Holdsworth; but Paul's Phillis has been understood specifically in ignorance of Virgil, Dante, and Manzoni, the shaping texts she studied and finally refuses. In the light of Phillis' learning, the ribbons and texts may be read as complementary emblems, respectively, of the sexual and intellectual bondage she mistook for fulfillment and liberation; to wear the ribbons is to enact her assigned role in the texts. Has experience taught her to reject those scripts? Phillis' readings chronicle a lineage of beribboned and betrayed Phillises. Tess' protest against Angel's offer to teach her history illuminates Phillis' position: "what's the use of learning that I am one of a long row only—finding out that there is set down in some old book somebody just like me, and to know that I shall only act her part" (*Tess*, p. 99).

Only Phillis' final lesson, which, significantly, Gaskell connects to Phillis' recovery and reserves for the ending of the story, fully asserts her independence from learned tutors and texts and establishes her individuality.[27] The unlettered Betty (who sleeps through prayers)

appeals directly to Phillis' sense of self: she must herself do something, fight her own way, says Betty. Unclouded by texts, Betty's "sharp eyes" (p. 354) have long seen that the Holmans are blind to their daughter, as she has also seen through Holdsworth's "beguiling ways" and Paul's limitations (pp. 336-37). Thus, while Gaskell will not permit Phillis fully to free herself from regressive nostalgia for the dependence of the "old days," she grants her life and the will to live. While this may appear a minimal assertion of independent will, it nonetheless establishes finally that Phillis is not merely "another," and it decisively rewrites the death-mandating scripts of Francesca, Maggie, Lydia, and Mollie, and especially of her namesakes, the suicidal Phillises from Ovid through Chaucer.

Notes

[1] Elizabeth Gaskell, "Cousin Phillis," in *Cousin Phillis and Other Tales,* ed. Angus Easson (Oxford: Oxford Univ. Press, 1981), p. 291. Subsequent quotations from "Cousin Phillis" are identified parenthetically in the text.

[2] Hilary M. Schor's survey of Gaskell criticism notes that the sophistication, learning, and allusiveness of Gaskell's fiction is largely unexplored (see "Elizabeth Gaskell: A Critical History and a Critical Revision," *Dickens Studies Annual,* 19 [1990], 360, 363). In *Scheherezade in the Marketplace: Elizabeth Gaskell and the Victorian Novel* (New York: Oxford Univ. Press, 1992) Schor demonstrates the importance of allusions and women's reading (especially in *Ruth, Cranford, Sylvia's Lovers,* and *Wives and Daughters*) to Gaskell's concerns as a woman writer. In "Elizabeth Gaskell and the Victorian Social Text," diss., Harvard Univ., 1991 (Ann Arbor: UMI, 1991) Deirdre d'Albertis also extends our knowledge of Gaskell's use of allusion in her discussion of *Wives and Daughters* (see pp. 186-226). Gaskell's literary allusions in "Cousin Phillis" have not been carefully read. In *Elizabeth Gaskell* (Bloomington and Indianapolis: Indiana Univ. Press, 1987) Patsy Stoneman views Phillis' shame as socially imposed, and calls attention to the "female models offered by literature," but does not connect Phillis' reading to her experience (see pp. 161-63). Angus Easson's useful account of Gaskell's reading suggests the broad range of her learning (see *Elizabeth Gaskell* [London: Routledge, 1979], pp. 19-32).

[3] See *The Mill on the Floss,* ed. Gordon S. Haight (Oxford: Clarendon Press, 1980), p. 251. Like Phillis, Maggie is distinguished by her height, beauty, intelligence, and pursuit of male wisdom. Pearl Brown usefully compares the Paul-Phillis and Tom-Maggie relationships (see "The Pastoral and Anti-Pastoral in Elizabeth Gaskell's "Cousin Phillis," *Victorian Newsletter,* no. 82 [1992], p. 24). See also Schor, *Scheherezade,* p. 164.
[4] *The Life of Charlotte Brontë,* ed. Alan Shelston (Lon-

don: Penguin, 1975), p. 197.

[5] This suggestive scene brings into sharper focus the projected frustration implicit in Gaskell's account in the *Life* of Emily Brontë's trying to study German grammar while kneading bread. Protesting too much, Gaskell insists that "no study, however interesting, interfered with the goodness of [Emily's] bread"; the Brontë sisters were "taught . . . that to take an active part in all household work was . . . woman's simple duty" (p. 159). Phillis similarly protests that "paring apples is nothing" ("Cousin Phillis," p. 283), but her actions evince suppressed frustration: Paul notes her "impetuosity of tone"; she "sighs" in annoyance with the difficulties of the texts and replies to Paul's question "almost petulantly" (p. 283). Both images express failed attempts to mask the conflicting demands of Gaskell's domestic and professional lives.

[6] Terry Lovell's assertions in *Consuming Fiction* (London: Verso, 1987), pp. 86, 89, that the private world of "Cousin Phillis" flatters its men, creating a comfortable place for male readers, and that Gaskell's fiction is "almost entirely innocent of irony at the expense of men" are, in my view, exactly wrong. Gaskell's irony is also unrecognized by Shelagh Hunter, who sees Paul Manning as an attractive, "completely unproblematic" narrator (see *Victorian Idyllic Fiction: Pastoral Strategies* [Atlantic Highlands, N.J.: Humanities Press, 1984], p. 93).

[7] See *The Inferno*, trans. John Ciardi (New Brunswick, N.J.: Rutgers Univ. Press, 1954), Canto V, ll. 73-140.

[8] *Virgil: Eclogues, Georgics, Aeneid I-IV*, rev. ed. (Loeb Classical Library), ed. G. P. Goold, trans. H. Rushton Fairclough (Cambridge, Mass.: Harvard Univ. Press, 1986), p. 81, l. 28.

[9] Cf. Philip Wakem's posing Maggie Tulliver for her portrait—"Please, turn your head this way" (*Mill*, p. 285)—which suggests Gaskell's further use of George Eliot.

[10] See *Tess of the d'Urbervilles: An Authoritative Text, Backgrounds and Sources, Criticism*, 3d ed., ed. Scott Elledge (New York: Norton, 1991), p. 103.

[11] In noting the conflict between Holman's classical learning and his role as minister through Brother Robinson's complaint that the minister's quotation from the *Georgics* "savoured of . . . heathenism" (p. 328), Gaskell alludes to a longstanding source of disagreement in the independent churches. The appropriateness of classical, and hence "heathen," education for ministers had been debated for more than two centuries. Far from individualizing Holman, his learning identifies him with a well-known conflict in the ideology of Dissent. For a useful history, see Barbara Kiefer Lewalski, "Milton on Learning and the Learned-Ministry Controversy," *Huntington Library Quarterly*, 24 (1961), 267-81.

[12] "To this day" in contemporary Italy alludes to Manzoni both in its hinted content and also in technique. The incompleted sentence is a markedly prominent stylistic device in *The Betrothed* (1840-42); Manzoni's narrator observes: "Ambiguous language, significant silences, sudden pauses in the middle of a sentence" all serve to mask dishonorable motives (*The Betrothed: "I Promessi Sposi": A Tale of Seventeenth-Century Milan*, trans. Archibald Colquhoun [London: Reprint Society, 1952], p. 251). Gaskell frequently employs incompleted or inaudible utterance to hint at what may not properly be spoken and thus to invite reader speculation. E.g., Holdsworth's exclamation, "What a sweet innocent face it is! and yet so—Oh, dear!" (p. 315); the minister's remark that "sermons though they be, they're . . . well, never mind!" (p. 277); Holdsworth's inaudible whisper to Phillis (p. 309), and his unexplained smile of pleasure (p. 304); and the multiple self-halving interruptions of Holman's welcome to Paul (p. 271).

[13] Gaskell frequently attracts the reader's attention to allusions by averting her characters' eyes from them. In *Cranford* Miss Pole inattentively counts crochet stitches and Miss Matty sleeps through Mr. Holbrook's reading of Tennyson's "Locksley Hall," missing the intensely misogynistic railing (ll. 147-53) about women's shallow brains, women as "lesser men," etc.—the evidence of Holbrook's resentment of Matty's rejection, the ultimate revelation of his character. Schor's discussion of this episodemmm (*Scheherezade*, pp. 102-4) nicely illuminates the subtle complexities of Gaskell's allusiveness.

[14] Holman's concern with Phillis' dress points especially to 1 Timothy 2:9-15.

[15] *Horace: The Odes and Epodes* (Loeb Classical Library), ed. T. E. Page, et al., trans. C. E. Bennett (Cambridge, Mass.: Harvard Univ. Press, 1952), p. 33, Book I, Ode II.

[16] Phillis, of course, is not herself in Paradise. She is introduced there as a negative instance of the burning passion that Folquet suffered prior to his repentance.

[17] John Lucas surprisingly claims that "Phillis is, of course, the classical name for the innocent country girl" (*The Literature of Change: Studies in the Nineteenth-Century Provincial Novel* [Sussex: Harvester Press, 1977], p. 27). Stoneman too says that Phillis' "name derives from a pastoral tradition in which shepherdesses were ornamental objects of idealised love" (p. 163). In *Sylvia's Lovers* (chap. 42) Gaskell alludes to the story of Countess Phillis in Richard Johnson's *Seven Champions of Christendom* (1597). As a model of wifely fidelity, this Phillis could be seen as a suitable source for the name. However, this proper Phillis also

proves to be "a fable at fault," a pretty story contradicted by Philip Hepburn's experience.

[18] Quoted in *The Myths of Hyginus,* ed. and trans. Mary Grant (Lawrence: Univ. of Kansas Press, 1960), p. 62. Hyginus has trees springing from Phyllis' grave. Ovid also refers to the dropping leaves (see *Ars Amatoria,* Book III, ll. 37-38; *Remedia Amoris,* ll. 591-608).

[19] "Meditations in a Grove," in *The Works of the Reverend and Learned Isaac Watts, D.D.,* ed. Jennings and Doddridge, 6 vols. (London: Barfield, 1810), IV, 450.

[20] See *The Poems of John Wilmot, Earl of Rochester,* ed. Keith Walker (Oxford: Shakespeare Head Press, 1984), pp. 45, 110.

[21] W. S. Gilbert, remembering Virgil, gave the name Phyllis to the heroine of *Iolanthe* (1882), a rustic beauty pursued by half the House of Lords, the Lord Chancellor, and, of course, Strephon.

[22] See *Ovid: Heroides and Amores,* 2d ed. (Loeb Classical Library), ed. G. P. Goold, trans. Grant Showerman (Cambridge, Mass.: Harvard Univ. Press, 1986), pp. 17-31. Except for Dante's allusion to Phillis in *Paradiso,* the other major retellings of the Phillis story preserve her as one of a group of more than a dozen women, including Dido, Ariadne, and Medea.

[23] Lucas claims that "there are no villains in this tale, nobody is to blame for the sadness and feeling of defeat that provide its dominant tone" (p. 27). Easson also insists that "none of them is to blame" (*Elizabeth Gaskell,* p. 225). Caroline Huber's astute reading of Holdsworth's behavior (see "'Complicated Matters': The Short Fiction of Elizabeth Gaskell," diss., Rutgers Univ., 1992 [Ann Arbor: UMI, 1993], pp. 185-86) and Pearl Brown (pp. 26-27) make cases for Holdsworth's culpability.

[24] In *Wives and Daughters* Gaskell's use of Scott's *The Bride of Lamermoor* (1819) as Molly Gibson's reading is closely analogous. As Schor observes in her analysis of the allusion, "the key lessons are all framed by books" (*Scheherezade,* p. 191).

[25] Mr. Manning's abandonment of Molly in the generation that precedes Phillis' may also be read as allusive to the *Heroides.* Demophoon, as the son of Theseus, merely repeats his father's betrayal of Ariadne, a circumstance that Ovid also notes in *Ars Amatoria,* Book III, ll. 459-60.

[26] Like Phillis', Lydia's name also associates her with a classical prototype. One assumes Gaskell chooses the name to elaborate Holman's allusion to Horace, with whom Lydia is traditionally associated (see, for example, Matthew Prior's "A Better Answer," ll. 26-28). Several of Horace's best-known odes are addressed to Lydia.

[27] This reading of the ending is supported by Schor's view of Gaskell as "a Victorian Scheherezade, writing her own endings to a story she inherited" (*Scheherezade,* p. 9). Rosemarie Bodenheimer's analysis of Gaskell's deviation from established patterns of unhappy endings (in *Ruth*) also makes a case for seeing such changes as critical resistance (see *The Politics of Story in Victorian Social Fiction* [Ithaca: Cornell Univ. Press, 1988], pp. 150-65).

Gabriele Helms (essay date 1995)

SOURCE: "The Coincidence of Biography and Autobiography: Elizabeth Gaskell's *The Life of Charlotte Brontë,*" in *Biography: An Interdisciplinary Quarterly,* Vol. 18, No. 4, Fall, 1995, pp. 339-59.

[*In the essay that follows, Helms considers the manner in which Gaskell comes to understand herself in relation to Charlotte Brontë and thus combines the genres of biography and autobiography.*]

The ongoing theoretical debates about the genres of biography and autobiography are often concerned with genre classifications, gender issues, intentions as well as techniques and methods, and a general rethinking of given paradigms. Many long-held categorizations and evaluations prove questionable in the context of post-structuralist and feminist theories. Victoria Glendinning has described the situation using an interesting image; she says that the "Berlin Wall between fiction and biography, between autobiography and biography, between politics and biography, has huge breaches in it" (4). I take Glendinning's assessment one step further—this Wall not only has breaches, it has actually collapsed. In this paper I want to find a way out of the ruins of the collapsed Wall. Instead of despairing because of blurred boundaries, unclear definitions, and questionable genre distinctions, I will attempt a revision of the theoretical approach to biography. My focus on the creation of the biographer-persona as a core device in biographical texts demonstrates that a biography can also be read as an autobiographical work about this persona. By examining the role and functions of the biographer-persona, I will shift the focus from the observed subject of the biography to its observing subject, the narrator. This shift in my approach from the traditional value criterion of "truthfulness" to the methods and devices employed in biographies derives from the larger theoretical and methodological framework of radical constructivism as applied to literary studies. In the second half of the paper Elizabeth Gaskell's *The Life of Charlotte Brontë* (1857) will serve as an example of how my approach can inform a new reading of a nineteenth-century text. I hope to show that applying a 1990s-understanding of auto/biography and its personae is not restricted to the analysis of contemporary literature. By separating the theoretical discussions about biography in general and the biographer-persona in particular from Gaskell's *The Life of Charlotte Brontë* as my case study, I hope to facilitate the transfer of my approach to other texts.

I suggest that the creation of a biographer-persona is one of the essential devices characterizing the genre of biography. Wilson Snipes has pointed out that the stance biographers establish for themselves through their personae is the basis of their craft and art (237). By necessity, if biographers want to tell a "life-story," they will have to invent a narrating voice in the text. This biographer-persona then presents the gathered material, establishes chronology, and suggests narrative connections.[1] Our awareness of the nature of language and its usage, of the nature of narrative, of themes and methodologies, renders it almost impossible to argue any longer that "the highest biographical art is the concealment of the biographer" (Kendall 12).

Critics have argued that because "[b]oth factual and fictional biographies . . . are made up, and in this sense are fictions" (Schabert 7), the difference between an auto/biography and a novel "lies not in the factuality of the one and fictiveness of the other" (Abbot 603). From this, one might assume that our twentieth-century decline of belief in the unmediated, ontological status of "reality" would have decisively influenced critics' approaches to biographical recognition. Even when this ontological dilemma is recognized, however, most critics will still maintain the fictional/factual distinction.[2] William H. Epstein has skillfully summarized how biographical recognition has been reluctant to abandon the "natural attitude" to events "as naturally discrete occurrences" (37) and to fact "as monumental or inflexible, as a cold, hard, silent thing" (46); we can conclude that "epistemological naivete is a distinctive feature of biographical recognition," which Epstein traces to the attempt to maintain "the natural" as one of the last strongholds of empirical knowledge (38). If, however, biography has lost its critical innocence (Frank 499), then Epstein's suggestions for a more radical approach to biographical recognition seem the most consistent, as such a perspective would see a life as culturally, not naturally, constituted and biographical recognition as an activity that authorizes "transformations between various processes of discursive encoding" (46).

To question the status of fact and fiction and thereby the objectivity of human knowledge involves discussion of concepts such as reality, knowledge, and truth. My own work on the biographer-persona, and thus my focus on the observing and constructing subject, is situated in the epistemological context of constructivism, a philosophi-

cal approach that postulates among other things that reality is not found but invented. Consequently, constructivism focuses on the subject and its cognitive activities, a focus markedly different from theories of cognition based on an objective reality independent of an observing subject.[3] Constructivist theory thus not only reformulates but also provides an empirical foundation for Immanuel Kant's idea of transcendentality. According to a constructivist theory of cognition, we do not have access to an objective reality; actually, "what becomes conscious has already been modelled and imprinted automatically by our brains" (Schmidt, "Construction of Fiction" 320). Thus, we cannot perceive anything that lies outside our own experience. Though constructivists do not deny, as a solipsist would, the existence of the ontological world, they do deny the possibility of making a statement about its "real" nature. Thus, an individual does not mirror "the" reality in the process of perception; rather, through neuronic activity of their brains, individuals construct models of the world in their cognitive domains.

The radicalness of constructivism lies in the assumption that all cognitive systems depend on processes of construction. When reality is not directly accessible and the term is instead used to refer to human perception and the models of reality constructed by human cognition, the focus shifts from the ontological world to the observer and the process of cognition itself. Instead of searching for an iconic representation or an objective copy of ontological reality, we begin to understand knowing as the attempt to find out "whether or not our constructs are viable in a problem-solving situation" (Schmidt, "Logic of Observation" 303). As Siegfried J. Schmidt has explained:

> By transforming the concept of "ontological objectivity" into that of "interactive intersubjectivity," the epistemological attention shifts from "the real world" to norms and criteria for consensuality and intersubjectivity in a social group or in a society as a whole, and to the language by which observers operate on events and activities in their consensual domains. ("Construction of Fiction" 322)

Radical constructivism has some important implications for literature and more specifically the biographer-persona. Since people produce their own models of the world through thoughts and language, descriptions in language, or fictions, actually constitute our reality, because the world is only accessible as a world in language. If we further pursue this idea of reality as a range of descriptions, as fictions, then all forms of literature are fictitious descriptions of a fiction, and literature is the description of a description, and literary research the description of a description of a description. . . . This is not mere wordplay; rather, within constructivist theory, literary critics are not interested in the objective content of descriptions but in the specific methods, devices, and so on that characterize literary forms. As Schmidt concludes:

> *Wenn dieser Dualismus [zwischen Kunst und Wirklichkeit] wegfällt, dann beginnt man zu begreifen, dass Literatur und Kunst zwei von vielen Kommunikations-und Beschreibungsmöglichkeiten für unsere Erfahrungen sind, die sich eben nicht durch ihre Konstruktivität, sondern nur durch den Gebrauch besonderer Verfahren von solchen wirklichkeitskonstruktiven Prozessen unterscheiden, die wir nicht als Kunst betrachten.* ("Der Radikale Konstruktivismus" 70)

> If this dualism [of fact and fiction] is gone, one starts to realize that literature and art are two of many possibilities to communicate and describe our experiences; they do not differ from those processes constructing reality which we do not consider art in terms of their constructedness, but in terms of the particular methods they use. (author's translation)

Let me now consider the implications of constructivism for traditional genre classifications. If everything is ultimately fictive, then the fictional/factual dichotomy can no longer help to differentiate between genres, such as novels versus auto/biographies. Can genre distinctions still be maintained? Yes, but we may have to acknowledge that genres themselves are constructions, and in this light reconsider what constitutes the differences between genres and what specific communicative, aesthetic, and political purposes these genres serve.[4] As Mary Jean Corbett assumes in her discussion of autobiographies, our generic expectations are historically determined and are produced by and produce cultural practices (5). Conventions of reading biographies as true portrayals of a person's life have been undermined by our growing epistemological skepticism. Biography therefore can best be regarded as a hybrid form that searches for a possible, plausible, but necessarily fictive, version of a life experience. Such a definition also accounts for autobiographical writing. Viewed in this light, the need for rigid genre distinctions between autobiography and biography becomes redundant, thus facilitating an exploration of what critics have referred to as "the murky area of biography-cum-autobiography" (Yalom 53).[5] This more flexible approach would encourage us to read for the autobiographical in a biography and vice versa, thereby enabling us to focus on issues of relative dominance and interplay, rather than binary differences.

Biographies cannot help being "colored by the subjective world of the biographer" and the persona this biographer creates in the text (Bell and Yalom 3). The selection and organization of material must be done by the biographer, whose perception of the subject is bound to be subjective—a constructed model of the other person. Thus, biographers' choices have to be autobio-graphically determined.[6] As Liz Stanley has summarized, "'the biographer' is a socially-located person, one who is sexed, raced, classed, aged, to mention no more, and is so every bit as much as an autobiographer is" (7). In what the biographer-personae reveal about their subjects, they evoke, reflect, and reveal themselves to the reader (Kuhn 13; Shelston 30): "the way one particular figure comments explicitly on another also contains elements of implicit self-characterization" (Pfister 186).[7] This, however, does not suggest that the author is identical with the storyteller, the biographer-persona, in the text.[8] To examine such a correlation responsibly would require studying the writer's own system of preconditions, which includes internalized values, norms, conventions, needs, intentions, motives, and knowledge.[9]

To avoid the biographical fallacy and to recognize the text as a construction in language, I will restrict my discussion to the information about the persona in the text. Problematizing the autobiographical dimension of biography even further, I want to draw on Robert Elbaz, who has convincingly argued that autobiography in turn can be read as biography (10-12).[10] To write autobiographically, writers have to create narratives of themselves; they have to make themselves into objects, personae, or a multiplicity of personae that can be examined and described from the outside: "just as we construct a *model* of a world, externalize it, and then treat it as though its existence were independent of our doing, so we construct a model of the entity that we call our 'self' and externalize it" (Glasersfeld 445-46). Viewed in this light, we can see that autobiography and biography are mutual and coincidental; neither is dependent or subordinate to the other.[11] The result is an amalgamation that defies the traditionally exclusive genre distinctions. Like a double image in perceptual psychology, auto/biography can be seen as an ambiguous stimulus pattern: the perceiver decides which element to concentrate on. A classification of genres less rigidly set in terms of dominance relations has no problems accounting for these forms of coincidence. By shifting the focus of biographical analyses to the biographer-personae, we recognize and emphasize the importance of biographers' own self-definitions, self-creations, and the coming to terms with themselves in the process of writing someone else's life-story.[12]

However, because of a lack of analytical tools, a broad gap exists between these theoretical explanations and existing textual analyses. In order to recognize where the biographer-personae reveal something about themselves in their observations of and revelations about their subjects, I will employ some ideas regarding the analysis of narrators' functions that Ansgar Nünning has developed in his communicative model of narrative transmission, and applied to George Eliot's novels (84-125). Appropriation of these ideas from narrative theory seems justifiable because biography in the form of the biographer-persona has a narrating voice that is very similar to a homo/heterodiegetic narrator.[13] Drawing on Jakobson's model of speech functions, Nünning identifies a spectrum of narrators that ranges from covert mediators to overt narrators (85). At the covert end the narrator mainly performs basic narrative functions that are obligatory and together create the narrated world. The information here constitutes the local, temporal, and personal deixis. In this category of narrative-diegetic statements, the biographer-personae reveal themselves through the means they use to establish the narrated world.

When the narrator becomes more explicit as a personalized character, nonobligatory or optional statements can serve additional analytical functions. Such remarks include explanatory-interpretive and evaluative comments on the characters, their actions, and their perspectives. Generalizations, reflections, and aphorisms that are not immediately related to the narrated world perform synthetic functions: they abstract and proceed from the particular to the general. Finally, statements that address the narrator's situation and the act of narration itself have reflexive or discursive functions. Here, the narrator moves into the foreground with expressive, appellative, phatic, and metanarrative comments. A speaking instance, a personalized narrator, is shaped through these optional statements with analytical, synthetic, and reflexive functions. They allow the reader to (re)construct the persona's underlying system of preconditions. In this way the narrators/biographer-personae most overtly reveal autobiographical information about themselves in the text.

I will now turn to Elizabeth Gaskell's biography *The Life of Charlotte Brontë* as a case study to indicate the interpretative value of my theoretical explorations and analytical categories. Primarily examined as a rendering of the details of Charlotte Brontë's life, and therefore usually read in connection with her life and works, it is less often examined to determine what the biographer has accomplished and how Elizabeth Gaskell has created that persona in the text. Some critical studies of Gaskell do not deal with *The Life of Charlotte Brontë* at all; others have severe difficulty in placing it within or alongside her novelistic oeuvre. Only Felicia Bonaparte, to my knowledge, has claimed that "*The Life of Charlotte Brontë* is less a biography than an autobiography" (232). Beginning to analyse the particular novelistic methods Gaskell employs, Ira Nadel similarly sees Gaskell using the biography indirectly to re-examine her own "goals and achievements through recounting those of her friend" (123). I do not intend to compare this biography with other biographies of Charlotte Brontë to establish a list of errors and omissions in Gaskell's work; instead, I will show how the theoretical basis developed in this paper can further expand and refine

Nadel's and Bonaparte's perspectives on *The Life of Charlotte Brontë,* shed brighter light on the autobiographical dimension of the text, and establish its rightful place among Gaskell's works.

The optional statements the biographer-persona makes in *The Life of Charlotte Brontë* show the most obvious autobiographical traces. To start, let me look more closely at one example for both evaluative and explanatory comments that have analytical functions:

> He [Mr. Brontë] never seemed quite to have lost the feeling that Charlotte was a child to be guided and ruled, when she was present; and she herself submitted to this with a quiet docility that half amused, half astonished me. But when she had to leave the room, then all his pride in her genius and fame came out. (508)

> I could not but deeply admire the patient docility which she displayed in her conduct towards her father. (511)

Patsy Stoneman has suggested that Gaskell's description of Mr. Brontë may well be exaggerated and that the astonishment expressed at Charlotte's patient docility towards her father reveals the persona's lack of experience of a similar situation herself (25). From the passage one can gather that the amusement and surprise the narrator feels are due to her own unfamiliarity with such behavior. The response implies that she is not to the same extent used to living in a patriarchal household where it is simply the woman's/child's duty to succumb to the man/father in the house. While the surprise may arise from a sense of unfamiliarity, the admiration leaves the reader with more problems. The fact that the biographer expresses admiration for this kind of docility conveys the impression that she values obedience but does not contemplate its implications of suppression.

A number of explanatory comments can be found in the accounts of Charlotte's childhood. The biographer describes and explains the children's loneliness by saying that "the children did not want society." That this is pointed out at all may suggest that the girls did not need anybody else because they were each other's best company: "They were all in all to each other." However, although admiring the sisters' interest in current newspapers, the biographer continues: "But I suspect that they had no 'children's books'" and later "[t]hey knew no other children." These observations suggest that the previous comment—"the children did not want society"—expresses the biographer's surprise and her desire to record an unusual seclusion that she cannot find "normal" for children. Thus, the statement reveals some of her internalized values and understandings about social life: children should grow up in the company of other children, read "children's books," maybe enjoy "infantine gaieties," and not be restricted to the company of adults who can only teach them grown-up "modes of thought" (93-95).

For other interpreting and judging comments, consider sentences such as these: "It appears strange that Mr Wilson should not have been informed by the teachers of the way in which the food was served up" at Cowan's Bridge School, which the Brontë sisters attended (103); "[i]t seems to me a daring experiment on the part of their teacher," that is of M. Héger, who prohibited French dictionaries and grammar books so that the students could learn "the spirit and rhythm rather from the ear and the heart" (233). The adjectives "strange" and "daring" hint at an underlying system of values, norms, and expectations. Both phrases suggest that a certain acceptable limit has been transgressed; both instances do not conform to the biographer-persona's own standards and expectations. According to her, the severity of the situation at school—the cook is described as "careless, dirty, and wasteful" (102)—would have called for the other teachers' intervention even if it was not their department of expertise or immediate responsibility. And in the case of M. Héger, his teaching methods not only contradict the persona's own training but they also set him apart as different, namely French.

Most of the biographer-persona's explicit comments serve reflexive and discursive functions. Exclamations indicate the biographer's personal and emotional involvement in the state of affairs she describes. "Poor misguided fellow!" she comments on Branwell, "this craving to see and know London, and that stronger craving after fame, were never to be satisfied" (156). As for Charlotte's and Emily's trip to Brussels, she exclaims: "What a contrast . . . must the Belgian capital have presented to those two young women thus left behind!" (225). In both cases the expressive statements show the persona's empathy with the people she is talking about. In describing their experiences, she is almost reliving them with them; the immediacy of emotions suggests to the reader the importance and significance of the affairs described.

Appellative statements appear prominently in Gaskell's *The Life of Charlotte Brontë:* "It will be interesting to some of my readers to know . . ." (119), "[l]et us somehow hope . . ." (269), "[t]he reader may remember the strange prophetic vision, which dictated a few words" (400).[14] Two of the most commonly used types of appellative statements appear here. Indirect addresses, which seem to impute certain attitudes to the readers and direct their attitudes and actions, are even more frequent than the pronoun "we," which suggests an alliance of narrator and fictive reader. The range of functions assigned to these appellations can be seen in the following example from the book's last paragraph:

But I turn from the critical, unsympathetic public—

inclined to judge harshly because they have only seen superficially and not thought deeply. I appeal to that larger and more solemn public, who know how to look with tender humility at faults and errors; how to admire generously extraordinary genius, and how to reverence with warm, full hearts all noble virtue. (526)

The biographer-persona tries to do two things at once. By identifying the intended readership for her portrayal of Charlotte Brontë, she thus reveals her own standards: a reading is good when it is deep and when it displays tolerance towards the writer. Second, she suggests to the readers that they exactly fit this description because they have already read the whole biography. By assuming similar value systems for herself and her readership, she reinforces her readers' standards, thus flattering their self-understanding and esteem. Hence, in addition to having an appellative character, these comments also serve phatic functions. By establishing common ground between herself and her readers, she ensures the openness of the communication channel and constantly reaffirms her readers' interest in her narrative. I want to suggest, however, that these types of appellative and phatic comments appear at exactly those points where the biographer faces problems in her presentation and feels a need to reassure herself of her readers' attention. While these statements pretend to say something about the personality of Charlotte Brontë, they say just as much about the biographer's own process of narrating the story of Charlotte's life.

The metanarrative and self-reflexive utterances make the biographer-persona stand out most clearly against the background of the life told in *The Life of Charlotte Brontë.* In these remarks, the persona explicitly draws attention to her own telling of Brontë's life, the act of narration itself, and the rewards and problems along the way. In doing so, she gives expression to her own feelings and attitudes. The focus thus very subtly shifts from Charlotte Brontë to the persona; very subtly indeed, because it is still the telling of Charlotte's life that triggers the persona's reactions.

Expressing and validating her own intentions are of primary concern to the biographer-persona from the beginning of her narration. She repeatedly emphasizes how seriously she takes the task of writing this biography, or as she says in the opening sentence of the second chapter, of presenting the "right understanding of the life of my dear friend, Charlotte Brontë" (60). The "right understanding" for the biographer has to include explanations and answers about how a life so devoid of social experience as Charlotte's could produce the novels hers did. It has to account for the harshness of Brontë's life, the way that Charlotte's sense of duty sustained her in the midst of all the labor and pain in the Brontë household, and the fact that her life was a triumph of spirit over suffering: "How I could show what a noble, true, and tender woman Charlotte Brontë really was" (490). The desire to provide these answers, at the same time, is accompanied by the wish "to arrive at the truth" (98), to give an "illustration of the truth" (131), and by her "resolution of writing truly" (490). The persona expresses a twofold reason for her way of approaching this biography. One is to prove the conclusion correct that a remarkable novel such as *Jane Eyre* supposes the existence of a remarkable person who wrote it. And second, the biography is a response to the criticism of Brontë as a woman writer and to the charges of coarseness against her writing.

Having determined the "right understanding" to be the primary goal of the narrator, I now want to explore the methods and techniques Gaskell's persona uses and problematizes in both collecting and presenting her material. To achieve this "right understanding," Gaskell does not choose the popular approach of a "Life and Work" biography. She does not give detailed information about Brontë's works, nor critical exegesis of her novels, nor hardly any critical evaluation. This in turn indicates that the persona assumes that the reader who takes up this account of Brontë's life will be familiar with the contents of her novels—that such familiarity is the very reason for interest and curiosity about Charlotte's life story: "I am not going to write an analysis of a book with which every one who reads this biography is sure to be acquainted" (326). Moreover, a positive assessment of Charlotte's novels would have been difficult for Gaskell, since she was quite critical of them, as her letters indicate (Nadel 125).

The material that is finally used and incorporated into *The Life of Charlotte Brontë* is diverse in both form and content. It includes extracts from letters to and from Charlotte's close friend Ellen Nussey (about 350 letters were given to Gaskell by Nussey herself); Brontë's publisher George Smith; his colleague William Smith Williams; Miss Wooler, her teacher and later employer at Roe Head; her schoolfriend Mary Taylor; and Robert Southey and George Henry Lewes as well. Other correspondence includes Charlotte's mother's letters to Patrick Brontë, Branwell's correspondence with William Wordsworth, and Anne's response to an invitation from friends. The biography also includes one of Charlotte Brontë's poems; two of her French exercises written in Brussels; Ellen Nussey's account of Anne's last days (which Gaskell slightly altered); extracts from Charlotte's own novels; and quotations from three biographies: Scatcherd's *History of Birstall*, Newton's *Life of Grimshaw*, and Hunter's *Life of Oliver Heywood*. Moreover, we are given the inscription on the Brontë family mural tablet found in their church. And last but not least, there are frequent references to oral communication, which is used as a source of information in the biography; in particular, the conversations with

Charlotte are presented as extremely precious because they are first-hand information and serve as proof of authenticity.[15]

With the strong emphasis on letters, Gaskell's biography can be seen squarely in the Victorian "Life and Letters" tradition, such as J. W. Cross's biography of George Eliot. Gaskell's biographer-persona explains that she wants to use Brontë's letters as much as possible: "Acting on the conviction, which I have all along entertained, that where Charlotte Brontë's own words could be used, no others ought to take their place" (288).[16] However, the biography does not strike the reader as a random collection. The persona presents herself as being extremely self-conscious and careful in the selection of each letter. It is almost as if she needs to justify each reprinting by stating the purpose of the quotation beforehand. The persona frequently introduces the letters with phrases like the following: "I have given this extract in order to explain the imaginary groundwork of a commotion" (57); "I have given this extract because I conceive it bears some reference to the life of Miss Brontë" (80); "I give it as a specimen of the remarkable poetical talent" (122); "[w]hat their plans were, let Charlotte explain" (156); and "[t]o fill up the account . . . I may add a few more extracts" (204).[17]

And yet, while the biographer explains the function of every letter and tries to give authenticity to her presentation of Charlotte's life by using her subject's "own words" as much as possible, the persona seems to be unaware of what her acts of quotation and her montage of texts do to the originals. As Meir Sternberg points out, any montage of texts, any use of quotation will change the function of the passage quoted: "whatever the units involved, to quote is to mediate, to mediate is to frame, and to frame is to interfere and exploit," since "[q]ua representational discourse, therefore, each act of quotation serves two masters" (145, 152). The letters, for instance, originally a means for Brontë to communicate with other people, in Gaskell's biography assume explanatory and complementary functions to illustrate Charlotte's life. The biographer subordinates the letters to serve her intentions. The organization of the letters also reflects her exertion of control and power: they become an expression of the persona's autobiographical choices and intentions. The reader may therefore get a strong sense that the montage of material does not allow free dialogic play between its elements, because the possible interactions take the preplanned form chosen by the governing biographer-persona.

In addition to problematizing the compilation of material and the act of narration, the biographer-persona overtly expresses doubts about her ability to evaluate the personalities and circumstances she presents:

> But I do not pretend to be able to harmonize points

of character, and account for them, and bring them all into one consistent and intelligible whole. The family with whom I have now to do shot their roots down deeper than I can penetrate. I cannot measure them, much less is it for me to judge them. (90)[18]

By acknowledging her own limitations and questioning her reliability as a narrator and biographer, Gaskell's persona reinforces some of the essential mystery connected with Charlotte Brontë's life. Although the persona claims to present a "right understanding," she thus creates a loophole for herself to escape accusations of misjudgment.[19]

And yet, although the biographer seems to admit that she "cannot measure or judge of such a character" as Charlotte's (526), the biographer undermines that statement by her own intention to provide the "right understanding" of her subject's life. Ultimately, she controls the readers' responses to Charlotte's life story, as her narrative sets Charlotte up as a moral exemplum—a purpose that is a judgment in itself. The same biographer who claims to refrain from judgment and measurement chooses and organizes her material very carefully. Aspects of Charlotte's life that would cause the persona to question her own admiration and undermine the picture of Charlotte as moral exemplum, such as her "purely imaginative writing" and her novels (119), or her strong attraction to M. Héger in Brussels, are either left out of the biography—here gaps speak for themselves—or they are assimilated to fit the purpose.[20] Inevitably, the biographer makes herself the measure against which she indirectly judges Charlotte and projects her own values in her justification of her friend.[21] The biographer's assessment of Charlotte's worth is thus closely linked to personal feelings about her subject. The "advantage of sympathy" leads to an expression of intimacy with and admiration for her subject that have been said to form the basis of the biographer-subject relationship.[22] Her admiration for Charlotte as dutiful model daughter, for instance, strongly suggests the biographer's own casting of herself in the surrogate mother's role—the mother who has to protect her child, if only from mistaken charges after Charlotte's death.

The biographer's attempt to separate Brontë the writer from Brontë the woman looms large in an autobiographical reading of *The Life of Charlotte Brontë*.[23] Bonaparte argues that Gaskell could only portray Brontë in a positive light—and defend her from charges of coarseness brought against her writing after her death—if she "disengaged the woman from her offending daemonic self," her fiction (242). The separation then reveals the biographer's primary interest in Brontë's life story: can a woman live the life of an artist?[24] The biographer-persona does not strive to show the blending of the two selves of author "Currer Bell" and woman "Charlotte Brontë"; rather, she reinforces the

disparity between the responsibility and duty of the household role versus the fulfilment and selfishness of the writer's role. While Nadel believes that Brontë "stimulated, challenged and confirmed the commitment of the biographer to the career of literature" and that the biography thus became "a striking self-proclamation on the part of the author" (129), I must agree with Bonaparte, who comes to a different conclusion: "If Gaskell, then, began the biography hoping to find through Charlotte Brontë the strength to assert that, although a woman, she had the right to be an artist, she did not succeed in convincing herself. Instead, she managed to turn Charlotte Brontë into an image of 'Mrs. Gaskell'" (250). While Gaskell kept writing—less controversial novels, as Nadel points out (130)—she never saw herself as a professional writer but as a woman who wrote (Bonaparte 248-49).

Although the biographer is at times conscious of her own limitations and trustworthiness, she does not seem to question the realibility of her central character, Charlotte Brontë. Charlotte herself seems to have imposed the fiction of her novels onto her own childhood, and thus her reality had been changed in the process of recalling it in her conversations with Gaskell. Gaskell's persona, however, presents Charlotte as her key witness and uses Charlotte's novels to support her oral testimony. She replicates Charlotte's own personal fiction of her life, and thus "truth" is recursively fictionalized. As presented to the reader through her biographer-persona, Gaskell's account of Brontë's life can therefore be seen as double-layered or double-voiced—Charlotte's rendering of how she felt about herself, her family, and so on, and the biographer's perception of it. And although the persona is aware that the "truth" she presents is inevitably a personal truth and that Charlotte's own truth is subjective, the persona is neither consistent in acknowledging the inevitability of subjective truth nor does she fully explore the implications of these realizations.[25] The title seems to provide the most obvious example in this context: *The Life of Charlotte Brontë*. If Gaskell had wanted to emphasize that her biography of Charlotte Brontë was only one version among many others, she could have avoided the definite article. It is open to speculation whether this decision was due to title conventions or a deliberate choice on the biographer's part.

Let me briefly reconsider the effects of the explicit statements of the biographer-persona through her revealing of autobiographical information. All of the examples discussed strongly emphasize the subjectiveness of the biographer's stance in her portrayal of Charlotte's life, the effect of which is threefold. First, through her interpretations and judgments and the ensuing selection and presentation of material, the biographer-persona creates a muted, "essentially one-dimensional portrait" of Charlotte (Bick 46). While the subjective filter has narrowing effects on the narration of

Charlotte's life, it reveals an additional layer of the biographer's position. Second, the strong presence of the biographer creates a sense of coherence, even if the material or information about Charlotte is rather weak, or if the biographer has doubts about her own abilities and reliability. Even the constant expression of doubt can create coherence. And third, the metanarrative nature of many of her comments destroys the attitude we are likely to adopt in reading a narrative literary biography, namely to "read narrative biographies much as we read a novel or watch a play or film—with a willing suspension of disbelief and submission to the illusion that we are perceiving an unmediated reality" (Frank 507). This illusion is destroyed by the biographer's explicit, necessarily autobiographical statements that introduce her own reflections.

This article has moved from a theoretical and abstract problematization of the biographer-persona as a central device in biographies to an analysis of this persona in Elizabeth Gaskell's *The Life of Charlotte Brontë.* I have shown that a more flexible approach to genre classification allows me to see the inevitable coincidence of biography and autobiography and to explore their mutual implications. Slightly modified ideas from narrative theory have provided the necessary analytical criteria to trace the biographer-persona in *The Life of Charlotte Brontë.* The persona's consciousness of the distortions wrought by a remembering ego that seeks to recreate the past of a friend reveals at least as much about the biographer as it reveals about the subject Charlotte Brontë. In observing and constructing her subject's life, the narrator assesses her own position in the act of telling and becomes a personalized character that stands out against Charlotte's life.

The collapse of the Berlin Wall between biography and autobiography, between fact and fiction, has brought initial problems of definition and classification. It has problematized the approach to and attraction of the genre of biography that used to lie in its being "a bastion of humanism safe from encroachment by the spirit of postmodernism" (Middlebrook 155). However, the gains seem to outweigh the losses. More than anything, the collapse has brought new freedom to reconsider and modify traditional concepts and categorizations, to shift the focus in biographical analyses from product to process and from the observed to the observing subject, and hence it has created an opening for (re-) readings from new perspectives.

Notes

[1] In this regard, consider Siegfried J. Schmidt: "With regard to biographies or autobiographies, we have to conclude from these hypotheses that the order of the narrated events stems from the narration and not from the order of events narrated" ("Past" 200).

[2] William R. Siebenschuh, for instance, concludes that

discussions of the role of fictional techniques in factual works, such as biography, autobiography, and history, are crucial, but that "simply because fictional techniques are used extensively," factual works are not "fictional in the sense that a novel or a poem is fictional" (148). Such techniques will not compromise the generic credibility of factual genres that are ultimately to be treated with "obviously different assumptions" (139). Ina Schabert ends up assigning the fictional and the factional different organizing principles, and H. Porter Abbot reintroduces these terms through a taxonomy of literary attitudes—truth standards in reader responses that range from fictive and autographic to factual. Ira B. Nadel acknowledges that biography cannot convey the "facts" in an objective manner (208), and therefore shifts his focus to the language and narrative modes used in biographies to get at the aesthetic and structural functions of fact in this genre.

[3] Unfortunately, I cannot elaborate here on the concept of constructivism. Following Schmidt, one can differentiate among four main constructivist approaches: neurobiological (H. R. Maturana, F. J. Varela); cybernetic (H. von Foerster); socio-philosophical (N. Luhmann); and psycho-philosophical (E. von Glasersfeld) ("Logic of Observation" 296). For other useful introductions to the ideas of (radical) constructivism, see Paul Watzlawick; and Schmidt "Der Radikale Konstruktivismus" and "On the Construction of Fiction."

[4] I have been assisted in formulating this point by Julia Watson and Sidonie Smith xviii. As an example, see David Amigoni, who explores how Victorian biography assisted in the construction of the academic disciplines of literature and history.

[5] Liz Stanley similarly argues that "the same analytic apparatus is required for engaging with all forms of life writing, for the same questions and problematics demand critical inquiry. This is not to deny that there are differences between different forms of life writing, but it is to argue that these differences are not *generic*" (3).

[6] Lois W. Banner affirms that "critics are coming to agree that no biographer can keep his or her own autobiography from the biography being written. For a biographer inevitably empathizes, either positively or negatively, with her or his subject: as in the process of psychological analysis, transference takes place, some sort of blurring of personal boundaries" (162). See also Linda Wagner-Martin 166-69 and especially the essays in *The Challenge of Feminist Biography* regarding the question of what further dimensions are added to the relation between writer and subject when a woman is writing about another woman (Aplern et al.).

[7] Manfred Pfister continues "[f]rom this it should be clear that the aim . . . is not to demonstrate how par-

ticular isolated units occur in individual sections of a text, but to expose certain processes in the way they constantly overlap or are superimposed on one another" (186).

[8] When I use the term biographer, it should be understood that I refer to the creation of the biographer-persona in the text.

[9] This has been exemplified in the context of empirical literary theory; see, for instance, Vera Nünning.

[10] Elbaz explains: "Indeed, autobiography is a discourse not about the 'I' but about a series of 'he's' [sic], because a 'he' does not conform to the mystified consistency and continuity of the 'I': the narrative is made up of a multiplicity of personae. The narrative is always a 'third person' phenomenon" (11). Banner also talks about writing a biographical autobiography, or an auto/biography (163).

[11] My idea of coincidence differs from Anna K. Kuhn's suggestion that we treat biography as a subcategory of autobiography (13). I see no need for a hierarchy of genres in this context.

[12] See Carol Hanberry McKay 79. Marilyn Yalom emphasizes these aspects especially in women's writing, when no other means of self-assertion, etc. were available to women (63).

[13] Siebenschuh (139), Nadel (170-75), and Wagner-Martin (166) have explicitly noted an analogy between the biographer-persona and the narrator in fiction.

[14] For more examples, see 60, 150, 211, 264, 283, 305, 334, 353, 379, 428, 434, 477, 526.

[15] For example: "I remember Miss Brontë once telling me" (61); "when Miss Brontë told me the tale" (92); "I have heard Charlotte say" (199).

[16] Consider also the following: "As to the rest, the letters speak for themselves, to those who know how to listen, far better than I can interpret their meaning into my poorer and weaker words" (328). Here we can see how the reflexive comment also has appellative-phatic functions; "those who know how to listen" clearly demarcates the readership and again is flattering to those who feel addressed.

[17] Similar explanations can be found on 114, 120, 128, 131, 141, 182, 187, 208, etc.

[18] Examples abound: "I do not know" (97); "which I find great difficulty in treating" (98); "I can hardly understand" (100); "but I do not know" (111); "I doubt whether" (182); "I am not aware for what reason" (196).

[19] Her loopholes, however, did not save Gaskell from numerous complaints about her infringement on privacy and a threatened lawsuit by Mrs. Robinson, which lead Gaskell to rewrite some sections for the third edition of the biography.

[20] Gaskell's strategy of assimilating information often cannot help but affirm what she is trying to downplay. Elsie B. Michie has noted this with regard to Charlotte's Irish ancestry. Michie explains that Gaskell ends up asserting Charlotte's father's "racial difference from the English at the moment she attempts to deny it" (57): "Mr Brontë has now no trace of his Irish origin remaining in his speech; he never could have shown his Celtic descent in the straight Greek lines and long oval of his face" (*The Life of Charlotte Brontë* 78).

[21] Note Angus Easson's critical view of the biographer's projections (*Elizabeth Gaskell* 132).

[22] See, for instance, Bell Gale Chevigny 358 and Blanche Wiesen Cook 398. The "advantage of sympathy" quotation is from Easson, "Domestic Romanticism" 174.

[23] Gaskell writes: "Charlotte Brontë's existence becomes divided into two parallel currents—her life as Currer Bell, the author; her life as Charlotte Brontë, the woman. There were separate duties belonging to each character—not opposing each other; not impossible, but difficult to be reconciled" (334).

[24] For discussions of the biographer's interest in the disparity between woman and writer, see Bick 35-37; Bonaparte, especially 241-53; Nadel 121-30; and Stoneman 21-44.

[25] In this context, consider the persona's note that even Charlotte "might have been apt, to the last, to take her deep belief in facts for the facts themselves—her conception of truth for the absolute truth" (98).

Works Cited

Abbot, H. Porter. "Autobiography, Autography, Fiction: Groundwork for a Taxonomy of Textual Categories." *New Literary History* 19.3 (Spring 1988): 597-615.

Alpern, Sara, Joyce Antler, Elisabeth Israels Perry, and Ingrid Winther Scobie, eds. *The Challenge of Feminist Biography: Writing the Lives of Modern American Women.* Urbana: U of Illinois P, 1992.

Amigoni, David. *Victorian Biography: Intellectuals and the Ordering of Discourse.* New York: Harvester Wheatsheaf, 1993.

Ascher, Carol, Louise DeSalva, and Sara Ruddick, eds. *Between Women: Biographers, Novelists, Critics, Teachers and Artists Write about Their Work on Women.* Boston: Beacon Hill, 1984.

Banner, Lois W. "Biography and Autobiography: Intermixing of Genres." *a/b: Auto/Biography Studies* 8.2 (1993): 159-78.

Bell, Susan Groag, and Marilyn Yalom, eds. *Revealing Lives: Autobiography, Biography, and Gender.* Albany: State U of New York P, 1990.

Bick, Suzann. "Clouding the 'Severe Truth': Elizabeth Gaskell's Strategy in *The Life of Charlotte Brontë.*" *Essays in Arts and Science* 11 (1982): 33-47.

Bonaparte, Felicia. *The Gypsy-Bachelor of Manchester: The Life of Mrs. Gaskell's Demon.* Charlottesville: UP of Virginia, 1992.

Chevigny, Bell Gale. "Daughters Writing." Ascher, DeSalva, and Ruddick. 357-79.

Cook, Blanche Wiesen. "Biographer and Subject: A Critical Connection." Ascher, DeSalva, and Ruddick. 397-411.

Corbett, Mary Jean. *Representing Femininity: Middle-Class Subjectivity in Victorian and Edwardian Women's Autobiographies.* New York: Oxford UP, 1992.

Easson, Angus. "Domestic Romanticism: Elizabeth Gaskell and *The Life of Charlotte Brontë.*" *Durham University Journal* 1981: 169-76.

———. *Elizabeth Gaskell.* London: Routledge, 1979.

Elbaz, Robert. *The Changing Nature of the Self: A Critical Study of the Autobiographical Discourse.* London: Croom Helm, 1988.

Epstein, William H. *Recognizing Biography.* Philadelphia: U of Pennsylvania P, 1987.

Frank, Katherine. "Writing Lives: Theory and Practice in Literary Biography." *Genre* 13 (Winter 1980): 499-516.

Gaskell, Elizabeth. *The Life of Charlotte Brontë.* 1857. Ed. Alan Shelston. London: Penguin, 1975.

Glasersfeld, Ernst von. "Facts and the self from a constructivist point of view." *Poetics* 18 (1989): 435-48.

Glendinning, Victoria. "The Truth about Biography." *Brick* 41 (1991): 4-9.

Kendall, Paul Murray. *The Art of Biography.* New York: Norton, 1965.

Kuhn, Anna K. "The 'Failure' of Biography and the Triumph of Women's Writing: Bettina von Arnim's *Die Günderode* and Christa Wolf's *The Quest for Christa T.*" Bell and Yalom. 13-28.

McKay, Carol Hanberry. "Biography as Reflected Autobiography: The Self-Creation of Anne Thackeray Ritchie." Bell and Yalom. 65-79.

Michie, Elsie B. *Outside the Pale: Cultural Exclusion, Gender Difference, and the Victorian Woman Writer.* Ithaca: Cornell UP, 1993.

Middlebrook, Diane Wood. "Postmodernism and the Biographer." Bell and Yalom. 155-65.

Nadel, Ira Bruce. *Biography: Fiction, Fact and Form.* London: Macmillan, 1984.

Nünning, Ansgar. *Grundzüge eines kommunikationstheoretischen Modells der erzählerischen Vermittlung. Die Funktionen der Erzählinstanz in den Romanen George Eliots.* Trier: Wissenschaftlicher Verlag, 1989.

Nünning, Vera. "Voraussetzungssystem und Produktionshandlungen Virginia Woolfs am Beispiel von *Orlando.*" *SPIEL* 7.2 (1988): 347-72.

Pfister, Manfred. *The Theory and Analysis of Drama.* Tr. John Halliday. Cambridge: Cambridge UP, 1988.

Schabert, Ina. "Fictional Biography, Factual Biography, and Their Contaminations." *Biography* 5.1 (Winter 1982): 1-16.

Schmidt, Siegfried J. "Der Radikale Konstruktivismus: Ein neues Paradigma im interdisziplinären Diskurs." *Der Diskurs des Radikalen Konstruktivismus.* Ed. Siegfried J. Schmidt. Frankfurt: Suhrkamp, 1987. 11-88.

———. "The Logic of Observation: An Introduction to Constructivism." *Canadian Review of Comparative Literature* 19.3 (September 1992): 295-311.

———. "On the Construction of Fiction and the Invention of Facts." *Poetics* 18 (1989): 319-35.

———. "Past: Notes on Memory and Narration." *Empirical Studies of the Arts* 7.2 (1989): 191-202.

Shelston, Alan. *Biography.* London: Methuen, 1977.

Siebenschuh, William R. *Fictional Techniques and Factual Works.* Athens: U of Georgia P, 1983.

Snipes, Wilson. "Authorial Typology in Literary Biography." *Biography* 13.3 (Summer 1990): 235-50.

Stanley, Liz. *The auto/biographical I: the theory and practice of feminist auto/biography.* Manchester: Manchester UP, 1992.

Sternberg, Meir. "Proteus in Quotation-Land: Mimesis and the Forms of Reported Discourse." *Poetics Today* 3.2 (Spring 1982): 107-56.

Stoneman, Patsy. *Elizabeth Gaskell.* Brighton: Harvester, 1987.

Wagner-Martin, Linda. *Telling Women's Lives: The New Biography.* New Brunswick: Rutgers UP, 1994.

Watson, Julia, and Sidonie Smith. "De/Colonization and the Politics of Discourse in Women's Autobiographical Practices." *De/Colonizing the Subject: The Politics of Gender in Women's Autobiography.* Ed. Sidonie Smith and Julia Watson. Minneapolis: U of Minnesota P, 1992. xiii-xxxi.

Watzlawick, Paul, ed. *The Invented Reality.* New York: Norton, 1984.

Yalom, Marilyn. "Biography as Autobiography: Adele Hugo, Witness of Her Husband's Life." Bell and Yalom. 53-63.

FURTHER READING

Bibliographies

Sanders, Gerald DeWitt, and Clark S. Northrup. *Elizabeth Gaskell.* New Haven: Yale University Press, 1929, 267p.

Includes a comprehensive biography and bibliography of secondary sources on Gaskell up to 1929.

Schor, Hilary M. "Elizabeth Gaskell: A Critical History and A Critical Revision." *Dickens Studies Annual: Essays on Victorian Fiction* 19 (1990): 345-69.

Provides a discussion of the primary editions of Gaskell's work and a historical overview of Gaskell criticism with a focus on recent studies.

Selig, Robert L. *Elizabeth Gaskell: A Reference Guide.* Boston: G. K. Hall, 1977, 431p.

Supplies an extensive annotated bibliography of Gaskell scholarship, from reviews published during her lifetime to the revival of interest in her work that followed the hundredth anniversary of her death (1965).

Welch, Jeffrey. *Elizabeth Gaskell: An Annotated Bibliography, 1929-1975.* New York: Garland Publishing, 1977, 139p.

Provides an annotated bibliography of scholarship on Gaskell; also includes lists of collected and individual editions of her works.

Weyant, Nancy S. *Elizabeth Gaskell: An Annotated Bibliography of English-Language Sources, 1976-1991.* Metuchen, N.J.: Scarecrow Press, 1994, 209p.

Annotated bibliography intended to serve as a supplement to Selig and Welch's bibliographies (both published in 1977).

Biographies

Bonaparte, Felicia. *The Gypsy-Bachelor of Manchester: The Life of Mrs. Gaskell's Demon.* Charlottesville: University Press of Virginia, 1992, 310p.

Examines the ways in which Gaskell's life and writing depart from the frequent perception of the author as having actualized the Victorian female ideal.

Easson, Angus. *Elizabeth Gaskell.* Boston: Routledge & Kegan Paul, 1979, 278p.

Stands as one of the more influential biographical studies of Gaskell, providing a biographical account of Gaskell and critical essays on each of her major works.

Hopkins, A. B. *Elizabeth Gaskell: Her Life and Work.* London: John Lehmann, 1952, 383p.

Provides a biographical study that draws primarily on the personal letters and other writings of Gaskell and her contemporaries.

Uglow, Jenny. *Elizabeth Gaskell: A Habit of Stories.* New York: Farrar Straus Giroux, 1993, 690p.

Gives a biographical account that concentrates on the interaction of Gaskell's life and writing.

Webb, R. K. "The Gaskells as Unitarians." In *Dickens and Other Victorians: Essays in Honour of Philip Collins,* edited by Joanne Shattock, pp. 144-71. London: Macmillan Press, 1988.

Describes religious influences on Gaskell's social-reform novels.

Criticism

Bick, Suzann. "Clouding the 'Severe Truth': Elizabeth Gaskell's Strategy in *The Life of Charlotte Brontë.*" *Essays in Arts and Sciences* 11 (September 1982): 33-47.

Discusses Gaskell's characterization of Charlotte Brontë as an "exemplar of conventional female virtue."

David, Deirdre. "Masters and Men and Ladies and Gentlemen." In *Fictions of Resolution in Three Victorian Novels: "North and South," "Our Mutual Friend," "Daniel Deronda,"* pp. 11-49. New York: Columbia University Press, 1981.

Emphasizes the significance of the struggle between the middle class and the working class in Gaskell's novels.

Easson, Angus, ed. *Elizabeth Gaskell: The Critical Heritage.* New York: Routledge, 1991, 595p.

Includes an anthology of critical reviews of Gaskell's major works, primarily those published contemporaneously with her own writing.

Flint, Kate. *Elizabeth Gaskell.* Plymouth, England: Northcote

House, 1995, 71p.
> Provides a biographical introduction, critical essays on the major novels, and a study of twentieth-century critical scholarship on Gaskell's work.

Fryckstedt, Monica Correa. *Elizabeth Gaskell's "Mary Barton" and "Ruth": A Challenge to Christian England.* Stockholm: Almqvist & Wiksell International, 1982, 213p.
> Examines Gaskell's concern with social injustice and social responsibility in her novels.

Lansbury, Coral. *Elizabeth Gaskell: The Novel of Social Crisis.* New York: Harper & Row, 1975, 230p.
> Traces Gaskell's psychological realism and understanding of social disparity through her major novels and the biography of Charlotte Brontë.

Lucas, John. "Mrs. Gaskell and Brotherhood." In *Tradition and Tolerance in Nineteenth-Century Fiction: Critical Essays on Some English and American Novels*, edited by David Howard, John Lucas, and John Goode, pp. 141-205. New York: Barnes & Noble, 1967.
> Contends that Gaskell's novels surpass the general mediocrity of nineteenth-century social reform novels.

Rubenius, Aina. *The Woman Question in Mrs. Gaskell's Life and Works.* Cambridge, Mass.: Harvard University Press, 1950, 370p.
> Discusses Gaskell's experience as a woman writer and her treatment of female characters in her novels.

Shelston, A. J. "*Ruth*: Mrs. Gaskell's Neglected Novel." *Bulletin of the John Rylands University Library* 58, No. 1 (Autumn 1975): 173-92.
> Argues that Gaskell's *Ruth* deserves a prominent place in Victorian literature studies due to the depth and intensity of the characterization of the novel's heroine.

Stone, Donald D. "Elizabeth Gaskell, Wordsworth, and the Burden of Reality." In *The Romantic Impulse in Victorian Fiction*, pp. 133-72. Cambridge, Mass.: Harvard University Press, 1980.
> Discusses the interplay of romanticism and realism at work in Gaskell's novels.

Wright, Edgar. *Mrs. Gaskell: The Basis for Reassessment.* New York: Oxford University Press, 1965, 285p.
> Stands as one of the more influential recent studies of Gaskell. Wright argues that Gaskell is an "important minor novelist" of the Victorian period.

Wright, Terence. *Elizabeth Gaskell, "We are not angels": Realism, Gender, Values.* London: Macmillan Press, 1995, 220p.
> Focuses on Gaskell's pragmatic realism in the novels and shorter fiction, which call attention to social injustice.

> **Additional coverage of Gaskell's life and career is contained in the following sources published by Gale Research:** *Concise Dictionary of British Literary Biography, 1832-1890; Dictionary of Literary Biography,* **Vols. 21, 144, 159;** *DISCovering Authors;* **and** *Short Story Criticism,* **Vol. 25.**

Leigh Hunt

1784–1859

(Born James Henry Leigh Hunt) English critic, essayist, journalist, poet, and playwright.

For additional information on Hunt's life and works, see *NCLC,* Volume 1.

INTRODUCTION

Although today he is remembered primarily as a minor poet and author of the frequently anthologized poem "Rondeau," commonly known as "Jenny kissed me," Hunt is important historically as a political essayist and literary critic who articulated the Romantic manifesto. He also played a vital role in encouraging and influencing the poets John Keats and Percy Bysshe Shelley.

Biographical Information

Hunt was born in England to Isaac and Mary Hunt, the only one of their seven children to be born in Great Britain. Although Hunt's parents were Americans, they were loyal to the English crown, and at the beginning of the Revolutionary War fled to England. As a child, Hunt attended Christ's Hospital School from 1791 to 1798, where he earned a solid education in the classics. He began writing at an early age, and his father collected and published his early poetry in *Juvenilia* (1801). Although this book is generally considered a derivative effort, Hunt regarded it as the first step toward his life as a man of letters. After the publication of this work, Hunt worked for a time as an apprentice to his brother Stephen who was a barrister; he was also a drama critic for *News,* a weekly published by his brother John. In 1808, Hunt and John established *The Examiner*, a weekly liberal newspaper. This began an editing career for Hunt which would encompass years of political and literary writing under the auspices of several popular journals. *The Examiner*, with the Hunts' attacks on the Prince Regent, also signaled the political opposition that earned jail sentences for each of the Hunts. While in jail, Hunt continued writing and frequently received visits from writers such as Lord Byron, Jeremy Bentham, and Charles Lamb. Upon his release from prison, Hunt became increasingly more involved in poetry, though he never gave up his political interests. Hunt died in Putney in August 1859.

Major Works

Hunt's pursuit of poetry resulted in *The Story of Rimini* (1816), an adaptation of the Paolo and Francesca story from Dante's *Divine Comedy*. This work was generally well received (although the attacks on Hunt by the reviewers for *Blackwood's Magazine* began soon after in 1817), and it fostered friendships with Keats and Shelley. Hunt's favorable reviews of these poets' early works, and his diligence in using his connections to publish them, helped establish Keats's and Shelley's reputations. Hunt's relationship with Byron deteriorated, however, especially after the death of Shelley in 1822—a great blow to Hunt, who considered Shelley his best friend. One of Hunt's best known nonpoetical works, *Lord Byron and Some of His Contemporaries* (1828), was actually a thinly veiled harangue against Byron. Though the book's controversial nature met with a cool reception, Hunt produced other works at this time which were commercial successes, including *The Poetical Works of Leigh Hunt* (1832). The nonpoetical *Imagination and Fancy* (1844) provided significant insight into the nature of Romantic tastes, and was favorably reviewed. Hunt continued to be prolific in his final years, and *The Autobiography of Leigh Hunt, with Reminiscences of Friends and Contemporaries* (1850), which retracted some of his earlier sharp criticism, indicates his pleasure at surviving years of literary warfare.

Critical Reception

Critical reception of Hunt's work, both contemporary and modern, has been uneven. While his poetry could inspire spirited attacks such as those appearing in *Blackwood's Magazine*, he was also praised as one of his generation's best-known literary figures. Poetry is widely held to have been the weakest of Hunt's undertakings, and he seems destined to remain a minor poet. Yet recent criticism favorably reviews the rococo aspects of his poetry, and his influence on other poets has never been questioned. Critical attention has been paid to his achievements as editor, essayist, teacher, and mentor. It is commonly accepted that he pioneered the contemporary journal and made invaluable contributions as political writer and dramatic critic. His current relative obscurity stems in part from the sheer volume of work he produced, which prevented him from concentrating on any one area. Ultimately, Hunt's personal contact with more prominent poets established him as a contributing force to a richly creative period.

PRINCIPAL WORKS

Juvenilia (poetry) 1801
Critical Essays on the Performers of the London Theatres, Including General Observations on the Practise and Genius of the Stage (criticism) 1807
The Examiner [editor] (journalism) 1808–21
The Feast of the Poets, with Notes, and Other Pieces in Verse (poetry) 1814
The Descent of Liberty (mask) 1815
The Story of Rimini (poetry) 1816
Foliage (poetry) 1818
Hero and Leander and Bacchus and Ariadne (poetry) 1819
The Indicator [editor] (journalism) 1819–21
The Liberal [editor] (journalism) 1822–23
Lord Byron and Some of His Contemporaries (essays) 1828
The Poetical Works of Leigh Hunt (poetry) 1832
Sir Ralph Esher; or Memoirs of a Gentleman of the Court of Charles II (novel) 1832

The Indicator and the Companion (essays) 1834
Captain Sword and Captain Pen (poetry) 1835
A Legend of Florence (drama) 1840
Imagination and Fancy [editor] (poetry and critical essays) 1844
Stories from the Italian Poets: with Lives of the Writers [translator and adapter] (poetry, biography, and criticism) 1846
Wit and Humour, Selected from the English Poets, with an Illustrative Essay, and Critical Comments [editor] (poetry and criticism) 1846
Men, Women and Books (sketches, essays, and memoirs) 1847
A Jar of Honey from Mount Hybla (essays) 1848
The Autobiography of Leigh Hunt, with Reminiscences of Friends and Contemporaries (autobiography) 1850
The Religion of the Heart (philosophy, prose) 1853
The Old Court Suburb; Or, Memorials of Kensington, Regal, Critical, and Anecdotal (sketches, memoirs) 1855
The Correspondence of Leigh Hunt (letters) 1862

CRITICISM

Leigh Hunt (essay date 1832)

SOURCE: "From the Author's Preface to the Editions of 1832," in *The Political Works of Leigh Hunt*, edited by H. S. Milford, Oxford University Press, 1923, pp. xvii-xxxi.

[*In the following excerpt from his preface to the first collected edition of his poems, Hunt introduces his work by explaining his philosophy of poetry.*]

I intended to write a very short preface to the volume here submitted to the public indulgence; but finding the small number of pages to which it amounted, compared with the price put upon it in the advertisement, I wished to do what I could towards bringing it to a becoming size. To add verses which I had rejected, would have been an injustice both to the readers and myself. It was suggested to me that a 'good *gossiping* preface' would not be ill received; and I therefore write one in the true spirit of that word, leaving it to their good nature to interpret it accordingly.

I am so aware that the world is rich in books of all sorts, and that its attention, beyond the moment, is not to be looked for by voluminous writers, except those of the first order, that I have done my best to render my verses as little unworthy of re-perusal, as correction and omission could make them. I have availed myself of the criticism both of friends and enemies; and have been so willing to construe in my disfavour any doubts which arose in my own mind, that the volume does not contain above a third of the verses I have written. I took for granted, that an author's self-love is pretty sure not to be too hard upon him, and adopted the principle of making the doubt itself a sentence of condemnation. Upon this I have acted in every instance, with the exception of the **"Fragments upon the Nymphs,"** the **"Sonnet on the Nile,"** and the passages out of the **"Bacchus in Tuscany."** The fragments, and the sonnet, a partial friend induced me not to discard: otherwise, with a doubt perhaps in favour of the second and eighth lines of the sonnet, I felt that they did not possess enough of the subtler and remoter spirit of poetry, demanded by the titles. Of the **"Bacchus"** I retained a few specimens, partly for the sake of old associations, and of the tune echoed into it from the Italian; but chiefly in consequence of discovering that it had found favour in unexpected quarters.

If it be asked, why I have not been as scrupulous with the whole volume, or whether I look upon the rest of it as being free from objection, I answer, that I only believe it to be as good as it was in the writer's power to make it. What that power may be, if any, is another matter. At all events, I cannot accuse myself of taking no pains to satisfy my own judgment, or to bespeak the reader's good wishes. I have not shovelled my verses out by cart-loads, leaving the public, much less another generation, to save me the trouble of selection! I do not believe that other generations will take the trouble to rake for jewels in much nobler dust than mine. Posterity is too rich and idle. The only hope I can have of coming into any one's hands, and exciting his attention beyond the moment, is by putting my workmanship, such as it is, into its best and compactest state.

The truth is, I have such a reverence for poetry, pre-eminently so called (by which I mean that which posterity and the greatest poets agree to call such), that I should not dare to apply the term to anything written by me in verse, were I not fortunate enough to be of opinion, that poetry, like the trees and flowers, is not of one class only; but that if the plant comes out of Nature's hands, and not the gauze-maker's, it is still a plant, and has ground for it. All houses are not palaces, nor every shrine a cathedral. *In domo patris mei* (not to speak it profanely) *mansiones multæ sunt.*

Poetry, in its highest sense, belongs exclusively to such men as Shakespeare, Spenser, and others, who possessed the deepest insight into the spirit and sympathies of all things; but poetry, in the most comprehensive application of the term, I take to be the flower of any kind of experience, rooted in truth, and issuing forth into beauty. All that the critic has a right to demand of it, according to its degree, is, that it should spring out of a real impulse, be consistent in its parts, and shaped into some characteristic harmony of verse.

Without these requisites (apart from fleeting and artificial causes), the world will scarcely look at any poetical production a second time; whereas, if it possess them, the humblest poetry stands a chance of surviving not only whatever is falsely so called, but much that contains, here and there, more poetical passages than itself; passages that are the fits and starts of a fancy without judgment—the incoherences of a nature, poetical only by convulsion, but prosaic in its ordinary strength.

Thus, in their several kinds, we have the poetry of thought and passion in Shakespeare and Chaucer; of poetical abstraction and enjoyment in Spenser; of scholarship and a rapt ambition in Milton; of courtliness in Waller (who writes like an inspired gentleman-usher); of gallantry in Suckling; of wit and satire in Pope; of heartiness in Burns; of the 'fat of the land' in Thomson; of a certain sequestered gentleness in Shenstone; and the poetry of prose itself in Dryden: not that he was a prosaic writer, but that what other people thought in prose, he could think in verse; and so made absolute poems of pamphlets and party-reasoning.

The first quality of a poet is imagination, or that faculty by which the subtlest idea is given us of the nature or condition of any one thing, by illustration from another, or by the inclusion of remote affinities: as when Shakspeare speaks of moonlight *sleeping* on a bank; or of nice customs *curtseying* to great kings (though the reader may, if he pleases, put this under the head of wit, or imagination in miniature); or where Milton speaks of towers *bosom'd* in trees, or of motes that *people* the sunbeams; or compares Satan on the wing at a distance, to a fleet of ships *hanging* in the clouds; or where Mr. Shelley (for I avoid quoting from living writers, lest it should be thought invidious towards such as are not quoted) puts that stately, superior, and comprehensive image, into the mouth of a speaker who is at once firm of soul, and yet anticipates a dreadful necessity—

I see, *as from a tower,* the *end of all:*

or lastly, where Mr. Keats tells us of the *realmless eyes* of old Saturn (as he sits musing after his dethronement); or of the two brothers and *their murdered man,* riding from Florence; that is to say, the man whom they were *about* to murder; or where, by one exquisite touch, he describes an important and affecting office of the god Mercury, and the effects of it upon the spectators in the lower world—calling him 'the *star* of Lethe;' by which we see that he was the only bright object which visited that dreary region. We behold him rising on its borders.

In proportion to the imagination, is the abstract poetical faculty: in proportion to extent of sympathy (for passion, which is everywhere in poetry, may be comparatively narrow and self-revolving), is the power of universality: in proportion to energy of temperament and variety of experience, is the power of embodying the conceptions in a greater or less amount of consistent and stirring action, whether narrative or dramatic. The greatest poets have the greatest amount of all these qualities conjoined: the next greatest are those who unite the first two: the next, those whose imagination is exquisite as far as it goes, but is confined to certain spheres of contemplation: then come the poets, who have less imagination, but more action--who are imaginative, as it were, in the mass, and with a certain vague enjoyment allied to the feelings of youth: then the purely artificial poets, or such as poetize in art rather than nature, or upon conventional beauty and propriety, as distinguished from beauty universal: and then follow the minor wits, the song-writers, burlesquers, &c. In every instance, the indispensable requisites are truth of feeling, freedom from superfluity (that is, absence of forced or unfitting thoughts), and beauty of result; and in proportion as these requisites are comprehensive, profound, and active, the poet is great. But it is always to be borne in mind, that the writers in any of these classes, who take lasting hold of the world's attention, are justly accounted superior to such as afford less evidences of power in a higher class. The pretension is nothing; the performance every thing. A good apple is better than an insipid peach. A song of Burns is (literally) worth half the poets in the collections.

Suckling's "Ballad on a Wedding" is a small and unambitious, yet unmisgiving and happy production, of no rank whatsoever considered with reference to the height of poetry; but so excellent of its kind for consistency, freshness, and relish, that it has survived hundreds of epithalamiums, and epics too; and will last as long as beauty has a lip, or gallantry frankness.

Shenstone's "School-mistress" is a poem of a very humble description in subject, style, and everything, except its humane and thoughtful sweetness: yet being founded in truth, and consistent, and desiring nothing but truth and consistency, it has survived in like manner. Compared with greater productions, it resembles the herbs which the author speaks of in its cottage-garden; but balm and mint have their flourishing, as well as the aloe; and like them, and its old heroine, it has secured its 'grey renown,' clean as her mob-cap, and laid up in lavender. Crashaw is a poet now scarcely known except to book-worms. Pope said of him, that his writing was 'a mixture of tender gentle thoughts and suitable expressions, of forced and inextricable conceits, and of needless fillers-up to the rest.' Crashaw had a morbid enthusiasm, which sometimes helped him to an apprehensiveness and depth of expression, perhaps beyond the voluntary power of his great critic; yet Pope, by writing nothing out of what the painters call 'keeping', or unworthy of himself, is justly reck-

oned worth a hundred Crashaws. Random thoughts and fillings-up are a poet's *felo de se*.

Far am I, in making these remarks, from pretending to claim any part or parcel in the fellowship of names consecrated by time. I can truly say, that, except when I look upon some others that get into the collections, consecrated by no hands but the book-jobbers, I do not know (after I have written them) whether my verses deserve to live a dozen days longer. The confession may be thought strong or weak, as it happens; but such is the fact. I have witnessed so much self-delusion in my time, and partaken of so much, and the older I grow, my veneration so increases for poetry not to be questioned, that all I can be sure of, is my admiration of genius in others. I cannot say how far I overvalue it, or even undervalue it, in myself. I am in the condition of a lover who is sure that he loves, and is therefore happy in the presence of the beloved object; but is uncertain how far he is worthy to be beloved. Perhaps the symptom is a bad one, and only better than that of a confident ignorance. Perhaps the many struggles of my life; the strange conflicting thoughts upon a thousand matters, into which I have been forced; the necessity of cultivating some modesty of self-knowledge, as a set-off to peremptoriness of public action; and the unceasing alternation of a melancholy and a cheerfulness, equally native to my blood—and the latter of which I have suffered to go its lengths, both as an innocent propensity and a means of resistance—have combined in me to baffle conclusion, and filled me full of these *perhapses,* which I have observed growing upon my writings for many years past. *Perhaps* the question is not worth a word I have said of it, except upon that principle of 'gossiping' with which my preface sets out, and which I hope will procure me the reader's pardon for starting it. All that I was going to say was, that if I cannot do in poetry what ought to be done, I know what ought not; and that if there is no truth in my verses, I look for no indulgence.

As I do write poetry however, such as it is, I must have my side of confidence as well as of misgiving; and when I am in the humour for thinking that I have done something that may dare hope to be called by the name, I fancy I know where my station is. I please myself with thinking, that had the circumstances of my life permitted it, I might have done something a little worthier of acceptance, in the way of a mixed kind of narrative poetry, part lively and part serious, somewhere between the longer poems of the Italians, and the *Fabliaux* of the old French. My propensity would have been (and, oh! had my duties permitted, how willingly would I have passed my life in it! how willingly now pass it!) to write 'eternal new stories' in verse, of no great length, but just sufficient to vent the pleasure with which I am stung on meeting with some touching adventure, and which haunts me till I can speak of it somehow. I would have dared to pretend to be a servant in the train of Ariosto, nay, of Chaucer,

   —and far off his skirts adore.

I sometimes look at the trusting animal spirits in which the following poems were written (for my doubts come after I have done writing, and not while I am about it), and wonder whether or not they are of a right sort. I know not. I cannot tell whether what pleased me at the moment, was mere pleasure taken in the subject, or whether it involved the power of communicating it to the reader. All I can be sure of is, that I was in earnest; that the feelings, whatever they were, which I pretended to have, I had. It was the mistake of the criticism of a northern climate, to think that the occasional quaintnesses and neologisms, which formerly disfigured the *Story of Rimini,* arose out of affectation. They were the sheer license of animal spirits. While I was writing them, I never imagined that they were not proper to be indulged in. I have tropical blood in my veins, inherited through many generations, and was too full of impulse and sincerity to pretend to anything I did not feel. Probably the criticisms were not altogether a matter of climate; for I was a writer of politics as well as verses, and the former (two years ago!) were as illegal as the sallies of phraseology. Be this as it may, I have here shown, that I have at any rate not enough of the vanity of affectation to hinder me from availing myself of experience, and ridding my volume both of superfluities of a larger sort, and of those petty anomalies of words and phrases which I never thought worth defending. I believe there are but two words remaining in the *Story of Rimini,* to which any body would think it worth while to object; and one of these (the word *swirl* in page 1)[1] I had marked to be taken out, but found it restored by a friend who saw the passage as it was going through the press (no stickler for neologisms), and who put a wondering *'quære'* why it should be omitted. I used it to express the entrance of a sailing boat into harbour, when it turns the corner of it, and comes round with a sweeping motion. 'Sweep' would have described the motion but not the figure. 'Wheel' appeared to me too mechanical, and to make the circle too complete. I could find, therefore, no other word for the mixed idea which I wished to convey; and as *swirl* is in the dictionaries, I had no hesitation in submitting to the query, and letting it remain. The other word is *'cored,'* at page 15[2], meaning something that has taken root in the heart of our consciousness. I give it up to the critic, if he dislikes it, having accidentally let the proof-sheet, which contained it, go to press beyond power of recal. I care no more for it, than if it had been the oldest and least venerable of commonplaces. I should beg the reader's pardon for detaining him so long with these trifles, did not my value for his good opinion in higher matters, make me wish not to be thought contemptuous of it in the smallest.

My verses having thus been corrected, as far as I saw occasion, and evidence enough (I hope) having been given to show that I have no overweening value for what I have written, merely because I *have* written it, I should prove indeed that I had no reason to doubt the measure of my pretensions, if I gave up the right of keeping my own opinion, upon points on which I did not feel it shaken. I have therefore retained in my versification, not only the triplets and alexandrines which some have objected to, because they have been rarely used in heroic poetry since the time of Dryden, but the double rhymes which have been disused since the days of Milton.

It has been said of the triplet, that it is only a temptation to add a needless line, to what ought to be comprised in two. This is manifestly a half-sighted objection; for at least the converse of the proposition may be as true; namely, that it comprises, in one additional line, what two might have needlessly extended. And undoubtedly compression is often obtained by the triplet, and should never be injured by it; but I take its true spirit to be this—that it carries onward the fervour of the poet's feeling; delivers him for the moment, and on the most suitable occasions, from the ordinary laws of his verse; and enables him to finish his impulse with triumph. In all instances, where the triplet is not used for the mere sake of convenience, it expresses continuity of some sort, whether for the purpose of extension, or inclusion; and this is the reason why the alexandrine so admirably suits it, the spirit of both being a sustained enthusiasm. In proportion as this enthusiasm is less, or the feeling to be conveyed is one of hurry in the midst of aggregation, the alexandrine is perhaps generally dropped. The continuity implied by the triplet, is one of four kinds: it is either an impatience of stopping, arising out of an eagerness to include; or it is the march of triumphant power; or it 'builds the lofty rhyme' for some staider shew of it; or lastly, it is the indulgence of a sense of luxury and beauty, a prolongation of delight. Dryden has fine specimens of all. . . .

If Dryden had had sentiment, he would have been as great a poet natural, as he was artificial. The want, it must be owned, is no trifle! It is idle, however, to wish the addition of these cubits to human stature. Let us be content with the greatness his genius gave him, and with our power to look up to it.

Pope denounced alexandrines in a celebrated couplet, in which he seems to confound length of line with slowness of motion; two very distinct things, as Mr. Lamb has shown in one of his masterly essays.

   A needless alexandrine ends the song,
     Which like a wounded snake, drags its slow
        length along.

And yet, in his no less celebrated eulogy upon the

versification of Dryden, he has attempted an imitation of his master's style, in which he has introduced both alexandrine and triplet.

> Waller was smooth; but Dryden taught to
> join
> The varying verse, the full majestic line,
> The long resounding march, and energy
> divine.

How comes it then, that he rejected both from his own poetry? The reason was, that he acted by a judicious instinct. He felt, that variety and energy were not what his muse would deal in, but beauties of a different sort; and he wisely confined himself to what he could do best. It is true, it seems strange that he should exalt Dryden's variety at the expense of Waller's smoothness. It looks like dispraising himself. But then he felt that he had more in him than Waller; and that if he had not Dryden's variety, neither had he his carelessness, but carried the rhyming heroic to what he thought a perfection superior to both, and justly purchased by the sacrifice of Dryden's inequality. Inferior indeed as Pope's versification is to Dryden's, upon every principle both of power and music, nobody can deny that it admirably suits the nicer point of his genius, and the subjects on which it was exercised. Dryden had a tranchant sword, which demanded stoutness in the sheath. Pope's weapon was a lancet enclosed in pearl.

Let it not be thought (as it has too often been unthinkingly asserted), that remarks of this kind are meant to disparage our great master of poetic wit; to whose genius I should think it a foppery to express even my homage, were it not for the sake of guarding against the imputation of a more preposterous immodesty. But, in endeavouring to ascertain critically what is best in general composition, one is sometimes obliged to notice what is not so good, except in specific instances.

I confess I like the very bracket that marks out the triplet to the reader's eye, and prepares him for the music of it. It has a look like the bridge of a lute.

. . . . .

It seems to me, that beautiful as are the compositions which the English language possesses in the heroic couplet, both by deceased and living writers, it remains for some poet hereafter to perfect the versification, by making a just compromise between the inharmonious freedom of our old poets in general (who were greatest in greater measures), and the regularity of Dryden himself; who, noble as his management of it is, beats, after all, too much upon the rhyme. It hinders his matter from having due pre-eminence before his manner. If any one could unite the vigour of Dryden with the ready and easy variety of pause in the works of the late Mr. Crabbe, and the lovely poetic consciousness in the "Lamia" of Keats, in which the lines seem to take pleasure in the progress of their own beauty, like sea-nymphs luxuriating through the water, he would be a perfect master of rhyming heroic verse.

To quit these considerations of the more bodily part of poetry, and say something of the spirit of the following pieces:—I took up the subject of the *Story of Rimini* at one of the happiest periods of my life; otherwise I confess I should have chosen a less melancholy one. Not that melancholy subjects are unpopular, or that pain, for any great purpose, is to be avoided; much less so sweet a one as that of pity. I am apt enough to think, with the poet's good-natured title to his play, that 'All's well that ends well'; and am as willing as any man to bear my share of suffering, for the purpose of bringing about that moral to human story. My life has been half made up of the effort. Neither is every tragical subject so melancholy as the word might be supposed to imply; for not to mention those balms of beauty and humanity with which great poets reconcile the sharpest wounds they give us, there are stories (*Hero and Leander* is one of them), in which the persons concerned are so innocent, and appear to have been happy for so long a time, that the most distressing termination of their felicity hardly hinders a secret conviction, that they might well suffer bitterly for so short a one. Their tragedy is the termination of happiness, and not the consummation of misery.

But besides the tendency I have from animal spirits, as well as from need of comfort, to indulge my fancy in happier subjects, it appears to me, that the world has become experienced enough to be capable of receiving its best profit through the medium of pleasurable, instead of painful, appeals to its reflection. There is an old philosophic conviction reviving among us as a popular one (and there could not be one more desirable), that it is time for those who would benefit their species, to put an end to recriminations, and denouncements, and threats, and agree to consider the sufferings of mankind as arising out of want of knowledge rather than defect of goodness,—as intimations which, like the physical pain of a wound, or a galling ligament, tell us that we are to set about removing the causes of pain, instead of venting the spleen of it.

Agreeably to this conviction, and to the good-nature of it, it appears desirable, that tragical stories should be so written, as to leave no chance of misconception with regard to the first discernible causes of the error that produced the tragedy. Now what is this first cause in the story which stands at the head of the present volume? Is it the crime committed by the father, in entrapping his daughter into a marriage unfit for her? No: it is not even that. It is the habit of falsehood which pervaded society around him, and which therefore enabled and encouraged him to lie for that purpose: in other words, it was the great social mistake, still the commonest among us, arising from want of better knowledge, and producing endless mistake, confusion, and a war of principle, in all the relations of life. Society lied, and taught lying, with contradictory tenets that drove the habit to desperation; and then, with the natural anger of inconvenienced folly, and after the fashion of the brute beasts we read of, who sit clawing their wounds, it took the last guilty sufferer for the first: and this it has been doing, more or less, ever since half-knowledge took itself for whole, or a partial perception of its ignorance exasperated and degraded it into spleen and bigotry. A secret uneasiness has accordingly pervaded all moral criticism, especially where the critic has not been wanting in a good measure of natural benevolence; nay, where the temperament has been violent, and the will greater than the reason, it has sometimes exasperated him and made him inhuman, in proportion to his very desire of sympathy. I remember I was never more astonished, than when some of the critics of the poem in question (not altogether impartial, however, on the political score), found out, that the hero and heroine had not suffered enough for the cause of good morals, and that they were too amiable! What would such critics have? Is it the unamiable alone who suffer, or who require to be warned against the perils they undergo? Or is it none but the amiable who are weak and thoughtless? Or must the cruellest temptations into which duplicity and error can bring people, be kept out of sight, purely to please the morbid fancies and social bad consciences of those who perpetuate them? Lastly, I would ask, whether a long train of misery, and a tragical death, are no calamities, or 'nothing to speak of'? I cannot answer, either for the misgivings of false morals, or for the strange fascinations of those, who might choose, for aught I know, to go and disobey their parents, and take to drinking poison, because last night they had seen the play of *Romeo and Juliet,* or the *Orphan!* But this I know, that I thought the catastrophe a very dreadful one when I wrote it, and the previous misery still worse; and that although I certainly intended no moral lesson, or thought about it, when I was led by the perusal of the story in Dante to attempt making a book of it, the subject gradually forced upon me the consideration of those first causes of error, of which I have been speaking. I thought of putting for a motto to the second edition, a passage out of the *Orlando Innamorato:*

> Bisogna ben guardare
> Al primo errore, ed inconveniente.

Guard well against the first, unfit mistake.

But so little did I suspect that any one could remain unimpressed with the catastrophe, that I doubted whether the motto itself would not be mixed up too exclusively with the principal sufferers. I am glad to think it is now likely to be otherwise, and that to those who choose to reflect on the tragedy of Dante's story, no link in the chain of moral causes need be lost sight of. It would be idle to reply, that, by bringing out a first cause, we cease to absorb attention upon the second, and endanger a just dread of it. Society only becomes the more bound to see into that first evil, without the existence of which we should not have so many others.

It is a great pleasure to me to reflect, that, before I had become aware of the inestimable value of the love of truth, as the foundation of every thing finally good, in poetry, philosophy, and the government of the world, I had unconsciously been giving a lesson upon it in a poetical form.

Of the like moral, in the story of the **"Gentle Armour,"** I was aware enough: but the reader is not bound to keep it in view, except as part of the story. My great object in writing the poem, was to vent my delight at the gallantry of a lover who could fight three armed people at once, with no other covering, than a sentiment in the shape of a piece of linen. All poetry, like every thing else in the world, contains a moral, whether intended or not; and, generally speaking, that which contains it least obviously, contains it most; because nature with her boundless instinct is speaking to us, and not the individual with his narrow experience. Yet sincerity of purpose is part of the truth of nature. People talk of trick and delusion, as if they were at the top of all things: whereas nothing is more certain, than that they are comprehended in something greater than themselves, and that nature must have been a good deal in earnest when she produced the mountains, and the stars, and sent the planets rolling in the everlasting hunger of their energy round the sun. Falsehood is the dreg in her operations, and is to be thrown off, as truth gathers that strength and concentration of movement, which the yearnings of philosophy and of human want equally shew that she intends for it. It becomes us, it is true, to reverence and think the best of all the operations of nature, including those yearnings, let them apparently terminate as they may. But it does not become us to assert—on the contrary, it may be very pernicious, and undesired by nature (except as matter of consolation and reconcilement to us, in default of our being able to do anything),—that she intends to perpetuate any mixture of evil or contradiction in her works; or that she cannot work without their aid. Better believe in a fugitive exception to good, however mysterious, generated by some convulsion in the great lapses of time, and of necessity worked off by the energy of the planet that suffers under it, till the star resumes the golden state of tranquillity natural to its heavenly brotherhood, than take for granted any kind of perpetuation, equally gratuitous, a great deal more contradictory, and infinitely more saddening. Where there is a choice of opinions, it is wise to adopt the best; especially when we consider that mankind has a natural impulse towards endeavour, and that nature herself has given us both the endeavour and the choice. But I am taking large measure, indeed, of the word 'gossiping', when a copy of verses makes me ramble after this fashion! when a butterfly leads me a chace among the stars!

"**The Gentle Armour**" is here published for the first time; and is the first poem of any length, which I have written for many years, having been debarred from that delight by ill health, and the constant necessity of writing prose. What I felt, when I found I could again recreate myself in this way, and when the verses came flowing again, I will not say; lest I should excite awkward comparisons between what I delight in doing, and what it amounts to when done. But as Gray wished that he could lie all his life upon sofas, reading 'eternal new novels of Marivaux and Crébillon,' so, notwithstanding the helps afforded us by the grander notions of the age, or rather in consequence of the very helps they afford, I can conceive no mode of existence more exquisite (apart from the affections) than after contributing a portion of one's morning to the furtherance of the common good—the better if in the same way—to devote the rest of one's time to reading romantic adventures, and versifying the best of them. What golden days would not such be for a builder of palaces 'with words!' What country-houses would he not possess in all quarters of the world—and of time! What flights not take from Greece to Araby, from Normandy to Cathay, from the Courts of Charlemagne and of Arthur, to the corners of the sea, and the House of Morpheus! With what transport not wake up, and find himself in the company of his beloved old books, content to be master of the world when he had his wings on, and to look for no better footing for the sole of his feet, than the hearth of an uninsulted poverty. *O felix ter et amplius!* No man ever deserved even to wish to be a poet, who could not think in this manner, or not think it as much at forty as at twenty.

The poem of *Hero and Leander,* as well as the *Story of Rimini,* I have corrected since it first appeared, the former indeed considerably altered; I hope with improvement to it as an unhalting and consistent narrative. They ought, it is true, to have been so written at first, as to require nothing which it was in my power to do for them afterwards; but I was conscious of letting some of the passages slip from me too carelessly. The long description, by the way, of the garden in the *Story of Rimini,* I have suffered to remain, though it may seem injurious to the progress of the action; but in spirit I thought it not so; because the heroine is to be prepared as gradually as possible for the change in her conduct; and a luxurious enjoyment of the works of nature, in the present perplexed condition of the world, is too often rendered an additional means of confusion, instead of being, as it ought to be, one of the final modes of the common good.[3] The great point

however is, whether the reader would rather have the description or not. Laws in poetry are nothing but the conclusions which critics have come to, respecting the means adopted by the best poets, for giving the greatest amount of pleasure. The appeal always lies from the law-makers to the reader's feeling. No laws whatever have yet been perfected, because in no art or science has the entire circle of truth been run round. There is one thing in Shakspeare himself which is unnatural, and it pervades almost all his plays; namely, the making his people talk so wonderfully well, with a profusion of thought and imagery to be found only in a mind like his own. It suits the excess of reflection in such characters as Hamlet and Lear, but scarcely any one else; and yet who would wish it away? Nature is *included* still, and that is sufficient. The drama itself is in nature: art is in nature: and provided no requisite beauty be omitted, it is a fine thing to see how far a poet can enrich his entertainment without oppressing delight.

The next composition, the *Feast of the Poets,* was the earliest of my grown productions in verse. I was full of animal spirits when I wrote it, and have a regard for it accordingly, like that for one's other associations of youth. It was however a good deal more personal than at present, and showed me the truth of what has been observed respecting the danger of a young writer's commencing his career with satire: for I have reason to believe, that its offences, both of commission and omission, gave rise to some of the most inveterate enmities I have experienced. I will honestly confess, especially as I had a nobler field of warfare to suffer in, that I would willingly not have aroused enmity by such means. I acknowledge also, that a young author was presumptuous in pronouncing judgment upon older men, some of whom made me blush afterwards with a better self-knowledge. I can only offer in excuse, that I had not at that time suffered enough myself, to be aware of the pain to be given in this way; and that I was a young student, full of my favourite writers, and regarding a satire as nothing but a pleasant thing in a book.

To omit this poem in the present collection, appeared to me, for various reasons, improper; but it has been altered to suit my present feelings; and if all the hostile passages have not been left out, the retention under the circumstances, is, I think, not unwarrantable. The passage on the late Mr. Gifford I have a value for, partly because Mr. Hazlitt liked it; but the chief reason why I let this and two others remain is, that if men have a right to quarrel personally with anything, it is with prosperous insincerity, and with inhumanities which neither age nor suffering do away. And I have another reason. I think it necessary, for the sake of many interests, to shew that I have still arms at my side. I have no desire to use them. Never had I so little. But my determination to use them, if insisted upon, never was so great. I have made amends, by long and patient forbearance, for a young mistake; but injuries affecting more than myself, I will repel. This is a grave piece of discourse upon so light a subject; but criticism and poetry are apt to be cloud and sunshine.

To the *Translations* the originals have been appended, partly out of a recollection of the pleasure I used to feel when a boy, at seeing the Latin under Pope's *Imitations of Horace;* partly from a willingness to shew the pains taken to do the originals justice. I have translated the whole of Tasso's *Amyntas,* of Redi's *Bacchus in Tuscany,* and of the *Lutrin* of Boileau: the *Bacchus,* from good will; the two other poems, from a less voluntary motive. The *Lutrin,* fortunately, has not been published; for I doubt whether it would have been better received than the Bacchus; and from the *Amyntas* I have retained only the "Ode to the Golden Age" which I fear is the only really fine thing in the original. Of the *Bacchus* and the *Lutrin,* I have given such specimens as I thought might afford the reader some gratification. I speak, of course, only of the translations: though I doubt, however well they might have been rendered, whether in England we could have received anything like such a pleasure from them, as the French and Italians do from the originals, owing to our want of intimacy with the same customs. The *Lutrin* has a 'catholic' relish with it; but not in the truly learned and universal sense of Sancho Panza's draught out of the flask; and Redi's wines become flat by importation.

Let me take this opportunity of saying, that with all the praise occasionally bestowed upon the serious powers of Theocritus, and his indications of a genius for epic poetry, I am not aware that justice has been done to the wonderful evidences he has given of a combination of faculties for the light and the passionate, the social and the sequestered, the humorous and the pathetic, the minute and the grand. This delightful poet courts a milk-maid or a sea-nymph with equal fitness of address; is a countryman and a townsman; a clown, a courtier, and a satirist; fills a house at midnight with ghastly phenomena; describes a piece of pugilism in a style to make the bones of the 'Fancy' crack under them; and makes us at once shudder and pity the great monster Polypheme, whom he reconciles to humanity by subduing with love. Then there is his Hylas, disappearing under the water like a falling star; and his lion at noon-day, with all the villagers indoors around him; and his infant Hercules, the little jovial potency, the true infant demi-god, tearless and sovereign, of whose encounter with the Serpents I have endeavoured to give some idea. If Theocritus had written an epic, the world would have had a poet unknown to it, a romance-writer equally great for abundance and concentration, a Greek Ariosto.

I fear I have indeed been gossiping in this preface, and that I shall be thought by some to have wasted a great many words upon rhyme and numbers, things a little too much forgotten perhaps in the general poetry of the age. There is enough romance however in my volume to save me from the charge of a mechanical impertinence, when I venture to congratulate the reader on the manifest failure of that prophecy, which announced the downfall of all poetry and fiction in the ascendancy of the steam engine, and would fain have persuaded us, that the heart, and imagination, and flesh and blood of man, were to quit him at the approach of science and utilitarianism, and leave him nothing but his ribs to reckon upon. O believe it not! Count it not feasible, or in nature! The very flowers on the tea-cups, the grace with which a ball of cotton is rolled up, might have shewn to the contrary. You must take colour out of the grass first, preference out of the fancy, passion out of the blood. Nay the more drought, the more thirst. The want makes the wish. You may make sects in opinion, and formalize a people for a while, here and there; but you cannot undo human nature. The very passion that makes them obstinate in what is formal, shall counteract itself in the blood of their children, and betray them back to imagination. Opinion may dogmatize; science may be mechanical in its operation; but in explaining one cause, it only throws us back upon another, and opens a wider and remoter world for the fancy to riot in. And the operators, by very reason of the solid footing they require, are apt to lose themselves most, if they do not hold fast. Newton himself got into strange borderlands of dissent. Pascal was a hypochondriacal dreamer. With the growth of this formidable mechanical epoch, that was to take all *dulce* out of the *utile,* we have had the wonderful works of Sir Walter Scott, the criticism of Hazlitt, the imagination of Keats, the tragedy and winged philosophy of Shelley, the passion of Byron, the wit and festivity of Moore, tales and novels endless, and Mr. Wordsworth has become a classic, and the Germans have poured forth every species of romance, and the very French have thought fit to Germanize, and our American brethren have written little but novels and verses, and Sir Humphry Davy has been dividing his time between coal-mines and fairy-land (no very remote regions); and the shop itself and the *Corn Laws* have given us a poet, and Mr. Crabbe has been versifying the very Parish Registers; and last, not least, the Utilitarians themselves are poetical! Dr. Bowring is not satisfied unless we hear of the poetry of the 'Maggyars'; and if you want a proper Bacchanalian uproar in a song, you must go to the author of '*Headlong* Hall', who will not advance utility itself, unless it be jovial. It is a moot point which he admires most, Bentham or Rossini.

The truth is, that if the literature of the age reminds us in any respect of the mechanical, it is in a certain irregularity and random thinking, and at the same time a want of animal spirits. There is something in it both of the turbulence and the melancholy of the manufactories, and it is traceable to the same causes, mixed with some portion of what is not exactly a passion for truth and simplicity; to wit, those which have made England itself the melancholy bankrupt of the wars of Europe. The poor have a right to complain; but if others have their collateral grievances, and must complain too, it would be better if they would handsomely merge them into that commoner stock, and thus mourn to some purpose. A man, who enjoys any of the reliefs of literature, and who sees what a beautiful world this is, and how all might enjoy it, if all would try for all, should be ashamed, however distressed or struggling, to mourn openly for himself. General endeavour, animated by particular, is the only thing at last that will do away individual trouble; and it is a pity that the comic philosopher mentioned at the close of my last paragraph, and the brilliant minstrel of Erin, who are almost the only writers whose animal spirits come out in strong relief from the general sombreness of our literature, cannot strike a little more vivacity into the blood of their countrymen, and help them to feel the value of it in proportion to the necessity for effort. It would enable 'us youth', who mix up something of the jovial with our very melancholy, to come in with a better grace under the shadow of their wing. Let us hope that as effort is unavoidable, cheerfulness will come with it. At present, we have become thinking enough to grow more tolerant, even towards those who hold pleasant teaching to be better than painful; but our determination, nevertheless, to be 'all unhappy together', is remarkable. The loudest and most ostentatious of the lively do but bluster, and even declare it an ostentation; the most successful betray the most melancholy opinions; the very happiest try hard at a misgiving. Poets novelists, critics, fine gentlemen, ladies, magazine-writers, annualists—all are in one common story of sorrowfulness, over all sorts of things that have surely been sufficiently sorrowed over, and tell us of little else but the vanity of their hopes and the error of their ways. Rich and poor, old and young, bookwriters, and stanza-writers, the necessitous and the easy, all are alike '*melancholy* and wise', and give us to understand that they shall consider it an impertinence and a proof of a shallow understanding, if we offer to comfort them. The ladies in particular, not having the fear of dullness and calumny before their eyes, make such a point of expatiating on the sad things they have become acquainted with, on the blighting effects of 'guilt', the lost happiness of their childhood, the peace which they must 'never hope for more', &c., that were it not for the very innocence of the lamentation, we should wonder that the parish-officers had not taken them all up, and brought them before the magistrate. However, out of all this dissatisfaction it is to be hoped there will come advancement. What an honest man might complain of, meanwhile, for his share of the grievance, is, that these fair mourners are so very clever, and look so well in their black, and afford him so many bewitching glimpses of their taste for felicity, that their refusal

to be consoled becomes doubly hard upon his sympathy.

Alas! (to borrow their style of lamentation when it is most used, namely, when there is least ground for it,) even 'gossiping' must have an end. I must terminate this long preface with again reminding the reader of its exordium, and with begging him to construe me, not as arrogating a right to be considered exemplary on any point of authorship of which it has spoken, nor as challenging a comparison with any person alluded to, but only as a writer who is 'nothing if not *social*', and who would willingly read other men's prefaces, if they were twice as long, and does read them.

I have one thing more, however, to allude to, but it is very fit that I should do it, and will be a still more becoming conclusion to this preface, which would not have been written but on the strength of it. It is to the subscription, by which this volume has been enabled to appear in its present shape. I was thinking of making a selection of my verses, in order to give them a chance of surviving me, at the moment when a kind friend came upon me with the project. There were reasons why I did not dare to say nay to him; and the mode of publication was reconciled to my self-love by many flattering recollections. To all the persons concerned in bringing it out, my friend in particular, and the publisher who has shewn himself a friend, and the printers who have taken such pains with it, and have indulged me in my 'brackets', and other interferences with the sightliness of their page, I return my best thanks. I dare not say much to the subscribers in general, lest in proportion as I seemed to make my book of no value, I should deprive all parties of a grace. It is impossible not to feel a strong moment of confidence and self-complacency (however it may give way, the next, to a sense of their good-nature), when a set of names, comprising almost the flower of existing literature, have not hesitated to give my pretensions, as a writer, the ornament of their recognition. Of opinions, I say nothing; except that it is an additional and delightful proof of the growth of one of the best of all opinions; namely, the right of their independence. I can truly say, that I have seldom felt greater pleasure, not only on my own account, but on that of my species, when I saw some of the names that came into the list. I will not enter into more particular reasons why, lest I should seem to flatter myself, more than honour them; which is assuredly not the case. I leave them to be guessed by those who know what political warfare is, and who might think these evidences of goodwill after the battle incompatible with it. I must say for myself, that I never was of that opinion, nor ever gave the world reason to think so; and therefore, so far, I am not as surprised as some may be, nor indeed surprised at all. I am only glad and confirmed. What was observed by one of these gentlemen, particularly delighted me. It amounted to saying, that he would gladly help in binding up my wounds, and the battle might be renewed afterwards. This is in true chivalrous style, and poetry in action. Let me add, that the end of all conflict, carried on in this spirit, and secured by the knowledge of the time, can only be good for all parties, and merge them in the great cause of mankind.

Notes

[1] [Canto I, line 24.]

[2] [Canto III, line 84.]

[3] In all which the writer intimates, here or in any other place, respecting the happiness which mankind may attain to in this life, he is far from wishing to imply any thing against the existence of another. He is of opinion with Selden in that matter, in his famous argument derived from the subject in hand—a garden; where he says, that he sees no reason why a man should not make himself as happy as possible in one beautiful place, because the giver of it has promised him another. If it be argued that evil here is necessary in order to enhance good in another world, so let it be

THE

AUTOBIOGRAPHY

OF

LEIGH HUNT;

WITH

REMINISCENCES

OF FRIENDS AND CONTEMPORARIES.

"Most men, when drawn to speak about themselves,
Are mov'd by little and little to say more
Than they first dreamt ; until at last they blush,
And can but hope to find secret excuse
In the self-knowledge of their auditors."

WALTER SCOTT's *Old Play.*

IN THREE VOLUMES.

VOL. I.

LONDON:

SMITH, ELDER AND CO., 65, CORNHILL.

1850.

argued; it is well and wise; but this consideration is for comfort, and not for action. No doctrines inculcate human endeavour, for the sake of the species and their improvement, more than those of Christianity.

Stephen F. Fogle (essay date 1958)

SOURCE: "Leigh Hunt and the Laureateship," in *Studies in Philology*, Vol. LV, No. 4, October, 1958, pp. 603-15.

[*In the following essay, Fogle examines Hunt's quest for the poet laureateship in light of Hunt's lifelong political rhetoric and writings concerning the royal family.*]

Twice during Leigh Hunt's career, there seemed, at least to him, a fair chance that he might be named poet laureate of England. Three times during his adult career as a man of letters, the office fell vacant: in 1813 on the death of Pye, in 1843 on the death of Southey, and in 1850 on the death of Wordsworth. It was of course manifestly impossible that the Prince Regent in 1813 would have offered the post to a journalist relatively little-known as a poet (for Hunt's best-known poems all come later) who was at the moment confined to Horsemonger Lane Gaol in Surrey after a conviction for libeling the Regent himself. And, also, Hunt had spent some of his space in *The Examiner* on making fun of the laureate and the laureateship. On January 24, 1808, he printed Pye's New Year's Ode, as performed to music adapted from Handel. In January 1810, he had reprinted the wretched New Year's Ode of the wretched Pye, calling it "a complete specimen, if not of the best Laureat writing, at least of the true Laureat flattery and fiction." He maintained further that, "In every point of view, the Laureatship is a ridiculous office [a phrase which was to rise again some thirty-three years later to haunt him]: if the monarch is a great prince, the hired poet degrades him; if an indifferent one, burlesques him; and if a bad one, renders both prince and poet execrable."[1] On the death of Pye in 1813, the editor of *The Examiner* indulged himself from jail in remarks on the vacant office: "The death of the Poet-Laureat, Mr. Pye, an opportunity of doing something not only politic, but sensible and manly; we mean in abolishing the very absurd office held by that gentleman."[2]

If Southey was named to the laureateship for political reasons, after Scott had refused the office, similar political reasons would operate against Hunt for the rest of his life. It is true that by the 1840's many of the measures recommended by Hunt twenty-five and thirty years earlier had been adopted by the Whigs and had become the law of the land, but Hunt retained his reputation of having been a dangerous man. Not only had he been imprisoned for libeling the Regent, but he had continued to write against the royal family for some years thereafter, under a variety of names. Hunt himself would distinguish between his treatment of the hated Georges and his treatment of other members of the family. On the death of the Princess Charlotte he had written first an **"Elegy on Our Lost Princess,"** which was published in *The Examiner*, December 28, 1817, under the name of Nelson Stratton, Beadle and Bellman for the year 1818, but later indexed as "By the Editor, as N. Stratton, Bellman." The poem, if commonplace, is nevertheless thoroughly respectful and does not draw clear distinction between the worthy dead and the unworthy parent left alive, a trick all too common among the political mourners of the day. This **"Elegy"** was followed the next year by a highly sentimental poem called **"His Departed Love to Prince Leopold,"** in which the spirit of the Princess Charlotte is made to sing a ghostly and saccharine consolation to the widower. Neither poem was reprinted during Hunt's lifetime, but a pencilled note in the handwriting of the late Luther A. Brewer, the noted collector of Huntiana, in his copy of *The Poetical Works of Leigh Hunt,* states that the poem was set to music by Vincent Novello.[3]

Leigh Hunt was understandably a little reluctant to identify himself as the author of topical satiric verse after his two-year stay in Horsemonger Lane and after having had to provide sureties for good conduct. The mask used for this category of his work was the name of Harry Brown, and by 1816 he had written enough "Harry Brown" poems in *The Examiner* and the Taunton *Courier,* to attempt to collect them and publish them in a volume. According to a letter from John Taylor, of the firm of Taylor and Hessey, it would seem that Hunt offered the volume as by "a lady" whom he did not further identify but for whom he was kind enough to act as agent.[4] There is no way of knowing to what extent Taylor and Hessey saw through this rather flimsy device, but at any rate the volume was refused, on the grounds that its contents were too topical and had already been seen through periodical publication by those who would be its natural audience.

Harry Brown continued to write in *The Examiner* until Hunt's departure for Italy at the end of 1821. There are poems on a number of political subjects, but the ones relating to the royal divorce and the trial of the queen are especially vitriolic. Hunt was of course, like most liberals, thoroughly on the queen's side of the case, or, perhaps more accurately, he was against the king. Two of the poems, **"Memory and Want of Memory, or Rather No Than Yes"** and **"An Excellent Scotch Parody,"** deal specifically with the trial. The first is in three parts, the examination of the Italian witness Majocchi first by the Counsel for the Plaintiff, then by the counsel for the Defendant, and a

final summary by Harry Brown himself. The poem is doggerel perhaps, but it is cuttingly satirical doggerel. From the first section:

> You swear, you swear—'Oh Signor, si'—
>   That through a double floor, eh,
> You've seen her *think* adulterously?
>   'Ver' true, Sir—Si, Signore.'
>
> I think, my Lords—'Oh Signor, si'—
>   That nothing's wanting more, eh,
> To show the Queen's as bad as we,
>   Aye, beats his sacred Majesty?—
>   'The thomper—Si, Signore.'

The second is built on the recurring *'Non mi ricordo'* of Majocchi's testimony and on the confusion into which he was thrown by the cross-questioning of the Queen's representative, Lord Brougham. The third section, the poet's comment, discusses the meaning of *Non mi ricordo:*

> Sometimes it means a woman's bad
>   And never sleeps alone-a,
> And when again examined, it
>   Shall call her *Donna buona*
>
> Sometimes it means a man is blind
>   And runs against th' Exchequer,
> And then again it signifies,
>   To see through a two-decker.
>
>   . . . . .
>
> Sometimes it stands for such a time
>   Betwixing and betweening,
> That being well interpreted
>   It means it has no meaning.
>
> It means a thief, it means some beef,
>   It means a shabby villain;
> It means 'mine host o' the Garter' here,
>   Who longs to bring his Bill in.

Presumably the juxtaposition of "shabby villain" and "mine host o' the Garter" would not be lost upon a contemporary audience as a none-too-veiled insult to the King.

The second song, **"An Excellent Scotch Parody, To Be Sung by All Loyal and Loving North Britons, from Maiden Kirk to John o' Groats,"** was printed in the *Examiner* on September 3, 1820, and was designed to be sung to the air of "Tibby Fowler of o' the Glen." It commences with "Cary Brunswick o' the Guelph, / There's ower mony swearing at her"; and ends with a bitter stanza:

> Be a lassie ne'er sae foul,
>   Gie her but the name of Regent,

And were her throne a cutty-stool,
  E'en Church wad be her maist obedient;
    Booing at her, wooing at her,
    Praying, Yea-ing, Nay-ing at her,
      Were she fatter than King Batter
    They wad a' be dressing at her.

These two songs were never reprinted by Hunt, but the third, **"Coronation Soliloquy of His Majesty King George the Fourth,"** was published first in *The Examiner* on July 29, 1821, and republished from a much revised and extended version in the volume of poems published in 1860 and prepared by Hunt for publication before his death. The original version was called merely **"A Lesson for Kings"** and was to be sung to the tune of *"Amo, Amas, / I love a lass, / As cedar tall and slender, &c."* The first and last stanzas of the original version will serve to make its tenor clear:

    Rego, regis,
    Good God, what's this!
    Only half my Peeries!
    Regas, regat,
    Good God, what's that!
    The voice is like my Deary's!
Chorus. Roar 'em, floor 'em,
    Shut the doorum,
    Hairum, scarum, strife O;
      Tag rag, merry derry, periwig, and
  cat's paw,
      Save us from our Wife O! , , ,

    See my Champy,
    Plumy, trampy,
    Sadler's Wells an't finer!
    Lord! he names me,
    And proclaims me,
    Never was lad *equiner!*

Chorus. Roarem, joram,
    Splash and pour 'em,
    Crown us, drown us, *vivo;*
      Wag mag, very merry, plethora, and
  flat man,
      Vivat Rex dead alive O

It seems from our distant point of view that any poet who had written about his king in this fashion, even though under a pseudonym, would be foolish ever to hope for preferment from any of the same dynasty. Actually Hunt was fortunate in having grants from the crown and finally a pension, even if he never attained the office he had hoped for. To many, the accession of Victoria seemed a happy beginning to a new era and the end of the bad old times. To Hunt, who, from the time of his sojourn in Italy, had turned to belles-lettres and to literary rather than political polemics, it seemed the dawn of a new day.

He had himself begun a new day, another of his many fresh starts, the editorship of the *Monthly Repository,* which was under his care from June 1837 until April 1838. As soon as the July issue, he was praising the Queen. The recent accession served as a point of departure for a few pages on **"The Female Sovereigns of England When Young,"** an essay which seems largely to have been compiled rather hastily by the process of leafing through a good many old books. It ends, however, with an address and compliment to Victoria:

> to make every reflecting heart regard her with a mixture of pitying tenderness and hopeful respect, and cordially to pray, that it may be consistent with the good of mankind, and best for it, whatever be their particular opinions meanwhile, to see her fair figure continue hovering over the advancing orb, like the embodied angel of the meaning of her name.[5]

This, it may be mentioned in passing, is approximately one half of the concluding sentence and may be noted as an example of Hunt's prose of the period, a style which always prefers a "reflecting heart" to a reflecting mind. In the same issue he produced three pages on **"Her Majesty's Name: and a Caution Thereon,"** full of complimentary punning passages, translations from Latin, Italian, and Portuguese in which the words *Victoria* or *Vittoria* had been used, and ending with a playful warning in which he arrogates to himself sole rights to pun upon the sovereign's name.

In the August issue there is an essay entitled simply **"The Queen,"** occasioned by standing in the crowd to watch Victoria coming home from the dissolution of Parliament. After analysing her features and noting that she appears to have every symptom which might be expected from her inheritance, he concludes the essay:

> We have mentioned the expressions used by the crowd. They were deep and general in the quarter where we stood, and therefore, we conclude, elsewhere. But there was no hurraing; no loss of the crowd's own self-possession; no violent outbreak of any sort. The feeling, as clearly as it could be expressed both by sound and silence, was to this effect:— "We love you, and wish you well with all our hearts; but we expect that you will maintain love with love, and be the proper sovereign for this new era, which knows the rights of people as well as sovereigns, and has broken up the delusion which sacrificed the many to the few."
>
> This is what the popular feeling said; and this is what we say ourselves, with all loving respect.[6]

The modern reader may suspect that the *New Yorker* would run this under the caption of "Feelings We

Doubt Ever Were Expressed by Sound and Silence," but at least it shows what Hunt thought he might hope for from the new regime.

By November, Hunt was beginning to be disillusioned. The working classes, through their London organization, had presented a petition to the Queen, necessarily through the medium of Lord John Russell, since the workers did not possess court dress and hence could not attend the levee to present it in person. Hunt, in reproducing the petition and the circumstances under which its presentation was hindred, is respectful toward Her Majesty and gives her all credit for good intentions in his essay on **"The Queen and the Working Classes."**

In December 1837 an essay on **"The Queen, the Opening of Parliament, and the Address of the Working Men on National Education"** shows a progressive disillusionment. The Queen is not personally blamed. He has been to watch the procession to open Parliament as he had watched the procession at the dissolution of the previous one.

> The hurrahs were louder than on the former occasion; but we did not hear any of those fervid exclamations of "God bless the Queen"—"God save your Majesty"; perhaps because we did not stand in the same place; perhaps because of the growing suspicion that the opinions at court are too merely conservative.[7]

He goes on to compare the speech from the throne with the address on National Education presented to the Queen by the working classes.

> Good God What a noble paper it is; and what a sign of the times! Compare it with the Speech put into the mouth of the good little Queen, and see (we say it not in disrespect towards anybody, but out of the force of truth, and a happy anticipation of better days for all) see indeed what a puppet royalty becomes by the side of it![8]

The condescending phrase "good little Queen" is in sharp contrast to "the embodied angel of the meaning of her name" about whom he had written six months previously. Now, one feels, he is making an effort to exonerate her from any blame in the actions of her ministers; she has become a "puppet."

Thus, Hunt's return to political writing, occasioned by a change of rulers, has resulted in disillusionment, and he ceases to write seriously about politics for some time. He does not, however, cease to write about royalty, and a change comes about. The change seems to have a double cause: Hunt twice received gifts of two hundred pounds from the Royal Bounty Fund[9] and the incumbent Laureate, Robert Southey, began to fail both mentally and physically. By August 4, 1839, Hunt was writing to Lord Melbourne to acknowledge the second

grant of money.[10] In 1838, Southey's intimates had begun to notice his deterioration; by 1839 gossip was spreading through the literary world. Under the date of 29 February 1840, Henry Crabb Robinson notes "Called on Miss Fenwick. . . . We talked about poor Southey. His death is now desired by his best friends."[11]

At any rate, Hunt in 1840 began to take over the duties of the laureate, publishing in the *Morning Chronicle* poems, as he calls them, "on occasions connected with the happiness of the Queen."[12] The series commenced well with a poem on the 28th of May, 1840, **"To the Queen, an Offering of Gratitude on Her Majesty's Birthday."** The poem is not a great one, and Hunt quotes its best lines in his *Autobiography*.[13] They run, in part,

> May she every day
> See some new good winning its gentle way
> By means of mild and unforbidden men!

In the September issue of the *Monthly Chronicle* there appeared another poem **"To the Queen,"** this one **"Upon the Strange Attempt Made on the Lives of Her Majesty and Prince Albert."** It opens:

> Recovering with one breath, one joy, one
>   prayer,
> From sudden horror, such as lifts the hair,
> Three kingdoms bless thee, lady, and thy life,

and goes on to:

> Great God! to picture what a pass was there!

There is no reason to suppose any insincerity on Hunt's part, but his picture of the royal couple, "The few months' wife, and mild and manly spouse," lacks any real distinction. It is in his verses to the royal children that Hunt comes most nearly a cropper. On Wednesday, November 25, 1840, there appeared just above the Court Circular in the *Morning Chronicle* an address **"To the Infant Princess Royal"** which begins

> Welcome, bud beside the rose,
> On whose stem our safety grows;
> Welcome, little Saxon Guelph;
> Welcome for thine own small self;
> Welcome for thy father, mother,
> Proud the one, and safe the other.
>
>   . . . . .
>
> Some have wished thee boy; and some
> Gladly wait till boy shall come,
> Counting it a genial sign
> When a lady leads the line.

So far as "occasions connected with the happiness of

the Queen" are concerned, there is now an hiatus, but the hopes for the laureateship did not grow less dim. A strong adherent had been enlisted, Macaulay, who endeavored to help Hunt as much as he could. Through his influence with MacVey Napier, Macaulay obtained some reviewing for Hunt from the *Edinburgh Review* and also himself reviewed in the *Edinburgh* Hunt's edition of the ***Dramatic Works of Wycherley, Congreve, Vanbrugh, and Farquhar.*** If the opening of Macaulay's review, "We have a kindness for Mr. Leigh Hunt . . . a very clever, a very honest, and a very good-natured man,"[14] strikes us as a little patronizing, a little condescending to a man some sixteen years the elder of the two, nevertheless any notice at this time could help Hunt. More, Macaulay interested himself actively in the question of the laureateship. On 27 March 1841 he wrote to Hunt from the War Office,

> I have just had a long conversation with Lord Melbourne, on whom I have pressed your claims with as much urgency as I thought myself justified in using. . . . At last he told me that he feared a pension was out of the question, but that he would try to do something for you. This is less than I wished, but more, I own, than I expected. . . .

> I heard the other day, from one of poor Southey's nephews, that he cannot live many weeks: I really do not see why you might not succeed him. The title of Poet Laureate is indeed ridiculous. But the salary ought to be left for the benefit of some man of letters. Should the present government be in office when a vacancy takes place, I really think that the matter might be managed.[15]

Here are Hunt's own words of 1810 about the ridiculousness of the laureateship, and they suggest a minor puzzle. Had Macaulay read them in one of the bound volumes of *The Examiner,* or had Hunt, in writing Macaulay about his hopes, quoted himself and attempted to reconcile his past statement with his present aspiration? But at least the promise of help was there.

Hunt was later to find out and state in his ***Autobiography*** "that Lord Melbourne considered it proper for no man to have a pension given him by one sovereign, who had been condemned in a court of law for opposing another."[16] However, Melbourne had at least mentioned Hunt's name in connection with a pension. In writing to Lord John Russell from Windsor Castle, July 18, 1841, some few months apparently after his discussion with Macaulay, Melbourne discussed what to do with the seven hundred pounds newly available for pensions. His list is a sardonic one and seems to consist only of people who should not receive aid.

> The list of applications which I have comprises Mrs. James, widow of the writer of the Naval History; Leigh Hunt, distinguished writer of seditions and

treasonable libels; Colonel Napier, historian of the war in Spain, conceited and dogmatic Radical, and grandson of a duke; Mr. Cary, translator of Dante, madman; Sheridan Knowles, man of great genius, but not old nor poor enough for a pension.[17]

It is at least interesting to see that Sheridan Knowles is valued more highly than either Hunt or Cary.

In the meantime, Southey sank further and further into mental and physical decay but did not die. Hunt was to have further opportunities for taking over the duties if not the office of the laureate. On the 8th of February, 1842, he contributed to the *Morning Chronicle* **"Three Visions Occasioned by the Birth and Christening of His Royal Highness, the Prince of Wales."** The third of the visions is of the Queen, seated with the new prince in her arms, resolving to do something for the poor. Like the other poems to the royal children, this is in tetrameter, the meter already made famous by Ambrose Philips in his verses to children.

A further attempt to establish himself as royalty's bard came in April of 1842 with the publication of *The Palfrey,* to which Hunt prefixed an Envoy, printed just after the title-page in most elaborate type. It was sent to the Queen via Lord Melbourne, to whom Hunt addressed a somewhat tactless letter, mentioning that he cannot be supposed to be self-seeking in addressing "one who is no longer Premier."[18] The letter is full of that embarrassment which usually affected Hunt in correspondence when he wanted a favor. Lord Melbourne sent the letter on to the Queen, with a short covering letter of his own. In spite of the sardonic way in which he had referred to Hunt in the previous year in his letter to Lord John Russell, already quoted, he is careful not to prejudice the Queen, saying merely that "it is a very gay and lively work, and has in it some wit and fun."[19]

Finally the blow fell. In February 1843 Southey suffered an apoplectic seizure and died on March 21. The laureateship was offered immediately to Wordsworth and was, after a first refusal, accepted. From this date, Hunt's opinion of Wordsworth was to sink, although he did not make any obvious attack upon the older man, and indeed got past his initial disappointment with some grace. Hunt must have been conscious that his attempts at carrying out the laureate's duties had attracted attention. A final poem, **"Lines on the Birth of Her Majesty's Third Child, a Princess, April 24th,"** appeared in the *Morning Chronicle* on the 5th of May, 1843. The opening verse paragraph has its own sad pride.

> Though the Laurel's courtly bough
> Boast again its poet now,
> One with verse, too, calm and stately,
> Fit to sing of greatness greatly,
> Granted yet be one last rhyme

To the Muse that sang meantime,
If for nought but to make known
That she sang for love alone;
That she sang from out a heart
Used to play no sordid part;
That howe'er a hope might rise,
Strange to her unprosperous eyes,
Ere the cloud came in between
All sweet harvests and their Queen,
Still the faith was not the fee,
Nor gratitude expectancy.
Oh! the soul that never thought
Meanly, when a throne it fought,
Was it not as far above
All that's mean, with one to love?

This is the first time for some years that Hunt has remembered in public that he had fought the throne, and it is the first public acknowledgment of what must have been all too clear to the literary world, that he had hoped for the laureateship. Although a fecund Queen continued to furnish occasions connected with her happiness for some years to come, they remained uncelebrated by Hunt.

In 1847, when Melbourne had been long out of power, Hunt was granted a pension, which, although it did not solve his financial problems—nothing could have done so—at least alleviated his recurrent distress. In these years after 1843, Hunt remained an extremely active literary man, producing at least a volume a year and meeting with considerable success. Then, the great opportunity recurred; Wordsworth died in April, 1850, and the laureateship was again to be disposed of. This time there was no one in office who would help him as Macaulay had attempted to do, and Hunt was forced to recommend himself. Hastily he set himself to produce an autobiography, and in doing so he produced his best-known work. He had been attempting to produce an autobiography ever since his first drafts of 1827 had resulted in a long and attractive portion of *Lord Byron and Some of His Contemporaries,* where the reminiscences had failed of their proper notice because of the storm raised by other portions of that hasty and ill-judged book. In 1847, Hunt had signed a contract with Smith, Elder and Company for an autobiography, but had accepted the down payment and failed to get to work. The publishers had been prodding him with the most effective instruments, further payments and the right to have a hack come in and revise Hunt's own work for immediate publication. Now he hastened to put together passages from his earlier work, and some of the Wishing-Cap papers he had sent back from Italy a quarter-century earlier, to write a great quantity of new material, and thus to produce a first-rate book. It had one great oddity, which has been generally obscured by the fact that modern editions are all based on the revision which came out in

1860, the year after Hunt's death. The final chapter as it originally stood is a clear bid for the laureateship.

He speaks of his "effusions of gratitude which constituted me for a time a 'volunteer laureate,' and which are thought by many to have given me a claim to the office."[20] He explains that he is not of the opinion himself which these 'many' hold and then goes ahead to explain that he would be a far better court poet than most, not merely in poetical qualities, which he admits that he possesses, but also in honest devotion to the monarch. There are however a few reasons why he should not have the office, "And had it been becoming in me to suppose that the laureateship would have been offered me on the death of Mr. Wordsworth (which has taken place but a short time before these words are written), I should have stated at once, in the proper quarters, what I am observing at this moment."[21] He then points out that he has not the proper aristocratical notions, although he is "a royalist of the only right English sort," nor the proper orthodoxy in religion, and refers very vaguely to "the fancied indecorum of appearing in a place, where any previous connexion of it, however different from its existing connexions, may have been set by him in a disadvantageous light."[22] It is hard to imagine a more nebulous reference to a conviction and imprisonment for libeling the sovereign. But all this delicacy was to go for nought. The laureateship was offered to Samuel Rogers, who refused on the score of age; it was rumored that Mrs. Browning would be named; and then, after the office had been vacant for six months, it was offered to Tennyson in November 1850. Samuel Rogers at least had some amusement and subject for conversation out of the affair, since Tennyson, like Wordsworth before him, borrowed Rogers' court dress in which to be presented.

Leigh Hunt, at sixty-six, could not hope for another opportunity during his lifetime. Later editions of the *Autobiography* omit all the argument stated above, and the occasion for the book is not clear in modern editions. If Hunt was to be disappointed in his hopes, at least the work that the longing for the laureateship stimulated into being has done more to keep his name alive than any other of his prose volumes.

Notes

1 *Examiner,* III, 34 (January 21, 1810).

2 *Examiner,* VI, 513 (August 15, 1813).

3 Ed. H. Milford (London: Oxford University Press, 1923), p. 319.

4 George Dumas Stout, "Leigh Hunt's Money Troubles: Some New Light," *Washington University Studies,*

Vol. XII, Humanistic Series, No. 2 (1925), p. 223. The letters quoted by Professor Stout are in the Pforzheimer Library.

5 *Monthly Repository,* 1837, p. 14.

6 *Ibid.,* p. 85.

7 *Ibid.,* p. 373.

8 *Ibid.,* p. 379.

9 *Lord Melbourne's Papers,* edited by Lloyd C. Sanders (London: Longmans, Green and Co., 1889), p. 509n. One of these grants had come during the reign of William IV, whom, rather curiously, Hunt claims to have regarded as a reformer and thus never attacked. Cf. *Autobiography,* edited by J. E. Morpurgo (London: Cresset Press, 1949), p. 421 and p. 443.

10 *Ibid.,* pp. 509-510.

11 *Henry Crabb Robinson on Books and Their Writers,* edited by Edith J. Morley (London: J. M. Dent and Sons, 1938), II, 579.

12 *Autobiography,* p. 449.

13 *Ibid.,* p. 450.

14 *Edinburgh Review,* LXXII (Jan., 1841), p. 490.

15 *The Correspondence of Leigh Hunt,* edited by His Eldest Son (London: Smith, Elder and Co., 1862), II, 9-10.

16 P. 443.

17 *Lord Melbourne's Papers,* p. 511.

18 *The Letters of Queen Victoria,* edited by A. C. Benson and Viscount Esher (London: John Murray, 1907), I, 517.

19 *Idem.*

20 *Autobiography of Leigh Hunt* (London: Smith, Elder and Co., 1850), III, 275. The actual copy consulted is the unique example in the Brewer Collection in the State University of Iowa library. This is from the library of Edmund Gosse and is specially bound in boards, having been made up of the first sheets, as a special volume for Alexander Elder, the publisher. Elder followed the same practice with other authors, such as the Brontes, published by his firm.

21 *Ibid.,* 275-276.

22 *Ibid.,* 276-277.

Hunt's remarks about Christmas in England (1817):

Christmas is a dreary business, compared with what it used to be in old times; and scarcely one of the other national holidays is alive. We shall give some accounts of them in the progress of our remarks; when the reader will be struck with the contrast as we were. The nation hardly appears to be the same. There is scarcely a vestige of the rural and out-of-door part of the festivities. In London particularly, nothing of that sort remains but the dancing of the chimney-sweepers on May-day, as if in mockery; and even at Christmas, every thing is withdrawn in doors, and done there with as little mirth as may be. Not even a bough appears in the windows, instead of the universal leafiness that used to take place, from the palace to the stall, as if a rural city had started up in the midst of winter. An air of constraint, and business, is thrown over every thing; and the holiday is rather transacted than enjoyed. There is a difference in different houses; but we are speaking generally. Personal character here and there prevails over custom; but the common amount of the merry-making consists of drawling through the morning either at church, or at home, or in some gaping *bit* of a walk,—having a dinner of roast-beef and plum-pudding, or mince-pies,—and sitting down in the evening to cards, which, in favour of the young people, are for once and a way made something like pleasure instead of profit, and allowed to be a round game. But even this pretended kind of holiday-keeping is by no means general.

Leigh Hunt, in "Christmas and Other Old National Merry-Makings Considered," December 21, 1817, reprinted in Leigh Hunt's Political and Occasional Essays, *edited by Lawrence Huston Houtchens and Carolyn Washburn Houtchens, Columbia University Press, 1962.*

Donald H. Reiman (essay date 1985)

SOURCE: "Leigh Hunt in Literary History: A Response," in *The Life & Times of Leigh Hunt,* edited by Robert A. McCown, Friends of the University of Iowa Libraries, 1985, pp. 73-100.

[*In the following essay, Reiman evaluates Hunt as one of the most influential Romantic writers—one who should be judged not just for his literary merits but also for his wide-ranging contributions to English culture.*]

William Charles Macready recorded in his diary for 30 March 1839 a dinner meeting of the Shakespeare Club when Dickens was in the chair. After a number of speeches, Macready writes, "Leigh Hunt was called up, being an honorary member and guest of the day, and in a rambling, conversational style talked of what

Shakespeare would think if he could walk into the room and ask on what man's account all this festivity and sympathy was raised, and how surprised and pleased he would be to learn that it was himself."[1] We may suppose that Leigh Hunt's own surprise and delight could not have been less than that he imagined for Shakespeare, should he have observed the festivities at Iowa City in his honor. Yet, as two papers in the symposium reminded us, Hunt was himself a center of controversy in his own lifetime and remains so today, insofar as he holds a place in the consciousness of students and teachers of literature. Forty pages earlier, Macready's diary records an evening when Hunt may have been the center of such a difference of opinion. On 19 June 1838, John Forster, Hunt's most loyal friend of that period, had invited Macready and two others to his rooms "to sup and hear Hunt's play" (*A Legend of Florence*). As Macready records the evening, "we supped and talked, not very harmoniously on the subject of the plan for opening the theatre next season. Forster quite lost his temper."[2] Hunt's dual power to elicit admiration and to stir contention will be evident in this paper.

When I began to write it, I intended simply to venture farther out on a limb than any of the four earlier speakers had chosen to go, by attempting to characterize and evaluate Hunt's entire career and his significance for English letters and society. I undertook this effort in full awareness of its ultimate impossibility. (The task reminds me of the professor of geology who asked his students to consider the Grand Canyon as a [w]hole.) But I did so secure in the knowledge that I was not being followed on the program by a respondent with a reputation for lancing the bubbles blown by other generalizers. One of the four papers, however, contains some problems that require closer examination. Therefore, my response will consist of three parts: in the first and third, I shall draw on the topics raised in the four papers to try to give an overview of Hunt's significance for English literature; in the second, I shall examine the problems raised in one of these four papers and adduce evidence that points to conclusions quite different from those reached by one of my colleagues.

I

My thesis is a simple one. Leigh Hunt was one of the dozen most important British writers of the Romantic period and, in addition, an important living cultural influence throughout the age of high Victorianism. The handful of his Romantic contemporaries who deserve to rank with him (and, in several cases, before him) are six poets, whose names I need not rehearse here,[3] the essayists Lamb and Hazlitt, and three novelists—Scott, Austen, and Godwin (the last being at least equally important for the impact of his nonfictional prose on the others I have mentioned). Being classified as one of a dozen may not seem high

praise until I name a few of the writers whom Hunt far exceeds in importance: De Quincey, Southey, Moore, Jeffrey, Cobbett, Lockhart, James Hogg, Peacock, Rogers, Campbell, George Crabbe, Beddoes, and John Clare. Some of these writers have been advanced as being better poets, superior prose writers, or more important cultural influences than Leigh Hunt. Yet I believe that my case would be easily proven, not only before an audience as ready to acquiesce to the proposition as you are, but even in a court of law.

Carl Woodring and Charles E. Robinson have spoken so cogently and forcefully of Hunt's merits as an essayist and his potential as a dramatist that there is little more to say. As a poet, during his years of fame at least, Hunt's example was important mainly in a negative sense. In his *Juvenilia* (1801), Hunt mastered the neo-classical conventions of the day. This mastery gave point to his later attacks on French models and neo-classical excesses in the poetry of such minor scions of the tradition gone to seed as William Hayley and Erasmus Darwin. Hunt's doctrine gave Keats and younger writers a rationale for their stylistic experiments. But Hunt's own poetry of the *Examiner* years ran to an opposite extreme of journalistic "jauntiness" that relied on facility, rather than judgment.[4] *The Story of Rimini* and the other longer poems on which his early reputation as a poet rested, gave way to the lax puerilities of the poems in *Foliage* that embarrassed both Keats and Shelley.[5] Thus Hunt's poetry is remembered chiefly for the reactions his verse aroused in his friends Byron and Keats and through the attacks and parodies of his enemies. Even Shelley became more of an artist after he saw the consequences of Hunt's failure to do so.

Hunt's reputation as a poet now rests on a few short anthology pieces, most written later in life, after his contemporary poetic fame was all but dead. These poems are written in very tight forms. Two earlier sonnets, **"To the Grasshopper and the Cricket"** and **"The Nile,"** written in competitions of poetic improvisation, the first with Keats, and the second, against both Keats and Shelley,[6] we read partly out of curiosity. We probably hope to vindicate the canon that we teach by seeing great poets outdistance an average one. But we find that, given the same limitations of time, theme, and form, a facile talent can compete with a great genius on almost even terms. This revelation sends us back to reexamine our definitions of genius and perhaps to wonder whether Thomas Edison might not have been right in ascribing a large part of genius to perspiration—to the working out of the initial conception with patient judgment. We also acknowledge that another distinguishing feature of the great geniuses is that they chose themes that lesser imaginations might not think of at all and worked them out in larger forms than a moderate talent is capable of managing.

Hunt's poems that seem destined to live outside the classroom include **"An Angel in the House,"** a sonnet in couplets; **"The Glove and the Lions,"** written in fourteener couplets, which reduce themselves to "common measure" (ballad stanzas); a **"Rondeau"** (**"Jenny kissed me,"** eight lines), and **"Abou Ben Adhem,"** of just nine closed—if metrically flexible—couplets. The first appeared in 1834, the next in 1836, and the last two in 1838. Thus, occasional verses of the mid-1830s seem to be the high-water mark of Hunt's lasting achievement as a poet.[7] Hunt's poetry was surpassed by several of the secondary writers I have mentioned, particularly Crabbe and Clare. Hunt's limitations as a poet arise from the very qualities that endear **"Jenny kissed me"** and **"Abou Ben Adhem"** to readers— namely, his spontaneity and his tolerance for all kinds of people. Jane Welsh Carlyle, whatever her virtues, was not one who frequently demonstrated, or inspired, such warmth and affection as this:

> Jenny kissed me when we met,
>   Jumping from the chair she sat in;
> Time, you thief, who love to get
>   Sweets into your list, put that in:
> Say I'm weary, say I'm sad,
>   Say that health and wealth have missed me,
> Say I'm growing old, but add,
>   Jenny kissed me.[8]

Loving one's fellow humans, as Abou ben Adhem does, rather than paying lip service to God, was a creed not widely advocated in England during the first half of Hunt's lifetime. This tolerance turns into weakness, however, in Hunt's poem entitled **"Godiva"** (1850), where he not only retells the story without mentioning "Peeping Tom," but even refuses to believe that anyone would be capable of such lascivious meanness.

> A prayer, a tear, a constant mind, a listening
>   ear that glowed,
> These may we dare to fancy there, on that
>   religious road.
>
> But who shall blind his heart with more? Who
>   dare, with lavish guess,
> Refuse the grace she hoped of us, in her
>   divine distress? (*P.W.,* p. 79)

Ultimately, Hunt's failure as a narrative poet results from this incapacity to portray the evil in human nature. (He mitigates this weakness in his dramas, because there the very form requires a conflict.) In Hunt's retelling of the story of **"The Glove and the Lions,"** he condemns the vanity of the lady in the court of Francis the First who purposely drops a glove into the lion pit and then asks her lover to retrieve it in order to display his love for her. But even there, the denouement produces little sense of human evil: the knight emerges unscathed and throws the glove in his lady's face, winning the king's approval. Hunt chooses stories that demonstrate the power of common sense over selfish vanity. He was incapable of writing a *Carmen,* in which human weakness and evil triumph and destroy true love and decency, or even a poem like "The Ruined Cottage," in which circumstances close fatally upon an innocent family. This inability to know what evil lurks in the hearts of men (and, of course, women) and to portray ordinary human suffering—a failure that Dickens exploits in his malicious portrait of Harold Skimpole—enabled Hunt to remain one of the most tolerant and sympathetic figures in English literary history and to applaud and encourage merit wherever he found it, even in such dyspeptic personalities as Benjamin Robert Haydon, William Hazlitt, Thomas Carlyle, and Walter Savage Landor.[9]

Hunt's failure to plumb human evil (which did not prevent him from recognizing and combating all kinds of injustice) cannot be attributed to a lack of intellect or even to some kind of impotence or weakness of character. Rather, a study of Hunt's early life and writings—particularly his *Juvenilia*[10]—suggests that the origins of his views on the nature of man (like the differing views of William Hazlitt) arose directly from the religious views of the parents he loved and tried to emulate. As the youngest and brightest child in a family (like that of Coleridge) made up of older brothers, Leigh Hunt was pampered enough during his childhood to believe that the world was generally a good place. In the early sketches for his *Autobiography,* edited by Stephen F. Fogle from the manuscripts in the Luther A. Brewer Collection, Hunt attributed this pampering to his ill-health when he was a small child, but implicit in the account is another reason—that he was in every sense the baby of the family:

> I was born nine years after my youngest brother now living, & subsequently to great care and sickness on the part of my mother;—the eighth of her children; & the only one of those born in England that have survived. We were of more delicate constitutions than the rest, my self in particular; which is the reason perhaps why I am alive, the greater necessity of the case demanding the greater care.
>
> I had almost every disorder to which infancy is exposed: so that it would be difficult to say whether the attentions necessary for me served to add to the other distresses now threatening my mother, or beguile her of them. . . . [11]

The list of subscribers to the third edition of Hunt's *Juvenilia* (1803) reveals that by the time he had reached early maturity, he had been patronized by British dukes, marquesses, earls, bishops, and nationally known clergymen of all ideological and political persuasions, by leading intellectuals of America and France, and even by such institutions as Harvard College, Columbia University, and the University of Pennsylvania. Such early attention and encouragement, rather than any psycho-sexual peculiarity he may (or may not) have had, can explain his feelings of benevolence and his virtual incapacity to hate. Just as a beaten child will often grow up to abuse even those nearest and dearest to him (or her), someone who receives as much recognition and support during his childhood as Leigh Hunt enjoyed may grow up to be a person of abnormally kind and trusting nature.

Hunt's sunny disposition produced a virtue that remains one of his claims to literary greatness. For he has an admirable record of privately encouraging and publicly praising and defending the best of contemporary writers, artists, actors, and musicians, as well as disseminating great writings of the past. His role as an influential journalist and cultural guru to the rising middle classes gave him an influence out of proportion to the originality of his judgments. But luckily his aesthetic taste (that least predictable of all human faculties) proved—at least on its positive side—to be superior to that of any other critic of the nineteenth century. As Thomas Babington Macaulay (neither a personal nor a political friend of Hunt) wrote in his well known essay in the *Edinburgh Review* on Hunt's edition of *The Dramatic Works of Wycherley, Congreve, Vanbrugh, and Farquhar* (1840), "In some respects, Mr. Leigh Hunt is excellently qualified for the task which he has now undertaken. . . . we find in him what is very rare in our time, the power of justly appreciating and heartily enjoying good things of very different kinds." Hunt not only introduced the developing British middle-class readership to the classics of their own culture and to the great writers of Greece, Rome, and Italy, but he also hailed and aided almost every English writer about whom we still care and who published during his tenure as a cultural influence; in most cases, he did so for reasons that we still find valid. Among his greater contemporaries, he praised the poetic power of Wordsworth before it was very fashionable to do so, saw the merits of Hazlitt's mind (and even Hazlitt's temper), valued Byron's poetry for the right reasons, and, of course, encouraged Shelley and Keats at crucial junctures in their careers. His concomitant weakness was that he praised and encouraged a number of other writers who, though his personal friends, did not deserve all the applause he gave them.

It is not claiming too much to assert that, without entering Hunt's circle and meeting Reynolds, Shelley, Haydon, and the many literary and artistic figures there, Keats might never have been able to pursue his destiny as a poet. Prior to his meeting with Hunt, Keats's nearest approximation to literary companions had been George Felton Mathew and Charles Cowden Clarke, the latter a disciple of Hunt. Robert Gittings points out that Keats's first great poem, "On first looking into Chapman's Homer," was inspired by "a book that was going the rounds of the Leigh Hunt circle" and that

Hunt had already praised in *The Examiner*, in his verse epistle to Charles Lamb (25 August 1816). The auspicious October of 1816, during which Cowden Clarke introduced Keats to Hunt and, through Hunt, Keats met Haydon and Reynolds, was followed by the publication (1 December) of Keats's sonnet on Chapman's Homer at the end of Hunt's notice praising three "Young Poets," Reynolds, Shelley, and Keats.[12] There followed a round of literary dinners and evenings that introduced Shelley and Keats, then arrangements (aided by Shelley) to publish Keats's first volume, through Hunt's friend Charles Ollier, and finally favorable notices both in *The Examiner* and by word of mouth throughout Hunt's circle. When response to that book went sour and Keats's relationship with the Ollier brothers ended, John Taylor and Augustus Hessey became Keats's publishers, probably by arrangements made through Reynolds.[13] Nor should we forget Hunt's kindness to Keats during his last illness, when Keats's other friends—most of whom had both greater resources and fewer responsibilities—neglected the dying poet. Only Keats's despair prevented him from appreciating fully what Hunt did in taking him into his house.

Hunt's friendship and encouragement of Shelley in 1816-17 helped Shelley maintain his equilibrium during the most trying months of his life, after the suicide of Harriet Shelley and throughout the Chancery trial for the custody of his children. Even Hunt's financial needs, which occupied part of Shelley's energies during 1817, gave Shelley a sense of worthy purpose that helped him extinguish part of the guilt aroused by Harriet's death. Hunt's childlike qualities, again satirized by Dickens in his portrait of Skimpole, are among those that helped to sustain or renew Shelley's very precarious faith that humanity contained enough good to be worth the sacrifice of oneself (and, sometimes, one's family). It remains a pertinent question whether or not Shelley would have had the spirit to write *Prometheus Unbound,* had he never known Hunt. Here, for example, is the tribute to Hunt in his "Letter to Maria Gisborne," which was written in June 1820, between the time *Prometheus Unbound* was completed and the date it was published. To the Gisbornes, in London, he portrays Hunt as he knew him in 1816-1818:

> You will see Hunt—one of those happy souls
> Who are the salt of the Earth, and without whom
> This world would smell like what it is, a tomb—
> Who is, what others seem—his room no doubt
> Is still adorned with a many a cast from Shout,
> With graceful flowers tastefully placed about
> And coronals of bay from ribbons hung,
> And brighter wreaths in neat disorder flung,
> The gifts of the most learn'd among some dozens
> Of female friends, sisters-in-law and cousins.
> And there is he with his eternal puns,
> Which beat the dullest brain for smiles, like duns

Thundering for money at a poet's door.
Alas, it is no use to say "I'm poor!"
Or oft in graver mood, when he will look
Things wiser than were ever read in book,
Except in Shakespeare's wisest tenderness.[14]

If Shelley had become disillusioned with Hunt, as many of Hunt's friends did, Shelley during his Italian exile might well have moved directly to the realism, satire, and cosmic irony of *Julian and Maddalo, Peter Bell the Third,* and "The Witch of Atlas" on his way to the darker vision informing his truncated final fragment, "The Triumph of Life." Hunt also fostered Mary Shelley's literary career, both through personal encouragement and public approval of her writings and with kindness and sympathy during her times of personal anguish.[15]

Before 1821, when Hunt left England for Italy, he encouraged such other writers as Lamb (whose *Works* he arranged for Ollier to publish in 1818) and some less worthy of his attention, including Bryan Waller Procter ("Barry Cornwall") and Cornelius Webb, whose derivative and flabby romanticism almost justified the harshness of Lockhart's strictures "On the Cockney School of Poetry."[16] In Italy, Hunt recognized the merits of the strangest amphibian of the time—Walter Savage Landor, some of whose manuscripts he later arranged to have published. Once back in England, even with his reputation tarnished and his self-esteem chastened, Leigh Hunt welcomed in his writings and with his friendship a new generation of writers, both major and minor: Tennyson, Carlyle, Elizabeth Barrett, Dickens, Robert Browning, and Thackeray, and such lesser lions as John Forster, R. H. Horne, and William Allingham. Whether or not Matthew Arnold recognized the affinity, Hunt—a reader who had mastered the matter, if not always the tone and moral depth, of the humanistic cultural tradition—had been his senior in the labor of seasoning the Hebraism of the British bourgeoisie with the Hellenism of sweetness and light. Edgar Johnson, Richard D. Altick, and Carl Woodring have all noted that Hunt had been "one of the formative influences of Dickens's own youth." And so he was for most people who entered careers in journalism between 1812 and 1850.[17]

For besides befriending, encouraging, and celebrating most of the major writers who emerged during the second, third, and fourth decades of the nineteenth century, Leigh Hunt was one of the most prominent and exemplary political journalists of the age. H. R. Fox Bourne wrote in his classic study *English Newspapers: Chapters in the History of Journalism:* "worthier Radicals than Cobbett, and a more important newspaper than 'The Political Register,' were coming to the front. The starting of 'The Examiner' by John and Leigh Hunt marks an epoch in the history of journalism."[18] Many journalists of the first half of the century emulated Hunt's example as a liberal writer (using liberal in both its political and educational meanings)—a defender of both the freedom of the press and of the rights of the people to enjoy the freedoms brought by enlarged knowledge. Among the many of Hunt's friend or disciples who were nationally or locally influential journalists were Thomas Barnes, a contributor to Hunt's *Reflector* who as editor of *The Times* of London developed that paper into "The Thunderer";[19] George Henry Lewes, who apart from his relationship with George Eliot was a leading man of letters who popularized both new developments in the sciences and Positivist ideas without neglecting to teach the merits of the arts;[20] John Chalk Claris, a young man of Canterbury, in his youth wrote talented, if derivative, poems in the vein of Byron and Shelley under the pseudonym "Arthur Brooke," but he spent most of his life—nearly forty years in all—as the editor of the *Kent Herald,* winning a local reputation both as a reformer and as a purveyor of his love for literature.[21] Many others also carried on the example of Hunt's early days as the very political, yet also cultural, editor of *The Examiner*—Laman Blanchard, W. J. Fox, S. C. Hall, H. B. Peacock, S. R. Townshend Mayer, and Thornton Hunt, Leigh Hunt's eldest son.[22] Among popularizing men and women of letters who were particularly devoted to Hunt were two couples whose careers have been traced and documented by Richard D. Altick and Carl Woodring—Charles and Mary Cowden Clarke and William and Mary Howitt.[23]

Hunt's example as an editor and journalist led in two directions: As editor and chief political writer for *The Examiner,* he taught the power of knowledge; as editor of *The Indicator, The Companion, The Tatler,* and their later reincarnations, he kept alive the essay periodical that made a study of belles lettres a socializing influence. Hunt styled himself "The Indicator" not only because his typographical sign manual in *The Examiner* was the pointing hand, or indicator; he had read about an African bird that was called the indicator bird because it pointed out to men where honey was to be found (sharing it with them when they had rid the tree of bees). He established that periodical (which Carl Woodring has rightly designated as the apex of his success as a personal essayist) to earn a little extra money when his income was reduced through a loss of circulation by *The Examiner,* because in that paper Hunt had gone to the defense of Richard Carlile's right to his unorthodox religious and political views.[24] During the period of Peterloo, when radicals of the right and left were gaining adherents at his expense, Hunt refused to choose any extreme. Though he remained political all his life, never renouncing or keeping quiet about his liberal opinions,[25] he also refused to compete with Carlile, Cobbett, or Thomas Wooler in demagoguery. Instead, he tried to point the way to the sweetness of more intelligent and higher ethical positions, often through the medium of a friendly chat about daily human experience, or through quotations from some writer of the past with whose opinions Hunt and his contemporaries concurred, as the writer's contemporaries had not. By employing his historical imagination, Hunt brought out the virtues of the writers of the past whom he loved, without attributing to them values that were unknown to their times and places.

Among the lesser literary figures of Hunt's time with whose names I began, William Cobbett thought the system had been corrupted by innovations in the eighteenth century that had overthrown the old yeomanry and squirarchy in favor of bankers, stockbrokers, and Jewish moneylenders. He felt that the whole rotten fabric would have to be torn down and burned to permit a return to the golden age of "Sweet Auburn, loveliest village of the plain." Robert Southey, on the other hand, in his mature years so feared the risks to public order attendant upon major political upheavals that he thought it best to join the establishment and work from within for improvements in the operation of the system; joining Southey in a kind of Janus-person was Francis Jeffrey, spokesman for the new commercial and professional classes, who wished to keep the old machinery of government, but to turn it over to forward-looking lawyers and political economists, who would know how to grease the wheels. Finally, somewhere in the middle, as a tertium quid, stood Coleridge, Shelley, and Hunt, each of whom feared to lose the old moral values in the rush toward material progress, yet who saw that an application of rationality and democracy to the political and social systems could yield great gains for the quality of life. Hunt and his followers kept alive the ideal of a humanistic community that had inspired Dante and Milton, an ideal combining a strong drive toward social justice and cohesiveness with an equally strong commitment to aesthetic values. The question that the more militant utilitarian and corn-law reformers asked in Hunt's time (as the Marxists did later) was whether modern societies could afford the luxury of such a devotion to nature and the arts.[26] That, I take it, is also one of the points of Dr. Carpenter's paper: Did Hunt's acknowledged aestheticism castrate him, so far as the manly values of muscular reformation were concerned? Was he another ineffectual angel, beautiful but irrelevant to greater social concerns?

II

Mary Wilson Carpenter's wide-ranging paper raises more issues than can be addressed in the limited space at my disposal. The original version of her paper, on which I based my response at the symposium, totaled seventy-six pages, including text, notes, and bibliographical appendix. In my initial response, I devoted a substantial portion of my time to considering her grounds for identifying as newly discovered works by Leigh Hunt some thirty-two articles on fine arts and other subjects in *Tait's Edinburgh Magazine,* dating from May 1832 through December 1844. I brought forward evidence from Leigh Hunt's letters, published and unpublished; internal evidence from portions of the articles that Dr. Carpenter quoted; and other evidence as to Hunt's interests, writing style, and even whereabouts on particular dates that did not jibe with his having written those particular articles. Finally, I quoted from Hunt's letters to Carlyle, in which he specifies exactly what he wrote—and did not write—for *Tait's,* clearly excluding no less than nineteen out of the thirty-two articles advanced as his in Dr. Carpenter's paper.[27] If I did not convince her, I did convince a substantial portion of the audience, including several of the scholars who had devoted the most time to the study of Hunt's writings. Rather than beat what I regard as a dead horse, in this paper I shall treat the issues Dr. Carpenter raises about Leigh Hunt's attitudes toward women, sexuality, and the aesthetic—what she chooses to characterize as Leigh Hunt's arrested state of "aesthetic fetishism."

As I read Dr. Carpenter's paper, she pushes her argument in several distinct—and, perhaps, not always mutually supportive—directions. She bases much of her argument about Leigh Hunt's attitudes toward female beauty and the relations between men and women on a few articles and poems that, I would say, are taken out of their historical contexts and creatively misread. She then characterizes Hunt's attitudes toward women and his psycho-sexual posture, which she denominates "aesthetic fetishism" and declares that this attitude betrays his "aesthetic impotence."

Those of us who have attempted psycho-sexual readings of literary lives and works know that any validity we may hope to achieve—any value that our perspective may possess—depends upon an absolutely Gibraltar-firm foundation of demonstrable biographical fact and an equally careful understanding of the conventional, as opposed to the individual, elements in the literary works we seek to explicate at their underlying, psycho-sexual levels. With Leigh Hunt's most carefully wrought works, written during the best documented periods of his life—such a poem as *The Story of Rimini,* for example—this kind of foundation in credible fact might be established. But for the early 1830s—the years that Dr. Carpenter has chosen to center on, the present inchoate state of Leigh Hunt scholarship, in which there is neither an adequate bibliography, nor a reliable edition of his poems, his prose, or his letters, nor even a reliable up-to-date biography, such a task is well nigh impossible. Many people who have spent a great deal more time studying Hunt's life and works than has Dr. Carpenter would avoid undertaking so formidable a challenge. I do not pretend to have read all of Hunt's published and unpublished poetry, prose, and letters of this period. But having worked for nineteen years in a library that has a collection of Leigh Hunt's manuscripts and books—and manuscripts written by Hunt's friends and members of his circle—second only to the

Luther A. Brewer Collection; and having edited and written about his life and art through those years in my work on *Shelley and his Circle,* I have had some opportunity to study his character and attitudes. My considered opinion is that Dr. Carpenter's paper takes views that Leigh Hunt expressed for a particular occasion quite out of their contexts in his life and career and invests them with meanings that further study would convince her do not essentially belong to them.[28]

It would prove valuable if someone were to analyze the popular press's treatment of women during the early decades of the nineteenth century to determine whether or not there was a shift in the conventions by which women were judged in British society between 1796, when Thomas Gisborne first published his *Enquiry into the Duties of the Female Sex* (which went into its fifth edition by 1801), and 1837, the date of Mrs. A. Walker's *Female Beauty, / as preserved and improved by / Regimen, Cleanliness, and Dress, / and especially by the / Adaptation, Colour and Arrangement of Dress, / as variously influencing the / Forms, Complexion, & Expression of Each Individual, / and rendering / Cosmetic Impositions Unnecessary. / . . .* [29] Or, why did one of the most intellectual and independent women-of-letters during the 1830s and 1840s edit an annual gift book entitled the *Book of Beauty?*[30] Such annuals and the monthly magazines were the mass media of the day; as such, they both helped to establish, and were subject to, conventions that were ultimately imposed at least as much by the consumers as by the producers of mass journalism. Had the women of England, during the course of those forty years, been reduced from being treated as moral agents, with specific responsibilities and privileges (as they were viewed by both Thomas Gisborne and Mary Wollstonecraft), to being viewed—and regarding themselves—primarily as aesthetic objects for the adornment of their husbands' dinner parties?[31] To explore this socio-psychological avenue would utilize the time-tested methods of research in depth exemplified by Richard D. Altick in *The English Common Reader,*[32] or might at least emulate the approach, deriving from Foucault, that is being developed in this country by such critics as Edward Said and Frank Lentricchia.[33]

Dr. Carpenter, however, does not dig into the contextual background at all to establish the milieu against which to judge the individuality of Leigh Hunt's treatment of women in his writings or in his life. Instead, she turns to Leigh Hunt's *Autobiography* in search of the origins of the sexual attitudes she finds in his *New Monthly Magazine* essay on female beauty. Ignoring thousands of pages of other writings by Hunt and numerous contemporary letters and memoirs detailing his attitudes and, above all, his *behavior* toward women—his wife, his sister-in-law, his daughters, his friends such as Mary Shelley, Clara and Mary Novello, and Jane Welsh Carlyle—Dr. Carpenter identifies as the epitomizing sign of Hunt's psycho-sexuality his expression of an innocent love for his

four- or five-year-old sister when Hunt was six or so, and Hunt's amusement at his tiny sister's ignorance of the French language that led her to think that *"lit"* was her brother's name, rather than the word for bed. Dr. Carpenter reads the anecdote and the fact that little Mary Hunt died soon afterwards, as a sign of Hunt's incestuous yet innocent/impotent love for his sister and an early symptom of his aesthetic fetishism, manifested in later life as an admiration of hair as a symbol of female beauty. This kind of symbolic psycho-biography—or semiotic reading of biographical anecdote—based on the narrowest evidence and in the face of a mass of unconsidered and, in this case, contradictory facts,[34] does not convince me of anything about Leigh Hunt, but rather leads me to doubt the validity of the methodology.

Hunt's anecdote about his childish singing to his young sister, both in its context in the final version of Hunt's *Autobiography* and in its earlier form and context, as edited by Stephen F. Fogle from Hunt's manuscripts in the Luther A. Brewer Collection, seems to me to project psycho-sexual meanings quite different from those that Dr. Carpenter elicits from it. The changes between the two extant versions, as well as an essay in *The Indicator* in which Hunt alludes to his dead sister, provide the key to its significance. In the early draft version, the song *Dans votre lit* is mentioned in connection with little Leigh Hunt's infatuation, not with his sister, but "Miss C. . . . . ., daughter of an eminent chymist, who used to encourage me to sing with her." The theme of the passage is that "the sex made an impression upon me very early. . . . "[35] When Hunt later prepared this passage for publication, perhaps heeding the advice of prudential friends, he downplayed his sexual precocity by placing the anecdote entirely among the innocent associations of his mother and the little sister who died in childhood. If there are Freudian overtones, they do not concern the sister (whose grave Hunt mentions in his *Indicator* essay of 5 April 1820 entitled "Deaths of Little Children," where she obviously functions as an example—symbol in the Coleridgean sense—of pre-sexual innocence[36]), but Hunt's Oedipal feelings for his mother, whose devotion to her youngest surviving child he repeatedly emphasizes. The change of the story from the early drafts to the first edition, designed to mask the strength of Hunt's sexuality, may not have succeeded, so far as most post-Freudian readers are concerned, but in the context of his whole life, aesthetic fetishism is not one of the hidden meanings suggested by his rewriting of the anecdote.

As my earlier evaluation of Hunt's career suggests, I do not believe that he was impotent as a writer; his ten children and the testimony of numerous women who met him go far toward affirming that he was an exceptionally attractive, charming, and virile man. One reason that he did not have to be *macho* in his writings was that he—unlike both Byron and Carlyle—had no reason to doubt his own masculinity.[37]

Charles Richard Sanders's study, "The Correspondence and Friendship of Thomas Carlyle and Leigh Hunt" (see note 9), not only surveys the entire warm and open relationship between the two men and their families, but it also treats in some depth their differing ideas of sexual behavior. Hunt's relations with Jane Welsh Carlyle may provide the focal point for the entire topic. Sanders writes of the occasion of **"Jenny Kissed Me"**:

> She was not given to kissing men other than her husband and close relations, but she enjoyed a flirtation and unquestionably found Leigh Hunt, like Tennyson, an extremely attractive man. Three years before [i.e., 1835] she had been greatly amused when her friend Susan Hunter, . . . later Mrs. J. H. Stirling, on a visit to her in Chelsea had been completely swept off her feet by Hunt's masculine charm.

At the end of a long letter to her husband, describing the behavior of her two friends, Jane Carlyle says:

> I believe they would have communicated their mutual experiences in a retired window seat till morning--*"God bless you Miss Hunter"* was repeated by Hunt three several times in tones of everincreasing pathos and tenderness as he handed her down stairs behind me. Susan for once in her life seemed of apt speech. At the bottom of the stairs a demur took place: I saw nothing but I heard . . . what think you?—a couple of handsome *smacks!* and then an almost inaudibly soft God bless you Miss Hunter! Now just remember what sort of looking woman is Susan Hunter and figure this transaction! If he had kissed me it would have been intelligible, but Susan Hunter of all people![38]

Later Sanders remarks, "Hunt undoubtedly had great admiration for Mrs. Carlyle and did much to spread her reputation as an extremely clever woman and talker," leading Carlyle's brother John to complain: "Leigh Hunt took to saying that she was really an eloquent woman, & Hunt's disciples (of whom he had always a considerable number) repeated the dictum, &, as usual, going further than their master, began to speak of her as quite a woman of genius. One . . . said that Mrs Carlyle was a Scotch Madame de Staël. 'Yes" rejoined W [?Wordsworth], '& a *very* Scotch one.'"[39]

Keeping in mind these openly affectionate feelings between Jane Carlyle and Hunt, one may find just a hint of jealousy or sexual rivalry in some of the arguments between the two men, as recounted by John Hunter, an Edinburgh lawyer (and Susan Hunter's brother); Hunter recorded in his diary for 8 April 1840, an evening of debate and discussion at the home of George L. Craik that was centered on these two men:

> Carlyle and Hunt were in great force, and came out in the course of the evening in their full strength. . . . I do not mean to make any attempt at giving an account of the conversation. That is out of the question in the present instance. It lasted without interruption from five till near twelve o'clock, and embraced the most multifarious subjects. We had the Scottish Kirk, Wordsworth, Petrarch, Burns, Knox and Hume, the Church of England, Dante, heaven and hell, all through our "glowing hands"; and strange work was made with most of them. . . . Carlyle . . . had been declaiming against Wordsworth, whom he represented as an inferior person to Cowper, adding that from the *débris* of Robert Burns a thousand Wordsworths might have been made. We laughed at all this, especially when we found that he had never read, or, at least, had no recollection of "Laodamia" and various other things in which Wordsworth's finest powers are exhibited. We next came to Petrarch, whom he crushed to sapless nothing in his grasp. I stood out a good while on this subject, as did Hunt and Craik. At last Carlyle said—"All I have to say is, that there is one son of Adam who has no sympathy with his weak, washy twaddle about another man's wife. I cast it from me as so much trash, unredeemed by any quality that speaks to my heart and soul. . . ."

John Hunter reports that he himself answered, "Then I would say of you that you are to be pitied for wanting a perception which I have, and which I think, and the world in general will think, I am the richer for possessing . . . ," and that he went on to compare Carlyle to a blind man; then:

> A slight shade passed over his face at this, and he said—"Well, I admit you are right to think so, whatever I may think of the politeness of your saying it as you have now done." Hunt interposed to the rescue with, "Well, that's very good. Carlyle knocks down all our idols with two or three sweeps of his arm, and having so far cleared his way to us, he winds up by knocking down ourselves; and when we cry out against this rough work, he begins to talk of—politeness!" This was followed by a peal of laughter, in which Carlyle joined with all his heart . . . (Sanders, pp. 60-61)

If we recall the story (from Diderot) that Miguel de Unamuno cites in *The Tragic Sense of Life,* in which the eunuch sent to learn the aesthetics of selecting beautiful girls for the harem admits that he is not equipped to learn that kind of aesthetics,[40] and we remember that Thomas Carlyle may have been impotent and Jane Welsh Carlyle a virgin, we may find Carlyle's inability to appreciate Petrarch's "twaddle about another man's wife" in an argument with the author of **"Jenny Kissed Me"** to be of more than passing semiotic significance. As Molly Tatchell reminds us, Leigh Hunt's philosophy always provided for free love, under the proper conditions (though he left it to his son Thornton to carry out the practice).[41] When Emerson visited England in 1848 and expressed displeasure at the number of prostitutes on the streets of Liverpool and London, Dickens upheld the custom of young men hurrying out to lose their virginity before marriage. Hunt was not present, but Dickens took it upon himself to convey his opinion: "Leigh Hunt," he said, "thought it indifferent."[42] But that is not the impression that Hunt himself gives in a letter to Carlyle dated 28 May 1833, about the latter's essay on Diderot. He writes:

> . . . do you not beg the question . . . in favour of that very odd & most on-all-hands-proposed "sacrament" of marriage? an experiment which I should hardly think can be said to have succeeded in the world, even in this chaste & hypocritical & Mamma-sacrificing country of England, where . . . I hate as hard as I can the *nation boutiquière,* with their love of pence & lords, & their sacrifice, in the metropolis, of a sixth part of the poor female sex for the convenience of prudential young gentlemen & the preservation of chastity in the five remaining classes of shrews & scolds, & women good & bad, & wives happy, unhappy, & crim-con-ical. . . . As to "Dennis" [Diderot], I hate his treatment of his wife, . . . & I cannot comprehend how he could write about his bodily ailments in that manner to his "Veneres Cupidinsque"; except that the French have an art of neutralizing the grossest things by putting on a face of impudent innocence about them.[43]

There his ideas about relations between the sexes seem to emphasize the need for a single standard of sexual conduct for men and women so that British society can stop exploiting thousands of young women as prostitutes—and stop giving young men the idea that women are to be used, rather than loved.

One of the best places to look for phallic images in Hunt's writings, to ascertain just how dismembered or fearful of castration he might have been, is in his little volume entitled *Captain Sword and Captain Pen* (1835). This volume combines a childlike poem by Hunt with simple illustrations by his son Thornton[44] and Hunt's powerful prose "Postscript; Containing Some Remarks on War and Military Statesmen." The work was, by the circumstances of its publication, an openly political act. Issued by Charles Knight, publisher for the Society for the Diffusion of Useful Knowledge, it was glowingly dedicated to Lord Brougham, the moving spirit of that Society, whom Hunt praises as "great in office for what he did for the world" and "greater out of it in calmly awaiting his time to do more. . . . " The dedication, dated 30 January 1835, clearly alludes to the governmental crisis that was to drive the Tory ministry of Robert Peel and the Duke of Wellington out of office in April 1835 and return the Whigs to power.[45]

The poem *Captain Sword and Captain Pen* strongly attacks military leaders, such as Wellington, who is the obvious object of much of the satire. Hunt makes much of the *macho* general's "manly pride" and the fact that "the ladies lov'd him more for his scorn, /

And thought him the noblest man ever born" (p. 3). After Captain Sword's great victory, he returns to hold "the hand of a fair ladye" (p. 13) and delights at a ball in dancing "the waltz, that loveth the lady's waist;"

> And the high-stepping minuet, face to face,
> Mutual worship of conscious grace;
> And all the shapes in which beauty goes
> Weaving motion with blithe repose.
> (p. 14).

Meanwhile, a poor woman and her daughter-in-law, mother and wife of a soldier at the front, hearing news of the "famous victory," imagine that their beloved young man is himself celebrating. But he has actually been wounded and left, with many other wounded men, on the field of battle to die of thirst or be pecked to death by ravens. (Such events actually occurred, as Hunt proves from eye-witness accounts of battlefields: "The field of Waterloo was not completely cleared of its dead and dying till nearly a week!"[46])

While recounting these horrors, Hunt turns to the women who have glorified the hero and tells them not to avert their eyes from the consequences of their admiration of brute force, as personified in Captain Sword, the military hero. This man of power, maddened with false ideas of his own importance, next tries to take control of the civilian government (as Wellington had already done on two occasions), but eventually Captain Pen, wielding a phallus of less deadly nature, wins over people through the power generated by knowledge. In the poem's final illustration, designed by Thornton Hunt, a third phallic symbol appears with the pen and the (now sheathed) sword—a large garden spade, being carried by the eldest son of the writer, who is portrayed in his study, surrounded by his children and his books.[47] Lest anyone think that Hunt himself was oblivious of the phallic significance of the symbols with which he armed his two Captains, the prose Postscript uses language that clearly reflects the issues of potency and masculinity that those symbols raise. In declaring the necessity of portraying graphically all the horrors of the battlefield, Hunt chides those who would hide the truth about war: "Moralists and preachers do not deal after this tender fashion with moral, or even physical consequences, resulting from other evils. Why should they spare these? Why refuse to look their own effeminacy in the face,—their own gaudy and overweening encouragement of what they dare not contemplate in its results?" (p. 51). Again, he writes: "To those who tell us that nations would grow cowardly and effeminate without war, we answer, 'Try a reasonable condition of peace first, and then prove it.'"[48] Nowhere, in the poem or in the long Postscript essay, does Hunt either avoid the implications of his phallic symbols, or substitute hair for them. As I mentioned earlier in another connection, at this period Hunt was fully aware of his own potency. On 29 June 1836 he wrote to John Watson

Dalby: "my pen never felt stronger for prose or verse (such as they are)—never so strong, I think, for the latter."[49]

Though collecting locks of hair was a widespread convention in those days before photographs, Hunt gathered an exceptionally fine collection of locks of hair of literary and historical figures.[50] But he treated them, so far as I can determine, just as Byron and Mary Shelley did—as relics and mementoes, not as fetishes. There is absolutely no evidence that he substituted viewing or touching hair for the sexual act, or even that hair turned him on more than it does other people. Like Shelley, Hunt praised women primarily for the intellectual qualities revealed through their *eyes,* as can be seen in his next lengthy poem written after *Captain Sword and Captain Pen.* Hunt's **"Blue-Stocking Revels; or, The Feast of the Violets"** (1837), is a mock-heroic take-off on his earlier mock-heroic *The Feast of the Poets* (1811, 1814, 1815). Here, in a poem devoted primarily to women, we should find evidence of Hunt's supposed preference for insipid beauty and lovely hair diluting his praise of intellectual women—Medusas to him, in Dr. Carpenter's reading—who were at this period his rivals not only for fame, but for the very bread to feed his family. But Hunt mentions hair only once, in a conventional classicist's allusion to that of "bright-haired Apollo."[51] Neither does he condescend to treat beauty as the primary attribute of any of those whom he introduces as intelligent people and significant writers (far more significant, in his estimate, than they were regarded by others in 1837 or are regarded now). In the general introductions, as each woman is greeted at the door and led into the room by Apollo, the host, Hunt writes:

> She walking, he gliding. It gave her such
> grace,
> And made the crowd happy to look in her
> face
> (For never did crowd gather yet at a door so);
> The plain became handsome, the handsomest
> moreso,
> If plain any face can be called that has eyes
> Such as almost all brain with its deep look
> supplies: (*P.W.,* p. 179)

And he introduces "the gorgeous Lady Blessington" (one of his rivals, as a memoirist of Lord Byron, and a woman whose reputation would have made her an easy target) in these words:

> "Lady Blessington!" cried the glad usher
> aloud,
> As she swam through the doorway, like moon
> from a cloud:
> I know not which most her face beamed with,—
> fine creature!
> Enjoyment, or judgment, or wit, or good-nature.

And even if he may be thought to have treated her fabled beauty rather lightly in the lines that follow, he comes across neither as a hair-fetishist nor as a man unmoved by fleshly female beauty.

> Perhaps you have known what it is to feel
> longings
> To pat silken shoulders at routs, and such
> throngings;—
> Well, think what it was at a vision like that!
> A Grace after dinner! A Venus grown fat!
> Some "Elderly Gentleman" risked an
> objection;
> But this only made us all swear her
> "perfection."
> His arms the host threw round the liberal
> bodice,
> And kissed her, exactly as god might do
> goddess.[52]

Hunt praises Sydney Owenson, now Lady Morgan, for her liberal politics:

> And dear Lady Morgan! Look, look how she
> comes,
> With her pulses all beating for freedom, like
> drums,—
> So Irish, so modish, so *mixtish,* so wild,
> So committing herself, as she talks, like a
> child,
> So trim yet so easy, polite yet big-hearted,
> That truth and she, try all she can, won't be
> parted. (*P.W.,* p. 183)

And when the guests are granted visions of the great writers of the past, Hunt mixes his knowledge of the traditions surrounding them with his own jaunty reverence for their greatness:

> I cannot name all who thus issued from air,
> As the god made us see them;—but Sappho
> was there,
> As brown as a berry, and little of size,
> But lord! with such midnight and love in her
> eyes! (*P.W.,* p. 187)

Finally, not only did Leigh Hunt treat the women he knew as individuals and with respect both for their intelligence and for other personal qualities, including their physical as well as their mental and moral charms, avoiding both a male chauvinistic assumption of masculine superiority and a macho need to beat his chest to show his masculinity. He had enough confidence in his whole humanity not only to defend Petrarch for coveting another man's wife (while he treated with patient sympathy his own alcoholic wife), but also to defend the sonnets of Shakespeare that his contemporaries felt nervous about. On 7 May 1838, Peter George Patmore recorded in his diary a dinner-party the previous night "at B——'s" (perhaps Thomas Barnes's) at which a number of editors and journalists, including William Jerdan, Samuel Laman Blanchard, and Leigh Hunt were present:

> The talk after dinner was chiefly *learned*. . . . In the course of this conversation, Hunt referred to some of the *crotchets* of the Greek and Latin poets, or rather versifiers; and to one in particular, who wrote a Latin poem, consisting of three hundred lines, every word of which begins with the letter P. . . .

> . . . towards the end of the evening, there was an admirable talk between B——, Hunt and Blanchard (*apropos* to a supposed contemporary portrait of Shakespeare), on the Shakespeare Sonnets—those at least addressed to Lord Southampton. It was chiefly carried on by Hunt, who gave an admirable (but somewhat *alarming*) account of them, with reference to the equivocal expressions in which they abound, under the supposition of their being addressed to a man. B—— seemed to think that there was no defending them on this point; but Hunt got through it with extraordinary eloquence and beauty, both of style, of thought, and of feeling. . . . There was also another very interesting discusion, in which he took a leading part, namely, on the character of Lord Bacon—the bad parts of which he defended nobly and beautifully, as did B—— also. . . . [53]

Here, as in the debates with Carlyle and his Scottish friends, Hunt held his own, and more. He certainly showed no tendency to circumscribe his intellectual conversation because of prudery or sentimental idealism—"aesthetic fetishism."

In short, Leigh Hunt's writings of the 1830s, as well as the conversations recorded at the time by eye-witnesses, make vividly clear that he did not take a coy or sentimental attitude toward human sexuality and that he neither feared nor patronized women, but appreciated them individually for their intelligence and wit, their character and principles, their talents, and, yes, their physical beauty, when they had any. He was neither a sexist nor a eunuch. William Hazlitt, whose published remarks about Hunt all have a touch of jealousy or rivalry, told the truth about him even as he probed his friend's obvious weaknesses, in his younger days, of fecklessness and vanity. In his essay "The Indian Jugglers," published in *Table-Talk* (1821), Hazlitt writes:

> I know an individual who if he had been born to an estate of five thousand a year, would have been the most accomplished gentleman of the age. He would have been the delight and envy of the circle in which he moved—would have graced by his manners the liberality flowing from the openness of his heart, would have laughed with the women, have argued with the men, have said good things and written agreeable ones, have taken a hand at piquet or the lead at the harpsichord, and have set and sung his

own verses—*nugae canorae*—with tenderness and spirit; a Rochester without a vice, a modern Surrey! As it is, all these capabilities of excellence stand in his way. He is too versatile for a professional man, not dull enough for a political drudge, too gay to be happy, too thoughtless to be rich.[54]

Hazlitt may have intended to belittle Hunt in this passage, by using him as the example of the "clever or ingenious man," as opposed to the "great man" (which appellation Hazlitt may have hoped would be appiled to himself). But Hunt lived on to see William Hazlitt, Jr., another of his younger journalist-disciples, dedicate the third edition of *Table-Talk* (1845) "To Leigh Hunt, whom the author alike admired and esteemed; the 'Rochester without the vice, the modern Surrey,' whom he celebrates in one of these Essays." Even had Hunt no higher tribute than Hazlitt's comparisons, students of the Renaissance and the Restoration would recognize (better, perhaps, than either Hazlitt) the quality of mind and artistic power, as well as goodness of soul and honorable character that Leigh Hunt embodied, according to the universal testimony of his contemporaries.

III

As the British historian G. R. Elton has observed, the student of history who has not mastered a historical period exhibits "a readiness to see the exceptional in the commonplace and to find the unusual ordinary . . . to find the past, or parts of it, quaint." A scholar becomes a "professional" in Elton's terms by "truly understanding an age from the inside—living with its attitudes and prejudices," capable of judging it, not as "a stranger, a visitor from Mars," but as "a contemporary. . . . "[55] To charge Leigh Hunt with a lack of awareness for not always sharing twentieth-century American attitudes about gender, race, religion, national origin, or sexual preference is equivalent to asking why he didn't try to raise his consciousness by watching some TV docu-dramas on those subjects. Leigh Hunt was a leader among his contemporaries in his attitudes on these and other questions, but he was still a man of his time. He did not drive a car or denounce British appropriation of the Falkland Islands; he did not blow-dry his hair or lead a fight for equal pay for equal work. Yet many of the social advances that we take for granted would have been impossible, had not Leigh Hunt and hundreds of liberal journalists who were influenced by his ideas and his example devoted their careers to extend the range of understanding and toleration for people and views differing from the accepted norms of the Victorian establishment.

Why was Leigh Hunt a more important literary figure than many of his contemporaries who bequeathed to us written works of equal, or even greater, power and polish? Because he combined in his various careers, as a political writer, critic of literature and the performing arts, playwright, essayist, poet, editor, and friend of younger writers, enough services to the culture of his time to have produced obvious benefits for our culture, to an extent not true of De Quincey, Southey, Peacock, Clare, and the others against whom we measure him. To those who are not familiar with the period in which Hunt lived and worked, I can try to convey the sense of his impact by analogies that, however imperfect, may help to stimulate historical imagination. Let us imagine a writer in our century who worked hard for almost fifty years to support a large and overdependent family. Imagine that his professional failures were due partly to political persecution (such as being imprisoned for contempt of Congress and blacklisted as a radical) and partly because he lacked a business head and financial prudence. Imagine that during his early years he edited a weekly called *The Saturday Review of Literature* and had the ear of the literate public to the extent that Norman Cousins did. Imagine that he also wrote popular poetry and both encouraged and provided publishing outlets for a whole generation of talented new poets, as Lawrence Ferlinghetti did at the City Lights Bookshop. Next, imagine that he wrote familiar essays for both magazines and daily newspapers that gained him the literary recognition of an E. B. White and the popular following of a Russell Baker. Combining these various careers would produce an approximate equivalent of Leigh Hunt, if twentieth-century America had as small and cohesive an intellectual community as did nineteenth-century Britain and if the impact of the written word were equivalent in the two centuries. But neither of these assumptions is true. In order to suggest the influence of Leigh Hunt in his milieu, we have to add such names as Edward R. Murrow and Eric Sevaried, Alistair Cooke, Bill Moyers, and Robert MacNeil.

Some thirty-five or forty-five years from now, students will look back on the protest movements of the 1960s and 1970s that championed equal rights for repressed or neglected groups in American society, and they will, no doubt, find it quaint that tempers once ran high over issues that by then appear so obvious that they generate no controversy. Those of our generations who survive will try to tell those students why we picketed and boycotted and marched in support of such causes. But, unless we can somehow stimulate their imaginations to put themselves back into the times we lived, they will never understand.

Whenever we apply rigid, categorical structures to the complex flow of human experience, we contribute to the tendency to isolate ourselves from both our ancestors and our posterity. Leigh Hunt, whose imaginative sympathies were greater than those of almost any of his contemporaries, would not attribute to ill-nature our tendency to judge him under foreign laws. But

even Leigh Hunt deserves advocates during his trial. In this volume, Hunt has received a strong defense out of the knowledge and eloquence of four other scholar-critics. My response is little more than a summation of the attitudes and the arguments adumbrated by Richard Altick, Carl Woodring, Charlie Robinson, and David Stam, either in this volume, or in other lectures and publications. The verdict on Hunt's place in literary history awaits the judgment of the readers of this volume and Hunt's readers over the next century—a posterity that will either learn to value his dedication to both truth and good-nature, or will doom itself to repeat a history it has failed to learn.

In a famous analysis of Leigh Hunt and his circle, Thornton Hunt characterized his father as "a devoted idealist" who "actually lived in the world of poetry, painting, and music; coming into the real world only to play his part . . . in the stern unprofitable business of constitutional politics. . . . " This view is not so far as might be thought from the judgment expressed by John Murray to Scott after Leigh Hunt had declined to contribute to the *Quarterly Review* for fear of compromising his political position: "Hunt is most vilely wrongheaded in politics, and has thereby been turned away from the path of elegant criticism, which might have led him to eminence and respectability."[56] It is easy to see Leigh Hunt in this role of a Don Quixote, as Thornton Hunt seems to do. But Mary Wollstonecraft Shelley, who had known Leigh Hunt through good times and bad and who had been given reasons to resent him, if she could, thought of him in 1838, not as a Don Quixote, but as the man of La Mancha who created Don Quixote. After completing her extensive life and critique of Cervantes for *Lardner's Cabinet Cyclopaedia,* Mary Shelley told Hunt as much in two letters. In the first, recently published from the manuscript in the Pforzheimer Library, she says: "In writing of Cervantes so much reminded me of you that I thought it would please you. . . . "[57] And when we turn to Mary Shelley's opening summary of Cervantes' character, we find this:

> For the honour of human nature, and to satisfy our own sense of gratitude, we desire to find that the author of "Don Quixote" enjoyed as much prosperity as is consistent with humanity. . . . This satisfaction being denied us—for he was "fallen on evil days," a poor and neglected man—we are anxious, even at this distance of time, to commiserate his misfortunes, and sympathise in his sorrows.[58]

The 1830s proved to be the nadir of Hunt's life (except for one blow later dealt him by a young novelist he had inspired and befriended). And we who a century and a half after those evil trials wish to commiserate his misfortunes, can also celebrate his strengths and his victories. These victories, true to his unworldliness, were not in the marketplace of best-sellers or popular adulation. But they were inscribed deeply in the annals of friendship. Thomas Carlyle began his famous "Memoranda," arguing that Leigh Hunt was deserving of a government pension, with words that speak of the man's strength and not his sorrows:

> . . . Mr. Hunt is a man of the most indisputedly superior worth; a *Man of Genius* in a very strict sense of that word, and in all the senses which it bears or implies; of brilliant varied gifts, of graceful fertility, of clearness, lovingness, truthfulness; of child-like open character; also of most pure and even exemplary private deportment; a man who can be other than *loved* only by those who have not seen him, or seen him from a distance through a false medium.[59]

Notes

[1] *The Diaries of William Charles Macready, 1833-1851,* ed. William Toynbee (New York: G. P. Putnam's Sons, 1912), I, 505.

[2] Macready, *Diaries,* ed. Toynbee, I, 465.

[3] For the record, the six poets are Blake, Wordsworth, Coleridge, Byron, Shelley, and Keats.

[4] The period of Hunt's greatest influence and attention was probably the decade from 1812, the year of his second trial for seditious libel, through 1821, when he left London for Italy. The controversy surrounding *The Liberal* (1822-1823), his dispute with his brother and nephew over the ownership of *The Examiner* (1824-25), and his attack on the memory of Byron in *Lord Byron and Some of His Contemporaries* (1828) lost Hunt several friends and destroyed much of his éclat among his literary and journalistic contemporaries. During these "Examiner years," Hunt wrote and published *The Feast of the Poets* (1811, 1814, 1815), *The Descent of Liberty: A Mask* (1815), *The Story of Rimini* (1816), *Foliage; or, Poems Original and Translated* (1818), *Hero and Leander, and Bocchus and Ariadne* (1819), *Amyntas: A Tale of the Woods* (translated from Tasso; 1820); he also wrote much ephemeral newspaper verse and *Ultra-Crepidarius: A Satire on William Gifford,* though he did not publish the last until 1823. The standard edition of Hunt's poetry—undoubtedly in need of a thorough revision, as soon as a new edition of his letters is published—is *The Poetical Works of Leigh Hunt,* ed. H. S. Milford (London: Humphrey Milford/Oxford University Press, 1923; hereafter cited as *"P.W."*).

[5] Keats's and Shelley's judgments of the volume must be inferred from the changes of their estimates of Hunt's poetic abilities as they read the poems published in *Foliage.* The day after Keats praised "The Nymphs" in his letter to Hunt of 10 May 1817, he wrote to Benjamin Robert Haydon that he did not think himself "deceived" about his poetic abilities "in the Manner that Hunt is" (Keats, *Letters,* ed. Rollins, I, 138-139, 143). In June 1818, after Hunt's volume appeared, Keats commented that "the Quarterly Reviewers . . . have *smothered* me in 'Foliage'" (*Letters,* I, 294). For Shelley's reactions, see his letter of 22 March 1818 and my comments on his reaction in *Shelley and his Circle,* VI (1973), 523-530, and other comments throughout volumes V, VI, and VII.

Henry Crabb Robinson, on the other hand, admired *Foliage,* "which for the first time had given me a good opinion of Hunt's poetic talents. Some sonnets Davis [Robinson's clerk] has copied for me: they are very beautiful both in thought and expression" (*Henry Crabb Robinson on Books and Their Writers,* ed. Edith J. Morley [London: J. M. Dent and Sons, 1938], I, 222).

[6] Hunt's "To the Grasshopper and the Cricket" (*P.W.,* p. 240) seems inferior to Keats's "On the Grasshopper and Cricket" (both written at Hunt's cottage in the Vale of Health, Hampstead, 30 December 1816), but his sonnet "The Nile" (*P.W.,* p. 248), is clearly superior to both Keats's and Shelley's sonnets "To the Nile," which were also written at the Vale of Health on 4 February 1818. Richard Woodhouse's note to Keats's poem indicates, however, that though the sonnets were to be finished in fifteen minutes and Shelley and Keats kept to this time limit, "Leigh Hunt remained up till 2 oClock in the morning before his was finished" (*John Keats, Complete Poems,* ed. Jack Stillinger [Cambridge: Harvard Univ. Press, 1982] p. 438). If true, this anecdote reinforces my thesis about the contribution of hard work and judgment to "genius," and we can only wish that Hunt had taken equal pains with his other poems before he published them. (Note that Hunt published his sonnet in *Foliage,* whereas neither Keats nor Shelley thought his own sonnet "To the Nile" worthy of publication.)

[7] Hunt himself was aware of his greater mastery—or care—in the composition of poetry during this period. On 29 June 1836, he wrote to John Watson Dalby: "my pen never felt stronger for prose or verse (such as they are)—never so strong, I think, for the latter" (*The Correspondence of Leigh Hunt,* ed. Thornton Hunt [London: Smith, Elder and Co., 1862], I, 289. This edition is hereafter cited as *"Correspondence."*)

[8] *P.W.,* p. 368.

[9] There is, surprisingly, no detailed account of Hazlitt's relations with Hunt, though information is available in the biographies, writings, and letters of the two men. Hunt's relations with Landor are best traced in R. H. Super's *Walter Savage Landor: A Biography* (New York: New York Univ. Press, 1954); with Carlyle in Charles Richard Sanders's two-part study, "The Correspondence and Friendship of Thomas Carlyle and Leigh

Hunt," *Bulletin of the John Rylands Library,* 45 (March 1963) 439-485; 46 (Sept. 1963), 179-216 (reprinted in Sanders's *Carlyle's Friendships and Other Studies* [Durham: Duke Univ. Press, 1977]); and with Haydon in my commentary in *Shelley and his Circle,* VII (Cambridge: Harvard Univ. Press, in press), 89-100.

[10] *Juvenilia; or a Collection of Poems written between the ages of twelve and sixteen.* London: Printed by J. Whiting, 1801.

[11] *Leigh Hunt's Autobiography: The Earliest Sketches,* ed. Stephen F. Fogle. University of Florida Monographs: Humanities, No. 2 (Fall 1959) [Gainesville: University of Florida Press], pp. 11-12.

[12] Gittings, *John Keats* (Boston: Little, Brown and Company, 1968), pp. 80-81. Earlier, on 5 May 1816, *The Examiner* had published Keats's sonnet beginning "O Solitude! if I must dwell with thee," the first of his poems to be published. The standard biographies of Keats by Aileen Ward, Walter Jackson Bate, and Robert Gittings all tell the story of Hunt's early encouragement of Keats; Hunt's encouragement of Shelley and the interaction between the two younger poets is detailed in *Shelley and his Circle,* particularly in my essay, "Keats and Shelley: Personal and Literary Relations," *Shelley and his Circle,* V (Cambridge: Harvard Univ. Press, 1973), 399-427.

[13] See Gittings, *John Keats,* pp. 117-118.

[14] *Shelley's Poetry and Prose,* ed. Donald H. Reiman and Sharon B. Powers, Norton Critical Edition (New York/London: W. W. Norton & Company, 1977) pp. 318-319. Among other relevant documents are: (1) Shelley's dedication of *The Cenci* to Hunt as the person he has known who is most "highly endowed . . . with all that it becomes a man to possess"; the most "gentle, honourable, innocent and brave"; of the most "exalted toleration for all who do and think evil, yet [the most] free from evil . . . "; and (2) Shelley's comments to Hunt in a letter of 10 April 1822, before they were reunited: "Perhaps time has corrupted me, and I am become, like those whom I formerly condemned, misanthropical and suspicious. If so, do you cure me; nor should I wonder, for if friendship is the medicine of such diseases . . . mine has been long neglected . . . " (see *Shelley and his Circle,* SC 739, Commentary; VIII, in press). Elsewhere I suggest that Shelley may have developed the mythopoeic mode that he first utilizes in the *Prometheus Unbound* volume from Hunt's example in "The Nymphs," for which "The Cloud" shows obvious affinities (see VI, 529-530). In July 1819, Hunt wrote to Shelley: "I had thoughts a little while ago of writing a poem myself, entitled Prometheus Throned; in which I intended to have described him as having lately taken possession of Jupiter's seat" (VI, 841). There are, in fact, formal and thematic parallels between

Shelley's "Lyrical Drama" and Hunt's earlier *The Descent of Liberty: A Mask.* Hunt may have worked out some of his ideas later in Captain Pen's overthrow of Captain Sword.

[15] Though Hunt and Mary Shelley treated one another as friends and equals from their very earliest acquaintance, perhaps Hunt's most important aid to Mary Shelley—"Marina" as he called her during Shelley's lifetime—came from July to November 1819, when he wrote frequent and sympathetic letters to Mary, then in despair because of the death of William, her last surviving child. For Hunt's kind—and effective—efforts to help Mary Shelley regain her spirits, see *Shelley and his Circle,* VI (1973), 839-916, 1080-94; for Mary Shelley's reaction, see *The Letters of Mary Wollstonecraft Shelley,* ed. Betty T. Bennett, I (Baltimore: Johns Hopkins Univ. Press, 1980), 101-115. During this same period, Hunt encouraged Mary Shelley's writing in various ways—once by taking a passage from her 24 September letter to him and publishing it as part of his essay, "Autumnal Commencement of Fires," in *The Indicator* for 20 October 1819.

[16] These articles appeared in *Blackwood's Edinburgh Magazine,* beginning in the issue for October 1817 and continuing in various articles and letters (not all under that series title) through October 1819; they have as their leading epigraph, lines from a poem by Cornelius Webb, in which he praises Byron, Wordsworth, Hunt, and Keats in that order. Most of the articles are reprinted in *The Romantics Reviewed,* ed. Donald H. Reiman (New York: Garland Publishing, 1972), Part C, I, 49-117. For a survey and evaluation of Webb's career, see the volume containing two volumes of his poems (as well as one by Charles Jeremiah Wells) in my series *The Romantic Context: Poetry* (New York: Garland Publishing, 1978).

[17] See Edgar Johnson, *Charles Dickens: His Tragedy and Triumph* (New York: Simon and Schuster, 1952), I, 220 and passim; see the papers by Altick and Woodring in this volume.

[18] Fox Bourne, *English Newspapers* (published, 1887; reissued, New York: Russell & Russell, 1966), I, 335 ff.

[19] See Derek Hudson, *Thomas Barnes of "The Times," with Selections from His Critical Essays Never before Reprinted,* ed. Harold Child (1944; reprinted, with a new Preface; Westport: Conn.: Greenwood Press, 1973).

[20] Lewes (1817-1878) planned to write a biography of Shelley as early as 1838, and he published important appreciations of Shelley in both the *Westminster Review* for April 1841 and in volume XXI of *The Penny Cyclopaedia* (1841; for the authorship of the latter and

the connections between the two, see Donald H. Reiman, "Shelley in the Encyclopedias," *Keats-Shelley Journal,* 7 [1963], 55-65). He is noted both for a major biography of Goethe (1855) and studies of the drama and for books of materialist psychology. A selection of Lewes's *Literary Criticism* was edited by A. R. Kaminsky (Lincoln: Univ. of Nebraska Press, 1964).

[21] For Claris, see my introduction to the two volumes in *The Romantic Context: Poetry* series that reprint "Brooke's" six published volumes of poetry (New York: Garland, 1977, 1978). The last of these six—*Elegy on the Death of Percy Bysshe Shelley* (London: C. and J. Ollier, 1822) contains this "Dedication": "To / LEIGH HUNT, ESQ. / The / companion and admirer of the illustrious/ deceased,—/ his friend and fellow-labourer,—/ these / STANZAS / are affectionately inscribed / by / THE AUTHOR./" In fact, a great deal of evidence indicates that Hunt's reputation and influence grew partly as a result of his associations with Shelley and Keats.

[22] All of these journalists except Peacock appear in the *DNB.* For further information on William Johnson Fox, see Ann Blainey, *The Farthing Poet: A Biography of Richard Hengist Horne, 1802-84, A Lesser Literary Lion* (London: Longmans, 1968) and Richard and Edward Garnett, *The Life of W. J. Fox, Public Teacher & Social Reformer* (London and New York: John Lane, 1910). On Samuel Carter Hall, see his *Retrospect of a Long Life: From 1815 to 1883* (2 vols., London: Richard Bentley & Son, 1883); on Thornton Leigh Hunt, see especially Molly Tatchell, *Leigh Hunt and His Family in Hammersmith* (London: Hammersmith Local History Group, 1969); on Samuel Ralph Townshend Mayer, see *Shelley and his Circle,* V (1973), 188; for Henry Barry Peacock (1801-1876), see *Shelley and his Circle,* VII (in press), 82.

[23] Altick, *The Cowden Clarkes* (London [etc.]: Geoffrey Cumberlege/Oxford University Press, 1948); Woodring, *Victorian Samplers: William and Mary Howitt* (Lawrence: Univ. of Kansas Press, 1952).

[24] On Hunt's naming of *The Indicator,* see *Shelley and his Circle,* VI, 912-916; for the negative effects on the circulation of *The Examiner* generated by its defense of Carlyle, see *Shelley and his Circle,* SC 700, Hunt to the Shelleys, "30" February 1820, (VIII, in press).

[25] See, for one example of many, Hunt's strong letter to the *Morning Chronicle,* 18 February 1835, denying the rumor that he has "been writing in a 'Conservative' paper.... Reform is endeared to me by the sufferings and consolations of a whole life; I have written much for it, never a syllable against it; and it is not likely that a cause which I loved in its adversity, and which I still love in my own, I should turn against, now that I have the comfort of seeing it prosper" (*Correspondence,* I, 283).

[26] The strongest statement I know characterizing this problem in Marxist orthodoxy appears in Heinrich Heine's preface to the French edition of his *Lutetia.* It reads, in English, thus: "This confession that the future belongs to the Communists . . . I made in a tone of anxiety and terror. . . . Indeed, I can only think with fear and trembling of the time when these gloomy iconoclasts will come to power. They will pitilessly break all the marble statues of Beauty with their calloused hands. . . . they will destory my groves of laurel and plant potatoes in their place. . . . they will drive away the nightingales, too, those useless singers, and—oh!—my Book of Songs will be used by the grocer to make paper bags into which to pour coffee and tobacco for the poor old ladies of the future" (quoted in *East German Short Stories,* trans. and ed., Peter E. and Evelyn S. Firchow [Boston: Twayne Publishers, 1979], p. xxiv).

[27] The crucial reference appears in the postscript of Hunt's letter to Carlyle date 29 July 1833: "Since 'The World of Books' [published May 1832], I have written nothing in Tait but 'Wishing-Caps'"—thus eliminating the nineteen "new attributions" by Dr. Carpenter that date between May 1832 and July 1833. In pursuing the subject since the 13 April symposium, I have run across what may be a clue to the authorship of at least some of those articles. In the Garnetts' *Life of W. J. Fox* (see note 22), there is mention of a series of letters to Fox from Harriet Martineau: "Her gratitude seems especially evoked by Fox's sympathy with essays written about the middle of 1832 for *Tait's Magazine,* which do not seem to be mentioned in her autobiography. One, relating to woman, she says she wrote with indescribable emotion" (p. 81). If that correspondence by Harriet Martineau to W. J. Fox survives, it may profitably be examined for further clues to the identity of Martineau's essays in *Tait's*—and perhaps the authorship of the essays in question.

[28] Dr. Carpenter has informed me that her paper was not meant to be psychobiographical, but rather a "semiotic" reading. I ask, in this regard: why are the intentions of semiotic critics more important than those of the great creative writers, whose much clearer intentions such critics ignore as a matter of policy?

[29] Gisborne, 5th ed., corrected. London: Printed by A. Strahan for T. Cadell Jun. and W. Davies, 1801. Mrs. A. Walker, London: Thomas Hurst, 1837. These are merely two of many such popular books for women collected by The Carl H. Pforzheimer Library.

[30] I refer, of course, to Lady Blessington, who was editor of *Heath's Book of Beauty* from 1834 to 1847. Lady Blessington's own beautiful portrait appears as the frontispiece for that annual for 1834. George Eliot, as her own portraits make clear, was not a person in a position to make an unbiased assessment of the role

that physical beauty might legitimately play in the appraisal of a woman; and her love for G. H. Lewes, whom Gordon Haight describes as "certainly one of the ugliest men in London" and whose unprepossessing appearance initially engendered in Marian Evans an aversion toward him, may not have given her liberty to speak frankly in her novels of her feelings about masculine good looks (see Gordon S. Haight, *George Eliot: A Biography* [Oxford: Clarendon Press, 1968], p. 128). Jane Austen, the Brontë sisters, and other intellectual women do not dismiss the value of such attributes.

[31] As a number of writers have noted, women at all levels of an agrarian society had more integral roles to play in the social and often in the economic system than the wives of the bourgeoisie in an urban society. Whereas for the aristocracy, antiquity of title or the loftiness of rank or a particularly honorable heritage might substitute for a show of wealth, for the nouveaux riches conspicuous consumption and material display were the only ways to assert their place in society—and a beautiful wife was an important part of such a display.

[32] *The English Common Reader: A Social History of the Mass Reading Public 1800-1900* (Chicago: Univ. of Chicago Press, 1957). Of Hunt's role in generating a veneration for books and literature among the new reading public, Altick wrote: "With men like Lamb and Leigh Hunt, books (especially old ones) aroused emotions almost as fervent as those with which Wordsworth regarded nature. To them, the book was a sacred object, not so much because it contained religious or practical wisdom as because it was the key by which the feelings could be unlocked and the imagination given the freedom it demanded. . . . At first this attitude had little currency beyond a small, select circle. But in the long course of time, popular writers and speakers, having acquired it from their reading of the essays of Lamb, Hunt, and Hazlitt, passed it on to their audiences . . . " (Phoenix Edition [1963], p. 139).

[33] See, especially, Edward W. Said, *The World, the Text, and the Critic* (Cambridge: Harvard Univ. Press, 1983), and Frank Lentricchia, *Criticism and Social Change* (Chicago: Univ. of Chicago Press, 1984).

[34] For example, as Dr. Carpenter's own quotations clearly show, Hunt never mentions hair in connection with his dead sister, but says specifically that the only physical attribute of hers that he can recall is "her blue eyes" (Hunt, *Autobiography* [London: Smith, Elder, 1850]. I, 80).

[35] Fogle, ed. (see note II), pp. 13-14.

[36] "We are writing, at this moment, just opposite a spot which contains the grave of one inexpressibly dear to

us. . . . And yet the sight of this spot does not give us pain. So far from it, it is the existence of that grave which doubles every charm of the spot; which links the pleasures of our childhood and manhood together; which puts a hushing tenderness in the winds, and a patient joy upon the landscape; which seems to unite heaven and earth, mortality and immortality, the grass of the tomb and the grass of the green field, and gives a more maternal aspect to the whole kindness of nature. It does not hinder gaiety itself. Happiness is what its tenant, through all her troubles, would have diffused. To diffuse happiness, and to enjoy it, is not only carrying on her wishes, but realizing her hopes; and gaiety, freed from its only pollutions, malignity and want of sympathy, is but a child playing about the knees of its mother." These words (*The Indicator,* I [5 April 1820], 202) obviously draw upon Wordsworth's early poems, such as "We Are Seven," but they prefigure such sentiments as these in *Adonais:* "a slope of green access / Where, like an infant's smile, over the dead, / A light of laughing flowers along the grass is spread" (stanza 49; *Shelley's Poetry and Prose,* p. 404).

[37] I refer, of course, to Byron's clear bisexuality and to Carlyle's reputed impotence.

[38] I quote Sanders's study (see note 9) from a pamphlet form of the two articles in *Bulletin of the John Rylands Library,* issued by that library, but paginated consecutively 1-85. The present quotation is from pp. 53-54.

[39] Sanders, p. 55.

[40] Miquel de Unamuno, *The Tragic Sense of Life in Men and Nations,* trans. Anthony Kerrigan (Bollingen Series LXXXV, vol. 4; Princeton: Princeton Univ. Press, 1972; paperback edition, 1977), p. III.

[41] See Tatchell, *Leigh Hunt and His Family in Hammersmith, pp.* 59-60, 66 ff.

[42] Quoted from Emerson's *Journals* in Sanders, p. 66.

[43] Sanders, pp. 15-16.

[44] Thornton Hunt, like Hazlitt, first failed in attempts to become a painter before he turned to journalism. The first edition of *Captain Sword and Captain Pen. A Poem, with some remarks on / War and Military Statesmen* (London: Charles Knight, 1835), has been reproduced in photofacsimile, with an introduction by Rhodes Dunlap (Iowa City: Friends of the University of Iowa Libraries, 1984)"To Mark the Bicentennial of the Author's Birth." Edmund Blunden, whose knowledge of the horrors of war entitled him to an opinion on the subject, admired this work, calling it "one of his most remarkable poems" (*Leigh Hunt: A Biography* [London: Cobden-Sanderson, 1930], pp. 266 ff.).

[45] Lord Melbourne's first administration, begun on 9 July 1834 with the retirement of Earl Grey, was dissolved by King William IV in November 1834 on the excuse of the resignation of the chancellor of the exchequer, Viscount Althorpe, when he succeeded to his father's title of Earl Spencer. Wellington had held the seals of office until Sir Robert Peel could be summoned from his travels in Italy; Peel took office as prime minister in December 1834. This government, widely regarded as an attempt by the king and oligarchy to foil the popular will, held on only till April 1835, when Melbourne's government returned. Brougham did not return as lord chancellor; having fought with his colleagues, he was pointedly excluded from the cabinet.

[46] *Captain Sword and Captain Pen* (1835), p. 52.

[47] This portrait of the eldest son more potent than his father (who is also shown as bald—possibly so that Hunt's book would be seen as being in praise of the writer in general, rather than of Hunt himself), may either have Oedipal implications or it may derive from the doctrine of work being expounded by Carlyle, whose writings young Thornton Hunt had been reading earlier.

[48] *Captain Sword and Captain Pen,* pp. 66-67.

[49] *Correspondence,* I, 289.

[50] Appendix 3 in Blunden's *Leigh Hunt* (pp. 368-373) lists the locks of hair and quotes Hunt's comments on them from his "Wishing-Cap" article in *Tait's Edinburgh Magazine* for January 1833. It will be seen that the locks of men's hair far outnumber those of women, and aside from Lucretia Borgia, a single hair of whom had been given to Hunt by Byron (who had pilfered or bribed it from the Ambrosian Library in Milan in October 1816; see *Byron's Letters and Journals,* ed. Leslie A. Marchand, V [Cambridge: Harvard Univ. Press, 1976], 116-118), the women were his literary friends Maria Edgeworth, Mary Shelley, and Elizabeth Barrett Browning.

[51] "Blue-Stocking Revels," Canto II, line 232; *P.W.,* p. 185.

[52] Canto II, 44-55; *P.W.,* p. 181. Hunt even works in a compliment to his wife Marianne, who though never a writer had tried her hand at sculpture and had done the bust of Shelley that Hunt later gave to the Carlyles. Hunt writes of Apollo: "But what pleased me hugely, he called to my wife, / And said, 'You have done Shelley's mood to the life'" (II, 84-85; *P.W.,* p. 182).

[53] Derek Hudson, *Thomas Barnes of "The Times"* (see note 19), pp. 99-101.

[54] *The Complete Works of William Hazlitt,* ed. P. P.

Howe, VIII (London and Toronto: J. M. Dent and Sons, 1931), 83-84; for the information on the third edition of *Table-Talk,* see Howe's note, VIII, 344.

[55] Elton, *The Practice of History* (New York: Thomas Y. Crowell, 1968; copyright 1967), pp. 16-18.

[56] For Thornton Hunt's characterization of his father (which much resembles Leigh Hunt's portrait of *his* father in his *Autobiography*), see Appendix 2 in Blunden's *Leigh Hunt,* pp. 358 ff.; for John Murray's letter to Walter Scott, see Samuel Smiles, *A Publisher and His Friends: Memoir and Correspondence of the Late John Murray* (London: John Murray; New York: Charles Scribners' Sons, 1891), I, 307-308.

[57] Mary Shelley, *Letters,* ed. Bennett, II, 292.

[58] "Cervantes," in *The Cabinet Cyclopaedia,* ed. Dionysius Lardner. *Biography: Eminent Literary and Scientific Men of Italy, Spain, and Portugal,* III (London: Longman, Orme, Brown, Green, & Longmans; and John Taylor, 1837), 120.

[59] Sanders, p. 64.

Timothy Webb (essay date 1992)

SOURCE: "Correcting the Irritability of His Temper: The Evolution of Leigh Hunt's Autobiography," in *Romantic Revisions,* edited by Robert Brinkley and Keith Hanley, Cambridge University Press, 1992, pp. 268-90.

[*In the following essay, Webb contends that Hunt used his* Autobiography *as an opportunity to revise earlier, more openly critical writings in order to express a generous, accepting philosophy.*]

Leigh Hunt was in the first place a circuitous autobiographer. This may have been a result, in part at least, of the rather unfortunate and compromised circumstances in which he was propelled towards his first extended contribution to the emerging genre. After the deaths of Shelley and of Byron, Hunt found himself trapped in Italy, a country which he found essentially uncongenial and harshly out of keeping with the pleasant images conjured up by Italian prints and the *Parnaso Italiano.* The publisher Henry Colburn rescued Hunt from impecunious and irritable exile; Colburn agreed to look after Hunt's financial needs on the understanding that Hunt would produce a 'selection' from his own writings, preceded by a biographical sketch.[1] Not untypically, perhaps, Hunt returned to England but did not honour his side of the bargain. When Colburn eventually pressed him, the original plan was altered in the interests of expediency. Hunt's account of the book's evolution is somewhat contradictory. In the

Preface to *Lord Byron and Some of his Contemporaries* (1828), which was the book's eventual title, Hunt at first seems to claim that the responsibility for the structural alterations was his own: 'I wished to make amends for loss of time: the plan of the book became altered; and I finally made up my mind to enlarge and enrich it with an account of Lord Byron.' The concluding paragraph suggests something rather different:

> The account of Lord Byron was not intended to stand first in the book. I should have kept it for a climax. My own reminiscences, I fear, coming after it, will be like bringing back the Moselle, after devils and Burgundy. Time also, as well as place, is violated: and the omission of a good part of the auto-biography, and substitution of detached portraits for inserted ones, have given altogether a different look to the publication from what was contemplated at first. But my publisher thought it best; perhaps it is so; and I have only to hope, that in adding to the attractions of the title-page, it will not make the greater part of the work seem unworthy of it.[2]

The product of this negotiation and rearrangement was a large, if miscellaneous, book in three volumes whose title reflects some confusion of purpose: *Lord Byron and Some of his Contemporaries; with Recollections of the Author's Life, and of his Visit to Italy* (hereafter referred to as *LBSC*). This new disposition of material was dictated by the generous but shrewd Colburn, who had recently published Thomas Medwin's *Conversations of Lord Byron* and the anonymous *Life and Writings of Lord Byron* and who must have sensed the commercial possibilities of Byron's name. Colburn attempted to capitalize on the devils and Burgundy by arranging for extracts to be printed in *The Athenaeum* in advance of publication. Although contemporary reviewers did not ignore the autobiographical element (*Blackwood's,* for one, maintained its savagely judicial perspective), *LBSC* is largely identified not with Hunt's account of his own life or of his travels but with his uncharacteristically intemperate attack on Byron.

Yet in a strangely roundabout way Hunt's *Autobiography* had its origins in the misconceived, unfortunate, and largely forgotten book 'which Colburn called Lord Byron and his Contemporaries' and to which 'for obvious reasons, my name was suffered to be attached'.[3] When Hunt eventually produced his *Autobiography* in 1850 he did not make a fresh beginning but turned for much of his material to the earlier work. The first volume of *LBSC,* which was devoted to Byron, provided the basis for those parts of Chapter 19 in *Autobiography* on 'Lord Byron in Italy' and on 'Pisa', for part of Chapter 20 on 'Genoa' and for a few pages of Chapter 15, 'Free Again—Shelley in England'. Most of the material which had scandalized the reading public of 1828 by its malicious indiscretions was excluded; the rest now took its place in a chronological sequence which largely followed the course of Hunt's own life,

while leaving room for chapters on 'Literary Acquaintance', 'Political Characters', and 'Keats, Lamb, and Coleridge', which were less obviously integrated into the narrative. These character sketches were based on the materials of the second volume of *LBSC,* where Hunt had given separate treatment to Moore, Shelley, Keats, Lamb, and Coleridge, and a composite chapter to Horace and James Smith, Fuseli and the others who feature under the heading of 'Literary Acquaintance'. The third volume of *LBSC* which bore the general title 'Recollections of the Author's Life', provided the foundation for the opening chapters of *Autobiography* and for the chapters on Hunt's 'Voyage to Italy' and on his 'Return to England'.

There were, of course, many other changes, exclusions, and additions. *Autobiography* is not in any simple sense that product of 1850 which many readers might take it to be. It draws on some but by no means all of those autobiographical materials whose exclusion from *LBSC* Hunt had so much regretted. It is also indebted to the *Letters from Abroad* which had appeared in *The Liberal* and to the two-part essay on the suburbs of Genoa and the country about London which had appeared in *The Literary Examiner* in 1823.[4] There are also various other self-borrowings from Hunt's periodical journalism and from letters. Yet in spite of these important exceptions, the book derives much of its being and its language from *LBSC,* of which it provides a revised and extended version.

LBSC is itself in many ways revisionary, and is often derived from Hunt's own earlier writings. For a number of years he had been in the habit of publishing essays in which he recorded various phases of his life or his experience. These might more properly be described as occasional memoirs rather than as exercises in autobiography, since for the most part they are concerned with impressions, character-sketches, and narratives and not with introspection, self-exploration, or auto-criticism.[5] At times, however, as in *The Wishing-Cap* essays for *The Examiner* (March-October 1824), they allowed Hunt to develop his autobiographical propensities while leaving room for 'any subject to which I feel an impulse, politics not excepted'. Although there is no fixed plan and no systematic development of autobiography, Hunt feels the need to defend at the outset the apparent egotism of the enterprise: 'I believe that if the first person we met in the street were to put down upon paper the experiences he has had in life, his schooldays, journeys, &c. they would be found interesting.' (This is only one example of what seems to have been a recurrent urge to apologize for the autobiographical vein and the use of the first person singular.)

The Wishing-Cap essays range over a wide variety of topics which feature both in *LBSC* and later in *Autobiography:* among other things, they touch briefly on musical evenings at Charles Lamb's house, the Volunteers (in which Hunt served), the literary dinners which Rowland Hunter inherited from Joseph Johnson the publisher, Christ's Hospital, the Thornton family in Austin Friars, Italian scenes, childhood memories of military music in St James's Park, and Hunt's imprisonment. All of these subjects are taken up in *LBSC,* quite often only glancingly but sometimes at greater length, and frequently the borrowing is direct. The longest and most impressive example of self-borrowing is provided by the two essays in which Hunt so memorably describes his imprisonment in Horsemonger Lane. Here for the first time he gave his celebrated account of how he transformed his grim surroundings into a pastoral *trompe-l'œil:* 'I papered the walls with a trellis of roses; I had the ceiling coloured with clouds and sky; the barred windows were screened with Venetian blinds; and when my book-cases were set up with their busts, and flowers and a piano-forte made their appearance, perhaps there was not a handsomer room on that side of the water.' This passage is usually quoted from the 1850 or, more usually, the 1859 version of *Autobiography* but it had first appeared in print as early as 1824. Even then, Hunt's frank response to the circumstances of his imprisonment had drawn upon a still earlier stratum of writings; his primary source was a remarkable sequence of leading articles for *The Examiner* which he had written from Horsemonger Lane immediately after his sentence and in which he had provided a very public reaction not only to his trial and sentence but to the everyday details of his incarceration.[6]

In addition to this, Hunt's portraits of contemporary writers drew heavily on the reviews and assessments of their work which he had published over the years. His accounts of Shelley, Keats, Lamb, Coleridge, Moore, and Campbell were a mixture of biography and criticism informed not only in their larger perspectives but in many of their phrases and formulations by the critical essays which he had contributed to *The Examiner.* The most complex and the most significant area of debt was constituted by the lengthy chapter in *LBSC* on Shelley. In composing this chapter Hunt was able to make use of a long sequence of essays and reviews in which he had defended Shelley against his critics and expounded the virtues of his life and work. These included a series of reviews in *The Examiner,* a number of which specifically defended Shelley against the moral strictures of *The Quarterly;* three further reviews which he had written in 1822 while waiting for calmer seas at Plymouth; passages from **'My Books'** and the second essay **'On the Suburbs of Genoa and the Country about London'** in *The Literary Examiner;* an essay intended for *The Liberal* but never published (and only recently identified); and a longer and quite different essay which was sent to *The Westminster Review* as a review of *Posthumous Poems* but was rejected.[7] The Shelley chapter was most heavily indebted to the re-

view for the *Westminster* but it brought all this material to a focus. As we shall see, Hunt's version of Shelley not only involved a rewriting and recapitulation of his own interpretations but also a corrective revision of the prejudiced and critical attitudes of those who had pronounced judgment on Shelley without any personal knowledge of his life.

Hunt was in the habit of working by means of accumulation and accretion. In the case of *LBSC* the pressure to meet his obligations to Colburn may have encouraged him to draw upon his own miscellaneous efforts at autobiography and reminiscence. No doubt there was an element of convenience in this, and an element of opportunism, but publication in book form and assimilation into a larger structure might also have seemed to offer a more authoritative status to the piecemeal products of periodical journalism. On the other hand, we must remember, too, Hunt's publicly stated disappointment in both the structure of *LBSC* and his inability to make use of many of the autobiographical materials which he had prepared. Although a selective and organizing process was involved, the incorporation of earlier materials into *LBSC* was more cumulative than revisionary. Yet any study of the revisionary practices of *Autobiography* must take into account the methods and the circumstances which generated *LBSC.* As we have seen, *LBSC* itself provided a foundation for much of what was to become the *Autobiography* while in the case of the *Autobiography* itself Hunt's use of his materials was consistently revisionary and reflected not only his dissatisfaction with *LBSC* but several major changes of perspective.

To begin with, Hunt was now in a position to correct various errors and imprecisions and to put the record straight in a number of cases where he had not been able to do so previously. Some of these changes were made for the 1850 edition of *Autobiography* and some for the revised edition of 1859 which continued the process.[8] So, for example, he deleted in 1850 this confusing passage about his brother John who had set up a paper called *The News:* 'I say, the paper was his own, but it is a singular instance of my incuriousness, that I do not know to this day, and most likely never did, whether he had any share in it or not. Upon reflection, my impression is, that he had not' (*LBSC,* p. 401). Here he relieves himself from the shadow of Harold Skimpole, who had yet to be invented by Dickens. Elsewhere, he is careful to define in one instance his parents not as 'Republicans and Unitarians' but simply as 'Unitarians' (*LBSC,* 317; *Autobiography* [hereafter *A*], I, p. 22) and in another to add the qualification that his mother had been 'perhaps' a Republican (*A,* I, p. 34). The text of *Autobiography* does not tell us, as *LBSC* does, that while he was in prison Hunt daily took a 'stout' walk in his cell 'of I dare say fourteen or fifteen miles' (*LBSC,* p. 422; *A,* 2, p. 145). *1850* still prints the anecdotes concerning Shelley's chivalry to the seduced young lady at the ball (*LBSC*, pp. 183-4) and Keats's admission on a bench at Hampstead that 'his heart was breaking' (*LBSC*, p. 267; *A*, 2, p. 210), but neither story was retained in 1859. Both *LBSC* and the 1850 version tell us that when Shelley took his final leave of Hunt to return by way of Leghorn he was going 'to sign his will in that city', but the 1859 version does not (*LBSC*, pp. 17-18, *A*, 3, p. 14).

A fascinating example of Hunt's corrections is provided by a detail of the Sunday which Shelley and Hunt spent together in Pisa on the eve of Shelley's fatal voyage. It comes at the end of a passage where Hunt has been claiming that 'with all his scepticism', Shelley exhibited what Hunt calls a 'natural piety'. At this point in *LBSC* Hunt directly attributes to Shelley a view which is precisely in accord both with his own philosophy and with his attitudes to the effect of organ music: 'He said to me in the Cathedral at Pisa, while the organ was playing, "What a divine religion might be found out, if charity were really made the principle of it, instead of faith!"' (p. 176).[9] Here he is quoting, with minor verbal alterations, the account which had been written little more than two years after the event and which he had intended for *The Westminster Review*. In *Autobiography* the authority for this statement has shifted significantly and Shelley's relation to it is much less uncomplicated: 'He assented warmly to an opinion which I expressed in the cathdral at Pisa . . .' (*A*, 3, p. 20). The passage of time may have acted as an obscuring agency but it may also have allowed Hunt a greater objectivity which enabled him to discriminate between his own opinions and those of Shelley.

If the passage of time enabled Hunt to make some corrections and adjustments, it also gave him the opportunity to become less self-revealing and to make his work less directly a register of his own feelings. Perhaps because of the urgency with which it had been composed, *LBSC* is often unguardedly and embarrassingly frank. For example, there is Hunt's admission that he preferred Shelley to Keats and that he himself was 'the dearest friend that [Shelley] had' (*LBSC*, p. 190). There is his reaction to the loss of Shelley; 'From that time, Italy was a black place to me' (*LBSC*, p. 18). There is the account of his emotions on first encountering Christ's Hospital: 'I was not prepared for so great a multitude; for the absence of the tranquillity and security of home; nor for those exhibitions of strange characters, conflicting wills, and violent, and, as they appeared to me, wicked passions, which were to be found, in little, in this epitome of the great world. I was confused, frightened and made solitary' (*LBSC*, p. 360). Above all, perhaps, there is his gratitude to those who had befriended him during his imprisonment: 'Why must I not say every thing upon this subject, showing my improvidence for a lesson, and their generosity for a comfort to mankind? . . . I might as soon thank my own heart. Their names are trembling

on my pen, as that is beating at the recollection' (*LBSC* p. 428). The image of Sir John Swinburne 'fills my whole frame with emotion. I could kneel before him and bring his hand upon my head, like a son asking his father's blessing' (*LBSC*, p. 427). Hunt reveals himself in the act of struggling against the desire to give thanks too openly: 'I am always afraid of talking about them, lest my tropical temperament should seem to render me too florid' (*LBSC*, p. 427).

None of these emotional outbursts was retained in *Autobiography*, and other uncomfortably self-revealing or self-regarding passages were also omitted. These changes are in keeping with a reticent polarity which was always in tension with the emotionalism of Hunt's 'tropical temperament' and with his autobiographical proclivities. The account of his life and character in *LBSC* may often seem disarmingly frank, yet it still is in some ways considerably less open and expressive than the manuscript narrative of his childhood and adolescence which he probably intended for Colburn before he was forced to compromise. Although this manuscript draft formed the basis for parts of *LBSC* and *Autobiography* and much of it was later translated into the printed text with minimal variations, many pages were abandoned and never published. Hunt is much more explicit in the draft about his adolescent infatuations; in *Autobiography* they are given a treatment which tends towards the composite and reduces their individuality and their interest. The draft is franker too about the sexual dangers of Hunt's tropical temperament (this phrase was one of his modes of referring to his West Indian origins, which he associated with indolence and sensuality).[10] Hunt also wrote '**An Attempt of the Author to Estimate his own Character**', which he seems to have intended for *LBSC*. Actually printed, apparently for the first edition, but then never published,[11] the '**Attempt**' contains 'matter, which no reputation for candour could render it agreeable to say, and which nothing could induce me to set down, if I did not believe that truth in society were the one thing needful'. Among other self-revelations, Hunt admits that 'I am not naturally a teller of truth. Impulse and fancy would tend to make me the reverse'; at the same time, he claims, 'I am more candid than others, and perhaps more voluptuous; but I demand also more refinement in my pleasures, and cannot separate them from sentiment and affection.' *Autobiography* does offer many insights into Hunt's character, but it is nonetheless significant that the '**Attempt**' which was so near to publication remained unavailable to the reading public. There seems to be some conflict between the impulse which caused Hunt to write it and the caution which led him to withhold it and to describe his *Autobiography* as a 'most involuntarily egotistical book' (*A*, 2, p. 3).

LBSC was completed with some urgency. It was permeated by a vindictive animosity which seems to have surprised even Hunt himself. The rancorous tone is most evident in the first volume which is concentrated on Byron, but it also leaves its mark on the later volumes. Simply by omitting most of the Byronic material, Hunt achieved a decisive transformation of tone while at the same time abandoning the scheme which had been planned by Colburn and shifting the axis of the book from Byron towards himself. This revisionary tactic is unsurprising; what is much more significant is the way in which Hunt recasts so many passages in keeping with a new attitude which is less edged, less bitterly outspoken and less sharply judgmental. This more generous, less pointed perspective conditions many of the revisions in 1850. It can be traced through numerous minor deletions and adjustments of phrase. So, for example, Hunt thinks better of an earlier parenthetical side-swipe against Ives, the Governor of Horsemonger Lane: in a *Wishing-Cap* essay and in *LBSC* Hunt had called him 'the jailer' and had continued in a spirit of mock deference, '(I beg pardon of his injured spirit—I ought to have called him Governor)' (p. 426). This impulse of animosity is not given voice in *Autobiography,* nor is an attack in the earlier texts on the stinginess of the Royal Family. In *LBSC* Hunt had analysed a central and paralysing paradox in the nature of Coleridge, who was 'a mighty intellect upon a sensual body': 'Two affirmatives in him make a negative. He is very metaphysical and very corporeal; and he does nothing' (p. 301). *Autobiography* necessarily adjusts the tenses but it also substitutes for the final phrase an emollient and hesitantly qualified extension of the original paradox: 'so in mooting everything, he said (so to speak) nothing' (*A,* 2, p. 224). Again, there is the case of Hazlitt, with whom Hunt's relations were far from easy although they had much in common. In *LBSC* Hunt wrote of 'A living writer, who, if he had been criticizing in another what he did himself, would have attributed it to an overweening opinion of his good word' (p. 404); the sting is slightly blunted by the courteous reluctance to use an identifying name. In 1850 the 'living writer', now dead for twenty years, was named as Hazlitt but the critical assessment was missing.

These small but indicative examples play their part in establishing through cumulative effect the ambience and native air of *LBSC* and of *Autobiography* respectively. Numerous changes are made on a larger scale and tend to arrange themselves around nuclear centres in the narrative. Byron, for example, not only plays a smaller role in *Autobiography* than in the book which bears his name but he also attracts far less authorial animosity when he does appear. Early in *LBSC* Hunt recalls how Byron had taken him into his confidence about his troubled relations with Lady Byron and had revealed that she had compared his own character to that of Giovanni in Hunt's recently published *Story of Rimini:* 'In all this I beheld only a generous nature, subject perhaps to ebullitions of ill temper, but candid,

sensitive, extremely to be pitied, and if a woman knew how, or was permitted by others to love him, extremely to be loved' (p. 5). After recording that Byron had shown him a very personal letter from his wife, Hunt delivers his own devaluation of Byron's flattering act of seemingly particular friendship: '[T]he case was extreme; and the compliment to me, in showing it, appeared the greater. I was not aware at that time, that with a singular incontinence, towards which it was lucky for a great many people that his friends were as singularly considerate, his Lordship was in the habit of making a confidant of every body he came nigh.' In *Autobiography* the first, more generous, passage has been omitted, while the second has been revised to read: '[A] certain over-communicativeness was one of those qualities of his Lordship, which, though it sometimes became the child-like simplicity of a poet, startled you at others in proportion as it led to disclosures of questionable propriety' (*A,* 2, p. 178). For the directly personal engagement of the earlier version, *Autobiography* here substitutes a judgment which presents itself as more balanced and more objective, while it invokes the generalized experience of 'you' in place of Hunt's own disillusioned innocence. The intemperate pounce of 'singular incontinence' is also replaced by 'disclosures of questionable propriety' where the abstraction is perhaps excessively dignified.

Here Hunt rewrote his original and negotiated a precarious treaty with his own bitterness and disillusionment. Another instance of this endeavour to restore a juster balance is provided by his account of Byron's sudden and unaccountable fluctuations of mood after Hunt's glimpses of 'the proper natural Byron' during congenial evenings at the Casa Lanfranchi. 'Next morning', says *LBSC,* 'it was all gone. His intimacy with the worst part of mankind had got him again in its chilling crust' (68). *Autobiography* not only omits this criticism of Byron and his degrading connections but points its moralizing finger at Hunt himself. Hunt used to think that 'there was not a sacrifice which I could not have made to keep him in that temper'. Now he reflects:

> But I ought to have made the sacrifice at once. I should have broken the ice between us which had been generated on points of literary predilection; and admired, and shown that I admired, as I ought to have done, his admirable genius. It was not only an oversight in me; it was a want of friendship. Friendship ought to have made me discover what less cordial feelings had kept me blind to. Next morning the happy moment had gone . . . (*A,* 3, p. 67)

It is as if Hunt were making compensation for his own animosities and failures of charity and publicly confessing his own shortcomings; so the whole moral balance is shifted from censure to tolerance and from comfortable superiority to a rather cloyingly humble and tortuous self-criticism. On other occasions Hunt simply removes all traces of his earlier feelings. So in *Autobiography,* the young Byron is classified as 'a warm politician, and earnest in the cause of liberty' (*A,* 2, p. 311); this straightforward eulogy has removed the barb from the *LBSC* version of Byron as 'a warm politician, and thought himself earnest in the cause of liberty' (p. 3).

Hunt's evacuation of anger is even more noticeable and more significant in his treatment of Shelley. In this case, it may also have influenced fundamentally the received portrait of Hunt's friend. In *LBSC* Shelley, like everybody else, except the author, is overshadowed by the giant presence of the eponymous Byron; in *Autobiography* Shelley becomes the hero, the true moral centre embodying values antithetical to those of a Byron who has largely been displaced. While Hunt's animosity had been directed towards Byron, Shelley had been entirely exempted; instead, Hunt's anger had been focused on those who had misunderstood Shelley or misrepresented him or who had helped to constitute the inhospitable social element which hampered, frustrated, and rejected his unorthodox but practical Christianity. Hunt openly acknowledged this habit of attacking Shelley's enemies: he once told Shelley, 'I reckon on your leaving your personal battles to me.' The protective practice seems to have had its roots in the unprovoked public attack on Shelley's morality carried out by John Taylor Coleridge under the licensed anonymity provided by *The Quarterly Review.* Quite correctly, Hunt traced a connection between the assault on Shelley's private life and the reception of *The Revolt of Islam;* he was himself deeply involved since the first attack on Shelley had been made in the course of a review of his own collection *Foliage* and he knew that gossip had linked Shelley's allegedly scandalous behaviour with his own. On 3 October 1819 he addressed himself in *The Examiner* to the compromised morality of the 'reviewing Scribes and Pharisees' who were responsible for such calumnies. Since *The Quarterly* had called into question Shelley's Christian virtues, Hunt now employed a set of Biblical criteria and the example of Christ himself to demonstrate the hypocrisy of the Tory reviewers, two of whom occupied prominent positions in public life:

> We will undertake to say that Mr Shelley knows more of the Bible, than all the priests who have anything to do with the Review or its writers. He does not abjure 'the pomps and vanities of this wicked world', only to put them on with the greater relish. To them, undoubtedly, the Bible is not a sealed book, in one sense. They open it to good profit enough. But in the sense which the Reviewer means, they contrive to have it sealed wherever the doctrines are inconvenient. What do they say to the injunctions against 'judging others that ye be not judged',—against revenge,—against tale-bearings,—against lying, hypocrisy, 'partiality', riches, pomps

and vanities, swearing, perjury (videlicet, Nolo-Episcopation), Pharisaical scorn, and every species of worldliness and malignity? Was Mr Canning (the parodist) a worthy follower of him that condoled with the lame and blind, when he joked upon a man's diseases? Was Mr Croker, (emphatically called 'the Admiralty Scribe') a worthy follower of him who denounced Scribes, Pharisees, and 'devourers of widows' houses', when he swallowed up all those widows' pensions? Was Mr Gifford a worthy follower of him who was the forgiver and friend of Mary Magdalen, when he ridiculed the very lameness and crutches of a Prince's discarded mistress? Men of this description are incapable of their own religion.[12]

Here Hunt's indignation is in full unrestrained satirical flow. He does not resist the argument *ad hominem* and his rhetoric derives much of its strength from the naming of names and the specificity of the examples. When *LBSC* appeared just over eight years later, Hunt was still protesting against the hypocrisy of Shelley's critics and the self-contradictions of the Christian establishment, but the tone had lost something of its ferocity and, though his analysis was precise, it was also more safely and more charitably generalized. He presented the social circumstances which provoked Shelley's rebellion, but he admitted that not everybody who submits to such an element is tainted irrevocably by its moral contradictions. In spite of bad moral influences, there are still 'the honourable part of the orthodox' and those who 'by dint of a genial nature . . . turn out decent members of society'. Having made such concessions, he continued:

> But how many others are spoilt for ever! How many victims to this confusion of truth and falsehood, apparently flourishing, but really callous or unhappy, are to be found in all quarters of the community; men who profess opinions which contradict their whole lives; takers of oaths, which they dispense with the very thought of; subscribers to articles which they doubt, or even despise: triflers with their hourly word for gain; statesmen of mere worldliness; ready hirelings of power; sneering disbelievers in good; teachers to their own children of what has spoilt themselves, and has rendered their existence a dull and selfish mockery. (*A,* 2, pp. 281-2)

In 1859 this analysis was removed from *Autobiography* together with Hunt's assertion that Shelley did not share the passivity of others who were prepared to 'see their fellow-creatures spoilt': 'He was a looker-on of a different nature.' Such a large deletion may have been motivated by the interests of verbal economy since the passage is largely a variation on a point which is powerfully enforced only two paragraphs earlier. Yet, for all the attempts at balance, this deletion also has the effect of limiting Hunt's own indignation and his tendency to identify with Shelley against 'the world'.

The passage in which Hunt partly anticipates this account of moral confusion and contradiction is, in fact, a satirical portrait of that English country society into which Shelley, the young idealist, had been born. Hunt's rhetorical strategy equated the poet confronted by this confusing clash of signals with the force of Truth itself:

> With what feelings is Truth to open its eyes upon this world among the most respectable of our mere party gentry? among licensed contradictions of all sorts? among the Christian doctrines and the worldly practices? among fox-hunters and their chaplains? among beneficed loungers, noli-episcoparian bishops, rakish old gentlemen, and more startling young ones, who are old in the folly of *knowingness?* In short, among all those professed demands of what is right and noble, mixed with real inculcations of what is wrong and full of hypocrisy, which have been so admirably exposed by Mr Bentham . . . (p. 179)

Most of this was in fact derived from the review of *Posthumous Poems* which had been rejected by *The Westminster.* There the practices were *carnal* rather than *worldly* and 'among placements, among livings for younger sons' had been included after *chaplains.* The passage in *LBSC* was largely incorporated into *Autobiography* where the self-cancelling bishops disappeared from the text and the exuberant thrust of the rhetoric was qualified by the substitution after *knowingness* of a piece of charitable exculpation: 'people not indeed bad in themselves, not so bad as their wholesale and unthinking decriers, much less their hypocritical decriers; many excellent by nature, but spoilt by those professed demands of what is right and noble, and those inculcations, at the same time, of what is false and wrong . . . ' (*A,* 2, p. 181). Such well-meaning and universal tolerance is hard to reconcile with the adversarial asperities of *The Examiner.* Whatever its moral virtue, Hunt's attempt to blame and not to blame remains unresolved. While *Autobiography* may be a more forgiving book than its predecessor, it tends to blur its own sharper perceptions through a desire to declare a general amnesty and forgiveness of sins.

The context of these passages is primarily religious rather than directly literary, since Hunt believed that many of the attacks on Shelley's poetry derived from a misunderstanding of his private life and especially of his attitude to Christianity. Hunt regularly claims that those who disapproved of Shelley's behaviour were not themselves true Christians whereas Shelley, paradoxically, was. This applied particularly to questions of sexual morality. Although Shelley was no libertine, his relations with Harriet were at the least a tragic tangle for which he bore heavy responsibility, yet Hunt, who had supported Shelley in the Chancery proceedings, entirely exonerated him from blame. In the *Posthumous Poems* review Hunt had even referred to Harriet as 'volatile and unfortunate' (in *LBSC* she was merely

'unfortunate' [p. 186]), and had treated her case so unsympathetically that this provided one of the main causes for the rejection of his review; yet this essay remained one of the main sources for the relevant pages in *LBSC*. In Hunt's eyes, Shelley was unhappy rather than culpable; culpability rested with the accusers to whom Hunt imputed precisely those moral enormities for which they had unjustly blamed Shelley. So in *LBSC* he exclaims with indignant and unsupported moral ferocity: 'Let the school-tyrants, the University refusers of argument, and the orthodox sowers of their wild oats, with myriads of unhappy women behind them, rise up in judgment against him' (p. 186).

In *Autobiography,* Hunt's essential position is still the same but the terms have been altered: 'Let the collegiate refusers of argument, and the conventional sowers of their wild oats . . . ' (*A,* 2, p. 190). Similar assumptions about wild oats and double standards of sexual morality inspire another passage in *LBSC:* 'Had he now behaved himself pardonably in the eyes of the orthodox, he would have gone to London with the resolution of sowing his wild oats, and becoming a decent member of society' (p. 184). In *Autobiography* 'conventional in those days' replaces *orthodox,* thus shifting the focus from a point of view which is specifically identified with religion towards a viewpoint which is social and which is historically determined. *Autobiography* also adds another of Hunt's absolving parentheses: 'for it is wonderful in how short a time honest discussion may be advanced by a court at once correct and unbigoted, and by a succession of calmly progressing ministries; and all classes are now beginning to permit the wisdom of every species of abuse to be doubted' (*A,* 2, p. 188). Here Hunt conveniently fuses three of the concerns of his later years. He suggests that those who disagreed with Shelley were the products of a specific historical context for which they cannot be held responsible. He expresses a faith in progress or evolutionary meliorism which is one of the controlling dynamics of *Autobiography* and of its revisionary process in both versions; indeed, the progress of *Autobiography* from its starting-point in *LBSC* to its final version in 1859 is not only conditioned by this philosophy but comes to embody it in its own transformations. Hunt's addendum also celebrates the virtues of a Victorian court in a way which reminds us both that it was Hunt's criticism of the Prince Regent which had caused his imprisonment and that *Autobiography* was, among other things, a *curriculum vitae* of a possible candidate for the Laureateship; its author made it clear that in spite of certain sympathies he was not a republican and he included in its later pages a list of his publications in praise of the Royal Family.[13]

Shelley's Christianity was founded on admiration for Christ, 'for whose truly divine spirit he entertained the greatest reverence' (*LBSC,* p. 191); in *Autobiography* this religious commitment is qualified when 'truly divine spirit' is replaced by the much more guarded 'beneficent intentions' (*A*, 2, p. 194). According to Hunt, Shelley's reviewers were embittered by his interest in the epistle of St James and the Sermon on the Mount and by 'his refusal to identify their superstitions and worldly use of the Christian doctrines with the just idea of a great Reformer and advocate of the many; one whom they would have been the first to cry out against, had he appeared now' (p. 191). This passage not only castigates the blind conservatism of *The Quarterly* and other reviews, but it also very clearly reveals Hunt's tendency to identify Shelley with Christ which also features in the essays for *The Liberal* and *The Westminster Review;* in 1850 it was removed. At this point *LBSC* had continued:

> His want of faith, indeed, in one sense of the word, and his exceeding faith in the existence of goodness and the great doctrine of charity, formed a comment, the one on the other, very formidable to the less troublesome constructions of the orthodox.

In 1850 this was subtly but significantly altered:

> His want of faith, indeed, in the letter, and his exceeding faith in the spirit, of Christianity, formed a comment, the one on the other, very formidable to those who chose to forget what Scripture itself observes on that point.

The effect of these changes is to make Shelley into a Christian of more specific orthodoxy while once again removing the heat of the criticism from the orthodox themselves to the less challengingly pointed target of 'those who chose to forget what Scripture itself observes'.

In *LBSC* the next paragraph begins with a further insight into the unpopularity of Shelley's brand of Christianity: 'Some alarmists at Marlow said, that if he went on at this rate, he would make all the poor people infidels. He went on, till ill health and calumny, and the love of his children, forced him abroad' (p. 192). This did not appear in *Autobiography*, which only printed a pruned account of Shelley's pragmatic charities during his stay at Marlow. So *Autobiography* did not tell its readers that 'It was not uncommon with him to give away all his ready money, and be compelled to take a journey on foot or on the top of a stage, no matter during what weather' (p. 192). Yet even the *LBSC* version is less explicit than the account which Hunt had written nine years earlier for *The Examiner* and which had recorded that Shelley 'visited (if necessary) *"the sick and the fatherless"*, to whom others gave Bibles and no help; wrote or studied again, or read to his wife and friends the whole evening; took a crust of bread or a glass of whey for his supper; and went early to bed'.[14] The frugalities of his life are also recorded, with slight variations, in *LBSC* and in *Auto-*

biography, but in these versions we are told that 'he visited the sick in their beds . . . and kept a regular list of industrious poor, whom he assisted with small sums to make up their accounts' (*LBSC*, pp. 186-7; *A*, 2, p. 190). In all cases Hunt is concerned to defend Shelley's reputation by claiming that, far from keeping a seraglio when he was at Marlow, he practised the Christian virtues.

In the earlier versions the tone is unmistakably controversial: Hunt is using the terms of Christianity against those unchristian Christians who have calumniated Shelley. One general effect of many of these changes is to make Hunt's account increasingly less adversarial, less immediately grounded in the urgently felt need to defend Shelley against his detractors. The most striking example of this is the story of how Shelley rescued a poor woman who was having convulsions near Hampstead Heath on a snowy winter's night. All the versions of this moral fable are centred on the contrast between the principled behaviour of the supposed atheist and the panic-stricken circumspection of a rich man whom Shelley approaches for help: '"God bless me, Sir! Dear me, Sir!" exclaimed the frightened wretch [the poor, frightened man (*Autobiography*)], and fluttered into his mansion' (*LBSC*, pp. 187-8; *A*, 2, pp. 198-200). In the *Literary Examiner* version Hunt had identified the house of this reluctant gentleman and had strongly hinted that it might be in his power to identify its owner, if he chose to remember his name. All the versions remark that 'the paucity of Christians is astonishing, considering the number of them' and that the 'real Christian had puzzled' the local gossips who hinted that Shelley, who was 'no Christian', had brought a disreputable female into the house. *The Literary Examiner* also remarked that 'their decent imaginations would never have got at the truth, had they carved it and Christianed it till doomsday'. Only *The Literary Examiner* and *LBSC* provided the moralizing conclusion: 'Now go, ye Pharisees of all sorts, and try if ye can still open your hearts and your doors like the good Samaritan. This man was himself too brought up in a splendid mansion, and might have revelled and rioted in all worldly goods. Yet this was one of the most ordinary of his actions.'[15] This address to the Pharisaical reader is in fact a development of a sentence in an essay on 'Fellow-Creatures Suffered to Die for Want' which had appeared in *The Examiner* on 30 November 1817. This essay had focused on the face of charity and had taken as its two leading examples of charity in action Hunt's mother (whose gift of a flannel petticoat to a poor woman on Blackfriars' Road is also celebrated in *LBSC* and *Autobiography*) and Samuel Johnson. Hunt's account of one example of Johnson's practical Christianity bears a remarkable similarity to Shelley's action at Hampstead:

> coming home one night, and finding a woman of the town in a most deplorable situation in the streets,

with none to help her, [he] did not stand gaping, or walk off shaking his head at negligence in the police, or even at vice, but finding that charity was to take some decided measures, fairly took his fellow-creature up in his arms, carried her to his lodging (which he could ill afford to share), put her to bed, had her sickness cured, and sent her home to her friends in the country. Go, ye anti-Jacobins and lovers of Orthodoxy, and do so likewise.[16]

The shape and the resonance of the final sentence seem to have combined with the similarity of the two acts of charity to produce Hunt's direct appeal to the Pharisees in 1823 (repeated again in **LBSC**).

Hunt's attempts to Christianize Shelley were the result partly of an element which can be genuinely identified in the work and life of the poet himself; they can also be traced partly to Hunt's desire to defend Shelley against his enemies, and partly to his own psychological need to deprive Shelley's views of their radical and sceptical edge and to make them conform to a reading of Christianity which was increasingly sentimentalized. Even at an early stage in their friendship Shelley had already acquired angelic attributes when in 1818 Hunt warned Mary not to let Shelley out too much in the Italian sun for fear he should 'burn his wings'.[17] After Shelley's death the angelic features become more pronounced so that Hunt can claim without any apparent hint of irony that 'looking at you attentively his aspect had a certain seraphical character that would have suited a portrait of John the Baptist, or the angel whom Milton describes as holding a reed "tipt with fire"' (**LBSC**, p. 175). The next sentence anticipates the reader's objections by adding, 'Nor would the most religious mind, had it known him, have objected to the comparison.' By stressing the general and visual rather than the contextual force of the allusion, Hunt represses the fact that Milton's angel is a rebel and a master of artillery whose posture is both threatening and undignified: 'at each behind / A Seraph stood, and in his hand a Reed / Stood waving tipt with fire' (*Paradise Lost* VI, 579-80). While Milton deflates the revolutionary glamour by the rhetorical placement of words such as *behind* and *orifice,* Hunt tames the radical Shelley by aestheticizing and sentimentalizing him and rendering him socially acceptable. So Shelley scandalized society by his life and his work, but the 'generous reader will be glad to hear, that the remains . . . were attended to their final abode by some of the most respectable English residents in Rome' (**LBSC**, p. 202).

Hunt's attitude to Shelley is crystallized by the status which he accords to Shelley's heart. Hunt had always shown a tendency to identify Shelley with his heart; so, defending his moral character against the strictures of *The Quarterly Review,* he claimed that 'we believe him, from the bottom of our hearts, to be one of the noblest hearts as well as heads which the world has

seen for a long time'.[18] The over-determination of this is symptomatic. Consequently, Hunt found himself in a peculiarly sensitive situation when he received for publication in *The Liberal* an account by Edward Trelawny of the cremation of Shelley's remains over which Trelawny had presided and in which Shelley's heart was rather publicly laid bare. Hunt himself wrote an essay which was intended as a framework for Trelawny's narrative; but, in the event, Hunt's own essay was never published and Trelawny's first appeared in **LBSC,** in a heavily edited and truncated version from which the physical details had been entirely eliminated. The manuscript in the British Library reveals a process which is more suggestive than this, since it shows Hunt's hand at work on Trelawny's prose. Here we can observe not the blank simplicity of total erasure but the much more indicative patterns of editorial intervention and revision.[19]

Hunt's main concern in this rewriting was to minimize the gruesome and the macabre, sometimes, perhaps, in the interests of accuracy but more often in the interests of good taste and tolerability. Trelawny is insistent and speculatively specific about the effect of fish on the watery corpses of Shelley and his friend Williams. For instance, he writes of Shelley that 'those parts exposed the face, hands, head had been so mauled by small fish so as not to leave a trace of what they had been' (*sic*). Hunt's version avoids the imprecision of *mauled* but also eliminates the fish altogether: 'though such parts of his flesh as were exposed, such as the face & hands, had been so destroyed & decomposed in the sea as not to leave a trace of what they had been'. Again, Trelawny's statement that the 'only parts of Williams's body eaten by the fish' were the hands, face, and head is tempered to read that these parts were the only ones 'disfigured or destroyed'. Likewise, where Trelawny records that the hands and one foot 'had been entirely eaten with all the flesh of the face by fish', Hunt emends the statement to read that the hands and feet 'were entirely gone'. It is likely that Hunt may have been motivated in part at least by stylistic considerations and by a desire to reduce the repetitive element in Trelawny's somewhat artless narration, but it is not without significance that the tendency of these revisions is to reduce the gruesomely physical specificity of the original.

This tendency is even more vividly in evidence in a larger intervention on Hunt's part. Trelawny offers a circumstantially detailed account both of the state of Shelley's body after it had been exhumed from its temporary place of burial in the sand and, most suggestively, of the reactions of the participants in the grim ritual:

> The body was in the worst state of putridity and very offensive: the soldiers employed, were obliged to strengthen their nerves continually by drinking

brandy and the officers retired from a sight so horrible. Both the legs were separated at the knees, the thigh bones bared and the flesh hung about in shreds; the hands were off and the arm bones protruded, the skull black & neither features nor face remaining.

Hunt's version of this is sanitized and deprived of its particularity: 'They were much decomposed & destroyed, like the others, from their long continuance in the sea.' Not only does this expurgate the anatomical comprehensiveness of the original but it also omits the gauge which Trelawny provides for measuring the intensity of the reactions experienced by those who actually participated. Nowhere else is the brandy mentioned or the withdrawal of the officers, and, once these details had been removed from the manuscript, they disappeared from the historical record as well.

Hunt's version of Trelawny also omitted a longish passage on the burning of Shelley's remains which pays particular attention to the durability of an organ which Trelawny identified as the heart:

> it remained unaltered; a quantity of thin fluid still flowing and occasioning a bright blue flame . . . I took the heart out to examine it, and the oily fluid flowed freely from it; the only visible effect the fire appeared to have had was to change its colour to a dingy blue.

That Hunt should have cancelled this passage is not at all surprising since not only is it unpleasantly physical but it also focuses on the organ to which Hunt accorded a passionate and almost neurotic veneration. Hunt's eagerness to claim the prize of Shelley's heart from the flames and his reluctance to restore it to the widow are only too well attested. His unwillingness to acknowledge the heart as physical and material in its substance is indicated by the exclusion from the text of the 'thin' and 'oily fluid'. On the other hand, he retains the next part of the passage which emphasizes its almost preternatural ability to survive:

> It is a curious circumstance that the heart, which was unusually large, together with some other vessels in that quarter seemed almost proof against fire, for it was still entire in figure and apparently in substance, though the intensity of heat was so great that harder substances were reduced to white dust.

Read in a context which minimizes the signs of physicality, these lines contribute to a sense of miracle. The tendency of Hunt's editing becomes even clearer when one notices that this is not precisely what Trelawny wrote. His version includes one minute but very significant variation: the heart was not, as Hunt would have it, 'unusually large' but rather it was 'unusually small'. What we are observing here is an editorial process, a consistent and extended metamorphosis whereby Shelley is dematerialized and his heart is transformed from an oleaginous organ to a symbolic property. This transformation may have answered to a psychological need; certainly, it was not impeded by the fact that Hunt was not present at the cremation but was safely ensconced in his carriage. This seclusion did not inhibit Hunt from correcting in Trelawny's version details of a scene which he had not witnessed. He consoled himself that through the circumstances of his death and cremation Shelley had escaped 'that gradual corruption of the body, which he seems to have contemplated with a dislike proportionate to his imagination'. Yet Shelley's imagination had allowed itself to dwell on the facts of bodily dissolution in *Adonais* and in his essay "On Life," while Hunt seems to have forgotten, or allowed himself to forget, that even if Shelley's temporary burial had hastened the process of decomposition, his remains presented a spectacle of putrefaction so potent that the soldiers were forced to stiffen their nerves with brandy. The elision is curious but crucial. Protected in this way from uncomfortable tokens of human frailty, Hunt was more easily able to initiate a cult of Shelley's heart and the 'heartly' qualities of his life and work. It seems entirely appropriate that the motto he invented for Shelley's tomb in Rome should turn out to be 'corcordium' (heart of hearts), not least because, whatever remains were interred in the Protestant cemetery in the shadow of the tomb of Caius Cestius, Shelley's heart was certainly not among them. In *Autobiography* but not in *LBSC* Shelley is characterized as 'that heart of hearts' (*A*, 2, p. 206) a figure of speech which both perpetuates the definition of the epitaph and simulates a characteristic Shelleyan trope ('soul of my soul').

The gradual dematerialization of Shelley and his translation into a disembodied organ of benevolence reflects the larger patterns of Hunt's own development. Thus he could respond to the demands of contemporary English politics in the year before the passage of the Reform Bill by claiming: 'The nobler morals of these times demand that a man should have a more enlarged heart, and a greater love of truth and his species.' It was no accident that when in the same year he issued a privately printed manual of devotion it should centre on the heart; when it was published in revised form in 1853 it was retitled *The Religion of the Heart*.[20] One of the features of this heterodox manual with its alternative Services and its 'exercises of the Heart in its Duties and Aspirations' was the inclusiveness of the texts which it recommended, not only more traditional writings but extracts from Wordsworth, Coleridge, Keats, Shelley, Tennyson, and Hunt himself.

Hunt's religion of the heart, with its emphasis on generosity and acceptance rather than on exclusiveness and judgment, is in keeping with his efforts both as a man and as a writer to eliminate anger and to cultivate charity and forgiveness. Hunt's writing shows a progressive tendency to invest in Shelley a set of values which were central to this philosophy. Shelley himself was not exempt from anger and it is fascinating to see the way in which Hunt negotiates this awkward (and too little acknowledged) fact. In the earlier accounts, Hunt had freely admitted that Shelley was susceptible to fits of temper. The essay intended for *The Liberal* put it this way:

> Mr Shelley was naturally hasty and passionate; but his anger was soon over and he so repented it, that as it was said of some other person whose name we forget, it was a good thing, on these occasions for a servant to have offended him, or come in his way. He had made a very solid apology to a domestic for something said hastily a little before he died; and the poor girl spoke of him to us with a flood of tears, turning away her head and wringing her hands.

The vividness of this seems to indicate some authenticity. This anecdote was not retained in the review of *Posthumous Poems* or in *LBSC* or in any later account of Shelley, but in the essay for *The Westminster Review* and in *LBSC* Hunt did make a revelation which was not available to readers of *Autobiography:* 'He [Shelley] was naturally irritable and violent; but had so mastered the infirmity, as to consider every body's inclinations before his own' (p. 213). Hunt also specifically referred to Shelley's temper in the context of *The Quarterly Review.* The anonymous reviewer (in fact John Taylor Coleridge) who had been Shelley's contemporary at Eton remembered Shelley setting trees on fire with a burning-glass, while, in Hunt's words, Shelley recollected him 'as one of the school-tyrants against whom he rose up, in opposition to the system of fagging'. After quoting a passage from *The Revolt of Islam* which was the target of Coleridge's hostile review, Hunt continued: 'Mr Shelley retained all his kindness and energy, but corrected, as he here aspires to do, the irritability of his temper. No man, by the account of all who lived with him, ever turned it into greater sweetness. The Reviewer, by the usual process of tyranny, became a slave' (pp. 180-1). This passage did not appear in *Autobiography.* Perhaps this shows that Hunt himself had corrected the irritability of his own temper but it also deprives the reader of a vital insight into the tensions and complexities of Shelley's character.

In a letter of June 1841, Hunt expressed regret for his critical remarks on Byron not because they were not true, 'for they were', but because 'a better knowledge of myself has taught me that no one frail human being has a right to sit in that manner in judgment on another'.[21] Again, in *Autobiography* his account of George III conceded that 'with all his faults' he was 'a more estimable man than many of his enemies' and was followed by a passage which begins: 'Whatever of any kind has taken place in the world, may have been best

for all of us in the long run. Nature permits us, retrospectively and for comfort's sake, though not in a different spirit, to entertain that conclusion among others' (*A,* 2, p. 56). Perhaps one is not being unjust in recognizing here something of that tone of voice which suggested to Dickens the character of Leonard (diplomatically altered to Harold) Skimpole. There is a striking contrast between this unfocused and all-embracing optimism and the pointed and energetically satirical accounts of the king which Hunt had contributed to *The Examiner.* As in other parts of *Autobiography,* the writing is compromised and weakened by the demands of the prevailing ideology: there is less and less of what Hazlitt had once pinpointed in Hunt's theatrical criticism as 'the true pineapple flavour'.[22] That Hunt himself was aware of this shifting of the balance is demonstrated by an essay which he published in *The Tatler* in April 1831: it gives an account of how in his younger days he had been bitten with admiration of wits and satirists but had been mellowed by suffering and experience.[23] In 1838 he provided another insight into his self-awareness when he wrote to S. C. Hall a letter which was intended as the basis for a biographical note in *The Book of Gems:* 'Time and suffering, without altering them, we understand, have blunted his exertions as a partisan, by showing him the excuses common and necessary to all men, but the zeal which he has lost as a partisan he no less evinces for the advancement of mankind.'[24]

This belief in a kind of evolutionary meliorism is evident both in his politics and in his religious philosophy of Universalism to which, as he tells us in *Autobiography,* both his parents had subscribed. The central tenet of Universalism was that in the final reckoning nobody would be condemned to hellfire or excluded from the circle of God's love. As Hunt himself put it in *The Religion of the Heart:* Universalism proclaimed 'the restoration of all mankind to happiness, without exception'.[25] The general tendency of Hunt's revisions both of *LBSC* and of *Autobiography* is in accord with this all-pardoning philosophy of Universalism and moves away from the censorious, the judgmental, and the satirical. Increasingly, it would seem, Hunt was driven by a desire to put the record straight which meant not so much a committed pursuit of historical authenticity as an understanding interpretation of what had once provoked his anger. Both versions of *Autobiography* retain passages which are sharply etched and which do not avoid satire or criticism, but there is a marked and progressive evolution towards what at the best is mellow and at the worst is bland. Hunt's philosophy of good cheer, the stoical optimism which carried him through the dark days of his imprisonment has now been translated into a kind of benevolent quietism which increasingly threatens though it never undermines the genuine achievement of *Autobiography.* This gradual process of revisionary evolution which is consummated by the closing pages of *Autobiography* (in both its versions) strongly suggests that for Hunt the process of revision was not only a matter of stylistics or even of truth to history and to self but an activity whose deepest resonances were moral and religious.

Notes

[1] Preface to *Lord Byron and Some of his Contemporaries* (London 1828), p. iii. Here and throughout this essay the text cited is the first edition folio which was also published in one quarto volume. The second edition, which was also published in 1828, was issued in three volumes with minimal textual variations from the first.

[2] Preface. See also: 'as to my own biography, I soon became tired of that. It is true, I should have entered into it in greater detail, and endeavoured to make the search into my thoughts and actions of some use, seeing that I had begun it at all; but I was warned off this ground as impossible on account of others, and gladly gave it up.'

[3] *The Correspondence of Leigh Hunt,* ed. Thornton Leigh Hunt (London, 1862), Vol. 2, p. 86; *The Autobiography of Leigh Hunt, with Reminiscences of Friends and Contemporaries* (London 1850), Vol. 2, p. 188.

[4] *The Liberal: Verse and Prose from the South* (London, 1822-3), Vol. 1, pp. 97-120, 269-88, Vol. 2, pp. 47-65, 251-64; *The Literary Examiner,* Nos. 7 and 8 (16 and 23 August 1823), pp. 97-105, 113-20.

[5] 'Coffee-Houses and Smoking', 16 (1826), p. 50; 'A Schoolmaster of the Old Leaven', 14 (1825), pp. 599-600. *The Indicator,* 35 (7 June 1820), p. 278; 36 (14 June, 1820), pp. 285-6.

[6] For the *Wishing-Cap* essays, see *The Examiner,* nos. 857, 859 (4, 18 July 1824), pp. 417-18, 449-51. For the earlier articles, see *The Examiner,* 259 (14 February 1813), pp. 97-99; 260 (21 February 1813), pp. 113-14; 261 (28 February 1813), pp. 129-30. While he was in prison, Hunt also prepared a memorandum which enabled him to rehearse on paper the topic of his imprisonment.

[7] *The Examiner,* 527, 530, 531, 613, 614, 615 (1 and 22 February, 1 March 1818, 26 September, 3 and 10 October 1819), reprinted in *Shelley: The Critical Heritage,* ed. James E. Barcus (London, 1975), pp. 106-14, 135-47; *The Examiner,* 751, 752, 754 (16 and 23 June, 7 July 1822), pp. 370-1, 389-90, 419-21; *The Literary Examiner,* 1 (5 July 1823), pp. 4, 6; 8 (23 August 1823), pp. 118-19; British Library, MS. Ashley 915, catalogued as 'MS. of Leigh Hunt's account of the cremation of P.B. Shelley', transcription to be published with commentary and notes by Timothy Webb in *The Keats-Shelley Review* (1992); Payson G. Gates,

'Leigh Hunt's Review of Shelley's *Posthumous Poems',* *Publications of the Bibliographical Society of America,* 42 (1948), pp. 1-40.

[8] Hunt died before he was able to complete his revisions of *Autobiography,* so the book was prepared for the press by his son Thornton, who added some notes of his own. *1859* is more economical than *1850,* does not print some of the primary materials (such as articles in *The Examiner*), is much more selective in its use of literary quotations, and is generally less discursive. Throughout this essay *Autobiography* is quoted from the text of 1850 unless otherwise specified.

[9] See, for example, Hunt's note to "The Book of Beginnings," *The Liberal,* Vol. 2, p. 118 where he refers to the organ in the Portuguese Ambassador's chapel in South Street, Grosvenor Square, which was played by his friend Vincent Novello:

> I, to wit, one of the 'Satanic School' (Oh Bob!) have stood in that chapel, under the influence of that organ, and . . . have felt the tears run down my cheeks at the crowd of thoughts that came upon me. 'Aye,' quoth the Laureat, 'you were sorry that you had no longer a faith.' Excuse me; I have a faith, though not in your damnatory one, or your verses: but I was struck to think of all the miseries and bloody wars that had accompanied the spread of the kindest of doctrines: and wondered how it was possible for men to look upon the altar-piece before me, and hear the music that melted towards it, and not find out, that to injure and damn one another to eternity, was unbecoming even the wrath of charity.

The conclusion of this note is informed, among other things, by Hunt's Universalist rejection of the concept of Hell.

[10] The manuscript now belongs to the Brewer-Leigh Hunt Collection in the University of Iowa Libraries. For a transcript and introduction, see *Leigh Hunt's Autobiography; the Earliest Sketches,* ed. Stephen Fogle (Gainesville, 1959).

[11] The original quarto half-sheet from which this brief essay in self-analysis was first reprinted in *The Athenaeum* in 1893 is now in the Forster Collection of the Victoria and Albert Museum. It was also reprinted by Roger Ingpen in his edition of *Autobiography* (London, 1903).

[12] Reprinted in *Shelley: The Critical Heritage,* p. 139.

[13] Stephen F. Fogle, 'Leigh Hunt and the Laureateship', *Studies in Philology,* 55 (1958), pp. 603-15. Hunt's attempt to present an effective candidature led him to the following evasive reference to his imprisonment: 'the fancied indecorum of appearing in a place, where any previous connexions of it, however differ-

ent from its existing connexions, may have been set by him in a disadvantageous light' (*A,* Vol. 3, p. 276; not in *1859*).

[14] *The Examiner,* 615 (10 October 1819), cited in *Shelley: The Critical Heritage,* p. 143.

[15] *The Literary Examiner,* 8 (23 August 1823), pp. 118-19; *LBSC,* pp. 187-8, where the anecdote is quoted in a footnote on the authority of *The Literary Examiner.*

[16] *The Examiner* 518 (30 November 1817), pp. 753-5; *LBSC,* pp. 324-5; *A,* Vol. 1, pp. 32-3. Thornton Hunt remembered that Shelley and the woman's son had 'brought her on from the inhospitable mansion [of the rich man] to our house in their arms'. He added: 'I believe that, the son's strength failing, for some way down the hill into the Vale of Health Shelley carried her on his back.' 'Shelley. By One Who Knew Him', *Atlantic Monthly,* 11 (1863), p. 186.

[17] *Correspondence,* Vol. 1, p. 116. See also, among numerous examples, references to Shelley's wings in *LBSC,* pp. 210, 212, and a letter to Horace Smith written shortly after Shelley's death: 'I cannot help thinking of him as if he were alive as much as ever, so unearthly he always appeared to me, and so seraphical a thing of the elements' (*Correspondence,* Vol. 1, p. 195).

[18] *The Examiner,* 615 (10 October 1819), cited in *Shelley: The Critical Heritage,* p. 143. See also the following reference to Shelley and Keats: 'Finer hearts, or more astonishing faculties never were broken up, than in those two. To paint any man's heart by the side of Shelley's, is alone an extraordinary panegyric.' *The Literary Examiner,* 8 (23 August 1823), pp. 117-18.

[19] Trelawny's manuscript is cited from British Library Add. MS. 39, 165, ff. 174-80; for permission to quote from this and from Hunt's essay I am indebted to the British Library. See also Leslie A. Marchand, 'Trelawny on the Death of Shelley', *Keats-Shelley Memorial Bulletin,* 4 (1952), pp. 9-34. A fuller account is included in my article for *Keats-Shelley Review* (see note 7 above).

[20] Originally issued under the title of *Christianism: or, Belief and Unbelief Reconciled; being Exercises and Meditations.*

[21] *Correspondence,* Vol. 2, p. 38.

[22] *The Complete Works of William Hazlitt,* ed. P. P. Howe, 21 vols. (London and Toronto, 1930-4), Vol. 18, p. 381.

[23] *The Tatler,* 195 (19 April, 1831), Vol. 2, p. 778.

[24] Quoted in S. C. Hall, *A Book of Memories of Great Men and Women of the Age,* (London, 1871), p. 242. For an external assessment, see Charles Lamb's observation in a letter to Southey which appeared in *The London Magazine* in October 1823. Lamb noted that 'his political asperities and petulancies' were 'wearing out with the heats and vanities of youth'. *The Works of Charles and Mary Lamb,* ed. E. V. Lucas, 7 vols. (London, 1903-5), Vol. 1, pp. 232-3.

[25] *Ibid.,* p. 219n.

Duncan Wu (essay date 1996)

SOURCE: "Leigh Hunt's 'Cockney' Aesthetics," in *The Keats-Shelley Review,* No. 10, Spring, 1996, pp. 77-96.

[*In the following essay, Wu examines Hunt's poetical aesthetics, his relations with Wordsworth as a critic, and his influence on Keats's poetry.*]

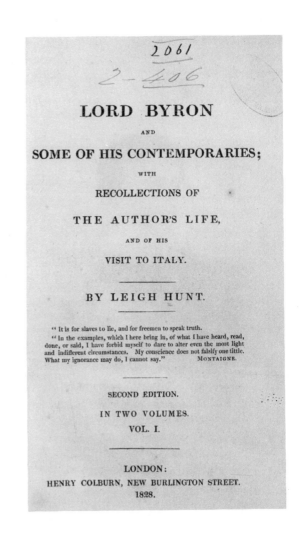

In October 1817 J. G. Lockhart launched his notorious attack in *Blackwood's Edinburgh Magazine* on what he christened the 'Cockney' school. 'Its chief Doctor and Professor', he wrote, 'is Mr Leigh Hunt, a man certainly of some talents, of extravagant pretensions both in wit, poetry, and politics, and withal of exquisitely bad taste, and extremely vulgar modes of thinking and manners in all respects.'[1] Most critical accounts of Hunt's influence on Keats approach the subject from the point of view of such detractors as the ideologically-motivated Tories who regarded it as their duty to attack such radicals as Hunt. In this paper I want to examine Hunt's 'Cockney' aesthetics through his eyes, using his own words. And I want to answer the questions: what were his guiding principles as a poet? And how influential were those principles on Keats?

Some of Hunt's most accomplished sonnets may be found in the series **"To Hampstead."**

> As one who after long and far-spent years
>   Comes on his mistress in an hour of sleep,
>   And half-surprised that he can silence keep
> Stands smiling o'er her through a flash of tears,
> So see how sweet and self-same she appears;
>   Till at his touch, with little moving creep
>   Of joy, she wakes from out her calmness deep,
> And then his heart finds voice, and dances round her ears—
> So I, first coming on my haunts again,
>   In pause and stillness of the early prime,
>   Stood thinking of the past and present time
> With earnest eyesight, scarcely crossed with pain;
>   Till the fresh moving leaves, and startling birds,
>   Loosened my long-suspended breath in words.[2]

If **"To Hampstead"** represents Hunt at his poetic best—as I think it does—the prevailing critical view would be that it does so in spite of itself. The sentimentality of the central metaphor, and self-conscious diction of such phrases as 'flash of tears' and 'little moving creep / of joy', are the very features that offended Hunt's early readers. And yet, if you detach yourself from the prejudices that have led to his decline on the literary stock market, you begin to feel more persuaded by the voice that addresses us—even, perhaps, touched by what it is trying to say. It may be, in fact, that **"To Hampstead,"** like all enduring verse, possesses the power to renew our responses at each reading. If we regard Hunt's technique as a matter of deliberation rather than as the result of incompetence, we may even suspect that its accumulation of adjectives and awkward constructions are the expression, surprisingly, of confidence—a confidence mediated through the assurance of tone and technical mastery. His most recent apologist, Rodney Stenning Edgecombe, has argued that the Huntian manner represents the beginning of 'a distinctive rococo *sensibility*' that culminated in the fairy tales of Oscar Wilde.[3] In this light, **"To Hampstead"** may be seen as one of Hunt's most accomplished works. From the opening word it knows exactly where it is taking us. The octave and sestet are no more than the two sides of a metaphor resolved only in the concluding line, with our emergence out of fantasy into Hampstead Health in early morning. But the poet cushions our descent to earth with that most evocative and moving of qualities: romantic possibility.

> So I, first coming on my haunts again,
>   In pause and stillness of the early prime,
>   Stood thinking of the past and present time
> With earnest eyesight, scarcely crossed with
>   pain;
>   Till the fresh moving leaves, and startling
>   birds,
>   Loosened my long-suspended breath in
>   words.

The aesthetic that mediates these impressive lines was not the result of either accident or vulgarity; it was the product of deliberation, the work of a mind that, to use Wordsworth's phrase, had thought long and deeply. In *Imagination and Fancy* (1832), Hunt spelled out his principles in an essay entitled "An answer to the question What Is Poetry?":

> Poetry is a passion, because it seeks the deepest impressions; and because it must undergo, in order to convey, them. . . . Poetry is imaginative passion . . . He who has thought, feeling, expression, imagination, action, character, and continuity, all in the largest amount and highest degree, is the greatest poet.[4]

These remarks sound familiar because Hunt is echoing Wordsworth who, as early as 1800, had said that 'the reader cannot be too often reminded that poetry is passion: it is the history or science of feelings'.[5] It was Wordsworth, too, who in the 1800 Preface to *Lyrical Ballads* had spoken of his 'deep impression of certain inherent and indestructible qualities of the human mind (and likewise of certain powers in the great and permanent objects that act upon it which are equally inherent and indestructible)'.[6] Hunt followed Wordsworth in tracing imaginative power back to the formative influence on the mind of intense emotional experience. That respect for the psychological integrity of the moment may be why the sonnet **"To Hampstead"** works when other, more fanciful poems such as **"The Nymphs,"** do not. It is curious enough that Hunt's poetry may be read in Wordsworthian terms at all; that he himself sought to explain it in those terms is remarkable. At a time when few, if any, critics, understood the principles set out in the Preface to *Lyrical Ballads,* Hunt was among a handful of people who advocated them. This is all the more surprising when one reflects that Hunt was a late convert to Wordsworth's poetry. He allied himself with Wordsworth's detractors as early as 1811, when, in *The Feast of the Poets,* first published in *The Reflector,* Hunt denied the elder poet a seat at the table of Apollo. At this comparatively early stage in his own publishing career, Wordsworth kept a close eye on his attackers, and probably read the *Feast* not long after publication; indeed, there was a copy of *The Reflector* at Rydal Mount in later years. However, when a second edition of the poem appeared in 1814, Hunt modified his earlier views in an extensive footnote. The first Wordsworth knew of this was when Sir George Beaumont, a mutual acquaintance, wrote to him on 2 June 1814: 'Leigh Hunt no great favourite of mine—after some severe sarcasms in verse has thought proper to do you some justice in a note which follows'.[7] On 23 June Wordsworth replied:

> Mr Lee Hunt whose 'amende honorable' you mention had not read a word of my Poems, at the time he wrote his sarcasms. This I know from an acquaintance of his; so that neither the censure nor the praise of such people is in *itself* of any value. It however affects the immediate sale of works, and authors who are tender of their own reputation would be glad to secure Mr Hunt's commendations. For my own part, my *dignity* absolutely requires an indifference upon this point.[8]

This frigid acknowledgement of Hunt's declared ignorance would hardly seem to provide the basis for a friendship. All the same, relations between the two warmed considerably in succeeding months. Wordsworth knew that Hunt had been imprisoned in the Surrey Jail since February 1813 for libelling the Prince Regent. On a visit to Lowther in September 1814 he met Hunt's defence counsel, Henry Brougham, who told Wordsworth that 'his writings were valued by Mr Hunt'.[9] In response Wordsworth sent Hunt a copy of his collected *Poems* (1815) the following February, just a few days after Hunt's release from prison, and Hunt went to some pains to pacify him when he complained about Hazlitt's comments on political apostasy in *The Examiner* later in 1815. Copies of Hunt's reprinted *Descent of Liberty: A Mask* were available by October[10] and Wordsworth was one of the earliest recipients of a copy bearing the author's presentation inscription.[11] In December Benjamin Robert Haydon, by then Wordsworth's principal informant on matters Huntian, told him that 'Leigh Hunt's respect for you seems to encrease daily—His Brother it is who has had your bust made'.[12] By spring 1816 Wordsworth was contributing sonnets to *The Examiner* and remarked to R. P. Gillies that 'I have great respect for the *Talents* of its Editor'.[13] From someone known for his scrupulous meanness with words of praise, this was no puff.

And yet, in the light of these unexpectedly cordial relations, Hunt's comments on Wordsworth in the 1814 *Feast of the Poets* are surprisingly equivocal. Admittedly, he does commend 'the greatness of Mr. Wordsworth's genius',[14] but goes on to characterise the author of *Lyrical Ballads* as subject to 'solitary morbidities':

> we get up, accompany the poet into his walks, and acknowledge them to be the best and most beautiful; but what do we meet there? Idiot Boys, Mad Mothers, Wandering Jews, Visitations of Ague, and Frenzied Mariners, who are fated to accost us with tales that almost make one's faculties topple over. . . . Let the reader observe that I am not objecting to these subjects on behalf of that cowardly self-love falsely called sensibility, or merely because they are of what is termed a distressing description, but because they are carried to an excess that defeats the poet's intention, and distresses to no purpose.[15]

Coming from someone as renowned for his committed radicalism as Hunt these criticisms are surprising, to say the least. Though he does not say it in so many words, the element of Wordsworth's poetry that causes him most disquiet is its preoccupation with social and political ills. Not that he objects to political poetry *per se;* he earlier expresses approval for *The Female Vagrant,* the radicalism of which dates from Wordsworth's infatuation with Godwinian philosophy in 1793. And *The Examiner* occasionally published poetry with an overtly political message, some of it by the editor. What offended Hunt was what he regarded as Wordsworth's morbid obsession with social outcasts; adverting to Wordsworth's attack in the Preface to *Lyrical Ballads* on sickly and stupid German tragedies, Hunt remarks:

> He wishes to turn aside our thirst for extraordinary intelligence to more genial sources of interest, and he gives us accounts of mothers who have gone mad at the loss of their children, of others who have killed their's in the most horrible manner, and of hard-hearted masters whose imaginations have revenged upon them the curses of the poor. In like manner, he would clear up and simplicize our thoughts; and he tells us tales of children that have no notion of death, of boys who would halloo to a landscape nobody knew why, and of an hundred inexpressible sensations, intended by nature no doubt to affect us, and even pleasurably so in the general feeling, but only calculated to perplex and sadden us in our attempts at analysis.

Wordsworth, he goes on, 'turns our thoughts away from society and men altogether, and nourishes that eremitical vagueness of sensation,—that making a business of reverie,—that despair of getting to any conclusion to any purpose, which is the next step to melancholy or indifference'.[16] Hunt criticizes not the determined radicalism of Wordsworth's poetry, but its apparent failure to produce anything besides perplexity and sadness. Few men of his time were more preoccupied with the need for political change, but poetry, for him, was the proper domain of truth, beauty, and power. To Hunt, these were not airy abstractions plucked out of chaos and old night; they were profoundly moral, with a solid foundation in real life. They were calculated also to produce pleasure. In the Preface to *Foliage* (1818), he insisted that 'a delight in rural luxury'— that is, the love of the natural world—was 'within the reach of every one, and much more beautiful in reality, than people's fondness for considering all poetry as fiction would imply. The poets only do with their imaginations what all might do with their practice,— live at as cheap, natural, easy, and truly pleasurable a rate as possible'.[17] In its way, this was as egalitarian in its aims as the millenarian brotherhood envisaged by Wordsworth and Coleridge during the 1790s. But Hunt never believed, with them, that didactic poetry was the key to political reform; instead, 'We should consider ourselves as we really are,—creatures made to enjoy more than to know'.[18] For him, the purpose of poetry was 'pleasure and exaltation'[19]—a crucial determinant not just of Hunt's critical judgements, but of the content of his own poetry. 'I do not write, I confess, for the sake of a moral only, nor even for that purpose principally:—I write to enjoy myself'.[20] That is why Hunt could publish **"To Hampstead"** in *The Examiner* for 14 May 1815, adjacent to reports of Napoleon's doings in Paris, the price of bread, and reports of what was euphemistically referred to as the King's illness: its very point was that it had nothing to say about those events. It was, like the poems by Keats that appeared in the same pages, a kind of light relief.

This may have been the only aesthetic principle over which they differed, but it is sufficient to explain why Hunt, beginning his review of Wordsworth's *Peter Bell* in 1819, could say: 'This is another didactic little horror of Mr. Wordsworth's'.[21] It was why he so admired Byron's *Don Juan,*[22] and why Wordsworth believed that the same poem 'will do more harm to the English character, than anything of our time'.[23] Wordsworth could never have sympathised with the view that poetry was primarily a form of entertainment. To him it was a weapon in the fight for the betterment of mankind, and—what may seem crazy to us—the means by which he would play his part in bringing about the millennium, Christ's 1000-year rule on earth.[24]

Keats could not have known this in October 1816, when he first met Hunt. It was at this period that he also met Reynolds, Haydon, and Shelley. But Hunt was his first poetic guide; he gave Keats the encouragement and support the younger man needed to postpone his training as an apothecary and embark on a literary career. The reassurance provided by Hunt in opposition to the pressures exerted by Keats' less sympathetic guardian, Richard Abbey, led to a period of intense closeness. As Walter Jackson Bate puts it, 'The autumn [of 1816] was altogether intoxicating.'[25] Keats often stayed overnight at Hunt's house in the Vale of

Health, to which Hunt had moved a year before Reviewing Keats' "Sleep and Poetry" in *The Examiner,* Hunt recalled that it 'originated in sleeping in a room adorned with busts and pictures'[26]—his own library. Charles Cowden Clarke also remembered the beginnings of Keats' poem: 'It was in the library at Hunt's cottage, where an extemporary bed had been made up for him on the sofa, that he composed the frame-work and many lines of the poem on "Sleep and Poetry"— the last sixty or seventy being an inventory of the art garniture of the room'.[27] During the months following their first meeting in October, Keats absorbed Hunt's aesthetic ideas; more intriguingly, Hunt in turn appropriated his young friend's writing as support for them.

This process of appropriation began with Hunt's review of Keats' *Poems,* published in *The Examiner* from 1 June-13 July 1817. Hunt begins by surveying the state of modern poetry, and commending Wordsworth 'who in spite of some morbidities as well as mistaken theories in other respects, has opened upon us a fund of thinking and imagination, that ranks him as the successor of the true and abundant poets of the older time' (i.e. Spenser and Milton).[28] Having given Wordsworth qualified praise, he introduces Keats in distinctly Wordsworthian terms: 'our author has all the sensitiveness of temperament requisite to receive these impressions [of the images of things]; and wherever he has turned hitherto, he has evidently felt them deeply'.[29] So far, so good; he then enlists Keats in support of the criticisms of Wordsworth published in *The Feast of the Poets* three years before:

> Mr. Keats takes an opportunity . . . to object to the morbidity that taints the productions of the Lake Poets. They might answer perhaps, generally, that they chuse to grapple with what is unavoidable, rather than pretend to be blind to it; but the more smiling Muse may reply, that half of the evils alluded to are produced by brooding over them . . . [30]

This is followed by a passage from "Sleep and Poetry"[31] which Hunt entitled 'Happy Poetry Preferred'— a heading that might be said to sum up his poetic credo. The extract begins by describing some poets' subject-matter as 'ugly clubs, the Poets Polyphemes / Disturbing the grand sea', and concludes by stating that poetry 'should be a friend / To sooth the cares, and lift the thoughts of man'. If this was Keats at his most Huntian, Hunt was nonetheless incorrect in framing it as an attack on Wordsworth; in fact, Richard Woodhouse, who had reason to know, recorded that as far as their author was concerned, Keats' criticisms were directed at Byron.[32] It was nonetheless convenient for Hunt to appropriate these lines as further support for his ideas. On the face of it, Keats might be expected to have acquiesced in his public enrolment as a disciple of Hunt's. After all, in lines from "Sleep and Poetry" not quoted in Hunt's review, he had proclaimed:

All hail delightful hopes!
As she was wont, th' imagination
Into most lovely labyrinths will be gone,
And they shall be accounted poet kings
Who simply tell the most heart-easing things.
    (ll. 264-8)

Only someone who had sat at Hunt's feet absorbing his theories could have proposed 'the most heart-easing things' as the fittest subject for the poet-king; it was a position Keats would soon repudiate. But if, in late 1816, when "Sleep and Poetry" was composed, he agreed with Hunt's central beliefs, there are no grounds for thinking that he enjoyed being implicated in Hunt's campaign against Wordsworthian morbidity. After all, Keats was more enthusiastic about Wordsworth than Hunt ever was. In 1818 Keats could tell Haydon: 'I am convinced that there are three things to rejoice at in this Age—The Excursion Your Pictures, and Hazlitt's depth of Taste';[33] it was a view Hunt would never share. Given the extent of the younger poet's admiration for Wordsworth, it would be remarkable if the *Examiner* article was not the cause of some strain between Keats and Hunt. The evidence indicates that it was; by 8 October, a few months after its publication, Hunt had compounded the appropriation of Keats in his review by his heavy-handed editing of *Endymion:* 'I am quite disgusted with literary Men and will never know another except Wordsworth',[34] Keats told Benjamin Bailey, 'after all I shall have the Reputation of Hunt's elevé—His corrections and amputations will by the knowing ones be trased in the Poem—This is to be sure the vexation of a day'.[35]

Every major poet, however immature, carries some distinctive element of his or her vision with them from the moment they start writing. Even when he met Hunt in 1816 Keats was sufficiently in possession of his talent to resist complete assimilation into Hunt's way of thinking. This is evident from the two sonnets on the grasshopper and cricket, which Keats and Hunt composed during one of their sonnet-writing contests on 30 December 1816.[36] They each completed their sonnets in 15 minutes, and the results appeared, side by side, in the *Examiner* for 21 September 1817.

TWO SONNETS ON THE GRASSHOPPER AND CRICKET.

I.

[FROM POEMS BY JOHN KEATS.]

The poetry of earth is never dead:
    When all the birds are faint with the hot sun,
    And hide in cooling trees, a voice will run
From hedge to hedge about the new-mown mead;
    That is the Grasshopper's;—he takes the lead

In summer luxury,—he has never done
    With his delights; for when tired out with fun,
He rests at ease beneath some pleasant weed.
The poetry of earth is ceasing never:
    On a lone winter evening, when the frost
    Has wrought a silence, from the stove there shrills
The Cricket's song, in warmth increasing ever,
    And seems to one, in drowsiness half lost,
    The Grasshopper's among some grassy hills.
December 30, 1816.

II.

BY LEIGH HUNT;—NEVER BEFORE PUBLISHED.

Green little vaulter in the sunny grass,
    Catching your heart up at the feel of June,
    Sole voice left stirring midst the lazy noon,
When ev'n the bees lag at the summoning brass;—
And you, warm little housekeeper, who class
    With those who think the candles come too soon,
    Loving the fire, and with your tricksome tune
Nick the glad silent moments as they pass;—
O sweet and tiny cousins, that belong,
    One to the fields, the other to the hearth,
Both have your sunshine; both though small are strong
    At your clear hearts; and both were sent on earth
To ring in thoughtful ears this natural song,
    —In doors and out,—summer and winter,—Mirth.
December 30, 1816.[37]

Keats' reference to 'summer luxury' picks up a term used often by Hunt, and indicates his acceptance of the Huntian faith in pleasure as a primary objective of poetry. Even so, his sonnet resolves itself very differently from his mentor's. Hunt's suggestion that both insects provide their listeners with 'Mirth' turns them into models of the poet himself, and concentrates our attention on the guiding principle underlying Hunt's poetry: as Edgecombe has observed, the poem offers 'a covert philosophical proposition—[Hunt's] philosophy of cheer'.[38] Keats' sonnet, by comparison, is more reserved; in his concluding sestet, the cricket transports the listener from the dead of winter into high summer, as its song is transformed by the musing mind into that of the grasshopper. The reverie that produces this transformation is, it might be argued, distinctively Huntian; after all, a similar reverie features in the sonnet **"To Hampstead."** But the Huntian sense of repletion is offset by the failure of the grasshopper to materialise before us. Hunt's poem presents both insects simultaneously; by contrast, Keats leaves them just offstage throughout the sestet: unseen, the cricket sings from the stove, while the grasshopper sounds from 'among some grassy hills'. They foreshadow that elusive nightingale, whose

> plaintive anthem fades
> Past the near meadows, over the still stream,
> Up the hill-side; and now 'tis buried deep
> In the next valley-glades . . .

Even at the height of their involvement, Keats stops short of the Huntian tendency fully to gratify the reader's expectations. The distinction may seem minor, but it was always characteristic of Keats, from that early celebration of tormented love, *Fill for me a brimming bowl* (composed August 1814), to the *Odes* of 1819. The one exception was, of course, *"The Eve of St Agnes"*—which Hunt regarded as 'the most delightful and complete specimen of his genius'.[39] The difference between Hunt and Keats is akin to that between the experience of hearing music, and merely straining to hear it. Keats is preoccupied with potentiality, capability, immanence; Hunt with indulgence and surfeit. Hence the listener of Keats' sonnet, 'in drowsiness half lost', only 'seems' to hear the cricket's song; in the Preface to *Poems* (1815), a copy of which was sitting in Hunt's library, Wordsworth had discoursed on the potency of the word 'seems' as used by Milton.[40] With that word, Keats' sonnet allows the imagination, as Wordsworth conceives it, to operate on the perceiving mind, as the listener turns the cricket's song into that of the grasshopper, thus turning winter to summer, and solitude into the hope of companionship. In that respect Keats' poem stands in a line of works in which the company of insects provides momentary reassurance to human onlookers, including Wordsworth's *Written in Germany, on one of the coldest days of the Century* and Burns' *To a Louse.*

The experience, it should be remembered, is apparent rather than actual, and that restraint leaves a psychological vacuum at the heart of the poem: the cricket is not a grasshopper; the nightingale's song is doomed to die away; the Grecian urn will always remain inscrutable. Keats specialises in the kind of emotional suspension that leaves the reader expectant and hopeful, as if there is something more to come after the poem has finished. Once again, it is an effect Keats has in common with Wordsworth, who at his most optimistic had written:

> Our destiny, our nature, and our home,
> Is with infinitude, and only there—
> With hope it is, hope that can never die,
> Effort, and expectation, and desire,
> And something evermore about to be.[41]

The ambiguity of this stance, the room it leaves for doubt and disappointment, is something Hunt would have deplored. Not only do Keats and Wordsworth wish to accommodate pain and suffering, but those 'morbid' elements are essential to their vision. This is what Keats meant when, in April 1819, he asked George and Georgiana Keats, 'Do you not see how necessary a world of pains and troubles is to school an intelligence and make it a soul, a place where the heart must feel and suffer in a thousand diverse ways?'[42] If Hunt would have answered, 'no', there can be little doubt that Keats would hardly have posed the question in the first place had he not been an admirer of the poet who had written: 'Suffering is permanent, obscure, and dark, / And shares the nature of infinity'.[43]

By October 1817 Keats was as aware of the limitations of Huntian aesthetics as he would ever be, the most significant being Hunt's emphasis on the pleasure-principle. Haydon anticipated this line of thought when, in November 1816, he confided to his diary: 'Such is the morbid sensibility of his temperament that the supposition he can be guilty of Sin gives gloomy pain & he must be kept in a continual excitement of pleasure & voluptuousness by amorous poems & bodily sensations to keep himself in a state of ordinary every day comfort'.[44] A few months later, in January 1817, he went further:

> . . . Hunt's imagination is naturally and inherently gloomy, and all his leafy bowers & clipsome waists & balmy bosoms proceed not from a lovely fancy shooting out without effort the beauties of its own superabundant brightness, but are the produce of a painful, hypochodriac Soul that struggles by dwelling on the *reverse* of its own *real* thoughts, perpetually to illumine its natural and forlorn dinginess; hence his painful wit, his struggling jokes, his hopeless puns; hence his wish to be surrounded by inferior intellects and being delighted to suck in their honey praise; hence his unwillingness to leave company or be left by them; hence his gloated trifling with Women, for in reality he has a contempt for them, for he says all women should submit to the infidelities of their husbands without feeling insulted; & hence his seeing only the gloomy prospects of damnation in believing Christianity, and hence his horror of being left alone *even for an hour!*[45]

Haydon, who had by then known Hunt for over a decade, traces Hunt's 'rococo' manner to its psychological roots in a desire to escape his 'morbid sensibility' and 'painful, hypochondriac Soul'. Crude though his conclusions may appear, they are to some extent corroborated by Hunt's attitude to Wordsworth, the main fault of whose poetry, Hunt had written, was that it was 'only calculated to perplex and sadden us', and 'distresses to no purpose'. In short, the constituent of Wordsworth's poetry that most repelled him was identical to that which, as Haydon saw it, Hunt was trying to evade in his own work. Of course, Haydon's perspective was coloured by the resentment that had grown up between him and Hunt during recent months, largely through their religious wranglings, but his interpretation is supported by Hunt's Preface to *Rimini,* which itself traces the preference for happy poetry to the need for healing, or, as he puts it, 'comfort':

> But besides the tendency I have from animal spirits, as well as from need of comfort, to indulge my fancy in happier subjects, it appears to me, that the world has become experienced enough to be capable of receiving its best profit through the medium of pleasurable, instead of painful, appeals to its reflection. There is an old philosophic conviction reviving among us as a popular one (and there could not be one more desirable), that it is time for those who would benefit their species, to put an end to recriminations, and denouncements, and threats, and agree to consider the sufferings of mankind as arising out of a want of knowledge rather than defect of goodness,—as intimations which, like the physical pain of a wound, or a galling ligament, tell us that we are to set about removing the causes of pain, instead of venting the spleen of it.[46]

Written in 1832, this retrospective justification of his poetic manner nonetheless foregrounds its limitations; to put suffering down to ignorance rather than evil, as Hunt contends, is to turn tragedy into farce. If the result is indeed to remove the cause of pain, it is also to view human nature only in the rosiest possible light. Spleen, like it or not, is as much a product of passion as any of the more pleasurable moods which Hunt prefers. For a poet to exclude it from his work is as restrictive as for a painter to decide not to use the colour red.

What distinguishes the case against Hunt, as made by both friends and enemies, is that in his case aesthetics were inextricably intertwined with morality. It is not hard to see why; after all, to eliminate malignancy from one's understanding of psychology renders moral judgements virtually impossible. If everyone is either good or ignorant, all human actions are effectively reduced to the same level. Of course, this discussion might have been carried on in such intellectual terms at the time, but in Hunt's case it was personalised from the outset. Haydon saw Hunt's position in the light of his resistance to formalised religion, reporting in his diary on 20 January 1817: '"The question is," said Hunt, "who are the wicked? It is difficult to tell, I believe." Alas, what must be the state of that man, he who sophisticates as to what is wicked & yet has dawnings he does not do *right,* who disbelieves Christianity and yet fears damnation.'[47] For Haydon, religion, morality and art were all of a piece. Doubt God, and that faithlessness would be expressed in your work. Which is why the painting with which Haydon was preoccupied at that moment, *Christ's Entry into Jerusalem,* which contained portraits of Keats and Wordsworth,

exemplifies so effectively both his religious faith and artistic convictions. Haydon believed that if you didn't know right from wrong, you were in no position to make critical judgements either. This was the argument of his letter to Wordsworth on 15 April, in which he complains about 'Leigh Hunt's weathercock estimation of you':

> When you were in Town you visited him—you remember what he said with an agitated mouth—'The longer I live, and the older I grow, I feel my respect for your Genius encrease, Sir.' These were *his words*—Before a month was over, I again perceived doubts & hums, and ha's, instead of the momentary enthusiasm for you displayed for about that time—Scott & I and all his Friends accounted for it in the usual way—knowing he never holds one opinion one month he does not sophisticate himself out of before the next is over . . . When first I knew Leigh Hunt, he was really a delightful fellow, ardent in virtue, & perceiving the right thing in everything but Religion . . . his great error is inordinate personal vanity—& he who pampers it not, is no longer received with affection—I am daily getting more estranged from him—and indeed all his old Friends, are dropping off . . . [48]

For Haydon, virtue is equivalent to constancy of judgement, just as its lack leads inevitably to a lack of perspective about oneself and the rest of the world. Significantly, Keats' letter to Haydon of 11 May takes the same line; in relation to Hunt, he observed that 'There is no greater Sin after the 7 deadly than to flatter oneself into an idea of being a great Poet'.[49]

What is so astonishing about Leigh Hunt is that in his case the criticisms of his friends and enemies were very similar. The Cockney school did not exist until J. G. Lockhart, writing as 'Z.', invented the term in *Blackwood's Edinburgh Magazine* and appointed Hunt as its ringleader. The first of his attacks, published in October 1817, concentrated on Hunt's alleged immorality, and takes the same line as Haydon—that ethics are directly related to art:

> Every man is, according to Mr Hunt, a dull potato-eating blockhead—of no greater value to God or man than any ox or drayhorse—who is not an admirer of Voltaire's *romans,* a worshipper of Lord Holland and Mr Haydon, and a quoter of John Buncle and Chaucer's Flower and Leaf. Every woman is useful only as a breeding machine, unless she is fond of reading Launcelot of the Lake, in an antique summer-house.

> How such a profligate creature as Mr Hunt can pretend to be an admirer of Mr Wordsworth, is to us a thing altogether inexplicable. One great charm of Wordsworth's noble compositions consists in the dignified purity of thought, and the patriarchal simplicity of feeling, with which they are throughout

penetrated and imbued. We can conceive a vicious man admiring with distant awe the spectacle of virtue and purity; but if he does so sincerely, he must also do so with the profoundest feeling of the error of his own ways, and the resolution to amend them. His admiration must be humble and silent, not pert and loquacious. Mr Hunt praises the purity of Wordsworth as if he himself were pure, his dignity as if he also were dignified.[50]

The most important feature of Lockhart's case is that it is ideologically motivated. One reason for targeting Hunt was his radicalism, and the adjectives used to describe him—'profligate', 'vicious', 'humble'—are calculated to appeal to the class prejudices of *Blackwood's* Tory readership; at the same time, Wordsworth's 'patriarchal' simplicity of feeling elevates him to the same level as the politicians whose fear of revolution led to the Peterloo massacre. The paragraph thus plays out a drama—that of the patrician poet besieged by the dissolute imitator of a lower class, desperate for a share of his fame. Repeated ascriptions of 'purity' almost suggest that Wordsworth is in danger of being raped. Hunt is alleged to worship Lord Holland[51] and Haydon in much the same way that he sullies the purity of Wordsworth; it is simply another example of a social reprobate getting above himself. But behind the histrionics, Lockhart is worrying away at an aesthetic matter, for the clues to Hunt's alleged depravity are literary: Voltaire, Chaucer, *John Buncle,* Launcelot of the Lake. For Lockhart, they are examples of either radical (in the case of Voltaire) or 'low' culture (as with Thomas Amory's novel, *John Buncle*). And why should *The Flower and the Leaf* be included in this list—at the time thought to have been written by Chaucer, but now ascribed to an anonymous female poet of the last quarter of the 15th century?[52] Because, only months before, on 16 March, *The Examiner* had published Keats' sonnet *Written on a Blank Space at the end of Chaucer's Tale of 'The Floure and the Lefe'.* Hunt had published it under a brief introductory note: 'The following exquisite Sonnet, as well as one or two others that have lately appeared under the same signature, is from the pen of the young poet (KEATS), who was mentioned not long since in this paper, and who may already lay true claim to that title:—"The youngest he, / That sits in shadow of Apollo's tree."'[53] The inclusion of *The Flower and the Leaf* in Lockhart's list reveals that he had noted Keats' poem and Hunt's proprietorial note, and, for those in the know, it suggests that Keats' strategy is no different from Hunt's—that of contaminating other writers by pretending to understand and admire them. More disturbing, Lockhart signals to Keats that he is next. Such was Keats' interpretation when, still in shock, he reported the article to Bailey on 3 November: 'There has been a flaming attack upon Hunt in the Endinburgh Magazine—I never read any thing so virulent accusing him of the greatest Crimes . . . I have no doubt that the second Number was intended for me'.[54]

Lockhart's essay upset Hunt sufficiently for him to challenge its anonymous author, in *The Examiner* for 16 November, to 'avow himself; which he cannot fail to do, unless to an utter disregard of all *Truth* and *Decency,* he adds the height of Meanness and COWARDICE.'[55] There were no less than three appeals in the *Examiner* to 'Z' to disclose his identity, none of which were heeded.[56] That his article was so obviously partisan should not obscure the fact that Lockhart's distortions were closer to the truth than he can have suspected. Hunt himself admitted that his literary principles arose out of ethical beliefs, and that his dislike of morbidity dictated a resistance to the kind of radical poetry composed by the young Wordsworth. Admittedly, this is not the position Lockhart criticises—his portrait of Hunt is caricature—but without being aware of it, he echoes anxieties current, for different reasons, among Hunt's associates, not least Haydon and Keats. And his central argument—that politics, morality, and literature are mutually determining—holds water; it is, in fact, a forerunner of the more ambitious propositions of today's new historicists.

Keats knew what was in store; his poetry received rough treatment from a number of reviewers, partly through his association with Hunt. Wielding the hatchet in August 1818, Lockhart took care to inform his colleagues that 'Keats belongs to the Cockney School of Politics, as well as the Cockney School of Poetry'.[57] Worse was to come, but Keats' reaction against Hunt was never as strong as it is sometimes claimed to be. Much as many critics would like to banish him from the story of Keats' development after 1818, the truth is that Keats' precocity owed much to the fact that he discovered his voice comparatively quickly, thanks to having worked alongside a literary personality so well defined as was Hunt's. That Huntian aesthetics permeate Keats' poetry right up to the end is ample proof of this. The central image in the 'Bright star' sonnet— that of the poet's head 'Pillowed upon my fair love's ripening breast'—is, of course, a Huntian luxury, just one step away from the intense emotion between the lovers in **"To Hampstead:"**

> Bright star! Would I were steadfast as thou art—
> Not in lone splendour hung aloft the night
> And watching, with eternal lids apart,
> Like nature's patient, sleepless eremite,
> The moving waters at their priestlike task
> Of pure ablution round earth's human shores,
> Or gazing on the new soft-fallen mask
> Of snow upon the mountains and the moors;
> No—yet still steadfast, still unchangeable,
> Pillowed upon my fair love's ripening breast,
> To feel for ever its soft fall and swell,
> Awake for ever in a sweet unrest,

Still, still to hear her tender-taken breath,
And so live ever—or else swoon to death.

Notes

1 'Z.' [J. G. Lockhart]. "On the Cockney School of Poetry No. 1," *Blackwood's Edinburgh Magazine* 2 (1817) 38-41, p. 38.

2 Text from *Romanticism: An Anthology* ed. Duncan Wu (Oxford: Blackwell, 1994), p. 668.

3 Rodney Stenning Edgecombe, *Leigh Hunt and the Poetry of Fancy* (London: Associated University Presses, 1994), p. 23.

4 *Imagination and Fancy* (1832), pp. 2-3.

5 *Romanticism*, p. 249.

6 *Romanticism*, p. 254.

7 This letter, hitherto unpublished, is retained at the Wordsworth Library, Grasmere. I am grateful to the Chairman and Trustees of the Library for permission to quote.

8 *The Letters of William and Dorothy Wordsworth: A Supplement of New Letters* ed. Alan G. Hill (Oxford: Clarendon Press, 1993), pp. 144-5; his italics.

9 *The Letters of William and Dorothy Wordsworth: The Middle Years 1806-20* ed. E. de Selincourt, rev. Mary Moorman and Alan G. Hill (2 vols., Oxford: Clarendon Press, 1969-70) (hereafter *MY*), ii 195.

10 Edmund Blunden, *Leigh Hunt: A Biography* (London: Cobden-Sanderson, 1930), p. 94.

11 Chester L. and Alice C. Shaver, *Wordsworth's Library* (New York, 1979), p. 133; *MY* ii 273.

12 Letter of 29 December 1815, now retained at the Wordsworth Library, Grasmere.

13 *MY* ii 299.

14 *Feast of the Poets* (1814), p. 89.

15 *Feast*, pp. 94-5.

16 *Feast*, pp 96-7.

17 *Foliage*, pp. 18-19.

18 *Foliage*, p. 16.

19 *Imagination and Fancy*, p. 1.

20 *Foliage*, p. 18.

21 *Examiner*, 2 May 1819, p. 282.

22 See his review of *Don Juan, The Examiner*, 31 October 1819, pp. 700-2.

23 *The Letters of William and Dorothy Wordsworth: The Later Years 1821-53* ed. E. de Selincourt, rev. Alan G. Hill (4 vols., Oxford: Clarendon Press, 1978-88) (hereafter *LY*), ii 579.

24 The best explication of the philosophy of *The Recluse* is provided by Jonathan Wordsworth, *The Borders of Vision* (Oxford: Clarendon Press, 1982), Epilogue.

25 Walter Jackson Bate, *John Keats* (London: The Hogarth Press, 1992), p. 111.

26 *Examiner*, 13 July 1817, p. 443.

27 Charles and Mary Cowden Clarke, *Recollections of Writers* (Fontwell: Centaur Press, 1969), pp. 133-4.

28 *Examiner*, 1 June 1817, p. 345.

29 *Examiner*, 6 July 1817, p. 428.

30 *Examiner* 13 July 1817, p. 443.

31 Lines 230-47.

32 See *The Poems of John Keats* ed. Miriam Allott (Harlow: Longman, 1970), p. 79, notes to ll. 231, 233-5, 241-2.

33 *The Letters of John Keats* ed. Hyder E. Rollins (2 vols., Cambridge, Mass.: Harvard University Press, 1958), i 203.

34 This statement seems to undermine Beth Lau's claim that 'It is therefore likely that the young poet at this time also adopted Hunt's opinion of Wordsworth's faults' (*Keats's Reading of the Romantic Poets* [Ann Arbor: University of Michigan Press, 1991], p. 21).

35 Rollins i 169-70.

36 The occasion is recalled by Clarke, *Recollections*, pp. 135-6.

37 *Examiner*, 21 September 1817, p. 599.

38 Edgecombe, p. 210.

39 *Imagination and Fancy*, p. 314.

40 See Wordsworth's commentary on *Paradise Lost* ii

642: '"So seemed": and to whom "seemed"? To the heavenly muse who dictates the poem, to the eye of the poet's mind, and to that of the reader, present at one moment in the wide Ethiopian, and the next in the solitudes, then first broken in upon, of the infernal regions!' (*Romanticism*, p. 479).

[41] *Thirteen-Book Prelude* vi 538-42; *Romanticism* p. 362.

[42] *Romanticism*, p. 1053.

[43] Wordsworth, *The Borderers* 1543-4; *The Poetical Works of William Wordsworth* ed. E. de Selincourt and Helen Darbishire (5 vols., Oxford: Clarendon Press, 1940-9), i 188.

[44] *The Diary of Benjamin Robert Haydon* ed. Willard Bissell Pope (5 vols., Cambridge, Mass.: Harvard University Press, 1960-3), ii 68.

[45] Pope, ii 81.

[46] *Leigh Hunt: Selected Writings* ed. David Jesson Dibley (Manchester: Carcanet, 1990), p. 17.

[47] Pope ii 87.

[48] Wordsworth Library, Grasmere. No doubt Haydon's letter influenced Wordsworth's later opinion: 'Mr Leigh Hunt is a Coxcomb, was a Coxcomb, and ever will be a Coxcomb' (*LY* ii 401).

[49] Rollins i 143.

[50] "On the Cockney School of Poetry No. 1", *Blackwood's Edinburgh Magazine* 2 (1817) 38-41, p. 40.

[51] Hunt's dealings with Holland were not extensive; in fact, if his *Autobiography* is to be believed, it was more a case of his being courted by Holland; see *The Autobiography of Leigh Hunt* ed. J. E. Morpurgo (London: Cresset Press, 1948), p. 226.

[52] For a full account of the arguments concerning the attribution of both works see Eleanor Prescott Hammond, *Chaucer: A Bibliographical Manual* (New York: Peter Smith, 1933), pp. 423-4, 408-9.

[53] *Examiner,* 16 March 1817, p. 173.

[54] Rollins i 180.

[55] *Examiner,* 16 November 1817, p. 729.

[56] On 2 November, 16 November, and 14 December, pp. 693, 729, 788.

[57] *Romanticism*, p. 1007.

FURTHER READING

Bibliography

Waltman, John L., and Gerald G. McDaniel. *Leigh Hunt: A Comprehensive Bibliography*. New York: Garland Publishing, Inc., 1985, 273 p.

Provides a complete bibliography of secondary materials about Hunt chronologically arranged by decade. Works cited include literary histories, newspaper and journal articles, biographies, and memorabilia.

Biographies

Blainey, Ann. *Immortal Boy: A Portrait of Leigh Hunt*. London: Croom Helm, 1985, 210 p.

Offers a portrait of the human side of Hunt. Relies on extensive collections of Hunt's personal letters.

Blunden, Edmund. *Leigh Hunt: A Biography*. London: Cobden-Sanderson, 1930, 402 p.

Stands as a classic work that presents a consistently favorable portrait of Hunt. Includes a comprehensive bibliography of Hunt's primary works.

Shaddy, Robert A. "Around the Library Table With Luther A. Brewer: Annual Reflections on Collecting Leigh Hunt." *Books at Iowa,* No. 57 (November 1992): 17–34.

Describes the philosophy and work of avid book-collector Luther Brewer, who assembled one of the world's finest collections of Hunt's writings.

Criticism

Barnard, John. "Leigh Hunt's Later Notes to *The Indicator*." *The Keats-Shelley Review*, No. 6 (Autumn 1991): 60–2.

Provides the text and context for several annotations Hunt included in a reprinting of *The Indicator*.

Cox, Jeffrey N. "Staging Hope: Genre, Myth, and Ideology in the Dramas of the Hunt Circle." *Texas Studies in Literature and Language* 38, Nos. 3–4 (Fall/Winter 1996): 245–64.

Explores the ideology of the group of dramatists that Hunt led, examining their use of mythological sources.

Edgecombe, Rodney Stenning. *Leigh Hunt and the Poetry of Fancy*. Cranbury, N.J.: Associated University Presses, 1994, 276 p.

Analyzes Hunt's poetry in terms of its rococo influences and ideas. Accepts other critics' characterization of Hunt as a minor poet but suggests a reevaluation of him as a rococo figure.

———. "Leigh Hunt and the Rococo." *The Keats-Shelley Journal* XLI (1992): 164–77.

Identifies rococo characteristics in Hunt's poetry, offering a favorable interpretation of Hunt as a rococo, not classical, poet.

Fogle, Stephen F. "Leigh Hunt and the End of Romantic Criticism." In *Some British Romantics: A Collection of Essays*, edited by James V. Logan, John E. Jordan, and Northrop Frye, pp. 117–39. Columbus, Ohio: Ohio State University Press, 1966.

Discusses Hunt's longest critical piece, suggesting that Hunt's failure to formulate consistent critical principles signaled the end of the creative period of Romantic criticism.

Gilmartin, Kevin. "'Victims of Argument, Slaves of Fact': Hunt, Hazlitt, Cobbett and the Literature of Opposition." *The Wordsworth Circle* XXI, No. 3 (Summer 1990): 90-6.

Discusses the political writings of Hunt and some of his contemporaries. Contends that while they claimed to be interested in independent truth, their work relied on constant political opposition.

Short, Clarice. "The Composition of Hunt's *The Story of Rimini*." *The Keats-Shelley Journal* XXI–XXII (1972–1973): 207–18.

Compares Hunt's rough drafts with the final, published form of *The Story of Rimini*, suggesting that the poet relied more on diligence than on poetical ability.

Trewin, J. C. "Leigh Hunt as a Dramatic Critic." *Keats-Shelley Memorial Bulletin* X (1959): 14–19.

Favorably characterizes Hunt's work as a theater critic, suggesting that it gives the modern reader a sharp and truthful look into the theater of Hunt's time.

Wheatley, Kim. "The *Blackwood's* Attacks on Leigh Hunt." *Nineteenth-Century Literature* 47, No. 1 (June 1992): 1–31.

Analyzes *Blackwood's Magazine*'s consistently unfavorable criticism of Hunt and his poetry. Suggests that the magazine's confusion of Hunt's real life with his fiction can be understood as a literary technique rather than a personal attack.

Woodring, Carl R. "Leigh Hunt as Political Essayist." In *Leigh Hunt's Political and Occasional Essays*, edited by Lawrence Huston Houtchens and Carolyn Washburn Houtchens, pp. 3–71. New York: Columbia University Press, 1962.

Provides an introduction to a collection of Hunt's political essays and analyzes Hunt's contributions to political journalism in the context of the historical period.

Jorge Ricardo Isaacs

1837-1895

Colombian poet, novelist, nonfiction writer, and politician.

INTRODUCTION

Isaacs is chiefly remembered for his tragic, romantic novel, *María* (1867), which is still widely read in Hispanic America. Isaacs was also a prolific poet, though his poetry has not received the same critical attention as *María*. In his nonfiction prose, Isaacs tended to espouse strong political positions. A liberal who believed in the separation of church and state, Isaacs took on such contentious issues as the treatment of Indians by Catholic missionaries. However, few of Isaacs's polemical writings remain in print.

Biographical Information

Isaacs was born in Cali, Colombia, in 1837, the son of a Jamaican man of Jewish descent and a Catholic, Colombian woman. Isaacs's father owned numerous ranches and a sugar-processing mill. Though educated in Bogotá, Isaacs did not graduate from high school. In 1856, after a brief stint in the army, Isaacs married Felisa González Umaña. He soon returned to the military, and there began writing his poetry. In 1861, Issacs left the military to run the family ranches and businesses, but he failed at this endeavor and by 1864 was forced to sell the ranches. Isaacs first achieved literary fame in 1864 with the publication of his poetry by the literary group "El Mosaico." He next worked as a construction inspector. This job required that he live in the jungles along the Pacific coast, away from his wife. There, he began writing his novel, *María*. Illness eventually led Isaacs to return to his family, and in 1866, Isaacs entered politics as the Cauca Valley's conservative representative. He soon switched to the liberal party, a move that coincided with his joining the Freemasons. This move gained Isaacs many political enemies, many of whom made much of Isaacs's Jewish ancestry in an attempt to discredit him. By 1870, however, Isaacs landed the prestigious post of consul to Chile. Returning to Colombia in 1873, Isaacs attempted ranching once more but once again failed. In 1875, having declared bankruptcy, Isaacs attempted to justify his business practices in *A Mis Amigos y a los Commerciantes del Cauca* (1875; *To My Friends and the Businessmen of the Cauca Valley*). Issacs was the subject of heavy criticism, both for his financial dealings and his continued liberal politics. His next occu-

pation, as general superintendent of public schools, was interrupted by civil war. Isaacs fought for the liberal government and by 1877 resumed teaching. For the next few years, Isaacs held a number of government positions, and among other causes, worked for Indian rights. For a few months in 1880, Isaacs declared himself president of the state of Antioquia until forced to resign. As a result, Isaacs was driven from the national congress and denounced as a revolutionary. That same year, he wrote a pamphlet, *La Revolución Radical en Antioquia* (1880; *The Radical Revolution in Antioquia*) in defense of his actions. In the next few years, Isaacs continued writing poetry and treatises and intermittently received government positions. He was again embroiled in his country's political upheaval in 1885 when he joined the revolution against the government. Escaping any serious repercussions, Isaacs received a government contract to mine coal deposits along the Atlantic coast. This venture, as Isaacs's other business attempts, yielded no profit in his lifetime. In 1893, Isaacs planned to write a trilogy of historical novels that, in the words of Donald McGrady, "were to glorify the heroism of those who had freed Colombia from the tyranny of Spain, to show the lack of political expertise of these liberators, and to denounce the powers of darkness (namely the Roman Catholic Church)." Isaacs died in 1895 before completing more than a fragment of just one of these novels, *Camilo* (1937).

Major Works

Although Isaacs's poetry and nonfiction offer insight into his life and times, Isaacs's masterpiece was his one finished novel, *María*. John Rosenberg calls *María* "a prototype of the Latin American romantic novel" and notes that Isaacs "invites us to read tearfully." The young narrator of the tale, Efraín, recounts his love for and separation from the beautiful María. María's eventual death, before Efraín can return to her, emphasizes the tragedy of the story. Donald McGrady writes that the sentimental nature of the novel "came as a breath of fresh air in a period suffocated by materialism and the spirit of Positivism." In *María*, Issacs explores the depths of human emotion and virtually ignores the political upheaval of his own time. *María* is also read as a partly autobiographical novel. María shared the Jewish ancestry of her creator, and the setting for the novel was inspired by one of Isaacs's childhood homes, "El Paraíso." Although neither explicitly historical or political, *María* does provide a view of mid-nineteenth century Colombia with Efraín accurately describing the landscape as he journeys through the jungles of Colombia. The interpolated story of Nay and Sinar, two African slaves, provided a glimpse of current racial stereotypes and the reality of South American slavery. Many of Isaacs's other works were more overtly political. Several of his poems deal with the Colombian civil wars. In his nonfiction prose, particularly *La Revolución Radical en Antioquia*, Isaacs explained his own political motivations. Other work was intensely personal: many of Isaacs's poems were dedicated to his wife and others describe possible extramarital affairs.

Critical Reception

Before the publication of *María*, Issacs was hailed as a budding poet. However, by 1877, as Donald McGrady notes, the president of Argentina was so disenchanted "that he called a meeting of his cabinet to consider the disparity between *María* and Isaacs' poetry." Following the opinion of Argentina's president, most critics confine their analysis to Isaacs's novel. *María* was an unmitigated success in its own time. Pirated editions of the novel appeared throughout Latin America and Spain during Isaacs's lifetime. Recently, critics have explored the significance of this novel beyond its romantic origins. The structure of the novel, as well as its depiction of women and of African slaves, has received a fair amount of attention. Critics have also noted that the tragedy of the novel moves beyond its depiction of María's death. Sylvia Molloy reads the novel as the "Spanish American model for the timeless *topos* of paradise lost," and Sharon Magnarelli argues in *The Lost Rib* that "Efraín writes to recapture this past, to reconquer this paradise."

PRINCIPAL WORKS

Poesías [*Poems*] (poetry) 1864
María (novel) 1867
A Mis Amigos y a los Commerciantes del Cauca [*To My Friends and the Businessmen of the Cauca Valley*] (manifesto) 1875
La Revolución Radical en Antioquia [*The Radical Revolution in Antioquia*] (manifesto) 1880
Saulo (unfinished epic poem) 1881
Estudio Sobre las Tribus Indígenas del Estado del Magdalena, antes Provincia de Santa Marta [*A Study of the Native Tribes of the State of Magdalena, Formerly the Province of Santa Marta*] (nonfiction) 1884
Camilo (unfinished novel of unfinished three-novel series) 1937
Poesías [*Poems*] (poetry) 1967

CRITICISM

Donald McGrady (essay date 1972)

SOURCE: "Isaacs' Poetry," in *Jorge Isaacs*, Twayne Publishers, Inc., 1972, pp. 33-58.

[*In the following excerpt, McGrady offers a survey of Isaacs's poetry.*]

I *Introduction*

Jorge Isaacs' poetry is much inferior to the high quality of his novel *María,* but is of sufficient merit to place him among Colombia's secondary poets. His poetry is, above all, a faithful reflection of his life. Precisely herein resides its chief importance: it throws additional light on the inward thoughts of the man who wrote *María.* For example, Isaacs' lyrical verses disclose his deep-rooted sensuality—a quality shared by the male protagonist of *María,* although the latter tries to obscure this aspect of his personality. Another trait evident in Isaacs' poetry, but which has been dissimulated somewhat in his novelistic double, is his spitefulness—his tendency to harbor a grudge, feeding his malice, rather than endeavoring to abate it.

Isaacs' poetry is not profound; it contains no hidden meanings or recondite symbols. Only an occasional image adorns the prosaic narratives and descriptions. It has been observed[1] that Isaacs' verses are as limpid as the crystalline waters of the rivers that abound in his work. Isaacs was primarily interested in the content of his verses, not in the form.[2] Therefore, the task of the critic is not that of discovering a meaning concealed by complicated or ambiguous technique, but simply consists in describing the content of Isaacs' poetry and showing its relationship to his life and to *María.*

It has been noted[3] that there are two periods in Isaacs' poetry. In his first stage of development, Isaacs made a cult of nature. In his second period, the poet's bitter disillusionment gives an introspective and melancholic tinge to his verses, which consequently lose the freshness and spontaneity of his earlier work. These two periods are clearly separated by three years of sterility, for Isaacs wrote no poetry from 1871 to 1873 (the compositions he published during these years had been written previously). This sterile period corresponds to the years that he was a consul in Chile (1871-72) and to the year of intense struggle on the "Guayabonegro" ranch. His most productive years were from 1860 to 1864, that is, when he was still at the home ranch and shortly thereafter. His ruinous management of the family estate (1861-63) can be attributed to the fact that Isaacs spent his time composing verses instead of supervising the production of sugar and the care of cattle.

There is little variety in the themes of Isaacs' poetry. His poetic production falls into four large categories: (1) autobiographical poetry, (2) narrative poems, (3) lyric poetry, and (4) descriptive verses. Naturally, some compositions contain elements from two categories (autobiographical and lyric, for example), but they can be classified in accordance with their predominant theme.

II *Autobiographic Poems*

There are autobiographical reminiscences in an unusually large proportion of Isaacs' poems. More than a dozen reflect the author's longing for the happiness of his childhood and youth, when the Isaacs family was prosperous and respected by all. Isaacs' autobiographical poems are characterized by the accuracy of the details concerning his life (on the other hand, the autobiographic references in *María* are often modified, or are purposefully left vague).

In **"Mayo,"** Isaacs recounts the tricks that he played, as a child, on his dog (this same pet appears in *María*). This poem contains one of the relatively few humorous notes in Isaacs' entire work:

Mayo was, according to many,
a pointer,
but never partridges
did he see even from afar.
Geese and chickens
he caught in the air
in marvelous fashion.

He persecuted like a white person
his own race,
and, like an aristocrat,
black faces.

(Mayo era, según muchos,
un perdiguero,
pero nunca perdices
vio ni de lejos.
Gansos y pollos
atrapaba en el aire
que era un asombro.

Persiguió como un blanco
su propia raza,
y, como un aristócrata,
las negras caras.[4])

This jocularity contrasts greatly with the melancholic part that the faithful canine plays in *María*. The trip which Isaacs made to Bogotá to commence his studies is portrayed with exact detail in **"Mayo"**:

When in eighteen hundred
and forty-eight

from my father's house
I departed crying . . .
After an absence of five years
I returned . . .

(Cuando en mil ochocientos
cuarenta y ocho
de la casa paterna
salí lloroso . . .
Tras un lustro de ausencia
volví . . .)

The exactness of these details differs considerably from the vagueness and inaccuracy of the corresponding quasi-autobiographical elements in *María:* "I was still a child when they sent me away from home in order that I should commence my studies . . ." (Chapter I); "after six years . . . they greeted me on my return to my native valley" (II).

Another family pet that evokes happy childhood memories for the poet is the troupial that gives title to **"El turpial."** In this poem, Isaacs mentions his father's return trip from Jamaica, names an old slave called Pedro, recalls the family ranch "La Rita," and speaks briefly of his five years of study in Bogotá. (All these autobiographical elements also occur in the first chapters of *María*.) Then follow distressing memories from the period of the family's economic decline. The story of the tropical bird's misfortunes over the years is used as a device to mirror the gradual financial deterioration of the Isaacs family.

The hendecasyllabic octaves of **"La oración" ("The Prayer")** likewise evoke "pleasant memories of the paternal home." These remembrances are always identified with the hills and rivers of the Cauca Valley. The poet strikes a typically Romantic pose as he contemplates the landscape from a hill at the twilight hour. Isaacs wrote **"¡Al mar!" ("To the Sea!")** when he was working on the road to Buenaventura, and he dedicated the piece to his co-workers. The poet notes with satisfaction that those who were enemies in the civil strife a short time before, now break their bread together. Isaacs prophesies that when the road is completed, it will produce great material benefits for his native state. Some years later, this same reasoning prompted the writer to acquire the "Guayabonegro" ranch.

"La casa paterna" ("The Paternal Home") is the most extensive autobiographical poem written by Isaacs. In it, the poet laments the economic difficulties that forced his family to abandon their country estate. In his imagination, he returns to the beloved scene of his childhood; his footsteps echo hollowly as he wanders through the deserted rooms. Certain strophes of the poem resemble closely the lyrical essay **"Leyendo a María" ("Reading María")**, where the author also returns in spirit to the former Isaacs mansion.[5] A considerable portion of the poem is devoted to his beloved wife **"Selfia"** (an anagram of Felisa), his faithful companion in the struggle against poverty; Isaacs recalls that their happiest moments were spent together at his father's house. In the last stanzas, the writer bids farewell to the cherished mansion, for he now has little hope of returning to it. In **"Clementina,"** the poet's small daughter serves as a vehicle to condemn the present owners of the ranches that belonged to the Isaacs. Little did the writer foresee that his poverty was to worsen with the years.

"A Henrique. ¡Ora y espera!" ("To Henrique. Pray and Hope!") is a curious piece dedicated to one of Isaacs' brothers. In the first half of the composition appear memories of their common childhood, while in the second part, the writer sympathizes with his brother regarding an unhappy love affair. **"El esclavo Pedro"** **("Pedro the Slave")** is dedicated to the same loyal servant that is a minor character in Chapters IV and V of *María*. The verse in which the slave takes leave of his small master upon the latter's departure for Bogotá ("I shall not see you, my master, when you are a man") is almost identical to his farewell in the novel ("My little master, I shall not see you again").

Isaacs also introduces autobiographical elements in some of his lyric poems. The note he reiterates most often is that of feeling ostracized, of being banished from his native city and state (examples are found in **"Felisa," "La oración," "Nima,"** and **"El gorrión"** [**"The Sparrow"**]). It would be only natural that the poet should speak in this manner after his economic failures of 1864 and 1874, or after his expulsion from Congress in 1880, for his financial and political activities created many enemies for him. The surprising thing is that all these poems bear the date of 1860. A Colombian critic has given a convincing explanation for this enigma: often poets who possess everything necessary for success invent for themselves a source of grief, as though they need to suffer in order to find inspiration for their work.[6] Such seems to be the case of Isaacs, who in 1860 had the prime requisites for happiness: a loving bride, a promising future as a writer, the prospect of wealth. Ironically, what Isaacs originally conceived as a poetic motive was to come all too true some years later.

Since Jorge Isaacs' autobiographical poems reproduce many real situations from his childhood and youth, it seems appropriate to examine his poetic works to see if they shed light on a problem that has been hotly debated in Colombia: Did María, the heroine of Isaacs' novel, really exist? As a matter of fact, there are allusions to a certain María in two of Isaacs' autobiographic poems, **"Mayo"** and **"La tarde azul" ("The Blue Evening")**. Certain stanzas of the latter poem, dated June, 1866, seem to allude to the Romantic hero-

ine, for they speak of a woman who is "a dream of my soul," a "delirium." However, another stanza contains details that make it clear that this is not the María of the novel:

> The first secret
> of a boy's love
> under the *gualanday* bushes
> along the gentle river . . .
> The first caress
> exchanged for doves
> by my María!

> (Primera confidencia
> de amor de niño
> bajo los gualandayes
> del manso río . . .
> ¡Primer caricia
> trocada por palomas
> a mi María!)

The expression, "boy's love," indicates that this love affair is much less deep and lasting than that of Efraín and María. And the "caress exchanged for doves" is the unequivocal sign of a mercenary love bought from a woman of inferior social status.

These conclusions are supported by evidence from the poem **"Mayo,"** written in 1860. Here a racy passage reveals that María protected the dog from little Jorge's pranks, but had less success in shielding herself from her young master's amorous attacks:

> From my fury
> María always saved him:
> I was so sly
> and she so pretty!
> Such was my destiny,
> from childhood to seek
> sensual things.[7]

> (De mi furor salvóle
> siempre María:
> yo era tan malicioso
> ¡y ella tan linda!
> Tal fue mi estrella,
> buscar desde chicuelo
> uvas y Evas.)

When the youth returned from his studies in Bogotá, he found that "now Clara and María were married."[8] This text makes evident that María was older than Jorge, that she exercised some kind of authority over him, and that she tolerated his not-so-innocent caresses. The logical conclusion is that in all probability this María was a servant in the Isaacs household. Although she was the poet's first "boy's love," this María could not possibly have inspired the chaste Romantic heroine of the novel.

The only poetic allusions to a woman resembling María appear in **"¡Ve, pensamiento!"** (**"Go, Thought!"**), a lyric (not autobiographical) poem dated 1867,[9] the year of publication of the novel:

> In the mountains
> there are lilies,
> Alas!, that no longer
> grow for her! . . .
> the garden . . .
> where at dawn,
> with fresh roses
> I saw her smilingly
> fill her apron . . .
> Lost Eden!
> Saintly innocence!
> Angel of a day
> on earth! . . .
> and withered roses
> which no longer adorn
> her black braids! . . .
> upon the grave
> where the weeds
> cover the slab,
> gray now,
> that my lips
> kiss with a sob.
>
> (En las montañas
> hay azucenas,
> ¡Ay! ¡que no nacen
> ya para ella! . . .
> los jardines . . .
> do en las auroras,
> de rosas frescas
> llenar su falda
> la vi risueña . . .
> ¡Edén perdido!
> ¡Santa inocencia!
> ¡Angel de un día
> sobre la tierra! . . .
> y rosas muertas . . .
> ¡que ya no adornan
> sus negras trenzas! . . .
> sobre el sepulcro
> do la maleza
> cubre la losa
> ya cenicienta
> que sollozantes
> mis labios besan.)

Although there is no mention of a girl's name here, the allusions to the lilies and the roses seem to refer to the flowers that Efraín brought from the mountain for María (Chapter X) and to those which María gathered for Efraín's room (III-IV). The descriptions of the tomb, made desolate by the weeds and grayed by the rain, and of the lover who casts himself sobbing upon the slab, appear in exactly this form in the last chapter of *María*.

The lack of references to a María in Isaacs' autobiographical poems is proof that the heroine of the novel did not exist in real life. It is inconceivable that a love so profound as Efraín's should not be reflected in poems that register such ephemeral sentimental incidents as the mercenary caresses of a servant, or the first kiss received from a cousin (see **"El primer beso"** [**"The First Kiss"**]). The fact that the only possible allusion to María is found in a lyric poem, not in an autobiographical one, clearly indicates that she existed only in Isaacs' imagination.[10]

III *Narrative Poems*

Narrative poems were very much in fashion during the years in which Jorge Isaacs was reading and composing poetry. In Spain, Ramón de Campoamor and Gaspar Núñez de Arce cultivated this type of poetry with great success, being universally applauded throughout the Spanish-speaking world. (Twentieth-century critics, however, have been less generous in their appraisal of these poets.) Isaacs' tastes coincided with those of his time: he enthusiastically hailed Núñez de Arce as "the greatest poet that Spain has had in the second half of this century."[11] Therefore, it is not surprising that he followed the example of Campoamor and Núñez de Arce, writing poems with a simple plot that portrayed contemporary life and manners.

The theme most often treated by Isaacs in his narrative poems is that of the Colombian civil wars, in several of which he took an active part. In all these poems, much stress is laid upon the tragedy that civil conflicts bring upon the recruits and their families.[12] In **"La montañera"** (**"The Moutain Girl"**), the poet describes the sadness of Gabriela, a peasant girl, whose suitor has died in the war:

> The mountain girl
> cries sitting
> upon the rocks,
> and in her sobs
> a name sounds
> like a sigh,
> like a lament.
>
> (La montañera
> llora sentada
> sobre las peñas,
> y en sus sollozos
> un nombre suena
> como un suspiro,
> como una queja.)

In **"La vuelta del recluta"** (**"The Return of the Recruit"**), the latter comes home and discovers that his sweetheart has married another, and that his family has disappeared. The protagonist of **"El cabo Muñoz"** (**"Corporal Muñoz"**) intends to marry the pretty peasant girl who has nursed his wounds, but he perishes in battle. **"La muerte del sargento" ("The Death of the Sergeant")** narrates the last melancholy moments of a soldier who leaves behind a widow and a son. In his **"Sonnet to My Country,"** Isaacs compares the warring parties to two lions that devour each other in the desert.

Another favorite theme of Isaacs' narrative poems is that of the unfortunate love affairs of a boy and girl of humble origin. In **"La aldeana infiel" ("The Unfaithful Village Girl"),** she forgets her fiancé and gives herself to a man of higher station. The latter casts her off after enjoying her, and the jilted lover goes to the war. On returning eight years later, the soldier encounters a blind beggar woman: it is the unfaithful village girl. This sentimental type of love story was common in Spanish Romanticism. A similar kind of tale occurs in **"Teresa":** a country girl leaves her peasant lover to marry a wealthier suitor, who is found murdered some time afterwards. In **"Martina y Jacinto,"** the lovers arrange a rendezvous by a river. Jacinto must swim across to join Martina, and dives into the storm-swollen waters. He drowns, and Martina does too when she tries to rescue her sweetheart. This poem bears an obvious resemblance to the Classical legend of Hero and Leander. A contrast with the former poems is provided by **"Amores de Soledad" ("Love Affairs of Soledad"),** which ends happily and takes place in a setting of pastoral innocence.

"La reina del campamento" ("The Queen of the Army Camp") contains a lively description of a pretty coquette who unabashedly provokes the desires of soldiers:

> As self-satisfied as a sergeant
> who has been promoted to officer,
> the torment of colonels,
> Tarcila goes passing by.
> Her shawl half hides
> her face full of charm and wit . . .
> And the ardent Creole keeps
> glancing backward,
> with eyes that say: sin!,
> and a criminal laugh.

> (Oronda como un sargento
> que han ascendido a oficial,
> tormento de coroneles,
> Tarcila pasando va.
> Su rebozo oculta a medias
> su rostro lleno de sal . . .
> Y sigue la ardiente criolla
> volviendo a ver hacia atrás,
> con ojos que dicen: ¡peca!
> y una risa criminal.)

The piquant dialogue exchanged between the flirt and the soldiers is a rhetorical fencing match in which she always parries their most vigorous thrusts. The bantering is sprinkled with provincialisms.

All the narrative poems mentioned so far were written between 1860 and 1864, and most utilize the rapid meters of the *romance* or *romancillo* (verse forms of eight syllables or less, with alternate lines in assonance). They are characterized by their use of peasant characters and by their depiction of customs and manners. Two subsequent poems, both dated 1870, offer different traits. In **"Un mundo por un soneto" ("A World for a Sonnet"),** a young writer exchanges a poem for a kiss. The charming simplicity of the ballad entitled **"Inocencia" ("Innocence")** immediately calls to mind the *serranillas* written by Iñigo de Mendoza (Marquis of Santillana) in fifteenth-century Spain. As in his medieval Spanish models, Isaacs describes the encounter, in a rustic setting, of a gentleman with a peasant girl. The traveler is captivated by the graceful and pure maiden, and wishes to take advantage of the situation:

> "Little girl, of the beautiful flowers
> that your apron hides,
> will you permit this traveler
> to take one, only one?"
> "They belong to the Virgin, sir,
> but there are many in the forests." . . .
> "Will you take me to the shady place
> where those waters murmur,
> and will you sing the songs
> that the doves listen to?"
> "Here is the path . . ."

> (—Niña, ¿de las bellas flores
> que tu delantar oculta
> permites a este viajero
> llevar una, sólo una?
> —Son de la Virgen, señor,
> pero en las selvas abundan." . . .
> —¿Quieres llevarme a la umbría
> donde esas aguas murmullan
> y cantarás las canciones
> que las palomas te escuchan?
> —He aquí la senda . . .")

But the gentleman controls himself in time and gives a piece of fatherly advice to the innocent maid: "flee from the gentlemen who traverse your green valley."

Isaacs wrote his shortest (only eight lines) narrative poem at an early age, in 1860, but apparently never published it. The composition is entitled **"En la tumba de Leopoldo . . ." ("At the Tomb of Leopoldo . . .")** and relates succinctly the supposedly true story of a youth of eighteen who took his life because of an unhappy love affair.[13] The third line of the poem, which calls the girl who motivated the suicide, "the virgin of your last amour," alludes to a picturesque Indian custom described by Chateaubriand in his famous novel, *Atala*.

IV *Lyric Poems*

The predominant theme in Jorge Isaacs' lyric poetry is, naturally enough, that of love. Several of his first amorous compositions are dedicated to his wife, Felisa. The poem entitled **"Felisa"** praises her beauty, charm, and virtue, by means of comparisons with the bucolic landscape of the Cauca Valley:

> I saw summer afternoons,
> afternoons in the Cauca Valley,
> voluptuous, smiling,
> and bedecked;
> and many days
> were less beautiful
> than my Felisa.
> Your night with a turban
> of blue and stars,
> embroidering with fireflies
> its black skirt,
> beloved homeland,
> never had the mystery
> of my Felisa.

> (Vi tardes de verano,
> tardes del Cauca,
> voluptuosas, risueñas,
> y engalanadas;
> y muchos días
> fueron menos hermosos
> que mi Felisa.
> Tu noche con turbante
> de azul y estrellas,
> bordando de cocuyos
> su falda negra,
> patria querida,
> nunca tuvo el misterio
> de mi Felisa.)

Isaacs was to utilize this same anthropomorphic technique in his novel when he described María: "Never were the dawns of July in the Cauca as beautiful as was María . . ." (Chapter XII . . .). . . . In **"El retrato de Felisa" ("Felisa's Picture"),** the far-away poet complains that the beautiful image of his wife seems cold and does not communicate to him her love. Here Isaacs uses for the first time the poetic name of Selfia, an anagram of Felisa, to refer to his spouse. **"Amor eterno" ("Eternal Love")** and **"Por ti suspiro" ("I Sigh for You")** are tender love poems undoubtedly inspired by Felisa, as is **"Los ojos pardos" ("Brown Eyes").** Isaacs never published two of his best poems to his wife, **"¿Sabéis por qué la amo?" ("Do You Know Why I Love Her?")** and **"Selfia,"** both written in 1866.

Curiously enough, at the same time that he was composing love poetry for his wife, Isaacs wrote a series of amorous poems dedicated to other women. Of 1861 is a poem of highly erotic content, entitled **"Elena":**

> On the green hills
> overlooking the neighboring river
> I spent with Elena
> part of a Sunday afternoon.
> More than ever complaisant
> she gave to my lips,
> delighted at my excitement,
> her own purple lips.
> She followed me to the plain,
> where the tranquil stream
> moistens the mature clusters
> of the white mulberries;
> she fled from me, laughing
> at my amorous ardor . . .
> but her small and agile foot
> was wounded by a hidden stalk
> beneath the white carpet
> of fallen orange blossoms.
> Her rose-colored foot
> at last she decided to show me,
> her alabaster arm
> around my neck,
> and the ardor of my kisses
> gave her such quick alleviation
> that the tears on her cheeks
> passed away like dew . . .

> (En las colinas verdes
> del comarcano río
> pasaba con Elena
> la siesta de un Domingo.
> Jamás tan complaciente
> brindó a los labios míos
> de mi emoción gozosa
> sus labios purpurinos.
> Siguióme hasta la vega
> donde el raudal tranquilo
> de las moreras moja
> los maduros racimos;
> huía de mí riendo
> de mi amoroso ahinco . . .
> mas su pie breve y ágil
> hirió tallo escondido
> bajo la blanca alfombra
> de azahares caídos.
> La sonrosada planta
> por fin mostrarme quiso,
> mi cuello rodeando
> su brazo alabastrino,
> y el fuego de mis besos
> la dio tan pronto alivio
> que el lloro en sus mejillas
> pasó como el rocío . . .)

The unusually rich imagery of this poem serves to underscore the sensual theme. The predominance of green coloring and the luxuriant vegetation evoke the Garden of Eden, the scene of the First Fall. The moisture found throughout constitutes an obvious note of sensuality, as does the allusion to the mature fruit. The fallen orange blossoms (the flower traditionally worn by the bride in Hispanic weddings) presage the impending consummation of the love affair. It is tempting to relate **"Elena"** to two other poems from Isaacs' first period, and to see in them different treatments of the same passionate and illicit love affair. Both **"¿Sólo amistad?" ("Only Friendship?")** and **"El último arrebol" ("The Last Sunset")** portray a "criminal" love, that is, one that cannot be legalized by marriage.[14] Both compositions share with **"Elena"** references to sunsets and to settings along rivers. These coincidences make it entirely possible that all three poems describe the same true love affair.

A different type of amour seems to be alluded to in **"Siempre contigo" ("Always with You")**. Here the poet laments that he was not able to marry a certain woman, and he affirms that all his feelings toward her are honorable. **"Siempre contigo"** may well be related to a rumor that Isaacs was disappointed by a childhood sweetheart, who married another.[15] A similar attitude of respect toward a married woman is contained in **"La 'Virginia' del Páez" ("The 'Virginia' of the Páez River")**. Isaacs did not publish this poem under his own name, but rather under the anagram of *Acasis*.[16] The probable cause for the use of the pseudonym is revealed by Isaacs' manuscript: the composition was written in honor of a married woman, Virginia Sánchez. Although the poem declares that Virginia was as pure as her name, Isaacs apparently deemed it wise not to arouse the jealousy of her husband—and that of his own wife.

In **"Hortensia Antomarchi,"** the poet discloses a feeling of guilt and repentance concerning his illicit love affairs:

> In the loving lips that my lips,
> thirsty for pleasure, have pressed,
> I found delight, but never happiness;
> after the fleeting enjoyment, nothingness and
>   disgust . . .
>
> (En los labios amantes que mis labios
> sedientos de placer han comprimido
> hallé deleites, mas la dicha nunca;
> tras de goce fugaz, nada y hastío . . .)

This sensation of guilt and disenchantment was to become more frequent in the poetry of Isaacs' second period.

Jorge Isaacs' biographers allude only vaguely to the poet's extramarital love affairs.[17] Nevertheless, the highly autobiographical quality of his poetry makes it possible to trace several of the writer's sentimental involvements. Indeed, it appears that, contrary to usual practice, Isaacs used the pronoun "I" in his poetry only when referring to his own experiences.[18]

Of Isaacs' non-amorous lyric poems, **"El gorrión" ("The Sparrow")**, **"Nima,"** and **"La visión del Castillo" ("The Vision of The Castle Ranch")**, all of 1860, deserve special mention. **"El gorrión"** is reminiscent of Edgar Allan Poe's "The Raven," for it too describes how a bird visits a lonely and sad poet, who laments the absence of his beloved. When the sparrow begins to peck at the flowers, the poet remembers that the blossoms were gathered by his dear wife, now far away. In **"Nima,"** named after a small river in the Cauca Valley, the author affirms that on the banks of this stream he has seen a beautiful and voluptuous undine. (In *María*, Efraín also claims to have seen water nymphs, much to his sweetheart's chagrin: Chapter XLVI.) Apparently, for Isaacs the undine represents "the dreams of my soul," because he saw her only during the happy years of his youth. In this poem abound references to local flora and fauna, and there is an extensive use of color.

"La visión del Castillo" is the composition that was most warmly applauded by the members of "El Mosaico" during Isaacs' reading of his poetry in May, 1864. It has been remarked[19] that the verses have an air of mystery which will perhaps never be deciphered. The poem at first seems to be in praise of the author's wife, but suddenly the thought and inspiration are elevated to a higher sphere. Professor Enrique Anderson Imbert believes that the piece is an elegy dedicated to the concept of Glory.[20] The poem can also be interpreted as a song addressed to Poetry itself, in which Isaacs implores his Muse to return to him the inspiration of days gone by:

> Return to my side, equally as smiling and
>   pure
> as other times I saw or imagined you,
> as you wandered in the dark forest
> luxurious with pensile flowers.
>
> (Vuelve a mi lado tan risueña y pura
> como otras veces te miré o fingí,
> como vagabas en la selva oscura
> lujosa con las flores del pensil.)

Many of the images and descriptions in this poem (the abstract ideal incarnated in the form of a woman, the use of mists and colors of vague hue, the frequent mention of the night and the moon) are reminiscent of the poetry of the Spanish Romantic, Gustavo Adolfo Bécquer, who dedicated some of his most inspired verses to the goddess Poetry.[21] In accordance with his custom, Isaacs uses the landscape of the Cauca Valley as a point of comparison to exalt the beauty of the figure that probably incarnates Poetry. In some verses, Poetry is identified with a woman of ideal loveliness; many of the similes employed here are identical to those that appear in the love poem, **"Felisa,"** cited earlier. In the second part of the poem, Isaacs changes from the hendecasyllabic form to the more solemn Alexandrine, and expresses in deeply felt lines his thirst for glory, the great ambition in his life:

> Oh! Be done with obscurity and a future
>   without a name,
> if so many have triumphed struggling, I will
>   struggle!
> I want my will to astonish the geniuses,
> to leave a sun for a beacon, where I found
>   only a reef.

> (¡Oh! Basta de tinieblas y porvenir sin
>   nombre,
> ¡si tantos han vencido luchando, lucharé!
> Yo quiero que a los genios mi voluntad
>   asombre,
> dejar un sol por faro donde el escollo hallé.)

In the last strophe, the bard makes his final supplication to his Muse, asking her for inspiration.

Very similar in tone and imagery to **"La visión del Castillo"** is **"Las noches en la montaña" ("The Nights in the Mountains"),** written in July, 1864, after Isaacs' triumphal reading before the "Mosaico" group. As in the earlier composition, the poet expresses a longing for an elusive abstraction that has many voluptuously feminine qualities. In the last verse, Isaacs reveals that the object of his yearning is Glory. In the latter portion of the poem, he alludes to his recent financial debacle, and bitterly condemns those who bought the ranches left mortgaged by his father. This personal attack upon James Eder, plus some more moderate censures of members of his own family, explain why Isaacs never published this poem. In spite of its invective, **"Las noches en la montaña"** is one of the poet's most artistic compositions.

"Si vienes a mi campo" ("If You Come to My Field), the only poem of Isaacs that bears the date of 1862, treats the Horatian *Beatus ille* theme, in which the virtuousness and simplicity of country life are contrasted with the depravity and vanity of city existence:

> If you come to the fields
> where I live happily,
> avoiding the ferocious instincts
> of mankind . . .

> you will inhale essences
> of roses and thyme,

perfumes that you do not have
in wealthy salons.

> (Si vienes a los campos
> do venturoso vivo
> burlando de los hombres
> los feroces instintos . . .

> aspirarás esencias
> de rosas y tomillos,
> perfumes que no tienes
> en los salones ricos.)

The religious element seldom takes on great importance in Isaacs' poetry. Usually, it consists merely of a rapid entreaty for God's help in his worldly affairs (**"Clementina," "A Henrique"**). However, in **"El Dios del siglo" ("The Contemporary God"),** Isaacs warns his enemies that God will avenge the injustices that he has suffered, and in **"Tu imagen de María" ("Your Image of Mary"),** he speaks of a medallion of the Virgin that he received from a friend and has worn for five years.

V *Descriptive Poems*

The type of poetry least cultivated by Jorge Isaacs is the purely descriptive. This is surprising, in view of the fact that in a large majority of his poems, regardless of subject, there are allusions to the landscape of the Cauca Valley. Isaacs' most famous descriptive poem is entitled **"Río Moro" ("The Moro River").** Antonio Gómez Restrepo, the Colombian critic, notes that this piece inspires "a solemn and mysterious impression, that produced by nature in the solitary observer, who finds motive for meditation and ecstasy in the beauty of the creation":[22]

> I came listening to your incessant murmur
> from the summit of a far-off mountain range;
> the echoes of the mountains repeated
> your thunder in their hidden caverns.
> By them I judged your volume, imagining
> your beauty underneath a vaporous veil . . .
> What a miserable fiction! Perhaps in my dreams
> I have traversed your lovely strands,
> during those hours in which the body dies
> and the soul worships God in His creation . . .

> (Tu incesante rumor vine escuchando
> desde la cumbre de lejana sierra;
> los ecos de los montes repetían
> tu trueno en sus recónditas cavernas.
> Juzgué por ellos tu raudal, fingíme
> tras vaporoso velo tu belleza . . .
> ¡Qué mísera ficción! Quizá en mis sueños
> he recorrido tus hermosas playas,
> en esas horas en que el cuerpo muere
> y adora a Dios en su creación el alma . . .)

The grandeur and timelessness of the river make Isaacs reflect upon the ephemerality of his own life and ambitions.

In a poem about another river, **"El Cauca,"** Isaacs uses the sonnet form to describe the stream that flows through his native city of Cali. The poet finds that the impassive and lazy river faithfully reflects the personality of the citizens that people its banks.

VI *The Poetry of Isaacs' Second Period*

The verses composed by Jorge Isaacs from 1874 to 1894 are characterized by their melancholy and disillusionment. The poetry of this period lacks the freshness and candor of earlier years, and deals almost exclusively with thoughts of a serious, philosophical nature. Obsessed by the idea of death, Isaacs meditates about the destiny of mankind. The change from light to transcendental themes is reflected in the poet's choice of meter: his mature poems are cast in long verse forms, not in the rapid *romancillos* and *seguidillas* that predominate in his first period. His later poetic production is much more limited than that of his first years, and, with a few notable exceptions (**"Ten piedad de mí"** [**"Have Compassion on Me"**], **"Resurrección,"** **"Elvira Silva"**) is inferior to his earlier work.

It would appear logical that Isaacs' increased self-absorption should be expressed in autobiographical poems, but such is not the case. In contrast to the many autobiographic compositions written between 1860 and 1870, there are relatively few for the years 1874-94. These scarce poems no longer treat agreeable childhood memories, but rather Isaacs' tribulations and failures. Eloquent proof of the poet's disenchantment with his fellow men is furnished by **"En la tortura"** (**"In Torture"**), written during his explorations on the Atlantic coast. Isaacs considers man to be a "human jaguar . . . cruel and vile." In his execrations of his enemies, the poet compares his own patience with that of Job, and likens the wickedness of his adversaries to that of Satan; Isaacs believes that God will finally intervene on behalf of the just. He contrasts the ill treatment he has received from his fellow whites with the cordial welcome accorded him by the natives during his explorations. In view of the poet's excoriating attack on his enemies in this composition, it is no wonder that **"En la tortura"** remained unpublished during his lifetime, and has been severely abridged by several editors of his poetic works.[23]

In addition, Isaacs published other poems in which he assailed his opponents in less direct fashion. For example, **"En las cumbres de Chisacá"** (**"On the Summits of Chisacá"**), contains a bitter censure of the Colombian government:

> Oh Fatherland! Oh mother! . . . inspiration of
> my life,
> you oppress me cruelly and with indifference .
> . .
> And youth, love, repose and happiness
> I offered to your glory!
>
> (¡Oh Patria! ¡Oh madre! . . . numen de mi
> vida,
> me oprimes sorda y cruel . . .
> Y juventud, amor, reposo y dicha
> ¡a tu gloria ofrendé!)

"Pro patria" (**"In Behalf of My Country"**), written in 1890, proves that Isaacs' disenchantment with things human even includes his poetry:

> Do not ask the gloomy desert dweller
> for elegant lyrics;
> from those infinite wastes
> I come with silence and shadows in my soul .
> . .
>
> (Al hosco morador de los desiertos
> no le pidas aún trovas galanas;
> de aquellas soledades infinitas
> traigo silencio y sombras en el alma . . .)

The author's disillusionment was sincere, for after **"Pro patria"** he penned only a half a dozen more poems.

Isaacs' disenchantment with life is evident even in the amorous poetry of this period, where it takes the form of repentance. The "cry of the conscience," caused by memories of illicit love, is graphically stated in a poem of violent passion entitled **"Zoraida"**:

> and this eternal pain that I devour,
> which is written on my ashamed forehead.
>
> (y este dolor eterno que devoro,
> que va en mi frente avergonzada escrito.)

Poems of ardent and unlawful love still flow from Isaacs' pen, but most of them end in the same somber manner—with sad reflections about the death of the companion in sin (**"¡Ella duerme!"** [**"She Sleeps!"**], **"A orillas del torrente"** [**"On the Banks of the Torrent"**], **"Nola"**).[24] The ending of **"Eliveria"** could well have been written by a medieval ascetic:

> How much . . . madness . . . gall . . . pain . . .
> noise
> was existence, and I am on your doorstep,
> oh Death, yearning for indifference and oblivion!
>
> (Cuánto . . . locura . . . hiel . . . dolor . . . ruido
> fue la existencia y tus umbrales huello,
> oh muerte, ansiando desamor y olvido!)

None of the amorous poems of Isaacs' second period is dedicated to his wife, although **"Amor eterno"** (**"Eternal Love"**) could be attributed to her inspiration. One of Isaacs' most beautiful lyric compositions, **"Ten piedad de mí,"** is addressed to a woman who has died. Many readers have supposed this figure to be María, the heroine of Isaacs' novel, and some editors have given the poem her name.

During the years 1880-85, Isaacs composed several poems dedicated to his children: **"A Virginia y Rufino"** (**"To V. and R."**), **"Adormeciendo a David"** (**"Lulling D. to Sleep"**), **"Albor"** (**"Whiteness"** or **"Dawn"**), **"A mi hija Clementina"** (**"To My Daughter C."**), **"La bella de noche"** (**"The Beautiful One at Night"**). During his first period, he had written **"El rey Ulises"** (**"King Ulysses"**) for one of his sons, but never published it. All these poems display Isaacs' affection for his offspring. Perhaps the most artistic is the one dedicated to David.

One of the best poems of Isaacs' second period is still little known. Entitled **"Resurrección,"** it constitutes a reply to a skeptical poem of the same title published in 1878 by the Colombian poet, Diógenes A. Arrieta. In his religiously polemical poem, Arrieta had declared: "Man dies, he does not arise again, and he will never return!" Isaacs picked up the gauntlet cast down by Arrieta and answered in deeply felt verses:

> Does man die, does he not arise again?
> Is not death a slumber
> in the fecund tomb of a tender mother?
> Is man mud and his tomb slime,
> and the mud in you feels and loves and
>   doubts?

> (¿Muere el hombre, no torna a levantarse?
> ¿Morirse no es dormir
> de madre tierna en el fecundo seno?
> ¿Es lodo el hombre y su sepulcro cieno,
> y el lodo siente y ama y duda en ti?)

Isaacs' wholly Christian reply to Arrieta's atheistic composition reveals that the author of *María* preserved his essential religiousness even during the years in which he was a Darwinist and Freemason.

As in his first period, several of Isaacs' latter works are narrative poems that comment upon the horrors of the Colombian civil conflicts. Both **"La agonía del héroe"** (**"The Agony of the Hero"**) and **"La tumba del soldado"** (**"The Soldier's Tomb"**) seem to be reflections on the author's personal experiences. Isaacs wrote **"Después de la victoria"** (**"After the Victory"**) shortly after the battle of Los Chancos (August 31, 1876), in which he took part. The atmosphere of this poem is appropriately one of nightmarish terror, in which Death approaches the poet's bed and bores deep into his soul with her "cold and black stare."

In **"Recuerdos de colegial"** (**"Remembrances of a High School Student"**), a young scholar discovers that the only way to appease his sweetheart, who is angry with him for dedicating verses to other women, is to make her jealous of another. The jocose tone of this piece contrasts decidedly with that of other poems printed at about the same time. It may possibly be an allegorical treatment of a fit of jealousy that Isaacs' wife could have had on account of his numerous love poems dedicated to other women. The feminine protagonist of **"Recuerdos"** stipulates that her lover not write more verses for a certain Nola; it is pertinent that Isaacs wrote an amorous poem with the very title of **"Nola"** at about the same time he penned **"Recuerdos."** The young poet in **"Recuerdos"** (perhaps Isaacs' double) maintains his innocence with the contention that his works were inspired by imaginary women. If the allegorical interpretation of this poem is correct, its light tone can be explained as an effort by Isaacs to humor his wife.

Isaacs displays the bigotry typical of impassioned Spanish-American Freemasons during the nineteenth century in **"El imperio chimila"** (**"The Empire of the Chimilas"**). The poet exalts this Indian nation, with which he had become acquainted during his explorations, because it has not come under the influence of the pope—the favorite target of the Freemasons.

One of Jorge Isaacs' most ambitious literary projects was the undertaking of a long epic poem, entitled *Saulo.* Like so many of his projects, however, the work remained unfinished. Isaacs completed only the first canto, which he published in 1881, dedicating it to General Julio Roca, then president of Argentina. The fragment is so confused that Antonio Gómez Restrepo stated that its meaning cannot be deciphered.[25] Fortunately, Isaacs confided to his friend Adriano Páez a detailed plan of his proposed epic poem, and Páez summarized the poet's project in article form.[26] The action was to be as follows: Two young lovers, Saulo and Olga, are sailing the Pacific from Chile to Colombia. Saulo is a poet, an unfortunate genius. Like Byron and his poetic creation, Childe Harold, Saulo has traversed the world repeatedly without finding rest for his tortured soul. Saulo has the same power of fascination over women as did Byron. Because of him, Olga has abandoned her family in Chile and is accompanying him to Colombia. Saulo breaks out in a song of impassioned love, directed equally to Olga and to Héloïse, the innocent Parisian girl who fell in love with Peter Abelard, the renowned philosopher and theologian, and who gave up all for him. In his poem, Saulo passes rapidly from one country and epoch to another, leaving Héloïse in order to evoke Jewish women of Old Testament times. The poem begins at the moment when Saulo and Olga have just finished reading the story of Héloïse. Saulo perceives the parallelism of the love of Héloïse and Abelard with Olga's and his own. He recalls other similar stories of love, such as that recounted by Rousseau in *La Nouvelle Héloïse (The New II.),* and another about Dioema and Rael, of biblical days.

Although Páez does not so state, **Saulo** evidently derives inspiration from the philosophical theory of eternal recurrence. The story of Saulo and Olga is a nineteenth-century reincarnation, in South America, of the same illicit passion that occurred between Dioema and Rael in Israel before the birth of Christ; between Héloïse and Abelard in France in the twelfth century; and again in France during the eighteenth century in Rousseau's novel. It seems apparent that the frenetic and unlawful love of Saulo and Olga will have a tragic ending, just as it did in the other incarnations.

The tone of **Saulo** is much more solemn and elevated than that of any of Isaacs' other poems. This is due partly to the long verse forms and partly to the rich imagery, most of which is of biblical inspiration. Unfortunately, the grandeur of the work is irremediably marred by its obscurity. The poem begins *in medias res,* but the beginning portion of the action is never presented. The setting in Chile and Colombia, the theme of unlicensed love, and the obvious Jewish ancestry of the protagonist, make one wonder if **Saulo** did not have an autobiographical basis in Isaacs' life during the period of his consulship in Chile. The initial situation, in which two sweethearts read a book that relates a love story that parallels their own relationship, is an obvious coincidence with Chapters XII-XIII of **María.** . . .

Jorge Isaacs had the sad opportunity to write elegies on the occasion of the deaths of two dear friends. The first poem of lamentation was **"La tumba de Belisario" ("The Tomb of B."),** written in honor of a faithful helper who accompanied Isaacs in his explorations on the Atlantic coast. The heartfelt verses of **"Elvira Silva"** rank among the best that the poet ever wrote. José Asunción Silva, the brother of Elvira, was so touched by the poem that he planned to publish it in an elegant edition in New York, although this did not materialize.[27] In the third section of the poem, Elvira appears, radiant in her beauty, in the company of her beloved brother:

> A vain dream, perhaps . . . Delirium and
> delight
> of the soul, which remembers or has a
> presentiment of
> immortal beauty . . . Tears blind
> the eyes that seek you, and
> groans answer the groans that call you . . .
> Alas! your laughter, your voice full of
> tenderness
> for your dearly loved and loving brother,
> one seems to hear it, and one imagines that on

> his breast,
> cherished child of your home, you recline
> your head like that of Psyche, on which
> snowy roses wither among black curls . . .
> and docile prisoner of his arms,
> you pretend to flee from him . . . Livid . . .
> Rigid!

> (Vano ensueño quizá . . . Delirio y gozo
> del alma que memora o que presiente
> la belleza inmortal . . . Lágrimas ciegan
> los ojos que te buscan, y responden
> al llamarte, gemidos a gemidos . . .
> ¡Ay! tus risas, tu voz de arrullos llena
> para el dilecto y amoroso hermano,
> escuchar se figura y que en su pecho,
> reina mimada del hogar, reclinas
> la cabeza de Psiquis en que aja
> las níveas rosas entre negros bucles . . .
> y dócil prisionera de sus brazos,
> finges huirle a él . . . Lívida . . . ¡Yerta!)

In subsequent stanzas, Isaacs emphasizes the purity of the great love that existed between Elvira and her brother, as if to contradict beforehand the rumors of incestuous love that were to start circulating after the publication of Silva's third "Nocturno." Isaacs dwells on the tragicalness of Elvira's demise, rather than expounding the typically Christian view of conformity with God's will. He calls upon God to raise her up again, as he did Lazarus, but God does not hear (this detail recalls Arrieta's "Resurrección," alluded to above). The emphasis upon the tragic human waste, instead of upon Christian resignation and upon the blessedness of the deceased's new abode in Heaven, may well be a concession to José A. Silva's atheistic beliefs. At the same time, Isaacs alludes to a peculiar kind of immortality, in his reference to the Platonic theory of a previous life, in which the soul has formed an idea of what beauty is (anamnesis).

Isaacs dedicated one of his last poems, **"La tierra de Córdoba,"** to the people of the state of Antioquia (the *antioqueños*). He praises the industriousness and other virtues of those to whom he would bequeath his mortal remains a few years later. The poet feels himself to be a racial brother of the only group who, he believes, has recognized his merits. Perhaps influenced somewhat by the hospitality he had received from the *antioqueños,* the poet repeats the popular belief that they are descendants of Jews (he expresses the same idea in Chapter IX of **María**). As in *Saulo,* Isaacs here utilizes extensively biblical imagery and names. While exalting the supposed Semitic origin of the natives of Antioquia, Isaacs makes bitter recriminations against the Spanish colonizers:

> What did Spain give them of the Nazarene?
> The law of peace and love?

She left the unburied bones of a hundred nations
. . .

(¿España qué les dio del Nazareno?
¿La ley de paz y amor?
Dejó de cien naciones los insepultos huesos . . .)

The violent attack against Spain—the prototype, for Isaacs, of the hated arch-Conservative and arch-Catholic country—was one of the principal themes in his last poems. Examples are found in the **"Himno de guerra colombiano" ("Colombian War Hymn"), "Colombia libre" ("Free C."),** and **"Estrofas libres" ("Free Strophes"),** in addition to **"La tierra de Córdoba."** The condemnation of the Spaniards and of the Conservative government in Colombia waxes so venomous in **"Estrofas libres"** that it is no wonder that the poem was not published during Isaacs' lifetime. As early as 1864-65, Isaacs had started censuring Spain in **"¡Al mar!"** and **"Al escudo de armas de N[ueva] G[ranada]" ("To the Coat of Arms of New Granada")** (the latter poem was also published only recently). And whenever Isaacs praised Colombian heroes, as in **"Caldas"** and in the two compositions named **"Ricaurte,"** he denigrated the mother country. It is apparent that Isaacs' censures of Spain were influenced by those of his Spanish friend, Núñez de Arce. However, Isaacs' last patriotic poem, **"Los inmortales" ("The Immortal Ones"),** dated July 20 (Colombia's Independence Day), 1894, is objective in its appraisal of Spain's work in Hispanic America. By this time, less than nine months before his death, Isaacs had put away political hatreds.

In his waning years, Isaacs wrote several poems of a philosophical nature: **"Insomnio" ("Insomnia"), "Lumbre de sombra" ("Light of Shadow"), "¿Qué? . . ." ("What? . . ."), "¡Sed buenos!" ("Be Good!"), "La tierra madre" ("Mother Earth").** "Insomnio" carries an epigraph from Goethe; in the poem, Isaacs asks himself the eternal question, whence do we come and where are we bound? Here Isaacs affirms his credence in the Darwinian theory of man's evolution from the monkey, but believes that mankind has progressed little beyond this animal as far as morality is concerned.

"¡Sed buenos!" is one of Isaacs' most embittered poems; its verses fairly ooze acrid rancor:

No, there is no pity or truce in the combat
with your legion of iniquitous persons, oh
  Fortune!
And the valiant fighter who falls,
let him expect scorn, but no pity. . . .
"We die of thirst." "Gall for the thirsty."
There are so many executioners, crosses and
  Calvaries!

(No, no hay piedad ni tregua en el combate

con tu legión de inicuos, ¡oh Fortuna!
Y el lidiador valiente que se abate
ludibrio espere, compasión . . . ninguna. . . .
—¡De sed morimos!—"Hiel a los sedientos."
¡Sobran verdugos, cruces y calvarios!)

Isaacs here compares his own misfortune with that of Christ; this somewhat megalomaniacal type of comparison had given the poet's enemies material with which to satirize him some ten years earlier, in 1880. . . . Elsewhere in the poem, Isaacs exhorts his children to lead upright lives, eschewing the examples of corruption and materialism that surround them. He proudly reminds them of their Jewish blood, which is also that of Jesus.

In **"La tierra madre"** (or **"Demeter"**), one of his last poems, Isaacs expresses the desire to return to the mother of all:

Aged by suffering, I now wish
to sleep in your lap, shady plain . . .

(Envejecido en el dolor, ya quiero
dormir en tu regazo, vega umbría . . .)

This conception of Earth as the mother of all mankind, plus an epigraph from Aeschylus, disclose that the poet became acquainted with Greek thought and literature toward the end of his life. The closing lines of **"La tierra madre"** show that Jorge Iasacs, like many other poets of all places and ages, foresaw that his fame was to prolong his life beyond the tomb:

Do not put the emblems of death
on the threshold of my future life;
the essence of immortal beings
was never dust, nor does it turn into dust . . .

(No pongáis los emblemas de la muerte
de mi vida futura en los umbrales:
ni polvo fue, ni en polvo se convierte
la esencia de los seres inmortales . . .)

VII *Conclusion*

Unlike his novel and his plays, Isaacs' poetry is not distinctively Romantic in tone.[28] On the one hand, it does not display the overriding passions, the revolt against society and its rules, the love of the exotic, and the bombastic rhetoric which is characteristic of much early Spanish Romanticism (particularly Espronceda). On the other, it reveals only sporadic influence of the low-key tone, the simplicity, the deep interior absorption, and the quiet musicality of the late Romantic, Bécquer. Isaacs translated poems from several English Romantics, but it is symptomatic that he was not attracted to the great poets (Wordsworth, Coleridge, Shelley, Keats), who formulated extremely complicated philosophies of creativity and theories of knowledge,[29] but to such secondary or tertiary authors as Moore, Wolfe, Hogg, and Bayly, or to minor pieces by Scott and Byron.[30] Neither does Isaacs' verse fit the three criteria which have been found central for the definition of European Romantic poetry: the idea of creative imagination, the organic view of nature, and the use of symbol and myth for poetic style.[31] True, Isaacs had a great feeling for nature, but his view of it is simply that of a man who was born and reared in the country and who appreciated the beauties of the garden spot that is the Cauca Valley. His poetry has none of the depth of the English, German, and French Romantics who saw in nature a system of hieroglyphics which the poet is destined to read, and who invented philosophical systems to relate themselves to nature and to explain the workings of the universe. The author of *María* simply contemplates his natural surroundings and paints them with word pictures.

Isaacs' simple-minded view of nature is not, then, especially Romantic. The same may be said of his egocentrism: it is not the Romantic's typically gloomy introspection and scrutiny of his tortured soul, but merely a reflection of the universal preoccupation with self. His spontaneity—the disregard for the themes and techniques of the great poets—is more the result of a limited acquaintance with the poetic masterworks of world literature than the Romantic's deliberate design of finding his inspiration within himself, rather than in the outside universe. In a word, Jorge Isaacs' verse is the work of a man mainly preoccupied with the problems of making a living, but who enjoyed reading some amount of light poetry by others, and who found pleasure in putting his own thoughts and reactions to concrete stimuli into rhyme.

Notes

[1] Ricardo Nieto, "La poesía de Jorge Isaacs," *El Relator,* no. 6098 (April 1, 1937), p. 13. See also Alfonso Méndez Plancarte, "Jorge Isaacs, un poeta. 1837-1937," *Abside* (México), no. 8 (August, 1937), pp. 29-45.

[2] Jorge Isaacs was not a metrical innovator, as numerous commentators have claimed. On the contrary, his verse forms are those found in manuals of versification, or those employed by other Romantic poets; see Romero Lozano, Introduction, ed. of Isaacs' *Poesías . . .*, p. xxxvi. Indeed, Isaacs himself stated in a letter that his knowledge of metrics was limited (Velasco Madriñán, *Jorge Isaacs,* p. 375). Jorge Roa, Isaacs' friend and publisher, reveals that the writer did not take special care to polish his verses, but often sent them directly to the press; see "Jorge Isaacs (Noticia biográfica y literaria)," *El Heraldo* (Bogotá), no. 507 (June 20, 1895), p. 1.

[3] R. Jiménez Triana, "Jorge Isaacs. Rasgos," *El Telegrama*

(Bogotá), IX, no. 2522 (April 24, 1895).

[4] Quotes are from Romero Lozano's edition of Isaacs' poetry, the most complete published to date; occasional faulty readings are corrected.

Several previous editors had attributed compositions by other poets to Isaacs, thereby creating the false impression that he was a precursor of Modernism in Latin American poetry.

[5] Published in *El Pasatiempo* (Bogotá), año III, no. 42 (August 14, 1880).

[6] Max Grillo, "Vida y obra de Isaacs," *Boletín de la Academia Colombiana,* II (1937), p. 186.

[7] The original humorous paronomasia "uvas y Evas" is lost in translation.

[8] In a copy of this poem, Isaacs later substituted the name of Lucía for that of María; see Luis Augusto Cuervo, "Apuntes sobre Jorge Isaacs," *Revista del Colegio Mayor de Nuestra Señora del Rosario* (Bogotá), XXIV (1929), p. 561. The poet probably made the change in order to avoid confusion of this María with the protagonist of the novel.

[9] In his edition of Isaacs' poetry, p. 126, Romero Lozano dates the poem 1864, but Isaacs dated it 1867 when he published it in *La Patria* (Bogotá), I (1877-1878), pp. 473-74.

Certain physical descriptions in "Teresa" and "La 'Virginia' del Páez" are reminiscent of those of María; see C. Enrique Pupo-Walker, "Relaciones internas entre la poesía y la novela de Jorge Isaacs," *Thesaurus* (Bogotá), XXII (1967), pp. 49-50. However, it is clear that the women who inspired these poems could not have been the spiritual models of María.

[10] For further details on the problem of the existence of María, see pp. 125-27 [of McGrady, *Jorge Isaacs,* 1972].

[11] Note *f* of his "La tierra de Córdoba," p. 284 in Romero Lozano's edition. Isaacs' friendship with Núñez de Arce . . . as well as the latter's high regard of *María* . . . possibly influenced this estimate of the Spaniard's worth as a poet.

[12] Many Colombian writers of the second half of the nineteenth century composed poems on this topic under the title of "El recluta"; perhaps the most famous version is that of José Asunción Silva.

[13] Luciano Rivera y Garrido, *Impresiones y recuerdos* (Bogotá: Librería Nueva, 1897), p. 571.

[14] The version of "El último arrebol" published by Romero Lozano is different from that printed by Isaacs in *El Cóndor* (Medellín), I (1870-1871), pp. 214-15, and in other reviews.

[15] Velasco Madriñán, *Jorge Isaacs,* pp. 150-51.

[16] It appeared in *El Iris* (Bogotá), II (1866), p. 152. The poem "Amores de Soledad" was later published in the same volume (pp. 180-82), also under the anagramatic pseudonym.

[17] But see Velasco Madriñán, *Jorge Isaacs,* p. 332, and Romero Lozano, ed. of *Poesías,* pp. xxxiv, xxxvii, 181.

[18] As noted above, in "Mayo," another poem recognized as being autobiographic, Isaacs alludes to his philandering tendencies. In "A Virginia y Rufino" ("To V. and R."), the poet mentions "the vague memory of an unhappy love affair." Other love poems which probably are autobiographical are: "Amor" ("Love"), "Ven a la vega solitaria" ("Come to the Solitary Plain"), "La flor de Popayán" ("The Flower of P."), "Tu amor es agua" ("Your Love Is Water"), "Tus ojos" ("Your Eyes"), "Rafaela," "A orillas del torrente" ("On the Banks of the Torrent"), "La patria del alma" ("The Homeland of the Soul"), "El primer soneto" ("The First Sonnet"), "Nola," "Débora mía" ("My D."), "La única patria" ("The Only Homeland").

[19] Víctor Sánchez Montenegro, "Jorge Isaacs y 'El Mosaico'," *Bolívar* (Bogotá), no. 19 (1953), p. 790.

[20] Prologue to *María* (México: Fondo de Cultura Económica, 1951), p. xxxiii.

[21] See *rimas* XI and XV. It is unlikely that Isaacs could have known Bécquer's poems in 1860, the supposed date of composition of "La visión del Castillo." There are two possible explanations to account for the similarity of Bécquer's and Isaacs' poems: (1) 1860 is not the true date of "La visión," or (2) both poets took inspiration from common sources in earlier Romantics. On Bécquer's indebtedness to preceding poets, and his influence on subsequent writers, see José Pedro Díaz, *Gustavo Adolfo Bécquer* (Madrid: Gredos, 1958), especially pp. 113-90, 325-61. Concha Meléndez, "El arte de Jorge Isaacs en *María,*" *Asomante* (San Juan, P.R.), I (1945), pp. 74-75, believes that Bécquer's poetry and prose influenced passages of *María.*

[22] "A propósito de Isaacs," *Boletin de la Academia Colombiana;* II (1937), p. 211.

[23] It is interesting that Carlos Arturo Torres, the Colombian essayist and poet, fused the first half of "En la tortura" with the latter portion of José Asunción

Silva's "Al pie de la estatua," and attributed the resulting apocryphal creation to Silva. See my article, "Sobre un poema atribuido a José Asunción Silva," *Thesaurus,* XXII (1967), pp. 359-68.

[24] Exceptions are "Débora mía" and "La única patria" (or "Isabel"), erotic poems probably dedicated to real women.

[25] "Sobre poemas," *Repertorio Colombiano,* XIII (1887), p. 157.

[26] "*Saulo.* Poema de Jorge Isaacs," *La Patria* (Bogotá), IV (1880), pp. 131-36.

[27] Velasco Madriñán, *Jorge Isaacs,* p. 366.

[28] Eduardo Ospina does not include Isaacs in his book, *El romanticismo: estudio de sus caracteres esenciales en la poesía lírica europea y colombiana* (Madrid: Editorial Voluntad, 1927).

[29] See the brilliant and very concise study by Albert Gerard, "On the Logic of Romanticism," *Essays in Criticism,* VII (1957), 262-73.

[30] The translations by Isaacs from English Romantics are found on pp. 326-50 of Romero Lozano's edition. Romero Lozano does not identify all the originals: "Lágrimas de felicidad" is an adaptation of Thomas Haynes Bayly's "Such Tears Are Bliss" and "El valiente trovador" is a somewhat expanded version of Scott's "The Troubadour"; the authorship of the remaining three poems has not been determined, possibly due to errors in the spelling of the writers' names (Dymon, Ryan, Van-Dick).

[31] René Wellek, "The Concept of Romanticism in Literary History," in *Concepts of Criticism* (New Haven and London: Yale University Press, 1963), pp. 128-98, especially pp. 160-61 and 196-97.

Selected Bibliography

Poesías, ed. Armando Romero Lozano. Calif Biblioteca de la Universidad del Valle, 1967. The most complete edition yet published of Isaacs' poems. Contains errata, omissions, and errors of transcription, and gives only a few variant readings of poems revised by Isaacs. Valuable Introduction and notes. This edition is complemented by the present author's review in *Thesaurus,* XXIV (1969), 292-306.

Velasco Madrinan, Luis Carlos. *Jorge Isaacs, el caballero de las lágrimas.* Cali: Editorial América, 1942. A poorly written and totally unscholarly work which is perhaps the most complete biography available. Though almost no bibliographical support is quoted, the information is generally reliable. . . .

Carol Beane (essay date 1984)

SOURCE: "Black Character: Toward a Dialectical Presentation in Three South American Novels," in *Voices from Under: Black Narrative in Latin America and the Caribbean*, edited by William Luis, Greenwood Press, 1984, pp. 181-200.

[*In the following excerpt, Beane discusses the African characters in Isaacs's* Maria.]

Fiction in which Blacks and Mulattoes are main characters "deals not with eternal essences or ideal forms of life, but with life lived in particular conditions."[1] Black characters and black character—a way of being—in Hispanic-American fiction reflect traits drawn from a social reality. Any discussion of black characters in literature must bear in mind that literary creation results from a complex interplay between historical and socioeconomic factors and imagination. The latter is the source of "all sorts of images of non-Western peoples and worlds which have flourished in our culture . . . images derived not from observation, experience and perceptible reality but from a psychological urge . . . that creates its own realities which are fully different from political realities."[2]

As literary subjects, Blacks and Mulattoes are charged with extraliterary associations. Slavery and oppression in the eighteenth century created stereotyped images, many of which appear in fiction.[3] Early portrayals were ostensibly sympathetic; later ones are less so. Blacks and Mulattoes have become the Other in relation to the society, or society is the Other in relation to the Blacks.[4] It is important to understand the origins of the stereotypes. However, equally important are the ways in which some writers, in their characterization of Blacks, have used stereotypes as a point of departure, disfiguring when not abandoning them. Such efforts express commitment to a truer image of the Black and to the artistic potential contained in the historical and cultural experience of being black.

This study is concerned with the characterization of Blacks and Mulattoes, two groups traditionally perceived as marginal in Western culture, even in South America, where they are a demographic and cultural presence. This is especially true in Colombia, Venezuela, certain parts of Peru and Ecuador, not to mention Brazil. Situations and experiences arising from a marginal state—slave until late in the nineteenth century, frustrated and oppressed laborer in the twentieth—form the material with which authors work. They attempt to give artistic expression to this marginality and the society's reactions to it. Conflict between the larger society and those outside it—inclusion and exclusion—sets the tone of their writing. . . .

Stanley E. Fish's *Self-Consuming Artifacts* categorizes literary presentations as being either rhetorical or dialectical. He defines a presentation as being rhetorical

> if it satisfies the needs of the readers. The work "satisfies" is meant literally here; for it is characteristic of a rhetorical form to mirror and present for approval the opinions its readers already hold. It follows then the experience of such a form will be flattering, for it tells the reader that what he has always thought about the world is true and that the ways of this thinking are sufficient. . . . Whatever one is told can be placed and contained within the categories and assumptions of received systems of knowledge.[5]

To the rhetorical presentation Fish opposes the dialectical, which is

> disturbing, for it requires of its readers a searching and vigorous scrutiny of everything they believe in and live by. It is didactic in a special sense; it does not preach the truth, but asks that its readers discover the truth themselves, and this discovery is often made at the expense not only of a reader's opinions and values, but of his self-esteem.[6]

Fish's classifications are useful as a critical approach to a general study of Afro-Hispanic literature. They are especially helpful in discussing the characterization of Blacks and Mulattoes and the ways in which authors establish the parameters of their identity. The issues are perception and presentation: complicated relationships between the author, his culture, the historical moment, the literary creation, its internal parts and the reader. When describing the rhetorical presentation, Fish speaks of the "needs of . . . readers." For the sake of this discussion, we shall postulate a reader who will react to either the rhetorical or the dialectical presentation. Such a reader will be a representative of the dominant society and committed to its prevailing attitudes and values.

The context in which a black character is defined may be exotic, picturesque, sociopolitical, psychological or some combination of these. For the most part, exotic and picturesque treatment of Blacks and Mulattoes to which the reader responds functions as part of what Fish calls the rhetorical presentation. Attention to the social, political and economic implications of the picturesque detail, however, obstructs a picturesque perception; such a presentation then becomes potentially dialectical.

The predominant social attitude toward Blacks and Mulattoes, especially since the eighteenth century, has been one of hostility, distancing, amusement and disenfranchisement.[7] It developed particularly in slave societies. The social structure of the large plantations engendered certain fictions about the nature of Blacks and their relations with Whites. These views appeared in literary fiction as social norms.

Prior to the nineteenth century, Blacks and Mulattoes in Hispanic-American fiction, for the most part, were treated in a picturesque way.[8] At the same time, the rigid codification of racial attitudes and categories of the eighteenth century and the restricted possibilities available for Blacks and Mulattoes can be seen as attempts to impose order and control in societies that were extremely dependent on their labor and participation.[9] It was, perhaps, faith in authority and security in a particular world view that enabled writers at this time to maintain an ethnocentric position.

In the early nineteenth century, religion and humanitarian sentiment, combined with a convenient failure of slavery as a viable economic system, influenced attitudes in favor of Blacks and Mulattoes. Portrayals of Blacks in antislavery literature—regardless of whether truly sympathetic or not—were created in reaction to the denigrating beliefs about Blacks current in nineteenth-century Hispanic-American society.[10]

The decline of slavery with the political instability that was occasioned by the wars of independence and continued into the post-independence period shook the old social order. Facing the prospect of greater and more formalized participation in society by groups theretofore excluded, society reacted. Pseudoscientific concepts of race such as those in Comte de Gobineau's *Essay on the Inequality of the Races* (1852-1853) were elaborated to rationalize the oppression of Blacks and Mulattoes. These ideas did not initiate negative beliefs but merely gave authority to existing sentiments. However, the terms of these new arguments were harsher and more dehumanizing than the commercial and legal ones of previous centuries—they exacerbated the negative attitudes about Blacks.

In nineteenth-century Hispanic-American characterizations of Blacks and Mulattoes, for example, one finds a duality of character types that clearly suggests an underlying ambivalence of that society. It seems apparent that character types such as the loyal slave, the maternal black woman, the amusing child and others are the more socially acceptable. Their counterparts are the rebellious, the lascivious, the sly and shiftless slave. Both types are creative expressions produced in a society attempting to identify and isolate elements that disrupt its social order. The "good" counterparts indicate efforts to accommodate Blacks rather than exclude them. However, the basis of the accommodation is exploitation. It is the perspective of the dominant society, the Other in relation to the black characters, that defines the types.

The uprising in Haiti in 1791 provided all slave owners in Latin America and the Caribbean with an example, long remembered, of the consequences of the rage of oppressed Blacks. Attempts to portray Blacks favorably in much nineteenth-century fiction share certain assumptions. The qualities that many authors attribute to Blacks and Mulattoes imply characters that must be made acceptable before readers will view them in a serious and sympathetic manner.

Characterizations of Blacks and Mulattoes in this period are based on a series of neutralizations. Neutralization is a way of coming to terms with those characteristics of which society disapproves. The writer eliminates the offending traits and substitutes them with others more agreeable to society. Those features most frequently neutralized are physical and psychological. Others, equally important, originate in the relationship between master and slave. They form the basis of the black character's identity.

We are interested in the elements that create the fictional identity of black characters: preoccupation with physical appearance, the external signs of identity; the types of rational and emotional responses attributed; the kinds of experiences allowed, the access that a character has to space and time.[11] The narrative voice that describes the black or mulatto character is also important. If this voice is hostile toward Blacks, we identify it as the voice of the dominant society, that of the Other. If a narrative voice is favorable to Blacks, we see it at odds with the dominant society. Black characters may also be described from their own perspective.

To present a Black or Mulatto characterizing positive affective language is not necessarily to portray him in a truly sympathetic way. Such presentations do not inevitably lead to a redefinition of black character in terms other than those set up by society. Indeed, the conditions of neutralization are those of the dominant society, revealing the extent to which authors share in the convictions of their culture. Portrayals of this kind seem to show a "desire to . . . merely expose and fight against . . . abuses in order to prevent deeper revolutionary upheavals."[12] The authors' characterizations also reflect the inferiority and undesirability of the Black and the Mulatto.

Maria, *A Rhetorical Presentation: Propagating The Stereotype*

Jorge Isaacs' *María* (1867),[13] is an example of the limitations of the picturesque placed on black characters. The episode in which the Africans, Nay and Sinar, appear provides an exotic interlude in this romantic novel. Although most of the action occurs in Africa, key incidents that define the black characters are to be found equally in the African and the American context.
This intercalated tale is the story of Nay and Sinar. She is the daughter of a famous Ashanti warrior; he, the son of a slain enemy chief, is captured by Nay's father and made a slave in his house. It tells of Nay's and Sinar's life in Africa, their love affair, their eventual capture by the slave traders, their separation, Sinar's

disappearance and Nay's passage to America. The account of her life in America as a member of the household of the novel's protagonist, Efraín, begins with his father buying Nay, freeing her and changing her name to Feliciana and concludes with her death.

Isaacs uses distance—geographic, historical, narrative, aesthetic—to create black characters the reader will accept. However, the conditions of acceptance are set by the larger society, limiting the extent to which new perceptions of these characters are possible. Given the nineteenth-century view held by Western culture about the inferiority of non-Western peoples in general, it is difficult to see how any new perceptions of Blacks and Mulattoes could occur. New perceptions arise from new understanding and reevaluation of historical and cultural material. Isaacs approached his black characters as one against the inhumanity of slavery who, in spite of himself, accepted the inferiority of Blacks.

The story of Nay and Sinar abounds in picturesque details. More than exotic paraphernalia, they delineate the cultural dislocation of the former slave, Feliciana, and establish a new cultural context for her by providing another identity: Nay is the African persona and Feliciana the American one. The new identity becomes the reference point for the retrogressive presentation of this character. As a dying woman, Feliciana first attracts the reader's attention; however, it is as Nay, her African manifestation, that she sustains this interest. Isaacs has carefully prepared this transference of identities and shift of the reader's focus by changing the narrator and the setting. The picturesque detail alerts the reader that certain black characters must be considered in a new social condition that antedates slavery.

Isaacs' choice of narrator for the Nay and Sinar episode reveals his intention to portray Blacks favorably. It reflects the possibilities that society and the prevailing literary mode—romanticism—offered. He substitutes Efraín, the first-person commentator of the novel, for Nay-Feliciana, who originally narrates the events in the story. In this way the author provides the reader with a familiar, sympathetic, "reliable" narrator for Nay's tale.[14] Changing the narrator also establishes a temporal distance that parallels the spatial distance created by the exotic setting. As narrator, Efraín tells Nay's story as he had heard it, as a bedtime tale.

As narrator of this episode, Efraín becomes the mediator between the Blacks and the white society. His sympathetic view of them intercedes with the reader on their behalf. The change of narrator, for example, affects the language with which the episode is presented. The reader will not learn of Nay's life in her language, which the author refers to as "clumsy and touching" ("rústico y patético lenguaje"). Instead Isaacs employs Efraín's language. His learned diction, Latinate lexicon and syntax are better able to rouse the reader's interest

and stimulate his sympathy. Furthermore, Efraín's language is a linguistic manifestation of socially approved authority; it invests the story it tells with dignity. His rendition of Nay's story has an elevated tone, associated with noble characters, the heroic, the epic. By avoiding Nay's common speech, Isaacs identifies her as a serious element of the novel. By not placing his black characters in comic positions, he does not subject them to a reduction based on limited roles and nonstandard speech or behavior ignorant of decorum.

On the one hand, Isaac's handling of narrator and language in the episode can be seen challenging images of Blacks as comic and inarticulate—images by which the dominant society dissociates itself from Blacks. On the other hand, the context in which Nay tells her story to the white character is marginal. It is domestic and occurs in the space of the least important members of the household, the children's quarters. This reinforces an image of Nay as Feliciana, the contented mammy figure. Her life and its significance to her is nullified, reduced to entertainment for the master's family.

In order to dispose the reader favorably toward black characters, Isaacs eliminates physical differences, making Nay and Sinar types that Whites accept, that is, more like themselves. Although Nay is Ashanti, she lacks kinky hair, a flat nose and thick lips.[15] Sinar, though not Ashanti, is one of the most beautiful young slaves Nay's father possesses. In neutralizing black skin color and other traits, Isaacs tacitly acknowledges them as undesirable, thereby confirming the attitude held by the larger society.

There are other instances of neutralization in this episode. Isaacs, attempting to portray the Black sympathetically, consistently selects the positive stereotypes. He avoids depicting slave women as sexually promiscuous, insisting on a maternal or domestic role for them, both of which are socially more acceptable. Sinar, a potential authority figure for Blacks in the New World, disappears. This eliminates the black male as a possible threat in the dominant society; there will be no Toussaint L'Ouvertures. The favorable image that the reader retains of Sinar, "young and handsome" (p. 234), is associated, nevertheless, with a character who, not unlike the novel's protagonist, always acquiesces to authority.

An implicit belief in authority underlies *María* Isaacs' black characters show great respect for the social sanctions of age, incest taboos, marital fidelity. Isaacs takes advantage of a possible cultural overlap—the importance of authority and social sanctions in African culture as well as in that of nineteenth-century Hispanic America. On the one hand, he validates the existence of this respect in black characters. However, he does not focus on it in a cultural context that is significant to them. Instead, Isaacs emphasizes respect for authority as a quality that the dominant society in the New World favors as a means of control in general and particularly for Blacks. Stressing the use of social sanctions and authority in maintaining order and defending legitimate social relationships, Isaacs tries to allay the negative reactions to fears about Blacks based on threats of insubordination. Loyalty, gratitude, obedience (based on respect and affection), passivity and acquiescence neutralize rebellion, mistrust and revenge.

Although neither white nor black characters challenge or reject authority in **María,** the relation of Blacks to authority is obviously more problematic for the society of that period than for Whites. Society felt that Blacks were subordinate and, therefore, had a "place" from which they were encouraged not to move. Isaacs allows his black characters to be rebellious only in situations in which isolation nullifies conventional social relations or in which rebellion can be easily pacified. For example, Sinar urges Nay to elope with him and return to his homeland. In pressing Nay to disobey, he encourages disloyalty, disregarding both her filial obligation and his own position as her father's slave. Nay, however, takes advantage of Sinar's love for her to persuade him to stay. By so doing, she overcomes his challenge to the patriarchal authority.

Defeats and failures are thematic motifs that link the Nay and Sinar episode to the main plot of Efraín and María. Losses that the black characters suffer parallel and anticipate those of the white protagonists. The most dramatic moment in Nay's story is when the slave traders capture her and Sinar. The episode's most memorable event becomes the one that represents their loss of freedom, their culture and each other. This image of their failure is then fixed in the reader's mind.

At the same time the black characters (in this episode and elsewhere) are the only ones who escape complete failure and psychological devastation. Unlike Efraín and his family, Blacks are compensated for their losses. Nay as Feliciana gains her freedom; her child by Sinar enjoys the "privileges" of a house slave. Isaacs leads the reader to feel more admiration for the adjustment the black characters have made than sympathy for their oppressed condition. He surrounds the incidents that expose the cruelties of slavery with idyllic situations: in Africa, Nay's privileged life; Sinar's position among the Ashantis as a favored slave; in the New World, the kindness of Efraín's father, who buys Nay and frees her; Nay's life on the estate so suggestively named "El Paraíso." Circumstances such as these distract the reader's attention from the unpleasant implications of slavery. By depicting the patriarchal society as benevolent to Blacks and destructive to Whites—Efraín is wretched, María dies—Isaacs affirms the prevailing sympathetic vision of the Black. The Black is victim; the Black is ward.

Both these designations imply inferiority. Society, regarding the Black "sympathetically," does penance for the wrongs of slavery. More importantly, it justifies keeping the Black subservient in order to do so.

Isaacs' presentation of black characters is essentially rhetorical. The needs and preoccupations of the dominant society define his black characters. The reader has no other perspective on them. The positive stereotypes to which Isaacs turns as he tries to validate the worth of Blacks to society serve only to reassure the anxious reader that his perception of the Black as inferior is valid.

Notes

[1] David Craig, *The Real Foundations: Literature and Social Change* (London: Chatto and Windus, 1973), p. 245.

[2] Henri Baudet, *Paradise on Earth: Some Thoughts on European Images of Non-European Man* (New Haven and London: Yale University Press, 1965), p. 6.

[3] For an analysis and discussion of race contact in the New World, see Magnus Morner's study, *Race Mixture in the History of Latin America* (Boston: Little, Brown, 1967); also Harmannus Hoetink, *Slavery and Race Relations in the Americas* (New York: Harper and Row, 1973).

[4] This point is well dealt with in Sylvia Wynter, "The Eye of the Other," in *Blacks in Hispanic Literature,* ed. Miriam DeCosta (Port Washington, N.Y.: Kennikat Press, 1977), pp. 27-39.

[5] Stanley E. Fish, *Self-Consuming Artifacts* (Berkeley and Los Angeles: University of California Press, 1972), pp. 1-2.

[6] Ibid.

[7] See Lemuel Johnson, *The Devil, the Gargoyle, and the Buffoon: The Negro as Metaphor in Western Literature* (Port Washington, N.Y.: Kennikat Press, 1971).

[8] Luis Monguió, "El negro en algunos poetas españoles y americanos anteriores a 1800," *Revista Iberoamericana* 22, no. 44 (1957): 245-59.

[9] Miguel Acosta Saignes, *Vida de los esclavos negros en Venezuela* (Havana: Casa de las Américas, 1978). This detailed study documents the role black slaves played in Venezuelan society through the end of the eighteenth century. It can serve as a model for other countries in Latin America insofar as the importance of Blacks to the economy and social organization is concerned.

[10] The principal antislavery novels were Anselmo Suárez y Romero's *Francisco,* written in 1839; Gertrudis Gómez de Avellaneda's *Sab* (1841); Antonio Zambrana's *El negro Francisco* (1873); Martín Morúa Delgado's *Sofía* (1891) and *La familia Unzúaza* (1901).

[11] In developing this point, Lemuel Johnson's analysis of space and time as significant indicators of attitudes toward black characters was particularly helpful. These ideas appeared in his paper read at the Medgar Evers Symposium on Afro-Hispanic Literature, New York, June 1980.

[12] Arnold Hauser, *The Social History of Art* (New York: Alfred A. Knopf, 1951), 4:118-19.

[13] Jorge Isaacs, *María,* ed. Donald McGrady (1867; reprint ed., Barcelona: Labor, 1970), p. 232. Further references will appear in the text.

[14] For a discussion of the "reliable" narrator, see Wayne Booth, *The Rhetoric of Fiction* (Chicago and London: University of Chicago Press, 1961), p. 250.

[15] Isaacs Cesar Cantú, author of an encyclopedia work *Storia universale* (1838-1846), is an authority on African tribes. Isaacs appears, however, to have rearranged certain items—creative license—to reinforce a white aesthetic. These are details of physical appearance.

Sharon Magnarelli (essay date 1985)

SOURCE: "The Love Story: Reading the Writing in Jorge Isaacs's *María,*" in *The Lost Rib: Female Characters in the Spanish-American Novel,* Bucknell University Press, 1985, pp. 19-37.

[*In the following excerpt, Magnarelli offers a feminist reading of Isaacs's* María *and analyzes the representation of the novel's title character.*]

Published in 1867 by Jorge Isaacs (Colombia, 1837-95), *María* is one of the earliest Spanish-American novels still widely read today. Generally relished by adolescents, *María* has been successively highly esteemed and discredited because of its maudlin romanticism. Numerous critics have demonstrated its close affiliation with European romanticism, and many have considered it but a poor copy of French works such as *Atala* and *Paul et Virginie.*[1] Nevertheless, some of the most important aspects of the text, especially those related to the title female, have been neglected. In the following pages, I shall examine *María* in terms of the dramatized narrative process and its portrayal of women. To date, scholars have focused principally on the story, analyzing it either as a reflection of Isaacs's own life or in terms of its rather insipid and terribly commonplace

love story.[2] What has all too often been overlooked (and what is both most interesting and most important) are the facts that, first, *María* is much more than a love story, and, secondly, the genre of the love story in and of itself is much more significant than we have previously acknowledged. That *María* is more than a simple love story is evidenced by the textual presentation and dramatization of the very important acts of reading and writing. *María* is not simply a tale of love, told in the third person; rather the story is developed within a framework which includes its own narration. We watch not only the unfolding of the story (the *énoncé*) but also the narrational process of that story (the *énonciation*) which forms a part of the fiction, and, as I shall demonstrate, this narration is but the reading and rewriting of a prior *énoncé,* those past and earlier signs.[3]

Recounting in the first person, Efraín focuses on a few months of his youth, on a significant pause between two of his journeys. The novel opens as he recalls his first departure from the family embrace. When he returned from that first educational journey, he found a paradise which apparently was even superior to the one he had remembered leaving behind four years before. A pure and innocent love unfolded between Efraín and María, although they both knew that his sojourn at home (and consequently his proximity to her) would be but the brief span of time before his next voyage. Having said goodbye to María and having promised to marry her upon his return, he departed on that second journey. Later, receiving urgent word to return home, he did so, expecting to repeat his previous return to paradise, but María had already died and the paradise had disintegrated.

The story, then, is trite—one of thousands of love stories told in countless languages. My interest in it stems not from the story itself, not from what it overtly tells us about the epoch in which it was written (its *costumbrismo*), nor from the character development. Instead, my curiosity about the text derives from its apparent misnomer and from its *énonciation;* the dramatized narrative gesture suggests very different conclusions about the novel from those of many of its earlier critics.

What is perhaps most intriguing about *María* is that its title, like that of so many Spanish-American novels, is misleading. Although the novel's title page promises a tale of a woman named María, in the final analysis, the novel is not essentially about María. Rather, it is an examination of the psychological state of Efraín, and, more importantly, a portrayal of his attempts to recapture those fleeting moments, already past, of childhood innocence and happiness. María may be the instrument and the stimulus of this innocence and happiness, much as she is portrayed as the inspiration for Efraín's narration, but she certainly is not the protagonist in the usual sense of the term.

Perhaps before one can consider the implications of the title of the novel, one needs to examine the significance of having baptized the young girl with the name María, rather than Juanita, Carmen, or some other suitable appellation. The name *María* of course, evokes an affiliation with the Virgin Mary and all the connotations of the religious virgin mother. In Western literature from the Middle Ages through the twentieth century, we find that many of the literary converts adopt the name María upon baptism, suggesting the belief or hope that the adoption of the name presumes the annexation of the characteristics associated with that name. Such is certainly the case with Isaacs's María.

However, María, born of Jewish parents, Salomón and Sara,[4] was originally named Ester. Ester, or Esther, is a particularly relevant name since it derives from the Hebrew Ishtar, who was the chief goddess of the Babylonians and the Assyrians. According to M. Esther Harding, Ishtar was a moon goddess and a goddess of fertility, "personification of that force of nature which shows itself in the giving and the taking of life."[5] She was a cyclic goddess who, like the Romans' Proserpina, spent part of the year in the sky giving life and part of the year in the underworld taking it away. Harding notes that during the period when Ishtar was in the land of noreturn, or the underworld, the "whole world is described as being sunk in a kind of hopeless inactivity, mourning for her return" (p. 159).[6] In addition, Ishtar, because of her cyclic nature, is the goddess of time.

Now, the evolution of the Christian Virgin Mary and her affiliation with the earlier moon goddesses, Ishtar and Isis, have been demonstrated by numerous scholars. Isaacs, however, overtly assigns both names to his character, thereby endowing her with what we might colloquially call the best of both worlds. The merging of the two goddess figures is patent in the fact that throughout the novel María is depicted in terms of both nature and motherhood (terms inexorably linked in earlier times but not necessarily considered related in Christianity); she is consistently found in Efraín's mother's room, and frequently acts as proxy mother to Juan. And she is always portrayed by Efraín in relation to nature—she brings the flowers, prepares the bath with flowers, etc.:[7] "María estaba bajo las enredaderas que adornaban las ventanas del aposento de mi madre" (p. 12) ("María was behind the creeper that climbed up by the windows of my mother's room," p. 2); "Soñé que María entraba a renovar las flores" (p. 16) ("I dreamed that María came in to renew the flowers on my table," p. 7).[8] In this respect María represents all that is fertile and life-giving but is refined by the Christian concept of purity, virginity, and holiness. She is, thus, the very representation of the "civilized" (some may call it patriarchal) progress from the more primitive mother goddesses to the contemporary Christian concept of perfect woman. This "progress" is echoed in her religious conversion from Judaism to Christianity and directly influences our reading of this text.

Although this seemingly simple and irrelevant modification of María's name may not appear to be of great significance, it does reflect and become a synecdoche for the attitude toward the portrayal of the female. First, the very fact that Isaacs felt it necessary to provide María with two names reflects an interest in language, naming, and finding just the right word or phrase to express the situation as he sees it, to which I referred in the introduction to this study. At the same time it also reflects the author's concern with time as I have discussed it. Just as the Bible provides two creation stories, one succeeding the other in time, the female character here is provided with two successive names (and, in some sense, births): she is first Ester and then María. As the later rib story persists, so does the name María. But even more importantly, the permutation highlights and underlines the primary concern in this study: the re-creation and supplementation of the female. María is born Ester, Hebrew. That is, her first presence in the world (within the confines of the fiction, of course) is a Jewish presence, but that "origin" is erased and reshaped by her conversion to Christianity. The re-creation of her being is thus reflected in her name as she apparently willingly gives up her original religion and name in exchange for the socially acceptable Catholicism and Catholic name. Suggestively, however, this "voluntary" conversion occurs when María is far too young to give what we would call today "informed consent."

In this regard, then, the female character here (on the level of the *énoncé;* I shall discuss the *énonciation* later) is a supplement, a mask, a negation of her former being, or carried one step further, she becomes a non-entity, a projection of another. After the name change, she is no longer Ester but assumes the prefabricated name and characteristics of the Virgin Mary, which the patriarchal society has deemed appropriate. Ironically, however, one must wonder how we are meant to interpret María's final illness and death. On some level it would seem that her new identity was inadequate to disguise and extinguish the old completely, for she does die from the weakness and illness inherited, significantly, from her mother, Sara. Somehow, the old family traits have persisted in spite of the name change.

At the same time, the substitution of the name becomes particularly relevant to the creation of an audience for the novel. As I suggested in the introduction, a novel frequently creates its own audience. There can be little doubt that a novel entitled *Ester* would attract and create quite a different audience than one entitled *María*. Ester would necessarily be "other" and alienated within the Catholic society that surrounds her, but María, via the change in appellation, on some level and to some extent eradicates, negates, or at least partially disguises her otherness.

Also important is the parallel between the relation of María to this text and that of the Virgin to Christianity or the Bible. The Virgin Mary, of course, maintains a curiously contradictory position. She is not one of the protagonists of the Christian text, for the main characters are all male: Father, Son, Holy Spirit.[9] But the Virgin is the instrument, the mediator, the stimulus in much the same way as María.[10] She cannot directly grant heavenly favors, but she can intercede and thus be the instrument of those favors. She has no power except that of intercession; she cannot act directly, but she can influence the acts of the male trinity.[11]

On another level one might understand the entire novel in terms of that "hopeless inactivity, mourning for her return" that occurs when Ishtar goes to the land of no-return (death), for what is the novel but a form of mourning for the return of María? The novel is clearly an obituary monument to her, and only at the conclusion of the narration can Efraín now begin some type of fruitful activity, for only then does the mourning period cease and life resume. Only at the conclusion of the text is the goddess or María in some sense returned, at least in the fictionalized form of a novel which presumably re-creates, re-presents, and depicts her anew. Her existence, literally and metaphorically, depends upon the reading of the novel.

Inasmuch as the novel attempts to recapture the pause between two journeys, the novel itself is a pause, a static product which arrests (or gives the illusion of arresting) the motion of time and life, the continuum. The novel thus signals a mythic view of life as a series of static medallions; one "journeys" from one medallion or stage to the next, but once there, all is basically and essentially static, unmoving, and unchanging until the moment arrives to travel on to the next medallion. Clearly, such a credence is a direct effort to deny or negate the continual movement of life, and this negation, although also mythic in origin, is contrary to the myth of Ishtar—a myth which inherently encompasses this motion.[12] But mankind's inability to cope with changes and unexpected contingency is a frequent theme in literature, and Efraín is not different from don Jerónimo of José Donoso's *El obsceno pájaro de la noche,* who not only tried to negate all that did not conform nicely with his perfect "medallón de piedra eterna" ("medallion of eternal stone")[13] but who also hired Humberto to write the history so that it would comply. Donoso even notes that it is the ritual which fixes life as in a medallion. Efraín, however, did not have to employ Humberto; he will write the story and make it static himself. Efraín, himself, will play the priestly role and perform that ritual (writing) which will inscribe the figures on the medallion.

Thus one can explain the name assigned to the female character and Efraín's role and goal as writer, but how does one explain the allocation of her name to the title of a book which might better be named *Efraín* or perhaps *Efraín y María?* As I have noted, *María* is only one of many Spanish-American novels whose titles belie their contents. José Mármol's *Amalia,* for example, written in approximately the same historical period as *María* centers even less than does *María* on the female character whose name is evoked in the title. *Amalia* a voluminous work, originally published in serial form, principally criticizes the atrocities of the Rosas regime in Argentina. The "love story" encompassed in *Amalia* forms a very loose and, in effect, superficial unifying factor for the rest of the novel. It is not gratuitous to consider *Amalia* in relation to *María,* and the former may indeed shed some light on the latter, for the two novels have several facets in common.

One of those common denominators is the temporal stance. *María* is narrated after the death of its heroine; in other words, the fictionalized present of the narration or *énonciation* affords a vantage point from which to look back upon the past of the story, or *énonce*. In a similar manner, *Amalia* pretends to be narrated *ex post facto*. Although the novel is written during the dictatorship of Rosas, the author specifically states in the "Explicación," "Pero el autor, *por una ficción calculada,* supone que escribe su obra con algunas generaciones de por medio entre él y aquéllos" ("But the author, *through a calculated fiction,* imagines that he is writing the work with several generations between himself and them").[14] He continues, "El autor ha creído que tal sistema convenía tanto a la mejor claridad de la narración" ("The author has believed that such a system contributes as much to the clarity of the narration"). In this respect, then, both novels focus on what is past and absent even though in *Amalia* the extranovelistic existence of the point of focus overtly underlines the fictionalization of that absence and nonexistence as they become products of that fiction. Through the process of fictionalization the center is thus distanced, removed, relegated to the past and in that sense made impotent and subsequently harmless.

But perhaps what is most important in the two novels is that they both embrace the underlying theme of language itself. Each is concerned with the problems of expression, of converting ideas, emotions, and events into language. In *María* this preoccupation is reflected in Efraín's early acknowledgment of the paucity of his language to express the depth of his emotions. As he notes, "Las grandes bellezas de la creación no pueden a un tiempo ser vistas y cantadas; es necesario que vuelvan al alma empalidecidas por la memoria infiel" (p. 13) ("The great beauties of nature cannot be sung at the same time they are seen; they must return to the soul, made dim by a faulty memory," p. 4); "su acento, sin dejar de tener aquella música que le era peculiar, se hacía lento y profundo al pronunciar palabras suavemente articuladas, que en vano probaría yo a recordar hoy: porque no he vuelto a oírlas, porque pronunciadas por otros labios no son las mismas, y escritas en estas páginas parecerían sin sentido. Pertenecen a otro idioma" (p. 35) ("her tones, without ceasing to have their peculiar music, would grow slow and solemn as she spoke words which it would be vain for me to try to recall now: I cannot hear them any more, and when they are uttered by other lips they are not the same; if they were written on this page they would seem meaningless. They belong to another language," p. 32); and "nuestra voz es impotente" (p. 13) ("our voices are powerless," p. 3). Similarly in *Amalia* the reader is repeatedly presented with reproduction or pseudo-reproduction of prior texts: letters, edicts, speeches, newspaper clippings, etc., in which the word is shown in its full ability to distort the facts, resuscitate emotions (especially inappropriate ones), and support the power structure. Consider, for example, the Rosas regime's repeated use of "¡Mueran los inmundos salvajes asquerosos unitarios!" ("Death to the filthy, savage, disgusting Unitarians!") and similar expressions. In this manner, the novel demonstrates how the Rosas regime uses language to distort, again signaling the distance between the word and the world. Thus, in both novels one finds a basic philosophy that Truth exists independently of language and that language is incapable of expressing or capturing the Truth.[15] And yet, ironically, one presumes that the "Truth" of María is reflected in her name.

In addition, while both titles are delusive to some degree, it appears that the title of *Amalia* is not only more misleading but also intentionally deceptive, for María certainly plays a greater role in the novel of her name than does Amalia in hers. Doubtlessly, the title of *Amalia* is designed to attract attention and readership—an audience which would not even begin to read a novel entitled *The Atrocities of Rosas* or something similar. Furthermore, I suspect that the love story buried in *Amalia* is also merely an artifice to entice readers and hold their interest in what is otherwise a prosaic, expository collection of political essays. In both novels the titles serve to distract attention from the true focus of the novel—political dissertations on one case, Efraín in the other.

It takes little imagination to understand why Mármol would want to shift the focus from the political writings, but might one assume a similar motive in Isaacs's novel? Certainly, the title *María* would captivate (at first, anyway) quite a different audience from that which would be attracted to the title of *Efraín*. *María* is most likely going to enjoy a predominately female audience, which would probably be Christian; when it tempts a male audience (usually adolescent) there remains nonetheless the underlying assumption that it is still a "girls' book," and in this respect, not to be taken too seriously. It is not fortuitous that throughout our Western literary tradition, the novels whose titles name males are those works which narrate the adventures of an appropriately "manly" protagonist—adventures of courage, conquest, and heroic feats. Consider, for example, *Amadís de Gaula, Gulliver's Travels, Guzmán de Alfarache,*[16] *Doctor Faustus, Nazarín, Zalacaín, Don Segundo Sombra,* and *Tom Jones.*[17] Patently, then, the feminine title does not announce the focus of the novel but rather functions, first, to attract a certain audience (perhaps the *lector hembra* or *desocupado*), secondly, to establish from the outset a certain attitude toward the text, and thirdly, to shift the attention away from the masculine actor and center. This final function suggests a strong social imposition of the ideal of what is suitably masculine and feminine. While Efraín may represent an adolescent ideal, he certainly cannot (and perhaps must not) reflect an adult male prototype.

Seen in this matter, then, *María* in specific and the love story in general must be recognized for what they truly represent: a rite of passage. *María* is still read, as noted above, for its story of youthful, pure love and devotion. Although the love story no doubt forms the basis for a large portion of popularly read "literature" (the majority of the rest of that "literature" probably revolves around the mystery or detective story), to my knowledge the love story per se (and particularly in terms of the rite of passage it becomes) has never been analyzed.[18] Northrop Frye has examined the notion of the hero-quest pattern which indubitably forms the nucleus of the love story, but there are distinctions.[19] Because the love story is the basis for so much literature for, about, and by women, it is an integral step in an analysis of their portrayal.

The basic ingredients of a love story are a male and a female, preferably young, who meet and try to overcome a series of obstacles to their love (social class, parental disapproval, geographical distance, rival loves, etc.). Although Frye defines the general category of romance in terms of three steps or stages: conflict, struggle, and discovery (p. 187), it seems that the love story, for the most part, evolves through five phases:

1. ENCOUNTER

2. CONQUEST

3. LOSS

4. STRUGGLE / PROOF

5. DEATH OR MARRIAGE

The first of these steps is the encounter; that is, boy meets girl, but for one reason or another, the relationship seems hopeless, bound to failure (without this basic futility or frustration there would be no story). The second stage is what I shall call the mini-conquest; the initial problems or obstacles are overcome or speciously eliminated. Girl appears to love boy, and the other barriers to their love are ostensibly resolved. Granted, some stories stop here, but most of them (in the interest of heightened emotion and reader involvement) continue. In phase three there is a new (real or imagined within the fiction) loss of the loved one. Owing to some development in the plot new obstacles are placed between the lovers: the new rival intervenes, a fortuitous event results in new geographical separation or parental disapproval. Whatever the circumstances, the new privation is felt much more acutely because it stands in contrast to the recent happiness and apparent fulfillment. Step four then involves the resurgent efforts to overcome these new problems (the labors or proofs), while step five is the conclusion, the result of these efforts. Clearly, there are only two possible conclusions to the love story: the difficulties are surmounted so boy and girl marry and "live happily ever after"; or, the impediments are not eliminated, and boy and girl (or the survivor, if one dies, as one often does) are relegated to a life of eternal isolation and separation from the loved one—at the very least, a symbolic form of death.

While this may seem simple enough, the true significance of the love story lies much deeper and is far more complex. First, the love story as I have already discussed in relation to *Amalia* and *María* is generally narrated *ex post facto* (as indeed are most stories). The story tells how boy won or lost the love of girl after that love has already been won or lost. In this sense, then, *María,* like fiction in general and love stories in particular, reflects an absence. Efrain writes of his sweetheart only after she has ceased to exist (even within the fiction)—only when she has become an absence. While each literary character is covertly an absence insofar as he is fictional and nonexistent, María is overtly so. María has already died before Efraín begins to narrate, so even within the text she has already been converted to a word, a sign whose referent can never be made present. And, the word here is static; its significance is already determined and cannot alter. There is no development of characters in the novel (as there rarely is in the love story), and even the evolution of a love between them is perhaps illusory in that not only is their love already past, but also it does not truly develop—it merely rises up from its latent state.

It is perhaps most interesting that in the stereotype of the love story, it is the male who pursues, woos, proves himself a worthy male, while the female sits back and watches. In other words, he is all activity, she unmoving. In general, the portrayals of men and women in

this novel are equally oppositional (speaking of men and women within the same social class). While men are shown as taking care of women, and women are represented as caring for men (each obviously in a different fashion), men are also portrayed as attending to the hunt and business, while women concern themselves with the home and religion. Men are physically stronger, while women are weak, although moral strength seems independent of gender. Men are better educated, more well-traveled, and thus more worldly and knowledgeable than women. Somewhat over simplified, it might be said that the men in this novel go out and do things (are active) while the women sit home and wait. Although Efraín's writing demonstrates a strong predilection for nouns, adjectives, and inactive verbs, we might surmise that men are principally portrayed by active verbs whereas women tend to be depicted by nouns, adjectives, and inactive verbs. Compare, for example, these two passages: "Las mujeres parecían vestidas con más esmero que de ordinario. Las muchachas, Lucía y Tránsito, llevaban enaguas de zaraza morada y camisas muy blancas. . . . Las trenzas de sus cabellos, gruesas y de color de azabache, les jugaban sobre sus espaldas. . . . Me hablaban con suma timidez. . . . Entonces se hicieron más joviales y risueñas; nos enlazaban amistosamente los recuerdos de los juegos infantiles" (p. 28) ("The women were dressed with more than usual care. Lucía and Tránsito, the girls, wore petticoats of violet-colored chintz, and fine white chemises. . . . Their thick, jet-black hair was arranged in braids, which danced upon their shoulders. . . . They addressed me with the greatest timidity. . . . Then they became more smilingly at ease; we were drawn to each other in the most friendly manner by the remembrance of games together as children," pp. 23-24); "José me condujo al río y me habló de sus siembras y cacerías, mientras yo me surmergía en el remanso diáfano desde el cual se lanzaban las aguas" (p. 29) ("José led me to the river, and talked to me about his crops and his hunting while I was taking a plunge in the transparent pool whence the stream fell over a small cascade," p. 24). This is not to suggest that the physical appearance of José is not described with the same detail as that of the girls, but the description of the girls is almost totally lacking active verbs; in fact, the most active verb in the entire passage, which is applied to the girls, is *servir,* the one activity definitely allowed women. And, the procedure is typical of the novel. (As Emigdio so pointedly expresses it, "¡Como si pudiera convenirme a mí el casarme con una señora para que resultara de todo que tuviera que servirle yo a ella en vez de ser servido!" [p. 63] ["How could I ever persuade myself to marry a lady, when it would simply result in my becoming her servant instead of her becoming mine?" p. 63].) What active verbs are present, for the most part are applied to masculine characters. As in other love stories, here too, the women wait while the men prove themselves.[20] Thus, many of the major portraits of María in the novel are static memories. Each is like a painting; in one Efraín remembers María standing, still as in a picture, by the window of their house as he departs on one of his journeys.[21] These memories, reiterated within the text, parallel the artistic capture of a fleeting instant, made eternal by the artist's presentation of it.

María then, even within the fiction, is never anything but a group of words, a conglomerate of adjectives, which are not even proper, not specific, insofar as they must be shared with the rest of humanity. For this reason Efraín mourns the paucity of his language to describe his love. She becomes for him, as well as for the reader, but a composite of nouns modified by adjectives. And ultimately, María, even within the fiction, functions in much the same way as any mass of written words, at once passive as they simply "lie" there, unmoving on the page, while simultaneously they act as agents, stimulating the reader to emotions and/or actions, just as María provided Efraín with the stimulus to write. In all these aspects, then, *María* reflects the genre of the love story.

Finally, since the protagonists of the love story are almost always youthful (in fact, the story very often centers on first love), the narration of the story reflects a nostalgia, a yearning for that past golden age of perfect and pure love. Thus, the end of the story, whether happy or sad, is inevitably a point of division and symbolic death, which, to paraphrase Neruda, cuts the duration of life into separate segments which can never meet. In this sense, the *énoncé* (like the *énonciation*) is inevitably a rite of passage. If the loved one dies, then, of course, the survivor dies in the symbolic sense that a "part of him" dies with her. It is the moment of her death and his realization or psychological acceptance of that death that signal his passage from an old state to a new state. That is, the youthful, idealistic dreamer (adolescent) gives way to the mature, wise man of the world who clearly can never again repeat the childlike innocence of the first love. In a similar manner, if the tale has a happy ending, then its conclusion is accordingly the ritual of marriage. While superficially marriage may appear a contradiction of the symbolic death, the fact is that the rite of marriage implies a similar death insofar as the marriage ceremony is the symbol of leaving one state and being reborn into another. That is, through the ritual the young man and woman leave the home of the parents (e.g., the father who "gives away" the bride), leave their childhood behind to become mature man and woman, heads of their own household and future parents. Clearly, whether the love itself succeeds or fails, the ritual has been performed, and the young man moves on to the next phase of life.

However, what is most significant, if indeed paradoxical, in *María* is that the passage is Efraín's and not hers, in spite of the title of the novel. If she matures, progresses, or "passes" at all, it is in the prehistory of the *énoncé* when she transforms from Ester to María. The writing freezes her in her innocent (i.e., prepassage) state.

Thus, we circle back to the notion that *María* in particular and the love story in general necessarily evoke that prepassage golden age, that ostensibly static period that precedes the journey. In evoking that golden age, two symbols, both female, emerge: the mother and the beloved. The idealized mother unquestionably symbolizes that golden age most perfectly, for she gives life and also affords protection, love, and nourishment. The beloved, on the other hand, maintains a more ambiguous position, for although she is closely related to the mother image, sometimes to the extent of providing a mother substitute (at the very least she is the future mother of his children), she encompasses a negative side also. She has the power to reject the suitor.[22] And, more importantly, her acceptance of the suitor necessarily separates him from his mother as, in effect, does the primitive rite of passage. That Efraín perceives María in direct relation to his mother, I have already shown; he even says at one point, speaking of María's welcome upon his return, "sus ojos [los de María] estaban humedecidos aún al sonreír a mi primera impresión afectuosa, como los de un niño cuyo llanto ha acallado una caricia materna" (p. 13) ("her eyes were yet moist when she smiled at my first affectionate word, like those of a child whose tears have been dried by a mother's caress," p. 4). The interrelationship and perhaps confusion between the two is further emphasized at the end of the novel; Efraín has returned after María's death and cruelly chastises his mother for having called him home when it was already too late. He hurls at her, "Así me engañaron . . . ¿A qué he venido?" ("So they deceived me! What have I come for?"), and she responds, "¿Y yo?" (p. 268) ("Haven't I suffered, too?" p. 289). . . .

Clearly, then, the evocation and re-creation of the lost paradise is the goal of the love story. While Frye has noted that the romance in general reflects a wish-fulfillment dream in which "the perennially childlike quality of romance is marked by its extraordinary persistent nostalgia, its search for some kind of imaginative golden age in time or space" (p. 186), the significant facet of the love story is that this golden age, while evoked, is simultaneously and necessarily depicted as no longer attainable. The love story indubitably centers on the inability to return as is demonstrated in the story of Nay and Sinar, interpolated within *María*. It is not coincidental that the tale of Nay and Sinar follows basically the same structure (story and narration) as the novel. The only difference is that the golden age evoked by Nay is remote not only in time but also in space. Nay, however, like Efraín, cannot return and cannot be reunited with the loved one; she, too, must resort to narrating her memories of this lost paradise. Her only consolation is her creation, her son, Juan Angel. In a similar manner, Efraín's only consolation will be his creation, the novel.

Earlier I noted that *María* begins with an apparently successful return which is never to be repeated. Clearly, the novel itself, that is the fictionalized *énonciation,* is an overt effort to repeat that return.[23] But what is most significant is not the desire to repeat a return, but the fiction of the return itself, for the first "return" of the novel is, in fact, not a reversion at all but the *illusion* of a regression. Efraín is disguising his forward movement in the pseudo return, much as he disguises the true focus of the novel with its feminine title. The fact that María and Efraín later feel an erotic love as opposed to the fraternal love they had previously experienced only underlines the illusory nature of this regression.[24]

The appeal of the love story, then, seems to rest in the dialectical nature of the text which simultaneously pulls us forward as it pushes us back (both temporally and spatially). In some sense, again one finds that the love story is the "best of both worlds," for one concurrently experiences all that is advantageous in the utopia while one continues to hold on to the positive attributes of progress, of moving ahead. There is little doubt that the nostalgia for any golden age is at least partially based on the knowledge that one is not locked into that phase. But María, unfortunately, is imprisoned in that stage. Just as she stayed behind as Efraín ventured off on his various educational journeys, so also she remains quiescent at the conclusion of the book, a static, fixed portrait, unchangeable for all eternity.

In addition, the evocation of the lost utopia, with its dialectical pseudo-movement, is directly related to the acts of reading and writing: acts of great importance throughout the text. The novel, in many ways, is the dramatization of the processes of reading and writing. There are many overt ways in which reading and writing are emphasized and shown to be among the prime concerns of the text. Not only does Efraín act as secretary for his father, in effect doing all his reading and writing for him, but also there are references to his interest in reading and writing poetry while away at school (p. 85). In fact, the act of reading is one of the most frequently repeated activities in the story. For example, early in the course of the action, Efraín appoints himself teacher for Emma and María. Curiously, and no doubt significantly, these "lessons," during which he reads and explains to the girls, become intricately identified with a nascent eroticism: María's "aliento, rozando mis cabellos, sus trenzas al rodar de sus hombros, turbaron mis explicaciones" (pp. 34-35) ("María's breath, grazing my hair, her braids, tossed on her shoulders, confused my explanations," omitted in English translation), and "mi corazón palpitaba

fuertemente" (p. 35) ("my heart was beating hard," omitted in English translation). Thus, Efraín "gives" the lessons as much for what he receives in sensual pleasure as for any more noble goal of enlightening the girls. The objective for "teaching" María, then, must be the development of her feminine sensuality, since little concern is demonstrated for the refinement of her intellect. In many ways, this whole question of the lessons reminds one of the writing lesson to be described by Lévi-Strauss nearly a century later. Intentionally or not, like the primitive described by Lévi-Strauss, Efraín uses the lessons as a means of establishing and reinforcing the power hierarchy.[25] And, like the origin of writing as explained by Jacques Derrida, these lessons respond to a need which is more sociological than intellectual,[26] as they cause both of the characters (and especially María, since she has less experience with books) to associate books and reading with physical awakening and desire. It is little wonder, then, that in a later chapter María suggests that reading is an activity which must be shared by two people. When asked by Efraín if she had read during his absence, she answers, "'No, porque me da tristeza leer sola'" (p. 135) ("'No, it makes me sad to read alone,'" p. 158).

Efraín continues in the following chapter to explain the effect his reading of Chateaubriand has had on María, an explanation which merits an attentive analysis:

> Las páginas de Chateaubriand iban claramente dando tintas a la imaginación de María. Ella, tan cristiana y tan llena de fe, se regocijaba al encontrar bellezas por ella presentidas en el culto católico. Su alma tomaba de la paleta que yo le ofrecía los más preciosos colores para hermosearlo todo, y el fuego poético, don del cielo que hace admirables a los hombres que lo poseen y diviniza a las mujeres que a su pesar lo revelan, daba a su semblante encantos desconocidos para mí hasta entonces en el rostro humano. Los pensamientos del poeta, acogidos en el alma de aquella mujer tan seductora en medio de su inocencia, volvían a mí como eco de una armonía lejana y conocida cuyas notas apaga la distancia y se pierden en la soledad. (P. 35)

> (The pages of Chateaubriand were clearly coloring María's imagination. So Christian and so full of faith, she delighted in finding the beauty which her religion had promised her. Her soul took the most precious colors from the palette I offered her in order to beautify everything, and the poetic fire, gift from Heaven which makes the men who possess it admirable and which sanctifies the women who reveal it in spite of themselves, gave her countenance charms which for me were heretofore unknown in the human face. The poet's ideas, received in the soul of that seductive but innocent woman, returned to me like the echo of a distant, familiar harmony whose notes are silenced by distance and lost in solitude. [Omitted in the English translation])

This passage, like many others in the book, simultaneously and discretely reflects the attitude of the narrator toward his subject, María, while it underlines the importance of reading within the novel. The first sentence of the passage clearly implies that María's mind is something of a tabula rasa, a blank, white space, waiting to be filled in and colored by Efraín (by the materials selected by him at the very least). Each sentence of the paragraph, through some type of reference to her faith, purity, and innocence, reinforces this image of a blank, white space insofar as these qualities are traditionally, metaphorically associated with whiteness. When we think of white spaces to be filled in, we immediately think of the blank white page, which, filled with suitable markings, will become a great work of literature. I suspect, in this regard, that it is not gratuitous that Isaacs (or Efraín, if you prefer) has chosen to use the word *"tintas"* (inks) rather than *matices, colores, tonos,* or some other suitable term. Thus, one is left with the impression that as he reads to her, Efraín will "write" on María's mind and imagination, and/or that the print of these literary works will become reimprinted on her. Thus, she is created.

One of the main ideas that surface in this passage is the influence of literature on life (a concept later to be posited by Borges). The implication is that the markings of one page can somehow magically be transposed (through the mediation of Efraín) onto María's blank or white imagination. Previously, the writings of Catholicism had influenced, become "imprinted" on, and helped to form the personality of María, and now, Romantic literature is completing the task. While alone, María read Christian writings (presumably offered her and encouraged by Efraín's parents), and, under the auspices of Efraín, she is now being offered the French Romanticists. Significantly, however, she does not, in fact, "read" the latter; rather they are read to her. Efraín, the teacher, molder, shaper, reader, and writer, is the "priest" of this cult called literature. This interpretation is reinforced a paragraph later when María is described, listening to Efraín read *Atala:* "medio arrodillada cerca de mí, no separaba sus miradas de mi rostro" (p. 36) ("half kneeling, close to me, she did not take her eyes off my face" omitted in English translation)—a portrayal which might be a verbal description of any one of dozens of paintings of biblical women kneeling before Christ. (Such a movement away from the source as a result of limitless repetitions clearly reflects the textual procedure in this novel, too.) Efraín, the priest, selects the literary works to which she is to be exposed, then reads or offers them to her (as he metaphorically expresses it), and, finally, provides the exegesis as he reads so that the less enlightened may comprehend a small part of the great mysteries. It further appears that she has been warned not to attempt to read or understand it all, for she complains, "'Iba a volver a leer *Atala* [significantly, the work he had been reading to her]; pero como me has dicho que tiene un pasaje no

sé como . . . '" (p. 135) ("'I was going to read some more of 'Atala,' but as you told me there is a passage in it not exactly—'" p. 158).

But, one must ask, why this combination of Catholic and Romantic readings? On the surface, these two bodies of literature would seem to be worlds apart. What do they have in common that allows them to be the only ones offered by the patriarchal society which surrounds the title character? The answer, undoubtedly, rests in the manner in which both of these great bodies of literary accomplishment present females. Each presents two distinctly dichotomous views of woman. In each, one possible portrayal is one of contempt (covert or overt) coupled with outright misogyny. Think, for example, of the early Judaic tradition and of St. Paul, to mention only two examples within biblical writings. In romanticism a similar misogyny and contempt is demonstrated by the Romantic figure par excellence, don Juan.[27] At the other extreme, we find an idealization of woman that distorts her beyond recognition as anything human (e.g., the Virgin Mary or the typical Romantic heroine)[28]—a distortion which ultimately may simply mask a latent misogyny inasmuch as such deification or wishful thinking may well be another expression of a contempt for the reality.[29] There is little doubt that most love stories, *María* included, are structured around the latter characterization—that is, an overidealization of the female character, a deification which demands of her the impossible, while maintaining her in a position totally divorced from reality. It is these love stories which, unfortunately, and as overtly demonstrated by *María* provide the principal reading material for the adolescent in her formative years and which, thus, introduce each girl to the model (absurd though it is) that she is to try to follow in the coming years.

Thus, first, María (perhaps like any adolescent girl) is a product of literature, and secondly, this literature is controlled by males, both in the sense that they have written it and in the sense that they have selected for her just what she will read or, more likely, have read and explicated to her by them. The patriarchal control, then, is very nearly complete, and the attitude expressed in the novel is not very different from that of the European anthropologists in their relations with the "primitives." Efraín's patronizing egoism and sense of superiority are patent in the cited passage; here, as in the rest of the novel, although the subject would ostensibly appear to be (and perhaps, in light of the title, should be) María, it is; in fact, Efraín. She may take only the possibilities he offers; to this extent her development and improvement are implemented by him and must be credited to him. He is, in every respect, then, her creator.

It is perhaps in the third sentence of the quoted passage that Efraín's sense of masculine superiority becomes most overt. In the previous paragraph he referred to the writing of the text we are reading and thus overtly accepted himself as a writer, a poet. In this paragraph, speaking of the *fuego poético,* a gift from heaven, he notes that it makes men admirable and deifies women who reveal it *"a su pesar."* "In spite of themselves" implies that such talent will either go unrecognized by women or was meant to be kept hidden and not revealed by them, although men, clearly, should manifest such abilities. At the same time, this phrase coupled with the next sentence which refers to María as simultaneously *seductora* and *inocente* suggest a superior (poetic) vision on the part of Efraín; he can see what others cannot—the *fuego poético* in María as well as the mixture of seductress and innocent virgin.

But, the final sentence of the paragraph brings together the principal leitmotifs of the novel. Here one sees not only that Efraín, his life, and his writings are also influenced by literature but that María provides something of a sounding board from which to reverberate the "notes" of the poet. As he explains, she absorbs the poet's thoughts and then echoes them back to him, thus projecting to him a harmony that time and distance have made dim. The terminology of the text, certainly, encourages one to think of the myth of Narcissus and Echo. Echo, of course, loved Narcissus but, much like María, was unable to initiate a conversation; she could only repeat what others said—María seldom says anything in the novel and seems to be a reflection (as the quotation suggests) of the thoughts of the poet (Efraín or Chateaubriand). Narcissus, on the other hand, fell in love with his own reflection and pined away. Are *María* and María not, in effect, the reflections of Efraín insomuch as he has created both, and does he not pine away because of an unrequited love that is only a reflection of himself? And is the novel itself not an echo of romanticism and other works of fiction just as it is an echo of the past golden age?

Thus, the reading of the French Romanticists forms an integral part of the novel as Efraín and María indubitably identify with the protagonists of these novels and unquestionably see all that surrounds them in terms of, or as a reflection of, these novels. The conclusion of *María* is clearly already written in *Atala,* and since Efraín's narrative task is to rewrite a Romantic novel, it is apropos that *María* dates from a moment in which romanticism was no longer considered stylish.

The book further portrays reading insofar as Efraín is continually "reading" signs or what he interprets as signs. He tries to read the meaning of certain looks or gestures on the part of María. He reads the absence of flowers in his room as an absence of love (p. 30, p. 27 in English); later he interprets her smile: "aquella sonrisa castísima que revela en las mujeres como María una felicidad que no les es posible ocultar" (p. 33)

("that most pure smile which reveals in women like María a happiness impossible to conceal," p. 31)—again, the priestly Efraín can see what is below the surface of María and that over which she presumably has no control. Also, he notes, "la luz de sus ojos . . . me decían . . . que en aquél era tan feliz como yo" (p. 134) ("The light in her eyes . . . told me, as they often had, that she was happy," p. 157). He also reads María's presence in nature and reads the blackbird as an evil omen. For Efraín, in fact, nature itself is but another language to be read and interpreted, a language which merely awaits his priestly, poetic intervention to tell us all. For example, during his final return to his homeland, he comments that the trees "parecían con sus rumores dar la bienvenida a un amigo no olvidado" (p. 252) ("with their sounds seemed to welcome a friend who had not been forgotten," omitted in English translation). Thus, there is nothing which is not open to his interpretation. Everything is comprehensible to one who reads, and the possibility that his "reading" might be erroneous is never considered within the text—the "priest" never errs.

What he seems to overlook in all of his reading, however, is the inevitable supplementation involved in the act; he reads María in nature only because he supplements nature with her—imposes her on nature. It is his own subjective state which allows him to see her there, and no form of presence or any purposefulness on the part of nature. One must wonder, then, if the enjoyment of the text *María,* on the part of readers today is not similarly a function of reader supplementation. Does one not enjoy *María* because in some manner one is able to read oneself into the text? And does not this imposition of the self on the text directly parallel the gesture of the chroniclers as they "read" the New World and then "wrote" it for their contemporaries? The book in this sense is a monument to María in much the same way as the stone over her grave is a monument to her. Like the written text, the latter is a white pedestal with black engraving.

If we accept, then, that the love story is essentially a rite of passage, we must at this point recognize that the narration or the writing of the story (especially when that *énonciation* forms an overt part of the fiction) is also a rite of passage. Writing is, indeed, a ritualistic, ceremonial sort of activity and like any ritual is subject to very definite, prescribed rules and formulae. Also like any other rite, it dramatically makes present that which is absent. In *María* however, the writing is very specifically a rite of passage as the narrator dramatizes his leaving behind of the past, female-dominated world. In fact, as Theodor Reik has noted, "one of the most important purposes of the puberty rites is to loosen the ties between boys and their mothers and to bind the novices to the society of men. This part of primitive education, marking the growth of boys into maturity, is accomplished by drastic means" (*The Creation of Woman* p. 123).

The narration or writing of *María* thus serves as a rite of passage for Efraín, who might be seen as both initiate and priest, and as a purification or exorcism of the past. María, now converted into a single, simple signifier, is immortalized and made permanent, impervious to the failings of future memory lapses. But, at the same time, she is distanced and made into an object, now separated from the subject. She can never change after she has been converted into the word, and that conversion distances her; she now forms a part of and, in fact, represents that golden age, fixed in the past, and paradisiacal because it is static, past, and unthreatening.

The very notion of a ritualistic or ceremonial writing is paralleled by another ritualistic activity directly portrayed in the text: the cutting of hair. As early as the second paragraph of the text the reader is presented with the first ceremonial haircut. Efraín is remembering the eve of his first departure when his sister entered his room "y sin decirme una sola palabra cariñosa . . . cortó de mi cabeza unos cabellos" (p. 11) ("without saying a single word . . . cut off a lock of my hair," p. 1). In the next paragraph he labels that hair "esa precaución del amor contra la muerte delante de tanta vida" ("that precaution of love against death, even in the presence of abounding life"). Toward the end of the novel a similar ritual is performed, again by the same agent, his sister. Apparently, María had requested that Emma cut her braids after her death and give them to Efraín. Superficially, both of these acts appear gratuitous or excessively emotional. Nevertheless, the repetition of the act implies significance, and I would suggest that the acts are symbolic. María's braids are her postmortuary gift to him. She was very vain about her hair, and the braids themselves are a sign of her femininity (men, of course, supposedly are neither vain about their hair nor do they wear braids). Interestingly, that the hair is indeed symbolic of femininity is demonstrated by the fact that in certain Greek rites, the women no longer sacrificed their virginity to the gods as had been the custom, but rather their hair, "as a sort of symbolic surrender of their womanhood" (Harding, p. 136). Most relevant is perhaps the supplementtal nature of the hair to these later women and of virginity to the earlier woman. In both cases, the sacrificed matter is viewed as something not essential to the inherent being, something additional, extra, and thus expendable.[30] María's braids are cut from her and separated from her essence, although they stand as a symbol of that essence in much the same way Efraín's writing is separated from that essence, that referent, although it too stands as a symbol of that paradise lost. The very biological fact that hair itself is dead matter reinforces the notion of the cutting of hair, like writing, as the separation from the vital, the essential, the living.

What one is left with then is narration and writing which are ritualistic attempts to simultaneously underline and negate the separation, while attempting to fill the void left by that separation. The ritualistic attempts in turn lead one directly back to the story of the creation of woman, which, like the rite of passage, attempts to negate the very real biological fact that man is born of woman, and not vice versa as the biblical story would like to imply. And, according to the story, that creation of woman left a void (which presumably can only be filled by man's reuniting with woman in the form of sacred matrimony). María and Eve, signs of past golden ages which no longer exist, never were anything but reflections, echoes, creations. Efraín writes to recapture this past, to reconquer this paradise. Thus, inexorably, the writing, itself fictionalized within the text, becomes a supplement of a supplement. To the extent that writing is inevitably supplemental, since it replaces, substitutes, and adds to a nonpresence, writing which portrays itself as it writes, writing which fictionalizes its own process of writing, must become doubly supplemental—just as even within the fiction, María is a supplement of a supplement, ultimately eternal absence.

Notes

[1] Some of the scholars who have commented on *María* include the following: Donald F. Brown, "Chateaubriand and the Story of Feliciana in Jorge Isaacs' *María*," *Modern Language Notes* 62 (1947): 326-29; Sonia Karson, "La estructura de *María* de Jorge Isaacs," *Revista Hispánica Moderna* 34 (July-October 1968): 685-89; Valerie Massón de Gómez, "Las flores como símbolos eróticos en la obra de Jorge Isaacs," *Thesaurus* 28:117-27; C. Enrique Pupo-Walker, "Relaciones internas entre la poesía y la novela de Jorge Isaacs," *Thesaurus* 22 (1967): 45-59; Seymour Menton, "La estructura dualística de *María*," *Thesaurus* 25 (1970): 251-77; Donald McGrady, "Función del episodio de Nay y Sinar en *María* de Isaacs," *Nueva Revista de Filología Hispánica* 18 (1965-66): 171-76; Mario Carvajal, *Vida y pasión de Jorge Isaacs* (Santiago de Chile: Ercilla, 1937); Ernesto Posada Delgado, "El paisaje en *María* y en *La vorágine*," *Boletín Cultural y Bibliográfico* (Bogotá) 10 (1967): 880-84; Germán Arciniegas, *Genio y figura de Jorge Isaacs* (Buenos Aires: Eudeba, 1970).

[2] Throughout, I shall be using the terms *story* and *narration* in a very specific and restricted sense. I shall use "story" in much the same sense it was used by the Russian formalists, that is, the history, the tale communicated by means of the narration. Thus "narration" will refer to the narrative process, the telling, the ordering of events, narrator interruptions, etc.

[3] Tzvetan Todorov develops the theory of *énoncé* as opposed to *énonciation* in *Littérature et signification* (Paris: Larousse, 1967). In this study I have sometimes used narration as a synonym for *énonciation* and narrative or story as a synonym for *énoncé*.

[4] In all probability these names are also symbolic. Salomon was the wise Hebrew king (wise enough to turn his only daughter over to Christians to be raised

properly?) and Sara was the wife of Abraham and mother of Isaac.

[5] See M. Esther Harding, *Woman's Mysteries* (New York: Putnam, 1971), p. 156. The first edition of this book dates from 1935.

[6] Helen Diner notes the same myth. *Mothers and Amazons* trans. and ed. John Phillip Lundin (New York: Doubleday, 1973), p. 29.

[7] See Valerie Massón de Gómez's study of the symbolism of the flowers, "Las flores."

[8] All quotations are from the Losada edition (Buenos Aires, 1966). English quotations are from the Harper edition (New York, 1890), trans. Rollo Ogden.

[9] Although technically the Holy Spirit is neither male nor female, "he" forms part of the otherwise male trinity, and it would rarely occur to anyone to depict or envision "him"/it as a female although it has on occasion been suggested that the god figure is a female.

[10] See Vicente Cicchitti, "María y su magnificat," in *La mujer símbolo del mundo nuevo* (Buenos Aires: Fernando García Cambeiro, 1976), pp. 11-18. In the same collection, see also Graciela Maturo, "La virgen, anunciadora del tiempo nuevo," pp. 32-50.

[11] Elizabeth Gould Davis develops an interesting theory which suggests that much of the early Church's success was a result of the incorporation of the virgin mother and her subsequent supplantation of the pagan virgin goddesses. See *The First Sex* (New York: Penguin, 1971), pp. 243-51.

[12] Many of the early moon goddesses were viewed as essentially tetramerous: the full moon, the waning crescent, the waxing crescent, and darkness. In this sense, they were the very symbol of temporal continuity and motion. See Helen Diner, *Mothers*.

[13] José Donoso, *El obsceno pájara de la noche* (Barcelona: Seix Barral, 1971), p. 182; *The Obscene Bird of Night*, trans. Hardie St. Martin and Leonard Mades (Boston: Nonpareil, 1979), p. 147.

[14] José Mármol, *Amalia* (México: Porrúa, 1974). First edition was in Buenos Aires, 1855. The emphasis is mine. The English translations are my own.

[15] Obviously, at this point in history it was not acceptable to think that perhaps there can be no Truth apart from language and that perhaps this Absolute Truth cannot exist.

[16] Even though the picaresque hero may not be totally admirable, he nonetheless encompasses many of those masculine virtues such as adventure, spirit, intelligence, etc.

[17] This statement, of course, ignores the ironic treatment of "heroes" which has predominated in much of the literature of the last thirty years.

[18] Throughout this essay I shall persist in using the term *love story* not in spite of, but rather because of, its popular connotations. Regardless of how we embellish it, the love story (at least today) is a tale of the people. I also use the term to avoid any confusion with the notion of romance (as discussed by Northrop Frye and others), which encompasses a much broader spectrum of adventures and themes than does the love story. Thus I shall understand as love story any verbal work (its actual form as a novel, short story, narrative poem, or drama is not relevant to my purposes) whose principal concern and purpose is the dramatization of the development (or frustration) of a strong emotional and eventually carnal tie (love) between two characters.

[19] See Northrop Frye, *Anatomy of Criticism* (Princeton, N.J.: Princeton University Press, 1957). Note, however, that when Frye uses the term *romance* he is not talking about the love story (although it would be included within Frye's notion of romance). Instead, he defines romance as "not the historical mode . . . but the tendency . . . to displace myth in a human direction and yet, in contrast to 'realism,' to conventionalize content in an idealized direction" (pp. 136-37).

[20] Madonna Kolbenschlag, *Kiss Sleeping Beauty Goodbye* (New York: Doubleday, 1979) focuses on the inert quality and waiting posture of the traditional fairy-tale heroine.

[21] Her position by the window is no doubt significant, although open to several interpretations. One might view her as guarding the opening of marital bliss and happy home life or as nearing the window which separates life from death.

[22] Interestingly, she does not reject him, for if she did then we would have no story, and the purpose of the story is to embellish her—her rejection would imply his unworthiness and thus defeat the purpose.

[23] A similar movement takes place in Alejo Carpentier's *Los pasos perdidos*. See Roberto González Echevarría, "The Parting of the Waters," in *The Pilgrim at Home* (Ithaca, N.Y.: Cornell, 1977), pp. 155-212.

[24] This movement from a fraternal to an amorous relationship underlines what might be seen as latent incestuous desire in the text. As Brooks has noted, "Throughout the Romantic tradition, it is perhaps most notably the image of incest (of the fraternal-sororal variety) which hovers as the sign of a passion interdicted be-

cause its fulfillment would be too perfect, a discharge indistinguishable from death. . ." See Peter Brooks, "Freud's Masterplot: Questions of Narrative," *Yale French Studies,* nos. 55-56 (1977): 297.

[25] See Claude Lévi-Strauss *Tristes tropiques* trans. John Russell (New York: Atheneum, 1972), pp. 286-97.

[26] Jacques Derrida, analyzing the "Writing Lesson," suggests, "'I' origine de l'écriture répondait à une nécessité plus 'sociologique' qu' 'intellectuelle.'" See *De la grammatologie,* p. 190.

[27] There can be little doubt that don Juan must be one of the most misogynous of literary characters. Curiously, Lederer implies that don Juan may also be most fearful of women: "because to them [the don Juans] love, the lasting commitment, stands for being swallowed up by woman." See Wolfgang Lederer, *The Fear of Women* (New York: Harcourt Brace Jovanovich, 1968), p. 236.

[28] Perhaps an all too typical example of this attitude can be found in Espronceda, who adored and exalted Teresa until he discovered that she could not live up to the superhuman expectations he had for her. Thus, because she did not meet the unrealistic and totally idealized concept he had created, he scorned and degraded her. "Mas ¡ay! que es la mujer angel caído,/o mujer nada más y lodo inmundo." See José de Espronceda, "Canto a Teresa," in *Presentación y antología de los siglos XVIII y XIX españoles,* ed. Lucía Bonilla and Juan Agudiez, vol. 1 (New York: Las Américas. 1966), p. 251.

[29] Katharine M. Rogers has noted, "The nineteenth-century idealization of self-sacrificing womanhood provided a vehicle for covert misogyny insofar as it assumed the subjugation of women and demanded self-renunciation from them." See *The Troublesome Helpmate,* p. 194.

[30] Ancient myths seem to suggest that virginity was not valued until fairly late in Western history. Elizabeth Gould Davis suggests that it was not valued until the advent of the patriarchal Judeo-Christian civilization (*First Sex,* p. 158).

Raymond L. Williams (essay date 1986)

SOURCE: "The Problem of Unity in Fiction: Narrator and Self in *María,*" in *MLN,* Vol. 101, No. 2, March, 1986, pp. 342-53.

[*In the following essay, Williams surveys earlier criticism of Isaacs's* María *and discusses narrative unity and fragmentation in the novel.*]

The assumptions underlying critical thought on Jorge

Isaacs' classic novel *María* (1867) have been quite traditional. During much of the twentieth century studies were limited to the sources of the book, comparisons or influences of European models or thematic and biographical investigations.[1] A moribund line of thought maintained that its numerous deviations from the principal story line undermined its effectiveness as a coherent novel.[2] A more recent reading by Seymour Menton has meticulously diagrammed relationships that demonstrate the book's unity.[3] The least traditional of these analyses is John S. Brushwood's explicitly Barthesian exposition of codes of character definition.[4] The present study will consider briefly both the assumptions embodied in critical thought on *María* and attempt to propose a new reading through the consideration of the function of the narrator and the self in the novel.

The fundamental assumption underlying the readings by Anderson Imbert and Menton is the desire and necessity for unity. As Hispanists writing in defense of one of Spanish America's most widely read novels, they argue convincingly that this classic writer did indeed effect an organizational plan conceived to evoke tears in a way comparable with those most capacious and renowned literary structures of the West. The former delineates relationships between the Efraín-María idyll and some episodes that might appear extraneous. Menton points out several paired relationships, identifying duality as the basic element in the novel's structure by means of a detailed analysis. These dualities involve "ternurapasión," "amor-muerte," "parejas de novios," "la naturaleza," "costumbrismo-conciencia social," "el tiempo novelístico," "romanticismo-modernismo," and "grupos binarios."[5] This procedure—both Isaacs' apparent conception of unity and Menton's discovery of it— allows the critic to conclude that *María* is the most outstanding of the Spanish and Spanish-American romantic novels. If the critic is willing to accept the necessity for unity as just a critical assumption, however, rather than a self-evident truth, the possibilities for reading *María* become more ample. Brushwood, for example, notes and then sets aside the question of unity or lack thereof in his delineation of five codes. He is more concerned with how these codes affect the reader's experience, particularly in the context of the reader's reaction to idyllic love and the delicacy of human emotions in this novel. His procedure becomes what Barthes calls "writerly"—*jouissance,* nonlinear.

A first step toward the problemization of this novel as a unity is a consideration of the first-person narrator. The distinction which Franz Stanzel has made between a "narrating-self" (a first-person narrator who tells a story in retrospection) and an "experiencing self" (a first-person narrator who tells the story as he experiences it) is a useful point of departure.[6] The first-person narrator in *María* is, technically speaking, of the "narrating-self" type: he tells the story of his loss of María with the advantage of retrospection. Several matters, however, complicate the narrative situation considerably. These include the narrator's use of retro-spection, the presence of a fictional editor, the changing relationship between the narrator and his surroundings, and the fact that the novel is partially autobiographical.

The basic narrative situation is as follows: an adult narrator relates in retrospective fashion the story of his adolescent love affair with María.[7] Despite the retrospective perspective, he does not use this temporal advantage to analyze his past circumstances. Rather, the narrative is a chronological reconstruction of the events and feelings of the moment. Brushwood points out that Isaacs does not write in a diary present that would be contemporary with the main events of the novel.[8] A dedication "A los hermanos de Efraín" suggests that an unidentified editor made the text on the basis of Efraín's memoirs. There are a few deviations from Isaacs' basic method. These variations appear in the form of interruptions in which the narrator reacts to these past events in the emotional framework of the present. For example, near the beginning of the novel the narrator interrupts his description of María's voice with the following response, a reaction to the situation he is describing: "¡Ay! Cuántas veces en mis sueños, un eco de ese mismo acento ha llegado a mi alma, y mis ojos han buscado en vano aquel huerto donde la vi tan bella en aquella mañana de agosto!"[9] Later he makes a similar type of exclamation that is a reaction to the state of affairs during the past which is the constant context of the narration: "Primer amor . . . Noble orgullo de sentirse amado; sacrificio dulce de todo lo que antes nos era caro a favor de la mujer querida; felicidad que, comprada para un día con las lágrimas de toda una existencia, recibimos como un don de Dios; perfume para todas las horas del porvenir, flor guardada en el alma y que no es dado a los desengaños marchitarla . . ." (p. 22). In addition, there is a variation in the narrator's distance from the fictional world he describes: in the majority of the novel he reacts intimately to the natural world to which he belongs; during the return trip he describes a new land with more distance.[10] During his trip up the river the story is technically Efraín's, but it is different from the voice in the other parts of the novel. It has an objective quality and is a description of something new, unlike the sensitive reactions to the land that characterize the earlier narration.

By taking this consideration of the intricacies of the narrative situation a step further, the reader approaches the problematics of the self, from technique to ideological-based structures and a questioning of the assumptions mentioned at the outset. An examination of the self further places the idea of unity in doubt. It should be noted that Isaacs wrote **María** from 1864 to 1866 while living in the mountains, isolated.[11] There is little question that he integrated experiences and anecdotes from his own personal life. For example, as a

child Isaacs was sent to Bogotá to study, just as the character in the novel. Setting aside the difficult and perhaps unimportant issue of the precise level of autobiographical content, we can note the textual evidence of instabilities created by the confluence of autobiography and creative process. The problematics of the self are established in the novel's first line: "Era yo niño cuando me alejaron de la casa paterna para que diera principio a mis estudios en el colegio de xxx, establecido en Bogotá hacía pocos años, y famoso en toda la República por aquel tiempo." First, we note the subject-verb relationship in this initial establishment of the "yo" as the supposed central object of the text. It would have been possible to begin the novel, of course, by inverting the subject and verb, probably a more natural structure: "Yo era niño . . ." Such a beginning would locate the "yo" as the primary and central focus of the narrative. There are inversions similar to the first sentence throughout the book. The third word of the sentence, "niño," presents more problems. Isaacs has confused the biographical and the narrating self: he identifies the narrator as *niño* because he has failed to distinguish clearly between the fourteen-year-

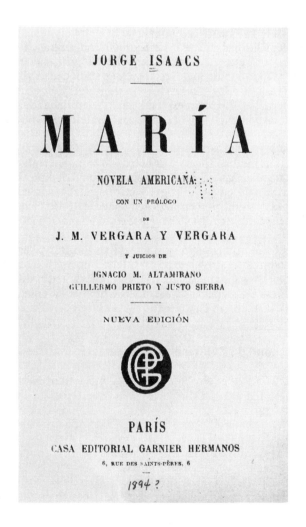

JORGE ISAACS

MARÍA

NOVELA AMERICANA:

CON UN PRÓLOGO

DE

J. M. VERGARA Y VERGARA

Y JUICIOS DE

IGNACIO M. ALTAMIRANO
GUILLERMO PRIETO Y JUSTO SIERRA

NUEVA EDICIÓN

PARÍS

CASA EDITORIAL GARNIER HERMANOS

6, RUE DES SAINTS-PÈRES, 6

1894 ?

old fictional character and the Jorge Isaacs who once studied in Bogotá at the age of eleven. At this point the reader with an acquaintance of the book can observe considerable ambiguity with respect to the self: it neither asserts itself as a well-defined entity who is the protagonist (as would be the case in "Yo era . . .") nor is it capable of identifying itself properly. The self functions in an ambiguous area which the narrator seems unable or unwilling to define. This identity places the situation squarely within the bounds of Todorov's proposition concerning the anonymity of the "I" narrator: "Le narrateur est innomable . . . il se réfugie . . . éternellement . . . dans l'anonymat."[12]

An additional factor that complicates the basic narrative situation is the presence of a fictional editor at the beginning of the book. This invented editor indicates that the book is dedicated "A los hermanos de Efraín." The text in theory contains both the sender and the receiver, narrator and narratee. Brushwood makes two important points related to this analysis of the narrative situation.[13] This first-person narrator certainly does not address himself exclusively to a group of sibling readers, because he makes many references that would be gratuitous if he were thinking only of members of his household. For example, most of the physical descriptions of María and the family would be unnecessary for the siblings. These observations lead us back to the speaker: if the receiver is unclear, the burden for this ambiguity ultimately leads the reader to question the identity of the sender. The term "hermanos" can also include persons like Efraín. Just as the sense of the dedication vacillates between the specific and general meanings, the reader's sense of the narrator has a similar ambiguity: is this narrator a brother or one of those creators with the broad vision of the writer of an epic? The answer to this question will be the former if read literally; on the other hand, those who suffer loss as Efraín did can consider themselves his "spiritual" siblings.

The confluence between personal biography and literary experience reaches a literal level of expression when one observes the changes effected by Isaacs in the four editions of the book. The author focussed his revisions on precisely the issue under consideration here: the presence of the self in the novel. The reader who observes the successive editions can note a tendency to change personal pronouns to impersonal ones (i.e. "mi sueño" to "el sueño").[14] Even more significantly, the revisions Isaacs makes include the omission of the personal pronoun "yo" from his text. Just as the author consciously or unconsciously chooses to mask his presence in the "yo era" / "era yo" inversion, and confuses himself with his narrator alter-ego with the misuse of the term "niño," his relationship to the narrating-self is blatantly unstable and even progressively moreso in the editions he

later revised. Considered within the context of the basic narrative situation, any unity of the self is questionable.

With respect to the relationship between the author and the narrating self and to the relationship between this self and the fictional world, one encounters more obstacles to the acceptance of the unified and coherent text proposed in the standard readings. The structure which establish this assumed unity operate from the assumption of an Efraín who is a clearly defined self and juxtapose this self with other characters in the fictional world. Leo Bersani has proposed that psychological complexity in fiction is often tolerated as long as it does not threaten an ideology of the self as a fundamentally intelligible structure unaffected by a history of fragmented, discontinuous desires.[15] Bersani has explained as follows:

> The exertion toward significant form in realistic fiction serves the cause of significant, coherently structured characters. The revealing incident makes personality intelligible; real beginnings and definitive endings provide a temporal frame in which individuals don't merely exist, but move purposefully from one stage of being to another . . . The richly detailed textures of characterization in realistic fiction seldom subvert the coherent wholeness of personality—or if they do, criticism has to deal with what we call "interesting" esthetic failures.[16]

The reading proposed in the present study reveals structured desires and desiring impulses sublimated into emotional "faculties" or passions and thereby providing the basis for the notion of a distinct and coherently unified personality. Rather than considering *María* an esthetic failure because of the tendencies which disrupt unity, the novel and its standard readings can be seen as part of a Western cultural habit of referring all experiences to centers or beginnings.[17]

The complex network of relationships between Efraín, his parents, and María set up the tension between the fulfillment and the sublimation of desire in this novel. The Oedipal structure is played out in both the most basic model involving the father, the son and mother triangle, in addition to certain variations involving substitutions. The horror of mother-son separation is announced in the first lines of the novel and repeated constantly in the first chapter. The first line deals specifically with the protagonist's separation from home: "Era yo niño cuando *me alejaron de la casa paterna* para que diera principio a mis estudios en el colegio de xxx, establecido en Bogotá hacía pocos años, y famoso en toda la República por aquel tiempo" (my emphasis, p. 11). The remainder of the chapter deals with the emotional trauma involved with this separation. For example, the night before his departure to Bogotá he wept in suffering: "Me dormí llorando y experimenté como un vago presentimiento de muchos pesares que debía sufrir después" (p. 11). The characterization of María in the initial chapters also emphasizes separation—the loss of her family. More specifically, in the sixth chapter the narrator explains the family history that resulted in María's loss of her parents in the Antilles and being sent to Colombia to live with her uncle's family. Separation from the mother will remain an underlying threat and consequently function as part of the Oedipal structure throughout the novel.

The playing out of the Oedipal triangle portrays the following situation: a son who spends the entire novel in an ambiguous state between boyhood and manhood (as suggested already in the analysis of the first line); a father who plays an overbearing role as dominator; a mother who subtly encourages incest; and, finally, a mother-like María who functions as Efraín's substitute for the desired mother. Efraín's characterization as a child instead of the adult-figure that he wishes to portray is a constant part of the book's dynamics. The following scene near the beginning of the story is revealing:

> Después de que mi madre me abrazó, Emma me abrazó, Emma me tendió la mano, y María, abandonándome por un instante la suya, sonrió como en la infancia me sonreía: esa sonrisa hoyuelada era la de la niña de mis amores infantiles sorprendida en el rostro de una virgen de Rafael. (p. 15)

First, we note that this mother embraces him in reaffirmation of the mother-child as opposed to a mother-adult relationship. Then the narrator-protagonist associates María's smile to "infantile loves." This image refers ostensibly to María; the substitution of "infantile love" for love of one's mother, however, is not an illogical or surprising substitution. In addition to this rather overt Oedipal revelation, the total context of this paragraph communicates an idealization of childhood; the ideal love is represented by a return to childhood and the security of the mother-child relationship.

Numerous incidents in subsequent chapters and remarks by the narrator underscore his characterization as a child. At times he describes childhood as a type of ideal. For example, early in the novel he makes the following remark:

> Una tarde, ya a puesta del sol, regresábamos de las labranzas a la fábrica, mi padre, Higinio (mayordomo) y yo. Ellos hablaban de trabajos hechos y por hacer; a mí me ocupaban cosas menos serias: pensaba en los días de mi infancia. El olor peculiar de los bosques derribados y el de las piñuelas en sazón; la geguería de los loros en los guadales y guayabales vecinos . . . (p. 18).

Later in the paragraph Efraín associates this childhood ideal with the presence of María. The protagonist evokes a similar idealized vision of childhood when he describes a scene in the country:

> Viajero años después por las montañas del país de José, he visto ya a puestas del sol llegar labradores alegres a la cabaña donde se me daba hospitalidad; luego que alababan a Dios ante el venerable jefe de la familia, esperaban en torno al hogar la cena que la anciana y cariñosa madre repartía: un plato bastaba a cada pareja de esposos, y los pequeñuelos hacían pinos apoyados en las rodillas de sus padres. Y he desviado mis miradas de estas escenas patriarcales, que me recordaban los últimos días felices de mi juventud . . . (p. 70).

Efraín's institutionally acceptable situations for overcoming childhood and assuming an adult role are his displays of masculinity in the wilderness hunting animals. His prizes of potentially ferocious prey seem impressive proof, with these societal ideals, of his genuine manliness. A brief analysis of these masculine ventures, however, reveals a character who is not convincingly effective in this traditional masculine role. Once in the wilderness, for example, Efraín does not seem to measure up to the hearty Emigdio. When the protagonist picks some flowers, for example, Emigdio warns him: "¿quieres que todo huela a rosas? El hombre debe oler a chivo" (p. 62). Once involved with the actual hunt, his prize is not the awesome bear that Efraín's father had demanded, but an effeminate cat. It is described in the dimunitive (*gatico*) and is wounded and weakened before Efraín finally delivers the death blow. Even this act does not involve the aggressive dominance that Efraín desires and believes he needs in order to perform his traditional role. Rather, he reacts spontaneously to the tiger's attack, happening to be the one with a rifle: "Entonces la fiera nos dio frente. Sólo mi escopeta estaba disponible; disparé: el tigre sentó sobre la cola, tambaleóse y cayó" (p. 74).

On the return trip from the hunt, his instrument of supposed aggression, his rifle, is appropriated by the person who substitutes in the true masculine role, José. José carries it on his shoulders: "Acomodada en las mochilas la piel, cabeza y patas del tigre, nos pusimos en camino para la posesión de José, el cual, tomando mi escopeta, la colocó en un mismo hombro con la suya, precediéndonos en la marcha y llamando a los perros" (p. 76). Having completed the adventure, the men unpack and restore order at home. Efraín, meanwhile, finds comfort in the return to the mother, explicitly evoked in nature as follows: " . . . la naturaleza es la más amorosa de las *madres* cuando el dolor se ha posesionado de nuestra alma; y si la felicidad nos acaricia, ella nos sonríe" (my emphasis, p. 77). The female-mother functions as a type of surrogate for the active male.

The second important character in the Oedipal triangle, the father, is an overwhelmingly dominant competitor for the child-like Efraín. Indeed, this father would represent formidable competition for even the most masculine and mature of Oedipally-inclined sons. One critic has observed that Efraín consistently speaks to his father in "lenguaje reverencial."[18] This language maintains a clearly defined distance between Efraín as child and the father as adult. The father is present as a constant barrier to Efraín's potential advances toward the mother/María. The father's physical presence precludes any communication with the women. An example of one of the numerous times the father's even non-verbal presence functions as an impediment takes places relatively early in the novel when Efraín happens to enter María's room:

> Olvidado de toda precaución, entré a la alcoba donde estaba María, y dominando el frenesí que me hubiera hecho estrecharla contra mi corazón para volverla a la vida, me acerqué desconcertado a su lecho. A los pies de éstos se hallaba sentado mi *padre;* fijó en mí una de sus miradas intensas . . . (my emphasis, p. 37).

His presence is a threat that remains constant throughout the novel. The father communicates the threat of María's death and remains associated with this possibility: "Mi padre me hacía las últimas indicaciones sobre los nuevos síntomas de la enfermedad . . ." (p. 39). The father's absence, in contrast, allows for the possibility of incestuous contact: scenes in which the father leaves the premises are those in which Efraín initiates dialogue with María. The father unequivocally determines the direction and limits of Efraín's incestuous desires: the father decides the necessary waiting period before any marriage can take place; the father announces the inauspicious notice with respect to María's health; the father plays the role of "dictator"—he who dictates to his son who writes in a passive manner. Finally, the father ultimately sends the son to England, definitely ending the threat of the son's consummation of his desire.

An understanding of Efraín's performance with respect to his mother depends upon the already-established association between the mother and María. This relationship is created from the first chapter, which ends with the image of María standing among the flowers adorning the mother's bedroom: "Dábamos ya la vuelta a una de las colinas de la vereda, en las que solían divisarse desde la casa viajeros deseados; volví la vista hacia ella buscando uno de tantos seres queridos; María estaba bajo las enredaderas que adornaban las ventanas del aposento de mi madre" (p. 12). In opposition to the father's rigid control over the triangle, the mother encourages Efraín's repressed and feeble initiatives. After the father has fixed stern regulations to control Efraín's relationship with María, the mother communicates her disapproval to the son. We note, importantly enough, within the context of a Freudian reading of this scene, that she breaks the symbolic space of the son's bedroom to make this statement: "Una mañana entró mi madre en mi cuarto, y sentándose a la cabacera de la cama, de la cual no había salido yo aún, me dijo:—Esto no puede ser; no debes seguir viviendo así; yo no me conformo" (p. 48). The isolation from María has been too extreme, according to the mother. That is, it is too excessive to permit the symbolic incest. At the end of the novel Efraín's relationship with his mother, despite his age and experience, is still of mother-child.

The relationship with María, of course, is considerably more elaborated in the text. The protagonist evokes images of María at the outset which associate her with the joy of childhood, as has been discussed briefly. She is also characterized as a mother-figure, as has been demonstrated by the example cited at the end of the first chapter. She will appear once again as the ideal mother in the third chapter: "María tomó en los brazos al niño que dormía en su regazo, y mis hermanas la siguieron a los aposentos: ellas la amaban mucho y se disputaban su dulce afecto" (pp. 14-15). As several critical studies have pointed out, the characterization of María is closely allied with nature and the evocation of sensorial images. Consequently, Efraín's emotional response to his physical surroundings is part of his sensitivity to the love relationship.

Two key chapters, twenty and thirty, are revealing with respect to their relationship. In chapter ten the intimacy of the relationship is solidified. Until then it had been only a potentially intimate and incestuous union. First, the father leaves the space occupied by the pair, creating the possibility of the son's expressing his desires. In terms of action, the chapter stands out as the one in which the duo articulate love vows for the first time. On a more subliminal level of exchange it is important to note that María initiates a type of physical contact and observes Efraín with his rifle, a type of phallic symbol. In this scene she serves him coffee, insists that he not load his rifle at that moment, and touches his cup. He assures her that he will respond to her contact with the cup by getting rid of the threatening rifle (p. 65). With all danger of the phallic object removed, they exchange vows of love in this chapter.

Chapter thirty features the full Oedipal traingle, with father, son, and María functioning as the mother-substitute. María cuts the father's hair, while he controls the entire situation. Mejía Duque reads the scene symbolically, but as a ritual of "autocastigo simbólico."[19] The scene begins with the classic dominant-father/passive-son situation: "En la mañana siguiente mi padre dictaba y yo escribía, mientras él se afeitaba, operación que nunca interrumpía los trabajos empezados, no obstante el esmero que en ello gastaba siempre" (p. 118). The father extends the domination to María with the demand that she cut his hair while he continues dictating to the passive and absolutely subservient son. His utter domination of María, parallel with the humiliation of the son, occurs at the end of the scene. His comments to the diligent Efraín are patronizing: "Cuidado, niño, con equivocarse" (p. 120). When María stoops to obediently clean up the father's hair trimmings, a rose falls from her hair. The father picks up the rose (symbolically dominating once again over Efraín) and places it in her hair, substituting for the enamored youth. Then the narrator notes that she "se mostraba deseosa de retirarse por *temor* de lo que él pudiera *añadir* (my emphasis, p. 120). What she might "añadir" is left ambiguous, but María's intensifying anxiety over this exchange makes it, symbolically, a direct sexual affront. The father not only diverts or appropriates any incestuous contact with the two mother figures, but also blatantly flaunts his sexual prowess before the helpless son.

María is an impressively well conceived and written novel for its period in Latin America. Discoveries of a certain level of unity and dualities attest to Issacs' mastery of the traditional craft of fiction. The function of the narrator and the self, however, reveal deeper structures that place into question the proposition of absolute unity. The narrator's striving for anonymity and ambiguity are one sign of his fragmentation. An analysis of his characterization reveals a protagonist who is far from the unified personality which the traditional unified text would require. The superficial psychic coherence of the type Efraín maintains involves a crippling of desire. He operates as the eternal *niño*, even within the rigid and traditional nineteenth-century societal structures within which he plays out his role. As such he remains incomplete—the potential writer who never dictates, the lover who never fulfills his desires.

Notes

1 See Donald F. Brown, "Chateaubriand and the Story of Feliciana in Jorge Isaacs' *María*," *Modern Language Notes* 62 (1947): 326-329; María J. Embeita, "El tema del amor imposible en *María* de Jorge Isaacs," *Revista Iberoamericana* 32, No. 61 (1966): 109-112; Alfonso Lopez Michelsen, "Ensayo sobre la influencia semítica en *María*," *Revista de las Indias* 20, No. 6 (1944): 5-10; Donald McGrady, "Las fuentes de *María* de Isaacs," *Hispano*, No. 24 (1966), pp. 43-54; Enrique Naranjo M, "Aldrededor de *María*," *Revista Iberoamericana* 5, No. 9 (1942): 103-108; Otto Olivera, "*María*, tema predilecto de Isaacs," *Symposium* 14 (1960): 7-25; Oscar Gerardo Ramos, "Mujer, paisaje y ambiente en la novela *María*," *Universidad de Antioquia*, No. 171 (1968), pp. 169-193; Victor Sánchez Montenegro, "Jorge Isaacs y 'El Mosaico'," *Bolívar*, No. 19 (Bogotá, 1953), pp. 669-800; Jacob Warshaw, "Jorge Isaacs' Library: New Light on Two *María* Problems," *The Romanic Review* 32 (1941): 389-398. For more recent readings of the novel see Sharon Magnarelli, "*María* and History," *Hispanic Review*, 49 (1981), pp. 209-217 and Jonathan Tittler, "Paisajes Figurales en Tres Novelas Colombianas," *El Café Literario*, 38 (1984), pp. 26-31.

2 See Enrique Anderson-Imbert, "Prólogo," *María* (Mexico: Fondo de Cultura Económica, 1951).

3 See Seymour Menton, "La estructura dualística de *María*," *Thesaurus* 25 (1970): 1-27. Reprinted in *La novela colombiana: planetas y satélites* (Bogotá: Plaza y Janés, 1977): 15-49.

4 John S. Brushwood's analysis is an experiment in the application of the type of study employed by Roland Barthes in *S / Z, An Essay* (New York: Hill and Wang, 1974). Brushwood establishes five codes in *María*: (1) María-Milieu, (2) Separation, (3) Omen, (4) Test, (5) Intensification. See "Codes of Character Definition: Jorge Isaacs's *María*," in *Genteel Barbarism: New Readings of Nineteenth-Century Spanish-American Novels* (Lincoln and Londón: University of Nebraska Press, 1981), pp. 82-106.

5 Menton, *op. cit.,* pp. 15-49.

6 Franz K. Stanzel, *Typische Formen des Romans* (Gottingen: Van der Koeken Ruprechl, 1964).

7 Brushwood characterizes the basic narrative situation as follows: "In general, the narration maintains the integrity of a first-person narrator who characterizes himself in terms of sensitivity to the loss he suffers. The narrative voice speaks retrospectively—that is, from a point in time that is later than the events of the story. What Efraín says about a given situation, therefore, is influenced by subsequent events. In such cases, the effect is to enhance Efrain's sensitivity. There are moments in the narration when the voice of Efraín might better give way to some other narrative voice— the story of Nay, for example." See *Genteel Barbarism*, p. 104. Brushwood makes an important and valid generalization about the narrative situation with this statement. The present study, however, questions the use of the phrase "integrity of the first-person narrator."

8 Brushwood, *op. cit.,* p. 89.

9 Jorge Isaacs, *María* (Buenos Aires: Losada, 1969), p. 17. Subsequent quotations are from this edition and are included in the text.

10 Brushwood, *op. cit.,* pp. 102-103.

11 See Jaime Mejía Duque, *Isaacs y María: el hambre y su novela* (Bogotá: La Carreta, 1979), p. 8.

12 Tzvetan Todorov, *Ou'est-ce que le structuralisme*

(Paris: Seuil, 1968), p. 21.

[13] Brushwood, *op. cit.,* p. 85.

[14] See Donald McGrady's discussion of the changes of personal pronouns in *Jorge Isaacs* (Boston: Twayne Publishers, Inc., 1972), pp. 59-60.

[15] Leo Bersani, *A Future for Astyanax* (Boston and Toronto: Little, Brown, and Co., 1969), pp. 55-56.

[16] Bersani, *op. cit.,* p. 55.

[17] Bersani cites the work of Jacques Derrida in exposing this cultural assumption of a center. Bersani states: "*Les Chants de Maldoror* is one of literature's most daring enterprises of decentralization. It is a major document among modern efforts to break away from what Jacques Derrida has been brilliantly anatomizing as the Western cultural habit of referring all experience to centers or beginnings, or origins of truth and being." *A Future for Astyanax,* p. 196. See also Jacques Derrida, *De la grammatologie* (Paris: Minuit, 1967).

[18] Jaime Mejía Duque offers the following explanation of the language Efraín directs to his father: "En casa de Efraín los actos son solemnes y esta solemnidad aparece oficiada por el padre, a quien Efraín se refiere a menudo en lenguaje reverencial, adecuado a ese ambiente de culto patriarcado: 'La noble fisonomía de mi padre mostraba . . . (Cap. XVI)'" (p. 107).

[19] Mejía Duque, *op. cit.,* p. 124.

Sylvia Molloy (essay date 1991)

SOURCE: "Childhood and Exile: The Cuban Paradise of the Countess of Merlin," in *At Face Value: Autobiographical Writing in Spanish America,* Cambridge University Press, 1991, pp. 79-96.

[*In the following excerpt, Molloy shows how Isaacs romanticizes the family in* María.]

Successive generations of readers have hailed Jorge Isaacs' novel as one of the highlights—perhaps the most brilliant—of nineteenth-century Spanish American fiction. Critics unanimously agree: *María,* they believe, arrived in a most timely way to legitimate a specific literary discourse, that of Romanticism. Most of those critics, however, have stopped short at this conclusion, unwilling to explore the reason for *María's* phenomenal success or to discover, precisely, what the novel gave legitimacy to. Thus the enormous impact of the novel has been reduced to the fact that it was a well-told story of ill-fated love, more or less in the tradition of Benjamin Constant, made all the more poignant of course by the foresee-

able death of the heroine. As a result of this reduction, the general criterion to judge *María* has been invariably lachrymose: tears are shed and those tears in some way ratify the novel's excellence. No one has stopped to consider other possible implications of this mournful stance, nor to inquire further into the reasons for *María's* favorable reception. For *María* is indeed a legitimating text—not merely of the Romantic sentimental novel, Spanish American style, but of an ideological posture that exceeds generic boundaries and affords a new look at the past. If tears flow in *María*—and they do: the author himself invites his readers to weep—they flow for more than a lost love. From the beginning, multiple signs point to a larger loss, one for which the death of the loved one (the María of the title) is but a token: it is the loss of a childhood paradise and, more concretely, the loss of the family home. Isaacs' novel, in a masterly gesture, incorporates the *petite histoire* of the immediate past—of his own immediate past, as we know, although it is not my purpose here to read *María* as an autobiography—and succeeds in giving it the stature of myth.[34]

The *petite histoire* that Isaacs recreates through the evocation of his first-person narrator is . . . embellished by longing and desire. The unsavory aspects of the family romance—notably the harshness of a thrifty father who cannot tolerate weakness and loss—are glossed over, never taken at face value; the ambiguous crisscrossings of desire and emotion within the family circle, striking even in those pre-Freudian times, are defused (or perhaps rendered blatant) by the sheer innocence with which they are evoked.[35] The past was good, the text tells us again and again, working against the evidence that it clearly was not, patiently building a lyric imposture of incredibly seductive power. And that past reconstructed so diligently coincides . . . with the most immediate, individual, past, the one left behind days, hours before. There is no future in *María* or rather its future is its past: from the very beginning the text is a protracted farewell. . . .

Isaacs has an eye for evocative trivia and knows how to anchor nostalgia with detailed, if selective, precision. He is a master of what Richard Coe calls *curiosa nostalgica:* "the minutiae of daily life, familiar to anyone of that generation but now unknown and unrecorded, are details of a manner of existence which was fundamentally acceptable and therefore *right;* and so their passing can inspire nothing but regret."[36] Thus the eminently satisfying recreation of objects, meals, everyday occupations and petty rituals gives structure to this idyllic past and, at the same time, makes it ageless. Protected from chronology, the past in *María* is akin to that cyclical time Bakhtin observes in ancient literatures: "an idealized, agricultural everyday life, one interwoven with the times of nature and myth."[37]

Isaacs' urge to reconstruct the childhood paradise does not stem . . . from geographic exile. Yet the theme of exile pervades this text: on an anecdotal level, it is significantly connected to the figure of the father and, on a metaphoric level, it is to be traced in the many forms of loss and banishment alluded to in the novel. One of the very real losses artfully concealed by textual legerdemain is a decisive *material* loss: the father suffers a financial setback the results of which (although only hinted at in the text) definitely jeopardize the family's security, its social standing and signal the replacement of one form of production by another. It is this reversal that shatters, as much as the tragically thwarted love story and perhaps even more, the family's harmony, threatening to banish its members from the patriarchal paradise.

I mention Isaacs' novel because I believe *María* has considerable bearing on Spanish American attitudes towards the past. Vindicating the *family history* in its most minute, though far from insignificant, detail, *María* provides a concrete, Spanish American mold for the timeless *topos* of paradise lost. It marks the inauguration of the patriarchal archive and makes the writer its guardian and record-keeper, establishes him, as it were, as an official *memorator*. Let it be remembered that *María* was published in 1867, a time of political and cultural reorganization throughout most Spanish American countries that led to a conversion from old to new ways of production. If not a period of political turmoil, it is—under the patina of order and progress—a period of deep, often disquieting, social and economic transformations, the ideological consequences of which will be decisive in the shaping of Spanish America. But it is also, after times of strife and anarchy, a period of relative calm, conducive to an ideological reassessment of the most recent past. *María,* with its prettified recreation of the family romance, comes as a consolation and a relief. As if endowed with talismanic power, it reassuringly provides the means to look at that past and to relish what it has to offer— which is, after all, what has been stored in it from the very beginning. Writing one's childhood can be a form of investment, a capitalistic gesture; husbanding the products of the past, as embellished by memory, can result in an act of power, an attribution of privilege. Indeed, the family tale is not unlike a personal fortune, to be shared with peers and preserved from outsiders. Not surprisingly, it will also often lead to a dreamy exercise in collective narcissism, a gazing into an officiously selective mirror that only flatters the onlooker and his look-alikes.

Notes

[34] For a lengthier discussion of *María* along these lines, see my "Paraíso perdido y economía terrenal en *María*," *Sin Nombre*, 14, 3 (1984), pp. 36-55. Also Doris Sommer's shrewd reading, "El mal de *María*: (Con)fusión en un romance nacional," *MLN,* 104, 2 (1989), pp. 439-474.

[35] The muted sexuality of the protagonist's contact with his mother does not escape Alfonso Reyes in his "Algunas notas sobre la *María* de Jorge Isaacs," *Obras completas,* VIII (Mexico: Fondo de Cultura Económica, 1958), pp. 271-273.

[36] Richard Coe, *When the Grass Was Taller: Autobiography and the Experience of Childhood* (New Haven: Yale University Press, 1984), p. 218.

[37] Mikhail Bakhtin, "Forms of Time and of the Chronotope in the Novel," *The Dialogic Imagination* (Austin: University of Texas Press, 1981), pp. 127-128.

John Rosenberg (essay date 1994)

SOURCE: "From Sentimentalism to Romanticism: Rereading *María*," in *The Latin American Literary Review,* Vol. XXII, No. 43, January-June, 1994, pp. 5-18.

[In the following essay, Rosenberg discusses the narrative structure of Isaacs's María.*]*

Jorge Isaacs's *María* is frequently found in the same category as Rostand's *Cyrano de Bergerac:* it is a novel to be read by the young and naive not yet disillusioned by the skepticism of experience. The fainting spells and tears in the tale of tragic and innocent love move the young reader after the model of Paolo and Francesca, all the while irritating cynics by evoking a past that in their maturity they are forced to admit never existed. As Sylvia Molloy notes, the traditional reading of Isaacs's text is that of "una novela lacrimógena en la cual se pretende reviviry compartir con el lector, la pérdida de un primer amor" (36). Nonhispanists have long maligned Hispanic Romanticism as a perversion of authentic romantic sentiment. *María* occupies the difficult position of being a prototype of the Latin American romantic novel and containing at the same time the most exaggerated sentimentality of all the "serious" literature in the Hispanic world. It is a text whose traditional or "romantic" readings have helped vilify Hispanic Romanticism as a whole. Ironically modern skeptical approaches, such as the one offered here, not only attempt to rescue the story from its carefully woven veil of tears but also offer a complex view of a movement filled with self-contradiction, irony, and dialogical tension.

Critical readers have thoroughly studied the novel's structure, notably in careful articles by Ernesto Porras Collantes, John Barta and Seymour Menton. Additionally, other provocative studies of the last twenty years investigate parallelism and opposition, the function of *costumbrismo,* the role of the Sinar episode and similarly related topics. Of special interest are the recent pieces by Jonathan Tittler, Sylvia Molloy and Valérie Massón de Gómez that provide exceptional symbolic readings of the novel's setting, and Raymond Williams's important essay on the novel's narrative structure and its relationship to identity. Studies of the novel's narrative design have been built on the premise that the reader must identify Efraín, the narrator of the story, with Efraín, the protagonist of the related history. In this sense, the narrator's words express an uncritical nostalgia for a past filled with error and pain, but a past which nevertheless can be recuperated within the pages of a book. This romantic or sentimental reading is the one that the narrator elicits consistently throughout his story. However, the fact that Efraín is engulfed by his own text (the character lives in the shadow of the narrator) emphasizes the unreliability inherent to all first-person narratives and places the truth of his tale in doubt. The structure explodes the naive myth expressed in Rousseau's *Confessions* of the possibility of discovering the "likeness" of Efraín "in all the truth of nature." Efraín's relationship with his first-person narrative is made even more complex by an external, editorial presence that comments, filters, and controls Efraín-narrator's voice from the "prologue" or introduction. The note, "A los hermanos de Efraín" removes the reader one step further from the world Efraín-narrator attempts to recover and makes the novel's voice even more unstable than it might have first appeared.

Many readers continue to assume that there is only one plausible reading of the text—a "romantic" reading. However, the editorial structure of the book and the implication of the first-person narrative suggest the possibility of a second reading that adds considerably to the story's complexity. The two narrators involved in the book invite the reader to interpret their words either romantically or "objectively." Efraín leads us toward an experience of controlled passion and tears. The editor appears to undermine much of Efraín's story and forces us to look unsympathetically at the main body of the text. By encasing the first person narrative within the framework of a controlling editor, the author creates what is in essence a novel within a novel. The implicit authors of the two "works" are at variance with one another and are rivals in their desire for the supremacy of their point of view. Similar to Pascual Duarte's inseparable and at times antagonistic relationship with his transcriber, the dynamic contact between Efraín and the editor provide the novel with energy that is lost if one limits interpretations of the book to simple romantic sentimentalism. Some may object that since the prefatory note contains only a few lines, it cannot be compared to more developed editorial structures like those of *Pascual Duarte*. However, we must acknowledge that the presence of any competing voice outside the primary text, regardless of how small or apparently unintrusive, seriously compromises the reliability of the central piece. It is on the basis of this

assumption regarding the complex relationship between "inner" and "outer" texts that this commentary proceeds.

From the beginning Efraín's text invites us to read tearfully. The romantic view of the book emphasizes sentiment, sobs, spells of fainting, and pallid countenances. Apparently influenced by works like *Atala,* the narrator draws his reader to dismiss the barrier between the reality of our world and the fiction of the storyteller and to weep in uncritical sympathy with the thwarted lovers. His goal is "hacer llorar al mundo" [make the world cry]. The dominant position of emotion, symbolized repetitively by tears, is expressed obsessively by Efraín in the latter parts of his story. Speaking of his tears he writes:

> Si las derramo aún al recordar los días que precedieron a mi viaje, pudieran servir para mojar esta pluma al historiarlos; si fuera posible a mi mente tan sólo una vez, por un instante siquiera, sorprender a mi corazón todo lo doloroso de su secreto para revelarlo, las líneas que voy a trazar serían bellas para los que mucho han llorado, pero acaso funestas para mí. No nos es dable deleitarnos por siempre con un pesar amado: como las de dolor, las horas de placer se van. Si alguna vez nos fuese concedido detenerlas, María hubiera logrado hacer más lentas las que antecedieron a nuestra despedida. Pero ¡ay! ¡todas, sordas a sus sollozos, ciegas ante sus lágrimas, volaron, y volaban prometiendo volver! (311)

> [If I continue to shed tears upon recalling the days leading up to my trip, perhaps those tears could serve to moisten the pen as I attempt to record that time; if it were possible for my mind even once, for but an instant, to reveal to my heart all of its painful secrets, the lines that I am going to write would be beautiful for those who have wept, though they would be distressing for me. We are not permitted to savor a beloved sadness forever: like the times of pleasure, the hours of pain also depart. If we were only allowed to hold them back, María would have been able to draw out those moments that preceded our farewell. But, oh, all the hours, deaf to her sobs, blind to her tears, flew, and continued to fly away promising to return.]

Efraín charges his narrative with emotional descriptions of solitary moments when "lloré largo tiempo rodeado de oscuridad"(313,224) [I cried at length enveloped in darkness], or "necesitaba llorar a solas. . . . ¡Ah! si ella hubiese podido saber cuántas brotaban de mi corazón en aquel instante" [I needed to cry alone. . . . Oh, if she could have known how many tears flowed from my heart at that moment.] Just as he and María were moved by the tragic story of Atala and Chactas, following the model of Dante's Paolo and Francesca, Efraín invites the reader to weep with him as he tells his story. Unlike Dante who condemned his characters for their inability to separate the world of literature from the world of reality, Efraín attempts to lull his readers into a passive, emotive interpretation of his history.

More difficult to define is the intent behind the insistence on sentimentalism. Perhaps this emotional approach develops a sympathetic relationship between the reader and narrator that shields the latter from a "violent" or critical interpretation of his actions. We are blinded by our tears to the extent that it becomes impossible to determine the "truth" of Efraín's nostalgic recreation of the past. The metaphor of tears expands to encompass more than emotion, since tears represent blindness, a restriction of vision that prevents Efraín from perceiving the reality of his own situation. Now that the moment of tragedy has passed and the painful despair been attenuated, Efraín, with clear eyes, attempts to understand things as they really were. He recognizes his weakness and moves to conceal them behind a veil of tears. His image of teary blindness finds expression at a particularly critical moment of the novel. While residing in London, Efraín receives a letter from María, whom he had left behind in Colombia. "Antes de desdoblarla [la carta], busqué en ella aquel perfume demasiado conocido para mí de la mano que la había escrito: aun lo conservaba; en sus pliegues iba un pedacito de cáliz de azucena. *Mis ojos nublados quisieron inútilmente leer las primer as líneas*" (313; emphasis mine). [Before opening the letter, I tried to sense the all too familiar perfume of the hand that had written it: it was still there; the fold of the letter held a small piece of calyx of a lily. *My teary eyes attempted in vain to read the first lines.*] Efraín's problems as a reader of María's text also point to a fundamental characteristic as the writer of his own text. Namely, he appears to rely on a nonintellectual sense, so to speak (smell—the perfume), in order to interpret the letter, and by extension, his world. The emotion preventing him from reading María's letter also inhibits the reader from reacting objectively to the details of the history.

The act of converting life into history also has a subversive and self-defensive purpose. History, even when told in an exemplary objective fashion (and in *María* it is not), can be reduced to a series of events related chronologically. We assume that since event B followed A that it was also a product of it (Nisbet 354). The metaphor of genealogy seems to be essential to all traditional literature and is manipulated well by Efraín in his self-defense. The notion of causality, that event A caused B and B caused C is important to Efraín's case. By setting himself within a historical framework that is dominated clearly by his father, the narrator represents his situation as a pawn caught in the unavoidable and irrepressible tide of events, thereby diluting his own responsibility for the resultant tragedy.

A careful reading of the novel reveals that Efraín has a number of things in his past to justify or obfuscate.

He shows himself to be submissive to his father's will. He gathers flowers for María but deliberately wounds her by refusing to give them to her upon finding that she had not placed the usual bouquet in his room (74). Although he dislikes his father's plans, he submits to his every capricious demand. Prior to Carlos's visit in search of María's hand in marriage, Efraín and his mother have the following exchange:

> —Tu padre insiste en que se dé cuenta a María de la pretensión de Carlos. ¿Crees tú también que debe hacerse así?
>
> —Creo que debe hacerse lo que mi padre disponga.
>
> —Se me figura que opinas de esa manera por obedecerle, no porque deje de impresionarte el que se tome tal resolución. (147-48)
>
> [—Your father insists that María be told of Carlos's intentions. Do you agree with his methods?
>
> —I think that whatever my father arranges should be done.
>
> —It seems to me you agree in order to obey him, not because you are not deeply affected by his plan of action.]

The mother's comments puzzle us. She appears to say that Efraín remains unconvinced about the plan to have María marry Carlos. What is it that she implicitly suggests? Disobedience? Her statements place Efraín in a double bind, caught between filiation and a conflicting triangular desire formed by his parents and himself. Later, after failing in his feeble attempt to dissuade his father from sending him abroad, Efraín responds with servility. "Haré cuanto esté a mi alcance, le contesté completamente desesperanzado ya,—haré cuanto pueda para corresponder a lo que usted espera de mí" (226). [I will do whatever is in my power, I answered him now completely without hope,—I will do all I can to meet your expectations of me.] His integrity and individuality—even his "author-ity"—are threatened by his submission to this "law of the father." Though he pictures himself as an exploited victim, we must recognize his demonstrated abulia and lack of determination.

Efraín turns life into history by his act of writing. Inevitably he is also responsible for the metamorphosis of history to fiction. Because of the essential temporal distance between the moment of acting and writing, personal intent and the fallibility of the written word, all writing becomes fiction to some extent. This process is evident in *María* in at least two ways. First, the narrator employs many lengthy dialogues to enliven his narrative. Obviously Efraín reconstructs conversations that his memory would not be able to reproduce. In other words, the lengthy dialogues are more products of the imagination than they are of any particular intratextual "reality." He consistently reports discussions in which he himself did not participate nor was he in a position to overhear. The structure of autobiographical fiction endows its narrator with a degree of omniscience not available to a living person.

Second, Efraín exercises control over his text (something he was unable to do over his own life) by imposing order upon the past that he transforms into writing. The process of selecting appropriate events for the story is essential to all fiction, but is especially significant in first-person narrative. An autobiography, far from being a reliable reproduction of the past, requires selection and ordering of events that are linked for aesthetic or rhetorical purposes. This processes of filtration and sequencing convert what has the appearance of history into fiction. By establishing order upon his own text, the narrator becomes his own god, at least symbolically. This assumption of divine power is reinforced by his slips into omniscience.

At the same time that Efraín claims for himself divine powers over his text, he converts his beloved into a creature who is even more explicitly divine. He transforms his story into an instrument of beatification for them both. Efraín associates María by name, physical description and character with the Virgin Mary. The reader frequently finds her playing the role of the Madonna; her maternal instincts appear to be as strong and inviolate as her chastity. The servant Tránsito christens her "la Virgen de la Silla" because "[ella] advirtió la notable semejanza entre el rostro de su futura madrina y el de una bella Madonna del oratorio de mi madre" (178) [she noted the remarkable similarity between the expression of her future mistress and that of a beautiful madonna in my mother's prayer chapel]. Reminiscent of the profanation of the sacred in courtly love poetry, *La Celestina,* and other texts, Efraín exalts his lady by describing her with words charged with religious significance.

> ¡Primer amor! . . . noble orgullo de sentirnos amados: *sacrificio* dulce de todo lo que antes nos era caro a favor de la mujer querida: felicidad que *comprada* para un día con las lágrimas de toda una existencia, recibirámos como un *don de Dios:* perfume para todas las horas del porvenir: *luz inextinguible* del pasado: flor guardada en *el alma* y que no es dado marchitar a los desengaños: único tesoro que no puede arrebatarnos la envidia de los hombres: delirio delicioso . . . *inspiración del cielo* . . . ¡María! ¡María! ¡Cuánto te amé! Cuánto te amara! (62, italics mine)

> [First love! . . . noble pride that comes from feeling loved: sweet *sacrifice* in behalf of the beloved of all that we held dear: happiness that, *purchased* for one day with a lifetime of tears, we accepted as if

it were *a gift from God:* perfume for all the future's hours: *everlasting light* of the past: flower held in *the soul* that cannot be wilted by disappointment: only treasure that cannot be carried away from us by man's jealousy: delicious delirium . . . *inspiration from heaven* . . . María! María! How much I loved you. Had I loved you more!]

The romantic reading, which involves the metaphor of tears, the narrator's careful manipulation of the event he records, and deification of principal characters remains the focus of Efraín's narrative intent. An alternate reading is also possible, based mainly on the information explicitly stated in the note "A los hermanos de Efraín" and subsequent inferences that can be made from it.

Autobiography finds itself at home in today's postmodern criticism of literature. Since the artist is also the subject of the artistic creation, autobiography inescapably turns inward. Francis Francis Hart comments: "The autobiography, more than any literary genre, tends to talk about itself: the development of the subject matter is so dependent upon psychological theory and ideas about documentation . . . that a discussion of the formation of autobiography almost always becomes part of the subject matter" (490). Elizabeth Bruss adds, "To speak in the first person is to identify oneself as the immediate source of the communication and to make of this a focal issue of that communication"(21). This textual inwardness becomes especially evident in Isaacs's prefatory note, "A los hermanos de Efraín." Here we gain our first insight into the mentality of the editor and his awareness of the mechanics and dynamics of the text he now controls. The introduction puts the reader at one remove from Efraín's text, allowing the reader to see it for what it really is: an attempt at establishing the truth of himself (of Efraín) by manipulating and converting the past into literature. The note in effect creates an ironic gap between the introduction and the text which allows the objective reading, thereby destabilizing the reading of tears elicited by the narrator's rhetoric. The reader's awareness of this gap makes possible the discovery of the alternate, nonromantic reading of the novel.

The editor's introduction suggests myriad details valuable to the interpretation of the body of the book. The editor immediately informs us of the identity of the implied readers: Efraín's brothers and sisters. We will assume that the "brothers and sisters" refer literally to the members of the family, although a looser interpretation is admissible. We are told that they loved him ("a quien tanto amásteis") and that, being aware of Efraín's writing, they have long awaited their arrival. Since many of the members of the family are mentioned in the main text, we draw the conclusion that the implied readers and some of the book's characters are the same people. Intimately aware of the tragic story (undoubtably knowledgeable about events that the narrator forgot or consciously eliminated from his history) the implied readers know that for them the novel is for them essentially an experience of rereading.

Rereading involves a process of discovery of details that had been overlooked in the first experience with the text. The deepest levels of meaning and intent often remain hidden after the first reading and can be revealed only upon subsequent investigation. Since second reading is necessarily removed temporally from the first (the actual experience and the reading experience), the implication is that during the lapse between experiences the reader has changed and therefore his perception of the work will also be modified. Usually it is only the reader who changes with time; the physical properties of the book, having no life of themselves independent of the reader, can evolve and metamorphose only when they come into contact with that reader's imagination. Books don't change, readers do; therefore, no two readings can ever be the same. *María* provides us with a different situation. The first reading was not literary, but literal (historical). The story was a dramatic production unfolding before them in which they, as witnesses, were somehow implicated. The "text" changed dramatically from the first to the second readings. Now written words, mediate between the implied readers and the experience with which they could formerly interact. Any influence they might have had over the action has been surrendered to the written text, to which they can react but can never alter.

Since words are imperfect bridges between meaning and object, the portrait left in written form must differ from the one experienced in the past. In addition, time has passed, dulling the sharpness of the details once felt acutely. The editor states explicitly that he has intentionally delayed the publication of the story, widening the already unavoidable temporal gap. Like the structural gap created by the presence of the introduction, this temporal gap serves to increase the reader's consciousness of the necessary fictionalization of the text. The extended lapse of time exaggerates the effects of forgetfulness and provides the editor with the opportunity to influence the second reading by physically altering Efraín's texts or by suggesting in his own ideas that cause the reader to revise his reading.

Both the motive and opportunity for editorial manipulation can be established by evidence provided by the story itself. The opportunity to tamper with Efraín's memoirs is verified by the editor's position relative to the rest of the text. He is always outside the novel. His introduction is external to the action and we must necessarily infer that he has control over the manuscript in his possession. He is free to alter what is written since he is solely responsible for its publication. In addition, the manuscript itself is unreliable. Quoting Efraín, the editor writes: "Lo que ahí falta tú lo sabes; podrás leer hasta lo que mis lágrimas han borrado." [You know what is missing; you can read up to what my tears have erased.] Like Pascual Duarte's disordered and illegible manuscript, or like the Arabic document containing the adventures of Don Quixote, Efraín's account of his fated love affair could not be published until acted upon by an intermediary. Girard's theory of the mediated desire finds in *María* an unexpected application. Rather than a meditation that produces the possibility of the fulfillment of romantic longings, the editor mediates between the principal narrator and his implied reader, making possible the success of the text. The editor appears to create from the romantic text, diluted and incomplete through the metaphor of tears, a new one free of tears, designed to suit his own purposes.

The rhetorical manipulation can be unraveled only upon identifying the person acting as the editor. It is impossible to identify who the author of the introduction is, due perhaps to the apparently intentional ambiguity of the subject pronouns used in the note. However, the editor's intimacy with the story's details, his self-exclusion from the group of Efraín's brothers and sisters and the fact that *he* has control over the manuscript suggest that the editor *may,* in fact, be Efraín's father.

A careful look at the triangular relationship—Efraín's father, Efraín and María—suggests the structural symmetry of the book that leads us to inferences about the editor's motives in controlling the text. Rivalry between the father and Efraín provides much of the energy that moves the action forward as it relates to those in the triangle. The father is always active, dominant and paternalistic both within his immediate family and with his servants and acquaintances. Efraín is his father's alter-ego. He is passive; he sees himself as the victim of his father's dominance. Frequently he is the direct object, not the subject, significantly in the book's opening sentence: "Era yo niño aún cuando me alejaron de la casa paterna para que diera principio a mis estudios en el colegio del doctor Lorenzo María Lleras" (49). [I was a child when they took me away from my father's house to begin my studies in Dr. Lorenzo María Lleras's school.] He measures every act by its possible repercussion with his father and despite his adult status is unable to tolerate any degree of friction or feeling of disapproval.

The father is an ambiguous figure. He appears to be too much the stereotype of the ideal parent and master. However, even Efraín, who usually fails, either through irony or self-deceit, to comprehend the inner workings of his father's mind, recognizes the ambivalence of his nature. "Mi padre, enternecido durante mi ausencia, me dirigía miradas de satisfacción, y sonreía con aquel su modo malicioso y dulce a un mismo tiempo, que no he visto nunca en otros labios" (53). [My father, softened during my absence, gazed at me with satisfaction, and he smiled in that way of his, malicious and sweet at the same time, that I have never seen on the lips of any other.]

The father's malice is fully revealed in his ambiguous relationship with María. Although his statements indicate an apparent interest in the lasting happiness of his son and niece, his actions suggest possible duplicity. He intentionally prevents the marriage of the two lovers. At first the pretext is age. Efraín is too young, claims the father, to rationally consider such an important step. "Hay algo en tu conducta que es preciso decirte no está bien: tú no tienes más que veinte años, y a esa edad un amor fomentado inconsideradamente podría hacer ilusorias todas las esperanzas de que acabo de hablarte (88). [I must tell you that something in the way you are acting is not right: you are barely twenty years old, and at that age an ill-conceived love could destroy all the hopes that I have just expressed for you]. Later, he complains that María is also too young to enter into marriage. However, his behavior is inconsistent in that he eventually allows Carlos, who is exactly the same age as Efraín, to ask for the hand of his adolescent protégé. The father's hypocrisy becomes more apparent when in a conversation with María he perhaps unwittingly, reveals, that he himself was the same age as Efraín at the time of his marriage and that his bride was only sixteen, just a year older than María. His words are filled with hubris at being able to accomplish what he now denies his son. "No hija, tenía veinte. Yo engañé a la señora (así llamaba a su suegra) temeroso de que me creyese muy muchacho" (222). [No, child, I was twenty. I deceived the *señora* (as he called his mother-in-law) fearing that she might think me too young.]

In addition, Efraín's father manipulates the circumstances surrounding María's illness to his advantage. Although the doctor visits the home frequently, the father is the one who initially makes the diagnosis and prescribes treatment. He describes María's attack as "el mismo mal de su madre, que había muerto muy joven atacada de una epilepsia incurable." (80) [the same sickness that afflicted her mother who at a young age had died from an attack of incurable epilepsy.] Although the doctor later announces that María's sickness is not related to her mother's infirmity, the father insists that the forced separation of the lovers is the only way to save the girl.

> Te ama hoy de tal manera, que emociones intensas, nuevas para ella, son las que según Mayn, han hecho aparecer los síntomas de la enfermedad: es decir que tu amor y el suyo necesitan precauciones, y que en adelante exijo me prometas, para tu bien, puesto que tanto así la amas, y para bien de ella que seguirás los consejos del doctor, dados por si llegaba este caso. (89)

> [Today she loves you in such a way that, these intense emotions, new to her, are those that, according to Mayn, have made the symptoms of her disease appear: that is to say that your love and hers require precautions, and I demand that in the future you promise me, considering that you love her so, and for her own good, that you will follow the advice of the doctor, given in the event this condition should arise.]

The doctor recommends that the family make every effort to avoid upsetting María emotionally. The father insists on what causes her the greatest pain of all: separation from Efraín. It is his cure, rather than the ostensibly inherited malady, as he would have us suppose, that leads directly to María's death.

Several hints in the novel suggest that the father, while vying for control over the household, also sees himself as Efraín's rival for María's affection (Williams 350-51). When she is present, the father is animated and in control. When she is absent, contrary to our expectations, he becomes lethargic and disinterested:

> No estaba María en el comedor. . . . Notando mi padre un asiento desocupado, preguntó por ella. . . . Procuré no mostrarme impresionado; haciendo todo esfuerzo porque la conversación fuera amena, hablé con entusiasmo de todas las mejoras que había encontrado en las fincas que acabábamos de visitar. Pero todo fue inútil: mi padre estaba más fatigado que yo, y se retiró temprano. . . . (66).

> [María was not in the dining room. . . . My father, noticing the vacant chair, asked about her. . . . I tried to control my emotions; doing my best to make pleasant conversation. I talked with enthusiasm about the improvements on the farms we had just visited. But it was useless: my father was more exhausted than I and retired early.]

Their conversations are emotional and are open to multiple interpretations. The father's language and gestures suggest affection that is inconsistent with his role as guardian:

> —¿Es decir, le preguntó mi padre . . . , . . . que no quieres casarte nunca?

>   . . . . .

> —Hija, ¿si tendrás ya visto algún novio? continuó mi padre: ¿no dices que no?

> —Sí digo, contestóle María muy asustada.

> —¿Será mejor que ese buen mozo que has desdeñado? Y al decir esto, mi padre le pasó la mano derecha por la frente para conseguir que la mirase. ¿Crees que eres muy linda?

> —¿Yo? no, señor.

> —Sí, y te lo habrá dicho muchas veces. (166)

[—You mean, my father asked her . . . , . . . that you do not ever want to marry?

. . . . .

—Child, you already have a boyfriend, don't you?, my father continued.

—Yes, María answered him, very frightened.

—Will he be better than the young man you have scorned? While saying this, my father passed his right hand across her forehead to get her to look at him. Do you think you are very pretty?

—Me? No, sir.

—Yes, and he must have told you so many times.]

The María-Efraín-father triangle rises to its highest emotional pitch in chapter xxx. It opens with a scene that recalls the father's insistence on his superiority over his son. Every action seems calculated to emphasize and verify the authority of the parental "I." The father dictates a letter, the son transcribes; the father creates and controls, the son copies. Later he asks María to enter the room and cut his hair. Just as she enters, the father makes a cruelly casual comment about Efraín's imminent departure, a comment he knows must cause her pain and humiliate her lover. "Puede que el Señor A*** escriba algo sobre su viaje en este correo: ya se demora en avisar para cuando debes estar listo" (174). [Perhaps Mr. A. will write something about his trip: he already is overdue in letting you know when you should be ready to leave.] This is precisely the type of emotional distress the doctor demands the girl be spared. "Ella entró dándonos los buenos días. Sea que hubiese oído las últimas palabras de mi padre sobre mi viaje, sea que no pudiese prescindir de su timidez genial delante de éste, con mayor razón desde que él le había hablado de nuestro amor, se puso algo pálida (175). [She greeted us as she entered the room. Perhaps because she had heard my father's talk of my trip, perhaps because she could not hide the shyness she felt in his presence, even more understandable since he had spoken to her of our love, she turned pale.] The father seems intent on aggravating the situation as further evidence of the influence he commands in the household. As María cuts the older man's hair he makes several comments filled with innuendo about their relationship. The scene contains an inversion of the Samson and Delilah myth (here the role of seducer is reversed). He boasts of his thick head of hair, alluding to his virility still in flower. Recalling that he used to bathe in "agua de Colonia" when he was young, María laughs and responds that he still maintains the habit, a piece of shared knowledge that is surprisingly intimate. The haircut scene, acted out in Efraín's presence as if challenging him, suggests the reification of the father's "yo" at the expense of his son's. It ends with the following situation highly suggestive of the father's rivalry for the girl's affection:

Cuando María se inclinó a sacudir los recortes de cabéllos que habían caído sobre el cuello de mi padre, la rosa que ella llevaba en una de las trenzas le cayó a él a los pies. Iba ella a alzarla, pero mi padre la había tomado ya. María volvió a ocupar su puesto tras de la silla, y él le dijo después de verse en el espejo detenidamente:

—Yo te la pondré ahora donde estaba, para recompensarte lo bien que lo has hecho; y acercándose a ella agregó, colocando la flor con tanta gracia como lo hubiera podido Emma: todavía se me puede *tener envidia*. (176, italics mine)

[When María bent over to brush off the hair clippings that had fallen on my father's neck, the rose that she wore in her braids fell at his feet. She was going to pick it up, but my father had already taken hold of it. María returned to her place behind the chair, and he said to her while gazing at himself in the mirror: "I will put it back now where it was, as a reward for your good work." And drawing close to her he added, placing the flower in her hair with as much grace as Emma might have shown: "I can still *inspire envy*."]

The father's words suggest an ambiguous close to the chapter. "Detuvo a María, que se mostraba deseosa de retirarse *por temor de lo que él pudiera añadir*, besóle la frente y le dijo en voz baja:—*Hoy no será como ayer; acabaremos temprano*" (176, italics mine). [He detained María, who appeared anxious to leave *for fear of what he might add*, he kissed her on the forehead and softly said to her, "*Tonight will not be like yesterday, we will finish early*.] In light of these details, is the older man suggesting that Efraín and María will that night have time to be together, or that he and María, unlike other nights, will have an abbreviated encounter? The symbolic suggestions and the unreadable gaps that flow from intimate knowledge, shared by the protagonists but denied the readers, fill the text with eloquent absences that reinforce the problematic relationship involving the controlling voices of the story and their shared object of desire.

Efraín's father's possible editorial participation in the book appears to be an effort to further demonstrate his control over his environment. By publishing the text he allows all to see his son's impotence in their rivalry. By encasing the son's manuscript within an editorial structure, he emphasizes textually that he is able to dominate not only in life but also in literature. As María cuts the father's hair he gazes into the mirror, narcissistically admiring the reflection of a still handsome man. The novel he produces is his ultimate act of self-love. He transforms the work which Efraín had written originally as an attempt to define himself into a text that degrades the central narrator for his abulia and exalts the father in a type of perverse dominance. He suggests two readings of the novel to those who persue its pages. "Leedlas, pues, y si suspendéis la lectura para llorar, ese llanto me probará que la he cumplido [la misión] fielmente (47). [Read them, and if you suspend your reading to cry, your tears will prove that I have faithfully completed my task.] A tearful reading, a romantic reading, is the one Efraín seeks. A reading without tears is demanded by the father in his final attempt at self-aggrandizement.

This objective reading permits us to perceive both the possible subversive motivations of the father as editor and the narrator's pathetic attempt to cover up a past with a series of rhetorical defenses. It must be noted, however, than we do not need to identify the editor as Efraín's father in order to make this point. It is just as plausible that Efraín himself may assume an editorial stance in order to distance himself from the naive, sentimental ("romantic") character who he would like us to believe "ya no existe" [no longer exists]. As such, the editor may be seen to escape from the past described in the autobiography in order to dramatize that his former self dies with María. Identifying the editor as Efraín places the main text in the same tenuous position we noted by seeing the father as editor. Efraín-editor now reflects on both Efraín-narrator and Efraín-character and demonstrates that the story is, in effect, a conversion. The text has metamorphosed progressively through the stages of memoir (the posited historical rendition of the events) to apology (Efraín's attempt to cover his weakness with a veil of tears) only to arrive at a confession: Efraín-editor attempts to reveal the truth of self as he depicts his newly discovered ironic self-consciousness. The structure of the novel thus seems to claim that the truth can only be perceived retrospectively, statically, outside the temporal frame of the artificial plot. The preface buries both the sentimental character and the insecure narrator, tacitly acknowledging the oppression of the "law of the father" and transforming the pain of the past into heightened self-awareness. As soon as the truth of self is perceived, however, the ironic self-consciousness that gave it birth forces the ego to recognize that this truth is just another level in an infinite regression of fictions. The essential dilemma that seems to resonate through the book's structure is whether it is ever possible to capture the historical integrity of the individual. Is there any way of using language to perceive, reconstruct, and represent either historical truth or truth of self? The continual and conflicting permutations of the figure called Efraín, whether the father or the protagonist are responsible for them, require a negative response to this fundamental question.

The superimposition of the objective reading on the romantic reading leads us to conclusions about the nature of romantic expression itself. Romantic texts, from the beginning, manifest an awareness of their own structure and the implications of that structure. From Rivas's *Don Alvaro,* through Larra's confessional cycle to Bécquer's metapoetry, the works appear to establish the identity of their voices while simultaneously subverting them. Isaacs's text initially posits the traditionally held view of Romanticism as unrestrained sentimentalism. In their attempt to create a rhetoric of tears, Efraín's pathetic confessions echo the hollow forms of that exaggerated Romanticism that, precisely because of their lack of an ideological referent, like the old Efraín, have ceased to exist. Paradoxically, the objective, "non-romantic" reading, then, becomes the most authentically romantic one. It is the one that draws our attention to itself, that dramatizes its own inconsistencies and structural tension. It is the one most concerned with the validation of the "I" and the one struggling most with its own voice. It resists certainty of interpretation and leaves us to deal with what is at heart a fundamentally ironic world. Perhaps this is why in an age that can no longer take *María*'s tears seriously, we can continue to peer behind her veil at a type of Romanticism that is very much with us today.

Works Cited

Bruss, Elizabeth. *Autobiographical Acts.* Baltimore: Johns Hopkins UP, 1976.

Barta, John. "La función estructural de los episodios costumbristas de María." *La literaturaiberoamericana del siglo XIX: Memoria del XV Congreso Internacional de Literatura Iberoamericana, Tucson Arizona, 21-24 de Enero de 1971.* Ed. Renato Rosaldo and Robert Anderson. Tucson: University of Arizona Press, 1971.

Freccero, John. "Zeno's Last Cigarette." *MLN* 72 (1962): 3-23.

Girard, René. *To Double Business Bound.* Baltimore: Johns Hopkins University Press, 1978.

Hart, Francis R. "Notes for an Anatomy of Modern Autobiography." *New Literary History* 1 (1970): 485-511.

Isaacs, Jorge. *María.* Ed. Donald McGrady. Barcelona: Labor, 1970.

Masson de Gómez, Valérie. "Las flores como símbolos eróticos en la obra de Jorge Isaacs." *Thesaurus* 28.1 (1973): 117-27.

Menton, Seymour. "La estructura dualística de María." *Thesaurus* 25.2 (1970): 251-77.

Molloy, Sylvia. "Paraíso perdidio y economía terrenal en María." *Sin Nombre* 14.3 (1984): 36-55.

Nisbet, Robert. "Genealogy, Growth and Other Metaphors." *New Literary History* 1 (1970): 351-64.

Porras Collantes, Ernesto. "Contemplación en la estructura de *María*." *Thesaurus* 31.2 (1976): 327-57.

Sayre, Robert F. *The Examined Self.* Princeton, N.J.: Princeton University Press, 1964.

Tittler, Jonathon. "Tropos tropicales: Paisajes figurados en *María, La vorágine y El otoño del patriarca*." *Discurso Literario: Revista de Temas Hispánicas.* 2.2 (1985): 507-518.

Williams, Raymond L. "The Problem of Unity in Fiction: Narrator and Self in *María*." *MLN* 101 (1986): 342-53.

FURTHER READING

Criticism

Brown, Donald F. "Chateaubriand and the Story of Feliciana in Jorge Isaacs' *María*." *Modern Language Notes* 62, No. 5 (May 1947): 326-29.

> Brown argues that the story of Nay and Sinar in *María* was directly influenced by Chateaubriand's *Atala*.

Brushwood, John S. "Codes of Character Definition: Jorge Isaacs's *María*." In *Genteel Barbarism: Experiments in Analysis of Nineteenth-Century Spanish-American Novels*, pp. 82-106. Lincoln: University of Nebraska Press, 1981.

> Interprets a series of passages from *María* by applying the theory of Roland Barthes.

Jackson, Shirley M. "Fact from Fiction: Another Look at Slavery in Three Spanish-American Novels." In *Blacks in Hispanic Literature: Critical Essays*, edited by Miriam DeCosta, pp.83-89. Port Washington, New York: Kennikat Press, 1977.

> Discusses the depictions of Spanish-American slavery in Isaacs's *María*, Cirilo Villaverde's *Cecilia Valdés,* and Gertrudis de Avellaneda's *Sab*.

Magnarelli, Sharon. "*María* and History." *Hispanic Review* 49, No. 2 (Spring 1981): 209-217.

> Magnarelli argues that Efraín, the narrator of *María*, adopts the stance of the historian in attempting to capture a lost past.

———. "Woman as Dramatized reader: *María* and *La Traichíon de Rita Hayworth*." *Hispanofila* 94, No. 1 (September 1988): 79-88.

> Offers a critical comparison of the female reading experience in these two novels.

McGrady, Donald. *Jorge Isaacs*. New York: Twayne Publishers, 1972, 172 p.

> Examines both Isaacs's life and work. McGrady also discusses contemporary responses to Isaacs's novel and poetry.

Warshaw, J. "Jorge Isaacs' Library: Light on Two *María* Problems." *The Romanic Review* 32, No. 4 (December 1941): 389-98.

> Warshaw lists the contents of Isaacs's library and discusses possible sources for *María*.

Brian Merriman

c. 1747-1805

(Bryan Merryman, Brian Mac Goilla Meidhre) Irish poet.

INTRODUCTION

Although today remembered as a poet, Merriman was known during his lifetime primarily as a teacher and a farmer. As such, he provides an interesting contrast to another poet of the early Romantic "Celtic fringe," Robert Burns. Whereas Burns, the "heaven-taught plowman," became the darling of the British *literati*, Merriman lived in relative obscurity. This is largely due to two factors: a language barrier and the social restraints placed on Irish Catholics by the British government at that time. Burns wrote in English and Scots, and although the latter was often difficult for English speakers to understand, it was nonetheless partially comprehensible. Merriman, however, wrote in Irish Gaelic, a language virtually unintelligible to English readers. Additionally, repressive British laws of the eighteenth century made it very difficult for Irish Catholics, particularly the rural poor who spoke Gaelic, to receive an education. As a result, the literate audience for which Gaelic-language poetry such as Merriman's might be published was very small. A small audience of potential readers meant low sales; this in turn made publishers unwilling to print Gaelic texts, and without a published text there was nothing to draw the attention of the patrons and subscribers whose support was necessary to launch a poet's career.

Biographical Information

Merriman was born around 1747 in or near Ennistimon, a village in western Ireland's rural County Clare. Based partially on one of the themes of his most famous poem, "Cúirt an Mheán-Oíche" (c. 1780; "The Midnight Court"), scholars often assert that he was the illegitimate son of a local landowner, but conclusive evidence is wanting. Various accounts relate that his father (or step-father) was either a traveling mason or a farmer who eventually settled in Feakle, another village in County Clare. There, sometime in his late teens, Merriman became a teacher in a local "hedge school," an educational institution unrecognized by the government because it defied the Penal Law that forbade Catholics from teaching. It was during this time that Merriman wrote "The Midnight Court." Merriman held the position until 1785, at which time he took up full-time farming, married a local woman named Kit

(Cit), and fathered two daughters, Kathleen (Caitlín) and Mary (Máire). As a farmer, Merriman was quite successful, winning two prizes for flax growing from the Royal Dublin Society in 1797. Five or six years later, Merriman and his family moved to the city of Limerick where he took a position teaching mathematics (the Penal Laws had been relaxed in the early 1790's). Merriman died in Limerick in 1805.

Major Works

Although Merriman wrote two other short lyrics, his reputation as a poet rests solely on "The Midnight Court." A comic epic of just over 1000 lines, the poem is a burlesque variant of the Irish *aisling* tradition of dream-vision poetry. In it, the poet-narrator falls asleep beside the waters of Loch Gréine, a lake in County Clare, and dreams of a fairy court ruled over by a figure named Aoibheal. The court has set itself the task of trying Irish men for their crime of not populating the countryside sufficiently. Two figures, a *spéirbhean*—a beautiful woman who is a traditional figure in Irish Gaelic poetry—and a cuckolded old man, give evidence from their personal experiences. In the process, the man argues that bastards (such, perhaps, as Merriman himself) can grow to be healthy members of society without married parents, so illegitimacy should not be considered a blemish of one's character. In turn, the woman argues that, because there are so few eligible men in Ireland, members of the clergy should be allowed to marry. The court's judgment is to allow women to seize upon any man of age twenty one or older and beat him until he submits to being married; older unmarried men are to be treated even more harshly. The poet is summarily seized by the court's bailiff and awakens just in time to escape punishment.

Critical Reception

"The Midnight Court" did not appear in English until the very end of the nineteenth century and was not widely available until the early twentieth. So, though a product of the late 1700's, it was almost completely unrecognized by non-Gaelic speakers for two centuries. As a result, scholars have had a difficult time determining the poem's proper position in literary history. The main topic of debate concerns the extent to which Merriman's poetry was shaped by such influential Enlightenment figures as Jonathon Swift, Richard Savage, Jean-Jacques Rousseau, and Voltaire. A related issue is the question of how much "The Midnight Court" is the product of a native Gaelic folk tradition and of how great a debt it owes to non-Gaelic forces. Another primary area of contention is the political theme of the poem. There is no critical consensus about whether Merriman's text follows the *aisling* tradition in its tacit desire for Irish independence (by explicitly calling for noncelibate clergy and implicitly questioning English common law through its recognition of illegitimate children), or is primarily a burlesque of that same tradition, questioning the foundations of its genre.

PRINCIPAL WORKS

*"Cúirt an Mheán Oíche" ["The Midnight Court"] (poetry) c. 1780
"An Macalla" ["The Echo"] (poetry) n.d.
"An Poitín" ["The Poteen"] (poetry) n.d.

*None of Merriman's poems appeared in print during his lifetime; the date given for "The Midnight Court" is the date of composition. Reliable information on the other two poems' dates of composition is not available.

PRINCIPAL ENGLISH TRANSLATIONS

The Midnight Court (translated by and privately printed for Michael C. O'Shea) 1897
Cúirt an Mheadoin Oidhche—The Midnight Court (translated, annotated, and edited for schools by F. W. O'Connell) 1909
The Midnight Court and The Adventures of a Luckless Fellow (translated by Percy Arland Ussher) 1926
The Midnight Court: A Rhythmical Bacchanalia (translated by Frank O'Connor) 1945
The Midnight Court—Cúirt an Mheadhon Oídhche (translated by David Marcus) 1953
Cúirt an Mhean-Oíche—The Midnight Court (translated by Patrick C. Power) 1971
The Penguin Book of Irish Verse (includes the O'Connor translation) 1979
The Midnight Court (translated by Cosslett Ó Cuinn) 1982

CRITICISM

W. B. Yeats (essay date 1926)

SOURCE: An introduction to *The Midnight Court and The Adventures of a Luckless Fellow*, by Brian Merriman and Denis Fellow, translated by Percy Arland Ussher, Jonathan Cape, 1926, pp. 5-12.

[*In this essay, Yeats, perhaps the most famous of Ireland's poets, connects "The Midnight Court" with Jonathan Swift's* Cadenus and Vanessa.]

Months ago Mr. Ussher asked me to introduce his translation of **The Midnight Court.** I had seen a few pages in an Irish magazine; praised its vitality; my words had been repeated; and because I could discover no reason for refusal that did not make me a little ashamed, I consented. Yet I could wish that a Gaelic scholar had been found, or failing that some man of known sobriety of manner and of mind—Professor Trench of Trinity College let us say—to introduce to the Irish reading public this vital, extravagant, immoral, preposterous poem.

Brian Mac Giolla Meidhre—or to put it in English, Brian Merriman—wrote in Gaelic, one final and three internal rhymes in every line, pouring all his mediaeval abundance into that narrow neck. He was born early in the eighteenth century, somewhere in Clare, even now the most turbulent of counties, and the countrymen of Clare and of many parts of Munster have repeated his poem down to our own day. Yet this poem which is so characteristically Gaelic and mediaeval is founded upon *Cadenus and Vanessa*,[1] read perhaps in some country gentleman's library. The shepherds and nymphs of Jonathan Swift plead by counsel before Venus:

> Accusing the false creature man.
> The brief with weighty crimes was charged
> On which the pleader much enlarged,
> That Cupid now has lost his art,
> Or blunt the point of every dart.

Men have made marriage mercenary and love an intrigue; but the shepherds' counsel answers that the fault lies with women who have changed love for 'gross desire' and care but for 'fops and fools and rakes.' Venus finds the matter so weighty that she calls the Muses and the Graces to her assistance and consults her books of law—Ovid, Virgil, Tibullus, Cowley, Waller—continuously adjourns the court for sixteen years, and then after the failure of an experiment gives the case in favour of the women. The experiment is the creation of Vanessa, who instead of becoming all men's idol and reformer, all women's example, repels both by her learning and falls in love with her tutor Swift.

The Gaelic poet changed a dead to a living mythology, and called men and women to plead before Eevell of Craglee, the chief of Munster Spirits, and gave her court reality by seeing it as a vision upon a mid-summer day under a Munster tree. No countryman of that time doubted, nor in all probability did the poet doubt, the existence of Eevell, a famous figure to every story-teller. The mediaeval convention of a dream or vision has served the turn of innumerable licentious rhymers in Gaelic and other languages, of Irish Jacobites who have substituted some personification of Ireland, some Dark Rosaleen, for a mortal mistress, of learned poets who call before our eyes an elaborate allegory of courtly love. I think of Chaucer's 'Romaunt of the Rose,' his 'Book of the Duchess,' and of two later poems that used to be called his, 'Chaucer's Dream' and 'The Complaint of the Black Knight.' But in all these the vision comes in May.

> That it was May, me thoughte tho,
> It is fyve yere or more ago;
> That it was May, thus dreamed me
> In tyme of love and jolitie
> That all things ginneth waxen gay.

One wonders if there is some Gaelic precedent for changing the spring festival for that of summer, the May-day singing of the birds to the silence of summer fields. Had Mac Giolla Meidhre before his mind the fires of St. John's Night, for all through Munster men and women leaped the fires that they might be fruitful, and after scattered the ashes that the fields might be fruitful also. Certainly it is not possible to read his verses without being shocked and horrified as city onlookers were perhaps shocked and horrified at the free speech and buffoonery of some traditional country festival.

He wrote at a moment of national discouragement, the penal laws were still in force though weakening, the old order was a vivid memory but with the failure of the last Jacobite rising hope of its return had vanished, and no new political dream had come. The state of Ireland is described: 'Her land purloined, her law decayed . . . pastures with weeds o'ergrown, her ground untilled . . . hirelings holding the upper hand,' and worst of all—and this the fairy court has been summoned to investigate—'the lads and lasses have left off breeding.' Are the men or the women to blame? A woman speaks first, and it is Swift's argument but uttered with voluble country extravagance, and as she speaks one calls up a Munster hearth, farmers sitting round at the day's end, some old farmer famous through all the countryside for this long recitation, speaking or singing with dramatic gesture. If a man marries, the girl declares, he does not choose a young girl but some rich scold 'with a hairless crown and a snotty nose.' Then she describes her own beauty and asks if she is not more fit for marriage? She has gone everywhere 'bedizened from top to toe,' but because she lacks money nobody will look at her and she is single still.

> After all I have spent upon readers of palms
> And tellers of tea-leaves and sellers of charms.

Then an old man replies, and heaps upon her and upon her poverty-stricken father and family all manner of abuse: he is the champion of the men, and he will show where the blame lies. He tells of his own marriage. He was a man of substance but has been ruined by his wife who gave herself up to every sort of dissipation—Swift's argument again. A child was born, but when he asked to see the child the women tried to cover it up, and when he did see it, it was too fine, too handsome and vigorous to be a child of his. And now Swift is forgotten and dramatic propriety, the poet speaks through the old man's mouth and asks Eevell of Craglee to abolish marriage that such children may be born in plenty.

> For why call a Priest in to bind and to bless
> Since Mary the Mother of God did conceive
> Without calling the Clergy or begging their
>   leave,
> The love-gotten children are famed as the
>   flower
> Of man's procreation and nature's power,
> For love is a lustier sire than law,
> And has made them sound without fault or
>   flaw
> And better and braver in heart and head
> Than the puny breed of the marriage bed.

The bastard's speech in Lear is floating through his mind mixed up doubtless with old stories of Diarmuid's and Cuchullain's loves, and old dialogues where Oisin railed at Patrick; but there is something more, an air of personal conviction that is of his age, something that makes his words—spoken to that audience—more than the last song of Irish paganism. One remembers that Burns is about to write his beautiful defiant 'Welcome to his love-begotten daughter' and that Blake who is defiant in thought alone meditates perhaps his 'Marriage of Heaven and Hell.' The girl replies to the old man that if he were not so old and crazed she would break his bones, and that if his wife is unfaithful what better could he expect seeing that she was starved into marrying him. However, she has her own solution. Let all the handsome young priests be compelled to marry. Then Eevell of Craglee gives her judgment, the Priests are left to the Pope who will order them into marriage one of these days, but let all other young men marry or be stripped and beaten by her spirits, and let all old bachelors be tortured by the spinsters. The poem ends by the girl falling upon the poet and beating him because he is unmarried. He is ugly and humped, she says, but might look as well as another in the dark.

Standish Hayes O'Grady has described the *Midnight Court* as the best poem written in Gaelic, and as I read Mr. Ussher's translation I have felt, without sharing what seems to me an extravagant opinion, that Giolla Meidhre, had political circumstances been different, might have founded a modern Gaelic literature. Mac

Conmara, or Macnamara, though his poem is of historical importance, does not interest me so much. He knew Irish and Latin only, knew nothing of his own age, saw vividly but could not reflect upon what he saw, and so remained an amusing provincial figure.

Notes

[1] Mr. Robin Flower pointed this out to me. *Cadenus and Vanessa,* which has the precision of fine prose, is the chief authority for the first meeting of Swift and Esther Vanhomrigh. I think it was Sir Walter Scott who first suggested 'a constitutional infirmity' to account for Swift's emotional entanglement, but this suggestion is not supported by Irish tradition. Some years ago a one-act play was submitted to the Abbey Theatre reading committee which showed Swift saved from English soldiers at the time of the 'Drapier letters' by a young harlot he was accustomed to visit. The author claimed that though the actual incident was his invention, his view of Swift was traditional, and inquiry proved him right. I had always known that stories of Swift and his serving man were folklore all over Ireland and now I learned from country friends why the man was once dismissed. Swift sent him out to fetch a woman and when Swift woke in the morning he found that she was a negress.

Frank O'Connor (essay date 1945)

SOURCE: A preface to *The Midnight Court: A Rhythmical Bacchanalia from the Irish of Bryan Merryman,* translated by Frank O'Connor, Maurice Fridberg, 1945, pp. 5-11.

[*In the following essay, O'Connor suggests that the humor of "The Midnight Court" conveys a social message in line with the theories of such contemporaries as Rousseau and Savage.*]

Architecturally, the little city of Limerick is one of the pleasantest spots in Ireland. The Georgian town stands at the other side of the river from the mediaeval town which has a castle with drum towers and a cathedral with a Transitional Cistercian core and a fifteenth century shell, all in curling papers of battlements. Across the bridge are the charming Custom House with its arcade cemented up by some genius from the Board of Works; Arthur's Quay falling into a ruin of tenements, and a fine long street of the purest Georgian which ends in a double crescent. There is no tablet in Clare Street to mark where Bryan Merryman, the author of *The Midnight Court* died, nor is there ever likely to be, for Limerick has a reputation for piety.

Merryman was born about the middle of the eighteenth century in a part of Ireland which must then have been as barbarous as any in Europe—it isn't exactly what one would call civilised today. He earned five or ten pounds a year by teaching school in a Godforsaken village called Feakle in the hills above the Shannon, eked it out with a little farming, and somehow or other managed to read and assimilate a great deal of contemporary literature, English and French. Even with compulsory education, the English language, and public libraries you would be hard set to find a young Clareman of Merryman's class today who knew as much of Lawrence and Gide as he knew of Savage, Swift, Goldsmith and, most of all, Rousseau. How he managed it in an Irish-speaking community is a mystery. He was undoubtedly a man of powerful objective intelligence; his obituary describes him as 'a teacher of mathematics' which may explain something; and though his use of *'Ego vos'* for the marriage service suggests a Catholic upbringing, the religious background of *The Midnight Court* is Protestant, which may explain more.

He certainly had intellectual independence. In *The Midnight Court* he imitated contemporary English verse, and it is clear that he had resolved to cut adrift entirely from traditional Gaelic forms. His language—that is its principal glory—is also a complete break with literary Irish. It is the spoken Irish of Clare. The handful of poems at the close of the book may suggest the best that literature before him had achieved—an occasional lyric of quality, but of drama, prose, criticism or narrative poetry there was nothing. Intellectually, Irish literature did not exist. What Merryman aimed at was something that had never even been guessed at in Gaelic Ireland; a perfectly proportioned work of art on a contemporary subject, with every detail subordinated to the central theme. The poem is as classical as the Limerick Custom House; and fortunately, the Board of Works has not been able to get at it.

The story of it is innocuous enough. The poet falls asleep, and in a dream is summoned to the fairy court, where the unmarried women of Munster are pleading their inability to get husbands. An old man replies by telling the story of his own marriage, and of how his young wife presented him with another man's child on his wedding night. The young girl rebuts the charge and tells the story of the marriage from the wife's point of view, and then the Fairy Queen sums up and gives judgment for the women, whose first victim is the poet himself.

His opening is as harmless as the story. The English Georgian poets had little feeling for Nature, and Merryman had none at all; he even forgets the season he is supposed to be writing of. Fairies also look a little gauche under a classical pediment; Merryman makes his fairy messenger twenty feet high which should satisfy the imaginative hunger of any true Celt. But the moment the young girl begins to speak, Merryman knows exactly where he is, and the whole picture instantly springs into focus. This girl goes to fortune tellers and experiments with white magic to get a man, and Merryman, the realist, has studied it all with the greatest care—most of the charms I have been quite unable to identify. As always when he deals with women's human needs, he puts real tenderness and beauty into the writing. My English cannot give the delicacy and fragrance of a line like *Ag súil trim chola le cogar ó'm chéile*. There is nothing remarkable about it which a romantic critic like Professor Corkery can seize on; no extravagance of imagery or language which you can translate; it is a pure classical beauty of vowels and consonants which you either hear or do not hear.

At this point the girl announces that for the future she is going in for black magic, and on that master-stroke the first part ends. With old Snarlygob's speech a new quality enters which is the characteristic quality of Merryman. He was supremely a realist, and this is his first opportunity of painting in the peasant background. He does it with a closeness of texture, a ruthless logic which will not allow him to dawdle over a line, and a mastery of language which extracts the maximum effect out of each. Snarlygob abuses the girl and describes the misery from which she came. Then after a terrific bit of rustic comedy in which the old man describes his marriage and his wedding night, comes a curious structural weakness—the first of several. Into the old man's mouth Merryman puts his great paean in praise of bastards. Critics who point out the inappropriateness of this also draw attention to the derivation from Savage, but to stress the borrowing seems to me to miss the point. The real inspiration of this passage is the implicit inspiration of the whole poem; not Savage so much as Rousseau; and the bastard is used as a symbol of natural innocence. The real hero of Merryman's poem is Nature as an eighteenth century Utopian saw her.

At this point he lashes out in an attack on marriage which all respectable critics insist on regarding as humorous merely because it is good-humoured, but again to miss the note of sincerity in Merryman is to miss his quality as a poet and treat him as Professor Corkery treats him, as a coarse jester. The sort of people 'who, lacking sensibility themselves, raise laughter by shocking it in others,' among whom Corkery classes Merryman, do not usually do so in poems of a thousand lines; and in general it is safer to assume that when a man expresses himself in this way he is more likely to do so because he is shocked himself rather than because he is anxious to shock others; and that it is the man of no sensibility who is most likely to be shocked by it.

With the girl's reply Merryman reverts to his natural realistic manner, though with deepening passion. There is something very like great poetry in this third canto. The girl's description of the old man's marriage begins in a mood of great tenderness; the tenderness Merryman always shows in dealing with women. In the Irish the lines are slow and halting, as the punctuation shows: *Bhí sí lag, gan ba, gan púnta; Bhí sí abhfad gan teas, gan clúda.*

> This girl was poor, she hadn't a home;
> Hadn't a thing to call her own . . .

From this it mounts into a perfect crescendo of frustrated sexual passion which I have had to suggest rather than to translate, though, like everything else in the poem, even this is held on a very tight rein, and is never allowed to become disproportionate to the total effect. To realise the true greatness of the eighteenth century and the way it imposed a common habit of thought on all the nations from Limerick to Leningrad, one has only to see how this village poet adopts the grand manner, and speaks as if he knew no boundaries to the human mind.

> The talk about women comes well from him
> Without hope in body or help in limb!
> If the creature that found him such a sell
> Has a lover today she deserves him well.

Then as the argument in favour of free love is developed, the girl bursts into a furious attack on clerical celibacy. This is where Merryman's audacity reaches its height, for, after all, he was writing in an Irish-speaking village in the eighteenth century things which even Yeats himself might have thought twice of writing in English-speaking Dublin of the twentieth, and yet he never once loses his bland and humane humour and is as full of pity for his well-fed canons and curates who have to conceal their indiscretions as he is for his young women. It is superb comedy, kept well in character; but then, once more we get the shifting of planes and the sudden intensity; the character of the woman drops away, and we are face to face with Bryan Merryman, the intellectual Protestant and disciple of Rousseau, with his appeal to Scripture.

After that, from the moment when the Queen gets up to deliver judgment, the poem falls away. Clearly this was intended to be the point at which Merryman would speak through her, and express his own convictions about life, but something went wrong. I have a suspicion that he found himself tied up in the mock-heroic machinery, and after the intensity of the previous cantos, felt it a rather ignominious expedient of comedy. Only once does he speak again in the grand manner; when he turns suddenly with a fine outburst of the old utopian passion and rends the men who desecrate human love; a curious passage from one of those unfortunate jesters, 'who, lacking sensibility themselves, raise laughter by shocking it in others.'

After that Merryman never wrote again. He went to live in Limerick with his daughter and her husband, a tailor, and died suddenly there in 1805. Why did he go there? Most probably because what Professor Corkery sneers at as 'his much-enlightened soul' longed for some sort of intellectual society, which in twentieth century Clare it might still long for. To say the man was 150 years before his time would be mere optimism—think of Professor Corkery! Did he expect to find among Limerick Protestants a cultured group who would understand him? If they ever heard of him they forgot to mention the fact. Perhaps it was their neglect which compelled him to realise the futility of trying to make Irish the language of contemporary thought. He had that sort of clear, objective intelligence which rarely attaches itself to lost causes, and he may well have turned with a wry smile from the dream of a modernised Gaelic Ireland to the teaching of trigonometry.

He has had no influence whatever on Irish life or Irish thought. Yeats, with one of those flashes of instinct by which poets recognise one another even through a veil, saw that he was a European poet, but even Yeats and Synge, for all their English blood, were wild Celts compared with this village schoolmaster with 'his much-enlightened soul.' The jeer may serve for an epitaph. It is the sort of soul that grows on one when the uproarious spirituality of Gaelic Ireland begins to pall. I have lived with it off and on for some years, and it isn't the sort one tires of easily. It is perhaps best suited to people of over thirty who have had some experience of life without being embittered by it. The verse it produces will never replace *Romeo and Juliet* by the bedside of an adolescent, but it may amuse a young woman whose children are growing up about her.

Merryman was ignored by Georgian society in Limerick, but in death he has taken a terrible revenge. The great, wine-coloured Georgian cliffs are being steadily eaten away by Rathmines Romanesque and Ruabon Renaissance. Nowhere else in Ireland has Irish Puritanism such power. Leaning over the bridge in the twilight, looking up the river at the wild hills of Clare from which old Merryman came down so long ago, you can hear a Gregorian choir chanting *Et expecto resurrectionem mortuorum,* and go back through the street where he walked, reflecting that in Limerick there isn't much else to expect.

R. A. Breatnach (essay date 1956)

SOURCE: "Ad 'Cúirt an Mheadhoin Oidhche' ll. 597-8," in *Eigse: A Journal of Irish Studies,* Vol. VIII, No. 2, 1956, pp. 140-43.

[*In the following essay, Breatnach demonstrates that traditional English translations of two lines of Merriman's "The Midnight Court" lead to misunderstandings about the poem's theme.*]

The lines in question have been seriously misunderstood.[1] In Stern's edition, CZ v. 220, they are as follows:—

Ó d'aibig an tadhbhar do bhronn mac Dé
Gan sagart ar domhan dá dtabhairt dá chéile.

The lines are metrically correct, because unstressed *Gan* may be read with *Dé* to rhyme with *chéile;* compare *ndiaig* followed by *A* in the next line rhyming with *fiadhaile,* l. 79, and there are several other cases of the same thing in the poem. Some MSS. have *dár* for *dá* in the second line, but *dá* is the reading of the majority, and I see no reason to reject it.

The words are spoken by the *seanduine* towards the end of his plea for the abolition of Matrimony. His speech, no more than Merriman's concept of his character, is not entirely self-consistent or logical. In the early part of it his plea is based on the ground that, being indissoluble, Matrimony inflicts a grave injustice on men like himself who have the misfortune to marry young women of easy virtue. At this later stage, however, while still desirous of saving those who have not been caught in the shackles (l. 588), he is expressly concerned to urge the advantages of *saorthoil síolraig.* His grievance forgotten, and fascinated by the physical perfection of his young wife's lovechild, he becomes something of a social reformer (see ll. 583-92, and 629-44). What has happened is that Merriman, with a touch of originality but perhaps with more daring than deftness, has made the traditional stock *seanduine* of folk-poetry the mouthpiece of a doctrine which could not benefit his impotent self.[2]

His case now centres round the child. The circumstances of its birth and the attempt to father it on himself have been related (530-70). A dozen lines (571-82) follow in which its physical perfection is described in detail. Then there is a fresh appeal for the setting aside of Marriage, this time in order to ensure that the land may be peopled by champions (583-92). The logical connection between this ground and the physical perfection of the child is self-evident. Clearly his purpose in next asking rhetorically 'what need is there for the tumult of the wedding-feast' (593) and all that goes with it (594-6) is simply to drive home the main point. Stern, misunderstanding the text, places a note of interrogation at the end of l. 596; but it is evident that ll. 597-8 are part of the rhetorical question and indeed state the reason which makes it rhetorical. It is to be noted that immediately after l. 598 there is a slight development in the thought, that ll. 599-606 extol the physical merits of natural children in general. But at l. 607 the *seanduine* returns again to the particular and, in a final bid for conviction, produces one such begotten *'le fonn na fola is le fortham na sláinte'* (628) for all to see and admire. There cannot be much doubt that the child is his wife's, though this is not expressly stated.[3] The passage ends at l. 628. The remainder of the speech (629-44) is a mere repetition in different words of the plea already made in ll. 583-92.

I have analysed the relevant part of the argument (530-644) in order to show that, in so far as Merriman is capable of sustained logical thought, the dominant idea throughout is the physical perfection of the love-child in particular and of its likes in general. From his particular knowledge the *seanduine* is made to argue to the general conclusion that *saor-thoil síolraig* gives the best results all round. The question of which ll. 597-8 form part is separated from the description of the child, which ends at l. 582, by only ten lines (583-92). The first six of these are a direct appeal to Aoibhioll and must be regarded as apostrophe, not as argument. The following four are clearly connected in the speaker's mind with the description of the child. They may be translated: 'if the human stock has become weak in the pleasant-hued, green land of Ireland, it is easy to fill the country again with champions without their (sc. the clergy's) useless and fruitless praying'. To anyone hearing this it would be obvious that the *seanduine* was referring obliquely to the begetting of the 'champion' to whom his wife gave birth. Hence when he exclaims 'what need is there for the tumult of the wedding-feast, etc.', implying clearly that there is no need whatever, and adds

> '*Ó d'aibig an tadhbhar do bhronn mac Dé*
> *Gan sagart ar domhan dá dtabhairt dá*
> *chéile*',

it would be natural for his hearers (as well as for readers of the poem) to understand these words as an explicit or less implicit reference to the idea which all the time is implicit in what he has been saying. To put it more directly: the *seanduine* is to be understood as referring here to the central fact on which his 'case' rests, viz. that his wife conceived and bore a perfect child without the help of the Sacrament of Matrimony.

There can be no doubt that this general interpretation is consistent with the analysis I have attempted to make of Merriman's thought. In regard to the precise sense of the two lines, the poem itself is our safest guide. The only real difficulties are the exact meaning of *d'aibig an tadhbhar* and the relationship, whether nominative or accusative, in which *adhbhar* stands to the relative sentence *do bhronn mac Dé*. The ordinary meanings of *adhbhar* are 'matter, stuff, material'[4]. Ideally, then, the word connotes something that is acted upon, and its use, as far as my observation goes, always reflects this fundamental idea. Therefore we may rule out the possibility that Irish *Sprachgefühl* would permit it to stand in a nominative relationship to the relative clause *do bhronn mac Dé*, the more so since the verb is followed by an 'animate' noun which denotes for all Christians the Son of the Agent *par*

excellemce. For these reasons *do bhronn mac Dé* can only mean 'which the Son of God bestowed'. The other difficulty disappears when we take into consideration l. 543: *bíoch nach bailioch a d'aibig an chré seo*. This was one of the whispers overheard by the *seanduine* on the night of the child's birth. I take it that *d'aibig an tadhbhar* is a re-echo of *d'aibig an chré*, the two words *adhbhar* and *cré*, as they may be in W. Kerry Irish, being synonymous, meaning loosely 'substance, stuff', and both referring to the child.[5] We note that the old man has more than once emphasized the maturity of the child; see ll. 573-82, and in particular: *Do aibig a shiúile us fiú a pholláirighe* (579); compare also ll. 607-28. Hence, as far as we can be sure of the meaning of anything that poets have written, we may take it as certain that Merriman meant *adhbhar* to refer to the child and we may translate *ó d'aibig an tadhbhar* 'since the substance (of the child) ripened'.

I have suggested that the child is explicitly referred to in the line just dealt with. In the following line there is no difficulty except to decide to whom the reference is in *dá dtabhairt dá chéile* 'giving them to each other'. No suitable referent has been mentioned in the preceding lines. If we accept the interpretation given to l. 597 we have no choice but to agree that by 'them' is meant the child's parents. Since their union is the prototype of the kind of union advocated by the old man because it has produced the perfect child, they must be just as much a part of his implicit thought as the child and the manner of its procreation are in ll. 589-92. In my opinion this is the most natural way to understand 'them'.

The two lines may be rendered: 'since the substance (*or simply* child) which the Son of God bestowed ripened (matured) without any priest at all giving them (*sc.* the parents) to each other'. But, it might be asked, why *mac Dé* and not *Dia*? Because *mac Dé* suits the metre. There is no theological difficulty: the attribution of creation to the Second Person is a commonplace. For instance, Tadhg Gaelach, a contemporary of Merriman's, addresses Christ as *A Íosa dhealbhaig talamh 's tréan-mhuir dúinn*.

Notes

[1] A poetic misinterpretation of them (Frank O'Connor, *The Midnight Court*, p. 33) took an important place in a controversy carried on in the columns of the *Irish Times*, Aug.-Sept., 1946.

[2] The subtlety of Merriman's irony here appears to have passed unnoticed, and it even has been mistaken for a 'note of sincerity'. In my view, it is the measure of the comic absurdity of the whole proposal.

[3] O'Rahilly, Gadelica, 194 n.4, suggests that there

may be a 'slightly veiled allusion to the poet himself'. But why should Merriman choose to vaunt his own (alleged) illegitimacy in such a way?

[4] Apparently it is a compound of *ad-* and the verbal stem *fer-* 'grant', 'supply', in which case its root sense would be something like 'provision'. See Ped. V. G. 721n.

[5] One frequently hears the expression *tá ana-chré (fir) ann* 'there is great stuff in him'. The word equates with L. *pulvis*.

Patrick C. Power (essay date 1971)

SOURCE: An introduction to *Cúirt an Mhea-Oiche: The Midnight Court* by Brian Merriman, translated by Patrick C. Power, The Mercier Press, 1971, pp. 6-8.

[*In the following essay, Power examines the structure of "The Midnight Court" and connects it with other examples of Irish poetry.*]

Cúirt an Mhean-oiche—The Midnight Court—written by Brian Merriman in 1780 is considered one of the most important contributions to Gaelic literature in the eighteenth century. The treatment of the theme, the richness of the diction and the length at which the poet successfully sustains his work, entitle it to the fame it has gained since it was composed.

The theme is the celebration of the right of woman to sex and marriage. In developing his theme, the poet satirizes unmarried men, old impotent suitors and older women married to young fellows. In addition to this he advocates the removal of the clerical law of celibacy in the Roman Catholic Church. He refers to the condition of Ireland under British-orientated rulers and—in a short passage—makes a scathing attack on the manner in which the administration of justice was conducted. The mood of the poem is basically serious but an earthy, goodhumoured mockery pervades it. This healthy laugh at sex and the idiosyncracies of men and women in sexual relationships is typically Irish, one feels, and it seems to find its finest expression in Gaelic literature. There is no puritanic prissiness nor prudery in *The Midnight Court* but, on the contrary, a wholesome attitude which strikes an artistic balance between simpering coyness and pornography. One recalls the spirit of the Middle-Irish *Aided Fergusa* and George Moore's *A Storyteller's Holiday* where the same rollicking mood prevails.

The richness of the language in this poem is part of a poetic tradition which went back over very many centuries. The style reflects a rural community. The poem opens with a description of mountain, lake, woods, swans, fish and birds together with a hunting scene.

Throughout the poem the rural community which Merriman knew so well is reflected: a description of a hovel, a lively delineation of a wedding-feast, a list of aphrodisiacal herbs, many references to farming as well as a passage describing some divinatory practices to enable girls to find a husband! This places the poem among what one might call 'peasant-poetry'. Merriman often indulges in a riot of adjectival description as, for example, when a lady speaks of her own beauty and when she describes the qualities of a satisfactory mate. These 'runs' of adjectives follow an old tradition in Gaelic literature and testify to the love of word-music and pure sound which was the delight of the eighteenth-century poets, above all.

One may describe the structure of *The Midnight Court* as that of the *aisling*. The *aisling* was very popular in the eighteenth century in Ireland and was a vision poem with Jacobite sympathies and, one might say, propaganda. Merriman follows the *aisling*-formula:

1. The poets walks at morning in the countryside and the setting is described. (lines 1-30)

2. He falls asleep and meets a lady in dream. (lines 31-60)

3. She represents to him the evils afflicting Ireland and stresses one—the number of unmarried ladies there. (lines 61-112)

4. She informs him that a court is in session where the fairies (the shee) discuss this problem and drags him there. (lines 113-166)

5. In the shee-court the problem is discussed by a lady and an old cuckold. This takes up the bulk of the poem. (lines 167-952)

6. The fairy-queen gives her decision to this problem and the unmarried poet is seized by the ladies as an example of the unmarried one reluctant to take a lady and he is flogged mercilessly. (lines 953-1094)

7. The poet awakes from his sleep and dream.

The metre and lively rhythm of *The Midnight Court* help in no small way to retain the interest of the reader. It is written in riming couplets, but it should be remembered that 'rime' in Gaelic verse is not the exact 'rime' as in English but assonance which is often a much more subtle ornamentation than the other when used by a skilful craftsman. Each line of the poem also has a pair of assonantal stressed syllables. The metre and rhythm is the nearest that Gaelic literature has to the octosyllabic couplets used by writers such as Dean Jonathan Swift whose work may have been known to Brian Merriman. Whether Swift influenced Merriman or otherwise is quite irrelevant, however, because in the matter of metrics Gaelic poetry is far richer than English ever was or is. *The Midnight Court* glides along on its impish way to gather in more than a thousand lines much of the fun and sense of humour which helped a dispossessed and depressed and deprived people to preserve their identity. This is some measure of Brian Merriman's achievement in this long poem.

Very little is known about the author and the correct form of his name in Gaelic has been disputed. He is said to have been a love-child. That the writer of such an unusual poem should have remained so obscure is very strange indeed because poets were honoured by the poor Gaelic-speaking people then and always. Whatever about Merriman, his poem became exceedingly popular in Munster and many of the old Gaelic speakers could quote long passages by heart and very often the whole poem. All we know definitely about Merriman is that he was a native of County Clare, where he appears to have been born in the middle of the eighteenth century; that he lived for a while in Feakle in that county and that he died in Limerick in 1805.

One may go through *The Midnight Court* and seek influences from English Literature and the love-poetry of the Middle Ages in Ireland, but it still remains a real Gaelic phenomenon which arose out of Irish life and Gaelic tradition; a work full of the good-humoured bawdiness which one may still hear in the countryside today over pints of porter in the company of men!

Margaret MacCurtain (essay date 1974)

SOURCE: "Pre-Famine Peasantry in Ireland: Definition and Theme," in *Irish University Review*, Vol. 4, No. 2, Autumn, 1974, pp. 190-92.

[*In the following excerpt, MacCurtain highlights the conflict between the courtly poetic genre of "The Midnight Court" and the poem's evocation of peasant culture.*]

From another angle (not quite that of Daniel Corkery[7]), there was a hidden Ireland that belonged to the peasantry who communicated with each other in the Irish language and through Irish customs. It was the rich Gaelic culture of **"The Midnight Court"**: passionate, earthy, explicit in its sexual imagery, belonging to a world where sexual experience was highly valued, a known way of enjoying life. But note that the ideal of good conduct which comes through in **"The Midnight Court"** is a healthy one, the peasant demand for proof of fecundity and virility expressed in the begetting of children (a direct relationship with land as earth and seed and fruit). Though the poem

has all the roystering spontaneity of great folk poetry, as Dr Ó Tuama points out in the introduction to the Ó hUaithne Gaelic version,[8] in its form and expression **"The Midnight Court"** belongs to the courtly traditions of western Europe. But Merriman was not the court-jester of a vanished civilisation as Daniel Corkery seems to imply; he was making a plea for an affirmation of life.

> I leave it to you, O Nut of Knowledge,
>   The girls at home and the boys in
>   college,
> You cannot persuade me it's a crime
>   If they make love while they still have
>   time,
> But you who for learning have no rival,
>   Tell us the teachings of the Bible;
> Where are we taught to pervert our senses
>   And make our natural needs offences?
> To fly from lust as in Saint Paul
>   Doesn't mean flight from life and all,
> But to leave home and friends behind
>   And stick to one who pleased one's
>   mind.[9]

Moreover, Merriman was making important statements about Irish peasant culture. Possibly because he was a Protestant school-teacher within that Gaelic culture, he felt the needs of the Catholic peasant world calling out more clearly to the Protestant in him. Already by the seventeen nineties the Catholic Church in Irish society had become a powerful instrument of persuasion in the moral sphere. In what he says of bastardy and clerical celibacy, Merriman explores aspects of life about which Catholics feel constrained. In his dialogue between the young girl and the old man there is a great deal of compassionate insight into the social significance of raising a family within peasant culture, and an understanding of the inability of the sexes to comprehend what they want to say to each other. Nor does one have to strain credibility to discover the mirror-image of the Big House and its inmates. It is there—in the setting of the Court—and the Irish version is even more explicit:

> A building aglow from floor to ceiling,
>   Lighted within by guttered torches
> Among massive walls and echoing arches.[10]

The attempt to live graciously on the model of the gentry is to be found in the striving towards gentility expressed by the girl in her endeavour to look fashionable and pretty at fair and hurleying-match, and in the defendant's evident pride in the wedding feast he had provided, "plenty for all and nothing borrowed."

Reality lies somewhere between the static *demi-monde* of [Maria Edworth's *Castle*] *Rackrent* peasantry and the teeming closed world of **"The Midnight Court"** (which is given its proper dimension in relation to townsfolk and farming class in the detached observations of Humphrey O'Sullivan's journal[11]).

Notes

[7] Daniel Corkery, *The Hidden Ireland* (Dublin: Gill and Son, 1925). See also Louis Cullen "The Hidden Ireland: Re-assessment of a Concept" in *Studia Hibernica 1969*, pp. 1-47.

[8] Brian Merriman, *Cúirt an Mheán Oíche*, ed. Ó hUaithne (Dublin: Dolmen Press, 1968), p. 8.

[9] "The Midnight Court", trans. Frank O'Connor in *Kings, Lords, & Commons* (London: Macmillan, 1959), pp. 136-66.

[10] O'Connor, op. cit., p. 140. In the Ó hUaithne Irish edition, p. 21:

> An Teaghlach taithneamhach maiseamhail
>   mórtach,
>   Soilseach seasamhach lannamhail lómrach,
> Taibhseach tathagach daingean dea-
>   dhóirseach.

[11] Tómas de Bhaldraithe (ed.), *Cín Lae Amhlaoibh* (Dublin: An Clóchomhar, 1970).

Seán Ó Tuama (essay date 1981)

SOURCE: "Brian Merriman and His Court," in *Irish University Review*, Vol. 11, No. 2, Autumn, 1981, pp. 149-64.

[*In the following article, Ó Tuama argues that, whereas the prologue and epilogue sections of "The Midnight Court" are based on the Anglo-French Court of Love tradition, the monologues that form the body of the poem come from the late-medieval tradition of popular Irish folk poetry. Ó Tuama then proceeds to connect the poem's examination of illegitimacy with the presumed illegitimacy of Merriman.*]

The emergence of an uniquely talented poet such as Brian Merriman in County Clare in the second half of the eighteenth century was in many ways an unlikely event. The renowned Irish literary figures of the previous century and a half had without exception come from counties east of the Shannon, and given what we know of the Clare literary tradition one would not have held out great hopes for a remarkable work of literature to emerge there in the last decades of the eighteenth century. There had been of course a good deal of traditional poetic and learned activity in County Clare right down through the eighteenth and into the first half of the nine-

teenth century, but the quality of the verse composed by even early eighteenth-century Clare poets was generally pedestrian.

What we know about the author of the Court is very little indeed, and in some ways only helps to deepen the mystery about the provenance of the poem. He was born somewhere in County Clare (probably in Ennistymon) about 1749. It is generally accepted that he was of illegitimate birth—indeed the untraditional Irish name of Merriman may indicate that. It would appear that his mother married a travelling mason who reared Brian as his own son. Afterwards the family settled down in Feakle where Brian later taught school and cultivated a small farm assiduously (winning two prizes for his flax crops in 1797). In the year 1787 he married, had two daughters, transferred to Limerick city in 1802-3, where he continued to teach until he died suddenly in July 1805. Unusually for an Irish poet of the time, his death was noted in the local newspaper. He was referred to however, not as a poet but as a teacher of "Mathematics, etc."

This general picture gives us no clear idea of the personality or thinking of Brian Merriman. We do not know what education he had, literary or otherwise. The two minor lyrics ascribed to him, apart from the Court, show no sign of special literary talent. He does not seem to have communicated with other poets, or joined with them in their courts of poetry. Indeed in a wry comment in *The Midnight Court* he seems to refer to himself not as one who is a familiar of the poets but as one who is a familiar of the privileged genty of the county.

The Midnight Court is undoubtedly one of the greatest comic works of literature, and certainly the greatest comic poem ever written in Ireland. Scores of copies of the original manuscript were made in the immediate years after its composition: it was read with avidity, discussed and frequently added to. But we know of no other Gaelic work similar to Merriman's poem in its overall structure.

The Midnight Court is, in fact, a *Court of Love* in the typical medieval West European mould. Literary parliaments, assemblies and courts were very much in vogue in western Europe between the twelfth and sixteenth centuries.[1] One finds courts of love in Provencal, French and Latin as early as the twelfth and thirteenth centuries. Later one comes on them in German, Italian and English. In English the genre is found in abundance from the time of Chaucer right down to Elizabethan times. Swift's *Cadenus and Vanessa* is one of the last to be written in English.

In Merriman's court illegitimates are extolled, free love and the marriage of the Catholic clergy are advocated. Because of such ideas the poem has been looked on in the past as a work of the eighteenth century Enlightenment, owing its inspiration to authors such as Rousseau, Voltaire and Swift. This view would scarcely be acceptable nowadays. Indeed it has been pointed out[2] that much of the thematic material in *The Midnight Court* is found already in that bawdy part of the courtly thirteenth century *Roman de la Rose* which was added on to the original by Jean de Meung. The *Roman,* which in itself contains the influences of the court of love convention, was the literary Bible of the Middle Ages; it was translated into other languages, and referred to incessantly in love-literature down to the end of the sixteenth century. It is extremely doubtful, however, if Brian Merriman would have read any part of the *Roman de la Rose* in either French or English. How then did a teacher of Mathematics in Feakle, County Clare in the year 1780 become familiar with the medieval court of love conventions and manage to encapsulate in his poem the spirit of Jean de Meung, the man who (as Helen Waddell puts it) "laid his not overclean hands upon the Rose"?

In attempting to find an answer to this problem one has to take into account that both the court of love conventions, and some of the basic thematic material used by Jean de Meung were common currency in various literary forms and works for some time before and for long centuries after the composition of the *Roman,* and could have been available to Brian Merriman in a variety of ways. His debt to the general European tradition is best understood by looking at the overall shape of the poem, and noting its affiliations with various medieval literary forms.

The Midnight Court may be said to consist formally of a Prologue, three dramatic monologues, and an Epilogue. In the Prologue Brian Merriman tells us first of all of a typical court poet's summer morning's vision:

> By the brink of the river I'd often walk,
> on a meadow fresh, in the heavy dew,
> along the woods, in the mountain's heart,
> happy and brisk in the brightening dawn.
> My heart would lighten to see Loch Gréine,
> the land, the view, the sky horizon,
> the sweet and delightful set of the
>   mountains
> looming their heads up over each other.

Later a woman appears and leads the poet to a splendid court where the fairy-goddess of Thomond, Aoibheall, supported by an assembly of women, is presiding over a love-debate. Elements of the literary apparatus of the Prologue are found at random throughout medieval courts of love. The love-debate is common to all. The splendid court is frequent. The summer morning's vision in a nature setting appears in the

Roman de la Rose, and in a host of other poems. The assembly of women—sometimes presided over by the goddess Venus—is a theme in several poems. (One of the earliest courts, the Latin *Council of Remiremont* from the twelfth century, was in fact an assembly of nuns.) Of special interest perhaps is the vision-woman who leads the poet to the place of assembly. W. A. Neilson tells us that "the business of the cicerone in medieval allegory, especially in France, is usually given to a maiden."[3] He then goes on to discuss some medieval instances in which such a woman takes on the appearance of an old woman or hag. 'Hag' is a mild description of the woman who appears in Merriman's *opus:*

> a frightful, fierce, fat, full-bummed female,
> thick-calved, bristling, bony and harsh,
> her height exact—if I guessed it right—
> six yards or seven, with something over.

The matter to be debated at court is why young men (like Merriman himself) were not getting married, thus leaving the women dissatisfied, and the country's population declining. The first person to take the witness stand is a young girl who in a long dramatic monologue complains of the lack of a husband. The young girl's *Complaincte* is a standard medieval popular form. There are examples of it to be found in traditional Irish literature which may have been composed before Merriman's time. Merriman's girl, however, makes her complaint very much in the extended burlesque tradition of the late sixteenth-century English or French ballad—and at the same time she speaks right out of the heart of the Irish eighteenth-century scene:

> I'm certainly always on display
> at every field where the game's fought hard,
> at dances, hurling, races, courting,
> bone-fires, gossip and dissipation,
> at fairs and markets and Sunday Mass—
> to see and be seen, and choose a man. . . .
> I never would settle me down to sleep
> without fruit in a sock beneath my ear;
> I found it no trouble to fast devoutly
> —a whole day I'd swallow no bite or sup:
> I'd rinse my shift against the stream
> for a whisper in dream from my future
>   spouse. . . .
> But the point and purpose of my tale
> Is I've done my best and I've still no
>   man—
> hence, alas, my long recital!
> In the knot of years I am tangled tight,
> I am heading hard for my days of grey
> and I fear that I'll die without anyone
>   asking. . . .

The second dramatic monologue is an old man's retort who points out to the court that the young girl's own poverty-stricken life and promiscuous habits are the cause of her trouble:

> It's a terrible scandal and show for the people
> that a wretch like yourself, without cattle or
>   sheep,
> should have shoes with a buckle, a silken cloak
> and a pocket hanky a-flap on the breeze!

The old man goes on to tell how he himself was deceived in marriage—a theme which got an airing in the *Roman de la Rose*, in a few courts of love, and in many other medieval literary works:

> My total loss that I failed to choke
> on the night I was christened!—or before I
>   lusted
> to bed with that woman who turned me grey
> and drove me wild, without friend or wits.
> Everyone old and young could tell me
> how game she was in the country pubs
> to drink and buy, as they beat the tables,
> and relax on her back for married or single.
>   . . .
> In gruesome fact, she gave me a son
> (no sinew of mine) before its time:
> I'd a fireside family after one night!

There is an English ballad of the seventeenth century, *The Lass of Lynn's new joy for finding a father for her child*, which tells of a situation very reminiscent of the old man's plight.

In support of his plea that love should be free and marriage abolished the old man finally embarks on a paean in praise of bastards. The message of free love was of course the principal message preached in the second part of *Roman de la Rose*, but the praise of bastards seems to surface principally in Elizabethan times in England. Shakespeare's famous passage in *King Lear* is a case in point. One contemporary of Shakespeare's had this to say: "It is so little feared that unless one hath had two or three bastardes a peece, they esteeme no man."[4]

An eighteenth-century poem by Richard Savage, *The Bastard*, published in Dublin in 1728, may have been a part of Merriman's reading; but the tone of Merriman's plea is very much the tone of sixteenth and seventeenth-century English ballads:

> The dull offspring of the marriage bed
> What is it but a human piece of lead?
> a sottish lump, ingendered of all ills
> Begot like cats, against their father's wills!

Those of illegitimate birth, however, are thought to be of more sterling quality:

> Hence spring the noble, fortunate and great
> Always begot in passion and in heat.[5]

This last line is echoed closely in Merriman's resounding couplet:

> . . . *crobhaire crothadh go cothrom gan
>   cháim é*
> *Le fonn na fola is le fothram na sláinte*

—lit., 'he is a stalwart fully-fashioned without blemish/in the heat of the blood and the resonance of health.'

In the third monologue the young woman gives a harrowing commentary on the old man's performance as a husband to the young woman he married. The material here is typical of the bawdy medieval song type called *chanson de la malmariée*, which appears frequently in French, Italian, Scottish and indeed Irish popular literature. A Clare poet, Seán Ó hUaithnín, who preceded Brian Merriman by almost fifty years, had written such a song, but Merriman's extension of the theme leaves all his predecessors in the shade:

> It was gloomy doings, the nightly joy
> —oppression and burden, trouble and fright:
> legs of lead, and skinny shoulders,
> iron knees as cold as ice,
> shrunken feet by embers scorched,
> an old man's ailing, wasting body. . . .
> She'd never complain at a night of work
> but give a brave slasher as good as she got.
> She'd never refuse any time or place
> on bone of her back with her eyes shut tight,
> with never a balk or immoderate sulk
> nor attack like a cat, nor scrape nor scratch,
> but stretched her all like a sheaf beside him
> flank on flank, with her legs around him,
> coaxing his thoughts by easy stages,
> fingering down on him, mouth on mouth,
> putting her leg the far side of him often
> rubbing her brush from waist to knee,
> or snatching the blanket and quilt from his
>   loins
> to fiddle and play with the juiceless lump.
> But useless to tickle or squeeze or rub
> or attack with her elbows, nails or heels
> —I'm ashamed to relate how she passed the
>   night
> squeezing the sluggard, shuddering, sprawling,
> tossing her limbs and the bedding beneath her,
> her teeth and her members all a-shiver,
> not sleeping a wink till the dawn of day,
> performing and tossing from side to side.

The young woman proceeds after this to plead that vigorous young men—and well-fed priests in particular—should be drafted into marriage. The advocacy of marriage for priests is somewhat unheralded in the poem, and is, perhaps, a little surprising. A similar theme, however, is to be found in a few medieval courts of love. In the *Council of Remiremont* the love of a clergyman was deemed much more satisfying than the love of a clerk, and any nun not acting according to this dictum was ordered to be promptly ex-communicated. Similarly a twelfth-century Court called *Clerus et Presbyter*—attended only by clergymen—decided that priests should have concubines:

> *Habebimus, clerici, duas concubinas*
> *Si tandem leges implebimus divinas.*

They looked to the Pope to free them from the dire rules of chastity, as indeed does the President of our *Midnight Court* in its concluding section, the Epilogue.

The typical Court of Love ends with judgment being given and statutes being passed. A French poem, for instance, written by Christine de Pisan in 1399 and translated into English by Thomas Hoccleve, reflects this convention. It is decided here by the God of Love that in order to protect womenfolk all villainous untrustworthy men should be seized, tied, and roughly treated.

In *The Midnight Court* judgment is similarly passed, decrees proposed, and the date noted. President Aoibheall's judgment, however, is unexpectedly on the conservative side. She would not advocate that the institution of marriage be abandoned, but would allow rather unsatisfactory provisions to enable young people to enjoy as much permissiveness as possible—hoping old people would lend their names to the illegitimate offspring. As for the matter of priests being permitted to marry, she counsels patience in the hope that the Pope "with full assent of a Council" would in time remove the restrictions on marriage for the clergy. The only specific decree she does propose is similar to that proposed in the poem by Christine de Pisan: that all young men of marriageable age such as Merriman himself, who had not taken wives unto themselves, should be seized, tied, and severely punished.

It is reasonably clear, then, whatever of the immediate provenance of *The Midnight Court,* that it is throughout closely related to medieval and late medieval conventions of thought and literary structure. The Court of Love apparatus is especially apparent in the Prologue and Epilogue. The love debate itself, carried out in the form of three burlesque dramatic monologues which one does not normally associate with a Court of Love, has close affiliations with late medieval popular songs and ballads. Simpler models of one or two of these song types may have existed in Irish folksong for several centuries previous to this, but it is questionable whether the particular burlesque models of these which appear in *The Midnight Court* had been established in Irish for very long before Merriman's time. It is quite likely indeed that the matter and models that Merriman

inherited, and radically transformed in his poem, belong more to the post-Elizabethan era in Ireland.[6]

The Midnight Court, in its conventions and themes, does, of course, emanate ultimately from a west-European literary love-movement which began to make a profound impact on poetry in various languages as early as the twelfth century, and continued to do so, in different waves and guises until a new love poetry appeared in the Renaissance period. In my book *An Grá in Amhráin na nDaoine* I make the case that Irish folkpoetry was greatly influenced by this medieval movement which began to wield its influence in Ireland in the wake of the Anglo-Norman invasion (1169). My main thesis was that a great many of the types of Irish love-song being sung in our *Gaeltachtaí* today were to be found in troubadour and *trouvère* literature of the twelfth and thirteenth centuries. This argument has frequently been misinterpreted as meaning that direct French influence on our folksong was unquestionably the dominant one. That is not necessarily so. Certainly, on the evidence available, it seems quite likely that in earlier medieval times (*c.* 1200-1400) the French influence was greater than that of English; but it seems equally likely that in later periods (after 1400) English influence on both our folk poetry and literary love-poetry began to supplant that of French. Consequently it need not surprise us that many of the elements which constitute the structure of *The Midnight Court* should have made their way into traditional Irish literature in the post-Elizabethan era. English influence at that period was all pervasive. Indeed eighteenth-century Gaelic poets such as Eoghan Rua Ó Súilleabháin, Seán Ó Tuama, Aindrias Mac Craith could themselves write fluent—though execrable—verses in English. Two poets who lived for a time near Ennis and were contemporaries of Merriman, Seán Lloyd and Tomás Ó Míocháin, wrote some of their work in English. In fact in the year 1780 Lloyd published in Ennis a small book of prose in English called *A Short Tour, or an Impartial and Accurate Description of the County of Clare.*

Merriman, who spent most of his life in East Clare—where literary activity in Irish was minimal compared to West Clare—lived in an area and an environment which was much more susceptible to English influence than that of many other parts of Munster. The Irish language was receding rapidly there as it was in the area across the Shannon, North Tipperary, with which it was closely linked. The colonial gentry and the anglicised Irish gentry whom, we presume, Merriman numbered amongst his friends, would have been in constant touch with external commercial and cultural matters, not only in the nearby city of Limerick but in Dublin as well. At the same time it must be remembered that there was probably a high degree of bilinguality at all levels of society at this period in East Clare. Hely Dutton in his *Statistical Survey of County Clare* could still say of County Clare in general nearly thirty years

*Cúirt an Mhean-Oíche
The Midnight Court*

BY

BRIAN MERRIMAN

Text and Translation

by

PATRICK C. POWER

THE MERCIER PRESS
CORK AND DUBLIN

after the composition of **The Midnight Court:** "Almost all the better kind of people speak Irish to the country people."

It is not at all easy, however, to envisage how the specific structural and thematic elements of **The Midnight Court** reached Brian Merriman in his East Clare *milieu.* The principal difficulty here is that (in terms of English literature) the Court of Love elements, as found in the Prologue and Epilogue, seem to belong to high literary tradition, whereas the monologues seem squarely in the late-medieval popular tradition. Did Brian Merriman then read some solemn English Court of Love and give his own comic Irish version of it, adding in the popular monologues (models for some of which might already have been assimilated into the Irish language by poets who preceded him)? Or did he in fact have as a model an English bawdy court of love containing, perhaps, burlesque elements of a kind already existing in the popular Irish literary tradition? Or, or, or . . . the permutations of the possibilities are endless. But it must be noted that, despite the affiliations between **The Midnight Court** and the general thematic material of medieval courts of love, there is no single Court of Love we know of, which resembles it in any detail.

The Prologue and Epilogue contain many Court of Love elements, for instance, which are not to be found in Swift's *Cadenus and Vanessa*—a work which has been suggested in the past as Merriman's model. If Merriman did, in fact, use a bawdy Court of Love in English as a complete or partial model for his **Midnight Court** it may have been a work such as the 'lost' *Court of Venus* which disappeared from circulation in England in the second half of the sixteenth century after Puritan Reformers had heaped 'universal opprobrium' on it because of its scandalous nature. There is a great deal of scholarly debate as to what this 'lost' *Court of Venus* really was,[7] but assuming it was in the traditional Court of Love form, it could possibly have been the starting point for Merriman's poem. It is not too extravagant to suggest that one of his friends amongst the gentry could have had such in his ancestral family library, or could have picked it up in a bookshop in Dublin or Limerick. All that, however, remains a mere hypothesis. . . .

The Midnight Court can, of course, be read with immense enjoyment and profit by a reader who has no knowledge whatever of its literary background and antecedents. It is a poem of gargantuan energy, moving clearly and pulsatingly along a simple story line, with a middle, a beginning and an end. For a poem of over one thousand lines it has few *longueurs.* It is full of tumultuous bouts of great good humour, verbal dexterity and rabelaisian ribaldry. It is a mammoth readable achievement with little need of gloss.

The literary critic does need to know, however, what exact conventions or thematic matter Merriman inherited, or grappled with, if he is to throw light on the poet's personal investment in his work. The originality of his new creation cannot be appreciated or put into focus until the nature of the old material is discovered.

It would be a help, then, in discussing Merriman's achievement to know whether he did or did not have an immediate model or models such as the 'lost' *Court of Venus.* At the same time, anyone who is familiar with the general literary background I have been describing, will be reasonably certain that all medieval themes and conventions as handled by Merriman were changed, transmuted utterly, and that a new demonic comic creation emerged which is absolutely eighteenth-century Irish. It says a great deal for the vigour and richness of the Irish literary tradition that, in a late eighteenth-century bilingual environment, it could still be manipulated so creatively and with such astonishing assimilating force. Material which remains conventional, inert, semi-abstract or solemn in medieval literature—material such as that of the young girl's complaint, the celibacy of the priests, the *chanson de la malmariée,* the vision-woman or Cicerone, the natural splendour of the illegitimate child—is developed and extended into extraordinary new dimensions. Part of the poet's success here is due to the manner and verve with which he merges significant human detail, contemporary and other, with old themes. For instance, the girl's complaint is full of exact and fascinating references to Irish superstitions and behaviour at the time. Similarly the old man's diatribe against her contains precise observation of County Clare fashions in the second half of the eighteenth century. Again, the old man's description of the poor hovel the girl lived in is both more moving and more immediate than any social historian's—and yet somehow is not at odds with the comic vein of the poem:

> The soot dripping wet and the rising damp,
> weeds appearing in great profusion
> and the signs of hens inscribed across it,
> a weakened ridge and bending beams
> and a brown downpour descending heavily.

Even the often criticised conventional summer morning opening of the poem has a good deal of human personal observation in it which saves it somewhat from being a tiresome old cliché.

Merriman's success was mainly due of course to his eloquence, his tumultuous, comic eloquence. It is virtually certain for instance that in no medieval text, lost or found, did the matter of clerical celibacy get the kind of virtuoso treatment it gets in *The Midnight Court.* The poet's eloquence could take different shapes as the requirements of the narrative or the dramatic monologues dictated. It is at its most effective when it flies into bawdy or bombast or vituperation; but (at the other end of the scale) it can also be quite effective in creating an animated conversational-type dramatic situation (as in the long section which portrays the gossips around the fireside dealing with the illegitimate child). Irish poetry has traditionally leaned towards the dramatic situational type of lyric structure; the bombastic vituperative vein has also been hugely cultivated. So in mentioning Merriman's stylistic achievements, one is also stressing that as a creative writer he is operating mainly within his own Gaelic literary tradition. The bombast, the adjectival rhetoric, may on occasion overshoot the mark. Generally speaking, however, it is an essential part of the outlandish quality of the poem.

The more one reads *The Midnight Court*—especially in the light of all the medieval themes and conventions which are found radically transformed in it—the more one is convinced that the poet is speaking of issues which are real to him; that a disturbing eighteenth-century revelation of some kind is taking place, or trying to take place. I have gone on record before this[8] as saying that the major defect of the poem is that it has no deep personal insights, or even interesting insights to offer on the problems broached (as one would expect in the works of the gifted comic writers from Aristophanes to Beckett). I should like to modify that view somewhat now and say that I feel the major defect

of the poem is that the insights and feelings about love and marriage which abound in the poem are not brought to proper artistic definition. Yet behind all the comic alarms and excursions, behind the somewhat ramshackle old-fashioned structure, it must be noted that there is a certain deep sense of conviction and a consistency of feeling.

The *leitmotif* of the poem at all main stages seems to be that human beings must not allow their basic sexual vigour or instincts to become arid or conventionalised: the human animal must at all costs fulfil himself—whatever the rules or mores of society ordain at any given time. The young girl complains at the outset, for instance, of her own wasted years, and later complains of the wasted years of a woman-friend who was married off to an old man. She also complains of how the rules of obligatory chastity lay waste the manhood of priests. The old man, despite his own experience—or more likely because of it?—appeals for an end to marriage, being an institution which thwarts people (when they have to await the requirements of legal and ecclesiastical ordinances) from propagating "as nature ordains".

The idea of sex as vigour abounds in *The Midnight Court;* but there is no concept of sex as love, no feeling of sexual love being a spiritual or even a romantic force. The romantic concept of sexual love was developed inordinately in Western literature from the time of the troubadours, in literary *Courts of Love,* as well as in love-poetry in general. But as Johan Huizanga points out, a more archaic viewpoint co-existed with this concept during the middle-ages:

> We should picture to ourselves two layers of civilization superimposed, co-existing though contradictory. Side by side with the courtly style of literary and rather recent origin, the primitive forms of erotic life kept all their force. . . . [This] vision of never-ending lust implies no less than the screwed-up system of courtly love, an attempt to substitute for the reality the dream of a happier life. It is once more the aspiration towards the life sublime, but this time viewed from the animal side. . . . [9]

The archaic viewpoint prevailed very much in older rooted rural communities, and it is obviously the viewpoint of Merriman in this poem. Romantic love inside or outside marriage scarcely exists as far as this poem is concerned. Communion of mind or spirit is not entertained. If put to express the matter; Merriman (to judge by this poem) might easily have said that 'love' was a game or artifice invented by human beings to mask the preponderant animal vigour in their natures, which in his view was one of the greatest of human gifts.

Whatever Merriman might have felt or said on matters

such as this, he didn't express it in his poem in any coherent way. The artistic indication of this is that the mounting feeling of indignation regarding the waste of our human animal potential peters out in the series of lukewarm conciliatory positions taken up in the final section of the poem. In Aoibheall's lack-lustre judgment, nothing insightful or memorable is proposed or felt. Frank O'Connor says:

> " . . . from the moment the Queen gets up to deliver judgment the poem falls away. Clearly this was intended to be the point at which Merriman would speak through her, and express his own convictions about life, but something went wrong!"[10]

What most likely went wrong was that Merriman had no ready answers to offer about life. In this, of course, he was no different from some of the greatest of writers or artists. Unfortunately for him, however, the *Court of Love* traditional concluding structure demanded balanced rational answers of a kind a real poet cannot give. It is quite probable, then, that the *Court of Love* apparatus finally ended up for him more a hindrance than a help. Some more irrational or surrealistic type of concluding structure might have helped Merriman to reveal more climactically his dark, archaic feelings.

These feelings were obviously quite closely linked to the matter of his own illegitimate birth. Indeed the emotional climax of the poem as it stands is the old man's plea for bastards. One senses here more than anywhere else in the poem Merriman's personal statement as he struggles to deal in comic terms with a grievous personal hurt. In fact he goes so far as to have himself proudly introduced by the old man to the court as a first-class advertisement for illegitimacy.

The ostensible reason for the whole love-debate is said by the vision-woman at the beginning to be the declining population of the country; but the pressing artistic reason most likely was the poet's need to dramatize and understand some profound inner disturbance emanating from the circumstances of his own birth. In this reading one is tempted to see the *Court of Love* structure used by the poet as a device by which he can put his own mother and (legal) father in the dock. For whether one looks on the young woman who speaks to the Court as Merriman's mother or not, she certainly presents the point of view of a (gadabout) girl who can't find a suitable mate (Monologue I), and later (in Monologue III), of a girl who, for whatever reason, is finally married off to an old man. And whether or not one looks on the old man who speaks to the Court as the travelling mason whom Merriman's mother married, he certainly presents the point of view of one who was harnessed in marriage to a young woman pregnant by some other man. President Aoibheall's judgment that young people should be free to couple freely, and old men ready to lend their names to illegitimates (and so

preserve the institution of marriage) is in a sense then a validation of Merriman's situation as a child reared by a father not his own.

In trying to understand the hurt inflicted on Merriman by his illegitimacy it would probably be a mistake to think of illegitimacy as inevitably carrying the same type of slur in eighteenth-century Ireland as it did in the nineteenth-century Ireland, especially in the post-Famine period. Merriman's feeling here must have been much nearer that of aristocratic Gaelic Ireland than of post-famine Victorian Ireland. Values and arrangements in matters connected with sex and marriage in aristocratic Gaelic Ireland remained to the end quite at odds with Christian teaching. Different types of marriage, divorce and so on, were allowed by the brehon laws. Bishops and priests had wives ('concubines'). What Christians stigmatise as illegitimacy didn't exist as a concept—women were often proud to 'name' their sons after their aristocratic lovers and requisite arrangements were made it seems for their future. All this reflects the values of the Irish 'heroic' (pagan) society which prevailed by and large against the assaults of Christianity right up at least to the first half of the seventeenth century. One cannot see Brian Merriman in the year 1780 in County Clare being unaffected by such values. After all it was only a little over a hundred years before the date of Merriman's birth that the British Parliament (1634) passed an act forbidding polygamy amongst the Irish. And it was less than a hundred years before the date of Merriman's birth that an Irish poet reports (*c.* 1655) that it was still the custom to be unchristianly flexible about matters of love and marriage: "bean isteach is amach ag aoinfhear."[11] Merriman may have been strongly influenced in the manner of his writing about these matters by *Court of Love* themes or Elizabethan ballads—he may even have been influenced by whatever he read or heard of the ideas of Rousseau and other writers of the age—but it seems virtually certain that the deeper feelings he is expressing throughout are the archaic feelings of his own traditional society. In fact it is expressly stated in **The Midnight Court** as a part of the old man's praise of bastards, that with the advent of free love an Irish heroic society would emerge again. Men would inherit the strength and body of a *Goll Mac Mórna,* says the old man, heroic vigour would burgeon anew in fruitfullness. "It is", as Huizanga said, "once more an aspiration towards the life sublime, but this time viewed from the animal side."

English Common Law—with increasing aid from the Catholic Church—was engaged during the seventeenth and eighteenth centuries in combating both the ideals and the old practical arrangements regarding love and marriage in Gaelic Ireland. Under the growing power of English law, the legal position of an illegitimate in County Clare in 1750 would, of course, be a far cry from the relatively favoured position of the illegitimate in older times. Local lore has it that Merriman's natural father was a minor aristocrat, a gentleman (*duine uasal*) called McNamara. In the old Irish dispensation Merriman might have been proudly calling himself McNamara (or whatever) and could have inherited land or been placed in a lucrative career. In the new dispensation his noble lineage was disparaged, and he ended up on a small farm of land with a travelling mason as father and the career of a hedgeschoolmaster possibly the only one open to him. Was it the diminution of status and prospects for a person of his birth—rather than the strong social stigma later on attached to illegitimacy—which wounded Merriman? It is virtually certain, I think, that it was. Such diminution might also account for his courting of the local gentry rather than the poets. It also might explain what appears to be an irrelevant non-comic harangue against English law in the Prologue to the poem, where it is stated that remnants of the old aristocracy now "have neither wealth nor freedom".

There is one more matter worth mentioning in relation to Merriman's trauma: that is the possibility that the gentleman who was his natural father may have been a priest or seminarian. (It has to be stated immediately, however, that there seems to be no suggestion whatever in local lore, or otherwise, that this was so.)

A priest being married or engaging in sex would have been no novel idea to anyone with a knowledge of traditional (including eighteenth-century) life in Ireland. Indeed the young woman states in the poem that priests whom she calls *mian ár gcroí* ('the desire of our hearts') were known for their philandering propensities, and that a number of their progeny existed bearing false names. I have no knowledge, however, that the question of marriage for priests was in any way a live issue in eighteenth-century Ireland; and except in the context of Merriman's natural father being a priest or seminarian can one make artistic or emotional sense of the elaborate and passionate plea made by the young girl (who I suggested may be expressing Merriman's mother's viewpoint) that priests should be allowed to marry, or understand the concern of Aoibheall when she assures the court that indeed they should, and would in time, be so allowed:

> the time will come with the Council's
>   sanction
> and the Pope applying his potent hand;
> a committee will sit on the country's ills
> and release to you all, under binding bonds,
> a torrent of blood, a storm of flesh,
> those ardent slashers—your heart's desire!

Whatever further evidence does emerge in time about either Merriman's personal trauma or the literary background to his poem, it is reasonably clear I think that a prodigious creative comic energy was unleashed by him as he endeavoured to articulate his grievance within a framework yoked together from medieval bits and pieces. There may be no "sense of the incommensurate" in the poem—as Daniel Corkery claimed—but there is certainly more than a hint of a somewhat uncomprehending hurt, half-struggling to reveal itself.

In the undistinguished Epilogue, perhaps the liveliest sections are those which deal with Merriman's punishment because of his not being married. Despite the alarming fear which the poem attributes to him in the face of that punishment, he did not in fact marry for some nine years after the composition of **The Midnight Court**. He was then somewhere around his fiftieth year; which, even in County Clare, is nearer the average age of death than marriage.

Notes

[1] For a detailed comparison between *The Midnight Court* and various medieval works of the Court of Love genre see my essay "Cúirt an Mheán Oíche", *Studia Hibernica* (Dublin, 1964), pp. 7-27.

[2] Máirín Ní Mhuirgheasa, *Feasta*, May, 1951.

[3] *The Origin and Sources of the Court of Love* (Boston, 1899), p. 214.

[4] Nina Epton, *Love and the English* (Penguin, 1964), p. 102.

[5] Ibid., p. 103.

[6] This speculation reverses a former suggestion of mine in "Cúirt an Mheán Oíche", *Studia Hibernica*, p. 19, that the Court of Love genre might have existed already in the fifteenth or sixteenth century Gaelic literary tradition.

[7] For various viewpoints see R. A. Fraser, *The Court of Venus* (Duke University Press, 1955) and C. A. Huttar, "Wyatt and the Several Editions of the *Court of Venus*", *Studies in Bibliography* XIX (1966), 181-95.

[8] Ibid., *Studia Hibernica*, p. 23.

[9] *The Waning of the Middle Ages* (Penguin, 1955), pp. 110-12.

[10] Frank O'Connor, *The Midnight Court* (London, 1945), p. 10.

[11] Cecile O'Rahilly, *Five Seventeenth Century Political Poems* (Dublin, 1952), p. 73.

Cosslett Ó Cuinn (essay date 1982)

SOURCE: "Merriman's Court," in *The Pleasures of Gaelic Poetry*, edited by Seán Mac Réamoinn, Allen Lane, 1982, pp. 111-26.

[*In the following essay, Ó Cuinn translates much of "The Midnight Court" into English, pointing out passages' connections to classical literature as he goes.*]

'Cúirt an Mheán Oíche' does not mean 'courting at midnight' as is said to have been assumed by whoever was responsible for refusing permission to erect a monument to Brian Merriman in Feakle graveyard in 1947. Just so, in 1957, the Archbishop refused to let the body of Nikos Kazantzakis lie in state in an Athenian Church. He, among a lot of other things, had written a sequel to Homer's *Odyssey* in a very countrified dialect of spoken Greek. There were so many words, collected from farmers and fishermen, and unintelligible to the urban lumpen-intelligentsia, that he had to provide a new dictionary. Again, the idylls of Theocritus were written not in Attic or Koine Greek but in a difficult Doric dialect. Peasant literature? Yes, but with a very ancient and living tradition behind it, both written and oral. And in these respects those two great masterpieces, two thousand years apart, were very similar to the Midnight law-court, or rather judicial enquiry with royalty on the bench; the word 'Cúirt' can suggest that, and maybe also remind you of the proverb 'If you go to a court or a castle, have a woman on your side'.

The author, Brian Merriman, was born about the year 1749 at Ennistimon, County Clare, the son of a travelling mason, who moved to Feakle some miles away. There Brian grew up, and taught for about twenty years (c. 1765-85) in a 'hedge-school', one of the clandestine rural academies of the Hidden Ireland. He had a little land, which he farmed successfully enough to win two prizes for flax crops from the (Royal) Dublin Society in 1797. He married a woman from the parish (c. 1787), and had two daughters, and the family moved to Limerick. There, after two or three years, he died in 1805. He was described in the press notices as 'Teacher of mathematics, etc.', as could also have been said of Lewis Carroll . . .

Seven years before his marriage, in 1780, Merriman had written his brief epic of 1026 lines. It circulated orally, and in copious manuscripts, and achieved a wide popularity, but was not printed till 1850. In 1905 Stern's edition, with German translation, introduced it to scholars all over Europe. Since then, English translations have been published by Percy Arland Ussher, the late Lord (Edward) Longford, Frank O'Connor, David Marcus, Patrick Power, and (in part) Brendan Behan. I am venturing to use a translation of my own in this essay: quotations from the original are taken from the revised text prepared by the late David Greene which was, until very recently, the best available (it has now been superseded by a definitive edition, the work of Liam Ó Murchú).

I also rely heavily on the research and judgement of Seán Ó Tuama. He has a fine passage on Merriman's *líofacht dhochreidte*, that incredible speed and gusto, that rolls along like a tidal wave, and yet is kept in control by the rider as if a stallion. But why does he find fault with Merriman for not being like Rabelais or Aristophanes? Why ask *poitín* to be like absinthe or ouzo? Abstract things, like 'deep personal insights' and 'criticisms of life' are found in books *about* writers. Let me be shockingly concrete: I have struggled with the difficult old-fashioned French of Rabelais, chosen fifty years ago as a Christmas present from a maiden aunt, and I'd suggest that the Abbey of Theleme, that co-educational College for students of both sexes with its motto 'Do as you like', is akin to Merriman. As for Aristophanes, he was a conservative, hankering for the pre-war status quo. He never tried to understand progressives like Euripides and Socrates, and poured out a lot of jeering propaganda against them which probably contributed to Socrates' fate. His plays were part of a pagan fertility rite in which bawdiness was a religious duty, but they contain some good fun and exquisite poetry. The 'New learning' advocated by Rabelais meant the study of those ancient classics. To Calvin, whose French is much more clear and lucid, it meant the study of the Greek New Testament. Satirists and Bishops are often better at looking back, and telling us what is wrong with the world. That's their job—but they must *not* try to quench the spirit, or silence the prophets. T. S. Eliot has well said that poetry is great through the width and precision of its expression of emotion, not through its intellectual framework.

Seán Ó Tuama shows that there are hardly any ideas (including the abolition of celibacy and marriage!) that were not discussed in the Courts of Love and associated literature between the thirteenth and sixteenth centuries. Merriman takes up these abstract themes and puts life and passion into them, as well as a certain bawdy humour, altogether in a medieval sort of way, not unlike Ariosto. He could do so in the Irish-speaking world; itself, in good as well as bad ways, a mainly oral tradition from still earlier times. The prologue to his 'Court' will be not unfamiliar to those who have read Chaucer or Langland.

The poet sets off on his favourite walk on a July day—surely barefoot:

> *Ba ghnáth mé ag siúl le ciumhais na*
> *habhann*
> *Ar bháinseach úr is an drúcht go*
> *trom . . .*

I choose the river path, where
  feet
In dewy grasses cool their heat.
Through a tree-fledged glen I
  edge my way
Made by the daylight brisk and
  gay.
Then my heart brightens into
  eyes
That see to where Lough Gréine
  lies.
Earth, land, and circumambient
  air
Are mirrored in its waters fair.
What a formidable beauty show
The mountain ranges, row on
  row,
Purple above, and green below!
The dry heart would grow
  bright again,
Long feelingless, or filled with
  pain,
One pauperized and penniless
Would cease to feel his bitterness
If he took time to stop and stare
Over the green treetops to
  where
The awkward squads of ducks
  look queer
Upon the mistless water clear,
As, slipping through their midst,
  a swan
Leads them majestically on.
Fish, full of fun, jump one perch
  high,
Their speckled bellies catch my
  eye.
Lake waters sport upon the
  shore,
Raising a great gay blue-waved
  roar.
On merry boughs the loud birds
  sing,
Near me the deer mid green
  shaws spring,
The huntsman's horn with
  merry sounds
Calls me to see the fox and
  hounds.
Yes, yestermorn did not betray
Dawn's promise of a cloudless
  day,
And Cancer topically let fly
One tropic day in late July;
Fresh from night's rest, the sun
  could play
At work, and burn all in its
  way,
But did not strike and had not

found me
Where treeleaves wrapped the
  green flag round me.

Then he finds a shady ditch amid the green growths, and sinks to sleep and dream. Amid an electric storm a huge Brobdignagian policewoman arrests him as a vagabond bachelor. She talks of oppression and mis-government and declining population (although it can be shown that the rural proletariat was rapidly increasing in numbers at the time). She hauls him off to the Fairy Palace of Magh Gréine, where Aoibheall of Craigléith, Queen of the Munster *Sídhe* (faery otherworld) is holding a Judicial Enquiry into the state of the country. The first witness is a *Cailín Domhnaigh* ('Sunday Girl')—always well dressed to attract men, yet always outdistanced by fat, ugly or smelly girls with dowries:

> *Táim in achrann daingean na*
>   *mblianta*
> *Ag tarraing go tréan ar na laethaibh*
>   *liatha*
>
> The years have crept up, held,
>   and caught me
> And gripped me fast: till day by
>   day
> I wither and grow old and grey.
> I've not had one proposal: I
> Lose hope of more before I die.
> Let me to no dim spinster fade
> Nor be a meaningless old maid
> Without her man to give
>   protection
> Or child or friend to lend
>   affection
> Huddled beside the fire, now
>   grown
> Unused to vistors, alone.

There is some real pathos there, over a subject usually a butt for raucous humour. But now the rebuttal: an old wheezy man staggers to his feet and rage fires him to a vigorous attack:

> *Is furas, dar liom, do chúl bheith*
>   *taibhseach*
> *Chonac lem shúile an chúl 'na*
>   *loigheann tú . . .*
>
> Your hair-dos do show easy
>   grace
> And many make-ups give you
>   face,
> But don't you air that high horse
>   head
> For I've seen where you make
>   your bed;
> No sheet, not even one coarse

spun thread
Of blanket, quilt or coverlet,
Only a tattered mattress set
Upon the floor, full of your wet,
In a dark filthy cabin where
There is no stool, bench, seat or
    chair;
The water oozes from the
    ground
And trickles down the walls all
    round.
Though weeds grow thick in
    rotting thatch
Full of the paths that lean hens
    scratch,
Though couples sag and ridge
    holes slip
And rafters have begun to dip,
The roof's still up to drop and
    drip.
Or if a rainstorm comes, to
    drown
All in a torrent of dark brown.

Where, he asks, did the girl get her finery? And answers himself: she got it for love. *He* married a similar young lady, who too speedily presented him with a fine healthy boy. So why not abolish marriage? It would save money, and remedy the depopulation, and all children would be equally legitimate or illegitimate, as among the animals. And here, like Shakespeare in *King Lear,* he gives vent to praise of bastards (in the old sense of the word). But the girl counter-attacks:

Oh it's easy to talk for old lepers
    like you
Of the woman you've never yet
    gone into:
That subject needs somebody
    strong and firm
And you are an old limp
    boneless worm . . .
If that modest matron's
    desperate need
Led to escapades, then her case I
    plead:
Is there fox on the hill, is there
    fish by the shore,
Are there eagles that sweep on
    their prey and soar
Or hinds that are blithe when
    the stags get gay,
That would go for a year or a
    single day
Without snatching pasture or
    catching prey:
'Twould be unnaturally absurd
For any animal or bird . . .

In the Irish the words are really winged, shooting out in parabolas in all directions like tracer bullets.

*An bhfuil sionnach ar sliabh, ná iasc i
    dtrá,
Ná fiolar le fiach, ná fia le fán,
Chomh fada gan chiall le bliain ná lá
A chaitheamh gan bia, 's a bhfiach le
    fáil.*

Notice the metre, with the double assonance *ia/ia* in the middle, and the vowel rhyme in *á* at the end of the line; it's much easier in Irish than in English to find the 'good bad rhyme' Yeats looked for. And Merriman varies not only the rhythm, but the weight and texture of his verses—'making the sound echo the sense'. A vaguer, more questioning rhythm leads on to another still relevant problem—not yet fully solved:

*Is mithid dom chroí bheith líonta ' e
    léithe
Is m'iongántas tríd gach smaointe
    baotha
Cad do bheir scaoilte ó chuíbhreach
    céile
In Eaglais sínsir suim na cléire . . .*

My head has hairs now turning
    grey
Wondering through wandering
    thoughts away,
The object of my fond research
Is in my old ancestral Church:
Why are its clergy woman-free
And given to celibacy? . . .
Some we'll do without, who'd
    require
Castrati from the papal choir,
Insects whose business is to ail,
Colts who know only how to
    stale!
But how can men whose
    manliest part
Could drive its nail straight in
    with art
Go idling off to dream and *Roam*
And shirk the work there is at
    home . . .
Their praise I've often heard,
    none mocks
But lauds such fathers of their
    flocks . . .
We've seen good fruits too of
    their games
In children bearing borrowed
    names . . .

If Merriman was one of *these*—not just illegitimate as Seán Ó Tuama has suggested, but if his father was in

fact a Roman Catholic priest—it explains the mixture
of indulgence and indignation and passion with which
he dwells on these matters.

Aoibheall takes up the subject with a final prophecy of
a Papal decision:

> Keep silent if you can't agree
> Don't contradict the Hierarchy
> Leave them since they're so
>   sensitive
> In that past age in which they
>   live
> Yet married men they still shall
>   be
> Whoever lives long enough to
>   see:
> Those red hot pokers go on duty
> To soothe the soft desires of
>   beauty.

As President of the Court, Aoibheall is a flop, a mere
chair-person who sums up what others have already
stated. But she enacts some Draconian legislation. Old
bachelors to be liquidated—with torture:

> Let me see agonies and groans
> Before you kill the old spent
>   drones!

Young ones, beginning with Merriman, to be stripped
and scourged (giving a chance of amendment of life)
by the ladies present!

> That babe who hated
>   spinsterhood
> Clenched her two fists as there
>   she stood
> Like one who's on to something
>   good:
> And then she jumped her own
>   full height
> Crying in rapturous delight
> I've got the object of my lust.
> How long I've longed you stale
>   old crust
> To have that seat of yours to
>   dust . . .
> You lazy slob, make no pretence
> To try to put up a defence.
> What woman witness will
>   advance
> Due proof of work as a free
>   lance?
> What good have you done in
>   your life?
> Show you've consoled one
>   lonely wife!
> With your permission I present

> Him, Maiden Ma'am Right
>   Reverent
> For medical examination
> Strip quick . . . commence the
>   operation . . .

There follows a portrait of the poet himself—unflatter-
ing at first, but admitting certain social qualities. Is it
a self-portrait—or a wry acknowledgement of what
Merriman assumed to be the popular view of him? We
can only speculate.

> He's palely puffy for a man
> I for my part prefer suntan
> He isn't married yet we see,
> Owing to some foul deformity
> He hides with much dexterity,
> —See how the cross slob scowls
>   at me—
> Which still, 't would seem has
>   left him free
> To enter high society
> A music maker and a sporter
> He's popular in every quarter
> Drinking, gambling without
>   cessation
> With cultured men of education
> And all his friends stand high in
>   station
> —But if I had him as a spouse
> I'd tame and I'd house-train that
>   louse—
> And I can give full proof that he
> Is of th'extremest villainy
> Merriman is this scoundrel's
>   name
> Yet he's impressive all the same
> And pleasant too when that's his
>   aim
> His solid qualities can claim
> Profits for others from his fame
> And merry witty airy game.

And now they set to execute the sentence—

> Bind his hands, Máire, behind
>   his back
> Let Maeve and Muirinn join the
>   pack,
> Sheila and Saiv the rope's end
>   crack:
> Come carry out with many a
>   whack
> The penalty our Queen
>   prescribes—
> Let every cord cut separate
>   kibes,
> Let the big pink pig squeal
>   afresh,

Each time they sink deep in his
 flesh,
Lavish all torments you can find
And don't spare Brian's big
 behind . . .
Cut deep, and pay him all we
 owe
Flay off his skin from top to toe
Round Ireland let the echoes go
Let all the bachelor hearts know
And tremble where they're lying
 low.

A believer in healthy sexual fertility, he very properly
denounced mass-produced celibacy, but was a bit blind
to the vocation and grace that can make virginity fruitful—the 'ideal of our Lady'.

But let him have the last word, and testify to the Faith
that was in him, as in an extraordinary passage he calls
on Aoibheall of the *Sídhe,* as an immortal who has
been an eyewitness of the incarnation:

Pearl, to whose perfect memory
The Great Event's contemporary
The Heavenly vision present
 sight
The History a mystery of light:
Set that eternal music free
Let words declare that victory.
O let the Lamb damn lies and
 say
Out truths that cannot pass away
It was no spinster made God
 human
God's mother was a married
 woman,
He through his prophets rules
 what's good
And highly favours
 womanhood.
Dia nárbh áil leis Máthair aonta
Is riail gach fáidhe i bhfábhar
 béithe . . .

So while they thus gloat gleefully over this poor victim, the secretary inscribes the date of the decree—
1780—

Slow she wrote the slow date,
 the Guard
Sat and watched me, their eyes
 were hard:
Then torment ends, the storm
 clouds break.
I jump up, rub my eyes and
 wake!

And so it ends. Seven years later, as we have noted,

Merriman married, and I'm sure was a good husband
and father. That one wild prophetic outburst preserved,
and also expressed, the sanity of an orthodox yet liberal traditionalist.

He could not claim the 'intellectual power of light-giving
imagination' of major poets like Shakespeare or Aeschylus
or Dante; but Dante shows some of Merriman's type of
humour when Virgil and he are 'protected' by a body-
guard of ten devils marching along to music furnished by
their leader's behind (so like some of our self-approved
protectors today!), and again Beatrice in Paradise talks to
him as a mother does to a cracked child. Dante, according to Boccaccio, suffered from *lussuria* in his maturer as
well as his younger years, and played with fire in the
form of a romantic passion for another man's wife, so as
to produce the most sublime of all jokes—the *Divine
Comedy.* Merriman played with a more fleshly fire of
drúis (which is the Irish brand of *lussuria*) by socializing
rather than sublimating it. It taught both of them humility, and a power to poke fun at themselves, that is rare
among poets. So I would suggest that **'The Midnight
Court'** is such a *kathartic*—smelly as it ought to be: not
porn, but anti-porn—a sort of karate in which the attacker
is allowed full momentum so that he may knock himself
out.

An chuid acu tá go táir 'na smaointe
Foireann nach foláir leo a gcáil
 bheith sínte . . .

Some think, whose minds are
 cruel and base,
They'll find distinction in
 disgrace,
Drop names of ladies whom
 they woo,
The public get a private view
Of everything they say they do.
They find it pleasant to act thus,
They even term it chivalrous.
Even she who has denied a
 favour
Will find denials cannot save her.
They've thus corrupted and
 betrayed
Many a chaste matron and
 young maid.
Yet it was not concupiscence
That was the cause of their
 offence,
Or heat of blood, or lust intense,
Or pleasure in the joys of sense,
Or a priapism too immense—
They want a noisy audience
That roars and gloats and licks
 its chaps,
They well deserve to get the
 claps.

At some no women set their
　caps,
Hundreds have never felt at all
The pleasure of their sex's call
Their manliness is just a loud
And empty boast before a
　crowd,
Incapable of any action
Which is to women's
　satisfaction,
Destructive female rage must
　follow,
Abolishing deceits so hollow.

Gearóid Ó Crualaoich (essay date 1983)

SOURCE: "The Vision of Liberation in Cúirt an Mheán Oíche," in *Folia Gadelica: Essays Presented by Former Students to R. A Breatnach*, edited by Pádraig de Brún, Seán Ó Coileáin, and P'adraig Ó Rianin, Cork University Press, 1983, pp. 95-104.

[*In the following article, Ó Crualaoich systematically analyzes the major arguments of the previous sixty years regarding "The Midnight Court" and situates Merriman's poem in its Irish and European historical contexts.*]

Cúirt an Mheán Oíche is surely the most genuinely popular poem in Irish known to us. Among ordinary people, of perhaps no very sophisticated literary tastes, it has been, and still is, a sort of instant success. The delights of its humour and its energetic fluency account for much of its popular appeal. For a people allegedly appreciative of verbal excellence *An Chúirt* constitutes a sort of test-piece. The attractiveness of its broad comedy is self-evidently not confined to Irish speakers only or indeed to the Irish people in general. The plain honesty and frankness with which Merriman deals with bodily appetite and the frustration of its satisfaction is guaranteed to have the widest appeal at the popular level where the niceties and reticences of 're-spectability' are commonly regarded as humbug and hypocrisy. In my view, however, the power of Merriman's vision, the message of the poem, if you like, must also play a role here. I know that other commentators have denied the existence of any such message or personal vision on the part of Brian Merriman as expressed, at least, in *The Midnight Court.*[1] I think they are wrong and that it is possible for us to see in the poem the expression of a personal vision that is at once large and psychologically very powerful. Seán Ó Tuama has spoken of the 'leitmotif of the poem' at all main stages as being its concern that human beings must not allow their basic sexual vigour or instincts to become arid or conventionalised and Ó Tuama sees a connection here with some kind of disturbing socio-political process in the poet's own late eighteenth-century world.[2] A main

purpose of this paper however is to show that such a concern is more than a motif in *The Midnight Court,* that it is, rather, the poet's chief assertion and the deepest strand of the poem's meaning; a meaning that strikes home in a very fundamental way to the ordinary Irish people (or that segment of them who are able to have access to it) who have been enduring the official respectability promoted by a largely English-speaking and increasingly Catholic middle-class establishment since Brian Merriman's day. One recalls Seán Ó Ríordáin's characterisation of the ordinary Irish people in the nineteenth century as a people so demoralised as to be prepared to believe that their reproductive organs were, *ipso facto,* an occasion of sin. Not only in the vigour of its language and the earthiness of its themes but also in the genuine liberalism and humanity of its vision of life *The Midnight Court* has represented a minor, and, of necessity, a subterranean kind of triumph for basic qualities of human living denied practically any positive recognition in the Ireland of the nineteenth and early twentieth century.

The banning in the 1940s of a translation of *The Midnight Court* into English would seem to support the view that Merriman's poem was officially then regarded as still dangerously subversive of propriety. The academic treatment of the poem in the twentieth century also demonstrates, I think, the continuing existence of some of the attitudes of mind to which the vision of the poem itself is diametrically opposed. I will mention T. F. O'Rahilly and Daniel Corkery as two scholars for whom the poem seems to have been in some senses an unfortunate creation, best dealt with firmly once, and then left alone. While granting Merriman credit for his inventiveness both critics deny his work any high poetic status. Corkery says that Merriman, having no contact with a School of Poetry, a Cúirt Éigse, was *unable* to achieve greatness, confined as he was to common speech and folk models; that his verse is vigorous rather than refined and that, in general, Merriman constitutes a sort of bridge between the truly 'literary' poets of Munster and the mere 'folk' poets of Connacht.[3] He does grant Merriman occasional flashes of the devastating bleakness that he recognises as a characteristic Gaelic strain, but he finds in the poem neither music nor charm, nor, as he puts it, 'any awareness of the incommensurable'. O'Rahilly takes something of the same line.[4] The poem, he says, 'roams, but it never soars'. 'It is brilliant but its brilliancy is that of prose.' Despite its splendid rhythmicality it lacks any 'Divine Afflatus'. One gets the impression that Brian Merriman's poem made these critics feel uncomfortable and liable to dismiss *The Midnight Court* with hardly-disguised distaste. Frank O'Connor, on the other hand, hailed the poem as a masterpiece on the grounds that it 'cut the navel-string of the new-born democracy' of late eighteenth-century Ireland in a way very close to that of contemporary English verse.[5] For O'Connor, Merriman's work is another sort of bridge, a bridge from the aristocratic, semi-feudal, Gaelic world into the enlightened world of late eighteenth-century English literature. For O'Connor, Merriman is a kind of intellectual Protestant writing urbane couplets regarding the civil dimensions of life—in all but language an Anglo-Irish man of letters. Piaras Béaslaí seems to me to have been the early critic who responded most acutely to *The Midnight Court,* seeing in it an attack on the suppression of Nature and the consequent evils to which such suppression gives rise.[6] He saw Merriman as a moralist, encouraging 'a spirit of health and mirth and vigour' but seems, along with the other early critics, to have missed seeing Merriman's unique poetic achievement in embodying this moral in a work simultaneously employing the European motifs of the medieval love-courts and the Irish motifs of an ancient Celtic sovereignty myth. The overall effect of the poem if we can see it like this is, I contend, profound both in its conception and, at least partially, in its execution. The effect of the invocation of the sovereignty myth, chiefly in the person of Aoibheall, and the relevance which Brian Merriman creates for it to the social realities of east Clare and much more of the Irish countryside in the last quarter of the eighteenth century have not been properly understood, and it is to this aspect of *The Midnight Court* and of Brian Merriman's poetic achievement that I especially want to call attention.

The Midnight Court's great indebtedness to the later medieval Court of Love tradition has been pretty obvious for a long time now, having been earlier shown by scholars like Gerard Murphy[7] and H. R. McAdoo.[8] Seán Ó Tuama has recently gone on from further demonstration of this to asking how specific elements of the poem, both thematic and structural, that are traditional medieval Love Court elements can have suggested themselves to Merriman in east Clare in the 1770s, and I am interested in his suggestion of a submanuscript level, popular borrowing of such elements from post-Elizabethan English literature into Irish popular tradition by Merriman's time.[9] The town of Gort, it has been suggested, is likely to have been a special location in the district for such coming together of eighteenth-century English and Irish traditional literatures, frequented as it was by sailors off ships calling to Kinvarra. And since local tradition has a gregarious Brian Merriman playing his fiddle at social gatherings of all kinds in the locality, we can see that in his case this kind of link up is indeed possible. The other area of Merriman's indebtedness as regards *The Midnight Court* that has been generally, though not universally, conceded is in relation to the poets and writers of the Enlightenment and of eighteenth-century English letters. Corkery would dispute that Merriman had to look an inch beyond traditional folk themes to discover models for his treatment of marriage, bastardy and clerical carnality,[10] but in general we are asked to believe that the author of *The Midnight Court* was on terms of good acquaintance with authors such

as Voltaire, Rousseau, Swift, Savage, Goldsmith and Burns. Oddly enough, nobody seems to have pointed out the specific elements of Merriman's poem that are derived from such writers, or identified the actual Merriman lines in question—with the exception of Frank O'Connor who has twice argued[11] that the famous passage in the first monologue where the young girl lists out the wiles she has employed to obtain a partner[12] has been translated by Merriman straight from the pages of Robert Burn's poem *Hallowe'en.* There is certainly a striking similarity in the lists, and one can think of a series of intriguing possibilities, among which are the following: (a) it was Burns who translated from Merriman; (b) there was at that time an uncommonly similar folk culture—at least in regard to the business in question—in the hinterlands of Feakle and Ayr; (c) some one single account of popular tradition somewhere supplied both poets with a common model; (d) O'Connor is right and the celebration in 1980 of the 'Court's' bicentenary was at least ten years too early, since the poem *Hallowe'en* was not published before 1790. There is even a Renaissance connection for *The Midnight Court,* since James Stewart has shown[13] that the use in late Gaelic literature of a female parliament or assembly to discuss and promote morality and moralistic views—as in An tAth. Domhnall Ó Colmáin's *Párliament na mBan* is something essentially derived from the didactic of Erasmus, who was certainly no medievalist but who, very interestingly, but no doubt entirely coincidentally, turns out to have been himself illegitimate and to have invented a romantically untrue account of the circumstances of his birth, *a lá* Richard Savage, another of the authors to whom Merriman is allegedly indebted. There is, obviously, plenty of scope here for the worst kind of literary scholarship on *The Midnight Court.* Basically, it seems to me that Merriman combined two models to produce the structure of his poem. One of these is undoubtedly the Court of Love, probably in the burlesque versions of the *Roman de la Rose* tradition. But he embedded all the Court elements in the framework of the Aisling tradition—in both its early native form, concerned with Love and Prophecy, *and* in its eighteenth-century allegorical form concerned with the restoration of political sovereignty. What he produced is a unique Irish poem which brings one of the deepest myths and traditions of Irish literature to bear in an extremely novel way on issues arising from the contemporary social and political scene. Though he writes in a sort of heroic couplet, Merriman is surely a mainstream Gaelic poet confronting the 'new world' with resources of language and metaphor rooted in the most ancient of Irish traditions. That we now must see him as the last of an old line rather than the first of a new, is something dictated by real events in the real world. As things turned out he brought no one with him into an educated and urban world of Gaelic letters in the 1800s, but he could have been a bridge, to use that metaphor a third time, if it were to be that the native literary tradition was to extend in other than a vestigial way into the increasingly town-orientated, commerce-dominated, Ireland of the nineteenth century.

Claims made concerning the 'revolutionary' nature of *The Midnight Court* in seeming to call for the abolition of marriage, for the exaltation of bastardy and for the casting aside of clerical celibacy have been refuted on the grounds that these themes are very frequently encountered both in the learned and popular traditions of medieval Europe. It is certainly true that their occurrence in his poem is not, in itself, solid evidence of Merriman's having been imbued with the notions of the European enlightenment. Yet the poem does seem to me to be extremely radical in another sense in regard to these matters. Merriman's concern throughout the poem is with the flowering of human sexuality and while this in itself is not a radical departure in literature, what is startling in the Irish literary tradition, is the informing of the call with the power and authority of the Gaelic sovereignty myth whose *bona fide* or writ in Ireland runs back to insular Celtic times. The use to which Merriman puts the myth in late eighteenth-century east Clare is, to my mind, truly revolutionary, in that he invokes its characters, its images and its power not in the cause of tribal or national sovereignty but in the cause of the civil and psychological liberation of the individual at the personal level.

It has been remarked that Romantic Love is absent from *The Midnight Court.* So it is, just as Romantic Love is absent from the earliest examples of the Aisling a thousand years previously and it is to this Aisling tradition stretching back far beyond the eighteenth-century allegorical variety of the genre that Merriman looks for the fundamental orientation of his poem. Early Irish, Proinsias Mac Cana tells us,[14] offers surprisingly little literature of love in the conventional medieval European sense. The 'wooings', the 'elopements' and other forms of early Irish love literature present us with lovers not in any personal roles but, instead, in mythological ones so that what is expressed in the text is the course of erotic encounter rather than the working out of personal relationship. This note, it seems to me, is struck again and struck very definitely in *The Midnight Court.* Once more the adjective 'revolutionary' can be used to describe what Merriman does to the Aisling tradition of his day. And he achieves his effect very simply. By locating his dramatic monologues, deriving partly from the burlesque version of the *Roman de la Rose* tradition, in a court presided over by Aoibheall of Craig Liath he is able by virtue of his poetic creativity of language, to transform the mythological tie between the sovereignty of Ireland and a rightful hereditary king into a relationship between woman and man and between both and the eighteenth-century Irish countryside at the social and psychological level. From time immemorial in Gaelic tradition, the mythological role of Love and Sexuality was bound up with the notion of the Divine Mother who personified the land and its well-being. For Irish poets from the earliest times to the eighteenth-century allegorists, the public welfare, the common good, of land and of people, was tied to the notion of mystical sovereignty and its embodiment in the person and authority of a rightful leader.[15] By the eighteenth century of course, real history had decreed that the liberation of Ireland as still envisaged by Aisling poets such as Aogán Ó Rathaille and Eoghan Rua Ó Súilleabháin—the return for instance of a Stuart king in place of a dispersed native nobility—was a hopeless dream. The Aisling poet Merriman also dreams of the liberation of the people but for him it is a civil and psychological liberation of the individual, at the carnal level first, that counts rather than some impossible political liberation in the terms of a bygone age. Both Ó Rathaille and Merriman each have a vision of a restored Ireland and of a restored Irish people and both deliver their visions with eloquence and with a profound sense of tradition. But they do so in very different ways indeed; the one with a backward-looking contemptuous regret, the other with a contemporary and dynamic comic gusto. It was not to any merely mortal royal liberator that Merriman looked for deliverance for country and people but to the older, supernatural, 'female' sovereignty of the spirit of the land itself. Thus he seeks to ensure the return and perpetuation of fertility and prosperity for all, not in the restoration of the Stuart or any other royal line but in the restoration of the primacy of 'fonn na fola agus fothrom na sláinte', the basic, healthy, animal, life instincts of the mature, adult, individual man and woman, free from conventional guilt or shame or repression. In effecting this transformation of the Aisling, Merriman liberates Sovereignty or Love—in the person of Aoibheall of Craig Liath—from its mythological role and brings it into play on the plane of the psychological and the naturalistic. In praising the allegorical Aisling poems, Daniel Corkery says that they are—by comparison with the Scottish Jacobite songs in English—in the heroic rather than the affectionate plane with the result that we are dazzled by the splendour of their art rather than moved by their intimacy.[16] It is my contention that Merriman deliberately chooses to move his Aisling away from this heroic plane, not, however, to indulge the affections but to liberate the psyche in a work that is full and fierce and carnal, and that yet is free of all sentimentality or shame, so that we his readers are ourselves humbled and liberated by his vision and by the maturity of its expression.

It is highly likely that contemporary eighteenth-century ideas regarding the freedom of the individual and the proper philosophical basis of social life influenced Merriman in writing his poetry, but the important point for me is that he expresses these ideas in a way that is so much within the traditional canon of Gaelic literature. Not for him any ideological celebration of the peasantry which was eventually the case with other leading intellectual and literary figures of the European Enlightenment. He picks up one of the oldest of traditional literary themes and by the invocation of its power and by the power of his own poetic imagination working through it he gives us a vision of a peasantry emancipated in a primary way, thereby presumably empowered to achieve other kinds of emancipation too.

It is interesting to note that of the eight motifs of the earliest form of the sovereignty-kingship myth listed by R. A. Breatnach,[17] Merriman uses four in *The Midnight Court*. These are: (1) the encounter with the *puella senilis* (the 'báille' of the Court being the old and ugly *alter ego* of the beautiful and gracious Aoibheall); (2) coition—which surely can be said to be rampant throughout the poem; (3) metamorphosis—it is the countryside itself and the future generations who will be transformed in fruitfulness and vigour rather than the mythological Aoibheall; (4) bestowal of sovereignty—it is the sovereignty of people over themselves that will be restored not that of any rightful or refugee king once Nature is set free and copulation flourishes in the countryside.

It is surely relevant that the 'spéirbhean' of *An Macalla*, Merriman's other Aisling-type poem, is also a personification of the countryside harping back to an older image than the 'spéirbhean' of the conventional eighteenth-century allegorical Aisling. *An Macalla* ends on a pious note with the poet appealing to the Lamb, an image of the Christian God, to grant release to all from their tribulations in a Heaven above. *The Midnight Court* has of course a tougher—if more immediately pleasurable—prescription for the winning of Joy.

As a voice of the hidden Ireland of the eighteenth century, Brian Merriman in his life—what we know of it—and in his poetry certainly represents the less rural, the 'urbanising' end of the social spectrum, though it is obvious that I am arguing that as a Gaelic man of letters he brings into this new world with him a feeling for, and a sympathy with, the oldest traditions of the Gaelic world. The transformation of the Irish countryside from a pre-capitalist and largely pastoral, political economy to an urban-dominated capitalist-industrial one is a process which, having begun to gather momentum in the late seventeenth century is, of course, not yet complete in our own day. The two great phases of this transformation that have relevance in the context of *The Midnight Court* are (1) the emergence throughout most of Ireland since the mid-seventeenth century of a new social world consisting of two great orders: a landowning, or land-holding, ascendancy on the one hand and a vastly more numerous order of tenant farmers and cottiers on the other; (2) the emergence of class distinctions within this new world as a result of population pressures and the competition for scarce resources in the course of the eighteenth century. These developments occur against a background of increased trading activity and the increased growth of towns whose influence, economic, social and cultural, permeates the countryside to an ever-greater degree. Ireland was, of course, not alone in undergoing such a social transformation, though the accompanying language shift gives the transformation of Ireland a tremendous finality, in cultural and psychological terms as well as in social. Right across Europe, however, from the Atlantic to the Urals and beyond, this transformation of society from being a hierarchy of orders—defined in terms of hereditary power or lack of it—to being a hierarchy of classes—defined in terms of accumulated wealth—is taking place throughout the eighteenth and nineteenth centuries. It is estimated that in the last quarter of the eighteenth century, 75% of the European population still lived on the land, and one historian speaks of the spectrum of subservience in what he calls 'the servile lands', running from France to Russia.[18] While all the British communities and to an even greater extent Ireland are peripheral to this whole process and need to be treated separately, nevertheless the remarks of the Russian historian, N. M. Karamzin, regarding the absence of any civil rights in Russia at the end of the eighteenth century seem apposite to the world of Brian Merriman in east Clare at this time. Writing in 1811, Karamzin says that Russians had no 'civil rights', properly speaking. 'We have only . . . the specific rights of the various estates of the realm; we have gentry, merchants, townsfolk, peasants and so forth—they all enjoy their specific rights, but they have no right in common, save for that of calling themselves Russians.'[19] When we add the Penal Laws to some such characterisation of the powerless and dispossessed state of the majority of the ordinary Irish people in Merriman's day—there had been 60 such laws enacted between 1695 and 1780—we can get some insight into the demoralisation that was still the lot of a majority of the Irish people in 1780. It was for these people at large that Merriman wrote, if he wrote for anyone other than himself, which is questionable, and his poem, his vision, struck some chord in them, if we are to judge by their response to it as reflected in its manuscript history, a chord that seems to have helped alleviate their distress and that provided them with a personal re-creation in the same way as Corkery rightly claims that Aogán's and Eoghan Rua's poems did also. My contention is that the chord struck was a deeper one than a simple delight in eloquence and comedy and that the popularity of *The Midnight Court* among the Irish people is a matter of their response to its author's vision, or message, as much as it is an appreciation of its humour and its fluency of expression.

Eighteenth-century Gaelic poets adapted in a wide range of ways to the transformation of Irish society as it affected them in their personal circumstances. We see someone like Aindrias Mac Cruitín, who lived until 1738, being *ollamh* to an O'Brien at the same time as he practised the trade of schoolmaster, and staying, so to speak, in the rural and less-urban setting of eighteenth-century Ireland. We see other poets, especially as the eighteenth century progresses, join Brian Merriman in crossing into the world of the town and the class society: Seán Ó Tuama an Ghrinn in Limerick, Donnchadh Caoch Ó Mathghamhna and Mícheál Óg Ó Longáin in Cork. The passage of time made it easier for the later eighteenth-century writers to accommodate; slowly but surely the world about them was becoming town-orientated and commercialised, whatever they felt about it. Where Aogán Ó Rathaille could hardly bear to contemplate the changes that were coming to pass in the world he knew:

> Tír gan eaglais chneasta ná cléirigh
> tír le mioscais, noch d'itheadar faolchoin
> tír do cuireadh go tubaisteach traochta
> fá smacht namhad is amhas is méirleach,

Eoghan Rua Ó Súilleabháin and Donnchadh Rua Mac Conmara and Tomás Ó Casaide can make the best of it, as it were, can accommodate somewhat and create their word-music and their songs to win popularity in the market place and the tavern. Brian Merriman, it seems to me, manages in his poem to possess or repossess, so to speak, this new Irish or Anglo-Irish world through the medium of the Irish language and to pass it through the furnace of his poetic imagination, so that *The Midnight Court* has vignettes of social life and custom in late eighteenth-century Clare that are startlingly alive and convincing as ethnographic description, though I think that it would be a great mistake to imagine that Merriman in any sense set out to write descriptive verse, or any kind of social documentary. Daniel Corkery accuses him of having no feeling for the literary mode and of knowing only the language of the commercial life of the market place. The implication is that Merriman compares unfavourably as a poet with the humble members of the 'Cúirteanna filíochta' who were in Corkery's phrase 'the visible blossoming of the ancient literary tradition'.[20] Corkery would also seem to approve of the latter's continued cultivation of the allegorical Aisling tradition with its dream of restoring the rightful leader to the throne. But if the poor peasant poets of the eighteenth-century Cúirteanna were genuinely seeking the restoration of the old *orders* of society then the question arises as to whether they were in fact victims of mystification by the very tradition they sought to protect and maintain. They were themselves, historically, now members of an increasingly class-orientated society where personal freedom and social mobility was at least a theoretical possibility. Merriman, for his part, seems to have consciously inhabited that contemporary emergent world and to have sought the maturity and independence of individuals in it rather than the restoration of some bygone order of things.

The charge is sometimes made that the complaint of the young woman plaintiff at the court of Aoibheall that spouses are hard, if not impossible, to find in the Irish society of the day cannot be true since the population of the country was burgeoning at the time, and that this somehow proves that Merriman is writing a pure fantasy with no relevance to the society of his time. The charge cannot, I think, be sustained if examination is made of the demographic facts in any detail.[21] Following the fall-off in population growth at the beginning of the eighteenth century the rate of increase grew rapidly again from mid-century on. The overall population figures have been put at 2½ million in 1700, 4½ million in 1780 and on to 8½ million in 1841, so that in Merriman's day there would seem to have been in theory no shortage of eligible young men and women. The fact is, however, that it was in the ranks of the landless labourers and the cottiers that evidence is found for the most frequent and earliest marriages. With the emergence of class differentiation and the competition for land and other resources, there was a tendency for farmers, tradesmen, the better-off in general to marry later, and there is a sizeable statistic of non-marriage within these groups at the time. The 'match', the arranged marriage with all its attendant dealing and bargaining and with 'every shilling brought into account', was starting to become more frequent in the relatively higher social grouping of later eighteenth-century rural Ireland. Merriman, perhaps to be seen as rising socially, certainly moving, at least partially, in the better-off circles would have been aware of this and would have noticed its discouraging effect on young people's marriage prospects as the increasingly market-orientated and class-stratified society developed. Such a class-defined mercenary constraint on the easy coupling of the sexes may well be the social reality that lies behind the young woman's complaint, which is after all the prime matter regarding which the Court of Aoibheall sits. It must be emphasised however that *Cúirt an Mheán Oíche* is primarily and unreservedly a work of the imagination. Its author ultimately requires no justifications other than those of his own creative impulses for any assertions in the mouths of its characters. Our perceptions today of the historical, and, more importantly, the cultural realities of Brain Merriman's world are, at best, only approximations to his and it is possible that much of what we would regard as having significance in the poem's contemporary Irish and European context is hidden from us. The personal and artistic relationship of Merriman himself to that context must remain an even deeper mystery.[22]

There remains the question of the relationship of *The Midnight Court* and the relationship of Brian Merriman to what is known since the mid-nineteenth century as folklore, but which is more properly called oral tradition or, in the older native term, *seanchas*.[23]

We might first look at Merriman's alleged relationship to Burns. In my view the relationship with Burns is the common circumstance of a poetic imagination exercising itself in the rapidly commercialising world of the late eighteenth-century post-Celtic hinterland. In the case of both poets it is the common people, their plight and their prospects, that engages that imagination and gives it impetus. In Burns's case critics have spoken of 'the animating life . . . the powerful outflow of genial and generous sympathies, the spirited independence and vigour of judgement, the warmth and generosity of regard for intrinsic human worth'[24] and these sentiments surely apply in Merriman's case also. On the part of both poets there is a 'natural recoil of sympathies against things that thwart the creative energies and potentialities of life and pervert the essential nature of man'.[25] Both poets employ the idiom of the people in their work, the speech of complex communities, a speech with its own very old traditional life.

> The words came skelpin' rank and file
> anainst before I ken.

Each poet's achievement in language starts from the conversational level—from small market town and village talk—and goes on to be a powerful antidote to sterility and barrenness not only in the lives, but in the minds and feelings of men and women. If the courtly motifs which Merriman uses are, as Seán Ó Tuama claims, found in popular tradition in Ireland, then too the gusto, the earthiness, the fluency with which he sets them forth is the gusto, the earthiness, the fluency of the people's own voice, the voice of the master *seanchaí*, the voice of folklore. In terms of content or motifs there is little if any 'folklore' in **The Midnight Court** but in important ways its voice and its message *are* those of folklore, not the folklore of the Indo-European *märchen* but the folklore of the native tradition, the world of Aoibheall and of Munster and of Ireland. Merriman, in his literary achievement, strangely echoes the achievement of the master *seanchaí* in creating a work consisting of virtuoso linguistic performance in which the plain people are vindicated. In theme and in execution **Cúirt an Mheán Oíche** is an example of how oral tradition in Ireland could at the end of the eighteenth century still inspire major literary artists in ways that seem impossible now.

Notes

[1] Cf. S. Ó Tuama, 'Cúirt an Mheán Oíche', *Studia Hibernica* 4 (1964) 7-27.

[2] Ideam, 'Brian Merriman and his Court', *Irish Times* 23 Aug. 1980.

[3] D. Corkery, *The hidden Ireland* (Dublin 1925) 237-56.

[4] Review of Ó Foghludha's edition of the poem in *Gadelica* 1 (1912-13) 190-204.

[5] *Leinster, Munster and Connaught* (London, n.d.) 219-33.

[6] Introduction to R. Ó Foghludha (ed.), *Cúirt an Mheadhon Oidhche* (Baile Átha Cliath 1912).

[7] 'Notes on Aisling poetry', *Eígse* 1 (1939) 40-50.

[8] 'Notes on the "Midnight Court" (Merryman)', *ibid.*, 167-72.

[9] Ó Tuama, *loc. cit.* (note 2).

[10] Corkery, *loc. cit.* (note 3).

[11] O'Connor, *loc. cit.* (note 5); idem, *Kings, lords and commons* (London 1962) preface.

[12] D. Ó hUaithne (ed.), *Cúirt an Mheán Oíche* (Baile Átha Cliath 1968) lines 287-306.

[13] 'Párliament na mBan', *Celtica* 7 (1966) 135-41.

[14] Cf. P. Mac Cana, *Celtic mythology* (London 1970) 85-96.

[15] Cf. *ibid.*, 117.

[16] Corkery (note 3), 133.

[17] R. A. Breatnach, 'The Lady and the King: a theme of Irish literature', *Studies* 43 (1953) 321-36. Another publication of Professor Breatnach's relating directly to Merriman's poem is 'Ad "Cúirt an Mheadhoin Oidhche" ll.597-8', *Eígse* 8/2 (1956) 140-43.

[18] J. Blum, *The end of the old order in Europe* (Princeton, N.J., 1978) introd.

[19] Ibid.

[20] Corkery (note 3), 104.

[21] Cf. K. H. Connell, 'The population of Ireland in the eighteenth century', *Economic Hist. Review* 16 (1946) 111-24; idem, 'Land and Population in Ireland, 1780-1845', *ibid.* 2nd series, 2 (1950) 278-89; idem, 'Peasant marriage in Ireland: its structure and development since the famine', *ibid.* 14 (1962) 502-523; M. Drake, 'Marriage and population growth in Ireland, 1750-1845', *ibid.* 16 (1963) 301-312; J. Lee, 'Marriage and population in pre-famine Ireland', *ibid.* 21 (1968) 283-95.

[22] See Murphy, *art. cit.* (note 7).

[23] For a recent discussion of the central importance of oral tradition in the transmission of Irish learning from the earliest times see P. Mac Cana, *The learned tales*

of medieval Ireland (Dublin 1980). The term *coimcne* would appear to be the one embracing most widely the various aspects of the tradition in question.

24 Cf. 'Burns and English literature', in B. Forde (ed.), *From Blake to Byron* (Pelican Guide to English Literature, Harmondsworth 1957) 94.

25 *Ibid.*

Kevin O'Neill (essay date 1984)

SOURCE: "A Demographer Looks at Cúirt an Mheán Oíche," in *Éire-Ireland*, Vol. XIX, No. 2, Summer, 1984, pp. 135-43.

[*In the following essay, O'Neill uses "The Midnight Court" to show that Irish marriage patterns associated with the post-Famine era actually arose in the late eighteenth century.*]

During the turbulent years of revolution and national consolidation, Daniel Corkery, novelist, literary critic and cultural historian, issued a call of central importance to the development of independent Irish intellectual life. Writing early in this century, under the influence of the Gaelic revival movement, Corkery urged a radical revaluation of intellectual perspectives. He argued that, as carried out by English-speaking, urban intellectuals, conventional academic study of Irish culture, society, and literature failed to pay adequate attention to Gaelic sources and subjects. Indeed, as the title of his foremost critical work, *The Hidden Ireland,* implies, Corkery believed an entire world lay beyond the vision and understanding of the Anglo-urban monoglots.[1] He believed that a combination of ignorance and hostility caused this Ireland to be overlooked, and he urged the young intellectuals of the emerging Irish nation to turn aggressively toward Gaelic sources to discover the hidden world of their culture. Much in Corkery might support a sort of reverse racism, a Gaelic chauvinism; but in many ways, some of them ironic, Corkery is a formidable figure in any discussion of Ireland's new social history.

Language was the central issue in Corkery's critique of the intellectual elite. It was hardly surprising that Anglo-Irish culture failed to respond intellectually or politically to the traditional, rural Gaelic world from which it had been cut off. But there were and are other obstacles that hinder the traditional academic's attempt to discover the realities of 18th-century Irish life. Even when the Gaelic-language material is accessible, the urban and English perspectives still wield strong influence. Because many academic observers have an imperfect understanding of the environment and of the social and economic complexity of this Gaelic world, they have difficulty interpreting it.

My research into one Irish peasant community indicates that the economic changes which, in the aggregate, created vast chaos and horrific human misery, also afforded Gaelic Ireland, a sizable minority, a preview of the "modern" world.[2] Market participation for profit, prosperity, and the post-Famine social and demographic regime—complete with delayed marriage and the dowry system—all coëxisted with the doomed world of the subsistence producer and landless laborer.[3] The exact relationships between the components of this economy remain unclear. The question of whether a commercial sector provided an escape—such as it was—for a subsistence sector, or whether it created the crisis of 19th-century Ireland, requires further quantitative research. Still, my own quantitative work on the social impact of these economic forces has encouraged me to offer the following hypothesis regarding the psychological landscape of late 18th-century Ireland.

The major narrative poem *Cúirt an Mheán Oíche* (**"The Midnight Court"**) by Brian Merriman, a teacher of mathematics, was written in the Irish language in 1780, and was nurtured and protected by the oral, Gaelic folk tradition until the 1890s when, under the influence of the early Gaelic revival movement, it was translated into English by an Irish exile in Boston.[4] Since then, numerous translations have been published. The one used here is by Frank O'Connor, a student of Daniel Corkery.[5] On the surface, the poem seems fairly straightforward, even to the literary critic. It is a lively, direct, humorous, and often rather explicit romp through the world of sexuality, gender, and marriage. A conventional court of love is held to examine the complaints of Irish women against Irish men.[6] One female character expounds: "Unless we get a spurt in procreation, / we can bid goodbye to the Irish nation." Her grievance is the plight of "all those girls whose charms miscarry, / throughout the land who'll never marry." Young men were avoiding marriage, and when a young man did seek a wife, she was not "some woman of his own sort," "But some pious old prude or dour defamer / Who sweated the couple of pounds that shame her." Most explicitly and directly, the poem attacks the sexual impotence of old men, ready and willing to marry:

> What possible use could she have at night
> For dourness, dropsy, bother and blight,
> A basket of bones with thighs of lead,
> Knees absconded from the dead,
> Fire-speckled shanks and temples whitening,
> Looking like one that was struck by lightning?
> Is there living a girl who could grow fat
> Tied to a travelling corpse like that
> Who twice a year wouldn't find a wish
> To see what she was, flesh or fish
> But dragged the clothes about his head
> Like a wintry wind to a woman in bed?

These lines are part of the poem's general attack on

the patriarchal system that includes late marriage, a high rate of lay celibacy and clerical celibacy, arranged matches, and a dowry system. As commentators have noted, these are all the elements strongly associated with the world of Charles Kickham, Cardinal Cullen, and, even, James Joyce.[7]

Yet, for the demographic historian—admittedly a rarity among literary critics—there is one great conundrum. The poem was written at a time when Ireland recorded probably the highest marital fertility rate in modern Europe; a time, according to many historians, when the average marriage age, after falling steadily for thirty years, may have approached a level typical of non-European society; and a time when some very "open" attitudes to sexuality were expressed in such practices as bundling, mock marriage for adolescents, and premarital pregnancy.[8] At first sight, the poem's world appears to differ from the image created by both statistical and qualitative evidence.

Of course, poets are not required to conform to "reality." Possibly, Merriman was being archaic, describing a world that may have existed decades earlier. Perhaps he was prophetic, using his intuition and understanding of social change to project an accurate image of the future; perhaps he was simply creating a world to fit his poetic theme. Or, perhaps all of those possibilities are true. But Irish poetry of the 18th century was, by necessity, a "people's poetry," dependent upon a popular audience both for patronage and for transmission to future generations.[9] Other popular poems such as Eoghan Rua Ó Súilleabháin's "Séamus, Light-hearted and Loving Friend of My Breast" carefully played on the tension between the poet's "heroic" status and the grim realities of plantation existence, as this excerpt indicates:

> Séamus, light-hearted and loving friend of
> my breast,
> Greek-Geraldine-blooded, valiant and terrible
> in arms,
> Supply in good order one smooth clean
> shaft for my spade
> And, to finish the show, add tastefully one
> foot-piece.[10]

In such an unusual poetic landscape we may be justified in suspending our "suspension of disbelief." This is a very "real" world. Furthermore, using the model of pre-Famine social interaction which my analytical work has produced, I can pose another explanation for our riddle.[11] Merriman's poem may be the most extraordinary piece of evidence of social change in 18th-century Ireland yet uncovered, as well as a significant document in the wider context of the European discussion of marriage, gender, and sexuality.

There is an internal key to understanding the poem. It rests upon two critical indications that the poem represents more than a battle betweeen the genders. They are the social identities of the male and female representatives and the original charge and verdict of the court.

The male and female protagonists provide both the dramatic confrontation and the social dynamic of the poem. The first of the two primary characters introduced is a young woman. She describes herself as the sort "a natural man desired," but she has failed to attract such a man by conventional means. In desperation, she has resorted to ancient folk practices to manipulate her world. She has placed a stocking of apples under her pillow. She has waded into the stream at its deepest and raised her shift. She has swept the wood stack bare, placed a flail up the chimney, burned bits of her frock, her finger nails, and her hair; and finally, she has even turned to the devil. All this magic fails. There is still no husband for her; the traditional world is malfunctioning.

The narrator, the only neutral voice in the poem—and a male one—describes the young woman briefly but favorably as "attractive, good-looking and shy." The poem explodes when the other important character, an old man, condemns the young woman:

> Damnation take you, you bastard's bitch,
> Got by a tinkerman under a ditch!
>   . . . Your seed and breed for all your brag
> Were tramps to a man with rag and bag;
> I knew your da and what passed for his
> wife,
> And he shouldered his traps to the end of
> his life,
> An aimless lout without friend or neighbour,
> Knowledge or niceness, wit or favour:
> The breeches he wore were riddled with
> holes,
> And his boots without a tack of the soles.
> Believe me, friends, if you sold at a fair,
> Himself and his wife, his kids and gear,
> When the costs were met, by the Holy
> Martyr,
> You'd still go short for a glass of porter.
> But the devil's child has the devil's cheek—
> You that never owned cow nor sheep . . .
> Now tell us the truth and don't be shy
> How long are you eating your dinner dry?
> A meal of spuds without butter or milk . . .
> I know too where you sleep at night,
> And blanket or quilt you never saw
> But a strip of old mat and a bundle of
> straw,
> In a hovel of mud without a seat,
> And slime that settles about your feet,
> A carpet of weeds from door to wall

And hens inscribing their tracks on all;
The rafters in with a broken back
And brown rain lashing through every crack. . . .

Clearly, this woman is very poor. Her lack of "cow or sheep," her "dry dinner," and the reference to "traps" enable us to be somewhat specific about her poverty: she seems to be of the landless poor, and the old man despises her for it. The significance of her social identity becomes clear when we compare it with that of the old man who lived . . .

Tilling my fields with an easy mind
Going wherever I felt inclined,
Welcomed by all as a man of price . . .
The neighbors listened, they couldn't refuse
For I'd money and stock to uphold my views.

Like his neighbors, the old man's wife could not refuse the power of his wealth. We learn:

This girl was poor, she hadn't a home
Or a single thing she could call her own
Drifting about in the saddest of lives,
Doing odd jobs for other men's wives,
As if for drudgery created
Begging a crust from women she hated.

The old man promised that, if she would marry him, he would give her cows of her own, a feather bed, and a decent home:

Flax and wool to weave and wind,
These were the things for which she pined.
Even her friends would not have said
That his looks took her head.
How else would he come by such a wife
But that ease was the alms she asked of life.

Holder of capital, stock and land, the old man belongs to the prosperous, or "strong" farming class. His experience differs vastly from the young woman's. Though he is still a "peasant" to the outside observer, he is not subject to the grinding poverty or the immobilizing insecurity usually associated with pre-Famine Ireland. We may view the conflict between him and the young woman as a metaphor for a larger social schism which had already assigned the homogeneous peasant world to the realm of memory. My quantitative work shows that prosperous farmers were conforming to the post-Famine marriage pattern in the 1830s; **"The Midnight Court"** suggests even earlier conformity. It is likely that the poem itself was a reaction to the introduction of a new moral and ethical system into the rural community, a system which reinforced the growing social differentiation within the community and which surprisingly antedates the church's efforts to "purify" Ireland.

I do not suggest that we view this poem as presenting a class rather than a gender conflict, though the poor woman's hatred of the farming women who employed her surely leads to the assumption that she preferred bondage to any man, even this wretched one, to servitude under wealthy women. I do suggest that we are witnessing a more fundamental and all-encompassing cultural collision. The traditional Gaelic world—one perceived by those within it as "natural"—based on a dynamic, though often volatile balance between the genders, was locked in a struggle with a new world marked by a materialistic concept of human relations. The dowry system stood at the heart of this concept and affected each gender and each class in very different ways, shifting social and gender power to the strong farming males.

Merriman sets forth his position at the beginning of the poem in the reference to the court and, at the end, in the court's verdict. Queen Eevul of the Grey Rock, a traditional female deity, takes an oath to the council:

To judge the women and the men,
Stand by the poor though all ignore them
And humble the pride of the rich before them;
Make might without right conceal its face
And use her might to give right its place.
Her favour money will not buy,
No lawyer will pull the truth awry. . . .

The parallel between rich and poor, and men and women, is clear, as is the identification of the "legitimate" system of law, an English import, as a vehicle for enforcing injustice. The poem climaxes with Eevul's formal sentencing of the offending male population:

I do enact according then
That all the present unmarried men
Shall be arrested by the guard,
Detained inside the chapel yard
And stripped and tied beside the gate
Until you decide upon their fate.

Each type of offense is considered separately. The old but celibate males, including the clergy, are turned over to the angry women with the instruction: "Roast or pickle them, some reflection / Will frame a suitable correction." Those who have used their power to prey upon the vulnerability of the young women face even more serious punishment: "if they won't reform, flay [them] alive." Merriman describes in detail their offenses against women and themselves:

But mostly those who sin from pride
With women whose names they do not hide,
Who keep their tally of ruined lives
In whispers, nudges, winks and gibes.
Was ever vanity more misplaced
Than in married women and girls disgraced?
It isn't desire that gives the thrust,

The smoking blood and the ache of lust,
Weakness of love and the body's blindness
But to punish the fools who show them
   kindness.
Thousands are born without a name
That braggarts may boast of their mother's
   shame—
Men lost to Nature through conceit,
And their manhood killed by their own deceit.

These men are condemned because they have abandoned the ethics and morality of traditional communal
society, both its natural sexuality and its reliance on
permanent relationships and shared responsibility.

Eevul makes an important exception, however. Not all
men are to be punished; indeed, she marks one group
for praise—the poor.

There are poor men working in rain and sleet,
Out of their minds with the troubles they
   meet,
But, men in name and in deed according,
They quarry their women at night and
   morning—
A fine traditional consolation!—
And these I would keep in circulation.

The "traditional" men are the poor, not yet contami-
nated by the advance of materialistic English culture.

Critics have not commented on these lines perhaps
because they make no sense if we assume the poem
simply presents a male-female confrontation. The linkage of poverty and traditional sexual morality turns in
logical opposition to the linkage of material wealth
and the old man's misogyny. I should note that the
"natural" sexuality of the poor is not the pagan amo-
rality alleged by some literary critics.[12] Merriman stages
a rather complicated confrontation between two moral
systems. The young woman describes the traditional
view of sexuality, when she informs the court:

I leave it to you, O Nut of Knowledge,
The girls at home and the boys in college,
You cannot persuade me it's a crime
If they make love while they still have time,
But you who for learning have no rival,
Tell us the teachings of the Bible;
Where are we taught to pervert our senses
And make our natural needs offenses?
To fly from lust as in Saint Paul
Doesn't mean flight from life and all,
But to leave home and friends behind
And stick to one who pleased one's mind.

It is the old man who pleads for amoral, or "free" love,
a system of sexual relations based on prostitution and
illegitimacy. He recognizes that the new materialism

empowers him, and men like him, to place women in
a new and more dependent position. Sexuality and
gender both are subordinated to materialism. It is not
the absence of sexuality in the new system which so
outrages the Gaelic folk, as other commentators have
argued, but its subordination to material concerns—
which, of course, explains the importance of gender
confrontation within the poem. With the shift from
Gaelic to English economic systems comes the shift in
power relations between men and women, a transformation in which sexuality is only one factor.

In the final analysis, **"The Midnight Court"** may offer
the most complete contemporary vision of the Gaelic
world's final cultural battle,[13] and as Corkery argued,
it probably reveals more about Ireland than any historical treatise on the 18th century yet published. Brian
Merriman documents the collision between two cultural systems and the penetration of the Gaelic order
by English concepts of wealth and social order, sexuality, gender, and of married life. Much more evidence
is necessary before this particular hypothesis may be
proved or disproved, and the production of such evidence will be a difficult and time-consuming task. Still,
it will be well worth the effort. Both demographers and
historians are finally beginning to appreciate Corkery's
argument that the realities of history and culture appear
most clearly in the life and thought of popular society.

Notes

[1] Daniel Corkery, *The Hidden Ireland, A Study of
Gaelic Munster in the Eighteenth Century* (Dublin:
Gill and Son, 1925).

[2] Kevin O'Neill, *Killashandra: A Local Study of Pre-
Famine Irish Agricultural and Demographic Change*,
forthcoming from the University of Wisconsin Press,
presents evidence which documents the transition of
a traditional subsistence community to a market-ori-
ented region. It demonstrates that the last decades of
the 18th century brought dramatic economic and demographic changes which affected different groups
within the traditional community in very different
ways.

[3] For example, large farmers—those with more than
25 acres under their control—already had a mean age
of first marriage of 28.42 by 1841. Landless laborers
married nearly four years younger on the average.

[4] Michael C. O'Shea, *The Midnight Court* (Boston,
1897), printed for the author.

[5] Brian Merriman, "The Midnight Court," trans. Frank
O'Connor, in *The Penguin Book of Irish Verse*, ed.
Brendan Kennelly (Penguin Books, 1979), pp. 91-118.

[6] Seán Ó Tuama illustrates the European context of the

poem's form in "Brian Merriman and his Court," *Irish University Review,* 11, 2 (Autumn 1981), 149-164.

[7] Margaret MacCurtain, in "Pre-Famine Peasantry in Ireland: Definition and Theme," *Irish University Review,* 4, 2 (Autumn, 1974), 188-198, provides the most subtle explanation of the poem as "an understanding of the inability of the sexes to comprehend what they want to say to each other." This essay suggests that this poor communication was a recent phenomenon tied to the anglicization of Gaelic society.

[8] See Kenneth Connell, *The Population of Ireland, 1750-1845* (Oxford University Press, 1950).

[9] See R. A. Breatnach, "The End of a Tradition: A Survey of Eighteenth Century Gaelic Literature," *Studia Hibernica,* 1 (Dublin, 1961), 128-150.

[10] Seán Ó Tuama and Thomas Kinsella, *An Duanaire: 1600-1900, Poems of the Dispossessed)* Portlaoise: The Dolmen Press, 1981), p. 183.

[11] Our model suggests that the agricultural changes necessitated by the British landlord system and markets caused the social differentiation of rural society into two great groups, the tenantry and the landless laborers. These groups had very different experiences during the late 18th century, as "The Midnight Court" and my quantitative work demonstrate.

[12] Ó Tuama and Kinsella, "Cúirt an Mheán Oíche" in *An Duanaire,* p. 243. Ó Tuama sees this decree as "unexpectedly on the conservative side" because it did not abolish marriage. This assumes, of course, that the old man represents the Gaelic community's morality, an interpretation at variance with the one put forward here. See Ó Tuama, "Brian Merriman and His Court," *Irish University Review,* 11, 2 (Autumn, 1981) 155.

[13] In many ways it echoes Dáibhí Ó Bruadair's *Tonnbhriseadh an tseanagháthaimh* ("cataclysm of the old order"). See Breatnach, *op. cit.,* p. 128.

Seamus Heaney (essay date 1995)

SOURCE: "Orpheus in Ireland: On Brian Merriman's *The Midnight Court,*" in *The Southern Review,* Louisana State University, Vol. 31, No. 3, July, 1995, pp. 786-806.

[*In the following essay (originally a lecture delivered at Oxford University), Heaney, the best known Irish poet of the late twentieth century, traces the political contexts of earlier interpretations of "The Midnight Court" and argues that the poem deserves greater recognition as a classic of world literature.*]

Joseph Brodsky once suggested that the highest goal human beings can set themselves is the creation of civilisation. What Brodsky had in mind was much the same thing, I assume, as W. B. Yeats had in mind when he spoke about the "profane perfection of mankind," a perfection that for Yeats depended on something he called, in another context, "the spiritual intellect's great work." In fact, in their own extravagant and undaunted ways, what both poets were really talking about was the central, epoch-making role that is always available in the world to poetry and the poet.

To occupy this role, of course, it is not necessary for the poet to cut a figure *in* the world. Emily Dickinson and Gerard Manley Hopkins contributed to the construction of a desirable civilisation without ever establishing themselves as notable presences in the minds of their contemporaries. The same could be said of Brian Merriman, author of *Cúirt an Mheáin Oidhche (The Midnight Court),* a poem written in Irish in 1780, a poem from beyond the Pale in all senses, but especially the literal sense. In Ireland, the Pale was that area around Dublin where the English language and an Anglocentric culture had been longest established, but Merriman lived and wrote in the province of Munster, where the Gaelic ethos continued to retain a considerable influence right down into the late eighteenth century. It was in Munster, for example, that another late, great poem of the Irish language appeared at almost the same moment as *The Midnight Court.* This was the extraordinary lamentation raised by Eibhlín Dhubh Ní Chonaill over the corpse of her husband, Art O'Laoghaire, an Irish captain whom English soldiers killed at Carriganimmy in County Cork in 1774. "Caoineadh Airt Uí Laoghaire" was a spontaneous keen uttered by a bereft widow, a poem that surged up out of an oral tradition and a mourning rite as old as Homer. It was also a poem that spoke out of and on behalf of the oppressed native Catholic population of Ireland, a Gaelic majority placed legally beyond the pale of official Anglo-Irish life by the operation of the Penal Laws—laws that forbade Catholics access to higher education and the professions and severely curtailed their right to own property, laws that were as scandalous in their day as the system of apartheid has been in ours.

Even so, Eibhlín Dhubh's poem was not primarily a political rallying cry. It was an outburst both heartbroken and formal, a howl of sorrow and a triumph of rhetoric. It was also a poem that proclaimed for almost the last time the integrity of the Gaelic order and the ordained place of poetry within that order, a place where there was a fortifying consonance between the personal and the communal voice. No wonder Peter Levi chose to focus on "Caoineadh Airt Uí Laoghaire" in his inaugural lecture as Oxford Professor of Poetry, in which he spoke about poetry's immemorial office to lament the dead. And no wonder, either, that it was from the family of such an impassioned silence-breaker that the great political silence-breaker of early-nine-teenth-century Ireland emerged. Daniel O'Connell was a nephew of Eibhlín Dhubh, and Daniel O'Connell was also the man who in 1829 achieved Catholic Emancipation for Ireland and earned himself the title of "The Liberator," then and in times to come.

If we were to think of sexual politics as opposed to national politics, we might well award the same title to Brian Merriman, for although his poem belonged in several important respects to the Irish past and to the literary conventions of medieval Europe, it can also be read as a tremor of the future. Certainly, as a text to be either repressed or promoted, it has featured signifi-cantly in the Irish literary tradition for more than two hundred years. Here I want to give an outline of the story it tells and then some account of ways it has been read at different critical moments during this century in Ireland. I also want to argue that within a category we might call "world literature," the poem has been insufficiently recognised as one of the most original and unexpected achievements of the eighteenth cen-tury; it is a comic work, vitally linked to its Irish time and place, but I shall try to amplify its claims by set-ting it within a European perspective that is even longer than the usual medieval one. In doing so, I shall also be suggesting that *The Midnight Court* contributes not only to the vitality of Irish culture but to the creation of that whole civilisation that the poets in their unmessianic way have always managed to envisage and augment.

The poet in question here lived between 1749 (or 1747) and 1805, but the other facts known about him are few. He was born in County Clare, probably into what we would nowadays call a single-parent family. Even-tually he acquired a stepfather when his mother mar-ried and settled in Feakle, where the poet would later teach a school and cultivate a small farm. His name appears, for example, in the records of a Dublin agri-cultural society for 1797, when he won two prizes for his flax crop. Also in 1797, he married, and five or six years later Merriman moved with his young family to the nearby city of Limerick. It was in Limerick that he died suddenly on July 27, 1805, an event noted in the *General Advertiser and Limerick Gazette* in a manner that gave little indication of what his real life-work had been: "Died on Saturday morning in Old Clare Street, after a few hours illness, Mr. Bryan Merryman, teacher of Mathematics, etc."

Merriman's poem, of course, is now the best-known thing about him. The large number of nineteenth-cen-tury manuscripts and twentieth-century translations is impressive evidence of its popularity from the begin-ning, and its relevance to contemporary issues is as lively now as it was in East Clare in the 1780s. What we are talking about is a work of just over a thousand lines, written in a hammer-and-tongs vernacular, in buoyant couplets, a poem that is to some extent a parody

of aspects of conventional Gaelic poetry and to some extent a transformation of them. It is a dream vision: the poet is discovered in an idealised landscape in the neighbourhood of Loch Gréine, where he promptly falls asleep and is peremptorily assailed by a dreadful fe-male grotesque, a bailiff who summonses him to a court in midnight session somewhere in the Feakle district. The president of the court is the fairy queen of Munster, Aoibheall of Craig Liath, and though its lo-cation is very firmly in the local world of County Clare, the setting does have an otherworldly radiance about it. Aoibheall is the guardian spirit of the country and guarantor among other things of its women's rights to sexual fulfilment and equality, and it is she who has organised this special sitting—special not only because it is a woman's court, but also because it is fair and just and incorruptible, a dream court that momentarily redresses the actual penal system under which the native population has to endure. But even so, Merriman, it must be said, exhibits little interest in protesting against prevailing political conditions. These are simply and scornfully noted as he quickly proceeds to the heart of his poetical matter, which is more psychosexual than national-patriotic.

Here perhaps it is worth noting a distinction critics used to make in the case of poems like *The Canterbury Tales* or *The Divine Comedy,* where it makes sense to separate Chaucer or Dante as author of the poem from Chaucer or Dante as character within his own compo-sition. Merriman also writes himself in as a participant in his narrative, and we can say about him as a char-acter in the poem what T. S. Eliot said about Tiresias in *The Waste Land,* namely, "what [he] witnesses is the substance of the poem." What Merriman (the char-acter) witnesses, then, is a debate between a young woman and an old man, a debate that is eventually adjudicated by Aoibheall; and Aoibheall's verdict on the case implicates him in the action and exposes him to accusation and punishment by the vindicated women.

The poem can be divided into three main parts. First (as I've just outlined) comes a description of the set-ting and the summons, during which the bailiff de-plores the condition of the country and focuses with particular rancour on the failure of young and mar-riageable men (including the poet) to mate or marry with the available and passionately languishing women. Then comes the main body of the work, the courtroom drama, which is composed of three long speeches. The first of these is a tirade by a young woman who com-plains of being sexually neglected and then goes on to boast vigorously and convincingly of her attributes and aptitudes as a sexual creature. Here is my translation of the opening of this central section, beginning with Merriman's description of the court:

> And there (I am sure) lit torches showed
> A handsome, grand, well-built abode,

A stately, steadfast, glittering space,
Accessible and commodious.
And I saw a lovely vision woman
Ensconced on the bench of law and freedom,
And saw her fierce, fleet guard of honour
Rank upon rank in throngs around her.
I saw then too rooms filling full,
Crowding with women from wall to wall,
And saw this other heavenly beauty
With her lazy eye, on her dignity,
Seductive, pouting, with curling locks,
Biding her time in the witness box.
Her hair spilled down, loosed tress on tress,
And a hurt expression marked her face;
She was full of fight, with a glinting eye,
Hot on the boil, ill-set and angry—
Yet for all her spasms, she couldn't speak,
For her hefts and huffing had made her weak.
She looked like death or a living death-wish
She was so cried out; but straight as a rush,
She stood to the fore as a witness stands,
Flailing and wailing and wringing hands.
And she kept it up; she raved and screeched
Till sighing restored her powers of speech.
Then her downlook went, her colour rose,
She dried her eyes and commenced as follows:
"A thousand welcomes! And bless Your
    Highness!
Aoibheall of Craig, our prophetess!
Our daylight's light, our moon forever,
Our hope of life when the weeping's over!
O head of all the hosted sisters,
Thomond can thole no more! Assist us!
My cause, my case, the reason why
My plea's prolonged so endlessly
Until I'm raving and round the twist
Like a maenad whirled in a swirl of mist—
The reason why is the unattached
And unprovided for, unmatched,
Women I know, like flowers in a bed
Nobody's dibbled or mulched or weeded
Or trimmed or watered or ever tended;
So here they are, unhusbanded,
Unasked, untouched, beyond conception—
And, needless to say, I'm no exception.
I'm scorched and tossed, a sorry case
Of nerves and drives and neediness,
Depressed, obsessed, awake at night,
Unused, unsoothed, disconsolate,
A throbbing ache, a dumb discord,
My mind and bed like a kneading board.
O Warden of the Craig, incline!
Observe the plight of Ireland's women,
For if things go on like this, then fuck it!
The men will have to be abducted!"

Why, she goes on to ask, do men have to marry hags and harridans when she and her like are throbbing with need? For it should be said that this poem is not about

romantic love but about sexual appetite and wasted sexual opportunity. Professor Seán Ó Tuama, one of the poem's most informed critics, makes this point and quotes to good effect an observation by Johan Huizinga. Ó Tuama sees in *The Midnight Court* a survival of unofficial, uncourtly, medieval genres that proceeded untouched by the sentiment of the troubadours, and he enriches his account of the poem by reference to Huizinga's claim that "We should picture to ourselves two layers of civilization superimposed, co-existing though contradictory. Side by side with the courtly style of literary and rather recent origin, the primitive forms of erotic life kept all their force. . . . " *The Midnight Court* does have this primitive basis, and nowhere is the melding of the archaic, the erotic, and the realistic more evident than at that point in the young woman's first speech when she lists the places she paraded, the fashions she wore, and the various superstitious rites she performed in order to attract the attention of a man. The following translation is by Frank O'Connor, revised by the author from a version first published in 1945 and banned for a while by the Censorship Board of the Irish Free State—although there would seem to be nothing in these particular lines that they could have objected to:

My hair was washed and combed and
    powdered,
My coif like snow and stiffly laundered;
I'd a little white hood with ribbons and ruff
On a spotted dress of the finest stuff,
And facings to show off the line
Of a cardinal cloak the colour of wine;
A cambric apron filled with showers
Of fruit and birds and trees and flowers;
Neatly-fitting, expensive shoes
With the highest of heels pegged up with
    screws;
Silken gloves, and myself in spangles
Of brooches, buckles, rings and bangles.
And you mustn't imagine I was shy,
The sort that slinks with a downcast eye,
Solitary, lonesome, cold and wild,
Like a mountainy girl or an only child.
I tossed my cap at the crowds of the races
And kept my head in the toughest places.

. . . . .

But I'm wasting my time on a wildgoose-
    chase,
And my spirit's broken—and that's my case!
After all my shaping, sulks and passions,
All my aping of styles and fashions,
All the times that my cards were spread
And my hands were read and my cup was
    read;
Every old rhyme, pishrogue and rune,
Crescent, full moon and harvest moon,

Whit and All Souls and the First of May,
I've nothing to show for all they say.
Every night when I went to bed
I'd a stocking of apples beneath my head;
I fasted three canonical hours
To try and come round the heavenly powers;
I washed my shift where the stream was deep
To hear a lover's voice in sleep;
Often I swept the woodstack bare,
Burned bits of my frock, my nails, my hair,
Up the chimney stuck the flail,
Slept with a spade without avail;
Hid my wool in the lime-kiln late
And my distaff behind the churchyard gate;
I had flax on the road to halt coach or
    carriage,
And haystacks stuffed with heads of cabbage,
And night and day on the proper occasions
Invoked Old Nick and all his legions;
But 'twas all no good and I'm broken-hearted
For here I'm back at the place I started;
And this is the cause of all my tears
I am fast in the rope of the rushing years,
With age and need in lessening span,
And death beyond, and no hopes of a man.

As soon as the young woman ends her complaint—
with a threat to use black magic if her luck doesn't
turn—a fierce old man springs into the witness box.
He speaks with demented rage about his marriage to a
young woman like the one who has just quit pleading.
He had been the victim of a conspiracy; on the wedding night he discovered he had brought to bed a wife
already pregnant and long notorious for her promiscu-
ity and venereal capacities. Marriage, he says, should
be abandoned; children born out of wedlock are far
healthier and more vigorous anyhow: doesn't he have
his wife's bastard to prove it? And he furthermore
insists that the evidence of the previous witness is
entirely suspect, for she is as untrustworthy and du-
plicitous as the woman he married. Snarlygob is Frank
O'Connor's name for this vigorous ancient, and the
name sits well with the venomous realism of the lines
where he contrasts the living conditions from which
the young woman witness has sprung with the finery
she parades in now because of sexual favors rendered:

Now tell us the truth and don't be shy
How long are you eating your dinner dry?
A meal of spuds without butter or milk,
And dirt in layers beneath the silk.
Bragging and gab are yours by right,
But I know too where you sleep at night,
And blanket or quilt you never saw
But a strip of old mat and a bundle of straw,
In a hovel of mud without a seat,
And slime that settles about your feet,
A carpet of weeds from door to wall
And hens inscribing their tracks on all;

The rafters in with a broken back
And brown rain lashing through every
    crack—
'Twas there you learned to look so nice,
But now may we ask how you came by the
    price?
We all admired the way you spoke,
But whisper, treasure, who paid for the
    cloak?
A sparrow with you would die of hunger—
How did you come by all the grandeur,
All the tassels and all the lace—
Would you have us believe they were got in
    grace?
The frock made a hole in somebody's pocket,
And it wasn't you that paid for the jacket;
But assuming that and the rest no news,
How the hell did you come by the shoes?

The "treasure" comes back at him, of course, and gives
as good as she has got. In a brilliant plea for sympathy
for all women like the ones spancelled to Snarlygob and
his ilk, she reels off an indignant and marvellously specific list of his inadequacies as a lover and of his wife's
attempts to overcome them. Why, she then asks in desperation, are the clergy not allowed to marry? Aren't
some of the most bullish and ebullient men in the country
going round in clerical clothes? Don't they leave their
mark here and there in houses and families already? Why
not give them their sexual heads and free them from their
vows of celibacy? And so on. The main body of the
poem ends on this powerful subversive note, and the
witnesses step back to hear the verdict from Aoibheall.
But since this verdict and its enactment are what I want
to talk about at the end of the essay, I shall postpone
discussion of them for now except to say that Merriman
(the character) is subject to Aoibheall's sentence and is
convicted with the rest of Ireland's males of insufficient
amorous drive and a failure of conjugal will.

I have been quoting in English because my own familiarity with the poem comes from reading it in translation. Anyone who wants to get to know it can find
representative passages in the standard anthologies of
Irish verse—Brendan Kennelly's *Penguin Book of Irish
Verse* prints O'Connor's version, John Montague's *Faber
Book of Irish Verse* gives examples of the treatment of
different passages by different translators, and Thomas
Kinsella has his own abbreviated and forthright version of the poem in the *Oxford Book of Irish Verse*,
which he edited. In the Republic of Ireland, of course,
most people learn the opening lines at school in the
original Irish. Yet even in translation, it is easy to
appreciate the fact that **Cúirt an Mheáin Oidhche**
has a thoroughly invigorating way with language. In
some places, to be sure, there is a copiousness that
amounts to overload in the Irish vocabulary; but elsewhere the language exhibits an abundance that is the
fine, surprising excess of poetic genius in full flight.

It is the parody, however, that is most in evidence near the beginning, in the description of the bailiff who enters the scene not only as her astonishing self—"Bony and huge, a terrible hallion"—but also as a send-up. Merriman's first audience would have recognised her as a burlesque of the visionary beauty who is a constant feature of an Irish poetic genre called the *aisling*. *Aisling* means vision, and the *aisling* genre evolved in Ireland during the late seventeenth and the eighteenth centuries; mostly it was a kind of Jacobite dream, a political fantasy about the future liberation of Ireland by the Stuarts, a compensatory response to the traumatic defeat that the native Gaelic order had suffered in the wake of the Cromwellian and Williamite campaigns. Typically, an *aisling* begins with the poet sleeping and encountering in his dream-vision a woman whose beauty drives him to diction and description of the most ardent sort; the woman is, of course, an image of Ireland, an allegorical representation of the country's subject state, and she goes on to tell of her rape by the foreigner, or her thraldom to the heretic, or whatever. But in the end she consoles herself and the poet by prophesying that her release will be effected by a young prince from overseas.

Merriman's bailiff is, among other things, a blast of surrealistic ridicule directed at such a fantasy. She comes on as both a literary and a political corrective to self-deception. She is a form of overkill whose purpose is to undermine. She directs attention to the demeaned realities of the here and now rather than deflecting the imagination into consoling reverie. But at the same time, she is also a manifestation of that fine excess that gives the poem its immense panache. Here is my version of her entry on the unsuspecting scene:

> Leafy branches were all around me,
> Shooting grasses and growths abounded;
> There were green plants climbing and worts
>   and weeds
> That would gladden your mind and clear your
>   head.
> I was tired out, dead sleepy and slack,
> So I lay at my length on the flat of my back
> With my head well propped, my limbs at ease
> In a nest in a ditch beside the trees. . . .
>
> But my rest was short for next there comes
> A sound from the ground like the roll of
>   drums,
> A wind from the north, a furious rout,
> And the lough in a sulphurous thunderlight.
> And then comes looming into view
> And steering towards me along the bay
> This hefty, menacing dangerwoman,
> Bony and huge, a terrible hallion.
> Her height, I'd say, to the nearest measure,
> Was six or seven yards or more,
> With a swatch of her shawl all japs and clabber

> Streeling behind in the muck and glar.
> It was awe-inspiring just to see her,
> So hatchet-faced and scarred and sour—
> With her ganting gums and her mouth in a
>   twist
> She'd have put the wind up man or beast.
> And Lord of Fates! Her hand was a vise
> Clamped on a towering staff or mace
> With a spike on top and a flange of brass
> That indicated her bailiff's powers.
> Her words were grim when she got started.
> "Get up," she said, "and on your feet!
> What do you think gives you the right
> To shun the crowds and the sitting court?
> A court of justice, truly founded,
> And not the usual rigged charade,
> But a fair and clement court of women
> Of the gentlest stock and regimen.
> The Irish race should be grateful always
> For such a bench, agreed and wise,
> In session now two days and a night
> In the spacious fort on Gréine Height. . . .
>
> "To add to which, the whole assembly
> Decreed on the Bible this very day:
> The youth has failed, declined, gone fallow—
> A censure, sir, that pertains to you.
> In living memory, with birth rates fallen
> And marriage in Ireland on the wane,
> The country's life has been dissipated,
> Pillage and death have worn it out.
> Blame arrogant kings, blame emigration,
> But it's you and your spunkless generation—
> You're a source blocked off that won't refill.
> You have failed your women, one and all."

The Midnight Court has a demonstrable relevance to the Ireland of its day, and in fact the poem has in recent decades been as much the locus of comment by social historians and folklorists as by literary critics; yet while this realism is one of its strengths, it is hard to feel that Merriman wrote in a realistic spirit. Admittedly, the comic phantasmagoria does constitute a definite, exhilarated retort to economic conditions and matrimonial patterns in East Clare in the late eighteenth century; but it would be hard to argue that the poem represents an act of civic concern on the poet's part. Indeed, one of the great triumphs of *The Midnight Court* is that it feels utterly unconstrained. There's an animating buzz of topicality in its inventions, but in no way does it read like a dated document; this is in large measure because the court set-up represents not a submission to the conditions of Merriman's world but a creative victory over them.

Merriman did not, in other words, devise the courtroom as a method of presenting evidence about the state of the sex war in County Clare or about the social and economic impediments to early marriage. You can imagine a documentary film team or an Open University sociology unit assembling the results of its research and questionnaires, then hitting upon the idea of a court case as a way of clarifying the topic. But with Merriman, as with any creative writer, the process is reversed. The image came first, and then the evidence supplied itself almost as a kind of spontaneous reflex. For Merriman the courtroom was not a method, but a stroke of genius; its real virtue lay in the way it released the flood of the poet's inventiveness.

Swift, for example, said that once he had thought of big men and little men, the whole of *Gulliver's Travels* was already more or less written; and Merriman could have claimed something similar when he hit upon the idea of burlesquing the *aisling* and the court of love, since this conception not only kick-started his poem but quickly sent it into vernacular overdrive. Professor Seán Ó Tuama is both persuasive and illuminating when he argues that Merriman was indeed working within this medieval literary convention of the love court, enshrined most influentially in Jean de Meung's *Roman de la Rose* and then dispersed in ballads and other more or less popular forms throughout Europe, England, and Norman and Gaelic Ireland. Ó Tuama shows that the young woman's speech, for example, belongs to a genre known as *chanson de la malmariée,* a form of lover's complaint that turns up all over the place; he notes how the praise of bastards is to be found in *King Lear* and in an eighteenth-century English poem by Richard Savage, and traces many other parallels between *The Midnight Court* and previous literature. Yet even Ó Tuama is at a loss to bring the scholarly record into an exact alignment with the imaginative origin of the poem. Every attempt to link Merriman directly to a literary source, he admits, has to operate on a hypothesis, and yet he believes the evidence does prove that the medieval themes were transmuted by Merriman into "a new demonic comic creation . . . which is absolutely eighteenth century Irish."

The court, then, is more a carnival where Merriman's imagination runs riot than a judicial inquiry into the rights and wrongs of the sexual mores of East Clare in the 1770s. Moreover, Merriman's most effective agent in summoning the volubility that distinguishes the proceedings is neither the bailiff who strides so commandingly into the poet's dream nor the bailiff's staff with its official insignia; the true motive force is the couplet, which gives the poem its metrical norm and its distinctive music:

> Ba ghnáth mé ag siúl le ciumhais na h-bhann,
> Ar bháinseach úr 'san drúcht go trom,
> In aice na gcoillte i gcoim an tsléibhe,
> Gan mhairg, gan mhoill le soilse an lae.

It's not that anything about these lines is especially original in point of language or technique; it's more that they establish a melody. They strike a tuning fork, and immediately a whole orchestra of possibility comes awake in the poet's ear and in the language itself. Another great unfettered event gets under way. Another unpredictable poetic intervention changes the contours of poetry itself. And this mixture of extravagance and inevitability distinguishes *Cúirt an Mheáin Oidhche* and makes it more than a gallery of rural sexual stereotypes. Obviously the success of the poem has also to do with the forceful pressure of urgent, credible human voices and with the huge inherent interest of the sexual game itself; much is at issue, and yet it is not only the perennial relevance of the theme that guarantees the poem's ongoing appeal. What makes it a work that can still, in Yeats's words, "engross the present and dominate memory" is Merriman's vital gift for "the stylistic arrangement of experience."

Not that anyone would want to deny the importance and interest of the liberating hullabaloo the poem raises about sexual matters. Or perhaps I should say gender matters, since gender rather than sex is where the flashpoint of the argument comes nowadays; and the poem's centrality to this debate is yet another example of the way it is able to subsume the social and intellectual preoccupations of different periods and to answer them by divulging new and timely meanings. If, therefore, we are prepared to make an artificial distinction between the poem's socio-political quotient and its artistic quotient, we could argue that during the first half and more of this century, *Cúirt an Mheáin Oidhche* was important because it sponsored a libertarian and adversarial stance against the repressive conditions that prevailed during those years in Irish life, public and private. We could further argue that in recent times its importance has shifted: from being an ally in the war against sexual repression and against a censorship obsessed with sexual morality, the poem has become a paradigm of the war initiated by the movement for women's empowerment, their restoration to the centre of language and consciousness, and thereby also to the centre of all the institutions and functionings of society.

This shifting and salubrious relationship between the poem and its world can be illustrated by looking briefly at its reception and interpretation at three different moments over the last hundred years. Seventy years ago, for example, when the Irish critic and cultural nationalist Daniel Corkery gave his account of the poem in *The Hidden Ireland,* he was fairly eager to play down Merriman's send-up of clerical celibacy and his advocacy of unconstrained heterosexual activity between consenting adults. Rather than saluting these extravagances as fantastic possibilities to be savoured in a spirit of hilarity and transgression, Corkery spoke with a certain primness of the poem's treatment of "curious questions" and attributed the pagan force of the thing to its ideas as such. It was as if he were anxious not to find the poet guilty of some form of un-Irish activity. Corkery inclined therefore to blame the poem's "irreligious ideas" on foreign influences: he favoured the old academic notion that these ideas came from Voltaire and Rousseau, and that Merriman had picked them up through reading the books of these Enlightenment *philosophes* in the houses of the gentry he was supposed to have been so fond of visiting. Yet Corkery could not help recognising that the poem's subversiveness derives in large measure from a native strain of paganism surviving unregenerate at different levels in Irish popular culture. But he fudged the issue, presumably because it would have been an embarrassment for a propagandist of the new self-Gaelicising Irish Free State to discover in the older Gaelic literature too gleeful an endorsement of anticlerical attitudes and too robust a promulgation of the desirability of promiscuous sexual behaviour.

Conditions have changed dramatically since Corkery's book appeared in 1924. The literary and moral constraints have clearly eased when an Irish-language woman poet like Nuala Ní Dhomhnaill can publish in Ireland—with an Irish publisher and to Irish acclaim—a poem like "Féar Suaithinseach," which implies that it is the sanctified male priest who is in need of the healing ministrations of the sexual woman and not the other way around; or when in another poem, called "Gan do Chuid Éadaigh," she expresses what might be called naked delight in imagining in erotic detail the body of a lover stripped of his clothes.

But even if Merriman's poem can be read now as a precursor of these free treatments of sexuality, and can be seen as one of a line of precursors that includes James Joyce's *Ulysses* and, indeed, Frank O'Connor's 1945 translation of *The Midnight Court* itself, it is still not immune to moralistic criticism of a more recent kind. The poem still stands in danger of being accused, for different reasons, under the terms of a new feminist consensus. For example, I discovered that the political activist Máirín de Búrca described it some thirteen years ago as "sexist rubbish." She did concede that men may mean well, but she nevertheless maintained that they "cannot write intelligently about women's oppression." This in itself sounds like a bit of sexist rubbish; and I would certainly argue that Brian Merriman should be immune to the common feminist castigation of Irish men poets for representing women (and Ireland) in the passive, submissive roles of maiden and mother. In fact, Merriman deserves a specially lenient hearing in the women's court, if only for having envisaged his own prosecution ahead of time and for having provided the outline of a case against himself. He was surely something of a progressive when it came to the representation of women. He gave them bodies and brains and let them speak as if they lived by them. He revised and implicitly criticised the *aisling* genre by burlesquing its idealised, victimised maiden in the fig-

ure of the beam-limbed bailiff; and he gave to the other young flesh-and-blood *spéirbhean* in the witness box a transfusion of emotional and rhetorical energy long denied to women by poets who had preceded him.

The poem is now probably read more in English than in Irish, and this means that the impression of machismo that surrounds it in the mind of the general reader has by no means lessened. Of the translations, Frank O'Connor's is probably the best and the best known, and since its emphatic bawdiness was meant to challenge the censor as much as to delight the reader, O'Connor very deliberately upped the sexual ante in a distinctly male idiom. In an introduction to the first edition of this version, he admits that there are qualities in the Irish that his own English, for better or worse, tended to coarsen:

> As always when he deals with women's human needs, [Merriman] puts real tenderness and beauty into the writing. My English cannot give the delicacy and fragrance of a line like *Ag súil trím chola le cogar ó'm chéile.* There is nothing remarkable about it . . . no extravagance of imagery or language which you can translate; it is a pure classical beauty of vowels and consonants which you either hear or do not hear.

This amounts to an admission by O'Connor that in his translation the surface noise of his own provocative anti-puritanical agenda is going to be more audible than the under-music of the women's voices—which means that those aspects of the poem most likely to offend a contemporary feminist are highlighted rather than mitigated by his treatment of them in English. A sensitised reader nowadays, man or woman, is going to be more uneasy than O'Connor was about, for example, the picture of the young woman setting her cap so assiduously for a man, or about the normative status that the poem—in spite of its subversive intent—grants to the state of marriage. So even though from a feminist viewpoint there has to be something admirable about the way Aoibheall of Craig Liath regulates the world of the poem (like a woman president in charge of the court and the country, a kind of *aisling* promise of Mary Robinson), and though there is a redemptive realism in the young witness's revelation that women can be every bit as sexually capable and cupidinous as men, it is nevertheless true that the poem places much emphasis on woman as a kind of human brooder and mostly ignores her potential as a being independent of her sexual attributes and her reproductive apparatus.

But all this has to be understood in the context of the poem's overall drive to celebrate the creaturely over the ethereal in human beings, male or female. As Gearóid Ó Cruadhlaoidh has argued, Merriman sees the country's deliverance and the return of fertility and prosperity for all in the restoration of "the basic, healthy, animal life instinct of the mature, adult individual man and woman, free from conventional guilt." And it is this same impulse to lift all kinds of bans and to break what Merriman's contemporary, William Blake, called "the mind-forged manacles," it is this anti-establishment animus that gives the original its great panache, even though it also gives a slightly too pronounced strut to O'Connor's English. His intention was to taunt, to affront the prudes and goad the Censorship Board. And in this respect O'Connor was influenced, I am certain, by the example of Yeats. He had known Yeats and worked with him closely during the 1930s, when many of Yeats's poems had the sort of upfront, histrionic sexuality and confrontational drive that distinguish O'Connor's translation. Indeed, we are almost certain to meet Crazy Jane on the road to O'Connor's midnight court. His purpose was to raise hackles, so he was prepared for his English to make slightly more of a racket than the Irish might have warranted.

All I'm doing here, of course, is stating the obvious; namely, that the loss of subtlety O'Connor noted in his translation had to do with the gain in audibility that he needed if the poem was to do its work of protest in the world he inhabited. And with this example of what we might call O'Connor's Hibernocentric enterprise, I hope I have given sufficient illustration of what I meant when I said in the beginning—perhaps a bit too rhetorically—that **The Midnight Court** had a role to play in the construction of a desirable civilisation. Without impairment to its artistic integrity, it has continued to sustain the praise and blame of generations of commentators and the interpretations of different translators, and in so doing, it has promoted those workings of the spirit and exercises of the intelligence that are good and desirable ends in themselves.

Before I conclude, I want to read the poem (as I promised I would) in an old poetic context rather than a new political one. This reading suggested itself because I have recently been involved in a project where I was commissioned to translate the story of Orpheus and Eurydice as it appears in Ovid's *Metamorphoses*. At the end of the story, when Orpheus has looked back and lost Eurydice to death all over again, Ovid says:

> The sun passed through the house
> Of Pisces three times then, and Orpheus
> Withdrew and turned away from loving
>   women—
> Perhaps because there only could be one
> Eurydice, or because the shock of loss
> Had changed his very nature. Nonetheless,
> Many women loved him and, denied
> Or not, adored.

Naturally I detected a faint, distant parallel between the situation of this classical poet-figure, desired by those he has spurned, and the eighteenth-century Irish poet as he appears at the end of *Cúirt an Mheáin Oidhche,* arraigned for still being a virgin when the country is full of women who'd be only too glad to ease him of his virtue. The parallel was reinforced when I realised that the portrait of Merriman as the jocund poet, playing his tunes the length and breadth of the country—the portrait that appears at the end of the Irish poem—is another manifestation of the traditional image of Orpheus as master poet of the lyre, the patron and sponsor of music and song. But what transposed the parallel from a minor to a major key was a further recognition of the way that the *death* of Orpheus, as related both by Ovid and by Virgil before him, provides an acoustic where the end of *Cúirt an Mheáin Oidhche* can be heard to new effect and where, indeed, some of the critical objections that have been voiced against the final section of the poem can be made sense of in a new way.

Both Frank O'Connor and Séan Ó Tuama are uneasy, for example, about the lack of poetic climax, the relatively conventional thinking and the relatively temperate tone of Aoibheall's final judgement. In his definitive 1981 account of the poem in *Irish University Review,* Ó Tuama writes: "It is quite probable, then, that the *Court of Love* apparatus finally ended up for him more a hindrance than a help. Some more irrational or surrealistic type of concluding structure might have helped Merriman to reveal more climactically his dark, archaic feelings."

What happens at the end of *Cúirt an Mheáin Oidhche* is that Aoibheall decrees that unmarried males of twenty-one and over are to be taken by women, tied to a tree beside a headstone in Feakle graveyard, and thoroughly whipped. She also decrees that the worn-out, sexually incapable husbands of sexually vigorous women should connive in the action when their wives take younger lovers, and should provide the legal cover of a family name when children arrive. She prophesies furthermore that a time will come when Rome will permit the Catholic clergy to marry, and ends with a passionate (if slightly moralistic) outburst against male sexual braggarts who are as inadequate as they are obnoxious. Then, after Aoibheall has delivered her verdict, the young woman plaintiff turns on the poet and rallies the women against him as a typical male offender; finally, just as they are about to put Aoibheall's sentence into action, the thing comes abruptly to an end as the poet starts up, awake and saved:

> "So hear me now, long-suffering judge!
> My own long hurt and ingrown grudge
> Have me desolated. I hereby claim
> A woman's right to punish him.
> And you, dear women, you must assist.
> So rope him, Una, and all the rest—
> Anna, Maura—take hold and bind him.

Double twist his arms behind him.
Remember all the sentence called for,
And execute it to the letter.
Maeve and Sive and Sheila! Maureen!
Knot the rope till it tears the skin.
Let Mr Brian take what we give,
Let him have it. Flay him alive,
And don't draw back when you're drawing
    blood.
Test all of your whips against his manhood.
Cut deep. No mercy. Make him squeal.
Leave him in strips from head to heel
Until every single mother's son
In the land of Ireland learns the lesson.

"And it only seems both right and fitting
To note the date of this special sitting,
So calm your nerves and start computing:
A thousand minus a hundred and ten—
Take what that gives you, double it, then
Your product's the year." She'd lifted her pen,
And her hand was poised to ratify
The fate that was looking me straight in the
    eye.
She was writing it down, the household guard
Sat at attention, staring hard
As I stared back. Then my dreaming ceased
And I started up, awake, released.

It is true that it is a blithe conclusion to a potentially baleful situation. What Ó Tuama calls the "archaic feelings" are efficiently aborted by the dream convention, yet there is a lingering sense that the nightmare scenario is truer to the psychic realities than the daylight world to which the poet is returned in the final couplet. Even the partial vengeance J. M. Synge allows Pegeen Mike and her cohorts to practise upon Christy Mahon at the end of *The Playboy of the Western World* is more genuinely scaresome than the actions carried out by Merriman's court. The good humour of it all can be explained, of course, by Merriman's very healthy sense of proportion and by the requirements of the court of love convention. But an archaic beast has indeed stirred under the poem's surface, and the reader experiences a vague need to see it unleashed into action—another way of saying that the Merriman poem has a mythic potency that its comic mode deflects and defuses. The myth in question is, of course, the myth of Orpheus, which Ovid renders fully in his account of the dismemberment of the bard at the hands of the frenzied maenads:

They circled him, still using as their weapons
Staffs they had twined with leaves and tipped
    with cones
That were never meant for duty such as this.
Some pelted him with clods, some stripped the
    branches
To scourge him raw, some stoned him with
    flintstones.

But as their frenzy peaked, they chanced upon
Far deadlier implements.

                Near at hand
Oxen in yokes pulled ploughshares through
    the ground
And sturdy farmers sweated as they dug—
Only to flee across their drills and rigs
When they saw the horde advancing. They
    downed tools
So there for the taking on the empty fields
Lay hoes and heavy mattocks and long
    spades.
The oxen lowered their horns, the squealing
    maenads
Cut them to pieces, then turned to rend the
    bard . . .

Ovid provides one possible explanation for this feral behaviour of the maenads by saying that after the loss of Eurydice, Orpheus had spurned the love of women and turned his amorous attention to young boys, the implication being that the maenads' action is a form of heterosexual revenge upon homosexual activity. But however we interpret the Latin or the Irish stories in relation to the sexual politics of their times, it seems to me that Merriman's poem is backlit in an especially illuminating way if it is read in relation to the much more violent outcome of the Orpheus episode in Ovid's *Metamorphoses*. Not only does its central action— namely, the summoning and arraignment of the male poet by a court of aggrieved women—take on a new resonance; but the perceived weaknesses of its conclusion are put into perspective, and the poem's claim to be considered in the context of what I called world literature is greatly enhanced. The poem remains, of course, what any vital work has to be, a response to the local conditions; but it becomes something more. Its power is augmented by being located within the force field of an archetype. The phallocentrism of its surface discourse can be reread as an aspect of male anxiety about suppressed female power, both sexual and political; and the weakness of its conclusion, namely the deflection of the threat to Brian—this tidy outcome can be seen as the price the satirical eighteenth-century mind was prepared to pay in order to keep the psychosexual demons of the unconscious at bay a while longer.

Still, given the down-to-earthness of this poem's cast of characters and the directness of their speech, this would be a rather elevated note on which to end. Perhaps I can convey the ongoing reality of the poem's life more simply by recollecting a Saturday evening last August when I had the privilege of unveiling a memorial to Brian Merriman on the shore of Loch Gréine in County Clare, where the opening scene of *The Midnight Court* is set. The memorial is a large stone quarried from a hill overlooking the lake, and the opening lines of the poem are carved on it in Irish.

The people who attended the ceremony were almost all from the local district, and they were eager to point out the exact corner of the nearby field where the poet had run his hedge-school, the spot on the lough shore where he had fallen asleep and had his vision. This was and is the first circle within which Merriman's poem flourished and continues to flourish. Later that evening, in a marquee a couple of miles farther down the road, we attended a performance by the Druid Theatre Company from Galway in which the poem was given a dramatic presentation with all the boost and blast-off that song and music and topical allusion could provide. Hundreds of local people were in the tent, shouting and taking sides like a football crowd as the old man and the young woman battled it out and the president of the court gave her judgement. The psychosexual demons were no longer at bay but rampant and fully recognized, so that the audience, at the end of the performance, came away from the experience every bit as accused and absolved as the poet himself at the end of his poem. The "profane perfection of mankind" was going ahead, and civilisation was being kept on course: in a ceremony that was entirely convincing and contemporary, Orpheus had been remembered in Ireland.

FURTHER READING

Corkery, Daniel. "Brian Merriman." In his *The Hidden Ireland: A Study of Gaelic Munster in the Eighteenth Century*, 2nd edition, pp. 237-56. Dublin: M. H. Gill and Son, 1925.

> Sets the little existing biographical information on Merriman in its historical context and offers a lengthy synopsis of "The Midnight Court," using lines of the Gaelic original alongside English translations.

Fahey, J. Noel. "Cúirt an Mheán Oíche—Clár Cinn [The Midnight Court—Home Page]." [http://www.homesteader.com/merriman/welcome.html]. 1998.

> An extensive web-site in both English and Irish Gaelic that includes a biography of Merriman, an introduction to "The Midnight Court," side-by-side English and Irish versions of the poem, and a bibliography of editions and translations.

O'Connor, Frank. "Clare." In his *Leinster, Munster and Connaught*, pp. 219-33. London: Robert Hale, 1950.

> Argues that "The Midnight Court" was written after 1790—not in 1780—and after the appearance of Robert Burns's *Poems*.

Nineteenth-Century Literature Criticism

Cumulative Indexes
Volumes 1-70

How to Use This Index

The main references

Calvino, Italo
1923–1985 .... CLC 5, 8, 11, 22, 33, 39,
73; SSC 3

list all author entries in the following Gale Literary Criticism series:

BLC = *Black Literature Criticism*
CLC = *Contemporary Literary Criticism*
CLR = *Children's Literature Review*
CMLC = *Classical and Medieval Literature Criticism*
DA = *DISCovering Authors*
DAB = *DISCovering Authors: British*
DAC = *DISCovering Authors: Canadian*
DAM = *DISCovering Authors: Modules*
    DRAM: *Dramatists Module*; *MST*: *Most-Studied Authors Module*;
    MULT: *Multicultural Authors Module*; *NOV*: *Novelists Module*;
    POET: *Poets Module*; *POP*: *Popular Fiction and Genre Authors Module*
DC = *Drama Criticism*
HLC = *Hispanic Literature Criticism*
LC = *Literature Criticism from 1400 to 1800*
NCLC = *Nineteenth-Century Literature Criticism*
PC = *Poetry Criticism*
SSC = *Short Story Criticism*
TCLC = *Twentieth-Century Literary Criticism*
WLC = *World Literature Criticism, 1500 to the Present*

The cross-references

See also CANR 23; CA 85-88;
   obituary CA116

list all author entries in the following Gale biographical and literary sources:

AAYA = *Authors & Artists for Young Adults*
AITN = *Authors in the News*
BEST = *Bestsellers*
BW = *Black Writers*
CA = *Contemporary Authors*
CAAS = *Contemporary Authors Autobiography Series*
CABS = *Contemporary Authors Bibliographical Series*
CANR = *Contemporary Authors New Revision Series*
CAP = *Contemporary Authors Permanent Series*
CDALB = *Concise Dictionary of American Literary Biography*
CDBLB = *Concise Dictionary of British Literary Biography*
DLB = *Dictionary of Literary Biography*
DLBD = *Dictionary of Literary Biography Documentary Series*
DLBY = *Dictionary of Literary Biography Yearbook*
HW = *Hispanic Writers*
JRDA = *Junior DISCovering Authors*
MAICYA = *Major Authors and Illustrators for Children and Young Adults*
MTCW = *Major 20th-Century Writers*
NNAL = *Native North American Literature*
SAAS = *Something about the Author Autobiography Series*
SATA = *Something about the Author*
YABC = *Yesterday's Authors of Books for Children*

Literary Criticism Series
Cumulative Author Index

185

Angelou, Maya 1928-**CLC 12, 35, 64, 77; BLC 1; DA; DAB; DAC; DAM MST, MULT, POET, POP; WLCS**
See also AAYA 7, 20; BW 2; CA 65-68; CANR 19, 42, 65; DLB 38; MTCW; SATA 49

Anna Comnena 1083-1153 **CMLC 25**

Annensky, Innokenty (Fyodorovich) 1856-1909 **TCLC 14**
See also CA 110; 155

Annunzio, Gabriele d'
See D'Annunzio, Gabriele

Anodos
See Coleridge, Mary E(lizabeth)

Anon, Charles Robert
See Pessoa, Fernando (Antonio Nogueira)

Anouilh, Jean (Marie Lucien Pierre) 1910-1987 **CLC 1, 3, 8, 13, 40, 50; DAM DRAM; DC 8**
See also CA 17-20R; 123; CANR 32; MTCW

Anthony, Florence
See Ai

Anthony, John
See Ciardi, John (Anthony)

Anthony, Peter
See Shaffer, Anthony (Joshua); Shaffer, Peter (Levin)

Anthony, Piers 1934- **CLC 35; DAM POP**
See also AAYA 11; CA 21-24R; CANR 28, 56; DLB 8; MTCW; SAAS 22; SATA 84

Antoine, Marc
See Proust, (Valentin-Louis-George-Eugene-) Marcel

Antoninus, Brother
See Everson, William (Oliver)

Antonioni, Michelangelo 1912- **CLC 20**
See also CA 73-76; CANR 45

Antschel, Paul 1920-1970
See Celan, Paul
See also CA 85-88; CANR 33, 61; MTCW

Anwar, Chairil 1922-1949 **TCLC 22**
See also CA 121

Apollinaire, Guillaume 1880-1918**TCLC 3, 8, 51; DAM POET; PC 7**
See also Kostrowitzki, Wilhelm Apollinaris de
See also CA 152

Appelfeld, Aharon 1932- **CLC 23, 47**
See also CA 112; 133

Apple, Max (Isaac) 1941- **CLC 9, 33**
See also CA 81-84; CANR 19, 54; DLB 130

Appleman, Philip (Dean) 1926- **CLC 51**
See also CA 13-16R; CAAS 18; CANR 6, 29, 56

Appleton, Lawrence
See Lovecraft, H(oward) P(hillips)

Apteryx
See Eliot, T(homas) S(tearns)

Apuleius, (Lucius Madaurensis) 125(?)-175(?) **CMLC 1**

Aquin, Hubert 1929-1977 **CLC 15**
See also CA 105; DLB 53

Aragon, Louis 1897-1982 **CLC 3, 22; DAM NOV, POET**
See also CA 69-72; 108; CANR 28; DLB 72; MTCW

Arany, Janos 1817-1882 **NCLC 34**

Arbuthnot, John 1667-1735 **LC 1**
See also DLB 101

Archer, Herbert Winslow
See Mencken, H(enry) L(ouis)

Archer, Jeffrey (Howard) 1940- **CLC 28; DAM POP**
See also AAYA 16; BEST 89:3; CA 77-80;

CANR 22, 52; INT CANR-22

Archer, Jules 1915- **CLC 12**
See also CA 9-12R; CANR 6; SAAS 5; SATA 4, 85

Archer, Lee
See Ellison, Harlan (Jay)

Arden, John 1930-**CLC 6, 13, 15; DAM DRAM**
See also CA 13-16R; CAAS 4; CANR 31, 65, 67; DLB 13; MTCW

Arenas, Reinaldo 1943-1990 **CLC 41; DAM MULT; HLC**
See also CA 124; 128; 133; DLB 145; HW

Arendt, Hannah 1906-1975 **CLC 66, 98**
See also CA 17-20R; 61-64; CANR 26, 60; MTCW

Aretino, Pietro 1492-1556 **LC 12**

Arghezi, Tudor **CLC 80**
See also Theodorescu, Ion N.

Arguedas, Jose Maria 1911-1969 **CLC 10, 18**
See also CA 89-92; DLB 113; HW

Argueta, Manlio 1936- **CLC 31**
See also CA 131; DLB 145; HW

Ariosto, Ludovico 1474-1533 **LC 6**

Aristides
See Epstein, Joseph

Aristophanes 450B.C.-385B.C. **CMLC 4; DA; DAB; DAC; DAM DRAM, MST; DC 2; WLCS**
See also DLB 176

Arlt, Roberto (Godofredo Christophersen) 1900-1942 **TCLC 29; DAM MULT; HLC**
See also CA 123; 131; CANR 67; HW

Armah, Ayi Kwei 1939- **CLC 5, 33; BLC 1; DAM MULT, POET**
See also BW 1; CA 61-64; CANR 21, 64; DLB 117; MTCW

Armatrading, Joan 1950- **CLC 17**
See also CA 114

Arnette, Robert
See Silverberg, Robert

Arnim, Achim von (Ludwig Joachim von Arnim) 1781-1831 **NCLC 5; SSC 29**
See also DLB 90

Arnim, Bettina von 1785-1859 **NCLC 38**
See also DLB 90

Arnold, Matthew 1822-1888**NCLC 6, 29; DA; DAB; DAC; DAM MST, POET; PC 5; WLC**
See also CDBLB 1832-1890; DLB 32, 57

Arnold, Thomas 1795-1842 **NCLC 18**
See also DLB 55

Arnow, Harriette (Louisa) Simpson 1908-1986 **CLC 2, 7, 18**
See also CA 9-12R; 118; CANR 14; DLB 6; MTCW; SATA 42; SATA-Obit 47

Arp, Hans
See Arp, Jean

Arp, Jean 1887-1966 **CLC 5**
See also CA 81-84; 25-28R; CANR 42

Arrabal
See Arrabal, Fernando

Arrabal, Fernando 1932- **CLC 2, 9, 18, 58**
See also CA 9-12R; CANR 15

Arrick, Fran **CLC 30**
See also Gaberman, Judie Angell

Artaud, Antonin (Marie Joseph) 1896-1948 **TCLC 3, 36; DAM DRAM**
See also CA 104; 149

Arthur, Ruth M(abel) 1905-1979 **CLC 12**
See also CA 9-12R; 85-88; CANR 4; SATA 7, 26

Artsybashev, Mikhail (Petrovich) 1878-1927 **TCLC 31**

Arundel, Honor (Morfydd) 1919-1973**CLC 17**
See also CA 21-22; 41-44R; CAP 2; CLR 35; SATA 4; SATA-Obit 24

Arzner, Dorothy 1897-1979 **CLC 98**

Asch, Sholem 1880-1957 **TCLC 3**
See also CA 105

Ash, Shalom
See Asch, Sholem

Ashbery, John (Lawrence) 1927- CLC 2, 3, 4, 6, 9, 13, 15, 25, 41, 77; DAM POET
See also CA 5-8R; CANR 9, 37, 66; DLB 5, 165; DLBY 81; INT CANR-9; MTCW

Ashdown, Clifford
See Freeman, R(ichard) Austin

Ashe, Gordon
See Creasey, John

Ashton-Warner, Sylvia (Constance) 1908-1984 **CLC 19**
See also CA 69-72; 112; CANR 29; MTCW

Asimov, Isaac 1920-1992 **CLC 1, 3, 9, 19, 26, 76, 92; DAM POP**
See also AAYA 13; BEST 90:2; CA 1-4R; 137; CANR 2, 19, 36, 60; CLR 12; DLB 8; DLBY 92; INT CANR-9; JRDA; MAICYA; MTCW; SATA 1, 26, 74

Assis, Joaquim Maria Machado de
See Machado de Assis, Joaquim Maria

Astley, Thea (Beatrice May) 1925- **CLC 41**
See also CA 65-68; CANR 11, 43

Aston, James
See White, T(erence) H(anbury)

Asturias, Miguel Angel 1899-1974 **CLC 3, 8, 13; DAM MULT, NOV; HLC**
See also CA 25-28; 49-52; CANR 32; CAP 2; DLB 113; HW; MTCW

Atares, Carlos Saura
See Saura (Atares), Carlos

Atheling, William
See Pound, Ezra (Weston Loomis)

Atheling, William, Jr.
See Blish, James (Benjamin)

Atherton, Gertrude (Franklin Horn) 1857-1948 **TCLC 2**
See also CA 104; 155; DLB 9, 78, 186

Atherton, Lucius
See Masters, Edgar Lee

Atkins, Jack
See Harris, Mark

Atkinson, Kate **CLC 99**

Attaway, William (Alexander) 1911-1986 **CLC 92; BLC 1; DAM MULT**
See also BW 2; CA 143; DLB 76

Atticus
See Fleming, Ian (Lancaster)

Atwood, Margaret (Eleanor) 1939- CLC 2, 3, 4, 8, 13, 15, 25, 44, 84; DA; DAB; DAC; DAM MST, NOV, POET; PC 8; SSC 2; WLC
See also AAYA 12; BEST 89:2; CA 49-52; CANR 3, 24, 33, 59; DLB 53; INT CANR-24; MTCW; SATA 50

Aubigny, Pierre d'
See Mencken, H(enry) L(ouis)

Aubin, Penelope 1685-1731(?) **LC 9**
See also DLB 39

Auchincloss, Louis (Stanton) 1917- CLC 4, 6, 9, 18, 45; DAM NOV; SSC 22
See also CA 1-4R; CANR 6, 29, 55; DLB 2; DLBY 80; INT CANR-29; MTCW

Auden, W(ystan) H(ugh) 1907-1973**CLC 1, 2, 3, 4, 6, 9, 11, 14, 43; DA; DAB; DAC; DAM DRAM, MST, POET; PC 1; WLC**
See also AAYA 18; CA 9-12R; 45-48; CANR

48; DAM POET
See also CA 9-12R; 135; CANR 7, 38; DLB 20; MTCW

Barker, Harley Granville
See Granville-Barker, Harley
See also DLB 10

Barker, Howard 1946-   **CLC 37**
See also CA 102; DLB 13

Barker, Pat(ricia) 1943-   **CLC 32, 94**
See also CA 117; 122; CANR 50; INT 122

Barlow, Joel 1754-1812   **NCLC 23**
See also DLB 37

Barnard, Mary (Ethel) 1909-   **CLC 48**
See also CA 21-22; CAP 2

Barnes, Djuna 1892-1982 **CLC 3, 4, 8, 11, 29; SSC 3**
See also CA 9-12R; 107; CANR 16, 55; DLB 4, 9, 45; MTCW

Barnes, Julian (Patrick) 1946- **CLC 42; DAB**
See also CA 102; CANR 19, 54; DLB 194; DLBY 93

Barnes, Peter 1931-   **CLC 5, 56**
See also CA 65-68; CAAS 12; CANR 33, 34, 64; DLB 13; MTCW

Baroja (y Nessi), Pio 1872-1956 **TCLC 8; HLC**
See also CA 104

Baron, David
See Pinter, Harold

Baron Corvo
See Rolfe, Frederick (William Serafino Austin Lewis Mary)

Barondess, Sue K(aufman) 1926-1977 **CLC 8**
See also Kaufman, Sue
See also CA 1-4R; 69-72; CANR 1

Baron de Teive
See Pessoa, Fernando (Antonio Nogueira)

Barres, (Auguste-) Maurice 1862-1923 **TCLC 47**
See also CA 164; DLB 123

Barreto, Afonso Henrique de Lima
See Lima Barreto, Afonso Henrique de

Barrett, (Roger) Syd 1946-   **CLC 35**

Barrett, William (Christopher) 1913-1992
CLC 27
See also CA 13-16R; 139; CANR 11, 67; INT CANR-11

Barrie, J(ames) M(atthew) 1860-1937 **TCLC 2; DAB; DAM DRAM**
See also CA 104; 136; CDBLB 1890-1914; CLR 16; DLB 10, 141, 156; MAICYA; YABC 1

Barrington, Michael
See Moorcock, Michael (John)

Barrol, Grady
See Bograd, Larry

Barry, Mike
See Malzberg, Barry N(athaniel)

Barry, Philip 1896-1949   **TCLC 11**
See also CA 109; DLB 7

Bart, Andre Schwarz
See Schwarz-Bart, Andre

Barth, John (Simmons) 1930-**CLC 1, 2, 3, 5, 7, 9, 10, 14, 27, 51, 89; DAM NOV; SSC 10**
See also AITN 1, 2; CA 1-4R; CABS 1; CANR 5, 23, 49, 64; DLB 2; MTCW

Barthelme, Donald 1931-1989**CLC 1, 2, 3, 5, 6, 8, 13, 23, 46, 59; DAM NOV; SSC 2**
See also CA 21-24R; 129; CANR 20, 58; DLB 2; DLBY 80, 89; MTCW; SATA 7; SATA-Obit 62

Barthelme, Frederick 1943-   **CLC 36**
See also CA 114; 122; DLBY 85; INT 122

Barthes, Roland (Gerard) 1915-1980**CLC 24,**

83
See also CA 130; 97-100; CANR 66; MTCW

Barzun, Jacques (Martin) 1907-   **CLC 51**
See also CA 61-64; CANR 22

Bashevis, Isaac
See Singer, Isaac Bashevis

Bashkirtseff, Marie 1859-1884   **NCLC 27**

Basho
See Matsuo Basho

Bass, Kingsley B., Jr.
See Bullins, Ed

Bass, Rick 1958-   **CLC 79**
See also CA 126; CANR 53

Bassani, Giorgio 1916-   **CLC 9**
See also CA 65-68; CANR 33; DLB 128, 177; MTCW

Bastos, Augusto (Antonio) Roa
See Roa Bastos, Augusto (Antonio)

Bataille, Georges 1897-1962   **CLC 29**
See also CA 101; 89-92

Bates, H(erbert) E(rnest) 1905-1974 **CLC 46; DAB; DAM POP; SSC 10**
See also CA 93-96; 45-48; CANR 34; DLB 162, 191; MTCW

Bauchart
See Camus, Albert

Baudelaire, Charles 1821-1867 **NCLC 6, 29, 55; DA; DAB; DAC; DAM MST, POET; PC 1; SSC 18; WLC**

Baudrillard, Jean 1929-   **CLC 60**

Baum, L(yman) Frank 1856-1919   **TCLC 7**
See also CA 108; 133; CLR 15; DLB 22; JRDA; MAICYA; MTCW; SATA 18

Baum, Louis F.
See Baum, L(yman) Frank

Baumbach, Jonathan 1933-   **CLC 6, 23**
See also CA 13-16R; CAAS 5; CANR 12, 66; DLBY 80; INT CANR-12; MTCW

Bausch, Richard (Carl) 1945-   **CLC 51**
See also CA 101; CAAS 14; CANR 43, 61; DLB 130

Baxter, Charles (Morley) 1947- **CLC 45, 78; DAM POP**
See also CA 57-60; CANR 40, 64; DLB 130

Baxter, George Owen
See Faust, Frederick (Schiller)

Baxter, James K(eir) 1926-1972   **CLC 14**
See also CA 77-80

Baxter, John
See Hunt, E(verette) Howard, (Jr.)

Bayer, Sylvia
See Glassco, John

Baynton, Barbara 1857-1929   **TCLC 57**

Beagle, Peter S(oyer) 1939-   **CLC 7, 104**
See also CA 9-12R; CANR 4, 51; DLBY 80; INT CANR-4; SATA 60

Bean, Normal
See Burroughs, Edgar Rice

Beard, Charles A(ustin) 1874-1948 **TCLC 15**
See also CA 115; DLB 17; SATA 18

Beardsley, Aubrey 1872-1898   **NCLC 6**

Beattie, Ann 1947-**CLC 8, 13, 18, 40, 63; DAM NOV, POP; SSC 11**
See also BEST 90:2; CA 81-84; CANR 53; DLBY 82; MTCW

Beattie, James 1735-1803   **NCLC 25**
See also DLB 109

Beauchamp, Kathleen Mansfield 1888-1923
See Mansfield, Katherine
See also CA 104; 134; DA; DAC; DAM MST

Beaumarchais, Pierre-Augustin Caron de 1732-1799   **DC 4**
See also DAM DRAM

Beaumont, Francis 1584(?)-1616 **LC 33; DC 6**
See also CDBLB Before 1660; DLB 58, 121

Beauvoir, Simone (Lucie Ernestine Marie Bertrand) de 1908-1986 **CLC 1, 2, 4, 8, 14, 31, 44, 50, 71; DA; DAB; DAC; DAM MST, NOV; WLC**
See also CA 9-12R; 118; CANR 28, 61; DLB 72; DLBY 86; MTCW

Becker, Carl (Lotus) 1873-1945   **TCLC 63**
See also CA 157; DLB 17

Becker, Jurek 1937-1997   **CLC 7, 19**
See also CA 85-88; 157; CANR 60; DLB 75

Becker, Walter 1950-   **CLC 26**

Beckett, Samuel (Barclay) 1906-1989 **CLC 1, 2, 3, 4, 6, 9, 10, 11, 14, 18, 29, 57, 59, 83; DA; DAB; DAC; DAM DRAM, MST, NOV; SSC 16; WLC**
See also CA 5-8R; 130; CANR 33, 61; CDBLB 1945-1960; DLB 13, 15; DLBY 90; MTCW

Beckford, William 1760-1844   **NCLC 16**
See also DLB 39

Beckman, Gunnel 1910-   **CLC 26**
See also CA 33-36R; CANR 15; CLR 25; MAICYA; SAAS 9; SATA 6

Becque, Henri 1837-1899   **NCLC 3**
See also DLB 192

Beddoes, Thomas Lovell 1803-1849 **NCLC 3**
See also DLB 96

Bede c. 673-735   **CMLC 20**
See also DLB 146

Bedford, Donald F.
See Fearing, Kenneth (Flexner)

Beecher, Catharine Esther 1800-1878 **NCLC 30**
See also DLB 1

Beecher, John 1904-1980   **CLC 6**
See also AITN 1; CA 5-8R; 105; CANR 8

Beer, Johann 1655-1700   **LC 5**
See also DLB 168

Beer, Patricia 1924-   **CLC 58**
See also CA 61-64; CANR 13, 46; DLB 40

Beerbohm, Max
See Beerbohm, (Henry) Max(imilian)

Beerbohm, (Henry) Max(imilian) 1872-1956
TCLC 1, 24
See also CA 104; 154; DLB 34, 100

Beer-Hofmann, Richard 1866-1945 **TCLC 60**
See also CA 160; DLB 81

Begiebing, Robert J(ohn) 1946-   **CLC 70**
See also CA 122; CANR 40

Behan, Brendan 1923-1964 **CLC 1, 8, 11, 15, 79; DAM DRAM**
See also CA 73-76; CANR 33; CDBLB 1945-1960; DLB 13; MTCW

Behn, Aphra 1640(?)-1689 **LC 1, 30; DA; DAB; DAC; DAM DRAM, MST, NOV, POET; DC 4; PC 13; WLC**
See also DLB 39, 80, 131

Behrman, S(amuel) N(athaniel) 1893-1973
CLC 40
See also CA 13-16; 45-48; CAP 1; DLB 7, 44

Belasco, David 1853-1931   **TCLC 3**
See also CA 104; DLB 7

Belcheva, Elisaveta 1893-   **CLC 10**
See also Bagryana, Elisaveta

Beldone, Phil "Cheech"
See Ellison, Harlan (Jay)

Beleno
See Azuela, Mariano

Belinski, Vissarion Grigoryevich 1811-1848
NCLC 5

Belitt, Ben 1911-   **CLC 22**
See also CA 13-16R; CAAS 4; CANR 7; DLB

5

Bell, Gertrude 1868-1926   **TCLC 67**
See also DLB 174

Bell, James Madison 1826-1902   **TCLC 43; BLC 1; DAM MULT**
See also BW 1; CA 122; 124; DLB 50

Bell, Madison Smartt 1957-   **CLC 41, 102**
See also CA 111; CANR 28, 54

Bell, Marvin (Hartley) 1937-CLC **8, 31; DAM POET**
See also CA 21-24R; CAAS 14; CANR 59; DLB 5; MTCW

Bell, W. L. D.
See Mencken, H(enry) L(ouis)

Bellamy, Atwood C.
See Mencken, H(enry) L(ouis)

Bellamy, Edward 1850-1898   **NCLC 4**
See also DLB 12

Bellin, Edward J.
See Kuttner, Henry

Belloc, (Joseph) Hilaire (Pierre Sebastien Rene Swanton) 1870-1953 **TCLC 7, 18; DAM POET**
See also CA 106; 152; DLB 19, 100, 141, 174; YABC 1

Belloc, Joseph Peter Rene Hilaire
See Belloc, (Joseph) Hilaire (Pierre Sebastien Rene Swanton)

Belloc, Joseph Pierre Hilaire
See Belloc, (Joseph) Hilaire (Pierre Sebastien Rene Swanton)

Belloc, M. A.
See Lowndes, Marie Adelaide (Belloc)

Bellow, Saul 1915-CLC **1, 2, 3, 6, 8, 10, 13, 15, 25, 33, 34, 63, 79; DA; DAB; DAC; DAM MST, NOV, POP; SSC 14; WLC**
See also AITN 2; BEST 89:3; CA 5-8R; CABS 1; CANR 29, 53; CDALB 1941-1968; DLB 2, 28; DLBD 3; DLBY 82; MTCW

Belser, Reimond Karel Maria de 1929-
See Ruyslinck, Ward
See also CA 152

Bely, Andrey   **TCLC 7; PC 11**
See also Bugayev, Boris Nikolayevich

Belyi, Andrei
See Bugayev, Boris Nikolayevich

Benary, Margot
See Benary-Isbert, Margot

Benary-Isbert, Margot 1889-1979   **CLC 12**
See also CA 5-8R; 89-92; CANR 4; CLR 12; MAICYA; SATA 2; SATA-Obit 21

Benavente (y Martinez), Jacinto 1866-1954 **TCLC 3; DAM DRAM, MULT**
See also CA 106; 131; HW; MTCW

Benchley, Peter (Bradford) 1940-   **CLC 4, 8; DAM NOV, POP**
See also AAYA 14; AITN 2; CA 17-20R; CANR 12, 35, 66; MTCW; SATA 3, 89

Benchley, Robert (Charles) 1889-1945 **TCLC 1, 55**
See also CA 105; 153; DLB 11

Benda, Julien 1867-1956   **TCLC 60**
See also CA 120; 154

Benedict, Ruth (Fulton) 1887-1948 **TCLC 60**
See also CA 158

Benedikt, Michael 1935-   **CLC 4, 14**
See also CA 13-16R; CANR 7; DLB 5

Benet, Juan 1927-   **CLC 28**
See also CA 143

Benet, Stephen Vincent 1898-1943   **TCLC 7; DAM POET; SSC 10**
See also CA 104; 152; DLB 4, 48, 102; DLBY 97; YABC 1

Benet, William Rose 1886-1950   **TCLC 28; DAM POET**
See also CA 118; 152; DLB 45

Benford, Gregory (Albert) 1941-   **CLC 52**
See also CA 69-72; CAAS 27; CANR 12, 24, 49; DLBY 82

Bengtsson, Frans (Gunnar) 1894-1954 TCLC 48

Benjamin, David
See Slavitt, David R(ytman)

Benjamin, Lois
See Gould, Lois

Benjamin, Walter 1892-1940   **TCLC 39**
See also CA 164

Benn, Gottfried 1886-1956   **TCLC 3**
See also CA 106; 153; DLB 56

Bennett, Alan 1934- CLC **45, 77; DAB; DAM MST**
See also CA 103; CANR 35, 55; MTCW

Bennett, (Enoch) Arnold 1867-1931 TCLC **5, 20**
See also CA 106; 155; CDBLB 1890-1914; DLB 10, 34, 98, 135

Bennett, Elizabeth
See Mitchell, Margaret (Munnerlyn)

Bennett, George Harold 1930-
See Bennett, Hal
See also BW 1; CA 97-100

Bennett, Hal   **CLC 5**
See also Bennett, George Harold
See also DLB 33

Bennett, Jay 1912-   **CLC 35**
See also AAYA 10; CA 69-72; CANR 11, 42; JRDA; SAAS 4; SATA 41, 87; SATA-Brief 27

Bennett, Louise (Simone) 1919-CLC **28; BLC 1; DAM MULT**
See also BW 2; CA 151; DLB 117

Benson, E(dward) F(rederic) 1867-1940 **TCLC 27**
See also CA 114; 157; DLB 135, 153

Benson, Jackson J. 1930-   **CLC 34**
See also CA 25-28R; DLB 111

Benson, Sally 1900-1972   **CLC 17**
See also CA 19-20; 37-40R; CAP 1; SATA 1, 35; SATA-Obit 27

Benson, Stella 1892-1933   **TCLC 17**
See also CA 117; 155; DLB 36, 162

Bentham, Jeremy 1748-1832   **NCLC 38**
See also DLB 107, 158

Bentley, E(dmund) C(lerihew) 1875-1956 **TCLC 12**
See also CA 108; DLB 70

Bentley, Eric (Russell) 1916-   **CLC 24**
See also CA 5-8R; CANR 6, 67; INT CANR-6

Beranger, Pierre Jean de 1780-1857NCLC 34

Berdyaev, Nicolas
See Berdyaev, Nikolai (Aleksandrovich)

Berdyaev, Nikolai (Aleksandrovich) 1874-1948 **TCLC 67**
See also CA 120; 157

Berdyayev, Nikolai (Aleksandrovich)
See Berdyaev, Nikolai (Aleksandrovich)

Berendt, John (Lawrence) 1939-   **CLC 86**
See also CA 146

Berger, Colonel
See Malraux, (Georges-)Andre

Berger, John (Peter) 1926-   **CLC 2, 19**
See also CA 81-84; CANR 51; DLB 14

Berger, Melvin H. 1927-   **CLC 12**
See also CA 5-8R; CANR 4; CLR 32; SAAS 2; SATA 5, 88

Berger, Thomas (Louis) 1924-CLC **3, 5, 8, 11, 18, 38; DAM NOV**
See also CA 1-4R; CANR 5, 28, 51; DLB 2; DLBY 80; INT CANR-28; MTCW

Bergman, (Ernst) Ingmar 1918- CLC **16, 72**
See also CA 81-84; CANR 33

Bergson, Henri 1859-1941   **TCLC 32**
See also CA 164

Bergstein, Eleanor 1938-   **CLC 4**
See also CA 53-56; CANR 5

Berkoff, Steven 1937-   **CLC 56**
See also CA 104

Bermant, Chaim (Icyk) 1929-   **CLC 40**
See also CA 57-60; CANR 6, 31, 57

Bern, Victoria
See Fisher, M(ary) F(rances) K(ennedy)

Bernanos, (Paul Louis) Georges 1888-1948 **TCLC 3**
See also CA 104; 130; DLB 72

Bernard, April 1956-   **CLC 59**
See also CA 131

Berne, Victoria
See Fisher, M(ary) F(rances) K(ennedy)

Bernhard, Thomas 1931-1989 **CLC 3, 32, 61**
See also CA 85-88; 127; CANR 32, 57; DLB 85, 124; MTCW

Bernhardt, Sarah (Henriette Rosine) 1844-1923 **TCLC 75**
See also CA 157

Berriault, Gina 1926-   **CLC 54, 109; SSC 30**
See also CA 116; 129; CANR 66; DLB 130

Berrigan, Daniel 1921-   **CLC 4**
See also CA 33-36R; CAAS 1; CANR 11, 43; DLB 5

Berrigan, Edmund Joseph Michael, Jr. 1934-1983
See Berrigan, Ted
See also CA 61-64; 110; CANR 14

Berrigan, Ted   **CLC 37**
See also Berrigan, Edmund Joseph Michael, Jr.
See also DLB 5, 169

Berry, Charles Edward Anderson 1931-
See Berry, Chuck
See also CA 115

Berry, Chuck   **CLC 17**
See also Berry, Charles Edward Anderson

Berry, Jonas
See Ashbery, John (Lawrence)

Berry, Wendell (Erdman) 1934- CLC **4, 6, 8, 27, 46; DAM POET**
See also AITN 1; CA 73-76; CANR 50; DLB 5, 6

Berryman, John 1914-1972CLC **1, 2, 3, 4, 6, 8, 10, 13, 25, 62; DAM POET**
See also CA 13-16; 33-36R; CABS 2; CANR 35; CAP 1; CDALB 1941-1968; DLB 48; MTCW

Bertolucci, Bernardo 1940-   **CLC 16**
See also CA 106

Berton, Pierre (Francis De Marigny) 1920- **CLC 104**
See also CA 1-4R; CANR 2, 56; DLB 68

Bertrand, Aloysius 1807-1841   **NCLC 31**

Bertran de Born c. 1140-1215   **CMLC 5**

Besant, Annie (Wood) 1847-1933   **TCLC 9**
See also CA 105

Bessie, Alvah 1904-1985   **CLC 23**
See also CA 5-8R; 116; CANR 2; DLB 26

Bethlen, T. D.
See Silverberg, Robert

Beti, Mongo   **CLC 27; BLC 1; DAM MULT**
See also Biyidi, Alexandre

Betjeman, John 1906-1984   **CLC 2, 6, 10, 34, 43; DAB; DAM MST, POET**

See also CA 9-12R; 112; CANR 33, 56; CDBLB 1945-1960; DLB 20; DLBY 84; MTCW

Bettelheim, Bruno 1903-1990 **CLC 79**
See also CA 81-84; 131; CANR 23, 61; MTCW

Betti, Ugo 1892-1953 **TCLC 5**
See also CA 104; 155

Betts, Doris (Waugh) 1932- **CLC 3, 6, 28**
See also CA 13-16R; CANR 9, 66; DLBY 82; INT CANR-9

Bevan, Alistair
See Roberts, Keith (John Kingston)

Bey, Pilaff
See Douglas, (George) Norman

Bialik, Chaim Nachman 1873-1934 **TCLC 25**

Bickerstaff, Isaac
See Swift, Jonathan

Bidart, Frank 1939- **CLC 33**
See also CA 140

Bienek, Horst 1930- **CLC 7, 11**
See also CA 73-76; DLB 75

Bierce, Ambrose (Gwinett) 1842-1914(?) **TCLC 1, 7, 44; DA; DAC; DAM MST; SSC 9; WLC**
See also CA 104; 139; CDALB 1865-1917; DLB 11, 12, 23, 71, 74, 186

Biggers, Earl Derr 1884-1933 **TCLC 65**
See also CA 108; 153

Billings, Josh
See Shaw, Henry Wheeler

Billington, (Lady) Rachel (Mary) 1942- **CLC 43**
See also AITN 2; CA 33-36R; CANR 44

Binyon, T(imothy) J(ohn) 1936- **CLC 34**
See also CA 111; CANR 28

Bioy Casares, Adolfo 1914-1984 **CLC 4, 8, 13, 88; DAM MULT; HLC; SSC 17**
See also CA 29-32R; CANR 19, 43, 66; DLB 113; HW; MTCW

Bird, Cordwainer
See Ellison, Harlan (Jay)

Bird, Robert Montgomery 1806-1854 **NCLC 1**

Birney, (Alfred) Earle 1904-1995 **CLC 1, 4, 6, 11; DAC; DAM MST, POET**
See also CA 1-4R; CANR 5, 20; DLB 88; MTCW

Bishop, Elizabeth 1911-1979 **CLC 1, 4, 9, 13, 15, 32; DA; DAC; DAM MST, POET; PC 3**
See also CA 5-8R; 89-92; CABS 2; CANR 26, 61; CDALB 1968-1988; DLB 5, 169; MTCW; SATA-Obit 24

Bishop, John 1935- **CLC 10**
See also CA 105

Bissett, Bill 1939- **CLC 18; PC 14**
See also CA 69-72; CAAS 19; CANR 15; DLB 53; MTCW

Bitov, Andrei (Georgievich) 1937- **CLC 57**
See also CA 142

Biyidi, Alexandre 1932-
See Beti, Mongo
See also BW 1; CA 114; 124; MTCW

Bjarme, Brynjolf
See Ibsen, Henrik (Johan)

Bjornson, Bjornstjerne (Martinius) 1832-1910 **TCLC 7, 37**
See also CA 104

Black, Robert
See Holdstock, Robert P.

Blackburn, Paul 1926-1971 **CLC 9, 43**
See also CA 81-84; 33-36R; CANR 34; DLB 16; DLBY 81

Black Elk 1863-1950 **TCLC 33; DAM MULT**

See also CA 144; NNAL

Black Hobart
See Sanders, (James) Ed(ward)

Blacklin, Malcolm
See Chambers, Aidan

Blackmore, R(ichard) D(oddridge) 1825-1900 **TCLC 27**
See also CA 120; DLB 18

Blackmur, R(ichard) P(almer) 1904-1965 **CLC 2, 24**
See also CA 11-12; 25-28R; CAP 1; DLB 63

Black Tarantula
See Acker, Kathy

Blackwood, Algernon (Henry) 1869-1951 **TCLC 5**
See also CA 105; 150; DLB 153, 156, 178

Blackwood, Caroline 1931-1996 **CLC 6, 9, 100**
See also CA 85-88; 151; CANR 32, 61, 65; DLB 14; MTCW

Blade, Alexander
See Hamilton, Edmond; Silverberg, Robert

Blaga, Lucian 1895-1961 **CLC 75**

Blair, Eric (Arthur) 1903-1950
See Orwell, George
See also CA 104; 132; DA; DAB; DAC; DAM MST, NOV; MTCW; SATA 29

Blais, Marie-Claire 1939- **CLC 2, 4, 6, 13, 22; DAC; DAM MST**
See also CA 21-24R; CAAS 4; CANR 38; DLB 53; MTCW

Blaise, Clark 1940- **CLC 29**
See also AITN 2; CA 53-56; CAAS 3; CANR 5, 66; DLB 53

Blake, Fairley
See De Voto, Bernard (Augustine)

Blake, Nicholas
See Day Lewis, C(ecil)
See also DLB 77

Blake, William 1757-1827 **NCLC 13, 37, 57; DA; DAB; DAC; DAM MST, POET; PC 12; WLC**
See also CDBLB 1789-1832; DLB 93, 163; MAICYA; SATA 30

Blasco Ibanez, Vicente 1867-1928 **TCLC 12; DAM NOV**
See also CA 110; 131; HW; MTCW

Blatty, William Peter 1928- **CLC 2; DAM POP**
See also CA 5-8R; CANR 9

Bleeck, Oliver
See Thomas, Ross (Elmore)

Blessing, Lee 1949- **CLC 54**

Blish, James (Benjamin) 1921-1975 **CLC 14**
See also CA 1-4R; 57-60; CANR 3; DLB 8; MTCW; SATA 66

Bliss, Reginald
See Wells, H(erbert) G(eorge)

Blixen, Karen (Christentze Dinesen) 1885-1962
See Dinesen, Isak
See also CA 25-28; CANR 22, 50; CAP 2; MTCW; SATA 44

Bloch, Robert (Albert) 1917-1994 **CLC 33**
See also CA 5-8R; 146; CAAS 20; CANR 5; DLB 44; INT CANR-5; SATA 12; SATA-Obit 82

Blok, Alexander (Alexandrovich) 1880-1921 **TCLC 5; PC 21**
See also CA 104

Blom, Jan
See Breytenbach, Breyten

Bloom, Harold 1930- **CLC 24, 103**
See also CA 13-16R; CANR 39; DLB 67

Bloomfield, Aurelius
See Bourne, Randolph S(illiman)

Blount, Roy (Alton), Jr. 1941- **CLC 38**
See also CA 53-56; CANR 10, 28, 61; INT CANR-28; MTCW

Bloy, Leon 1846-1917 **TCLC 22**
See also CA 121; DLB 123

Blume, Judy (Sussman) 1938- **CLC 12, 30; DAM NOV, POP**
See also AAYA 3; CA 29-32R; CANR 13, 37, 66; CLR 2, 15; DLB 52; JRDA; MAICYA; MTCW; SATA 2, 31, 79

Blunden, Edmund (Charles) 1896-1974 **CLC 2, 56**
See also CA 17-18; 45-48; CANR 54; CAP 2; DLB 20, 100, 155; MTCW

Bly, Robert (Elwood) 1926- **CLC 1, 2, 5, 10, 15, 38; DAM POET**
See also CA 5-8R; CANR 41; DLB 5; MTCW

Boas, Franz 1858-1942 **TCLC 56**
See also CA 115

Bobette
See Simenon, Georges (Jacques Christian)

Boccaccio, Giovanni 1313-1375 **CMLC 13; SSC 10**

Bochco, Steven 1943- **CLC 35**
See also AAYA 11; CA 124; 138

Bodenheim, Maxwell 1892-1954 **TCLC 44**
See also CA 110; DLB 9, 45

Bodker, Cecil 1927- **CLC 21**
See also CA 73-76; CANR 13, 44; CLR 23; MAICYA; SATA 14

Boell, Heinrich (Theodor) 1917-1985 **CLC 2, 3, 6, 9, 11, 15, 27, 32, 72; DA; DAB; DAC; DAM MST, NOV; SSC 23; WLC**
See also CA 21-24R; 116; CANR 24; DLB 69; DLBY 85; MTCW

Boerne, Alfred
See Doeblin, Alfred

Boethius 480(?)-524(?) **CMLC 15**
See also DLB 115

Bogan, Louise 1897-1970 **CLC 4, 39, 46, 93; DAM POET; PC 12**
See also CA 73-76; 25-28R; CANR 33; DLB 45, 169; MTCW

Bogarde, Dirk **CLC 19**
See also Van Den Bogarde, Derek Jules Gaspard Ulric Niven
See also DLB 14

Bogosian, Eric 1953- **CLC 45**
See also CA 138

Bograd, Larry 1953- **CLC 35**
See also CA 93-96; CANR 57; SAAS 21; SATA 33, 89

Boiardo, Matteo Maria 1441-1494 **LC 6**

Boileau-Despreaux, Nicolas 1636-1711 **LC 3**

Bojer, Johan 1872-1959 **TCLC 64**

Boland, Eavan (Aisling) 1944- **CLC 40, 67; DAM POET**
See also CA 143; CANR 61; DLB 40

Boll, Heinrich
See Boell, Heinrich (Theodor)

Bolt, Lee
See Faust, Frederick (Schiller)

Bolt, Robert (Oxton) 1924-1995 **CLC 14; DAM DRAM**
See also CA 17-20R; 147; CANR 35, 67; DLB 13; MTCW

Bombet, Louis-Alexandre-Cesar
See Stendhal

Bomkauf
See Kaufman, Bob (Garnell)

Bonaventura **NCLC 35**
See also DLB 90

Bond, Edward 1934- **CLC 4, 6, 13, 23; DAM**

See also CA 125; CANR 50

Campana, Dino 1885-1932   **TCLC 20**
See also CA 117; DLB 114

Campanella, Tommaso 1568-1639   **LC 32**

Campbell, John W(ood, Jr.) 1910-1971   **CLC 32**
See also CA 21-22; 29-32R; CANR 34; CAP 2; DLB 8; MTCW

Campbell, Joseph 1904-1987   **CLC 69**
See also AAYA 3; BEST 89:2; CA 1-4R; 124; CANR 3, 28, 61; MTCW

Campbell, Maria 1940-   **CLC 85; DAC**
See also CA 102; CANR 54; NNAL

Campbell, (John) Ramsey 1946- **CLC 42; SSC 19**
See also CA 57-60; CANR 7; INT CANR-7

Campbell, (Ignatius) Roy (Dunnachie) 1901-1957   **TCLC 5**
See also CA 104; 155; DLB 20

Campbell, Thomas 1777-1844   **NCLC 19**
See also DLB 93; 144

Campbell, Wilfred   **TCLC 9**
See also Campbell, William

Campbell, William 1858(?)-1918
See Campbell, Wilfred
See also CA 106; DLB 92

Campion, Jane   **CLC 95**
See also CA 138

Campos, Alvaro de
See Pessoa, Fernando (Antonio Nogueira)

Camus, Albert 1913-1960 CLC **1, 2, 4, 9, 11, 14, 32, 63, 69; DA; DAB; DAC; DAM DRAM, MST, NOV; DC 2; SSC 9; WLC**
See also CA 89-92; DLB 72; MTCW

Canby, Vincent 1924-   **CLC 13**
See also CA 81-84

Cancale
See Desnos, Robert

Canetti, Elias 1905-1994 CLC **3, 14, 25, 75, 86**
See also CA 21-24R; 146; CANR 23, 61; DLB 85, 124; MTCW

Canin, Ethan 1960-   **CLC 55**
See also CA 131; 135

Cannon, Curt
See Hunter, Evan

Cao, Lan 1961-   **CLC 109**
See also CA 165

Cape, Judith
See Page, P(atricia) K(athleen)

Capek, Karel 1890-1938   **TCLC 6, 37; DA; DAB; DAC; DAM DRAM, MST, NOV; DC 1; WLC**
See also CA 104; 140

Capote, Truman 1924-1984 CLC **1, 3, 8, 13, 19, 34, 38, 58; DA; DAB; DAC; DAM MST, NOV, POP; SSC 2; WLC**
See also CA 5-8R; 113; CANR 18, 62; CDALB 1941-1968; DLB 2, 185; DLBY 80, 84; MTCW; SATA 91

Capra, Frank 1897-1991   **CLC 16**
See also CA 61-64; 135

Caputo, Philip 1941-   **CLC 32**
See also CA 73-76; CANR 40

Caragiale, Ion Luca 1852-1912   **TCLC 76**
See also CA 157

Card, Orson Scott 1951- CLC **44, 47, 50; DAM POP**
See also AAYA 11; CA 102; CANR 27, 47; INT CANR-27; MTCW; SATA 83

Cardenal, Ernesto 1925-   **CLC 31; DAM MULT, POET; HLC; PC 22**
See also CA 49-52; CANR 2, 32, 66; HW; MTCW

Cardozo, Benjamin N(athan) 1870-1938   **TCLC 65**
See also CA 117; 164

Carducci, Giosue (Alessandro Giuseppe) 1835-1907   **TCLC 32**
See also CA 163

Carew, Thomas 1595(?)-1640   **LC 13**
See also DLB 126

Carey, Ernestine Gilbreth 1908-   **CLC 17**
See also CA 5-8R; SATA 2

Carey, Peter 1943-   **CLC 40, 55, 96**
See also CA 123; 127; CANR 53; INT 127; MTCW; SATA 94

Carleton, William 1794-1869   **NCLC 3**
See also DLB 159

Carlisle, Henry (Coffin) 1926-   **CLC 33**
See also CA 13-16R; CANR 15

Carlsen, Chris
See Holdstock, Robert P.

Carlson, Ron(ald F.) 1947-   **CLC 54**
See also CA 105; CANR 27

Carlyle, Thomas 1795-1881   **NCLC 70; DA; DAB; DAC; DAM MST**
See also CDBLB 1789-1832; DLB 55; 144

Carman, (William) Bliss 1861-1929 TCLC **7; DAC**
See also CA 104; 152; DLB 92

Carnegie, Dale 1888-1955   **TCLC 53**

Carossa, Hans 1878-1956   **TCLC 48**
See also DLB 66

Carpenter, Don(ald Richard) 1931-1995 CLC **41**
See also CA 45-48; 149; CANR 1

Carpentier (y Valmont), Alejo 1904-1980 **CLC 8, 11, 38, 110; DAM MULT; HLC**
See also CA 65-68; 97-100; CANR 11; DLB 113; HW

Carr, Caleb 1955(?)-   **CLC 86**
See also CA 147

Carr, Emily 1871-1945   **TCLC 32**
See also CA 159; DLB 68

Carr, John Dickson 1906-1977   **CLC 3**
See also Fairbairn, Roger
See also CA 49-52; 69-72; CANR 3, 33, 60; MTCW

Carr, Philippa
See Hibbert, Eleanor Alice Burford

Carr, Virginia Spencer 1929-   **CLC 34**
See also CA 61-64; DLB 111

Carrere, Emmanuel 1957-   **CLC 89**

Carrier, Roch 1937- CLC **13, 78; DAC; DAM MST**
See also CA 130; CANR 61; DLB 53

Carroll, James P. 1943(?)-   **CLC 38**
See also CA 81-84

Carroll, Jim 1951-   **CLC 35**
See also AAYA 17; CA 45-48; CANR 42

Carroll, Lewis   **NCLC 2, 53; PC 18; WLC**
See also Dodgson, Charles Lutwidge
See also CDBLB 1832-1890; CLR 2, 18; DLB 18, 163, 178; JRDA

Carroll, Paul Vincent 1900-1968   **CLC 10**
See also CA 9-12R; 25-28R; DLB 10

Carruth, Hayden 1921- CLC **4, 7, 10, 18, 84; PC 10**
See also CA 9-12R; CANR 4, 38, 59; DLB 5, 165; INT CANR-4; MTCW; SATA 47

Carson, Rachel Louise 1907-1964   **CLC 71; DAM POP**
See also CA 77-80; CANR 35; MTCW; SATA 23

Carter, Angela (Olive) 1940-1992 **CLC 5, 41, 76; SSC 13**

See also CA 53-56; 136; CANR 12, 36, 61; DLB 14; MTCW; SATA 66; SATA-Obit 70

Carter, Nick
See Smith, Martin Cruz

Carver, Raymond 1938-1988 CLC **22, 36, 53, 55; DAM NOV; SSC 8**
See also CA 33-36R; 126; CANR 17, 34, 61; DLB 130; DLBY 84, 88; MTCW

Cary, Elizabeth, Lady Falkland 1585-1639   **LC 30**

Cary, (Arthur) Joyce (Lunel) 1888-1957   **TCLC 1, 29**
See also CA 104; 164; CDBLB 1914-1945; DLB 15, 100

Casanova de Seingalt, Giovanni Jacopo 1725-1798   **LC 13**

Casares, Adolfo Bioy
See Bioy Casares, Adolfo

Casely-Hayford, J(oseph) E(phraim) 1866-1930   **TCLC 24; BLC 1; DAM MULT**
See also BW 2; CA 123; 152

Casey, John (Dudley) 1939-   **CLC 59**
See also BEST 90:2; CA 69-72; CANR 23

Casey, Michael 1947-   **CLC 2**
See also CA 65-68; DLB 5

Casey, Patrick
See Thurman, Wallace (Henry)

Casey, Warren (Peter) 1935-1988   **CLC 12**
See also CA 101; 127; INT 101

Casona, Alejandro   **CLC 49**
See also Alvarez, Alejandro Rodriguez

Cassavetes, John 1929-1989   **CLC 20**
See also CA 85-88; 127

Cassian, Nina 1924-   **PC 17**

Cassill, R(onald) V(erlin) 1919-   **CLC 4, 23**
See also CA 9-12R; CAAS 1; CANR 7, 45; DLB 6

Cassirer, Ernst 1874-1945   **TCLC 61**
See also CA 157

Cassity, (Allen) Turner 1929-   **CLC 6, 42**
See also CA 17-20R; CAAS 8; CANR 11; DLB 105

Castaneda, Carlos 1931(?)-   **CLC 12**
See also CA 25-28R; CANR 32, 66; HW; MTCW

Castedo, Elena 1937-   **CLC 65**
See also CA 132

Castedo-Ellerman, Elena
See Castedo, Elena

Castellanos, Rosario 1925-1974 CLC **66; DAM MULT; HLC**
See also CA 131; 53-56; CANR 58; DLB 113; HW

Castelvetro, Lodovico 1505-1571   **LC 12**

Castiglione, Baldassare 1478-1529   **LC 12**

Castle, Robert
See Hamilton, Edmond

Castro, Guillen de 1569-1631   **LC 19**

Castro, Rosalia de 1837-1885 NCLC **3; DAM MULT**

Cather, Willa
See Cather, Willa Sibert

Cather, Willa Sibert 1873-1947   TCLC **1, 11, 31; DA; DAB; DAC; DAM MST, NOV; SSC 2; WLC**
See also AAYA 24; CA 104; 128; CDALB 1865-1917; DLB 9, 54, 78; DLBD 1; MTCW; SATA 30

Catherine, Saint 1347-1380   **CMLC 27**

Cato, Marcus Porcius 234B.C.-149B.C.   **CMLC 21**

Catton, (Charles) Bruce 1899-1978   **CLC 35**
See also AITN 1; CA 5-8R; 81-84; CANR 7;

DLB 17; SATA 2; SATA-Obit 24
Catullus c. 84B.C.-c. 54B.C. **CMLC 18**
Cauldwell, Frank
  See King, Francis (Henry)
Caunitz, William J. 1933-1996 **CLC 34**
  See also BEST 89:3; CA 125; 130; 152; INT
  130
Causley, Charles (Stanley) 1917- **CLC 7**
  See also CA 9-12R; CANR 5, 35; CLR 30; DLB
  27; MTCW; SATA 3, 66
Caute, (John) David 1936- **CLC 29; DAM
  NOV**
  See also CA 1-4R; CAAS 4; CANR 1, 33, 64;
  DLB 14
Cavafy, C(onstantine) P(eter) 1863-1933
  TCLC 2, 7; DAM POET
  See also Kavafis, Konstantinos Petrou
  See also CA 148
Cavallo, Evelyn
  See Spark, Muriel (Sarah)
Cavanna, Betty **CLC 12**
  See also Harrison, Elizabeth Cavanna
  See also JRDA; MAICYA; SAAS 4; SATA 1,
  30
Cavendish, Margaret Lucas 1623-1673 **LC 30**
  See also DLB 131
Caxton, William 1421(?)-1491(?) **LC 17**
  See also DLB 170
Cayer, D. M.
  See Duffy, Maureen
Cayrol, Jean 1911- **CLC 11**
  See also CA 89-92; DLB 83
Cela, Camilo Jose 1916- CLC 4, 13, 59; **DAM
  MULT; HLC**
  See also BEST 90:2; CA 21-24R; CAAS 10;
  CANR 21, 32; DLBY 89; HW; MTCW
Celan, Paul **CLC 10, 19, 53, 82; PC 10**
  See also Antschel, Paul
  See also DLB 69
Celine, Louis-Ferdinand CLC 1, 3, 4, 7, 9, 15,
  47
  See also Destouches, Louis-Ferdinand
  See also DLB 72
Cellini, Benvenuto 1500-1571 **LC 7**
Cendrars, Blaise 1887-1961 **CLC 18, 106**
  See also Sauser-Hall, Frederic
Cernuda (y Bidon), Luis 1902-1963 **CLC 54;
  DAM POET**
  See also CA 131; 89-92; DLB 134; HW
Cervantes (Saavedra), Miguel de 1547-1616
  **LC 6, 23; DA; DAB; DAC; DAM MST,
  NOV; SSC 12; WLC**
Cesaire, Aime (Fernand) 1913- **CLC 19, 32;
  BLC 1; DAM MULT, POET**
  See also BW 2; CA 65-68; CANR 24, 43;
  MTCW
Chabon, Michael 1963- **CLC 55**
  See also CA 139; CANR 57
Chabrol, Claude 1930- **CLC 16**
  See also CA 110
Challans, Mary 1905-1983
  See Renault, Mary
  See also CA 81-84; 111; SATA 23; SATA-Obit
  36
Challis, George
  See Faust, Frederick (Schiller)
Chambers, Aidan 1934- **CLC 35**
  See also CA 25-28R; CANR 12, 31, 58; JRDA;
  MAICYA; SAAS 12; SATA 1, 69
Chambers, James 1948-
  See Cliff, Jimmy
  See also CA 124
Chambers, Jessie

See Lawrence, D(avid) H(erbert Richards)
Chambers, Robert W. 1865-1933 **TCLC 41**
  See also CA 165
Chandler, Raymond (Thornton) 1888-1959
  TCLC 1, 7; SSC 23
  See also AAYA 25; CA 104; 129; CANR 60;
  CDALB 1929-1941; DLBD 6; MTCW
Chang, Eileen 1921- **SSC 28**
Chang, Jung 1952- **CLC 71**
  See also CA 142
Channing, William Ellery 1780-1842 **NCLC
  17**
  See also DLB 1, 59
Chaplin, Charles Spencer 1889-1977 **CLC 16**
  See also Chaplin, Charlie
  See also CA 81-84; 73-76
Chaplin, Charlie
  See Chaplin, Charles Spencer
  See also DLB 44
Chapman, George 1559(?)-1634 **LC 22; DAM
  DRAM**
  See also DLB 62, 121
Chapman, Graham 1941-1989 **CLC 21**
  See also Monty Python
  See also CA 116; 129; CANR 35
Chapman, John Jay 1862-1933 **TCLC 7**
  See also CA 104
Chapman, Lee
  See Bradley, Marion Zimmer
Chapman, Walker
  See Silverberg, Robert
Chappell, Fred (Davis) 1936- **CLC 40, 78**
  See also CA 5-8R; CAAS 4; CANR 8, 33, 67;
  DLB 6, 105
Char, Rene(-Emile) 1907-1988 **CLC 9, 11, 14,
  55; DAM POET**
  See also CA 13-16R; 124; CANR 32; MTCW
Charby, Jay
  See Ellison, Harlan (Jay)
Chardin, Pierre Teilhard de
  See Teilhard de Chardin, (Marie Joseph) Pierre
Charles I 1600-1649 **LC 13**
Charriere, Isabelle de 1740-1805 **NCLC 66**
Charyn, Jerome 1937- **CLC 5, 8, 18**
  See also CA 5-8R; CAAS 1; CANR 7, 61;
  DLBY 83; MTCW
Chase, Mary (Coyle) 1907-1981 **DC 1**
  See also CA 77-80; 105; SATA 17; SATA-Obit
  29
Chase, Mary Ellen 1887-1973 **CLC 2**
  See also CA 13-16; 41-44R; CAP 1; SATA 10
Chase, Nicholas
  See Hyde, Anthony
Chateaubriand, Francois Rene de 1768-1848
  NCLC 3
  See also DLB 119
Chatterje, Sarat Chandra 1876-1936(?)
  See Chatterji, Saratchandra
  See also CA 109
Chatterji, Bankim Chandra 1838-1894**NCLC
  19**
Chatterji, Saratchandra **TCLC 13**
  See also Chatterje, Sarat Chandra
Chatterton, Thomas 1752-1770 **LC 3; DAM
  POET**
  See also DLB 109
Chatwin, (Charles) Bruce 1940-1989 **CLC 28,
  57, 59; DAM POP**
  See also AAYA 4; BEST 90:1; CA 85-88; 127;
  DLB 194
Chaucer, Daniel
  See Ford, Ford Madox
Chaucer, Geoffrey 1340(?)-1400 **LC 17; DA;**

**DAB; DAC; DAM MST, POET; PC 19;
  WLCS**
  See also CDBLB Before 1660; DLB 146
Chaviaras, Strates 1935-
  See Haviaras, Stratis
  See also CA 105
Chayefsky, Paddy **CLC 23**
  See also Chayefsky, Sidney
  See also DLB 7, 44; DLBY 81
Chayefsky, Sidney 1923-1981
  See Chayefsky, Paddy
  See also CA 9-12R; 104; CANR 18; DAM
  DRAM
Chedid, Andree 1920- **CLC 47**
  See also CA 145
Cheever, John 1912-1982 CLC 3, 7, 8, 11, 15,
  25, 64; DA; DAB; DAC; DAM MST, NOV,
  POP; SSC 1; WLC
  See also CA 5-8R; 106; CABS 1; CANR 5, 27;
  CDALB 1941-1968; DLB 2, 102; DLBY 80,
  82; INT CANR-5; MTCW
Cheever, Susan 1943- **CLC 18, 48**
  See also CA 103; CANR 27, 51; DLBY 82; INT
  CANR-27
Chekhonte, Antosha
  See Chekhov, Anton (Pavlovich)
Chekhov, Anton (Pavlovich) 1860-1904**TCLC
  3, 10, 31, 55; DA; DAB; DAC; DAM
  DRAM, MST; SSC 2, 28; WLC**
  See also CA 104; 124; SATA 90
Chernyshevsky, Nikolay Gavrilovich 1828-
  1889 **NCLC 1**
Cherry, Carolyn Janice 1942-
  See Cherryh, C. J.
  See also CA 65-68; CANR 10
Cherryh, C. J. **CLC 35**
  See also Cherry, Carolyn Janice
  See also AAYA 24; DLBY 80; SATA 93
Chesnutt, Charles W(addell) 1858-1932
  TCLC 5, 39; BLC 1; DAM MULT; SSC 7
  See also BW 1; CA 106; 125; DLB 12, 50, 78;
  MTCW
Chester, Alfred 1929(?)-1971 **CLC 49**
  See also CA 33-36R; DLB 130
Chesterton, G(ilbert) K(eith) 1874-1936
  TCLC 1, 6, 64; DAM NOV, POET; SSC 1
  See also CA 104; 132; CDBLB 1914-1945;
  DLB 10, 19, 34, 70, 98, 149, 178; MTCW;
  SATA 27
Chiang Pin-chin 1904-1986
  See Ding Ling
  See also CA 118
Ch'ien Chung-shu 1910- **CLC 22**
  See also CA 130; MTCW
Child, L. Maria
  See Child, Lydia Maria
Child, Lydia Maria 1802-1880 **NCLC 6**
  See also DLB 1, 74; SATA 67
Child, Mrs.
  See Child, Lydia Maria
Child, Philip 1898-1978 **CLC 19, 68**
  See also CA 13-14; CAP 1; SATA 47
Childers, (Robert) Erskine 1870-1922 **TCLC
  65**
  See also CA 113; 153; DLB 70
Childress, Alice 1920-1994**CLC 12, 15, 86, 96;
  BLC 1; DAM DRAM, MULT, NOV; DC 4**
  See also AAYA 8; BW 2; CA 45-48; 146;
  CANR 3, 27, 50; CLR 14; DLB 7, 38; JRDA;
  MAICYA; MTCW; SATA 7, 48, 81
Chin, Frank (Chew, Jr.) 1940- **DC 7**
  See also CA 33-36R; DAM MULT
Chislett, (Margaret) Anne 1943- **CLC 34**

See also CA 151

Chitty, Thomas Willes 1926-   **CLC 11**
See also Hinde, Thomas
See also CA 5-8R

Chivers, Thomas Holley 1809-1858 **NCLC 49**
See also DLB 3

Chomette, Rene Lucien 1898-1981
See Clair, Rene
See also CA 103

Chopin, Kate **TCLC 5, 14; DA; DAB; SSC 8;
WLCS**
See also Chopin, Katherine
See also CDALB 1865-1917; DLB 12, 78

Chopin, Katherine 1851-1904
See Chopin, Kate
See also CA 104; 122; DAC; DAM MST, NOV

Chretien de Troyes c. 12th cent. - **CMLC 10**

Christie
See Ichikawa, Kon

Christie, Agatha (Mary Clarissa) 1890-1976
**CLC 1, 6, 8, 12, 39, 48, 110; DAB; DAC;
DAM NOV**
See also AAYA 9; AITN 1, 2; CA 17-20R; 61-
64; CANR 10, 37; CDBLB 1914-1945; DLB
13, 77; MTCW; SATA 36

Christie, (Ann) Philippa
See Pearce, Philippa
See also CA 5-8R; CANR 4

Christine de Pizan 1365(?)-1431(?)   **LC 9**

Chubb, Elmer
See Masters, Edgar Lee

Chulkov, Mikhail Dmitrievich 1743-1792 **LC
2**
See also DLB 150

Churchill, Caryl 1938-   **CLC 31, 55; DC 5**
See also CA 102; CANR 22, 46; DLB 13;
MTCW

Churchill, Charles 1731-1764   **LC 3**
See also DLB 109

Chute, Carolyn 1947-   **CLC 39**
See also CA 123

Ciardi, John (Anthony) 1916-1986 **CLC 10,
40, 44; DAM POET**
See also CA 5-8R; 118; CAAS 2; CANR 5, 33;
CLR 19; DLB 5; DLBY 86; INT CANR-5;
MAICYA; MTCW; SAAS 26; SATA 1, 65;
SATA-Obit 46

Cicero, Marcus Tullius 106B.C.-43B.C.
CMLC 3

Cimino, Michael 1943-   **CLC 16**
See also CA 105

Cioran, E(mil) M. 1911-1995   **CLC 64**
See also CA 25-28R; 149

Cisneros, Sandra 1954- **CLC 69; DAM MULT;
HLC**
See also AAYA 9; CA 131; CANR 64; DLB
122, 152; HW

Cixous, Helene 1937-   **CLC 92**
See also CA 126; CANR 55; DLB 83; MTCW

Clair, Rene   **CLC 20**
See also Chomette, Rene Lucien

Clampitt, Amy 1920-1994   **CLC 32; PC 19**
See also CA 110; 146; CANR 29; DLB 105

Clancy, Thomas L., Jr. 1947-
See Clancy, Tom
See also CA 125; 131; CANR 62; INT 131;
MTCW

Clancy, Tom   **CLC 45; DAM NOV, POP**
See also Clancy, Thomas L., Jr.
See also AAYA 9; BEST 89:1, 90:1

Clare, John 1793-1864 **NCLC 9; DAB; DAM
POET**
See also DLB 55, 96

Clarin
See Alas (y Urena), Leopoldo (Enrique Garcia)

Clark, Al C.
See Goines, Donald

Clark, (Robert) Brian 1932-   **CLC 29**
See also CA 41-44R; CANR 67

Clark, Curt
See Westlake, Donald E(dwin)

Clark, Eleanor 1913-1996   **CLC 5, 19**
See also CA 9-12R; 151; CANR 41; DLB 6

Clark, J. P.
See Clark, John Pepper
See also DLB 117

Clark, John Pepper 1935-   **CLC 38; BLC 1;
DAM DRAM, MULT; DC 5**
See also Clark, J. P.
See also BW 1; CA 65-68; CANR 16

Clark, M. R.
See Clark, Mavis Thorpe

Clark, Mavis Thorpe 1909-   **CLC 12**
See also CA 57-60; CANR 8, 37; CLR 30;
MAICYA; SAAS 5; SATA 8, 74

Clark, Walter Van Tilburg 1909-1971**CLC 28**
See also CA 9-12R; 33-36R; CANR 63; DLB
9; SATA 8

Clarke, Arthur C(harles) 1917- **CLC 1, 4, 13,
18, 35; DAM POP; SSC 3**
See also AAYA 4; CA 1-4R; CANR 2, 28, 55;
JRDA; MAICYA; MTCW; SATA 13, 70

Clarke, Austin 1896-1974   **CLC 6, 9; DAM
POET**
See also CA 29-32; 49-52; CAP 2; DLB 10, 20

Clarke, Austin C(hesterfield) 1934-**CLC 8, 53;
BLC 1; DAC; DAM MULT**
See also BW 1; CA 25-28R; CAAS 16; CANR
14, 32, 68; DLB 53, 125

Clarke, Gillian 1937-   **CLC 61**
See also CA 106; DLB 40

Clarke, Marcus (Andrew Hislop) 1846-1881
NCLC 19

Clarke, Shirley 1925-   **CLC 16**

Clash, The
See Headon, (Nicky) Topper; Jones, Mick;
Simonon, Paul; Strummer, Joe

Claudel, Paul (Louis Charles Marie) 1868-1955
TCLC 2, 10
See also CA 104; 165; DLB 192

Clavell, James (duMaresq) 1925-1994 **CLC 6,
25, 87; DAM NOV, POP**
See also CA 25-28R; 146; CANR 26, 48;
MTCW

Cleaver, (Leroy) Eldridge 1935-**CLC 30; BLC
1; DAM MULT**
See also BW 1; CA 21-24R; CANR 16

Cleese, John (Marwood) 1939-   **CLC 21**
See also Monty Python
See also CA 112; 116; CANR 35; MTCW

Cleishbotham, Jebediah
See Scott, Walter

Cleland, John 1710-1789   **LC 2**
See also DLB 39

Clemens, Samuel Langhorne 1835-1910
See Twain, Mark
See also CA 104; 135; CDALB 1865-1917; DA;
DAB; DAC; DAM MST, NOV; DLB 11, 12,
23, 64, 74, 186, 189; JRDA; MAICYA;
YABC 2

Cleophil
See Congreve, William

Clerihew, E.
See Bentley, E(dmund) C(lerihew)

Clerk, N. W.
See Lewis, C(live) S(taples)

Cliff, Jimmy   **CLC 21**
See also Chambers, James

Clifton, (Thelma) Lucille 1936- **CLC 19, 66;
BLC 1; DAM MULT, POET; PC 17**
See also BW 2; CA 49-52; CANR 2, 24, 42;
CLR 5; DLB 5, 41; MAICYA; MTCW;
SATA 20, 69

Clinton, Dirk
See Silverberg, Robert

Clough, Arthur Hugh 1819-1861   **NCLC 27**
See also DLB 32

Clutha, Janet Paterson Frame 1924-
See Frame, Janet
See also CA 1-4R; CANR 2, 36; MTCW

Clyne, Terence
See Blatty, William Peter

Cobalt, Martin
See Mayne, William (James Carter)

Cobb, Irvin S. 1876-1944   **TCLC 77**
See also DLB 11, 25, 86

Cobbett, William 1763-1835   **NCLC 49**
See also DLB 43, 107, 158

Coburn, D(onald) L(ee) 1938-   **CLC 10**
See also CA 89-92

Cocteau, Jean (Maurice Eugene Clement)
1889-1963**CLC 1, 8, 15, 16, 43; DA; DAB;
DAC; DAM DRAM, MST, NOV; WLC**
See also CA 25-28; CANR 40; CAP 2; DLB
65; MTCW

Codrescu, Andrei 1946-**CLC 46; DAM POET**
See also CA 33-36R; CAAS 19; CANR 13, 34,
53

Coe, Max
See Bourne, Randolph S(illiman)

Coe, Tucker
See Westlake, Donald E(dwin)

Coen, Ethan 1958-   **CLC 108**
See also CA 126

Coen, Joel 1955-   **CLC 108**
See also CA 126

The Coen Brothers
See Coen, Ethan; Coen, Joel

Coetzee, J(ohn) M(ichael) 1940- **CLC 23, 33,
66; DAM NOV**
See also CA 77-80; CANR 41, 54; MTCW

Coffey, Brian
See Koontz, Dean R(ay)

Cohan, George M(ichael) 1878-1942**TCLC 60**
See also CA 157

Cohen, Arthur A(llen) 1928-1986   **CLC 7, 31**
See also CA 1-4R; 120; CANR 1, 17, 42; DLB
28

Cohen, Leonard (Norman) 1934-   **CLC 3, 38;
DAC; DAM MST**
See also CA 21-24R; CANR 14; DLB 53;
MTCW

Cohen, Matt 1942-   **CLC 19; DAC**
See also CA 61-64; CAAS 18; CANR 40; DLB
53

Cohen-Solal, Annie 19(?)-   **CLC 50**

Colegate, Isabel 1931-   **CLC 36**
See also CA 17-20R; CANR 8, 22; DLB 14;
INT CANR-22; MTCW

Coleman, Emmett
See Reed, Ishmael

Coleridge, M. E.
See Coleridge, Mary E(lizabeth)

Coleridge, Mary E(lizabeth) 1861-1907**TCLC
73**
See also CA 116; DLB 19, 98

Coleridge, Samuel Taylor 1772-1834**NCLC 9,
54; DA; DAB; DAC; DAM MST, POET;
PC 11; WLC**

Coupland, Douglas 1961-**CLC 85; DAC; DAM POP**
See also CA 142; CANR 57

Court, Wesli
See Turco, Lewis (Putnam)

Courtenay, Bryce 1933- **CLC 59**
See also CA 138

Courtney, Robert
See Ellison, Harlan (Jay)

Cousteau, Jacques-Yves 1910-1997 **CLC 30**
See also CA 65-68; 159; CANR 15, 67; MTCW; SATA 38, 98

Cowan, Peter (Walkinshaw) 1914- **SSC 28**
See also CA 21-24R; CANR 9, 25, 50

Coward, Noel (Peirce) 1899-1973**CLC 1, 9, 29, 51; DAM DRAM**
See also AITN 1; CA 17-18; 41-44R; CANR 35; CAP 2; CDBLB 1914-1945; DLB 10; MTCW

Cowley, Abraham 1618-1667 **LC 43**
See also DLB 131, 151

Cowley, Malcolm 1898-1989 **CLC 39**
See also CA 5-8R; 128; CANR 3, 55; DLB 4, 48; DLBY 81, 89; MTCW

Cowper, William 1731-1800 **NCLC 8; DAM POET**
See also DLB 104, 109

Cox, William Trevor 1928- **CLC 9, 14, 71; DAM NOV**
See also Trevor, William
See also CA 9-12R; CANR 4, 37, 55; DLB 14; INT CANR-37; MTCW

Coyne, P. J.
See Masters, Hilary

Cozzens, James Gould 1903-1978 **CLC 1, 4, 11, 92**
See also CA 9-12R; 81-84; CANR 19; CDALB 1941-1968; DLB 9; DLBD 2; DLBY 84, 97; MTCW

Crabbe, George 1754-1832 **NCLC 26**
See also DLB 93

Craddock, Charles Egbert
See Murfree, Mary Noailles

Craig, A. A.
See Anderson, Poul (William)

Craik, Dinah Maria (Mulock) 1826-1887 **NCLC 38**
See also DLB 35, 163; MAICYA; SATA 34

Cram, Ralph Adams 1863-1942 **TCLC 45**
See also CA 160

Crane, (Harold) Hart 1899-1932 **TCLC 2, 5, 80; DA; DAB; DAC; DAM MST, POET; PC 3; WLC**
See also CA 104; 127; CDALB 1917-1929; DLB 4, 48; MTCW

Crane, R(onald) S(almon) 1886-1967 **CLC 27**
See also CA 85-88; DLB 63

Crane, Stephen (Townley) 1871-1900 **TCLC 11, 17, 32; DA; DAB; DAC; DAM MST, NOV, POET; SSC 7; WLC**
See also AAYA 21; CA 109; 140; CDALB 1865-1917; DLB 12, 54, 78; YABC 2

Crase, Douglas 1944- **CLC 58**
See also CA 106

Crashaw, Richard 1612(?)-1649 **LC 24**
See also DLB 126

Craven, Margaret 1901-1980 **CLC 17; DAC**
See also CA 103

Crawford, F(rancis) Marion 1854-1909**TCLC 10**
See also CA 107; DLB 71

Crawford, Isabella Valancy 1850-1887**NCLC 12**

See also DLB 92

Crayon, Geoffrey
See Irving, Washington

Creasey, John 1908-1973 **CLC 11**
See also CA 5-8R; 41-44R; CANR 8, 59; DLB 77; MTCW

Crebillon, Claude Prosper Jolyot de (fils) 1707-1777 **LC 28**

Credo
See Creasey, John

Credo, Alvaro J. de
See Prado (Calvo), Pedro

Creeley, Robert (White) 1926- **CLC 1, 2, 4, 8, 11, 15, 36, 78; DAM POET**
See also CA 1-4R; CAAS 10; CANR 23, 43; DLB 5, 16, 169; MTCW

Crews, Harry (Eugene) 1935- **CLC 6, 23, 49**
See also AITN 1; CA 25-28R; CANR 20, 57; DLB 6, 143, 185; MTCW

Crichton, (John) Michael 1942- **CLC 2, 6, 54, 90; DAM NOV, POP**
See also AAYA 10; AITN 2; CA 25-28R; CANR 13, 40, 54; DLBY 81; INT CANR-13; JRDA; MTCW; SATA 9, 88

Crispin, Edmund **CLC 22**
See also Montgomery, (Robert) Bruce
See also DLB 87

Cristofer, Michael 1945(?)- **CLC 28; DAM DRAM**
See also CA 110; 152; DLB 7

Croce, Benedetto 1866-1952 **TCLC 37**
See also CA 120; 155

Crockett, David 1786-1836 **NCLC 8**
See also DLB 3, 11

Crockett, Davy
See Crockett, David

Crofts, Freeman Wills 1879-1957 **TCLC 55**
See also CA 115; DLB 77

Croker, John Wilson 1780-1857 **NCLC 10**
See also DLB 110

Crommelynck, Fernand 1885-1970 **CLC 75**
See also CA 89-92

Cromwell, Oliver 1599-1658 **LC 43**

Cronin, A(rchibald) J(oseph) 1896-1981 **CLC 32**
See also CA 1-4R; 102; CANR 5; DLB 191; SATA 47; SATA-Obit 25

Cross, Amanda
See Heilbrun, Carolyn G(old)

Crothers, Rachel 1878(?)-1958 **TCLC 19**
See also CA 113; DLB 7

Croves, Hal
See Traven, B.

Crow Dog, Mary (Ellen) (?)- **CLC 93**
See also Brave Bird, Mary
See also CA 154

Crowfield, Christopher
See Stowe, Harriet (Elizabeth) Beecher

Crowley, Aleister **TCLC 7**
See also Crowley, Edward Alexander

Crowley, Edward Alexander 1875-1947
See Crowley, Aleister
See also CA 104

Crowley, John 1942- **CLC 57**
See also CA 61-64; CANR 43; DLBY 82; SATA 65

Crud
See Crumb, R(obert)

Crumarums
See Crumb, R(obert)

Crumb, R(obert) 1943- **CLC 17**
See also CA 106

Crumbum

See Crumb, R(obert)

Crumski
See Crumb, R(obert)

Crum the Bum
See Crumb, R(obert)

Crunk
See Crumb, R(obert)

Crustt
See Crumb, R(obert)

Cryer, Gretchen (Kiger) 1935- **CLC 21**
See also CA 114; 123

Csath, Geza 1887-1919 **TCLC 13**
See also CA 111

Cudlip, David 1933- **CLC 34**

Cullen, Countee 1903-1946**TCLC 4, 37; BLC 1; DA; DAC; DAM MST, MULT, POET; PC 20; WLCS**
See also BW 1; CA 108; 124; CDALB 1917-1929; DLB 4, 48, 51; MTCW; SATA 18

Cum, R.
See Crumb, R(obert)

Cummings, Bruce F(rederick) 1889-1919
See Barbellion, W. N. P.
See also CA 123

Cummings, E(dward) E(stlin) 1894-1962**CLC 1, 3, 8, 12, 15, 68; DA; DAB; DAC; DAM MST, POET; PC 5; WLC 2**
See also CA 73-76; CANR 31; CDALB 1929-1941; DLB 4, 48; MTCW

Cunha, Euclides (Rodrigues Pimenta) da 1866-1909 **TCLC 24**
See also CA 123

Cunningham, E. V.
See Fast, Howard (Melvin)

Cunningham, J(ames) V(incent) 1911-1985 **CLC 3, 31**
See also CA 1-4R; 115; CANR 1; DLB 5

Cunningham, Julia (Woolfolk) 1916- **CLC 12**
See also CA 9-12R; CANR 4, 19, 36; JRDA; MAICYA; SAAS 2; SATA 1, 26

Cunningham, Michael 1952- **CLC 34**
See also CA 136

Cunninghame Graham, R(obert) B(ontine) 1852-1936 **TCLC 19**
See also Graham, R(obert) B(ontine) Cunninghame
See also CA 119; DLB 98

Currie, Ellen 19(?)- **CLC 44**

Curtin, Philip
See Lowndes, Marie Adelaide (Belloc)

Curtis, Price
See Ellison, Harlan (Jay)

Cutrate, Joe
See Spiegelman, Art

Cynewulf c. 770-c. 840 **CMLC 23**

Czaczkes, Shmuel Yosef
See Agnon, S(hmuel) Y(osef Halevi)

Dabrowska, Maria (Szumska) 1889-1965**CLC 15**
See also CA 106

Dabydeen, David 1955- **CLC 34**
See also BW 1; CA 125; CANR 56

Dacey, Philip 1939- **CLC 51**
See also CA 37-40R; CAAS 17; CANR 14, 32, 64; DLB 105

Dagerman, Stig (Halvard) 1923-1954 **TCLC 17**
See also CA 117; 155

Dahl, Roald 1916-1990**CLC 1, 6, 18, 79; DAB; DAC; DAM MST, NOV, POP**
See also AAYA 15; CA 1-4R; 133; CANR 6, 32, 37, 62; CLR 1, 7, 41; DLB 139; JRDA; MAICYA; MTCW; SATA 1, 26, 73; SATA-

76; DAM NOV, POP
See also BEST 89:1; CA 81-84; CANR 21;
DLB 6, 173; MTCW
de Lisser, H. G.
See De Lisser, H(erbert) G(eorge)
See also DLB 117
De Lisser, H(erbert) G(eorge) 1878-1944
TCLC 12
See also de Lisser, H. G.
See also BW 2; CA 109; 152
Deloney, Thomas 1560-1600   **LC 41**
Deloria, Vine (Victor), Jr. 1933-   **CLC 21;**
DAM MULT
See also CA 53-56; CANR 5, 20, 48; DLB 175;
MTCW; NNAL; SATA 21
Del Vecchio, John M(ichael) 1947-   **CLC 29**
See also CA 110; DLBD 9
de Man, Paul (Adolph Michel) 1919-1983
CLC 55
See also CA 128; 111; CANR 61; DLB 67;
MTCW
De Marinis, Rick 1934-   **CLC 54**
See also CA 57-60; CAAS 24; CANR 9, 25, 50
Dembry, R. Emmet
See Murfree, Mary Noailles
Demby, William 1922-CLC 53; BLC 1; DAM
MULT
See also BW 1; CA 81-84; DLB 33
de Menton, Francisco
See Chin, Frank (Chew, Jr.)
Demijohn, Thom
See Disch, Thomas M(ichael)
de Montherlant, Henry (Milon)
See Montherlant, Henry (Milon) de
Demosthenes 384B.C.-322B.C.   **CMLC 13**
See also DLB 176
de Natale, Francine
See Malzberg, Barry N(athaniel)
Denby, Edwin (Orr) 1903-1983   **CLC 48**
See also CA 138; 110
Denis, Julio
See Cortazar, Julio
Denmark, Harrison
See Zelazny, Roger (Joseph)
Dennis, John 1658-1734   **LC 11**
See also DLB 101
Dennis, Nigel (Forbes) 1912-1989   **CLC 8**
See also CA 25-28R; 129; DLB 13, 15; MTCW
Dent, Lester 1904(?)-1959   **TCLC 72**
See also CA 112; 161
De Palma, Brian (Russell) 1940-   **CLC 20**
See also CA 109
De Quincey, Thomas 1785-1859   **NCLC 4**
See also CDBLB 1789-1832; DLB 110; 144
Deren, Eleanora 1908(?)-1961
See Deren, Maya
See also CA 111
Deren, Maya 1917-1961   **CLC 16, 102**
See also Deren, Eleanora
Derleth, August (William) 1909-1971 CLC 31
See also CA 1-4R; 29-32R; CANR 4; DLB 9;
SATA 5
Der Nister 1884-1950   **TCLC 56**
de Routisie, Albert
See Aragon, Louis
Derrida, Jacques 1930-   **CLC 24, 87**
See also CA 124; 127
Derry Down Derry
See Lear, Edward
Dersonnes, Jacques
See Simenon, Georges (Jacques Christian)
Desai, Anita 1937-CLC 19, 37, 97; DAB; DAM
NOV

See also CA 81-84; CANR 33, 53; MTCW;
SATA 63
de Saint-Luc, Jean
See Glassco, John
de Saint Roman, Arnaud
See Aragon, Louis
Descartes, Rene 1596-1650   **LC 20, 35**
De Sica, Vittorio 1901(?)-1974   **CLC 20**
See also CA 117
Desnos, Robert 1900-1945   **TCLC 22**
See also CA 121; 151
Destouches, Louis-Ferdinand 1894-1961 CLC
9, 15
See also Celine, Louis-Ferdinand
See also CA 85-88; CANR 28; MTCW
de Tolignac, Gaston
See Griffith, D(avid Lewelyn) W(ark)
Deutsch, Babette 1895-1982   **CLC 18**
See also CA 1-4R; 108; CANR 4; DLB 45;
SATA 1; SATA-Obit 33
Devenant, William 1606-1649   **LC 13**
Devkota, Laxmiprasad 1909-1959 TCLC 23
See also CA 123
De Voto, Bernard (Augustine) 1897-1955
TCLC 29
See also CA 113; 160; DLB 9
De Vries, Peter 1910-1993 CLC 1, 2, 3, 7, 10,
28, 46; DAM NOV
See also CA 17-20R; 142; CANR 41; DLB 6;
DLBY 82; MTCW
Dexter, John
See Bradley, Marion Zimmer
Dexter, Martin
See Faust, Frederick (Schiller)
Dexter, Pete 1943-   **CLC 34, 55; DAM POP**
See also BEST 89:2; CA 127; 131; INT 131;
MTCW
Diamano, Silmang
See Senghor, Leopold Sedar
Diamond, Neil 1941-   **CLC 30**
See also CA 108
Diaz del Castillo, Bernal 1496-1584   **LC 31**
di Bassetto, Corno
See Shaw, George Bernard
Dick, Philip K(indred) 1928-1982CLC 10, 30,
72; DAM NOV, POP
See also AAYA 24; CA 49-52; 106; CANR 2,
16; DLB 8; MTCW
Dickens, Charles (John Huffam) 1812-1870
NCLC 3, 8, 18, 26, 37, 50; DA; DAB; DAC;
DAM MST, NOV; SSC 17; WLC
See also AAYA 23; CDBLB 1832-1890; DLB
21, 55, 70, 159, 166; JRDA; MAICYA;
SATA 15
Dickey, James (Lafayette) 1923-1997 CLC 1,
2, 4, 7, 10, 15, 47, 109; DAM NOV, POET,
POP
See also AITN 1, 2; CA 9-12R; 156; CABS 2;
CANR 10, 48, 61; CDALB 1968-1988; DLB
5, 193; DLBD 7; DLBY 82, 93, 96, 97; INT
CANR-10; MTCW
Dickey, William 1928-1994   **CLC 3, 28**
See also CA 9-12R; 145; CANR 24; DLB 5
Dickinson, Charles 1951-   **CLC 49**
See also CA 128
Dickinson, Emily (Elizabeth) 1830-1886
NCLC 21; DA; DAB; DAC; DAM MST,
POET; PC 1; WLC
See also AAYA 22; CDALB 1865-1917; DLB
1; SATA 29
Dickinson, Peter (Malcolm) 1927-CLC 12, 35
See also AAYA 9; CA 41-44R; CANR 31, 58;
CLR 29; DLB 87, 161; JRDA; MAICYA;

SATA 5, 62, 95
Dickson, Carr
See Carr, John Dickson
Dickson, Carter
See Carr, John Dickson
Diderot, Denis 1713-1784   **LC 26**
Didion, Joan 1934- CLC 1, 3, 8, 14, 32; DAM
NOV
See also AITN 1; CA 5-8R; CANR 14, 52;
CDALB 1968-1988; DLB 2, 173, 185;
DLBY 81, 86; MTCW
Dietrich, Robert
See Hunt, E(verette) Howard, (Jr.)
Dillard, Annie 1945- CLC 9, 60; DAM NOV
See also AAYA 6; CA 49-52; CANR 3, 43, 62;
DLBY 80; MTCW; SATA 10
Dillard, R(ichard) H(enry) W(ilde) 1937-
CLC 5
See also CA 21-24R; CAAS 7; CANR 10; DLB
5
Dillon, Eilis 1920-1994   **CLC 17**
See also CA 9-12R; 147; CAAS 3; CANR 4,
38; CLR 26; MAICYA; SATA 2, 74; SATA-
Obit 83
Dimont, Penelope
See Mortimer, Penelope (Ruth)
Dinesen, Isak   **CLC 10, 29, 95; SSC 7**
See also Blixen, Karen (Christentze Dinesen)
Ding Ling   **CLC 68**
See also Chiang Pin-chin
Disch, Thomas M(ichael) 1940-   **CLC 7, 36**
See also AAYA 17; CA 21-24R; CAAS 4;
CANR 17, 36, 54; CLR 18; DLB 8;
MAICYA; MTCW; SAAS 15; SATA 92
Disch, Tom
See Disch, Thomas M(ichael)
d'Isly, Georges
See Simenon, Georges (Jacques Christian)
Disraeli, Benjamin 1804-1881   **NCLC 2, 39**
See also DLB 21, 55
Ditcum, Steve
See Crumb, R(obert)
Dixon, Paige
See Corcoran, Barbara
Dixon, Stephen 1936-   **CLC 52; SSC 16**
See also CA 89-92; CANR 17, 40, 54; DLB
130
Doak, Annie
See Dillard, Annie
Dobell, Sydney Thompson 1824-1874 NCLC
43
See also DLB 32
Doblin, Alfred   **TCLC 13**
See also Doeblin, Alfred
Dobrolyubov, Nikolai Alexandrovich 1836-
1861   **NCLC 5**
Dobson, Austin 1840-1921   **TCLC 79**
See also DLB 35; 144
Dobyns, Stephen 1941-   **CLC 37**
See also CA 45-48; CANR 2, 18
Doctorow, E(dgar) L(aurence) 1931- CLC 6,
11, 15, 18, 37, 44, 65; DAM NOV, POP
See also AAYA 22; AITN 2; BEST 89:3; CA
45-48; CANR 2, 33, 51; CDALB 1968-1988;
DLB 2, 28, 173; DLBY 80; MTCW
Dodgson, Charles Lutwidge 1832-1898
See Carroll, Lewis
See also CLR 2; DA; DAB; DAC; DAM MST,
NOV, POET; MAICYA; YABC 2
Dodson, Owen (Vincent) 1914-1983 CLC 79;
BLC 1; DAM MULT
See also BW 1; CA 65-68; 110; CANR 24; DLB
76

Doeblin, Alfred 1878-1957   **TCLC 13**
  See also Doblin, Alfred
  See also CA 110; 141; DLB 66
Doerr, Harriet 1910-   **CLC 34**
  See also CA 117; 122; CANR 47; INT 122
Domecq, H(onorio) Bustos
  See Bioy Casares, Adolfo; Borges, Jorge Luis
Domini, Rey
  See Lorde, Audre (Geraldine)
Dominique
  See Proust, (Valentin-Louis-George-Eugene-)
  Marcel
Don, A
  See Stephen, SirLeslie
Donaldson, Stephen R. 1947- **CLC 46; DAM POP**
  See also CA 89-92; CANR 13, 55; INT CANR-13
Donleavy, J(ames) P(atrick) 1926-**CLC 1, 4, 6, 10, 45**
  See also AITN 2; CA 9-12R; CANR 24, 49, 62; DLB 6, 173; INT CANR-24; MTCW
Donne, John 1572-1631 **LC 10, 24; DA; DAB; DAC; DAM MST, POET; PC 1**
  See also CDBLB Before 1660; DLB 121, 151
Donnell, David 1939(?)-   **CLC 34**
Donoghue, P. S.
  See Hunt, E(verette) Howard, (Jr.)
Donoso (Yanez), Jose 1924-1996**CLC 4, 8, 11, 32, 99; DAM MULT; HLC**
  See also CA 81-84; 155; CANR 32; DLB 113; HW; MTCW
Donovan, John 1928-1992   **CLC 35**
  See also AAYA 20; CA 97-100; 137; CLR 3; MAICYA; SATA 72; SATA-Brief 29
Don Roberto
  See Cunninghame Graham, R(obert) B(ontine)
Doolittle, Hilda 1886-1961**CLC 3, 8, 14, 31, 34, 73; DA; DAC; DAM MST, POET; PC 5; WLC**
  See also H. D.
  See also CA 97-100; CANR 35; DLB 4, 45; MTCW
Dorfman, Ariel 1942-   **CLC 48, 77; DAM MULT; HLC**
  See also CA 124; 130; CANR 67; HW; INT 130
Dorn, Edward (Merton) 1929-   **CLC 10, 18**
  See also CA 93-96; CANR 42; DLB 5; INT 93-96
Dorris, Michael (Anthony) 1945-1997 **CLC 109; DAM MULT, NOV**
  See also AAYA 20; BEST 90:1; CA 102; 157; CANR 19, 46; DLB 175; NNAL; SATA 75; SATA-Obit 94
Dorris, Michael A.
  See Dorris, Michael (Anthony)
Dorsan, Luc
  See Simenon, Georges (Jacques Christian)
Dorsange, Jean
  See Simenon, Georges (Jacques Christian)
Dos Passos, John (Roderigo) 1896-1970 **CLC 1, 4, 8, 11, 15, 25, 34, 82; DA; DAB; DAC; DAM MST, NOV; WLC**
  See also CA 1-4R; 29-32R; CANR 3; CDALB 1929-1941; DLB 4, 9; DLBD 1, 15; DLBY 96; MTCW
Dossage, Jean
  See Simenon, Georges (Jacques Christian)
Dostoevsky, Fedor Mikhailovich 1821-1881 **NCLC 2, 7, 21, 33, 43; DA; DAB; DAC; DAM MST, NOV; SSC 2; WLC**
Doughty, Charles M(ontagu) 1843-1926

TCLC 27
  See also CA 115; DLB 19, 57, 174
Douglas, Ellen   **CLC 73**
  See also Haxton, Josephine Ayres; Williamson, Ellen Douglas
Douglas, Gavin 1475(?)-1522   **LC 20**
Douglas, George
  See Brown, George Douglas
Douglas, Keith (Castellain) 1920-1944 **TCLC 40**
  See also CA 160; DLB 27
Douglas, Leonard
  See Bradbury, Ray (Douglas)
Douglas, Michael
  See Crichton, (John) Michael
Douglas, (George) Norman 1868-1952 **TCLC 68**
  See also CA 119; 157; DLB 34, 195
Douglas, William
  See Brown, George Douglas
Douglass, Frederick 1817(?)-1895**NCLC 7, 55; BLC 1; DA; DAC; DAM MST, MULT; WLC**
  See also CDALB 1640-1865; DLB 1, 43, 50, 79; SATA 29
Dourado, (Waldomiro Freitas) Autran 1926- **CLC 23, 60**
  See also CA 25-28R; CANR 34
Dourado, Waldomiro Autran
  See Dourado, (Waldomiro Freitas) Autran
Dove, Rita (Frances) 1952-**CLC 50, 81; BLCS; DAM MULT, POET; PC 6**
  See also BW 2; CA 109; CAAS 19; CANR 27, 42, 68; DLB 120
Doveglion
  See Villa, Jose Garcia
Dowell, Coleman 1925-1985   **CLC 60**
  See also CA 25-28R; 117; CANR 10; DLB 130
Dowson, Ernest (Christopher) 1867-1900 **TCLC 4**
  See also CA 105; 150; DLB 19, 135
Doyle, A. Conan
  See Doyle, Arthur Conan
Doyle, Arthur Conan 1859-1930**TCLC 7; DA; DAB; DAC; DAM MST, NOV; SSC 12; WLC**
  See also AAYA 14; CA 104; 122; CDBLB 1890-1914; DLB 18, 70, 156, 178; MTCW; SATA 24
Doyle, Conan
  See Doyle, Arthur Conan
Doyle, John
  See Graves, Robert (von Ranke)
Doyle, Roddy 1958(?)-   **CLC 81**
  See also AAYA 14; CA 143; DLB 194
Doyle, Sir A. Conan
  See Doyle, Arthur Conan
Doyle, Sir Arthur Conan
  See Doyle, Arthur Conan
Dr. A
  See Asimov, Isaac; Silverstein, Alvin
Drabble, Margaret 1939-**CLC 2, 3, 5, 8, 10, 22, 53; DAB; DAC; DAM MST, NOV, POP**
  See also CA 13-16R; CANR 18, 35, 63; CDBLB 1960 to Present; DLB 14, 155; MTCW; SATA 48
Drapier, M. B.
  See Swift, Jonathan
Drayham, James
  See Mencken, H(enry) L(ouis)
Drayton, Michael 1563-1631   **LC 8; DAM POET**
  See also DLB 121

Dreadstone, Carl
  See Campbell, (John) Ramsey
Dreiser, Theodore (Herman Albert) 1871-1945 **TCLC 10, 18, 35; DA; DAC; DAM MST, NOV; SSC 30; WLC**
  See also CA 106; 132; CDALB 1865-1917; DLB 9, 12, 102, 137; DLBD 1; MTCW
Drexler, Rosalyn 1926-   **CLC 2, 6**
  See also CA 81-84; CANR 68
Dreyer, Carl Theodor 1889-1968   **CLC 16**
  See also CA 116
Drieu la Rochelle, Pierre(-Eugene) 1893-1945 **TCLC 21**
  See also CA 117; DLB 72
Drinkwater, John 1882-1937   **TCLC 57**
  See also CA 109; 149; DLB 10, 19, 149
Drop Shot
  See Cable, George Washington
Droste-Hulshoff, Annette Freiin von 1797-1848 **NCLC 3**
  See also DLB 133
Drummond, Walter
  See Silverberg, Robert
Drummond, William Henry 1854-1907**TCLC 25**
  See also CA 160; DLB 92
Drummond de Andrade, Carlos 1902-1987 **CLC 18**
  See also Andrade, Carlos Drummond de
  See also CA 132; 123
Drury, Allen (Stuart) 1918-   **CLC 37**
  See also CA 57-60; CANR 18, 52; INT CANR-18
Dryden, John 1631-1700 **LC 3, 21; DA; DAB; DAC; DAM DRAM, MST, POET; DC 3; WLC**
  See also CDBLB 1660-1789; DLB 80, 101, 131
Duberman, Martin (Bauml) 1930-   **CLC 8**
  See also CA 1-4R; CANR 2, 63
Dubie, Norman (Evans) 1945-   **CLC 36**
  See also CA 69-72; CANR 12; DLB 120
Du Bois, W(illiam) E(dward) B(urghardt) 1868-1963 **CLC 1, 2, 13, 64, 96; BLC 1; DA; DAC; DAM MST, MULT, NOV; WLC**
  See also BW 1; CA 85-88; CANR 34; CDALB 1865-1917; DLB 47, 50, 91; MTCW; SATA 42
Dubus, Andre 1936- **CLC 13, 36, 97; SSC 15**
  See also CA 21-24R; CANR 17; DLB 130; INT CANR-17
Duca Minimo
  See D'Annunzio, Gabriele
Ducharme, Rejean 1941-   **CLC 74**
  See also CA 165; DLB 60
Duclos, Charles Pinot 1704-1772   **LC 1**
Dudek, Louis 1918-   **CLC 11, 19**
  See also CA 45-48; CAAS 14; CANR 1; DLB 88
Duerrenmatt, Friedrich 1921-1990 **CLC 1, 4, 8, 11, 15, 43, 102; DAM DRAM**
  See also CA 17-20R; CANR 33; DLB 69, 124; MTCW
Duffy, Bruce (?)-   **CLC 50**
Duffy, Maureen 1933-   **CLC 37**
  See also CA 25-28R; CANR 33, 68; DLB 14; MTCW
Dugan, Alan 1923-   **CLC 2, 6**
  See also CA 81-84; DLB 5
du Gard, Roger Martin
  See Martin du Gard, Roger
Duhamel, Georges 1884-1966   **CLC 8**
  See also CA 81-84; 25-28R; CANR 35; DLB 65; MTCW

See also CA 89-92; 150; CANR 17, 46; DLB 40; MTCW

Ewers, Hanns Heinz 1871-1943　　**TCLC 12**
See also CA 109; 149

Ewing, Frederick R.
See Sturgeon, Theodore (Hamilton)

Exley, Frederick (Earl) 1929-1992 **CLC 6, 11**
See also AITN 2; CA 81-84; 138; DLB 143; DLBY 81

Eynhardt, Guillermo
See Quiroga, Horacio (Sylvestre)

Ezekiel, Nissim 1924-　　　　　　**CLC 61**
See also CA 61-64

Ezekiel, Tish O'Dowd 1943-　　　**CLC 34**
See also CA 129

Fadeyev, A.
See Bulgya, Alexander Alexandrovich

Fadeyev, Alexander　　　　　　　**TCLC 53**
See also Bulgya, Alexander Alexandrovich

Fagen, Donald 1948-　　　　　　**CLC 26**

Fainzilberg, Ilya Arnoldovich 1897-1937
See Ilf, Ilya
See also CA 120; 165

Fair, Ronald L. 1932-　　　　　　**CLC 18**
See also BW 1; CA 69-72; CANR 25; DLB 33

Fairbairn, Roger
See Carr, John Dickson

Fairbairns, Zoe (Ann) 1948-　　　**CLC 32**
See also CA 103; CANR 21

Falco, Gian
See Papini, Giovanni

Falconer, James
See Kirkup, James

Falconer, Kenneth
See Kornbluth, C(yril) M.

Falkland, Samuel
See Heijermans, Herman

Fallaci, Oriana 1930-　　　　**CLC 11, 110**
See also CA 77-80; CANR 15, 58; MTCW

Faludy, George 1913-　　　　　　**CLC 42**
See also CA 21-24R

Faludy, Gyoergy
See Faludy, George

Fanon, Frantz 1925-1961　　**CLC 74; BLC 2; DAM MULT**
See also BW 1; CA 116; 89-92

Fanshawe, Ann 1625-1680　　　　**LC 11**

Fante, John (Thomas) 1911-1983　**CLC 60**
See also CA 69-72; 109; CANR 23; DLB 130; DLBY 83

Farah, Nuruddin 1945-**CLC 53; BLC 2; DAM MULT**
See also BW 2; CA 106; DLB 125

Fargue, Leon-Paul 1876(?)-1947　**TCLC 11**
See also CA 109

Farigoule, Louis
See Romains, Jules

Farina, Richard 1936(?)-1966　　　**CLC 9**
See also CA 81-84; 25-28R

Farley, Walter (Lorimer) 1915-1989 **CLC 17**
See also CA 17-20R; CANR 8, 29; DLB 22; JRDA; MAICYA; SATA 2, 43

Farmer, Philip Jose 1918-　　　**CLC 1, 19**
See also CA 1-4R; CANR 4, 35; DLB 8; MTCW; SATA 93

Farquhar, George 1677-1707　**LC 21; DAM DRAM**
See also DLB 84

Farrell, J(ames) G(ordon) 1935-1979 **CLC 6**
See also CA 73-76; 89-92; CANR 36; DLB 14; MTCW

Farrell, James T(homas) 1904-1979**CLC 1, 4, 8, 11, 66; SSC 28**

See also CA 5-8R; 89-92; CANR 9, 61; DLB 4, 9, 86; DLBD 2; MTCW

Farren, Richard J.
See Betjeman, John

Farren, Richard M.
See Betjeman, John

Fassbinder, Rainer Werner 1946-1982　**CLC 20**
See also CA 93-96; 106; CANR 31

Fast, Howard (Melvin) 1914-　**CLC 23; DAM NOV**
See also AAYA 16; CA 1-4R; CAAS 18; CANR 1, 33, 54; DLB 9; INT CANR-33; SATA 7

Faulcon, Robert
See Holdstock, Robert P.

Faulkner, William (Cuthbert) 1897-1962**CLC 1, 3, 6, 8, 9, 11, 14, 18, 28, 52, 68; DA; DAB; DAC; DAM MST, NOV; SSC 1; WLC**
See also AAYA 7; CA 81-84; CANR 33; CDALB 1929-1941; DLB 9, 11, 44, 102; DLBD 2; DLBY 86, 97; MTCW

Fauset, Jessie Redmon 1884(?)-1961 **CLC 19, 54; BLC 2; DAM MULT**
See also BW 1; CA 109; DLB 51

Faust, Frederick (Schiller) 1892-1944(?) **TCLC 49; DAM POP**
See also CA 108; 152

Faust, Irvin 1924-　　　　　　　**CLC 8**
See also CA 33-36R; CANR 28, 67; DLB 2, 28; DLBY 80

Fawkes, Guy
See Benchley, Robert (Charles)

Fearing, Kenneth (Flexner) 1902-1961　**CLC 51**
See also CA 93-96; CANR 59; DLB 9

Fecamps, Elise
See Creasey, John

Federman, Raymond 1928-　　**CLC 6, 47**
See also CA 17-20R; CAAS 8; CANR 10, 43; DLBY 80

Federspiel, J(uerg) F. 1931-　　**CLC 42**
See also CA 146

Feiffer, Jules (Ralph) 1929-　**CLC 2, 8, 64; DAM DRAM**
See also AAYA 3; CA 17-20R; CANR 30, 59; DLB 7, 44; INT CANR-30; MTCW; SATA 8, 61

Feige, Hermann Albert Otto Maximilian
See Traven, B.

Feinberg, David B. 1956-1994　　**CLC 59**
See also CA 135; 147

Feinstein, Elaine 1930-　　　　**CLC 36**
See also CA 69-72; CAAS 1; CANR 31, 68; DLB 14, 40; MTCW

Feldman, Irving (Mordecai) 1928-　**CLC 7**
See also CA 1-4R; CANR 1; DLB 169

Felix-Tchicaya, Gerald
See Tchicaya, Gerald Felix

Fellini, Federico 1920-1993　　**CLC 16, 85**
See also CA 65-68; 143; CANR 33

Felsen, Henry Gregor 1916-　　**CLC 17**
See also CA 1-4R; CANR 1; SAAS 2; SATA 1

Fenno, Jack
See Calisher, Hortense

Fenton, James Martin 1949-　　**CLC 32**
See also CA 102; DLB 40

Ferber, Edna 1887-1968　　　**CLC 18, 93**
See also AITN 1; CA 5-8R; 25-28R; CANR 68; DLB 9, 28, 86; MTCW; SATA 7

Ferguson, Helen
See Kavan, Anna

Ferguson, Samuel 1810-1886　　**NCLC 33**
See also DLB 32

Fergusson, Robert 1750-1774　　**LC 29**
See also DLB 109

Ferling, Lawrence
See Ferlinghetti, Lawrence (Monsanto)

Ferlinghetti, Lawrence (Monsanto) 1919(?)-**CLC 2, 6, 10, 27; DAM POET; PC 1**
See also CA 5-8R; CANR 3, 41; CDALB 1941-1968; DLB 5, 16; MTCW

Fernandez, Vicente Garcia Huidobro
See Huidobro Fernandez, Vicente Garcia

Ferrer, Gabriel (Francisco Victor) Miro
See Miro (Ferrer), Gabriel (Francisco Victor)

Ferrier, Susan (Edmonstone) 1782-1854　**NCLC 8**
See also DLB 116

Ferrigno, Robert 1948(?)-　　　　**CLC 65**
See also CA 140

Ferron, Jacques 1921-1985　　**CLC 94; DAC**
See also CA 117; 129; DLB 60

Feuchtwanger, Lion 1884-1958　　**TCLC 3**
See also CA 104; DLB 66

Feuillet, Octave 1821-1890　　　**NCLC 45**
See also DLB 192

Feydeau, Georges (Leon Jules Marie) 1862-1921　　　　　**TCLC 22; DAM DRAM**
See also CA 113; 152; DLB 192

Fichte, Johann Gottlieb 1762-1814 **NCLC 62**
See also DLB 90

Ficino, Marsilio 1433-1499　　　　**LC 12**

Fiedeler, Hans
See Doeblin, Alfred

Fiedler, Leslie A(aron) 1917-　**CLC 4, 13, 24**
See also CA 9-12R; CANR 7, 63; DLB 28, 67; MTCW

Field, Andrew 1938-　　　　　　**CLC 44**
See also CA 97-100; CANR 25

Field, Eugene 1850-1895　　　　**NCLC 3**
See also DLB 23, 42, 140; DLBD 13; MAICYA; SATA 16

Field, Gans T.
See Wellman, Manly Wade

Field, Michael　　　　　　　　**TCLC 43**

Field, Peter
See Hobson, Laura Z(ametkin)

Fielding, Henry 1707-1754　**LC 1; DA; DAB; DAC; DAM DRAM, MST, NOV; WLC**
See also CDBLB 1660-1789; DLB 39, 84, 101

Fielding, Sarah 1710-1768　　　　**LC 1**
See also DLB 39

Fields, W. C. 1880-1946　　　　**TCLC 80**
See also DLB 44

Fierstein, Harvey (Forbes) 1954-　**CLC 33; DAM DRAM, POP**
See also CA 123; 129

Figes, Eva 1932-　　　　　　　**CLC 31**
See also CA 53-56; CANR 4, 44; DLB 14

Finch, Anne 1661-1720　　　**LC 3; PC 21**
See also DLB 95

Finch, Robert (Duer Claydon) 1900- **CLC 18**
See also CA 57-60; CANR 9, 24, 49; DLB 88

Findley, Timothy 1930-　**CLC 27, 102; DAC; DAM MST**
See also CA 25-28R; CANR 12, 42; DLB 53

Fink, William
See Mencken, H(enry) L(ouis)

Firbank, Louis 1942-
See Reed, Lou
See also CA 117

Firbank, (Arthur Annesley) Ronald 1886-1926　**TCLC 1**
See also CA 104; DLB 36

Fisher, M(ary) F(rances) K(ennedy) 1908-1992　**CLC 76, 87**

See also CA 118

Frazer, Robert Caine
See Creasey, John

Frazer, Sir James George
See Frazer, J(ames) G(eorge)

Frazier, Charles 1950-   **CLC 109**
See also CA 161

Frazier, Ian 1951-   **CLC 46**
See also CA 130; CANR 54

Frederic, Harold 1856-1898   **NCLC 10**
See also DLB 12, 23; DLBD 13

Frederick, John
See Faust, Frederick (Schiller)

Frederick the Great 1712-1786   **LC 14**

Fredro, Aleksander 1793-1876   **NCLC 8**

Freeling, Nicolas 1927-   **CLC 38**
See also CA 49-52; CAAS 12; CANR 1, 17, 50; DLB 87

Freeman, Douglas Southall 1886-1953 **TCLC 11**
See also CA 109; DLB 17

Freeman, Judith 1946-   **CLC 55**
See also CA 148

Freeman, Mary Eleanor Wilkins 1852-1930
TCLC 9; SSC 1
See also CA 106; DLB 12, 78

Freeman, R(ichard) Austin 1862-1943 **TCLC 21**
See also CA 113; DLB 70

French, Albert 1943-   **CLC 86**

French, Marilyn 1929-   CLC 10, 18, 60; **DAM DRAM, NOV, POP**
See also CA 69-72; CANR 3, 31; INT CANR-31; MTCW

French, Paul
See Asimov, Isaac

Freneau, Philip Morin 1752-1832   **NCLC 1**
See also DLB 37, 43

Freud, Sigmund 1856-1939   **TCLC 52**
See also CA 115; 133; MTCW

Friedan, Betty (Naomi) 1921-   **CLC 74**
See also CA 65-68; CANR 18, 45; MTCW

Friedlander, Saul 1932-   **CLC 90**
See also CA 117; 130

Friedman, B(ernard) H(arper) 1926- **CLC 7**
See also CA 1-4R; CANR 3, 48

Friedman, Bruce Jay 1930-   **CLC 3, 5, 56**
See also CA 9-12R; CANR 25, 52; DLB 2, 28; INT CANR-25

Friel, Brian 1929-   **CLC 5, 42, 59; DC 8**
See also CA 21-24R; CANR 33; DLB 13; MTCW

Friis-Baastad, Babbis Ellinor 1921-1970 CLC 12
See also CA 17-20R; 134; SATA 7

Frisch, Max (Rudolf) 1911-1991CLC 3, 9, 14, 18, 32, 44; **DAM DRAM, NOV**
See also CA 85-88; 134; CANR 32; DLB 69, 124; MTCW

Fromentin, Eugene (Samuel Auguste) 1820-1876   **NCLC 10**
See also DLB 123

Frost, Frederick
See Faust, Frederick (Schiller)

Frost, Robert (Lee) 1874-1963 **CLC 1, 3, 4, 9, 10, 13, 15, 26, 34, 44; DA; DAB; DAC; DAM MST, POET; PC 1; WLC**
See also AAYA 21; CA 89-92; CANR 33; CDALB 1917-1929; DLB 54; DLBD 7; MTCW; SATA 14

Froude, James Anthony 1818-1894 NCLC 43
See also DLB 18, 57, 144

Froy, Herald

See Waterhouse, Keith (Spencer)

Fry, Christopher 1907- CLC 2, 10, 14; **DAM DRAM**
See also CA 17-20R; CAAS 23; CANR 9, 30; DLB 13; MTCW; SATA 66

Frye, (Herman) Northrop 1912-1991CLC 24, 70
See also CA 5-8R; 133; CANR 8, 37; DLB 67, 68; MTCW

Fuchs, Daniel 1909-1993   **CLC 8, 22**
See also CA 81-84; 142; CAAS 5; CANR 40; DLB 9, 26, 28; DLBY 93

Fuchs, Daniel 1934-   **CLC 34**
See also CA 37-40R; CANR 14, 48

Fuentes, Carlos 1928-CLC 3, 8, 10, 13, 22, 41, 60; **DA; DAB; DAC; DAM MST, MULT, NOV; HLC; SSC 24; WLC**
See also AAYA 4; AITN 2; CA 69-72; CANR 10, 32, 68; DLB 113; HW; MTCW

Fuentes, Gregorio Lopez y
See Lopez y Fuentes, Gregorio

Fugard, (Harold) Athol 1932-CLC 5, 9, 14, 25, 40, 80; **DAM DRAM; DC 3**
See also AAYA 17; CA 85-88; CANR 32, 54; MTCW

Fugard, Sheila 1932-   **CLC 48**
See also CA 125

Fuller, Charles (H., Jr.) 1939-CLC 25; BLC 2; **DAM DRAM, MULT; DC 1**
See also BW 2; CA 108; 112; DLB 38; INT 112; MTCW

Fuller, John (Leopold) 1937-   **CLC 62**
See also CA 21-24R; CANR 9, 44; DLB 40

Fuller, Margaret   **NCLC 5, 50**
See also Ossoli, Sarah Margaret (Fuller marchesa d')

Fuller, Roy (Broadbent) 1912-1991CLC 4, 28
See also CA 5-8R; 135; CAAS 10; CANR 53; DLB 15, 20; SATA 87

Fulton, Alice 1952-   **CLC 52**
See also CA 116; CANR 57; DLB 193

Furphy, Joseph 1843-1912   **TCLC 25**
See also CA 163

Fussell, Paul 1924-   **CLC 74**
See also BEST 90:1; CA 17-20R; CANR 8, 21, 35; INT CANR-21; MTCW

Futabatei, Shimei 1864-1909   **TCLC 44**
See also CA 162; DLB 180

Futrelle, Jacques 1875-1912   **TCLC 19**
See also CA 113; 155

Gaboriau, Emile 1835-1873   **NCLC 14**

Gadda, Carlo Emilio 1893-1973   **CLC 11**
See also CA 89-92; DLB 177

Gaddis, William 1922- CLC 1, 3, 6, 8, 10, 19, 43, 86
See also CA 17-20R; CANR 21, 48; DLB 2; MTCW

Gage, Walter
See Inge, William (Motter)

Gaines, Ernest J(ames) 1933- CLC 3, 11, 18, 86; **BLC 2; DAM MULT**
See also AAYA 18; AITN 1; BW 2; CA 9-12R; CANR 6, 24, 42; CDALB 1968-1988; DLB 2, 33, 152; DLBY 80; MTCW; SATA 86

Gaitskill, Mary 1954-   **CLC 69**
See also CA 128; CANR 61

Galdos, Benito Perez
See Perez Galdos, Benito

Gale, Zona 1874-1938 **TCLC 7; DAM DRAM**
See also CA 105; 153; DLB 9, 78

Galeano, Eduardo (Hughes) 1940-   **CLC 72**
See also CA 29-32R; CANR 13, 32; HW

Galiano, Juan Valera y Alcala

See Valera y Alcala-Galiano, Juan

Gallagher, Tess 1943-   CLC 18, 63; **DAM POET; PC 9**
See also CA 106; DLB 120

Gallant, Mavis 1922-   CLC 7, 18, 38; **DAC; DAM MST; SSC 5**
See also CA 69-72; CANR 29; DLB 53; MTCW

Gallant, Roy A(rthur) 1924-   **CLC 17**
See also CA 5-8R; CANR 4, 29, 54; CLR 30; MAICYA; SATA 4, 68

Gallico, Paul (William) 1897-1976   **CLC 2**
See also AITN 1; CA 5-8R; 69-72; CANR 23; DLB 9, 171; MAICYA; SATA 13

Gallo, Max Louis 1932-   **CLC 95**
See also CA 85-88

Gallois, Lucien
See Desnos, Robert

Gallup, Ralph
See Whitemore, Hugh (John)

Galsworthy, John 1867-1933TCLC 1, 45; **DA; DAB; DAC; DAM DRAM, MST, NOV; SSC 22; WLC 2**
See also CA 104; 141; CDBLB 1890-1914; DLB 10, 34, 98, 162; DLBD 16

Galt, John 1779-1839   **NCLC 1**
See also DLB 99, 116, 159

Galvin, James 1951-   **CLC 38**
See also CA 108; CANR 26

Gamboa, Federico 1864-1939   **TCLC 36**

Gandhi, M. K.
See Gandhi, Mohandas Karamchand

Gandhi, Mahatma
See Gandhi, Mohandas Karamchand

Gandhi, Mohandas Karamchand 1869-1948
TCLC 59; DAM MULT
See also CA 121; 132; MTCW

Gann, Ernest Kellogg 1910-1991   **CLC 23**
See also AITN 1; CA 1-4R; 136; CANR 1

Garcia, Cristina 1958-   **CLC 76**
See also CA 141

Garcia Lorca, Federico 1898-1936TCLC 1, 7, 49; **DA; DAB; DAC; DAM DRAM, MST, MULT, POET; DC 2; HLC; PC 3; WLC**
See also CA 104; 131; DLB 108; HW; MTCW

Garcia Marquez, Gabriel (Jose) 1928-CLC 2, 3, 8, 10, 15, 27, 47, 55, 68; **DA; DAB; DAC; DAM MST, MULT, NOV, POP; HLC; SSC 8; WLC**
See also AAYA 3; BEST 89:1, 90:4; CA 33-36R; CANR 10, 28, 50; DLB 113; HW; MTCW

Gard, Janice
See Latham, Jean Lee

Gard, Roger Martin du
See Martin du Gard, Roger

Gardam, Jane 1928-   **CLC 43**
See also CA 49-52; CANR 2, 18, 33, 54; CLR 12; DLB 14, 161; MAICYA; MTCW; SAAS 9; SATA 39, 76; SATA-Brief 28

Gardner, Herb(ert) 1934-   **CLC 44**
See also CA 149

Gardner, John (Champlin), Jr. 1933-1982
CLC 2, 3, 5, 7, 8, 10, 18, 28, 34; **DAM NOV, POP; SSC 7**
See also AITN 1; CA 65-68; 107; CANR 33; DLB 2; DLBY 82; MTCW; SATA 40; SATA-Obit 31

Gardner, John (Edmund) 1926-   **CLC 30; DAM POP**
See also CA 103; CANR 15; MTCW

Gardner, Miriam
See Bradley, Marion Zimmer

Gardner, Noel

See Kuttner, Henry
Gardons, S. S.
  See Snodgrass, W(illiam) D(e Witt)
Garfield, Leon 1921-1996   **CLC 12**
  See also AAYA 8; CA 17-20R; 152; CANR 38,
    41; CLR 21; DLB 161; JRDA; MAICYA;
    SATA 1, 32, 76; SATA-Obit 90
Garland, (Hannibal) Hamlin 1860-1940
    TCLC 3; SSC 18
  See also CA 104; DLB 12, 71, 78, 186
Garneau, (Hector de) Saint-Denys 1912-1943
    TCLC 13
  See also CA 111; DLB 88
Garner, Alan 1934-**CLC 17; DAB; DAM POP**
  See also AAYA 18; CA 73-76; CANR 15, 64;
    CLR 20; DLB 161; MAICYA; MTCW;
    SATA 18, 69
Garner, Hugh 1913-1979   **CLC 13**
  See also CA 69-72; CANR 31; DLB 68
Garnett, David 1892-1981   **CLC 3**
  See also CA 5-8R; 103; CANR 17; DLB 34
Garos, Stephanie
  See Katz, Steve
Garrett, George (Palmer) 1929-**CLC 3, 11, 51;**
    SSC 30
  See also CA 1-4R; CAAS 5; CANR 1, 42, 67;
    DLB 2, 5, 130, 152; DLBY 83
Garrick, David 1717-1779   **LC 15; DAM**
    DRAM
  See also DLB 84
Garrigue, Jean 1914-1972   **CLC 2, 8**
  See also CA 5-8R; 37-40R; CANR 20
Garrison, Frederick
  See Sinclair, Upton (Beall)
Garth, Will
  See Hamilton, Edmond; Kuttner, Henry
Garvey, Marcus (Moziah, Jr.) 1887-1940
    TCLC 41; BLC 2; DAM MULT
  See also BW 1; CA 120; 124
Gary, Romain   **CLC 25**
  See also Kacew, Romain
  See also DLB 83
Gascar, Pierre   **CLC 11**
  See also Fournier, Pierre
Gascoyne, David (Emery) 1916-   **CLC 45**
  See also CA 65-68; CANR 10, 28, 54; DLB
    20; MTCW
Gaskell, Elizabeth Cleghorn 1810-1865**NCLC**
    70; DAB; DAM MST; SSC 25
  See also CDBLB 1832-1890; DLB 21, 144, 159
Gass, William H(oward) 1924-**CLC 1, 2, 8, 11,**
    15, 39; SSC 12
  See also CA 17-20R; CANR 30; DLB 2;
    MTCW
Gasset, Jose Ortega y
  See Ortega y Gasset, Jose
Gates, Henry Louis, Jr. 1950-**CLC 65; BLCS;**
    DAM MULT
  See also BW 2; CA 109; CANR 25, 53; DLB
    67
Gautier, Theophile 1811-1872   **NCLC 1, 59;**
    DAM POET; PC 18; SSC 20
  See also DLB 119
Gawsworth, John
  See Bates, H(erbert) E(rnest)
Gay, Oliver
  See Gogarty, Oliver St. John
Gaye, Marvin (Penze) 1939-1984   **CLC 26**
  See also CA 112
Gebler, Carlo (Ernest) 1954-   **CLC 39**
  See also CA 119; 133
Gee, Maggie (Mary) 1948-   **CLC 57**
  See also CA 130

Gee, Maurice (Gough) 1931-   **CLC 29**
  See also CA 97-100; CANR 67; SATA 46
Gelbart, Larry (Simon) 1923-   **CLC 21, 61**
  See also CA 73-76; CANR 45
Gelber, Jack 1932-   **CLC 1, 6, 14, 79**
  See also CA 1-4R; CANR 2; DLB 7
Gellhorn, Martha (Ellis) 1908-1998 **CLC 14,**
    60
  See also CA 77-80; 164; CANR 44; DLBY 82
Genet, Jean 1910-1986**CLC 1, 2, 5, 10, 14, 44,**
    46; DAM DRAM
  See also CA 13-16R; CANR 18; DLB 72;
    DLBY 86; MTCW
Gent, Peter 1942-   **CLC 29**
  See also AITN 1; CA 89-92; DLBY 82
Gentlewoman in New England, A
  See Bradstreet, Anne
Gentlewoman in Those Parts, A
  See Bradstreet, Anne
George, Jean Craighead 1919-   **CLC 35**
  See also AAYA 8; CA 5-8R; CANR 25; CLR
    1; DLB 52; JRDA; MAICYA; SATA 2, 68
George, Stefan (Anton) 1868-1933**TCLC 2, 14**
  See also CA 104
Georges, Georges Martin
  See Simenon, Georges (Jacques Christian)
Gerhardi, William Alexander
  See Gerhardie, William Alexander
Gerhardie, William Alexander 1895-1977
    CLC 5
  See also CA 25-28R; 73-76; CANR 18; DLB
    36
Gerstler, Amy 1956-   **CLC 70**
  See also CA 146
Gertler, T.   **CLC 34**
  See also CA 116; 121; INT 121
Ghalib   **NCLC 39**
  See also Ghalib, Hsadullah Khan
Ghalib, Hsadullah Khan 1797-1869
  See Ghalib
  See also DAM POET
Ghelderode, Michel de 1898-1962 **CLC 6, 11;**
    DAM DRAM
  See also CA 85-88; CANR 40
Ghiselin, Brewster 1903-   **CLC 23**
  See also CA 13-16R; CAAS 10; CANR 13
Ghose, Zulfikar 1935-   **CLC 42**
  See also CA 65-68; CANR 67
Ghosh, Amitav 1956-   **CLC 44**
  See also CA 147
Giacosa, Giuseppe 1847-1906   **TCLC 7**
  See also CA 104
Gibb, Lee
  See Waterhouse, Keith (Spencer)
Gibbon, Lewis Grassic   **TCLC 4**
  See also Mitchell, James Leslie
Gibbons, Kaye 1960- **CLC 50, 88; DAM POP**
  See also CA 151
Gibran, Kahlil 1883-1931   **TCLC 1, 9; DAM**
    POET, POP; PC 9
  See also CA 104; 150
Gibran, Khalil
  See Gibran, Kahlil
Gibson, William 1914-   **CLC 23; DA; DAB;**
    DAC; DAM DRAM, MST
  See also CA 9-12R; CANR 9, 42; DLB 7; SATA
    66
Gibson, William (Ford) 1948-   **CLC 39, 63;**
    DAM POP
  See also AAYA 12; CA 126; 133; CANR 52
Gide, Andre (Paul Guillaume) 1869-1951
    TCLC 5, 12, 36; DA; DAB; DAC; DAM
    MST, NOV; SSC 13; WLC

See also CA 104; 124; DLB 65; MTCW
Gifford, Barry (Colby) 1946-   **CLC 34**
  See also CA 65-68; CANR 9, 30, 40
Gilbert, Frank
  See De Voto, Bernard (Augustine)
Gilbert, W(illiam) S(chwenck) 1836-1911
    TCLC 3; DAM DRAM, POET
  See also CA 104; SATA 36
Gilbreth, Frank B., Jr. 1911-   **CLC 17**
  See also CA 9-12R; SATA 2
Gilchrist, Ellen 1935-**CLC 34, 48; DAM POP;**
    SSC 14
  See also CA 113; 116; CANR 41, 61; DLB 130;
    MTCW
Giles, Molly 1942-   **CLC 39**
  See also CA 126
Gill, Patrick
  See Creasey, John
Gilliam, Terry (Vance) 1940-   **CLC 21**
  See also Monty Python
  See also AAYA 19; CA 108; 113; CANR 35;
    INT 113
Gillian, Jerry
  See Gilliam, Terry (Vance)
Gilliatt, Penelope (Ann Douglass) 1932-1993
    CLC 2, 10, 13, 53
  See also AITN 2; CA 13-16R; 141; CANR 49;
    DLB 14
Gilman, Charlotte (Anna) Perkins (Stetson)
    1860-1935   **TCLC 9, 37; SSC 13**
  See also CA 106; 150
Gilmour, David 1949-   **CLC 35**
  See also CA 138; 147
Gilpin, William 1724-1804   **NCLC 30**
Gilray, J. D.
  See Mencken, H(enry) L(ouis)
Gilroy, Frank D(aniel) 1925-   **CLC 2**
  See also CA 81-84; CANR 32, 64; DLB 7
Gilstrap, John 1957(?)-   **CLC 99**
  See also CA 160
Ginsberg, Allen 1926-1997**CLC 1, 2, 3, 4, 6, 13,**
    36, 69, 109; DA; DAB; DAC; DAM MST,
    POET; PC 4; WLC 3
  See also AITN 1; CA 1-4R; 157; CANR 2, 41,
    63; CDALB 1941-1968; DLB 5, 16, 169;
    MTCW
Ginzburg, Natalia 1916-1991**CLC 5, 11, 54, 70**
  See also CA 85-88; 135; CANR 33; DLB 177;
    MTCW
Giono, Jean 1895-1970   **CLC 4, 11**
  See also CA 45-48; 29-32R; CANR 2, 35; DLB
    72; MTCW
Giovanni, Nikki 1943- **CLC 2, 4, 19, 64; BLC**
    2; DA; DAB; DAC; DAM MST, MULT,
    POET; PC 19; WLCS
  See also AAYA 22; AITN 1; BW 2; CA 29-
    32R; CAAS 6; CANR 18, 41, 60; CLR 6;
    DLB 5, 41; INT CANR-18; MAICYA;
    MTCW; SATA 24
Giovene, Andrea 1904-   **CLC 7**
  See also CA 85-88
Gippius, Zinaida (Nikolayevna) 1869-1945
  See Hippius, Zinaida
  See also CA 106
Giraudoux, (Hippolyte) Jean 1882-1944
    TCLC 2, 7; DAM DRAM
  See also CA 104; DLB 65
Gironella, Jose Maria 1917-   **CLC 11**
  See also CA 101
Gissing, George (Robert) 1857-1903 **TCLC 3,**
    24, 47
  See also CA 105; DLB 18, 135, 184
Giurlani, Aldo

See Palazzeschi, Aldo

Gladkov, Fyodor (Vasilyevich) 1883-1958
TCLC 27

Glanville, Brian (Lester) 1931- **CLC 6**
See also CA 5-8R; CAAS 9; CANR 3; DLB
15, 139; SATA 42

Glasgow, Ellen (Anderson Gholson) 1873-1945
TCLC 2, 7
See also CA 104; 164; DLB 9, 12

Glaspell, Susan 1882(?)-1948 **TCLC 55**
See also CA 110; 154; DLB 7, 9, 78; YABC 2

Glassco, John 1909-1981 **CLC 9**
See also CA 13-16R; 102; CANR 15; DLB 68

Glasscock, Amnesia
See Steinbeck, John (Ernst)

Glasser, Ronald J. 1940(?)- **CLC 37**

Glassman, Joyce
See Johnson, Joyce

Glendinning, Victoria 1937- **CLC 50**
See also CA 120; 127; CANR 59; DLB 155

Glissant, Edouard 1928- **CLC 10, 68; DAM
MULT**
See also CA 153

Gloag, Julian 1930- **CLC 40**
See also AITN 1; CA 65-68; CANR 10

Glowacki, Aleksander
See Prus, Boleslaw

Gluck, Louise (Elisabeth) 1943-**CLC 7, 22, 44,
81; DAM POET; PC 16**
See also CA 33-36R; CANR 40; DLB 5

Glyn, Elinor 1864-1943 **TCLC 72**
See also DLB 153

Gobineau, Joseph Arthur (Comte) de 1816-
1882 **NCLC 17**
See also DLB 123

Godard, Jean-Luc 1930- **CLC 20**
See also CA 93-96

Godden, (Margaret) Rumer 1907- **CLC 53**
See also AAYA 6; CA 5-8R; CANR 4, 27, 36,
55; CLR 20; DLB 161; MAICYA; SAAS 12;
SATA 3, 36

Godoy Alcayaga, Lucila 1889-1957
See Mistral, Gabriela
See also BW 2; CA 104; 131; DAM MULT;
HW; MTCW

Godwin, Gail (Kathleen) 1937- **CLC 5, 8, 22,
31, 69; DAM POP**
See also CA 29-32R; CANR 15, 43; DLB 6;
INT CANR-15; MTCW

Godwin, William 1756-1836 **NCLC 14**
See also CDBLB 1789-1832; DLB 39, 104,
142, 158, 163

Goebbels, Josef
See Goebbels, (Paul) Joseph

Goebbels, (Paul) Joseph 1897-1945 **TCLC 68**
See also CA 115; 148

Goebbels, Joseph Paul
See Goebbels, (Paul) Joseph

Goethe, Johann Wolfgang von 1749-1832
**NCLC 4, 22, 34; DA; DAB; DAC; DAM
DRAM, MST, POET; PC 5; WLC 3**
See also DLB 94

Gogarty, Oliver St. John 1878-1957 **TCLC 15**
See also CA 109; 150; DLB 15, 19

Gogol, Nikolai (Vasilyevich) 1809-1852**NCLC
5, 15, 31; DA; DAB; DAC; DAM DRAM,
MST; DC 1; SSC 4, 29; WLC**

Goines, Donald 1937(?)-1974**CLC 80; BLC 2;
DAM MULT, POP**
See also AITN 1; BW 1; CA 124; 114; DLB 33

Gold, Herbert 1924- **CLC 4, 7, 14, 42**
See also CA 9-12R; CANR 17, 45; DLB 2;
DLBY 81

Goldbarth, Albert 1948- **CLC 5, 38**
See also CA 53-56; CANR 6, 40; DLB 120

Goldberg, Anatol 1910-1982 **CLC 34**
See also CA 131; 117

Goldemberg, Isaac 1945- **CLC 52**
See also CA 69-72; CAAS 12; CANR 11, 32;
HW

Golding, William (Gerald) 1911-1993 **CLC 1,
2, 3, 8, 10, 17, 27, 58, 81; DA; DAB; DAC;
DAM MST, NOV; WLC**
See also AAYA 5; CA 5-8R; 141; CANR 13,
33, 54; CDBLB 1945-1960; DLB 15, 100;
MTCW

Goldman, Emma 1869-1940 **TCLC 13**
See also CA 110; 150

Goldman, Francisco 1954- **CLC 76**
See also CA 162

Goldman, William (W.) 1931- **CLC 1, 48**
See also CA 9-12R; CANR 29; DLB 44

Goldmann, Lucien 1913-1970 **CLC 24**
See also CA 25-28; CAP 2

Goldoni, Carlo 1707-1793**LC 4; DAM DRAM**

Goldsberry, Steven 1949- **CLC 34**
See also CA 131

Goldsmith, Oliver 1728-1774**LC 2; DA; DAB;
DAC; DAM DRAM, MST, NOV, POET;
DC 8; WLC**
See also CDBLB 1660-1789; DLB 39, 89, 104,
109, 142; SATA 26

Goldsmith, Peter
See Priestley, J(ohn) B(oynton)

Gombrowicz, Witold 1904-1969**CLC 4, 7, 11,
49; DAM DRAM**
See also CA 19-20; 25-28R; CAP 2

Gomez de la Serna, Ramon 1888-1963 **CLC 9**
See also CA 153; 116; HW

Goncharov, Ivan Alexandrovich 1812-1891
NCLC 1, 63

Goncourt, Edmond (Louis Antoine Huot) de
1822-1896 **NCLC 7**
See also DLB 123

Goncourt, Jules (Alfred Huot) de 1830-1870
NCLC 7
See also DLB 123

Gontier, Fernande 19(?)- **CLC 50**

Gonzalez Martinez, Enrique 1871-1952
TCLC 72
See also HW

Goodman, Paul 1911-1972 **CLC 1, 2, 4, 7**
See also CA 19-20; 37-40R; CANR 34; CAP
2; DLB 130; MTCW

Gordimer, Nadine 1923- **CLC 3, 5, 7, 10, 18,
33, 51, 70; DA; DAB; DAC; DAM MST,
NOV; SSC 17; WLCS**
See also CA 5-8R; CANR 3, 28, 56; INT
CANR-28; MTCW

Gordon, Adam Lindsay 1833-1870 **NCLC 21**

Gordon, Caroline 1895-1981**CLC 6, 13, 29, 83;
SSC 15**
See also CA 11-12; 103; CANR 36; CAP 1;
DLB 4, 9, 102; DLBY 81; MTCW

Gordon, Charles William 1860-1937
See Connor, Ralph
See also CA 109

Gordon, Mary (Catherine) 1949- **CLC 13, 22**
See also CA 102; CANR 44; DLB 6; DLBY
81; INT 102; MTCW

Gordon, N. J.
See Bosman, Herman Charles

Gordon, Sol 1923- **CLC 26**
See also CA 53-56; CANR 4; SATA 11

Gordone, Charles 1925-1995 **CLC 1, 4; DAM
DRAM; DC 8**

See also BW 1; CA 93-96; 150; CANR 55; DLB
7; INT 93-96; MTCW

Gore, Catherine 1800-1861 **NCLC 65**
See also DLB 116

Gorenko, Anna Andreevna
See Akhmatova, Anna

Gorky, Maxim 1868-1936**TCLC 8; DAB; SSC
28; WLC**
See also Peshkov, Alexei Maximovich

Goryan, Sirak
See Saroyan, William

Gosse, Edmund (William) 1849-1928 **TCLC
28**
See also CA 117; DLB 57, 144, 184

Gotlieb, Phyllis Fay (Bloom) 1926- **CLC 18**
See also CA 13-16R; CANR 7; DLB 88

Gottesman, S. D.
See Kornbluth, C(yril) M.; Pohl, Frederik

Gottfried von Strassburg fl. c. 1210- **CMLC
10**
See also DLB 138

Gould, Lois **CLC 4, 10**
See also CA 77-80; CANR 29; MTCW

Gourmont, Remy (-Marie-Charles) de 1858-
1915 **TCLC 17**
See also CA 109; 150

Govier, Katherine 1948- **CLC 51**
See also CA 101; CANR 18, 40

Goyen, (Charles) William 1915-1983 **CLC 5,
8, 14, 40**
See also AITN 2; CA 5-8R; 110; CANR 6; DLB
2; DLBY 83; INT CANR-6

Goytisolo, Juan 1931- **CLC 5, 10, 23; DAM
MULT; HLC**
See also CA 85-88; CANR 32, 61; HW; MTCW

Gozzano, Guido 1883-1916 **PC 10**
See also CA 154; DLB 114

Gozzi, (Conte) Carlo 1720-1806 **NCLC 23**

Grabbe, Christian Dietrich 1801-1836 **NCLC
2**
See also DLB 133

Grace, Patricia 1937- **CLC 56**

Gracian y Morales, Baltasar 1601-1658**LC 15**

Gracq, Julien **CLC 11, 48**
See also Poirier, Louis
See also DLB 83

Grade, Chaim 1910-1982 **CLC 10**
See also CA 93-96; 107

Graduate of Oxford, A
See Ruskin, John

Grafton, Garth
See Duncan, Sara Jeannette

Graham, John
See Phillips, David Graham

Graham, Jorie 1951- **CLC 48**
See also CA 111; CANR 63; DLB 120

Graham, R(obert) B(ontine) Cunninghame
See Cunninghame Graham, R(obert) B(ontine)
See also DLB 98, 135, 174

Graham, Robert
See Haldeman, Joe (William)

Graham, Tom
See Lewis, (Harry) Sinclair

Graham, W(illiam) S(ydney) 1918-1986 **CLC
29**
See also CA 73-76; 118; DLB 20

Graham, Winston (Mawdsley) 1910- **CLC 23**
See also CA 49-52; CANR 2, 22, 45, 66; DLB
77

Grahame, Kenneth 1859-1932**TCLC 64; DAB**
See also CA 108; 136; CLR 5; DLB 34, 141,
178; MAICYA; YABC 1

Grant, Skeeter

Guillen, Nicolas (Cristobal) 1902-1989 **CLC 48, 79; BLC 2; DAM MST, MULT, POET; HLC**
  See also BW 2; CA 116; 125; 129; HW
Guillevic, (Eugene) 1907- **CLC 33**
  See also CA 93-96
Guillois
  See Desnos, Robert
Guillois, Valentin
  See Desnos, Robert
Guiney, Louise Imogen 1861-1920 **TCLC 41**
  See also CA 160; DLB 54
Guiraldes, Ricardo (Guillermo) 1886-1927 **TCLC 39**
  See also CA 131; HW; MTCW
Gumilev, Nikolai (Stepanovich) 1886-1921 **TCLC 60**
  See also CA 165
Gunesekera, Romesh 1954- **CLC 91**
  See also CA 159
Gunn, Bill **CLC 5**
  See also Gunn, William Harrison
  See also DLB 38
Gunn, Thom(son William) 1929-**CLC 3, 6, 18, 32, 81; DAM POET**
  See also CA 17-20R; CANR 9, 33; CDBLB 1960 to Present; DLB 27; INT CANR-33; MTCW
Gunn, William Harrison 1934(?)-1989
  See Gunn, Bill
  See also AITN 1; BW 1; CA 13-16R; 128; CANR 12, 25
Gunnars, Kristjana 1948- **CLC 69**
  See also CA 113; DLB 60
Gurdjieff, G(eorgei) I(vanovich) 1877(?)-1949 **TCLC 71**
  See also CA 157
Gurganus, Allan 1947- **CLC 70; DAM POP**
  See also BEST 90:1; CA 135
Gurney, A(lbert) R(amsdell), Jr. 1930- **CLC 32, 50, 54; DAM DRAM**
  See also CA 77-80; CANR 32, 64
Gurney, Ivor (Bertie) 1890-1937 **TCLC 33**
Gurney, Peter
  See Gurney, A(lbert) R(amsdell), Jr.
Guro, Elena 1877-1913 **TCLC 56**
Gustafson, James M(oody) 1925- **CLC 100**
  See also CA 25-28R; CANR 37
Gustafson, Ralph (Barker) 1909- **CLC 36**
  See also CA 21-24R; CANR 8, 45; DLB 88
Gut, Gom
  See Simenon, Georges (Jacques Christian)
Guterson, David 1956- **CLC 91**
  See also CA 132
Guthrie, A(lfred) B(ertram), Jr. 1901-1991 **CLC 23**
  See also CA 57-60; 134; CANR 24; DLB 6; SATA 62; SATA-Obit 67
Guthrie, Isobel
  See Grieve, C(hristopher) M(urray)
Guthrie, Woodrow Wilson 1912-1967
  See Guthrie, Woody
  See also CA 113; 93-96
Guthrie, Woody **CLC 35**
  See also Guthrie, Woodrow Wilson
Guy, Rosa (Cuthbert) 1928- **CLC 26**
  See also AAYA 4; BW 2; CA 17-20R; CANR 14, 34; CLR 13; DLB 33; JRDA; MAICYA; SATA 14, 62
Gwendolyn
  See Bennett, (Enoch) Arnold
H. D. **CLC 3, 8, 14, 31, 34, 73; PC 5**
  See also Doolittle, Hilda

H. de V.
  See Buchan, John
Haavikko, Paavo Juhani 1931- **CLC 18, 34**
  See also CA 106
Habbema, Koos
  See Heijermans, Herman
Habermas, Juergen 1929- **CLC 104**
  See also CA 109
Habermas, Jurgen
  See Habermas, Juergen
Hacker, Marilyn 1942- **CLC 5, 9, 23, 72, 91; DAM POET**
  See also CA 77-80; CANR 68; DLB 120
Haeckel, Ernst Heinrich (Philipp August) 1834-1919 **TCLC 80**
  See also CA 157
Haggard, H(enry) Rider 1856-1925 **TCLC 11**
  See also CA 108; 148; DLB 70, 156, 174, 178; SATA 16
Hagiosy, L.
  See Larbaud, Valery (Nicolas)
Hagiwara Sakutaro 1886-1942 **TCLC 60; PC 18**
Haig, Fenil
  See Ford, Ford Madox
Haig-Brown, Roderick (Langmere) 1908-1976 **CLC 21**
  See also CA 5-8R; 69-72; CANR 4, 38; CLR 31; DLB 88; MAICYA; SATA 12
Hailey, Arthur 1920-**CLC 5; DAM NOV, POP**
  See also AITN 2; BEST 90:3; CA 1-4R; CANR 2, 36; DLB 88; DLBY 82; MTCW
Hailey, Elizabeth Forsythe 1938- **CLC 40**
  See also CA 93-96; CAAS 1; CANR 15, 48; INT CANR-15
Haines, John (Meade) 1924- **CLC 58**
  See also CA 17-20R; CANR 13, 34; DLB 5
Hakluyt, Richard 1552-1616 **LC 31**
Haldeman, Joe (William) 1943- **CLC 61**
  See also CA 53-56; CAAS 25; CANR 6; DLB 8; INT CANR-6
Haley, Alex(ander Murray Palmer) 1921-1992 **CLC 8, 12, 76; BLC 2; DA; DAB; DAC; DAM MST, MULT, POP**
  See also BW 2; CA 77-80; 136; CANR 61; DLB 38; MTCW
Haliburton, Thomas Chandler 1796-1865 **NCLC 15**
  See also DLB 11, 99
Hall, Donald (Andrew, Jr.) 1928- **CLC 1, 13, 37, 59; DAM POET**
  See also CA 5-8R; CAAS 7; CANR 2, 44, 64; DLB 5; SATA 23, 97
Hall, Frederic Sauser
  See Sauser-Hall, Frederic
Hall, James
  See Kuttner, Henry
Hall, James Norman 1887-1951 **TCLC 23**
  See also CA 123; SATA 21
Hall, (Marguerite) Radclyffe 1886-1943 **TCLC 12**
  See also CA 110; 150
Hall, Rodney 1935- **CLC 51**
  See also CA 109
Halleck, Fitz-Greene 1790-1867 **NCLC 47**
  See also DLB 3
Halliday, Michael
  See Creasey, John
Halpern, Daniel 1945- **CLC 14**
  See also CA 33-36R
Hamburger, Michael (Peter Leopold) 1924- **CLC 5, 14**
  See also CA 5-8R; CAAS 4; CANR 2, 47; DLB

27
Hamill, Pete 1935- **CLC 10**
  See also CA 25-28R; CANR 18
Hamilton, Alexander 1755(?)-1804 **NCLC 49**
  See also DLB 37
Hamilton, Clive
  See Lewis, C(live) S(taples)
Hamilton, Edmond 1904-1977 **CLC 1**
  See also CA 1-4R; CANR 3; DLB 8
Hamilton, Eugene (Jacob) Lee
  See Lee-Hamilton, Eugene (Jacob)
Hamilton, Franklin
  See Silverberg, Robert
Hamilton, Gail
  See Corcoran, Barbara
Hamilton, Mollie
  See Kaye, M(ary) M(argaret)
Hamilton, (Anthony Walter) Patrick 1904-1962 **CLC 51**
  See also CA 113; DLB 10
Hamilton, Virginia 1936- **CLC 26; DAM MULT**
  See also AAYA 2, 21; BW 2; CA 25-28R; CANR 20, 37; CLR 1, 11, 40; DLB 33, 52; INT CANR-20; JRDA; MAICYA; MTCW; SATA 4, 56, 79
Hammett, (Samuel) Dashiell 1894-1961 **CLC 3, 5, 10, 19, 47; SSC 17**
  See also AITN 1; CA 81-84; CANR 42; CDALB 1929-1941; DLBD 6; DLBY 96; MTCW
Hammon, Jupiter 1711(?)-1800(?) **NCLC 5; BLC 2; DAM MULT, POET; PC 16**
  See also DLB 31, 50
Hammond, Keith
  See Kuttner, Henry
Hamner, Earl (Henry), Jr. 1923- **CLC 12**
  See also AITN 2; CA 73-76; DLB 6
Hampton, Christopher (James) 1946- **CLC 4**
  See also CA 25-28R; DLB 13; MTCW
Hamsun, Knut **TCLC 2, 14, 49**
  See also Pedersen, Knut
Handke, Peter 1942-**CLC 5, 8, 10, 15, 38; DAM DRAM, NOV**
  See also CA 77-80; CANR 33; DLB 85, 124; MTCW
Hanley, James 1901-1985 **CLC 3, 5, 8, 13**
  See also CA 73-76; 117; CANR 36; DLB 191; MTCW
Hannah, Barry 1942- **CLC 23, 38, 90**
  See also CA 108; 110; CANR 43, 68; DLB 6; INT 110; MTCW
Hannon, Ezra
  See Hunter, Evan
Hansberry, Lorraine (Vivian) 1930-1965**CLC 17, 62; BLC 2; DA; DAB; DAC; DAM DRAM, MST, MULT; DC 2**
  See also AAYA 25; BW 1; CA 109; 25-28R; CABS 3; CANR 58; CDALB 1941-1968; DLB 7, 38; MTCW
Hansen, Joseph 1923- **CLC 38**
  See also CA 29-32R; CAAS 17; CANR 16, 44, 66; INT CANR-16
Hansen, Martin A. 1909-1955 **TCLC 32**
Hanson, Kenneth O(stlin) 1922- **CLC 13**
  See also CA 53-56; CANR 7
Hardwick, Elizabeth 1916- **CLC 13; DAM NOV**
  See also CA 5-8R; CANR 3, 32; DLB 6; MTCW
Hardy, Thomas 1840-1928**TCLC 4, 10, 18, 32, 48, 53, 72; DA; DAB; DAC; DAM MST, NOV, POET; PC 8; SSC 2; WLC**
  See also CA 104; 123; CDBLB 1890-1914;

DLB 18, 19, 135; MTCW
Hare, David 1947- **CLC 29, 58**
See also CA 97-100; CANR 39; DLB 13;
MTCW
Harewood, John
See Van Druten, John (William)
Harford, Henry
See Hudson, W(illiam) H(enry)
Hargrave, Leonie
See Disch, Thomas M(ichael)
Harjo, Joy 1951- **CLC 83; DAM MULT**
See also CA 114; CANR 35, 67; DLB 120, 175;
NNAL
Harlan, Louis R(udolph) 1922- **CLC 34**
See also CA 21-24R; CANR 25, 55
Harling, Robert 1951(?)- **CLC 53**
See also CA 147
Harmon, William (Ruth) 1938- **CLC 38**
See also CA 33-36R; CANR 14, 32, 35; SATA
65
Harper, F. E. W.
See Harper, Frances Ellen Watkins
Harper, Frances E. W.
See Harper, Frances Ellen Watkins
Harper, Frances E. Watkins
See Harper, Frances Ellen Watkins
Harper, Frances Ellen
See Harper, Frances Ellen Watkins
Harper, Frances Ellen Watkins 1825-1911
**TCLC 14; BLC 2; DAM MULT, POET;
PC 21**
See also BW 1; CA 111; 125; DLB 50
Harper, Michael S(teven) 1938- **CLC 7, 22**
See also BW 1; CA 33-36R; CANR 24; DLB
41
Harper, Mrs. F. E. W.
See Harper, Frances Ellen Watkins
Harris, Christie (Lucy) Irwin 1907- **CLC 12**
See also CA 5-8R; CANR 6; CLR 47; DLB 88;
JRDA; MAICYA; SAAS 10; SATA 6, 74
Harris, Frank 1856-1931 **TCLC 24**
See also CA 109; 150; DLB 156
Harris, George Washington 1814-1869**NCLC
23**
See also DLB 3, 11
Harris, Joel Chandler 1848-1908 **TCLC 2;
SSC 19**
See also CA 104; 137; CLR 49; DLB 11, 23,
42, 78, 91; MAICYA; YABC 1
Harris, John (Wyndham Parkes Lucas) Beynon
1903-1969
See Wyndham, John
See also CA 102; 89-92
Harris, MacDonald **CLC 9**
See also Heiney, Donald (William)
Harris, Mark 1922- **CLC 19**
See also CA 5-8R; CAAS 3; CANR 2, 55; DLB
2; DLBY 80
Harris, (Theodore) Wilson 1921- **CLC 25**
See also BW 2; CA 65-68; CAAS 16; CANR
11, 27; DLB 117; MTCW
Harrison, Elizabeth Cavanna 1909-
See Cavanna, Betty
See also CA 9-12R; CANR 6, 27
Harrison, Harry (Max) 1925- **CLC 42**
See also CA 1-4R; CANR 5, 21; DLB 8; SATA
4
Harrison, James (Thomas) 1937- **CLC 6, 14,
33, 66; SSC 19**
See also CA 13-16R; CANR 8, 51; DLBY 82;
INT CANR-8
Harrison, Jim
See Harrison, James (Thomas)

Harrison, Kathryn 1961- **CLC 70**
See also CA 144; CANR 68
Harrison, Tony 1937- **CLC 43**
See also CA 65-68; CANR 44; DLB 40; MTCW
Harriss, Will(ard Irvin) 1922- **CLC 34**
See also CA 111
Harson, Sley
See Ellison, Harlan (Jay)
Hart, Ellis
See Ellison, Harlan (Jay)
Hart, Josephine 1942(?)- **CLC 70; DAM POP**
See also CA 138
Hart, Moss 1904-1961 **CLC 66; DAM DRAM**
See also CA 109; 89-92; DLB 7
Harte, (Francis) Bret(t) 1836(?)-1902**TCLC 1,
25; DA; DAC; DAM MST; SSC 8; WLC**
See also CA 104; 140; CDALB 1865-1917;
DLB 12, 64, 74, 79, 186; SATA 26
Hartley, L(eslie) P(oles) 1895-1972 **CLC 2, 22**
See also CA 45-48; 37-40R; CANR 33; DLB
15, 139; MTCW
Hartman, Geoffrey H. 1929- **CLC 27**
See also CA 117; 125; DLB 67
Hartmann, Sadakichi 1867-1944 **TCLC 73**
See also CA 157; DLB 54
Hartmann von Aue c. 1160-c. 1205 **CMLC 15**
See also DLB 138
Hartmann von Aue 1170-1210 **CMLC 15**
Haruf, Kent 1943- **CLC 34**
See also CA 149
Harwood, Ronald 1934- **CLC 32; DAM
DRAM, MST**
See also CA 1-4R; CANR 4, 55; DLB 13
Hasegawa Tatsunosuke
See Futabatei, Shimei
Hasek, Jaroslav (Matej Frantisek) 1883-1923
TCLC 4
See also CA 104; 129; MTCW
Hass, Robert 1941- **CLC 18, 39, 99; PC 16**
See also CA 111; CANR 30, 50; DLB 105;
SATA 94
Hastings, Hudson
See Kuttner, Henry
Hastings, Selina **CLC 44**
Hathorne, John 1641-1717 **LC 38**
Hatteras, Amelia
See Mencken, H(enry) L(ouis)
Hatteras, Owen **TCLC 18**
See also Mencken, H(enry) L(ouis); Nathan,
George Jean
Hauptmann, Gerhart (Johann Robert) 1862-
1946 **TCLC 4; DAM DRAM**
See also CA 104; 153; DLB 66, 118
Havel, Vaclav 1936- **CLC 25, 58, 65; DAM
DRAM; DC 6**
See also CA 104; CANR 36, 63; MTCW
Haviaras, Stratis **CLC 33**
See also Chaviaras, Strates
Hawes, Stephen 1475(?)-1523(?) **LC 17**
Hawkes, John (Clendennin Burne, Jr.) 1925-
CLC 1, 2, 3, 4, 7, 9, 14, 15, 27, 49
See also CA 1-4R; CANR 2, 47, 64; DLB 2, 7;
DLBY 80; MTCW
Hawking, S. W.
See Hawking, Stephen W(illiam)
Hawking, Stephen W(illiam) 1942- **CLC 63,
105**
See also AAYA 13; BEST 89:1; CA 126; 129;
CANR 48
Hawthorne, Julian 1846-1934 **TCLC 25**
See also CA 165
Hawthorne, Nathaniel 1804-1864 **NCLC 39;
DA; DAB; DAC; DAM MST, NOV; SSC

3, 29; WLC**
See also AAYA 18; CDALB 1640-1865; DLB
1, 74; YABC 2
Haxton, Josephine Ayres 1921-
See Douglas, Ellen
See also CA 115; CANR 41
Hayaseca y Eizaguirre, Jorge
See Echegaray (y Eizaguirre), Jose (Maria
Waldo)
Hayashi Fumiko 1904-1951 **TCLC 27**
See also CA 161; DLB 180
Haycraft, Anna
See Ellis, Alice Thomas
See also CA 122
Hayden, Robert E(arl) 1913-1980 **CLC 5, 9,
14, 37; BLC 2; DA; DAC; DAM MST,
MULT, POET; PC 6**
See also BW 1; CA 69-72; 97-100; CABS 2;
CANR 24; CDALB 1941-1968; DLB 5, 76;
MTCW; SATA 19; SATA-Obit 26
Hayford, J(oseph) E(phraim) Casely
See Casely-Hayford, J(oseph) E(phraim)
Hayman, Ronald 1932- **CLC 44**
See also CA 25-28R; CANR 18, 50; DLB 155
Haywood, Eliza (Fowler) 1693(?)-1756 **LC 1**
Hazlitt, William 1778-1830 **NCLC 29**
See also DLB 110, 158
Hazzard, Shirley 1931- **CLC 18**
See also CA 9-12R; CANR 4; DLBY 82;
MTCW
Head, Bessie 1937-1986 **CLC 25, 67; BLC 2;
DAM MULT**
See also BW 2; CA 29-32R; 119; CANR 25;
DLB 117; MTCW
Headon, (Nicky) Topper 1956(?)- **CLC 30**
Heaney, Seamus (Justin) 1939- **CLC 5, 7, 14,
25, 37, 74, 91; DAB; DAM POET; PC 18;
WLCS**
See also CA 85-88; CANR 25, 48; CDBLB
1960 to Present; DLB 40; DLBY 95; MTCW
Hearn, (Patricio) Lafcadio (Tessima Carlos)
1850-1904 **TCLC 9**
See also CA 105; DLB 12, 78
Hearne, Vicki 1946- **CLC 56**
See also CA 139
Hearon, Shelby 1931- **CLC 63**
See also AITN 2; CA 25-28R; CANR 18, 48
Heat-Moon, William Least **CLC 29**
See also Trogdon, William (Lewis)
See also AAYA 9
Hebbel, Friedrich 1813-1863**NCLC 43; DAM
DRAM**
See also DLB 129
Hebert, Anne 1916-**CLC 4, 13, 29; DAC; DAM
MST, POET**
See also CA 85-88; DLB 68; MTCW
Hecht, Anthony (Evan) 1923- **CLC 8, 13, 19;
DAM POET**
See also CA 9-12R; CANR 6; DLB 5, 169
Hecht, Ben 1894-1964 **CLC 8**
See also CA 85-88; DLB 7, 9, 25, 26, 28, 86
Hedayat, Sadeq 1903-1951 **TCLC 21**
See also CA 120
Hegel, Georg Wilhelm Friedrich 1770-1831
NCLC 46
See also DLB 90
Heidegger, Martin 1889-1976 **CLC 24**
See also CA 81-84; 65-68; CANR 34; MTCW
Heidenstam, (Carl Gustaf) Verner von 1859-
1940 **TCLC 5**
See also CA 104
Heifner, Jack 1946- **CLC 11**
See also CA 105; CANR 47

Heijermans, Herman 1864-1924   TCLC 24
See also CA 123
Heilbrun, Carolyn G(old) 1926-   CLC 25
See also CA 45-48; CANR 1, 28, 58
Heine, Heinrich 1797-1856   NCLC 4, 54
See also DLB 90
Heinemann, Larry (Curtiss) 1944- CLC 50
See also CA 110; CAAS 21; CANR 31; DLBD
9; INT CANR-31
Heiney, Donald (William) 1921-1993
See Harris, MacDonald
See also CA 1-4R; 142; CANR 3, 58
Heinlein, Robert A(nson) 1907-1988CLC 1, 3,
8, 14, 26, 55; DAM POP
See also AAYA 17; CA 1-4R; 125; CANR 1,
20, 53; DLB 8; JRDA; MAICYA; MTCW;
SATA 9, 69; SATA-Obit 56
Helforth, John
See Doolittle, Hilda
Hellenhofferu, Vojtech Kapristian z
See Hasek, Jaroslav (Matej Frantisek)
Heller, Joseph 1923-CLC 1, 3, 5, 8, 11, 36, 63;
DA; DAB; DAC; DAM MST, NOV, POP;
WLC
See also AAYA 24; AITN 1; CA 5-8R; CABS
1; CANR 8, 42, 66; DLB 2, 28; DLBY 80;
INT CANR-8; MTCW
Hellman, Lillian (Florence) 1906-1984CLC 2,
4, 8, 14, 18, 34, 44, 52; DAM DRAM; DC 1
See also AITN 1, 2; CA 13-16R; 112; CANR
33; DLB 7; DLBY 84; MTCW
Helprin, Mark 1947-CLC 7, 10, 22, 32; DAM
NOV, POP
See also CA 81-84; CANR 47, 64; DLBY 85;
MTCW
Helvetius, Claude-Adrien 1715-1771   LC 26
Helyar, Jane Penelope Josephine 1933-
See Poole, Josephine
See also CA 21-24R; CANR 10, 26; SATA 82
Hemans, Felicia 1793-1835   NCLC 29
See also DLB 96
Hemingway, Ernest (Miller) 1899-1961 CLC
1, 3, 6, 8, 10, 13, 19, 30, 34, 39, 41, 44, 50,
61, 80; DA; DAB; DAC; DAM MST, NOV;
SSC 25; WLC
See also AAYA 19; CA 77-80; CANR 34;
CDALB 1917-1929; DLB 4, 9, 102; DLBD
1, 15, 16; DLBY 81, 87, 96; MTCW
Hempel, Amy 1951-   CLC 39
See also CA 118; 137
Henderson, F. C.
See Mencken, H(enry) L(ouis)
Henderson, Sylvia
See Ashton-Warner, Sylvia (Constance)
Henderson, Zenna (Chlarson) 1917-1983 SSC
29
See also CA 1-4R; 133; CANR 1; DLB 8; SATA
5
Henley, Beth   CLC 23; DC 6
See also Henley, Elizabeth Becker
See also CABS 3; DLBY 86
Henley, Elizabeth Becker 1952-
See Henley, Beth
See also CA 107; CANR 32; DAM DRAM,
MST; MTCW
Henley, William Ernest 1849-1903   TCLC 8
See also CA 105; DLB 19
Hennissart, Martha
See Lathen, Emma
See also CA 85-88; CANR 64
Henry, O.   TCLC 1, 19; SSC 5; WLC
See also Porter, William Sydney
Henry, Patrick 1736-1799   LC 25

Henryson, Robert 1430(?)-1506(?)   LC 20
See also DLB 146
Henry VIII 1491-1547   LC 10
Henschke, Alfred
See Klabund
Hentoff, Nat(han Irving) 1925-   CLC 26
See also AAYA 4; CA 1-4R; CAAS 6; CANR
5, 25; CLR 1; INT CANR-25; JRDA;
MAICYA; SATA 42, 69; SATA-Brief 27
Heppenstall, (John) Rayner 1911-1981 CLC
10
See also CA 1-4R; 103; CANR 29
Heraclitus c. 540B.C.-c. 450B.C.   CMLC 22
See also DLB 176
Herbert, Frank (Patrick) 1920-1986 CLC 12,
23, 35, 44, 85; DAM POP
See also AAYA 21; CA 53-56; 118; CANR 5,
43; DLB 8; INT CANR-5; MTCW; SATA
9, 37; SATA-Obit 47
Herbert, George 1593-1633   LC 24; DAB;
DAM POET; PC 4
See also CDBLB Before 1660; DLB 126
Herbert, Zbigniew 1924-   CLC 9, 43; DAM
POET
See also CA 89-92; CANR 36; MTCW
Herbst, Josephine (Frey) 1897-1969   CLC 34
See also CA 5-8R; 25-28R; DLB 9
Hergesheimer, Joseph 1880-1954   TCLC 11
See also CA 109; DLB 102, 9
Herlihy, James Leo 1927-1993   CLC 6
See also CA 1-4R; 143; CANR 2
Hermogenes fl. c. 175-   CMLC 6
Hernandez, Jose 1834-1886   NCLC 17
Herodotus c. 484B.C.-429B.C.   CMLC 17
See also DLB 176
Herrick, Robert 1591-1674 LC 13; DA; DAB;
DAC; DAM MST, POP; PC 9
See also DLB 126
Herring, Guilles
See Somerville, Edith
Herriot, James 1916-1995CLC 12; DAM POP
See also Wight, James Alfred
See also AAYA 1; CA 148; CANR 40; SATA
86
Herrmann, Dorothy 1941-   CLC 44
See also CA 107
Herrmann, Taffy
See Herrmann, Dorothy
Hersey, John (Richard) 1914-1993CLC 1, 2, 7,
9, 40, 81, 97; DAM POP
See also CA 17-20R; 140; CANR 33; DLB 6,
185; MTCW; SATA 25; SATA-Obit 76
Herzen, Aleksandr Ivanovich 1812-1870
NCLC 10, 61
Herzl, Theodor 1860-1904   TCLC 36
Herzog, Werner 1942-   CLC 16
See also CA 89-92
Hesiod c. 8th cent. B.C.-   CMLC 5
See also DLB 176
Hesse, Hermann 1877-1962CLC 1, 2, 3, 6, 11,
17, 25, 69; DA; DAB; DAC; DAM MST,
NOV; SSC 9; WLC
See also CA 17-18; CAP 2; DLB 66; MTCW;
SATA 50
Hewes, Cady
See De Voto, Bernard (Augustine)
Heyen, William 1940-   CLC 13, 18
See also CA 33-36R; CAAS 9; DLB 5
Heyerdahl, Thor 1914-   CLC 26
See also CA 5-8R; CANR 5, 22, 66; MTCW;
SATA 2, 52
Heym, Georg (Theodor Franz Arthur) 1887-
1912   TCLC 9

See also CA 106
Heym, Stefan 1913-   CLC 41
See also CA 9-12R; CANR 4; DLB 69
Heyse, Paul (Johann Ludwig von) 1830-1914
TCLC 8
See also CA 104; DLB 129
Heyward, (Edwin) DuBose 1885-1940 TCLC
59
See also CA 108; 157; DLB 7, 9, 45; SATA 21
Hibbert, Eleanor Alice Burford 1906-1993
CLC 7; DAM POP
See also BEST 90:4; CA 17-20R; 140; CANR
9, 28, 59; SATA 2; SATA-Obit 74
Hichens, Robert (Smythe) 1864-1950   TCLC
64
See also CA 162; DLB 153
Higgins, George V(incent) 1939-CLC 4, 7, 10,
18
See also CA 77-80; CAAS 5; CANR 17, 51;
DLB 2; DLBY 81; INT CANR-17; MTCW
Higginson, Thomas Wentworth 1823-1911
TCLC 36
See also CA 162; DLB 1, 64
Highet, Helen
See MacInnes, Helen (Clark)
Highsmith, (Mary) Patricia 1921-1995CLC 2,
4, 14, 42, 102; DAM NOV, POP
See also CA 1-4R; 147; CANR 1, 20, 48, 62;
MTCW
Highwater, Jamake (Mamake) 1942(?)- CLC
12
See also AAYA 7; CA 65-68; CAAS 7; CANR
10, 34; CLR 17; DLB 52; DLBY 85; JRDA;
MAICYA; SATA 32, 69; SATA-Brief 30
Highway, Tomson 1951-CLC 92; DAC; DAM
MULT
See also CA 151; NNAL
Higuchi, Ichiyo 1872-1896   NCLC 49
Hijuelos, Oscar 1951- CLC 65; DAM MULT,
POP; HLC
See also AAYA 25; BEST 90:1; CA 123;
CANR 50; DLB 145; HW
Hikmet, Nazim 1902(?)-1963   CLC 40
See also CA 141; 93-96
Hildegard von Bingen 1098-1179   CMLC 20
See also DLB 148
Hildesheimer, Wolfgang 1916-1991   CLC 49
See also CA 101; 135; DLB 69, 124
Hill, Geoffrey (William) 1932-   CLC 5, 8, 18,
45; DAM POET
See also CA 81-84; CANR 21; CDBLB 1960
to Present; DLB 40; MTCW
Hill, George Roy 1921-   CLC 26
See also CA 110; 122
Hill, John
See Koontz, Dean R(ay)
Hill, Susan (Elizabeth) 1942-   CLC 4; DAB;
DAM MST, NOV
See also CA 33-36R; CANR 29; DLB 14, 139;
MTCW
Hillerman, Tony 1925-   CLC 62; DAM POP
See also AAYA 6; BEST 89:1; CA 29-32R;
CANR 21, 42, 65; SATA 6
Hillesum, Etty 1914-1943   TCLC 49
See also CA 137
Hilliard, Noel (Harvey) 1929-   CLC 15
See also CA 9-12R; CANR 7
Hillis, Rick 1956-   CLC 66
See also CA 134
Hilton, James 1900-1954   TCLC 21
See also CA 108; DLB 34, 77; SATA 34
Himes, Chester (Bomar) 1909-1984 CLC 2, 4,
7, 18, 58, 108; BLC 2; DAM MULT

Author Index

CLC 11
See also CA 77-80; 126; CANR 58; DLB 87;
SATA 14; SATA-Obit 59

Housman, A(lfred) E(dward) 1859-1936
**TCLC 1, 10; DA; DAB; DAC; DAM MST,
POET; PC 2; WLCS**
See also CA 104; 125; DLB 19; MTCW

Housman, Laurence 1865-1959   **TCLC 7**
See also CA 106; 155; DLB 10; SATA 25

Howard, Elizabeth Jane 1923-   **CLC 7, 29**
See also CA 5-8R; CANR 8, 62

Howard, Maureen 1930-   **CLC 5, 14, 46**
See also CA 53-56; CANR 31; DLBY 83; INT
CANR-31; MTCW

Howard, Richard 1929-   **CLC 7, 10, 47**
See also AITN 1; CA 85-88; CANR 25; DLB
5; INT CANR-25

Howard, Robert E(rvin) 1906-1936   **TCLC 8**
See also CA 105; 157

Howard, Warren F.
See Pohl, Frederik

Howe, Fanny 1940-   **CLC 47**
See also CA 117; CAAS 27; SATA-Brief 52

Howe, Irving 1920-1993   **CLC 85**
See also CA 9-12R; 141; CANR 21, 50; DLB
67; MTCW

Howe, Julia Ward 1819-1910   **TCLC 21**
See also CA 117; DLB 1, 189

Howe, Susan 1937-   **CLC 72**
See also CA 160; DLB 120

Howe, Tina 1937-   **CLC 48**
See also CA 109

Howell, James 1594(?)-1666   **LC 13**
See also DLB 151

Howells, W. D.
See Howells, William Dean

Howells, William D.
See Howells, William Dean

Howells, William Dean 1837-1920   **TCLC 7,
17, 41**
See also CA 104; 134; CDALB 1865-1917;
DLB 12, 64, 74, 79, 189

Howes, Barbara 1914-1996   **CLC 15**
See also CA 9-12R; 151; CAAS 3; CANR 53;
SATA 5

Hrabal, Bohumil 1914-1997   **CLC 13, 67**
See also CA 106; 156; CAAS 12; CANR 57

Hsun, Lu
See Lu Hsun

Hubbard, L(afayette) Ron(ald) 1911-1986
CLC 43; DAM POP
See also CA 77-80; 118; CANR 52

Huch, Ricarda (Octavia) 1864-1947 **TCLC 13**
See also CA 111; DLB 66

Huddle, David 1942-   **CLC 49**
See also CA 57-60; CAAS 20; DLB 130

Hudson, Jeffrey
See Crichton, (John) Michael

Hudson, W(illiam) H(enry) 1841-1922 **TCLC
29**
See also CA 115; DLB 98, 153, 174; SATA 35

Hueffer, Ford Madox
See Ford, Ford Madox

Hughart, Barry 1934-   **CLC 39**
See also CA 137

Hughes, Colin
See Creasey, John

Hughes, David (John) 1930-   **CLC 48**
See also CA 116; 129; DLB 14

Hughes, Edward James
See Hughes, Ted
See also DAM MST, POET

Hughes, (James) Langston 1902-1967 **CLC 1,**
5, 10, 15, 35, 44, 108; BLC 2; DA; DAB;
DAC; DAM DRAM, MST, MULT, POET;
DC 3; PC 1; SSC 6; WLC
See also AAYA 12; BW 1; CA 1-4R; 25-28R;
CANR 1, 34; CDALB 1929-1941; CLR 17;
DLB 4, 7, 48, 51, 86; JRDA; MAICYA;
MTCW; SATA 4, 33

Hughes, Richard (Arthur Warren) 1900-1976
CLC 1, 11; DAM NOV
See also CA 5-8R; 65-68; CANR 4; DLB 15,
161; MTCW; SATA 8; SATA-Obit 25

Hughes, Ted 1930- **CLC 2, 4, 9, 14, 37; DAB;
DAC; PC 7**
See also Hughes, Edward James
See also CA 1-4R; CANR 1, 33, 66; CLR 3;
DLB 40, 161; MAICYA; MTCW; SATA 49;
SATA-Brief 27

Hugo, Richard F(ranklin) 1923-1982 **CLC 6,
18, 32; DAM POET**
See also CA 49-52; 108; CANR 3; DLB 5

Hugo, Victor (Marie) 1802-1885 **NCLC 3, 10,
21; DA; DAB; DAC; DAM DRAM, MST,
NOV, POET; PC 17; WLC**
See also DLB 119, 192; SATA 47

Huidobro, Vicente
See Huidobro Fernandez, Vicente Garcia

Huidobro Fernandez, Vicente Garcia 1893-
1948   **TCLC 31**
See also CA 131; HW

Hulme, Keri 1947-   **CLC 39**
See also CA 125; INT 125

Hulme, T(homas) E(rnest) 1883-1917 **TCLC
21**
See also CA 117; DLB 19

Hume, David 1711-1776   **LC 7**
See also DLB 104

Humphrey, William 1924-1997   **CLC 45**
See also CA 77-80; 160; CANR 68; DLB 6

Humphreys, Emyr Owen 1919-   **CLC 47**
See also CA 5-8R; CANR 3, 24; DLB 15

Humphreys, Josephine 1945-   **CLC 34, 57**
See also CA 121; 127; INT 127

Huneker, James Gibbons 1857-1921 **TCLC 65**
See also DLB 71

Hungerford, Pixie
See Brinsmead, H(esba) F(ay)

Hunt, E(verette) Howard, (Jr.) 1918- **CLC 3**
See also AITN 1; CA 45-48; CANR 2, 47

Hunt, Kyle
See Creasey, John

Hunt, Leigh 1784-1859   **NCLC 70**
See also DLB 96, 110, 144

Hunt, (James Henry) Leigh 1784-1859 **NCLC
1; DAM POET**

Hunt, Marsha 1946-   **CLC 70**
See also BW 2; CA 143

Hunt, Violet 1866-1942   **TCLC 53**
See also DLB 162

Hunter, E. Waldo
See Sturgeon, Theodore (Hamilton)

Hunter, Evan 1926- **CLC 11, 31; DAM POP**
See also CA 5-8R; CANR 5, 38, 62; DLBY 82;
INT CANR-5; MTCW; SATA 25

Hunter, Kristin (Eggleston) 1931-   **CLC 35**
See also AITN 1; BW 1; CA 13-16R; CANR
13; CLR 3; DLB 33; INT CANR-13;
MAICYA; SAAS 10; SATA 12

Hunter, Mollie 1922-   **CLC 21**
See also McIlwraith, Maureen Mollie Hunter
See also AAYA 13; CANR 37; CLR 25; DLB
161; JRDA; MAICYA; SAAS 7; SATA 54

Hunter, Robert (?)-1734   **LC 7**

Hurston, Zora Neale 1903-1960 **CLC 7, 30, 61;**
BLC 2; DA; DAC; DAM MST, MULT,
NOV; SSC 4; WLCS
See also AAYA 15; BW 1; CA 85-88; CANR
61; DLB 51, 86; MTCW

Huston, John (Marcellus) 1906-1987 **CLC 20**
See also CA 73-76; 123; CANR 34; DLB 26

Hustvedt, Siri 1955-   **CLC 76**
See also CA 137

Hutten, Ulrich von 1488-1523   **LC 16**
See also DLB 179

Huxley, Aldous (Leonard) 1894-1963 **CLC 1,
3, 4, 5, 8, 11, 18, 35, 79; DA; DAB; DAC;
DAM MST, NOV; WLC**
See also AAYA 11; CA 85-88; CANR 44;
CDBLB 1914-1945; DLB 36, 100, 162, 195;
MTCW; SATA 63

Huxley, T(homas) H(enry) 1825-1895 **NCLC
67**
See also DLB 57

Huysmans, Joris-Karl 1848-1907 **TCLC 7, 69**
See also CA 104; 165; DLB 123

Hwang, David Henry 1957-   **CLC 55; DAM
DRAM; DC 4**
See also CA 127; 132; INT 132

Hyde, Anthony 1946-   **CLC 42**
See also CA 136

Hyde, Margaret O(ldroyd) 1917-   **CLC 21**
See also CA 1-4R; CANR 1, 36; CLR 23;
JRDA; MAICYA; SAAS 8; SATA 1, 42, 76

Hynes, James 1956(?)-   **CLC 65**
See also CA 164

Ian, Janis 1951-   **CLC 21**
See also CA 105

Ibanez, Vicente Blasco
See Blasco Ibanez, Vicente

Ibarguengoitia, Jorge 1928-1983   **CLC 37**
See also CA 124; 113; HW

Ibsen, Henrik (Johan) 1828-1906 **TCLC 2, 8,
16, 37, 52; DA; DAB; DAC; DAM DRAM,
MST; DC 2; WLC**
See also CA 104; 141

Ibuse Masuji 1898-1993   **CLC 22**
See also CA 127; 141; DLB 180

Ichikawa, Kon 1915-   **CLC 20**
See also CA 121

Idle, Eric 1943-   **CLC 21**
See also Monty Python
See also CA 116; CANR 35

Ignatow, David 1914-1997 **CLC 4, 7, 14, 40**
See also CA 9-12R; 162; CAAS 3; CANR 31,
57; DLB 5

Ihimaera, Witi 1944-   **CLC 46**
See also CA 77-80

Ilf, Ilya   **TCLC 21**
See also Fainzilberg, Ilya Arnoldovich

Illyes, Gyula 1902-1983   **PC 16**
See also CA 114; 109

Immermann, Karl (Lebrecht) 1796-1840
NCLC 4, 49
See also DLB 133

Inchbald, Elizabeth 1753-1821   **NCLC 62**
See also DLB 39, 89

Inclan, Ramon (Maria) del Valle
See Valle-Inclan, Ramon (Maria) del

Infante, G(uillermo) Cabrera
See Cabrera Infante, G(uillermo)

Ingalls, Rachel (Holmes) 1940-   **CLC 42**
See also CA 123; 127

Ingamells, Rex 1913-1955   **TCLC 35**

Inge, William (Motter) 1913-1973 **CLC 1, 8,
19; DAM DRAM**
See also CA 9-12R; CDALB 1941-1968; DLB
7; MTCW

Jimenez Mantecon, Juan
  See Jimenez (Mantecon), Juan Ramon
Jin, Ha 1956-   **CLC 109**
  See also CA 152
Joel, Billy   **CLC 26**
  See also Joel, William Martin
Joel, William Martin 1949-
  See Joel, Billy
  See also CA 108
John, Saint 7th cent. -   **CMLC 27**
John of the Cross, St. 1542-1591   **LC 18**
Johnson, B(ryan) S(tanley William) 1933-1973
  CLC 6, 9
  See also CA 9-12R; 53-56; CANR 9; DLB 14,
  40
Johnson, Benj. F. of Boo
  See Riley, James Whitcomb
Johnson, Benjamin F. of Boo
  See Riley, James Whitcomb
Johnson, Charles (Richard) 1948- CLC 7, 51,
  65; BLC 2; DAM MULT
  See also BW 2; CA 116; CAAS 18; CANR 42,
  66; DLB 33
Johnson, Denis 1949-   **CLC 52**
  See also CA 117; 121; DLB 120
Johnson, Diane 1934-   **CLC 5, 13, 48**
  See also CA 41-44R; CANR 17, 40, 62; DLBY
  80; INT CANR-17; MTCW
Johnson, Eyvind (Olof Verner) 1900-1976
  CLC 14
  See also CA 73-76; 69-72; CANR 34
Johnson, J. R.
  See James, C(yril) L(ionel) R(obert)
Johnson, James Weldon 1871-1938 TCLC 3,
  19; BLC 2; DAM MULT, POET
  See also BW 1; CA 104; 125; CDALB 1917-
  1929; CLR 32; DLB 51; MTCW; SATA 31
Johnson, Joyce 1935-   **CLC 58**
  See also CA 125; 129
Johnson, Lionel (Pigot) 1867-1902 **TCLC 19**
  See also CA 117; DLB 19
Johnson, Mel
  See Malzberg, Barry N(athaniel)
Johnson, Pamela Hansford 1912-1981 CLC 1,
  7, 27
  See also CA 1-4R; 104; CANR 2, 28; DLB 15;
  MTCW
Johnson, Robert 1911(?)-1938   **TCLC 69**
Johnson, Samuel 1709-1784LC 15; DA; DAB;
  DAC; DAM MST; WLC
  See also CDBLB 1660-1789; DLB 39, 95, 104,
  142
Johnson, Uwe 1934-1984   **CLC 5, 10, 15, 40**
  See also CA 1-4R; 112; CANR 1, 39; DLB 75;
  MTCW
Johnston, George (Benson) 1913-   **CLC 51**
  See also CA 1-4R; CANR 5, 20; DLB 88
Johnston, Jennifer 1930-   **CLC 7**
  See also CA 85-88; DLB 14
Jolley, (Monica) Elizabeth 1923-CLC 46; SSC
  19
  See also CA 127; CAAS 13; CANR 59
Jones, Arthur Llewellyn 1863-1947
  See Machen, Arthur
  See also CA 104
Jones, D(ouglas) G(ordon) 1929-   **CLC 10**
  See also CA 29-32R; CANR 13; DLB 53
Jones, David (Michael) 1895-1974CLC 2, 4, 7,
  13, 42
  See also CA 9-12R; 53-56; CANR 28; CDBLB
  1945-1960; DLB 20, 100; MTCW
Jones, David Robert 1947-
  See Bowie, David

See also CA 103
Jones, Diana Wynne 1934-   **CLC 26**
  See also AAYA 12; CA 49-52; CANR 4, 26,
  56; CLR 23; DLB 161; JRDA; MAICYA;
  SAAS 7; SATA 9, 70
Jones, Edward P. 1950-   **CLC 76**
  See also BW 2; CA 142
Jones, Gayl 1949-   **CLC 6, 9; BLC 2; DAM
  MULT**
  See also BW 2; CA 77-80; CANR 27, 66; DLB
  33; MTCW
Jones, James 1921-1977   **CLC 1, 3, 10, 39**
  See also AITN 1, 2; CA 1-4R; 69-72; CANR 6;
  DLB 2, 143; MTCW
Jones, John J.
  See Lovecraft, H(oward) P(hillips)
Jones, LeRoi   **CLC 1, 2, 3, 5, 10, 14**
  See also Baraka, Amiri
Jones, Louis B.   **CLC 65**
  See also CA 141
Jones, Madison (Percy, Jr.) 1925-   **CLC 4**
  See also CA 13-16R; CAAS 11; CANR 7, 54;
  DLB 152
Jones, Mervyn 1922-   **CLC 10, 52**
  See also CA 45-48; CAAS 5; CANR 1; MTCW
Jones, Mick 1956(?)-   **CLC 30**
Jones, Nettie (Pearl) 1941-   **CLC 34**
  See also BW 2; CA 137; CAAS 20
Jones, Preston 1936-1979   **CLC 10**
  See also CA 73-76; 89-92; DLB 7
Jones, Robert F(rancis) 1934-   **CLC 7**
  See also CA 49-52; CANR 2, 61
Jones, Rod 1953-   **CLC 50**
  See also CA 128
Jones, Terence Graham Parry 1942- CLC 21
  See also Jones, Terry; Monty Python
  See also CA 112; 116; CANR 35; INT 116
Jones, Terry
  See Jones, Terence Graham Parry
  See also SATA 67; SATA-Brief 51
Jones, Thom 1945(?)-   **CLC 81**
  See also CA 157
Jong, Erica 1942-   **CLC 4, 6, 8, 18, 83; DAM
  NOV, POP**
  See also AITN 1; BEST 90:2; CA 73-76; CANR
  26, 52; DLB 2, 5, 28, 152; INT CANR-26;
  MTCW
Jonson, Ben(jamin) 1572(?)-1637   **LC 6, 33;
  DA; DAB; DAC; DAM DRAM, MST,
  POET; DC 4; PC 17; WLC**
  See also CDBLB Before 1660; DLB 62, 121
Jordan, June 1936-   **CLC 5, 11, 23; BLCS;
  DAM MULT, POET**
  See also AAYA 2; BW 2; CA 33-36R; CANR
  25; CLR 10; DLB 38; MAICYA; MTCW;
  SATA 4
Jordan, Neil (Patrick) 1950-   **CLC 110**
  See also CA 124; 130; CANR 54; INT 130
Jordan, Pat(rick M.) 1941-   **CLC 37**
  See also CA 33-36R
Jorgensen, Ivar
  See Ellison, Harlan (Jay)
Jorgenson, Ivar
  See Silverberg, Robert
Josephus, Flavius c. 37-100   **CMLC 13**
Josipovici, Gabriel 1940-   **CLC 6, 43**
  See also CA 37-40R; CAAS 8; CANR 47; DLB
  14
Joubert, Joseph 1754-1824   **NCLC 9**
Jouve, Pierre Jean 1887-1976   **CLC 47**
  See also CA 65-68
Jovine, Francesco 1902-1950   **TCLC 79**
Joyce, James (Augustine Aloysius) 1882-1941

TCLC 3, 8, 16, 35, 52; DA; DAB; DAC;
  **DAM MST, NOV, POET; PC 22; SSC 3,
  26; WLC**
  See also CA 104; 126; CDBLB 1914-1945;
  DLB 10, 19, 36, 162; MTCW
Jozsef, Attila 1905-1937   **TCLC 22**
  See also CA 116
Juana Ines de la Cruz 1651(?)-1695   **LC 5**
Judd, Cyril
  See Kornbluth, C(yril) M.; Pohl, Frederik
Julian of Norwich 1342(?)-1416(?)   **LC 6**
  See also DLB 146
Junger, Sebastian 1962-   **CLC 109**
  See also CA 165
Juniper, Alex
  See Hospital, Janette Turner
Junius
  See Luxemburg, Rosa
Just, Ward (Swift) 1935-   **CLC 4, 27**
  See also CA 25-28R; CANR 32; INT CANR-
  32
Justice, Donald (Rodney) 1925-   **CLC 6, 19,
  102; DAM POET**
  See also CA 5-8R; CANR 26, 54; DLBY 83;
  INT CANR-26
Juvenal c. 55-c. 127   **CMLC 8**
Juvenis
  See Bourne, Randolph S(illiman)
Kacew, Romain 1914-1980
  See Gary, Romain
  See also CA 108; 102
Kadare, Ismail 1936-   **CLC 52**
  See also CA 161
Kadohata, Cynthia   **CLC 59**
  See also CA 140
Kafka, Franz 1883-1924TCLC 2, 6, 13, 29, 47,
  **53; DA; DAB; DAC; DAM MST, NOV;
  SSC 5, 29; WLC**
  See also CA 105; 126; DLB 81; MTCW
Kahanovitsch, Pinkhes
  See Der Nister
Kahn, Roger 1927-   **CLC 30**
  See also CA 25-28R; CANR 44; DLB 171;
  SATA 37
Kain, Saul
  See Sassoon, Siegfried (Lorraine)
Kaiser, Georg 1878-1945   **TCLC 9**
  See also CA 106; DLB 124
Kaletski, Alexander 1946-   **CLC 39**
  See also CA 118; 143
Kalidasa fl. c. 400-   **CMLC 9; PC 22**
Kallman, Chester (Simon) 1921-1975 **CLC 2**
  See also CA 45-48; 53-56; CANR 3
Kaminsky, Melvin 1926-
  See Brooks, Mel
  See also CA 65-68; CANR 16
Kaminsky, Stuart M(elvin) 1934-   **CLC 59**
  See also CA 73-76; CANR 29, 53
Kane, Francis
  See Robbins, Harold
Kane, Paul
  See Simon, Paul (Frederick)
Kane, Wilson
  See Bloch, Robert (Albert)
Kanin, Garson 1912-   **CLC 22**
  See also AITN 1; CA 5-8R; CANR 7; DLB 7
Kaniuk, Yoram 1930-   **CLC 19**
  See also CA 134
Kant, Immanuel 1724-1804   **NCLC 27, 67**
  See also DLB 94
Kantor, MacKinlay 1904-1977   **CLC 7**
  See also CA 61-64; 73-76; CANR 60, 63; DLB
  9, 102

Kaplan, David Michael 1946- **CLC 50**

Kaplan, James 1951- **CLC 59**
See also CA 135

Karageorge, Michael
See Anderson, Poul (William)

Karamzin, Nikolai Mikhailovich 1766-1826
NCLC 3
See also DLB 150

Karapanou, Margarita 1946- **CLC 13**
See also CA 101

Karinthy, Frigyes 1887-1938 **TCLC 47**

Karl, Frederick R(obert) 1927- **CLC 34**
See also CA 5-8R; CANR 3, 44

Kastel, Warren
See Silverberg, Robert

Kataev, Evgeny Petrovich 1903-1942
See Petrov, Evgeny
See also CA 120

Kataphusin
See Ruskin, John

Katz, Steve 1935- **CLC 47**
See also CA 25-28R; CAAS 14, 64; CANR 12;
DLBY 83

Kauffman, Janet 1945- **CLC 42**
See also CA 117; CANR 43; DLBY 86

Kaufman, Bob (Garnell) 1925-1986 **CLC 49**
See also BW 1; CA 41-44R; 118; CANR 22;
DLB 16, 41

Kaufman, George S. 1889-1961 **CLC 38; DAM DRAM**
See also CA 108; 93-96; DLB 7; INT 108

Kaufman, Sue **CLC 3, 8**
See also Barondess, Sue K(aufman)

Kavafis, Konstantinos Petrou 1863-1933
See Cavafy, C(onstantine) P(eter)
See also CA 104

Kavan, Anna 1901-1968 **CLC 5, 13, 82**
See also CA 5-8R; CANR 6, 57; MTCW

Kavanagh, Dan
See Barnes, Julian (Patrick)

Kavanagh, Patrick (Joseph) 1904-1967 **CLC 22**
See also CA 123; 25-28R; DLB 15, 20; MTCW

Kawabata, Yasunari 1899-1972 **CLC 2, 5, 9, 18, 107; DAM MULT; SSC 17**
See also CA 93-96; 33-36R; DLB 180

Kaye, M(ary) M(argaret) 1909- **CLC 28**
See also CA 89-92; CANR 24, 60; MTCW;
SATA 62

Kaye, Mollie
See Kaye, M(ary) M(argaret)

Kaye-Smith, Sheila 1887-1956 **TCLC 20**
See also CA 118; DLB 36

Kaymor, Patrice Maguilene
See Senghor, Leopold Sedar

Kazan, Elia 1909- **CLC 6, 16, 63**
See also CA 21-24R; CANR 32

Kazantzakis, Nikos 1883(?)-1957 **TCLC 2, 5, 33**
See also CA 105; 132; MTCW

Kazin, Alfred 1915- **CLC 34, 38**
See also CA 1-4R; CAAS 7; CANR 1, 45; DLB 67

Keane, Mary Nesta (Skrine) 1904-1996
See Keane, Molly
See also CA 108; 114; 151

Keane, Molly **CLC 31**
See also Keane, Mary Nesta (Skrine)
See also INT 114

Keates, Jonathan 1946(?)- **CLC 34**
See also CA 163

Keaton, Buster 1895-1966 **CLC 20**

Keats, John 1795-1821 **NCLC 8; DA; DAB;**
DAC; DAM MST, POET; PC 1; WLC
See also CDBLB 1789-1832; DLB 96, 110

Keene, Donald 1922- **CLC 34**
See also CA 1-4R; CANR 5

Keillor, Garrison **CLC 40**
See also Keillor, Gary (Edward)
See also AAYA 2; BEST 89:3; DLBY 87;
SATA 58

Keillor, Gary (Edward) 1942-
See Keillor, Garrison
See also CA 111; 117; CANR 36, 59; DAM
POP; MTCW

Keith, Michael
See Hubbard, L(afayette) Ron(ald)

Keller, Gottfried 1819-1890 **NCLC 2; SSC 26**
See also DLB 129

Keller, Nora Okja **CLC 109**

Kellerman, Jonathan 1949- **CLC 44; DAM POP**
See also BEST 90:1; CA 106; CANR 29, 51;
INT CANR-29

Kelley, William Melvin 1937- **CLC 22**
See also BW 1; CA 77-80; CANR 27; DLB 33

Kellogg, Marjorie 1922- **CLC 2**
See also CA 81-84

Kellow, Kathleen
See Hibbert, Eleanor Alice Burford

Kelly, M(ilton) T(erry) 1947- **CLC 55**
See also CA 97-100; CAAS 22; CANR 19, 43

Kelman, James 1946- **CLC 58, 86**
See also CA 148; DLB 194

Kemal, Yashar 1923- **CLC 14, 29**
See also CA 89-92; CANR 44

Kemble, Fanny 1809-1893 **NCLC 18**
See also DLB 32

Kemelman, Harry 1908-1996 **CLC 2**
See also AITN 1; CA 9-12R; 155; CANR 6;
DLB 28

Kempe, Margery 1373(?)-1440(?) **LC 6**
See also DLB 146

Kempis, Thomas a 1380-1471 **LC 11**

Kendall, Henry 1839-1882 **NCLC 12**

Keneally, Thomas (Michael) 1935- **CLC 5, 8, 10, 14, 19, 27, 43; DAM NOV**
See also CA 85-88; CANR 10, 50; MTCW

Kennedy, Adrienne (Lita) 1931- **CLC 66; BLC 2; DAM MULT; DC 5**
See also BW 2; CA 103; CAAS 20; CABS 3;
CANR 26, 53; DLB 38

Kennedy, John Pendleton 1795-1870 **NCLC 2**
See also DLB 3

Kennedy, Joseph Charles 1929-
See Kennedy, X. J.
See also CA 1-4R; CANR 4, 30, 40; SATA 14, 86

Kennedy, William 1928- **CLC 6, 28, 34, 53;**
DAM NOV
See also AAYA 1; CA 85-88; CANR 14, 31;
DLB 143; DLBY 85; INT CANR-31;
MTCW; SATA 57

Kennedy, X. J. **CLC 8, 42**
See also Kennedy, Joseph Charles
See also CAAS 9; CLR 27; DLB 5; SAAS 22

Kenny, Maurice (Francis) 1929- **CLC 87;**
DAM MULT
See also CA 144; CAAS 22; DLB 175; NNAL

Kent, Kelvin
See Kuttner, Henry

Kenton, Maxwell
See Southern, Terry

Kenyon, Robert O.
See Kuttner, Henry

Kerouac, Jack **CLC 1, 2, 3, 5, 14, 29, 61**
See also Kerouac, Jean-Louis Lebris de
See also AAYA 25; CDALB 1941-1968; DLB
2, 16; DLBD 3; DLBY 95

Kerouac, Jean-Louis Lebris de 1922-1969
See Kerouac, Jack
See also AITN 1; CA 5-8R; 25-28R; CANR 26,
54; DA; DAB; DAC; DAM MST, NOV,
POET, POP; MTCW; WLC

Kerr, Jean 1923- **CLC 22**
See also CA 5-8R; CANR 7; INT CANR-7

Kerr, M. E. **CLC 12, 35**
See also Meaker, Marijane (Agnes)
See also AAYA 2, 23; CLR 29; SAAS 1

Kerr, Robert **CLC 55**

Kerrigan, (Thomas) Anthony 1918- **CLC 4, 6**
See also CA 49-52; CAAS 11; CANR 4

Kerry, Lois
See Duncan, Lois

Kesey, Ken (Elton) 1935- **CLC 1, 3, 6, 11, 46, 64; DA; DAB; DAC; DAM MST, NOV, POP; WLC**
See also AAYA 25; CA 1-4R; CANR 22, 38,
66; CDALB 1968-1988; DLB 2, 16; MTCW;
SATA 66

Kesselring, Joseph (Otto) 1902-1967 **CLC 45;**
DAM DRAM, MST
See also CA 150

Kessler, Jascha (Frederick) 1929- **CLC 4**
See also CA 17-20R; CANR 8, 48

Kettelkamp, Larry (Dale) 1933- **CLC 12**
See also CA 29-32R; CANR 16; SAAS 3;
SATA 2

Key, Ellen 1849-1926 **TCLC 65**

Keyber, Conny
See Fielding, Henry

Keyes, Daniel 1927- **CLC 80; DA; DAC; DAM**
MST, NOV
See also AAYA 23; CA 17-20R; CANR 10, 26,
54; SATA 37

Keynes, John Maynard 1883-1946 **TCLC 64**
See also CA 114; 162, 163; DLBD 10

Khanshendel, Chiron
See Rose, Wendy

Khayyam, Omar 1048-1131 **CMLC 11; DAM**
POET; PC 8

Kherdian, David 1931- **CLC 6, 9**
See also CA 21-24R; CAAS 2; CANR 39; CLR
24; JRDA; MAICYA; SATA 16, 74

Khlebnikov, Velimir **TCLC 20**
See also Khlebnikov, Viktor Vladimirovich

Khlebnikov, Viktor Vladimirovich 1885-1922
See Khlebnikov, Velimir
See also CA 117

Khodasevich, Vladislav (Felitsianovich) 1886-
1939 **TCLC 15**
See also CA 115

Kielland, Alexander Lange 1849-1906 **TCLC 5**
See also CA 104

Kiely, Benedict 1919- **CLC 23, 43**
See also CA 1-4R; CANR 2; DLB 15

Kienzle, William X(avier) 1928- **CLC 25;**
DAM POP
See also CA 93-96; CAAS 1; CANR 9, 31, 59;
INT CANR-31; MTCW

Kierkegaard, Soren 1813-1855 **NCLC 34**

Killens, John Oliver 1916-1987 **CLC 10**
See also BW 2; CA 77-80; 123; CAAS 2;
CANR 26; DLB 33

Killigrew, Anne 1660-1685 **LC 4**
See also DLB 131

Kim
See Simenon, Georges (Jacques Christian)

Kincaid, Jamaica 1949- **CLC 43, 68; BLC 2; DAM MULT, NOV**
See also AAYA 13; BW 2; CA 125; CANR 47, 59; DLB 157
King, Francis (Henry) 1923-**CLC 8, 53; DAM NOV**
See also CA 1-4R; CANR 1, 33; DLB 15, 139; MTCW
King, Kennedy
See Brown, George Douglas
King, Martin Luther, Jr. 1929-1968 **CLC 83; BLC 2; DA; DAB; DAC; DAM MST, MULT; WLCS**
See also BW 2; CA 25-28; CANR 27, 44; CAP 2; MTCW; SATA 14
King, Stephen (Edwin) 1947- **CLC 12, 26, 37, 61; DAM NOV, POP; SSC 17**
See also AAYA 1, 17; BEST 90:1; CA 61-64; CANR 1, 30, 52; DLB 143; DLBY 80; JRDA; MTCW; SATA 9, 55
King, Steve
See King, Stephen (Edwin)
King, Thomas 1943- **CLC 89; DAC; DAM MULT**
See also CA 144; DLB 175; NNAL; SATA 96
Kingman, Lee **CLC 17**
See also Natti, (Mary) Lee
See also SAAS 3; SATA 1, 67
Kingsley, Charles 1819-1875 **NCLC 35**
See also DLB 21, 32, 163, 190; YABC 2
Kingsley, Sidney 1906-1995 **CLC 44**
See also CA 85-88; 147; DLB 7
Kingsolver, Barbara 1955-**CLC 55, 81; DAM POP**
See also AAYA 15; CA 129; 134; CANR 60; INT 134
Kingston, Maxine (Ting Ting) Hong 1940- **CLC 12, 19, 58; DAM MULT, NOV; WLCS**
See also AAYA 8; CA 69-72; CANR 13, 38; DLB 173; DLBY 80; INT CANR-13; MTCW; SATA 53
Kinnell, Galway 1927- **CLC 1, 2, 3, 5, 13, 29**
See also CA 9-12R; CANR 10, 34, 66; DLB 5; DLBY 87; INT CANR-34; MTCW
Kinsella, Thomas 1928- **CLC 4, 19**
See also CA 17-20R; CANR 15; DLB 27; MTCW
Kinsella, W(illiam) P(atrick) 1935- **CLC 27, 43; DAC; DAM NOV, POP**
See also AAYA 7; CA 97-100; CAAS 7; CANR 21, 35, 66; INT CANR-21; MTCW
Kipling, (Joseph) Rudyard 1865-1936 **TCLC 8, 17; DA; DAB; DAC; DAM MST, POET; PC 3; SSC 5; WLC**
See also CA 105; 120; CANR 33; CDBLB 1890-1914; CLR 39; DLB 19, 34, 141, 156; MAICYA; MTCW; YABC 2
Kirkup, James 1918- **CLC 1**
See also CA 1-4R; CAAS 4; CANR 2; DLB 27; SATA 12
Kirkwood, James 1930(?)-1989 **CLC 9**
See also AITN 2; CA 1-4R; 128; CANR 6, 40
Kirshner, Sidney
See Kingsley, Sidney
Kis, Danilo 1935-1989 **CLC 57**
See also CA 109; 118; 129; CANR 61; DLB 181; MTCW
Kivi, Aleksis 1834-1872 **NCLC 30**
Kizer, Carolyn (Ashley) 1925-**CLC 15, 39, 80; DAM POET**
See also CA 65-68; CAAS 5; CANR 24; DLB 5, 169

Klabund 1890-1928 **TCLC 44**
See also CA 162; DLB 66
Klappert, Peter 1942- **CLC 57**
See also CA 33-36R; DLB 5
Klein, A(braham) M(oses) 1909-1972**CLC 19; DAB; DAC; DAM MST**
See also CA 101; 37-40R; DLB 68
Klein, Norma 1938-1989 **CLC 30**
See also AAYA 2; CA 41-44R; 128; CANR 15, 37; CLR 2, 19; INT CANR-15; JRDA; MAICYA; SAAS 1; SATA 7, 57
Klein, T(heodore) E(ibon) D(onald) 1947- **CLC 34**
See also CA 119; CANR 44
Kleist, Heinrich von 1777-1811 **NCLC 2, 37; DAM DRAM; SSC 22**
See also DLB 90
Klima, Ivan 1931- **CLC 56; DAM NOV**
See also CA 25-28R; CANR 17, 50
Klimentov, Andrei Platonovich 1899-1951
See Platonov, Andrei
See also CA 108
Klinger, Friedrich Maximilian von 1752-1831 **NCLC 1**
See also DLB 94
Klingsor the Magician
See Hartmann, Sadakichi
Klopstock, Friedrich Gottlieb 1724-1803 **NCLC 11**
See also DLB 97
Knapp, Caroline 1959- **CLC 99**
See also CA 154
Knebel, Fletcher 1911-1993 **CLC 14**
See also AITN 1; CA 1-4R; 140; CAAS 3; CANR 1, 36; SATA 36; SATA-Obit 75
Knickerbocker, Diedrich
See Irving, Washington
Knight, Etheridge 1931-1991**CLC 40; BLC 2; DAM POET; PC 14**
See also BW 1; CA 21-24R; 133; CANR 23; DLB 41
Knight, Sarah Kemble 1666-1727 **LC 7**
See also DLB 24
Knister, Raymond 1899-1932 **TCLC 56**
See also DLB 68
Knowles, John 1926- **CLC 1, 4, 10, 26; DA; DAC; DAM MST, NOV**
See also AAYA 10; CA 17-20R; CANR 40; CDALB 1968-1988; DLB 6; MTCW; SATA 8, 89
Knox, Calvin M.
See Silverberg, Robert
Knox, John c. 1505-1572 **LC 37**
See also DLB 132
Knye, Cassandra
See Disch, Thomas M(ichael)
Koch, C(hristopher) J(ohn) 1932- **CLC 42**
See also CA 127
Koch, Christopher
See Koch, C(hristopher) J(ohn)
Koch, Kenneth 1925- **CLC 5, 8, 44; DAM POET**
See also CA 1-4R; CANR 6, 36, 57; DLB 5; INT CANR-36; SATA 65
Kochanowski, Jan 1530-1584 **LC 10**
Kock, Charles Paul de 1794-1871 **NCLC 16**
Koda Shigeyuki 1867-1947
See Rohan, Koda
See also CA 121
Koestler, Arthur 1905-1983**CLC 1, 3, 6, 8, 15, 33**
See also CA 1-4R; 109; CANR 1, 33; CDBLB 1945-1960; DLBY 83; MTCW

Kogawa, Joy Nozomi 1935- **CLC 78; DAC; DAM MST, MULT**
See also CA 101; CANR 19, 62
Kohout, Pavel 1928- **CLC 13**
See also CA 45-48; CANR 3
Koizumi, Yakumo
See Hearn, (Patricio) Lafcadio (Tessima Carlos)
Kolmar, Gertrud 1894-1943 **TCLC 40**
Komunyakaa, Yusef 1947-**CLC 86, 94; BLCS**
See also CA 147; DLB 120
Konrad, George
See Konrad, Gyoergy
Konrad, Gyoergy 1933- **CLC 4, 10, 73**
See also CA 85-88
Konwicki, Tadeusz 1926- **CLC 8, 28, 54**
See also CA 101; CAAS 9; CANR 39, 59; MTCW
Koontz, Dean R(ay) 1945- **CLC 78; DAM NOV, POP**
See also AAYA 9; BEST 89:3, 90:2; CA 108; CANR 19, 36, 52; MTCW; SATA 92
Kopit, Arthur (Lee) 1937-**CLC 1, 18, 33; DAM DRAM**
See also AITN 1; CA 81-84; CABS 3; DLB 7; MTCW
Kops, Bernard 1926- **CLC 4**
See also CA 5-8R; DLB 13
Kornbluth, C(yril) M. 1923-1958 **TCLC 8**
See also CA 105; 160; DLB 8
Korolenko, V. G.
See Korolenko, Vladimir Galaktionovich
Korolenko, Vladimir
See Korolenko, Vladimir Galaktionovich
Korolenko, Vladimir G.
See Korolenko, Vladimir Galaktionovich
Korolenko, Vladimir Galaktionovich 1853-1921 **TCLC 22**
See also CA 121
Korzybski, Alfred (Habdank Skarbek) 1879-1950 **TCLC 61**
See also CA 123; 160
Kosinski, Jerzy (Nikodem) 1933-1991 **CLC 1, 2, 3, 6, 10, 15, 53, 70; DAM NOV**
See also CA 17-20R; 134; CANR 9, 46; DLB 2; DLBY 82; MTCW
Kostelanetz, Richard (Cory) 1940- **CLC 28**
See also CA 13-16R; CAAS 8; CANR 38
Kostrowitzki, Wilhelm Apollinaris de 1880-1918
See Apollinaire, Guillaume
See also CA 104
Kotlowitz, Robert 1924- **CLC 4**
See also CA 33-36R; CANR 36
Kotzebue, August (Friedrich Ferdinand) von 1761-1819 **NCLC 25**
See also DLB 94
Kotzwinkle, William 1938- **CLC 5, 14, 35**
See also CA 45-48; CANR 3, 44; CLR 6; DLB 173; MAICYA; SATA 24, 70
Kowna, Stancy
See Szymborska, Wislawa
Kozol, Jonathan 1936- **CLC 17**
See also CA 61-64; CANR 16, 45
Kozoll, Michael 1940(?)- **CLC 35**
Kramer, Kathryn 19(?)- **CLC 34**
Kramer, Larry 1935-**CLC 42; DAM POP; DC 8**
See also CA 124; 126; CANR 60
Krasicki, Ignacy 1735-1801 **NCLC 8**
Krasinski, Zygmunt 1812-1859 **NCLC 4**
Kraus, Karl 1874-1936 **TCLC 5**
See also CA 104; DLB 118
Kreve (Mickevicius), Vincas 1882-1954**TCLC**

27

Kristeva, Julia 1941-   **CLC 77**
See also CA 154
Kristofferson, Kris 1936-   **CLC 26**
See also CA 104
Krizanc, John 1956-   **CLC 57**
Krleza, Miroslav 1893-1981   **CLC 8**
See also CA 97-100; 105; CANR 50; DLB 147
Kroetsch, Robert 1927- **CLC 5, 23, 57; DAC;**
DAM POET
See also CA 17-20R; CANR 8, 38; DLB 53;
MTCW
Kroetz, Franz
See Kroetz, Franz Xaver
Kroetz, Franz Xaver 1946-   **CLC 41**
See also CA 130
Kroker, Arthur (W.) 1945-   **CLC 77**
See also CA 161
Kropotkin, Peter (Aleksieevich) 1842-1921
TCLC 36
See also CA 119
Krotkov, Yuri 1917-   **CLC 19**
See also CA 102
Krumb
See Crumb, R(obert)
Krumgold, Joseph (Quincy) 1908-1980 **CLC**
12
See also CA 9-12R; 101; CANR 7; MAICYA;
SATA 1, 48; SATA-Obit 23
Krumwitz
See Crumb, R(obert)
Krutch, Joseph Wood 1893-1970   **CLC 24**
See also CA 1-4R; 25-28R; CANR 4; DLB 63
Krutzch, Gus
See Eliot, T(homas) S(tearns)
Krylov, Ivan Andreevich 1768(?)-1844 **NCLC**
1
See also DLB 150
Kubin, Alfred (Leopold Isidor) 1877-1959
TCLC 23
See also CA 112; 149; DLB 81
Kubrick, Stanley 1928-   **CLC 16**
See also CA 81-84; CANR 33; DLB 26
Kumin, Maxine (Winokur) 1925- **CLC 5, 13,**
28; DAM POET; PC 15
See also AITN 2; CA 1-4R; CAAS 8; CANR 1,
21; DLB 5; MTCW; SATA 12
Kundera, Milan 1929- **CLC 4, 9, 19, 32, 68;**
DAM NOV; SSC 24
See also AAYA 2; CA 85-88; CANR 19, 52;
MTCW
Kunene, Mazisi (Raymond) 1930-   **CLC 85**
See also BW 1; CA 125; DLB 117
Kunitz, Stanley (Jasspon) 1905-**CLC 6, 11, 14;**
PC 19
See also CA 41-44R; CANR 26, 57; DLB 48;
INT CANR-26; MTCW
Kunze, Reiner 1933-   **CLC 10**
See also CA 93-96; DLB 75
Kuprin, Aleksandr Ivanovich 1870-1938
TCLC 5
See also CA 104
Kureishi, Hanif 1954(?)-   **CLC 64**
See also CA 139; DLB 194
Kurosawa, Akira 1910-**CLC 16; DAM MULT**
See also AAYA 11; CA 101; CANR 46
Kushner, Tony 1957(?)-**CLC 81; DAM DRAM**
See also CA 144
Kuttner, Henry 1915-1958   **TCLC 10**
See also Vance, Jack
See also CA 107; 157; DLB 8
Kuzma, Greg 1944-   **CLC 7**
See also CA 33-36R

Kuzmin, Mikhail 1872(?)-1936   **TCLC 40**
Kyd, Thomas 1558-1594**LC 22; DAM DRAM;**
DC 3
See also DLB 62
Kyprianos, Iossif
See Samarakis, Antonis
La Bruyere, Jean de 1645-1696   **LC 17**
Lacan, Jacques (Marie Emile) 1901-1981
CLC 75
See also CA 121; 104
Laclos, Pierre Ambroise Francois Choderlos de
1741-1803   **NCLC 4**
La Colere, Francois
See Aragon, Louis
Lacolere, Francois
See Aragon, Louis
La Deshabilleuse
See Simenon, Georges (Jacques Christian)
Lady Gregory
See Gregory, Isabella Augusta (Persse)
Lady of Quality, A
See Bagnold, Enid
La Fayette, Marie (Madelaine Pioche de la
Vergne Comtes 1634-1693   **LC 2**
Lafayette, Rene
See Hubbard, L(afayette) Ron(ald)
Laforgue, Jules 1860-1887**NCLC 5, 53; PC 14;**
SSC 20
Lagerkvist, Paer (Fabian) 1891-1974 **CLC 7,**
10, 13, 54; DAM DRAM, NOV
See also Lagerkvist, Par
See also CA 85-88; 49-52; MTCW
Lagerkvist, Par   **SSC 12**
See also Lagerkvist, Paer (Fabian)
Lagerloef, Selma (Ottiliana Lovisa) 1858-1940
TCLC 4, 36
See also Lagerlof, Selma (Ottiliana Lovisa)
See also CA 108; SATA 15
Lagerlof, Selma (Ottiliana Lovisa)
See Lagerloef, Selma (Ottiliana Lovisa)
See also CLR 7; SATA 15
La Guma, (Justin) Alex(ander) 1925-1985
CLC 19; BLCS; DAM NOV
See also BW 1; CA 49-52; 118; CANR 25; DLB
117; MTCW
Laidlaw, A. K.
See Grieve, C(hristopher) M(urray)
Lainez, Manuel Mujica
See Mujica Lainez, Manuel
See also HW
Laing, R(onald) D(avid) 1927-1989   **CLC 95**
See also CA 107; 129; CANR 34; MTCW
Lamartine, Alphonse (Marie Louis Prat) de
1790-1869**NCLC 11; DAM POET; PC 16**
Lamb, Charles 1775-1834   **NCLC 10; DA;**
DAB; DAC; DAM MST; WLC
See also CDBLB 1789-1832; DLB 93, 107,
163; SATA 17
Lamb, Lady Caroline 1785-1828   **NCLC 38**
See also DLB 116
Lamming, George (William) 1927- **CLC 2, 4,**
66; BLC 2; DAM MULT
See also BW 2; CA 85-88; CANR 26; DLB 125;
MTCW
L'Amour, Louis (Dearborn) 1908-1988 **CLC**
25, 55; DAM NOV, POP
See also AAYA 16; AITN 2; BEST 89:2; CA
1-4R; 125; CANR 3, 25, 40; DLBY 80;
MTCW
Lampedusa, Giuseppe (Tomasi) di 1896-1957
TCLC 13
See also Tomasi di Lampedusa, Giuseppe
See also CA 164; DLB 177

Lampman, Archibald 1861-1899   **NCLC 25**
See also DLB 92
Lancaster, Bruce 1896-1963   **CLC 36**
See also CA 9-10; CAP 1; SATA 9
Lanchester, John   **CLC 99**
Landau, Mark Alexandrovich
See Aldanov, Mark (Alexandrovich)
Landau-Aldanov, Mark Alexandrovich
See Aldanov, Mark (Alexandrovich)
Landis, Jerry
See Simon, Paul (Frederick)
Landis, John 1950-   **CLC 26**
See also CA 112; 122
Landolfi, Tommaso 1908-1979   **CLC 11, 49**
See also CA 127; 117; DLB 177
Landon, Letitia Elizabeth 1802-1838 **NCLC**
15
See also DLB 96
Landor, Walter Savage 1775-1864 **NCLC 14**
See also DLB 93, 107
Landwirth, Heinz 1927-
See Lind, Jakov
See also CA 9-12R; CANR 7
Lane, Patrick 1939- **CLC 25; DAM POET**
See also CA 97-100; CANR 54; DLB 53; INT
97-100
Lang, Andrew 1844-1912   **TCLC 16**
See also CA 114; 137; DLB 98, 141, 184;
MAICYA; SATA 16
Lang, Fritz 1890-1976   **CLC 20, 103**
See also CA 77-80; 69-72; CANR 30
Lange, John
See Crichton, (John) Michael
Langer, Elinor 1939-   **CLC 34**
See also CA 121
Langland, William 1330(?)-1400(?)   **LC 19;**
DA; DAB; DAC; DAM MST, POET
See also DLB 146
Langstaff, Launcelot
See Irving, Washington
Lanier, Sidney 1842-1881   **NCLC 6; DAM**
POET
See also DLB 64; DLBD 13; MAICYA; SATA
18
Lanyer, Aemilia 1569-1645   **LC 10, 30**
See also DLB 121
Lao Tzu   **CMLC 7**
Lapine, James (Elliot) 1949-   **CLC 39**
See also CA 123; 130; CANR 54; INT 130
Larbaud, Valery (Nicolas) 1881-1957**TCLC 9**
See also CA 106; 152
Lardner, Ring
See Lardner, Ring(gold) W(ilmer)
Lardner, Ring W., Jr.
See Lardner, Ring(gold) W(ilmer)
Lardner, Ring(gold) W(ilmer) 1885-1933
TCLC 2, 14
See also CA 104; 131; CDALB 1917-1929;
DLB 11, 25, 86; DLBD 16; MTCW
Laredo, Betty
See Codrescu, Andrei
Larkin, Maia
See Wojciechowska, Maia (Teresa)
Larkin, Philip (Arthur) 1922-1985**CLC 3, 5, 8,**
9, 13, 18, 33, 39, 64; DAB; DAM MST,
POET; PC 21
See also CA 5-8R; 117; CANR 24, 62; CDBLB
1960 to Present; DLB 27; MTCW
Larra (y Sanchez de Castro), Mariano Jose de
1809-1837   **NCLC 17**
Larsen, Eric 1941-   **CLC 55**
See also CA 132
Larsen, Nella 1891-1964   **CLC 37; BLC 2;**

DAM MULT
See also BW 1; CA 125; DLB 51

Larson, Charles R(aymond) 1938-   **CLC 31**
See also CA 53-56; CANR 4

Larson, Jonathan 1961-1996   **CLC 99**
See also CA 156

Las Casas, Bartolome de 1474-1566   **LC 31**

Lasch, Christopher 1932-1994   **CLC 102**
See also CA 73-76; 144; CANR 25; MTCW

Lasker-Schueler, Else 1869-1945   **TCLC 57**
See also DLB 66, 124

Laski, Harold 1893-1950   **TCLC 79**

Latham, Jean Lee 1902-1995   **CLC 12**
See also AITN 1; CA 5-8R; CANR 7; CLR 50;
MAICYA; SATA 2, 68

Latham, Mavis
See Clark, Mavis Thorpe

Lathen, Emma   **CLC 2**
See also Hennissart, Martha; Latsis, Mary J(ane)

Lathrop, Francis
See Leiber, Fritz (Reuter, Jr.)

Latsis, Mary J(ane) 1927(?)-1997
See Lathen, Emma
See also CA 85-88; 162

Lattimore, Richmond (Alexander) 1906-1984
CLC 3
See also CA 1-4R; 112; CANR 1

Laughlin, James 1914-1997   **CLC 49**
See also CA 21-24R; 162; CAAS 22; CANR 9,
47; DLB 48; DLBY 96, 97

Laurence, (Jean) Margaret (Wemyss) 1926-
1987   **CLC 3, 6, 13, 50, 62; DAC; DAM
MST; SSC 7**
See also CA 5-8R; 121; CANR 33; DLB 53;
MTCW; SATA-Obit 50

Laurent, Antoine 1952-   **CLC 50**

Lauscher, Hermann
See Hesse, Hermann

Lautreamont, Comte de 1846-1870 NCLC 12;
SSC 14

Laverty, Donald
See Blish, James (Benjamin)

Lavin, Mary 1912-1996 CLC 4, 18, 99; SSC 4
See also CA 9-12R; 151; CANR 33; DLB 15;
MTCW

Lavond, Paul Dennis
See Kornbluth, C(yril) M.; Pohl, Frederik

Lawler, Raymond Evenor 1922-   **CLC 58**
See also CA 103

Lawrence, D(avid) H(erbert Richards) 1885-
1930 TCLC 2, 9, 16, 33, 48, 61; DA; DAB;
DAC; DAM MST, NOV, POET; SSC 4, 19;
WLC
See also CA 104; 121; CDBLB 1914-1945;
DLB 10, 19, 36, 98, 162, 195; MTCW

Lawrence, T(homas) E(dward) 1888-1935
TCLC 18
See also Dale, Colin
See also CA 115; DLB 195

Lawrence of Arabia
See Lawrence, T(homas) E(dward)

Lawson, Henry (Archibald Hertzberg) 1867-
1922   **TCLC 27; SSC 18**
See also CA 120

Lawton, Dennis
See Faust, Frederick (Schiller)

Laxness, Halldor   **CLC 25**
See also Gudjonsson, Halldor Kiljan

Layamon fl. c. 1200-   **CMLC 10**
See also DLB 146

Laye, Camara 1928-1980 CLC 4, 38; BLC 2;
DAM MULT
See also BW 1; CA 85-88; 97-100; CANR 25;

MTCW

Layton, Irving (Peter) 1912- CLC 2, 15; DAC;
DAM MST, POET
See also CA 1-4R; CANR 2, 33, 43, 66; DLB
88; MTCW

Lazarus, Emma 1849-1887   **NCLC 8**

Lazarus, Felix
See Cable, George Washington

Lazarus, Henry
See Slavitt, David R(ytman)

Lea, Joan
See Neufeld, John (Arthur)

Leacock, Stephen (Butler) 1869-1944 TCLC 2;
DAC; DAM MST
See also CA 104; 141; DLB 92

Lear, Edward 1812-1888   **NCLC 3**
See also CLR 1; DLB 32, 163, 166; MAICYA;
SATA 18

Lear, Norman (Milton) 1922-   **CLC 12**
See also CA 73-76

Leavis, F(rank) R(aymond) 1895-1978   **CLC
24**
See also CA 21-24R; 77-80; CANR 44; MTCW

Leavitt, David 1961-   **CLC 34; DAM POP**
See also CA 116; 122; CANR 50, 62; DLB 130;
INT 122

Leblanc, Maurice (Marie Emile) 1864-1941
TCLC 49
See also CA 110

Lebowitz, Fran(ces Ann) 1951(?)- CLC 11, 36
See also CA 81-84; CANR 14, 60; INT CANR-
14; MTCW

Lebrecht, Peter
See Tieck, (Johann) Ludwig

le Carre, John   **CLC 3, 5, 9, 15, 28**
See also Cornwell, David (John Moore)
See also BEST 89:4; CDBLB 1960 to Present;
DLB 87

Le Clezio, J(ean) M(arie) G(ustave) 1940-
CLC 31
See also CA 116; 128; DLB 83

Leconte de Lisle, Charles-Marie-Rene 1818-
1894   **NCLC 29**

Le Coq, Monsieur
See Simenon, Georges (Jacques Christian)

Leduc, Violette 1907-1972   **CLC 22**
See also CA 13-14; 33-36R; CAP 1

Ledwidge, Francis 1887(?)-1917   **TCLC 23**
See also CA 123; DLB 20

Lee, Andrea 1953-   **CLC 36; BLC 2; DAM
MULT**
See also BW 1; CA 125

Lee, Andrew
See Auchincloss, Louis (Stanton)

Lee, Chang-rae 1965-   **CLC 91**
See also CA 148

Lee, Don L.   **CLC 2**
See also Madhubuti, Haki R.

Lee, George W(ashington) 1894-1976 CLC 52;
BLC 2; DAM MULT
See also BW 1; CA 125; DLB 51

Lee, (Nelle) Harper 1926-   **CLC 12, 60; DA;
DAB; DAC; DAM MST, NOV; WLC**
See also AAYA 13; CA 13-16R; CANR 51;
CDALB 1941-1968; DLB 6; MTCW; SATA
11

Lee, Helen Elaine 1959(?)-   **CLC 86**
See also CA 148

Lee, Julian
See Latham, Jean Lee

Lee, Larry
See Lee, Lawrence

Lee, Laurie 1914-1997 CLC 90; DAB; DAM
POP
See also CA 77-80; 158; CANR 33; DLB 27;
MTCW

Lee, Lawrence 1941-1990   **CLC 34**
See also CA 131; CANR 43

Lee, Manfred B(ennington) 1905-1971   **CLC
11**
See also Queen, Ellery
See also CA 1-4R; 29-32R; CANR 2; DLB 137

Lee, Shelton Jackson 1957(?)-   **CLC 105;
BLCS; DAM MULT**
See also Lee, Spike
See also BW 2; CA 125; CANR 42

Lee, Spike
See Lee, Shelton Jackson
See also AAYA 4

Lee, Stan 1922-   **CLC 17**
See also AAYA 5; CA 108; 111; INT 111

Lee, Tanith 1947-   **CLC 46**
See also AAYA 15; CA 37-40R; CANR 53;
SATA 8, 88

Lee, Vernon   **TCLC 5**
See also Paget, Violet
See also DLB 57, 153, 156, 174, 178

Lee, William
See Burroughs, William S(eward)

Lee, Willy
See Burroughs, William S(eward)

Lee-Hamilton, Eugene (Jacob) 1845-1907
TCLC 22
See also CA 117

Leet, Judith 1935-   **CLC 11**

Le Fanu, Joseph Sheridan 1814-1873 NCLC 9,
58; DAM POP; SSC 14
See also DLB 21, 70, 159, 178

Leffland, Ella 1931-   **CLC 19**
See also CA 29-32R; CANR 35; DLBY 84; INT
CANR-35; SATA 65

Leger, Alexis
See Leger, (Marie-Rene Auguste) Alexis Saint-
Leger

**Leger, (Marie-Rene Auguste) Alexis Saint-
Leger** 1887-1975 CLC 11; DAM POET
See also Perse, St.-John
See also CA 13-16R; 61-64; CANR 43; MTCW

Leger, Saintleger
See Leger, (Marie-Rene Auguste) Alexis Saint-
Leger

Le Guin, Ursula K(roeber) 1929- CLC 8, 13,
22, 45, 71; DAB; DAC; DAM MST, POP;
SSC 12
See also AAYA 9; AITN 1; CA 21-24R; CANR
9, 32, 52; CDALB 1968-1988; CLR 3, 28;
DLB 8, 52; INT CANR-32; JRDA;
MAICYA; MTCW; SATA 4, 52

Lehmann, Rosamond (Nina) 1901-1990 CLC 5
See also CA 77-80; 131; CANR 8; DLB 15

Leiber, Fritz (Reuter, Jr.) 1910-1992 CLC 25
See also CA 45-48; 139; CANR 2, 40; DLB 8;
MTCW; SATA 45; SATA-Obit 73

Leibniz, Gottfried Wilhelm von 1646-1716 LC
35
See also DLB 168

Leimbach, Martha 1963-
See Leimbach, Marti
See also CA 130

Leimbach, Marti   **CLC 65**
See also Leimbach, Martha

Leino, Eino   **TCLC 24**
See also Loennbohm, Armas Eino Leopold

Leiris, Michel (Julien) 1901-1990   **CLC 61**
See also CA 119; 128; 132

Leithauser, Brad 1953-   **CLC 27**

See also CA 107; CANR 27; DLB 120

Lelchuk, Alan 1938-   **CLC 5**
See also CA 45-48; CAAS 20; CANR 1

Lem, Stanislaw 1921-   **CLC 8, 15, 40**
See also CA 105; CAAS 1; CANR 32; MTCW

Lemann, Nancy 1956-   **CLC 39**
See also CA 118; 136

Lemonnier, (Antoine Louis) Camille 1844-1913
TCLC 22
See also CA 121

Lenau, Nikolaus 1802-1850   **NCLC 16**

L'Engle, Madeleine (Camp Franklin) 1918-
CLC 12; DAM POP
See also AAYA 1; AITN 2; CA 1-4R; CANR
3, 21, 39, 66; CLR 1, 14; DLB 52; JRDA;
MAICYA; MTCW; SAAS 15; SATA 1, 27,
75

Lengyel, Jozsef 1896-1975   **CLC 7**
See also CA 85-88; 57-60

Lenin 1870-1924
See Lenin, V. I.
See also CA 121

Lenin, V. I.   **TCLC 67**
See also Lenin

Lennon, John (Ono) 1940-1980   **CLC 12, 35**
See also CA 102

Lennox, Charlotte Ramsay 1729(?)-1804
NCLC 23
See also DLB 39

Lentricchia, Frank (Jr.) 1940-   **CLC 34**
See also CA 25-28R; CANR 19

Lenz, Siegfried 1926-   **CLC 27**
See also CA 89-92; DLB 75

Leonard, Elmore (John, Jr.) 1925-   **CLC 28,
34, 71; DAM POP**
See also AAYA 22; AITN 1; BEST 89:1, 90:4;
CA 81-84; CANR 12, 28, 53; DLB 173; INT
CANR-28; MTCW

Leonard, Hugh   **CLC 19**
See Byrne, John Keyes
See also DLB 13

Leonov, Leonid (Maximovich) 1899-1994
CLC 92; DAM NOV
See also CA 129; MTCW

Leopardi, (Conte) Giacomo 1798-1837 **NCLC
22**

Le Reveler
See Artaud, Antonin (Marie Joseph)

Lerman, Eleanor 1952-   **CLC 9**
See also CA 85-88

Lerman, Rhoda 1936-   **CLC 56**
See also CA 49-52

Lermontov, Mikhail Yuryevich 1814-1841
NCLC 47; PC 18

Leroux, Gaston 1868-1927   **TCLC 25**
See also CA 108; 136; SATA 65

Lesage, Alain-Rene 1668-1747   **LC 28**

Leskov, Nikolai (Semyonovich) 1831-1895
NCLC 25

Lessing, Doris (May) 1919- **CLC 1, 2, 3, 6, 10,
15, 22, 40, 94; DA; DAB; DAC; DAM
MST, NOV; SSC 6; WLCS**
See also CA 9-12R; CAAS 14; CANR 33, 54;
CDBLB 1960 to Present; DLB 15, 139;
DLBY 85; MTCW

Lessing, Gotthold Ephraim 1729-1781 **LC 8**
See also DLB 97

Lester, Richard 1932-   **CLC 20**

Lever, Charles (James) 1806-1872 **NCLC 23**
See also DLB 21

Leverson, Ada 1865(?)-1936(?)   **TCLC 18**
See also Elaine
See also CA 117; DLB 153

Levertov, Denise 1923-1997 **CLC 1, 2, 3, 5, 8,
15, 28, 66; DAM POET; PC 11**
See also CA 1-4R; 163; CAAS 19; CANR 3,
29, 50; DLB 5, 165; INT CANR-29; MTCW

Levi, Jonathan   **CLC 76**

Levi, Peter (Chad Tigar) 1931-   **CLC 41**
See also CA 5-8R; CANR 34; DLB 40

Levi, Primo 1919-1987   **CLC 37, 50; SSC 12**
See also CA 13-16R; 122; CANR 12, 33, 61;
DLB 177; MTCW

Levin, Ira 1929-   **CLC 3, 6; DAM POP**
See also CA 21-24R; CANR 17, 44; MTCW;
SATA 66

Levin, Meyer 1905-1981   **CLC 7; DAM POP**
See also AITN 1; CA 9-12R; 104; CANR 15;
DLB 9, 28; DLBY 81; SATA 21; SATA-Obit
27

Levine, Norman 1924-   **CLC 54**
See also CA 73-76; CAAS 23; CANR 14; DLB
88

Levine, Philip 1928-   **CLC 2, 4, 5, 9, 14, 33;
DAM POET; PC 22**
See also CA 9-12R; CANR 9, 37, 52; DLB 5

Levinson, Deirdre 1931-   **CLC 49**
See also CA 73-76

Levi-Strauss, Claude 1908-   **CLC 38**
See also CA 1-4R; CANR 6, 32, 57; MTCW

Levitin, Sonia (Wolff) 1934-   **CLC 17**
See also AAYA 13; CA 29-32R; CANR 14, 32;
JRDA; MAICYA; SAAS 2; SATA 4, 68

Levon, O. U.
See Kesey, Ken (Elton)

Levy, Amy 1861-1889   **NCLC 59**
See also DLB 156

Lewes, George Henry 1817-1878   **NCLC 25**
See also DLB 55, 144

Lewis, Alun 1915-1944   **TCLC 3**
See also CA 104; DLB 20, 162

Lewis, C. Day
See Day Lewis, C(ecil)

Lewis, C(live) S(taples) 1898-1963 **CLC 1, 3, 6,
14, 27; DA; DAB; DAC; DAM MST, NOV,
POP; WLC**
See also AAYA 3; CA 81-84; CANR 33;
CDBLB 1945-1960; CLR 3, 27; DLB 15,
100, 160; JRDA; MAICYA; MTCW; SATA
13

Lewis, Janet 1899-   **CLC 41**
See also Winters, Janet Lewis
See also CA 9-12R; CANR 29, 63; CAP 1;
DLBY 87

Lewis, Matthew Gregory 1775-1818 **NCLC 11,
62**
See also DLB 39, 158, 178

Lewis, (Harry) Sinclair 1885-1951   **TCLC 4,
13, 23, 39; DA; DAB; DAC; DAM MST,
NOV; WLC**
See also CA 104; 133; CDALB 1917-1929;
DLB 9, 102; DLBD 1; MTCW

Lewis, (Percy) Wyndham 1882(?)-1957 **TCLC
2, 9**
See also CA 104; 157; DLB 15

Lewisohn, Ludwig 1883-1955   **TCLC 19**
See also CA 107; DLB 4, 9, 28, 102

Lewton, Val 1904-1951   **TCLC 76**

Leyner, Mark 1956-   **CLC 92**
See also CA 110; CANR 28, 53

Lezama Lima, Jose 1910-1976 **CLC 4, 10, 101;
DAM MULT**
See also CA 77-80; DLB 113; HW

>Heureux, John (Clarke)

1934-   **CLC 52**
See also CA 13-16R; CANR 23, 45

Liddell, C. H.
See Kuttner, Henry

Lie, Jonas (Lauritz Idemil) 1833-1908(?)
TCLC 5
See also CA 115

Lieber, Joel 1937-1971   **CLC 6**
See also CA 73-76; 29-32R

Lieber, Stanley Martin
See Lee, Stan

Lieberman, Laurence (James) 1935- **CLC 4,
36**
See also CA 17-20R; CANR 8, 36

Lieh Tzu fl. 7th cent. B.C.-5th cent. B.C.
CMLC 27

Lieksman, Anders
See Haavikko, Paavo Juhani

Li Fei-kan 1904-
See Pa Chin
See also CA 105

Lifton, Robert Jay 1926-   **CLC 67**
See also CA 17-20R; CANR 27; INT CANR-
27; SATA 66

Lightfoot, Gordon 1938-   **CLC 26**
See also CA 109

Lightman, Alan P(aige) 1948-   **CLC 81**
See also CA 141; CANR 63

Ligotti, Thomas (Robert) 1953- **CLC 44; SSC
16**
See also CA 123; CANR 49

Li Ho 791-817   **PC 13**

Liliencron, (Friedrich Adolf Axel) Detlev von
1844-1909   **TCLC 18**
See also CA 117

Lilly, William 1602-1681   **LC 27**

Lima, Jose Lezama
See Lezama Lima, Jose

Lima Barreto, Afonso Henrique de 1881-1922
TCLC 23
See also CA 117

Limonov, Edward 1944-   **CLC 67**
See also CA 137

Lin, Frank
See Atherton, Gertrude (Franklin Horn)

Lincoln, Abraham 1809-1865   **NCLC 18**

Lind, Jakov   **CLC 1, 2, 4, 27, 82**
See also Landwirth, Heinz
See also CAAS 4

Lindbergh, Anne (Spencer) Morrow 1906-
CLC 82; DAM NOV
See also CA 17-20R; CANR 16; MTCW; SATA
33

Lindsay, David 1878-1945   **TCLC 15**
See also CA 113

Lindsay, (Nicholas) Vachel 1879-1931 **TCLC
17; DA; DAC; DAM MST, POET; WLC**
See also CA 114; 135; CDALB 1865-1917;
DLB 54; SATA 40

Linke-Poot
See Doeblin, Alfred

Linney, Romulus 1930-   **CLC 51**
See also CA 1-4R; CANR 40, 44

Linton, Eliza Lynn 1822-1898   **NCLC 41**
See also DLB 18

Li Po 701-763   **CMLC 2**

Lipsius, Justus 1547-1606   **LC 16**

Lipsyte, Robert (Michael) 1938- **CLC 21; DA;
DAC; DAM MST, NOV**
See also AAYA 7; CA 17-20R; CANR 8, 57;
CLR 23; JRDA; MAICYA; SATA 5, 68

Lish, Gordon (Jay) 1934-   **CLC 45; SSC 18**

See also CA 113; 117; DLB 130; INT 117
Lispector, Clarice 1925-1977   **CLC 43**
  See also CA 139; 116; DLB 113
Littell, Robert 1935(?)-   **CLC 42**
  See also CA 109; 112; CANR 64
Little, Malcolm 1925-1965
  See Malcolm X
  See also BW 1; CA 125; 111; DA; DAB; DAC;
    DAM MST, MULT; MTCW
Littlewit, Humphrey Gent.
  See Lovecraft, H(oward) P(hillips)
Litwos
  See Sienkiewicz, Henryk (Adam Alexander
    Pius)
Liu E 1857-1909   **TCLC 15**
  See also CA 115
Lively, Penelope (Margaret) 1933- **CLC 32,**
  50; DAM NOV
  See also CA 41-44R; CANR 29, 67; CLR 7;
    DLB 14, 161; JRDA; MAICYA; MTCW;
    SATA 7, 60
Livesay, Dorothy (Kathleen) 1909-**CLC 4, 15,**
  79; DAC; DAM MST, POET
  See also AITN 2; CA 25-28R; CAAS 8; CANR
    36, 67; DLB 68; MTCW
Livy c. 59B.C.-c. 17   **CMLC 11**
Lizardi, Jose Joaquin Fernandez de 1776-1827
  NCLC 30
Llewellyn, Richard
  See Llewellyn Lloyd, Richard Dafydd Vivian
  See also DLB 15
Llewellyn Lloyd, Richard Dafydd Vivian 1906-
  1983   **CLC 7, 80**
  See also Llewellyn, Richard
  See also CA 53-56; 111; CANR 7; SATA 11;
    SATA-Obit 37
Llosa, (Jorge) Mario (Pedro) Vargas
  See Vargas Llosa, (Jorge) Mario (Pedro)
Lloyd, Manda
  See Mander, (Mary) Jane
Lloyd Webber, Andrew 1948-
  See Webber, Andrew Lloyd
  See also AAYA 1; CA 116; 149; DAM DRAM;
    SATA 56
Llull, Ramon c. 1235-c. 1316   **CMLC 12**
Locke, Alain (Le Roy) 1886-1954   **TCLC 43;**
  BLCS
  See also BW 1; CA 106; 124; DLB 51
Locke, John 1632-1704   **LC 7, 35**
  See also DLB 101
Locke-Elliott, Sumner
  See Elliott, Sumner Locke
Lockhart, John Gibson 1794-1854   **NCLC 6**
  See also DLB 110, 116, 144
Lodge, David (John) 1935-   **CLC 36; DAM**
  POP
  See also BEST 90:1; CA 17-20R; CANR 19,
    53; DLB 14, 194; INT CANR-19; MTCW
Lodge, Thomas 1558-1625   **LC 41**
  See also DLB 172
Lodge, Thomas 1558-1625   **LC 41**
Loennbohm, Armas Eino Leopold 1878-1926
  See Leino, Eino
  See also CA 123
Loewinsohn, Ron(ald William) 1937- **CLC 52**
  See also CA 25-28R
Logan, Jake
  See Smith, Martin Cruz
Logan, John (Burton) 1923-1987   **CLC 5**
  See also CA 77-80; 124; CANR 45; DLB 5
Lo Kuan-chung 1330(?)-1400(?)   **LC 12**
Lombard, Nap
  See Johnson, Pamela Hansford

London, Jack   **TCLC 9, 15, 39; SSC 4; WLC**
  See also London, John Griffith
  See also AAYA 13; AITN 2; CDALB 1865-
    1917; DLB 8, 12, 78; SATA 18
London, John Griffith 1876-1916
  See London, Jack
  See also CA 110; 119; DA; DAB; DAC; DAM
    MST, NOV; JRDA; MAICYA; MTCW
Long, Emmett
  See Leonard, Elmore (John, Jr.)
Longbaugh, Harry
  See Goldman, William (W.)
Longfellow, Henry Wadsworth 1807-1882
  NCLC 2, 45; DA; DAB; DAC; DAM MST,
  POET; WLCS
  See also CDALB 1640-1865; DLB 1, 59; SATA
    19
Longinus c. 1st cent. -   **CMLC 27**
  See also DLB 176
Longley, Michael 1939-   **CLC 29**
  See also CA 102; DLB 40
Longus fl. c. 2nd cent. -   **CMLC 7**
Longway, A. Hugh
  See Lang, Andrew
Lonnrot, Elias 1802-1884   **NCLC 53**
Lopate, Phillip 1943-   **CLC 29**
  See also CA 97-100; DLBY 80; INT 97-100
Lopez Portillo (y Pacheco), Jose 1920-**CLC 46**
  See also CA 129; HW
Lopez y Fuentes, Gregorio 1897(?)-1966 **CLC**
  32
  See also CA 131; HW
Lorca, Federico Garcia
  See Garcia Lorca, Federico
Lord, Bette Bao 1938-   **CLC 23**
  See also BEST 90:3; CA 107; CANR 41; INT
    107; SATA 58
Lord Auch
  See Bataille, Georges
Lord Byron
  See Byron, George Gordon (Noel)
Lorde, Audre (Geraldine) 1934-1992**CLC 18,**
  71; BLC 2; DAM MULT, POET; PC 12
  See also BW 1; CA 25-28R; 142; CANR 16,
    26, 46; DLB 41; MTCW
Lord Houghton
  See Milnes, Richard Monckton
Lord Jeffrey
  See Jeffrey, Francis
Lorenzini, Carlo 1826-1890
  See Collodi, Carlo
  See also MAICYA; SATA 29
Lorenzo, Heberto Padilla
  See Padilla (Lorenzo), Heberto
Loris
  See Hofmannsthal, Hugo von
Loti, Pierre   **TCLC 11**
  See also Viaud, (Louis Marie) Julien
  See also DLB 123
Louie, David Wong 1954-   **CLC 70**
  See also CA 139
Louis, Father M.
  See Merton, Thomas
Lovecraft, H(oward) P(hillips) 1890-1937
  TCLC 4, 22; DAM POP; SSC 3
  See also AAYA 14; CA 104; 133; MTCW
Lovelace, Earl 1935-   **CLC 51**
  See also BW 2; CA 77-80; CANR 41; DLB 125;
    MTCW
Lovelace, Richard 1618-1657   **LC 24**
  See also DLB 131
Lowell, Amy 1874-1925   **TCLC 1, 8; DAM**
  POET; PC 13

See also CA 104; 151; DLB 54, 140
Lowell, James Russell 1819-1891   **NCLC 2**
  See also CDALB 1640-1865; DLB 1, 11, 64,
    79, 189
Lowell, Robert (Traill Spence, Jr.) 1917-1977
  CLC 1, 2, 3, 4, 5, 8, 9, 11, 15, 37; DA; DAB;
  DAC; DAM MST, NOV; PC 3; WLC
  See also CA 9-12R; 73-76; CABS 2; CANR
    26, 60; DLB 5, 169; MTCW
Lowndes, Marie Adelaide (Belloc) 1868-1947
  TCLC 12
  See also CA 107; DLB 70
Lowry, (Clarence) Malcolm 1909-1957**TCLC**
  6, 40
  See also CA 105; 131; CANR 62; CDBLB
    1945-1960; DLB 15; MTCW
Lowry, Mina Gertrude 1882-1966
  See Loy, Mina
  See also CA 113
Loxsmith, John
  See Brunner, John (Kilian Houston)
Loy, Mina   **CLC 28; DAM POET; PC 16**
  See also Lowry, Mina Gertrude
  See also DLB 4, 54
Loyson-Bridet
  See Schwob, (Mayer Andre) Marcel
Lucas, Craig 1951-   **CLC 64**
  See also CA 137
Lucas, E(dward) V(errall) 1868-1938   **TCLC**
  73
  See also DLB 98, 149, 153; SATA 20
Lucas, George 1944-   **CLC 16**
  See also AAYA 1, 23; CA 77-80; CANR 30;
    SATA 56
Lucas, Hans
  See Godard, Jean-Luc
Lucas, Victoria
  See Plath, Sylvia
Ludlam, Charles 1943-1987   **CLC 46, 50**
  See also CA 85-88; 122
Ludlum, Robert 1927-   **CLC 22, 43; DAM**
  NOV, POP
  See also AAYA 10; BEST 89:1, 90:3; CA 33-
    36R; CANR 25, 41, 68; DLBY 82; MTCW
Ludwig, Ken   **CLC 60**
Ludwig, Otto 1813-1865   **NCLC 4**
  See also DLB 129
Lugones, Leopoldo 1874-1938   **TCLC 15**
  See also CA 116; 131; HW
Lu Hsun 1881-1936   **TCLC 3; SSC 20**
  See also Shu-Jen, Chou
Lukacs, George   **CLC 24**
  See also Lukacs, Gyorgy (Szegeny von)
Lukacs, Gyorgy (Szegeny von) 1885-1971
  See Lukacs, George
  See also CA 101; 29-32R; CANR 62
Luke, Peter (Ambrose Cyprian) 1919-1995
  CLC 38
  See also CA 81-84; 147; DLB 13
Lunar, Dennis
  See Mungo, Raymond
Lurie, Alison 1926-   **CLC 4, 5, 18, 39**
  See also CA 1-4R; CANR 2, 17, 50; DLB 2;
    MTCW; SATA 46
Lustig, Arnost 1926-   **CLC 56**
  See also AAYA 3; CA 69-72; CANR 47; SATA
    56
Luther, Martin 1483-1546   **LC 9, 37**
  See also DLB 179
Luxemburg, Rosa 1870(?)-1919   **TCLC 63**
  See also CA 118
Luzi, Mario 1914-   **CLC 13**
  See also CA 61-64; CANR 9; DLB 128

Lyly, John 1554(?)-1606**LC 41; DAM DRAM; DC 7**
See also DLB 62, 167
L'Ymagier
See Gourmont, Remy (-Marie-Charles) de
Lynch, B. Suarez
See Bioy Casares, Adolfo; Borges, Jorge Luis
Lynch, David (K.) 1946-   **CLC 66**
See also CA 124; 129
Lynch, James
See Andreyev, Leonid (Nikolaevich)
Lynch Davis, B.
See Bioy Casares, Adolfo; Borges, Jorge Luis
Lyndsay, Sir David 1490-1555   **LC 20**
Lynn, Kenneth S(chuyler) 1923-   **CLC 50**
See also CA 1-4R; CANR 3, 27, 65
Lynx
See West, Rebecca
Lyons, Marcus
See Blish, James (Benjamin)
Lyre, Pinchbeck
See Sassoon, Siegfried (Lorraine)
Lytle, Andrew (Nelson) 1902-1995   **CLC 22**
See also CA 9-12R; 150; DLB 6; DLBY 95
Lyttelton, George 1709-1773   **LC 10**
Maas, Peter 1929-   **CLC 29**
See also CA 93-96; INT 93-96
Macaulay, Rose 1881-1958   **TCLC 7, 44**
See also CA 104; DLB 36
Macaulay, Thomas Babington 1800-1859
     NCLC 42
See also CDBLB 1832-1890; DLB 32, 55
MacBeth, George (Mann) 1932-1992**CLC 2, 5, 9**
See also CA 25-28R; 136; CANR 61, 66; DLB 40; MTCW; SATA 4; SATA-Obit 70
MacCaig, Norman (Alexander) 1910-**CLC 36; DAB; DAM POET**
See also CA 9-12R; CANR 3, 34; DLB 27
MacCarthy, (Sir Charles Otto) Desmond 1877-1952   **TCLC 36**
MacDiarmid, Hugh CLC 2, 4, 11, 19, 63; PC 9
See also Grieve, C(hristopher) M(urray)
See also CDBLB 1945-1960; DLB 20
MacDonald, Anson
See Heinlein, Robert A(nson)
Macdonald, Cynthia 1928-   **CLC 13, 19**
See also CA 49-52; CANR 4, 44; DLB 105
MacDonald, George 1824-1905   **TCLC 9**
See also CA 106; 137; DLB 18, 163, 178; MAICYA; SATA 33
Macdonald, John
See Millar, Kenneth
MacDonald, John D(ann) 1916-1986   **CLC 3, 27, 44; DAM NOV, POP**
See also CA 1-4R; 121; CANR 1, 19, 60; DLB 8; DLBY 86; MTCW
Macdonald, John Ross
See Millar, Kenneth
Macdonald, Ross   CLC 1, 2, 3, 14, 34, 41
See also Millar, Kenneth
See also DLBD 6
MacDougal, John
See Blish, James (Benjamin)
MacEwen, Gwendolyn (Margaret) 1941-1987 **CLC 13, 55**
See also CA 9-12R; 124; CANR 7, 22; DLB 53; SATA 50; SATA-Obit 55
Macha, Karel Hynek 1810-1846   **NCLC 46**
Machado (y Ruiz), Antonio 1875-1939 **TCLC 3**
See also CA 104; DLB 108
Machado de Assis, Joaquim Maria 1839-1908
     TCLC 10; BLC 2; SSC 24
See also CA 107; 153
Machen, Arthur   TCLC 4; SSC 20
See also Jones, Arthur Llewellyn
See also DLB 36, 156, 178
Machiavelli, Niccolo 1469-1527**LC 8, 36; DA; DAB; DAC; DAM MST; WLCS**
MacInnes, Colin 1914-1976   **CLC 4, 23**
See also CA 69-72; 65-68; CANR 21; DLB 14; MTCW
MacInnes, Helen (Clark) 1907-1985 **CLC 27, 39; DAM POP**
See also CA 1-4R; 117; CANR 1, 28, 58; DLB 87; MTCW; SATA 22; SATA-Obit 44
Mackay, Mary 1855-1924
See Corelli, Marie
See also CA 118
Mackenzie, Compton (Edward Montague) 1883-1972   **CLC 18**
See also CA 21-22; 37-40R; CAP 2; DLB 34, 100
Mackenzie, Henry 1745-1831   **NCLC 41**
See also DLB 39
Mackintosh, Elizabeth 1896(?)-1952
See Tey, Josephine
See also CA 110
MacLaren, James
See Grieve, C(hristopher) M(urray)
Mac Laverty, Bernard 1942-   **CLC 31**
See also CA 116; 118; CANR 43; INT 118
MacLean, Alistair (Stuart) 1922(?)-1987 **CLC 3, 13, 50, 63; DAM POP**
See also CA 57-60; 121; CANR 28, 61; MTCW; SATA 23; SATA-Obit 50
Maclean, Norman (Fitzroy) 1902-1990   **CLC 78; DAM POP; SSC 13**
See also CA 102; 132; CANR 49
MacLeish, Archibald 1892-1982**CLC 3, 8, 14, 68; DAM POET**
See also CA 9-12R; 106; CANR 33, 63; DLB 4, 7, 45; DLBY 82; MTCW
MacLennan, (John) Hugh 1907-1990   **CLC 2, 14, 92; DAC; DAM MST**
See also CA 5-8R; 142; CANR 33; DLB 68; MTCW
MacLeod, Alistair 1936-**CLC 56; DAC; DAM MST**
See also CA 123; DLB 60
Macleod, Fiona
See Sharp, William
MacNeice, (Frederick) Louis 1907-1963 **CLC 1, 4, 10, 53; DAB; DAM POET**
See also CA 85-88; CANR 61; DLB 10, 20; MTCW
MacNeill, Dand
See Fraser, George MacDonald
Macpherson, James 1736-1796   **LC 29**
See also DLB 109
Macpherson, (Jean) Jay 1931-   **CLC 14**
See also CA 5-8R; DLB 53
MacShane, Frank 1927-   **CLC 39**
See also CA 9-12R; CANR 3, 33; DLB 111
Macumber, Mari
See Sandoz, Mari(e Susette)
Madach, Imre 1823-1864   **NCLC 19**
Madden, (Jerry) David 1933-   **CLC 5, 15**
See also CA 1-4R; CAAS 3; CANR 4, 45; DLB 6; MTCW
Maddern, Al(an)
See Ellison, Harlan (Jay)
Madhubuti, Haki R. 1942-**CLC 6, 73; BLC 2; DAM MULT, POET; PC 5**
See also Lee, Don L.

See also BW 2; CA 73-76; CANR 24, 51; DLB 5, 41; DLBD 8
Maepenn, Hugh
See Kuttner, Henry
Maepenn, K. H.
See Kuttner, Henry
Maeterlinck, Maurice 1862-1949   **TCLC 3; DAM DRAM**
See also CA 104; 136; DLB 192; SATA 66
Maginn, William 1794-1842   **NCLC 8**
See also DLB 110, 159
Mahapatra, Jayanta 1928-   **CLC 33; DAM MULT**
See also CA 73-76; CAAS 9; CANR 15, 33, 66
Mahfouz, Naguib (Abdel Aziz Al-Sabilgi) 1911(?)-
See Mahfuz, Najib
See also BEST 89:2; CA 128; CANR 55; DAM NOV; MTCW
Mahfuz, Najib   CLC 52, 55
See also Mahfouz, Naguib (Abdel Aziz Al-Sabilgi)
See also DLBY 88
Mahon, Derek 1941-   **CLC 27**
See also CA 113; 128; DLB 40
Mailer, Norman 1923-**CLC 1, 2, 3, 4, 5, 8, 11, 14, 28, 39, 74; DA; DAB; DAC; DAM MST, NOV, POP**
See also AITN 2; CA 9-12R; CABS 1; CANR 28; CDALB 1968-1988; DLB 2, 16, 28, 185; DLBD 3; DLBY 80, 83; MTCW
Maillet, Antonine 1929-   **CLC 54; DAC**
See also CA 115; 120; CANR 46; DLB 60; INT 120
Mais, Roger 1905-1955   **TCLC 8**
See also BW 1; CA 105; 124; DLB 125; MTCW
Maistre, Joseph de 1753-1821   **NCLC 37**
Maitland, Frederic 1850-1906   **TCLC 65**
Maitland, Sara (Louise) 1950-   **CLC 49**
See also CA 69-72; CANR 13, 59
Major, Clarence 1936-**CLC 3, 19, 48; BLC 2; DAM MULT**
See also BW 2; CA 21-24R; CAAS 6; CANR 13, 25, 53; DLB 33
Major, Kevin (Gerald) 1949-   **CLC 26; DAC**
See also AAYA 16; CA 97-100; CANR 21, 38; CLR 11; DLB 60; INT CANR-21; JRDA; MAICYA; SATA 32, 82
Maki, James
See Ozu, Yasujiro
Malabaila, Damiano
See Levi, Primo
Malamud, Bernard 1914-1986 **CLC 1, 2, 3, 5, 8, 9, 11, 18, 27, 44, 78, 85; DA; DAB; DAC; DAM MST, NOV, POP; SSC 15; WLC**
See also AAYA 16; CA 5-8R; 118; CABS 1; CANR 28, 62; CDALB 1941-1968; DLB 2, 28, 152; DLBY 80, 86; MTCW
Malan, Herman
See Bosman, Herman Charles; Bosman, Herman Charles
Malaparte, Curzio 1898-1957   **TCLC 52**
Malcolm, Dan
See Silverberg, Robert
Malcolm X   CLC 82; BLC 2; WLCS
See also Little, Malcolm
Malherbe, Francois de 1555-1628   **LC 5**
Mallarme, Stephane 1842-1898 **NCLC 4, 41; DAM POET; PC 4**
Mallet-Joris, Francoise 1930-   **CLC 11**
See also CA 65-68; CANR 17; DLB 83
Malley, Ern
See McAuley, James Phillip

Mallowan, Agatha Christie
  See Christie, Agatha (Mary Clarissa)
Maloff, Saul 1922-   **CLC 5**
  See also CA 33-36R
Malone, Louis
  See MacNeice, (Frederick) Louis
Malone, Michael (Christopher) 1942-**CLC 43**
  See also CA 77-80; CANR 14, 32, 57
Malory, (Sir) Thomas 1410(?)-1471(?) **LC 11;**
  DA; DAB; DAC; DAM MST; WLCS
  See also CDBLB Before 1660; DLB 146; SATA
  59; SATA-Brief 33
Malouf, (George Joseph) David 1934-**CLC 28,**
  86
  See also CA 124; CANR 50
Malraux, (Georges-)Andre 1901-1976 **CLC 1,**
  4, 9, 13, 15, 57; DAM NOV
  See also CA 21-22; 69-72; CANR 34, 58; CAP
  2; DLB 72; MTCW
Malzberg, Barry N(athaniel) 1939-   **CLC 7**
  See also CA 61-64; CAAS 4; CANR 16; DLB
  8
Mamet, David (Alan) 1947-**CLC 9, 15, 34, 46,**
  91; DAM DRAM; DC 4
  See also AAYA 3; CA 81-84; CABS 3; CANR
  15, 41, 67; DLB 7; MTCW
Mamoulian, Rouben (Zachary) 1897-1987
  CLC 16
  See also CA 25-28R; 124
Mandelstam, Osip (Emilievich) 1891(?)-1938(?)
  TCLC 2, 6; PC 14
  See also CA 104; 150
Mander, (Mary) Jane 1877-1949   **TCLC 31**
  See also CA 162
Mandeville, John fl. 1350-   **CMLC 19**
  See also DLB 146
Mandiargues, Andre Pieyre de   **CLC 41**
  See also Pieyre de Mandiargues, Andre
  See also DLB 83
Mandrake, Ethel Belle
  See Thurman, Wallace (Henry)
Mangan, James Clarence 1803-1849**NCLC 27**
Maniere, J.-E.
  See Giraudoux, (Hippolyte) Jean
Manley, (Mary) Delariviere 1672(?)-1724 **LC**
  1
  See also DLB 39, 80
Mann, Abel
  See Creasey, John
Mann, Emily 1952-   **DC 7**
  See also CA 130; CANR 55
Mann, (Luiz) Heinrich 1871-1950   **TCLC 9**
  See also CA 106; 164; DLB 66
Mann, (Paul) Thomas 1875-1955 **TCLC 2, 8,**
  14, 21, 35, 44, 60; DA; DAB; DAC; DAM
  MST, NOV; SSC 5; WLC
  See also CA 104; 128; DLB 66; MTCW
Mannheim, Karl 1893-1947   **TCLC 65**
Manning, David
  See Faust, Frederick (Schiller)
Manning, Frederic 1887(?)-1935   **TCLC 25**
  See also CA 124
Manning, Olivia 1915-1980   **CLC 5, 19**
  See also CA 5-8R; 101; CANR 29; MTCW
Mano, D. Keith 1942-   **CLC 2, 10**
  See also CA 25-28R; CAAS 6; CANR 26, 57;
  DLB 6
Mansfield, KatherineTCLC 2, 8, 39; DAB; SSC
  9, 23; WLC
  See also Beauchamp, Kathleen Mansfield
  See also DLB 162
Manso, Peter 1940-   **CLC 39**
  See also CA 29-32R; CANR 44

Mantecon, Juan Jimenez
  See Jimenez (Mantecon), Juan Ramon
Manton, Peter
  See Creasey, John
Man Without a Spleen, A
  See Chekhov, Anton (Pavlovich)
Manzoni, Alessandro 1785-1873   **NCLC 29**
Mapu, Abraham (ben Jekutiel) 1808-1867
  NCLC 18
Mara, Sally
  See Queneau, Raymond
Marat, Jean Paul 1743-1793   **LC 10**
Marcel, Gabriel Honore 1889-1973   **CLC 15**
  See also CA 102; 45-48; MTCW
Marchbanks, Samuel
  See Davies, (William) Robertson
Marchi, Giacomo
  See Bassani, Giorgio
Margulies, Donald   **CLC 76**
Marie de France c. 12th cent. - **CMLC 8; PC**
  22
Marie de l'Incarnation 1599-1672   **LC 10**
Marier, Captain Victor
  See Griffith, D(avid Lewelyn) W(ark)
Mariner, Scott
  See Pohl, Frederik
Marinetti, Filippo Tommaso 1876-1944
  TCLC 10
  See also CA 107; DLB 114
Marivaux, Pierre Carlet de Chamblain de
  1688-1763   **LC 4; DC 7**
Markandaya, Kamala   **CLC 8, 38**
  See also Taylor, Kamala (Purnaiya)
Markfield, Wallace 1926-   **CLC 8**
  See also CA 69-72; CAAS 3; DLB 2, 28
Markham, Edwin 1852-1940   **TCLC 47**
  See also CA 160; DLB 54, 186
Markham, Robert
  See Amis, Kingsley (William)
Marks, J
  See Highwater, Jamake (Mamake)
Marks-Highwater, J
  See Highwater, Jamake (Mamake)
Markson, David M(errill) 1927-   **CLC 67**
  See also CA 49-52; CANR 1
Marley, Bob   **CLC 17**
  See also Marley, Robert Nesta
Marley, Robert Nesta 1945-1981
  See Marley, Bob
  See also CA 107; 103
Marlowe, Christopher 1564-1593 **LC 22; DA;**
  DAB; DAC; DAM DRAM, MST; DC 1;
  WLC
  See also CDBLB Before 1660; DLB 62
Marlowe, Stephen 1928-
  See Queen, Ellery
  See also CA 13-16R; CANR 6, 55
Marmontel, Jean-Francois 1723-1799   **LC 2**
Marquand, John P(hillips) 1893-1960 **CLC 2,**
  10
  See also CA 85-88; DLB 9, 102
Marques, Rene 1919-1979   **CLC 96; DAM**
  MULT; HLC
  See also CA 97-100; 85-88; DLB 113; HW
Marquez, Gabriel (Jose) Garcia
  See Garcia Marquez, Gabriel (Jose)
Marquis, Don(ald Robert Perry) 1878-1937
  TCLC 7
  See also CA 104; DLB 11, 25
Marric, J. J.
  See Creasey, John
Marryat, Frederick 1792-1848   **NCLC 3**
  See also DLB 21, 163

Marsden, James
  See Creasey, John
Marsh, (Edith) Ngaio 1899-1982 **CLC 7, 53;**
  DAM POP
  See also CA 9-12R; CANR 6, 58; DLB 77;
  MTCW
Marshall, Garry 1934-   **CLC 17**
  See also AAYA 3; CA 111; SATA 60
Marshall, Paule 1929-   **CLC 27, 72; BLC 3;**
  DAM MULT; SSC 3
  See also BW 2; CA 77-80; CANR 25; DLB 157;
  MTCW
Marsten, Richard
  See Hunter, Evan
Marston, John 1576-1634**LC 33; DAM DRAM**
  See also DLB 58, 172
Martha, Henry
  See Harris, Mark
Marti, Jose 1853-1895   **NCLC 63; DAM**
  MULT; HLC
Martial c. 40-c. 104   **PC 10**
Martin, Ken
  See Hubbard, L(afayette) Ron(ald)
Martin, Richard
  See Creasey, John
Martin, Steve 1945-   **CLC 30**
  See also CA 97-100; CANR 30; MTCW
Martin, Valerie 1948-   **CLC 89**
  See also BEST 90:2; CA 85-88; CANR 49
Martin, Violet Florence 1862-1915 **TCLC 51**
Martin, Webber
  See Silverberg, Robert
Martindale, Patrick Victor
  See White, Patrick (Victor Martindale)
Martin du Gard, Roger 1881-1958 **TCLC 24**
  See also CA 118; DLB 65
Martineau, Harriet 1802-1876   **NCLC 26**
  See also DLB 21, 55, 159, 163, 166, 190;
  YABC 2
Martines, Julia
  See O'Faolain, Julia
Martinez, Enrique Gonzalez
  See Gonzalez Martinez, Enrique
Martinez, Jacinto Benavente y
  See Benavente (y Martinez), Jacinto
Martinez Ruiz, Jose 1873-1967
  See Azorin; Ruiz, Jose Martinez
  See also CA 93-96; HW
Martinez Sierra, Gregorio 1881-1947**TCLC 6**
  See also CA 115
Martinez Sierra, Maria (de la O'LeJarraga)
  1874-1974   **TCLC 6**
  See also CA 115
Martinsen, Martin
  See Follett, Ken(neth Martin)
Martinson, Harry (Edmund) 1904-1978 **CLC**
  14
  See also CA 77-80; CANR 34
Marut, Ret
  See Traven, B.
Marut, Robert
  See Traven, B.
Marvell, Andrew 1621-1678   **LC 4, 43; DA;**
  DAB; DAC; DAM MST, POET; PC 10;
  WLC
  See also CDBLB 1660-1789; DLB 131
Marx, Karl (Heinrich) 1818-1883   **NCLC 17**
  See also DLB 129
Masaoka Shiki   **TCLC 18**
  See also Masaoka Tsunenori
Masaoka Tsunenori 1867-1902
  See Masaoka Shiki
  See also CA 117

See also CA 25-28R; CANR 61; DLB 14

McIlwraith, Maureen Mollie Hunter
See Hunter, Mollie
See also SATA 2

McInerney, Jay 1955- **CLC 34; DAM POP**
See also AAYA 18; CA 116; 123; CANR 45, 68; INT 123

McIntyre, Vonda N(eel) 1948- **CLC 18**
See also CA 81-84; CANR 17, 34; MTCW

McKay, Claude TCLC 7, 41; BLC 3; DAB; PC 2
See also McKay, Festus Claudius
See also DLB 4, 45, 51, 117

McKay, Festus Claudius 1889-1948
See McKay, Claude
See also BW 1; CA 104; 124; DA; DAC; DAM MST, MULT, NOV, POET; MTCW; WLC

McKuen, Rod 1933- **CLC 1, 3**
See also AITN 1; CA 41-44R; CANR 40

McLoughlin, R. B.
See Mencken, H(enry) L(ouis)

McLuhan, (Herbert) Marshall 1911-1980 **CLC 37, 83**
See also CA 9-12R; 102; CANR 12, 34, 61; DLB 88; INT CANR-12; MTCW

McMillan, Terry (L.) 1951- **CLC 50, 61; BLCS; DAM MULT, NOV, POP**
See also AAYA 21; BW 2; CA 140; CANR 60

McMurtry, Larry (Jeff) 1936- **CLC 2, 3, 7, 11, 27, 44; DAM NOV, POP**
See also AAYA 15; AITN 2; BEST 89:2; CA 5-8R; CANR 19, 43, 64; CDALB 1968-1988; DLB 2, 143; DLBY 80, 87; MTCW

McNally, T. M. 1961- **CLC 82**

McNally, Terrence 1939- **CLC 4, 7, 41, 91; DAM DRAM**
See also CA 45-48; CANR 2, 56; DLB 7

McNamer, Deirdre 1950- **CLC 70**

McNeile, Herman Cyril 1888-1937
See Sapper
See also DLB 77

McNickle, (William) D'Arcy 1904-1977 **CLC 89; DAM MULT**
See also CA 9-12R; 85-88; CANR 5, 45; DLB 175; NNAL; SATA-Obit 22

McPhee, John (Angus) 1931- **CLC 36**
See also BEST 90:1; CA 65-68; CANR 20, 46, 64; DLB 185; MTCW

McPherson, James Alan 1943- **CLC 19, 77; BLCS**
See also BW 1; CA 25-28R; CAAS 17; CANR 24; DLB 38; MTCW

McPherson, William (Alexander) 1933- **CLC 34**
See also CA 69-72; CANR 28; INT CANR-28

Mead, Margaret 1901-1978 **CLC 37**
See also AITN 1; CA 1-4R; 81-84; CANR 4; MTCW; SATA-Obit 20

Meaker, Marijane (Agnes) 1927-
See Kerr, M. E.
See also CA 107; CANR 37, 63; INT 107; JRDA; MAICYA; MTCW; SATA 20, 61

Medoff, Mark (Howard) 1940- **CLC 6, 23; DAM DRAM**
See also AITN 1; CA 53-56; CANR 5; DLB 7; INT CANR-5

Medvedev, P. N.
See Bakhtin, Mikhail Mikhailovich

Meged, Aharon
See Megged, Aharon

Meged, Aron
See Megged, Aharon

Megged, Aharon 1920- **CLC 9**

See also CA 49-52; CAAS 13; CANR 1

Mehta, Ved (Parkash) 1934- **CLC 37**
See also CA 1-4R; CANR 2, 23; MTCW

Melanter
See Blackmore, R(ichard) D(oddridge)

Melikow, Loris
See Hofmannsthal, Hugo von

Melmoth, Sebastian
See Wilde, Oscar (Fingal O'Flahertie Wills)

Meltzer, Milton 1915- **CLC 26**
See also AAYA 8; CA 13-16R; CANR 38; CLR 13; DLB 61; JRDA; MAICYA; SAAS 1; SATA 1, 50, 80

Melville, Herman 1819-1891 **NCLC 3, 12, 29, 45, 49; DA; DAB; DAC; DAM MST, NOV; SSC 1, 17; WLC**
See also AAYA 25; CDALB 1640-1865; DLB 3, 74; SATA 59

Menander c. 342B.C.-c. 292B.C. **CMLC 9; DAM DRAM; DC 3**
See also DLB 176

Mencken, H(enry) L(ouis) 1880-1956 **TCLC 13**
See also CA 105; 125; CDALB 1917-1929; DLB 11, 29, 63, 137; MTCW

Mendelsohn, Jane 1965(?)- **CLC 99**
See also CA 154

Mercer, David 1928-1980 **CLC 5; DAM DRAM**
See also CA 9-12R; 102; CANR 23; DLB 13; MTCW

Merchant, Paul
See Ellison, Harlan (Jay)

Meredith, George 1828-1909 **TCLC 17, 43; DAM POET**
See also CA 117; 153; CDBLB 1832-1890; DLB 18, 35, 57, 159

Meredith, William (Morris) 1919- **CLC 4, 13, 22, 55; DAM POET**
See also CA 9-12R; CAAS 14; CANR 6, 40; DLB 5

Merezhkovsky, Dmitry Sergeyevich 1865-1941 **TCLC 29**

Merimee, Prosper 1803-1870 **NCLC 6, 65; SSC 7**
See also DLB 119, 192

Merkin, Daphne 1954- **CLC 44**
See also CA 123

Merlin, Arthur
See Blish, James (Benjamin)

Merrill, James (Ingram) 1926-1995 **CLC 2, 3, 6, 8, 13, 18, 34, 91; DAM POET**
See also CA 13-16R; 147; CANR 10, 49, 63; DLB 5, 165; DLBY 85; INT CANR-10; MTCW

Merriman, Alex
See Silverberg, Robert

Merriman, Brian 1747-1805 **NCLC 70**

Merritt, E. B.
See Waddington, Miriam

Merton, Thomas 1915-1968 **CLC 1, 3, 11, 34, 83; PC 10**
See also CA 5-8R; 25-28R; CANR 22, 53; DLB 48; DLBY 81; MTCW

Merwin, W(illiam) S(tanley) 1927- **CLC 1, 2, 3, 5, 8, 13, 18, 45, 88; DAM POET**
See also CA 13-16R; CANR 15, 51; DLB 5, 169; INT CANR-15; MTCW

Metcalf, John 1938- **CLC 37**
See also CA 113; DLB 60

Metcalf, Suzanne
See Baum, L(yman) Frank

Mew, Charlotte (Mary) 1870-1928 **TCLC 8**

See also CA 105; DLB 19, 135

Mewshaw, Michael 1943- **CLC 9**
See also CA 53-56; CANR 7, 47; DLBY 80

Meyer, June
See Jordan, June

Meyer, Lynn
See Slavitt, David R(ytman)

Meyer-Meyrink, Gustav 1868-1932
See Meyrink, Gustav
See also CA 117

Meyers, Jeffrey 1939- **CLC 39**
See also CA 73-76; CANR 54; DLB 111

Meynell, Alice (Christina Gertrude Thompson) 1847-1922 **TCLC 6**
See also CA 104; DLB 19, 98

Meyrink, Gustav **TCLC 21**
See also Meyer-Meyrink, Gustav
See also DLB 81

Michaels, Leonard 1933- **CLC 6, 25; SSC 16**
See also CA 61-64; CANR 21, 62; DLB 130; MTCW

Michaux, Henri 1899-1984 **CLC 8, 19**
See also CA 85-88; 114

Micheaux, Oscar 1884-1951 **TCLC 76**
See also DLB 50

Michelangelo 1475-1564 **LC 12**

Michelet, Jules 1798-1874 **NCLC 31**

Michener, James A(lbert) 1907(?)-1997 **CLC 1, 5, 11, 29, 60, 109; DAM NOV, POP**
See also AITN 1; BEST 90:1; CA 5-8R; 161; CANR 21, 45, 68; DLB 6; MTCW

Mickiewicz, Adam 1798-1855 **NCLC 3**

Middleton, Christopher 1926- **CLC 13**
See also CA 13-16R; CANR 29, 54; DLB 40

Middleton, Richard (Barham) 1882-1911 **TCLC 56**
See also DLB 156

Middleton, Stanley 1919- **CLC 7, 38**
See also CA 25-28R; CAAS 23; CANR 21, 46; DLB 14

Middleton, Thomas 1580-1627 **LC 33; DAM DRAM, MST; DC 5**
See also DLB 58

Migueis, Jose Rodrigues 1901- **CLC 10**

Mikszath, Kalman 1847-1910 **TCLC 31**

Miles, Jack **CLC 100**

Miles, Josephine (Louise) 1911-1985 **CLC 1, 2, 14, 34, 39; DAM POET**
See also CA 1-4R; 116; CANR 2, 55; DLB 48

Militant
See Sandburg, Carl (August)

Mill, John Stuart 1806-1873 **NCLC 11, 58**
See also CDBLB 1832-1890; DLB 55, 190

Millar, Kenneth 1915-1983 **CLC 14; DAM POP**
See also Macdonald, Ross
See also CA 9-12R; 110; CANR 16, 63; DLB 2; DLBD 6; DLBY 83; MTCW

Millay, E. Vincent
See Millay, Edna St. Vincent

Millay, Edna St. Vincent 1892-1950 **TCLC 4, 49; DA; DAB; DAC; DAM MST, POET; PC 6; WLCS**
See also CA 104; 130; CDALB 1917-1929; DLB 45; MTCW

Miller, Arthur 1915- **CLC 1, 2, 6, 10, 15, 26, 47, 78; DA; DAB; DAC; DAM DRAM, MST; DC 1; WLC**
See also AAYA 15; AITN 1; CA 1-4R; CABS 3; CANR 2, 30, 54; CDALB 1941-1968; DLB 7; MTCW

Miller, Henry (Valentine) 1891-1980 **CLC 1, 2, 4, 9, 14, 43, 84; DA; DAB; DAC; DAM**

MST, NOV; WLC
See also CA 9-12R; 97-100; CANR 33, 64;
CDALB 1929-1941; DLB 4, 9; DLBY 80;
MTCW

Miller, Jason 1939(?)-   **CLC 2**
See also AITN 1; CA 73-76; DLB 7

Miller, Sue 1943-   **CLC 44; DAM POP**
See also BEST 90:3; CA 139; CANR 59; DLB
143

Miller, Walter M(ichael, Jr.) 1923- **CLC 4, 30**
See also CA 85-88; DLB 8

Millett, Kate 1934-   **CLC 67**
See also AITN 1; CA 73-76; CANR 32, 53;
MTCW

Millhauser, Steven (Lewis) 1943- **CLC 21, 54,
109**
See also CA 110; 111; CANR 63; DLB 2; INT
111

Millin, Sarah Gertrude 1889-1968   **CLC 49**
See also CA 102; 93-96

Milne, A(lan) A(lexander) 1882-1956**TCLC 6;
DAB; DAC; DAM MST**
See also CA 104; 133; CLR 1, 26; DLB 10, 77,
100, 160; MAICYA; MTCW; YABC 1

Milner, Ron(ald) 1938-**CLC 56; BLC 3; DAM
MULT**
See also AITN 1; BW 1; CA 73-76; CANR 24;
DLB 38; MTCW

Milnes, Richard Monckton 1809-1885 **NCLC
61**
See also DLB 32, 184

Milosz, Czeslaw 1911- **CLC 5, 11, 22, 31, 56,
82; DAM MST, POET; PC 8; WLCS**
See also CA 81-84; CANR 23, 51; MTCW

Milton, John 1608-1674 **LC 9, 43; DA; DAB;
DAC; DAM MST, POET; PC 19; WLC**
See also CDBLB 1660-1789; DLB 131, 151

Min, Anchee 1957-   **CLC 86**
See also CA 146

Minehaha, Cornelius
See Wedekind, (Benjamin) Frank(lin)

Miner, Valerie 1947-   **CLC 40**
See also CA 97-100; CANR 59

Minimo, Duca
See D'Annunzio, Gabriele

Minot, Susan 1956-   **CLC 44**
See also CA 134

Minus, Ed 1938-   **CLC 39**

Miranda, Javier
See Bioy Casares, Adolfo

Mirbeau, Octave 1848-1917   **TCLC 55**
See also DLB 123, 192

Miro (Ferrer), Gabriel (Francisco Victor) 1879-
1930   **TCLC 5**
See also CA 104

Mishima, Yukio 1925-1970**CLC 2, 4, 6, 9, 27;
DC 1; SSC 4**
See also Hiraoka, Kimitake
See also DLB 182

Mistral, Frederic 1830-1914   **TCLC 51**
See also CA 122

Mistral, Gabriela   **TCLC 2; HLC**
See also Godoy Alcayaga, Lucila

Mistry, Rohinton 1952-   **CLC 71; DAC**
See also CA 141

Mitchell, Clyde
See Ellison, Harlan (Jay); Silverberg, Robert

Mitchell, James Leslie 1901-1935
See Gibbon, Lewis Grassic
See also CA 104; DLB 15

Mitchell, Joni 1943-   **CLC 12**
See also CA 112

Mitchell, Joseph (Quincy) 1908-1996 **CLC 98**

See also CA 77-80; 152; DLB 185; DLBY 96

Mitchell, Margaret (Munnerlyn) 1900-1949
TCLC 11; DAM NOV, POP
See also AAYA 23; CA 109; 125; CANR 55;
DLB 9; MTCW

Mitchell, Peggy
See Mitchell, Margaret (Munnerlyn)

Mitchell, S(ilas) Weir 1829-1914   **TCLC 36**
See also CA 165

Mitchell, W(illiam) O(rmond) 1914-1998**CLC
25; DAC; DAM MST**
See also CA 77-80; 165; CANR 15, 43; DLB
88

Mitford, Mary Russell 1787-1855   **NCLC 4**
See also DLB 110, 116

Mitford, Nancy 1904-1973   **CLC 44**
See also CA 9-12R; DLB 191

Miyamoto, Yuriko 1899-1951   **TCLC 37**
See also DLB 180

Miyazawa, Kenji 1896-1933   **TCLC 76**
See also CA 157

Mizoguchi, Kenji 1898-1956   **TCLC 72**

Mo, Timothy (Peter) 1950(?)-   **CLC 46**
See also CA 117; DLB 194; MTCW

Modarressi, Taghi (M.) 1931-   **CLC 44**
See also CA 121; 134; INT 134

Modiano, Patrick (Jean) 1945-   **CLC 18**
See also CA 85-88; CANR 17, 40; DLB 83

Moerck, Paal
See Roelvaag, O(le) E(dvart)

Mofolo, Thomas (Mokopu) 1875(?)-1948
TCLC 22; BLC 3; DAM MULT
See also CA 121; 153

Mohr, Nicholasa 1938-**CLC 12; DAM MULT;
HLC**
See also AAYA 8; CA 49-52; CANR 1, 32, 64;
CLR 22; DLB 145; HW; JRDA; SAAS 8;
SATA 8, 97

Mojtabai, A(nn) G(race) 1938- **CLC 5, 9, 15,
29**
See also CA 85-88

Moliere 1622-1673   **LC 28; DA; DAB; DAC;
DAM DRAM, MST; WLC**

Molin, Charles
See Mayne, William (James Carter)

Molnar, Ferenc 1878-1952   **TCLC 20; DAM
DRAM**
See also CA 109; 153

Momaday, N(avarre) Scott 1934- **CLC 2, 19,
85, 95; DA; DAB; DAC; DAM MST,
MULT, NOV, POP; WLCS**
See also AAYA 11; CA 25-28R; CANR 14, 34,
68; DLB 143, 175; INT CANR-14; MTCW;
NNAL; SATA 48; SATA-Brief 30

Monette, Paul 1945-1995   **CLC 82**
See also CA 139; 147

Monroe, Harriet 1860-1936   **TCLC 12**
See also CA 109; DLB 54, 91

Monroe, Lyle
See Heinlein, Robert A(nson)

Montagu, Elizabeth 1917-   **NCLC 7**
See also CA 9-12R

Montagu, Mary (Pierrepont) Wortley 1689-
1762   **LC 9; PC 16**
See also DLB 95, 101

Montagu, W. H.
See Coleridge, Samuel Taylor

Montague, John (Patrick) 1929- **CLC 13, 46**
See also CA 9-12R; CANR 9; DLB 40; MTCW

Montaigne, Michel (Eyquem) de 1533-1592
   LC 8; DA; DAB; DAC; DAM MST; WLC

Montale, Eugenio 1896-1981**CLC 7, 9, 18; PC
13**

See also CA 17-20R; 104; CANR 30; DLB 114;
MTCW

Montesquieu, Charles-Louis de Secondat 1689-
1755   **LC 7**

Montgomery, (Robert) Bruce 1921-1978
See Crispin, Edmund
See also CA 104

Montgomery, L(ucy) M(aud) 1874-1942
TCLC 51; DAC; DAM MST
See also AAYA 12; CA 108; 137; CLR 8; DLB
92; DLBD 14; JRDA; MAICYA; YABC 1

Montgomery, Marion H., Jr. 1925-   **CLC 7**
See also AITN 1; CA 1-4R; CANR 3, 48; DLB
6

Montgomery, Max
See Davenport, Guy (Mattison, Jr.)

Montherlant, Henry (Milon) de 1896-1972
CLC 8, 19; DAM DRAM
See also CA 85-88; 37-40R; DLB 72; MTCW

Monty Python
See Chapman, Graham; Cleese, John
(Marwood); Gilliam, Terry (Vance); Idle,
Eric; Jones, Terence Graham Parry; Palin,
Michael (Edward)
See also AAYA 7

Moodie, Susanna (Strickland) 1803-1885
NCLC 14
See also DLB 99

Mooney, Edward 1951-
See Mooney, Ted
See also CA 130

Mooney, Ted   **CLC 25**
See also Mooney, Edward

Moorcock, Michael (John) 1939-**CLC 5, 27, 58**
See also CA 45-48; CAAS 5; CANR 2, 17, 38,
64; DLB 14; MTCW; SATA 93

Moore, Brian 1921- **CLC 1, 3, 5, 7, 8, 19, 32,
90; DAB; DAC; DAM MST**
See also CA 1-4R; CANR 1, 25, 42, 63; MTCW

Moore, Edward
See Muir, Edwin

Moore, George Augustus 1852-1933 **TCLC 7;
SSC 19**
See also CA 104; DLB 10, 18, 57, 135

Moore, Lorrie   **CLC 39, 45, 68**
See also Moore, Marie Lorena

Moore, Marianne (Craig) 1887-1972**CLC 1, 2,
4, 8, 10, 13, 19, 47; DA; DAB; DAC; DAM
MST, POET; PC 4; WLCS**
See also CA 1-4R; 33-36R; CANR 3, 61;
CDALB 1929-1941; DLB 45; DLBD 7;
MTCW; SATA 20

Moore, Marie Lorena 1957-
See Moore, Lorrie
See also CA 116; CANR 39

Moore, Thomas 1779-1852   **NCLC 6**
See also DLB 96, 144

Morand, Paul 1888-1976   **CLC 41; SSC 22**
See also CA 69-72; DLB 65

Morante, Elsa 1918-1985   **CLC 8, 47**
See also CA 85-88; 117; CANR 35; DLB 177;
MTCW

Moravia, Alberto 1907-1990**CLC 2, 7, 11, 27,
46; SSC 26**
See also Pincherle, Alberto
See also DLB 177

More, Hannah 1745-1833   **NCLC 27**
See also DLB 107, 109, 116, 158

More, Henry 1614-1687   **LC 9**
See also DLB 126

More, Sir Thomas 1478-1535   **LC 10, 32**

Moreas, Jean   **TCLC 18**
See also Papadiamantopoulos, Johannes

Morgan, Berry 1919-　　　　CLC 6
　See also CA 49-52; DLB 6
Morgan, Claire
　See Highsmith, (Mary) Patricia
Morgan, Edwin (George) 1920-　　CLC 31
　See also CA 5-8R; CANR 3, 43; DLB 27
Morgan, (George) Frederick 1922-　CLC 23
　See also CA 17-20R; CANR 21
Morgan, Harriet
　See Mencken, H(enry) L(ouis)
Morgan, Jane
　See Cooper, James Fenimore
Morgan, Janet 1945-　　　　CLC 39
　See also CA 65-68
Morgan, Lady 1776(?)-1859　　NCLC 29
　See also DLB 116, 158
Morgan, Robin (Evonne) 1941-　　CLC 2
　See also CA 69-72; CANR 29, 68; MTCW;
　　SATA 80
Morgan, Scott
　See Kuttner, Henry
Morgan, Seth 1949(?)-1990　　CLC 65
　See also CA 132
Morgenstern, Christian 1871-1914　TCLC 8
　See also CA 105
Morgenstern, S.
　See Goldman, William (W.)
Moricz, Zsigmond 1879-1942　　TCLC 33
　See also CA 165
Morike, Eduard (Friedrich) 1804-1875NCLC
　10
　See also DLB 133
Moritz, Karl Philipp 1756-1793　　LC 2
　See also DLB 94
Morland, Peter Henry
　See Faust, Frederick (Schiller)
Morren, Theophil
　See Hofmannsthal, Hugo von
Morris, Bill 1952-　　　　CLC 76
Morris, Julian
　See West, Morris L(anglo)
Morris, Steveland Judkins 1950(?)-
　See Wonder, Stevie
　See also CA 111
Morris, William 1834-1896　　NCLC 4
　See also CDBLB 1832-1890; DLB 18, 35, 57,
　　156, 178, 184
Morris, Wright 1910-　　CLC 1, 3, 7, 18, 37
　See also CA 9-12R; CANR 21; DLB 2; DLBY
　　81; MTCW
Morrison, Arthur 1863-1945　　TCLC 72
　See also CA 120; 157; DLB 70, 135
Morrison, Chloe Anthony Wofford
　See Morrison, Toni
Morrison, James Douglas 1943-1971
　See Morrison, Jim
　See also CA 73-76; CANR 40
Morrison, Jim　　　　　　CLC 17
　See also Morrison, James Douglas
Morrison, Toni 1931-CLC 4, 10, 22, 55, 81, 87;
　　BLC 3; DA; DAB; DAC; DAM MST,
　　MULT, NOV, POP
　See also AAYA 1, 22; BW 2; CA 29-32R;
　　CANR 27, 42, 67; CDALB 1968-1988; DLB
　　6, 33, 143; DLBY 81; MTCW; SATA 57
Morrison, Van 1945-　　　　CLC 21
　See also CA 116
Morrissy, Mary 1958-　　　　CLC 99
Mortimer, John (Clifford) 1923- CLC 28, 43;
　　DAM DRAM, POP
　See also CA 13-16R; CANR 21; CDBLB 1960
　　to Present; DLB 13; INT CANR-21; MTCW
Mortimer, Penelope (Ruth) 1918-　　CLC 5

See also CA 57-60; CANR 45
Morton, Anthony
　See Creasey, John
Mosca, Gaetano 1858-1941　　TCLC 75
Mosher, Howard Frank 1943-　　CLC 62
　See also CA 139; CANR 65
Mosley, Nicholas 1923-　　　CLC 43, 70
　See also CA 69-72; CANR 41, 60; DLB 14
Mosley, Walter 1952- CLC 97; BLCS; DAM
　　MULT, POP
　See also AAYA 17; BW 2; CA 142; CANR 57
Moss, Howard 1922-1987 CLC 7, 14, 45, 50;
　　DAM POET
　See also CA 1-4R; 123; CANR 1, 44; DLB 5
Mossgiel, Rab
　See Burns, Robert
Motion, Andrew (Peter) 1952-　　CLC 47
　See also CA 146; DLB 40
Motley, Willard (Francis) 1909-1965 CLC 18
　See also BW 1; CA 117; 106; DLB 76, 143
Motoori, Norinaga 1730-1801　　NCLC 45
Mott, Michael (Charles Alston) 1930-CLC 15,
　34
　See also CA 5-8R; CAAS 7; CANR 7, 29
Mountain Wolf Woman 1884-1960　CLC 92
　See also CA 144; NNAL
Moure, Erin 1955-　　　　CLC 88
　See also CA 113; DLB 60
Mowat, Farley (McGill) 1921- CLC 26; DAC;
　　DAM MST
　See also AAYA 1; CA 1-4R; CANR 4, 24, 42,
　　68; CLR 20; DLB 68; INT CANAR-24;
　　JRDA; MAICYA; MTCW; SATA 3, 55
Moyers, Bill 1934-　　　　CLC 74
　See also AITN 2; CA 61-64; CANR 31, 52
Mphahlele, Es'kia
　See Mphahlele, Ezekiel
　See also DLB 125
Mphahlele, Ezekiel 1919-1983 CLC 25; BLC
　　3; DAM MULT
　See also Mphahlele, Es'kia
　See also BW 2; CA 81-84; CANR 26
Mqhayi, S(amuel) E(dward) K(rune Loliwe)
　1875-1945TCLC 25; BLC 3; DAM MULT
　See also CA 153
Mrozek, Slawomir 1930-　　　CLC 3, 13
　See also CA 13-16R; CAAS 10; CANR 29;
　　MTCW
Mrs. Belloc-Lowndes
　See Lowndes, Marie Adelaide (Belloc)
Mtwa, Percy (?)-　　　　　CLC 47
Mueller, Lisel 1924-　　　　CLC 13, 51
　See also CA 93-96; DLB 105
Muir, Edwin 1887-1959　　　TCLC 2
　See also CA 104; DLB 20, 100, 191
Muir, John 1838-1914　　　TCLC 28
　See also CA 165; DLB 186
Mujica Lainez, Manuel 1910-1984　CLC 31
　See also Lainez, Manuel Mujica
　See also CA 81-84; 112; CANR 32; HW
Mukherjee, Bharati 1940-CLC 53; DAM NOV
　See also BEST 89:2; CA 107; CANR 45; DLB
　　60; MTCW
Muldoon, Paul 1951-CLC 32, 72; DAM POET
　See also CA 113; 129; CANR 52; DLB 40; INT
　　129
Mulisch, Harry 1927-　　　　CLC 42
　See also CA 9-12R; CANR 6, 26, 56
Mull, Martin 1943-　　　　CLC 17
　See also CA 105
Mulock, Dinah Maria
　See Craik, Dinah Maria (Mulock)
Munford, Robert 1737(?)-1783　　LC 5

See also DLB 31
Mungo, Raymond 1946-　　　CLC 72
　See also CA 49-52; CANR 2
Munro, Alice 1931-　　CLC 6, 10, 19, 50, 95;
　　DAC; DAM MST, NOV; SSC 3; WLCS
　See also AITN 2; CA 33-36R; CANR 33, 53;
　　DLB 53; MTCW; SATA 29
Munro, H(ector) H(ugh) 1870-1916
　See Saki
　See also CA 104; 130; CDBLB 1890-1914; DA;
　　DAB; DAC; DAM MST, NOV; DLB 34,
　　162; MTCW; WLC
Murasaki, Lady　　　　　CMLC 1
Murdoch, (Jean) Iris 1919-CLC 1, 2, 3, 4, 6, 8,
　　11, 15, 22, 31, 51; DAB; DAC; DAM MST,
　　NOV
　See also CA 13-16R; CANR 8, 43, 68; CDBLB
　　1960 to Present; DLB 14, 194; INT CANR-
　　8; MTCW
Murfree, Mary Noailles 1850-1922　SSC 22
　See also CA 122; DLB 12, 74
Murnau, Friedrich Wilhelm
　See Plumpe, Friedrich Wilhelm
Murphy, Richard 1927-　　　CLC 41
　See also CA 29-32R; DLB 40
Murphy, Sylvia 1937-　　　CLC 34
　See also CA 121
Murphy, Thomas (Bernard) 1935-　CLC 51
　See also CA 101
Murray, Albert L. 1916-　　　CLC 73
　See also BW 2; CA 49-52; CANR 26, 52; DLB
　　38
Murray, Judith Sargent 1751-1820 NCLC 63
　See also DLB 37
Murray, Les(lie) A(llan) 1938-CLC 40; DAM
　　POET
　See also CA 21-24R; CANR 11, 27, 56
Murry, J. Middleton
　See Murry, John Middleton
Murry, John Middleton 1889-1957 TCLC 16
　See also CA 118; DLB 149
Musgrave, Susan 1951-　　　CLC 13, 54
　See also CA 69-72; CANR 45
Musil, Robert (Edler von) 1880-1942 TCLC
　　12, 68; SSC 18
　See also CA 109; CANR 55; DLB 81, 124
Muske, Carol 1945-　　　　CLC 90
　See also Muske-Dukes, Carol (Anne)
Muske-Dukes, Carol (Anne) 1945-
　See Muske, Carol
　See also CA 65-68; CANR 32
Musset, (Louis Charles) Alfred de 1810-1857
　NCLC 7
　See also DLB 192
My Brother's Brother
　See Chekhov, Anton (Pavlovich)
Myers, L(eopold) H(amilton) 1881-1944
　TCLC 59
　See also CA 157; DLB 15
Myers, Walter Dean 1937-　CLC 35; BLC 3;
　　DAM MULT, NOV
　See also AAYA 4, 23; BW 2; CA 33-36R;
　　CANR 20, 42, 67; CLR 4, 16, 35; DLB 33;
　　INT CANR-20; JRDA; MAICYA; SAAS 2;
　　SATA 41, 71; SATA-Brief 27
Myers, Walter M.
　See Myers, Walter Dean
Myles, Symon
　See Follett, Ken(neth Martin)
Nabokov, Vladimir (Vladimirovich) 1899-1977
　　CLC 1, 2, 3, 6, 8, 11, 15, 23, 44, 46, 64;
　　DA; DAB; DAC; DAM MST, NOV; SSC
　　11; WLC

See Shute, Nevil
See also CA 102; 93-96
Norwid, Cyprian Kamil 1821-1883 **NCLC 17**
Nosille, Nabrah
See Ellison, Harlan (Jay)
Nossack, Hans Erich 1901-1978 **CLC 6**
See also CA 93-96; 85-88; DLB 69
Nostradamus 1503-1566 **LC 27**
Nosu, Chuji
See Ozu, Yasujiro
Notenburg, Eleanora (Genrikhovna) von
See Guro, Elena
Nova, Craig 1945- **CLC 7, 31**
See also CA 45-48; CANR 2, 53
Novak, Joseph
See Kosinski, Jerzy (Nikodem)
Novalis 1772-1801 **NCLC 13**
See also DLB 90
Novis, Emile
See Weil, Simone (Adolphine)
Nowlan, Alden (Albert) 1933-1983 **CLC 15;**
DAC; DAM MST
See also CA 9-12R; CANR 5; DLB 53
Noyes, Alfred 1880-1958 **TCLC 7**
See also CA 104; DLB 20
Nunn, Kem **CLC 34**
See also CA 159
Nye, Robert 1939- **CLC 13, 42; DAM NOV**
See also CA 33-36R; CANR 29, 67; DLB 14;
MTCW; SATA 6
Nyro, Laura 1947- **CLC 17**
Oates, Joyce Carol 1938-CLC 1, 2, 3, 6, 9, 11,
15, 19, 33, 52, 108; DA; DAB; DAC; DAM
MST, NOV, POP; SSC 6; WLC
See also AAYA 15; AITN 1; BEST 89:2; CA
5-8R; CANR 25, 45; CDALB 1968-1988;
DLB 2, 5, 130; DLBY 81; INT CANR-25;
MTCW
O'Brien, Darcy 1939- **CLC 11**
See also CA 21-24R; CANR 8, 59
O'Brien, E. G.
See Clarke, Arthur C(harles)
O'Brien, Edna 1936- **CLC 3, 5, 8, 13, 36, 65;**
DAM NOV; SSC 10
See also CA 1-4R; CANR 6, 41, 65; CDBLB
1960 to Present; DLB 14; MTCW
O'Brien, Fitz-James 1828-1862 **NCLC 21**
See also DLB 74
O'Brien, Flann **CLC 1, 4, 5, 7, 10, 47**
See also O Nuallain, Brian
O'Brien, Richard 1942- **CLC 17**
See also CA 124
O'Brien, (William) Tim(othy) 1946- **CLC 7,**
19, 40, 103; DAM POP
See also AAYA 16; CA 85-88; CANR 40, 58;
DLB 152; DLBD 9; DLBY 80
Obstfelder, Sigbjoern 1866-1900 **TCLC 23**
See also CA 123
O'Casey, Sean 1880-1964 CLC 1, 5, 9, 11, 15,
88; DAB; DAC; DAM DRAM, MST;
WLCS
See also CA 89-92; CANR 62; CDBLB 1914-
1945; DLB 10; MTCW
O'Cathasaigh, Sean
See O'Casey, Sean
Ochs, Phil 1940-1976 **CLC 17**
See also CA 65-68
O'Connor, Edwin (Greene) 1918-1968CLC 14
See also CA 93-96; 25-28R
O'Connor, (Mary) Flannery 1925-1964 CLC
1, 2, 3, 6, 10, 13, 15, 21, 66, 104; DA; DAB;
DAC; DAM MST, NOV; SSC 1, 23; WLC
See also AAYA 7; CA 1-4R; CANR 3, 41;

CDALB 1941-1968; DLB 2, 152; DLBD 12;
DLBY 80; MTCW
O'Connor, Frank **CLC 23; SSC 5**
See also O'Donovan, Michael John
See also DLB 162
O'Dell, Scott 1898-1989 **CLC 30**
See also AAYA 3; CA 61-64; 129; CANR 12,
30; CLR 1, 16; DLB 52; JRDA; MAICYA;
SATA 12, 60
Odets, Clifford 1906-1963CLC 2, 28, 98; DAM
DRAM; DC 6
See also CA 85-88; CANR 62; DLB 7, 26;
MTCW
O'Doherty, Brian 1934- **CLC 76**
See also CA 105
O'Donnell, K. M.
See Malzberg, Barry N(athaniel)
O'Donnell, Lawrence
See Kuttner, Henry
O'Donovan, Michael John 1903-1966CLC 14
See also O'Connor, Frank
See also CA 93-96
Oe, Kenzaburo 1935- **CLC 10, 36, 86; DAM**
NOV; SSC 20
See also CA 97-100; CANR 36, 50; DLB 182;
DLBY 94; MTCW
O'Faolain, Julia 1932- **CLC 6, 19, 47, 108**
See also CA 81-84; CAAS 2; CANR 12, 61;
DLB 14; MTCW
O'Faolain, Sean 1900-1991 **CLC 1, 7, 14, 32,**
70; SSC 13
See also CA 61-64; 134; CANR 12, 66; DLB
15, 162; MTCW
O'Flaherty, Liam 1896-1984CLC 5, 34; SSC 6
See also CA 101; 113; CANR 35; DLB 36, 162;
DLBY 84; MTCW
Ogilvy, Gavin
See Barrie, J(ames) M(atthew)
O'Grady, Standish (James) 1846-1928 **TCLC**
5
See also CA 104; 157
O'Grady, Timothy 1951- **CLC 59**
See also CA 138
O'Hara, Frank 1926-1966 **CLC 2, 5, 13, 78;**
DAM POET
See also CA 9-12R; 25-28R; CANR 33; DLB
5, 16, 193; MTCW
O'Hara, John (Henry) 1905-1970CLC 1, 2, 3,
6, 11, 42; DAM NOV; SSC 15
See also CA 5-8R; 25-28R; CANR 31, 60;
CDALB 1929-1941; DLB 9, 86; DLBD 2;
MTCW
O Hehir, Diana 1922- **CLC 41**
See also CA 93-96
Okigbo, Christopher (Ifenayichukwu) 1932-
1967 **CLC 25, 84; BLC 3; DAM MULT,**
POET; PC 7
See also BW 1; CA 77-80; DLB 125; MTCW
Okri, Ben 1959- **CLC 87**
See also BW 2; CA 130; 138; CANR 65; DLB
157; INT 138
Olds, Sharon 1942- **CLC 32, 39, 85; DAM**
POET; PC 22
See also CA 101; CANR 18, 41, 66; DLB 120
Oldstyle, Jonathan
See Irving, Washington
Olesha, Yuri (Karlovich) 1899-1960 **CLC 8**
See also CA 85-88
Oliphant, Laurence 1829(?)-1888 **NCLC 47**
See also DLB 18, 166
Oliphant, Margaret (Oliphant Wilson) 1828-
1897 **NCLC 11, 61; SSC 25**
See also DLB 18, 159, 190

Oliver, Mary 1935- **CLC 19, 34, 98**
See also CA 21-24R; CANR 9, 43; DLB 5, 193
Olivier, Laurence (Kerr) 1907-1989 **CLC 20**
See also CA 111; 150; 129
Olsen, Tillie 1913-CLC 4, 13; DA; DAB; DAC;
DAM MST; SSC 11
See also CA 1-4R; CANR 1, 43; DLB 28;
DLBY 80; MTCW
Olson, Charles (John) 1910-1970 CLC 1, 2, 5,
6, 9, 11, 29; DAM POET; PC 19
See also CA 13-16; 25-28R; CABS 2; CANR
35, 61; CAP 1; DLB 5, 16, 193; MTCW
Olson, Toby 1937- **CLC 28**
See also CA 65-68; CANR 9, 31
Olyesha, Yuri
See Olesha, Yuri (Karlovich)
Ondaatje, (Philip) Michael 1943- CLC 14, 29,
51, 76; DAB; DAC; DAM MST
See also CA 77-80; CANR 42; DLB 60
Oneal, Elizabeth 1934-
See Oneal, Zibby
See also CA 106; CANR 28; MAICYA; SATA
30, 82
Oneal, Zibby **CLC 30**
See also Oneal, Elizabeth
See also AAYA 5; CLR 13; JRDA
O'Neill, Eugene (Gladstone) 1888-1953TCLC
1, 6, 27, 49; DA; DAB; DAC; DAM DRAM,
MST; WLC
See also AITN 1; CA 110; 132; CDALB 1929-
1941; DLB 7; MTCW
Onetti, Juan Carlos 1909-1994 **CLC 7, 10;**
DAM MULT, NOV; SSC 23
See also CA 85-88; 145; CANR 32, 63; DLB
113; HW; MTCW
O Nuallain, Brian 1911-1966
See O'Brien, Flann
See also CA 21-22; 25-28R; CAP 2
Ophuls, Max 1902-1957 **TCLC 79**
See also CA 113
Opie, Amelia 1769-1853 **NCLC 65**
See also DLB 116, 159
Oppen, George 1908-1984 **CLC 7, 13, 34**
See also CA 13-16R; 113; CANR 8; DLB 5,
165
Oppenheim, E(dward) Phillips 1866-1946
TCLC 45
See also CA 111; DLB 70
Opuls, Max
See Ophuls, Max
Origen c. 185-c. 254 **CMLC 19**
Orlovitz, Gil 1918-1973 **CLC 22**
See also CA 77-80; 45-48; DLB 2, 5
Orris
See Ingelow, Jean
Ortega y Gasset, Jose 1883-1955 **TCLC 9;**
DAM MULT; HLC
See also CA 106; 130; HW; MTCW
Ortese, Anna Maria 1914- **CLC 89**
See also DLB 177
Ortiz, Simon J(oseph) 1941- **CLC 45; DAM**
MULT, POET; PC 17
See also CA 134; DLB 120, 175; NNAL
Orton, Joe **CLC 4, 13, 43; DC 3**
See also Orton, John Kingsley
See also CDBLB 1960 to Present; DLB 13
Orton, John Kingsley 1933-1967
See Orton, Joe
See also CA 85-88; CANR 35, 66; DAM
DRAM; MTCW
Orwell, George **TCLC 2, 6, 15, 31, 51; DAB;**
WLC
See also Blair, Eric (Arthur)

Pavic, Milorad 1929- **CLC 60**
See also CA 136; DLB 181
Payne, Alan
See Jakes, John (William)
Paz, Gil
See Lugones, Leopoldo
Paz, Octavio 1914-1998**CLC 3, 4, 6, 10, 19, 51, 65; DA; DAB; DAC; DAM MST, MULT, POET; HLC; PC 1; WLC**
See also CA 73-76; 165; CANR 32, 65; DLBY 90; HW; MTCW
p'Bitek, Okot 1931-1982 **CLC 96; BLC 3; DAM MULT**
See also BW 2; CA 124; 107; DLB 125; MTCW
Peacock, Molly 1947- **CLC 60**
See also CA 103; CAAS 21; CANR 52; DLB 120
Peacock, Thomas Love 1785-1866 **NCLC 22**
See also DLB 96, 116
Peake, Mervyn 1911-1968 **CLC 7, 54**
See also CA 5-8R; 25-28R; CANR 3; DLB 15, 160; MTCW; SATA 23
Pearce, Philippa **CLC 21**
See also Christie, (Ann) Philippa
See also CLR 9; DLB 161; MAICYA; SATA 1, 67
Pearl, Eric
See Elman, Richard (Martin)
Pearson, T(homas) R(eid) 1956- **CLC 39**
See also CA 120; 130; INT 130
Peck, Dale 1967- **CLC 81**
See also CA 146
Peck, John 1941- **CLC 3**
See also CA 49-52; CANR 3
Peck, Richard (Wayne) 1934- **CLC 21**
See also AAYA 1, 24; CA 85-88; CANR 19, 38; CLR 15; INT CANR-19; JRDA; MAICYA; SAAS 2; SATA 18, 55, 97
Peck, Robert Newton 1928- **CLC 17; DA; DAC; DAM MST**
See also AAYA 3; CA 81-84; CANR 31, 63; CLR 45; JRDA; MAICYA; SAAS 1; SATA 21, 62
Peckinpah, (David) Sam(uel) 1925-1984 **CLC 20**
See also CA 109; 114
Pedersen, Knut 1859-1952
See Hamsun, Knut
See also CA 104; 119; CANR 63; MTCW
Peeslake, Gaffer
See Durrell, Lawrence (George)
Peguy, Charles Pierre 1873-1914 **TCLC 10**
See also CA 107
Pena, Ramon del Valle y
See Valle-Inclan, Ramon (Maria) del
Pendennis, Arthur Esquir
See Thackeray, William Makepeace
Penn, William 1644-1718 **LC 25**
See also DLB 24
PEPECE
See Prado (Calvo), Pedro
Pepys, Samuel 1633-1703 **LC 11; DA; DAB; DAC; DAM MST; WLC**
See also CDBLB 1660-1789; DLB 101
Percy, Walker 1916-1990**CLC 2, 3, 6, 8, 14, 18, 47, 65; DAM NOV, POP**
See also CA 1-4R; 131; CANR 1, 23, 64; DLB 2; DLBY 80, 90; MTCW
Perec, Georges 1936-1982 **CLC 56**
See also CA 141; DLB 83
Pereda (y Sanchez de Porrua), Jose Maria de 1833-1906 **TCLC 16**
See also CA 117

Pereda y Porrua, Jose Maria de
See Pereda (y Sanchez de Porrua), Jose Maria de
Peregoy, George Weems
See Mencken, H(enry) L(ouis)
Perelman, S(idney) J(oseph) 1904-1979 **CLC 3, 5, 9, 15, 23, 44, 49; DAM DRAM**
See also AITN 1, 2; CA 73-76; 89-92; CANR 18; DLB 11, 44; MTCW
Peret, Benjamin 1899-1959 **TCLC 20**
See also CA 117
Peretz, Isaac Loeb 1851(?)-1915 **TCLC 16; SSC 26**
See also CA 109
Peretz, Yitzhkok Leibush
See Peretz, Isaac Loeb
Perez Galdos, Benito 1843-1920 **TCLC 27**
See also CA 125; 153; HW
Perrault, Charles 1628-1703 **LC 2**
See also MAICYA; SATA 25
Perry, Brighton
See Sherwood, Robert E(mmet)
Perse, St.-John **CLC 4, 11, 46**
See also Leger, (Marie-Rene Auguste) Alexis Saint-Leger
Perutz, Leo 1882-1957 **TCLC 60**
See also DLB 81
Peseenz, Tulio F.
See Lopez y Fuentes, Gregorio
Pesetsky, Bette 1932- **CLC 28**
See also CA 133; DLB 130
Peshkov, Alexei Maximovich 1868-1936
See Gorky, Maxim
See also CA 105; 141; DA; DAC; DAM DRAM, MST, NOV
Pessoa, Fernando (Antonio Nogueira) 1898-1935 **TCLC 27; HLC; PC 20**
See also CA 125
Peterkin, Julia Mood 1880-1961 **CLC 31**
See also CA 102; DLB 9
Peters, Joan K(aren) 1945- **CLC 39**
See also CA 158
Peters, Robert L(ouis) 1924- **CLC 7**
See also CA 13-16R; CAAS 8; DLB 105
Petofi, Sandor 1823-1849 **NCLC 21**
Petrakis, Harry Mark 1923- **CLC 3**
See also CA 9-12R; CANR 4, 30
Petrarch 1304-1374 **CMLC 20; DAM POET; PC 8**
Petrov, Evgeny **TCLC 21**
See also Kataev, Evgeny Petrovich
Petry, Ann (Lane) 1908-1997 **CLC 1, 7, 18**
See also BW 1; CA 5-8R; 157; CAAS 6; CANR 4, 46; CLR 12; DLB 76; JRDA; MAICYA; MTCW; SATA 5; SATA-Obit 94
Petursson, Halligrimur 1614-1674 **LC 8**
Phaedrus 18(?)B.C.-55(?) **CMLC 25**
Philips, Katherine 1632-1664 **LC 30**
See also DLB 131
Philipson, Morris H. 1926- **CLC 53**
See also CA 1-4R; CANR 4
Phillips, Caryl 1958- **CLC 96; BLCS; DAM MULT**
See also BW 2; CA 141; CANR 63; DLB 157
Phillips, David Graham 1867-1911 **TCLC 44**
See also CA 108; DLB 9, 12
Phillips, Jack
See Sandburg, Carl (August)
Phillips, Jayne Anne 1952-**CLC 15, 33; SSC 16**
See also CA 101; CANR 24, 50; DLBY 80; INT CANR-24; MTCW
Phillips, Richard
See Dick, Philip K(indred)

Phillips, Robert (Schaeffer) 1938- **CLC 28**
See also CA 17-20R; CAAS 13; CANR 8; DLB 105
Phillips, Ward
See Lovecraft, H(oward) P(hillips)
Piccolo, Lucio 1901-1969 **CLC 13**
See also CA 97-100; DLB 114
Pickthall, Marjorie L(owry) C(hristie) 1883-1922 **TCLC 21**
See also CA 107; DLB 92
Pico della Mirandola, Giovanni 1463-1494**LC 15**
Piercy, Marge 1936- **CLC 3, 6, 14, 18, 27, 62**
See also CA 21-24R; CAAS 1; CANR 13, 43, 66; DLB 120; MTCW
Piers, Robert
See Anthony, Piers
Pieyre de Mandiargues, Andre 1909-1991
See Mandiargues, Andre Pieyre de
See also CA 103; 136; CANR 22
Pilnyak, Boris **TCLC 23**
See also Vogau, Boris Andreyevich
Pincherle, Alberto 1907-1990 **CLC 11, 18; DAM NOV**
See also Moravia, Alberto
See also CA 25-28R; 132; CANR 33, 63; MTCW
Pinckney, Darryl 1953- **CLC 76**
See also BW 2; CA 143
Pindar 518B.C.-446B.C. **CMLC 12; PC 19**
See also DLB 176
Pineda, Cecile 1942- **CLC 39**
See also CA 118
Pinero, Arthur Wing 1855-1934 **TCLC 32; DAM DRAM**
See also CA 110; 153; DLB 10
Pinero, Miguel (Antonio Gomez) 1946-1988 **CLC 4, 55**
See also CA 61-64; 125; CANR 29; HW
Pinget, Robert 1919-1997 **CLC 7, 13, 37**
See also CA 85-88; 160; DLB 83
Pink Floyd
See Barrett, (Roger) Syd; Gilmour, David; Mason, Nick; Waters, Roger; Wright, Rick
Pinkney, Edward 1802-1828 **NCLC 31**
Pinkwater, Daniel Manus 1941- **CLC 35**
See also Pinkwater, Manus
See also AAYA 1; CA 29-32R; CANR 12, 38; CLR 4; JRDA; MAICYA; SAAS 3; SATA 46, 76
Pinkwater, Manus
See Pinkwater, Daniel Manus
See also SATA 8
Pinsky, Robert 1940-**CLC 9, 19, 38, 94; DAM POET**
See also CA 29-32R; CAAS 4; CANR 58; DLBY 82
Pinta, Harold
See Pinter, Harold
Pinter, Harold 1930-**CLC 1, 3, 6, 9, 11, 15, 27, 58, 73; DA; DAB; DAC; DAM DRAM, MST; WLC**
See also CA 5-8R; CANR 33, 65; CDBLB 1960 to Present; DLB 13; MTCW
Piozzi, Hester Lynch (Thrale) 1741-1821 **NCLC 57**
See also DLB 104, 142
Pirandello, Luigi 1867-1936**TCLC 4, 29; DA; DAB; DAC; DAM DRAM, MST; DC 5; SSC 22; WLC**
See also CA 104; 153
Pirsig, Robert M(aynard) 1928-**CLC 4, 6, 73; DAM POP**

See also CA 53-56; CANR 42; MTCW; SATA 39

Pisarev, Dmitry Ivanovich 1840-1868 **NCLC 25**

Pix, Mary (Griffith) 1666-1709   **LC 8**
See also DLB 80

Pixerecourt, (Rene Charles) Guilbert de 1773-1844   **NCLC 39**
See also DLB 192

Plaatje, Sol(omon) T(shekisho) 1876-1932 **TCLC 73; BLCS**
See also BW 2; CA 141

Plaidy, Jean
See Hibbert, Eleanor Alice Burford

Planche, James Robinson 1796-1880 **NCLC 42**

Plant, Robert 1948-   **CLC 12**

Plante, David (Robert) 1940- **CLC 7, 23, 38; DAM NOV**
See also CA 37-40R; CANR 12, 36, 58; DLBY 83; INT CANR-12; MTCW

Plath, Sylvia 1932-1963 **CLC 1, 2, 3, 5, 9, 11, 14, 17, 50, 51, 62; DA; DAB; DAC; DAM MST, POET; PC 1; WLC**
See also AAYA 13; CA 19-20; CANR 34; CAP 2; CDALB 1941-1968; DLB 5, 6, 152; MTCW; SATA 96

Plato 428(?)B.C.-348(?)B.C.   **CMLC 8; DA; DAB; DAC; DAM MST; WLCS**
See also DLB 176

Platonov, Andrei   **TCLC 14**
See also Klimentov, Andrei Platonovich

Platt, Kin 1911-   **CLC 26**
See also AAYA 11; CA 17-20R; CANR 11; JRDA; SAAS 17; SATA 21, 86

Plautus c. 251B.C.-184B.C. **CMLC 24; DC 6**

Plick et Plock
See Simenon, Georges (Jacques Christian)

Plimpton, George (Ames) 1927-   **CLC 36**
See also AITN 1; CA 21-24R; CANR 32; DLB 185; MTCW; SATA 10

Pliny the Elder c. 23-79   **CMLC 23**

Plomer, William Charles Franklin 1903-1973 **CLC 4, 8**
See also CA 21-22; CANR 34; CAP 2; DLB 20, 162, 191; MTCW; SATA 24

Plowman, Piers
See Kavanagh, Patrick (Joseph)

Plum, J.
See Wodehouse, P(elham) G(renville)

Plumly, Stanley (Ross) 1939-   **CLC 33**
See also CA 108; 110; DLB 5, 193; INT 110

Plumpe, Friedrich Wilhelm 1888-1931 **TCLC 53**
See also CA 112

Po Chu-i 772-846   **CMLC 24**

Poe, Edgar Allan 1809-1849 **NCLC 1, 16, 55; DA; DAB; DAC; DAM MST, POET; PC 1; SSC 1, 22; WLC**
See also AAYA 14; CDALB 1640-1865; DLB 3, 59, 73, 74; SATA 23

Poet of Titchfield Street, The
See Pound, Ezra (Weston Loomis)

Pohl, Frederik 1919-   **CLC 18; SSC 25**
See also AAYA 24; CA 61-64; CAAS 1; CANR 11, 37; DLB 8; INT CANR-11; MTCW; SATA 24

Poirier, Louis 1910-
See Gracq, Julien
See also CA 122; 126

Poitier, Sidney 1927-   **CLC 26**
See also BW 1; CA 117

Polanski, Roman 1933-   **CLC 16**
See also CA 77-80

Poliakoff, Stephen 1952-   **CLC 38**
See also CA 106; DLB 13

Police, The
See Copeland, Stewart (Armstrong); Summers, Andrew James; Sumner, Gordon Matthew

Polidori, John William 1795-1821 **NCLC 51**
See also DLB 116

Pollitt, Katha 1949-   **CLC 28**
See also CA 120; 122; CANR 66; MTCW

Pollock, (Mary) Sharon 1936- **CLC 50; DAC; DAM DRAM, MST**
See also CA 141; DLB 60

Polo, Marco 1254-1324   **CMLC 15**

Polonsky, Abraham (Lincoln) 1910- **CLC 92**
See also CA 104; DLB 26; INT 104

Polybius c. 200B.C.-c. 118B.C.   **CMLC 17**
See also DLB 176

Pomerance, Bernard 1940-   **CLC 13; DAM DRAM**
See also CA 101; CANR 49

Ponge, Francis (Jean Gaston Alfred) 1899-1988 **CLC 6, 18; DAM POET**
See also CA 85-88; 126; CANR 40

Pontoppidan, Henrik 1857-1943   **TCLC 29**

Poole, Josephine   **CLC 17**
See Helyar, Jane Penelope Josephine
See also SAAS 2; SATA 5

Popa, Vasko 1922-1991   **CLC 19**
See also CA 112; 148; DLB 181

Pope, Alexander 1688-1744 **LC 3; DA; DAB; DAC; DAM MST, POET; WLC**
See also CDBLB 1660-1789; DLB 95, 101

Porter, Connie (Rose) 1959(?)-   **CLC 70**
See also BW 2; CA 142; SATA 81

Porter, Gene(va Grace) Stratton 1863(?)-1924 **TCLC 21**
See also CA 112

Porter, Katherine Anne 1890-1980 **CLC 1, 3, 7, 10, 13, 15, 27, 101; DA; DAB; DAC; DAM MST, NOV; SSC 4**
See also AITN 2; CA 1-4R; 101; CANR 1, 65; DLB 4, 9, 102; DLBD 12; DLBY 80; MTCW; SATA 39; SATA-Obit 23

Porter, Peter (Neville Frederick) 1929- **CLC 5, 13, 33**
See also CA 85-88; DLB 40

Porter, William Sydney 1862-1910
See Henry, O.
See also CA 104; 131; CDALB 1865-1917; DA; DAB; DAC; DAM MST; DLB 12, 78, 79; MTCW; YABC 2

Portillo (y Pacheco), Jose Lopez
See Lopez Portillo (y Pacheco), Jose

Post, Melville Davisson 1869-1930 **TCLC 39**
See also CA 110

Potok, Chaim 1929- **CLC 2, 7, 14, 26; DAM NOV**
See also AAYA 15; AITN 1, 2; CA 17-20R; CANR 19, 35, 64; DLB 28, 152; INT CANR-19; MTCW; SATA 33

Potter, (Helen) Beatrix 1866-1943
See Webb, (Martha) Beatrice (Potter)
See also MAICYA

Potter, Dennis (Christopher George) 1935-1994 **CLC 58, 86**
See also CA 107; 145; CANR 33, 61; MTCW

Pound, Ezra (Weston Loomis) 1885-1972 **CLC 1, 2, 3, 4, 5, 7, 10, 13, 18, 34, 48, 50; DA; DAB; DAC; DAM MST, POET; PC 4; WLC**
See also CA 5-8R; 37-40R; CANR 40; CDALB 1917-1929; DLB 4, 45, 63; DLBD 15; MTCW

Povod, Reinaldo 1959-1994   **CLC 44**
See also CA 136; 146

Powell, Adam Clayton, Jr. 1908-1972 **CLC 89; BLC 3; DAM MULT**
See also BW 1; CA 102; 33-36R

Powell, Anthony (Dymoke) 1905- **CLC 1, 3, 7, 9, 10, 31**
See also CA 1-4R; CANR 1, 32, 62; CDBLB 1945-1960; DLB 15; MTCW

Powell, Dawn 1897-1965   **CLC 66**
See also CA 5-8R; DLBY 97

Powell, Padgett 1952-   **CLC 34**
See also CA 126; CANR 63

Power, Susan 1961-   **CLC 91**

Powers, J(ames) F(arl) 1917- **CLC 1, 4, 8, 57; SSC 4**
See also CA 1-4R; CANR 2, 61; DLB 130; MTCW

Powers, John J(ames) 1945-
See Powers, John R.
See also CA 69-72

Powers, John R.   **CLC 66**
See also Powers, John J(ames)

Powers, Richard (S.) 1957-   **CLC 93**
See also CA 148

Pownall, David 1938-   **CLC 10**
See also CA 89-92; CAAS 18; CANR 49; DLB 14

Powys, John Cowper 1872-1963 **CLC 7, 9, 15, 46**
See also CA 85-88; DLB 15; MTCW

Powys, T(heodore) F(rancis) 1875-1953 **TCLC 9**
See also CA 106; DLB 36, 162

Prado (Calvo), Pedro 1886-1952   **TCLC 75**
See also CA 131; HW

Prager, Emily 1952-   **CLC 56**

Pratt, E(dwin) J(ohn) 1883(?)-1964 **CLC 19; DAC; DAM POET**
See also CA 141; 93-96; DLB 92

Premchand   **TCLC 21**
See also Srivastava, Dhanpat Rai

Preussler, Otfried 1923-   **CLC 17**
See also CA 77-80; SATA 24

Prevert, Jacques (Henri Marie) 1900-1977 **CLC 15**
See also CA 77-80; 69-72; CANR 29, 61; MTCW; SATA-Obit 30

Prevost, Abbe (Antoine Francois) 1697-1763 **LC 1**

Price, (Edward) Reynolds 1933- **CLC 3, 6, 13, 43, 50, 63; DAM NOV; SSC 22**
See also CA 1-4R; CANR 1, 37, 57; DLB 2; INT CANR-37

Price, Richard 1949-   **CLC 6, 12**
See also CA 49-52; CANR 3; DLBY 81

Prichard, Katharine Susannah 1883-1969 **CLC 46**
See also CA 11-12; CANR 33; CAP 1; MTCW; SATA 66

Priestley, J(ohn) B(oynton) 1894-1984 **CLC 2, 5, 9, 34; DAM DRAM, NOV**
See also CA 9-12R; 113; CANR 33; CDBLB 1914-1945; DLB 10, 34, 77, 100, 139; DLBY 84; MTCW

Prince 1958(?)-   **CLC 35**

Prince, F(rank) T(empleton) 1912- **CLC 22**
See also CA 101; CANR 43; DLB 20

Prince Kropotkin
See Kropotkin, Peter (Alekseievich)

Prior, Matthew 1664-1721   **LC 4**
See also DLB 95

Prishvin, Mikhail 1873-1954   **TCLC 75**

Pritchard, William H(arrison) 1932- **CLC 34**
See also CA 65-68; CANR 23; DLB 111
Pritchett, V(ictor) S(awdon) 1900-1997 **CLC
5, 13, 15, 41; DAM NOV; SSC 14**
See also CA 61-64; 157; CANR 31, 63; DLB
15, 139; MTCW
Private 19022
See Manning, Frederic
Probst, Mark 1925- **CLC 59**
See also CA 130
Prokosch, Frederic 1908-1989 **CLC 4, 48**
See also CA 73-76; 128; DLB 48
Prophet, The
See Dreiser, Theodore (Herman Albert)
Prose, Francine 1947- **CLC 45**
See also CA 109; 112; CANR 46
Proudhon
See Cunha, Euclides (Rodrigues Pimenta) da
Proulx, Annie
See Proulx, E(dna) Annie
Proulx, E(dna) Annie 1935- **CLC 81; DAM
POP**
See also CA 145; CANR 65
**Proust, (Valentin-Louis-George-Eugene-)
Marcel** 1871-1922 **TCLC 7, 13, 33; DA;
DAB; DAC; DAM MST, NOV; WLC**
See also CA 104; 120; DLB 65; MTCW
Prowler, Harley
See Masters, Edgar Lee
Prus, Boleslaw 1845-1912 **TCLC 48**
Pryor, Richard (Franklin Lenox Thomas)
1940- **CLC 26**
See also CA 122
Przybyszewski, Stanislaw 1868-1927**TCLC 36**
See also CA 160; DLB 66
Pteleon
See Grieve, C(hristopher) M(urray)
See also DAM POET
Puckett, Lute
See Masters, Edgar Lee
Puig, Manuel 1932-1990 **CLC 3, 5, 10, 28, 65;
DAM MULT; HLC**
See also CA 45-48; CANR 2, 32, 63; DLB 113;
HW; MTCW
Pulitzer, Joseph 1847-1911 **TCLC 76**
See also CA 114; DLB 23
Purdy, Al(fred Wellington) 1918- **CLC 3, 6,
14, 50; DAC; DAM MST, POET**
See also CA 81-84; CAAS 17; CANR 42, 66;
DLB 88
Purdy, James (Amos) 1923- **CLC 2, 4, 10, 28,
52**
See also CA 33-36R; CAAS 1; CANR 19, 51;
DLB 2; INT CANR-19; MTCW
Pure, Simon
See Swinnerton, Frank Arthur
Pushkin, Alexander (Sergeyevich) 1799-1837
**NCLC 3, 27; DA; DAB; DAC; DAM
DRAM, MST, POET; PC 10; SSC 27;
WLC**
See also SATA 61
P'u Sung-ling 1640-1715 **LC 3**
Putnam, Arthur Lee
See Alger, Horatio, Jr.
Puzo, Mario 1920-**CLC 1, 2, 6, 36, 107; DAM
NOV, POP**
See also CA 65-68; CANR 4, 42, 65; DLB 6;
MTCW
Pygge, Edward
See Barnes, Julian (Patrick)
Pyle, Ernest Taylor 1900-1945
See Pyle, Ernie
See also CA 115; 160

Pyle, Ernie 1900-1945 **TCLC 75**
See also Pyle, Ernest Taylor
See also DLB 29
Pym, Barbara (Mary Crampton) 1913-1980
CLC 13, 19, 37
See also CA 13-14; 97-100; CANR 13, 34; CAP
1; DLB 14; DLBY 87; MTCW
Pynchon, Thomas (Ruggles, Jr.) 1937-**CLC 2,
3, 6, 9, 11, 18, 33, 62, 72; DA; DAB; DAC;
DAM MST, NOV, POP; SSC 14; WLC**
See also BEST 90:2; CA 17-20R; CANR 22,
46; DLB 2, 173; MTCW
Pythagoras c. 570B.C.-c. 500B.C. **CMLC 22**
See also DLB 176
Qian Zhongshu
See Ch'ien Chung-shu
Qroll
See Dagerman, Stig (Halvard)
Quarrington, Paul (Lewis) 1953- **CLC 65**
See also CA 129; CANR 62
Quasimodo, Salvatore 1901-1968 **CLC 10**
See also CA 13-16; 25-28R; CAP 1; DLB 114;
MTCW
Quay, Stephen 1947- **CLC 95**
Quay, Timothy 1947- **CLC 95**
Queen, Ellery **CLC 3, 11**
See also Dannay, Frederic; Davidson, Avram;
Lee, Manfred B(ennington); Marlowe,
Stephen; Sturgeon, Theodore (Hamilton);
Vance, John Holbrook
Queen, Ellery, Jr.
See Dannay, Frederic; Lee, Manfred
B(ennington)
Queneau, Raymond 1903-1976 **CLC 2, 5, 10,
42**
See also CA 77-80; 69-72; CANR 32; DLB 72;
MTCW
Quevedo, Francisco de 1580-1645 **LC 23**
Quiller-Couch, SirArthur Thomas 1863-1944
TCLC 53
See also CA 118; DLB 135, 153, 190
Quin, Ann (Marie) 1936-1973 **CLC 6**
See also CA 9-12R; 45-48; DLB 14
Quinn, Martin
See Smith, Martin Cruz
Quinn, Peter 1947- **CLC 91**
Quinn, Simon
See Smith, Martin Cruz
Quiroga, Horacio (Sylvestre) 1878-1937
TCLC 20; DAM MULT; HLC
See also CA 117; 131; HW; MTCW
Quoirez, Francoise 1935- **CLC 9**
See also Sagan, Francoise
See also CA 49-52; CANR 6, 39; MTCW
Raabe, Wilhelm 1831-1910 **TCLC 45**
See also DLB 129
Rabe, David (William) 1940- **CLC 4, 8, 33;
DAM DRAM**
See also CA 85-88; CABS 3; CANR 59; DLB
7
Rabelais, Francois 1483-1553**LC 5; DA; DAB;
DAC; DAM MST; WLC**
Rabinovitch, Sholem 1859-1916
See Aleichem, Sholom
See also CA 104
Rachilde 1860-1953 **TCLC 67**
See also DLB 123, 192
Racine, Jean 1639-1699 **LC 28; DAB; DAM
MST**
Radcliffe, Ann (Ward) 1764-1823**NCLC 6, 55**
See also DLB 39, 178
Radiguet, Raymond 1903-1923 **TCLC 29**
See also CA 162; DLB 65

Radnoti, Miklos 1909-1944 **TCLC 16**
See also CA 118
Rado, James 1939- **CLC 17**
See also CA 105
Radvanyi, Netty 1900-1983
See Seghers, Anna
See also CA 85-88; 110
Rae, Ben
See Griffiths, Trevor
Raeburn, John (Hay) 1941- **CLC 34**
See also CA 57-60
Ragni, Gerome 1942-1991 **CLC 17**
See also CA 105; 134
Rahv, Philip 1908-1973 **CLC 24**
See also Greenberg, Ivan
See also DLB 137
Raimund, Ferdinand Jakob 1790-1836**NCLC
69**
See also DLB 90
Raine, Craig 1944- **CLC 32, 103**
See also CA 108; CANR 29, 51; DLB 40
Raine, Kathleen (Jessie) 1908- **CLC 7, 45**
See also CA 85-88; CANR 46; DLB 20; MTCW
Rainis, Janis 1865-1929 **TCLC 29**
Rakosi, Carl 1903- **CLC 47**
See also Rawley, Callman
See also CAAS 5; DLB 193
Raleigh, Richard
See Lovecraft, H(oward) P(hillips)
Raleigh, Sir Walter 1554(?)-1618 **LC 31, 39**
See also CDBLB Before 1660; DLB 172
Rallentando, H. P.
See Sayers, Dorothy L(eigh)
Ramal, Walter
See de la Mare, Walter (John)
Ramon, Juan
See Jimenez (Mantecon), Juan Ramon
Ramos, Graciliano 1892-1953 **TCLC 32**
Rampersad, Arnold 1941- **CLC 44**
See also BW 2; CA 127; 133; DLB 111; INT
133
Rampling, Anne
See Rice, Anne
Ramsay, Allan 1684(?)-1758 **LC 29**
See also DLB 95
Ramuz, Charles-Ferdinand 1878-1947 **TCLC
33**
See also CA 165
Rand, Ayn 1905-1982 **CLC 3, 30, 44, 79; DA;
DAC; DAM MST, NOV, POP; WLC**
See also AAYA 10; CA 13-16R; 105; CANR
27; MTCW
Randall, Dudley (Felker) 1914-**CLC 1; BLC 3;
DAM MULT**
See also BW 1; CA 25-28R; CANR 23; DLB
41
Randall, Robert
See Silverberg, Robert
Ranger, Ken
See Creasey, John
Ransom, John Crowe 1888-1974 **CLC 2, 4, 5,
11, 24; DAM POET**
See also CA 5-8R; 49-52; CANR 6, 34; DLB
45, 63; MTCW
Rao, Raja 1909- **CLC 25, 56; DAM NOV**
See also CA 73-76; CANR 51; MTCW
Raphael, Frederic (Michael) 1931- **CLC 2, 14**
See also CA 1-4R; CANR 1; DLB 14
Ratcliffe, James P.
See Mencken, H(enry) L(ouis)
Rathbone, Julian 1935- **CLC 41**
See also CA 101; CANR 34
Rattigan, Terence (Mervyn) 1911-1977 **CLC**

7; DAM DRAM
See also CA 85-88; 73-76; CDBLB 1945-1960; DLB 13; MTCW
Ratushinskaya, Irina 1954-   **CLC 54**
See also CA 129; CANR 68
Raven, Simon (Arthur Noel) 1927-   **CLC 14**
See also CA 81-84
Ravenna, Michael
See Welty, Eudora
Rawley, Callman 1903-
See Rakosi, Carl
See also CA 21-24R; CANR 12, 32
Rawlings, Marjorie Kinnan 1896-1953 **TCLC 4**
See also AAYA 20; CA 104; 137; DLB 9, 22, 102; JRDA; MAICYA; YABC 1
Ray, Satyajit 1921-1992   **CLC 16, 76; DAM MULT**
See also CA 114; 137
Read, Herbert Edward 1893-1968   **CLC 4**
See also CA 85-88; 25-28R; DLB 20, 149
Read, Piers Paul 1941-   **CLC 4, 10, 25**
See also CA 21-24R; CANR 38; DLB 14; SATA 21
Reade, Charles 1814-1884   **NCLC 2**
See also DLB 21
Reade, Hamish
See Gray, Simon (James Holliday)
Reading, Peter 1946-   **CLC 47**
See also CA 103; CANR 46; DLB 40
Reaney, James 1926-   **CLC 13; DAC; DAM MST**
See also CA 41-44R; CAAS 15; CANR 42; DLB 68; SATA 43
Rebreanu, Liviu 1885-1944   **TCLC 28**
See also CA 165
Rechy, John (Francisco) 1934- **CLC 1, 7, 14, 18, 107; DAM MULT; HLC**
See also CA 5-8R; CAAS 4; CANR 6, 32, 64; DLB 122; DLBY 82; HW; INT CANR-6
Redcam, Tom 1870-1933   **TCLC 25**
Reddin, Keith   **CLC 67**
Redgrove, Peter (William) 1932- **CLC 6, 41**
See also CA 1-4R; CANR 3, 39; DLB 40
Redmon, Anne   **CLC 22**
See also Nightingale, Anne Redmon
See also DLBY 86
Reed, Eliot
See Ambler, Eric
Reed, Ishmael 1938-**CLC 2, 3, 5, 6, 13, 32, 60; BLC 3; DAM MULT**
See also BW 2; CA 21-24R; CANR 25, 48; DLB 2, 5, 33, 169; DLBD 8; MTCW
Reed, John (Silas) 1887-1920   **TCLC 9**
See also CA 106
Reed, Lou   **CLC 21**
See also Firbank, Louis
Reeve, Clara 1729-1807   **NCLC 19**
See also DLB 39
Reich, Wilhelm 1897-1957   **TCLC 57**
Reid, Christopher (John) 1949-   **CLC 33**
See also CA 140; DLB 40
Reid, Desmond
See Moorcock, Michael (John)
Reid Banks, Lynne 1929-
See Banks, Lynne Reid
See also CA 1-4R; CANR 6, 22, 38; CLR 24; JRDA; MAICYA; SATA 22, 75
Reilly, William K.
See Creasey, John
Reiner, Max
See Caldwell, (Janet Miriam) Taylor (Holland)
Reis, Ricardo

See Pessoa, Fernando (Antonio Nogueira)
Remarque, Erich Maria 1898-1970 **CLC 21; DA; DAB; DAC; DAM MST, NOV**
See also CA 77-80; 29-32R; DLB 56; MTCW
Remizov, A.
See Remizov, Aleksei (Mikhailovich)
Remizov, A. M.
See Remizov, Aleksei (Mikhailovich)
Remizov, Aleksei (Mikhailovich) 1877-1957 **TCLC 27**
See also CA 125; 133
Renan, Joseph Ernest 1823-1892   **NCLC 26**
Renard, Jules 1864-1910   **TCLC 17**
See also CA 117
Renault, Mary   **CLC 3, 11, 17**
See also Challans, Mary
See also DLBY 83
Rendell, Ruth (Barbara) 1930- **CLC 28, 48; DAM POP**
See also Vine, Barbara
See also CA 109; CANR 32, 52; DLB 87; INT CANR-32; MTCW
Renoir, Jean 1894-1979   **CLC 20**
See also CA 129; 85-88
Resnais, Alain 1922-   **CLC 16**
Reverdy, Pierre 1889-1960   **CLC 53**
See also CA 97-100; 89-92
Rexroth, Kenneth 1905-1982 **CLC 1, 2, 6, 11, 22, 49; DAM POET; PC 20**
See also CA 5-8R; 107; CANR 14, 34, 63; CDALB 1941-1968; DLB 16, 48, 165; DLBY 82; INT CANR-14; MTCW
Reyes, Alfonso 1889-1959   **TCLC 33**
See also CA 131; HW
Reyes y Basoalto, Ricardo Eliecer Neftali
See Neruda, Pablo
Reymont, Wladyslaw (Stanislaw) 1868(?)-1925 **TCLC 5**
See also CA 104
Reynolds, Jonathan 1942-   **CLC 6, 38**
See also CA 65-68; CANR 28
Reynolds, Joshua 1723-1792   **LC 15**
See also DLB 104
Reynolds, Michael Shane 1937-   **CLC 44**
See also CA 65-68; CANR 9
Reznikoff, Charles 1894-1976   **CLC 9**
See also CA 33-36; 61-64; CAP 2; DLB 28, 45
Rezzori (d'Arezzo), Gregor von 1914-**CLC 25**
See also CA 122; 136
Rhine, Richard
See Silverstein, Alvin
Rhodes, Eugene Manlove 1869-1934**TCLC 53**
R'hoone
See Balzac, Honore de
Rhys, Jean 1890(?)-1979 **CLC 2, 4, 6, 14, 19, 51; DAM NOV; SSC 21**
See also CA 25-28R; 85-88; CANR 35, 62; CDBLB 1945-1960; DLB 36, 117, 162; MTCW
Ribeiro, Darcy 1922-1997   **CLC 34**
See also CA 33-36R; 156
Ribeiro, Joao Ubaldo (Osorio Pimentel) 1941- **CLC 10, 67**
See also CA 81-84
Ribman, Ronald (Burt) 1932-   **CLC 7**
See also CA 21-24R; CANR 46
Ricci, Nino 1959-   **CLC 70**
See also CA 137
Rice, Anne 1941-   **CLC 41; DAM POP**
See also AAYA 9; BEST 89:2; CA 65-68; CANR 12, 36, 53
Rice, Elmer (Leopold) 1892-1967 **CLC 7, 49; DAM DRAM**

See also CA 21-22; 25-28R; CAP 2; DLB 4, 7; MTCW
Rice, Tim(othy Miles Bindon) 1944- **CLC 21**
See also CA 103; CANR 46
Rich, Adrienne (Cecile) 1929-**CLC 3, 6, 7, 11, 18, 36, 73, 76; DAM POET; PC 5**
See also CA 9-12R; CANR 20, 53; DLB 5, 67; MTCW
Rich, Barbara
See Graves, Robert (von Ranke)
Rich, Robert
See Trumbo, Dalton
Richard, Keith   **CLC 17**
See also Richards, Keith
Richards, David Adams 1950- **CLC 59; DAC**
See also CA 93-96; CANR 60; DLB 53
Richards, I(vor) A(rmstrong) 1893-1979 **CLC 14, 24**
See also CA 41-44R; 89-92; CANR 34; DLB 27
Richards, Keith 1943-
See Richard, Keith
See also CA 107
Richardson, Anne
See Roiphe, Anne (Richardson)
Richardson, Dorothy Miller 1873-1957**TCLC 3**
See also CA 104; DLB 36
Richardson, Ethel Florence (Lindesay) 1870-1946
See Richardson, Henry Handel
See also CA 105
Richardson, Henry Handel   **TCLC 4**
See also Richardson, Ethel Florence (Lindesay)
Richardson, John 1796-1852 **NCLC 55; DAC**
See also DLB 99
Richardson, Samuel 1689-1761   **LC 1; DA; DAB; DAC; DAM MST, NOV; WLC**
See also CDBLB 1660-1789; DLB 39
Richler, Mordecai 1931-**CLC 3, 5, 9, 13, 18, 46, 70; DAC; DAM MST, NOV**
See also AITN 1; CA 65-68; CANR 31, 62; CLR 17; DLB 53; MAICYA; MTCW; SATA 44, 98; SATA-Brief 27
Richter, Conrad (Michael) 1890-1968**CLC 30**
See also AAYA 21; CA 5-8R; 25-28R; CANR 23; DLB 9; MTCW; SATA 3
Ricostranza, Tom
See Ellis, Trey
Riddell, Charlotte 1832-1906   **TCLC 40**
See also CA 165; DLB 156
Riding, Laura   **CLC 3, 7**
See also Jackson, Laura (Riding)
Riefenstahl, Berta Helene Amalia 1902-
See Riefenstahl, Leni
See also CA 108
Riefenstahl, Leni   **CLC 16**
See also Riefenstahl, Berta Helene Amalia
Riffe, Ernest
See Bergman, (Ernst) Ingmar
Riggs, (Rolla) Lynn 1899-1954   **TCLC 56; DAM MULT**
See also CA 144; DLB 175; NNAL
Riis, Jacob A(ugust) 1849-1914   **TCLC 80**
See also CA 113; DLB 23
Riley, James Whitcomb 1849-1916 **TCLC 51; DAM POET**
See also CA 118; 137; MAICYA; SATA 17
Riley, Tex
See Creasey, John
Rilke, Rainer Maria 1875-1926**TCLC 1, 6, 19; DAM POET; PC 2**
See also CA 104; 132; CANR 62; DLB 81;

110, 116, 159, 178; SATA 29

Shelley, Percy Bysshe 1792-1822 **NCLC 18; DA; DAB; DAC; DAM MST, POET; PC 14; WLC**
See also CDBLB 1789-1832; DLB 96, 110, 158

Shepard, Jim 1956- **CLC 36**
See also CA 137; CANR 59; SATA 90

Shepard, Lucius 1947- **CLC 34**
See also CA 128; 141

Shepard, Sam 1943- CLC 4, 6, 17, 34, 41, 44; **DAM DRAM; DC 5**
See also AAYA 1; CA 69-72; CABS 3; CANR 22; DLB 7; MTCW

Shepherd, Michael
See Ludlum, Robert

Sherburne, Zoa (Morin) 1912- **CLC 30**
See also AAYA 13; CA 1-4R; CANR 3, 37; MAICYA; SAAS 18; SATA 3

Sheridan, Frances 1724-1766 **LC 7**
See also DLB 39, 84

Sheridan, Richard Brinsley 1751-1816 NCLC 5; DA; DAB; DAC; DAM DRAM, MST; DC 1; WLC
See also CDBLB 1660-1789; DLB 89

Sherman, Jonathan Marc **CLC 55**

Sherman, Martin 1941(?)- **CLC 19**
See also CA 116; 123

Sherwin, Judith Johnson 1936- **CLC 7, 15**
See also CA 25-28R; CANR 34

Sherwood, Frances 1940- **CLC 81**
See also CA 146

Sherwood, Robert E(mmet) 1896-1955 TCLC 3; DAM DRAM
See also CA 104; 153; DLB 7, 26

Shestov, Lev 1866-1938 **TCLC 56**

Shevchenko, Taras 1814-1861 **NCLC 54**

Shiel, M(atthew) P(hipps) 1865-1947 TCLC 8
See also Holmes, Gordon
See also CA 106; 160; DLB 153

Shields, Carol 1935- **CLC 91; DAC**
See also CA 81-84; CANR 51

Shields, David 1956- **CLC 97**
See also CA 124; CANR 48

Shiga, Naoya 1883-1971 **CLC 33; SSC 23**
See also CA 101; 33-36R; DLB 180

Shilts, Randy 1951-1994 **CLC 85**
See also AAYA 19; CA 115; 127; 144; CANR 45; INT 127

Shimazaki, Haruki 1872-1943
See Shimazaki Toson
See also CA 105; 134

Shimazaki Toson 1872-1943 **TCLC 5**
See also Shimazaki, Haruki
See also DLB 180

Sholokhov, Mikhail (Aleksandrovich) 1905-1984 **CLC 7, 15**
See also CA 101; 112; MTCW; SATA-Obit 36

Shone, Patric
See Hanley, James

Shreve, Susan Richards 1939- **CLC 23**
See also CA 49-52; CAAS 5; CANR 5, 38; MAICYA; SATA 46, 95; SATA-Brief 41

Shue, Larry 1946-1985 **CLC 52; DAM DRAM**
See also CA 145; 117

Shu-Jen, Chou 1881-1936
See Lu Hsun
See also CA 104

Shulman, Alix Kates 1932- **CLC 2, 10**
See also CA 29-32R; CANR 43; SATA 7

Shuster, Joe 1914- **CLC 21**

Shute, Nevil **CLC 30**
See also Norway, Nevil Shute

Shuttle, Penelope (Diane) 1947- **CLC 7**

See also CA 93-96; CANR 39; DLB 14, 40

Sidney, Mary 1561-1621 **LC 19, 39**

Sidney, Sir Philip 1554-1586 LC 19, 39; DA; **DAB; DAC; DAM MST, POET**
See also CDBLB Before 1660; DLB 167

Siegel, Jerome 1914-1996 **CLC 21**
See also CA 116; 151

Siegel, Jerry
See Siegel, Jerome

Sienkiewicz, Henryk (Adam Alexander Pius) 1846-1916 **TCLC 3**
See also CA 104; 134

Sierra, Gregorio Martinez
See Martinez Sierra, Gregorio

Sierra, Maria (de la O'LeJarraga) Martinez
See Martinez Sierra, Maria (de la O'LeJarraga)

Sigal, Clancy 1926- **CLC 7**
See also CA 1-4R

Sigourney, Lydia Howard (Huntley) 1791-1865 **NCLC 21**
See also DLB 1, 42, 73

Siguenza y Gongora, Carlos de 1645-1700 L C 8

Sigurjonsson, Johann 1880-1919 **TCLC 27**

Sikelianos, Angelos 1884-1951 **TCLC 39**

Silkin, Jon 1930- **CLC 2, 6, 43**
See also CA 5-8R; CAAS 5; DLB 27

Silko, Leslie (Marmon) 1948-CLC 23, 74; DA; **DAC; DAM MST, MULT, POP; WLCS**
See also AAYA 14; CA 115; 122; CANR 45, 65; DLB 143, 175; NNAL

Sillanpaa, Frans Eemil 1888-1964 **CLC 19**
See also CA 129; 93-96; MTCW

Sillitoe, Alan 1928- **CLC 1, 3, 6, 10, 19, 57**
See also AITN 1; CA 9-12R; CAAS 2; CANR 8, 26, 55; CDBLB 1960 to Present; DLB 14, 139; MTCW; SATA 61

Silone, Ignazio 1900-1978 **CLC 4**
See also CA 25-28; 81-84; CANR 34; CAP 2; MTCW

Silver, Joan Micklin 1935- **CLC 20**
See also CA 114; 121; INT 121

Silver, Nicholas
See Faust, Frederick (Schiller)

Silverberg, Robert 1935- **CLC 7; DAM POP**
See also AAYA 24; CA 1-4R; CAAS 3; CANR 1, 20, 36; DLB 8; INT CANR-20; MAICYA; MTCW; SATA 13, 91

Silverstein, Alvin 1933- **CLC 17**
See also CA 49-52; CANR 2; CLR 25; JRDA; MAICYA; SATA 8, 69

Silverstein, Virginia B(arbara Opshelor) 1937- **CLC 17**
See also CA 49-52; CANR 2; CLR 25; JRDA; MAICYA; SATA 8, 69

Sim, Georges
See Simenon, Georges (Jacques Christian)

Simak, Clifford D(onald) 1904-1988CLC 1, 55
See also CA 1-4R; 125; CANR 1, 35; DLB 8; MTCW; SATA-Obit 56

Simenon, Georges (Jacques Christian) 1903-1989 **CLC 1, 2, 3, 8, 18, 47; DAM POP**
See also CA 85-88; 129; CANR 35; DLB 72; DLBY 89; MTCW

Simic, Charles 1938- **CLC 6, 9, 22, 49, 68; DAM POET**
See also CA 29-32R; CAAS 4; CANR 12, 33; 52, 61; DLB 105

Simmel, Georg 1858-1918 **TCLC 64**
See also CA 157

Simmons, Charles (Paul) 1924- **CLC 57**
See also CA 89-92; INT 89-92

Simmons, Dan 1948- **CLC 44; DAM POP**

See also AAYA 16; CA 138; CANR 53

Simmons, James (Stewart Alexander) 1933- **CLC 43**
See also CA 105; CAAS 21; DLB 40

Simms, William Gilmore 1806-1870 NCLC 3
See also DLB 3, 30, 59, 73

Simon, Carly 1945- **CLC 26**
See also CA 105

Simon, Claude 1913-1984 CLC 4, 9, 15, 39; **DAM NOV**
See also CA 89-92; CANR 33; DLB 83; MTCW

Simon, (Marvin) Neil 1927-CLC 6, 11, 31, 39, **70; DAM DRAM**
See also AITN 1; CA 21-24R; CANR 26, 54; DLB 7; MTCW

Simon, Paul (Frederick) 1941(?)- **CLC 17**
See also CA 116; 153

Simonon, Paul 1956(?)- **CLC 30**

Simpson, Harriette
See Arnow, Harriette (Louisa) Simpson

Simpson, Louis (Aston Marantz) 1923-CLC 4, **7, 9, 32; DAM POET**
See also CA 1-4R; CAAS 4; CANR 1, 61; DLB 5; MTCW

Simpson, Mona (Elizabeth) 1957- **CLC 44**
See also CA 122; 135; CANR 68

Simpson, N(orman) F(rederick) 1919-CLC 29
See also CA 13-16R; DLB 13

Sinclair, Andrew (Annandale) 1935- CLC 2, **14**
See also CA 9-12R; CAAS 5; CANR 14, 38; DLB 14; MTCW

Sinclair, Emil
See Hesse, Hermann

Sinclair, Iain 1943- **CLC 76**
See also CA 132

Sinclair, Iain MacGregor
See Sinclair, Iain

Sinclair, Irene
See Griffith, D(avid Lewelyn) W(ark)

Sinclair, Mary Amelia St. Clair 1865(?)-1946
See Sinclair, May
See also CA 104

Sinclair, May **TCLC 3, 11**
See also Sinclair, Mary Amelia St. Clair
See also DLB 36, 135

Sinclair, Roy
See Griffith, D(avid Lewelyn) W(ark)

Sinclair, Upton (Beall) 1878-1968 CLC 1, 11, **15, 63; DA; DAB; DAC; DAM MST, NOV; WLC**
See also CA 5-8R; 25-28R; CANR 7; CDALB 1929-1941; DLB 9; INT CANR-7; MTCW; SATA 9

Singer, Isaac
See Singer, Isaac Bashevis

Singer, Isaac Bashevis 1904-1991 CLC 1, 3, 6, **9, 11, 15, 23, 38, 69; DA; DAB; DAC; DAM MST, NOV; SSC 3; WLC**
See also AITN 1, 2; CA 1-4R; 134; CANR 1, 39; CDALB 1941-1968; CLR 1; DLB 6, 28, 52; DLBY 91; JRDA; MAICYA; MTCW; SATA 3, 27; SATA-Obit 68

Singer, Israel Joshua 1893-1944 **TCLC 33**

Singh, Khushwant 1915- **CLC 11**
See also CA 9-12R; CAAS 9; CANR 6

Singleton, Ann
See Benedict, Ruth (Fulton)

Sinjohn, John
See Galsworthy, John

Sinyavsky, Andrei (Donatevich) 1925-1997 **CLC 8**
See also CA 85-88; 159

Sirin, V.
See Nabokov, Vladimir (Vladimirovich)
Sissman, L(ouis) E(dward) 1928-1976 CLC 9, 18
See also CA 21-24R; 65-68; CANR 13; DLB 5
Sisson, C(harles) H(ubert) 1914- CLC 8
See also CA 1-4R; CAAS 3; CANR 3, 48; DLB 27
Sitwell, Dame Edith 1887-1964 CLC 2, 9, 67; DAM POET; PC 3
See also CA 9-12R; CANR 35; CDBLB 1945-1960; DLB 20; MTCW
Siwaarmill, H. P.
See Sharp, William
Sjoewall, Maj 1935- CLC 7
See also CA 65-68
Sjowall, Maj
See Sjoewall, Maj
Skelton, Robin 1925-1997 CLC 13
See also AITN 2; CA 5-8R; 160; CAAS 5; CANR 28; DLB 27, 53
Skolimowski, Jerzy 1938- CLC 20
See also CA 128
Skram, Amalie (Bertha) 1847-1905 TCLC 25
See also CA 165
Skvorecky, Josef (Vaclav) 1924- CLC 15, 39, 69; DAC; DAM NOV
See also CA 61-64; CAAS 1; CANR 10, 34, 63; MTCW
Slade, Bernard CLC 11, 46
See also Newbound, Bernard Slade
See also CAAS 9; DLB 53
Slaughter, Carolyn 1946- CLC 56
See also CA 85-88
Slaughter, Frank G(ill) 1908- CLC 29
See also AITN 2; CA 5-8R; CANR 5; INT CANR-5
Slavitt, David R(ytman) 1935- CLC 5, 14
See also CA 21-24R; CAAS 3; CANR 41; DLB 5, 6
Slesinger, Tess 1905-1945 TCLC 10
See also CA 107; DLB 102
Slessor, Kenneth 1901-1971 CLC 14
See also CA 102; 89-92
Slowacki, Juliusz 1809-1849 NCLC 15
Smart, Christopher 1722-1771 LC 3; DAM POET; PC 13
See also DLB 109
Smart, Elizabeth 1913-1986 CLC 54
See also CA 81-84; 118; DLB 88
Smiley, Jane (Graves) 1949-CLC 53, 76; DAM POP
See also CA 104; CANR 30, 50; INT CANR-30
Smith, A(rthur) J(ames) M(arshall) 1902-1980 CLC 15; DAC
See also CA 1-4R; 102; CANR 4; DLB 88
Smith, Adam 1723-1790 LC 36
See also DLB 104
Smith, Alexander 1829-1867 NCLC 59
See also DLB 32, 55
Smith, Anna Deavere 1950- CLC 86
See also CA 133
Smith, Betty (Wehner) 1896-1972 CLC 19
See also CA 5-8R; 33-36R; DLBY 82; SATA 6
Smith, Charlotte (Turner) 1749-1806 NCLC 23
See also DLB 39, 109
Smith, Clark Ashton 1893-1961 CLC 43
See also CA 143
Smith, Dave CLC 22, 42
See also Smith, David (Jeddie)

See also CAAS 7; DLB 5
Smith, David (Jeddie) 1942-
See Smith, Dave
See also CA 49-52; CANR 1, 59; DAM POET
Smith, Florence Margaret 1902-1971
See Smith, Stevie
See also CA 17-18; 29-32R; CANR 35; CAP 2; DAM POET; MTCW
Smith, Iain Crichton 1928- CLC 64
See also CA 21-24R; DLB 40, 139
Smith, John 1580(?)-1631 LC 9
Smith, Johnston
See Crane, Stephen (Townley)
Smith, Joseph, Jr. 1805-1844 NCLC 53
Smith, Lee 1944- CLC 25, 73
See also CA 114; 119; CANR 46; DLB 143; DLBY 83; INT 119
Smith, Martin
See Smith, Martin Cruz
Smith, Martin Cruz 1942- CLC 25; DAM MULT, POP
See also BEST 89:4; CA 85-88; CANR 6, 23, 43, 65; INT CANR-23; NNAL
Smith, Mary-Ann Tirone 1944- CLC 39
See also CA 118; 136
Smith, Patti 1946- CLC 12
See also CA 93-96; CANR 63
Smith, Pauline (Urmson) 1882-1959TCLC 25
Smith, Rosamond
See Oates, Joyce Carol
Smith, Sheila Kaye
See Kaye-Smith, Sheila
Smith, Stevie CLC 3, 8, 25, 44; PC 12
See also Smith, Florence Margaret
See also DLB 20
Smith, Wilbur (Addison) 1933- CLC 33
See also CA 13-16R; CANR 7, 46, 66; MTCW
Smith, William Jay 1918- CLC 6
See also CA 5-8R; CANR 44; DLB 5; MAICYA; SAAS 22; SATA 2, 68
Smith, Woodrow Wilson
See Kuttner, Henry
Smolenskin, Peretz 1842-1885 NCLC 30
Smollett, Tobias (George) 1721-1771 LC 2
See also CDBLB 1660-1789; DLB 39, 104
Snodgrass, W(illiam) D(e Witt) 1926- CLC 2, 6, 10, 18, 68; DAM POET
See also CA 1-4R; CANR 6, 36, 65; DLB 5; MTCW
Snow, C(harles) P(ercy) 1905-1980 CLC 1, 4, 6, 9, 13, 19; DAM NOV
See also CA 5-8R; 101; CANR 28; CDBLB 1945-1960; DLB 15, 77; MTCW
Snow, Frances Compton
See Adams, Henry (Brooks)
Snyder, Gary (Sherman) 1930-CLC 1, 2, 5, 9, 32; DAM POET; PC 21
See also CA 17-20R; CANR 30, 60; DLB 5, 16, 165
Snyder, Zilpha Keatley 1927- CLC 17
See also AAYA 15; CA 9-12R; CANR 38; CLR 31; JRDA; MAICYA; SAAS 2; SATA 1, 28, 75
Soares, Bernardo
See Pessoa, Fernando (Antonio Nogueira)
Sobh, A.
See Shamlu, Ahmad
Sobol, Joshua CLC 60
Socrates 469B.C.-399B.C. CMLC 27
Soderberg, Hjalmar 1869-1941 TCLC 39
Sodergran, Edith (Irene)
See Soedergran, Edith (Irene)
Soedergran, Edith (Irene) 1892-1923 TCLC

31
Softly, Edgar
See Lovecraft, H(oward) P(hillips)
Softly, Edward
See Lovecraft, H(oward) P(hillips)
Sokolov, Raymond 1941- CLC 7
See also CA 85-88
Solo, Jay
See Ellison, Harlan (Jay)
Sologub, Fyodor TCLC 9
See also Teternikov, Fyodor Kuzmich
Solomons, Ikey Esquir
See Thackeray, William Makepeace
Solomos, Dionysios 1798-1857 NCLC 15
Solwoska, Mara
See French, Marilyn
Solzhenitsyn, Aleksandr I(sayevich) 1918-
CLC 1, 2, 4, 7, 9, 10, 18, 26, 34, 78; DA;
DAB; DAC; DAM MST, NOV; WLC
See also AITN 1; CA 69-72; CANR 40, 65;
MTCW
Somers, Jane
See Lessing, Doris (May)
Somerville, Edith 1858-1949 TCLC 51
See also DLB 135
Somerville & Ross
See Martin, Violet Florence; Somerville, Edith
Sommer, Scott 1951- CLC 25
See also CA 106
Sondheim, Stephen (Joshua) 1930- CLC 30, 39; DAM DRAM
See also AAYA 11; CA 103; CANR 47, 68
Song, Cathy 1955- PC 21
See also CA 154; DLB 169
Sontag, Susan 1933-CLC 1, 2, 10, 13, 31, 105;
DAM POP
See also CA 17-20R; CANR 25, 51; DLB 2, 67; MTCW
Sophocles 496(?)B.C.-406(?)B.C. CMLC 2;
DA; DAB; DAC; DAM DRAM, MST; DC 1; WLCS
See also DLB 176
Sordello 1189-1269 CMLC 15
Sorel, Julia
See Drexler, Rosalyn
Sorrentino, Gilbert 1929-CLC 3, 7, 14, 22, 40
See also CA 77-80; CANR 14, 33; DLB 5, 173;
DLBY 80; INT CANR-14
Soto, Gary 1952- CLC 32, 80; DAM MULT;
HLC
See also AAYA 10; CA 119; 125; CANR 50;
CLR 38; DLB 82; HW; INT 125; JRDA;
SATA 80
Soupault, Philippe 1897-1990 CLC 68
See also CA 116; 147; 131
Souster, (Holmes) Raymond 1921-CLC 5, 14;
DAC; DAM POET
See also CA 13-16R; CAAS 14; CANR 13, 29, 53; DLB 88; SATA 63
Southern, Terry 1924(?)-1995 CLC 7
See also CA 1-4R; 150; CANR 1, 55; DLB 2
Southey, Robert 1774-1843 NCLC 8
See also DLB 93, 107, 142; SATA 54
Southworth, Emma Dorothy Eliza Nevitte 1819-1899 NCLC 26
Souza, Ernest
See Scott, Evelyn
Soyinka, Wole 1934-CLC 3, 5, 14, 36, 44; BLC 3; DA; DAB; DAC; DAM DRAM, MST, MULT; DC 2; WLC
See also BW 2; CA 13-16R; CANR 27, 39; DLB 125; MTCW
Spackman, W(illiam) M(ode) 1905-1990 CLC

46
See also CA 81-84; 132
Spacks, Barry (Bernard) 1931- **CLC 14**
See also CA 154; CANR 33; DLB 105
Spanidou, Irini 1946- **CLC 44**
Spark, Muriel (Sarah) 1918-CLC 2, 3, 5, 8, 13,
18, 40, 94; DAB; DAC; DAM MST, NOV;
SSC 10
See also CA 5-8R; CANR 12, 36; CDBLB
1945-1960; DLB 15, 139; INT CANR-12;
MTCW
Spaulding, Douglas
See Bradbury, Ray (Douglas)
Spaulding, Leonard
See Bradbury, Ray (Douglas)
Spence, J. A. D.
See Eliot, T(homas) S(tearns)
Spencer, Elizabeth 1921- **CLC 22**
See also CA 13-16R; CANR 32, 65; DLB 6;
MTCW; SATA 14
Spencer, Leonard G.
See Silverberg, Robert
Spencer, Scott 1945- **CLC 30**
See also CA 113; CANR 51; DLBY 86
Spender, Stephen (Harold) 1909-1995 CLC 1,
2, 5, 10, 41, 91; DAM POET
See also CA 9-12R; 149; CANR 31, 54;
CDBLB 1945-1960; DLB 20; MTCW
Spengler, Oswald (Arnold Gottfried) 1880-1936
TCLC 25
See also CA 118
Spenser, Edmund 1552(?)-1599LC 5, 39; DA;
DAB; DAC; DAM MST, POET; PC 8;
WLC
See also CDBLB Before 1660; DLB 167
Spicer, Jack 1925-1965 **CLC 8, 18, 72; DAM
POET**
See also CA 85-88; DLB 5, 16, 193
Spiegelman, Art 1948- **CLC 76**
See also AAYA 10; CA 125; CANR 41, 55
Spielberg, Peter 1929- **CLC 6**
See also CA 5-8R; CANR 4, 48; DLBY 81
Spielberg, Steven 1947- **CLC 20**
See also AAYA 8, 24; CA 77-80; CANR 32;
SATA 32
Spillane, Frank Morrison 1918-
See Spillane, Mickey
See also CA 25-28R; CANR 28, 63; MTCW;
SATA 66
Spillane, Mickey **CLC 3, 13**
See also Spillane, Frank Morrison
Spinoza, Benedictus de 1632-1677 **LC 9**
Spinrad, Norman (Richard) 1940- **CLC 46**
See also CA 37-40R; CAAS 19; CANR 20;
DLB 8; INT CANR-20
Spitteler, Carl (Friedrich Georg) 1845-1924
TCLC 12
See also CA 109; DLB 129
Spivack, Kathleen (Romola Drucker) 1938-
CLC 6
See also CA 49-52
Spoto, Donald 1941- **CLC 39**
See also CA 65-68; CANR 11, 57
Springsteen, Bruce (F.) 1949- **CLC 17**
See also CA 111
Spurling, Hilary 1940- **CLC 34**
See also CA 104; CANR 25, 52
Spyker, John Howland
See Elman, Richard (Martin)
Squires, (James) Radcliffe 1917-1993 CLC 51
See also CA 1-4R; 140; CANR 6, 21
Srivastava, Dhanpat Rai 1880(?)-1936
See Premchand

See also CA 118
Stacy, Donald
See Pohl, Frederik
Stael, Germaine de 1766-1817
See Stael-Holstein, Anne Louise Germaine
Necker Baronn
See also DLB 119
**Stael-Holstein, Anne Louise Germaine Necker
Baronn** 1766-1817 **NCLC 3**
See also Stael, Germaine de
See also DLB 192
Stafford, Jean 1915-1979CLC 4, 7, 19, 68; SSC
26
See also CA 1-4R; 85-88; CANR 3, 65; DLB
2, 173; MTCW; SATA-Obit 22
Stafford, William (Edgar) 1914-1993 **CLC 4,
7, 29; DAM POET**
See also CA 5-8R; 142; CAAS 3; CANR 5, 22;
DLB 5; INT CANR-22
Stagnelius, Eric Johan 1793-1823 **NCLC 61**
Staines, Trevor
See Brunner, John (Kilian Houston)
Stairs, Gordon
See Austin, Mary (Hunter)
Stannard, Martin 1947- **CLC 44**
See also CA 142; DLB 155
Stanton, Elizabeth Cady 1815-1902 TCLC 73
See also DLB 79
Stanton, Maura 1946- **CLC 9**
See also CA 89-92; CANR 15; DLB 120
Stanton, Schuyler
See Baum, L(yman) Frank
Stapledon, (William) Olaf 1886-1950 **TCLC
22**
See also CA 111; 162; DLB 15
Starbuck, George (Edwin) 1931-1996CLC 53;
DAM POET
See also CA 21-24R; 153; CANR 23
Stark, Richard
See Westlake, Donald E(dwin)
Staunton, Schuyler
See Baum, L(yman) Frank
Stead, Christina (Ellen) 1902-1983 CLC 2, 5,
8, 32, 80
See also CA 13-16R; 109; CANR 33, 40;
MTCW
Stead, William Thomas 1849-1912 TCLC 48
Steele, Richard 1672-1729 **LC 18**
See also CDBLB 1660-1789; DLB 84, 101
Steele, Timothy (Reid) 1948- **CLC 45**
See also CA 93-96; CANR 16, 50; DLB 120
Steffens, (Joseph) Lincoln 1866-1936 **TCLC
20**
See also CA 117
Stegner, Wallace (Earle) 1909-1993 **CLC 9,
49, 81; DAM NOV; SSC 27**
See also AITN 1; BEST 90:3; CA 1-4R; 141;
CAAS 9; CANR 1, 21, 46; DLB 9; DLBY
93; MTCW
Stein, Gertrude 1874-1946TCLC 1, 6, 28, 48;
DA; DAB; DAC; DAM MST, NOV, POET;
PC 18; WLC
See also CA 104; 132; CDALB 1917-1929;
DLB 4, 54, 86; DLBD 15; MTCW
Steinbeck, John (Ernst) 1902-1968 CLC 1, 5,
9, 13, 21, 34, 45, 75; DA; DAB; DAC; DAM
DRAM, MST, NOV; SSC 11; WLC
See also AAYA 12; CA 1-4R; 25-28R; CANR
1, 35; CDALB 1929-1941; DLB 7, 9; DLBD
2; MTCW; SATA 9
Steinem, Gloria 1934- **CLC 63**
See also CA 53-56; CANR 28, 51; MTCW
Steiner, George 1929- **CLC 24; DAM NOV**

See also CA 73-76; CANR 31, 67; DLB 67;
MTCW; SATA 62
Steiner, K. Leslie
See Delany, Samuel R(ay, Jr.)
Steiner, Rudolf 1861-1925 **TCLC 13**
See also CA 107
Stendhal 1783-1842 NCLC 23, 46; DA; DAB;
DAC; DAM MST, NOV; SSC 27; WLC
See also DLB 119
Stephen, Adeline Virginia
See Woolf, (Adeline) Virginia
Stephen, SirLeslie 1832-1904 **TCLC 23**
See also CA 123; DLB 57, 144, 190
Stephen, Sir Leslie
See Stephen, SirLeslie
Stephen, Virginia
See Woolf, (Adeline) Virginia
Stephens, James 1882(?)-1950 **TCLC 4**
See also CA 104; DLB 19, 153, 162
Stephens, Reed
See Donaldson, Stephen R.
Steptoe, Lydia
See Barnes, Djuna
Sterchi, Beat 1949- **CLC 65**
Sterling, Brett
See Bradbury, Ray (Douglas); Hamilton,
Edmond
Sterling, Bruce 1954- **CLC 72**
See also CA 119; CANR 44
Sterling, George 1869-1926 **TCLC 20**
See also CA 117; 165; DLB 54
Stern, Gerald 1925- **CLC 40, 100**
See also CA 81-84; CANR 28; DLB 105
Stern, Richard (Gustave) 1928- **CLC 4, 39**
See also CA 1-4R; CANR 1, 25, 52; DLBY 87;
INT CANR-25
Sternberg, Josef von 1894-1969 **CLC 20**
See also CA 81-84
Sterne, Laurence 1713-1768 **LC 2; DA; DAB;
DAC; DAM MST, NOV; WLC**
See also CDBLB 1660-1789; DLB 39
Sternheim, (William Adolf) Carl 1878-1942
TCLC 8
See also CA 105; DLB 56, 118
Stevens, Mark 1951- **CLC 34**
See also CA 122
Stevens, Wallace 1879-1955 TCLC 3, 12, 45;
DA; DAB; DAC; DAM MST, POET; PC
6; WLC
See also CA 104; 124; CDALB 1929-1941;
DLB 54; MTCW
Stevenson, Anne (Katharine) 1933-CLC 7, 33
See also CA 17-20R; CAAS 9; CANR 9, 33;
DLB 40; MTCW
Stevenson, Robert Louis (Balfour) 1850-1894
NCLC 5, 14, 63; DA; DAB; DAC; DAM
MST, NOV; SSC 11; WLC
See also AAYA 24; CDBLB 1890-1914; CLR
10, 11; DLB 18, 57, 141, 156, 174; DLBD
13; JRDA; MAICYA; YABC 2
Stewart, J(ohn) I(nnes) M(ackintosh) 1906-
1994 **CLC 7, 14, 32**
See also CA 85-88; 147; CAAS 3; CANR 47;
MTCW
Stewart, Mary (Florence Elinor) 1916-CLC 7,
35; DAB
See also CA 1-4R; CANR 1, 59; SATA 12
Stewart, Mary Rainbow
See Stewart, Mary (Florence Elinor)
Stifle, June
See Campbell, Maria
Stifter, Adalbert 1805-1868NCLC 41; SSC 28
See also DLB 133

Still, James 1906-   **CLC 49**
    See also CA 65-68; CAAS 17; CANR 10, 26;
    DLB 9; SATA 29
Sting
    See Sumner, Gordon Matthew
Stirling, Arthur
    See Sinclair, Upton (Beall)
Stitt, Milan 1941-   **CLC 29**
    See also CA 69-72
Stockton, Francis Richard 1834-1902
    See Stockton, Frank R.
    See also CA 108; 137; MAICYA; SATA 44
Stockton, Frank R.   **TCLC 47**
    See also Stockton, Francis Richard
    See also DLB 42, 74; DLBD 13; SATA-Brief
    32
Stoddard, Charles
    See Kuttner, Henry
Stoker, Abraham 1847-1912
    See Stoker, Bram
    See also CA 105; 150; DA; DAC; DAM MST,
    NOV; SATA 29
Stoker, Bram 1847-1912 **TCLC 8; DAB; WLC**
    See also Stoker, Abraham
    See also AAYA 23; CDBLB 1890-1914; DLB
    36, 70, 178
Stolz, Mary (Slattery) 1920-   **CLC 12**
    See also AAYA 8; AITN 1; CA 5-8R; CANR
    13, 41; JRDA; MAICYA; SAAS 3; SATA
    10, 71
Stone, Irving 1903-1989   **CLC 7; DAM POP**
    See also AITN 1; CA 1-4R; 129; CAAS 3;
    CANR 1, 23; INT CANR-23; MTCW; SATA
    3; SATA-Obit 64
Stone, Oliver (William) 1946-   **CLC 73**
    See also AAYA 15; CA 110; CANR 55
Stone, Robert (Anthony) 1937- **CLC 5, 23, 42**
    See also CA 85-88; CANR 23, 66; DLB 152;
    INT CANR-23; MTCW
Stone, Zachary
    See Follett, Ken(neth Martin)
Stoppard, Tom 1937-**CLC 1, 3, 4, 5, 8, 15, 29,
    34, 63, 91; DA; DAB; DAC; DAM DRAM,
    MST; DC 6; WLC**
    See also CA 81-84; CANR 39, 67; CDBLB
    1960 to Present; DLB 13; DLBY 85; MTCW
Storey, David (Malcolm) 1933-**CLC 2, 4, 5, 8;
    DAM DRAM**
    See also CA 81-84; CANR 36; DLB 13, 14;
    MTCW
Storm, Hyemeyohsts 1935-   **CLC 3; DAM
    MULT**
    See also CA 81-84; CANR 45; NNAL
Storm, (Hans) Theodor (Woldsen) 1817-1888
    NCLC 1; SSC 27
    See also DLB 129
Storni, Alfonsina 1892-1938   **TCLC 5; DAM
    MULT; HLC**
    See also CA 104; 131; HW
Stoughton, William 1631-1701   **LC 38**
    See also DLB 24
Stout, Rex (Todhunter) 1886-1975   **CLC 3**
    See also AITN 2; CA 61-64
Stow, (Julian) Randolph 1935-   **CLC 23, 48**
    See also CA 13-16R; CANR 33; MTCW
Stowe, Harriet (Elizabeth) Beecher 1811-1896
    **NCLC 3, 50; DA; DAB; DAC; DAM MST,
    NOV; WLC**
    See also CDALB 1865-1917; DLB 1, 12, 42,
    74, 189; JRDA; MAICYA; YABC 1
Strachey, (Giles) Lytton 1880-1932 **TCLC 12**
    See also CA 110; DLB 149; DLBD 10
Strand, Mark 1934- **CLC 6, 18, 41, 71; DAM
    POET**
    See also CA 21-24R; CANR 40, 65; DLB 5;
    SATA 41
Straub, Peter (Francis) 1943-   **CLC 28, 107;
    DAM POP**
    See also BEST 89:1; CA 85-88; CANR 28, 65;
    DLBY 84; MTCW
Strauss, Botho 1944-   **CLC 22**
    See also CA 157; DLB 124
Streatfeild, (Mary) Noel 1895(?)-1986**CLC 21**
    See also CA 81-84; 120; CANR 31; CLR 17;
    DLB 160; MAICYA; SATA 20; SATA-Obit
    48
Stribling, T(homas) S(igismund) 1881-1965
    CLC 23
    See also CA 107; DLB 9
Strindberg, (Johan) August 1849-1912 **TCLC
    1, 8, 21, 47; DA; DAB; DAC; DAM DRAM,
    MST; WLC**
    See also CA 104; 135
Stringer, Arthur 1874-1950   **TCLC 37**
    See also CA 161; DLB 92
Stringer, David
    See Roberts, Keith (John Kingston)
Stroheim, Erich von 1885-1957   **TCLC 71**
Strugatskii, Arkadii (Natanovich) 1925-1991
    CLC 27
    See also CA 106; 135
Strugatskii, Boris (Natanovich) 1933-**CLC 27**
    See also CA 106
Strummer, Joe 1953(?)-   **CLC 30**
Stuart, Don A.
    See Campbell, John W(ood, Jr.)
Stuart, Ian
    See MacLean, Alistair (Stuart)
Stuart, Jesse (Hilton) 1906-1984**CLC 1, 8, 11,
    14, 34**
    See also CA 5-8R; 112; CANR 31; DLB 9, 48,
    102; DLBY 84; SATA 2; SATA-Obit 36
Sturgeon, Theodore (Hamilton) 1918-1985
    CLC 22, 39
    See also Queen, Ellery
    See also CA 81-84; 116; CANR 32; DLB 8;
    DLBY 85; MTCW
Sturges, Preston 1898-1959   **TCLC 48**
    See also CA 114; 149; DLB 26
Styron, William 1925-**CLC 1, 3, 5, 11, 15, 60;
    DAM NOV, POP; SSC 25**
    See also BEST 90:4; CA 5-8R; CANR 6, 33;
    CDALB 1968-1988; DLB 2, 143; DLBY 80;
    INT CANR-6; MTCW
Suarez Lynch, B.
    See Bioy Casares, Adolfo; Borges, Jorge Luis
Su Chien 1884-1918
    See Su Man-shu
    See also CA 123
Suckow, Ruth 1892-1960   **SSC 18**
    See also CA 113; DLB 9, 102
Sudermann, Hermann 1857-1928   **TCLC 15**
    See also CA 107; DLB 118
Sue, Eugene 1804-1857   **NCLC 1**
    See also DLB 119
Sueskind, Patrick 1949-   **CLC 44**
    See also Suskind, Patrick
Sukenick, Ronald 1932-   **CLC 3, 4, 6, 48**
    See also CA 25-28R; CAAS 8; CANR 32; DLB
    173; DLBY 81
Suknaski, Andrew 1942-   **CLC 19**
    See also CA 101; DLB 53
Sullivan, Vernon
    See Vian, Boris
Sully Prudhomme 1839-1907   **TCLC 31**
Su Man-shu   **TCLC 24**
    See also Su Chien
Summerforest, Ivy B.
    See Kirkup, James
Summers, Andrew James 1942-   **CLC 26**
Summers, Andy
    See Summers, Andrew James
Summers, Hollis (Spurgeon, Jr.) 1916- **CLC
    10**
    See also CA 5-8R; CANR 3; DLB 6
Summers, (Alphonsus Joseph-Mary Augustus)
    Montague 1880-1948   **TCLC 16**
    See also CA 118; 163
Sumner, Gordon Matthew 1951-   **CLC 26**
Surtees, Robert Smith 1803-1864   **NCLC 14**
    See also DLB 21
Susann, Jacqueline 1921-1974   **CLC 3**
    See also AITN 1; CA 65-68; 53-56; MTCW
Su Shih 1036-1101   **CMLC 15**
Suskind, Patrick
    See Sueskind, Patrick
    See also CA 145
Sutcliff, Rosemary 1920-1992 **CLC 26; DAB;
    DAC; DAM MST, POP**
    See also AAYA 10; CA 5-8R; 139; CANR 37;
    CLR 1, 37; JRDA; MAICYA; SATA 6, 44,
    78; SATA-Obit 73
Sutro, Alfred 1863-1933   **TCLC 6**
    See also CA 105; DLB 10
Sutton, Henry
    See Slavitt, David R(ytman)
Svevo, Italo 1861-1928 **TCLC 2, 35; SSC 25**
    See also Schmitz, Aron Hector
Swados, Elizabeth (A.) 1951-   **CLC 12**
    See also CA 97-100; CANR 49; INT 97-100
Swados, Harvey 1920-1972   **CLC 5**
    See also CA 5-8R; 37-40R; CANR 6; DLB 2
Swan, Gladys 1934-   **CLC 69**
    See also CA 101; CANR 17, 39
Swarthout, Glendon (Fred) 1918-1992**CLC 35**
    See also CA 1-4R; 139; CANR 1, 47; SATA
    26
Sweet, Sarah C.
    See Jewett, (Theodora) Sarah Orne
Swenson, May 1919-1989 **CLC 4, 14, 61, 106;
    DA; DAB; DAC; DAM MST, POET; PC
    14**
    See also CA 5-8R; 130; CANR 36, 61; DLB 5;
    MTCW; SATA 15
Swift, Augustus
    See Lovecraft, H(oward) P(hillips)
Swift, Graham (Colin) 1949-   **CLC 41, 88**
    See also CA 117; 122; CANR 46; DLB 194
Swift, Jonathan 1667-1745   **LC 1; DA; DAB;
    DAC; DAM MST, NOV, POET; PC 9;
    WLC**
    See also CDBLB 1660-1789; DLB 39, 95, 101;
    SATA 19
Swinburne, Algernon Charles 1837-1909
    **TCLC 8, 36; DA; DAB; DAC; DAM MST,
    POET; WLC**
    See also CA 105; 140; CDBLB 1832-1890;
    DLB 35, 57
Swinfen, Ann   **CLC 34**
Swinnerton, Frank Arthur 1884-1982**CLC 31**
    See also CA 108; DLB 34
Swithen, John
    See King, Stephen (Edwin)
Sylvia
    See Ashton-Warner, Sylvia (Constance)
Symmes, Robert Edward
    See Duncan, Robert (Edward)
Symonds, John Addington 1840-1893 **NCLC
    34**

See also DLB 57, 144

Symons, Arthur 1865-1945 **TCLC 11**
See also CA 107; DLB 19, 57, 149

Symons, Julian (Gustave) 1912-1994 **CLC 2, 14, 32**
See also CA 49-52; 147; CAAS 3; CANR 3, 33, 59; DLB 87, 155; DLBY 92; MTCW

Synge, (Edmund) J(ohn) M(illington) 1871-1909 **TCLC 6, 37; DAM DRAM; DC 2**
See also CA 104; 141; CDBLB 1890-1914; DLB 10, 19

Syruc, J.
See Milosz, Czeslaw

Szirtes, George 1948- **CLC 46**
See also CA 109; CANR 27, 61

Szymborska, Wislawa 1923- **CLC 99**
See also CA 154; DLBY 96

T. O., Nik
See Annensky, Innokenty (Fyodorovich)

Tabori, George 1914- **CLC 19**
See also CA 49-52; CANR 4

Tagore, Rabindranath 1861-1941 **TCLC 3, 53; DAM DRAM, POET; PC 8**
See also CA 104; 120; MTCW

Taine, Hippolyte Adolphe 1828-1893 **NCLC 15**

Talese, Gay 1932- **CLC 37**
See also AITN 1; CA 1-4R; CANR 9, 58; DLB 185; INT CANR-9; MTCW

Tallent, Elizabeth (Ann) 1954- **CLC 45**
See also CA 117; DLB 130

Tally, Ted 1952- **CLC 42**
See also CA 120; 124; INT 124

Tamayo y Baus, Manuel 1829-1898 **NCLC 1**

Tammsaare, A(nton) H(ansen) 1878-1940 **TCLC 27**
See also CA 164

Tam'si, Tchicaya U
See Tchicaya, Gerald Felix

Tan, Amy (Ruth) 1952-**CLC 59; DAM MULT, NOV, POP**
See also AAYA 9; BEST 89:3; CA 136; CANR 54; DLB 173; SATA 75

Tandem, Felix
See Spitteler, Carl (Friedrich Georg)

Tanizaki, Jun'ichiro 1886-1965**CLC 8, 14, 28; SSC 21**
See also CA 93-96; 25-28R; DLB 180

Tanner, William
See Amis, Kingsley (William)

Tao Lao
See Storni, Alfonsina

Tarassoff, Lev
See Troyat, Henri

Tarbell, Ida M(inerva) 1857-1944 **TCLC 40**
See also CA 122; DLB 47

Tarkington, (Newton) Booth 1869-1946 **TCLC 9**
See also CA 110; 143; DLB 9, 102; SATA 17

Tarkovsky, Andrei (Arsenyevich) 1932-1986 **CLC 75**
See also CA 127

Tartt, Donna 1964(?)- **CLC 76**
See also CA 142

Tasso, Torquato 1544-1595 **LC 5**

Tate, (John Orley) Allen 1899-1979 **CLC 2, 4, 6, 9, 11, 14, 24**
See also CA 5-8R; 85-88; CANR 32; DLB 4, 45, 63; MTCW

Tate, Ellalice
See Hibbert, Eleanor Alice Burford

Tate, James (Vincent) 1943- **CLC 2, 6, 25**
See also CA 21-24R; CANR 29, 57; DLB 5,

169

Tavel, Ronald 1940- **CLC 6**
See also CA 21-24R; CANR 33

Taylor, C(ecil) P(hilip) 1929-1981 **CLC 27**
See also CA 25-28R; 105; CANR 47

Taylor, Edward 1642(?)-1729 **LC 11; DA; DAB; DAC; DAM MST, POET**
See also DLB 24

Taylor, Eleanor Ross 1920- **CLC 5**
See also CA 81-84

Taylor, Elizabeth 1912-1975 **CLC 2, 4, 29**
See also CA 13-16R; CANR 9; DLB 139; MTCW; SATA 13

Taylor, Frederick Winslow 1856-1915 **TCLC 76**

Taylor, Henry (Splawn) 1942- **CLC 44**
See also CA 33-36R; CAAS 7; CANR 31; DLB 5

Taylor, Kamala (Purnaiya) 1924-
See Markandaya, Kamala
See also CA 77-80

Taylor, Mildred D. **CLC 21**
See also AAYA 10; BW 1; CA 85-88; CANR 25; CLR 9; DLB 52; JRDA; MAICYA; SAAS 5; SATA 15, 70

Taylor, Peter (Hillsman) 1917-1994**CLC 1, 4, 18, 37, 44, 50, 71; SSC 10**
See also CA 13-16R; 147; CANR 9, 50; DLBY 81, 94; INT CANR-9; MTCW

Taylor, Robert Lewis 1912- **CLC 14**
See also CA 1-4R; CANR 3, 64; SATA 10

Tchekhov, Anton
See Chekhov, Anton (Pavlovich)

Tchicaya, Gerald Felix 1931-1988 **CLC 101**
See also CA 129; 125

Tchicaya U Tam'si
See Tchicaya, Gerald Felix

Teasdale, Sara 1884-1933 **TCLC 4**
See also CA 104; 163; DLB 45; SATA 32

Tegner, Esaias 1782-1846 **NCLC 2**

Teilhard de Chardin, (Marie Joseph) Pierre 1881-1955 **TCLC 9**
See also CA 105

Temple, Ann
See Mortimer, Penelope (Ruth)

Tennant, Emma (Christina) 1937-**CLC 13, 52**
See also CA 65-68; CAAS 9; CANR 10, 38, 59; DLB 14

Tenneshaw, S. M.
See Silverberg, Robert

Tennyson, Alfred 1809-1892 **NCLC 30, 65; DA; DAB; DAC; DAM MST, POET; PC 6; WLC**
See also CDBLB 1832-1890; DLB 32

Teran, Lisa St. Aubin de **CLC 36**
See also St. Aubin de Teran, Lisa

Terence 195(?)B.C.-159B.C. **CMLC 14; DC 7**

Teresa de Jesus, St. 1515-1582 **LC 18**

Terkel, Louis 1912-
See Terkel, Studs
See also CA 57-60; CANR 18, 45, 67; MTCW

Terkel, Studs **CLC 38**
See also Terkel, Louis
See also AITN 1

Terry, C. V.
See Slaughter, Frank G(ill)

Terry, Megan 1932- **CLC 19**
See also CA 77-80; CABS 3; CANR 43; DLB 7

Tertz, Abram
See Sinyavsky, Andrei (Donatevich)

Tesich, Steve 1943(?)-1996 **CLC 40, 69**
See also CA 105; 152; DLBY 83

Teternikov, Fyodor Kuzmich 1863-1927
See Sologub, Fyodor
See also CA 104

Tevis, Walter 1928-1984 **CLC 42**
See also CA 113

Tey, Josephine **TCLC 14**
See also Mackintosh, Elizabeth
See also DLB 77

Thackeray, William Makepeace 1811-1863 **NCLC 5, 14, 22, 43; DA; DAB; DAC; DAM MST, NOV; WLC**
See also CDBLB 1832-1890; DLB 21, 55, 159, 163; SATA 23

Thakura, Ravindranatha
See Tagore, Rabindranath

Tharoor, Shashi 1956- **CLC 70**
See also CA 141

Thelwell, Michael Miles 1939- **CLC 22**
See also BW 2; CA 101

Theobald, Lewis, Jr.
See Lovecraft, H(oward) P(hillips)

Theodorescu, Ion N. 1880-1967
See Arghezi, Tudor
See also CA 116

Theriault, Yves 1915-1983 **CLC 79; DAC; DAM MST**
See also CA 102; DLB 88

Theroux, Alexander (Louis) 1939- **CLC 2, 25**
See also CA 85-88; CANR 20, 63

Theroux, Paul (Edward) 1941- **CLC 5, 8, 11, 15, 28, 46; DAM POP**
See also BEST 89:4; CA 33-36R; CANR 20, 45; DLB 2; MTCW; SATA 44

Thesen, Sharon 1946- **CLC 56**
See also CA 163

Thevenin, Denis
See Duhamel, Georges

Thibault, Jacques Anatole Francois 1844-1924
See France, Anatole
See also CA 106; 127; DAM NOV; MTCW

Thiele, Colin (Milton) 1920- **CLC 17**
See also CA 29-32R; CANR 12, 28, 53; CLR 27; MAICYA; SAAS 2; SATA 14, 72

Thomas, Audrey (Callahan) 1935-**CLC 7, 13, 37, 107; SSC 20**
See also AITN 2; CA 21-24R; CAAS 19; CANR 36, 58; DLB 60; MTCW

Thomas, D(onald) M(ichael) 1935- **CLC 13, 22, 31**
See also CA 61-64; CAAS 11; CANR 17, 45; CDBLB 1960 to Present; DLB 40; INT CANR-17; MTCW

Thomas, Dylan (Marlais) 1914-1953 **TCLC 1, 8, 45; DA; DAB; DAC; DAM DRAM, MST, POET; PC 2; SSC 3; WLC**
See also CA 104; 120; CANR 65; CDBLB 1945-1960; DLB 13, 20, 139; MTCW; SATA 60

Thomas, (Philip) Edward 1878-1917 **TCLC 10; DAM POET**
See also CA 106; 153; DLB 19

Thomas, Joyce Carol 1938- **CLC 35**
See also AAYA 12; BW 2; CA 113; 116; CANR 48; CLR 19; DLB 33; INT 116; JRDA; MAICYA; MTCW; SAAS 7; SATA 40, 78

Thomas, Lewis 1913-1993 **CLC 35**
See also CA 85-88; 143; CANR 38, 60; MTCW

Thomas, Paul
See Mann, (Paul) Thomas

Thomas, Piri 1928- **CLC 17**
See also CA 73-76; HW

Thomas, R(onald) S(tuart) 1913- **CLC 6, 13, 48; DAB; DAM POET**

See also CA 89-92; CAAS 4; CANR 30;
CDBLB 1960 to Present; DLB 27; MTCW
Thomas, Ross (Elmore) 1926-1995   **CLC 39**
See also CA 33-36R; 150; CANR 22, 63
Thompson, Francis Clegg
See Mencken, H(enry) L(ouis)
Thompson, Francis Joseph 1859-1907 **TCLC 4**
See also CA 104; CDBLB 1890-1914; DLB 19
Thompson, Hunter S(tockton) 1939-   **CLC 9,**
17, 40, 104; DAM POP
See also BEST 89:1; CA 17-20R; CANR 23,
46; DLB 185; MTCW
Thompson, James Myers
See Thompson, Jim (Myers)
Thompson, Jim (Myers) 1906-1977(?) **CLC 69**
See also CA 140
Thompson, Judith   **CLC 39**
Thomson, James 1700-1748   **LC 16, 29, 40;**
DAM POET
See also DLB 95
Thomson, James 1834-1882 **NCLC 18; DAM**
POET
See also DLB 35
Thoreau, Henry David 1817-1862 **NCLC 7, 21,**
61; DA; DAB; DAC; DAM MST; WLC
See also CDALB 1640-1865; DLB 1
Thornton, Hall
See Silverberg, Robert
Thucydides c. 455B.C.-399B.C.   **CMLC 17**
See also DLB 176
Thurber, James (Grover) 1894-1961 **CLC 5,**
11, 25; DA; DAB; DAC; DAM DRAM,
MST, NOV; SSC 1
See also CA 73-76; CANR 17, 39; CDALB
1929-1941; DLB 4, 11, 22, 102; MAICYA;
MTCW; SATA 13
Thurman, Wallace (Henry) 1902-1934 **TCLC**
6; BLC 3; DAM MULT
See also BW 1; CA 104; 124; DLB 51
Ticheburn, Cheviot
See Ainsworth, William Harrison
Tieck, (Johann) Ludwig 1773-1853 **NCLC 5,**
46
See also DLB 90
Tiger, Derry
See Ellison, Harlan (Jay)
Tilghman, Christopher 1948(?)-   **CLC 65**
See also CA 159
Tillinghast, Richard (Williford) 1940- **CLC 29**
See also CA 29-32R; CAAS 23; CANR 26, 51
Timrod, Henry 1828-1867   **NCLC 25**
See also DLB 3
Tindall, Gillian (Elizabeth) 1938-   **CLC 7**
See also CA 21-24R; CANR 11, 65
Tiptree, James, Jr.   **CLC 48, 50**
See also Sheldon, Alice Hastings Bradley
See also DLB 8
Titmarsh, Michael Angelo
See Thackeray, William Makepeace
Tocqueville, Alexis (Charles Henri Maurice
Clerel Comte) 1805-1859   **NCLC 7, 63**
Tolkien, J(ohn) R(onald) R(euel) 1892-1973
CLC 1, 2, 3, 8, 12, 38; DA; DAB; DAC;
DAM MST, NOV, POP; WLC
See also AAYA 10; AITN 1; CA 17-18; 45-48;
CANR 36; CAP 2; CDBLB 1914-1945; DLB
15, 160; JRDA; MAICYA; MTCW; SATA
2, 32; SATA-Obit 24
Toller, Ernst 1893-1939   **TCLC 10**
See also CA 107; DLB 124
Tolson, M. B.
See Tolson, Melvin B(eaunorus)
Tolson, Melvin B(eaunorus) 1898(?)-1966

CLC 36, 105; BLC 3; DAM MULT, POET
See also BW 1; CA 124; 89-92; DLB 48, 76
Tolstoi, Aleksei Nikolaevich
See Tolstoy, Alexey Nikolaevich
Tolstoy, Alexey Nikolaevich 1882-1945 **TCLC**
18
See also CA 107; 158
Tolstoy, Count Leo
See Tolstoy, Leo (Nikolaevich)
Tolstoy, Leo (Nikolaevich) 1828-1910 **TCLC**
4, 11, 17, 28, 44, 79; DA; DAB; DAC; DAM
MST, NOV; SSC 9, 30; WLC
See also CA 104; 123; SATA 26
Tomasi di Lampedusa, Giuseppe 1896-1957
See Lampedusa, Giuseppe (Tomasi) di
See also CA 111
Tomlin, Lily   **CLC 17**
See also Tomlin, Mary Jean
Tomlin, Mary Jean 1939(?)-
See Tomlin, Lily
See also CA 117
Tomlinson, (Alfred) Charles 1927- **CLC 2, 4,**
6, 13, 45; DAM POET; PC 17
See also CA 5-8R; CANR 33; DLB 40
Tomlinson, H(enry) M(ajor) 1873-1958 **TCLC**
71
See also CA 118; 161; DLB 36, 100, 195
Tonson, Jacob
See Bennett, (Enoch) Arnold
Toole, John Kennedy 1937-1969 **CLC 19, 64**
See also CA 104; DLBY 81
Toomer, Jean 1894-1967   **CLC 1, 4, 13, 22;**
BLC 3; DAM MULT; PC 7; SSC 1; WLCS
See also BW 1; CA 85-88; CDALB 1917-1929;
DLB 45, 51; MTCW
Torley, Luke
See Blish, James (Benjamin)
Tornimparte, Alessandra
See Ginzburg, Natalia
Torre, Raoul della
See Mencken, H(enry) L(ouis)
Torrey, E(dwin) Fuller 1937-   **CLC 34**
See also CA 119
Torsvan, Ben Traven
See Traven, B.
Torsvan, Benno Traven
See Traven, B.
Torsvan, Berick Traven
See Traven, B.
Torsvan, Berwick Traven
See Traven, B.
Torsvan, Bruno Traven
See Traven, B.
Torsvan, Traven
See Traven, B.
Tournier, Michel (Edouard) 1924- **CLC 6, 23,**
36, 95
See also CA 49-52; CANR 3, 36; DLB 83;
MTCW; SATA 23
Tournimparte, Alessandra
See Ginzburg, Natalia
Towers, Ivar
See Kornbluth, C(yril) M.
Towne, Robert (Burton) 1936(?)-   **CLC 87**
See also CA 108; DLB 44
Townsend, Sue   **CLC 61**
See also Townsend, Susan Elaine
See also SATA 55, 93; SATA-Brief 48
Townsend, Susan Elaine 1946-
See Townsend, Sue
See also CA 119; 127; CANR 65; DAB; DAC;
DAM MST
Townshend, Peter (Dennis Blandford) 1945-

CLC 17, 42
See also CA 107
Tozzi, Federigo 1883-1920   **TCLC 31**
See also CA 160
Traill, Catharine Parr 1802-1899 **NCLC 31**
See also DLB 99
Trakl, Georg 1887-1914   **TCLC 5; PC 20**
See also CA 104; 165
Transtroemer, Tomas (Goesta) 1931- **CLC 52,**
65; DAM POET
See also CA 117; 129; CAAS 17
Transtromer, Tomas Gosta
See Transtroemer, Tomas (Goesta)
Traven, B. (?)-1969   **CLC 8, 11**
See also CA 19-20; 25-28R; CAP 2; DLB 9,
56; MTCW
Treitel, Jonathan 1959-   **CLC 70**
Tremain, Rose 1943-   **CLC 42**
See also CA 97-100; CANR 44; DLB 14
Tremblay, Michel 1942- **CLC 29, 102; DAC;**
DAM MST
See also CA 116; 128; DLB 60; MTCW
Trevanian   **CLC 29**
See also Whitaker, Rod(ney)
Trevor, Glen
See Hilton, James
Trevor, William 1928- **CLC 7, 9, 14, 25, 71;**
SSC 21
See also Cox, William Trevor
See also DLB 14, 139
Trifonov, Yuri (Valentinovich) 1925-1981
CLC 45
See also CA 126; 103; MTCW
Trilling, Lionel 1905-1975   **CLC 9, 11, 24**
See also CA 9-12R; 61-64; CANR 10; DLB 28,
63; INT CANR-10; MTCW
Trimball, W. H.
See Mencken, H(enry) L(ouis)
Tristan
See Gomez de la Serna, Ramon
Tristram
See Housman, A(lfred) E(dward)
Trogdon, William (Lewis) 1939-
See Heat-Moon, William Least
See also CA 115; 119; CANR 47; INT 119
Trollope, Anthony 1815-1882   **NCLC 6, 33;**
DA; DAB; DAC; DAM MST, NOV; SSC
28; WLC
See also CDBLB 1832-1890; DLB 21, 57, 159;
SATA 22
Trollope, Frances 1779-1863   **NCLC 30**
See also DLB 21, 166
Trotsky, Leon 1879-1940   **TCLC 22**
See also CA 118
Trotter (Cockburn), Catharine 1679-1749 **LC**
8
See also DLB 84
Trout, Kilgore
See Farmer, Philip Jose
Trow, George W. S. 1943-   **CLC 52**
See also CA 126
Troyat, Henri 1911-   **CLC 23**
See also CA 45-48; CANR 2, 33, 67; MTCW
Trudeau, G(arretson) B(eekman) 1948-
See Trudeau, Garry B.
See also CA 81-84; CANR 31; SATA 35
Trudeau, Garry B.   **CLC 12**
See also Trudeau, G(arretson) B(eekman)
See also AAYA 10; AITN 2
Truffaut, Francois 1932-1984 **CLC 20, 101**
See also CA 81-84; 113; CANR 34
Trumbo, Dalton 1905-1976   **CLC 19**
See also CA 21-24R; 69-72; CANR 10; DLB

Walker, Margaret (Abigail) 1915- **CLC 1, 6; BLC; DAM MULT; PC 20**
See also BW 2; CA 73-76; CANR 26, 54; DLB 76, 152; MTCW

Walker, Ted **CLC 13**
See also Walker, Edward Joseph
See also DLB 40

Wallace, David Foster 1962- **CLC 50**
See also CA 132; CANR 59

Wallace, Dexter
See Masters, Edgar Lee

Wallace, (Richard Horatio) Edgar 1875-1932 **TCLC 57**
See also CA 115; DLB 70

Wallace, Irving 1916-1990 **CLC 7, 13; DAM NOV, POP**
See also AITN 1; CA 1-4R; 132; CAAS 1; CANR 1, 27; INT CANR-27; MTCW

Wallant, Edward Lewis 1926-1962 **CLC 5, 10**
See also CA 1-4R; CANR 22; DLB 2, 28, 143; MTCW

Walley, Byron
See Card, Orson Scott

Walpole, Horace 1717-1797 **LC 2**
See also DLB 39, 104

Walpole, Hugh (Seymour) 1884-1941 **TCLC 5**
See also CA 104; 165; DLB 34

Walser, Martin 1927- **CLC 27**
See also CA 57-60; CANR 8, 46; DLB 75, 124

Walser, Robert 1878-1956 **TCLC 18; SSC 20**
See also CA 118; 165; DLB 66

Walsh, Jill Paton **CLC 35**
See also Paton Walsh, Gillian
See also AAYA 11; CLR 2; DLB 161; SAAS 3

Walter, Villiam Christian
See Andersen, Hans Christian

Wambaugh, Joseph (Aloysius, Jr.) 1937- **CLC 3, 18; DAM NOV, POP**
See also AITN 1; BEST 89:3; CA 33-36R; CANR 42, 65; DLB 6; DLBY 83; MTCW

Wang Wei 699(?)-761(?) **PC 18**

Ward, Arthur Henry Sarsfield 1883-1959
See Rohmer, Sax
See also CA 108

Ward, Douglas Turner 1930- **CLC 19**
See also BW 1; CA 81-84; CANR 27; DLB 7, 38

Ward, Mary Augusta
See Ward, Mrs. Humphry

Ward, Mrs. Humphry 1851-1920 **TCLC 55**
See also DLB 18

Ward, Peter
See Faust, Frederick (Schiller)

Warhol, Andy 1928(?)-1987 **CLC 20**
See also AAYA 12; BEST 89:4; CA 89-92; 121; CANR 34

Warner, Francis (Robert le Plastrier) 1937- **CLC 14**
See also CA 53-56; CANR 11

Warner, Marina 1946- **CLC 59**
See also CA 65-68; CANR 21, 55; DLB 194

Warner, Rex (Ernest) 1905-1986 **CLC 45**
See also CA 89-92; 119; DLB 15

Warner, Susan (Bogert) 1819-1885 **NCLC 31**
See also DLB 3, 42

Warner, Sylvia (Constance) Ashton
See Ashton-Warner, Sylvia (Constance)

Warner, Sylvia Townsend 1893-1978 **CLC 7, 19; SSC 23**
See also CA 61-64; 77-80; CANR 16, 60; DLB 34, 139; MTCW

Warren, Mercy Otis 1728-1814 **NCLC 13**
See also DLB 31

Warren, Robert Penn 1905-1989 **CLC 1, 4, 6, 8, 10, 13, 18, 39, 53, 59; DA; DAB; DAC; DAM MST, NOV, POET; SSC 4; WLC**
See also AITN 1; CA 13-16R; 129; CANR 10, 47; CDALB 1968-1988; DLB 2, 48, 152; DLBY 80, 89; INT CANR-10; MTCW; SATA 46; SATA-Obit 63

Warshofsky, Isaac
See Singer, Isaac Bashevis

Warton, Thomas 1728-1790 **LC 15; DAM POET**
See also DLB 104, 109

Waruk, Kona
See Harris, (Theodore) Wilson

Warung, Price 1855-1911 **TCLC 45**

Warwick, Jarvis
See Garner, Hugh

Washington, Alex
See Harris, Mark

Washington, Booker T(aliaferro) 1856-1915 **TCLC 10; BLC 3; DAM MULT**
See also BW 1; CA 114; 125; SATA 28

Washington, George 1732-1799 **LC 25**
See also DLB 31

Wassermann, (Karl) Jakob 1873-1934 **TCLC 6**
See also CA 104; DLB 66

Wasserstein, Wendy 1950- **CLC 32, 59, 90; DAM DRAM; DC 4**
See also CA 121; 129; CABS 3; CANR 53; INT 129; SATA 94

Waterhouse, Keith (Spencer) 1929- **CLC 47**
See also CA 5-8R; CANR 38, 67; DLB 13, 15; MTCW

Waters, Frank (Joseph) 1902-1995 **CLC 88**
See also CA 5-8R; 149; CAAS 13; CANR 3, 18, 63; DLBY 86

Waters, Roger 1944- **CLC 35**

Watkins, Frances Ellen
See Harper, Frances Ellen Watkins

Watkins, Gerrold
See Malzberg, Barry N(athaniel)

Watkins, Gloria 1955(?)-
See hooks, bell
See also BW 2; CA 143

Watkins, Paul 1964- **CLC 55**
See also CA 132; CANR 62

Watkins, Vernon Phillips 1906-1967 **CLC 43**
See also CA 9-10; 25-28R; CAP 1; DLB 20

Watson, Irving S.
See Mencken, H(enry) L(ouis)

Watson, John H.
See Farmer, Philip Jose

Watson, Richard F.
See Silverberg, Robert

Waugh, Auberon (Alexander) 1939- **CLC 7**
See also CA 45-48; CANR 6, 22; DLB 14, 194

Waugh, Evelyn (Arthur St. John) 1903-1966 **CLC 1, 3, 8, 13, 19, 27, 44, 107; DA; DAB; DAC; DAM MST, NOV, POP; WLC**
See also CA 85-88; 25-28R; CANR 22; CDBLB 1914-1945; DLB 15, 162, 195; MTCW

Waugh, Harriet 1944- **CLC 6**
See also CA 85-88; CANR 22

Ways, C. R.
See Blount, Roy (Alton), Jr.

Waystaff, Simon
See Swift, Jonathan

Webb, (Martha) Beatrice (Potter) 1858-1943 **TCLC 22**
See also Potter, (Helen) Beatrix
See also CA 117

Webb, Charles (Richard) 1939- **CLC 7**
See also CA 25-28R

Webb, James H(enry), Jr. 1946- **CLC 22**
See also CA 81-84

Webb, Mary (Gladys Meredith) 1881-1927 **TCLC 24**
See also CA 123; DLB 34

Webb, Mrs. Sidney
See Webb, (Martha) Beatrice (Potter)

Webb, Phyllis 1927- **CLC 18**
See also CA 104; CANR 23; DLB 53

Webb, Sidney (James) 1859-1947 **TCLC 22**
See also CA 117; 163; DLB 190

Webber, Andrew Lloyd **CLC 21**
See also Lloyd Webber, Andrew

Weber, Lenora Mattingly 1895-1971 **CLC 12**
See also CA 19-20; 29-32R; CAP 1; SATA 2; SATA-Obit 26

Weber, Max 1864-1920 **TCLC 69**
See also CA 109

Webster, John 1579(?)-1634(?) **LC 33; DA; DAB; DAC; DAM DRAM, MST; DC 2; WLC**
See also CDBLB Before 1660; DLB 58

Webster, Noah 1758-1843 **NCLC 30**

Wedekind, (Benjamin) Frank(lin) 1864-1918 **TCLC 7; DAM DRAM**
See also CA 104; 153; DLB 118

Weidman, Jerome 1913- **CLC 7**
See also AITN 2; CA 1-4R; CANR 1; DLB 28

Weil, Simone (Adolphine) 1909-1943 **TCLC 23**
See also CA 117; 159

Weinstein, Nathan
See West, Nathanael

Weinstein, Nathan von Wallenstein
See West, Nathanael

Weir, Peter (Lindsay) 1944- **CLC 20**
See also CA 113; 123

Weiss, Peter (Ulrich) 1916-1982 **CLC 3, 15, 51; DAM DRAM**
See also CA 45-48; 106; CANR 3; DLB 69, 124

Weiss, Theodore (Russell) 1916- **CLC 3, 8, 14**
See also CA 9-12R; CAAS 2; CANR 46; DLB 5

Welch, (Maurice) Denton 1915-1948 **TCLC 22**
See also CA 121; 148

Welch, James 1940- **CLC 6, 14, 52; DAM MULT, POP**
See also CA 85-88; CANR 42, 66; DLB 175; NNAL

Weldon, Fay 1931- **CLC 6, 9, 11, 19, 36, 59; DAM POP**
See also CA 21-24R; CANR 16, 46, 63; CDBLB 1960 to Present; DLB 14, 194; INT CANR-16; MTCW

Wellek, Rene 1903-1995 **CLC 28**
See also CA 5-8R; 150; CAAS 7; CANR 8; DLB 63; INT CANR-8

Weller, Michael 1942- **CLC 10, 53**
See also CA 85-88

Weller, Paul 1958- **CLC 26**

Wellershoff, Dieter 1925- **CLC 46**
See also CA 89-92; CANR 16, 37

Welles, (George) Orson 1915-1985 **CLC 20, 80**
See also CA 93-96; 117

Wellman, Mac 1945- **CLC 65**

Wellman, Manly Wade 1903-1986 **CLC 49**
See also CA 1-4R; 118; CANR 6, 16, 44; SATA 6; SATA-Obit 47

Wells, Carolyn 1869(?)-1942 **TCLC 35**
See also CA 113; DLB 11

Wells, H(erbert) G(eorge) 1866-1946 **TCLC 6,**

12, 19; DA; DAB; DAC; DAM MST, NOV; SSC 6; WLC
See also AAYA 18; CA 110; 121; CDBLB 1914-1945; DLB 34, 70, 156, 178; MTCW; SATA 20

Wells, Rosemary 1943-   CLC 12
See also AAYA 13; CA 85-88; CANR 48; CLR 16; MAICYA; SAAS 1; SATA 18, 69

Welty, Eudora 1909- CLC 1, 2, 5, 14, 22, 33, 105; DA; DAB; DAC; DAM MST, NOV; SSC 1, 27; WLC
See also CA 9-12R; CABS 1; CANR 32, 65; CDALB 1941-1968; DLB 2, 102, 143; DLBD 12; DLBY 87; MTCW

Wen I-to 1899-1946   TCLC 28

Wentworth, Robert
See Hamilton, Edmond

Werfel, Franz (Viktor) 1890-1945   TCLC 8
See also CA 104; 161; DLB 81, 124

Wergeland, Henrik Arnold 1808-1845 NCLC 5

Wersba, Barbara 1932-   CLC 30
See also AAYA 2; CA 29-32R; CANR 16, 38; CLR 3; DLB 52; JRDA; MAICYA; SAAS 2; SATA 1, 58

Wertmueller, Lina 1928-   CLC 16
See also CA 97-100; CANR 39

Wescott, Glenway 1901-1987   CLC 13
See also CA 13-16R; 121; CANR 23; DLB 4, 9, 102

Wesker, Arnold 1932-   CLC 3, 5, 42; DAB; DAM DRAM
See also CA 1-4R; CAAS 7; CANR 1, 33; CDBLB 1960 to Present; DLB 13; MTCW

Wesley, Richard (Errol) 1945-   CLC 7
See also BW 1; CA 57-60; CANR 27; DLB 38

Wessel, Johan Herman 1742-1785   LC 7

West, Anthony (Panther) 1914-1987 CLC 50
See also CA 45-48; 124; CANR 3, 19; DLB 15

West, C. P.
See Wodehouse, P(elham) G(renville)

West, (Mary) Jessamyn 1902-1984 CLC 7, 17
See also CA 9-12R; 112; CANR 27; DLB 6; DLBY 84; MTCW; SATA-Obit 37

West, Morris L(anglo) 1916-   CLC 6, 33
See also CA 5-8R; CANR 24, 49, 64; MTCW

West, Nathanael 1903-1940   TCLC 1, 14, 44; SSC 16
See also CA 104; 125; CDALB 1929-1941; DLB 4, 9, 28; MTCW

West, Owen
See Koontz, Dean R(ay)

West, Paul 1930-   CLC 7, 14, 96
See also CA 13-16R; CAAS 7; CANR 22, 53; DLB 14; INT CANR-22

West, Rebecca 1892-1983   CLC 7, 9, 31, 50
See also CA 5-8R; 109; CANR 19; DLB 36; DLBY 83; MTCW

Westall, Robert (Atkinson) 1929-1993CLC 17
See also AAYA 12; CA 69-72; 141; CANR 18, 68; CLR 13; JRDA; MAICYA; SAAS 2; SATA 23, 69; SATA-Obit 75

Westlake, Donald E(dwin) 1933- CLC 7, 33; DAM POP
See also CA 17-20R; CAAS 13; CANR 16, 44, 65; INT CANR-16

Westmacott, Mary
See Christie, Agatha (Mary Clarissa)

Weston, Allen
See Norton, Andre

Wetcheek, J. L.
See Feuchtwanger, Lion

Wetering, Janwillem van de

See van de Wetering, Janwillem

Wetherell, Elizabeth
See Warner, Susan (Bogert)

Whale, James 1889-1957   TCLC 63

Whalen, Philip 1923-   CLC 6, 29
See also CA 9-12R; CANR 5, 39; DLB 16

Wharton, Edith (Newbold Jones) 1862-1937 TCLC 3, 9, 27, 53; DA; DAB; DAC; DAM MST, NOV; SSC 6; WLC
See also AAYA 25; CA 104; 132; CDALB 1865-1917; DLB 4, 9, 12, 78, 189; DLBD 13; MTCW

Wharton, James
See Mencken, H(enry) L(ouis)

Wharton, William (a pseudonym) CLC 18, 37
See also CA 93-96; DLBY 80; INT 93-96

Wheatley (Peters), Phillis 1754(?)-1784 LC 3; BLC 3; DA; DAC; DAM MST, MULT, POET; PC 3; WLC
See also CDALB 1640-1865; DLB 31, 50

Wheelock, John Hall 1886-1978   CLC 14
See also CA 13-16R; 77-80; CANR 14; DLB 45

White, E(lwyn) B(rooks) 1899-1985 CLC 10, 34, 39; DAM POP
See also AITN 2; CA 13-16R; 116; CANR 16, 37; CLR 1, 21; DLB 11, 22; MAICYA; MTCW; SATA 2, 29; SATA-Obit 44

White, Edmund (Valentine III) 1940-CLC 27, 110; DAM POP
See also AAYA 7; CA 45-48; CANR 3, 19, 36, 62; MTCW

White, Patrick (Victor Martindale) 1912-1990 CLC 3, 4, 5, 7, 9, 18, 65, 69
See also CA 81-84; 132; CANR 43; MTCW

White, Phyllis Dorothy James 1920-
See James, P. D.
See also CA 21-24R; CANR 17, 43, 65; DAM POP; MTCW

White, T(erence) H(anbury) 1906-1964 CLC 30
See also AAYA 22; CA 73-76; CANR 37; DLB 160; JRDA; MAICYA; SATA 12

White, Terence de Vere 1912-1994   CLC 49
See also CA 49-52; 145; CANR 3

White, Walter F(rancis) 1893-1955 TCLC 15
See also White, Walter
See also BW 1; CA 115; 124; DLB 51

White, William Hale 1831-1913
See Rutherford, Mark
See also CA 121

Whitehead, E(dward) A(nthony) 1933-CLC 5
See also CA 65-68; CANR 58

Whitemore, Hugh (John) 1936-   CLC 37
See also CA 132; INT 132

Whitman, Sarah Helen (Power) 1803-1878 NCLC 19
See also DLB 1

Whitman, Walt(er) 1819-1892   NCLC 4, 31; DA; DAB; DAC; DAM MST, POET; PC 3; WLC
See also CDALB 1640-1865; DLB 3, 64; SATA 20

Whitney, Phyllis A(yame) 1903-   CLC 42; DAM POP
See also AITN 2; BEST 90:3; CA 1-4R; CANR 3, 25, 38, 60; JRDA; MAICYA; SATA 1, 30

Whittemore, (Edward) Reed (Jr.) 1919- CLC 4
See also CA 9-12R; CAAS 8; CANR 4; DLB 5

Whittier, John Greenleaf 1807-1892 NCLC 8, 59
See also DLB 1

Whittlebot, Hernia
See Coward, Noel (Peirce)

Wicker, Thomas Grey 1926-
See Wicker, Tom
See also CA 65-68; CANR 21, 46

Wicker, Tom   CLC 7
See also Wicker, Thomas Grey

Wideman, John Edgar 1941- CLC 5, 34, 36, 67; BLC 3; DAM MULT
See also BW 2; CA 85-88; CANR 14, 42, 67; DLB 33, 143

Wiebe, Rudy (Henry) 1934-   CLC 6, 11, 14; DAC; DAM MST
See also CA 37-40R; CANR 42, 67; DLB 60

Wieland, Christoph Martin 1733-1813 NCLC 17
See also DLB 97

Wiene, Robert 1881-1938   TCLC 56

Wieners, John 1934-   CLC 7
See also CA 13-16R; DLB 16

Wiesel, Elie(zer) 1928- CLC 3, 5, 11, 37; DA; DAB; DAC; DAM MST, NOV; WLCS 2
See also AAYA 7; AITN 1; CA 5-8R; CAAS 4; CANR 8, 40, 65; DLB 83; DLBY 87; INT CANR-8; MTCW; SATA 56

Wiggins, Marianne 1947-   CLC 57
See also BEST 89:3; CA 130; CANR 60

Wight, James Alfred 1916-1995
See Herriot, James
See also CA 77-80; SATA 55; SATA-Brief 44

Wilbur, Richard (Purdy) 1921- CLC 3, 6, 9, 14, 53, 110; DA; DAB; DAC; DAM MST, POET
See also CA 1-4R; CABS 2; CANR 2, 29; DLB 5, 169; INT CANR-29; MTCW; SATA 9

Wild, Peter 1940-   CLC 14
See also CA 37-40R; DLB 5

Wilde, Oscar (Fingal O'Flahertie Wills) 1854(?)-1900TCLC 1, 8, 23, 41; DA; DAB; DAC; DAM DRAM, MST, NOV; SSC 11; WLC
See also CA 104; 119; CDBLB 1890-1914; DLB 10, 19, 34, 57, 141, 156, 190; SATA 24

Wilder, Billy   CLC 20
See also Wilder, Samuel
See also DLB 26

Wilder, Samuel 1906-
See Wilder, Billy
See also CA 89-92

Wilder, Thornton (Niven) 1897-1975 CLC 1, 5, 6, 10, 15, 35, 82; DA; DAB; DAC; DAM DRAM, MST, NOV; DC 1; WLC
See also AITN 2; CA 13-16R; 61-64; CANR 40; DLB 4, 7, 9; DLBY 97; MTCW

Wilding, Michael 1942-   CLC 73
See also CA 104; CANR 24, 49

Wiley, Richard 1944-   CLC 44
See also CA 121; 129

Wilhelm, Kate   CLC 7
See also Wilhelm, Katie Gertrude
See also AAYA 20; CAAS 5; DLB 8; INT CANR-17

Wilhelm, Katie Gertrude 1928-
See Wilhelm, Kate
See also CA 37-40R; CANR 17, 36, 60; MTCW

Wilkins, Mary
See Freeman, Mary Eleanor Wilkins

Willard, Nancy 1936-   CLC 7, 37
See also CA 89-92; CANR 10, 39, 68; CLR 5; DLB 5, 52; MAICYA; MTCW; SATA 37, 71; SATA-Brief 30

Williams, C(harles) K(enneth) 1936- CLC 33,

56; DAM POET
  See also CA 37-40R; CAAS 26; CANR 57;
  DLB 5
Williams, Charles
  See Collier, James L(incoln)
Williams, Charles (Walter Stansby) 1886-1945
  TCLC 1, 11
  See also CA 104; 163; DLB 100, 153
Williams, (George) Emlyn 1905-1987CLC 15;
  DAM DRAM
  See also CA 104; 123; CANR 36; DLB 10, 77;
  MTCW
Williams, Hugo 1942-   CLC 42
  See also CA 17-20R; CANR 45; DLB 40
Williams, J. Walker
  See Wodehouse, P(elham) G(renville)
Williams, John A(lfred) 1925-CLC 5, 13; BLC
  3; DAM MULT
  See also BW 2; CA 53-56; CAAS 3; CANR 6,
  26, 51; DLB 2, 33; INT CANR-6
Williams, Jonathan (Chamberlain) 1929-
  CLC 13
  See also CA 9-12R; CAAS 12; CANR 8; DLB
  5
Williams, Joy 1944-   CLC 31
  See also CA 41-44R; CANR 22, 48
Williams, Norman 1952-   CLC 39
  See also CA 118
Williams, Sherley Anne 1944-CLC 89; BLC 3;
  DAM MULT, POET
  See also BW 2; CA 73-76; CANR 25; DLB 41;
  INT CANR-25; SATA 78
Williams, Shirley
  See Williams, Sherley Anne
Williams, Tennessee 1911-1983CLC 1, 2, 5, 7,
  8, 11, 15, 19, 30, 39, 45, 71; DA; DAB;
  DAC; DAM DRAM, MST; DC 4; WLC
  See also AITN 1, 2; CA 5-8R; 108; CABS 3;
  CANR 31; CDALB 1941-1968; DLB 7;
  DLBD 4; DLBY 83; MTCW
Williams, Thomas (Alonzo) 1926-1990 CLC
  14
  See also CA 1-4R; 132; CANR 2
Williams, William C.
  See Williams, William Carlos
Williams, William Carlos 1883-1963CLC 1, 2,
  5, 9, 13, 22, 42, 67; DA; DAB; DAC; DAM
  MST, POET; PC 7
  See also CA 89-92; CANR 34; CDALB 1917-
  1929; DLB 4, 16, 54, 86; MTCW
Williamson, David (Keith) 1942-   CLC 56
  See also CA 103; CANR 41
Williamson, Ellen Douglas 1905-1984
  See Douglas, Ellen
  See also CA 17-20R; 114; CANR 39
Williamson, Jack   CLC 29
  See also Williamson, John Stewart
  See also CAAS 8; DLB 8
Williamson, John Stewart 1908-
  See Williamson, Jack
  See also CA 17-20R; CANR 23
Willie, Frederick
  See Lovecraft, H(oward) P(hillips)
Willingham, Calder (Baynard, Jr.) 1922-1995
  CLC 5, 51
  See also CA 5-8R; 147; CANR 3; DLB 2, 44;
  MTCW
Willis, Charles
  See Clarke, Arthur C(harles)
Willy
  See Colette, (Sidonie-Gabrielle)
Willy, Colette
  See Colette, (Sidonie-Gabrielle)

Wilson, A(ndrew) N(orman) 1950-   CLC 33
  See also CA 112; 122; DLB 14, 155, 194
Wilson, Angus (Frank Johnstone) 1913-1991
  CLC 2, 3, 5, 25, 34; SSC 21
  See also CA 5-8R; 134; CANR 21; DLB 15,
  139, 155; MTCW
Wilson, August 1945-CLC 39, 50, 63; BLC 3;
  DA; DAB; DAC; DAM DRAM, MST,
  MULT; DC 2; WLCS
  See also AAYA 16; BW 2; CA 115; 122; CANR
  42, 54; MTCW
Wilson, Brian 1942-   CLC 12
Wilson, Colin 1931-   CLC 3, 14
  See also CA 1-4R; CAAS 5; CANR 1, 22, 33;
  DLB 14, 194; MTCW
Wilson, Dirk
  See Pohl, Frederik
Wilson, Edmund 1895-1972CLC 1, 2, 3, 8, 24
  See also CA 1-4R; 37-40R; CANR 1, 46; DLB
  63; MTCW
Wilson, Ethel Davis (Bryant) 1888(?)-1980
  CLC 13; DAC; DAM POET
  See also CA 102; DLB 68; MTCW
Wilson, John 1785-1854   NCLC 5
Wilson, John (Anthony) Burgess 1917-1993
  See Burgess, Anthony
  See also CA 1-4R; 143; CANR 2, 46; DAC;
  DAM NOV; MTCW
Wilson, Lanford 1937-   CLC 7, 14, 36; DAM
  DRAM
  See also CA 17-20R; CABS 3; CANR 45; DLB
  7
Wilson, Robert M. 1944-   CLC 7, 9
  See also CA 49-52; CANR 2, 41; MTCW
Wilson, Robert McLiam 1964-   CLC 59
  See also CA 132
Wilson, Sloan 1920-   CLC 32
  See also CA 1-4R; CANR 1, 44
Wilson, Snoo 1948-   CLC 33
  See also CA 69-72
Wilson, William S(mith) 1932-   CLC 49
  See also CA 81-84
Wilson, Woodrow 1856-1924   TCLC 79
  See also DLB 47
Winchilsea, Anne (Kingsmill) Finch Counte
  1661-1720
  See Finch, Anne
Windham, Basil
  See Wodehouse, P(elham) G(renville)
Wingrove, David (John) 1954-   CLC 68
  See also CA 133
Wintergreen, Jane
  See Duncan, Sara Jeannette
Winters, Janet Lewis   CLC 41
  See also Lewis, Janet
  See also DLBY 87
Winters, (Arthur) Yvor 1900-1968 CLC 4, 8,
  32
  See also CA 11-12; 25-28R; CAP 1; DLB 48;
  MTCW
Winterson, Jeanette 1959-CLC 64; DAM POP
  See also CA 136; CANR 58
Winthrop, John 1588-1649   LC 31
  See also DLB 24, 30
Wiseman, Frederick 1930-   CLC 20
  See also CA 159
Wister, Owen 1860-1938   TCLC 21
  See also CA 108; 162; DLB 9, 78, 186; SATA
  62
Witkacy
  See Witkiewicz, Stanislaw Ignacy
Witkiewicz, Stanislaw Ignacy 1885-1939
  TCLC 8

See also CA 105; 162
Wittgenstein, Ludwig (Josef Johann) 1889-1951
  TCLC 59
  See also CA 113; 164
Wittig, Monique 1935(?)-   CLC 22
  See also CA 116; 135; DLB 83
Wittlin, Jozef 1896-1976   CLC 25
  See also CA 49-52; 65-68; CANR 3
Wodehouse, P(elham) G(renville) 1881-1975
  CLC 1, 2, 5, 10, 22; DAB; DAC; DAM
  NOV; SSC 2
  See also AITN 2; CA 45-48; 57-60; CANR 3,
  33; CDBLB 1914-1945; DLB 34, 162;
  MTCW; SATA 22
Woiwode, L.
  See Woiwode, Larry (Alfred)
Woiwode, Larry (Alfred) 1941-   CLC 6, 10
  See also CA 73-76; CANR 16; DLB 6; INT
  CANR-16
Wojciechowska, Maia (Teresa) 1927- CLC 26
  See also AAYA 8; CA 9-12R; CANR 4, 41;
  CLR 1; JRDA; MAICYA; SAAS 1; SATA
  1, 28, 83
Wolf, Christa 1929-   CLC 14, 29, 58
  See also CA 85-88; CANR 45; DLB 75; MTCW
Wolfe, Gene (Rodman) 1931- CLC 25; DAM
  POP
  See also CA 57-60; CAAS 9; CANR 6, 32, 60;
  DLB 8
Wolfe, George C. 1954-   CLC 49; BLCS
  See also CA 149
Wolfe, Thomas (Clayton) 1900-1938 TCLC 4,
  13, 29, 61; DA; DAB; DAC; DAM MST,
  NOV; WLC
  See also CA 104; 132; CDALB 1929-1941;
  DLB 9, 102; DLBD 2, 16; DLBY 85, 97;
  MTCW
Wolfe, Thomas Kennerly, Jr. 1931-
  See Wolfe, Tom
  See also CA 13-16R; CANR 9, 33; DAM POP;
  DLB 185; INT CANR-9; MTCW
Wolfe, Tom   CLC 1, 2, 9, 15, 35, 51
  See also Wolfe, Thomas Kennerly, Jr.
  See also AAYA 8; AITN 2; BEST 89:1; DLB
  152
Wolff, Geoffrey (Ansell) 1937-   CLC 41
  See also CA 29-32R; CANR 29, 43
Wolff, Sonia
  See Levitin, Sonia (Wolff)
Wolff, Tobias (Jonathan Ansell) 1945- CLC
  39, 64
  See also AAYA 16; BEST 90:2; CA 114; 117;
  CAAS 22; CANR 54; DLB 130; INT 117
Wolfram von Eschenbach c. 1170-c. 1220
  CMLC 5
  See also DLB 138
Wolitzer, Hilma 1930-   CLC 17
  See also CA 65-68; CANR 18, 40; INT CANR-
  18; SATA 31
Wollstonecraft, Mary 1759-1797   LC 5
  See also CDBLB 1789-1832; DLB 39, 104, 158
Wonder, Stevie   CLC 12
  See also Morris, Steveland Judkins
Wong, Jade Snow 1922-   CLC 17
  See also CA 109
Woodberry, George Edward 1855-1930
  TCLC 73
  See also CA 165; DLB 71, 103
Woodcott, Keith
  See Brunner, John (Kilian Houston)
Woodruff, Robert W.
  See Mencken, H(enry) L(ouis)
Woolf, (Adeline) Virginia 1882-1941TCLC 1,

Zuk, Georges
  See Skelton, Robin
Zukofsky, Louis 1904-1978 CLC 1, 2, 4, 7, 11,
    18; DAM POET; PC 11
  See also CA 9-12R; 77-80; CANR 39; DLB 5,
    165; MTCW
Zweig, Paul 1935-1984   CLC 34, 42
  See also CA 85-88; 113
Zweig, Stefan 1881-1942   TCLC 17
  See also CA 112; DLB 81, 118
Zwingli, Huldreich 1484-1531   LC 37
  See also DLB 179

Literary Criticism Series
Cumulative Topic Index

This index lists all topic entries in Gale's *Classical and Medieval Literature Criticism, Contemporary Literary Criticism, Literature Criticism from 1400 to 1800, Nineteenth-Century Literature Criticism,* and *Twentieth-Century Literary Criticism.*

Topic Index

Topic Index

Topic Index

NCLC Cumulative Nationality Index

Nationality Index

Title Index

ISBN 0-7876-1910-8

90000

9 780787 619107